Multiple View Geometry in Computer Vision

Second Edition

Richard Hartley
Australian National University,
Canberra, Australia

Andrew Zisserman
University of Oxford, UK

CAMBRIDGE
UNIVERSITY PRESS

CAMBRIDGE
UNIVERSITY PRESS

University Printing House, Cambridge CB2 8BS, United Kingdom

One Liberty Plaza, 20th Floor, New York, NY 10006, USA

477 Williamstown Road, Port Melbourne, VIC 3207, Australia

314-321, 3rd Floor, Plot 3, Splendor Forum, Jasola District Centre, New Delhi - 110025, India

79 Anson Road, #06-04/06, Singapore 079906

Cambridge University Press is part of the University of Cambridge.

It furthers the University's mission by disseminating knowledge in the pursuit of education, learning and research at the highest international levels of excellence.

www.cambridge.org
Information on this title: www.cambridge.org/9780521540513

First published 2000
Reprinted 2001, 2002
Second Edition 2003
17th printing 2018

A catalogue record for this publication is available from the British Library

ISBN 978-0-521-54051-3 Paperback

Dedication

This book is dedicated to Joe Mundy whose vision and constant search for new ideas led us into this field.

Contents

Foreword

By Olivier Faugeras

Making a computer see was something that leading experts in the field of Artificial Intelligence thought to be at the level of difficulty of a summer student's project back in the sixties. Forty years later the task is still unsolved and seems formidable. A whole field, called Computer Vision, has emerged as a discipline in itself with strong connections to mathematics and computer science and looser connections to physics, the psychology of perception and the neuro sciences.

One of the likely reasons for this half-failure is the fact that researchers had overlooked the fact, perhaps because of this plague called naive introspection, that perception in general and visual perception in particular are far more complex in animals and humans than was initially thought. There is of course no reason why we should pattern Computer Vision algorithms after biological ones, but the fact of the matter is that

(i) the way biological vision works is still largely unknown and therefore hard to emulate on computers, and
(ii) attempts to ignore biological vision and reinvent a sort of silicon-based vision have not been so successful as initially expected.

Despite these negative remarks, Computer Vision researchers have obtained some outstanding successes, both practical and theoretical.

On the side of practice, and to single out one example, the possibility of guiding vehicles such as cars and trucks on regular roads or on rough terrain using computer vision technology was demonstrated many years ago in Europe, the USA and Japan. This requires capabilities for real-time three-dimensional dynamic scene analysis which are quite elaborate. Today, car manufacturers are slowly incorporating some of these functions in their products.

On the theoretical side some remarkable progress has been achieved in the area of what one could call geometric Computer Vision. This includes the description of the way the appearance of objects changes when viewed from different viewpoints as a function of the objects' shape and the cameras parameters. This endeavour would not have been achieved without the use of fairly sophisticated mathematical techniques encompassing many areas of geometry, ancient and novel. This book deals in particular with the intricate and beautiful geometric relations that exist between the images of objects in the world. These relations are important to analyze for their own sake because this is one of the goals of science to provide explanations for appearances; they are also important to analyze because of the range of applications their understanding opens up.

The book has been written by two pioneers and leading experts in geometric Computer Vision. They have succeeded in what was something of a challenge, namely to convey in a simple and easily accessible way the mathematics that is necessary for understanding the underlying geometric concepts, to be quite exhaustive in the coverage of the results that have been obtained by them and other researchers worldwide, to analyze the interplay between the geometry and the fact that the image measurements are necessarily noisy, to express many of these theoretical results in algorithmic form so that they can readily be transformed into computer code, and to present many real examples that illustrate the concepts and show the range of applicability of the theory.

Returning to the original holy grail of making a computer see we may wonder whether this kind of work is a step in the right direction. I must leave the readers of the book to answer this question, and be content with saying that no designer of systems using cameras hooked to computers that will be built in the foreseeable future can ignore this work. This is perhaps a step in the direction of defining what it means for a computer to see.

Preface

Over the past decade there has been a rapid development in the understanding and modelling of the geometry of multiple views in computer vision. The theory and practice have now reached a level of maturity where excellent results can be achieved for problems that were certainly unsolved a decade ago, and often thought unsolvable. These tasks and algorithms include:

- Given two images, and no other information, compute matches between the images, and the 3D position of the points that generate these matches and the cameras that generate the images.
- Given three images, and no other information, similarly compute the matches between images of points and lines, and the position in 3D of these points and lines and the cameras.
- Compute the epipolar geometry of a stereo rig, and trifocal geometry of a trinocular rig, without requiring a calibration object.
- Compute the internal calibration of a camera from a sequence of images of natural scenes (i.e. calibration "on the fly").

The distinctive flavour of these algorithms is that they are *uncalibrated* — it is not necessary to know or first need to compute the camera internal parameters (such as the focal length).

Underpinning these algorithms is a new and more complete theoretical understanding of the geometry of multiple uncalibrated views: the number of parameters involved, the constraints between points and lines imaged in the views; and the retrieval of cameras and 3-space points from image correspondences. For example, to determine the epipolar geometry of a stereo rig requires specifying only seven parameters, the camera calibration is not required. These parameters are determined from the correspondence of seven or more image point correspondences. Contrast this uncalibrated route, with the previous calibrated route of a decade ago: each camera would first be calibrated from the image of a carefully engineered calibration object with known geometry. The calibration involves determining 11 parameters for each camera. The epipolar geometry would then have been computed from these two sets of 11 parameters.

This example illustrates the importance of the uncalibrated (projective) approach – using the appropriate representation of the geometry makes explicit the parameters that are required at each stage of a computation. This avoids computing parameters that have no effect on the final result, and results in simpler algorithms. It is also worth correcting a possible misconception. In the uncalibrated framework, entities (for instance point positions in 3-space) are often recovered to within a precisely defined ambiguity. This ambiguity does not mean that the points are poorly estimated.

More practically, it is often not possible to calibrate cameras once-and-for-all; for instance where cameras are moved (on a mobile vehicle) or internal parameters are changed (a surveillance camera with zoom). Furthermore, calibration information is simply not available in some circumstances. Imagine computing the motion of a camera from a video sequence, or building a virtual reality model from archive film footage where both motion and internal calibration information are unknown.

The achievements in multiple view geometry have been possible because of developments in our theoretical understanding, but also because of improvements in estimating mathematical objects from images. The first improvement has been an attention to the error that should be minimized in over-determined systems – whether it be algebraic, geometric or statistical. The second improvement has been the use of robust estimation algorithms (such as RANSAC), so that the estimate is unaffected by "outliers" in the data. Also these techniques have generated powerful search and matching algorithms.

Many of the problems of reconstruction have now reached a level where we may claim that they are solved. Such problems include:

(i) Estimation of the multifocal tensors from image point correspondences, particularly the fundamental matrix and trifocal tensors (the quadrifocal tensor having not received so much attention).
(ii) Extraction of the camera matrices from these tensors, and subsequent projective reconstruction from two, three and four views.

Other significant successes have been achieved, though there may be more to learn about these problems. Examples include:

(i) Application of bundle adjustment to solve more general reconstruction problems.
(ii) Metric (Euclidean) reconstruction given minimal assumptions on the camera matrices.
(iii) Automatic detection of correspondences in image sequences, and elimination of outliers and false matches using the multifocal tensor relationships.

Roadplan. The book is divided into six parts and there are seven short appendices. Each part introduces a new geometric relation: the homography for background, the camera matrix for single view, the fundamental matrix for two views, the trifocal tensor for three views, and the quadrifocal tensor for four views. In each case there is a chapter describing the relation, its properties and applications, and a companion chapter describing algorithms for its estimation from image measurements. The estimation algorithms described range from cheap, simple, approaches through to the optimal algorithms which are currently believed to be the best available.

Part 0: Background. This part is more tutorial than the others. It introduces the central ideas in the projective geometry of 2-space and 3-space (for example ideal points, and the absolute conic); how this geometry may be represented, manipulated, and estimated; and how the geometry relates to various objectives in computer vision such as rectifying images of planes to remove perspective distortion.

Part 1: Single view geometry. Here the various cameras that model the perspective projection from 3-space to an image are defined and their anatomy explored. Their estimation using traditional techniques of calibration objects is described, as well as camera calibration from vanishing points and vanishing lines.

Part 2: Two view geometry. This part describes the epipolar geometry of two cameras, projective reconstruction from image point correspondences, methods of resolving the projective ambiguity, optimal triangulation, transfer between views via planes.

Part 3: Three view geometry. Here the trifocal geometry of three cameras is described, including transfer of a point correspondence from two views to a third, and similarly transfer for a line correspondence; computation of the geometry from point and line correspondences, retrieval of the camera matrices.

Part 4: N-views. This part has two purposes. First, it extends three view geometry to four views (a minor extension) and describes estimation methods applicable to N-views, such as the factorization algorithm of Tomasi and Kanade for computing structure and motion simultaneously from multiple images. Second, it covers themes that have been touched on in earlier chapters, but can be understood more fully and uniformly by emphasising their commonality. Examples include deriving multi-linear view constraints on correspondences, auto-calibration, and ambiguous solutions.

Appendices. These describe further background material on tensors, statistics, parameter estimation, linear and matrix algebra, iterative estimation, the solution of sparse matrix systems, and special projective transformations.

Acknowledgements. We have benefited enormously from ideas and discussions with our colleagues: Paul Beardsley, Stefan Carlsson, Olivier Faugeras, Andrew Fitzgibbon, Jitendra Malik, Steve Maybank, Amnon Shashua, Phil Torr, Bill Triggs.

If there are only a countable number of errors in this book then it is due to Antonio Criminisi, David Liebowitz and Frederik Schaffalitzky who have with great energy and devotion read most of it, and made numerous suggestions for improvements. Similarly both Peter Sturm and Bill Triggs have suggested many improvements to various chapters. We are grateful to other colleagues who have read individual chapters: David Capel, Lourdes de Agapito Vicente, Bob Kaucic, Steve Maybank, Peter Tu.

We are particularly grateful to those who have provided multiple figures: Paul Beardsley, Antonio Criminisi, Andrew Fitzgibbon, David Liebowitz, and Larry Shapiro; and for individual figures from: Martin Armstrong, David Capel, Lourdes de Agapito Vicente, Eric Hayman, Phil Pritchett, Luc Robert, Cordelia Schmid, and others who are explicitly acknowledged in figure captions.

At Cambridge University Press we thank David Tranah for his constant source of advice and patience, and Michael Behrend for excellent copy editing.

A small number of minor errors have been corrected in the reprinted editions, and we thank the following readers for pointing these out: Luis Baumela, Niclas Borlin, Mike Brooks, Jun ho. Choi, Wojciech Chojnacki, Carlo Colombo, Nicolas Dano, Andrew Fitzgibbon, Bogdan Georgescu, Fredrik Kahl, Bob Kaucic, Jae-Hak Kim, Hansung Lee, Dennis Maier, Karsten Muelhmann, David Nister, Andreas Olsson, Stéphane Paris, Frederik Schaffalitzky, Bill Severson, Pedro Lopez de Teruel Alcolea, Bernard Thiesse, Ken Thornton, Magdalena Urbanek, Gergely Vass, Eugene Vendrovsky, Sui Wei, and Tomáš Werner.

The second edition. This new paperback edition has been expanded to include some of the developments since the original version of July 2000. For example, the book now covers the discovery of a closed form factorization solution in the projective case when a plane is visible in the scene, and the extension of affine factorization to non-rigid scenes. We have also extended the discussion of single view geometry (chapter 8) and three view geometry (chapter 15), and added an appendix on parameter estimation.

In preparing this second edition we are very grateful to colleagues who have made suggestion for improvements and additions. These include Marc Pollefeys, Bill Triggs and in particular Tomáš Werner who provided excellent and comprehensive comments. We also thank Antonio Criminisi, Andrew Fitzgibbon, Rob Fergus, David Liebowitz, and particularly Josef Šivic, for proof reading and very helpful comments on parts of the new material. As always we are grateful to David Tranah of CUP.

The figures appearing in this book can be downloaded from

`http://www.robots.ox.ac.uk/~vgg/hzbook.html`

This site also includes Matlab code for several of the algorithms, and lists the errata of earlier printings.

I am never forget the day my first book is published. Every chapter I stole from somewhere else. Index I copy from old Vladivostok telephone directory. This book, this book was sensational!

Excerpts from "Nikolai Ivanovich Lobachevsky" by Tom Lehrer.

1

Introduction – a Tour of Multiple View Geometry

This chapter is an introduction to the principal ideas covered in this book. It gives an *informal* treatment of these topics. Precise, unambiguous definitions, careful algebra, and the description of well honed estimation algorithms is postponed until chapter 2 and the following chapters in the book. Throughout this introduction we will generally not give specific forward pointers to these later chapters. The material referred to can be located by use of the index or table of contents.

1.1 Introduction – the ubiquitous projective geometry

We are all familiar with projective transformations.When we look at a picture, we see squares that are not squares, or circles that are not circles. The transformation that maps these planar objects onto the picture is an example of a projective transformation.

So what properties of geometry are preserved by projective transformations? Certainly, shape is not, since a circle may appear as an ellipse. Neither are lengths since two perpendicular radii of a circle are stretched by different amounts by the projective transformation. Angles, distance, ratios of distances – none of these are preserved, and it may appear that very little geometry is preserved by a projective transformation. However, a property that is preserved is that of straightness. It turns out that this is the most general requirement on the mapping, and we may define a projective transformation of a plane as any mapping of the points on the plane that preserves straight lines.

To see why we will require projective geometry we start from the familiar Euclidean geometry. This is the geometry that describes angles and shapes of objects. Euclidean geometry is troublesome in one major respect – we need to keep making an exception to reason about some of the basic concepts of the geometry – such as intersection of lines. Two lines (we are thinking here of 2-dimensional geometry) almost always meet in a point, but there are some pairs of lines that do not do so – those that we call parallel. A common linguistic device for getting around this is to say that parallel lines meet "at infinity". However this is not altogether convincing, and conflicts with another dictum, that infinity does not exist, and is only a convenient fiction. We can get around this by enhancing the Euclidean plane by the addition of these points at infinity where parallel lines meet, and resolving the difficulty with infinity by calling them "ideal points."

By adding these points at infinity, the familiar Euclidean space is transformed into a new type of geometric object, projective space. This is a very useful way of thinking, since we are familiar with the properties of Euclidean space, involving concepts such as distances, angles, points, lines and incidence. There is nothing very mysterious about projective space – it is just an extension of Euclidean space in which two lines always meet in a point, though sometimes at mysterious points at infinity.

Coordinates. A point in Euclidean 2-space is represented by an ordered pair of real numbers, (x, y). We may add an extra coordinate to this pair, giving a triple $(x, y, 1)$, that we declare to represent the same point. This seems harmless enough, since we can go back and forward from one representation of the point to the other, simply by adding or removing the last coordinate. We now take the important conceptual step of asking why the last coordinate needs to be 1 – after all, the others two coordinates are not so constrained. What about a coordinate triple $(x, y, 2)$. It is here that we make a definition and say that $(x, y, 1)$ and $(2x, 2y, 2)$ represent the same point, and furthermore, (kx, ky, k) represents the same point as well, for any non-zero value k. Formally, points are represented by *equivalence classes* of coordinate triples, where two triples are equivalent when they differ by a common multiple. These are called the *homogeneous coordinates* of the point. Given a coordinate triple (kx, ky, k), we can get the original coordinates back by dividing by k to get (x, y).

The reader will observe that although $(x, y, 1)$ represents the same point as the coordinate pair (x, y), there is no point that corresponds to the triple $(x, y, 0)$. If we try to divide by the last coordinate, we get the point $(x/0, y/0)$ which is infinite. This is how the points at infinity arise then. They are the points represented by homogeneous coordinates in which the last coordinate is zero.

Once we have seen how to do this for 2-dimensional Euclidean space, extending it to a projective space by representing points as homogeneous vectors, it is clear that we can do the same thing in any dimension. The Euclidean space $\mathbb{R}^n$ can be extended to a projective space $\mathbb{P}^n$ by representing points as homogeneous vectors. It turns out that the points at infinity in the two-dimensional projective space form a line, usually called the *line at infinity*. In three-dimensions they form the *plane at infinity*.

Homogeneity. In classical Euclidean geometry all points are the same. There is no distinguished point. The whole of the space is homogeneous. When coordinates are added, one point is seemingly picked out as the origin. However, it is important to realize that this is just an accident of the particular coordinate frame chosen. We could just as well find a different way of coordinatizing the plane in which a different point is considered to be the origin. In fact, we can consider a change of coordinates for the Euclidean space in which the axes are shifted and rotated to a different position. We may think of this in another way as the space itself translating and rotating to a different position. The resulting operation is known as a Euclidean transform.

A more general type of transformation is that of applying a linear transformation to $\mathbb{R}^n$, followed by a Euclidean transformation moving the origin of the space. We may think of this as the space moving, rotating and finally *stretching* linearly possibly by different ratios in different directions. The resulting transformation is known as an *affine* transformation.

The result of either a Euclidean or an affine transformation is that points at infinity remain at infinity. Such points are in some way preserved, at least as a set, by such transformations. They are in some way distinguished, or special in the context of Euclidean or *affine* geometry.

From the point of view of projective geometry, points at infinity are not any different from other points. Just as Euclidean space is uniform, so is projective space. The property that points at infinity have final coordinate zero in a homogeneous coordinate representation is nothing other than an accident of the choice of coordinate frame. By analogy with Euclidean or affine transformations, we may define a *projective transformation* of projective space. A linear transformation of Euclidean space $\mathbb{R}^n$ is represented by matrix multiplication applied to the coordinates of the point. In just the same way a projective transformation of projective space $\mathbb{P}^n$ is a mapping of the homogeneous coordinates representing a point (an $(n+1)$-vector), in which the coordinate vector is multiplied by a non-singular matrix. Under such a mapping, points at infinity (with final coordinate zero) are mapped to arbitrary other points. The points at infinity are not preserved. Thus, a projective transformation of projective space $\mathbb{P}^n$ is represented by a linear transformation of homogeneous coordinates

$$\mathbf{X}' = \mathtt{H}_{(n+1)\times(n+1)}\mathbf{X}.$$

In computer vision problems, projective space is used as a convenient way of representing the real 3D world, by extending it to the 3-dimensional (3D) projective space. Similarly images, usually formed by projecting the world onto a 2-dimensional representation, are for convenience extended to be thought of as lying in the 2-dimensional projective space. In reality, the real world, and images of it do not contain points at infinity, and we need to keep our finger on which are the fictitious points, namely the line at infinity in the image and the plane at infinity in the world. For this reason, although we usually work with the projective spaces, we are aware that the line and plane at infinity are in some way special. This goes against the spirit of pure projective geometry, but makes it useful for our practical problems. Generally we try to have it both ways by treating all points in projective space as equals when it suits us, and singling out the line at infinity in space or the plane at infinity in the image when that becomes necessary.

1.1.1 Affine and Euclidean Geometry

We have seen that projective space can be obtained from Euclidean space by adding a line (or plane) at infinity. We now consider the reverse process of going backwards. This discussion is mainly concerned with two and three-dimensional projective space.

Affine geometry. We will take the point of view that the projective space is initially homogeneous, with no particular coordinate frame being preferred. In such a space, there is no concept of parallelism of lines, since parallel lines (or planes in the three-dimensional case) are ones that meet at infinity. However, in projective space, there is no concept of which points are at infinity – all points are created equal. We say that parallelism is not a concept of projective geometry. It is simply meaningless to talk about it.

In order for such a concept to make sense, we need to pick out some particular line, and decide that this is the line at infinity. This results in a situation where although all points are created equal, some are more equal than others. Thus, start with a blank sheet of paper, and imagine that it extends to infinity and forms a projective space $\mathbb{P}^2$. What we see is just a small part of the space, that looks a lot like a piece of the ordinary Euclidean plane. Now, let us draw a straight line on the paper, and declare that this is the line at infinity. Next, we draw two other lines that intersect at this distinguished line. Since they meet at the "line at infinity" we define them as being parallel. The situation is similar to what one sees by looking at an infinite plane. Think of a photograph taken in a very flat region of the earth. The points at infinity in the plane show up in the image as the horizon line. Lines, such as railway tracks show up in the image as lines meeting at the horizon. Points in the image lying above the horizon (the image of the sky) apparently do not correspond to points on the world plane. However, if we think of extending the corresponding ray backwards behind the camera, it will meet the plane at a point behind the camera. Thus there is a one-to-one relationship between points in the image and points in the world plane. The points at infinity in the world plane correspond to a real horizon line in the image, and parallel lines in the world correspond to lines meeting at the horizon. From our point of view, the world plane and its image are just alternative ways of viewing the geometry of a projective plane, plus a distinguished line. The geometry of the projective plane and a distinguished line is known as *affine geometry* and any projective transformation that maps the distinguished line in one space to the distinguished line of the other space is known as an *affine transformation.*

By identifying a special line as the "line at infinity" we are able to define parallelism of straight lines in the plane. However, certain other concepts make sense as well, as soon as we can define parallelism. For instance, we may define equalities of intervals between two points on parallel lines. For instance, if A, B, C and D are points, and the lines AB and CD are parallel, then we define the two intervals AB and CD to have *equal length* if the lines AC and BD are also parallel. Similarly, two intervals on the same line are equal if there exists another interval on a parallel line that is equal to both.

Euclidean geometry. By distinguishing a special line in a projective plane, we gain the concept of parallelism and with it *affine geometry.* Affine geometry is seen as specialization of projective geometry, in which we single out a particular line (or plane – according to the dimension) and call it the line at infinity.

Next, we turn to Euclidean geometry and show that by singling out some special feature of the line or plane at infinity affine geometry becomes Euclidean geometry. In doing so, we introduce one of the most important concepts of this book, the *absolute conic*.

We begin by considering two-dimensional geometry, and start with circles. Note that a circle is not a concept of affine geometry, since arbitrary stretching of the plane, which preserves the line at infinity, turns the circle into an ellipse. Thus, affine geometry does not distinguish between circles and ellipses.

In Euclidean geometry however, they are distinct, and have an important difference. Algebraically, an ellipse is described by a second-degree equation. It is therefore expected, and true that two ellipses will most generally intersect in four points. However, it is geometrically evident that two distinct circles can not intersect in more than two points. Algebraically, we are intersecting two second-degree curves here, or equivalently solving two quadratic equations. We should expect to get four solutions. The question is, what is special about circles that they only intersect in two points.

The answer to this question is of course that there exist two other solutions, the two circles meeting in two other *complex* points. We do not have to look very far to find these two points.

The equation for a circle in homogeneous coordinates (x, y, w) is of the form

$$(x - aw)^2 + (y - bw)^2 = r^2w^2$$

This represents the circle with centre represented in homogeneous coordinates as $(x_0, y_0, w_0)^\mathsf{T} = (a, b, 1)^\mathsf{T}$. It is quickly verified that the points $(x, y, w)^\mathsf{T} = (1, \pm i, 0)^\mathsf{T}$ lie on every such circle. To repeat this interesting fact, every circle passes through the points $(1, \pm i, 0)^\mathsf{T}$, and therefore they lie in the intersection of any two circles. Since their final coordinate is zero, these two points lie on the line at infinity. For obvious reasons, they are called the *circular points* of the plane. Note that although the two circular points are complex, they satisfy a pair of real equations: $x^2 + y^2 = 0$; $w = 0$.

This observation gives the clue of how we may define Euclidean geometry. Euclidean geometry arises from projective geometry by singling out first a line at infinity and subsequently, two points called *circular points* lying on this line. Of course the circular points are complex points, but for the most part we do not worry too much about this. Now, we may define a circle as being any conic (a curve defined by a second-degree equation) that passes through the two circular points. Note that in the standard Euclidean coordinate system, the circular points have the coordinates $(1, \pm i, 0)^\mathsf{T}$. In assigning a Euclidean structure to a projective plane, however, we may designate any line and any two (complex) points on that line as being the line at infinity and the circular points.

As an example of applying this viewpoint, we note that a general conic may be found passing through five arbitrary points in the plane, as may be seen by counting the number of coefficients of a general quadratic equation $ax^2 + by^2 + \ldots + fw^2 = 0$. A circle on the other hand is defined by only three points. Another way of looking at this is that it is a conic passing through two special points, the circular points, as well as three other points, and hence as any other conic, it requires five points to specify it uniquely.

It should not be a surprise that as a result of singling out two circular points one obtains the whole of the familiar Euclidean geometry. In particular, concepts such as angle and length ratios may be defined in terms of the circular points. However, these concepts are most easily defined in terms of some coordinate system for the Euclidean plane, as will be seen in later chapters.

3D Euclidean geometry. We saw how the Euclidean plane is defined in terms of the projective plane by specifying a line at infinity and a pair of circular points. The same idea may be applied to 3D geometry. As in the two-dimensional case, one may look carefully at spheres, and how they intersect. Two spheres intersect in a circle, and not in a general fourth-degree curve, as the algebra suggests, and as two general ellipsoids (or other *quadric* surfaces) do. This line of thought leads to the discovery that in homogeneous coordinates $(\mathrm{X}, \mathrm{Y}, \mathrm{Z}, \mathrm{T})^\mathsf{T}$ all spheres intersect the plane at infinity in a curve with the equations: $\mathrm{X}^2 + \mathrm{Y}^2 + \mathrm{Z}^2 = 0$; $\mathrm{T} = 0$. This is a second-degree curve (a conic) lying on the plane at infinity, and consisting only of complex points. It is known as the *absolute conic* and is one of the key geometric entities in this book, most particularly because of its connection to camera calibration, as will be seen later.

The absolute conic is defined by the above equations only in the Euclidean coordinate system. In general we may consider 3D Euclidean space to be derived from projective space by singling out a particular plane as the plane at infinity and specifying a particular conic lying in this plane to be the absolute conic. These entities may have quite general descriptions in terms of a coordinate system for the projective space.

We will not here go into details of how the absolute conic determines the complete Euclidean 3D geometry. A single example will serve. Perpendicularity of lines in space is not a valid concept in affine geometry, but belongs to Euclidean geometry. The perpendicularity of lines may be defined in terms of the absolute conic, as follows. By extending the lines until they meet the plane at infinity, we obtain two points called the directions of the two lines. Perpendicularity of the lines is defined in terms of the relationship of the two directions to the absolute conic. The lines are perpendicular if the two directions are conjugate points with respect to the absolute conic (see figure 3.8(*p*83)). The geometry and algebraic representation of conjugate points are defined in section 2.8.1(*p*58). Briefly, if the absolute conic is represented by a 3×3 symmetric matrix Ω_∞, and the directions are the points $\mathbf{d}_1$ and $\mathbf{d}_2$, then they are conjugate with respect to Ω_∞ if $\mathbf{d}_1^\mathsf{T} \Omega_\infty \mathbf{d}_2 = 0$. More generally, angles may be defined in terms of the absolute conic in any arbitrary coordinate system, as expressed by (3.23–*p*82).

1.2 Camera projections

One of the principal topics of this book is the process of image formation, namely the formation of a two-dimensional representation of a three-dimensional world, and what we may deduce about the 3D structure of what appears in the images.

The drop from three-dimensional world to a two-dimensional image is a projection process in which we lose one dimension. The usual way of modelling this process is by *central projection* in which a ray from a point in space is drawn from a 3D world point through a fixed point in space, the *centre of projection*. This ray will intersect a specific plane in space chosen as the *image plane*. The intersection of the ray with the image plane represents the image of the point. If the 3D structure lies on a plane then there is no drop in dimension.

This model is in accord with a simple model of a camera, in which a ray of light from a point in the world passes through the lens of a camera and impinges on a film or digital device, producing an image of the point. Ignoring such effects as focus and lens thickness, a reasonable approximation is that all the rays pass through a single point, the centre of the lens.

In applying projective geometry to the imaging process, it is customary to model the world as a 3D projective space, equal to $\mathbb{R}^3$ along with points at infinity. Similarly the model for the image is the 2D projective plane $\mathbb{P}^2$. Central projection is simply a map from $\mathbb{P}^3$ to $\mathbb{P}^2$. If we consider points in $\mathbb{P}^3$ written in terms of homogeneous coordinates $(\mathtt{X}, \mathtt{Y}, \mathtt{Z}, \mathtt{T})^\mathsf{T}$ and let the centre of projection be the origin $(0, 0, 0, 1)^\mathsf{T}$, then we see that the set of all points $(\mathtt{X}, \mathtt{Y}, \mathtt{Z}, \mathtt{T})^\mathsf{T}$ for fixed $\mathtt{X}$, $\mathtt{Y}$ and $\mathtt{Z}$, but varying $\mathtt{T}$ form a single ray passing through the point centre of projection, and hence all mapping to the same point. Thus, the final coordinate of $(\mathtt{X}, \mathtt{Y}, \mathtt{Z}, \mathtt{T})$ is irrelevant to where the point is imaged. In fact, the image point is the point in $\mathbb{P}^2$ with homogeneous coordinates $(\mathtt{X}, \mathtt{Y}, \mathtt{Z})^\mathsf{T}$. Thus, the mapping may be represented by a mapping of 3D homogeneous coordinates, represented by a 3×4 matrix $\mathtt{P}$ with the block structure $\mathtt{P} = [\mathtt{I}_{3\times 3} | \mathbf{0}_3]$, where $\mathtt{I}_{3\times 3}$ is the 3×3 identity matrix and $\mathbf{0}_3$ a zero 3-vector. Making allowance for a different centre of projection, and a different projective coordinate frame in the image, it turns out that the most general imaging projection is represented by an arbitrary 3×4 matrix of rank 3, acting on the homogeneous coordinates of the point in $\mathbb{P}^3$ mapping it to the imaged point in $\mathbb{P}^2$. This matrix $\mathtt{P}$ is known as the camera matrix.

In summary, the action of a projective camera on a point in space may be expressed in terms of a linear mapping of homogeneous coordinates as

$$\begin{pmatrix} x \\ y \\ w \end{pmatrix} = \mathtt{P}_{3\times 4} \begin{pmatrix} \mathtt{X} \\ \mathtt{Y} \\ \mathtt{Z} \\ \mathtt{T} \end{pmatrix}$$

Furthermore, if all the points lie on a plane (we may choose this as the plane $\mathtt{Z} = 0$) then the linear mapping reduces to

$$\begin{pmatrix} x \\ y \\ w \end{pmatrix} = \mathtt{H}_{3\times 3} \begin{pmatrix} \mathtt{X} \\ \mathtt{Y} \\ \mathtt{T} \end{pmatrix}$$

which is a projective transformation.

Cameras as points. In a central projection, points in $\mathbb{P}^3$ are mapped to points in $\mathbb{P}^2$, all points in a ray passing through the centre of projection projecting to the same point in an image. For the purposes of image projection, it is possible to consider all points along such a ray as being equal. We can go one step further, and think of the ray through the projection centre as representing the image point. Thus, the set of all image points is the same as the set of rays through the camera centre. If we represent

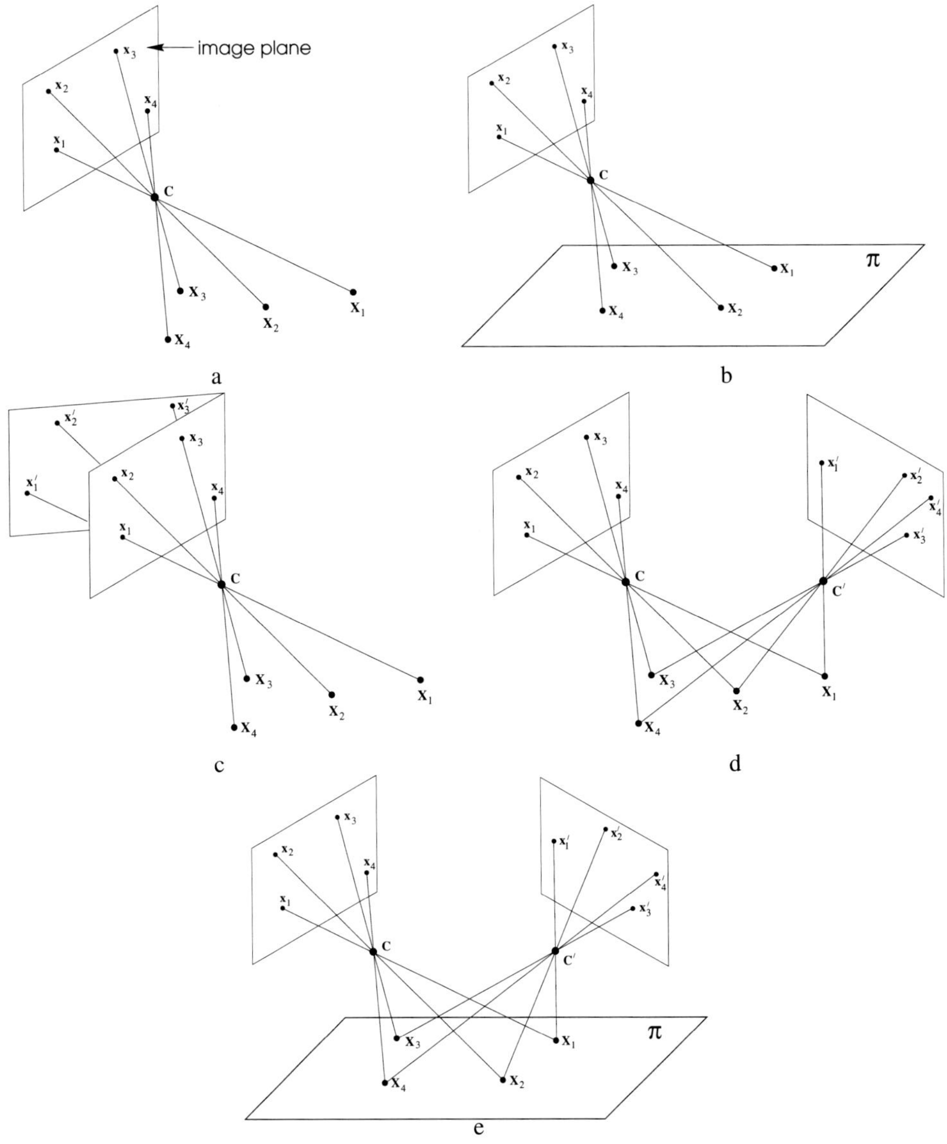

Fig. 1.1. **The camera centre is the essence.** *(a) Image formation: the image points $\mathbf{x}_i$ are the intersection of a plane with rays from the space points $\mathbf{X}_i$ through the camera centre $\mathbf{C}$. (b) If the space points are coplanar then there is a projective transformation between the world and image planes, $\mathbf{x}_i = \mathtt{H}_{3\times3}\mathbf{X}_i$. (c) All images with the same camera centre are related by a projective transformation, $\mathbf{x}'_i = \mathtt{H}'_{3\times3}\mathbf{x}_i$. Compare (b) and (c) – in both cases planes are mapped to one another by rays through a centre. In (b) the mapping is between a scene and image plane, in (c) between two image planes. (d) If the camera centre moves, then the images are in general not related by a projective transformation, unless (e) all the space points are coplanar.*

the ray from $(0, 0, 0, 1)^\mathsf{T}$ through the point $(\mathrm{X}, \mathrm{Y}, \mathrm{Z}, \mathrm{T})^\mathsf{T}$ by its first three coordinates $(\mathrm{X}, \mathrm{Y}, \mathrm{Z})^\mathsf{T}$, it is easily seen that for any constant k, the ray $k(\mathrm{X}, \mathrm{Y}, \mathrm{Z})^\mathsf{T}$ represents the same ray. Thus the rays themselves are represented by homogeneous coordinates. In fact they make up a 2-dimensional space of rays. The set of rays themselves may be thought of as a representation of the image space $\mathbb{P}^2$. In this representation of the image, all that is important is the camera centre, for this alone determines the set of rays forming the image. Different camera matrices representing the image formation from the same centre of projection reflect only different coordinate frames for the set of rays forming the image. Thus two images taken from the same point in space are projectively equivalent. It is only when we start to measure points in an image, that a particular coordinate frame for the image needs to be specified. Only then does it become necessary to specify a particular camera matrix. In short, modulo field-of-view which we ignore for now, all images acquired with the same camera centre are equivalent – they can be mapped onto each other by a projective transformation without any information about the 3D points or position of the camera centre. These issues are illustrated in figure 1.1.

Calibrated cameras. To understand fully the Euclidean relationship between the image and the world, it is necessary to express their relative Euclidean geometry. As we have seen, the Euclidean geometry of the 3D world is determined by specifying a particular plane in $\mathbb{P}^3$ as being the plane at infinity, and a specific conic Ω in that plane as being the absolute conic. For a camera not located on the plane at infinity, the plane at infinity in the world maps one-to-one onto the image plane. This is because any point in the image defines a ray in space that meets the plane at infinity in a single point. Thus, the plane at infinity in the world does not tell us anything new about the image. The absolute conic, however being a conic in the plane at infinity must project to a conic in the image. The resulting image curve is called the Image of the Absolute Conic, or IAC. If the location of the IAC is known in an image, then we say that the camera is *calibrated.*

In a calibrated camera, it is possible to determine the angle between the two rays back-projected from two points in the image. We have seen that the angle between two lines in space is determined by where they meet the plane at infinity, relative to the absolute conic. In a calibrated camera, the plane at infinity and the absolute conic Ω_∞ are projected one-to-one onto the image plane and the IAC, denoted $\boldsymbol{\omega}$. The projective relationship between the two image points and $\boldsymbol{\omega}$ is exactly equal to the relationship between the intersections of the back-projected rays with the plane at infinity, and Ω_∞. Consequently, knowing the IAC, one can measure the angle between rays by direct measurements in the image. Thus, for a calibrated camera, one can measure angles between rays, compute the field of view represented by an image patch or determine whether an ellipse in the image back-projects to a circular cone. Later on, we will see that it helps us to determine the *Euclidean structure* of a reconstructed scene.

Example 1.1. 3D reconstructions from paintings
Using techniques of projective geometry, it is possible in many instances to reconstruct scenes from a single image. This cannot be done without some assumptions being made about the imaged scene. Typical techniques involve the analysis of features such as parallel lines and vanishing points to determine the affine structure of the scene, for

Fig. 1.2. **Single view reconstruction.** *(a) Original painting – St. Jerome in his study, 1630, Hendrick van Steenwijck (1580-1649), Joseph R. Ritman Private Collection, Amsterdam, The Netherlands. (b) (c)(d) Views of the 3D model created from the painting. Figures courtesy of Antonio Criminisi.*

example by determining the line at infinity for observed planes in the image. Knowledge (or assumptions) about angles observed in the scene, most particularly orthogonal lines or planes, can be used to upgrade the affine reconstruction to Euclidean.

It is not yet possible for such techniques to be fully automatic. However, projective geometric knowledge may be built into a system that allows user-guided single-view reconstruction of the scene.

Such techniques have been used to reconstruct 3D texture mapped graphical models derived from old-master paintings. Starting in the Renaissance, paintings with extremely accurate perspective were produced. In figure 1.2 a reconstruction carried out from such a painting is shown. △

1.3 Reconstruction from more than one view

We now turn to one of the major topics in the book – that of reconstructing a scene from several images. The simplest case is that of two images, which we will consider first. As a mathematical abstraction, we restrict the discussion to "scenes" consisting of points only.

The usual input to many of the algorithms given in this book is a set of point correspondences. In the two-view case, therefore, we consider a set of correspondences

$\mathbf{x}_i \leftrightarrow \mathbf{x}'_i$ in two images. It is assumed that there exist some camera matrices, $\mathtt{P}$ and $\mathtt{P}'$ and a set of 3D points $\mathbf{X}_i$ that give rise to these image correspondences in the sense that $\mathtt{P}\mathbf{X}_i = \mathbf{x}_i$ and $\mathtt{P}'\mathbf{X}_i = \mathbf{x}'_i$. Thus, the point $\mathbf{X}_i$ projects to the two given data points. However, neither the cameras (represented by projection matrices $\mathtt{P}$ and $\mathtt{P}'$), nor the points $\mathbf{X}_i$ are known. It is our task to determine them.

It is clear from the outset that it is impossible to determine the positions of the points uniquely. This is a general ambiguity that holds however many images we are given, and even if we have more than just point correspondence data. For instance, given several images of a cube, it is impossible to tell its absolute position (is it located in a night-club in Addis Ababa, or the British Museum), its orientation (which face is facing north) or its scale. We express this by saying that the reconstruction is possible at best up to a similarity transformation of the world. However, it turns out that unless something is known about the calibration of the two cameras, the ambiguity in the reconstruction is expressed by a more general class of transformations – projective transformations.

This ambiguity arises because it is possible to apply a projective transformation (represented by a 4×4 matrix $\mathtt{H}$) to each point $\mathbf{X}_i$, and on the right of each camera matrix $\mathtt{P}_j$, without changing the projected image points, thus:

$$\mathtt{P}_j\mathbf{X}_i = (\mathtt{P}_j\mathtt{H}^{-1})(\mathtt{H}\mathbf{X}_i). \tag{1.1}$$

There is no compelling reason to choose one set of points and camera matrices over the other. The choice of $\mathtt{H}$ is essentially arbitrary, and we say that the reconstruction has a projective ambiguity, or is a *projective reconstruction*.

However, the good news is that this is the worst that can happen. It is possible to reconstruct a set of points from two views, up to an unavoidable projective ambiguity. Well, to be able to say this, we need to make a few qualifications; there must be sufficiently many points, at least seven, and they must not lie in one of various well-defined *critical configurations*.

The basic tool in the reconstruction of point sets from two views is the *fundamental matrix*, which represents the constraint obeyed by image points $\mathbf{x}$ and $\mathbf{x}'$ if they are to be images of the same 3D point. This constraint arises from the coplanarity of the camera centres of the two views, the images points and the space point. Given the fundamental matrix $\mathtt{F}$, a pair of matching points $\mathbf{x}_i \leftrightarrow \mathbf{x}'_i$ must satisfy

$$\mathbf{x}'^{\mathsf{T}}_i \mathtt{F} \mathbf{x}_i = 0$$

where $\mathtt{F}$ is a 3×3 matrix of rank 2. These equations are linear in the entries of the matrix $\mathtt{F}$, which means that if $\mathtt{F}$ is unknown, then it can be computed from a set of point correspondences.

A pair of camera matrices $\mathtt{P}$ and $\mathtt{P}'$ uniquely determine a fundamental matrix $\mathtt{F}$, and conversely, the fundamental matrix determines the pair of camera matrices, up to a 3D projective ambiguity. Thus, the fundamental matrix encapsulates the complete projective geometry of the pair of cameras, and is unchanged by projective transformation of 3D.

The fundamental-matrix method for reconstructing the scene is very simple, consisting of the following steps:

(i) Given several point correspondences $\mathbf{x}_i \leftrightarrow \mathbf{x}'_i$ across two views, form linear equations in the entries of $\mathtt{F}$ based on the coplanarity equations $\mathbf{x}'^{\mathsf{T}}_i \mathtt{F} \mathbf{x}_i = 0$.
(ii) Find $\mathtt{F}$ as the solution to a set of linear equations.
(iii) Compute a pair of camera matrices from $\mathtt{F}$ according to the simple formula given in section 9.5(*p*253).
(iv) Given the two cameras $(\mathtt{P}, \mathtt{P}')$ and the corresponding image point pairs $\mathbf{x}_i \leftrightarrow \mathbf{x}'_i$, find the 3D point $\mathbf{X}_i$ that projects to the given image points. Solving for $\mathbf{X}$ in this way is known as *triangulation*.

The algorithm given here is an outline only, and each part of it is examined in detail in this book. The algorithm should not be implemented directly from this brief description.

1.4 Three-view geometry

In the last section it was discussed how reconstruction of a set of points, and the relative placement of the cameras, is possible from two views of a set of points. The reconstruction is possible only up to a projective transformation of space, and the corresponding adjustment to the camera matrices.

In this section, we consider the case of three views. Whereas for two views, the basic algebraic entity is the fundamental matrix, for three views this role is played by the trifocal tensor. The trifocal tensor is a $3 \times 3 \times 3$ array of numbers that relate the coordinates of corresponding points or lines in three views. Just as the fundamental matrix is determined by the two camera matrices, and determines them up to projective transformation, so in three views, the trifocal tensor is determined by the three camera matrices, and in turn determines them, again up to projective transformation. Thus, the trifocal tensor encapsulates the relative projective geometry of the three cameras.

For reasons that will be explained in chapter 15 it is usual to write some of the indices of a tensor as lower and some as upper indices. These are referred to as the covariant and contravariant indices. The trifocal tensor is of the form $\mathcal{T}_i^{jk}$, having two upper and one lower index.

The most basic relationship between image entities in three views concerns a correspondence between two lines and a point. We consider a correspondence $\mathbf{x} \leftrightarrow \mathbf{l}' \leftrightarrow \mathbf{l}''$ between a point $\mathbf{x}$ in one image and two lines $\mathbf{l}'$ and $\mathbf{l}''$ in the other two images. This relationship means that there is a point $\mathbf{X}$ in space that maps to $\mathbf{x}$ in the first image, and to points $\mathbf{x}'$ and $\mathbf{x}''$ lying on the lines $\mathbf{l}'$ and $\mathbf{l}''$ in the other two images. The coordinates of these three images are then related via the trifocal tensor relationship:

$$\sum_{ijk} x^i l'_j l''_k \mathcal{T}_i^{jk} = 0. \tag{1.2}$$

This relationship gives a single linear relationship between the elements of the tensor. With sufficiently many such correspondences, it is possible to solve linearly for the elements of the tensor. Fortunately, one can obtain more equations from a point correspondence $\mathbf{x} \leftrightarrow \mathbf{x}' \leftrightarrow \mathbf{x}''$. In fact, in this situation, one can choose any lines $\mathbf{l}'$ and $\mathbf{l}''$ passing through the points $\mathbf{x}'$ and $\mathbf{x}''$ and generate a relation of the sort (1.2). Since it is possible to choose two independent lines passing through $\mathbf{x}'$, and two others passing through $\mathbf{x}''$, one can obtain four independent equations in this way. A total of seven point correspondences are sufficient to compute the trifocal tensor linearly in this way. It can be computed from a minimum of six point correspondences using a non-linear method.

The 27 elements of the tensor are not independent, however, but are related by a set of so called *internal constraints*. These constraints are quite complicated, but tensors satisfying the constraints can be computed in various ways, for instance by using the 6 point non-linear method. The fundamental matrix (which is a 2-view tensor) also satisfies an internal constraint but a relatively simple one: the elements obey $\det \mathtt{F} = 0$.

As with the fundamental matrix, once the trifocal tensor is known, it is possible to extract the three camera matrices from it, and thereby obtain a reconstruction of the scene points and lines. As ever, this reconstruction is unique only up to a 3D projective transformation; it is a projective reconstruction.

Thus, we are able to generalize the method for two views to three views. There are several advantages to using such a three-view method for reconstruction.

(i) It is possible to use a mixture of line and point correspondences to compute the projective reconstruction. With two views, only point correspondences can be used.
(ii) Using three views gives greater stability to the reconstruction, and avoids unstable configurations that may occur using only two views for the reconstruction.

1.5 Four view geometry and n-view reconstruction

It is possible to go one more step with tensor-based methods and define a quadrifocal tensor relating entities visible in four views. This method is seldom used, however, because of the relative difficulty of computing a quadrifocal tensor that obey its internal constraints. Nevertheless, it does provide a non-iterative method for computing a projective reconstruction based on four views. The tensor method does not extend to more than four views, however, and so reconstruction from more than four views becomes more difficult.

Many methods have been considered for reconstruction from several views, and we consider a few of these in the book. One way to proceed is to reconstruct the scene bit by bit, using three-view or two-view techniques. Such a method may be applied to any image sequence, and with care in selecting the right triples to use, it will generally succeed.

There are methods that can be used in specific circumstances. The task of reconstruction becomes easier if we are able to apply a simpler camera model, known as the *affine camera*. This camera model is a fair approximation to perspective projection whenever the distance to the scene is large compared with the difference in depth between the back and front of the scene. If a set of points are visible in all of a set of n views involving an affine camera, then a well-known algorithm, the *factorization algorithm*, can be used to compute both the structure of the scene, and the specific camera models in one step using the Singular Value Decomposition. This algorithm is very reliable and simple to implement. Its main difficulties are the use of the affine camera model, rather than a full projective model, and the requirement that all the points be visible in all views.

This method has been extended to projective cameras in a method known as projective factorization. Although this method is generally satisfactory, it can not be proven to converge to the correct solution in all cases. Besides, it also requires all points to be visible in all images.

Other methods for n-view reconstruction involve various assumptions, such as knowledge of four coplanar points in the world visible in all views, or six or seven points that are visible in all images in the sequence. Methods that apply to specific motion sequences, such as linear motion, planar motion or single axis (turntable) motion have also been developed.

The dominant methodology for the general reconstruction problem is *bundle adjustment*. This is an iterative method, in which one attempts to fit a non-linear model to the measured data (the point correspondences). The advantage of bundle-adjustment is that it is a very general method that may be applied to a wide range of reconstruction and optimization problems. It may be implemented in such a way that the discovered solution is the Maximum Likelihood solution to the problem, that is a solution that is in some sense optimal in terms of a model for the inaccuracies of image measurements.

Unfortunately, bundle adjustment is an iterative process, which can not be guaranteed to converge to the optimal solution from an arbitrary starting point. Much research in reconstruction methods seeks easily computable non-optimal solutions that can be used as a starting point for bundle adjustment. An initialization step followed by bundle adjustment is the generally preferred technique for reconstruction. A common impression is that bundle-adjustment is necessarily a slow technique. The truth is that it is quite efficient when implemented carefully. A lengthy appendix in this book deals with efficient methods of bundle adjustment.

Using n-view reconstruction techniques, it is possible to carry out reconstructions automatically from quite long sequences of images. An example is given in figure 1.3, showing a reconstruction from 700 frames.

1.6 Transfer

We have discussed 3D reconstruction from a set of images. Another useful application of projective geometry is that of *transfer*: given the position of a point in one (or more) image(s), determine where it will appear in all other images of the set. To do this, we must first establish the relationship between the cameras using (for instance) a set of auxiliary point correspondences. Conceptually transfer is straightforward given that a reconstruction is possible. For instance, suppose the point is identified in two views (at $\mathbf{x}$ and $\mathbf{x}'$) and we wish to know its position $\mathbf{x}''$ in a third, then this may be computed by the following steps:

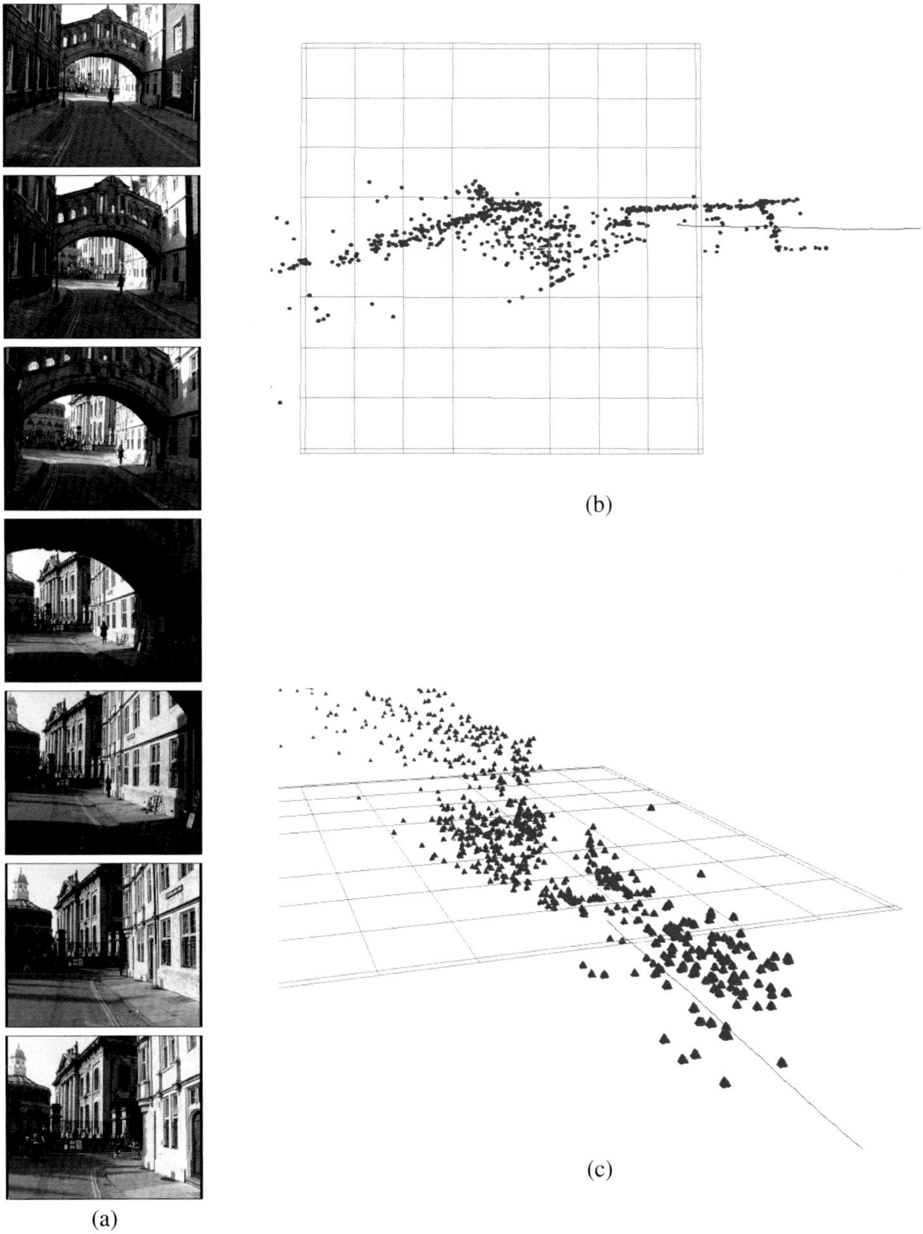

Fig. 1.3. **Reconstruction.** *(a) Seven frames of a 700 frame sequence acquired by a hand held camera whilst walking down a street in Oxford. (b)(c) Two views of the reconstructed point cloud and camera path (the red curve). Figures courtesy of David Capel and 2d3 (*`www.2d3.com`*).*

Fig. 1.4. **Projective ambiguity:** *Reconstructions of a mug (shown with the true shape in the centre) under 3D projective transformations in the* Z *direction. Five examples of the cup with different degrees of projective distortion are shown. The shapes are quite different from the original.*

(i) Compute the camera matrices of the three views $\mathtt{P}, \mathtt{P}', \mathtt{P}''$ from other point correspondences $\mathbf{x}_i \leftrightarrow \mathbf{x}'_i \leftrightarrow \mathbf{x}''_i$.

(ii) Triangulate the 3D point $\mathbf{X}$ from $\mathbf{x}$ and $\mathbf{x}'$ using $\mathtt{P}$ and $\mathtt{P}'$.

(iii) Project the 3D point into the third view as $\mathbf{x}'' = \mathtt{P}''\mathbf{X}$.

This procedure only requires projective information. An alternative procedure is to use the multi-view tensors (the fundamental matrix and trifocal tensor) to transfer the point directly without an explicit 3D reconstruction. Both methods have their advantages.

Suppose the camera rotates about its centre or that all the scene points of interest lie on a plane. Then the appropriate multiple view relations are the planar projective transformations between the images. In this case, a point seen in just one image can be transferred to any other image.

1.7 Euclidean reconstruction

So far we have considered the reconstruction of a scene, or transfer, for images taken with a set of uncalibrated cameras. For such cameras, important parameters such as the focal length, the geometric centre of the image (the principal point) and possibly the aspect ratio of the pixels in the image are unknown. If a complete calibration of each of the cameras is known then it is possible to remove some of the ambiguity of the reconstructed scene.

So far, we have discussed projective reconstruction, which is all that is possible without knowing something about the calibration of the cameras or the scene. Projective reconstruction is insufficient for many purposes, such as application to computer graphics, since it involves distortions of the model that appear strange to a human used to viewing a Euclidean world. For instance, the distortions that projective transformations induce in a simple object are shown in figure 1.4. Using the technique of projective reconstruction, there is no way to choose between any of the possible shapes of the mug in figure 1.4, and a projective reconstruction algorithm is as likely to come up with any one of the reconstructions shown there as any other. Even more severely distorted models may arise from projective reconstruction.

In order to obtain a reconstruction of the model in which objects have their correct (Euclidean) shape, it is necessary to determine the calibration of the cameras. It is easy to see that this is sufficient to determine the Euclidean structure of the scene. As we have seen, determining the Euclidean structure of the world is equivalent to specifying the plane at infinity and the absolute conic. In fact, since the absolute conic lies in a plane, the plane at infinity, it is enough to find the absolute conic in space. Now, suppose that we have computed a projective reconstruction of the world, using calibrated cameras. By definition, this means that the IAC is known in each of the images; let it be denoted by $\boldsymbol{\omega}_i$ in the i-th image. The back-projection of each $\boldsymbol{\omega}_i$ is a cone in space, and the absolute conic must lie in the intersection of all the cones. Two cones in general intersect in a fourth-degree curve, but given that they must intersect in a conic, this curve must split into two conics. Thus, reconstruction of the absolute conic from two images is not unique – rather, there are two possible solutions in general. However, from three or more images, the intersection of the cones is unique in general. Thus the absolute conic is determined and with it the Euclidean structure of the scene.

Of course, if the Euclidean structure of the scene is known, then so is the position of the absolute conic. In this case we may project it back into each of the images, producing the IAC in each image, and hence calibrating the cameras. Thus knowledge of the camera calibration is equivalent to being able to determine the Euclidean structure of the scene.

1.8 Auto-calibration

Without any knowledge of the calibration of the cameras, it is impossible to do better than projective reconstruction. There is no information in a set of feature correspondences across any number of views that can help us find the image of the absolute conic, or equivalently the calibration of the cameras. However, if we know just a little about the calibration of the cameras then we may be able to determine the position of the absolute conic.

Suppose, for instance that it is known that the calibration is the same for each of the cameras used in reconstructing a scene from an image sequence. By this we mean the following. In each image a coordinate system is defined, in which we have measured the image coordinates of corresponding features used to do projective reconstruction. Suppose that in all these image coordinate systems, the IAC is the same, but just where it is located is unknown. From this knowledge, we wish to compute the position of the absolute conic.

One way to find the absolute conic is to hypothesize the position of the IAC in one image; by hypothesis, its position in the other images will be the same. The back-projection of each of the conics will be a cone in space. If the three cones all meet in a single conic, then this must be a possible solution for the position of the absolute conic, consistent with the reconstruction.

Note that this is a conceptual description only. The IAC is of course a conic containing only complex points, and its back-projection will be a complex cone. However, algebraically, the problem is more tractable. Although it is complex, the IAC may be described by a real quadratic form (represented by a real symmetric matrix). The back-projected cone is also represented by a real quadratic form. For some value of the IAC, the three back-projected cones will meet in a conic curve in space.

Generally given three cameras known to have the same calibration, it is possible to determine the absolute conic, and hence the calibration of the cameras. However, although various methods have been proposed for this, it remains quite a difficult problem.

Knowing the plane at infinity. One method of auto-calibration is to proceed in steps by first determining the plane on which it lies. This is equivalent to identifying the plane at infinity in the world, and hence to determining the affine geometry of the world. In a second step, one locates the position of the absolute conic on the plane to determine the Euclidean geometry of space. Assuming one knows the plane at infinity, one can back-project a hypothesised IAC from each of a sequence of images and intersect the resulting cones with the plane at infinity. If the IAC is chosen correctly, the intersection curve is the absolute conic. Thus, from each pair of images one has a condition that the back-projected cones meet in the same conic curve on the plane at infinity. It turns out that this gives a linear constraint on the entries of the matrix representing the IAC. From a set of linear equations, one can determine the IAC, and hence the absolute conic. Thus, auto-calibration is relatively simple, once the plane at infinity has been identified. The identification of the plane at infinity itself is substantially more difficult.

Auto-calibration given square pixels in the image. If the cameras are partially calibrated, then it is possible to complete the calibration starting from a projective reconstruction. One can make do with quite minimal conditions on the calibration of the cameras, represented by the IAC. One interesting example is the square-pixel constraint on the cameras. What this means is that a Euclidean coordinate system is known in each image. In this case, the absolute conic, lying in the plane at infinity in the world must meet the image plane in its two circular points. The circular points in a plane are the two points where the absolute conic meets that plane. The back-projected rays through the circular points of the image plane must intersect the absolute conic. Thus, each image with square pixels determines two rays that must meet the absolute conic. Given n images, the autocalibration task then becomes that of determining a space conic (the absolute conic) that meets a set of $2n$ rays in space. An equivalent geometric picture is to intersect the set of rays with a plane and require that the set of intersection points lie on a conic. By a simple counting argument one may see that there are only a finite number of conics that meet eight prescribed rays in space. Therefore, from four images one may determine the calibration, albeit up to a finite number of possibilities.

1.9 The reward I : 3D graphical models

We have now described all the ingredients necessary to compute realistic graphics models from image sequences. From point matches between images, it is possible to carry out first a projective reconstruction of the point set, and determine the motion of the camera in the chosen projective coordinate frame.

Using auto-calibration techniques, assuming some restrictions on the calibration of the camera that captured the image sequence, the camera may be calibrated, and the scene subsequently transformed to its true Euclidean structure.

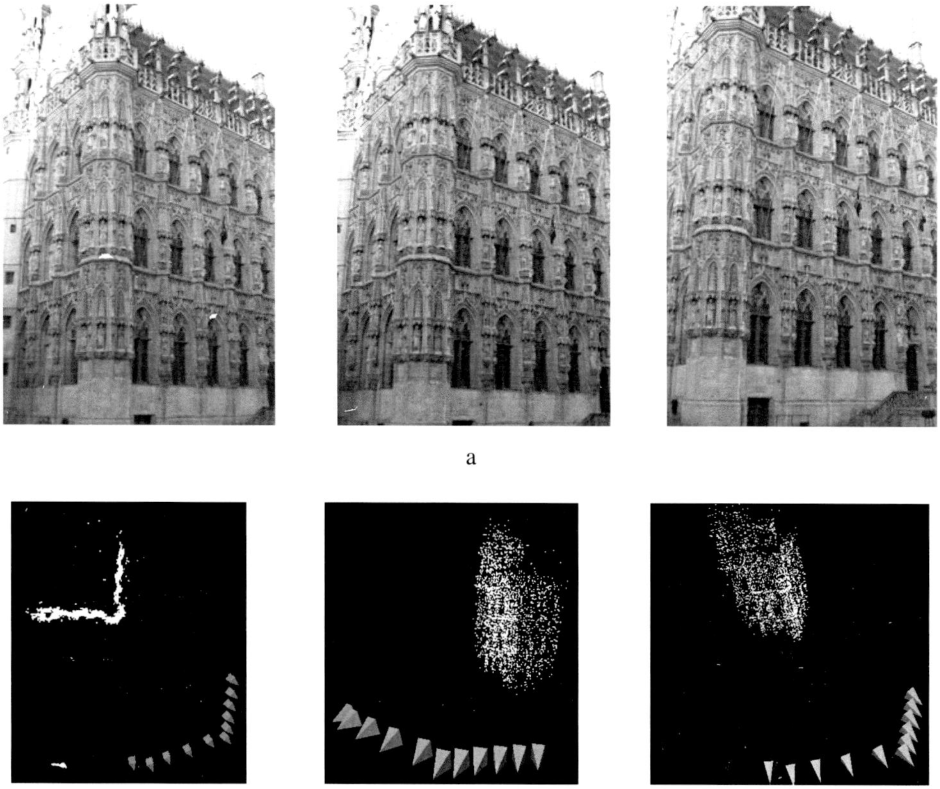

a

b

Fig. 1.5. *(a) Three high resolution images (3000 × 2000 pixels) from a set of eleven of the cityhall in Leuven, Belgium. (b) Three views of a Euclidean reconstruction computed from the image set showing the 11 camera positions and point cloud.*

Knowing the projective structure of the scene, it is possible to find the epipolar geometry relating pairs of images and this restricts the correspondence search for further matches to a line – a point in one image defines a line in the other image on which the (as yet unknown) corresponding point must lie. In fact for suitable scenes, it is possible to carry out a dense point match between images and create a dense 3D model of the imaged scene. This takes the form of a triangulated shape model that is subsequently shaded or texture-mapped from the supplied images and used to generate novel views. The steps of this process are illustrated in figure 1.5 and figure 1.6.

1.10 The reward II: video augmentation

We finish this introduction with a further application of reconstruction methods to computer graphics. Automatic reconstruction techniques have recently become widely used in the film industry as a means for adding artificial graphics objects in real video sequences. Computer analysis of the motion of the camera is replacing the previously used manual methods for correctly aligning the artificial inserted object.

The most important requirement for realistic insertion of an artificial object in a video

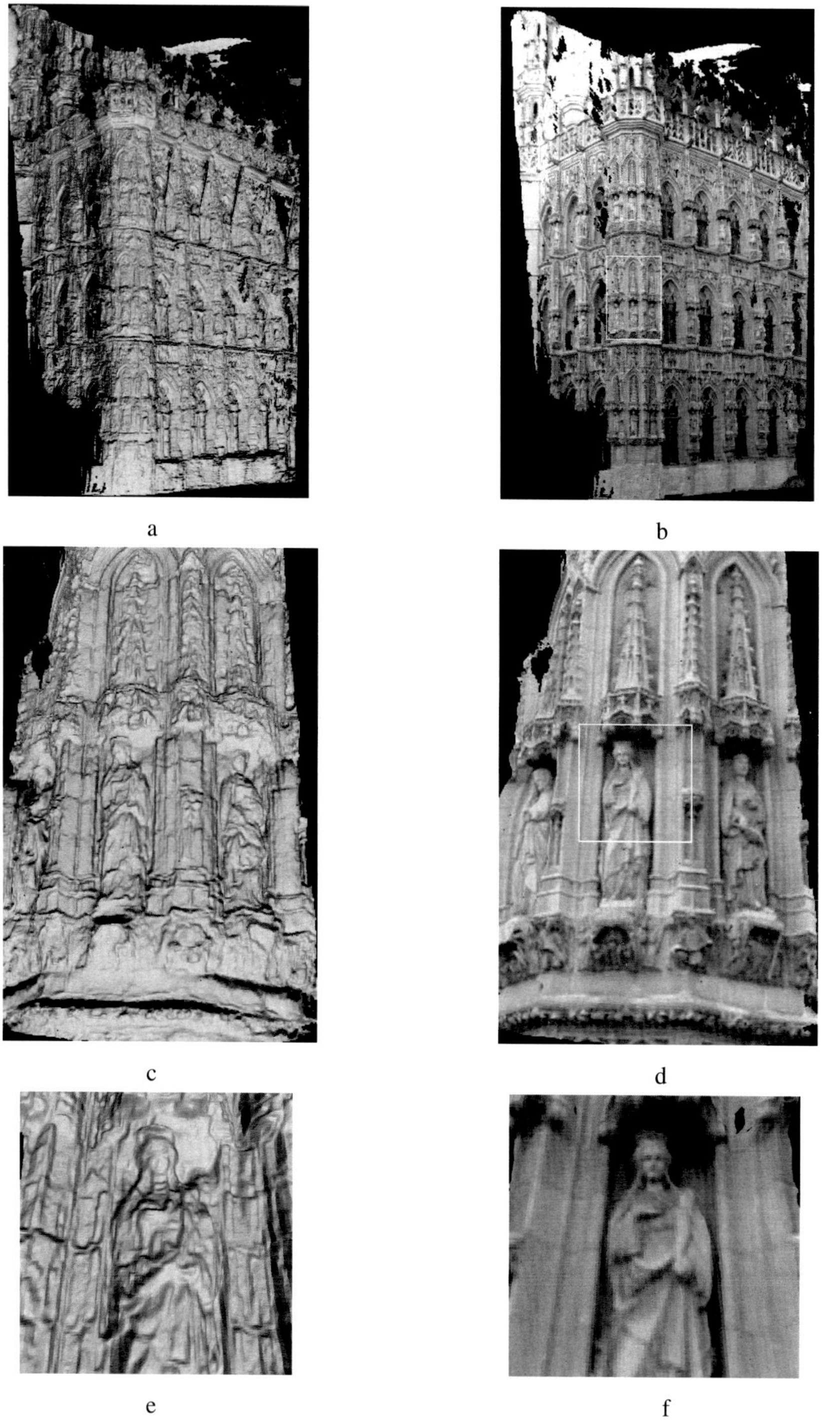

Fig. 1.6. **Dense reconstructions.** *These are computed from the cameras and image of figure 1.5. (a) Untextured and (b) textured reconstruction of the full scene. (c) Untextured and (d) textured close up of the area shown in the white rectangle of (b). (e) Untextured and (f) textured close up of the area shown in the white rectangle of (d). The dense surface is computed using the three-view stereo algorithm described in [Strecha-02]. Figures courtesy of Christoph Strecha, Frank Verbiest, and Luc Van Gool.*

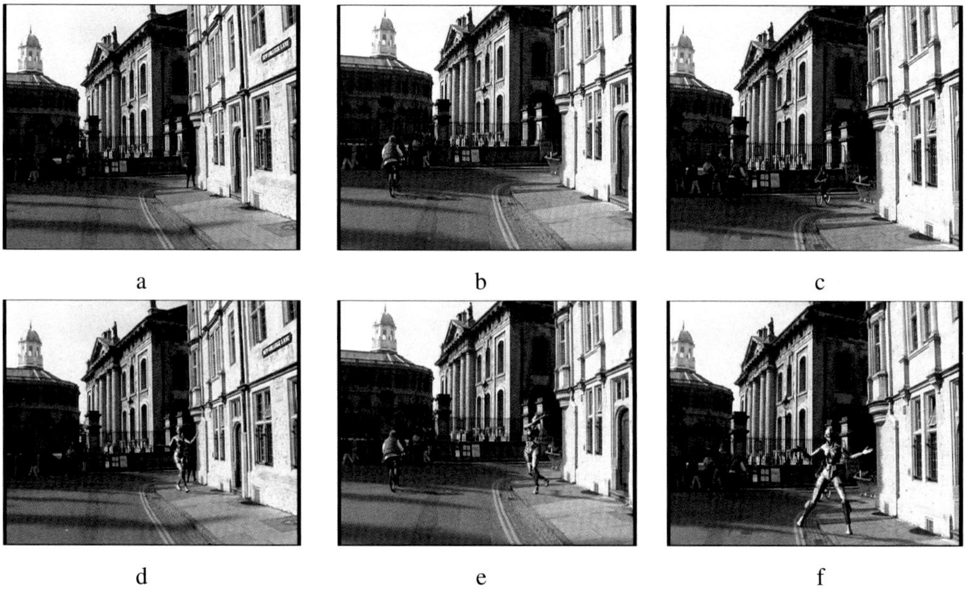

Fig. 1.7. **Augmented video.** *The animated robot is inserted into the scene and rendered using the computed cameras of figure 1.3. (a)-(c) Original frames from the sequence. (d)-(f) The augmented frames. Figures courtesy of 2d3 (*`www.2d3.com`*).*

sequence is to compute the correct motion of the camera. Unless the camera motion is correctly determined, it is impossible to generate the correct sequences of views of the graphics model in a way that will appear consistent with the background video. Generally, it is only the motion of the camera that is important here; we do not need to reconstruct the scene, since it is already present in the existing video, and novel views of the scene visible in the video are not required. The only requirement is to be able to generate correct perspective views of the graphics model.

It is essential to compute the motion of the camera in a Euclidean frame. It is not enough merely to know the projective motion of the camera. This is because a Euclidean object is to be placed in the scene. Unless this graphics object and the cameras are known in the same coordinate frame, then generated views of the inserted object will be seen to distort with respect to the perceived structure of the scene seen in the existing video.

Once the correct motion of the camera, and its calibration are known the inserted object may be rendered into the scene in a realistic manner. If the change of the camera calibration from frame to frame is correctly determined, then the camera may change focal length (zoom) during the sequence. It is even possible for the principal point to vary during the sequence through cropping.

In inserting the rendered model into the video, the task is relatively straight-forward if it lies in front of all the existing scene. Otherwise the possibility of occlusions arises, in which the scene may obscure parts of the model. An example of video augmentation is shown in figure 1.7.

Part 0

The Background: Projective Geometry, Transformations and Estimation

La reproduction interdite (The Forbidden Reproduction), 1937, René Magritte.
Courtesy of Museum Boijmans van Beuningen, Rotterdam.

Outline

The four chapters in this part lay the foundation for the representations, terminology, and notation that will be used in the subsequent parts of the book. The ideas and notation of projective geometry are central to an analysis of multiple view geometry. For example, the use of homogeneous coordinates enables non-linear mappings (such as perspective projection) to be represented by linear matrix equations, and points at infinity to be represented quite naturally avoiding the awkward necessity of taking limits.

Chapter 2 introduces projective transformations of 2-space. These are the transformations that arise when a plane is imaged by a perspective camera. This chapter is more introductory and sets the scene for the geometry of 3-space. Most of the concepts can be more easily understood and visualized in 2D than in 3D. Specializations of projective transformations are introduced, including affine and similarity transformations. Particular attention is focussed on the recovery of affine properties (e.g. parallel lines) and metric properties (e.g. angles between lines) from a perspective image.

Chapter 3 covers the projective geometry of 3-space. This geometry develops in much the same manner as that of 2-space, though of course there are extra properties arising from the additional dimension. The main new geometry here is the plane at infinity and the absolute conic.

Chapter 4 introduces *estimation* of geometry from image measurements, which is one of the main topics of this book. The example of estimating a projective transformation from point correspondences is used to illustrate the basis and motivation for the algorithms that will be used throughout the book. The important issue of what should be minimized in a cost function, e.g. algebraic or geometric or statistical measures, is described at length. The chapter also introduces the idea of robust estimation, and the use of such techniques in the automatic estimation of transformations.

Chapter 5 describes how the results of estimation algorithms may be evaluated. In particular how the covariance of an estimation may be computed.

2

Projective Geometry and Transformations of 2D

This chapter introduces the main geometric ideas and notation that are required to understand the material covered in this book. Some of these ideas are relatively familiar, such as vanishing point formation or representing conics, whilst others are more esoteric, such as using circular points to remove perspective distortion from an image. These ideas can be understood more easily in the planar (2D) case because they are more easily visualized here. The geometry of 3-space, which is the subject of the later parts of this book, is only a simple generalization of this planar case.

In particular, the chapter covers the geometry of projective transformations of the plane. These transformations model the geometric distortion which arises when a plane is imaged by a perspective camera. Under perspective imaging certain geometric properties are preserved, such as collinearity (a straight line is imaged as a straight line), whilst others are not, for example parallel lines are not imaged as parallel lines in general. Projective geometry models this imaging and also provides a mathematical representation appropriate for computations.

We begin by describing the representation of points, lines and conics in homogeneous notation, and how these entities map under projective transformations. The line at infinity and the circular points are introduced, and it is shown that these capture the affine and metric properties of the plane. Algorithms for rectifying planes are then given which enable affine and metric properties to be computed from images. We end with a description of fixed points under projective transformations.

2.1 Planar geometry

The basic concepts of planar geometry are familiar to anyone who has studied mathematics even at an elementary level. In fact, they are so much a part of our everyday experience that we take them for granted. At an elementary level, geometry is the study of points and lines and their relationships.

To the purist, the study of geometry ought properly to be carried out from a "geometric" or coordinate-free viewpoint. In this approach, theorems are stated and proved in terms of geometric primitives only, without the use of algebra. The classical approach of Euclid is an example of this method. Since Descartes, however, it has been seen that geometry may be algebraicized, and indeed the theory of geometry may be developed from an algebraic viewpoint. Our approach in this book will be a hybrid approach, sometimes using geometric, and sometimes algebraic methods. In the algebraic approach, geometric entities are described in terms of coordinates and algebraic entities. Thus, for instance a point is identified with a vector in terms of some coordinate basis. A line is also identified with a vector, and a conic section (more briefly, a conic) is represented by a symmetric matrix. In fact, we often carry this identification so far as to consider that the vector actually *is* a point, or the symmetric matrix *is* a conic, at least for convenience of language. A significant advantage of the algebraic approach to geometry is that results derived in this way may more easily be used to derive algorithms and practical computational methods. Computation and algorithms are a major concern in this book, which justifies the use of the algebraic method.

2.2 The 2D projective plane

As we all know, a point in the plane may be represented by the pair of coordinates (x, y) in $\mathbb{R}^2$. Thus, it is common to identify the plane with $\mathbb{R}^2$. Considering $\mathbb{R}^2$ as a vector space, the coordinate pair (x, y) is a vector – a point is identified as a vector. In this section we introduce the *homogeneous* notation for points and lines on a plane.

Row and column vectors. Later on, we will want to consider linear mappings between vector spaces, and represent such mappings as matrices. In the usual manner, the product of a matrix and a vector is another vector, the image under the mapping. This brings up the distinction between "column" and "row" vectors, since a matrix may be multiplied on the right by a column and on the left by a row vector. Geometric entities will by default be represented by column vectors. A bold-face symbol such as $\mathbf{x}$ always represents a column vector, and its transpose is the row vector $\mathbf{x}^{\mathsf{T}}$. In accordance with this convention, a point in the plane will be represented by the column vector $(x, y)^{\mathsf{T}}$, rather than its transpose, the row vector (x, y). We write $\mathbf{x} = (x, y)^{\mathsf{T}}$, both sides of this equation representing column vectors.

2.2.1 Points and lines

Homogeneous representation of lines. A line in the plane is represented by an equation such as $ax + by + c = 0$, different choices of a, b and c giving rise to different lines. Thus, a line may naturally be represented by the vector $(a, b, c)^{\mathsf{T}}$. The correspondence between lines and vectors $(a, b, c)^{\mathsf{T}}$ is not one-to-one, since the lines $ax + by + c = 0$ and $(ka)x + (kb)y + (kc) = 0$ are the same, for any non-zero constant k. Thus, the vectors $(a, b, c)^{\mathsf{T}}$ and $k(a, b, c)^{\mathsf{T}}$ represent the same line, for any non-zero k. In fact, two such vectors related by an overall scaling are considered as being equivalent. An equivalence class of vectors under this equivalence relationship is known as a *homogeneous* vector. Any particular vector $(a, b, c)^{\mathsf{T}}$ is a representative of the equivalence class. The set of equivalence classes of vectors in $\mathbb{R}^3 - (0, 0, 0)^{\mathsf{T}}$ forms the *projective space* $\mathbb{P}^2$. The notation $-(0, 0, 0)^{\mathsf{T}}$ indicates that the vector $(0, 0, 0)^{\mathsf{T}}$, which does not correspond to any line, is excluded.

Homogeneous representation of points. A point $\mathbf{x} = (x, y)^\mathsf{T}$ lies on the line $\mathbf{l} = (a, b, c)^\mathsf{T}$ if and only if $ax + by + c = 0$. This may be written in terms of an inner product of vectors representing the point as $(x, y, 1)(a, b, c)^\mathsf{T} = (x, y, 1)\mathbf{l} = 0$; that is the point $(x, y)^\mathsf{T}$ in $\mathbb{R}^2$ is represented as a 3-vector by adding a final coordinate of 1. Note that for any non-zero constant k and line $\mathbf{l}$ the equation $(kx, ky, k)\mathbf{l} = 0$ if and only if $(x, y, 1)\mathbf{l} = 0$. It is natural, therefore, to consider the set of vectors $(kx, ky, k)^\mathsf{T}$ for varying values of k to be a representation of the point $(x, y)^\mathsf{T}$ in $\mathbb{R}^2$. Thus, just as with lines, points are represented by homogeneous vectors. An arbitrary homogeneous vector representative of a point is of the form $\mathbf{x} = (x_1, x_2, x_3)^\mathsf{T}$, representing the point $(x_1/x_3, x_2/x_3)^\mathsf{T}$ in $\mathbb{R}^2$. Points, then, as homogeneous vectors are also elements of $\mathbb{P}^2$.

One has a simple equation to determine when a point lies on a line, namely

Result 2.1. *The point* $\mathbf{x}$ *lies on the line* $\mathbf{l}$ *if and only if* $\mathbf{x}^\mathsf{T}\mathbf{l} = 0$.

Note that the expression $\mathbf{x}^\mathsf{T}\mathbf{l}$ is just the inner or scalar product of the two vectors $\mathbf{l}$ and $\mathbf{x}$. The scalar product $\mathbf{x}^\mathsf{T}\mathbf{l} = \mathbf{l}^\mathsf{T}\mathbf{x} = \mathbf{x}.\mathbf{l}$. In general, the transpose notation $\mathbf{l}^\mathsf{T}\mathbf{x}$ will be preferred, but occasionally, we will use a . to denote the inner product. We distinguish between the *homogeneous coordinates* $\mathbf{x} = (x_1, x_2, x_3)^\mathsf{T}$ of a point, which is a 3-vector, and the *inhomogeneous* coordinates $(x, y)^\mathsf{T}$, which is a 2-vector.

Degrees of freedom (dof). It is clear that in order to specify a point two values must be provided, namely its x- and y-coordinates. In a similar manner a line is specified by two parameters (the two independent ratios $\{a : b : c\}$) and so has two degrees of freedom. For example, in an inhomogeneous representation, these two parameters could be chosen as the gradient and y intercept of the line.

Intersection of lines. Given two lines $\mathbf{l} = (a, b, c)^\mathsf{T}$ and $\mathbf{l}' = (a', b', c')^\mathsf{T}$, we wish to find their intersection. Define the vector $\mathbf{x} = \mathbf{l} \times \mathbf{l}'$, where $\times$ represents the vector or cross product. From the triple scalar product identity $\mathbf{l}.(\mathbf{l} \times \mathbf{l}') = \mathbf{l}'.(\mathbf{l} \times \mathbf{l}') = 0$, we see that $\mathbf{l}^\mathsf{T}\mathbf{x} = \mathbf{l}'^\mathsf{T}\mathbf{x} = 0$. Thus, if $\mathbf{x}$ is thought of as representing a point, then $\mathbf{x}$ lies on both lines $\mathbf{l}$ and $\mathbf{l}'$, and hence is the intersection of the two lines. This shows:

Result 2.2. *The intersection of two lines* $\mathbf{l}$ *and* $\mathbf{l}'$ *is the point* $\mathbf{x} = \mathbf{l} \times \mathbf{l}'$.

Note that the simplicity of this expression for the intersection of the two lines is a direct consequence of the use of homogeneous vector representations of lines and points.

Example 2.3. Consider the simple problem of determining the intersection of the lines $x = 1$ and $y = 1$. The line $x = 1$ is equivalent to $-1x + 1 = 0$, and thus has homogeneous representation $\mathbf{l} = (-1, 0, 1)^\mathsf{T}$. The line $y = 1$ is equivalent to $-1y+1 = 0$, and thus has homogeneous representation $\mathbf{l}' = (0, -1, 1)^\mathsf{T}$. From result 2.2 the intersection point is

$$\mathbf{x} = \mathbf{l} \times \mathbf{l}' = \begin{vmatrix} \mathbf{i} & \mathbf{j} & \mathbf{k} \\ -1 & 0 & 1 \\ 0 & -1 & 1 \end{vmatrix} = \begin{pmatrix} 1 \\ 1 \\ 1 \end{pmatrix}$$

which is the inhomogeneous point $(1, 1)^\mathsf{T}$ as required. △

Line joining points. An expression for the line passing through two points $\mathbf{x}$ and $\mathbf{x}'$ may be derived by an entirely analogous argument. Defining a line $\mathbf{l}$ by $\mathbf{l} = \mathbf{x} \times \mathbf{x}'$, it may be verified that both points $\mathbf{x}$ and $\mathbf{x}'$ lie on $\mathbf{l}$. Thus

Result 2.4. *The line through two points* $\mathbf{x}$ *and* $\mathbf{x}'$ *is* $\mathbf{l} = \mathbf{x} \times \mathbf{x}'$.

2.2.2 Ideal points and the line at infinity

Intersection of parallel lines. Consider two lines $ax+by+c = 0$ and $ax+by+c' = 0$. These are represented by vectors $\mathbf{l} = (a, b, c)^\mathsf{T}$ and $\mathbf{l}' = (a, b, c')^\mathsf{T}$ for which the first two coordinates are the same. Computing the intersection of these lines gives no difficulty, using result 2.2. The intersection is $\mathbf{l} \times \mathbf{l}' = (c' - c)(b, -a, 0)^\mathsf{T}$, and ignoring the scale factor $(c' - c)$, this is the point $(b, -a, 0)^\mathsf{T}$.

Now if we attempt to find the inhomogeneous representation of this point, we obtain $(b/0, -a/0)^\mathsf{T}$, which makes no sense, except to suggest that the point of intersection has infinitely large coordinates. In general, points with homogeneous coordinates $(x, y, 0)^\mathsf{T}$ do not correspond to any finite point in $\mathbb{R}^2$. This observation agrees with the usual idea that parallel lines meet at infinity.

Example 2.5. Consider the two lines $x = 1$ and $x = 2$. Here the two lines are parallel, and consequently intersect "at infinity". In homogeneous notation the lines are $\mathbf{l} = (-1, 0, 1)^\mathsf{T}$, $\mathbf{l}' = (-1, 0, 2)^\mathsf{T}$, and from result 2.2 their intersection point is

$$\mathbf{x} = \mathbf{l} \times \mathbf{l}' = \begin{vmatrix} \mathbf{i} & \mathbf{j} & \mathbf{k} \\ -1 & 0 & 1 \\ -1 & 0 & 2 \end{vmatrix} = \begin{pmatrix} 0 \\ 1 \\ 0 \end{pmatrix}$$

which is the point at infinity in the direction of the y-axis. △

Ideal points and the line at infinity. Homogeneous vectors $\mathbf{x} = (x_1, x_2, x_3)^\mathsf{T}$ such that $x_3 \neq 0$ correspond to finite points in $\mathbb{R}^2$. One may augment $\mathbb{R}^2$ by adding points with last coordinate $x_3 = 0$. The resulting space is the set of all homogeneous 3-vectors, namely the projective space $\mathbb{P}^2$. The points with last coordinate $x_3 = 0$ are known as *ideal* points, or points at infinity. The set of all ideal points may be written $(x_1, x_2, 0)^\mathsf{T}$, with a particular point specified by the ratio $x_1 : x_2$. Note that this set lies on a single line, the *line at infinity*, denoted by the vector $\mathbf{l}_\infty = (0, 0, 1)^\mathsf{T}$. Indeed, one verifies that $(0, 0, 1)(x_1, x_2, 0)^\mathsf{T} = 0$.

Using result 2.2 one finds that a line $\mathbf{l} = (a, b, c)^\mathsf{T}$ intersects $\mathbf{l}_\infty$ in the ideal point $(b, -a, 0)^\mathsf{T}$ (since $(b, -a, 0)\mathbf{l} = 0$). A line $\mathbf{l}' = (a, b, c')^\mathsf{T}$ *parallel* to $\mathbf{l}$ intersects $\mathbf{l}_\infty$ in the same ideal point $(b, -a, 0)^\mathsf{T}$ irrespective of the value of c'. In inhomogeneous notation $(b, -a)^\mathsf{T}$ is a vector tangent to the line, and orthogonal to the line normal (a, b), and so represents the line's *direction*. As the line's direction varies the ideal point $(b, -a, 0)^\mathsf{T}$ varies over $\mathbf{l}_\infty$. For these reasons the line at infinity can be thought of as the set of directions of lines in the plane.

Note how the introduction of the concept of points at infinity serves to simplify the intersection properties of points and lines. In the projective plane $\mathbb{P}^2$, one may state without qualification that two distinct lines meet in a single point and two distinct

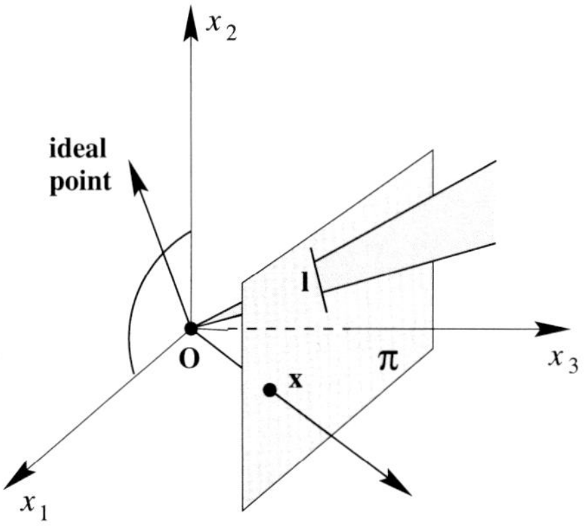

Fig. 2.1. **A model of the projective plane.** *Points and lines of* $\mathbb{P}^2$ *are represented by rays and planes, respectively, through the origin in* $\mathbb{R}^3$. *Lines lying in the* x_1x_2*-plane represent ideal points, and the* x_1x_2*-plane represents* $\mathbf{l}_\infty$.

points lie on a single line. This is not true in the standard Euclidean geometry of $\mathbb{R}^2$, in which parallel lines form a special case.

The study of the geometry of $\mathbb{P}^2$ is known as projective geometry. In a coordinate-free purely geometric study of projective geometry, one does not make any distinction between points at infinity (ideal points) and ordinary points. It will, however, serve our purposes in this book sometimes to distinguish between ideal points and non-ideal points. Thus, the line at infinity will at times be considered as a special line in projective space.

A model for the projective plane. A fruitful way of thinking of $\mathbb{P}^2$ is as a set of rays in $\mathbb{R}^3$. The set of all vectors $k(x_1, x_2, x_3)^\mathsf{T}$ as k varies forms a ray through the origin. Such a ray may be thought of as representing a single point in $\mathbb{P}^2$. In this model, the lines in $\mathbb{P}^2$ are planes passing through the origin. One verifies that two non-identical rays lie on exactly one plane, and any two planes intersect in one ray. This is the analogue of two distinct points uniquely defining a line, and two lines always intersecting in a point.

Points and lines may be obtained by intersecting this set of rays and planes by the plane $x_3 = 1$. As illustrated in figure 2.1 the rays representing ideal points and the plane representing $\mathbf{l}_\infty$ are parallel to the plane $x_3 = 1$.

Duality. The reader has probably noticed how the role of points and lines may be interchanged in statements concerning the properties of lines and points. In particular, the basic incidence equation $\mathbf{l}^\mathsf{T}\mathbf{x} = 0$ for line and point is symmetric, since $\mathbf{l}^\mathsf{T}\mathbf{x} = 0$ implies $\mathbf{x}^\mathsf{T}\mathbf{l} = 0$, in which the positions of line and point are swapped. Similarly, result 2.2 and result 2.4 giving the intersection of two lines and the line through two points are essentially the same, with the roles of points and lines swapped. One may enunciate a general principle, the *duality principle* as follows:

Result 2.6. Duality principle. *To any theorem of 2-dimensional projective geometry there corresponds a dual theorem, which may be derived by interchanging the roles of points and lines in the original theorem.*

In applying this principle, concepts of incidence must be appropriately translated as well. For instance, the line through two points is dual to the point through (that is the point of intersection of) two lines.

Note that is it not necessary to prove the dual of a given theorem once the original theorem has been proved. The proof of the dual theorem will be the dual of the proof of the original theorem.

2.2.3 Conics and dual conics

A conic is a curve described by a second-degree equation in the plane. In Euclidean geometry conics are of three main types: hyperbola, ellipse, and parabola (apart from so-called degenerate conics, to be defined later). Classically these three types of conic arise as conic sections generated by planes of differing orientation (the degenerate conics arise from planes which contain the cone vertex). However, it will be seen that in 2D projective geometry all non-degenerate conics are equivalent under projective transformations.

The equation of a conic in inhomogeneous coordinates is

$$ax^2 + bxy + cy^2 + dx + ey + f = 0$$

i.e. a polynomial of degree 2. "Homogenizing" this by the replacements: $x \mapsto x_1/x_3,\ y \mapsto x_2/x_3$ gives

$$a{x_1}^2 + bx_1x_2 + c{x_2}^2 + dx_1x_3 + ex_2x_3 + f{x_3}^2 = 0 \tag{2.1}$$

or in matrix form

$$\mathbf{x}^{\mathsf{T}}\mathtt{C}\mathbf{x} = 0 \tag{2.2}$$

where the conic coefficient matrix $\mathtt{C}$ is given by

$$\mathtt{C} = \begin{bmatrix} a & b/2 & d/2 \\ b/2 & c & e/2 \\ d/2 & e/2 & f \end{bmatrix}. \tag{2.3}$$

Note that the conic coefficient matrix is symmetric. As in the case of the homogeneous representation of points and lines, only the ratios of the matrix elements are important, since multiplying $\mathtt{C}$ by a non-zero scalar does not affect the above equations. Thus $\mathtt{C}$ is a homogeneous representation of a conic. The conic has five degrees of freedom which can be thought of as the ratios $\{a : b : c : d : e : f\}$ or equivalently the six elements of a symmetric matrix less one for scale.

Five points define a conic. Suppose we wish to compute the conic which passes through a set of points, $\mathbf{x}_i$. How many points are we free to specify before the conic is determined uniquely? The question can be answered constructively by providing an algorithm to determine the conic. From (2.1) each point $\mathbf{x}_i$ places one constraint on the conic coefficients, since if the conic passes through (x_i, y_i) then

$$a{x_i}^2 + bx_iy_i + c{y_i}^2 + dx_i + ey_i + f = 0.$$

This constraint can be written as

$$\begin{pmatrix} x_i^2 & x_iy_i & y_i^2 & x_i & y_i & 1 \end{pmatrix} \mathbf{c} = 0$$

where $\mathbf{c} = (a, b, c, d, e, f)^\mathsf{T}$ is the conic $\mathtt{C}$ represented as a 6-vector.

Stacking the constraints from five points we obtain

$$\begin{bmatrix} x_1^2 & x_1y_1 & y_1^2 & x_1 & y_1 & 1 \\ x_2^2 & x_2y_2 & y_2^2 & x_2 & y_2 & 1 \\ x_3^2 & x_3y_3 & y_3^2 & x_3 & y_3 & 1 \\ x_4^2 & x_4y_4 & y_4^2 & x_4 & y_4 & 1 \\ x_5^2 & x_5y_5 & y_5^2 & x_5 & y_5 & 1 \end{bmatrix} \mathbf{c} = \mathbf{0} \tag{2.4}$$

and the conic is the null vector of this 5×6 matrix. This shows that a conic is determined uniquely (up to scale) by five points in general position. The method of fitting a geometric entity (or relation) by determining a null space will be used frequently in the computation chapters throughout this book.

Tangent lines to conics. The line $\mathbf{l}$ tangent to a conic at a point $\mathbf{x}$ has a particularly simple form in homogeneous coordinates:

Result 2.7. *The line* $\mathbf{l}$ *tangent to* $\mathtt{C}$ *at a point* $\mathbf{x}$ *on* $\mathtt{C}$ *is given by* $\mathbf{l} = \mathtt{C}\mathbf{x}$.

Proof. The line $\mathbf{l} = \mathtt{C}\mathbf{x}$ passes through $\mathbf{x}$, since $\mathbf{l}^\mathsf{T}\mathbf{x} = \mathbf{x}^\mathsf{T}\mathtt{C}\mathbf{x} = 0$. If $\mathbf{l}$ has one-point contact with the conic, then it is a tangent, and we are done. Otherwise suppose that $\mathbf{l}$ meets the conic in another point $\mathbf{y}$. Then $\mathbf{y}^\mathsf{T}\mathtt{C}\mathbf{y} = 0$ and $\mathbf{x}^\mathsf{T}\mathtt{C}\mathbf{y} = \mathbf{l}^\mathsf{T}\mathbf{y} = 0$. From this it follows that $(\mathbf{x} + \alpha\mathbf{y})^\mathsf{T}\mathtt{C}(\mathbf{x} + \alpha\mathbf{y}) = 0$ for all α, which means that the whole line $\mathbf{l} = \mathtt{C}\mathbf{x}$ joining $\mathbf{x}$ and $\mathbf{y}$ lies on the conic $\mathtt{C}$, which is therefore degenerate (see below). □

Dual conics. The conic $\mathtt{C}$ defined above is more properly termed a *point* conic, as it defines an equation on points. Given the duality result 2.6 of $\mathbb{P}^2$ it is not surprising that there is also a conic which defines an equation on lines. This *dual* (or line) conic is also represented by a 3×3 matrix, which we denote as $\mathtt{C}^*$. A line $\mathbf{l}$ *tangent* to the conic $\mathtt{C}$ satisfies $\mathbf{l}^\mathsf{T}\mathtt{C}^*\mathbf{l} = 0$. The notation $\mathtt{C}^*$ indicates that $\mathtt{C}^*$ is the adjoint matrix of $\mathtt{C}$ (the adjoint is defined in section A4.2(*p*580) of appendix 4(*p*578)). For a non-singular symmetric matrix $\mathtt{C}^* = \mathtt{C}^{-1}$ (up to scale).

The equation for a dual conic is straightforward to derive in the case that $\mathtt{C}$ has full rank: From result 2.7, at a point $\mathbf{x}$ on $\mathtt{C}$ the tangent is $\mathbf{l} = \mathtt{C}\mathbf{x}$. Inverting, we find the point $\mathbf{x}$ at which the line $\mathbf{l}$ is tangent to $\mathtt{C}$ is $\mathbf{x} = \mathtt{C}^{-1}\mathbf{l}$. Since $\mathbf{x}$ satisfies $\mathbf{x}^\mathsf{T}\mathtt{C}\mathbf{x} = 0$ we obtain $(\mathtt{C}^{-1}\mathbf{l})^\mathsf{T}\mathtt{C}(\mathtt{C}^{-1}\mathbf{l}) = \mathbf{l}^\mathsf{T}\mathtt{C}^{-1}\mathbf{l} = 0$, the last step following from $\mathtt{C}^{-\mathsf{T}} = \mathtt{C}^{-1}$ because $\mathtt{C}$ is symmetric.

Dual conics are also known as conic envelopes, and the reason for this is illustrated

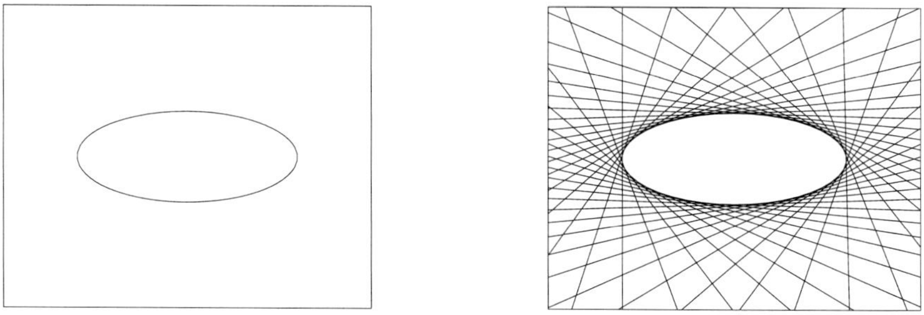

a b

Fig. 2.2. *(a) Points* $\mathbf{x}$ *satisfying* $\mathbf{x}^{\mathsf{T}}\mathtt{C}\mathbf{x} = 0$ *lie on a point conic. (b) Lines* $\mathbf{l}$ *satisfying* $\mathbf{l}^{\mathsf{T}}\mathtt{C}^{*}\mathbf{l} = 0$ *are tangent to the point conic* $\mathtt{C}$. *The conic* $\mathtt{C}$ *is the envelope of the lines* $\mathbf{l}$.

in figure 2.2. A dual conic has five degrees of freedom. In a similar manner to points defining a point conic, it follows that five lines in general position define a dual conic.

Degenerate conics. If the matrix $\mathtt{C}$ is not of full rank, then the conic is termed degenerate. Degenerate point conics include two lines (rank 2), and a repeated line (rank 1).

Example 2.8. The conic

$$\mathtt{C} = \mathbf{l}\mathbf{m}^{\mathsf{T}} + \mathbf{m}\mathbf{l}^{\mathsf{T}}$$

is composed of two lines $\mathbf{l}$ and $\mathbf{m}$. Points on $\mathbf{l}$ satisfy $\mathbf{l}^{\mathsf{T}}\mathbf{x} = 0$, and are on the conic since $\mathbf{x}^{\mathsf{T}}\mathtt{C}\mathbf{x} = (\mathbf{x}^{\mathsf{T}}\mathbf{l})(\mathbf{m}^{\mathsf{T}}\mathbf{x}) + (\mathbf{x}^{\mathsf{T}}\mathbf{m})(\mathbf{l}^{\mathsf{T}}\mathbf{x}) = 0$. Similarly, points satisfying $\mathbf{m}^{\mathsf{T}}\mathbf{x} = 0$ also satisfy $\mathbf{x}^{\mathsf{T}}\mathtt{C}\mathbf{x} = 0$. The matrix $\mathtt{C}$ is symmetric and has rank 2. The null vector is $\mathbf{x} = \mathbf{l} \times \mathbf{m}$ which is the intersection point of $\mathbf{l}$ and $\mathbf{m}$. $\triangle$

Degenerate *line* conics include two points (rank 2), and a repeated point (rank 1). For example, the line conic $\mathtt{C}^{*} = \mathbf{x}\mathbf{y}^{\mathsf{T}} + \mathbf{y}\mathbf{x}^{\mathsf{T}}$ has rank 2 and consists of lines passing through either of the two points $\mathbf{x}$ and $\mathbf{y}$. Note that for matrices that are not invertible $(\mathtt{C}^{*})^{*} \neq \mathtt{C}$.

2.3 Projective transformations

In the view of geometry set forth by Felix Klein in his famous "Erlangen Program", [Klein-39], geometry is the study of properties invariant under groups of transformations. From this point of view, 2D projective geometry is the study of properties of the projective plane $\mathbb{P}^2$ that are invariant under a group of transformations known as *projectivities*.

A projectivity is an invertible mapping from points in $\mathbb{P}^2$ (that is homogeneous 3-vectors) to points in $\mathbb{P}^2$ that maps lines to lines. More precisely,

Definition 2.9. A *projectivity* is an invertible mapping h from $\mathbb{P}^2$ to itself such that three points $\mathbf{x}_1$, $\mathbf{x}_2$ and $\mathbf{x}_3$ lie on the same line if and only if $h(\mathbf{x}_1)$, $h(\mathbf{x}_2)$ and $h(\mathbf{x}_3)$ do.

Projectivities form a group since the inverse of a projectivity is also a projectivity, and so is the composition of two projectivities. A projectivity is also called a *collineation* (a helpful name), a *projective transformation* or a *homography*: the terms are synonymous.

In definition 2.9, a projectivity is defined in terms of a coordinate-free geometric concept of point line incidence. An equivalent algebraic definition of a projectivity is possible, based on the following result.

Theorem 2.10. *A mapping $h : \mathbb{P}^2 \rightarrow \mathbb{P}^2$ is a projectivity if and only if there exists a non-singular 3×3 matrix $\mathtt{H}$ such that for any point in $\mathbb{P}^2$ represented by a vector $\mathbf{x}$ it is true that $h(\mathbf{x}) = \mathtt{H}\mathbf{x}$.*

To interpret this theorem, any point in $\mathbb{P}^2$ is represented as a homogeneous 3-vector, $\mathbf{x}$, and $\mathtt{H}\mathbf{x}$ is a linear mapping of homogeneous coordinates. The theorem asserts that any projectivity arises as such a linear transformation in homogeneous coordinates, and that conversely any such mapping is a projectivity. The theorem will not be proved in full here. It will only be shown that any invertible linear transformation of homogeneous coordinates is a projectivity.

Proof. Let $\mathbf{x}_1$, $\mathbf{x}_2$ and $\mathbf{x}_3$ lie on a line $\mathbf{l}$. Thus $\mathbf{l}^{\mathsf{T}}\mathbf{x}_i = 0$ for $i = 1, \ldots, 3$. Let $\mathtt{H}$ be a non-singular 3×3 matrix. One verifies that $\mathbf{l}^{\mathsf{T}}\mathtt{H}^{-1}\mathtt{H}\mathbf{x}_i = 0$. Thus, the points $\mathtt{H}\mathbf{x}_i$ all lie on the line $\mathtt{H}^{-\mathsf{T}}\mathbf{l}$, and collinearity is preserved by the transformation.

The converse is considerably harder to prove, namely that each projectivity arises in this way. □

As a result of this theorem, one may give an alternative definition of a projective transformation (or collineation) as follows.

Definition 2.11. Projective transformation. A planar projective transformation is a linear transformation on homogeneous 3-vectors represented by a non-singular 3×3 matrix:

$$\begin{pmatrix} x'_1 \\ x'_2 \\ x'_3 \end{pmatrix} = \begin{bmatrix} h_{11} & h_{12} & h_{13} \\ h_{21} & h_{22} & h_{23} \\ h_{31} & h_{32} & h_{33} \end{bmatrix} \begin{pmatrix} x_1 \\ x_2 \\ x_3 \end{pmatrix}, \qquad (2.5)$$

or more briefly, $\mathbf{x}' = \mathtt{H}\mathbf{x}$.

Note that the matrix $\mathtt{H}$ occurring in this equation may be changed by multiplication by an arbitrary non-zero scale factor without altering the projective transformation. Consequently we say that $\mathtt{H}$ is a *homogeneous* matrix, since as in the homogeneous representation of a point, only the ratio of the matrix elements is significant. There are eight independent ratios amongst the nine elements of $\mathtt{H}$, and it follows that a projective transformation has eight degrees of freedom.

A projective transformation projects every figure into a projectively equivalent figure, leaving all its projective properties invariant. In the ray model of figure 2.1 a projective transformation is simply a linear transformation of $\mathbb{R}^3$.

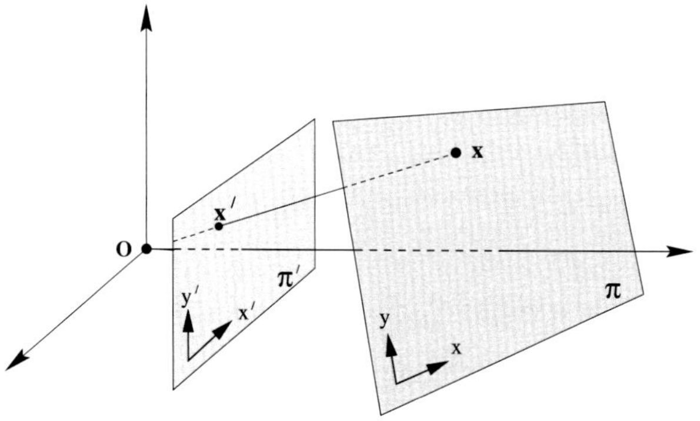

Fig. 2.3. **Central projection maps points on one plane to points on another plane.** *The projection also maps lines to lines as may be seen by considering a plane through the projection centre which intersects with the two planes* π *and* π'. *Since lines are mapped to lines, central projection is a projectivity and may be represented by a linear mapping of homogeneous coordinates* $\mathbf{x}' = \mathtt{H}\mathbf{x}$.

Mappings between planes. As an example of how theorem 2.10 may be applied, consider figure 2.3. Projection along rays through a common point (the centre of projection) defines a mapping from one plane to another. It is evident that this point-to-point mapping preserves lines in that a line in one plane is mapped to a line in the other. If a coordinate system is defined in each plane and points are represented in homogeneous coordinates, then the *central projection* mapping may be expressed by $\mathbf{x}' = \mathtt{H}\mathbf{x}$ where $\mathtt{H}$ is a non-singular 3×3 matrix. Actually, if the two coordinate systems defined in the two planes are both Euclidean (rectilinear) coordinate systems then the mapping defined by central projection is more restricted than an arbitrary projective transformation. It is called a *perspectivity* rather than a full projectivity, and may be represented by a transformation with six degrees of freedom. We return to perspectivities in section A7.4(*p*632).

Example 2.12. Removing the projective distortion from a perspective image of a plane.

Shape is distorted under perspective imaging. For instance, in figure 2.4a the windows are not rectangular in the image, although the originals are. In general parallel lines on a scene plane are not parallel in the image but instead converge to a finite point. We have seen that a central projection image of a plane (or section of a plane) is related to the original plane via a projective transformation, and so the image is a projective distortion of the original. It is possible to "undo" this projective transformation by computing the inverse transformation and applying it to the image. The result will be a new synthesized image in which the objects in the plane are shown with their correct geometric shape. This will be illustrated here for the front of the building of figure 2.4a. Note that since the ground and the front are not in the same plane, the projective transformation that must be applied to rectify the front is not the same as the one used for the ground.

Computation of a projective transformation from point-to-point correspondences will be considered in great detail in chapter 4. For now, a method for computing the trans-

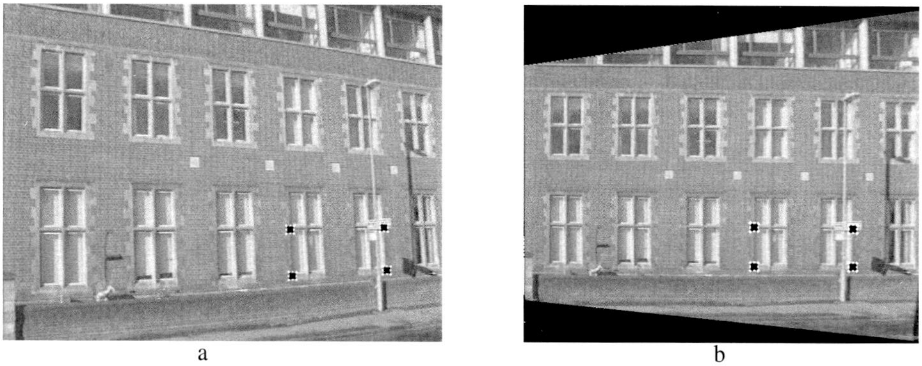

Fig. 2.4. **Removing perspective distortion.** *(a) The original image with perspective distortion – the lines of the windows clearly converge at a finite point. (b) Synthesized frontal orthogonal view of the front wall. The image (a) of the wall is related via a projective transformation to the true geometry of the wall. The inverse transformation is computed by mapping the four imaged window corners to corners of an appropriately sized rectangle. The four point correspondences determine the transformation. The transformation is then applied to the whole image. Note that sections of the image of the ground are subject to a further projective distortion. This can also be removed by a projective transformation.*

formation is briefly indicated. One begins by selecting a section of the image corresponding to a planar section of the world. Local 2D image and world coordinates are selected as shown in figure 2.3. Let the inhomogeneous coordinates of a pair of matching points $\mathbf{x}$ and $\mathbf{x}'$ in the world and image plane be (x, y) and (x', y') respectively. We use inhomogeneous coordinates here instead of the homogeneous coordinates of the points, because it is these inhomogeneous coordinates that are measured directly from the image and from the world plane. The projective transformation of (2.5) can be written in inhomogeneous form as

$$x' = \frac{x'_1}{x'_3} = \frac{h_{11}x + h_{12}y + h_{13}}{h_{31}x + h_{32}y + h_{33}}, \qquad y' = \frac{x'_2}{x'_3} = \frac{h_{21}x + h_{22}y + h_{23}}{h_{31}x + h_{32}y + h_{33}}.$$

Each point correspondence generates two equations for the elements of $\mathtt{H}$, which after multiplying out are

$$\begin{aligned} x'\left(h_{31}x + h_{32}y + h_{33}\right) &= h_{11}x + h_{12}y + h_{13} \\ y'\left(h_{31}x + h_{32}y + h_{33}\right) &= h_{21}x + h_{22}y + h_{23}. \end{aligned}$$

These equations are *linear* in the elements of $\mathtt{H}$. Four point correspondences lead to eight such linear equations in the entries of $\mathtt{H}$, which are sufficient to solve for $\mathtt{H}$ up to an insignificant multiplicative factor. The only restriction is that the four points must be in "general position", which means that no three points are collinear. The inverse of the transformation $\mathtt{H}$ computed in this way is then applied to the whole image to undo the effect of perspective distortion on the selected plane. The results are shown in figure 2.4b. △

Three remarks concerning this example are appropriate: first, the computation of the rectifying transformation $\mathtt{H}$ in this way does not require knowledge of *any* of the camera's parameters or the pose of the plane; second, it is not always necessary to

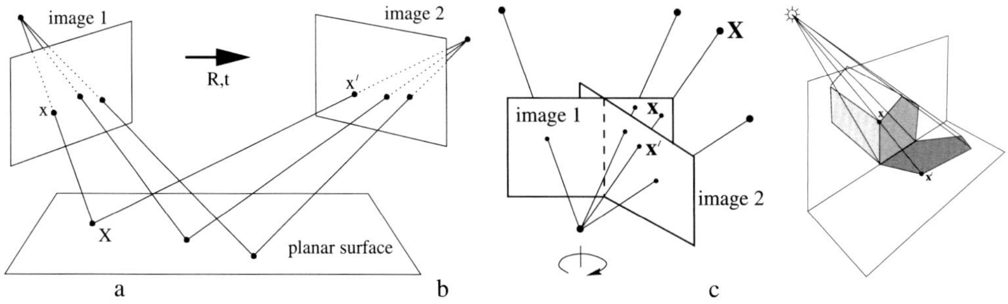

Fig. 2.5. **Examples of a projective transformation, $\mathbf{x}' = \mathtt{H}\mathbf{x}$, arising in perspective images.** *(a) The projective transformation between two images induced by a world plane (the concatenation of two projective transformations is a projective transformation); (b) The projective transformation between two images with the same camera centre (e.g. a camera rotating about its centre or a camera varying its focal length); (c) The projective transformation between the image of a plane (the end of the building) and the image of its shadow onto another plane (the ground plane). Figure (c) courtesy of Luc Van Gool.*

know coordinates for four points in order to remove projective distortion: alternative approaches, which are described in section 2.7, require less, and different types of, information; third, superior (and preferred) methods for computing projective transformations are described in chapter 4.

Projective transformations are important mappings representing many more situations than the perspective imaging of a world plane. A number of other examples are illustrated in figure 2.5. Each of these situations is covered in more detail later in the book.

2.3.1 Transformations of lines and conics

Transformation of lines. It was shown in the proof of theorem 2.10 that if points $\mathbf{x}_i$ lie on a line $\mathbf{l}$, then the transformed points $\mathbf{x}'_i = \mathtt{H}\mathbf{x}_i$ under a projective transformation lie on the line $\mathbf{l}' = \mathtt{H}^{-\mathsf{T}}\mathbf{l}$. In this way, incidence of points on lines is preserved, since $\mathbf{l}'^{\mathsf{T}}\mathbf{x}'_i = \mathbf{l}^{\mathsf{T}}\mathtt{H}^{-1}\mathtt{H}\mathbf{x}_i = 0$. This gives the transformation rule for lines:
Under the point transformation $\mathbf{x}' = \mathtt{H}\mathbf{x}$, a line transforms as

$$\mathbf{l}' = \mathtt{H}^{-\mathsf{T}}\mathbf{l}. \tag{2.6}$$

One may alternatively write $\mathbf{l}'^{\mathsf{T}} = \mathbf{l}^{\mathsf{T}}\mathtt{H}^{-1}$. Note the fundamentally different way in which lines and points transform. Points transform according to $\mathtt{H}$, whereas lines (as rows) transform according to $\mathtt{H}^{-1}$. This may be explained in terms of "covariant" or "contravariant" behaviour. One says that points transform *contravariantly* and lines transform *covariantly*. This distinction will be taken up again, when we discuss tensors in chapter 15 and is fully explained in appendix 1(*p*562).

Transformation of conics. Under a point transformation $\mathbf{x}' = \mathtt{H}\mathbf{x}$, (2.2) becomes

$$\begin{aligned} \mathbf{x}^{\mathsf{T}}\mathtt{C}\mathbf{x} &= \mathbf{x}'^{\mathsf{T}}[\mathtt{H}^{-1}]^{\mathsf{T}}\mathtt{C}\mathtt{H}^{-1}\mathbf{x}' \\ &= \mathbf{x}'^{\mathsf{T}}\mathtt{H}^{-\mathsf{T}}\mathtt{C}\mathtt{H}^{-1}\mathbf{x}' \end{aligned}$$

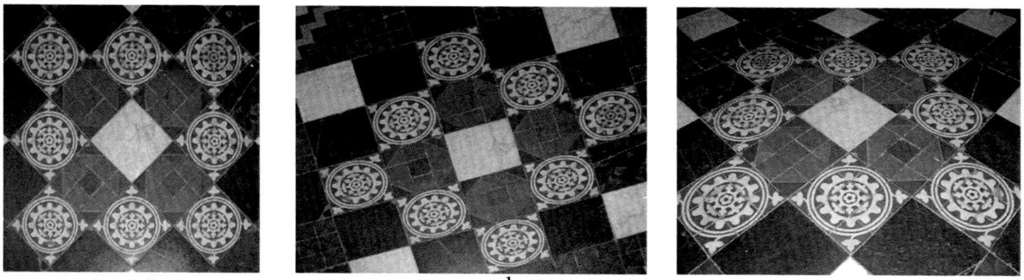

a b c

Fig. 2.6. **Distortions arising under central projection.** *Images of a tiled floor. (a)* **Similarity***: the circular pattern is imaged as a circle. A square tile is imaged as a square. Lines which are parallel or perpendicular have the same relative orientation in the image. (b)* **Affine***: The circle is imaged as an ellipse. Orthogonal world lines are not imaged as orthogonal lines. However, the sides of the square tiles, which are parallel in the world are parallel in the image. (c)* **Projective***: Parallel world lines are imaged as converging lines. Tiles closer to the camera have a larger image than those further away.*

which is a quadratic form $\mathbf{x}'^{\mathsf{T}}\mathtt{C}'\mathbf{x}'$ with $\mathtt{C}' = \mathtt{H}^{-\mathsf{T}}\mathtt{C}\mathtt{H}^{-1}$. This gives the transformation rule for a conic:

Result 2.13. *Under a point transformation* $\mathbf{x}' = \mathtt{H}\mathbf{x}$, *a conic* $\mathtt{C}$ *transforms to* $\mathtt{C}' = \mathtt{H}^{-\mathsf{T}}\mathtt{C}\mathtt{H}^{-1}$.

The presence of $\mathtt{H}^{-1}$ in this equation may be expressed by saying that a conic transforms *covariantly*. The transformation rule for a dual conic is derived in a similar manner. This gives:

Result 2.14. *Under a point transformation* $\mathbf{x}' = \mathtt{H}\mathbf{x}$, *a dual conic* $\mathtt{C}^*$ *transforms to* $\mathtt{C}^{*\prime} = \mathtt{H}\mathtt{C}^*\mathtt{H}^{\mathsf{T}}$.

2.4 A hierarchy of transformations

In this section we describe the important specializations of a projective transformation and their geometric properties. It was shown in section 2.3 that projective transformations form a group. This group is called the *projective linear group*, and it will be seen that these specializations are *subgroups* of this group.

The group of invertible $n \times n$ matrices with real elements is the (real) general linear group on n dimensions, or $GL(n)$. To obtain the projective linear group the matrices related by a scalar multiplier are identified, giving $PL(n)$ (this is a quotient group of $GL(n)$). In the case of projective transformations of the plane $n = 3$.

The important subgroups of $PL(3)$ include the *affine group*, which is the subgroup of $PL(3)$ consisting of matrices for which the last row is $(0, 0, 1)$, and the *Euclidean group*, which is a subgroup of the affine group for which in addition the upper left hand 2×2 matrix is orthogonal. One may also identify the *oriented Euclidean group* in which the upper left hand 2×2 matrix has determinant 1.

We will introduce these transformations starting from the most specialized, the isometries, and progressively generalizing until projective transformations are reached.

This defines a *hierarchy* of transformations. The distortion effects of various transformations in this hierarchy are shown in figure 2.6.

Some transformations of interest are not groups, for example, perspectivities (because the composition of two perspectivities is a projectivity, not a perspectivity). This point is covered in section A7.4(*p*632).

Invariants. An alternative to describing the transformation *algebraically*, i.e. as a matrix acting on coordinates of a point or curve, is to describe the transformation in terms of those elements or quantities that are preserved or *invariant*. A (scalar) invariant of a geometric configuration is a function of the configuration whose value is unchanged by a particular transformation. For example, the separation of two points is unchanged by a Euclidean transformation (translation and rotation), but not by a similarity (e.g. translation, rotation and isotropic scaling). Distance is thus a Euclidean, but not similarity invariant. The angle between two lines is both a Euclidean and a similarity invariant.

2.4.1 Class I: Isometries

Isometries are transformations of the plane $\mathbb{R}^2$ that preserve Euclidean distance (from *iso* = same, *metric* = measure). An isometry is represented as

$$\begin{pmatrix} x' \\ y' \\ 1 \end{pmatrix} = \begin{bmatrix} \epsilon\cos\theta & -\sin\theta & t_x \\ \epsilon\sin\theta & \cos\theta & t_y \\ 0 & 0 & 1 \end{bmatrix} \begin{pmatrix} x \\ y \\ 1 \end{pmatrix}$$

where $\epsilon = \pm 1$. If $\epsilon = 1$ then the isometry is *orientation-preserving* and is a *Euclidean* transformation (a composition of a translation and rotation). If $\epsilon = -1$ then the isometry reverses orientation. An example is the composition of a reflection, represented by the matrix $\text{diag}(-1, 1, 1)$, with a Euclidean transformation.

Euclidean transformations model the motion of a rigid object. They are by far the most important isometries in practice, and we will concentrate on these. However, the orientation reversing isometries often arise as ambiguities in structure recovery.

A planar Euclidean transformation can be written more concisely in block form as

$$\mathbf{x}' = \mathtt{H}_\mathrm{E}\mathbf{x} = \begin{bmatrix} \mathtt{R} & \mathbf{t} \\ \mathbf{0}^\mathsf{T} & 1 \end{bmatrix} \mathbf{x} \tag{2.7}$$

where $\mathtt{R}$ is a 2×2 rotation matrix (an orthogonal matrix such that $\mathtt{R}^\mathsf{T}\mathtt{R} = \mathtt{R}\mathtt{R}^\mathsf{T} = \mathtt{I}$), $\mathbf{t}$ a translation 2-vector, and $\mathbf{0}$ a null 2-vector. Special cases are a pure rotation (when $\mathbf{t} = \mathbf{0}$) and a pure translation (when $\mathtt{R} = \mathtt{I}$). A Euclidean transformation is also known as a *displacement*.

A planar Euclidean transformation has three degrees of freedom, one for the rotation and two for the translation. Thus three parameters must be specified in order to define the transformation. The transformation can be computed from two point correspondences.

Invariants. The invariants are very familiar, for instance: length (the distance between two points), angle (the angle between two lines), and area.

Groups and orientation. An isometry is orientation-preserving if the upper left hand 2×2 matrix has determinant 1. Orientation-*preserving* isometries form a group, orientation-*reversing* ones do not. This distinction applies also in the case of similarity and affine transformations which now follow.

2.4.2 Class II: Similarity transformations

A similarity transformation (or more simply a *similarity*) is an isometry composed with an isotropic scaling. In the case of a Euclidean transformation composed with a scaling (i.e. no reflection) the similarity has matrix representation

$$\begin{pmatrix} x' \\ y' \\ 1 \end{pmatrix} = \begin{bmatrix} s\cos\theta & -s\sin\theta & t_x \\ s\sin\theta & s\cos\theta & t_y \\ 0 & 0 & 1 \end{bmatrix} \begin{pmatrix} x \\ y \\ 1 \end{pmatrix}. \tag{2.8}$$

This can be written more concisely in block form as

$$\mathbf{x}' = \mathtt{H}_{\mathrm{S}}\mathbf{x} = \begin{bmatrix} s\mathtt{R} & \mathbf{t} \\ \mathbf{0}^{\mathsf{T}} & 1 \end{bmatrix} \mathbf{x} \tag{2.9}$$

where the scalar s represents the isotropic scaling. A similarity transformation is also known as an *equi-form* transformation, because it preserves "shape" (form). A planar similarity transformation has four degrees of freedom, the scaling accounting for one more degree of freedom than a Euclidean transformation. A similarity can be computed from two point correspondences.

Invariants. The invariants can be constructed from Euclidean invariants with suitable provision being made for the additional scaling degree of freedom. Angles between lines are not affected by rotation, translation or isotropic scaling, and so are similarity invariants. In particular parallel lines are mapped to parallel lines. The length between two points is not a similarity invariant, but the *ratio* of two lengths is an invariant, because the scaling of the lengths cancels out. Similarly a ratio of areas is an invariant because the scaling (squared) cancels out.

Metric structure. A term that will be used frequently in the discussion on reconstruction (chapter 10) is *metric*. The description *metric structure* implies that the structure is defined up to a similarity.

2.4.3 Class III: Affine transformations

An affine transformation (or more simply an *affinity*) is a non-singular linear transformation followed by a translation. It has the matrix representation

$$\begin{pmatrix} x' \\ y' \\ 1 \end{pmatrix} = \begin{bmatrix} a_{11} & a_{12} & t_x \\ a_{21} & a_{22} & t_y \\ 0 & 0 & 1 \end{bmatrix} \begin{pmatrix} x \\ y \\ 1 \end{pmatrix} \tag{2.10}$$

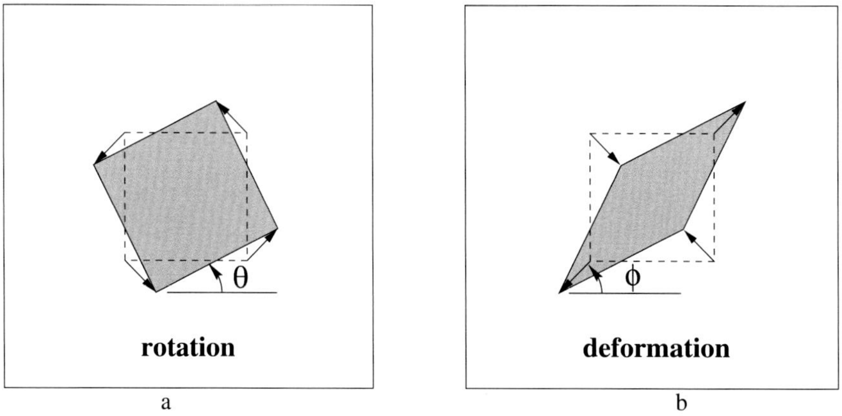

Fig. 2.7. **Distortions arising from a planar affine transformation.** *(a) Rotation by* $\mathtt{R}(\theta)$. *(b) A deformation* $\mathtt{R}(-\phi)\,\mathtt{D}\,\mathtt{R}(\phi)$. *Note, the scaling directions in the deformation are orthogonal.*

or in block form

$$\mathbf{x}' = \mathtt{H}_\mathrm{A}\mathbf{x} = \begin{bmatrix} \mathtt{A} & \mathbf{t} \\ \mathbf{0}^\mathsf{T} & 1 \end{bmatrix} \mathbf{x} \tag{2.11}$$

with $\mathtt{A}$ a 2×2 non-singular matrix. A planar affine transformation has six degrees of freedom corresponding to the six matrix elements. The transformation can be computed from three point correspondences.

A helpful way to understand the geometric effects of the linear component $\mathtt{A}$ of an affine transformation is as the composition of two fundamental transformations, namely rotations and non-isotropic scalings. The affine matrix $\mathtt{A}$ can always be decomposed as

$$\mathtt{A} \;=\; \mathtt{R}(\theta)\,\mathtt{R}(-\phi)\,\mathtt{D}\,\mathtt{R}(\phi) \tag{2.12}$$

where $\mathtt{R}(\theta)$ and $\mathtt{R}(\phi)$ are rotations by θ and ϕ respectively, and $\mathtt{D}$ is a diagonal matrix:

$$\mathtt{D} = \begin{bmatrix} \lambda_1 & 0 \\ 0 & \lambda_2 \end{bmatrix}.$$

This decomposition follows directly from the SVD (section A4.4(*p*585)): writing $\mathtt{A} = \mathtt{UDV}^\mathsf{T} = (\mathtt{UV}^\mathsf{T})(\mathtt{VDV}^\mathsf{T}) = \mathtt{R}(\theta)\,(\mathtt{R}(-\phi)\,\mathtt{D}\,\mathtt{R}(\phi))$, since $\mathtt{U}$ and $\mathtt{V}$ are orthogonal matrices.

The affine matrix $\mathtt{A}$ is hence seen to be the concatenation of a rotation (by ϕ); a scaling by λ_1 and λ_2 respectively in the (rotated) x and y directions; a rotation back (by $-\phi$); and finally another rotation (by θ). The only "new" geometry, compared to a similarity, is the non-isotropic scaling. This accounts for the two extra degrees of freedom possessed by an affinity over a similarity. They are the angle ϕ specifying the scaling direction, and the ratio of the scaling parameters $\lambda_1 : \lambda_2$. The essence of an affinity is this scaling in orthogonal directions, oriented at a particular angle. Schematic examples are given in figure 2.7.

Invariants. Because an affine transformation includes non-isotropic scaling, the similarity invariants of length ratios and angles between lines are not preserved under an affinity. Three important invariants are:

(i) **Parallel lines.** Consider two parallel lines. These intersect at a point $(x_1, x_2, 0)^\mathsf{T}$ at infinity. Under an affine transformation this point is mapped to another point at infinity. Consequently, the parallel lines are mapped to lines which still intersect at infinity, and so are parallel after the transformation.

(ii) **Ratio of lengths of parallel line segments.** The length scaling of a line segment depends only on the angle between the line direction and scaling directions. Suppose the line is at angle α to the x-axis of the orthogonal scaling direction, then the scaling magnitude is $\sqrt{\lambda_1^2 \cos^2 \alpha + \lambda_2^2 \sin^2 \alpha}$. This scaling is common to all lines with the same direction, and so cancels out in a ratio of parallel segment lengths.

(iii) **Ratio of areas.** This invariance can be deduced directly from the decomposition (2.12). Rotations and translations do not affect area, so only the scalings by λ_1 and λ_2 matter here. The effect is that area is scaled by $\lambda_1 \lambda_2$ which is equal to $\det \mathtt{A}$. Thus the area of any shape is scaled by $\det \mathtt{A}$, and so the scaling cancels out for a ratio of areas. It will be seen that this does not hold for a projective transformation.

An affinity is orientation-preserving or -reversing according to whether $\det \mathtt{A}$ is positive or negative respectively. Since $\det \mathtt{A} = \lambda_1 \lambda_2$ the property depends only on the sign of the scalings.

2.4.4 Class IV: Projective transformations

A projective transformation was defined in (2.5). It is a general non-singular linear transformation of *homogeneous* coordinates. This generalizes an affine transformation, which is the composition of a general non-singular linear transformation of *inhomogeneous* coordinates and a translation. We have earlier seen the action of a projective transformation (in section 2.3). Here we examine its block form

$$\mathbf{x}' = \mathtt{H}_\mathrm{P}\mathbf{x} = \begin{bmatrix} \mathtt{A} & \mathbf{t} \\ \mathbf{v}^\mathsf{T} & v \end{bmatrix} \mathbf{x} \tag{2.13}$$

where the vector $\mathbf{v} = (v_1, v_2)^\mathsf{T}$. The matrix has nine elements with only their ratio significant, so the transformation is specified by eight parameters. Note, it is not always possible to scale the matrix such that v is unity since v might be zero. A projective transformation between two planes can be computed from four point correspondences, with no three collinear on either plane. See figure 2.4.

Unlike the case of affinities, it is not possible to distinguish between orientation preserving and orientation reversing projectivities in $\mathbb{P}^2$. We will return to this point in section 2.6.

Invariants. The most fundamental projective invariant is the cross ratio of four collinear points: a ratio of lengths on a line is invariant under affinities, but not under projectivities. However, a ratio of ratios or *cross ratio* of lengths on a line is a projective invariant. We return to properties of this invariant in section 2.5.

2.4.5 Summary and comparison

Affinities (6 dof) occupy the middle ground between similarities (4 dof) and projectivities (8 dof). They generalize similarities in that angles are not preserved, so that shapes are skewed under the transformation. On the other hand their action is homogeneous over the plane: for a given affinity the $\det \mathtt{A}$ scaling in area of an object (e.g. a square) is the same anywhere on the plane; and the orientation of a transformed line depends only on its initial orientation, not on its position on the plane. In contrast, for a given projective transformation, area scaling varies with position (e.g. under perspective a more distant square on the plane has a smaller image than one that is nearer, as in figure 2.6); and the orientation of a transformed line depends on both the orientation and position of the source line (however, it will be seen later in section 8.6(p213) that a line's vanishing point depends only on line orientation, not position).

The key difference between a projective and affine transformation is that the vector $\mathbf{v}$ is not null for a projectivity. This is responsible for the non-linear effects of the projectivity. Compare the mapping of an ideal point $(x_1, x_2, 0)^\mathsf{T}$ under an affinity and projectivity: First the affine transformation

$$\begin{bmatrix} \mathtt{A} & \mathbf{t} \\ \mathbf{0}^\mathsf{T} & 1 \end{bmatrix} \begin{pmatrix} x_1 \\ x_2 \\ 0 \end{pmatrix} = \begin{pmatrix} \mathtt{A} \begin{pmatrix} x_1 \\ x_2 \end{pmatrix} \\ 0 \end{pmatrix}. \tag{2.14}$$

Second the projective transformation

$$\begin{bmatrix} \mathtt{A} & \mathbf{t} \\ \mathbf{v}^\mathsf{T} & v \end{bmatrix} \begin{pmatrix} x_1 \\ x_2 \\ 0 \end{pmatrix} = \begin{pmatrix} \mathtt{A} \begin{pmatrix} x_1 \\ x_2 \end{pmatrix} \\ v_1 x_1 + v_2 x_2 \end{pmatrix}. \tag{2.15}$$

In the first case the ideal point remains ideal (i.e. at infinity). In the second it is mapped to a finite point. It is this ability which allows a projective transformation to model vanishing points.

2.4.6 Decomposition of a projective transformation

A projective transformation can be decomposed into a chain of transformations, where each matrix in the chain represents a transformation higher in the hierarchy than the previous one.

$$\mathtt{H} = \mathtt{H}_\mathrm{S}\, \mathtt{H}_\mathrm{A}\, \mathtt{H}_\mathrm{P} = \begin{bmatrix} s\mathtt{R} & \mathbf{t} \\ \mathbf{0}^\mathsf{T} & 1 \end{bmatrix} \begin{bmatrix} \mathtt{K} & \mathbf{0} \\ \mathbf{0}^\mathsf{T} & 1 \end{bmatrix} \begin{bmatrix} \mathtt{I} & \mathbf{0} \\ \mathbf{v}^\mathsf{T} & v \end{bmatrix} = \begin{bmatrix} \mathtt{A} & \mathbf{t} \\ \mathbf{v}^\mathsf{T} & v \end{bmatrix} \tag{2.16}$$

with $\mathtt{A}$ a non-singular matrix given by $\mathtt{A} = s\mathtt{RK} + \mathbf{t}\mathbf{v}^\mathsf{T}$, and $\mathtt{K}$ an upper-triangular matrix normalized as $\det \mathtt{K} = 1$. This decomposition is valid provided $v \neq 0$, and is unique if s is chosen positive.

Each of the matrices $\mathtt{H}_S, \mathtt{H}_A, \mathtt{H}_P$ is the "essence" of a transformation of that type (as indicated by the subscripts S, A, P). Consider the process of rectifying the perspective image of a plane as in example 2.12: $\mathtt{H}_P$ (2 dof) moves the line at infinity; $\mathtt{H}_A$ (2 dof) affects the affine properties, but does not move the line at infinity; and finally, $\mathtt{H}_S$ is a general similarity transformation (4 dof) which does not affect the affine or projective properties. The transformation $\mathtt{H}_P$ is an *elation*, described in section A7.3(*p*631).

Example 2.15. The projective transformation

$$\mathtt{H} = \begin{bmatrix} 1.707 & 0.586 & 1.0 \\ 2.707 & 8.242 & 2.0 \\ 1.0 & 2.0 & 1.0 \end{bmatrix}$$

may be decomposed as

$$\mathtt{H} = \begin{bmatrix} 2\cos 45^\circ & -2\sin 45^\circ & 1 \\ 2\sin 45^\circ & 2\cos 45^\circ & 2 \\ 0 & 0 & 1 \end{bmatrix} \begin{bmatrix} 0.5 & 1 & 0 \\ 0 & 2 & 0 \\ 0 & 0 & 1 \end{bmatrix} \begin{bmatrix} 1 & 0 & 0 \\ 0 & 1 & 0 \\ 1 & 2 & 1 \end{bmatrix}.$$

△

This decomposition can be employed when the objective is to only partially determine the transformation. For example, if one wants to measure length ratios from the perspective image of a plane, then it is only necessary to determine (rectify) the transformation up to a similarity. We return to this approach in section 2.7.

Taking the inverse of $\mathtt{H}$ in (2.16) gives $\mathtt{H}^{-1} = \mathtt{H}_P^{-1}\,\mathtt{H}_A^{-1}\,\mathtt{H}_S^{-1}$. Since $\mathtt{H}_P^{-1}, \mathtt{H}_A^{-1}$ and $\mathtt{H}_S^{-1}$ are still projective, affine and similarity transformations respectively, a general projective transformation may also be decomposed in the form

$$\mathtt{H} = \mathtt{H}_P\,\mathtt{H}_A\,\mathtt{H}_S = \begin{bmatrix} \mathtt{I} & \mathbf{0} \\ \mathbf{v}^\mathsf{T} & 1 \end{bmatrix} \begin{bmatrix} \mathtt{K} & \mathbf{0} \\ \mathbf{0}^\mathsf{T} & 1 \end{bmatrix} \begin{bmatrix} s\mathtt{R} & \mathbf{t} \\ \mathbf{0}^\mathsf{T} & 1 \end{bmatrix} \tag{2.17}$$

Note that the actual values of $\mathtt{K}$, $\mathtt{R}$, $\mathbf{t}$ and $\mathbf{v}$ will be different from those of (2.16).

2.4.7 The number of invariants

The question naturally arises as to how many invariants there are for a given geometric configuration under a particular transformation. First the term "number" needs to be made more precise, for if a quantity is invariant, such as length under Euclidean transformations, then any function of that quantity is invariant. Consequently, we seek a counting argument for the number of functionally independent invariants. By considering the number of transformation parameters that must be eliminated in order to form an invariant, it can be seen that:

Result 2.16. *The number of functionally independent invariants is equal to, or greater than, the number of degrees of freedom of the configuration less the number of degrees of freedom of the transformation.*

Group	Matrix	Distortion	Invariant properties
Projective 8 dof	$\begin{bmatrix} h_{11} & h_{12} & h_{13} \\ h_{21} & h_{22} & h_{23} \\ h_{31} & h_{32} & h_{33} \end{bmatrix}$	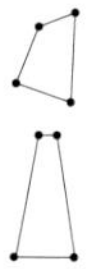	Concurrency, collinearity, **order of contact**: intersection (1 pt contact); tangency (2 pt contact); inflections (3 pt contact with line); tangent discontinuities and cusps. cross ratio (ratio of ratio of lengths).
Affine 6 dof	$\begin{bmatrix} a_{11} & a_{12} & t_x \\ a_{21} & a_{22} & t_y \\ 0 & 0 & 1 \end{bmatrix}$	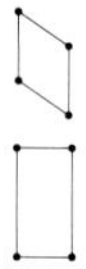	Parallelism, ratio of areas, ratio of lengths on collinear or parallel lines (e.g. midpoints), linear combinations of vectors (e.g. centroids). The line at infinity, $\mathbf{l}_\infty$.
Similarity 4 dof	$\begin{bmatrix} sr_{11} & sr_{12} & t_x \\ sr_{21} & sr_{22} & t_y \\ 0 & 0 & 1 \end{bmatrix}$	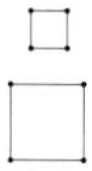	Ratio of lengths, angle. The circular points, **I**, **J** (see section 2.7.3).
Euclidean 3 dof	$\begin{bmatrix} r_{11} & r_{12} & t_x \\ r_{21} & r_{22} & t_y \\ 0 & 0 & 1 \end{bmatrix}$	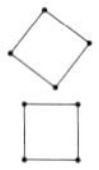	Length, area

Table 2.1. **Geometric properties invariant to commonly occurring *planar* transformations.** *The matrix* $\mathtt{A} = [a_{ij}]$ *is an invertible* 2×2 *matrix,* $\mathtt{R} = [r_{ij}]$ *is a 2D rotation matrix, and* (t_x, t_y) *a 2D translation. The distortion column shows typical effects of the transformations on a square. Transformations higher in the table can produce all the actions of the ones below. These range from Euclidean, where only translations and rotations occur, to projective where the square can be transformed to any arbitrary quadrilateral (provided no three points are collinear).*

For example, a configuration of four points in general position has 8 degrees of freedom (2 for each point), and so 4 similarity, 2 affinity and zero projective invariants since these transformations have respectively 4, 6 and 8 degrees of freedom.

Table 2.1 summarizes the 2D transformation groups and their invariant properties. Transformations lower in the table are specializations of those above. A transformation lower in the table inherits the invariants of those above.

2.5 The projective geometry of 1D

The development of the projective geometry of a line, $\mathbb{P}^1$, proceeds in much the same way as that of the plane. A point x on the line is represented by homogeneous coordinates $(x_1, x_2)^\mathsf{T}$, and a point for which $x_2 = 0$ is an ideal point of the line. We will use the notation $\bar{\mathbf{x}}$ to represent the 2-vector $(x_1, x_2)^\mathsf{T}$. A projective transformation of a line is represented by a 2×2 homogeneous matrix,

$$\bar{\mathbf{x}}' = \mathtt{H}_{2\times 2}\bar{\mathbf{x}}$$

and has 3 degrees of freedom corresponding to the four elements of the matrix less one for overall scaling. A projective transformation of a line may be determined from three corresponding points.

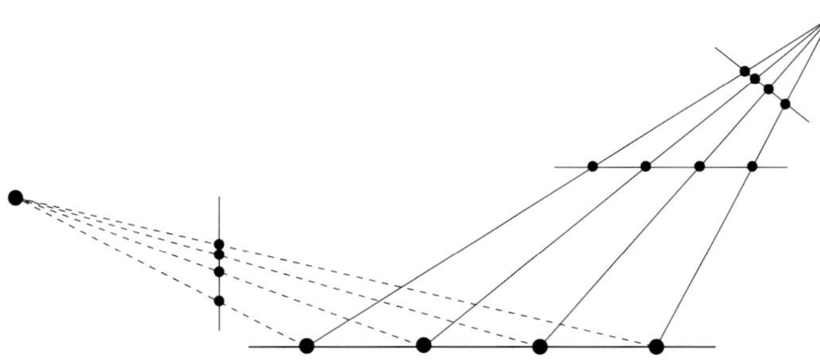

Fig. 2.8. **Projective transformations between lines.** *There are four sets of four collinear points in this figure. Each set is related to the others by a line-to-line projectivity. Since the cross ratio is an invariant under a projectivity, the cross ratio has the same value for all the sets shown.*

The cross ratio. The cross ratio is the basic projective invariant of $\mathbb{P}^1$. Given 4 points $\bar{\mathbf{x}}_i$ the *cross ratio* is defined as

$$\text{Cross}(\bar{\mathbf{x}}_1, \bar{\mathbf{x}}_2, \bar{\mathbf{x}}_3, \bar{\mathbf{x}}_4) = \frac{|\bar{\mathbf{x}}_1\bar{\mathbf{x}}_2||\bar{\mathbf{x}}_3\bar{\mathbf{x}}_4|}{|\bar{\mathbf{x}}_1\bar{\mathbf{x}}_3||\bar{\mathbf{x}}_2\bar{\mathbf{x}}_4|}$$

where

$$|\bar{\mathbf{x}}_i\bar{\mathbf{x}}_j| = \det \begin{bmatrix} x_{i1} & x_{j1} \\ x_{i2} & x_{j2} \end{bmatrix}.$$

A few comments on the cross ratio:

(i) The value of the cross ratio is not dependent on which particular homogeneous representative of a point $\bar{\mathbf{x}}_i$ is used, since the scale cancels between numerator and denominator.

(ii) If each point $\bar{\mathbf{x}}_i$ is a finite point and the homogeneous representative is chosen such that $x_2 = 1$, then $|\bar{\mathbf{x}}_i\bar{\mathbf{x}}_j|$ represents the signed distance from $\bar{\mathbf{x}}_i$ to $\bar{\mathbf{x}}_j$.

(iii) The definition of the cross ratio is also valid if one of the points $\bar{\mathbf{x}}_i$ is an ideal point.

(iv) The value of the cross ratio is invariant under any projective transformation of the line: if $\bar{\mathbf{x}}' = \mathtt{H}_{2\times 2}\bar{\mathbf{x}}$ then

$$\text{Cross}(\bar{\mathbf{x}}'_1, \bar{\mathbf{x}}'_2, \bar{\mathbf{x}}'_3, \bar{\mathbf{x}}'_4) = \text{Cross}(\bar{\mathbf{x}}_1, \bar{\mathbf{x}}_2, \bar{\mathbf{x}}_3, \bar{\mathbf{x}}_4). \quad (2.18)$$

The proof is left as an exercise. Equivalently stated, the cross ratio is invariant to the projective coordinate frame chosen for the line.

Figure 2.8 illustrates a number of projective transformations between lines with equivalent cross ratios.

Under a projective transformation of the plane, a 1D projective transformation is induced on any line in the plane.

Concurrent lines. A configuration of concurrent lines is dual to collinear points on a line. This means that concurrent lines on a plane also have the geometry $\mathbb{P}^1$. In particular four concurrent lines have a cross ratio as illustrated in figure 2.9a.

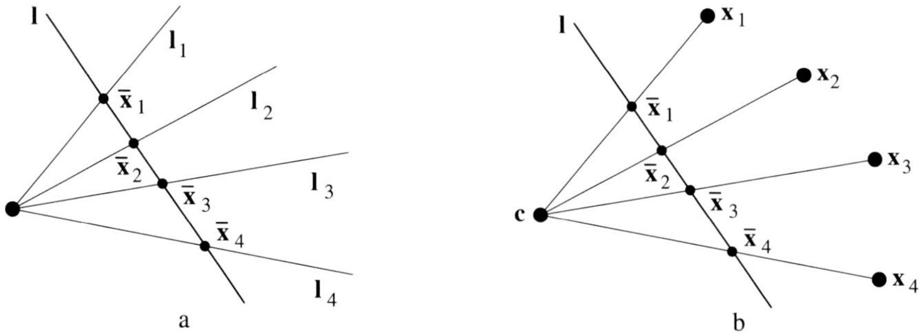

Fig. 2.9. **Concurrent lines.** *(a) Four concurrent lines $\mathbf{l}_i$ intersect the line $\mathbf{l}$ in the four points $\bar{\mathbf{x}}_i$. The cross ratio of these lines is an invariant to projective transformations of the plane. Its value is given by the cross ratio of the points, Cross$(\bar{\mathbf{x}}_1, \bar{\mathbf{x}}_2, \bar{\mathbf{x}}_3, \bar{\mathbf{x}}_4)$. (b) Coplanar points $\mathbf{x}_i$ are imaged onto a line $\mathbf{l}$ (also in the plane) by a projection with centre $\mathbf{c}$. The cross ratio of the image points $\bar{\mathbf{x}}_i$ is invariant to the position of the image line $\mathbf{l}$.*

Note how figure 2.9b may be thought of as representing projection of points in $\mathbb{P}^2$ into a 1-dimensional image. In particular, if $\mathbf{c}$ represents a camera centre, and the line $\mathbf{l}$ represents an image line (1D analogue of the image plane), then the points $\bar{\mathbf{x}}_i$ are the projections of points $\mathbf{x}_i$ into the image. The cross ratio of the points $\bar{\mathbf{x}}_i$ characterizes the projective configuration of the four image points. Note that the actual position of the image line is irrelevant as far as the projective configuration of the four image points is concerned – different choices of image line give rise to projectively equivalent configurations of image points.

The projective geometry of concurrent lines is important to the understanding of the projective geometry of epipolar lines in chapter 9.

2.6 Topology of the projective plane

We make brief mention of the topology of $\mathbb{P}^2$. Understanding of this section is not required for following the rest of the book.

We have seen that the projective plane $\mathbb{P}^2$ may be thought of as the set of all homogeneous 3-vectors. A vector of this type $\mathbf{x} = (x_1, x_2, x_3)^\mathsf{T}$ may be normalized by multiplication by a non-zero factor so that $x_1^2 + x_2^2 + x_3^2 = 1$. Such a point lies on the unit sphere in $\mathbb{R}^3$. However, any vector $\mathbf{x}$ and $-\mathbf{x}$ represent the same point in $\mathbb{P}^2$, since they differ by a multiplicative factor, -1. Thus, there is a two-to-one correspondence between the unit sphere S^2 in $\mathbb{R}^3$ and the projective plane $\mathbb{P}^2$. The projective plane may be pictured as the unit sphere with opposite points identified. In this representation, a line in $\mathbb{P}^2$ is modelled as a great circle on the unit sphere (as ever, with opposite points identified). One may verify that any two distinct (non-antipodal) points on the sphere lie on exactly one great circle, and any two great circles intersect in one point (since antipodal points are identified).

In the language of topology, the sphere S^2 is a 2-sheeted covering space of $\mathbb{P}^2$. This implies that $\mathbb{P}^2$ is not *simply-connected*, which means that there are loops in $\mathbb{P}^2$ which cannot be contracted to a point inside $\mathbb{P}^2$. To be technical, the fundamental group of $\mathbb{P}^2$ is the cyclic group of order 2.

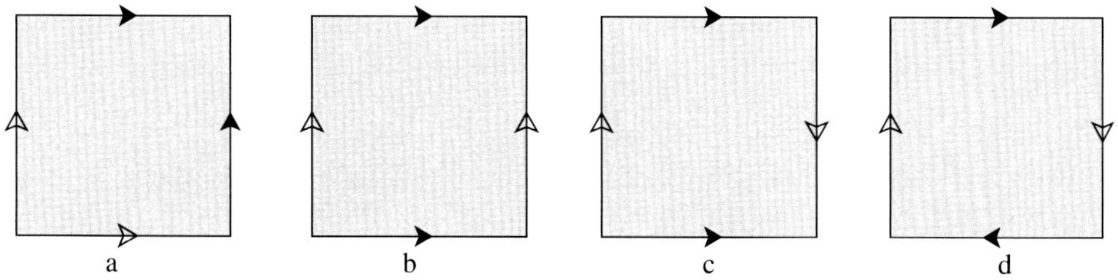

Fig. 2.10. **Topology of surfaces.** *Common surfaces may be constructed from a paper square (topologically a disk) with edges glued together. In each case, the matching arrow edges of the square are to be glued together in such a way that the directions of the arrows match. One obtains (a) a sphere, (b) a torus, (c) a Klein bottle and (d) a projective plane. Only the sphere and torus are actually realizable with a real sheet of paper. The sphere and torus are orientable but the projective plane and Klein bottle are not.*

In the model for the projective plane as a sphere with opposite points identified one may dispense with the lower hemisphere of S^2, since points in this hemisphere are the same as the opposite points in the upper hemisphere. In this case, $\mathbb{P}^2$ may be constructed from the upper hemisphere by identifying opposite points on the equator. Since the upper hemisphere of S^2 is topologically the same as a disk, $\mathbb{P}^2$ is simply a disk with opposite points on its boundary identified, or glued together. This is not physically possible. Constructing topological spaces by gluing the boundary of a disk is a common method in topology, and in fact any 2-manifold may be constructed in this way. This is illustrated in figure 2.10.

A notable feature of the projective plane $\mathbb{P}^2$ is that it is non-orientable. This means that it is impossible to define a local orientation (represented for instance by a pair of oriented coordinate axes) that is consistent over the whole surface. This is illustrated in figure 2.11 in which it is shown that the projective plane contains an orientation-reversing path.

The topology of $\mathbb{P}^1$. In a similar manner, the 1-dimensional projective line may be identified as a 1-sphere S^1 (that is, a circle) with opposite points identified. If we omit the lower half of the circle, as being duplicated by the top half, then the top half of a circle is topologically equivalent to a line segment. Thus $\mathbb{P}^1$ is topologically equivalent to a line segment with the two endpoints identified – namely a circle, S^1.

2.7 Recovery of affine and metric properties from images

We return to the example of projective rectification of example 2.12(*p*34) where the aim was to remove the projective distortion in the perspective image of a plane to the extent that similarity properties (angles, ratios of lengths) could be measured on the original plane. In that example the projective distortion was completely removed by specifying the position of four reference points on the plane (a total of 8 degrees of freedom), and explicitly computing the transformation mapping the reference points to their images. In fact this overspecifies the geometry – a projective transformation has only 4 degrees of freedom more than a similarity, so it is only necessary to specify 4

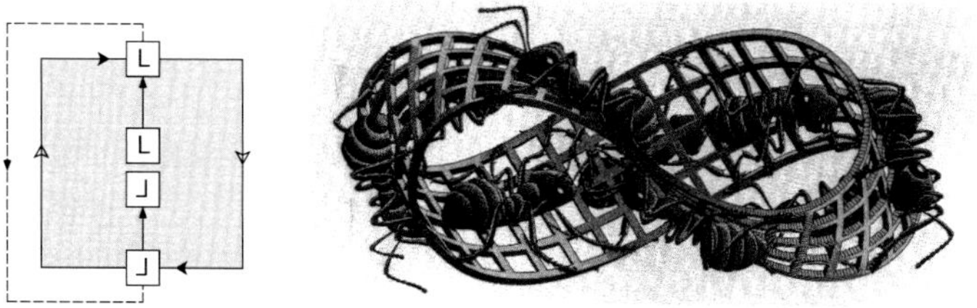

a b

Fig. 2.11. **Orientation of surfaces.** *A coordinate frame (represented by an L in the diagram) may be transported along a path in the surface eventually coming back to the point where it started. (a) represents a projective plane. In the path shown, the coordinate frame (represented by a pair of axes) is reversed when it returns to the same point, since the identification at the boundary of the square swaps the direction of one of the axes. Such a path is called an orientation-reversing path, and a surface that contains such a path is called non-orientable. (b) shows the well known example of a Möbius strip obtained by joining two opposite edges of a rectangle (M.C. Escher's "Moebius Strip II [Red Ants]", 1963. ©2000 Cordon Art B.V. – Baarn-Holland. All rights reserved). As can be verified, a path once around the strip is orientation-reversing.*

degrees of freedom (not 8) in order to determine metric properties. In projective geometry these 4 degrees of freedom are given "physical substance" by being associated with geometric objects: the line at infinity $\mathbf{l}_\infty$ (2 dof), and the two *circular points* (2 dof) on $\mathbf{l}_\infty$. This association is often a more intuitive way of reasoning about the problem than the equivalent description in terms of specifying matrices in the decomposition chain (2.16).

In the following it is shown that the projective distortion may be removed once the image of $\mathbf{l}_\infty$ is specified, and the affine distortion removed once the image of the circular points is specified. Then the only remaining distortion is a similarity.

2.7.1 The line at infinity

Under a projective transformation ideal points may be mapped to finite points (2.15), and consequently $\mathbf{l}_\infty$ is mapped to a finite line. However, if the transformation is an affinity, then $\mathbf{l}_\infty$ is not mapped to a finite line, but remains at infinity. This is evident directly from the line transformation (2.6–*p*36):

$$\mathbf{l}'_\infty = \mathtt{H}_\mathrm{A}^{-\mathsf{T}}\mathbf{l}_\infty = \begin{bmatrix} \mathtt{A}^{-\mathsf{T}} & \mathbf{0} \\ -\mathbf{t}^\mathsf{T}\mathtt{A}^{-\mathsf{T}} & 1 \end{bmatrix}\begin{pmatrix} 0 \\ 0 \\ 1 \end{pmatrix} = \begin{pmatrix} 0 \\ 0 \\ 1 \end{pmatrix} = \mathbf{l}_\infty.$$

The converse is also true, i.e. an affine transformation is the most general linear transformation that fixes $\mathbf{l}_\infty$, and may be seen as follows. We require that a point at infinity, say $\mathbf{x} = (1, 0, 0)^\mathsf{T}$, be mapped to a point at infinity. This requires that $h_{31} = 0$. Similarly, $h_{32} = 0$, so the transformation is an affinity. To summarize,

Result 2.17. *The line at infinity, $\mathbf{l}_\infty$, is a fixed line under the projective transformation* $\mathtt{H}$ *if and only if* $\mathtt{H}$ *is an affinity.*

However, $\mathbf{l}_\infty$ is not fixed pointwise under an affine transformation: (2.14) showed that under an affinity a point on $\mathbf{l}_\infty$ (an ideal point) is mapped to a point on $\mathbf{l}_\infty$, but

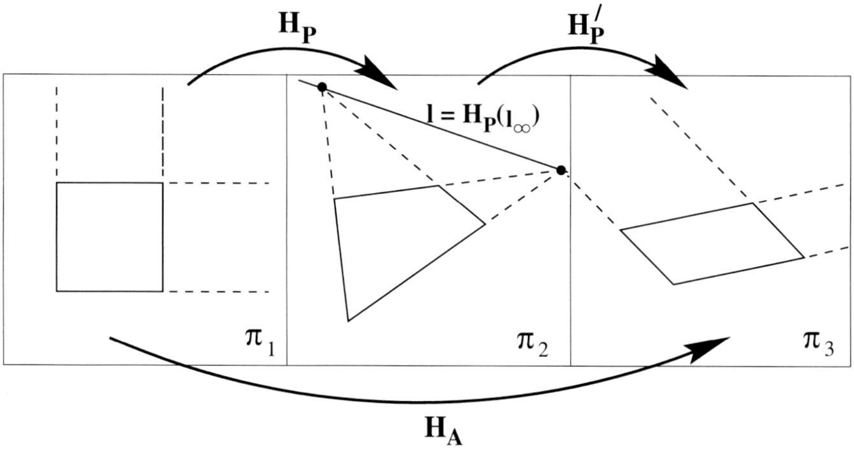

Fig. 2.12. **Affine rectification.** *A projective transformation maps l_∞ from $(0, 0, 1)^\mathsf{T}$ on a Euclidean plane π_1 to a finite line l on the plane π_2. If a projective transformation is constructed such that l is mapped back to $(0, 0, 1)^\mathsf{T}$ then from result 2.17 the transformation between the first and third planes* must be an affine transformation *since the canonical position of l_∞ is preserved. This means that affine properties of the first plane can be measured from the third, i.e. the third plane is within an affinity of the first.*

it is not the same point unless $\mathtt{A}(x_1, x_2)^\mathsf{T} = k(x_1, x_2)^\mathsf{T}$. It will now be shown that identifying l_∞ allows the recovery of affine properties (parallelism, ratio of areas).

2.7.2 Recovery of affine properties from images

Once the imaged line at infinity is identified in an image of a plane, it is then possible to make affine measurements on the original plane. For example, lines may be identified as parallel on the original plane if the imaged lines intersect on the imaged l_∞. This follows because parallel lines on the Euclidean plane intersect on l_∞, and after a projective transformation the lines still intersect on the imaged l_∞ since intersections are preserved by projectivities. Similarly, once l_∞ is identified a length ratio on a line may be computed from the cross ratio of the three points specifying the lengths together with the intersection of the line with l_∞ (which provides the fourth point for the cross ratio), and so forth.

However, a less tortuous path which is better suited to computational algorithms is simply to transform the identified l_∞ to its canonical position of $l_\infty = (0, 0, 1)^\mathsf{T}$. The (projective) matrix which achieves this transformation can be applied to every point in the image in order to affinely rectify the image, i.e. after the transformation, affine measurements can be made directly from the rectified image. The key idea here is illustrated in figure 2.12.

If the imaged line at infinity is the line $l = (l_1, l_2, l_3)^\mathsf{T}$, then provided $l_3 \neq 0$ a suitable projective point transformation which will map l back to $l_\infty = (0, 0, 1)^\mathsf{T}$ is

$$\mathtt{H} = \mathtt{H}_\mathtt{A} \begin{bmatrix} 1 & 0 & 0 \\ 0 & 1 & 0 \\ l_1 & l_2 & l_3 \end{bmatrix} \tag{2.19}$$

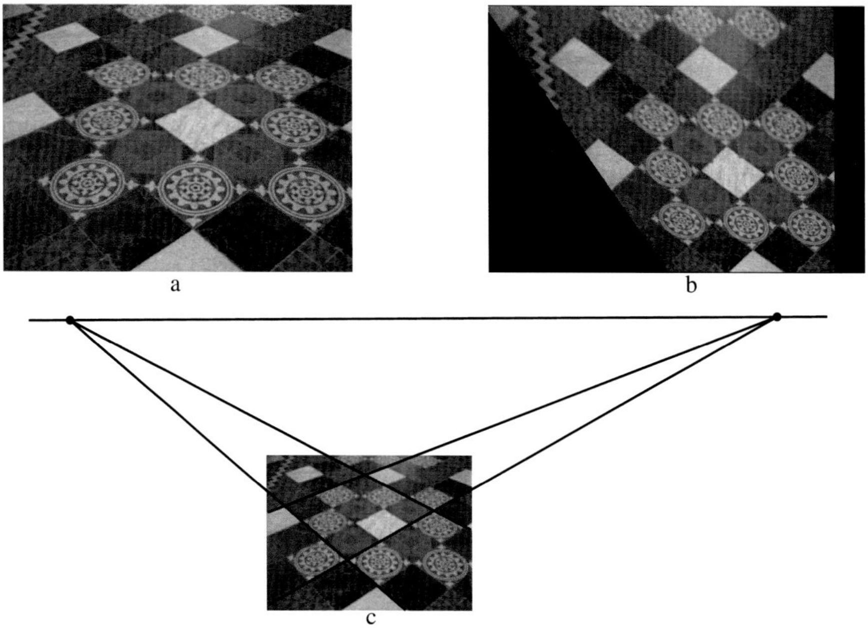

Fig. 2.13. **Affine rectification via the vanishing line.** *The vanishing line of the plane imaged in (a) is computed (c) from the intersection of two sets of imaged parallel lines. The image is then projectively warped to produce the affinely rectified image (b). In the affinely rectified image parallel lines are now parallel. However, angles do not have their veridical world value since they are affinely distorted. See also figure 2.17.*

where $\mathtt{H}_\mathrm{A}$ is any affine transformation (the last row of $\mathtt{H}$ is $\mathbf{l}^\mathsf{T}$). One can verify that under the line transformation (2.6–*p*36) $\mathtt{H}^{-\mathsf{T}}(l_1, l_2, l_3)^\mathsf{T} = (0, 0, 1)^\mathsf{T} = \mathbf{l}_\infty$.

Example 2.18. Affine rectification
In a perspective image of a plane, the line at infinity on the world plane is imaged as the vanishing line of the plane. This is discussed in more detail in chapter 8. As illustrated in figure 2.13 the vanishing line $\mathbf{l}$ may be computed by intersecting imaged parallel lines. The image is then rectified by applying a projective warping (2.19) such that $\mathbf{l}$ is mapped to its canonical position $\mathbf{l}_\infty = (0, 0, 1)^\mathsf{T}$. △

This example shows that affine properties may be recovered by simply specifying a line (2 dof). It is equivalent to specifying only the projective component of the transformation decomposition chain (2.16). Conversely if affine properties are known, these may be used to determine points and the line at infinity. This is illustrated in the following example.

Example 2.19. Computing a vanishing point from a length ratio. Given two intervals on a line with a known length ratio, the point at infinity on the line may be determined. A typical case is where three points $\mathbf{a}'$, $\mathbf{b}'$ and $\mathbf{c}'$ are identified on a line in an image. Suppose $\mathbf{a}$, $\mathbf{b}$ and $\mathbf{c}$ are the corresponding collinear points on the world line, and the length ratio $d(\mathbf{a}, \mathbf{b}) : d(\mathbf{b}, \mathbf{c}) = a : b$ is known (where $d(\mathbf{x}, \mathbf{y})$ is the Euclidean

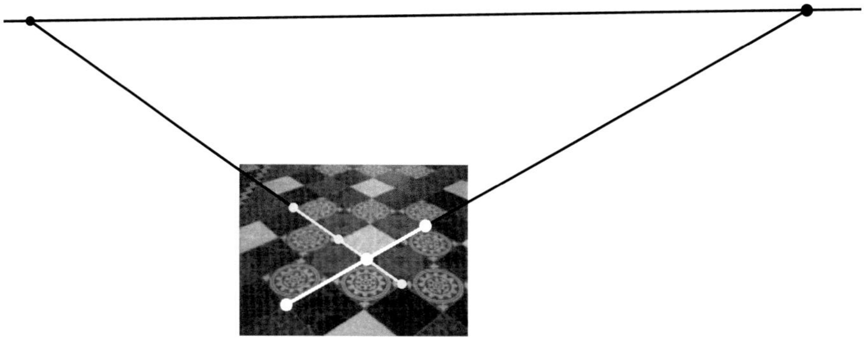

Fig. 2.14. *Two examples of using equal length ratios on a line to determine the point at infinity. The line intervals used are shown as the thin and thick white lines delineated by points. This construction determines the vanishing line of the plane. Compare with figure 2.13c.*

distance between the points $\mathbf{x}$ and $\mathbf{y}$). It is possible to find the vanishing point using the cross ratio. Equivalently, one may proceed as follows:

(i) Measure the distance ratio in the image, $d(\mathbf{a}', \mathbf{b}') : d(\mathbf{b}', \mathbf{c}') = a' : b'$.

(ii) Points $\mathbf{a}$, $\mathbf{b}$ and $\mathbf{c}$ may be represented as coordinates 0, a and $a+b$ in a coordinate frame on the line $\langle \mathbf{a}, \mathbf{b}, \mathbf{c} \rangle$. For computational purposes, these points are represented by homogeneous 2-vectors $(0, 1)^\mathsf{T}$, $(a, 1)^\mathsf{T}$ and $(a + b, 1)^\mathsf{T}$. Similarly, $\mathbf{a}'$, $\mathbf{b}'$ and $\mathbf{c}'$ have coordinates 0, a' and $a' + b'$, which may also be expressed as homogeneous vectors.

(iii) Relative to these coordinate frames, compute the 1D projective transformation $\mathtt{H}_{2\times 2}$ mapping $\mathbf{a} \mapsto \mathbf{a}'$, $\mathbf{b} \mapsto \mathbf{b}'$ and $\mathbf{c} \mapsto \mathbf{c}'$.

(iv) The image of the point at infinity (with coordinates $(1, 0)^\mathsf{T}$) under $\mathtt{H}_{2\times 2}$ is the vanishing point on the line $\langle \mathbf{a}', \mathbf{b}', \mathbf{c}' \rangle$.

An example of vanishing points computed in this manner is shown in figure 2.14. △

Example 2.20. Geometric construction of vanishing points from a length ratio. The vanishing points shown in figure 2.14 may also be computed by a purely geometric construction consisting of the following steps:

(i) Given: three collinear points, $\mathbf{a}'$, $\mathbf{b}'$ and $\mathbf{c}'$, in an image corresponding to collinear world points with interval ratio $a : b$.

(ii) Draw any line $\mathbf{l}$ through $\mathbf{a}'$ (not coincident with the line $\mathbf{a}'\mathbf{c}'$), and mark off points $\mathbf{a} = \mathbf{a}'$, $\mathbf{b}$ and $\mathbf{c}$ such that the line segments $\langle \mathbf{ab} \rangle$, $\langle \mathbf{bc} \rangle$ have length ratio $a : b$.

(iii) Join $\mathbf{bb}'$ and $\mathbf{cc}'$ and intersect in $\mathbf{o}$.

(iv) The line through $\mathbf{o}$ parallel to $\mathbf{l}$ meets the line $\mathbf{a}'\mathbf{c}'$ in the vanishing point $\mathbf{v}'$.

This construction is illustrated in figure 2.15. △

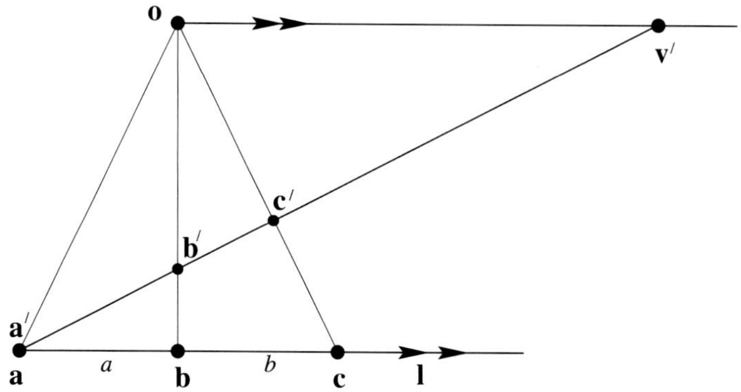

Fig. 2.15. *A geometric construction to determine the image of the point at infinity on a line given a known length ratio. The details are given in the text.*

2.7.3 The circular points and their dual

Under any similarity transformation there are two points on $\mathbf{l}_\infty$ which are fixed. These are the *circular points* (also called the *absolute points*) $\mathbf{I}, \mathbf{J}$, with canonical coordinates

$$\mathbf{I} = \begin{pmatrix} 1 \\ i \\ 0 \end{pmatrix} \qquad \mathbf{J} = \begin{pmatrix} 1 \\ -i \\ 0 \end{pmatrix}.$$

The circular points are a pair of complex conjugate ideal points. To see that they are fixed under an orientation-preserving similarity:

$$\begin{aligned} \mathbf{I}' &= \mathtt{H}_S \mathbf{I} \\ &= \begin{bmatrix} s\cos\theta & -s\sin\theta & t_x \\ s\sin\theta & s\cos\theta & t_y \\ 0 & 0 & 1 \end{bmatrix} \begin{pmatrix} 1 \\ i \\ 0 \end{pmatrix} \\ &= se^{-i\theta} \begin{pmatrix} 1 \\ i \\ 0 \end{pmatrix} = \mathbf{I} \end{aligned}$$

with an analogous proof for $\mathbf{J}$. A reflection swaps $\mathbf{I}$ and $\mathbf{J}$. The converse is also true, i.e. if the circular points are fixed then the linear transformation is a similarity. The proof is left as an exercise. To summarize,

Result 2.21. *The circular points, $\mathbf{I}, \mathbf{J}$, are fixed points under the projective transformation $\mathtt{H}$ if and only if $\mathtt{H}$ is a similarity.*

The name "circular points" arises because every circle intersects $\mathbf{l}_\infty$ at the circular points. To see this, start from equation (2.1–*p*30) for a conic. In the case that the conic is a circle: $a = c$ and $b = 0$. Then

$$x_1^2 + x_2^2 + dx_1x_3 + ex_2x_3 + fx_3^2 = 0$$

where a has been set to unity. This conic intersects $\mathbf{l}_\infty$ in the (ideal) points for which $x_3 = 0$, namely

$$x_1^2 + x_2^2 = 0$$

with solution $\mathbf{I} = (1, i, 0)^\mathsf{T}$, $\mathbf{J} = (1, -i, 0)^\mathsf{T}$, i.e. any circle intersects $\mathbf{l}_\infty$ in the circular points. In Euclidean geometry it is well known that a circle is specified by three points. The circular points enable an alternative computation. A circle can be computed using the general formula for a conic defined by five points (2.4–*p*31), where the five points are the three points augmented with the two circular points.

In section 2.7.5 it will be shown that identifying the circular points (or equivalently their dual, see below) allows the recovery of similarity properties (angles, ratios of lengths). Algebraically, the circular points are the orthogonal directions of Euclidean geometry, $(1, 0, 0)^\mathsf{T}$ and $(0, 1, 0)^\mathsf{T}$, packaged into a single complex conjugate entity, e.g.

$$\mathbf{I} = (1, 0, 0)^\mathsf{T} + i(0, 1, 0)^\mathsf{T}.$$

Consequently, it is not so surprising that once the circular points are identified, orthogonality, and other metric properties, are then determined.

The conic dual to the circular points. The conic

$$\mathtt{C}_\infty^* = \mathbf{IJ}^\mathsf{T} + \mathbf{JI}^\mathsf{T} \tag{2.20}$$

is dual to the circular points. The conic $\mathtt{C}_\infty^*$ is a degenerate (rank 2) line conic (see section 2.2.3), which consists of the two circular points. In a Euclidean coordinate system it is given by

$$\mathtt{C}_\infty^* = \begin{pmatrix} 1 \\ i \\ 0 \end{pmatrix} \begin{pmatrix} 1 & -i & 0 \end{pmatrix} + \begin{pmatrix} 1 \\ -i \\ 0 \end{pmatrix} \begin{pmatrix} 1 & i & 0 \end{pmatrix} = \begin{bmatrix} 1 & 0 & 0 \\ 0 & 1 & 0 \\ 0 & 0 & 0 \end{bmatrix}.$$

The conic $\mathtt{C}_\infty^*$ is fixed under similarity transformations in an analogous fashion to the fixed properties of circular points. A conic is fixed if the same matrix results (up to scale) under the transformation rule. Since $\mathtt{C}_\infty^*$ is a dual conic it transforms according to result 2.14(*p*37) ($\mathtt{C}^{*\prime} = \mathtt{H}\mathtt{C}^*\mathtt{H}^\mathsf{T}$), and one can verify that under the point transformation $\mathbf{x}' = \mathtt{H}_\mathrm{S}\mathbf{x}$,

$$\mathtt{C}_\infty^{*\,\prime} = \mathtt{H}_\mathrm{S}\mathtt{C}_\infty^*\mathtt{H}_\mathrm{S}^\mathsf{T} = \mathtt{C}_\infty^*.$$

The converse is also true, and we have

Result 2.22. *The dual conic* $\mathtt{C}_\infty^*$ *is fixed under the projective transformation* $\mathtt{H}$ *if and only if* $\mathtt{H}$ *is a similarity.*

Some properties of $\mathtt{C}_\infty^*$ in any projective frame:

(i) $\mathtt{C}_\infty^*$ has 4 degrees of freedom: a 3×3 homogeneous symmetric matrix has 5 degrees of freedom, but the constraint $\det \mathtt{C}_\infty^* = 0$ reduces the degrees of freedom by 1.

(ii) $\mathbf{l}_\infty$ is the null vector of $\mathtt{C}^*_\infty$. This is clear from the definition: the circular points lie on $\mathbf{l}_\infty$, so that $\mathbf{I}^\mathsf{T}\mathbf{l}_\infty = \mathbf{J}^\mathsf{T}\mathbf{l}_\infty = 0$; then

$$\mathtt{C}^*_\infty \mathbf{l}_\infty = (\mathbf{I}\mathbf{J}^\mathsf{T} + \mathbf{J}\mathbf{I}^\mathsf{T})\mathbf{l}_\infty = \mathbf{I}(\mathbf{J}^\mathsf{T}\mathbf{l}_\infty) + \mathbf{J}(\mathbf{I}^\mathsf{T}\mathbf{l}_\infty) = \mathbf{0}.$$

2.7.4 Angles on the projective plane

In Euclidean geometry the angle between two lines is computed from the dot product of their normals. For the lines $\mathbf{l} = (l_1, l_2, l_3)^\mathsf{T}$ and $\mathbf{m} = (m_1, m_2, m_3)^\mathsf{T}$ with normals parallel to $(l_1, l_2)^\mathsf{T}$, $(m_1, m_2)^\mathsf{T}$ respectively, the angle is

$$\cos\theta = \frac{l_1 m_1 + l_2 m_2}{\sqrt{(l_1^2 + l_2^2)(m_1^2 + m_2^2)}}. \tag{2.21}$$

The problem with this expression is that the first two components of $\mathbf{l}$ and $\mathbf{m}$ do not have well defined transformation properties under projective transformations (they are not tensors), and so (2.21) cannot be applied after an affine or projective transformation of the plane. However, an analogous expression to (2.21) which is invariant to projective transformations is

$$\cos\theta = \frac{\mathbf{l}^\mathsf{T}\mathtt{C}^*_\infty\mathbf{m}}{\sqrt{(\mathbf{l}^\mathsf{T}\mathtt{C}^*_\infty\mathbf{l})(\mathbf{m}^\mathsf{T}\mathtt{C}^*_\infty\mathbf{m})}} \tag{2.22}$$

where $\mathtt{C}^*_\infty$ is the conic dual to the circular points. It is clear that in a Euclidean coordinate system (2.22) reduces to (2.21). It may be verified that (2.22) is invariant to projective transformations by using the transformation rules for lines (2.6–*p*36) ($\mathbf{l}' = \mathtt{H}^{-\mathsf{T}}\mathbf{l}$) and dual conics (result 2.14(*p*37)) ($\mathtt{C}^{*\prime} = \mathtt{H}\mathtt{C}^*\mathtt{H}^\mathsf{T}$) under the point transformation $\mathbf{x}' = \mathtt{H}\mathbf{x}$. For example, the numerator transforms as

$$\mathbf{l}^\mathsf{T}\mathtt{C}^*_\infty\mathbf{m} \mapsto \mathbf{l}^\mathsf{T}\mathtt{H}^{-1}\mathtt{H}\mathtt{C}^*_\infty\mathtt{H}^\mathsf{T}\mathtt{H}^{-\mathsf{T}}\mathbf{m} = \mathbf{l}^\mathsf{T}\mathtt{C}^*_\infty\mathbf{m}.$$

It may also be verified that the scale of the homogeneous objects cancels between the numerator and denominator. Thus (2.22) is indeed invariant to the projective frame. To summarize, we have shown

Result 2.23. *Once the conic $\mathtt{C}^*_\infty$ is identified on the projective plane then Euclidean angles may be measured by (2.22).*

Note, as a corollary,

Result 2.24. *Lines $\mathbf{l}$ and $\mathbf{m}$ are orthogonal if $\mathbf{l}^\mathsf{T}\mathtt{C}^*_\infty\mathbf{m} = 0$.*

Geometrically, if $\mathbf{l}$ and $\mathbf{m}$ satisfy $\mathbf{l}^\mathsf{T}\mathtt{C}^*_\infty\mathbf{m} = 0$, then the lines are conjugate (see section 2.8.1) with respect to the conic $\mathtt{C}^*_\infty$.

Length ratios may also be measured once $\mathtt{C}^*_\infty$ is identified. Consider the triangle shown in figure 2.16 with vertices $\mathbf{a}, \mathbf{b}, \mathbf{c}$. From the standard trigonometric sine rule the ratio of lengths $d(\mathbf{b}, \mathbf{c}) : d(\mathbf{a}, \mathbf{c}) = \sin\alpha : \sin\beta$, where $d(\mathbf{x}, \mathbf{y})$ denotes the Euclidean distance between the points $\mathbf{x}$ and $\mathbf{y}$. Using (2.22), both $\cos\alpha$ and $\cos\beta$ may be computed from the lines $\mathbf{l}' = \mathbf{a}' \times \mathbf{b}'$, $\mathbf{m}' = \mathbf{c}' \times \mathbf{a}'$ and $\mathbf{n}' = \mathbf{b}' \times \mathbf{c}'$ for any

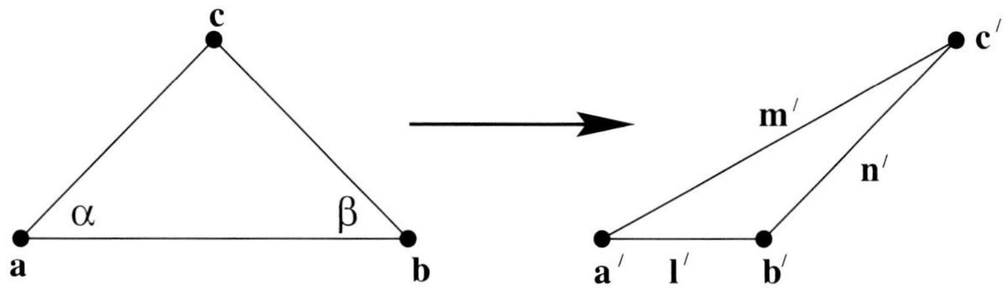

Fig. 2.16. **Length ratios.** *Once C^*_∞ is identified the Euclidean length ratio $d(\mathbf{b}, \mathbf{c}) : d(\mathbf{a}, \mathbf{c})$ may be measured from the projectively distorted figure. See text for details.*

projective frame in which C^*_∞ is specified. Consequently both $\sin\alpha$, $\sin\beta$, and thence the ratio $d(\mathbf{a}, \mathbf{b}) : d(\mathbf{c}, \mathbf{a})$, may be determined from the projectively mapped points.

2.7.5 Recovery of metric properties from images

A completely analogous approach to that of section 2.7.2 and figure 2.12, where affine properties are recovered by specifying $\mathbf{l}_\infty$, enables metric properties to be recovered from an image of a plane by transforming the circular points to their canonical position. Suppose the circular points are identified in an image, and the image is then rectified by a projective transformation H that maps the imaged circular points to their canonical position (at $(1, \pm i, 0)^\mathsf{T}$) on $\mathbf{l}_\infty$. From result 2.21 the transformation between the world plane and the rectified image is then a similarity since it is projective and the circular points are fixed.

Metric rectification using C^*_∞. The dual conic C^*_∞ neatly packages all the information required for a metric rectification. It enables both the projective and affine components of a projective transformation to be determined, leaving only similarity distortions. This is evident from its transformation under a projectivity. If the point transformation is $\mathbf{x}' = H\mathbf{x}$, where the $\mathbf{x}$-coordinate frame is Euclidean and $\mathbf{x}'$ projective, C^*_∞ transforms according to result 2.14(*p*37) ($C^{*\prime} = HC^*H^\mathsf{T}$). Using the decomposition chain (2.17–*p*43) for H

$$\begin{aligned} C^{*\,\prime}_\infty &= (H_P\, H_A\, H_S)\, C^*_\infty\, (H_P\, H_A\, H_S)^\mathsf{T} = (H_P\, H_A)\left(H_S\, C^*_\infty H_S^\mathsf{T}\right)\left(H_A^\mathsf{T}\, H_P^\mathsf{T}\right) \\ &= (H_P\, H_A)\, C^*_\infty \left(H_A^\mathsf{T}\, H_P^\mathsf{T}\right) \\ &= \begin{bmatrix} KK^\mathsf{T} & KK^\mathsf{T}\mathbf{v} \\ \mathbf{v}^\mathsf{T}KK^\mathsf{T} & \mathbf{v}^\mathsf{T}KK^\mathsf{T}\mathbf{v} \end{bmatrix}. \end{aligned} \tag{2.23}$$

It is clear that the projective ($\mathbf{v}$) and affine (K) components are determined directly from the image of C^*_∞, but (since C^*_∞ is invariant to similarity transformation by result 2.22) the similarity component is undetermined. Consequently,

Result 2.25. *Once the conic C^*_∞ is identified on the projective plane then projective distortion may be rectified up to a similarity.*

Actually, a suitable rectifying homography may be obtained directly from the identified $C^{*\,\prime}_\infty$ in an image using the SVD (section A4.4(*p*585)): writing the SVD of $C^{*\,\prime}_\infty$

as

$$C_\infty^{*\prime} = U \begin{bmatrix} 1 & 0 & 0 \\ 0 & 1 & 0 \\ 0 & 0 & 0 \end{bmatrix} U^\top$$

then by inspection from (2.23) the rectifying projectivity is $H = U$ up to a similarity.

The following two examples show typical situations where C_∞^* may be identified in an image, and thence a metric rectification obtained.

Example 2.26. Metric rectification I
Suppose an image has been affinely rectified (as in example 2.18 above), then we require two constraints to specify the 2 degrees of freedom of the circular points in order to determine a metric rectification. These two constraints may be obtained from two imaged right angles on the world plane.

Suppose the lines $\mathbf{l}', \mathbf{m}'$ in the affinely rectified image correspond to an orthogonal line pair $\mathbf{l}, \mathbf{m}$ on the world plane. From result 2.24 $\mathbf{l}'^\top C_\infty^{*\prime}\mathbf{m}' = 0$, and using (2.23) with $\mathbf{v} = \mathbf{0}$

$$\begin{pmatrix} l'_1 & l'_2 & l'_3 \end{pmatrix} \begin{bmatrix} KK^\top & \mathbf{0} \\ \mathbf{0}^\top & 0 \end{bmatrix} \begin{pmatrix} m'_1 \\ m'_2 \\ m'_3 \end{pmatrix} = 0$$

which is a *linear* constraint on the 2×2 matrix $S = KK^\top$. The matrix $S = KK^\top$ is symmetric with three independent elements, and thus 2 degrees of freedom (as the overall scaling is unimportant). The orthogonality condition reduces to the equation $(l'_1, l'_2)S(m'_1, m'_2)^\top = 0$ which may be written as

$$(l'_1 m'_1, l'_1 m'_2 + l'_2 m'_1, l'_2 m'_2)\,\mathbf{s} = 0,$$

where $\mathbf{s} = (s_{11}, s_{12}, s_{22})^\top$ is S written as a 3-vector. Two such orthogonal line pairs provide two constraints which may be stacked to give a 2×3 matrix with $\mathbf{s}$ determined as the null vector. Thus S, and hence K, is obtained up to scale (by Cholesky decomposition, section A4.2.1(*p*582)). Figure 2.17 shows an example of two orthogonal line pairs being used to metrically rectify the affinely rectified image computed in figure 2.13. △

Alternatively, the two constraints required for metric rectification may be obtained from an imaged circle or two known length ratios. In the case of a circle, the image conic is an ellipse in the affinely rectified image, and the intersection of this ellipse with the (known) $\mathbf{l}_\infty$ directly determines the imaged circular points.

The conic C_∞^* can alternatively be identified directly in a perspective image, without first identifying $\mathbf{l}_\infty$, as is illustrated in the following example.

Example 2.27. Metric rectification II
We start here from the original perspective image of the plane (not the affinely rectified image of example 2.26). Suppose lines $\mathbf{l}$ and $\mathbf{m}$ are images of orthogonal lines on the world plane; then from result 2.24 $\mathbf{l}^\top C_\infty^* \mathbf{m} = 0$, and in a similar manner to constraining

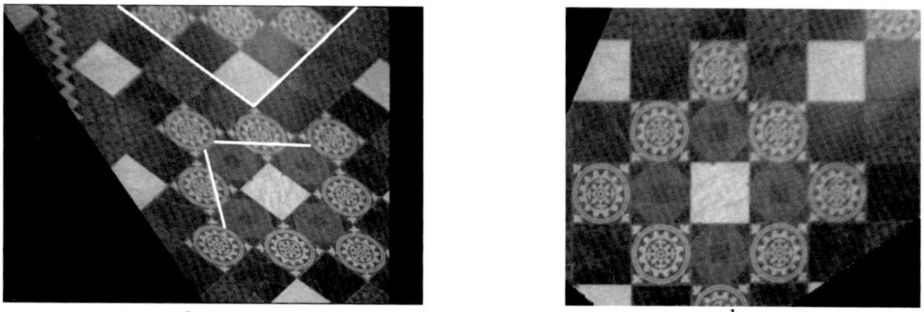

Fig. 2.17. **Metric rectification via orthogonal lines I.** *The affine transformation required to metrically rectify an affine image may be computed from imaged orthogonal lines. (a) Two (non-parallel) line pairs identified on the affinely rectified image (figure 2.13) correspond to orthogonal lines on the world plane. (b) The metrically rectified image. Note that in the metrically rectified image all lines orthogonal in the world are orthogonal, world squares have unit aspect ratio, and world circles are circular.*

Fig. 2.18. **Metric rectification via orthogonal lines II.** *(a) The conic C^*_∞ is determined on the perspectively imaged plane (the front wall of the building) using the five orthogonal line pairs shown. The conic C^*_∞ determines the circular points, and equivalently the projective transformation necessary to metrically rectify the image (b). The image shown in (a) is the same perspective image as that of figure 2.4(p35), where the perspective distortion was removed by specifying the world position of four image points.*

a conic to contain a point (2.4–*p*31), this provides a linear constraint on the elements of C^*_∞, namely

$$(l_1m_1, (l_1m_2 + l_2m_1)/2, l_2m_2, (l_1m_3 + l_3m_1)/2, (l_2m_3 + l_3m_2)/2, l_3m_3)\,\mathbf{c} = 0$$

where $\mathbf{c} = (a, b, c, d, e, f)^\mathsf{T}$ is the conic matrix (2.3–*p*30) of C^*_∞ written as a 6-vector. Five such constraints can be stacked to form a 5×6 matrix, and $\mathbf{c}$, and hence C^*_∞, is obtained as the null vector. This shows that C^*_∞ can be determined linearly from the images of five line pairs which are orthogonal on the world plane. An example of metric rectification using such line pair constraints is shown in figure 2.18. △

Stratification. Note, in example 2.27 the affine and projective distortions are determined in one step by specifying C^*_∞. In the previous example 2.26 first the projective and subsequently the affine distortions were removed. This two-step approach is termed *stratified*. Analogous approaches apply in 3D, and are employed in chapter 10

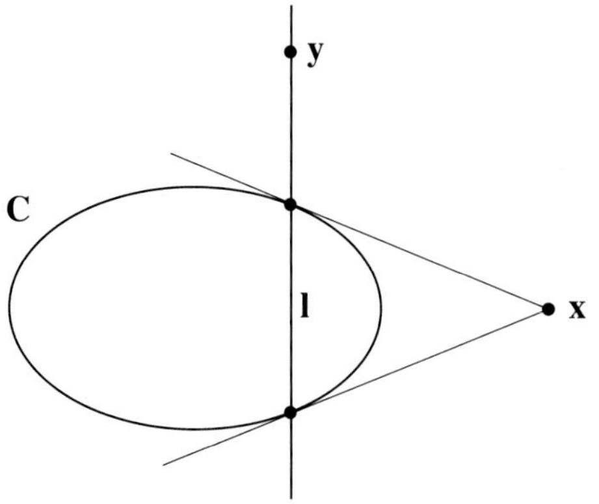

Fig. 2.19. **The pole–polar relationship.** *The line* $\mathbf{l} = \mathtt{C}\mathbf{x}$ *is the* polar *of the point* $\mathbf{x}$ *with respect to the conic* $\mathtt{C}$*, and the point* $\mathbf{x} = \mathtt{C}^{-1}\mathbf{l}$ *is the* pole *of* $\mathbf{l}$ *with respect to* $\mathtt{C}$*. The polar of* $\mathbf{x}$ *intersects the conic at the points of tangency of lines from* $\mathbf{x}$*. If* $\mathbf{y}$ *is on* $\mathbf{l}$ *then* $\mathbf{y}^\mathsf{T}\mathbf{l} = \mathbf{y}^\mathsf{T}\mathtt{C}\mathbf{x} = 0$*. Points* $\mathbf{x}$ *and* $\mathbf{y}$ *which satisfy* $\mathbf{y}^\mathsf{T}\mathtt{C}\mathbf{x} = 0$ *are* conjugate.

on 3D reconstruction and chapter 19 on auto-calibration, when obtaining a metric from a 3D projective reconstruction.

2.8 More properties of conics

We now introduce an important geometric relation between a point, line and conic, which is termed *polarity*. Applications of this relation (to the representation of orthogonality) are given in chapter 8.

2.8.1 The pole–polar relationship

A point $\mathbf{x}$ and conic $\mathtt{C}$ define a line $\mathbf{l} = \mathtt{C}\mathbf{x}$. The line $\mathbf{l}$ is called the *polar* of $\mathbf{x}$ with respect to $\mathtt{C}$, and the point $\mathbf{x}$ is the *pole* of $\mathbf{l}$ with respect to $\mathtt{C}$.

- *The polar line* $\mathbf{l} = \mathtt{C}\mathbf{x}$ *of the point* $\mathbf{x}$ *with respect to a conic* $\mathtt{C}$ *intersects the conic in two points. The two lines tangent to* $\mathtt{C}$ *at these points intersect at* $\mathbf{x}$*.*

This relationship is illustrated in figure 2.19.

Proof. Consider a point $\mathbf{y}$ on $\mathtt{C}$. The tangent line at $\mathbf{y}$ is $\mathtt{C}\mathbf{y}$, and this line contains $\mathbf{x}$ if $\mathbf{x}^\mathsf{T}\mathtt{C}\mathbf{y} = 0$. Using the symmetry of $\mathtt{C}$, the condition $\mathbf{x}^\mathsf{T}\mathtt{C}\mathbf{y} = (\mathtt{C}\mathbf{x})^\mathsf{T}\mathbf{y} = 0$ is that the point $\mathbf{y}$ lies on the line $\mathtt{C}\mathbf{x}$. Thus the polar line $\mathtt{C}\mathbf{x}$ intersects the conic in the point $\mathbf{y}$ at which the tangent line contains $\mathbf{x}$. □

As the point $\mathbf{x}$ approaches the conic the tangent lines become closer to collinear, and their contact points on the conic also become closer. In the limit that $\mathbf{x}$ lies on $\mathtt{C}$, the polar line has two-point contact at $\mathbf{x}$, and we have:

- *If the point* $\mathbf{x}$ *is on* $\mathtt{C}$ *then the polar is the tangent line to the conic at* $\mathbf{x}$*.*

See result 2.7(*p*31).

Example 2.28. A circle of radius r centred on the x-axis at $x = a$ has the equation $(x-a)^2 + y^2 = r^2$, and is represented by the conic matrix

$$\mathtt{C} = \begin{bmatrix} 1 & 0 & -a \\ 0 & 1 & 0 \\ -a & 0 & a^2 - r^2 \end{bmatrix}.$$

The polar line of the origin is given by $\mathbf{l} = \mathtt{C}(0,0,1)^\mathsf{T} = (-a, 0, a^2 - r^2)^\mathsf{T}$. This is a vertical line at $x = (a^2 - r^2)/a$. If $r = a$ the origin lies on the circle. In this case the polar line is the y-axis and is tangent to the circle. △

It is evident that the conic induces a map between points and lines of $\mathbb{P}^2$. This map is a projective construction since it involves only intersections and tangency, both properties that are preserved under projective transformations. A projective map between points and lines is termed a *correlation* (an unfortunate name, given its more common usage).

Definition 2.29. A *correlation* is an invertible mapping from points of $\mathbb{P}^2$ to lines of $\mathbb{P}^2$. It is represented by a 3×3 non-singular matrix $\mathtt{A}$ as $\mathbf{l} = \mathtt{A}\mathbf{x}$.

A correlation provides a systematic way to dualize relations involving points and lines. It need not be represented by a symmetric matrix, but we will only consider symmetric correlations here, because of the association with conics.

- **Conjugate points.** *If the point* $\mathbf{y}$ *is on the line* $\mathbf{l} = \mathtt{C}\mathbf{x}$ *then* $\mathbf{y}^\mathsf{T}\mathbf{l} = \mathbf{y}^\mathsf{T}\mathtt{C}\mathbf{x} = 0$. *Any two points* $\mathbf{x}, \mathbf{y}$ *satisfying* $\mathbf{y}^\mathsf{T}\mathtt{C}\mathbf{x} = 0$ *are* conjugate *with respect to the conic* $\mathtt{C}$.

  The conjugacy relation is symmetric:

- *If* $\mathbf{x}$ *is on the polar of* $\mathbf{y}$ *then* $\mathbf{y}$ *is on the polar of* $\mathbf{x}$.

This follows simply because of the symmetry of the conic matrix – the point $\mathbf{x}$ is on the polar of $\mathbf{y}$ if $\mathbf{x}^\mathsf{T}\mathtt{C}\mathbf{y} = 0$, and the point $\mathbf{y}$ is on the polar of $\mathbf{x}$ if $\mathbf{y}^\mathsf{T}\mathtt{C}\mathbf{x} = 0$. Since $\mathbf{x}^\mathsf{T}\mathtt{C}\mathbf{y} = \mathbf{y}^\mathsf{T}\mathtt{C}\mathbf{x}$, if one form is zero, then so is the other. There is a dual conjugacy relationship for lines: two lines $\mathbf{l}$ and $\mathbf{m}$ are conjugate if $\mathbf{l}^\mathsf{T}\mathtt{C}^*\mathbf{m} = 0$.

2.8.2 Classification of conics

This section describes the projective and affine classification of conics.

Projective normal form for a conic. Since $\mathtt{C}$ is a symmetric matrix it has real eigenvalues, and may be decomposed as a product $\mathtt{C} = \mathtt{U}^\mathsf{T}\mathtt{D}\mathtt{U}$ (see section A4.2(*p*580)), where $\mathtt{U}$ is an orthogonal matrix, and $\mathtt{D}$ is diagonal. Applying the projective transformation represented by $\mathtt{U}$, conic $\mathtt{C}$ is transformed to another conic $\mathtt{C}' = \mathtt{U}^{-\mathsf{T}}\mathtt{C}\mathtt{U}^{-1} = \mathtt{U}^{-\mathsf{T}}\mathtt{U}^\mathsf{T}\mathtt{D}\mathtt{U}\mathtt{U}^{-1} = \mathtt{D}$. This shows that any conic is equivalent under projective transformation to one with a diagonal matrix. Let $\mathtt{D} = \mathrm{diag}(\epsilon_1 d_1, \epsilon_2 d_2, \epsilon_3 d_3)$ where $\epsilon_i = \pm 1$ or 0 and each $d_i > 0$. Thus, $\mathtt{D}$ may be written in the form

$$\mathtt{D} = \mathrm{diag}(s_1, s_2, s_3)^\mathsf{T}\mathrm{diag}(\epsilon_1, \epsilon_2, \epsilon_3)\mathrm{diag}(s_1, s_2, s_3)$$

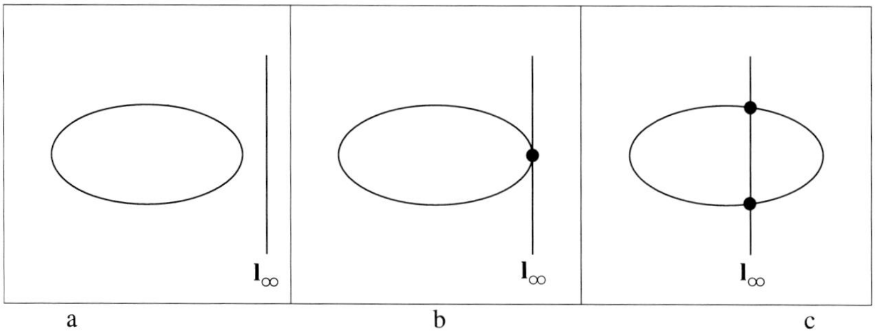

Fig. 2.20. **Affine classification of point conics.** *A conic is an (a) ellipse, (b) parabola, or (c) hyperbola; according to whether it (a) has no real intersection, (b) is tangent to (2-point contact), or (c) has 2 real intersections with $\mathbf{l}_\infty$. Under an affine transformation $\mathbf{l}_\infty$ is a fixed line, and intersections are preserved. Thus this classification is unaltered by an affinity.*

where $s_i^2 = d_i$. Note that $\text{diag}(s_1, s_2, s_3)^\mathsf{T} = \text{diag}(s_1, s_2, s_3)$. Now, transforming once more by the transformation $\text{diag}(s_1, s_2, s_3)$, the conic $\mathtt{D}$ is transformed to a conic with matrix $\text{diag}(\epsilon_1, \epsilon_2, \epsilon_3)$, with each $\epsilon_i = \pm 1$ or 0. Further transformation by permutation matrices may be carried out to ensure that values $\epsilon_i = 1$ occur before values $\epsilon_i = -1$ which in turn precede values $\epsilon_i = 0$. Finally, by multiplying by -1 if necessary, one may ensure that there are at least as many $+1$ entries as -1. The various types of conics may now be enumerated, and are shown in table 2.2.

Diagonal	Equation	Conic type
$(1, 1, 1)$	$x^2 + y^2 + w^2 = 0$	Improper conic – no real points.
$(1, 1, -1)$	$x^2 + y^2 - w^2 = 0$	Circle
$(1, 1, 0)$	$x^2 + y^2 = 0$	Single real point $(0, 0, 1)^\mathsf{T}$
$(1, -1, 0)$	$x^2 - y^2 = 0$	Two lines $x = \pm y$
$(1, 0, 0)$	$x^2 = 0$	Single line $x = 0$ counted twice.

Table 2.2. **Projective classification of point conics.** *Any plane conic is projectively equivalent to one of the types shown in this table. Those conics for which $\epsilon_i = 0$ for some i are known as degenerate conics, and are represented by a matrix of rank less than 3. The conic type column only describes the real points of the conics – for example as a complex conic $x^2 + y^2 = 0$ consists of the line pair $x = \pm iy$.*

Affine classification of conics. The classification of (non-degenerate, proper) conics in Euclidean geometry into hyperbola, ellipse and parabola is well known. As shown above in projective geometry these three types of conic are projectively equivalent to a circle. However, in affine geometry the Euclidean classification is still valid because it depends only on the relation of $\mathbf{l}_\infty$ to the conic. The relation for the three types of conic is illustrated in figure 2.20.

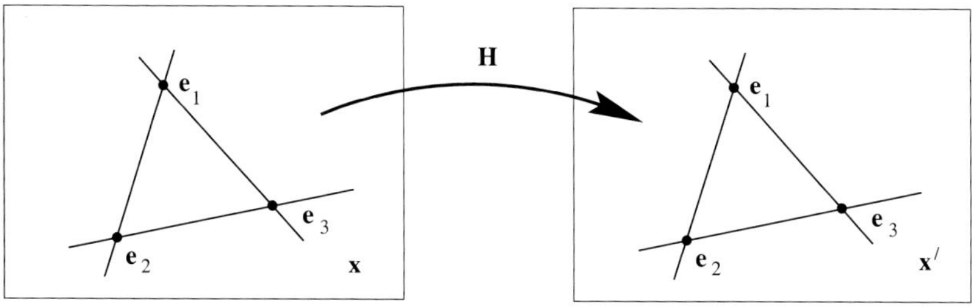

Fig. 2.21. **Fixed points and lines of a plane projective transformation.** *There are three fixed points, and three fixed lines through these points. The fixed lines and points may be complex. Algebraically, the fixed points are the eigenvectors,* $\mathbf{e}_i$, *of the point transformation* ($\mathbf{x}' = \mathtt{H}\mathbf{x}$), *and the fixed lines eigenvectors of the line transformation* ($\mathbf{l}' = \mathtt{H}^{-\mathsf{T}}\mathbf{l}$). *Note, the fixed line is* not *fixed pointwise: under the transformation, points on the line are mapped to other points on the line; only the fixed points are mapped to themselves.*

2.9 Fixed points and lines

We have seen, by the examples of $\mathbf{l}_\infty$ and the circular points, that points and lines may be fixed under a projective transformation. In this section the idea is investigated more thoroughly.

Here, the source and destination planes are identified (the same) so that the transformation maps points $\mathbf{x}$ to points $\mathbf{x}'$ in the same coordinate system. The key idea is that an *eigenvector* corresponds to a *fixed point* of the transformation, since for an eigenvector $\mathbf{e}$ with eigenvalue λ,

$$\mathtt{H}\mathbf{e} = \lambda\mathbf{e}$$

and $\mathbf{e}$ and $\lambda\mathbf{e}$ represent the same point. Often the eigenvector and eigenvalue have physical or geometric significance in computer vision applications.

A 3×3 matrix has three eigenvalues and consequently a plane projective transformation has up to three fixed points, if the eigenvalues are distinct. Since the characteristic equation is a cubic in this case, one or three of the eigenvalues, and corresponding eigenvectors, is real. A similar development can be given for *fixed lines*, which, since lines transform as (2.6–*p*36) $\mathbf{l}' = \mathtt{H}^{-\mathsf{T}}\mathbf{l}$, correspond to the eigenvectors of $\mathtt{H}^{\mathsf{T}}$.

The relationship between the fixed points and fixed lines is shown in figure 2.21. Note the lines are fixed as a set, not fixed pointwise, i.e. a point on the line is mapped to another point on the line, but in general the source and destination points will differ. There is nothing mysterious here: The projective transformation of the plane induces a 1D projective transformation on the line. A 1D projective transformation is represented by a 2×2 homogeneous matrix (section 2.5). This 1D projectivity has two fixed points corresponding to the two eigenvectors of the 2×2 matrix. These fixed points are those of the 2D projective transformation.

A further specialization concerns repeated eigenvalues. Suppose two of the eigenvalues (λ_2, λ_3 say) are identical, and that there are two distinct eigenvectors ($\mathbf{e}_2, \mathbf{e}_3$), corresponding to $\lambda_2 = \lambda_3$. Then the line containing the eigenvectors $\mathbf{e}_2, \mathbf{e}_3$ will be fixed pointwise, i.e. it is a line of fixed points. For suppose $\mathbf{x} = \alpha\mathbf{e}_2 + \beta\mathbf{e}_3$; then

$$\mathtt{H}\mathbf{x} = \lambda_2\alpha\mathbf{e}_2 + \lambda_2\beta\mathbf{e}_3 = \lambda_2\mathbf{x}$$

i.e. a point on the line through two degenerate eigenvectors is mapped to itself (only differing by scale). Another possibility is that $\lambda_2 = \lambda_3$, but that there is only one corresponding eigenvector. In this case, the eigenvector has *algebraic dimension* equal to two, but *geometric dimension* equal to one. Then there is one fewer fixed point (2 instead of 3). Various cases of repeated eigenvalues are discussed further in appendix 7(*p*628).

We now examine the fixed points and lines of the hierarchy of projective transformation subgroups of section 2.4. Affine transformations, and the more specialized forms, have two eigenvectors which are ideal points ($x_3 = 0$), and which correspond to the eigenvectors of the upper left 2×2 matrix. The third eigenvector is finite in general.

A Euclidean matrix. The two ideal fixed points are the complex conjugate pair of circular points $\mathbf{I}, \mathbf{J}$, with corresponding eigenvalues $\{e^{i\theta}, e^{-i\theta}\}$, where θ is the rotation angle. The third eigenvector, which has unit eigenvalue, is called the *pole*. The Euclidean transformation is equal to a pure rotation by θ about this point with no translation.

A special case is that of a pure translation (i.e. where $\theta = 0$). Here the eigenvalues are triply degenerate. The line at infinity is fixed pointwise, and there is a pencil of fixed lines through the point $(t_x, t_y, 0)^\mathsf{T}$ which corresponds to the translation direction. Consequently lines parallel to $\mathbf{t}$ are fixed. This is an example of an elation (see section A7.3(*p*631)).

A similarity matrix. The two ideal fixed points are again the circular points. The eigenvalues are $\{1, se^{i\theta}, se^{-i\theta}\}$. The action can be understood as a rotation and isotropic scaling by s about the finite fixed point. Note that the eigenvalues of the circular points again encode the angle of rotation.

An affine matrix. The two ideal fixed points can be real or complex conjugates, but the fixed line $\mathbf{l}_\infty = (0, 0, 1)^\mathsf{T}$ through these points is real in either case.

2.10 Closure

2.10.1 The literature

A gentle introduction to plane projective geometry, written for computer vision researchers, is given in the appendix of Mundy and Zisserman [Mundy-92]. A more formal approach is that of Semple and Kneebone [Semple-79], but [Springer-64] is more readable.

On the recovery of affine and metric scene properties for an imaged plane, Collins and Beveridge [Collins-93] use the vanishing line to recover affine properties from satellite images, and Liebowitz and Zisserman [Liebowitz-98] use metric information on the plane, such as right angles, to recover the metric geometry.

2.10.2 Notes and exercises

(i) **Affine transformations.**

(a) Show that an affine transformation can map a circle to an ellipse, but cannot map an ellipse to a hyperbola or parabola.

(b) Prove that under an affine transformation the ratio of lengths on parallel line segments is an invariant, but that the ratio of two lengths that are not parallel is not.

(ii) **Projective transformations.** Show that there is a three-parameter family of projective transformations which fix (as a set) a unit circle at the origin, i.e. a unit circle at the origin is mapped to a unit circle at the origin (hint, use result 2.13(*p*37) to compute the transformation). What is the geometric interpretation of this family?

(iii) **Isotropies.** Show that two lines have an invariant under a similarity transformation; and that two lines and two points have an invariant under a projective transformation. In both cases the equality case of the counting argument (result 2.16(*p*43)) is violated. Show that for these two cases the respective transformation cannot be fully determined, although it is partially determined.

(iv) **Invariants.** Using the transformation rules for points, lines and conics show:

(a) Two lines, $\mathbf{l}_1$, $\mathbf{l}_2$, and two points, $\mathbf{x}_1$, $\mathbf{x}_2$, not lying on the lines have the invariant

$$I = \frac{(\mathbf{l}_1^{\mathsf{T}}\mathbf{x}_1)(\mathbf{l}_2^{\mathsf{T}}\mathbf{x}_2)}{(\mathbf{l}_1^{\mathsf{T}}\mathbf{x}_2)(\mathbf{l}_2^{\mathsf{T}}\mathbf{x}_1)}$$

(see the previous question).

(b) A conic $\mathtt{C}$ and two points, $\mathbf{x}_1$ and $\mathbf{x}_2$, in general position have the invariant

$$I = \frac{(\mathbf{x}_1^{\mathsf{T}}\mathtt{C}\mathbf{x}_2)^2}{(\mathbf{x}_1^{\mathsf{T}}\mathtt{C}\mathbf{x}_1)(\mathbf{x}_2^{\mathsf{T}}\mathtt{C}\mathbf{x}_2)}.$$

(c) Show that the projectively invariant expression for measuring angles (2.22) is equivalent to Laguerre's projectively invariant expression involving a cross ratio with the circular points (see [Springer-64]).

(v) **The cross ratio.** Prove the invariance of the cross ratio of four collinear points under projective transformations of the line (2.18–*p*45). Hint, start with the transformation of two points on the line written as $\bar{\mathbf{x}}'_i = \lambda_i \mathtt{H}_{2\times2}\bar{\mathbf{x}}_i$ and $\bar{\mathbf{x}}'_j = \lambda_j \mathtt{H}_{2\times2}\bar{\mathbf{x}}_j$, where equality is *not* up to scale, then from the properties of determinants show that $|\bar{\mathbf{x}}'_i\bar{\mathbf{x}}'_j| = \lambda_i\lambda_j \det \mathtt{H}_{2\times2}|\bar{\mathbf{x}}_i\bar{\mathbf{x}}_j|$ and continue from here. An alternative derivation method is given in [Semple-79].

(vi) **Polarity.** Figure 2.19 shows the geometric construction of the polar line for a point $\mathbf{x}$ *outside* an ellipse. Give a geometric construction for the polar when the point is inside. Hint, start by choosing any line through $\mathbf{x}$. The pole of this line is a point on the polar of $\mathbf{x}$.

(vii) **Conics.** If the sign of the conic matrix $\mathtt{C}$ is chosen such that two eigenvalues are positive and one negative, then internal and external points may be distinguished according to the sign of $\mathbf{x}^{\mathsf{T}}\mathtt{C}\mathbf{x}$: the point $\mathbf{x}$ is inside/on/outside the conic

C if $\mathbf{x}^\mathsf{T}\mathtt{C}\mathbf{x}$ is negative/zero/positive respectively. This can seen by example from a circle $\mathtt{C} = \text{diag}(1, 1, -1)$. Under projective transformations internality is invariant, though its interpretation requires care in the case of an ellipse being transformed to a hyperbola (see figure 2.20).

(viii) **Dual conics.** Show that the matrix $[\mathbf{l}]_\times \mathtt{C} [\mathbf{l}]_\times$ represents a rank 2 dual conic which consists of the two points at which the line $\mathbf{l}$ intersects the (point) conic C (the notation $[\mathbf{l}]_\times$ is defined in (A4.5–*p*581)).

(ix) **Special projective transformations.** Suppose points on a scene plane are related by reflection in a line: for example, a plane object with bilateral symmetry. Show that in a perspective image of the plane the points are related by a projectivity H satisfying $\mathtt{H}^2 = \mathtt{I}$. Furthermore, show that under H there is a line of fixed points corresponding to the imaged reflection line, and that H has an eigenvector, not lying on this line, which is the vanishing point of the reflection direction (H is a planar harmonic homology, see section A7.2(*p*629)).
Now suppose that the points are related by a finite rotational symmetry: for example, points on a hexagonal bolt head. Show in this case that $\mathtt{H}^n = \mathtt{I}$, where n is the order of rotational symmetry (6 for a hexagonal symmetry), that the eigenvalues of H determine the rotation angle, and that the eigenvector corresponding to the real eigenvalue is the image of the centre of the rotational symmetry.

3

Projective Geometry and Transformations of 3D

This chapter describes the properties and entities of projective 3-space, or $\mathbb{P}^3$. Many of these are straightforward generalizations of those of the projective plane, described in chapter 2. For example, in $\mathbb{P}^3$ Euclidean 3-space is augmented with a set of ideal points which are on a *plane* at infinity, $\boldsymbol{\pi}_\infty$. This is the analogue of $\mathbf{l}_\infty$ in $\mathbb{P}^2$. Parallel lines, and now parallel *planes*, intersect on $\boldsymbol{\pi}_\infty$. Not surprisingly, homogeneous coordinates again play an important role, here with all dimensions increased by one. However, additional properties appear by virtue of the extra dimension. For example, two lines always intersect on the projective plane, but they need not intersect in 3-space.

The reader should be familiar with the ideas and notation of chapter 2 before reading this chapter. We will concentrate here on the differences and additional geometry introduced by adding the extra dimension, and will not repeat the bulk of the material of the previous chapter.

3.1 Points and projective transformations

A point $\mathbf{X}$ in 3-space is represented in homogeneous coordinates as a 4-vector. Specifically, the homogeneous vector $\mathbf{X} = (\mathrm{X}_1, \mathrm{X}_2, \mathrm{X}_3, \mathrm{X}_4)^\mathsf{T}$ with $\mathrm{X}_4 \neq 0$ represents the point $(\mathrm{X}, \mathrm{Y}, \mathrm{Z})^\mathsf{T}$ of $\mathbb{R}^3$ with inhomogeneous coordinates

$$\mathrm{X} = \mathrm{X}_1/\mathrm{X}_4, \quad \mathrm{Y} = \mathrm{X}_2/\mathrm{X}_4, \quad \mathrm{Z} = \mathrm{X}_3/\mathrm{X}_4.$$

For example, a homogeneous representation of $(\mathrm{X}, \mathrm{Y}, \mathrm{Z})^\mathsf{T}$ is $\mathbf{X} = (\mathrm{X}, \mathrm{Y}, \mathrm{Z}, 1)^\mathsf{T}$. Homogeneous points with $\mathrm{X}_4 = 0$ represent points at infinity.

A projective transformation acting on $\mathbb{P}^3$ is a linear transformation on homogeneous 4-vectors represented by a non-singular 4×4 matrix: $\mathbf{X}' = \mathtt{H}\mathbf{X}$. The matrix $\mathtt{H}$ representing the transformation is homogeneous and has 15 degrees of freedom. The degrees of freedom follow from the 16 elements of the matrix less one for overall scaling.

As in the case of planar projective transformations, the map is a collineation (lines are mapped to lines), which preserves incidence relations such as the intersection point of a line with a plane, and order of contact.

3.2 Representing and transforming planes, lines and quadrics

In $\mathbb{P}^3$ points and *planes* are dual, and their representation and development is analogous to the point–line duality in $\mathbb{P}^2$. Lines are self-dual in $\mathbb{P}^3$.

3.2.1 Planes

A plane in 3-space may be written as

$$\pi_1 \mathrm{X} + \pi_2 \mathrm{Y} + \pi_3 \mathrm{Z} + \pi_4 = 0. \tag{3.1}$$

Clearly this equation is unaffected by multiplication by a non-zero scalar, so only the three independent ratios $\{\pi_1 : \pi_2 : \pi_3 : \pi_4\}$ of the plane coefficients are significant. It follows that a plane has 3 degrees of freedom in 3-space. The homogeneous representation of the plane is the 4-vector $\boldsymbol{\pi} = (\pi_1, \pi_2, \pi_3, \pi_4)^\mathsf{T}$.

Homogenizing (3.1) by the replacements $\mathrm{X} \mapsto \mathrm{X}_1/\mathrm{X}_4$, $\mathrm{Y} \mapsto \mathrm{X}_2/\mathrm{X}_4$, $\mathrm{Z} \mapsto \mathrm{X}_3/\mathrm{X}_4$ gives

$$\pi_1 \mathrm{X}_1 + \pi_2 \mathrm{X}_2 + \pi_3 \mathrm{X}_3 + \pi_4 \mathrm{X}_4 = 0$$

or more concisely

$$\boldsymbol{\pi}^\mathsf{T} \mathbf{X} = 0 \tag{3.2}$$

which expresses that the point $\mathbf{X}$ is on the plane $\boldsymbol{\pi}$.

The first 3 components of $\boldsymbol{\pi}$ correspond to the plane normal of Euclidean geometry – using inhomogeneous notation (3.2) becomes the familiar plane equation written in 3-vector notation as $\mathbf{n}.\widetilde{\mathbf{X}} + d = 0$, where $\mathbf{n} = (\pi_1, \pi_2, \pi_3)^\mathsf{T}$, $\widetilde{\mathbf{X}} = (\mathrm{X}, \mathrm{Y}, \mathrm{Z})^\mathsf{T}$, $\mathrm{X}_4 = 1$ and $d = \pi_4$. In this form $d/\|\mathbf{n}\|$ is the distance of the plane from the origin.

Join and incidence relations. In $\mathbb{P}^3$ there are numerous geometric relations between planes and points and lines. For example,

(i) A plane is defined uniquely by the join of three points, or the join of a line and point, in general position (i.e. the points are not collinear or incident with the line in the latter case).

(ii) Two distinct planes intersect in a unique line.

(iii) Three distinct planes intersect in a unique point.

These relations have algebraic representations which will now be developed in the case of points and planes. The representations of the relations involving lines are not as simple as those arising from 3D vector algebra of $\mathbb{P}^2$ (e.g. $\mathbf{l} = \mathbf{x} \times \mathbf{y}$), and are postponed until line representations are introduced in section 3.2.2.

Three points define a plane. Suppose three points $\mathbf{X}_i$ are incident with the plane $\boldsymbol{\pi}$. Then each point satisfies (3.2) and thus $\boldsymbol{\pi}^\mathsf{T}\mathbf{X}_i = 0, \;\; i = 1, \ldots, 3$. Stacking these equations into a matrix gives

$$\begin{bmatrix} \mathbf{X}_1^\mathsf{T} \\ \mathbf{X}_2^\mathsf{T} \\ \mathbf{X}_3^\mathsf{T} \end{bmatrix} \boldsymbol{\pi} = \mathbf{0}. \tag{3.3}$$

Since three points $\mathbf{X}_1, \mathbf{X}_2$ and $\mathbf{X}_3$ in general position are linearly independent, it follows that the 3×4 matrix composed of the points as rows has rank 3. The plane $\boldsymbol{\pi}$ defined by the points is thus obtained uniquely (up to scale) as the 1-dimensional (right) null-space. If the matrix has only a rank of 2, and consequently the null-space is 2-dimensional, then the points are collinear, and define a pencil of planes with the line of collinear points as axis.

In $\mathbb{P}^2$, where points are dual to lines, a line $\mathbf{l}$ through two points $\mathbf{x}, \mathbf{y}$ can similarly be obtained as the null-space of the 2×3 matrix with $\mathbf{x}^\mathsf{T}$ and $\mathbf{y}^\mathsf{T}$ as rows. However, a more convenient direct formula $\mathbf{l} = \mathbf{x} \times \mathbf{y}$ is also available from vector algebra. In $\mathbb{P}^3$ the analogous expression is obtained from properties of determinants and minors.

We start from the matrix $\mathtt{M} = [\mathbf{X}, \mathbf{X}_1, \mathbf{X}_2, \mathbf{X}_3]$ which is composed of a general point $\mathbf{X}$ and the three points $\mathbf{X}_i$ which define the plane $\boldsymbol{\pi}$. The determinant $\det \mathtt{M} = 0$ when $\mathbf{X}$ lies on $\boldsymbol{\pi}$ since the point $\mathbf{X}$ is then expressible as a linear combination of the points $\mathbf{X}_i, i = 1, \ldots, 3$. Expanding the determinant about the column $\mathbf{X}$ we obtain

$$\det \mathtt{M} = \mathrm{X}_1 D_{234} - \mathrm{X}_2 D_{134} + \mathrm{X}_3 D_{124} - \mathrm{X}_4 D_{123}$$

where D_{jkl} is the determinant formed from the jkl rows of the 4×3 matrix $[\mathbf{X}_1, \mathbf{X}_2, \mathbf{X}_3]$. Since $\det \mathtt{M} = 0$ for points on $\boldsymbol{\pi}$ we can then read off the plane coefficients as

$$\boldsymbol{\pi} = (D_{234}, -D_{134}, D_{124}, -D_{123})^\mathsf{T}. \tag{3.4}$$

This is the solution vector (the null-space) of (3.3) above.

Example 3.1. Suppose the three points defining the plane are

$$\mathbf{X}_1 = \begin{pmatrix} \widetilde{\mathbf{X}}_1 \\ 1 \end{pmatrix} \quad \mathbf{X}_2 = \begin{pmatrix} \widetilde{\mathbf{X}}_2 \\ 1 \end{pmatrix} \quad \mathbf{X}_3 = \begin{pmatrix} \widetilde{\mathbf{X}}_3 \\ 1 \end{pmatrix}$$

where $\widetilde{\mathbf{X}} = (\mathrm{X}, \mathrm{Y}, \mathrm{Z})^\mathsf{T}$. Then

$$D_{234} = \begin{vmatrix} \mathrm{Y}_1 & \mathrm{Y}_2 & \mathrm{Y}_3 \\ \mathrm{Z}_1 & \mathrm{Z}_2 & \mathrm{Z}_3 \\ 1 & 1 & 1 \end{vmatrix} = \begin{vmatrix} \mathrm{Y}_1 - \mathrm{Y}_3 & \mathrm{Y}_2 - \mathrm{Y}_3 & \mathrm{Y}_3 \\ \mathrm{Z}_1 - \mathrm{Z}_3 & \mathrm{Z}_2 - \mathrm{Z}_3 & \mathrm{Z}_3 \\ 0 & 0 & 1 \end{vmatrix} = \left((\widetilde{\mathbf{X}}_1 - \widetilde{\mathbf{X}}_3) \times (\widetilde{\mathbf{X}}_2 - \widetilde{\mathbf{X}}_3)\right)_1$$

and similarly for the other components, giving

$$\boldsymbol{\pi} = \begin{pmatrix} (\widetilde{\mathbf{X}}_1 - \widetilde{\mathbf{X}}_3) \times (\widetilde{\mathbf{X}}_2 - \widetilde{\mathbf{X}}_3) \\ -\widetilde{\mathbf{X}}_3^\mathsf{T}(\widetilde{\mathbf{X}}_1 \times \widetilde{\mathbf{X}}_2) \end{pmatrix}.$$

This is the familiar result from Euclidean vector geometry where, for example, the plane normal is computed as $(\widetilde{\mathbf{X}}_1 - \widetilde{\mathbf{X}}_3) \times (\widetilde{\mathbf{X}}_2 - \widetilde{\mathbf{X}}_3)$. △

Three planes define a point. The development here is dual to the case of three points defining a plane. The intersection point $\mathbf{X}$ of three planes $\boldsymbol{\pi}_i$ can be computed straightforwardly as the (right) null-space of the 3×4 matrix composed of the planes as rows:

$$\begin{bmatrix} \boldsymbol{\pi}_1^\mathsf{T} \\ \boldsymbol{\pi}_2^\mathsf{T} \\ \boldsymbol{\pi}_3^\mathsf{T} \end{bmatrix} \mathbf{X} = \mathbf{0}. \tag{3.5}$$

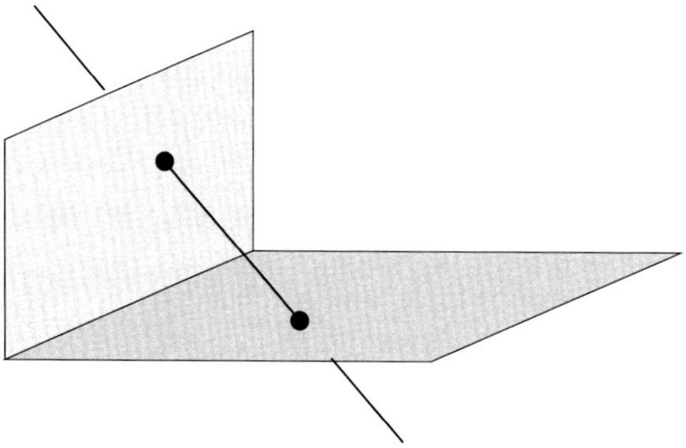

Fig. 3.1. *A line may be specified by its points of intersection with two orthogonal planes. Each intersection point has 2 degrees of freedom, which demonstrates that a line in* $\mathbb{P}^3$ *has a total of 4 degrees of freedom.*

A direct solution for $\mathbf{X}$, in terms of determinants of 3×3 submatrices, is obtained as an analogue of (3.4), though computationally a numerical solution would be obtained by algorithm A5.1(*p*589).

The two following results are direct analogues of their 2D counterparts.

Projective transformation. Under the point transformation $\mathbf{X}' = \mathtt{H}\mathbf{X}$, a plane transforms as

$$\boldsymbol{\pi}' = \mathtt{H}^{-\mathsf{T}}\boldsymbol{\pi}. \tag{3.6}$$

Parametrized points on a plane. The points $\mathbf{X}$ on the plane $\boldsymbol{\pi}$ may be written as

$$\mathbf{X} = \mathtt{M}\mathbf{x} \tag{3.7}$$

where the columns of the 4×3 matrix $\mathtt{M}$ generate the rank 3 null-space of $\boldsymbol{\pi}^{\mathsf{T}}$, i.e. $\boldsymbol{\pi}^{\mathsf{T}}\mathtt{M} = \mathbf{0}$, and the 3-vector $\mathbf{x}$ (which is a point on the projective plane $\mathbb{P}^2$) parametrizes points on the plane $\boldsymbol{\pi}$. $\mathtt{M}$ is not unique, of course. Suppose the plane is $\boldsymbol{\pi} = (a, b, c, d)^{\mathsf{T}}$ and a is non-zero, then $\mathtt{M}^{\mathsf{T}}$ can be written as $\mathtt{M}^{\mathsf{T}} = [\mathbf{p} \mid \mathtt{I}_{3\times3}]$, where $\mathbf{p} = (-b/a, -c/a, -d/a)^{\mathsf{T}}$.

This parametrized representation is simply the analogue in 3D of a line $\mathbf{l}$ in $\mathbb{P}^2$ defined as a linear combination of its 2D null-space as $\mathbf{x} = \mu\mathbf{a} + \lambda\mathbf{b}$, where $\mathbf{l}^{\mathsf{T}}\mathbf{a} = \mathbf{l}^{\mathsf{T}}\mathbf{b} = 0$.

3.2.2 Lines

A line is defined by the *join* of two points or the intersection of two planes. Lines have 4 degrees of freedom in 3-space. A convincing way to count these degrees of freedom is to think of a line as defined by its intersection with two orthogonal planes, as in figure 3.1. The point of intersection on each plane is specified by two parameters, producing a total of 4 degrees of freedom for the line.

Lines are very awkward to represent in 3-space since a natural representation for an object with 4 degrees of freedom would be a homogeneous 5-vector. The problem is that a homogeneous 5 vector cannot easily be used in mathematical expressions together with the 4-vectors representing points and planes. To overcome this problem a number of line representations have been proposed, and these differ in their mathematical complexity. We survey three of these representations. In each case the representation provides mechanisms for a line to be defined by: the join of two points, a dual version where the line is defined by the intersection of two planes, and also a map between the two definitions. The representations also enable join and incidence relations to be computed, for example the point at which a line intersects a plane.

I. Null-space and span representation. This representation builds on the intuitive geometric notion that a line is a pencil (one-parameter family) of collinear points, and is defined by any two of these points. Similarly, a line is the axis of a pencil of planes, and is defined by the intersection of any two planes from the pencil. In both cases the actual points or planes are not important (in fact two points have 6 degrees of freedom and are represented by two 4-vectors – far too many parameters). This notion is captured mathematically by representing a line as the *span* of two vectors. Suppose $\mathbf{A}, \mathbf{B}$ are two (non-coincident) space points. Then the line joining these points is represented by the span of the row space of the 2×4 matrix $\mathtt{W}$ composed of $\mathbf{A}^\mathsf{T}$ and $\mathbf{B}^\mathsf{T}$ as rows:

$$\mathtt{W} = \begin{bmatrix} \mathbf{A}^\mathsf{T} \\ \mathbf{B}^\mathsf{T} \end{bmatrix}.$$

Then:

(i) The span of $\mathtt{W}^\mathsf{T}$ is the pencil of points $\lambda\mathbf{A} + \mu\mathbf{B}$ on the line.
(ii) The span of the 2-dimensional right null-space of $\mathtt{W}$ is the pencil of planes with the line as axis.

It is evident that two other points, $\mathbf{A}'^\mathsf{T}$ and $\mathbf{B}'^\mathsf{T}$, on the line will generate a matrix $\mathtt{W}'$ with the same span as $\mathtt{W}$, so that the span, and hence the representation, is independent of the particular points used to define it.

To prove the null-space property, suppose that $\mathbf{P}$ and $\mathbf{Q}$ are a basis for the null-space. Then $\mathtt{W}\mathbf{P} = \mathbf{0}$ and consequently $\mathbf{A}^\mathsf{T}\mathbf{P} = \mathbf{B}^\mathsf{T}\mathbf{P} = 0$, so that $\mathbf{P}$ is a plane containing the points $\mathbf{A}$ and $\mathbf{B}$. Similarly, $\mathbf{Q}$ is a distinct plane also containing the points $\mathbf{A}$ and $\mathbf{B}$. Thus $\mathbf{A}$ and $\mathbf{B}$ lie on both the (linearly independent) planes $\mathbf{P}$ and $\mathbf{Q}$, so the line defined by $\mathtt{W}$ is the plane intersection. Any plane of the pencil, with the line as axis, is given by the span $\lambda'\mathbf{P} + \mu'\mathbf{Q}$.

The dual representation of a line as the intersection of two planes, $\mathbf{P}, \mathbf{Q}$, follows in a similar manner. The line is represented as the span (of the row space) of the 2×4 matrix $\mathtt{W}^*$ composed of $\mathbf{P}^\mathsf{T}$ and $\mathbf{Q}^\mathsf{T}$ as rows:

$$\mathtt{W}^* = \begin{bmatrix} \mathbf{P}^\mathsf{T} \\ \mathbf{Q}^\mathsf{T} \end{bmatrix}$$

with the properties

(i) The span of $\mathtt{W}^{*\mathsf{T}}$ is the pencil of planes $\lambda'\mathbf{P} + \mu'\mathbf{Q}$ with the line as axis.
(ii) The span of the 2-dimensional null-space of $\mathtt{W}^*$ is the pencil of points on the line.

The two representations are related by $\mathtt{W}^* \mathtt{W}^\mathsf{T} = \mathtt{W}\mathtt{W}^{*\mathsf{T}} = 0_{2\times2}$, where $0_{2\times2}$ is a 2×2 null matrix.

Example 3.2. The X-axis is represented as

$$\mathtt{W} = \begin{bmatrix} 0 & 0 & 0 & 1 \\ 1 & 0 & 0 & 0 \end{bmatrix} \qquad \mathtt{W}^* = \begin{bmatrix} 0 & 0 & 1 & 0 \\ 0 & 1 & 0 & 0 \end{bmatrix}$$

where the points $\mathbf{A}$ and $\mathbf{B}$ are here the origin and ideal point in the X-direction, and the planes $\mathbf{P}$ and $\mathbf{Q}$ are the XY- and XZ-planes respectively. △

Join and incidence relations are also computed from null-spaces.

(i) The plane $\boldsymbol{\pi}$ defined by the join of the point $\mathbf{X}$ and line W is obtained from the null-space of

$$\mathtt{M} = \begin{bmatrix} \mathtt{W} \\ \mathbf{X}^\mathsf{T} \end{bmatrix}.$$

If the null-space of M is 2-dimensional then $\mathbf{X}$ is on W, otherwise $\mathtt{M}\boldsymbol{\pi} = \mathbf{0}$.

(ii) The point $\mathbf{X}$ defined by the intersection of the line W with the plane $\boldsymbol{\pi}$ is obtained from the null-space of

$$\mathtt{M} = \begin{bmatrix} \mathtt{W}^* \\ \boldsymbol{\pi}^\mathsf{T} \end{bmatrix}.$$

If the null-space of M is 2-dimensional then the line W is on $\boldsymbol{\pi}$, otherwise $\mathtt{M}\mathbf{X} = \mathbf{0}$.

These properties can be derived almost by inspection. For example, the first is equivalent to three points defining a plane (3.3).

The span representation is very useful in practical numerical implementations where null-spaces can be computed simply by using the SVD algorithm (see section A4.4-(p585)) available with most matrix packages. The representation is also useful in estimation problems, where it is often not a problem that the entity being estimated is over-parametrized (see the discussion of section 4.5(p110)).

II. Plücker matrices. Here a line is represented by a 4×4 skew-symmetric homogeneous matrix. In particular, the line joining the two points $\mathbf{A}, \mathbf{B}$ is represented by the matrix L with elements

$$l_{ij} = A_i B_j - B_i A_j$$

or equivalently in vector notation as

$$\mathtt{L} = \mathbf{A}\mathbf{B}^\mathsf{T} - \mathbf{B}\mathbf{A}^\mathsf{T} \tag{3.8}$$

First a few properties of L:

(i) L has rank 2. Its 2-dimensional null-space is spanned by the pencil of planes with the line as axis (in fact $\mathtt{L}\mathtt{W}^{*\mathsf{T}} = 0$, with 0 a 4×2 null-matrix).

(ii) The representation has the required 4 degrees of freedom for a line. This is accounted as follows: the skew-symmetric matrix has 6 independent non-zero elements, but only their 5 ratios are significant, and furthermore because $\det \mathtt{L} = 0$ the elements satisfy a (quadratic) constraint (see below). The net number of degrees of freedom is then 4.

(iii) The relation $\mathtt{L} = \mathbf{A}\mathbf{B}^{\mathsf{T}} - \mathbf{B}\mathbf{A}^{\mathsf{T}}$ is the generalization to 4-space of the vector product formula $\mathbf{l} = \mathbf{x} \times \mathbf{y}$ of $\mathbb{P}^2$ for a line $\mathbf{l}$ defined by two points $\mathbf{x}, \mathbf{y}$ all represented by 3-vectors.

(iv) The matrix $\mathtt{L}$ is independent of the points $\mathbf{A}, \mathbf{B}$ used to define it, since if a different point $\mathbf{C}$ on the line is used, with $\mathbf{C} = \mathbf{A} + \mu\mathbf{B}$, then the resulting matrix is

$$\begin{aligned} \hat{\mathtt{L}} &= \mathbf{A}\mathbf{C}^{\mathsf{T}} - \mathbf{C}\mathbf{A}^{\mathsf{T}} = \mathbf{A}(\mathbf{A}^{\mathsf{T}} + \mu\mathbf{B}^{\mathsf{T}}) - (\mathbf{A} + \mu\mathbf{B})\mathbf{A}^{\mathsf{T}} \\ &= \mathbf{A}\mathbf{B}^{\mathsf{T}} - \mathbf{B}\mathbf{A}^{\mathsf{T}} = \mathtt{L}. \end{aligned}$$

(v) Under the point transformation $\mathbf{X}' = \mathtt{H}\mathbf{X}$, the matrix transforms as $\mathtt{L}' = \mathtt{H}\mathtt{L}\mathtt{H}^{\mathsf{T}}$, i.e. it is a valency-2 tensor (see appendix 1(*p*562)).

Example 3.3. From (3.8) the X-axis is represented as

$$\mathtt{L} = \begin{pmatrix} 0 \\ 0 \\ 0 \\ 1 \end{pmatrix} \begin{pmatrix} 1 & 0 & 0 & 0 \end{pmatrix} - \begin{pmatrix} 1 \\ 0 \\ 0 \\ 0 \end{pmatrix} \begin{pmatrix} 0 & 0 & 0 & 1 \end{pmatrix} = \begin{bmatrix} 0 & 0 & 0 & -1 \\ 0 & 0 & 0 & 0 \\ 0 & 0 & 0 & 0 \\ 1 & 0 & 0 & 0 \end{bmatrix}$$

where the points $\mathbf{A}$ and $\mathbf{B}$ are (as in the previous example) the origin and ideal point in the X-direction respectively. △

A dual Plücker representation $\mathtt{L}^*$ is obtained for a line formed by the intersection of two planes $\mathbf{P}, \mathbf{Q}$,

$$\mathtt{L}^* = \mathbf{P}\mathbf{Q}^{\mathsf{T}} - \mathbf{Q}\mathbf{P}^{\mathsf{T}} \tag{3.9}$$

and has similar properties to $\mathtt{L}$. Under the point transformation $\mathbf{X}' = \mathtt{H}\mathbf{X}$, the matrix $\mathtt{L}^*$ transforms as $\mathtt{L}^{*\prime} = \mathtt{H}^{-\mathsf{T}}\mathtt{L}\mathtt{H}^{-1}$. The matrix $\mathtt{L}^*$ can be obtained directly from $\mathtt{L}$ by a simple rewrite rule:

$$l_{12} : l_{13} : l_{14} : l_{23} : l_{42} : l_{34} = l^*_{34} : l^*_{42} : l^*_{23} : l^*_{14} : l^*_{13} : l^*_{12}. \tag{3.10}$$

The correspondence rule is very simple: the indices of the dual and original component always include all the numbers $\{1, 2, 3, 4\}$, so if the original is ij then the dual is those numbers of $\{1, 2, 3, 4\}$ which are not ij. For example $12 \mapsto 34$.

Join and incidence properties are very nicely represented in this notation:

(i) The plane defined by the join of the point $\mathbf{X}$ and line $\mathtt{L}$ is

$$\boldsymbol{\pi} = \mathtt{L}^*\mathbf{X}$$

and $\mathtt{L}^*\mathbf{X} = \mathbf{0}$ if, and only if, $\mathbf{X}$ is on $\mathtt{L}$.

(ii) The point defined by the intersection of the line $\mathtt{L}$ with the plane $\boldsymbol{\pi}$ is

$$\mathbf{X} = \mathtt{L}\boldsymbol{\pi}$$

and $\mathtt{L}\boldsymbol{\pi} = \mathbf{0}$ if, and only if, $\mathtt{L}$ is on $\boldsymbol{\pi}$.

The properties of two (or more) lines $\mathtt{L}_1, \mathtt{L}_2, \ldots$ can be obtained from the null-space of the matrix $\mathtt{M} = [\mathtt{L}_1, \mathtt{L}_2, \ldots]$. For example if the lines are coplanar then $\mathtt{M}^{\mathsf{T}}$ has a 1-dimensional null-space corresponding to the plane $\boldsymbol{\pi}$ of the lines.

Example 3.4. The intersection of the X-axis with the plane $X = 1$ is given by $\mathbf{X} = \mathtt{L}\boldsymbol{\pi}$ as

$$\mathbf{X} = \begin{bmatrix} 0 & 0 & 0 & -1 \\ 0 & 0 & 0 & 0 \\ 0 & 0 & 0 & 0 \\ 1 & 0 & 0 & 0 \end{bmatrix} \begin{pmatrix} 1 \\ 0 \\ 0 \\ -1 \end{pmatrix} = \begin{pmatrix} 1 \\ 0 \\ 0 \\ 1 \end{pmatrix}$$

which is the inhomogeneous point $(X, Y, Z)^{\mathsf{T}} = (1, 0, 0)^{\mathsf{T}}$. △

III. Plücker line coordinates. The Plücker line coordinates are the six non-zero elements of the 4×4 skew-symmetric Plücker matrix (3.8) $\mathtt{L}$, namely[1]

$$\mathcal{L} = \{l_{12}, l_{13}, l_{14}, l_{23}, l_{42}, l_{34}\}. \tag{3.11}$$

This is a homogeneous 6-vector, and thus is an element of $\mathbb{P}^5$. It follows from evaluating $\det \mathtt{L} = 0$ that the coordinates satisfy the equation

$$l_{12}l_{34} + l_{13}l_{42} + l_{14}l_{23} = 0. \tag{3.12}$$

A 6-vector $\mathcal{L}$ only corresponds to a line in 3-space if it satisfies (3.12). The geometric interpretation of this constraint is that the lines of $\mathbb{P}^3$ define a (co-dimension 1) surface in $\mathbb{P}^5$ which is known as the *Klein quadric*, a quadric because the terms of (3.12) are quadratic in the Plücker line coordinates.

Suppose two lines $\mathcal{L}$, $\hat{\mathcal{L}}$ are the joins of the points $\mathbf{A}, \mathbf{B}$ and $\widehat{\mathbf{A}}, \widehat{\mathbf{B}}$ respectively. The lines intersect if and only if the four points are coplanar. A necessary and sufficient condition for this is that $\det[\mathbf{A}, \mathbf{B}, \widehat{\mathbf{A}}, \widehat{\mathbf{B}}] = 0$. It can be shown that the determinant expands as

$$\begin{aligned} \det[\mathbf{A}, \mathbf{B}, \widehat{\mathbf{A}}, \widehat{\mathbf{B}}] &= l_{12}\hat{l}_{34} + \hat{l}_{12}l_{34} + l_{13}\hat{l}_{42} + \hat{l}_{13}l_{42} + l_{14}\hat{l}_{23} + \hat{l}_{14}l_{23} \\ &= (\mathcal{L}|\hat{\mathcal{L}}). \end{aligned} \tag{3.13}$$

Since the Plücker coordinates are independent of the particular points used to define them, the bilinear product $(\mathcal{L}|\hat{\mathcal{L}})$ is independent of the points used in the derivation and only depends on the lines $\mathcal{L}$ and $\hat{\mathcal{L}}$. Then we have

Result 3.5. *Two lines $\mathcal{L}$ and $\hat{\mathcal{L}}$ are coplanar (and thus intersect) if and only if* $(\mathcal{L}|\hat{\mathcal{L}}) = 0$.

This product appears in a number of useful formulae:

[1] The element l_{42} is conventionally used instead of l_{24} as it eliminates negatives in many of the subsequent formulae.

(i) A 6-vector $\mathcal{L}$ only represents a line in $\mathbb{P}^3$ if $(\mathcal{L}|\mathcal{L}) = 0$. This is simply repeating the Klein quadric constraint (3.12) above.

(ii) Suppose two lines $\mathcal{L}$, $\hat{\mathcal{L}}$ are the intersections of the planes $\mathbf{P}$, $\mathbf{Q}$ and $\widehat{\mathbf{P}}$, $\widehat{\mathbf{Q}}$ respectively. Then

$$(\mathcal{L}|\hat{\mathcal{L}}) = \det[\mathbf{P}, \mathbf{Q}, \widehat{\mathbf{P}}, \widehat{\mathbf{Q}}]$$

and again the lines intersect if and only if $(\mathcal{L}|\hat{\mathcal{L}}) = 0$.

(iii) If $\mathcal{L}$ is the intersection of two planes $\mathbf{P}$ and $\mathbf{Q}$ and $\hat{\mathcal{L}}$ is the join of two points $\mathbf{A}$ and $\mathbf{B}$, then

$$(\mathcal{L}|\hat{\mathcal{L}}) = (\mathbf{P}^\mathsf{T}\mathbf{A})(\mathbf{Q}^\mathsf{T}\mathbf{B}) - (\mathbf{Q}^\mathsf{T}\mathbf{A})(\mathbf{P}^\mathsf{T}\mathbf{B}). \tag{3.14}$$

Plücker coordinates are useful in algebraic derivations. They will be used in defining the map from a line in 3-space to its image in chapter 8.

3.2.3 Quadrics and dual quadrics

A quadric is a surface in $\mathbb{P}^3$ defined by the equation

$$\mathbf{X}^\mathsf{T}\mathtt{Q}\mathbf{X} = 0 \tag{3.15}$$

where $\mathtt{Q}$ is a symmetric 4×4 matrix. Often the matrix $\mathtt{Q}$ and the quadric surface it defines are not distinguished, and we will simply refer to the quadric $\mathtt{Q}$.

Many of the properties of quadrics follow directly from those of conics in section 2.2.3(*p*30). To highlight a few:

(i) A quadric has 9 degrees of freedom. These correspond to the ten independent elements of a 4×4 symmetric matrix less one for scale.

(ii) Nine points in general position define a quadric.

(iii) If the matrix $\mathtt{Q}$ is singular, then the quadric is *degenerate*, and may be defined by fewer points.

(iv) A quadric defines a polarity between a point and a plane, in a similar manner to the polarity defined by a conic between a point and a line (section 2.8.1). The plane $\boldsymbol{\pi} = \mathtt{Q}\mathbf{X}$ is the polar plane of $\mathbf{X}$ with respect to $\mathtt{Q}$. In the case that $\mathtt{Q}$ is non-singular and $\mathbf{X}$ is outside the quadric, the polar plane is defined by the points of contact with $\mathtt{Q}$ of the cone of rays through $\mathbf{X}$ tangent to $\mathtt{Q}$. If $\mathbf{X}$ lies on $\mathtt{Q}$, then $\mathtt{Q}\mathbf{X}$ is the tangent plane to $\mathtt{Q}$ at $\mathbf{X}$.

(v) The intersection of a plane $\boldsymbol{\pi}$ with a quadric $\mathtt{Q}$ is a conic $\mathtt{C}$. Computing the conic can bc tricky because it requires a coordinate system for the plane. Recall from (3.7) that a coordinate system for the plane can be defined by the complement space to $\boldsymbol{\pi}$ as $\mathbf{X} = \mathtt{M}\mathbf{x}$. Points on $\boldsymbol{\pi}$ are on $\mathtt{Q}$ if $\mathbf{X}^\mathsf{T}\mathtt{Q}\mathbf{X} = \mathbf{x}^\mathsf{T}\mathtt{M}^\mathsf{T}\mathtt{Q}\mathtt{M}\mathbf{x} = 0$. These points lie on a conic $\mathtt{C}$, since $\mathbf{x}^\mathsf{T}\mathtt{C}\mathbf{x} = 0$, with $\mathtt{C} = \mathtt{M}^\mathsf{T}\mathtt{Q}\mathtt{M}$.

(vi) Under the point transformation $\mathbf{X}' = \mathtt{H}\mathbf{X}$, a (point) quadric transforms as

$$\mathtt{Q}' = \mathtt{H}^{-\mathsf{T}}\mathtt{Q}\mathtt{H}^{-1}. \tag{3.16}$$

The dual of a quadric is also a quadric. Dual quadrics are equations on planes: the tangent planes $\boldsymbol{\pi}$ to the point quadric $\mathtt{Q}$ satisfy $\boldsymbol{\pi}^\mathsf{T}\mathtt{Q}^*\boldsymbol{\pi} = 0$, where $\mathtt{Q}^* = \text{adjoint}\ \mathtt{Q}$, or $\mathtt{Q}^{-1}$ if $\mathtt{Q}$ is invertible. Under the point transformation $\mathbf{X}' = \mathtt{H}\mathbf{X}$, a dual quadric transforms as

$$\mathtt{Q}^{*\prime} = \mathtt{H}\mathtt{Q}^{*}\mathtt{H}^{\mathsf{T}}. \tag{3.17}$$

The algebra of imaging a quadric is far simpler for a dual quadric than a point quadric. This is detailed in chapter 8.

3.2.4 Classification of quadrics

Since the matrix, $\mathtt{Q}$, representing a quadric is symmetric, it may be decomposed as $\mathtt{Q} = \mathtt{U}^{\mathsf{T}}\mathtt{D}\mathtt{U}$ where $\mathtt{U}$ is a real orthogonal matrix and $\mathtt{D}$ is a real diagonal matrix. Further, by appropriate scaling of the rows of $\mathtt{U}$, one may write $\mathtt{Q} = \mathtt{H}^{\mathsf{T}}\mathtt{D}\mathtt{H}$ where $\mathtt{D}$ is diagonal with entries equal to $0, 1$, or -1. We may further ensure that the zero entries of $\mathtt{D}$ appear last along the diagonal, and that the $+1$ entries appear first. Now, replacement of $\mathtt{Q} = \mathtt{H}^{\mathsf{T}}\mathtt{D}\mathtt{H}$ by $\mathtt{D}$ is equivalent to a projective transformation effected by the matrix $\mathtt{H}$ (see (3.16)). Thus, up to projective equivalence, we may assume that the quadric is represented by a matrix $\mathtt{D}$ of the given simple form.

The *signature* of a diagonal matrix $\mathtt{D}$, denoted $\sigma(\mathtt{D})$, is defined to be the number of $+1$ entries minus the number of -1 entries. This definition is extended to arbitrary real symmetric matrices $\mathtt{Q}$ by defining $\sigma(\mathtt{Q}) = \sigma(\mathtt{D})$ such that $\mathtt{Q} = \mathtt{H}^{\mathsf{T}}\mathtt{D}\mathtt{H}$, where $\mathtt{H}$ is a real matrix. It may be proved that the signature is well defined, being independent of the particular choice of $\mathtt{H}$. Since the matrix representing a quadric is defined only up to sign, we may assume that its signature is non-negative. Then, the projective type of a quadric is uniquely determined by its rank and signature. This will allow us to enumerate the different projective equivalence classes of quadrics.

A quadric represented by a diagonal matrix $\mathrm{diag}(d_1, d_2, d_3, d_4)$ corresponds to a set of points satisfying an equation $d_1\mathrm{X}^2 + d_2\mathrm{Y}^2 + d_3\mathrm{Z}^2 + d_4\mathrm{T}^2 = 0$. One may set $\mathrm{T} = 1$ to get an equation for the non-infinite points on the quadric. See table 3.1. Examples of quadric surfaces are shown in figure 3.2 – figure 3.4.

Rank	σ	Diagonal	Equation	Realization
4	4	$(1,1,1,1)$	$\mathrm{X}^2+\mathrm{Y}^2+\mathrm{Z}^2+1=0$	No real points
	2	$(1,1,1,-1)$	$\mathrm{X}^2+\mathrm{Y}^2+\mathrm{Z}^2=1$	Sphere
	0	$(1,1,-1,-1)$	$\mathrm{X}^2+\mathrm{Y}^2=\mathrm{Z}^2+1$	Hyperboloid of one sheet
3	3	$(1,1,1,0)$	$\mathrm{X}^2+\mathrm{Y}^2+\mathrm{Z}^2=0$	One point $(0,0,0,1)^{\mathsf{T}}$
	1	$(1,1,-1,0)$	$\mathrm{X}^2+\mathrm{Y}^2=\mathrm{Z}^2$	Cone at the origin
2	2	$(1,1,0,0)$	$\mathrm{X}^2+\mathrm{Y}^2=0$	Single line (Z-axis)
	0	$(1,-1,0,0)$	$\mathrm{X}^2=\mathrm{Y}^2$	Two planes $\mathrm{X}=\pm\mathrm{Y}$
1	1	$(1,0,0,0)$	$\mathrm{X}^2=0$	The plane $\mathrm{X}=0$

Table 3.1. *Categorization of point quadrics.*

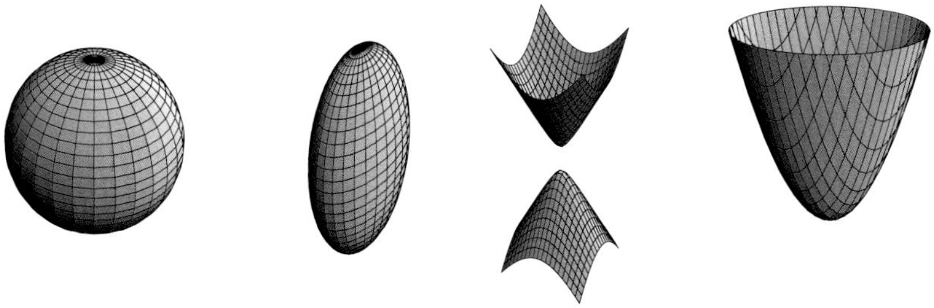

Fig. 3.2. **Non-ruled quadrics.** *This shows plots of a sphere, ellipsoid, hyperboloid of two sheets and paraboloid. They are all projectively equivalent.*

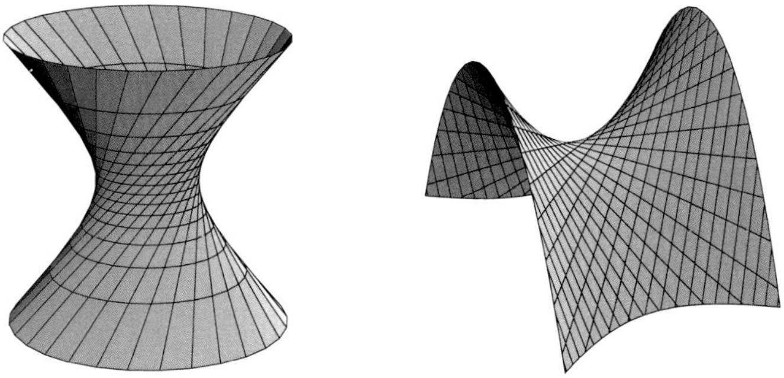

Fig. 3.3. **Ruled quadrics.** *Two examples of a hyperboloid of one sheet are given. These surfaces are given by equations* $\mathrm{X}^2 + \mathrm{Y}^2 = \mathrm{Z}^2 + 1$ *and* $\mathrm{XY} = \mathrm{Z}$ *respectively, and are projectively equivalent. Note that these two surfaces are made up of two sets of disjoint straight lines, and that each line from one set meets each line from the other set. The two quadrics shown here are projectively (though not affinely) equivalent.*

Ruled quadrics. Quadrics fall into two classes – ruled and unruled quadrics. A ruled quadric is one that contains a straight line. More particularly, as shown in figure 3.3, the non-degenerate ruled quadric (hyperboloid of one sheet) contains two families of straight lines called *generators*. For more properties of ruled quadrics, refer to [Semple-79].

The most interesting of the quadrics are the two quadrics of rank 4. Note that these two quadrics differ even in their topological type. The quadric of signature 2 (the sphere) is (obviously enough) topologically a sphere. On the other hand, the hyperboloid of 1 sheet is *not* topologically equivalent (homeomorphic) to a sphere. In fact, it is topologically a torus (topologically equivalent to $S^1 \times S^1$). This gives the clearest indication that they are not projectively equivalent.

3.3 Twisted cubics

The twisted cubic may be considered to be a 3-dimensional analogue of a 2D conic (although in other ways it is a quadric surface which is the 3-dimensional analogue of a 2D conic.)

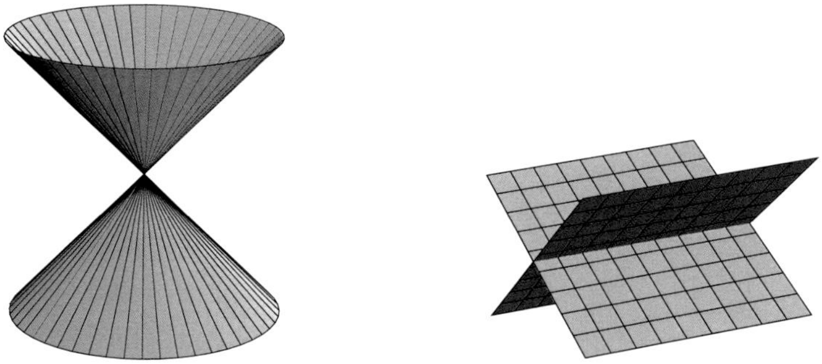

Fig. 3.4. **Degenerate quadrics.** *The two most important degenerate quadrics are shown, the cone and two planes. Both these quadrics are ruled. The matrix representing the cone has rank 3, and the null-vector represents the nodal point of the cone. The matrix representing the two (non-coincident) planes has rank 2, and the two generators of the rank 2 null-space are two points on the intersection line of the planes.*

A conic in the 2-dimensional projective plane may be described as a parametrized curve given by the equation

$$\begin{pmatrix} x_1 \\ x_2 \\ x_3 \end{pmatrix} = \mathtt{A}\begin{pmatrix} 1 \\ \theta \\ \theta^2 \end{pmatrix} = \begin{pmatrix} a_{11} + a_{12}\theta + a_{13}\theta^2 \\ a_{21} + a_{22}\theta + a_{23}\theta^2 \\ a_{31} + a_{32}\theta + a_{33}\theta^2 \end{pmatrix} \tag{3.18}$$

where $\mathtt{A}$ is a non-singular 3×3 matrix.

In an analogous manner, a twisted cubic is defined to be a curve in $\mathbb{P}^3$ given in parametric form as

$$\begin{pmatrix} X_1 \\ X_2 \\ X_3 \\ X_4 \end{pmatrix} = \mathtt{A}\begin{pmatrix} 1 \\ \theta \\ \theta^2 \\ \theta^3 \end{pmatrix} = \begin{pmatrix} a_{11} + a_{12}\theta + a_{13}\theta^2 + a_{14}\theta^3 \\ a_{21} + a_{22}\theta + a_{23}\theta^2 + a_{24}\theta^3 \\ a_{31} + a_{32}\theta + a_{33}\theta^2 + a_{34}\theta^3 \\ a_{41} + a_{42}\theta + a_{43}\theta^2 + a_{44}\theta^3 \end{pmatrix} \tag{3.19}$$

where $\mathtt{A}$ is a non-singular 4×4 matrix.

Since a twisted cubic is perhaps an unfamiliar object, various views of the curve are shown in figure 3.5. In fact, a twisted cubic is a quite benign space curve.

Properties of a twisted cubic. Let $\mathbf{c}$ be a non-singular twisted cubic. Then $\mathbf{c}$ is not contained within any plane of $\mathbb{P}^3$; it intersects a general plane at three distinct points. A twisted cubic has 12 degrees of freedom (counted as 15 for the matrix $\mathtt{A}$, less 3 for a 1D projectivity on the parametrization θ, which leaves the curve unaltered). Requiring the curve to pass through a point $\mathbf{X}$ places two constraints on $\mathbf{c}$, since $\mathbf{X} = \mathtt{A}(1, \theta, \theta^2, \theta^3)^\mathsf{T}$ is three independent ratios, but only two constraints once θ is eliminated. Thus, there is a unique $\mathbf{c}$ through six points in general position. Finally, all non-degenerate twisted cubics are projectively equivalent. This is clear from the definition (3.19): a projective transformation $\mathtt{A}^{-1}$ maps $\mathbf{c}$ to the standard form $\mathbf{c}(\theta') = (1, \theta', \theta'^2, \theta'^3)^\mathsf{T}$, and since

Fig. 3.5. *Various views of the twisted cubic* $(t^3, t^2, t,)^\mathsf{T}$. *The curve is thickened to a tube to aid in visualization.*

all twisted cubics can be mapped to this curve, it follows that all twisted cubics are projectively equivalent.

A classification of the various special cases of a twisted cubic, such as a conic and coincident line, are given in [Semple-79]. The twisted cubic makes an appearance as the horopter for two-view geometry (chapter 9), and plays the central role in defining the degenerate set for camera resectioning (chapter 22).

3.4 The hierarchy of transformations

There are a number of specializations of a projective transformation of 3-space which will appear frequently throughout this book. The specializations are analogous to the strata of section 2.4(*p*37) for planar transformations. Each specialization is a subgroup, and is identified by its matrix form, or equivalently by its invariants. These are summarized in table 3.2. This table lists only the *additional* properties of the 3-space transformations over their 2-space counterparts – the transformations of 3-space also have the invariants listed in table 2.1(*p*44) for the corresponding 2-space transformations.

The 15 degrees of freedom of a projective transformation are accounted for as seven for a similarity (three for rotation, three for translation, one for isotropic scaling), five for affine scalings, and three for the projective part of the transformation.

Two of the most important characterizations of these transformations are parallelism and angles. For example, after an affine transformation lines which were originally parallel remain parallel, but angles are skewed; and after a projective transformation parallelism is lost.

In the following we briefly describe a decomposition of a Euclidean transformation that will be useful when discussing special motions later in this book.

3.4.1 The screw decomposition

A Euclidean transformation on the plane may be considered as a specialization of a Euclidean transformation of 3-space with the restrictions that the translation vector $\mathbf{t}$ lies in the plane, and the rotation axis is perpendicular to the plane. However, Euclidean actions on 3-space are more general than this because the rotation axis and translation are not perpendicular in general. The screw decomposition enables any Euclidean

Group	Matrix	Distortion	Invariant properties
Projective 15 dof	$\begin{bmatrix} \mathtt{A} & \mathbf{t} \\ \mathbf{v}^\mathsf{T} & v \end{bmatrix}$	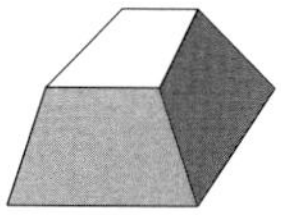	Intersection and tangency of surfaces in contact. Sign of Gaussian curvature.
Affine 12 dof	$\begin{bmatrix} \mathtt{A} & \mathbf{t} \\ \mathbf{0}^\mathsf{T} & 1 \end{bmatrix}$	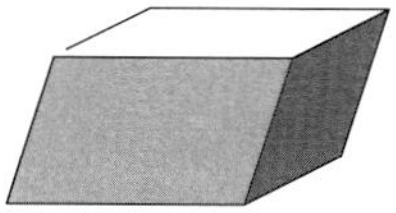	Parallelism of planes, volume ratios, centroids. The plane at infinity, $\boldsymbol{\pi}_\infty$, (see section 3.5).
Similarity 7 dof	$\begin{bmatrix} s\mathtt{R} & \mathbf{t} \\ \mathbf{0}^\mathsf{T} & 1 \end{bmatrix}$	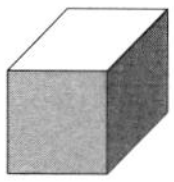	The absolute conic, Ω_∞, (see section 3.6).
Euclidean 6 dof	$\begin{bmatrix} \mathtt{R} & \mathbf{t} \\ \mathbf{0}^\mathsf{T} & 1 \end{bmatrix}$	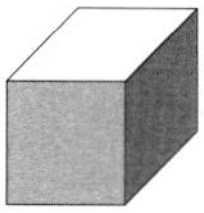	Volume.

Table 3.2. **Geometric properties invariant to commonly occurring transformations of 3-space.** *The matrix* $\mathtt{A}$ *is an invertible* 3×3 *matrix,* $\mathtt{R}$ *is a 3D rotation matrix,* $\mathbf{t} = (t_\mathrm{X}, t_\mathrm{Y}, t_\mathrm{Z})^\mathsf{T}$ *a 3D translation,* $\mathbf{v}$ *a general 3-vector,* v *a scalar, and* $\mathbf{0} = (0,0,0)^\mathsf{T}$ *a null 3-vector. The distortion column shows typical effects of the transformations on a cube. Transformations higher in the table can produce all the actions of the ones below. These range from Euclidean, where only translations and rotations occur, to projective where five points can be transformed to any other five points (provided no three points are collinear, or four coplanar).*

action (a rotation composed with a translation) to be reduced to a situation almost as simple as the 2D case. The screw decomposition is that

Result 3.6. *Any particular translation and rotation is equivalent to a rotation about a* screw axis *together with a translation along the screw axis. The screw axis is parallel to the rotation axis.*

In the case of a translation and an *orthogonal* rotation axis (termed *planar motion*), the motion is equivalent to a rotation *alone* about the screw axis.

Proof. We will sketch a constructive geometric proof that can easily be visualized. Consider first the 2D case – a Euclidean transformation on the plane. It is evident from figure 3.6 that a screw axis exists for such 2D transformations. For the 3D case, decompose the translation $\mathbf{t}$ into two components $\mathbf{t} = \mathbf{t}_\parallel + \mathbf{t}_\perp$, parallel and orthogonal respectively to the rotation axis direction ($\mathbf{t}_\parallel = (\mathbf{t}.\mathbf{a})\mathbf{a}$, $\mathbf{t}_\perp = \mathbf{t} - (\mathbf{t}.\mathbf{a})\mathbf{a}$).
Then the Euclidean motion is partitioned into two parts: first a rotation about the screw

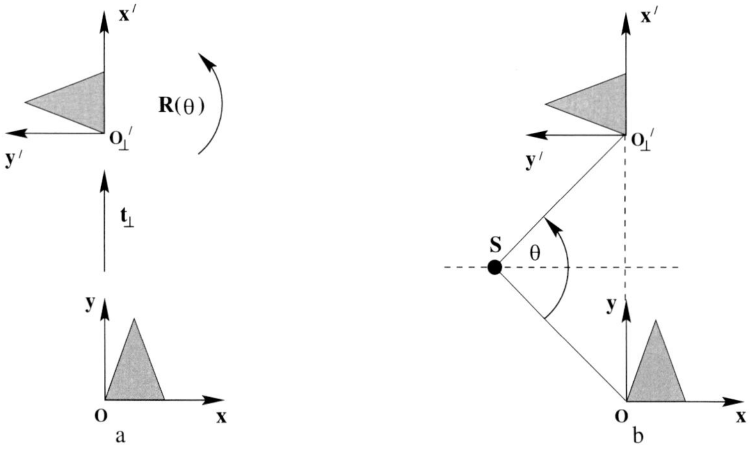

Fig. 3.6. **2D Euclidean motion and a "screw" axis.** *(a) The frame $\{x, y\}$ undergoes a translation $\mathbf{t}_\perp$ and a rotation by θ to reach the frame $\{x', y'\}$. The motion is in the plane orthogonal to the rotation axis. (b) This motion is equivalent to a single rotation about the screw axis $\mathbf{S}$. The screw axis lies on the perpendicular bisector of the line joining corresponding points, such that the angle between the lines joining $\mathbf{S}$ to the corresponding points is θ. In the figure the corresponding points are the two frame origins and θ has the value $90°$.*

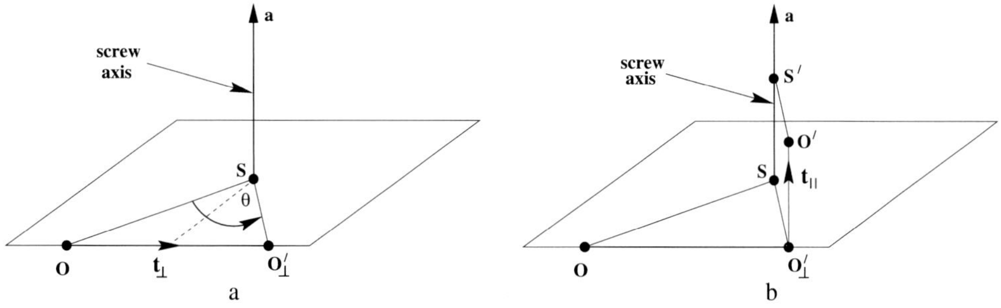

Fig. 3.7. **3D Euclidean motion and the screw decomposition.** *Any Euclidean rotation $\mathtt{R}$ and translation $\mathbf{t}$ may be achieved by (a) a rotation about the screw axis, followed by (b) a translation along the screw axis by $\mathbf{t}_{||}$. Here $\mathbf{a}$ is the (unit) direction of the rotation axis (so that $\mathtt{R}\mathbf{a} = \mathbf{a}$), and $\mathbf{t}$ is decomposed as $\mathbf{t} = \mathbf{t}_{||} + \mathbf{t}_\perp$, which are vector components parallel and orthogonal respectively to the rotation axis direction The point $\mathbf{S}$ is closest to $\mathbf{O}$ on the screw axis (so that the line from $\mathbf{S}$ to $\mathbf{O}$ is perpendicular to the direction of $\mathbf{a}$). Similarly $\mathbf{S}'$ is the point on the screw axis closest to $\mathbf{O}'$.*

axis, which covers the rotation and $\mathbf{t}_\perp$; second a translation by $\mathbf{t}_{||}$ along the screw axis. The complete motion is illustrated in figure 3.7. □

The screw decomposition can be determined from the fixed points of the 4×4 matrix representing the Euclidean transformation. This idea is examined in the exercises at the end of the chapter.

3.5 The plane at infinity

In planar projective geometry identifying the line at infinity, $\mathbf{l}_\infty$, allowed affine properties of the plane to be measured. Identifying the circular points on $\mathbf{l}_\infty$ then allowed the measurement of metric properties. In the projective geometry of 3-space the corresponding geometric entities are the plane at infinity, π_∞, and the absolute conic, Ω_∞.

The plane at infinity has the canonical position $\pi_\infty = (0, 0, 0, 1)^\mathsf{T}$ in affine 3-space. It contains the directions $\mathbf{D} = (\mathrm{X}_1, \mathrm{X}_2, \mathrm{X}_3, 0)^\mathsf{T}$, and enables the identification of affine properties such as parallelism. In particular:

- Two planes are parallel if, and only if, their line of intersection is on π_∞.
- A line is parallel to another line, or to a plane, if the point of intersection is on π_∞.

We then have in $\mathbb{P}^3$ that any pair of planes intersect in a line, with parallel planes intersecting in a line on the plane at infinity.

The plane π_∞ is a geometric representation of the 3 degrees of freedom required to specify affine properties in a projective coordinate frame. In loose terms, the plane at infinity is a fixed plane under any affine transformation, but "sees" (is moved by) a projective transformation. The 3 degrees of freedom of π_∞ thus measure the projective component of a general homography – they account for the 15 degrees of freedom of this general transformation compared to an affinity (12 dof). More formally:

Result 3.7. *The plane at infinity, π_∞, is a fixed plane under the projective transformation $\mathtt{H}$ if, and only if, $\mathtt{H}$ is an affinity.*

The proof is the analogue of the derivation of result 2.17(*p*48). It is worth clarifying two points:

(i) The plane π_∞ is, in general, only fixed as a set under an affinity; it is not fixed pointwise.

(ii) Under a particular affinity (for example a Euclidean motion) there may be planes in addition to π_∞ which are fixed. However, only π_∞ is fixed under any affinity.

These points are illustrated in more detail by the following example.

Example 3.8. Consider the Euclidean transformation represented by the matrix

$$\mathtt{H}_\mathrm{E} = \begin{bmatrix} \mathtt{R} & \mathbf{0} \\ \mathbf{0}^\mathsf{T} & 1 \end{bmatrix} = \begin{bmatrix} \cos\theta & -\sin\theta & 0 & 0 \\ \sin\theta & \cos\theta & 0 & 0 \\ 0 & 0 & 1 & 0 \\ 0 & 0 & 0 & 1 \end{bmatrix}. \tag{3.20}$$

This is a rotation by θ about the Z-axis with a zero translation (it is a planar screw motion, see section 3.4.1). Geometrically it is evident that the family of XY-planes orthogonal to the rotation axis are simply rotated about the Z-axis by this transformation. This means that there is a pencil of fixed planes orthogonal to the Z-axis. The planes are fixed as sets, but not pointwise as any (finite) point (not on the axis) is rotated in horizontal circles by this Euclidean action. Algebraically, the fixed planes of $\mathtt{H}$ are the eigenvectors of $\mathtt{H}^\mathsf{T}$ (refer to section 2.9). In this case the eigenvalues are $\{e^{i\theta}, e^{-i\theta}, 1, 1\}$

and the corresponding eigenvectors of $\mathtt{H}_{\mathrm{E}}^{\mathsf{T}}$ are

$$\mathbf{E}_1 = \begin{pmatrix} 1 \\ i \\ 0 \\ 0 \end{pmatrix} \quad \mathbf{E}_2 = \begin{pmatrix} 1 \\ -i \\ 0 \\ 0 \end{pmatrix} \quad \mathbf{E}_3 = \begin{pmatrix} 0 \\ 0 \\ 1 \\ 0 \end{pmatrix} \quad \mathbf{E}_4 = \begin{pmatrix} 0 \\ 0 \\ 0 \\ 1 \end{pmatrix}.$$

The eigenvectors $\mathbf{E}_1$ and $\mathbf{E}_2$ do not correspond to real planes, and will not be discussed further here. The eigenvectors $\mathbf{E}_3$ and $\mathbf{E}_4$ are degenerate. Thus there is a pencil of fixed planes which is spanned by these eigenvectors. The axis of this pencil is the line of intersection of the the planes (perpendicular to the Z-axis) with $\boldsymbol{\pi}_\infty$, and the pencil includes $\boldsymbol{\pi}_\infty$. △

The example also illustrates the connection between the geometry of the projective plane, $\mathbb{P}^2$, and projective 3-space, $\mathbb{P}^3$. A plane $\boldsymbol{\pi}$ intersects $\boldsymbol{\pi}_\infty$ in a line which is the line at infinity, $\mathbf{l}_\infty$, of the plane $\boldsymbol{\pi}$. A projective transformation of $\mathbb{P}^3$ induces a *subordinate* plane projective transformation on $\boldsymbol{\pi}$.

Affine properties of a reconstruction. In later chapters on reconstruction, for example chapter 10, it will be seen that the projective coordinates of the (Euclidean) scene can be reconstructed from multiple views. Once $\boldsymbol{\pi}_\infty$ is identified in projective 3-space, i.e. its projective coordinates are known, it is then possible to determine affine properties of the reconstruction such as whether geometric entities are parallel – they are parallel if they intersect on $\boldsymbol{\pi}_\infty$.

A more algorithmic approach is to transform $\mathbb{P}^3$ so that the identified $\boldsymbol{\pi}_\infty$ is moved to its canonical position at $\boldsymbol{\pi}_\infty = (0,0,0,1)^{\mathsf{T}}$. After this mapping we then have the situation that the Euclidean scene, where $\boldsymbol{\pi}_\infty$ has the coordinates $(0,0,0,1)^{\mathsf{T}}$, and our reconstruction are related by a projective transformation that fixes $\boldsymbol{\pi}_\infty$ at $(0,0,0,1)^{\mathsf{T}}$. It follows from result 3.7 that the scene and reconstruction are related by an affine transformation. Thus affine properties can now be measured directly from the coordinates of the entities.

3.6 The absolute conic

The absolute conic, Ω_∞, is a (point) conic on $\boldsymbol{\pi}_\infty$. In a metric frame $\boldsymbol{\pi}_\infty = (0,0,0,1)^{\mathsf{T}}$, and points on Ω_∞ satisfy

$$\left.\begin{matrix} \mathrm{X}_1^2 + \mathrm{X}_2^2 + \mathrm{X}_3^2 \\ \mathrm{X}_4 \end{matrix}\right\} = 0. \tag{3.21}$$

Note that two equations are required to define Ω_∞.

For directions on $\boldsymbol{\pi}_\infty$ (i.e. points with $\mathrm{X}_4 = 0$) the defining equation can be written

$$(\mathrm{X}_1, \mathrm{X}_2, \mathrm{X}_3)\mathtt{I}(\mathrm{X}_1, \mathrm{X}_2, \mathrm{X}_3)^{\mathsf{T}} = 0$$

so that Ω_∞ corresponds to a conic $\mathtt{C}$ with matrix $\mathtt{C} = \mathtt{I}$. It is thus a conic of purely imaginary points on $\boldsymbol{\pi}_\infty$.

The conic Ω_∞ is a geometric representation of the 5 additional degrees of freedom that are required to specify metric properties in an affine coordinate frame. A key property of Ω_∞ is that it is a fixed conic under any similarity transformation. More formally:

Result 3.9. *The absolute conic, Ω_∞, is a fixed conic under the projective transformation $\mathtt{H}$ if, and only if, $\mathtt{H}$ is a similarity transformation.*

Proof. Since the absolute conic lies in the plane at infinity, a transformation fixing it must fix the plane at infinity, and hence must be affine. Such a transformation is of the form

$$\mathtt{H}_\mathtt{A} = \begin{bmatrix} \mathtt{A} & \mathbf{t} \\ \mathbf{0}^\mathsf{T} & 1 \end{bmatrix}.$$

Restricting to the plane at infinity, the absolute conic is represented by the matrix $\mathtt{I}_{3\times3}$, and since it is fixed by $\mathtt{H}_\mathtt{A}$, one has $\mathtt{A}^{-\mathsf{T}}\mathtt{I}\mathtt{A}^{-1} = \mathtt{I}$ (up to scale), and taking inverses gives $\mathtt{A}\mathtt{A}^\mathsf{T} = \mathtt{I}$. This means that $\mathtt{A}$ is orthogonal, hence a scaled rotation, or scaled rotation with reflection. This completes the proof. □

Even though Ω_∞ does not have any real points, it shares the properties of any conic – such as that a line intersects a conic in two points; the pole–polar relationship etc. Here are a few particular properties of Ω_∞:

(i) Ω_∞ is only fixed as a set by a general similarity; it is not fixed pointwise. This means that under a similarity a point on Ω_∞ may travel to another point on Ω_∞, but it is not mapped to a point off the conic.

(ii) All circles intersect Ω_∞ in two points. Suppose the support plane of the circle is π. Then π intersects π_∞ in a line, and this line intersects Ω_∞ in two points. These two points are the circular points of π.

(iii) All spheres intersect π_∞ in Ω_∞.

Metric properties. Once Ω_∞ (and its support plane π_∞) have been identified in projective 3-space then metric properties, such as angles and relative lengths, can be measured.

Consider two lines with directions (3-vectors) $\mathbf{d}_1$ and $\mathbf{d}_2$. The angle between these directions in a Euclidean world frame is given by

$$\cos\theta = \frac{(\mathbf{d}_1^\mathsf{T}\mathbf{d}_2)}{\sqrt{(\mathbf{d}_1^\mathsf{T}\mathbf{d}_1)(\mathbf{d}_2^\mathsf{T}\mathbf{d}_2)}}. \tag{3.22}$$

This may be written as

$$\cos\theta = \frac{(\mathbf{d}_1^\mathsf{T}\Omega_\infty\mathbf{d}_2)}{\sqrt{(\mathbf{d}_1^\mathsf{T}\Omega_\infty\mathbf{d}_1)(\mathbf{d}_2^\mathsf{T}\Omega_\infty\mathbf{d}_2)}} \tag{3.23}$$

where $\mathbf{d}_1$ and $\mathbf{d}_2$ are the points of intersection of the lines with the plane π_∞ containing the conic Ω_∞, and Ω_∞ is the matrix representation of the absolute conic in that plane.

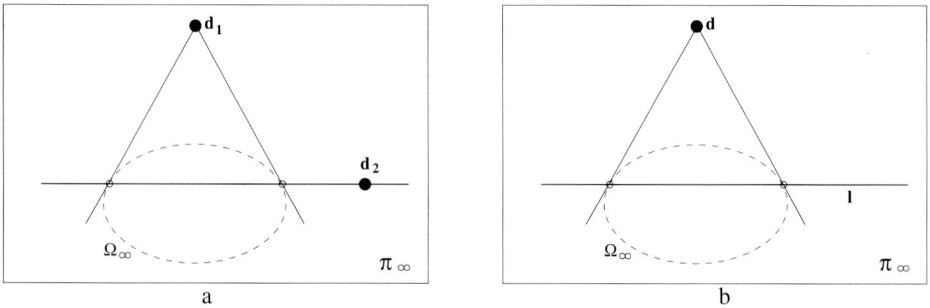

Fig. 3.8. **Orthogonality and Ω_∞.** *(a) On π_∞ orthogonal directions $\mathbf{d}_1$, $\mathbf{d}_2$ are conjugate with respect to Ω_∞. (b) A plane normal direction* $\mathbf{d}$ *and the intersection line* $\mathbf{l}$ *of the plane with π_∞ are in pole–polar relation with respect to Ω_∞.*

The expression (3.23) reduces to (3.22) in a Euclidean world frame where $\Omega_\infty = \mathtt{I}$. However, the expression is valid in any projective coordinate frame as may be verified from the transformation properties of points and conics (see (iv)(b) on page 63).

There is no simple formula for the angle between two planes computed from the directions of their surface normals.

Orthogonality and polarity. We now give a geometric representation of orthogonality in a projective space based on the absolute conic. The main device will be the pole–polar relationship between a point and line induced by a conic.

An immediate consequence of (3.23) is that two directions $\mathbf{d}_1$ and $\mathbf{d}_2$ are orthogonal if $\mathbf{d}_1^\mathsf{T}\Omega_\infty\mathbf{d}_2 = 0$. Thus orthogonality is encoded by *conjugacy* with respect to Ω_∞. The great advantage of this is that conjugacy is a projective relation, so that in a projective frame (obtained by a projective transformation of Euclidean 3-space) directions can be identified as orthogonal if they are conjugate with respect to Ω_∞ in that frame (in general the matrix of Ω_∞ is not $\mathtt{I}$ in a projective frame). The geometric representation of orthogonality is shown in figure 3.8.

This representation is helpful when considering orthogonality between rays in a camera, for example in determining the normal to a plane through the camera centre (see section 8.6(*p*213)). If image points are conjugate with respect to the *image* of Ω_∞ then the corresponding rays are orthogonal.

Again, a more algorithmic approach is to projectively transform the coordinates so that Ω_∞ is mapped to its canonical position (3.21), and then metric properties can be determined directly from coordinates.

3.7 The absolute dual quadric

Recall that Ω_∞ is defined by *two* equations – it is a conic on the plane at infinity. The dual of the absolute conic Ω_∞ is a degenerate dual *quadric* in 3-space called the *absolute dual quadric*, and denoted $\mathtt{Q}_\infty^*$. Geometrically $\mathtt{Q}_\infty^*$ consists of the planes tangent to Ω_∞, so that Ω_∞ is the "rim" of $\mathtt{Q}_\infty^*$. This is called a *rim quadric*. Think of the set of planes tangent to an ellipsoid, and then squash the ellipsoid to a pancake.

Algebraically $\mathtt{Q}_\infty^*$ is represented by a 4×4 homogeneous matrix of rank 3, which in metric 3-space has the canonical form

$$\mathtt{Q}^*_\infty = \begin{bmatrix} \mathtt{I} & \mathbf{0} \\ \mathbf{0}^\mathsf{T} & 0 \end{bmatrix}. \tag{3.24}$$

We will show that any plane in the dual absolute quadric envelope is indeed tangent to Ω_∞, so the $\mathtt{Q}^*_\infty$ is truly a dual of Ω_∞. Consider a plane represented by $\boldsymbol{\pi} = (\mathbf{v}^\mathsf{T}, k)^\mathsf{T}$. This plane is in the envelope defined by $\mathtt{Q}^*_\infty$ if and only if $\boldsymbol{\pi}^\mathsf{T}\mathtt{Q}^*_\infty\boldsymbol{\pi} = 0$, which given the form (3.24) is equivalent to $\mathbf{v}^\mathsf{T}\mathbf{v} = 0$. Now, (see section 8.6(*p*213)) $\mathbf{v}$ represents the line in which the plane $(\mathbf{v}^\mathsf{T}, k)^\mathsf{T}$ meets the plane at infinity. This line is tangent to the absolute conic if and only if $\mathbf{v}^\mathsf{T}\mathtt{I}\mathbf{v} = 0$. Thus, the envelope of $\mathtt{Q}^*_\infty$ is made up of just those planes tangent to the absolute conic.

Since this is an important fact, we consider it from another angle. Consider the absolute conic as the limit of a series of squashed ellipsoids, namely quadrics represented by the matrix $\mathtt{Q} = \mathrm{diag}(1, 1, 1, k)$. As $k \to \infty$, these quadrics become increasingly close to the plane at infinity, and in the limit the only points they contain are the points $(\mathrm{X}_1, \mathrm{X}_2, \mathrm{X}_3, 0)^\mathsf{T}$ with $\mathrm{X}_1^2 + \mathrm{X}_2^2 + \mathrm{X}_3^2 = 0$, that is points on the absolute conic. However, the dual of $\mathtt{Q}$ is the quadric $\mathtt{Q}^* = \mathtt{Q}^{-1} = \mathrm{diag}(1, 1, 1, k^{-1})$, which in the limit becomes the absolute dual quadric $\mathtt{Q}^*_\infty = \mathrm{diag}(1, 1, 1, 0)$.

The dual quadric $\mathtt{Q}^*_\infty$ is a degenerate quadric and has 8 degrees of freedom (a symmetric matrix has 10 independent elements, but the irrelevant scale and zero determinant condition each reduce the degrees of freedom by 1). It is a geometric representation of the 8 degrees of freedom that are required to specify metric properties in a projective coordinate frame. $\mathtt{Q}^*_\infty$ has a significant advantage over Ω_∞ in algebraic manipulations because both $\boldsymbol{\pi}_\infty$ and Ω_∞ are contained in a single geometric object (unlike Ω_∞ which requires two equations (3.21) in order to specify it). In the following we give its three most important properties.

Result 3.10. *The absolute dual quadric, $\mathtt{Q}^*_\infty$, is fixed under the projective transformation $\mathtt{H}$ if, and only if, $\mathtt{H}$ is a similarity.*

Proof. This follows directly from the invariance of the absolute conic under a similarity transform, since the planar tangency relationship between $\mathtt{Q}^*_\infty$ and Ω_∞ is transformation invariant. Nevertheless, we give an independent direct proof.
Since $\mathtt{Q}^*_\infty$ is a dual quadric, it transforms according to (3.17–*p*74), so it is fixed under $\mathtt{H}$ if and only if $\mathtt{Q}^*_\infty = \mathtt{H}\mathtt{Q}^*_\infty\mathtt{H}^\mathsf{T}$. Applying this with an arbitrary transform

$$\mathtt{H} = \begin{bmatrix} \mathtt{A} & \mathbf{t} \\ \mathbf{v}^\mathsf{T} & k \end{bmatrix}$$

we find

$$\begin{aligned} \begin{bmatrix} \mathtt{I} & \mathbf{0} \\ \mathbf{0}^\mathsf{T} & 0 \end{bmatrix} &= \begin{bmatrix} \mathtt{A} & \mathbf{t} \\ \mathbf{v}^\mathsf{T} & k \end{bmatrix} \begin{bmatrix} \mathtt{I} & \mathbf{0} \\ \mathbf{0}^\mathsf{T} & 0 \end{bmatrix} \begin{bmatrix} \mathtt{A}^\mathsf{T} & \mathbf{v} \\ \mathbf{t}^\mathsf{T} & k \end{bmatrix} \\ &= \begin{bmatrix} \mathtt{A}\mathtt{A}^\mathsf{T} & \mathtt{A}\mathbf{v} \\ \mathbf{v}^\mathsf{T}\mathtt{A}^\mathsf{T} & \mathbf{v}^\mathsf{T}\mathbf{v} \end{bmatrix} \end{aligned}$$

which must be true up to scale. By inspection, this equation holds if and only if $\mathbf{v} = \mathbf{0}$ and $\mathtt{A}$ is a scaled orthogonal matrix (scaling, rotation and possible reflection). In other words, $\mathtt{H}$ is a similarity transform. □

Result 3.11. *The plane at infinity* $\boldsymbol{\pi}_\infty$ *is the null-vector of* $\mathtt{Q}^*_\infty$.

This is easily verified when $\mathtt{Q}^*_\infty$ has its canonical form (3.24) in a metric frame since then, with $\boldsymbol{\pi}_\infty = (0,0,0,1)^\mathsf{T}$, $\mathtt{Q}^*_\infty\boldsymbol{\pi}_\infty = \mathbf{0}$. This property holds in any frame as may be readily seen algebraically from the transformation properties of planes and dual quadrics: if $\mathbf{X}' = \mathtt{H}\mathbf{X}$, then $\mathtt{Q}^{*\,\prime}_\infty = \mathtt{H}\,\mathtt{Q}^*_\infty\,\mathtt{H}^\mathsf{T}$, $\boldsymbol{\pi}'_\infty = \mathtt{H}^{-\mathsf{T}}\boldsymbol{\pi}_\infty$, and

$$\mathtt{Q}^{*\,\prime}_\infty\boldsymbol{\pi}'_\infty = (\mathtt{H}\,\mathtt{Q}^*_\infty\,\mathtt{H}^\mathsf{T})\mathtt{H}^{-\mathsf{T}}\boldsymbol{\pi}_\infty = \mathtt{H}\mathtt{Q}^*_\infty\boldsymbol{\pi}_\infty = \mathbf{0}.$$

Result 3.12. *The angle between two planes* $\boldsymbol{\pi}_1$ *and* $\boldsymbol{\pi}_2$ *is given by*

$$\cos\theta = \frac{\boldsymbol{\pi}_1^\mathsf{T}\mathtt{Q}^*_\infty\boldsymbol{\pi}_2}{\sqrt{(\boldsymbol{\pi}_1^\mathsf{T}\mathtt{Q}^*_\infty\boldsymbol{\pi}_1)\,(\boldsymbol{\pi}_2^\mathsf{T}\mathtt{Q}^*_\infty\boldsymbol{\pi}_2)}}. \tag{3.25}$$

Proof. Consider two planes with Euclidean coordinates $\boldsymbol{\pi}_1 = (\mathbf{n}_1^\mathsf{T}, d_1)^\mathsf{T}$, $\boldsymbol{\pi}_2 = (\mathbf{n}_2^\mathsf{T}, d_2)^\mathsf{T}$. In a Euclidean frame, $\mathtt{Q}^*_\infty$ has the form (3.24), and (3.25) reduces to

$$\cos\theta = \frac{\mathbf{n}_1^\mathsf{T}\mathbf{n}_2}{\sqrt{(\mathbf{n}_1^\mathsf{T}\mathbf{n}_1)\,(\mathbf{n}_2^\mathsf{T}\mathbf{n}_2)}}$$

which is the angle between the planes expressed in terms of a scalar product of their normals.

If the planes and $\mathtt{Q}^*_\infty$ are projectively transformed, (3.25) will still determine the angle between planes due to the (covariant) transformation properties of planes and dual quadrics. □

The details of the last part of the proof are left as an exercise, but are a direct 3D analogue of the derivation of result 2.23(*p*54) on the angle between two lines in $\mathbb{P}^2$ computed using the dual of the circular points. Planes in $\mathbb{P}^3$ are the analogue of lines in $\mathbb{P}^2$, and the absolute dual quadric is the analogue of the dual of the circular points.

3.8 Closure

3.8.1 The literature

The textbooks cited in chapter 2 are also relevant here. See also [Boehm-94] for a general background from the perspective of descriptive geometry, and Hilbert and Cohn-Vossen [Hilbert-56] for many clearly explained properties of curves and surfaces.

An important representation for points, lines and planes in $\mathbb{P}^3$, which is omitted in this chapter, is the Grassmann–Cayley algebra. In this representation geometric operations such as incidence and joins are represented by a "bracket algebra" based on matrix determinants. A good introduction to this area is given by [Carlsson-94], and its application to multiple view tensors is illustrated in [Triggs-95].

Faugeras and Maybank [Faugeras-90] introduced Ω_∞ into the computer vision literature (in order to determine the multiplicity of solutions for relative orientation), and Triggs introduced $\mathtt{Q}^*_\infty$ in [Triggs-97] for use in auto-calibration.

3.8.2 Notes and exercises

(i) **Plücker coordinates.**

(a) Using Plücker line coordinates, $\mathcal{L}$, write an expression for the point of intersection of a line with a plane, and the plane defined by a point and a line.
(b) Now derive the condition for a point to be on a line, and a line to be on a plane.
(c) Show that parallel planes intersect in a line on π_∞. Hint, start from (3.9–p71) to determine the line of intersection of two parallel planes $\mathtt{L}^*$.
(d) Show that parallel lines intersect on π_∞.

(ii) **Projective transformations.** Show that a (real) projective transformation of 3-space can map an ellipsoid to a paraboloid or hyperboloid of two sheets, but cannot map an ellipsoid to a hyperboloid of one sheet (i.e. a surface with real rulings).

(iii) **Screw decomposition.** Show that the 4×4 matrix representing the Euclidean transformation $\{\mathtt{R}, \mathbf{t}\}$ (with $\mathbf{a}$ the direction of the rotation axis, i.e. $\mathtt{R}\mathbf{a} = \mathbf{a}$) has two complex conjugate eigenvalues, and two equal real eigenvalues, and the following eigenvector structure:

(a) if $\mathbf{a}$ is perpendicular to $\mathbf{t}$, then the eigenvectors corresponding to the real eigenvalues are distinct;
(b) otherwise, the eigenvectors corresponding to the real eigenvalues are coincident, and on π_∞.

(E.g. choose simple cases such as (3.20), another case is given on page 495). In the first case the two real points corresponding to the real eigenvalues define a line of fixed points. This is the screw axis for planar motion. In the second case, the direction of the screw axis is defined, but it is not a line of fixed points. What do the eigenvectors corresponding to the complex eigenvalues represent?

4

Estimation – 2D Projective Transformations

In this chapter, we consider the problem of estimation. In the present context this will be taken to mean the computation of some transformation or other mathematical quantity, based on measurements of some nature. This definition is somewhat vague, so to make it more concrete, here are a number of estimation problems of the type that we would like to consider.

(i) **2D homography.** Given a set of points $\mathbf{x}_i$ in $\mathbb{P}^2$ and a corresponding set of points $\mathbf{x}'_i$ likewise in $\mathbb{P}^2$, compute the projective transformation that takes each $\mathbf{x}_i$ to $\mathbf{x}'_i$. In a practical situation, the points $\mathbf{x}_i$ and $\mathbf{x}'_i$ are points in two images (or the same image), each image being considered as a projective plane $\mathbb{P}^2$.

(ii) **3D to 2D camera projection.** Given a set of points $\mathbf{X}_i$ in 3D space, and a set of corresponding points $\mathbf{x}_i$ in an image, find the 3D to 2D projective mapping that maps $\mathbf{X}_i$ to $\mathbf{x}_i$. Such a 3D to 2D projection is the mapping carried out by a projective camera, as discussed in chapter 6.

(iii) **Fundamental matrix computation.** Given a set of points $\mathbf{x}_i$ in one image, and corresponding points $\mathbf{x}'_i$ in another image, compute the fundamental matrix $\mathtt{F}$ consistent with these correspondences. The fundamental matrix, discussed in chapter 9, is a singular 3×3 matrix $\mathtt{F}$ satisfying $\mathbf{x}'^{\mathsf{T}}_i \mathtt{F} \mathbf{x}_i = 0$ for all i.

(iv) **Trifocal tensor computation.** Given a set of point correspondences $\mathbf{x}_i \leftrightarrow \mathbf{x}'_i \leftrightarrow \mathbf{x}''_i$ across three images, compute the trifocal tensor. The trifocal tensor, discussed in chapter 15, is a tensor $\mathcal{T}_i^{jk}$ relating points or lines in three views.

These problems have many features in common, and the considerations that relate to one of the problems are also relevant to each of the others. Therefore, in this chapter, the first of these problems will be considered in detail. What we learn about ways of solving this problem will teach us how to proceed in solving each of the other problems as well.

Apart from being important for illustrative purposes, the problem of estimating 2D projective transformations is of importance in its own right. We consider a set of point correspondences $\mathbf{x}_i \leftrightarrow \mathbf{x}'_i$ between two images. Our problem is to compute a 3×3 matrix $\mathtt{H}$ such that $\mathtt{H}\mathbf{x}_i = \mathbf{x}'_i$ for each i.

Number of measurements required. The first question to consider is how many corresponding points $\mathbf{x}_i \leftrightarrow \mathbf{x}'_i$ are required to compute the projective transformation $\mathtt{H}$. A lower bound is available by a consideration of the number of degrees of freedom and number of constraints. On the one hand, the matrix $\mathtt{H}$ contains 9 entries, but is defined only up to scale. Thus, the total number of degrees of freedom in a 2D projective transformation is 8. On the other hand, each point-to-point correspondence accounts for two constraints, since for each point $\mathbf{x}_i$ in the first image the two degrees of freedom of the point in the second image must correspond to the mapped point $\mathtt{H}\mathbf{x}_i$. A 2D point has two degrees of freedom corresponding to the x and y components, each of which may be specified separately. Alternatively, the point is specified as a homogeneous 3-vector, which also has two degrees of freedom since scale is arbitrary. As a consequence, it is necessary to specify four point correspondences in order to constrain $\mathtt{H}$ fully.

Approximate solutions. It will be seen that if exactly four correspondences are given, then an exact solution for the matrix $\mathtt{H}$ is possible. This is the *minimal* solution. Such solutions are important as they define the size of the subsets required in robust estimation algorithms, such as RANSAC, described in section 4.7. However, since points are measured inexactly ("noise"), if more than four such correspondences are given, then these correspondences may not be fully compatible with any projective transformation, and one will be faced with the task of determining the "best" transformation given the data. This will generally be done by finding the transformation $\mathtt{H}$ that minimizes some cost function. Different cost functions will be discussed during this chapter, together with methods for minimizing them. There are two main categories of cost function: those based on minimizing an algebraic error; and those based on minimizing a geometric or statistical image distance. These two categories are described in section 4.2.

The Gold Standard algorithm. There will usually be one cost function which is optimal in the sense that the $\mathtt{H}$ that minimizes it gives the best possible estimate of the transformation under certain assumptions. The computational algorithm that enables this cost function to be minimized is called the "Gold Standard" algorithm. The results of other algorithms are assessed by how well they compare to this Gold Standard. In the case of estimating a homography between two views the cost function is (4.8), the assumptions for optimality are given in section 4.3, and the Gold Standard is algorithm 4.3(p114).

4.1 The Direct Linear Transformation (DLT) algorithm

We begin with a simple linear algorithm for determining $\mathtt{H}$ given a set of four 2D to 2D point correspondences, $\mathbf{x}_i \leftrightarrow \mathbf{x}'_i$. The transformation is given by the equation $\mathbf{x}'_i = \mathtt{H}\mathbf{x}_i$. Note that this is an equation involving homogeneous vectors; thus the 3-vectors $\mathbf{x}'_i$ and $\mathtt{H}\mathbf{x}_i$ are not equal, they have the same direction but may differ in magnitude by a non-zero scale factor. The equation may be expressed in terms of the vector cross product as $\mathbf{x}'_i \times \mathtt{H}\mathbf{x}_i = \mathbf{0}$. This form will enable a simple linear solution for $\mathtt{H}$ to be derived.

If the j-th row of the matrix $\mathtt{H}$ is denoted by $\mathbf{h}^{j\mathsf{T}}$, then we may write

$$\mathtt{H}\mathbf{x}_i = \begin{pmatrix} \mathbf{h}^{1\mathsf{T}}\mathbf{x}_i \\ \mathbf{h}^{2\mathsf{T}}\mathbf{x}_i \\ \mathbf{h}^{3\mathsf{T}}\mathbf{x}_i \end{pmatrix}.$$

Writing $\mathbf{x}'_i = (x'_i, y'_i, w'_i)^\mathsf{T}$, the cross product may then be given explicitly as

$$\mathbf{x}'_i \times \mathtt{H}\mathbf{x}_i = \begin{pmatrix} y'_i\mathbf{h}^{3\mathsf{T}}\mathbf{x}_i - w'_i\mathbf{h}^{2\mathsf{T}}\mathbf{x}_i \\ w'_i\mathbf{h}^{1\mathsf{T}}\mathbf{x}_i - x'_i\mathbf{h}^{3\mathsf{T}}\mathbf{x}_i \\ x'_i\mathbf{h}^{2\mathsf{T}}\mathbf{x}_i - y'_i\mathbf{h}^{1\mathsf{T}}\mathbf{x}_i \end{pmatrix}.$$

Since $\mathbf{h}^{j\mathsf{T}}\mathbf{x}_i = \mathbf{x}_i^\mathsf{T}\mathbf{h}^j$ for $j = 1, \ldots, 3$, this gives a set of three equations in the entries of $\mathtt{H}$, which may be written in the form

$$\begin{bmatrix} \mathbf{0}^\mathsf{T} & -w'_i\mathbf{x}_i^\mathsf{T} & y'_i\mathbf{x}_i^\mathsf{T} \\ w'_i\mathbf{x}_i^\mathsf{T} & \mathbf{0}^\mathsf{T} & -x'_i\mathbf{x}_i^\mathsf{T} \\ -y'_i\mathbf{x}_i^\mathsf{T} & x'_i\mathbf{x}_i^\mathsf{T} & \mathbf{0}^\mathsf{T} \end{bmatrix} \begin{pmatrix} \mathbf{h}^1 \\ \mathbf{h}^2 \\ \mathbf{h}^3 \end{pmatrix} = \mathbf{0}. \quad (4.1)$$

These equations have the form $\mathtt{A}_i\mathbf{h} = \mathbf{0}$, where $\mathtt{A}_i$ is a 3×9 matrix, and $\mathbf{h}$ is a 9-vector made up of the entries of the matrix $\mathtt{H}$,

$$\mathbf{h} = \begin{pmatrix} \mathbf{h}^1 \\ \mathbf{h}^2 \\ \mathbf{h}^3 \end{pmatrix}, \qquad \mathtt{H} = \begin{bmatrix} h_1 & h_2 & h_3 \\ h_4 & h_5 & h_6 \\ h_7 & h_8 & h_9 \end{bmatrix} \quad (4.2)$$

with h_i the i–th element of $\mathbf{h}$. Three remarks regarding these equations are in order here.

(i) The equation $\mathtt{A}_i\mathbf{h} = \mathbf{0}$ is an equation *linear* in the unknown $\mathbf{h}$. The matrix elements of $\mathtt{A}_i$ are quadratic in the known coordinates of the points.

(ii) Although there are three equations in (4.1), only two of them are linearly independent (since the third row is obtained, up to scale, from the sum of x'_i times the first row and y'_i times the second). Thus each point correspondence gives two equations in the entries of $\mathtt{H}$. It is usual to omit the third equation in solving for $\mathtt{H}$ ([Sutherland-63]). Then (for future reference) the set of equations becomes

$$\begin{bmatrix} \mathbf{0}^\mathsf{T} & -w'_i\mathbf{x}_i^\mathsf{T} & y'_i\mathbf{x}_i^\mathsf{T} \\ w'_i\mathbf{x}_i^\mathsf{T} & \mathbf{0}^\mathsf{T} & -x'_i\mathbf{x}_i^\mathsf{T} \end{bmatrix} \begin{pmatrix} \mathbf{h}^1 \\ \mathbf{h}^2 \\ \mathbf{h}^3 \end{pmatrix} = \mathbf{0}. \quad (4.3)$$

This will be written

$$\mathtt{A}_i\mathbf{h} = \mathbf{0}$$

where $\mathtt{A}_i$ is now the 2×9 matrix of (4.3).

(iii) The equations hold for any homogeneous coordinate representation $(x'_i, y'_i, w'_i)^\mathsf{T}$ of the point $\mathbf{x}'_i$. One may choose $w'_i = 1$, which means that (x'_i, y'_i) are the coordinates measured in the image. Other choices are possible, however, as will be seen later.

Solving for $\mathtt{H}$

Each point correspondence gives rise to two independent equations in the entries of $\mathtt{H}$. Given a set of four such point correspondences, we obtain a set of equations $\mathtt{A}\mathbf{h} = \mathbf{0}$, where $\mathtt{A}$ is the matrix of equation coefficients built from the matrix rows $\mathtt{A}_i$ contributed from each correspondence, and $\mathbf{h}$ is the vector of unknown entries of $\mathtt{H}$. We seek a non-zero solution $\mathbf{h}$, since the obvious solution $\mathbf{h} = \mathbf{0}$ is of no interest to us. If (4.1) is used then $\mathtt{A}$ has dimension 12×9, and if (4.3) the dimension is 8×9. In either case $\mathtt{A}$ has rank 8, and thus has a 1-dimensional null-space which provides a solution for $\mathbf{h}$. Such a solution $\mathbf{h}$ can only be determined up to a non-zero scale factor. However, $\mathtt{H}$ is in general only determined up to scale, so the solution $\mathbf{h}$ gives the required $\mathtt{H}$. A scale may be arbitrarily chosen for $\mathbf{h}$ by a requirement on its norm such as $\|\mathbf{h}\| = 1$.

4.1.1 Over-determined solution

If more than four point correspondences $\mathbf{x}_i \leftrightarrow \mathbf{x}'_i$ are given, then the set of equations $\mathtt{A}\mathbf{h} = \mathbf{0}$ derived from (4.3) is over-determined. If the position of the points is exact then the matrix $\mathtt{A}$ will still have rank 8, a one dimensional null-space, and there is an exact solution for $\mathbf{h}$. This will not be the case if the measurement of image coordinates is inexact (generally termed *noise*) – there will not be an exact solution to the over-determined system $\mathtt{A}\mathbf{h} = \mathbf{0}$ apart from the zero solution. Instead of demanding an exact solution, one attempts to find an approximate solution, namely a vector $\mathbf{h}$ that minimizes a suitable cost function. The question that naturally arises then is: what should be minimized? Clearly, to avoid the solution $\mathbf{h} = \mathbf{0}$ an additional constraint is required. Generally, a condition on the norm is used, such as $\|\mathbf{h}\| = 1$. The value of the norm is unimportant since $\mathtt{H}$ is only defined up to scale. Given that there is no exact solution to $\mathtt{A}\mathbf{h} = \mathbf{0}$, it seems natural to attempt to minimize the norm $\|\mathtt{A}\mathbf{h}\|$ instead, subject to the usual constraint, $\|\mathbf{h}\| = 1$. This is identical to the problem of finding the minimum of the quotient $\|\mathtt{A}\mathbf{h}\|/\|\mathbf{h}\|$. As shown in section A5.3(*p*592) the solution is the (unit) eigenvector of $\mathtt{A}^\mathsf{T}\mathtt{A}$ with least eigenvalue. Equivalently, the solution is the unit singular vector corresponding to the smallest singular value of $\mathtt{A}$. The resulting algorithm, known as the basic DLT algorithm, is summarized in algorithm 4.1.

4.1.2 Inhomogeneous solution

An alternative to solving for $\mathbf{h}$ directly as a homogeneous vector is to turn the set of equations (4.3) into a inhomogeneous set of linear equations by imposing a condition $h_j = 1$ for some entry of the vector $\mathbf{h}$. Imposing the condition $h_j = 1$ is justified by the observation that the solution is determined only up to scale, and this scale can be chosen such that $h_j = 1$. For example, if the last element of $\mathbf{h}$, which corresponds to $\mathtt{H}_{33}$, is chosen as unity then the resulting equations derived from (4.3) are

$$\begin{bmatrix} 0 & 0 & 0 & -x_i w'_i & -y_i w'_i & -w_i w'_i & x_i y'_i & y_i y'_i \\ x_i w'_i & y_i w'_i & w_i w'_i & 0 & 0 & 0 & -x_i x'_i & -y_i x'_i \end{bmatrix} \tilde{\mathbf{h}} = \begin{pmatrix} -w_i y'_i \\ w_i x'_i \end{pmatrix}$$

where $\tilde{\mathbf{h}}$ is an 8-vector consisting of the first 8 components of $\mathbf{h}$. Concatenating the equations from four correspondences then generates a matrix equation of the form

Objective

Given $n \geq 4$ 2D to 2D point correspondences $\{\mathbf{x}_i \leftrightarrow \mathbf{x}'_i\}$, determine the 2D homography matrix $\mathtt{H}$ such that $\mathbf{x}'_i = \mathtt{H}\mathbf{x}_i$.

Algorithm

(i) For each correspondence $\mathbf{x}_i \leftrightarrow \mathbf{x}'_i$ compute the matrix $\mathtt{A}_i$ from (4.1). Only the first two rows need be used in general.

(ii) Assemble the n 2×9 matrices $\mathtt{A}_i$ into a single $2n \times 9$ matrix $\mathtt{A}$.

(iii) Obtain the SVD of $\mathtt{A}$ (section A4.4(*p*585)). The unit singular vector corresponding to the smallest singular value is the solution $\mathbf{h}$. Specifically, if $\mathtt{A} = \mathtt{UDV}^\mathsf{T}$ with $\mathtt{D}$ diagonal with positive diagonal entries, arranged in descending order down the diagonal, then $\mathbf{h}$ is the last column of $\mathtt{V}$.

(iv) The matrix $\mathtt{H}$ is determined from $\mathbf{h}$ as in (4.2).

Algorithm 4.1. *The basic DLT for* $\mathtt{H}$ *(but see algorithm 4.2(*p109*) which includes normalization).*

$\mathtt{M}\tilde{\mathbf{h}} = \mathbf{b}$, where $\mathtt{M}$ has 8 columns and $\mathbf{b}$ is an 8-vector. Such an equation may be solved for $\tilde{\mathbf{h}}$ using standard techniques for solving linear equations (such as Gaussian elimination) in the case where $\mathtt{M}$ contains just 8 rows (the minimum case), or by least-squares techniques (section A5.1(*p*588)) in the case of an over-determined set of equations.

However, if in fact $h_j = 0$ is the true solution, then no multiplicative scale k can exist such that $kh_j = 1$. This means that the true solution cannot be reached. For this reason, this method can be expected to lead to unstable results in the case where the chosen h_j is close to zero. Consequently, this method is *not* recommended in general.

Example 4.1. It will be shown that $h_9 = \mathtt{H}_{33}$ is zero if the coordinate origin is mapped to a point at infinity by $\mathtt{H}$. Since $(0,0,1)^\mathsf{T}$ represents the coordinate origin $\mathbf{x}_0$, and also $(0,0,1)^\mathsf{T}$ represents the line at infinity $\mathbf{l}$, this condition may be written as $\mathbf{l}^\mathsf{T}\mathtt{H}\mathbf{x}_0 = (0,0,1)\mathtt{H}(0,0,1)^\mathsf{T} = 0$, thus $\mathtt{H}_{33} = 0$. In a perspective image of a scene plane the line at infinity is imaged as the vanishing line of the plane (see chapter 8), for example the horizon is the vanishing line of the ground plane. It is not uncommon for the horizon to pass through the image centre, and for thc coordinate origin to coincide with the image centre. In this case the mapping that takes the image to the world plane maps the origin to the line at infinity, so that the true solution has $\mathtt{H}_{33} = h_9 = 0$. Consequently, an $h_9 = 1$ normalization can be a serious failing in practical situations. △

4.1.3 Degenerate configurations

Consider a minimal solution in which a homography is computed using four point correspondences, and suppose that three of the points $\mathbf{x}_1, \mathbf{x}_2, \mathbf{x}_3$ are collinear. The question is whether this is significant. If the corresponding points $\mathbf{x}'_1, \mathbf{x}'_2, \mathbf{x}'_3$ are also collinear then one might suspect that the homography is not sufficiently constrained, and there will exist a family of homographies mapping $\mathbf{x}_i$ to $\mathbf{x}'_i$. On the other hand, if the corresponding points $\mathbf{x}'_1, \mathbf{x}'_2, \mathbf{x}'_3$ are not collinear then clearly there can be no transformation $\mathtt{H}$ taking $\mathbf{x}_i$ to $\mathbf{x}'_i$, since a projective transformation must preserve collinearity. Nevertheless the set of eight homogeneous equations derived from (4.3) must have a non-zero solution, giving rise to a matrix $\mathtt{H}$. How is this apparent contradiction to be resolved?

The equations (4.3) express the condition that $\mathbf{x}'_i \times \mathtt{H}\mathbf{x}_i = \mathbf{0}$ for $i = 1, \ldots, 4$, and so the matrix $\mathtt{H}$ found by solving the system of 8 equations will satisfy this condition. Suppose that $\mathbf{x}_1, \ldots, \mathbf{x}_3$ are collinear and let $\mathbf{l}$ be the line that they lie on, so that $\mathbf{l}^\mathsf{T}\mathbf{x}_i = 0$ for $i = 1, \ldots, 3$. Now define $\mathtt{H}^* = \mathbf{x}'_4\mathbf{l}^\mathsf{T}$, which is a 3×3 matrix of rank 1. In this case, one verifies that $\mathtt{H}^*\mathbf{x}_i = \mathbf{x}'_4(\mathbf{l}^\mathsf{T}\mathbf{x}_i) = \mathbf{0}$ for $i = 1, \ldots, 3$, since $\mathbf{l}^\mathsf{T}\mathbf{x}_i = 0$. On the other hand, $\mathtt{H}^*\mathbf{x}_4 = \mathbf{x}'_4(\mathbf{l}^\mathsf{T}\mathbf{x}_4) = k\mathbf{x}'_4$. Therefore the condition $\mathbf{x}'_i \times \mathtt{H}^*\mathbf{x}_i = \mathbf{0}$ is satisfied for all i. Note that the vector $\mathbf{h}^*$ corresponding to $\mathtt{H}^*$ is given by $\mathbf{h}^{*\mathsf{T}} = (x_4\mathbf{l}^\mathsf{T}, y_4\mathbf{l}^\mathsf{T}, w_4\mathbf{l}^\mathsf{T})$, and one easily verifies that this vector satisfies (4.3) for all i. The problem with this solution for $\mathtt{H}^*$ is that $\mathtt{H}^*$ is a rank 1 matrix and hence does not represent a projective transformation. As a consequence the points $\mathtt{H}^*\mathbf{x}_i = \mathbf{0}$ for $i = 1, \ldots, 3$ are not well defined.

We showed that if $\mathbf{x}_1, \mathbf{x}_2, \mathbf{x}_3$ are collinear then $\mathtt{H}^* = \mathbf{x}'_4\mathbf{l}^\mathsf{T}$ is a solution to (4.1). There are two cases: either $\mathtt{H}^*$ is the unique solution (up to scale) or there is a further solution $\mathtt{H}$. In the first case, since $\mathtt{H}^*$ is a singular matrix, there exists no transformation taking each $\mathbf{x}_i$ to $\mathbf{x}'_i$. This occurs when $\mathbf{x}_1, \ldots, \mathbf{x}_3$ are collinear but $\mathbf{x}'_1, \ldots, \mathbf{x}'_3$ are not. In the second case, where a further solution $\mathtt{H}$ exists, then any matrix of the form $\alpha\,\mathtt{H}^* + \beta\,\mathtt{H}$ is a solution. Thus a 2-dimensional family of transformations exist, and it follows that the 8 equations derived from (4.3) are not independent.

A situation where a configuration does not determine a unique solution for a particular class of transformation is termed *degenerate*. Note that the definition of degeneracy involves both the configuration and the type of transformation. The degeneracy problem is not limited to a minimal solution, however. If additional (perfect, i.e. error-free) correspondences are supplied which are also collinear (lie on $\mathbf{l}$), then the degeneracy is not resolved.

4.1.4 Solutions from lines and other entities

The development to this point, and for the rest of the chapter, is exclusively in terms of computing homographies from point correspondences. However, an identical development can be given for computing homographies from line correspondences. Starting from the line transformation $\mathbf{l}_i = \mathtt{H}^\mathsf{T}\mathbf{l}'_i$, a matrix equation of the form $\mathtt{A}\mathbf{h} = \mathbf{0}$ can be derived, with a minimal solution requiring four lines in general position. Similarly, a homography may be computed from conic correspondences and so forth.

There is the question then of how many correspondences are required to compute the homography (or any other relation). The general rule is that the number of constraints must equal or exceed the number of degrees of freedom of the transformation. For example, in 2D each corresponding point or line generates two constraints on $\mathtt{H}$, in 3D each corresponding point or plane generates three constraints. Thus in 2D the correspondence of four points or four lines is sufficient to compute $\mathtt{H}$, since $4 \times 2 = 8$, with 8 the number of degrees of freedom of the homography. In 3D a homography has 15 degrees of freedom, and five points or five planes are required. For a planar affine transformation (6 dof) only three corresponding points or lines are required, and so on. A conic provides five constraints on a 2D homography.

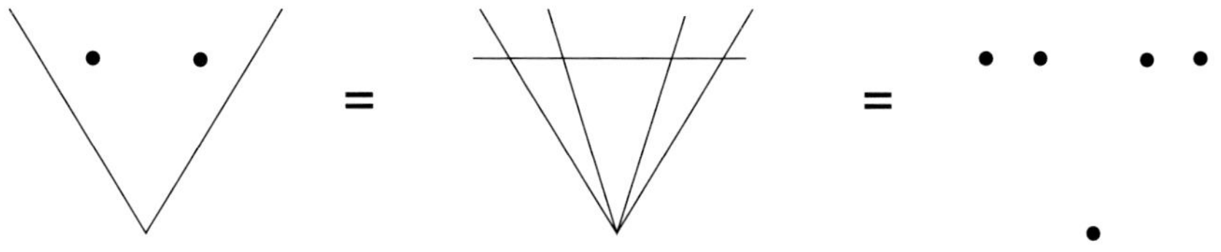

Fig. 4.1. **Geometric equivalence of point–line configurations.** *A configuration of two points and two lines is equivalent to five lines with four concurrent, or five points with four collinear.*

Care has to be taken when computing H from correspondences of mixed type. For example, a 2D homography cannot be determined uniquely from the correspondences of two points and two lines, but can from three points and one line or one point and three lines, even though in each case the configuration has 8 degrees of freedom. The case of three lines and one point is geometrically equivalent to four points, since the three lines define a triangle and the vertices of the triangle uniquely define three points. We have seen that the correspondence of four points in general position uniquely determines a homography, which means that the correspondence of three lines and one point also uniquely determines a homography. Similarly the case of three points and a line is equivalent to four lines, and again the correspondence of four lines in general position (i.e. no three concurrent) uniquely determines a homography. However, as a quick sketch shows (figure 4.1), the case of two points and two lines is equivalent to five lines with four concurrent, or five points with four collinear. As shown in the previous section, this configuration is degenerate and a one-parameter family of homographies map the two-point and two-line configuration to the corresponding configuration.

4.2 Different cost functions

We will now describe a number of cost functions which may be minimized in order to determine H for over-determined solutions. Methods of minimizing these functions are described later in the chapter.

4.2.1 Algebraic distance

The DLT algorithm minimizes the norm $\|\mathtt{A}\mathbf{h}\|$. The vector $\boldsymbol{\epsilon} = \mathtt{A}\mathbf{h}$ is called the residual vector and it is the norm of this error vector that is minimized. The components of this vector arise from the individual correspondences that generate each row of the matrix A. Each correspondence $\mathbf{x}_i \leftrightarrow \mathbf{x}'_i$ contributes a partial error vector $\boldsymbol{\epsilon}_i$ from (4.1) or (4.3) towards the full error vector $\boldsymbol{\epsilon}$. This vector $\boldsymbol{\epsilon}_i$ is the *algebraic error vector* associated with the point correspondence $\mathbf{x}_i \leftrightarrow \mathbf{x}'_i$ and the homography H. The norm of this vector is a scalar which is called the *algebraic distance*:

$$d_{\text{alg}}(\mathbf{x}'_i, \mathtt{H}\mathbf{x}_i)^2 = \|\boldsymbol{\epsilon}_i\|^2 = \left\| \begin{bmatrix} \mathbf{0}^{\mathsf{T}} & -w'_i\mathbf{x}_i^{\mathsf{T}} & y'_i\mathbf{x}_i^{\mathsf{T}} \\ w'_i\mathbf{x}_i^{\mathsf{T}} & \mathbf{0}^{\mathsf{T}} & -x'_i\mathbf{x}_i^{\mathsf{T}} \end{bmatrix} \mathbf{h} \right\|^2 . \tag{4.4}$$

More generally, and briefly, for any two vectors $\mathbf{x}_1$ and $\mathbf{x}_2$ we may write

$$d_{\text{alg}}(\mathbf{x}_1, \mathbf{x}_2)^2 = a_1^2 + a_2^2 \text{ where } \mathbf{a} = (a_1, a_2, a_3)^{\mathsf{T}} = \mathbf{x}_1 \times \mathbf{x}_2.$$

The relation of this distance to a geometric distance is described in section 4.2.4.

Given a set of correspondences, the quantity $\epsilon = \mathtt{A}\mathbf{h}$ is the algebraic error vector for the complete set, and one sees that

$$\sum_i d_{\text{alg}}(\mathbf{x}'_i, \mathtt{H}\mathbf{x}_i)^2 = \sum_i \|\epsilon_i\|^2 = \|\mathtt{A}\mathbf{h}\|^2 = \|\epsilon\|^2. \tag{4.5}$$

The concept of algebraic distance originated in the conic-fitting work of Bookstein [Bookstein-79]. Its disadvantage is that the quantity that is minimized is not geometrically or statistically meaningful. As Bookstein demonstrated, the solutions that minimize algebraic distance may not be those expected intuitively. Nevertheless, with a good choice of normalization (as will be discussed in section 4.4) methods which minimize algebraic distance do give very good results. Their particular advantages are a linear (and thus a unique) solution, and computational cheapness. Often solutions based on algebraic distance are used as a starting point for a non-linear minimization of a geometric or statistical cost function. The non-linear minimization gives the solution a final "polish".

4.2.2 Geometric distance

Next we discuss alternative error functions based on the measurement of geometric distance in the image, and minimization of the difference between the measured and estimated image coordinates.

Notation. Vectors $\mathbf{x}$ represent the *measured* image coordinates; $\hat{\mathbf{x}}$ represent estimated values of the points and $\bar{\mathbf{x}}$ represent true values of the points.

Error in one image. We start by considering error only in the second image, with points in the first measured perfectly. Clearly, this will not be true in most practical situations with images. An example where the assumption is more reasonable is in estimating the projective transformation between a calibration pattern or a world plane, where points are measured to a very high accuracy, and its image. The appropriate quantity to be minimized is the *transfer* error. This is the Euclidean image distance in the second image between the measured point $\mathbf{x}'$ and the point $\mathtt{H}\bar{\mathbf{x}}$ at which the corresponding point $\bar{\mathbf{x}}$ is mapped from the first image. We use the notation $d(\mathbf{x}, \mathbf{y})$ to represent the Euclidean distance between the inhomogeneous points represented by $\mathbf{x}$ and $\mathbf{y}$. Then the transfer error for the set of correspondences is

$$\sum_i d(\mathbf{x}'_i, \mathtt{H}\bar{\mathbf{x}}_i)^2. \tag{4.6}$$

The estimated homography $\hat{\mathtt{H}}$ is the one for which the error (4.6) is minimized.

Symmetric transfer error. In the more realistic case where image measurement errors occur in both the images, it is preferable that errors be minimized in both images, and not solely in the one. One way of constructing a more satisfactory error function is to consider the forward (H) and backward ($\mathtt{H}^{-1}$) transformation, and sum the geometric errors corresponding to each of these two transformations. Thus, the error is

$$\sum_i d(\mathbf{x}_i, \mathtt{H}^{-1}\mathbf{x}'_i)^2 + d(\mathbf{x}'_i, \mathtt{H}\mathbf{x}_i)^2. \tag{4.7}$$

The first term in this sum is the transfer error in the first image, and the second term is the transfer error in the second image. Again the estimated homography $\hat{\mathtt{H}}$ is the one for which (4.7) is minimized.

4.2.3 Reprojection error – both images

An alternative method of quantifying error in each of the two images involves estimating a "correction" for each correspondence. One asks how much it is necessary to correct the measurements in each of the two images in order to obtain a perfectly matched set of image points. One should compare this with the geometric one-image transfer error (4.6) which measures the correction that it is necessary to make to the measurements in one image (the second image) in order to get a set of perfectly matching points.

In the present case, we are seeking a homography $\hat{\mathtt{H}}$ and pairs of *perfectly* matched points $\hat{\mathbf{x}}_i$ and $\hat{\mathbf{x}}'_i$ that minimize the total error function

$$\sum_i d(\mathbf{x}_i, \hat{\mathbf{x}}_i)^2 + d(\mathbf{x}'_i, \hat{\mathbf{x}}'_i)^2 \quad \text{subject to } \hat{\mathbf{x}}'_i = \hat{\mathtt{H}}\hat{\mathbf{x}}_i \;\; \forall i. \tag{4.8}$$

Minimizing this cost function involves determining both $\hat{\mathtt{H}}$ *and* a set of subsidiary correspondences $\{\hat{\mathbf{x}}_i\}$ and $\{\hat{\mathbf{x}}'_i\}$. This estimation models, for example, the situation that measured correspondences $\mathbf{x}_i \leftrightarrow \mathbf{x}'_i$ arise from images of points on a world plane. We wish to estimate a point on the world plane $\widehat{\mathbf{X}}_i$ from $\mathbf{x}_i \leftrightarrow \mathbf{x}'_i$ which is then *reprojected* to the estimated perfectly matched correspondence $\hat{\mathbf{x}}_i \leftrightarrow \hat{\mathbf{x}}'_i$.

This reprojection error function is compared with the symmetric error function in figure 4.2. It will be seen in section 4.3 that (4.8) is related to the Maximum Likelihood estimation of the homography and correspondences.

4.2.4 Comparison of geometric and algebraic distance

We return to the case of errors only in the second image. Let $\mathbf{x}'_i = (x'_i, y'_i, w'_i)^\mathsf{T}$ and define a vector $(\hat{x}'_i, \hat{y}'_i, \hat{w}'_i)^\mathsf{T} = \hat{\mathbf{x}}'_i = \mathtt{H}\bar{\mathbf{x}}_i$. Using this notation, the left hand side of (4.3) becomes

$$\mathtt{A}_i\mathbf{h} = \boldsymbol{\epsilon}_i = \begin{pmatrix} y'_i\hat{w}'_i - w'_i\hat{y}'_i \\ w'_i\hat{x}'_i - x'_i\hat{w}'_i \end{pmatrix}.$$

This vector is the *algebraic error vector* associated with the point correspondence $\mathbf{x}_i \leftrightarrow \mathbf{x}'_i$ and the camera mapping H. Thus,

$$d_{\text{alg}}(\mathbf{x}'_i, \hat{\mathbf{x}}'_i)^2 = (y'_i\hat{w}'_i - w'_i\hat{y}'_i)^2 + (w'_i\hat{x}'_i - x'_i\hat{w}'_i)^2.$$

For points $\mathbf{x}'_i$ and $\hat{\mathbf{x}}'_i$ the geometric distance is

$$d(\mathbf{x}'_i, \hat{\mathbf{x}}'_i) \;=\; \left((x'_i/w'_i - \hat{x}'_i/\hat{w}'_i)^2 + (y'_i/w'_i - \hat{y}'_i/\hat{w}'_i)^2\right)^{1/2}$$

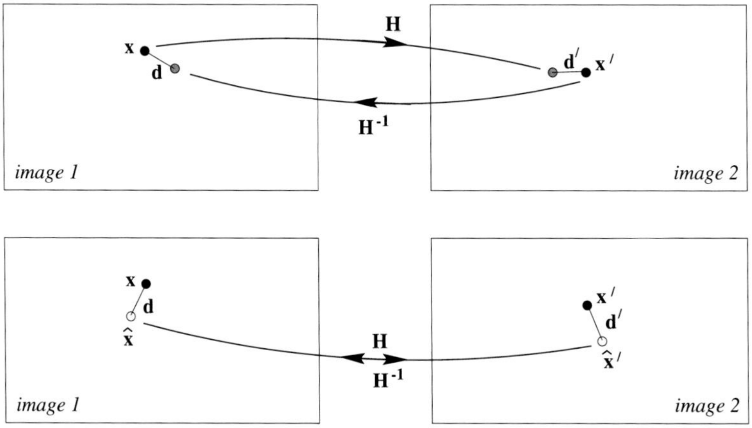

Fig. 4.2. *A comparison between symmetric transfer error (upper) and reprojection error (lower) when estimating a homography. The points* $\mathbf{x}$ *and* $\mathbf{x}'$ *are the measured (noisy) points. Under the estimated homography the points* $\mathbf{x}'$ *and* $\mathtt{H}\mathbf{x}$ *do* not *correspond perfectly (and neither do the points* $\mathbf{x}$ *and* $\mathtt{H}^{-1}\mathbf{x}'$*). However, the estimated points,* $\hat{\mathbf{x}}$ *and* $\hat{\mathbf{x}}'$*, do correspond perfectly by the homography* $\hat{\mathbf{x}}' = \mathtt{H}\hat{\mathbf{x}}$*. Using the notation* $d(\mathbf{x}, \mathbf{y})$ *for the Euclidean image distance between* $\mathbf{x}$ *and* $\mathbf{y}$*, the symmetric transfer error is* $d(\mathbf{x}, \mathtt{H}^{-1}\mathbf{x}')^2 + d(\mathbf{x}', \mathtt{H}\mathbf{x})^2$*; the reprojection error is* $d(\mathbf{x}, \hat{\mathbf{x}})^2 + d(\mathbf{x}', \hat{\mathbf{x}}')^2$.

$$= d_{\text{alg}}(\mathbf{x}'_i, \hat{\mathbf{x}}'_i)/\hat{w}'_i w'_i.$$

Thus, geometric distance is related to, but not quite the same as, algebraic distance. Note, though, that if $\hat{w}'_i = w'_i = 1$, then the two distances are identical.

One can always assume that $w_i = 1$, thus expressing the points $\mathbf{x}_i$ in the usual form $\mathbf{x}_i = (x_i, y_i, 1)^\mathsf{T}$. For one important class of 2D homographies, the values of $\hat{w}'_i$ will always be 1 as well. A 2D *affine* transformation is represented by a matrix of the form (2.10–*p*39)

$$\mathtt{H}_\text{A} = \begin{bmatrix} h_{11} & h_{12} & h_{13} \\ h_{21} & h_{22} & h_{23} \\ 0 & 0 & 1 \end{bmatrix}. \tag{4.9}$$

One verifies immediately from $\hat{\mathbf{x}}'_i = \mathtt{H}_\text{A}\bar{\mathbf{x}}_i$ that $\hat{w}'_i = 1$ if $w_i = 1$. This demonstrates that in the case of an affine transformation geometric distance and algebraic distance are identical. The DLT algorithm is easily adapted to enforce the condition that the last row of $\mathtt{H}$ has the form $(0, 0, 1)$ by setting $h_7 = h_8 = 0$. Hence, for affine transformations, geometric distance can be minimized by the linear DLT algorithm based on algebraic distance.

4.2.5 Geometric interpretation of reprojection error

The estimation of a homography between two planes can be thought of as fitting a "surface" to points in a 4D space, $\mathbb{R}^4$. Each pair of image points $\mathbf{x}$, $\mathbf{x}'$ defines a single point denoted $\mathbf{X}$ in a measurement space $\mathbb{R}^4$, formed by concatenating the inhomogeneous coordinates of $\mathbf{x}$ and $\mathbf{x}'$. For a given specific homography $\mathtt{H}$, the image correspondences $\mathbf{x} \leftrightarrow \mathbf{x}'$ that satisfy $\mathbf{x}' \times (\mathtt{H}\mathbf{x}) = \mathbf{0}$ define an algebraic variety[1] $\mathcal{V}_\mathtt{H}$ in $\mathbb{R}^4$ which is the

[1] A *variety* is the simultaneous zero-set of one or more multivariate polynomials defined in $\mathbb{R}^N$.

intersection of two quadric hypersurfaces. The surface is a quadric in $\mathbb{R}^4$ because each row of (4.1) is a degree 2 polynomial in x, y, x', y'. The elements of $\mathtt{H}$ determine the coefficient of each term of the polynomial, and so $\mathtt{H}$ specifies the particular quadric. The two independent equations of (4.1) define two such quadrics.

Given points $\mathbf{X}_i = (x_i, y_i, x'_i, y'_i)^\mathsf{T}$ in $\mathbb{R}^4$, the task of estimating a homography becomes the task of finding a variety $\mathcal{V}_\mathtt{H}$ that passes (or most nearly passes) through the points $\mathbf{X}_i$. In general, of course, it will not be possible to fit a variety precisely. In this case, let $\mathcal{V}_\mathtt{H}$ be some variety corresponding to a transformation $\mathtt{H}$, and for each point $\mathbf{X}_i$, let $\widehat{\mathbf{X}}_i = (\hat{x}_i, \hat{y}_i, \hat{x}'_i, \hat{y}'_i)^\mathsf{T}$ be the closest point to $\mathbf{X}_i$ lying on the variety $\mathcal{V}_\mathtt{H}$. One sees immediately that

$$\begin{aligned} \|\mathbf{X}_i - \widehat{\mathbf{X}}_i\|^2 &= (x_i - \hat{x}_i)^2 + (y_i - \hat{y}_i)^2 + (x'_i - \hat{x}'_i)^2 + (y'_i - \hat{y}'_i)^2 \\ &= d(\mathbf{x}_i, \hat{\mathbf{x}}_i)^2 + d(\mathbf{x}'_i, \hat{\mathbf{x}}'_i)^2. \end{aligned}$$

Thus geometric distance in $\mathbb{R}^4$ is equivalent to the reprojection error measured in both the images, and finding the variety $\mathcal{V}_\mathtt{H}$ and points $\widehat{\mathbf{X}}_i$ on $\mathcal{V}_\mathtt{H}$ that minimize the squared sum of distances to the measured points $\mathbf{X}_i$ is equivalent to finding the homography $\hat{\mathtt{H}}$ and the estimated points $\hat{\mathbf{x}}_i$ and $\hat{\mathbf{x}}'_i$ that minimize the reprojection error function (4.8).

The point $\widehat{\mathbf{X}}$ on $\mathcal{V}_\mathtt{H}$ that lies closest to a measured point $\mathbf{X}$ is a point where the line between $\mathbf{X}$ and $\widehat{\mathbf{X}}$ is perpendicular to the tangent plane to $\mathcal{V}_\mathtt{H}$ at $\widehat{\mathbf{X}}$. Thus

$$d(\mathbf{x}_i, \hat{\mathbf{x}}_i)^2 + d(\mathbf{x}'_i, \hat{\mathbf{x}}'_i)^2 = d_\perp(\mathbf{X}_i, \mathcal{V}_\mathtt{H})^2$$

where $d_\perp(\mathbf{X}, \mathcal{V}_\mathtt{H})$ is the perpendicular distance of the point $\mathbf{X}$ to the variety $\mathcal{V}_\mathtt{H}$. As may be seen from the conic-fitting analogue discussed below, there may be more than one such perpendicular from $\mathbf{X}$ to $\mathcal{V}_\mathtt{H}$.

The distance $d_\perp(\mathbf{X}, \mathcal{V}_\mathtt{H})$ is invariant to rigid transformations of $\mathbb{R}^4$, and this includes as a special case rigid transformations of the coordinates (x, y), (x', y') of each image individually. This point is returned to in section 4.4.3.

Conic analogue. Before proceeding further we will first sketch an analogous estimation problem that can be visualized more easily. The problem is fitting a conic to 2D points, which occupies a useful intermediate position between fitting a straight line (no curvature, too simple) and fitting a homography (four dimensions, with non-zero curvature).

Consider the problem of fitting a conic to a set of $n > 5$ points $(x_i, y_i)^\mathsf{T}$ on the plane such that an error based on geometric distance is minimized. The points may be thought of as "correspondences" $x_i \leftrightarrow y_i$. The transfer distance and reprojection (perpendicular) distance are illustrated in figure 4.3. It is clear from this figure that $d_\perp$ is less than or equal to the transfer error.

The algebraic distance of a point $\mathbf{x}$ from a conic $\mathtt{C}$ is defined as $d_{\text{alg}}(\mathbf{x}, \mathtt{C})^2 = \mathbf{x}^\mathsf{T}\mathtt{C}\mathbf{x}$. A linear solution for $\mathtt{C}$ can be obtained by minimizing $\sum_i d_{\text{alg}}(\mathbf{x}_i, \mathtt{C})^2$ with a suitable normalization on $\mathtt{C}$. There is no linear expression for the perpendicular distance of a point (x, y) to a conic $\mathtt{C}$, since through each point in $\mathbb{R}^2$ there are up to 4 lines perpendicular to $\mathtt{C}$. The solution can be obtained from the roots of a quartic. However, a function $d_\perp(\mathbf{x}, \mathtt{C})$ may be defined which returns the shortest distance between a conic

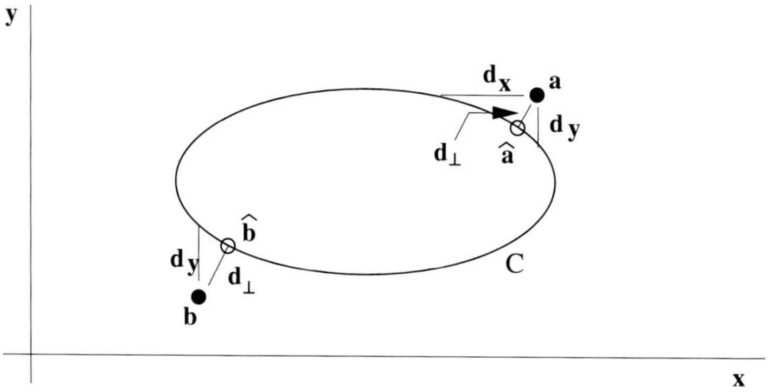

Fig. 4.3. *A conic may be estimated from a set of 2D points by minimizing "symmetric transfer error" $d_x^2 + d_y^2$ or the sum of squared perpendicular distances $d_\perp^2$. The analogue of transfer error is to consider x as perfect and measure the distance d_y to the conic in the y direction, and similarly for d_x. For point* $\mathbf{a}$ *it is clear that $d_\perp \le d_x$ and $d_\perp \le d_y$. Also $d_\perp$ is more stable than d_x or d_y as illustrated by point* $\mathbf{b}$ *where d_x cannot be defined.*

and a point. A conic can then be estimated by minimizing $\sum_i d_\perp(\mathbf{x}_i, \mathtt{C})^2$ over the five parameters of $\mathtt{C}$, though this cannot be achieved by a linear solution. Given a conic $\mathtt{C}$ and a measured point $\mathbf{x}$, a corrected point $\hat{\mathbf{x}}$ is obtained simply by choosing the closest point on $\mathtt{C}$.

We return now to estimating a homography. In the case of an affine transformation the variety is the intersection of two hyperplanes, i.e. it is a linear subspace of dimension 2. This follows from the form (4.9) of the affine matrix which for $\mathbf{x}' = \mathtt{H}_\mathtt{A}\mathbf{x}$ yields one linear constraint between x, x', y and another between x, y, y', each of which defines a hyperplane in $\mathbb{R}^4$. An analogue of this situation is line fitting to points on the plane. In both cases the relation (affine transformation or line) may be estimated by minimizing the perpendicular distance of points to the variety. In both cases there is a closed form solution as discussed in the following section.

4.2.6 Sampson error

The geometric error (4.8) is quite complex in nature, and minimizing it requires the simultaneous estimation of both the homography matrix and the points $\hat{\mathbf{x}}_i, \hat{\mathbf{x}}'_i$. This non-linear estimation problem will be discussed further in section 4.5. Its complexity contrasts with the simplicity of minimizing the algebraic error (4.4). The geometric interpretation of geometric error given in section 4.2.5 leads to a further cost function that lies between the algebraic and geometric cost functions in terms of complexity, but gives a close approximation to geometric error. We will refer to this cost function as *Sampson error* since Sampson [Sampson-82] used this approximation for conic fitting.

As described in section 4.2.5, the vector $\widehat{\mathbf{X}}$ that minimizes the geometric error $\|\mathbf{X} - \widehat{\mathbf{X}}\|^2$ is the closest point on the variety $\mathcal{V}_\mathtt{H}$ to the measurement $\mathbf{X}$. This point can not be estimated directly except via iteration, because of the non-linear nature of the variety $\mathcal{V}_\mathtt{H}$. The idea of the Sampson error function is to estimate a first-order approximation to the point $\widehat{\mathbf{X}}$, assuming that the cost function is well approximated linearly in the neighbourhood of the estimated point. The discussion to follow is related directly to the 2D homography estimation problem, but applies substantially unchanged to the other estimation problems discussed in this book.

For a given homography $\mathtt{H}$, any point $\mathbf{X} = (x, y, x', y')^\mathsf{T}$ that lies on $\mathcal{V}_\mathtt{H}$ will satisfy the equation (4.3–p89), or $\mathtt{A}\mathbf{h} = \mathbf{0}$. To emphasize the dependency on $\mathbf{X}$ we will write this instead as $\mathcal{C}_\mathtt{H}(\mathbf{X}) = \mathbf{0}$, where $\mathcal{C}_\mathtt{H}(\mathbf{X})$ is in this case a 2-vector. To first order, this cost function may be approximated by a Taylor expansion

$$\mathcal{C}_\mathtt{H}(\mathbf{X} + \boldsymbol{\delta}_\mathbf{X}) = \mathcal{C}_\mathtt{H}(\mathbf{X}) + \frac{\partial \mathcal{C}_\mathtt{H}}{\partial \mathbf{X}} \boldsymbol{\delta}_\mathbf{X}. \tag{4.10}$$

If we write $\boldsymbol{\delta}_\mathbf{X} = \widehat{\mathbf{X}} - \mathbf{X}$ and desire $\widehat{\mathbf{X}}$ to lie on the variety $\mathcal{V}_\mathtt{H}$ so that $\mathcal{C}_\mathtt{H}(\widehat{\mathbf{X}}) = \mathbf{0}$, then the result is $\mathcal{C}_\mathtt{H}(\mathbf{X}) + (\partial \mathcal{C}_\mathtt{H}/\partial \mathbf{X})\boldsymbol{\delta}_\mathbf{X} = \mathbf{0}$, which we will henceforth write as $\mathtt{J}\boldsymbol{\delta}_\mathbf{X} = -\boldsymbol{\epsilon}$ where $\mathtt{J}$ is the partial-derivative matrix, and $\boldsymbol{\epsilon}$ is the cost $\mathcal{C}_\mathtt{H}(\mathbf{X})$ associated with $\mathbf{X}$. The minimization problem that we now face is to find the smallest $\boldsymbol{\delta}_\mathbf{X}$ that satisfies this equation, namely:

- *Find the vector $\boldsymbol{\delta}_\mathbf{X}$ that minimizes $\|\boldsymbol{\delta}_\mathbf{X}\|$ subject to $\mathtt{J}\boldsymbol{\delta}_\mathbf{X} = -\boldsymbol{\epsilon}$.*

The standard way to solve problems of this type is to use Lagrange multipliers. A vector $\boldsymbol{\lambda}$ of Lagrange multipliers is introduced, and the problem reduces to that of finding the extrema of $\boldsymbol{\delta}_\mathbf{X}^\mathsf{T}\boldsymbol{\delta}_\mathbf{X} - 2\boldsymbol{\lambda}^\mathsf{T}(\mathtt{J}\boldsymbol{\delta}_\mathbf{X} + \boldsymbol{\epsilon})$, where the factor 2 is simply introduced for convenience. Taking derivatives with respect to $\boldsymbol{\delta}_\mathbf{X}$ and equating to zero gives

$$2\boldsymbol{\delta}_\mathbf{X}^\mathsf{T} - 2\boldsymbol{\lambda}^\mathsf{T}\mathtt{J} = \mathbf{0}^\mathsf{T}$$

from which we obtain $\boldsymbol{\delta}_\mathbf{X} = \mathtt{J}^\mathsf{T}\boldsymbol{\lambda}$. The derivative with respect to $\boldsymbol{\lambda}$ gives $\mathtt{J}\boldsymbol{\delta}_\mathbf{X} + \boldsymbol{\epsilon} = \mathbf{0}$, the original constraint. Substituting for $\boldsymbol{\delta}_\mathbf{X}$ leads to

$$\mathtt{J}\mathtt{J}^\mathsf{T}\boldsymbol{\lambda} = -\boldsymbol{\epsilon}$$

which may be solved for $\boldsymbol{\lambda}$ giving $\boldsymbol{\lambda} = -(\mathtt{J}\mathtt{J}^\mathsf{T})^{-1}\boldsymbol{\epsilon}$, and so finally

$$\boldsymbol{\delta}_\mathbf{X} = -\mathtt{J}^\mathsf{T}(\mathtt{J}\mathtt{J}^\mathsf{T})^{-1}\boldsymbol{\epsilon}, \tag{4.11}$$

and $\widehat{\mathbf{X}} = \mathbf{X} + \boldsymbol{\delta}_\mathbf{X}$. The norm $\|\boldsymbol{\delta}_\mathbf{X}\|^2$ is the Sampson error:

$$\|\boldsymbol{\delta}_\mathbf{X}\|^2 = \boldsymbol{\delta}_\mathbf{X}^\mathsf{T}\boldsymbol{\delta}_\mathbf{X} = \boldsymbol{\epsilon}^\mathsf{T}(\mathtt{J}\mathtt{J}^\mathsf{T})^{-1}\boldsymbol{\epsilon}. \tag{4.12}$$

Example 4.2. Sampson approximation for a conic

We will compute the Sampson approximation to the geometric distance $d_\perp(\mathbf{x}, \mathtt{C})$ between a point $\mathbf{x}$ and conic $\mathtt{C}$ shown in figure 4.3. In this case the conic variety $\mathcal{V}_\mathtt{C}$ is defined by the equation $\mathbf{x}^\mathsf{T}\mathtt{C}\mathbf{x} = 0$, so that $\mathbf{X} = (x, y)^\mathsf{T}$ is a 2-vector, $\epsilon = \mathbf{x}^\mathsf{T}\mathtt{C}\mathbf{x}$ is a scalar, and $\mathtt{J}$ is the 1×2 matrix given by

$$\mathtt{J} = \left[\frac{\partial(\mathbf{x}^\mathsf{T}\mathtt{C}\mathbf{x})}{\partial x}, \frac{\partial(\mathbf{x}^\mathsf{T}\mathtt{C}\mathbf{x})}{\partial y}\right].$$

This means that $\mathtt{J}\mathtt{J}^\mathsf{T}$ is a scalar. The elements of $\mathtt{J}$ may be computed by the chain rule as

$$\frac{\partial(\mathbf{x}^\mathsf{T}\mathtt{C}\mathbf{x})}{\partial x} = \frac{\partial(\mathbf{x}^\mathsf{T}\mathtt{C}\mathbf{x})}{\partial \mathbf{x}}\frac{\partial \mathbf{x}}{\partial x} = 2\mathbf{x}^\mathsf{T}\mathtt{C}(1,0,0)^\mathsf{T} = 2(\mathtt{C}\mathbf{x})_1$$

where $(\mathtt{C}\mathbf{x})_i$ denotes the i-th component of the 3-vector $\mathtt{C}\mathbf{x}$. Then from (4.12)

$$d_\perp^2 = \|\boldsymbol{\delta}_\mathbf{X}\|^2 = \boldsymbol{\epsilon}^\mathsf{T}(\mathtt{J}\mathtt{J}^\mathsf{T})^{-1}\boldsymbol{\epsilon} = \frac{\boldsymbol{\epsilon}^\mathsf{T}\boldsymbol{\epsilon}}{\mathtt{J}\mathtt{J}^\mathsf{T}} = \frac{(\mathbf{x}^\mathsf{T}\mathtt{C}\mathbf{x})^2}{4((\mathtt{C}\mathbf{x})_1^2 + (\mathtt{C}\mathbf{x})_2^2)}$$

△

A few points to note:

(i) For the 2D homography estimation problem, $\mathbf{X} = (x, y, x', y')^\mathsf{T}$ where the 2D measurements are $\mathbf{x} = (x, y, 1)^\mathsf{T}$ and $\mathbf{x}' = (x', y', 1)^\mathsf{T}$.

(ii) $\boldsymbol{\epsilon} = \mathcal{C}_\mathtt{H}(\mathbf{X})$ is the algebraic error vector $\mathtt{A}_i\mathbf{h}$ – a 2-vector – and $\mathtt{A}_i$ is defined in (4.3–*p*89).

(iii) $\mathtt{J} = \partial\mathcal{C}_\mathtt{H}(\mathbf{X})/\partial\mathbf{X}$ is a 2×4 matrix. For example

$$J_{11} = \partial(-w_i'\mathbf{x}_i^\mathsf{T}\mathbf{h}^2 + y_i'\mathbf{x}_i^\mathsf{T}\mathbf{h}^3)/\partial x = -w_i'h_{21} + y_i'h_{31}.$$

(iv) Note the similarity of (4.12) to the algebraic error $\|\boldsymbol{\epsilon}\| = \boldsymbol{\epsilon}^\mathsf{T}\boldsymbol{\epsilon}$. The Sampson error may be interpreted as being the Mahalanobis norm (see section A2.1-(*p*565)), $\|\boldsymbol{\epsilon}\|_{\mathtt{J}\mathtt{J}^\mathsf{T}}$.

(v) One could alternatively use $\mathtt{A}$ defined by (4.1–*p*89), in which case $\mathtt{J}$ has dimension 3×4 and $\boldsymbol{\epsilon}$ is a 3-vector. However, in general the Sampson error, and consequently the solution $\boldsymbol{\delta}_\mathbf{X}$, will be independent of whether (4.1–*p*89) or (4.3–*p*89) is used.

The Sampson error (4.12) is derived here for a single point pair. In applying this to the estimation of a 2D homography $\mathtt{H}$ from several point correspondences $\mathbf{x}_i \leftrightarrow \mathbf{x}_i'$, the errors corresponding to all the point correspondences must be summed, giving

$$\mathcal{D}_\perp = \sum_i \boldsymbol{\epsilon}_i^\mathsf{T}(\mathtt{J}_i\mathtt{J}_i^\mathsf{T})^{-1}\boldsymbol{\epsilon}_i \tag{4.13}$$

where $\boldsymbol{\epsilon}$ and $\mathtt{J}$ both depend on $\mathtt{H}$. To estimate $\mathtt{H}$, this expression must be minimized over all values of $\mathtt{H}$. This is a simple minimization problem in which the set of variable parameters consists only of the entries (or some other parametrization) of $\mathtt{H}$.

This derivation of the Sampson error assumed that each point had isotropic (circular) error distribution, the same in each image. The appropriate formulae for more general Gaussian error distributions are given in the exercises at the end of this chapter.

Linear cost function

The algebraic error vector $\mathcal{C}_\mathtt{H}(\mathbf{X}) = \mathtt{A}(\mathbf{X})\mathbf{h}$ is typically multilinear in the entries of $\mathbf{X}$. The case where $\mathtt{A}(\mathbf{X})\mathbf{h}$ is *linear* is, however, important in its own right. The first point to note is that in this case, the first-order approximation to geometric error given by the Taylor expansion in (4.10) is exact (the higher order terms are zero), which means that *the Sampson error is identical to geometric error.*

In addition, the variety $\mathcal{V}_\mathtt{H}$ defined by the equation $\mathcal{C}_\mathtt{H}(\mathbf{X}) = \mathbf{0}$, a set of linear equations, is a hyperplane depending on $\mathtt{H}$. The problem of finding $\mathtt{H}$ now becomes a hyperplane fitting problem – find the best fit to the data $\mathbf{X}_i$ among the hyperplanes parametrized by $\mathtt{H}$.

As an example of this idea a *linear* algorithm which minimizes geometric error (4.8) for an affine transformation is developed in the exercises at the end of this chapter.

4.2.7 Another geometric interpretation

It was shown in section 4.2.5 that finding a homography that takes a set of points $\mathbf{x}_i$ to another set $\mathbf{x}'_i$ is equivalent to the problem of fitting a variety of a given type to a set of points in $\mathbb{R}^4$. We now consider a different interpretation in which the set of all measurements is represented by a single point in a measurement space $\mathbb{R}^N$.

The estimation problems we consider may all be fitted into a common framework. In abstract terms the estimation problem has two components,

- a *measurement space* $\mathbb{R}^N$ consisting of *measurement vectors* $\mathbf{X}$, and
- a *model*, which in abstract terms may be thought of simply as a subset S of points in $\mathbb{R}^N$. A measurement vector $\mathbf{X}$ that lies inside this subset is said to *satisfy the model.* Typically the subspace that satisfies the model is a submanifold, or variety in $\mathbb{R}^N$.

Now, given a measurement vector $\mathbf{X}$ in $\mathbb{R}^N$, the estimation problem is to find the vector $\widehat{\mathbf{X}}$, closest to $\mathbf{X}$, that satisfies the model.

It will now be pointed out how the 2D homography estimation problem fits into this framework.

Error in both images. Let $\{\mathbf{x}_i \leftrightarrow \mathbf{x}'_i\}$ be a set of measured matched points for $i = 1, \ldots, n$. In all, there are $4n$ measurements, namely two coordinates in each of two images for n points. Thus, the set of matched points represents a point in $\mathbb{R}^N$, where $N = 4n$. The vector made up of the coordinates of all the matched points in both images will be denoted $\mathbf{X}$.

Of course, not all sets of point pairs $\mathbf{x}_i \leftrightarrow \mathbf{x}'_i$ are related via a homography $\mathtt{H}$. A set of point correspondences $\{\mathbf{x}_i \leftrightarrow \mathbf{x}'_i\}$ for which there exists a projective transformation $\mathtt{H}$ satisfying $\mathbf{x}'_i = \mathtt{H}\mathbf{x}_i$ for all i constitutes the subset of $\mathbb{R}^N$ satisfying the model. In general, this set of points will form a submanifold S in $\mathbb{R}^N$ (in fact a variety) of some dimension. The dimension of this submanifold is equal to the minimal number of parameters that may be used to parametrize the submanifold.

One may arbitrarily choose n points $\hat{\mathbf{x}}_i$ in the first image. In addition, a homography $\mathtt{H}$ may be chosen arbitrarily. Once these choices have been made, the points $\hat{\mathbf{x}}'_i$ in the second image are determined by $\hat{\mathbf{x}}'_i = \mathtt{H}\hat{\mathbf{x}}_i$. Thus, a feasible choice of points is determined by a set of $2n + 8$ parameters: the $2n$ coordinates of the points $\hat{\mathbf{x}}_i$, plus the 8 independent parameters (degrees of freedom) of the transformation $\mathtt{H}$. Thus, the submanifold $S \subset \mathbb{R}^N$ has dimension $2n + 8$, and hence codimension $2n - 8$.

Given a set of measured point pairs $\{\mathbf{x}_i \leftrightarrow \mathbf{x}'_i\}$, corresponding to a point $\mathbf{X}$ in $\mathbb{R}^N$, and an estimated point $\widehat{\mathbf{X}} \in \mathbb{R}^N$ lying on S, one easily verifies that

$$\|\mathbf{X} - \widehat{\mathbf{X}}\|^2 = \sum_i d(\mathbf{x}_i, \hat{\mathbf{x}}_i)^2 + d(\mathbf{x}'_i, \hat{\mathbf{x}}'_i)^2.$$

Thus, finding the point $\widehat{\mathbf{X}}$ on S lying closest to $\mathbf{X}$ in $\mathbb{R}^N$ is equivalent to minimizing the cost function given by (4.8). The estimated correct correspondences $\hat{\mathbf{x}}_i \leftrightarrow \hat{\mathbf{x}}'_i$ are those corresponding to the closest surface point $\widehat{\mathbf{X}}$ in $\mathbb{R}^N$. Once $\widehat{\mathbf{X}}$ is known $\mathtt{H}$ may be computed.

Error in one image only. In the case of error in one image, one has a set of correspondences $\{\bar{\mathbf{x}}_i \leftrightarrow \mathbf{x}'_i\}$. The points $\bar{\mathbf{x}}_i$ are assumed perfect. The inhomogeneous coordinates of the $\mathbf{x}'_i$ constitute the measurement vector $\mathbf{X}$. Hence, in this case the measurement space has dimension $N = 2n$. The vector $\widehat{\mathbf{X}}$ consists of the inhomogeneous coordinates of the mapped perfect points $\{\mathtt{H}\bar{\mathbf{x}}_1, \mathtt{H}\bar{\mathbf{x}}_2, \ldots, \mathtt{H}\bar{\mathbf{x}}_n\}$. The set of measurement vectors satisfying the model is the set $\widehat{\mathbf{X}}$ as $\mathtt{H}$ varies over the set of all homography matrices. Once again this subspace is a variety. Its dimension is 8, since this is the total number of degrees of freedom of the homography matrix $\mathtt{H}$. As with the previous case, the codimension is $2n - 8$. One verifies that

$$\|\mathbf{X} - \widehat{\mathbf{X}}\|^2 = \sum_i d(\mathbf{x}'_i, \mathtt{H}\bar{\mathbf{x}}_i)^2.$$

Thus, finding the closest point on S to the measurement vector $\mathbf{X}$ is equivalent to minimizing the cost function (4.6).

4.3 Statistical cost functions and Maximum Likelihood estimation

In section 4.2, various cost functions were considered that were related to geometric distance between estimated and measured points in an image. The use of such cost functions is now justified and then generalized by a consideration of error statistics of the point measurements in an image.

In order to obtain a best (optimal) estimate of $\mathtt{H}$ it is necessary to have a model for the measurement error (the "noise"). We are assuming here that in the absence of measurement error the true points exactly satisfy a homography, i.e. $\bar{\mathbf{x}}'_i = \mathtt{H}\bar{\mathbf{x}}_i$. A common assumption is that image coordinate measurement errors obey a Gaussian (or normal) probability distribution. This assumption is surely not justified in general, and takes no account of the presence of outliers (grossly erroneous measurements) in the measured data. Methods for detecting and removing outliers will be discussed later in section 4.7. Once outliers have been removed, the assumption of a Gaussian error model, if still not strictly justified, becomes more tenable. Therefore, for the present, we assume that image measurement errors obey a zero-mean isotropic Gaussian distribution. This distribution is described in section A2.1(*p*565).

Specifically we assume that the noise is Gaussian on each image coordinate with zero mean and uniform standard deviation σ. This means that $x = \bar{x} + \Delta x$, with Δx obeying a Gaussian distribution with variance σ^2. If it is further assumed that the noise on each measurement is independent, then, if the true point is $\bar{\mathbf{x}}$, the probability density function (PDF) of each measured point $\mathbf{x}$ is

$$\Pr(\mathbf{x}) = \left(\frac{1}{2\pi\sigma^2}\right) e^{-d(\mathbf{x},\bar{\mathbf{x}})^2/(2\sigma^2)}. \tag{4.14}$$

Error in one image. First we consider the case where the errors are only in the second image. The probability of obtaining the set of correspondences $\{\bar{\mathbf{x}}_i \leftrightarrow \mathbf{x}'_i\}$ is simply the product of their individual PDFs, since the errors on each point are assumed independent. Then the PDF of the noise-perturbed data is

$$\Pr(\{\mathbf{x}'_i\}|\mathtt{H}) = \prod_i \left(\frac{1}{2\pi\sigma^2}\right) e^{-d(\mathbf{x}'_i, \mathtt{H}\bar{\mathbf{x}}_i)^2/(2\sigma^2)} \ . \tag{4.15}$$

The symbol $\Pr(\{\mathbf{x}'_i\}|\mathtt{H})$ is to be interpreted as meaning the probability of obtaining the measurements $\{\mathbf{x}'_i\}$ given that the true homography is $\mathtt{H}$. The *log-likelihood* of the set of correspondences is

$$\log \Pr(\{\mathbf{x}'_i\}|\mathtt{H}) = -\frac{1}{2\sigma^2}\sum_i d(\mathbf{x}'_i, \mathtt{H}\bar{\mathbf{x}}_i)^2 + \text{ constant.}$$

The *Maximum Likelihood estimate* (MLE) of the homography, $\hat{\mathtt{H}}$, maximizes this log-likelihood, i.e. minimizes

$$\sum_i d(\mathbf{x}'_i, \mathtt{H}\bar{\mathbf{x}}_i)^2.$$

Thus, we note that ML estimation is equivalent to minimizing the geometric error function (4.6).

Error in both images. Following a similar development to the above, if the true correspondences are $\{\bar{\mathbf{x}}_i \leftrightarrow \mathtt{H}\bar{\mathbf{x}}_i = \bar{\mathbf{x}}'_i\}$, then the PDF of the noise-perturbed data is

$$\Pr(\{\mathbf{x}_i, \mathbf{x}'_i\}|\mathtt{H}, \{\bar{\mathbf{x}}_i\}) = \prod_i \left(\frac{1}{2\pi\sigma^2}\right) e^{-\left(d(\mathbf{x}_i, \bar{\mathbf{x}}_i)^2 + d(\mathbf{x}'_i, \mathtt{H}\bar{\mathbf{x}}_i)^2\right)/(2\sigma^2)}.$$

The additional complication here is that we have to seek "corrected" image measurements that play the role of the true measurements ($\mathtt{H}\bar{\mathbf{x}}$ above). Thus the ML estimate of the projective transformation $\mathtt{H}$ *and* the correspondences $\{\mathbf{x}_i \leftrightarrow \mathbf{x}'_i\}$, is the homography $\hat{\mathtt{H}}$ and corrected correspondences $\{\hat{\mathbf{x}}_i \leftrightarrow \hat{\mathbf{x}}'_i\}$ that minimize

$$\sum_i d(\mathbf{x}_i, \hat{\mathbf{x}}_i)^2 + d(\mathbf{x}'_i, \hat{\mathbf{x}}'_i)^2$$

with $\hat{\mathbf{x}}'_i = \hat{\mathtt{H}}\hat{\mathbf{x}}_i$. Note that in this case, the ML estimate is identical with minimizing the reprojection error function (4.8).

Mahalanobis distance. In the general Gaussian case, one may assume a vector of measurements $\mathbf{X}$ satisfying a Gaussian distribution function with covariance matrix Σ. The cases above are equivalent to a covariance matrix which is a multiple of the identity.

Maximizing the log-likelihood is then equivalent to minimizing the Mahalanobis distance (see section A2.1(*p*565))

$$\|\mathbf{X} - \bar{\mathbf{X}}\|_\Sigma^2 = (\mathbf{X} - \bar{\mathbf{X}})^\mathsf{T}\Sigma^{-1}(\mathbf{X} - \bar{\mathbf{X}}).$$

In the case where there is error in each image, but assuming that errors in one image are independent of the error in the other image, the appropriate cost function is

$$\|\mathbf{X} - \bar{\mathbf{X}}\|_\Sigma^2 + \|\mathbf{X}' - \bar{\mathbf{X}}'\|_{\Sigma'}^2$$

where Σ and Σ' are the covariance matrices of the measurements in the two images.

Finally, if we assume that the errors for all the points $\mathbf{x}_i$ and $\mathbf{x}'_i$ are independent, with individual covariance matrices Σ_i and Σ'_i respectively, then the above expression expands to

$$\sum \|\mathbf{x}_i - \bar{\mathbf{x}}_i\|^2_{\Sigma_i} + \sum \|\mathbf{x}'_i - \bar{\mathbf{x}}'_i\|^2_{\Sigma'_i} \tag{4.16}$$

This equation allows the incorporation of the type of anisotropic covariance matrices that arise for point locations computed as the intersection of two non-perpendicular lines. In the case where the points are known exactly in one of the two images, errors being confined to the other image, one of the two summation terms in (4.16) disappears.

4.4 Transformation invariance and normalization

We now start to discuss the properties and performance of the DLT algorithm of section 4.1 and how it compares with algorithms minimizing geometric error. The first topic is the invariance of the algorithm to different choices of coordinates in the image. It is clear that it would generally be undesirable for the result of an algorithm to be dependent on such arbitrary choices as the origin and scale, or even orientation, of the coordinate system in an image.

4.4.1 Invariance to image coordinate transformations

Image coordinates are sometimes given with the origin at the top-left of the image, and sometimes with the origin at the centre. The question immediately occurs whether this makes a difference to the results of computing the transformation. Similarly, if the units used to express image coordinates are changed by multiplication by some factor, then is it possible that the result of the algorithm changes also? More generally, to what extent is the result of an algorithm that minimizes a cost function to estimate a homography dependent on the choice of coordinates in the image? Suppose, for instance, that the image coordinates are changed by some similarity, affine or even projective transformation before running the algorithm. Will this materially change the result?

Formally, suppose that coordinates $\mathbf{x}$ in one image are replaced by $\tilde{\mathbf{x}} = \mathtt{T}\mathbf{x}$, and coordinates $\mathbf{x}'$ in the other image are replaced by $\tilde{\mathbf{x}}' = \mathtt{T}'\mathbf{x}'$, where $\mathtt{T}$ and $\mathtt{T}'$ are 3×3 homographies. Substituting in the equation $\mathbf{x}' = \mathtt{H}\mathbf{x}$, we derive the equation $\tilde{\mathbf{x}}' = \mathtt{T}'\mathtt{H}\mathtt{T}^{-1}\tilde{\mathbf{x}}$. This relation implies that $\tilde{\mathtt{H}} = \mathtt{T}'\mathtt{H}\mathtt{T}^{-1}$ is the transformation matrix for the point correspondences $\tilde{\mathbf{x}} \leftrightarrow \tilde{\mathbf{x}}'$. An alternative method of finding the transformation taking $\mathbf{x}_i$ to $\mathbf{x}'_i$ is therefore suggested, as follows.

(i) Transform the image coordinates according to transformations $\tilde{\mathbf{x}}_i = \mathtt{T}\mathbf{x}_i$ and $\tilde{\mathbf{x}}'_i = \mathtt{T}'\mathbf{x}'_i$.
(ii) Find the transformation $\tilde{\mathtt{H}}$ from the correspondences $\tilde{\mathbf{x}}_i \leftrightarrow \tilde{\mathbf{x}}'_i$.
(iii) Set $\mathtt{H} = \mathtt{T}'^{-1}\tilde{\mathtt{H}}\mathtt{T}$.

The transformation matrix $\mathtt{H}$ found in this way applies to the original untransformed point correspondences $\mathbf{x}_i \leftrightarrow \mathbf{x}'_i$. What choice should be made for the transformations $\mathtt{T}$ and $\mathtt{T}'$ will be left unspecified for now. The question to be decided now is whether the outcome of this algorithm is independent of the transformations $\mathtt{T}$ and $\mathtt{T}'$ being applied. Ideally it ought to be, at least when $\mathtt{T}$ and $\mathtt{T}'$ are similarity transformations, since the choice of a different scale, orientation or coordinate origin in the images should not materially affect the outcome of the algorithm.

In the subsequent sections it will be shown that an algorithm that minimizes geometric error is invariant to similarity transformations. On the other hand, for the DLT algorithm as described in section 4.1, the result unfortunately is not invariant to similarity transformations. The solution is to apply a normalizing transformation to the data before applying the DLT algorithm. This normalizing transformation will nullify the effect of the arbitrary selection of origin and scale in the coordinate frame of the image, and will mean that the combined algorithm is invariant to a similarity transformation of the image. Appropriate normalizing transformations will be discussed later.

4.4.2 Non-invariance of the DLT algorithm

Consider a set of correspondences $\mathbf{x}_i \leftrightarrow \mathbf{x}'_i$ and a matrix $\mathtt{H}$ that is the result of the DLT algorithm applied to this set of corresponding points. Consider further a related set of correspondences $\tilde{\mathbf{x}}_i \leftrightarrow \tilde{\mathbf{x}}'_i$ where $\tilde{\mathbf{x}}_i = \mathtt{T}\mathbf{x}_i$ and $\tilde{\mathbf{x}}'_i = \mathtt{T}'\mathbf{x}'_i$, and let $\tilde{\mathtt{H}}$ be defined by $\tilde{\mathtt{H}} = \mathtt{T}'\mathtt{H}\mathtt{T}^{-1}$. Following section 4.4.1, the question to be decided here is the following:

- *Does the DLT algorithm applied to the correspondence set $\tilde{\mathbf{x}}_i \leftrightarrow \tilde{\mathbf{x}}'_i$ yield the transformation $\tilde{\mathtt{H}}$?*

We will use the following notation: Matrix $\mathtt{A}_i$ is the DLT equation matrix (4.3–*p*89) derived from a point correspondence $\mathbf{x}_i \leftrightarrow \mathbf{x}'_i$, and $\mathtt{A}$ is the $2n \times 9$ matrix formed by stacking the $\mathtt{A}_i$. Matrix $\tilde{\mathtt{A}}_i$ is similarly defined in terms of the correspondences $\tilde{\mathbf{x}}_i \leftrightarrow \tilde{\mathbf{x}}'_i$, where $\tilde{\mathbf{x}}_i = \mathtt{T}\mathbf{x}_i$ and $\tilde{\mathbf{x}}'_i = \mathtt{T}'\mathbf{x}'_i$ for some projective transformations $\mathtt{T}$ and $\mathtt{T}'$.

Result 4.3. *Let $\mathtt{T}'$ be a similarity transformation with scale factor s, and let $\mathtt{T}$ be an arbitrary projective transformation. Further, suppose $\mathtt{H}$ is any 2D homography and let $\tilde{\mathtt{H}}$ be defined by $\tilde{\mathtt{H}} = \mathtt{T}'\mathtt{H}\mathtt{T}^{-1}$. Then $\|\tilde{\mathtt{A}}\tilde{\mathbf{h}}\| = s\|\mathtt{A}\mathbf{h}\|$ where $\mathbf{h}$ and $\tilde{\mathbf{h}}$ are the vectors of entries of $\mathtt{H}$ and $\tilde{\mathtt{H}}$.*

Proof. Define the vector $\boldsymbol{\epsilon}_i = \mathbf{x}'_i \times \mathtt{H}\mathbf{x}_i$. Note that $\mathtt{A}_i\mathbf{h}$ is the vector consisting of the first two entries of $\boldsymbol{\epsilon}_i$. Let $\tilde{\boldsymbol{\epsilon}}_i$ be similarly defined in terms of the transformed quantities as $\tilde{\boldsymbol{\epsilon}}_i = \tilde{\mathbf{x}}'_i \times \tilde{\mathtt{H}}\tilde{\mathbf{x}}_i$. One computes:

$$\begin{aligned}\tilde{\boldsymbol{\epsilon}}_i &= \tilde{\mathbf{x}}'_i \times \tilde{\mathtt{H}}\tilde{\mathbf{x}}_i = \mathtt{T}'\mathbf{x}'_i \times (\mathtt{T}'\mathtt{H}\mathtt{T}^{-1})\mathtt{T}\mathbf{x}_i \\ &= \mathtt{T}'\mathbf{x}'_i \times \mathtt{T}'\mathtt{H}\mathbf{x}_i = \mathtt{T}'^{*}(\mathbf{x}'_i \times \mathtt{H}\mathbf{x}_i) \\ &= \mathtt{T}'^{*}\boldsymbol{\epsilon}_i\end{aligned}$$

where $\mathtt{T}'^{*}$ represents the cofactor matrix of $\mathtt{T}'$ and the second-last equality follows from lemma A4.2(*p*581). For a general transformation $\mathtt{T}$, the error vectors $\mathtt{A}_i\mathbf{h}$ and $\tilde{\mathtt{A}}_i\tilde{\mathbf{h}}$ (namely the first two components of $\boldsymbol{\epsilon}_i$ and $\tilde{\boldsymbol{\epsilon}}_i$) are not simply related. However, in the special case where $\mathtt{T}'$ is a similarity transformation, one may write $\mathtt{T}' = \begin{bmatrix} s\mathtt{R} & \mathbf{t} \\ \mathbf{0}^{\mathsf{T}} & 1 \end{bmatrix}$ where $\mathtt{R}$ is a rotation matrix, $\mathbf{t}$ is a translation and s is a scaling factor. In this case, we see that $\mathtt{T}'^* = s\begin{bmatrix} \mathtt{R} & \mathbf{0} \\ -\mathbf{t}^\mathsf{T}\mathtt{R} & s \end{bmatrix}$. Applying $\mathtt{T}'^*$ just to the first two components of $\boldsymbol{\epsilon}_i$, one sees that

$$\tilde{\mathtt{A}}_i\tilde{\mathbf{h}} = (\tilde{\epsilon}_{i1}, \tilde{\epsilon}_{i2})^\mathsf{T} = s\mathtt{R}(\epsilon_{i1}, \epsilon_{i2})^\mathsf{T} = s\mathtt{R}\mathtt{A}_i\mathbf{h}.$$

Since rotation does not affect vector norms, one sees that $\|\tilde{\mathtt{A}}\tilde{\mathbf{h}}\| = s\|\mathtt{A}\mathbf{h}\|$, as required. This result may be expressed in terms of algebraic error as

$$d_{\text{alg}}(\tilde{\mathbf{x}}'_i, \tilde{\mathtt{H}}\tilde{\mathbf{x}}_i) = s d_{\text{alg}}(\mathbf{x}'_i, \mathtt{H}\mathbf{x}_i).$$

□

Thus, there is a one-to-one correspondence between $\mathtt{H}$ and $\tilde{\mathtt{H}}$ giving rise to the same error, except for constant scale. It may appear therefore that the matrices $\mathtt{H}$ and $\tilde{\mathtt{H}}$ minimizing the algebraic error will be related by the formula $\tilde{\mathtt{H}} = \mathtt{T}'\mathtt{H}\mathtt{T}^{-1}$, and hence one may retrieve $\mathtt{H}$ as the product $\mathtt{T}'^{-1}\tilde{\mathtt{H}}\mathtt{T}$. This conclusion is **false** however. For, although $\mathtt{H}$ and $\tilde{\mathtt{H}}$ so defined give rise to the same error ϵ, the condition $\|\mathtt{H}\| = 1$, imposed as a constraint on the solution, is not equivalent to the condition $\|\tilde{\mathtt{H}}\| = 1$. Specifically, $\|\mathtt{H}\|$ and $\|\tilde{\mathtt{H}}\|$ are not related in any simple manner. Thus, there is no one-to-one correspondence between $\mathtt{H}$ and $\tilde{\mathtt{H}}$ giving rise to the same error ϵ, subject to the constraint $\|\mathtt{H}\| = \|\tilde{\mathtt{H}}\| = 1$. Specifically,

$$\begin{aligned} & \text{minimize} \sum_i d_{\text{alg}}(\mathbf{x}'_i, \mathtt{H}\mathbf{x}_i)^2 \text{ subject to } \|\mathtt{H}\| = 1 \\ \Leftrightarrow\ & \text{minimize} \sum_i d_{\text{alg}}(\tilde{\mathbf{x}}'_i, \tilde{\mathtt{H}}\tilde{\mathbf{x}}_i)^2 \text{ subject to } \|\mathtt{H}\| = 1 \\ \not\Leftrightarrow\ & \text{minimize} \sum_i d_{\text{alg}}(\tilde{\mathbf{x}}'_i, \tilde{\mathtt{H}}\tilde{\mathbf{x}}_i)^2 \text{ subject to } \|\tilde{\mathtt{H}}\| = 1. \end{aligned}$$

Thus, the method of transformation leads to a different solution for the computed transformation matrix. This is a rather undesirable feature of the DLT algorithm as it stands, that the result is changed by a change of coordinates, or even simply a change of the origin of coordinates. If the constraint under which the norm $\|\mathtt{A}\mathbf{h}\|$ is minimized is invariant under the transformation, however, then one sees that the computed matrices $\mathtt{H}$ and $\tilde{\mathtt{H}}$ are related in the right way. Examples of minimization conditions for which $\mathtt{H}$ is transformation-invariant are discussed in the exercises at the end of this chapter.

4.4.3 Invariance of geometric error

It will be shown now that minimizing geometric error to find $\mathtt{H}$ is invariant under similarity (scaled Euclidean) transformations. As before, consider a point correspondence $\mathbf{x} \leftrightarrow \mathbf{x}'$ and a transformation matrix $\mathtt{H}$. Also, define a related set of correspondences $\tilde{\mathbf{x}} \leftrightarrow \tilde{\mathbf{x}}'$ where $\tilde{\mathbf{x}} = \mathtt{T}\mathbf{x}$ and $\tilde{\mathbf{x}}' = \mathtt{T}'\mathbf{x}'$, and let $\tilde{\mathtt{H}}$ be defined by $\tilde{\mathtt{H}} = \mathtt{T}'\mathtt{H}\mathtt{T}^{-1}$. Suppose that $\mathtt{T}$ and $\mathtt{T}'$ represent Euclidean transformations of $\mathbb{P}^2$. One verifies that

$$d(\tilde{\mathbf{x}}', \tilde{\mathtt{H}}\tilde{\mathbf{x}}) = d(\mathtt{T}'\mathbf{x}', \mathtt{T}'\mathtt{H}\mathtt{T}^{-1}\mathtt{T}\mathbf{x}) = d(\mathtt{T}'\mathbf{x}', \mathtt{T}'\mathtt{H}\mathbf{x}) = d(\mathbf{x}', \mathtt{H}\mathbf{x})$$

where the last equality holds because Euclidean distance is unchanged under a Euclidean transformation such as $\mathtt{T}'$. This shows that if $\mathtt{H}$ minimizes the geometric error for a set of correspondences, then $\widetilde{\mathrm{H}}$ minimizes the geometric error for the transformed set of correspondences, and so minimizing geometric error is invariant under Euclidean transformations.

For similarity transformations, geometric error is multiplied by the scale factor of the transformation, hence the minimizing transformations correspond in the same way as in the Euclidean transformation case. Minimizing geometric error is invariant to similarity transformations.

4.4.4 Normalizing transformations

As was shown in section 4.4.2, the result of the DLT algorithm for computing 2D homographies depends on the coordinate frame in which points are expressed. In fact the result is not invariant to similarity transformations of the image. This suggests the question whether some coordinate systems are in some way better than others for computing a 2D homography. The answer to this is an emphatic *yes*. In this section a method of normalization of the data is described, consisting of translation and scaling of image coordinates. This normalization should be carried out before applying the DLT algorithm. Subsequently an appropriate correction to the result expresses the computed H with respect to the original coordinate system.

Apart from improved accuracy of results, data normalization provides a second desirable benefit, namely that an algorithm that incorporates an initial data normalization step will be invariant with respect to arbitrary choices of the scale and coordinate origin. This is because the normalization step undoes the effect of coordinate changes, by effectively choosing a canonical coordinate frame for the measurement data. Thus, algebraic minimization is carried out in a fixed canonical frame, and the DLT algorithm is in practice invariant to similarity transformations.

Isotropic scaling. As a first step of normalization, the coordinates in each image are translated (by a different translation for each image) so as to bring the centroid of the set of all points to the origin. The coordinates are also scaled so that on the average a point $\mathbf{x}$ is of the form $\mathbf{x} = (x, y, w)^{\mathsf{T}}$, with each of x, y and w having the same average magnitude. Rather than choose different scale factors for each coordinate direction, an isotropic scaling factor is chosen so that the x and y-coordinates of a point are scaled equally. To this end, we choose to scale the coordinates so that the average distance of a point $\mathbf{x}$ from the origin is equal to $\sqrt{2}$. This means that the "average" point is equal to $(1, 1, 1)^{\mathsf{T}}$. In summary the transformation is as follows:

(i) The points are translated so that their centroid is at the origin.
(ii) The points are then scaled so that the average distance from the origin is equal to $\sqrt{2}$.
(iii) This transformation is applied to each of the two images independently.

Why is normalization essential? The recommended version of the DLT algorithm with data normalization is given in algorithm 4.2. We will now motivate why this version of the algorithm, incorporating data normalization, should be used in preference to the basic DLT of algorithm 4.1(*p*91). Note that normalization is also called *pre-conditioning* in the numerical literature.

The DLT method of algorithm 4.1 uses the SVD of $\mathtt{A} = \mathtt{UDV}^\mathsf{T}$ to obtain a solution to the overdetermined set of equations $\mathtt{A}\mathbf{h} = \mathbf{0}$. These equations do not have an exact solution (since the $2n \times 9$ matrix $\mathtt{A}$ will not have rank 8 for noisy data), but the vector $\mathbf{h}$, given by the last column of $\mathtt{V}$, provides a solution which minimizes $\|\mathtt{A}\mathbf{h}\|$ (subject to $\|\mathbf{h}\| = 1$). This is equivalent to finding the rank 8 matrix $\hat{\mathtt{A}}$ which is closest to $\mathtt{A}$ in Frobenius norm and obtaining $\mathbf{h}$ as the exact solution of $\hat{\mathtt{A}}\mathbf{h} = \mathbf{0}$. The matrix $\hat{\mathtt{A}}$ is given by $\hat{\mathtt{A}} = \mathtt{U}\hat{\mathtt{D}}\mathtt{V}^\mathsf{T}$ where $\hat{\mathtt{D}}$ is $\mathtt{D}$ with the smallest singular value set to zero. The matrix $\hat{\mathtt{A}}$ has rank 8 and minimizes the difference to $\mathtt{A}$ in Frobenius norm because

$$\|\mathtt{A} - \hat{\mathtt{A}}\|_\mathrm{F} = \|\mathtt{UDV}^\mathsf{T} - \mathtt{U}\hat{\mathtt{D}}\mathtt{V}^\mathsf{T}\|_\mathrm{F} = \|\mathtt{D} - \hat{\mathtt{D}}\|_\mathrm{F}.$$

where $\|.\|_\mathrm{F}$ is the Frobenius norm, i.e. the square root of the sum of squares of all entries.

Without normalization typical image points $\mathbf{x}_i, \mathbf{x}'_i$ are of the order $(x, y, w)^\mathsf{T} = (100, 100, 1)^\mathsf{T}$, i.e., x, y are much larger than w. In $\mathtt{A}$ the entries xx', xy', yx', yy' will be of order 10^4, entries xw', yw' etc. of order 10^2, and entries ww' will be unity. Replacing $\mathtt{A}$ by $\hat{\mathtt{A}}$ means that some entries are increased and others decreased such that the square sum of differences of these changes is minimal (and the resulting matrix has rank 8). However, and this is the key point, increasing the term ww' by 100 means a huge change in the image points, whereas increasing the term xx' by 100 means only a slight change. This is the reason why all entries in $\mathtt{A}$ must have similar magnitude and why normalization is essential.

The effect of normalization is related to the condition number of the set of DLT equations, or more precisely the ratio d_1/d_{n-1} of the first to the second-last singular value of the equation matrix $\mathtt{A}$. This point is investigated in more detail in [Hartley-97c]. For the present it is sufficient to say that for exact data and infinite precision arithmetic the results will be independent of the normalizing transformation. However, in the presence of noise the solution will diverge from the correct result. The effect of a large condition number is to amplify this divergence. This is true even for infinite-precision arithmetic – this is not a round-off error effect.

The effect that this data normalization has on the results of the DLT algorithm is shown graphically in figure 4.4. The conclusion to be drawn here is that data normalization gives dramatically better results. The examples shown in the figure are chosen to make the effect easily visible. However, a marked advantage remains even in cases of computation from larger numbers of point correspondences, with points more widely distributed. To emphasize this point we remark:

- *Data normalization is an* essential *step in the DLT algorithm. It must* not *be considered optional.*

Data normalization becomes even more important for less well conditioned problems, such as the DLT computation of the fundamental matrix or the trifocal tensor, which will be considered in later chapters.

Objective

Given $n \geq 4$ 2D to 2D point correspondences $\{\mathbf{x}_i \leftrightarrow \mathbf{x}'_i\}$, determine the 2D homography matrix $\mathtt{H}$ such that $\mathbf{x}'_i = \mathtt{H}\mathbf{x}_i$.

Algorithm

(i) **Normalization of $\mathbf{x}$:** Compute a similarity transformation $\mathtt{T}$, consisting of a translation and scaling, that takes points $\mathbf{x}_i$ to a new set of points $\tilde{\mathbf{x}}_i$ such that the centroid of the points $\tilde{\mathbf{x}}_i$ is the coordinate origin $(0,0)^\mathsf{T}$, and their average distance from the origin is $\sqrt{2}$.

(ii) **Normalization of $\mathbf{x}'$:** Compute a similar transformation $\mathtt{T}'$ for the points in the second image, transforming points $\mathbf{x}'_i$ to $\tilde{\mathbf{x}}'_i$.

(iii) **DLT:** Apply algorithm 4.1(*p*91) to the correspondences $\tilde{\mathbf{x}}_i \leftrightarrow \tilde{\mathbf{x}}'_i$ to obtain a homography $\tilde{\mathtt{H}}$.

(iv) **Denormalization:** Set $\mathtt{H} = \mathtt{T}'^{-1}\tilde{\mathtt{H}}\mathtt{T}$.

Algorithm 4.2. *The normalized DLT for 2D homographies.*

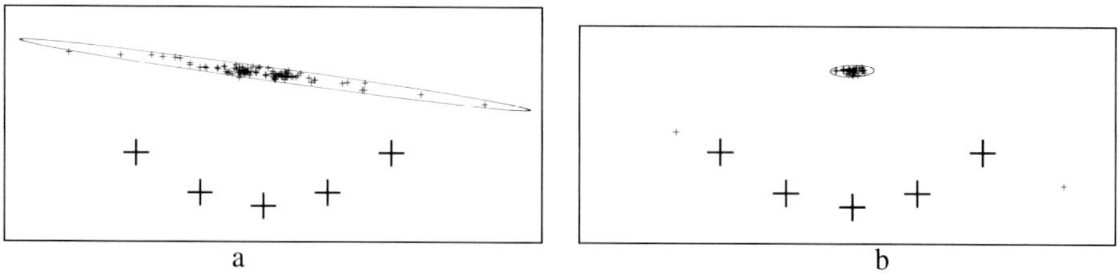

Fig. 4.4. *Results of Monte Carlo simulation (see section 5.3(p149) of computation of 2D homographies). A set of 5 points (denoted by large crosses) was used to compute a 2D homography. Each of the 5 points is mapped (in the noise-free case) to the point with the same coordinates, so that homography* $\mathtt{H}$ *is the identity mapping. Now, 100 trials were made with each point being subject to 0.1 pixel Gaussian noise in one image. (For reference, the large crosses are 4 pixels across.) The mapping* $\mathtt{H}$ *computed using the DLT algorithm was then applied to transfer a further point into the second image. The 100 projections of this point are shown with small crosses and the 95% ellipse computed from their scatter matrix is also shown. (a) are the results without data normalization, and (b) the results with normalization. The left- and rightmost reference points have (unnormalized) coordinates* $(130, 108)$ *and* $(170, 108)$.

Non-isotropic scaling. Other methods of scaling are also possible. In non-isotropic scaling, the centroid of the points is translated to the origin as before. After this translation the points form a cloud about the origin. Scaling is then carried out so that the two principal moments of the set of points are both equal to unity. Thus, the set of points will form an approximately symmetric circular cloud of points of radius 1 about the origin. Experimental results given in [Hartley-97c] suggest that the extra effort required for non-isotropic scaling does not lead to significantly better results than isotropic scaling.

A further variant on scaling was discussed in [Muehlich-98], based on a statistical analysis of the estimator, its bias and variance. In that paper it was observed that some columns of $\mathtt{A}$ are not affected by noise. This applies to the third and sixth columns in (4.3–*p*89), corresponding to the entry $w_i w'_i = 1$. Such error-free entries in $\mathtt{A}$ should not be varied in finding $\hat{\mathtt{A}}$, the closest rank-deficient approximation to $\mathtt{A}$. A method known as Total Least Squares - Fixed Columns is used to find the best solution. For estimation of the fundamental matrix (see chapter 11), [Muehlich-98] reports slightly improved results compared with non-isotropic scaling.

Scaling with points near infinity. Consider the case of estimation of a homography between an infinite plane and an image. If the viewing direction is sufficiently oblique, then very distant points in the plane may be visible in the image – even points at infinity (vanishing points) if the horizon is visible. In this case it makes no sense to normalize the coordinates of points in the infinite plane by setting the centroid at the origin, since the centroid may have very large coordinates, or be undefined. An approach to normalization in this case is considered in exercise (iii) on page 128.

4.5 Iterative minimization methods

This section describes methods for minimizing the various geometric cost functions developed in section 4.2 and section 4.3. Minimizing such cost functions requires the use of iterative techniques. This is unfortunate, because iterative techniques tend to have certain disadvantages compared to linear algorithms such as the normalized DLT algorithm 4.2:

(i) They are slower.
(ii) They generally need an initial estimate at which to start the iteration.
(iii) They risk not converging, or converging to a local minimum instead of the global minimum.
(iv) Selection of a stopping criterion for iteration may be tricky.

Consequently, iterative techniques generally require more careful implementation.

The technique of iterative minimization generally consists of five steps:

(i) **Cost function.** A cost function is chosen as the basis for minimization. Different possible cost functions were discussed in section 4.2.
(ii) **Parametrization.** The transformation (or other entity) to be computed is expressed in terms of a finite number of parameters. It is not in general necessary that this be a minimum set of parameters, and there are in fact often advantages to over-parametrization. (See the discussion below.)
(iii) **Function specification.** A function must be specified that expresses the cost in terms of the set of parameters.
(iv) **Initialization.** A suitable initial parameter estimate is computed. This will generally be done using a linear algorithm such as the DLT algorithm.
(v) **Iteration.** Starting from the initial solution, the parameters are iteratively refined with the goal of minimizing the cost function.

A word about parametrization

For a given cost function, there are often several choices of parametrization. The general strategy that guides parametrization is to select a set of parameters that cover the complete space over which one is minimizing, while at the same time allowing one to compute the cost function in a convenient manner. For example, H may be parametrized by 9 parameters – that is, it is over-parametrized, since there are really only 8 degrees of freedom, overall scale not being significant. A *minimal* parametrization (i.e. the same number of parameters as degrees of freedom) would involve only 8 parameters.

In general no bad effects are likely to occur if a minimization problem of this type is over-parametrized, as long as for all choices of parameters the corresponding object is of the desired type. In particular for homogeneous objects, such as the 3×3 projection matrix encountered here, it is usually not necessary or advisable to attempt to use a minimal parametrization by removing the scale-factor ambiguity.

The reasoning is the following: it is not *necessary* to use minimal parametrization because a well-performing non-linear minimization algorithm will "notice" that it is not necessary to move in redundant directions, such as the matrix scaling direction. The algorithm described in Gill and Murray [Gill-78], which is a modification of the Gauss–Newton method, has an effective strategy for discarding redundant combinations of the parameters. Similarly, the Levenberg-Marquardt algorithm (see section A6.2(*p*600)) handles redundant parametrizations easily. It is not *advisable* because it is found empirically that the cost function surface is more complicated when minimal parametrizations are used. There is then a greater possibility of becoming stuck in a local minimum.

One other issue that arises in choosing a parametrization is that of restricting the transformation to a particular class. For example, suppose H is known to be a homology, then as described in section A7.2(*p*629) it may be parametrized as

$$\mathtt{H} = \mathtt{I} + (\mu - 1)\frac{\mathbf{v}\mathbf{a}^{\mathsf{T}}}{\mathbf{v}^{\mathsf{T}}\mathbf{a}}$$

where μ is a scalar, and $\mathbf{v}$ and $\mathbf{a}$ 3-vectors. A homology has 5 degrees of freedom which correspond here to the scalar μ and the directions of $\mathbf{v}$ and $\mathbf{a}$. If H is parametrized by its 9 matrix entries, then the estimated H is unlikely to exactly be a homology. However, if H is parametrized by μ, $\mathbf{v}$ and $\mathbf{a}$ (a total of 7 parameters) then the estimated H is guaranteed to be a homology. This parametrization is *consistent* with a homology (it is also an over-parametrization). We will return to the issues of consistent, local, minimal and over-parametrization in later chapters. The issues are also discussed further in appendix A6.9(*p*623).

Function specification

It has been seen in section 4.2.7 that a general class of estimation problems is concerned with a measurement space $\mathbb{R}^N$ containing a model surface S. Given a measurement $\mathbf{X} \in \mathbb{R}^N$ the estimation task is to find the point $\widehat{\mathbf{X}}$ lying on S closest to $\mathbf{X}$. In the case where a non-isotropic Gaussian error distribution is imposed on $\mathbb{R}^N$, the word *closest* is to be interpreted in terms of Mahalanobis distance. Iterative minimization methods will now be described in terms of this estimation model. In iterative estimation through parameter fitting, the model surface S is locally parametrized, and the parameters are allowed to vary to minimize the distance to the measured point. More specifically,

(i) One has a *measurement vector* $\mathbf{X} \in \mathbb{R}^N$ with covariance matrix Σ.

(ii) A set of parameters are represented as a vector $\mathbf{P} \in \mathbb{R}^M$.

(iii) A mapping $f : \mathbb{R}^M \rightarrow \mathbb{R}^N$ is defined. The range of this mapping is (at least locally) the model surface S in $\mathbb{R}^N$ representing the set of allowable measurements.

(iv) The cost function to be minimized is the squared Mahalanobis distance

$$\|\mathbf{X} - f(\mathbf{P})\|_\Sigma^2 = (\mathbf{X} - f(\mathbf{P}))^\mathsf{T}\Sigma^{-1}(\mathbf{X} - f(\mathbf{P})).$$

In effect, we are attempting to find a set of parameters $\mathbf{P}$ such that $f(\mathbf{P}) = \mathbf{X}$, or failing that, to bring $f(\mathbf{P})$ as close to $\mathbf{X}$ as possible, with respect to Mahalanobis distance. The Levenberg–Marquardt algorithm is a general tool for iterative minimization, when the cost function to be minimized is of this type. We will now show how the various different types of cost functions described in this chapter fit into this format.

Error in one image. Here one fixes the coordinates of points $\mathbf{x}_i$ in the first image, and varies $\mathtt{H}$ so as to minimize cost function (4.6–*p*94), namely

$$\sum_i d(\mathbf{x}'_i, \mathtt{H}\bar{\mathbf{x}}_i)^2.$$

The measurement vector $\mathbf{X}$ is made up of the $2n$ inhomogeneous coordinates of the points $\mathbf{x}'_i$. One may choose as parameters the vector $\mathbf{h}$ of entries of the homography matrix $\mathtt{H}$. The function f is defined by

$$f : \mathbf{h} \mapsto (\mathtt{H}\mathbf{x}_1, \mathtt{H}\mathbf{x}_2, \ldots, \mathtt{H}\mathbf{x}_n)$$

where it is understood that here, and in the functions below, $\mathtt{H}\mathbf{x}_i$ indicates the inhomogeneous coordinates. One verifies that $\|\mathbf{X} - f(\mathbf{h})\|^2$ is equal to (4.6–*p*94).

Symmetric transfer error. In the case of the symmetric cost function (4.7–*p*95)

$$\sum_i d(\mathbf{x}_i, \mathtt{H}^{-1}\mathbf{x}'_i)^2 + d(\mathbf{x}'_i, \mathtt{H}\mathbf{x}_i)^2$$

one chooses as measurement vector $\mathbf{X}$ the $4n$-vector made up of the inhomogeneous coordinates of the points $\mathbf{x}_i$ followed by the inhomogeneous coordinates of the points $\mathbf{x}'_i$. The parameter vector as before is the vector $\mathbf{h}$ of entries of $\mathtt{H}$, and the function f is defined by

$$f : \mathbf{h} \mapsto (\mathtt{H}^{-1}\mathbf{x}'_1, \ldots, \mathtt{H}^{-1}\mathbf{x}'_n, \mathtt{H}\mathbf{x}_1, \ldots, \mathtt{H}\mathbf{x}_n).$$

As before, we find that $\|\mathbf{X} - f(\mathbf{h})\|^2$ is equal to (4.7–*p*95).

Reprojection error. Minimizing the cost function (4.8–*p*95) is more complex. The difficulty is that it requires a simultaneous minimization over all choices of points $\hat{\mathbf{x}}_i$ as well as the entries of the transformation matrix $\mathtt{H}$. If there are many point correspondences, then this becomes a very large minimization problem. Thus, the problem may be parametrized by the coordinates of the points $\hat{\mathbf{x}}_i$ and the entries of the matrix $\hat{\mathtt{H}}$ – a total of $2n + 9$ parameters. The coordinates of $\hat{\mathbf{x}}'_i$ are not required, since they are related to the other parameters by $\hat{\mathbf{x}}'_i = \hat{\mathtt{H}}\hat{\mathbf{x}}_i$. The parameter vector is therefore

$\mathbf{P} = (\mathbf{h}, \hat{\mathbf{x}}_1, \ldots, \hat{\mathbf{x}}_n)$. The measurement vector contains the inhomogeneous coordinates of all the points $\mathbf{x}_i$ and $\mathbf{x}'_i$. The function f is defined by

$$f : (\mathbf{h}, \hat{\mathbf{x}}_1, \ldots, \hat{\mathbf{x}}_n) \mapsto (\hat{\mathbf{x}}_1, \hat{\mathbf{x}}'_1, \ldots, \hat{\mathbf{x}}_n, \hat{\mathbf{x}}'_n)$$

where $\hat{\mathbf{x}}'_i = \mathtt{H}\hat{\mathbf{x}}_i$. One verifies that $\|\mathbf{X} - f(\mathbf{P})\|^2$, with $\mathbf{X}$ a $4n$-vector, is equal to the cost function (4.8–*p*95). This cost function must be minimized over all $2n + 9$ parameters.

Sampson approximation. In contrast with $2n + 9$ parameters of reprojection error, minimizing the error in one image (4.6–*p*94) or symmetric transfer error (4.7–*p*95) requires a minimization over the 9 entries of the matrix $\mathtt{H}$ only – in general a more tractable problem. The Sampson approximation to reprojection error enables reprojection error also to be minimized with only 9 parameters.

This is an important consideration, since the iterative solution of an m-parameter non-linear minimization problem using a method such as Levenberg–Marquardt involves the solution of an $m \times m$ set of linear equations at each iteration step. This is a problem with complexity $O(m^3)$. Hence, it is appropriate to keep the size of m low.

The Sampson error avoids minimizing over the $2n + 9$ parameters of reprojection error because effectively it determines the $2n$ variables $\{\hat{\mathbf{x}}_i\}$ for each particular choice of $\mathbf{h}$. Consequently the minimization then only requires the 9 parameters of $\mathbf{h}$. In practice this approximation gives excellent results provided the errors are small compared to the measurements.

Initialization

An initial estimate for the parametrization may be found by employing a linear technique. For example, the normalized DLT algorithm 4.2 directly provides $\mathtt{H}$ and thence the 9-vector $\mathbf{h}$ used to parametrize the iterative minimization. In general if there are $n \geq 4$ correspondences, then all will be used in the linear solution. However, as will be seen in section 4.7 on robust estimation, when the correspondences contain outliers it may be advisable to use a carefully selected minimal set of correspondences (i.e. four correspondences). Linear techniques or minimal solutions are the two initialization techniques recommended in this book.

An alternative method that is sometimes used (for instance see [Horn-90, Horn-91]) is to carry out a sufficiently dense sampling of parameter space, iterating from each sampled starting point and retaining the best result. This is only possible if the dimension of the parameter space is sufficiently small. Sampling of parameter space may be done either randomly, or else according to some pattern. Another initialization method is simply to do without any effective initialization at all, starting the iteration at a given fixed point in parameter space. This method is not often viable. Iteration is very likely to fall into a false minimum or not converge. Even in the best case, the number of iteration steps required will increase the further one starts from the final solution. For this reason using a good initialization method is the best plan.

Objective

Given $n > 4$ image point correspondences $\{\mathbf{x}_i \leftrightarrow \mathbf{x}'_i\}$, determine the Maximum Likelihood estimate $\hat{\mathtt{H}}$ of the homography mapping between the images.

The MLE involves also solving for a set of subsidiary points $\{\hat{\mathbf{x}}_i\}$, which minimize

$$\sum_i d(\mathbf{x}_i, \hat{\mathbf{x}}_i)^2 + d(\mathbf{x}'_i, \hat{\mathbf{x}}'_i)^2$$

where $\hat{\mathbf{x}}'_i = \hat{\mathtt{H}}\hat{\mathbf{x}}_i$.

Algorithm

(i) **Initialization**: Compute an initial estimate of $\hat{\mathtt{H}}$ to provide a starting point for the geometric minimization. For example, use the linear normalized DLT algorithm 4.2, or use RANSAC (section 4.7.1) to compute $\hat{\mathtt{H}}$ from four point correspondences.

(ii) **Geometric minimization of – either Sampson error:**

- Minimize the Sampson approximation to the geometric error (4.12–*p*99).
- The cost is minimized using the Newton algorithm of section A6.1(*p*597) or Levenberg–Marquardt algorithm of section A6.2(*p*600) over a suitable parametrization of $\hat{\mathtt{H}}$. For example the matrix may be parametrized by its 9 entries.

or Gold Standard error:

- Compute an initial estimate of the subsidiary variables $\{\hat{\mathbf{x}}_i\}$ using the measured points $\{\mathbf{x}_i\}$ or (better) the Sampson correction to these points given by (4.11–*p*99).
- Minimize the cost

$$\sum_i d(\mathbf{x}_i, \hat{\mathbf{x}}_i)^2 + d(\mathbf{x}'_i, \hat{\mathbf{x}}'_i)^2$$

  over $\hat{\mathtt{H}}$ and $\hat{\mathbf{x}}_i, i = 1, \ldots, n$. The cost is minimized using the Levenberg–Marquardt algorithm over $2n+9$ variables: $2n$ for the n 2D points $\hat{\mathbf{x}}_i$, and 9 for the homography matrix $\hat{\mathtt{H}}$.
- If the number of points is large then the sparse method of minimizing this cost function given in section A6.4(*p*607) is the recommended approach.

Algorithm 4.3. *The Gold Standard algorithm and variations for estimating* $\mathtt{H}$ *from image correspondences. The Gold Standard algorithm is preferred to the Sampson method for 2D homography computation.*

Iteration methods

There are various iterative methods for minimizing the chosen cost function, of which the most popular are Newton iteration and the Levenberg–Marquardt method. These methods are described in appendix 6(*p*597). Other general methods for minimizing a cost function are available, such as Powell's method and the simplex method both described in [Press-88].

Summary. The ideas in this section are collected together in algorithm 4.3, which describes the Gold Standard and Sampson methods for estimating the homography mapping between point correspondences in two images.

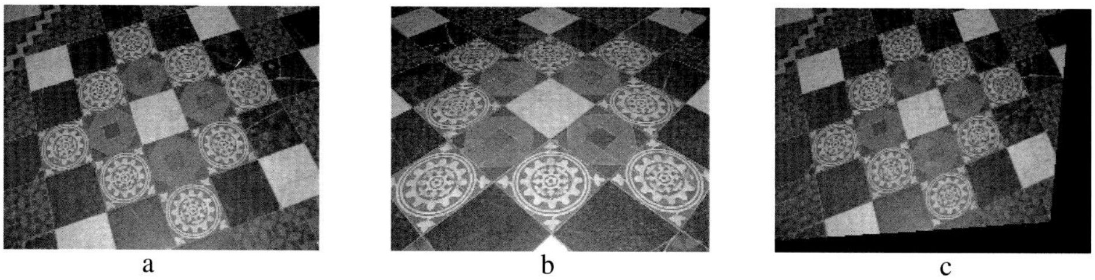

a b c

Fig. 4.5. *Three images of a plane which are used to compare methods of computing projective transformations from corresponding points.*

Method	Pair 1 figure 4.5 a & b	Pair 2 figure 4.5 a & c
Linear normalized	0.4078	0.6602
Gold Standard	0.4078	0.6602
Linear unnormalized	0.4080	26.2056
Homogeneous scaling	0.5708	0.7421
Sampson	0.4077	0.6602
Error in 1 view	0.4077	0.6602
Affine	6.0095	2.8481
Theoretical optimal	0.5477	0.6582

Table 4.1. *Residual errors in pixels for the various algorithms.*

4.6 Experimental comparison of the algorithms

The algorithms are compared for the images shown in figure 4.5. Table 4.1 shows the results of testing several of the algorithms described in this chapter. Residual error is shown for two pairs of images. The methods used are fairly self-explanatory, with a few exceptions. The method "affine" was an attempt to fit the projective transformation with an optimal affine mapping. The "optimal" is the ML estimate assuming a noise level of one pixel.

The first pair of images are (a) and (b) of figure 4.5, with 55 point correspondences. It appears that all methods work almost equally well (except the affine method). The optimal residual is greater than the achieved results, because the noise level (unknown) is less than one pixel.

Image (c) of figure 4.5 was produced synthetically by resampling (a), and the second pair consists of (a) and (c) with 20 point correspondences. In this case, almost all methods perform almost optimally, as shown in the table 4.1. The exception is the affine method (expected to perform badly, since it is not an affine transformation) and the unnormalized linear method. The unnormalized method is expected to perform badly (though maybe not this badly). Just why it performs well in the first pair and very badly for the second pair is not understood. In any case, it is best to avoid this method and use a normalized linear or Gold Standard method.

A further evaluation is presented in figure 4.6. The transformation to be estimated is the one that maps the chessboard image shown here to a square grid aligned with the

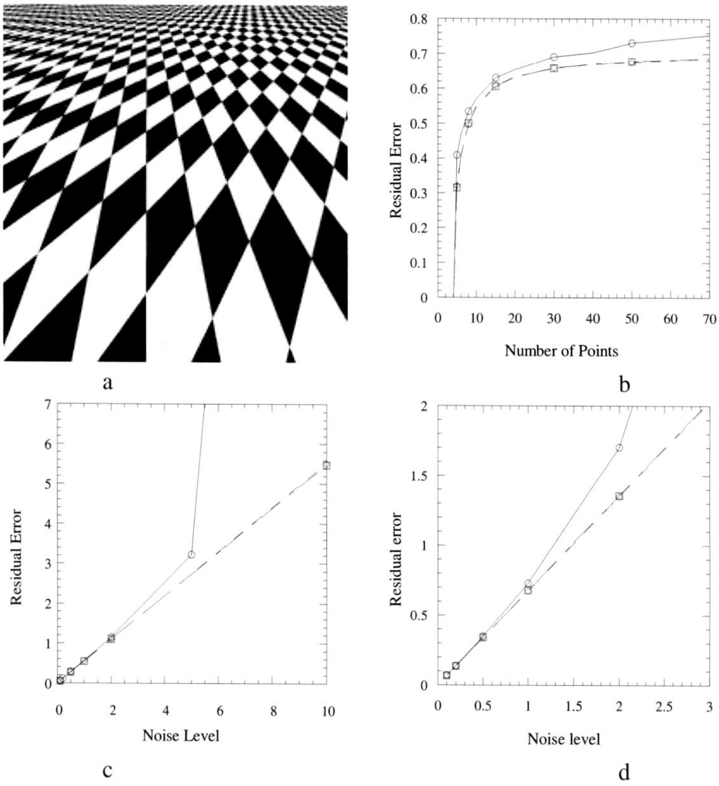

Fig. 4.6. **Comparison of the DLT and Gold Standard algorithms to the theoretically optimal residual error.** *(a) The homography is computed between a chessboard and this image. In all three graphs, the result for the Gold Standard algorithm overlap and are indistinguishable from the theoretical minimum. (b) Residual error as a function of the number of points. (c) The effect of varying noise level for 10 points, and (d) 50 points.*

axes. As may be seen, the image is substantially distorted, with respect to a square grid. For the experiments, randomly selected points in the image were chosen and matched with the corresponding point on the square grid. The (normalized) DLT algorithm and the Gold Standard algorithm are compared to the theoretical minimum or residual error (see chapter 5). Note that for noise up to 5 pixels, the DLT algorithm performs adequately. However, for a noise level of 10 pixels it fails. Note however that in a 200-pixel image, an error of 10 pixels is extremely high. For less severe homographies, closer to the identity map, the DLT performs almost as well as the Gold Standard algorithm.

4.7 Robust estimation

Up to this point it has been assumed that we have been presented with a set of correspondences, $\{\mathbf{x}_i \leftrightarrow \mathbf{x}'_i\}$, where the only source of error is in the measurement of the point's position, which follows a Gaussian distribution. In many practical situations this assumption is not valid because points are mismatched. The mismatched points are *outliers* to the Gaussian error distribution. These outliers can severely disturb the

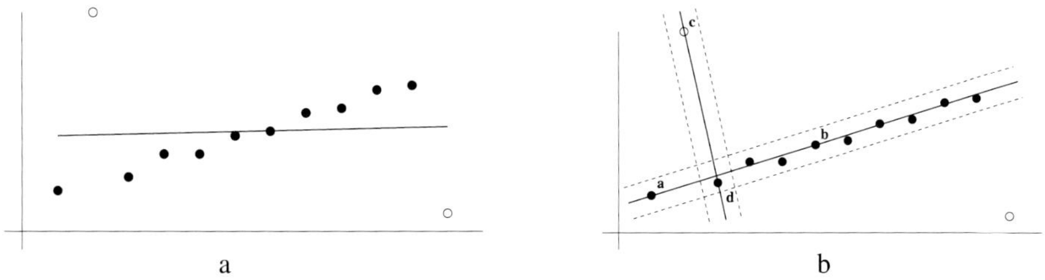

Fig. 4.7. **Robust line estimation.** *The solid points are inliers, the open points outliers. (a) A least-squares (orthogonal regression) fit to the point data is severely affected by the outliers. (b) In the RANSAC algorithm the support for lines through randomly selected point pairs is measured by the number of points within a threshold distance of the lines. The dotted lines indicate the threshold distance. For the lines shown the support is 10 for line* $\langle \mathbf{a}, \mathbf{b} \rangle$ *(where both of the points* $\mathbf{a}$ *and* $\mathbf{b}$ *are inliers); and 2 for line* $\langle \mathbf{c}, \mathbf{d} \rangle$ *where the point* $\mathbf{c}$ *is an outlier.*

estimated homography, and consequently should be identified. The goal then is to determine a set of *inliers* from the presented "correspondences" so that the homography can then be estimated in an optimal manner from these inliers using the algorithms described in the previous sections. This is *robust estimation* since the estimation is robust (tolerant) to outliers (measurements following a different, and possibly unmodelled, error distribution).

4.7.1 RANSAC

We start with a simple example that can easily be visualized – estimating a straight line fit to a set of 2-dimensional points. This can be thought of as estimating a 1-dimensional affine transformation, $x' = ax + b$, between corresponding points lying on two lines.

The problem, which is illustrated in figure 4.7a, is the following: given a set of 2D data points, find the line which minimizes the sum of squared perpendicular distances (orthogonal regression), subject to the condition that none of the valid points deviates from this line by more than t units. This is actually two problems: a line fit to the data; and a classification of the data into inliers (valid points) and outliers. The threshold t is set according to the measurement noise (for example $t = 3\sigma$), and is discussed below. There are many types of robust algorithms and which one to use depends to some extent on the proportion of outliers. For example, if it is known that there is only one outlier, then each point can be deleted in turn and the line estimated from the remainder. Here we describe in detail a general and very successful robust estimator – the RANdom SAmple Consensus (RANSAC) algorithm of Fischler and Bolles [Fischler-81]. The RANSAC algorithm is able to cope with a large proportion of outliers.

The idea is very simple: two of the points are selected randomly; these points define a line. The *support* for this line is measured by the number of points that lie within a distance threshold. This random selection is repeated a number of times and the line with most support is deemed the robust fit. The points within the threshold distance are the inliers (and constitute the eponymous *consensus* set). The intuition is that if one of the points is an outlier then the line will not gain much support, see figure 4.7b.

Furthermore, scoring a line by its support has the additional advantage of favouring better fits. For example, the line $\langle \mathbf{a}, \mathbf{b} \rangle$ in figure 4.7b has a support of 10, whereas the line $\langle \mathbf{a}, \mathbf{d} \rangle$, where the sample points are neighbours, has a support of only 4. Consequently, even though both samples contain no outliers, the line $\langle \mathbf{a}, \mathbf{b} \rangle$ will be selected.

More generally, we wish to fit a *model*, in this case a line, to data, and the random *sample* consists of a minimal subset of the data, in this case two points, sufficient to determine the model. If the model is a planar homography, and the data a set of 2D point correspondences, then the minimal subset consists of four correspondences. The application of RANSAC to the estimation of a homography is described below.

As stated by Fischler and Bolles [Fischler-81] "The RANSAC procedure is opposite to that of conventional smoothing techniques: Rather than using as much of the data as possible to obtain an initial solution and then attempting to eliminate the invalid data points, RANSAC uses as small an initial data set as feasible and enlarges this set with consistent data when possible".

The RANSAC algorithm is summarized in algorithm 4.4. Three questions immediately arise:

Objective

Robust fit of a model to a data set S which contains outliers.

Algorithm

(i) Randomly select a sample of s data points from S and instantiate the model from this subset.
(ii) Determine the set of data points S_i which are within a distance threshold t of the model. The set S_i is the consensus set of the sample and defines the inliers of S.
(iii) If the size of S_i (the number of inliers) is greater than some threshold T, re-estimate the model using all the points in S_i and terminate.
(iv) If the size of S_i is less than T, select a new subset and repeat the above.
(v) After N trials the largest consensus set S_i is selected, and the model is re-estimated using all the points in the subset S_i.

Algorithm 4.4. *The RANSAC robust estimation algorithm, adapted from [Fischler-81]. A minimum of s data points are required to instantiate the free parameters of the model. The three algorithm thresholds t, T, and N are discussed in the text.*

1. What is the distance threshold? We would like to choose the distance threshold, t, such that with a probability α the point is an inlier. This calculation requires the probability distribution for the distance of an inlier from the model. In practice the distance threshold is usually chosen empirically. However, if it is assumed that the measurement error is Gaussian with zero mean and standard deviation σ, then a value for t may be computed. In this case the square of the point distance, $d_\perp^2$, is a sum of squared Gaussian variables and follows a χ_m^2 distribution with m degrees of freedom, where m equals the codimension of the model. For a line the codimension is 1 – only the perpendicular distance to the line is measured. If the model is a point the codimension is 2, and the square of the distance is the sum of squared x and y measurement errors.

The probability that the value of a χ^2_m random variable is less than k^2 is given by the cumulative chi-squared distribution, $F_m(k^2) = \int_0^{k^2} \chi^2_m(\xi)d\xi$. Both of these distributions are described in section A2.2(*p*566). From the cumulative distribution

$$\begin{cases} \text{inlier} & d_\perp^2 < t^2 \\ \text{outlier} & d_\perp^2 \geq t^2 \end{cases} \text{ with } t^2 = F_m^{-1}(\alpha)\sigma^2. \tag{4.17}$$

Usually α is chosen as 0.95, so that there is a 95% probability that the point is an inlier. This means that an inlier will only be incorrectly rejected 5% of the time. Values of t for $\alpha = 0.95$ and for the models of interest in this book are tabulated in table 4.2.

Codimension m	Model	t^2
1	line, fundamental matrix	$3.84\ \sigma^2$
2	homography, camera matrix	$5.99\ \sigma^2$
3	trifocal tensor	$7.81\ \sigma^2$

Table 4.2. *The distance threshold $t^2 = F_m^{-1}(\alpha)\sigma^2$ for a probability of $\alpha = 0.95$ that the point (correspondence) is an inlier.*

2. How many samples? It is often computationally infeasible and unnecessary to try every possible sample. Instead the number of samples N is chosen sufficiently high to ensure with a probability, p, that at least one of the random samples of s points is free from outliers. Usually p is chosen at 0.99. Suppose w is the probability that any selected data point is an inlier, and thus $\epsilon = 1 - w$ is the probability that it is an outlier. Then at least N selections (each of s points) are required, where $(1 - w^s)^N = 1 - p$, so that

$$N = \log(1 - p)/\log(1 - (1 - \epsilon)^s). \tag{4.18}$$

Table 4.3 gives examples of N for $p = 0.99$ for a given s and ϵ.

Sample size	Proportion of outliers ϵ						
s	5%	10%	20%	25%	30%	40%	50%
2	2	3	5	6	7	11	17
3	3	4	7	9	11	19	35
4	3	5	9	13	17	34	72
5	4	6	12	17	26	57	146
6	4	7	16	24	37	97	293
7	4	8	20	33	54	163	588
8	5	9	26	44	78	272	1177

Table 4.3. *The number N of samples required to ensure, with a probability $p = 0.99$, that at least one sample has no outliers for a given size of sample, s, and proportion of outliers, ϵ.*

Example 4.4. For the line-fitting problem of figure 4.7 there are $n = 12$ data points, of which two are outliers so that $\epsilon = 2/12 = 1/6$. From table 4.3 for a minimal subset of size $s = 2$, at least $N = 5$ samples are required. This should be compared with the cost of exhaustively trying every point pair, in which case $\binom{12}{2} = 66$ samples are required (the notation $\binom{n}{2}$ means the number of choices of 2 among n, specifically, $\binom{n}{2} = n(n-1)/2$). △

Note

(i) The number of samples is linked to the proportion rather than number of outliers. This means that the number of samples required may be smaller than the number of outliers. Consequently the computational cost of the sampling can be acceptable even when the number of outliers is large.
(ii) The number of samples increases with the size of the minimal subset (for a given ϵ and p). It might be thought that it would be advantageous to use more than the minimal subset, three or more points in the case of a line, because then a better estimate of the line would be obtained, and the measured support would more accurately reflect the true support. However, this possible advantage in measuring support is generally outweighed by the severe increase in computational cost incurred by the increase in the number of samples.

3. How large is an acceptable consensus set? A rule of thumb is to terminate if the size of the consensus set is similar to the number of inliers believed to be in the data set, given the assumed proportion of outliers, i.e. for n data points $T = (1 - \epsilon)n$. For the line-fitting example of figure 4.7 a conservative estimate of ϵ is $\epsilon = 0.2$, so that $T = (1.0 - 0.2)12 = 10$.

Determining the number of samples adaptively. It is often the case that ϵ, the fraction of data consisting of outliers, is unknown. In such cases the algorithm is initialized using a worst case estimate of ϵ, and this estimate can then be updated as larger consistent sets are found. For example, if the worst case guess is $\epsilon = 0.5$ and a consensus set with 80% of the data is found as inliers, then the updated estimate is $\epsilon = 0.2$.

This idea of "probing" the data via the consensus sets can be applied repeatedly in order to adaptively determine the number of samples, N. To continue the example above, the worst case estimate of $\epsilon = 0.5$ determines an initial N according to (4.18). When a consensus set containing more than 50% of the data is found, we then know that there is at least that proportion of inliers. This updated estimate of ϵ determines a reduced N from (4.18). This update is repeated at each sample, and whenever a consensus set with ϵ lower than the current estimate is found, then N is again reduced. The algorithm terminates as soon as N samples have been performed. It may occur that a sample is found for which ϵ determines an N less than the number of samples that have already been performed. In such a case sufficient samples have been performed and the algorithm terminates. In pseudo-code the adaptive computation of N is summarized in algorithm 4.5.

This adaptive approach works very well and in practice covers the questions of both

- $N = \infty$, sample_count= 0.
- While $N >$ sample_count Repeat
  - Choose a sample and count the number of inliers.
  - Set $\epsilon = 1 - (\text{number of inliers})/(\text{total number of points})$
  - Set N from ϵ and (4.18) with $p = 0.99$.
  - Increment the sample_count by 1.
- Terminate.

Algorithm 4.5. *Adaptive algorithm for determining the number of RANSAC samples.*

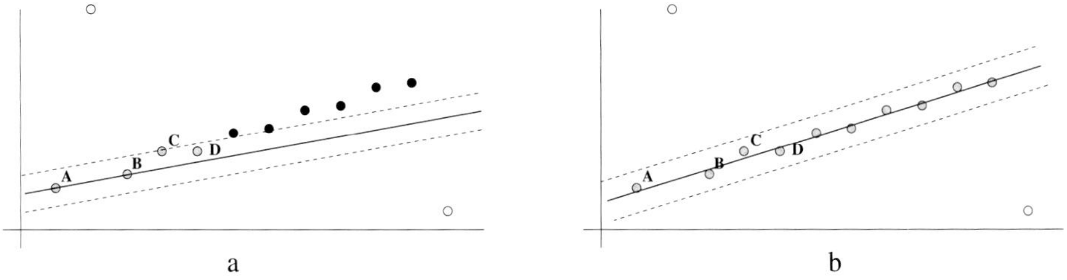

Fig. 4.8. **Robust ML estimation.** *The grey points are classified as inliers to the line. (a) A line defined by points* $\langle \mathbf{A}, \mathbf{B} \rangle$ *has a support of four (from points* $\{\mathbf{A}, \mathbf{B}, \mathbf{C}, \mathbf{D}\}$*). (b) The ML line fit (orthogonal least-squares) to the four points. This is a much improved fit over that defined by* $\langle \mathbf{A}, \mathbf{B} \rangle$*. 10 points are classified as inliers.*

the number of samples and terminating the algorithm. The initial ϵ can be chosen as 1.0, in which case the initial N will be infinite. It is wise to use a conservative probability p such as 0.99 in (4.18). Table 4.4 on page 127 gives example ϵ's and N's when computing a homography.

4.7.2 Robust Maximum Likelihood estimation

The RANSAC algorithm partitions the data set into inliers (the largest consensus set) and outliers (the rest of the data set), and also delivers an estimate of the model, M_0, computed from the minimal set with greatest support. The final step of the RANSAC algorithm is to re-estimate the model using all the inliers. This re-estimation should be optimal and will involve minimizing a ML cost function, as described in section 4.3. In the case of a line, ML estimation is equivalent to orthogonal regression, and a closed form solution is available. In general, though, the ML estimation involves iterative minimization, and the minimal set estimate, M_0, provides the starting point.

The only drawback with this procedure, which is often the one adopted, is that the inlier–outlier classification is irrevocable. After the model has been optimally fitted to the consensus set, there may well be additional points which would now be classified as inliers if the distance threshold was applied to the new model. For example, suppose the line $\langle \mathbf{A}, \mathbf{B} \rangle$ in figure 4.8 was selected by RANSAC. This line has a support of four points, all inliers. After the optimal fit to these four points, there are now 10 points which would correctly be classified as inliers. These two steps: optimal fit to inliers; re-classify inliers using (4.17); can then be iterated until the number of inliers converges.

A least-squares fit with inliers weighted by their distance to the model is often used at this stage.

Robust cost function. An alternative to minimizing $\mathcal{C} = \sum_i d_{\perp i}^2$ over the inliers is to minimize a robust version including all data. A suitable robust cost function is

$$\mathcal{D} = \sum_i \gamma\left(d_{\perp i}\right) \qquad \text{with } \gamma(e) = \begin{cases} e^2 & e^2 < t^2 \quad \text{inlier} \\ t^2 & e^2 \geq t^2 \quad \text{outlier} \end{cases} \tag{4.19}$$

Here $d_{\perp i}$ are point errors and $\gamma(e)$ is a robust cost function [Huber-81] where outliers are given a fixed cost. The χ^2 motivation for the threshold is the same as that of (4.17), where t^2 is defined. The quadratic cost for inliers arises from the Gaussian error model, as described in section 4.3. The constant cost for outliers in the robust cost function arises from the assumption that outliers follow a diffuse or uniform distribution, the log-likelihood of which is a constant. It might be thought that outliers could be excluded from the cost function by simply thresholding on $d_{\perp i}$. The problem with thresholding alone is that it would result in only outliers being included because they would incur no cost.

The cost function $\mathcal{D}$ allows the minimization to be conducted on all points whether they are outliers or inliers. At the start of the iterative minimization $\mathcal{D}$ differs from $\mathcal{C}$ only by a constant (given by 4 times the number of outliers). However, as the minimization progresses outliers can be redesignated inliers, and this typically occurs in practice. A discussion and comparison of cost functions is given in appendix A6.8-(*p*616).

4.7.3 Other robust algorithms

In RANSAC a model instantiated from a minimal set is scored by the number of data points within a threshold distance. An alternative is to score the model by the median of the distances to all points in the data. The model with least median is then selected. This is Least Median of Squares (LMS) estimation, where, as in RANSAC, minimum size subset samples are selected randomly with the number of samples obtained from (4.18). The advantage of LMS is that it requires *no* setting of thresholds or *a priori* knowledge of the variance of the error. The disadvantage of LMS is that it fails if more than half the data is outlying, for then the median distance will be to an outlier. The solution is to use the proportion of outliers to determine the selection distance. For example if there are 50% outliers then a distance below the median value (the quartile say) should be used.

Both the RANSAC and LMS algorithms are able to cope with a large proportion of outliers. If the number of outliers is small, then other robust methods may well be more efficient. These include case deletion, where each point in turn is deleted and the model fitted to the remaining data; and iterative weighted least-squares, where a data point's influence on the fit is weighted inversely by its residual. Generally these methods are **not** recommended. Both Torr [Torr-95b] and Xu and Zhang [Xu-96] describe and compare various robust estimators for estimating the fundamental matrix.

Objective

Compute the 2D homography between two images.

Algorithm

(i) **Interest points:** Compute interest points in each image.
(ii) **Putative correspondences:** Compute a set of interest point matches based on proximity and similarity of their intensity neighbourhood.
(iii) **RANSAC robust estimation:** Repeat for N samples, where N is determined adaptively as in algorithm 4.5:
   (a) Select a random sample of 4 correspondences and compute the homography H.
   (b) Calculate the distance $d_\perp$ for each putative correspondence.
   (c) Compute the number of inliers consistent with H by the number of correspondences for which $d_\perp < t = \sqrt{5.99}\,\sigma$ pixels.

   Choose the H with the largest number of inliers. In the case of ties choose the solution that has the lowest standard deviation of inliers.
(iv) **Optimal estimation:** re-estimate H from all correspondences classified as inliers, by minimizing the ML cost function (4.8–*p*95) using the Levenberg–Marquardt algorithm of section A6.2(*p*600).
(v) **Guided matching:** Further interest point correspondences are now determined using the estimated H to define a search region about the transferred point position.

The last two steps can be iterated until the number of correspondences is stable.

Algorithm 4.6. *Automatic estimation of a homography between two images using RANSAC.*

4.8 Automatic computation of a homography

This section describes an algorithm to automatically compute a homography between two images. The input to the algorithm is simply the images, with no other *a priori* information required; and the output is the estimated homography together with a set of interest points in correspondence. The algorithm might be applied, for example, to two images of a planar surface or two images acquired by rotating a camera about its centre.

The first step of the algorithm is to compute interest points in each image. We are then faced with a "chicken and egg" problem: once the correspondence between the interest points is established the homography can be computed; conversely, given the homography the correspondence between the interest points can easily be established. This problem is resolved by using robust estimation, here RANSAC, as a "search engine". The idea is first to obtain by some means a set of putative point correspondences. It is expected that a proportion of these correspondences will in fact be mismatches. RANSAC is designed to deal with exactly this situation – estimate the homography and also a set of inliers consistent with this estimate (the true correspondences), and outliers (the mismatches).

The algorithm is summarized in algorithm 4.6, with an example of its use shown in figure 4.9, and the steps described in more detail below. Algorithms with essentially the same methodology enable the automatic computation of the fundamental matrix and trifocal tensor directly from image pairs and triplets respectively. This computation is described in chapter 11 and chapter 16.

Determining putative correspondences. The aim, in the absence of any knowledge of the homography, is to provide an initial point correspondence set. A good proportion of these correspondences should be correct, but the aim is not perfect matching, since RANSAC will later be used to eliminate the mismatches. Think of these as "seed" correspondences. These putative correspondences are obtained by detecting interest points independently in each image, and then matching these interest points using a combination of proximity and similarity of intensity neighbourhoods as follows. For brevity, the interest points will be referred to as 'corners'. However, these corners need not be images of physical corners in the scene. The corners are defined by a minimum of the image auto-correlation function.

For each corner at (x, y) in image 1 the match with highest neighbourhood cross-correlation in image 2 is selected within a square search region centred on (x, y). Symmetrically, for each corner in image 2 the match is sought in image 1. Occasionally there will be a conflict where a corner in one image is "claimed" by more than one corner in the other. In such cases a "winner takes all" scheme is applied and only the match with highest cross-correlation is retained.

A variation on the similarity measure is to use Squared Sum of intensity Differences (SSD) instead of (normalized) Cross-Correlation (CC). CC is invariant to the affine mapping of the intensity values (i.e. $I \mapsto \alpha I + \beta$, scaling plus offset) which often occurs in practice between images. SSD is not invariant to this mapping. However, SSD is often preferred when there is small variation in intensity between images, because it is a more sensitive measure than CC and is computationally cheaper.

RANSAC for a homography. The RANSAC algorithm is applied to the putative correspondence set to estimate the homography and the (inlier) correspondences which are consistent with this estimate. The sample size is four, since four correspondences determine a homography. The number of samples is set adaptively as the proportion of outliers is determined from each consensus set, as described in algorithm 4.5.

There are two issues: what is the "distance" in this case? and how should the samples be selected?

(i) **Distance measure**: The simplest method of assessing the error of a correspondence from a homography $\mathtt{H}$ is to use the symmetric transfer error, i.e. $d^2_{\text{transfer}} = d(\mathbf{x}, \mathtt{H}^{-1}\mathbf{x}')^2 + d(\mathbf{x}', \mathtt{H}\mathbf{x})^2$, where $\mathbf{x} \leftrightarrow \mathbf{x}'$ is the point correspondence. A better, though more expensive, distance measure is the reprojection error, $d^2_\perp = d(\mathbf{x}, \hat{\mathbf{x}})^2 + d(\mathbf{x}', \hat{\mathbf{x}}')^2$, where $\hat{\mathbf{x}}' = \mathtt{H}\hat{\mathbf{x}}$ is the perfect correspondence. This measure is more expensive because $\hat{\mathbf{x}}$ must also be computed. A further alternative is Sampson error.

(ii) **Sample selection**: There are two issues here. First, degenerate samples should be disregarded. For example, if three of the four points are collinear then a homography cannot be computed; second, the sample should consist of points with a good spatial distribution over the image. This is because of the extrapolation problem – an estimated homography will accurately map the region straddled by the computation points, but the accuracy generally deteriorates with distance from this region (think of four points in the very top corner of the image). Distributed spatial sampling can be implemented by tiling the image and ensuring, by a suitable weighting of the random sampler, that samples with points lying in different tiles are the more likely.

Robust ML estimation and guided matching. The aim of this final stage is two-fold: first, to obtain an improved estimate of the homography by using all the inliers in the estimation (rather than only the four points of the sample); second, to obtain more inlying matches from the putative correspondence set because a more accurate homography is available. An improved estimate of the homography is then computed from the inliers by minimizing an ML cost function. This final stage can be implemented in two ways. One way is to carry out an ML estimation on the inliers, then recompute the inliers using the new estimated $\mathtt{H}$, and repeat this cycle until the number of inliers converges. The ML cost function minimization is carried out using the Levenberg–Marquardt algorithm described in section A6.2(*p*600). The alternative is to estimate the homography and inliers simultaneously by minimizing a robust ML cost function of (4.19) as described in section 4.7.2. The disadvantage of the simultaneous approach is the computational effort incurred in the minimization of the cost function. For this reason the cycle approach is usually the more attractive.

4.8.1 Application domain

The algorithm requires that interest points can be recovered fairly uniformly across the image, and this in turn requires scenes and resolutions which support this requirement. Scenes should be lightly textured – images of blank walls are not ideal.

The search window proximity constraint places an upper limit on the image motion of corners (the *disparity*) between views. However, the algorithm is not defeated if this constraint is not applied, and in practice the main role of the proximity constraint is to reduce computational complexity, as a smaller search window means that fewer corner matches must be evaluated.

Ultimately the scope of the algorithm is limited by the success of the corner neighbourhood similarity measure (SSD or CC) in providing disambiguation between correspondences. Failure generally results from lack of spatial invariance: the measures are only invariant to image translation, and are severely degraded by transformations outside this class such as image rotation or significant differences in foreshortening between images. One solution is to use measures with a greater invariance to the homography mapping between images, for example measures which are rotationally invariant. An alternative solution is to use an initial estimate of the homography to map between intensity neighbourhoods. Details are beyond the scope of this discussion, but are provided in [Pritchett-98, Schmid-98]. The use of robust estimation confers moderate immunity to independent motion, changes in shadows, partial occlusions etc.

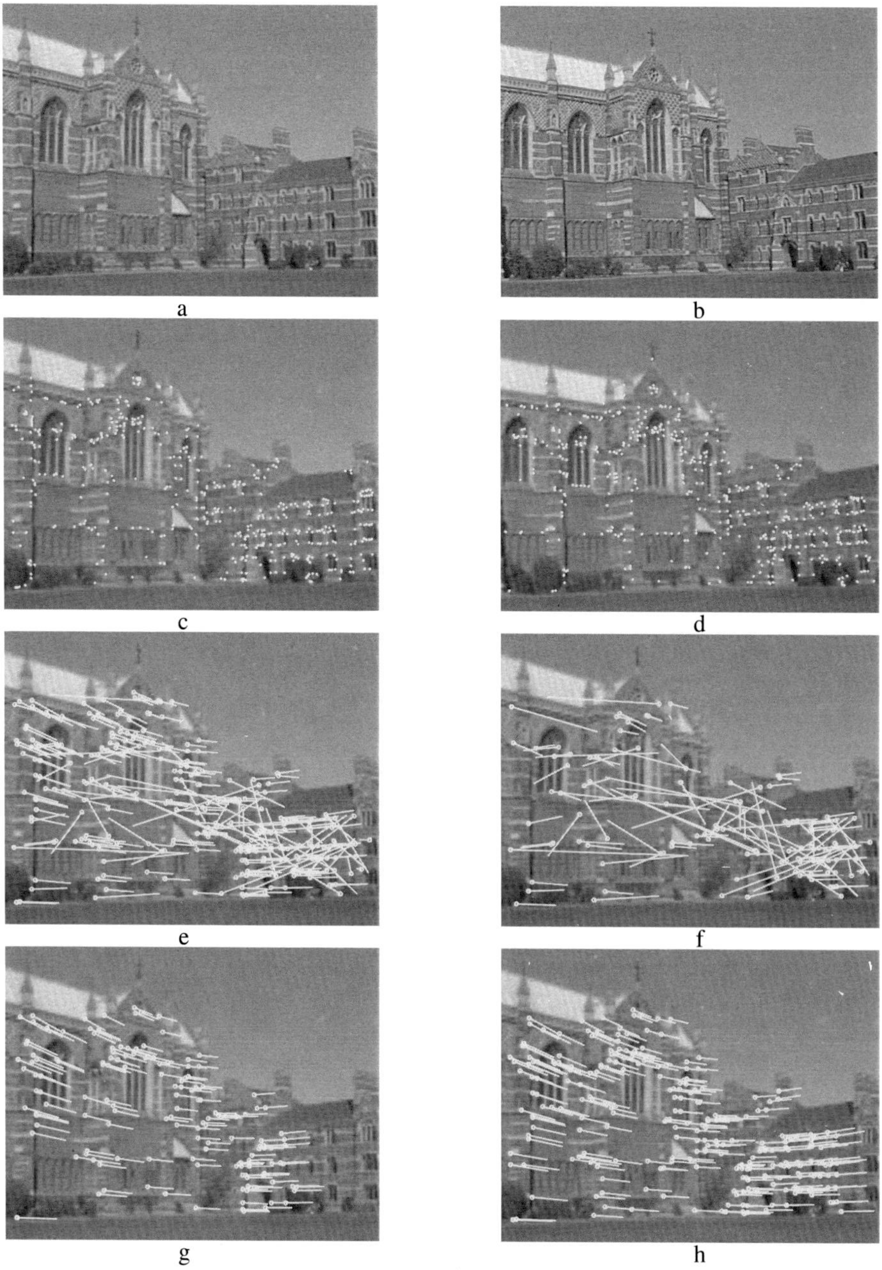

Fig. 4.9. **Automatic computation of a homography between two images using RANSAC.** *The motion between views is a rotation about the camera centre so the images are exactly related by a homography. (a) (b) left and right images of Keble College, Oxford. The images are* 640×480 *pixels. (c) (d) detected corners superimposed on the images. There are approximately 500 corners on each image. The following results are superimposed on the left image: (e) 268 putative matches shown by the line linking corners, note the clear mismatches; (f) outliers – 117 of the putative matches; (g) inliers – 151 correspondences consistent with the estimated* $\mathtt{H}$*; (h) final set of 262 correspondences after guided matching and MLE.*

4.8.2 Implementation and run details

Interest points are obtained using the Harris [Harris-88] corner detector. This detector localizes corners to sub-pixel accuracy, and it has been found empirically that the correspondence error is usually less than a pixel [Schmid-98].

When obtaining seed correspondences, in the putative correspondence stage of the algorithm, the threshold on the neighbourhood similarity measure for match acceptance is deliberately conservative to minimize incorrect matches (the SSD threshold is 20). For the guided matching stage this threshold is relaxed (it is doubled) so that additional putative correspondences are available.

Number of inliers	$1 - \epsilon$	Adaptive N
6	2%	20,028,244
10	3%	2,595,658
44	16%	6,922
58	21%	2,291
73	26%	911
151	56%	43

Table 4.4. *The results of the adaptive algorithm 4.5 used during RANSAC to compute the homography for figure 4.9. N is the total number of samples required as the algorithm runs for $p = 0.99$ probability of no outliers in the sample. The algorithm terminated after 43 samples.*

For the example of figure 4.9 the images are 640×480 pixels, and the search window ± 320 pixels, i.e. the entire image. Of course a much smaller search window could have been used given the actual point disparities in this case. Often in video sequences a search window of ± 40 pixels suffices (i.e. a square of side 80 centred on the current position). The inlier threshold was $t = 1.25$ pixels.

A total of 43 samples were required, with the sampling run as shown in table 4.4. The guided matching required two iterations of the MLE–inlier classification cycle. The RMS values for $d_\perp$ pixel error were 0.23 before the MLE and 0.19 after. The Levenberg–Marquardt algorithm required 10 iterations.

4.9 Closure

This chapter has illustrated the issues and techniques that apply to estimating the tensors representing multiple view relations. These ideas will reoccur in each of the computation chapters throughout the book. In each case there are a minimal number of correspondences required; degenerate configurations that should be avoided; algebraic and geometric errors that can be minimized when more than the minimal number of correspondences are available; parametrizations that enforce internal constraints on the tensor etc.

4.9.1 The literature

The DLT algorithm dates back at least to Sutherland [Sutherland-63]. Sampson's classic paper on conic fitting (an improvement on the equally classic Bookstein algorithm) appeared in [Sampson-82]. Normalization was made public in the Computer Vision literature by Hartley [Hartley-97c].

Related reading on numerical methods may be found in the excellent *Numerical Recipes in C* [Press-88], and also Gill and Murray [Gill-78] for iterative minimization.

Fischler and Bolles' [Fischler-81] RANSAC was one of the earliest robust algorithms, and in fact was developed to solve a Computer Vision problem (pose from 3 points). The original paper is very clearly argued and well worth reading. Other background material on robustness may be found in Rousseeuw [Rousseeuw-87]. The primary application of robust estimation in computer vision was to estimating the fundamental matrix (chapter 11), by Torr and Murray [Torr-93] using RANSAC, and, Zhang *et al.* [Zhang-95] using LMS. The automatic ML estimation of a homography was described by Torr and Zisserman [Torr-98].

4.9.2 Notes and exercises

(i) **Computing homographies of $\mathbb{P}^n$.** The derivation of (4.1–*p*89) and (4.3–*p*89) assumed that the dimension of $\mathbf{x}'_i$ is three, so that the cross-product is defined. However, (4.3) may be derived in a way that generalizes to all dimensions. Assuming that $w'_i = 1$, we may solve for the unknown scale factor explicitly by writing $\mathtt{H}\mathbf{x}_i = k(x_i, y_i, 1)^\mathsf{T}$. From the third coordinate we obtain $k = \mathbf{h}^{3\mathsf{T}}\mathbf{x}_i$, and substituting this into the original equation gives

$$\begin{pmatrix} \mathbf{h}^{1\mathsf{T}}\mathbf{x}_i \\ \mathbf{h}^{2\mathsf{T}}\mathbf{x}_i \end{pmatrix} = \begin{pmatrix} x'_i\mathbf{h}^{3\mathsf{T}}\mathbf{x}_i \\ y'_i\mathbf{h}^{3\mathsf{T}}\mathbf{x}_i \end{pmatrix}$$

which leads directly to (4.3).

(ii) **Computing homographies for ideal points.** If one of the points $\mathbf{x}'_i$ is an ideal point, so that $w'_i = 0$, then the pair of equations (4.3) collapses to a single equation although (4.1) does contain two independent equations. To avoid such degeneracy, while including only the minimum number of equations, a good way to proceed is as follows. We may rewrite the equation $\mathbf{x}'_i = \mathtt{H}\mathbf{x}_i$ as

$$[\mathbf{x}'_i]^\perp \mathtt{H}\mathbf{x}_i = \mathbf{0}$$

where $[\mathbf{x}'_i]^\perp$ is a matrix with rows orthogonal to $\mathbf{x}'_i$ so that $[\mathbf{x}'_i]^\perp\mathbf{x}'_i = \mathbf{0}$. Each row of $[\mathbf{x}'_i]^\perp$ leads to a separate linear equation in the entries of $\mathtt{H}$. The matrix $[\mathbf{x}'_i]^\perp$ may be obtained by deleting the first row of an orthogonal matrix $\mathtt{M}$ satisfying $\mathtt{M}\mathbf{x}'_i = (1, 0, \ldots, 0)^\mathsf{T}$. A Householder matrix (see section A4.1.2(*p*580)) is an easily constructed matrix with the desired property.

(iii) **Scaling unbounded point sets.** In the case of points at or near infinity in a plane, it is neither reasonable nor feasible to normalize coordinates using the isotropic (or non-isotropic) scaling schemes presented in this chapter, since the centroid and scale are infinite or near infinite. A method that seems to give good results is to normalize the set of points $\mathbf{x}_i = (x_i, y_i, w_i)^\mathsf{T}$ such that

$$\sum_i x_i = \sum_i y_i = 0 \ ; \ \sum_i x_i^2 + y_i^2 = 2\sum_i w_i^2 \ ; \ x_i^2 + y_i^2 + w_i^2 = 1 \forall i$$

Note that the coordinates x_i and y_i appearing here are the homogeneous coordinates, and the conditions no longer imply that the centroid is at the origin. Investigate methods of achieving this normalization, and evaluate its properties.

(iv) **Transformation invariance of DLT.** We consider computation of a 2D homography by minimizing algebraic error $\|\mathtt{A}\mathbf{h}\|$ (see (4.5–*p*94)) subject to various constraints. Prove the following cases:

(a) If $\|\mathtt{A}\mathbf{h}\|$ is minimized subject to the constraint $h_9 = \mathtt{H}_{33} = 1$, then the result is invariant under change of scale but *not* translation of coordinates.

(b) If instead the constraint is $\mathtt{H}_{31}^2 + \mathtt{H}_{32}^2 = 1$ then the result is similarity invariant.

(c) **Affine case:** The same is true for the constraint $\mathtt{H}_{31} = \mathtt{H}_{32} = 0;\ \mathtt{H}_{33} = 1$.

(v) **Expressions for image coordinate derivatives.** For the map $\mathbf{x}' = (x', y', w')^\mathsf{T} = \mathtt{H}\mathbf{x}$, derive the following expressions (where $\tilde{\mathbf{x}}' = (\tilde{x}', \tilde{y}')^\mathsf{T} = (x'/w', y'/w')^\mathsf{T}$ are the inhomogeneous coordinates of the image point):

(a) Derivative wrt $\mathbf{x}$

$$\partial\tilde{\mathbf{x}}'/\partial\mathbf{x} = \frac{1}{w'}\begin{bmatrix} \mathbf{h}^{1\mathsf{T}} - \tilde{x}'\mathbf{h}^{3\mathsf{T}} \\ \mathbf{h}^{2\mathsf{T}} - \tilde{y}'\mathbf{h}^{3\mathsf{T}} \end{bmatrix} \tag{4.20}$$

where $\mathbf{h}^{j\mathsf{T}}$ is the j–th row of $\mathtt{H}$.

(b) Derivative wrt $\mathtt{H}$

$$\partial\tilde{\mathbf{x}}'/\partial\mathbf{h} = \frac{1}{w'}\begin{bmatrix} \mathbf{x}^\mathsf{T} & 0 & -\tilde{x}'\mathbf{x}^\mathsf{T} \\ 0 & \mathbf{x}^\mathsf{T} & -\tilde{y}'\mathbf{x}^\mathsf{T} \end{bmatrix} \tag{4.21}$$

with $\mathbf{h}$ as defined in (4.2–*p*89).

(vi) **Sampson error with non-isotropic error distributions.** The derivation of Sampson error in section 4.2.6(*p*98) assumed that points were measured with circular error distributions. In the case where the point $\mathbf{X} = (x, y, x', y')$ is measured with covariance matrix $\Sigma_\mathbf{X}$ it is appropriate instead to minimize the Mahalanobis norm $\|\boldsymbol{\delta}_\mathbf{X}\|^2_{\Sigma_\mathbf{X}} = \boldsymbol{\delta}_\mathbf{X}^\mathsf{T}\Sigma_\mathbf{X}^{-1}\boldsymbol{\delta}_\mathbf{X}$. Show that in this case the formulae corresponding to (4.11–*p*99) and (4.12–*p*99) are

$$\boldsymbol{\delta}_\mathbf{X} = -\Sigma_\mathbf{X}\mathtt{J}^\mathsf{T}(\mathtt{J}\Sigma_\mathbf{X}\mathtt{J}^\mathsf{T})^{-1}\boldsymbol{\epsilon} \tag{4.22}$$

and

$$\|\boldsymbol{\delta}_\mathbf{X}\|^2_{\Sigma_\mathbf{X}} = \boldsymbol{\epsilon}^\mathsf{T}(\mathtt{J}\Sigma_\mathbf{X}J^\mathsf{T})^{-1}\boldsymbol{\epsilon}. \tag{4.23}$$

Note that if the measurements in the two images are independent, then the covariance matrix $\Sigma_\mathbf{X}$ will be block-diagonal with two 2×2 diagonal blocks corresponding to the two images.

(vii) **Sampson error programming hint.** In the case of 2D homography estimation, and in fact every other similar problem considered in this book, the cost function $\mathcal{C}_\mathtt{H}(\mathbf{X}) = \mathtt{A}(\mathbf{X})\mathbf{h}$ of section 4.2.6(*p*98) is multilinear in the coordinates

Objective

Given $n \geq 4$ image point correspondences $\{\mathbf{x}_i \leftrightarrow \mathbf{x}'_i\}$, determine the affine homography $\mathtt{H}_\mathrm{A}$ which minimizes reprojection error in both images (4.8–*p*95).

Algorithm

(a) Express points as inhomogeneous 2-vectors. Translate the points $\mathbf{x}_i$ by a translation $\mathbf{t}$ so that their centroid is at the origin. Do the same to the points $\mathbf{x}'_i$ by a translation $\mathbf{t}'$. Henceforth work with the translated coordinates.

(b) Form the $n \times 4$ matrix $\mathtt{A}$ whose rows are the vectors

$$\mathbf{X}_i^\mathsf{T} = (\mathbf{x}_i^\mathsf{T}, \mathbf{x}_i'^\mathsf{T}) = (x_i, y_i, x'_i, y'_i).$$

(c) Let $\mathbf{V}_1$ and $\mathbf{V}_2$ be the right singular-vectors of $\mathtt{A}$ corresponding to the two largest (sic) singular values.

(d) Let $\mathtt{H}_{2\times 2} = \mathtt{CB}^{-1}$, where $\mathtt{B}$ and $\mathtt{C}$ are the 2×2 blocks such that

$$[\mathbf{V}_1 \mathbf{V}_2] = \begin{bmatrix} \mathtt{B} \\ \mathtt{C} \end{bmatrix}.$$

(e) The required homography is

$$\mathtt{H}_\mathrm{A} = \begin{bmatrix} \mathtt{H}_{2\times 2} & \mathtt{H}_{2\times 2}\mathbf{t} - \mathbf{t}' \\ \mathbf{0}^\mathsf{T} & 1 \end{bmatrix},$$

and the corresponding estimate of the image points is given by

$$\widehat{\mathbf{X}}_i = (\mathbf{V}_1\mathbf{V}_1^\mathsf{T} + \mathbf{V}_2\mathbf{V}_2^\mathsf{T})\mathbf{X}_i$$

Algorithm 4.7. *The Gold Standard Algorithm for estimating an* affine *homography* $\mathtt{H}_\mathrm{A}$ *from image correspondences.*

of $\mathbf{X}$. This means that the partial derivative $\partial \mathcal{C}_\mathtt{H}(\mathbf{X})/\partial \mathbf{X}$ may be very simply computed. For instance, the derivative

$$\partial \mathcal{C}_\mathtt{H}(x, y, x', y')/\partial x = \mathcal{C}_\mathtt{H}(x+1, y, x', y') - \mathcal{C}_\mathtt{H}(x, y, x', y')$$

is *exact*, not a finite difference approximation. This means that for programming purposes, one does not need to code a special routine for taking derivatives – the routine for computing $\mathcal{C}_\mathtt{H}(\mathbf{X})$ will suffice. Denoting by $\mathbf{E}_i$ the vector containing 1 in the i-th position, and otherwise 0, one sees that $\partial \mathcal{C}_\mathtt{H}(\mathbf{X})/\partial X_i = \mathcal{C}_\mathtt{H}(\mathbf{X} + \mathbf{E}_i) - \mathcal{C}_\mathtt{H}(\mathbf{X})$, and further

$$\mathtt{JJ}^\mathsf{T} = \sum_i \left(\mathcal{C}_\mathtt{H}(\mathbf{X} + \mathbf{E}_i) - \mathcal{C}_\mathtt{H}(\mathbf{X})\right)\left(\mathcal{C}_\mathtt{H}(\mathbf{X} + \mathbf{E}_i) - \mathcal{C}_\mathtt{H}(\mathbf{X})\right)^\mathsf{T}.$$

Also note that computationally it is more efficient to solve $\mathtt{JJ}^\mathsf{T}\boldsymbol{\lambda} = -\boldsymbol{\epsilon}$ directly for $\boldsymbol{\lambda}$, rather than take the inverse as $\boldsymbol{\lambda} = -(\mathtt{JJ}^\mathsf{T})^{-1}\boldsymbol{\epsilon}$.

(viii) **Minimizing geometric error for affine transformations.** Given a set of correspondences $(x_i, y_i) \leftrightarrow (x'_i, y'_i)$, find an affine transformation $\mathtt{H}_\mathrm{A}$ that minimizes geometric error (4.8–*p*95). We will step through the derivation of a linear algorithm based on Sampson's approximation which is exact in this case. The complete method is summarized in algorithm 4.7.

(a) Show that the optimum affine transformation takes the centroid of the $\mathbf{x}_i$ to the centroid of $\mathbf{x}'_i$, so by translating the points to have their centroid at the origin, the translation part of the transformation is determined. It is only necessary then to determine the upper-left 2×2 submatrix $\mathtt{H}_{2\times 2}$ of $\mathtt{H}_A$, which represents the linear part of the transformation.
(b) The point $\mathbf{X}_i = (\mathbf{x}_i^\mathsf{T}, \mathbf{x}_i'^\mathsf{T})^\mathsf{T}$ lies on $\mathcal{V}_\mathtt{H}$ if and only if $[\mathtt{H}_{2\times 2}| - \mathtt{I}_{2\times 2}]\mathbf{X} = \mathbf{0}$. So $\mathcal{V}_\mathtt{H}$ is a codimension-2 subspace of $\mathbb{R}^4$.
(c) Any codimension-2 subspace may be expressed as $[\mathtt{H}_{2\times 2}| - \mathtt{I}]\mathbf{X} = \mathbf{0}$ for suitable $\mathtt{H}_{2\times 2}$. Thus given measurements $\mathbf{X}_i$, the estimation task is equivalent to finding the best-fitting codimension-2 subspace.
(d) Given a matrix $\mathtt{M}$ with rows $\mathbf{X}_i^\mathsf{T}$, the best-fitting subspace to the $\mathbf{X}_i$ is spanned by the singular vectors $\mathbf{V}_1$ and $\mathbf{V}_2$ corresponding to the two largest singular values of $\mathtt{M}$.
(e) The $\mathtt{H}_{2\times 2}$ corresponding to the subspace spanned by $\mathbf{V}_1$ and $\mathbf{V}_2$ is found by solving the equations $[\mathtt{H}_{2\times 2}| - \mathtt{I}][\mathbf{V}_1\mathbf{V}_2] = \mathtt{0}$.

(ix) **Computing homographies of $\mathbb{P}^3$ from line correspondences.** Consider computing a 4×4 homography $\mathtt{H}$ from lines correspondences alone, assuming the lines are in general position in $\mathbb{P}^3$. There are two questions: how many correspondences are required?, and how to formulate the algebraic constraints to obtain a solution for $\mathtt{H}$? It might be thought that four line correspondences would be sufficient because each line in $\mathbb{P}^3$ has four degrees of freedom, and thus four lines should provide $4 \times 4 = 16$ constraints on the 15 degrees of freedom of $\mathtt{H}$. However, a configuration of four lines is degenerate (see section 4.1.3(*p*91)) for computing the transformation, as there is a 2D isotropy subgroup. This is discussed further in [Hartley-94c]. Equations linear in $\mathtt{H}$ can be obtained in the following way:

$$\boldsymbol{\pi}_i^\mathsf{T}\mathtt{H}\mathbf{X}_j = 0\,, \quad i = 1, 2,\ j = 1, 2\,,$$

where $\mathtt{H}$ transfers a line defined by the two points $(\mathbf{X}_1, \mathbf{X}_2)$ to a line defined by the intersection of the two planes $(\boldsymbol{\pi}_1, \boldsymbol{\pi}_2)$. This method was derived in [Oskarsson-02], where more details are to be found.

5

Algorithm Evaluation and Error Analysis

This chapter describes methods for assessing and quantifying the results of estimation algorithms. Often it is not sufficient to simply have an estimate of a variable or transformation. Instead some measure of confidence or uncertainty is also required.

Two methods for computing this uncertainty (covariance) are outlined here. The first is based on linear approximations and involves concatenating various Jacobian expressions. The second is the easier to implement Monte Carlo method.

5.1 Bounds on performance

Once an algorithm has been developed for the estimation of a certain type of transformation it is time to test its performance. This may be done by testing it on real or on synthetic data. In this section, testing on synthetic data will be considered, and a methodology for testing will be sketched.

We recall the notational convention:

- A quantity such as $\mathbf{x}$ represents a measured image point.
- Estimated quantities are represented by a hat, such as $\hat{\mathbf{x}}$ or $\hat{\mathtt{H}}$.
- True values are represented by a bar, such as $\bar{\mathbf{x}}$ or $\bar{\mathtt{H}}$.

Typically, testing will begin with the synthetic generation of a set of image correspondences $\bar{\mathbf{x}}_i \leftrightarrow \bar{\mathbf{x}}'_i$ between two images. The number of such correspondences will vary. Corresponding points will be chosen in such a way that they correspond via a given fixed projective transformation $\bar{\mathtt{H}}$, and the correspondence is exact, in the sense that $\bar{\mathbf{x}}'_i = \bar{\mathtt{H}}\bar{\mathbf{x}}_i$ precisely, up to machine accuracy.

Next, artificial Gaussian noise will be added to the image measurements by perturbing both the x- and y-coordinates of the point by a zero-mean Gaussian random variable with known variance. The resulting noisy points are denoted $\mathbf{x}_i$ and $\mathbf{x}'_i$. A suitable Gaussian random number generator is given in [Press-88]. The estimation algorithm is then run to compute the estimated quantity. For the 2D projective transformation problem considered in chapter 4, this means the projective transformation itself, and also perhaps estimates of the correct original noise-free image points. The algorithm is then evaluated according to how closely the computed model matches the (noisy) input data, or alternatively, how closely the estimated model agrees with the original noise-free data. This procedure should be carried out many times with different noise (i.e. a different seed for the random number generator, though each time with the same noise variance) in order to obtain a statistically meaningful performance evaluation.

5.1.1 Error in one image

To illustrate this, we continue our investigation of the problem of 2D homography estimation. For simplicity we consider the case where noise is added to the coordinates of the second image only. Thus, $\mathbf{x}_i = \bar{\mathbf{x}}_i$ for all i. Let $\mathbf{x}_i \leftrightarrow \mathbf{x}'_i$ be a set of noisy matched points between two images, generated from a perfectly matched set of data by injection of Gaussian noise with variance σ^2 in each of the two coordinates of the second (primed) image. Let there be n such matched points. From this data, a projective transformation $\hat{\mathtt{H}}$ is estimated using any one of the algorithms described in chapter 4. Obviously, the estimated transformation $\hat{\mathtt{H}}$ will not generally map $\mathbf{x}_i$ to $\mathbf{x}'_i$, nor $\bar{\mathbf{x}}_i$ to $\bar{\mathbf{x}}'_i$ precisely, because of the injected noise in the coordinates of $\mathbf{x}'_i$. The RMS (root-mean-squared) residual error

$$\epsilon_{\text{res}} = \left(\frac{1}{2n} \sum_{i=1}^{n} d(\mathbf{x}'_i, \hat{\mathbf{x}}'_i)^2 \right)^{1/2} \tag{5.1}$$

measures the average difference between the noisy input data ($\mathbf{x}'_i$) and the estimated points $\hat{\mathbf{x}}'_i = \hat{\mathtt{H}}\bar{\mathbf{x}}_i$. It is therefore appropriately called *residual error*. It measures how well the computed transformation matches the input data, and as such is a suitable quality measure for the estimation procedure.

The value of the residual error is *not* in itself an absolute measure of the quality of the solution obtained. For instance, consider the 2D projectivity problem in the case where the input data consists of just 4 matched points. Since a projective transformation is defined uniquely and exactly by 4 point correspondences, any reasonable algorithm will compute an $\hat{\mathtt{H}}$ that matches the points exactly, in the sense that $\mathbf{x}'_i = \hat{\mathtt{H}}\mathbf{x}_i$. This means that the residual error is zero. One cannot expect any better performance from an algorithm than this.

Note that $\hat{\mathtt{H}}$ matches the projected points to the input data $\mathbf{x}'_i$, and not to the original noise-free data, $\bar{\mathbf{x}}'_i$. In fact, since the difference between the noise-free and the noisy coordinates has variance σ^2, in the minimal four-point case the residual difference between projected points $\hat{\mathtt{H}}\mathbf{x}_i$ and the noise-free data $\bar{\mathbf{x}}'_i$ also has variance σ^2. Thus, in the case of 4 points, the model fits the noisy input data perfectly (i.e. the residual is zero), but does not give a very close approximation to the true noise-free values.

With more than 4 point matches, the value of the residual error will increase. In fact, intuitively, one expects that as the number of measurements (matched points) increases, the estimated model should agree more and more closely with the noise-free true values. Asymptotically, the variance should decrease in inverse proportion to the number of point matches. At the same time, the residual error will increase.

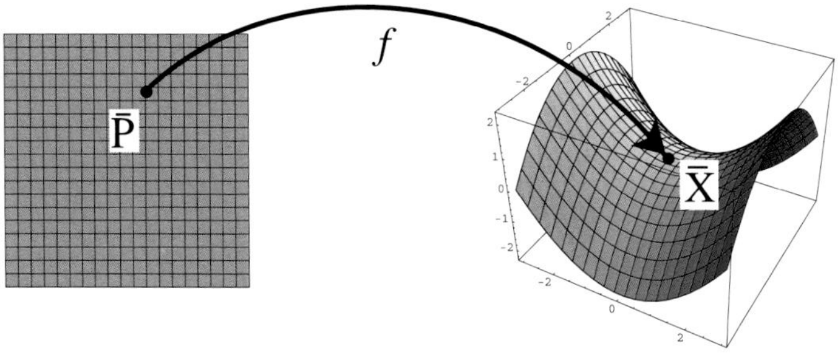

Fig. 5.1. *As the values of the parameters* $\mathbf{P}$ *vary, the function image traces out a surface* S_M *through the true value* $\overline{\mathbf{X}}$.

5.1.2 Error in both images

In the case of error in both images, the residual error is

$$\epsilon_{\text{res}} = \frac{1}{\sqrt{4n}} \left(\sum_{i=1}^{n} d(\mathbf{x}_i, \hat{\mathbf{x}}_i)^2 + \sum_{i=1}^{n} d(\mathbf{x}'_i, \hat{\mathbf{x}}'_i)^2 \right)^{1/2} \tag{5.2}$$

where $\hat{\mathbf{x}}_i$ and $\hat{\mathbf{x}}'_i$ are estimated points such that $\hat{\mathbf{x}}'_i = \hat{\mathtt{H}}\hat{\mathbf{x}}_i$.

5.1.3 Optimal estimators (MLE)

Bounds for estimation performance will be considered in a general framework, and then specialized to the two cases of error in one or both images. The goal is to derive formulae for the expected residual error of the Maximum Likelihood Estimate (MLE). As described previously, minimization of geometric error is equivalent to MLE, and so the goal of any algorithm implementing minimization of geometric error should be to achieve the theoretical bound given for the MLE. Another algorithm minimizing a different cost function (such as algebraic error) can be judged according to how close it gets to the bound given by the MLE.

A general estimation problem is concerned with a function f from $\mathbb{R}^M$ to $\mathbb{R}^N$ as described in section 4.2.7(p101), where $\mathbb{R}^M$ is a parameter space, and $\mathbb{R}^N$ is a space of measurements. Consider now a point $\overline{\mathbf{X}} \in \mathbb{R}^N$ for which there exists a vector of parameters $\overline{\mathbf{P}} \in \mathbb{R}^M$ such that $f(\overline{\mathbf{P}}) = \overline{\mathbf{X}}$ (i.e. a point $\overline{\mathbf{X}}$ in the range of f with preimage $\overline{\mathbf{P}}$). In the context of 2D projectivities with measurements in the second image only, this corresponds to a noise-free set of points $\bar{\mathbf{x}}'_i = \overline{\mathtt{H}}\bar{\mathbf{x}}_i$. The x- and y-components of the n points $\bar{\mathbf{x}}'_i, i = 1, \ldots, n$ constitute the N-vector $\overline{\mathbf{X}}$ with $N = 2n$, and the parameters of the homography constitute the vector $\overline{\mathbf{P}}$ which may be an 8- or 9-vector depending on the parametrization of $\overline{\mathtt{H}}$.

Let $\mathbf{X}$ be a measurement vector chosen according to an isotropic Gaussian distribution with mean the true measurement $\overline{\mathbf{X}}$ and variance $N\sigma^2$ (this notation means that each of the N components has variance σ^2). As the value of the parameter vector $\mathbf{P}$ varies in a neighbourhood of the point $\overline{\mathbf{P}}$, the value of the function $f(\mathbf{P})$ traces out a surface S_M in $\mathbb{R}^N$ through the point $\overline{\mathbf{X}}$. This is illustrated in figure 5.1. The surface S_M

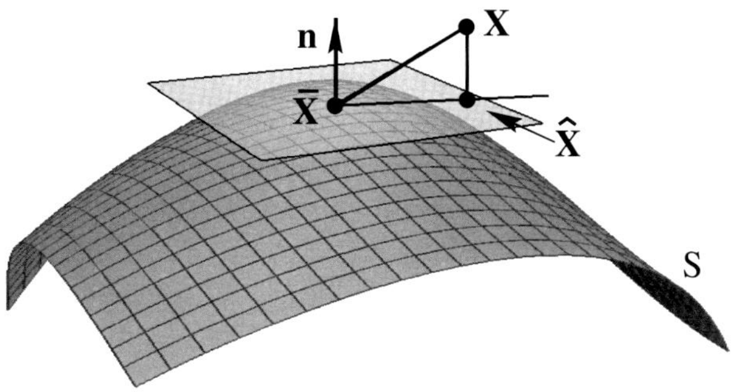

Fig. 5.2. *Geometry of the errors in measurement space using the tangent plane approximation to* S_{M}. *The estimated point* $\widehat{\mathbf{X}}$ *is the closest point on* S_{M} *to the measured point* $\mathbf{X}$. *The residual error is the distance between the measured point* $\mathbf{X}$ *and* $\widehat{\mathbf{X}}$. *The estimation error is the distance from* $\widehat{\mathbf{X}}$ *to the true point* $\overline{\mathbf{X}}$.

is given by the range of f. The dimension of the surface as a submanifold of $\mathbb{R}^N$ is equal to d, where d is the number of essential parameters (that is the number of degrees of freedom, or minimum number of parameters). In the single-image error case, this equals 8, since the mapping determined by the matrix $\mathtt{H}$ is independent of scale.

Now, given a measurement vector $\mathbf{X}$, the maximum likelihood (ML) estimate $\widehat{\mathbf{X}}$ is the point on S_{M} closest to $\mathbf{X}$. The ML estimator is the one that returns this closest point to $\mathbf{X}$ that lies on this surface. Denote this ML estimate by $\widehat{\mathbf{X}}$.

We now assume that in the neighbourhood of $\overline{\mathbf{X}}$, the surface is essentially planar and is well approximated by the tangent surface – at least for neighbourhoods around $\overline{\mathbf{X}}$ of the order of magnitude of noise variance. In this linear approximation, the ML estimate $\widehat{\mathbf{X}}$ is the foot of the perpendicular from $\mathbf{X}$ onto the tangent plane. The residual error is the distance from the point $\mathbf{X}$ to the estimated value $\widehat{\mathbf{X}}$. Furthermore, the distance from $\widehat{\mathbf{X}}$ to (the unknown) $\overline{\mathbf{X}}$ is the distance from the optimally estimated value to the true value as seen in figure 5.2. Our task is to compute the expected value of these errors.

Computing the expected ML residual error has now been abstracted to a geometric problem as follows. The *total variance* of an N-dimensional Gaussian distribution is the trace of the covariance matrix, that is the sum of variances in each of the axial directions. This is, of course, unchanged by a change of orthogonal coordinate frame. For an N-dimensional isotropic Gaussian distribution with independent variances σ^2 in each variable, the total variance is $N\sigma^2$. Now, given an isotropic Gaussian random variable defined on $\mathbb{R}^N$ with total variance $N\sigma^2$ and mean the true point $\overline{\mathbf{X}}$, we wish to compute the expected distance of the random variable from a dimension d hyperplane passing through $\overline{\mathbf{X}}$. The projection of a Gaussian random variable in $\mathbb{R}^N$ onto the d-dimensional tangent plane gives the distribution of the *estimation error* (the difference between the estimated value and the true result). Projection onto the

$(N-d)$-dimensional normal to the tangent surface gives the distribution of the residual error.

By a rotation of axes if necessary, one may assume, without loss of generality, that the tangent surface coincides with the first d coordinate axes. Integration over the remaining axial directions provides the following result.

Result 5.1. *The projection of an isotropic Gaussian distribution defined on $\mathbb{R}^N$ with total variance $N\sigma^2$ onto a subspace of dimension s is an isotropic Gaussian distribution with total variance $s\sigma^2$.*

The proof of this is straightforward, and is omitted. We apply this in the two cases where $s = d$ and $s = N - d$ to obtain the following results.

Result 5.2. *Consider an estimation problem where N measurements are to be modelled by a function depending on a set of d essential parameters. Suppose the measurements are subject to independent Gaussian noise with standard deviation σ in each measurement variable.*

(i) *The RMS* **residual error** *(distance of the measured from the estimated value) for the ML estimator is*

$$\epsilon_{\text{res}} = E[\|\widehat{\mathbf{X}} - \mathbf{X}\|^2/N]^{1/2} = \sigma(1 - d/N)^{1/2} \tag{5.3}$$

(ii) *The RMS* **estimation error** *(distance of the estimated from the true value) for the ML estimator is*

$$\epsilon_{\text{est}} = E[\|\widehat{\mathbf{X}} - \overline{\mathbf{X}}\|^2/N]^{1/2} = \sigma(d/N)^{1/2} \tag{5.4}$$

where $\mathbf{X}$, $\widehat{\mathbf{X}}$ and $\overline{\mathbf{X}}$ are respectively the measured, estimated and true values of the measurement vector.

Result 5.2 follows directly from result 5.1 by dividing by N to get the variance per measurement, then taking a square root to get standard deviation, instead of variance.

These values give lower bounds for residual error against which a particular estimation algorithm may be measured.

2D homography – error in one image. For the 2D projectivity estimation problem considered in this chapter, assuming error in the second image only, we have $d = 8$ and $N = 2n$, where n is the number of point matches. Thus, we have for this problem

$$\begin{aligned} \epsilon_{\text{res}} &= \sigma\,(1 - 4/n)^{1/2} \\ \epsilon_{\text{est}} &= \sigma\,(4/n)^{1/2}. \end{aligned} \tag{5.5}$$

Graphs of these errors as n varies are shown in figure 5.3.

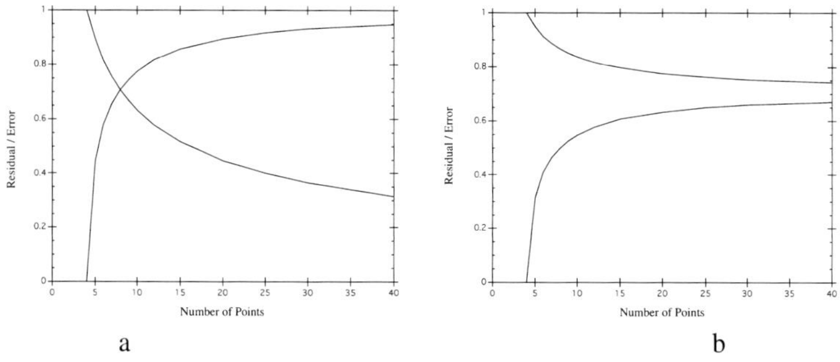

Fig. 5.3. *Optimal error when noise is present in (a) one image, and in (b) both images as the number of points varies. An error level of one pixel is assumed. The descending curve shows the estimation error* ϵ_{est} *and the ascending curve shows the residual error* ϵ_{res}.

Error in both images. In this case, $N = 4n$ and $d = 2n + 8$. As before, assuming linearity of the tangent surface in the neighbourhood of the true measurement vector $\widehat{\mathbf{X}}$, result 5.2 gives the following expected errors.

$$\begin{aligned} \epsilon_{\text{res}} &= \sigma \left(\frac{n-4}{2n} \right)^{1/2} \\ \epsilon_{\text{est}} &= \sigma \left(\frac{n+4}{2n} \right)^{1/2} . \end{aligned} \tag{5.6}$$

Graphs of these errors as n varies are also shown in Figure 5.3.

An interesting observation to be made from this graph is that the asymptotic error with respect to the true values is $\sigma/\sqrt{2}$, and not 0 as in the case of error in one image. This result is expected, since in effect, one has two measurements of the position of each point, one in each image, related by the projective transformation. With two measurements of a point the variance in the estimate of the point position decreases by a factor of $\sqrt{2}$. By contrast, in the previous case where errors occur in one image only, one has one exact measurement for each point (i.e. in the first image). Thus, as the transformation $\mathtt{H}$ is estimated with greater and greater accuracy, the exact position of the point in the second image becomes known with uncertainty asymptotically approaching 0.

Mahalanobis distance. The formulae quoted above were derived under the assumption that the error distribution in measurement space was an isotropic Gaussian distribution, meaning that errors in each coordinate were independent. This assumption is not essential. We may assume any Gaussian distribution of error, with covariance matrix Σ. The formulae of result 5.2 remain true with ϵ being replaced with the expected Mahalanobis distance $E[\|\widehat{\mathbf{X}} - \mathbf{X}\|_{\Sigma}^{2}/N]^{1/2}$. The standard deviation σ also disappears, since it is taken care of by the Mahalanobis distance.

This follows from a simple change of coordinates in the measurement space $\mathbb{R}^N$ to make the covariance matrix equal to the identity. In this new coordinate frame, Mahalanobis distance becomes the same as Euclidean distance.

5.1.4 Determining the correct convergence of an algorithm

The relations given in (5.3) and (5.4) give a simple way of determining correct convergence of an estimation algorithm, without the need to determine the number of degrees of freedom of the problem. As seen in figure 5.2, the measurement space corresponding to the model specified by the parameter vector $\mathbf{P}$ forms a surface S_{M}. If near the noise-free data $\overline{\mathbf{X}}$ the surface is nearly planar, then it may be approximated by its tangent plane, and the three points $\widehat{\mathbf{X}}$, $\mathbf{X}$ and $\overline{\mathbf{X}}$ form a right-angled triangle. In most estimation problems this assumption of planarity will be very close to correct at the scale set by typical noise magnitude. In this case, the Pythagorean equality may be written as

$$\|\mathbf{X} - \overline{\mathbf{X}}\|^2 = \|\mathbf{X} - \widehat{\mathbf{X}}\|^2 + \|\overline{\mathbf{X}} - \widehat{\mathbf{X}}\|^2 \tag{5.7}$$

In evaluating an algorithm with synthetic data, this equality allows a simple test to see whether the algorithm has converged to the optimal value. If the estimated value $\widehat{\mathbf{X}}$ satisfies this equality, then it is a strong indication that the algorithm has found the true global minimum. Note that it is unnecessary in applying this test to determine the number of degrees of freedom of the problem. A few more properties are listed:

- This test can be used to determine on a run-by-run basis whether the algorithm has succeeded. Thus, with repeated runs, it allows an estimate of the percentage success rate for the algorithm.
- This test can only be used for synthetic data, or at least data for which the true measurements $\overline{\mathbf{X}}$ are known.
- The equality (5.7) depends on the assumption that the surface S_{M} consisting of valid measurements is locally planar. If the equality is not satisfied for a particular run of the estimation algorithm, then this is because the surface is not planar, or (far more likely) because the algorithm is failing to find the best solution.
- The test (5.7) is a test for the algorithm finding the global, not a local solution. If $\widehat{\mathbf{X}}$ settles to a local cost minimum, then the right-hand-side of (5.7) is likely to be much larger than the left-hand-side. The condition is unlikely to be satisfied entirely by chance if the algorithm finds the incorrect point $\widehat{\mathbf{X}}$.

5.2 Covariance of the estimated transformation

In the previous section the ML estimate was considered, and how its expected average error may be computed. Comparing the achieved residual error or estimation error of an algorithm against the ML error is a good way of evaluating the performance of a particular estimation algorithm, since it compares the results of the algorithm against the best that may be achieved (the optimum estimate) in the absence of any other prior information.

Nevertheless, the chief concern is how accurately the transformation itself has been computed. The uncertainty of the estimated transformation depends on many factors, including the number of points used to compute it, the accuracy of the given point matches, as well as the configuration of the points in question. To illustrate the importance of the configuration suppose the points used to compute the transformation are close to a degenerate configuration; then the transformation may not be computed with great accuracy. For instance, if the transformation is computed from a set of points that lie close to a straight line, then the behaviour of the transformation in the dimension perpendicular to that line is not accurately determined. Thus, whereas the achievable residual error and estimation error were seen to be dependent only on the number of point correspondences and their accuracy, by contrast, the accuracy of the computed transformation is dependent on the particular points. The uncertainty of the computed transformation is conveniently captured in the *covariance matrix* of the transformation. Since $\mathtt{H}$ is a matrix with 9 entries, its covariance matrix will be a 9×9 matrix. In this section it will be seen how this covariance matrix may be computed.

5.2.1 Forward propagation of covariance

The covariance matrix behaves in a pleasantly simple manner under affine transformations, as described in the following theorem.

Result 5.3. *Let* $\mathbf{v}$ *be a random vector in* $\mathbb{R}^M$ *with mean* $\bar{\mathbf{v}}$ *and covariance matrix* Σ, *and suppose that* $f : \mathbb{R}^M \rightarrow \mathbb{R}^N$ *is an affine mapping defined by* $f(\mathbf{v}) = f(\bar{\mathbf{v}}) + \mathtt{A}(\mathbf{v} - \bar{\mathbf{v}})$. *Then* $f(\mathbf{v})$ *is a random variable with mean* $f(\bar{\mathbf{v}})$ *and covariance matrix* $\mathtt{A}\Sigma\mathtt{A}^\mathsf{T}$.

Note that it is not assumed that $\mathtt{A}$ is a square matrix. Instead of giving a proof of this theorem, we give an example.

Example 5.4. Let x and y be independent random variables with mean 0 and standard deviations of 1 and 2 respectively. What are the mean and standard deviation of $x' = f(x, y) = 3x + 2y - 7$?

The mean is $\bar{x}' = f(0, 0) = -7$. Next we compute the variance of x'. In this case, Σ is the matrix $\begin{bmatrix} 1 & 0 \\ 0 & 4 \end{bmatrix}$ and $\mathtt{A}$ is the matrix $[3\ 2]$. Thus, the variance of x' is $\mathtt{A}\Sigma\mathtt{A}^\mathsf{T} = 25$. Thus $3x + 2y - 7$ has standard deviation 5. △

Example 5.5. Let $x' = 3x + 2y$ and $y' = 3x - 2y$. Find the covariance matrix of (x', y'), given that x and y have the same distribution as before.

In this case, the matrix $\mathtt{A} = \begin{bmatrix} 3 & 2 \\ 3 & -2 \end{bmatrix}$. One computes $\mathtt{A}\Sigma\mathtt{A}^\mathsf{T} = \begin{bmatrix} 25 & -7 \\ -7 & 25 \end{bmatrix}$. Thus, one sees that both x' and y' have variance 25 (standard deviation 5), whereas x' and y' are negatively correlated, with covariance $E[x'y'] = -7$. △

Non-linear propagation. If $\mathbf{v}$ is a random vector in $\mathbb{R}^M$ and $f : \mathbb{R}^M \rightarrow \mathbb{R}^N$ is a non-linear function acting on $\mathbf{v}$, then we may compute an approximation to the mean and covariance of $f(\mathbf{v})$ by assuming that f is approximately affine in the vicinity of the mean of the distribution. The affine approximation to f is $f(\mathbf{v}) \approx f(\bar{\mathbf{v}}) + \mathtt{J}(\mathbf{v} - \bar{\mathbf{v}})$, where $\mathtt{J}$ is the partial derivative (Jacobian) matrix $\partial f / \partial \mathbf{v}$ evaluated at $\bar{\mathbf{v}}$. Note that $\mathtt{J}$ has dimension $N \times M$. Then we have the following result.

Result 5.6. *Let* $\mathbf{v}$ *be a random vector in* $\mathbb{R}^M$ *with mean* $\bar{\mathbf{v}}$ *and covariance matrix* Σ, *and let $f : \mathbb{R}^M \rightarrow \mathbb{R}^N$ be differentiable in a neighbourhood of $\bar{\mathbf{v}}$. Then up to a first-order approximation, $f(\mathbf{v})$ is a random variable with mean $f(\bar{\mathbf{v}})$ and covariance $\mathtt{J}\Sigma\mathtt{J}^\mathsf{T}$, where $\mathtt{J}$ is the Jacobian matrix of f, evaluated at $\bar{\mathbf{v}}$.*

The extent to which this result gives a good approximation to the actual mean and variance of $f(\bar{\mathbf{v}})$ depends on how closely the function f is approximated by a linear function in a region about $\bar{\mathbf{v}}$ commensurate in size with the support of the probability distribution of $\mathbf{v}$.

Example 5.7. Let $\mathbf{x} = (x, y)^\mathsf{T}$ be a Gaussian random vector with mean $(0, 0)^\mathsf{T}$ and covariance matrix $\sigma^2\text{diag}(1, 4)$. Let $x' = f(x, y) = x^2 + 3x - 2y + 5$. Then one may compute the true values of the mean and standard deviation of $f(x, y)$ according to the formulae

$$\begin{aligned}\bar{x}' &= \int\int_{-\infty}^{\infty} P(x,y)f(x,y)dxdy \\ \sigma_{x'}^2 &= \int\int_{-\infty}^{\infty} P(x,y)(f(x,y) - \bar{x}')^2 dxdy\end{aligned}$$

where

$$P(x, y) = \frac{1}{4\pi\sigma^2} e^{-(x^2+y^2/4)/2\sigma^2}$$

is the Gaussian probability distribution (A2.1–*p*565). One obtains

$$\begin{aligned}\bar{x}' &= 5 + \sigma^2 \\ \sigma_{x'}^2 &= 25\sigma^2 + 2\sigma^4.\end{aligned}$$

Applying the approximation given by result 5.6, and noting that $\mathtt{J} = [3 \ \ -2]$, we find that the estimated values are

$$\begin{aligned}\bar{x}' &= 5 \\ \sigma_{x'}^2 &= \sigma^2[3 \ \ -2]\begin{bmatrix} 1 & \\ & 4 \end{bmatrix}[3 \ \ -2]^\mathsf{T} = 25\sigma^2.\end{aligned}$$

Thus, as long as σ is small, this is a close approximation to the correct values of the mean and variance of x'. The following table shows the true and approximated values for the mean and standard deviation of $f(x, y)$ for two different values of σ.

	$\sigma = 0.25$		$\sigma = 0.5$	
	$\bar{x}'$	$\sigma_{x'}$	$\bar{x}'$	$\sigma_{x'}$
estimate	5.0000	1.25000	5.00	2.5000
true	5.0625	1.25312	5.25	2.5249

For reference, in the case $\sigma = 0.25$, one sees that as long as $|x| < 2\sigma$ (about 95% of the total distribution) the value $f(x, y) = x^2 + 3x - 2y + 5$ differs from its linear approximation $3x - 2y + 5$ by no more than $x^2 < 0.25$. $\triangle$

Example 5.8. More generally, assuming that x and y are independent zero-mean Gaussian random variables, one may compute that for the function $f(x,y) = ax^2 + bxy + cy^2 + dx + ey + f$,

$$\begin{aligned} \text{mean} &= a\sigma_x^2 + c\sigma_y^2 + f \\ \text{variance} &= 2a^2\sigma_x^4 + b^2\sigma_x^2\sigma_y^2 + 2c^2\sigma_y^4 + d^2\sigma_x^2 + e^2\sigma_y^2 \end{aligned}$$

which are close to the estimated values mean $= f$, variance $= d^2\sigma_x^2 + e^2\sigma_y^2$ as long as σ_x and σ_y are small. △

5.2.2 Backward propagation of covariance

The material in this and the following section 5.2.3 is more advanced. The examples in section 5.2.4 show the straightforward application of the results of these sections, and can be read first.

Consider a differentiable mapping f from a "parameter space", $\mathbb{R}^M$ to a "measurement space" $\mathbb{R}^N$, and let a Gaussian probability distribution be defined on $\mathbb{R}^N$ with covariance matrix Σ. Let S_{M} be the image of the mapping f. We assume that $M < N$ and that S_{M} has the same dimension M as the parameter space $\mathbb{R}^M$. Thus we are not considering the over-parametrized case at present. A vector $\mathbf{P}$ in $\mathbb{R}^M$ represents a parametrization of the point $f(\mathbf{P})$ on S_{M}. Finding the point on S_{M} closest in Mahalanobis distance to a given point $\mathbf{X}$ in $\mathbb{R}^N$ defines a map from $\mathbb{R}^N$ to the surface S_{M}. We call this mapping $\eta : \mathbb{R}^N \rightarrow S_{\mathrm{M}}$. Now, f is by assumption invertible on the surface S_{M}, and we define $f^{-1} : S_{\mathrm{M}} \rightarrow \mathbb{R}^M$ to be the inverse function.

By composing the map $\eta : \mathbb{R}^N \rightarrow S_{\mathrm{M}}$ and $f^{-1} : S_{\mathrm{M}} \rightarrow \mathbb{R}^M$ we have a mapping $f^{-1} \circ \eta : \mathbb{R}^N \rightarrow \mathbb{R}^M$. This mapping assigns to a measurement vector $\mathbf{X}$, the set of parameters $\mathbf{P}$ corresponding to the ML estimate $\widehat{\mathbf{X}}$. In principle we may propagate the covariance of the probability distribution in the measurement space $\mathbb{R}^N$ to compute a covariance matrix for the set of parameters $\mathbf{P}$ corresponding to ML estimation. Our goal is to apply result 5.3 or result 5.6.

We consider first the case where the mapping f is an affine mapping from $\mathbb{R}^M$ into $\mathbb{R}^N$. We will show next that the mapping $f^{-1} \circ \eta$ is also an affine mapping, and a specific form will be given for $f^{-1} \circ \eta$, thereby allowing us to apply result 5.3 to compute the covariance of the estimated parameters $\widehat{\mathbf{P}} = f^{-1} \circ \eta(\mathbf{X})$.

Since f is affine, we may write $f(\mathbf{P}) = f(\overline{\mathbf{P}}) + \mathtt{J}(\mathbf{P} - \overline{\mathbf{P}})$, where $f(\overline{\mathbf{P}}) = \overline{\mathbf{X}}$ is the mean of the probability distribution on $\mathbb{R}^N$. Since we are assuming that the surface $S_{\mathrm{M}} = f(\mathbb{R}^M)$ has dimension M, the rank of $\mathtt{J}$ is equal to its column dimension. Given a measurement vector $\mathbf{X}$, the ML estimate $\widehat{\mathbf{X}}$ minimizes $\|\mathbf{X} - \widehat{\mathbf{X}}\|_\Sigma = \|\mathbf{X} - f(\widehat{\mathbf{P}})\|_\Sigma$. Thus, we seek $\widehat{\mathbf{P}}$ to minimize this latter quantity. However,

$$\|\mathbf{X} - f(\widehat{\mathbf{P}})\|_\Sigma = \|(\mathbf{X} - \overline{\mathbf{X}}) - \mathtt{J}(\widehat{\mathbf{P}} - \overline{\mathbf{P}})\|_\Sigma$$

and this is minimized (see (A5.2–*p*591) in section A5.2.1(*p*591)) when

$$(\widehat{\mathbf{P}} - \overline{\mathbf{P}}) = (\mathtt{J}^\mathsf{T}\Sigma^{-1}\mathtt{J})^{-1}\mathtt{J}^\mathsf{T}\Sigma^{-1}(\mathbf{X} - \overline{\mathbf{X}}) \ .$$

Writing $\overline{\mathbf{P}} = f^{-1}\overline{\mathbf{X}}$ and $\widehat{\mathbf{P}} = f^{-1}\widehat{\mathbf{X}}$, we see that

$$\begin{aligned} f^{-1} \circ \eta(\mathbf{X}) &= \widehat{\mathbf{P}} \\ &= (\mathtt{J}^\mathsf{T}\Sigma^{-1}\mathtt{J})^{-1}\mathtt{J}^\mathsf{T}\Sigma^{-1}(\mathbf{X} - \overline{\mathbf{X}}) + f^{-1}(\overline{\mathbf{X}}) \\ &= (\mathtt{J}^\mathsf{T}\Sigma^{-1}\mathtt{J})^{-1}\mathtt{J}^\mathsf{T}\Sigma^{-1}(\mathbf{X} - \overline{\mathbf{X}}) + f^{-1} \circ \eta(\overline{\mathbf{X}}) \ . \end{aligned}$$

This shows that $f^{-1} \circ \eta$ is affine and $(\mathtt{J}^\mathsf{T}\Sigma^{-1}\mathtt{J})^{-1}\mathtt{J}^\mathsf{T}\Sigma^{-1}$ is its linear part. Applying result 5.3, we see that the covariance matrix for $\widehat{\mathbf{P}}$ is

$$\begin{aligned} \left[(\mathtt{J}^\mathsf{T}\Sigma^{-1}\mathtt{J})^{-1}\mathtt{J}^\mathsf{T}\Sigma^{-1}\right]\Sigma\left[(\mathtt{J}^\mathsf{T}\Sigma^{-1}\mathtt{J})^{-1}\mathtt{J}^\mathsf{T}\Sigma^{-1}\right]^\mathsf{T} &= (\mathtt{J}^\mathsf{T}\Sigma^{-1}\mathtt{J})^{-1}\mathtt{J}^\mathsf{T}\Sigma^{-1}\Sigma\Sigma^{-1}\mathtt{J}(\mathtt{J}^\mathsf{T}\Sigma^{-1}\mathtt{J})^{-1} \\ &= (\mathtt{J}^\mathsf{T}\Sigma^{-1}\mathtt{J})^{-1}, \end{aligned}$$

recalling that Σ is symmetric. We have proved the following theorem.

Result 5.9 Backward transport of covariance – affine case. *Let $f : \mathbb{R}^M \rightarrow \mathbb{R}^N$ be an affine mapping of the form $f(\mathbf{P}) = f(\overline{\mathbf{P}}) + \mathtt{J}(\mathbf{P} - \overline{\mathbf{P}})$, where $\mathtt{J}$ has rank M. Let $\mathbf{X}$ be a random variable in $\mathbb{R}^N$ with mean $\overline{\mathbf{X}} = f(\overline{\mathbf{P}})$ and covariance matrix Σ. Let $f^{-1} \circ \eta : \mathbb{R}^N \rightarrow \mathbb{R}^M$ be the mapping that maps a measurement $\mathbf{X}$ to the set of parameters corresponding to the ML estimate $\widehat{\mathbf{X}}$. Then $\widehat{\mathbf{P}} = f^{-1} \circ \eta(\mathbf{X})$ is a random variable with mean $\overline{\mathbf{P}}$ and covariance matrix*

$$\Sigma_\mathbf{P} = (\mathtt{J}^\mathsf{T}\Sigma_\mathbf{X}^{-1}\mathtt{J})^{-1}. \tag{5.8}$$

In the case where f is not affine, an approximation to the mean and covariance may be obtained by approximating f by an affine function in the usual way, as follows.

Result 5.10 Backward transport of covariance – non-linear case. *Let $f : \mathbb{R}^M \rightarrow \mathbb{R}^N$ be a differentiable mapping and let $\mathtt{J}$ be its Jacobian matrix evaluated at a point $\overline{\mathbf{P}}$. Suppose that $\mathtt{J}$ has rank M. Then f is one-to-one in a neighbourhood of $\overline{\mathbf{P}}$. Let $\mathbf{X}$ be a random variable in $\mathbb{R}^N$ with mean $\overline{\mathbf{X}} = f(\overline{\mathbf{P}})$ and covariance matrix $\Sigma_\mathbf{X}$. Let $f^{-1} \circ \eta : \mathbb{R}^N \rightarrow \mathbb{R}^M$ be the mapping that maps a measurement $\mathbf{X}$ to the set of parameters corresponding to the ML estimate $\widehat{\mathbf{X}}$. Then to first-order, $\widehat{\mathbf{P}} = f^{-1} \circ \eta(\mathbf{X})$ is a random variable with mean $\overline{\mathbf{P}}$ and covariance matrix $(\mathtt{J}^\mathsf{T}\Sigma_\mathbf{X}^{-1}\mathtt{J})^{-1}$.*

5.2.3 Over-parametrization

One may generalize result 5.9 and result 5.10 to the case of redundant sets of parameters – the over-parametrized case. In this case, the mapping f from the parameter space $\mathbb{R}^M$ to measurement space $\mathbb{R}^N$ is not locally one-to-one. For instance, in the case of estimating a 2D homography as discussed in section 4.5(p110) there is a mapping $f(\mathbf{P})$ where $\mathbf{P}$ is a 9-vector representing the entries of the homography matrix $\mathtt{H}$. Since the homography has only 8 degrees of freedom, the mapping f is not one-to-one. In particular, for any constant k, the matrix $k\mathtt{H}$ represents the same map, and so the image coordinate vectors $f(\mathbf{P})$ and $f(k\mathbf{P})$ are equal.

In the general case of a mapping $f : \mathbb{R}^M \rightarrow \mathbb{R}^N$ the Jacobian matrix $\mathtt{J}$ does not have full rank M, but rather a smaller rank $d < M$. This rank d is called the number of *essential parameters*. The matrix $\mathtt{J}^\mathsf{T}\Sigma_\mathbf{X}^{-1}\mathtt{J}$ in this case has dimension M but rank

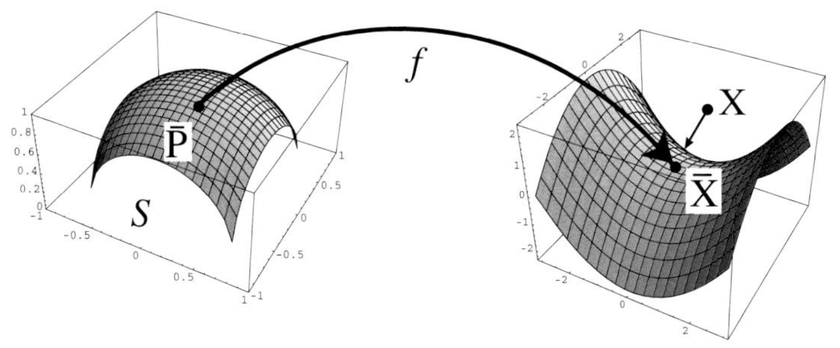

Fig. 5.4. **Back propagation (over-parametrized).** *Mapping f maps constrained parameter surface to measurement space. A measurement $\mathbf{X}$ is mapped (by a mapping η) to the closest point on the surface $f(S_\mathrm{P})$ and then back via f^{-1} to the parameter space, providing the ML estimate of the parameters. The covariance of $\mathbf{X}$ is transferred via $f^{-1} \circ \eta$ to a covariance of the parameters.*

$d < M$. The formula (5.8), $\Sigma_\mathbf{P} = (\mathtt{J}^\mathsf{T}\Sigma_\mathbf{X}^{-1}\mathtt{J})^{-1}$, clearly does not hold, since the matrix on the right side is not invertible.

In fact, it is clear that without any further restriction, the elements of the estimated vector $\widehat{\mathbf{P}}$ may vary without bound, namely through multiplication by an arbitrary constant k. Hence the elements have infinite variance. It is usual to restrict the estimated homography matrix $\mathtt{H}$ or more generally the parameter vector $\mathbf{P}$ by imposing some constraint. The usual constraint is that $\|\mathbf{P}\| = 1$ though other constraints are possible, such as demanding that the last parameter should equal 1 (see section 4.4.2(p105)). Thus, the parameter vector $\mathbf{P}$ is constrained to lie on a surface in the parameter space $\mathbb{R}^9$, or generally $\mathbb{R}^M$. In the first case the surface $\|\mathbf{P}\| = 1$ is the unit sphere in $\mathbb{R}^M$. The constraint $P_m = 1$ represents a plane in $\mathbb{R}^M$. In the general case we may assume that the estimated vector $\mathbf{P}$ lies on some submanifold of $\mathbb{R}^M$ as in the following theorem.

Result 5.11. Backward transport of covariance – over-parametrized case. *Let $f : \mathbb{R}^M \rightarrow \mathbb{R}^N$ be a differentiable mapping taking a parameter vector $\overline{\mathbf{P}}$ to a measurement vector $\overline{\mathbf{X}}$. Let S_P be a smooth manifold of dimension d embedded in $\mathbb{R}^M$ passing through point $\overline{\mathbf{P}}$, and such that the map f is one-to-one on the manifold S_P in a neighbourhood of $\overline{\mathbf{P}}$, mapping S_P locally to a manifold $f(S_\mathrm{P})$ in $\mathbb{R}^N$. The function f has a local inverse, denoted f^{-1}, restricted to the surface $f(S_\mathrm{P})$ in a neighbourhood of $\overline{\mathbf{X}}$. Let a Gaussian distribution on $\mathbb{R}^N$ be defined with mean $\overline{\mathbf{X}}$ and covariance matrix $\Sigma_\mathbf{X}$ and let $\eta : \mathbb{R}^N \rightarrow f(S_\mathrm{P})$ be the mapping that takes a point in $\mathbb{R}^N$ to the closest point on $f(S_\mathrm{P})$ with respect to Mahalanobis norm $\| \cdot \|_{\Sigma_\mathbf{X}}$. Via $f^{-1} \circ \eta$ the probability distribution on $\mathbb{R}^N$ with covariance matrix $\Sigma_\mathbf{X}$ induces a probability distribution on $\mathbb{R}^M$ with covariance matrix, to first-order equal to*

$$\Sigma_\mathbf{P} = (\mathtt{J}^\mathsf{T}\Sigma_\mathbf{X}^{-1}\mathtt{J})^{+\mathtt{A}} = \mathtt{A}(\mathtt{A}^\mathsf{T}\mathtt{J}^\mathsf{T}\Sigma_\mathbf{X}^{-1}\mathtt{J}\mathtt{A})^{-1}\mathtt{A}^\mathsf{T} \tag{5.9}$$

where $\mathtt{A}$ is any $m \times d$ matrix whose column vectors span the tangent space to S_P at $\overline{\mathbf{P}}$.

This is illustrated in figure 5.4. The notation $(\mathtt{J}^\mathsf{T}\Sigma_\mathbf{X}^{-1}\mathtt{J})^{+\mathtt{A}}$, defined by (5.9), is discussed further in section A5.2(p590).

Proof. The proof of result 5.11 is straightforward. Let d be the number of essential parameters. One defines a map $g : \mathbb{R}^d \to \mathbb{R}^M$ mapping an open neighbourhood U in $\mathbb{R}^d$ to an open set of S_P containing the point $\overline{\mathbf{P}}$. Then the combined mapping $f \circ g : \mathbb{R}^d \to \mathbb{R}^N$ is one-to-one on the neighbourhood U. Let us denote the partial derivative matrices of f by $\mathtt{J}$ and of g by $\mathtt{A}$. The matrix of partial derivatives of $f \circ g$ is then $\mathtt{JA}$. Result 5.10 now applies, and one sees that the probability distribution function with covariance matrix Σ on $\mathbb{R}^N$ may be transported backwards to a covariance matrix $(\mathtt{A}^\mathsf{T}\mathtt{J}^\mathsf{T}\Sigma^{-1}\mathtt{JA})^{-1}$ on $\mathbb{R}^d$. Transporting this forwards again to $\mathbb{R}^M$, applying result 5.6, we arrive at the covariance matrix $\mathtt{A}(\mathtt{A}^\mathsf{T}\mathtt{J}^\mathsf{T}\Sigma^{-1}\mathtt{JA})^{-1}\mathtt{A}^\mathsf{T}$ on S_P. This matrix, which will be denoted here by $(\mathtt{J}^\mathsf{T}\Sigma^{-1}\mathtt{J})^{+\mathtt{A}}$, is related to the pseudo-inverse of $(\mathtt{J}^\mathsf{T}\Sigma^{-1}\mathtt{J})$ as defined in section A5.2(*p*590). The expression (5.9) is not dependent on the particular choice of the matrix $\mathtt{A}$ as long as the column span of $\mathtt{A}$ is unchanged. In particular, if $\mathtt{A}$ is replaced by $\mathtt{AB}$ for any invertible $d \times d$ matrix $\mathtt{B}$, then the value of (5.9) does not change. Thus, any matrix $\mathtt{A}$ whose columns span the tangent space of S_P at $\overline{\mathbf{P}}$ will do. □

Note that the proof gives a specific way of computing a matrix $\mathtt{A}$ spanning the tangent space – namely the Jacobian matrix of g. In many instances, as we will see, there are easier ways of finding $\mathtt{A}$. Note that the covariance matrix (5.9) is singular. In particular, it has dimension M and rank $d < M$. This is because the variance of the estimated parameter set in directions orthogonal to the constraint surface S_P is zero – there can be no variation in that direction. Note that whereas $\mathtt{J}^\mathsf{T}\Sigma^{-1}\mathtt{J}$ is non-invertible, the $d \times d$ matrix $\mathtt{A}^\mathsf{T}\mathtt{J}^\mathsf{T}\Sigma^{-1}\mathtt{JA}$ has rank d and is invertible.

An important case occurs when the constraint surface is locally orthogonal to the null-space of the Jacobian matrix. Denote by $N_L(\mathtt{X})$ the left null-space of matrix $\mathtt{X}$, namely the space of all vectors $\mathbf{x}$ such that $\mathbf{x}^\mathsf{T}\mathtt{X} = \mathbf{0}$. Then (as shown in section A5.2-(*p*590)), the *pseudo-inverse* $\mathtt{X}^+$ is given by

$$\mathtt{X}^+ = \mathtt{X}^{+\mathtt{A}} = \mathtt{A}(\mathtt{A}^\mathsf{T}\mathtt{XA})^{-1}\mathtt{A}^\mathsf{T}$$

if and only if $N_L(\mathtt{A}) = N_L(\mathtt{X})$. The following result then derives directly from result 5.11.

Result 5.12. *Let $f : \mathbb{R}^M \to \mathbb{R}^N$ be a differentiable mapping taking $\overline{\mathbf{P}}$ to $\overline{\mathbf{X}}$, and let $\mathtt{J}$ be the Jacobian matrix of f. Let a Gaussian distribution on $\mathbb{R}^N$ be defined at $\overline{\mathbf{X}}$ with covariance matrix $\Sigma_\mathbf{X}$ and let $f^{-1} \circ \eta : \mathbb{R}^N \to \mathbb{R}^M$ as in result 5.11 be the mapping taking a measurement $\mathbf{X}$ to the MLE parameter vector $\mathtt{P}$ constrained to lie on a surface S_P locally orthogonal to the null-space of $\mathtt{J}$. Then $f^{-1} \circ \eta$ induces a distribution on $\mathbb{R}^M$ with covariance matrix, to first-order equal to*

$$\Sigma_\mathbf{P} = (\mathtt{J}^\mathsf{T}\Sigma_\mathbf{X}^{-1}\mathtt{J})^+. \tag{5.10}$$

Note that the restriction that $\mathbf{P}$ be constrained to lie on a surface locally orthogonal to the null-space of $\mathtt{J}$ is in many cases the natural constraint. For instance, if $\mathbf{P}$ is a *homogeneous* parameter vector (such as the entries of a homogeneous matrix), the restriction is satisfied for the usual constraint $\|\mathbf{P}\| = 1$. In such a case, the constraint surface is the unit sphere, and the tangent plane at any point is perpendicular to the parameter vector. On the other hand, since $\mathtt{P}$ is a homogeneous vector, the function

$f(\mathtt{P})$ is invariant to changes of scale, and so J has a null-vector in the radial direction, thus perpendicular to the constraint surface.

In other cases, it is often not critical what restriction we place on the parameter set for the purpose of computing the covariance matrix of the parameters. In addition, since the pseudo-inversion operation is its own inverse, we can retrieve the original matrix from its pseudo-inverse, according to $\mathtt{J}^\mathsf{T}\Sigma_{\mathbf{X}}^{-1}\mathtt{J} = \Sigma_{\mathbf{P}}^{+}$. One can then compute the covariance matrix corresponding to any other subspace, according to

$$(\mathtt{J}^\mathsf{T}\Sigma_{\mathbf{X}}^{-1}\mathtt{J})^{+\mathtt{A}} = (\Sigma_{\mathbf{P}}^{+})^{+\mathtt{A}}$$

where the columns of A span the constrained subspace of parameter space.

5.2.4 Application and examples

Error in one image. Let us consider the application of this theory to the problem of finding the covariance of an estimated 2D homography H. First, we look at the case where the error is limited to the second image. The 3×3 matrix H is represented by a 9-dimensional parameter vector which will be denoted by $\mathbf{h}$ instead of $\mathbf{P}$ so as to remind us that it is made up of the entries of H. The covariance of the estimated $\hat{\mathbf{h}}$ is a 9×9 symmetric matrix. We are given a set of matched points $\bar{\mathbf{x}}_i \leftrightarrow \mathbf{x}'_i$. The points $\bar{\mathbf{x}}_i$ are fixed true values, and the points $\mathbf{x}'_i$ are considered as random variables subject to Gaussian noise with variance σ^2 in each component, or if desired, with a more general covariance. The function $f : \mathbb{R}^9 \rightarrow \mathbb{R}^{2n}$ is defined as mapping a 9-vector $\mathbf{h}$ representing a matrix H to the $2n$-vector made up of the coordinates of the points $\mathbf{x}'_i = \mathtt{H}\bar{\mathbf{x}}_i$. The coordinates of $\mathbf{x}'_i$ make up a composite vector in $\mathbb{R}^N$, which we denote by $\mathbf{X}'$. As we have seen, as $\mathbf{h}$ varies, the point $f(\mathbf{h})$ traces out an 8-dimensional surface S_{P} in $\mathbb{R}^{2n}$. Each point $\mathbf{X}'$ on the surface represents a set of points $\mathbf{x}'_i$ consistent with the first-image points $\bar{\mathbf{x}}_i$. Given a vector of measurements $\mathbf{X}'$, one selects the closest point $\hat{\mathbf{X}}'$ on the surface S_{P} with respect to Mahalanobis distance. The pre-image $\hat{\mathbf{h}} = f^{-1}(\hat{\mathbf{X}}')$, subject to constraint $\|\mathbf{h}\| = 1$, represents the estimated homography matrix $\hat{\mathtt{H}}$, estimated using the ML estimator. From the probability distribution of values of $\mathbf{X}'$ one wishes to derive the distribution of the estimated $\hat{\mathbf{h}}$. The covariance matrix $\Sigma_{\mathbf{h}}$ is given by result 5.12. This covariance matrix corresponds to the constraint $\|\mathbf{h}\| = 1$.

Thus, a procedure for computing the covariance matrix of the estimated transformation is as follows.

(i) Estimate the transformation $\hat{\mathtt{H}}$ from the given data.
(ii) Compute the Jacobian matrix $\mathtt{J}_f = \partial\mathbf{X}'/\partial\mathbf{h}$, evaluated at $\hat{\mathbf{h}}$.
(iii) The covariance matrix of the estimated $\mathbf{h}$ is given by (5.10): $\Sigma_{\mathbf{h}} = (\mathtt{J}_f^\mathsf{T}\Sigma_{\mathbf{X}'}^{-1}\mathtt{J}_f)^+$.

We investigate the two last steps of this method in slightly more detail.

Computation of the derivative matrix. Consider first the Jacobian matrix $\mathtt{J} = \partial\mathbf{X}'/\partial\mathbf{h}$. This matrix has a natural decomposition into blocks so that $\mathtt{J} = (\mathtt{J}_1^\mathsf{T}, \mathtt{J}_2^\mathsf{T}, \ldots, \mathtt{J}_i^\mathsf{T}, \ldots, \mathtt{J}_n^\mathsf{T})^\mathsf{T}$ where $\mathtt{J}_i = \partial\mathbf{x}'_i/\partial\mathbf{h}$. A formula for $\partial\mathbf{x}'_i/\partial\mathbf{h}$ is given in

(4.21–*p*129):

$$\mathtt{J}_i = \partial \mathbf{x}'_i / \partial \mathbf{h} = \frac{1}{w'_i} \begin{bmatrix} \tilde{\mathbf{x}}_i^{\mathsf{T}} & \mathbf{0}^{\mathsf{T}} & -x'_i \tilde{\mathbf{x}}_i^{\mathsf{T}} \\ \mathbf{0}^{\mathsf{T}} & \tilde{\mathbf{x}}_i^{\mathsf{T}} & -y'_i \tilde{\mathbf{x}}_i^{\mathsf{T}} \end{bmatrix} \tag{5.11}$$

where $\tilde{\mathbf{x}}_i^{\mathsf{T}}$ represents the vector $(x_i, y_i, 1)$.

Stacking these matrices on top of each other for all points $\mathbf{x}_i$ gives the derivative matrix $\partial \mathbf{X}' / \partial \mathbf{h}$. An important case is when the image measurements $\mathbf{x}'_i$ are independent random vectors. In this case $\Sigma = \operatorname{diag}(\Sigma_1, \ldots, \Sigma_n)$ where each Σ_i is the 2×2 covariance matrix of the i-th measured point $\mathbf{x}'_i$. Then one computes

$$\Sigma_{\mathbf{h}} = (\mathtt{J}^{\mathsf{T}} \Sigma_{\mathbf{X}'}^{-1} \mathtt{J})^{+} = \left(\sum_i \mathtt{J}_i^{\mathsf{T}} \Sigma_i^{-1} \mathtt{J}_i \right)^{+} . \tag{5.12}$$

Example 5.13. We consider the simple numerical example of a point correspondence containing just 4 points as follows:

$$\begin{aligned} \mathbf{x}_1 = (1, 0)^{\mathsf{T}} &\leftrightarrow (1, 0)^{\mathsf{T}} = \mathbf{x}'_1 \\ \mathbf{x}_2 = (0, 1)^{\mathsf{T}} &\leftrightarrow (0, 1)^{\mathsf{T}} = \mathbf{x}'_2 \\ \mathbf{x}_3 = (-1, 0)^{\mathsf{T}} &\leftrightarrow (-1, 0)^{\mathsf{T}} = \mathbf{x}'_3 \\ \mathbf{x}_4 = (0, -1)^{\mathsf{T}} &\leftrightarrow (0, -1)^{\mathsf{T}} = \mathbf{x}'_4 \end{aligned}$$

namely, the identity map on the points of a projective basis. We assume that points $\mathbf{x}_i$ are known exactly, and points $\mathbf{x}'_i$ have one pixel standard deviation in each coordinate direction. This means that the covariance matrix $\Sigma_{\mathbf{x}'_i}$ is the identity.

Obviously, the computed homography will be the identity map. For simplicity we normalize (scale it) so that it is indeed the identity matrix, and hence $\|\mathtt{H}\|^2 = 3$ instead of the usual normalization $\|\mathtt{H}\| = 1$. In this case, all the w'_i in (5.11) are equal to 1. The matrix $\mathtt{J}$ is easily computed from (5.11) to equal

$$\mathtt{J} = \left[\begin{array}{ccc|ccc|ccc} 1 & 0 & 1 & 0 & 0 & 0 & -1 & 0 & -1 \\ 0 & 0 & 0 & 1 & 0 & 1 & 0 & 0 & 0 \\ \hline 0 & 1 & 1 & 0 & 0 & 0 & 0 & 0 & 0 \\ 0 & 0 & 0 & 0 & 1 & 1 & 0 & -1 & -1 \\ \hline -1 & 0 & 1 & 0 & 0 & 0 & -1 & 0 & 1 \\ 0 & 0 & 0 & -1 & 0 & 1 & 0 & 0 & 0 \\ \hline 0 & -1 & 1 & 0 & 0 & 0 & 0 & 0 & 0 \\ 0 & 0 & 0 & 0 & -1 & 1 & 0 & -1 & 1 \end{array} \right] .$$

Then

$$\mathtt{J}^{\mathsf{T}}\mathtt{J} = \left[\begin{array}{ccc|ccc|ccc} 2 & 0 & 0 & 0 & 0 & 0 & 0 & 0 & -2 \\ 0 & 2 & 0 & 0 & 0 & 0 & 0 & 0 & 0 \\ 0 & 0 & 4 & 0 & 0 & 0 & -2 & 0 & 0 \\ \hline 0 & 0 & 0 & 2 & 0 & 0 & 0 & 0 & 0 \\ 0 & 0 & 0 & 0 & 2 & 0 & 0 & 0 & -2 \\ 0 & 0 & 0 & 0 & 0 & 4 & 0 & -2 & 0 \\ \hline 0 & 0 & -2 & 0 & 0 & 0 & 2 & 0 & 0 \\ 0 & 0 & 0 & 0 & 0 & -2 & 0 & 2 & 0 \\ -2 & 0 & 0 & 0 & -2 & 0 & 0 & 0 & 4 \end{array} \right] . \tag{5.13}$$

To take the pseudo-inverse of this matrix, we may use (5.9) where $\mathtt{A}$ is a matrix with columns spanning the tangent plane to the constraint surface. Since $\mathtt{H}$ is computed subject to the condition $\|\mathtt{H}\|^2 = 3$, which represents a hypersphere, the constraint surface is perpendicular to the vector $\mathbf{h}$ corresponding to the computed homography $\mathtt{H}$. A Householder matrix $\mathtt{A}$ (see section A4.1.2(p580)) corresponding to the vector $\mathbf{h}$ has the property that $\mathtt{A}\mathbf{h} = (0, \ldots, 0, 1)^\mathsf{T}$, so the first 8 columns of $\mathtt{A}$ (denoted $\mathtt{A}_1$)are perpendicular to $\mathbf{h}$ as required. This allows the pseudo-inverse to be computed exactly without using SVD. Applying (5.9) the pseudo-inverse is computed to be

$$\Sigma_\mathbf{h} = (\mathtt{J}^\mathsf{T}\mathtt{J})^{+\mathtt{A}_1} = \mathtt{A}_1(\mathtt{A}_1^\mathsf{T}(\mathtt{J}^\mathsf{T}\mathtt{J})\mathtt{A}_1)^{-1}\mathtt{A}_1^\mathsf{T} = \frac{1}{18}\left[\begin{array}{ccc|ccc|ccc} 5 & 0 & 0 & 0 & -4 & 0 & 0 & 0 & -1 \\ 0 & 9 & 0 & 0 & 0 & 0 & 0 & 0 & 0 \\ 0 & 0 & 9 & 0 & 0 & 0 & 9 & 0 & 0 \\ \hline 0 & 0 & 0 & 9 & 0 & 0 & 0 & 0 & 0 \\ -4 & 0 & 0 & 0 & 5 & 0 & 0 & 0 & -1 \\ 0 & 0 & 0 & 0 & 0 & 9 & 0 & 9 & 0 \\ \hline 0 & 0 & 9 & 0 & 0 & 0 & 18 & 0 & 0 \\ 0 & 0 & 0 & 0 & 0 & 9 & 0 & 18 & 0 \\ -1 & 0 & 0 & 0 & -1 & 0 & 0 & 0 & 2 \end{array}\right]. \tag{5.14}$$

The diagonals give the individual variances of the entries of $\mathtt{H}$. △

This computed covariance is used to assess the accuracy of point transfer in example 5.14.

5.2.5 Error in both images

In the case of error in both images, computation of the covariance of the transformation is a bit more complicated. As seen in section 4.2.7(p101), one may define a set of $2n+8$ parameters, where 8 parameters describe the transformation matrix and $2n$ parameters $\hat{\mathbf{x}}_i$ represent estimates of the points in the first image. More conveniently, one may over-parametrize by using 9 parameters for the transformation $\mathtt{H}$. The Jacobian matrix naturally splits up into two parts as $\mathtt{J} = [\mathtt{A} \mid \mathtt{B}]$ where $\mathtt{A}$ and $\mathtt{B}$ are the derivatives with respect to the camera parameters and the points $\mathbf{x}_i$ respectively. Applying (5.10) one computes

$$\mathtt{J}^\mathsf{T}\Sigma_\mathbf{X}^{-1}\mathtt{J} = \begin{bmatrix} \mathtt{A}^\mathsf{T}\Sigma_\mathbf{X}^{-1}\mathtt{A} & \mathtt{A}^\mathsf{T}\Sigma_\mathbf{X}^{-1}\mathtt{B} \\ \mathtt{B}^\mathsf{T}\Sigma_\mathbf{X}^{-1}\mathtt{A} & \mathtt{B}^\mathsf{T}\Sigma_\mathbf{X}^{-1}\mathtt{B} \end{bmatrix}.$$

The pseudo-inverse of this matrix is thc covariancc of thc parameter set and the top-left block of this pseudo-inverse is the covariance of the entries of $\mathtt{H}$. A detailed discussion of this is given in section A6.4.1(p608), where it is shown how one can make use of the block structure of the Jacobian to simplify the computation.

In example 5.13 on estimating the covariance of $\mathtt{H}$ from four points in the previous section, the covariance turns out to be $\Sigma_\mathbf{h} = 2(\mathtt{J}^\mathsf{T}\Sigma_{\mathbf{X}'}^{-1}\mathtt{J})^+$, namely twice the covariance computed for noise in one image only. This assumes that points are measured with the same covariance in both images. This simple relationship between the covariances in the one and two-image cases does not generally hold.

5.2.6 Using the covariance matrix in point transfer

Once one has the covariance, one may compute the uncertainty associated with a given point transfer. Consider a new point $\mathbf{x}$ in the first image, not used in the computation of the transformation, $\mathtt{H}$. The corresponding point in the second image is $\mathbf{x}' = \mathtt{H}\mathbf{x}$. However, because of the uncertainty in the estimation of $\mathtt{H}$, the correct location of the point $\mathbf{x}'$ will also have associated uncertainty. One may compute this uncertainty from the covariance matrix of $\mathtt{H}$.

The covariance matrix for the point $\mathbf{x}'$ is given by the formula

$$\Sigma_{\mathbf{x}'} = \mathtt{J}_{\mathbf{h}} \Sigma_{\mathbf{h}} \mathtt{J}_{\mathbf{h}}^{\mathsf{T}} \tag{5.15}$$

where $\mathtt{J}_{\mathbf{h}} = \partial \mathbf{x}'/\partial \mathbf{h}$. A formula for $\partial \mathbf{x}'/\partial \mathbf{h}$ is given in (4.21–p129).

If in addition, the point $\mathbf{x}$ itself is measured with some uncertainty, then one has instead

$$\Sigma_{\mathbf{x}'} = \mathtt{J}_{\mathbf{h}} \Sigma_{\mathbf{h}} \mathtt{J}_{\mathbf{h}}^{\mathsf{T}} + \mathtt{J}_{\mathbf{x}} \Sigma_{\mathbf{x}} \mathtt{J}_{\mathbf{x}}^{\mathsf{T}} \tag{5.16}$$

assuming that there is no cross-correlation between $\mathbf{x}$ and $\mathbf{h}$, which is reasonable, since point $\mathbf{x}$ is assumed to be a new point not used in the computation of the transformation $\mathtt{H}$. A formula for the Jacobian matrix $\mathtt{J}_{\mathbf{x}} = \partial \mathbf{x}'/\partial \mathbf{x}$ is given in (4.20–p129).

The covariance matrix $\Sigma_{\mathbf{x}'}$ given by (5.15) is expressed in terms of the covariance matrix $\Sigma_{\mathbf{h}}$ of the transformation $\mathtt{H}$. We have seen that this covariance matrix $\Sigma_{\mathbf{h}}$ depends on the particular constraint used in estimating $\mathtt{H}$, according to (5.9). It may therefore appear that $\Sigma_{\mathbf{x}'}$ also depends on the particular method used to constrain $\mathtt{H}$. It may however be verified that these formulae are independent of the particular constraint $\mathtt{A}$ used to compute the covariance matrix $\Sigma_{\mathbf{P}} = (\mathtt{J}^{\mathsf{T}} \Sigma_{\mathbf{X}}^{-1} \mathtt{J})^{+\mathtt{A}}$.

Example 5.14. To continue example 5.13, let the computed 2D homography $\mathtt{H}$ be given by the identity matrix, with covariance matrix $\Sigma_{\mathbf{h}}$ as in (5.14). Consider an arbitrary point (x, y) mapped to the point $\mathbf{x}' = \mathtt{H}\mathbf{x}$. In this case the covariance matrix $\Sigma_{\mathbf{x}'} = \mathtt{J}_{\mathbf{h}} \Sigma_{\mathbf{h}} \mathtt{J}_{\mathbf{h}}^{\mathsf{T}}$ may be computed symbolically to equal

$$\Sigma_{\mathbf{x}'} = \begin{bmatrix} \sigma_{x'x'} & \sigma_{x'y'} \\ \sigma_{x'y'} & \sigma_{y'y'} \end{bmatrix} = \frac{1}{4} \begin{bmatrix} 2 - x^2 + x^4 + y^2 + x^2y^2 & xy(x^2 + y^2 - 2) \\ xy(x^2 + y^2 - 2) & 2 - y^2 + y^4 + x^2 + x^2y^2 \end{bmatrix}.$$

Note that $\sigma_{x'x'}$ and $\sigma_{y'y'}$ are even functions of x and y, whereas $\sigma_{x'y'}$ is an odd function. This is a consequence of the symmetry about the x and y axes of the point set used to compute $\mathtt{H}$. Also note that $\sigma_{x'x'}$ and $\sigma_{y'y'}$ differ by swapping x and y, which is a further consequence of the symmetry of the defining point set.

As may be seen, the variance $\sigma_{x'x'}$ varies as the fourth power of x, and hence the standard deviation varies as the square. This shows that extrapolating the values of transformed points $\mathbf{x}' = \mathtt{H}\mathbf{x}$ far beyond the set of points used to compute $\mathtt{H}$ is not reliable. More specifically, the RMS uncertainty of the position of $\mathbf{x}'$ is equal to $(\sigma_{x'x'} + \sigma_{y'y'})^{1/2} = \sqrt{\mathrm{trace}(\Sigma_{\mathbf{x}'})}$ which one finds is equal to $(1 + (x^2 + y^2)^2)^{1/2} = (1 + r^4)^{1/2}$, where r is the radial distance from the origin. Note the interesting fact that the RMS error is only dependent on the radial distance. In fact, one may verify that the probability distribution for point $\mathbf{x}'$ depends only on the radial distance of $\mathbf{x}'$, its

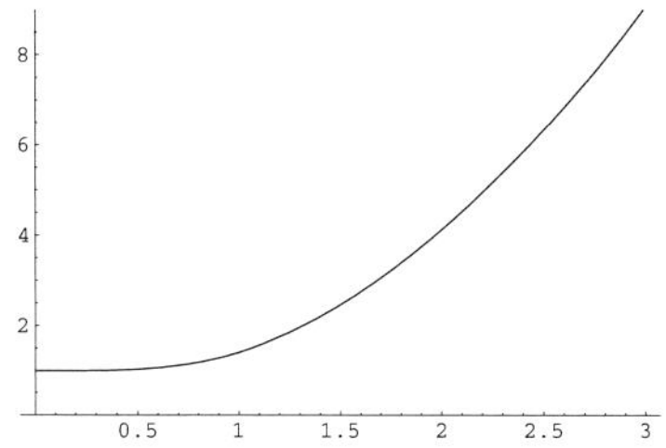

Fig. 5.5. *RMS error in the position of a projected point* $\mathbf{x}'$ *as a function of radial distance of* $\mathbf{x}'$ *from the origin. The homography* H *is computed from 4 evenly spaced points on a unit circle around the origin with errors in the second image only. The RMS error is proportional to the assumed error in the points used to compute* H*, and the vertical axis is calibrated in terms of this assumed error.*

two principal axes pointing radially and tangentially. Figure 5.5 shows the graph of the RMS error in $\mathbf{x}'$ as a function of r. △

This example has computed the covariance of a transferred point in the minimal case of four point correspondences. For more than four correspondences, the situation is not substantially different. Extrapolation beyond the set of points used to compute the homography is unreliable. In fact, one may show that if H is computed from n points evenly spaced around a unit circle (instead of 4 as in the computation above) then the RMS error is equal to $\sigma_{x'x'} + \sigma_{y'y'} = 4(1 + r^4)/n$, so the error exhibits the same quadratic growth.

5.3 Monte Carlo estimation of covariance

The method of estimating covariance discussed in the previous sections has relied on an assumption of linearity. In other words, it has been assumed that the surface $f(\mathbf{h})$ is locally flat in the vicinity of the estimated point, at least over a region corresponding to the approximate extent of the noise distribution. It has also been assumed that the method of estimation of the transformation H was the Maximum Likelihood Estimate. If the surface is not entirely flat then the estimate of covariance may be incorrect. In addition, a particular estimation method may be inferior to the ML estimate, thereby introducing additional uncertainty in the values of the estimated transformation H.

A general (though expensive) method of getting an estimate of the covariance is by exhaustive simulation. Assuming that the noise is drawn from a given noise distribution, one starts with a set of point matches corresponding perfectly to a given transformation. One then adds noise to the points and computes the corresponding transformation using the chosen estimation procedure. The covariance of the transformation H or a further transferred point is then computed statistically from multiple trials with noise drawn from the assumed noise distribution. This is illustrated for the case of the identity mapping in figure 5.6.

Both the analytical and the Monte Carlo methods of estimating covariance of the transformation H may be applied to the estimation of covariance from real data for which one does not know the true value of H. From the given data, an estimate of H and the corresponding true values of the points $\mathbf{x}'_i$ and $\mathbf{x}_i$ are computed. Then the

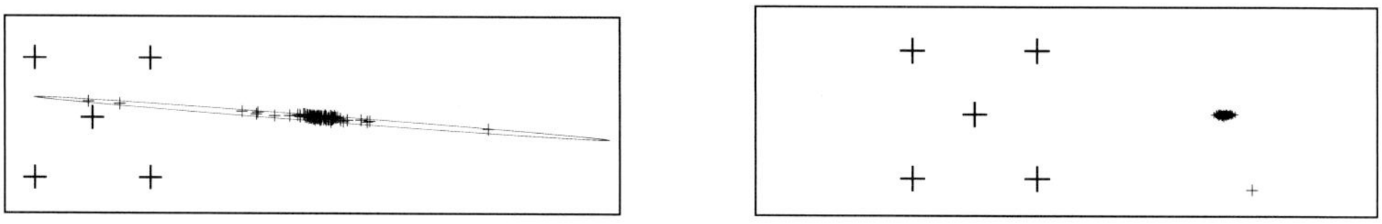

Fig. 5.6. *Transfer of a point under the identity mapping for the normalized and unnormalized DLT algorithm. See also figure 4.4*(p*109*) *for further explanation.*

covariance is computed as if the estimated values were the true values of the matched data points and the transformation. The resulting covariance matrix is assumed to be the covariance of the true transformation. This identification is based on the assumption that the true values of the data points are sufficiently close to the estimated values that the covariance matrix is essentially unaffected.

5.4 Closure

An extended discussion of bias and variance of estimated parameters is given in appendix 3(*p*568).

5.4.1 The literature

The derivations throughout this chapter have been considerably simplified by only using first-order Taylor expansions, and assuming Gaussian error distributions. Similar ideas (ML, covariance ...) can be developed for other distributions by using the Fisher Information matrix. Related reading may be found in Kanatani [Kanatani-96], Press *et al.* [Press-88], and other statistical textbooks.

Criminisi *et al.* [Criminisi-99b] give many examples of the computed covariances in point transfer as the correspondences used to determine the homography vary in number and position.

5.4.2 Notes and exercises

(i) Consider the problem of computing a best line fit to a set of 2D points in the plane using orthogonal regression. Suppose that N points are measured with independent standard deviations of σ in each coordinate. What is the expected RMS distance of each point from a fitted line? **Answer :** $\sigma\left((n-2)/n\right)^{1/2}$.

(ii) (Harder) : In section 18.5.2(*p*450) a method is given for computing a projective reconstruction from a set of $n+4$ point correspondences across m views, where 4 of the point correspondences are presumed to be known to be from a plane. Suppose the 4 planar correspondences are known exactly, and the other n image points are measured with 1 pixel error (each coordinate in each image). What is the expected residual error of $\|\mathbf{x}_j^i - \hat{\mathtt{P}}^i \mathbf{X}_j\|$?

Part I

Camera Geometry and Single View Geometry

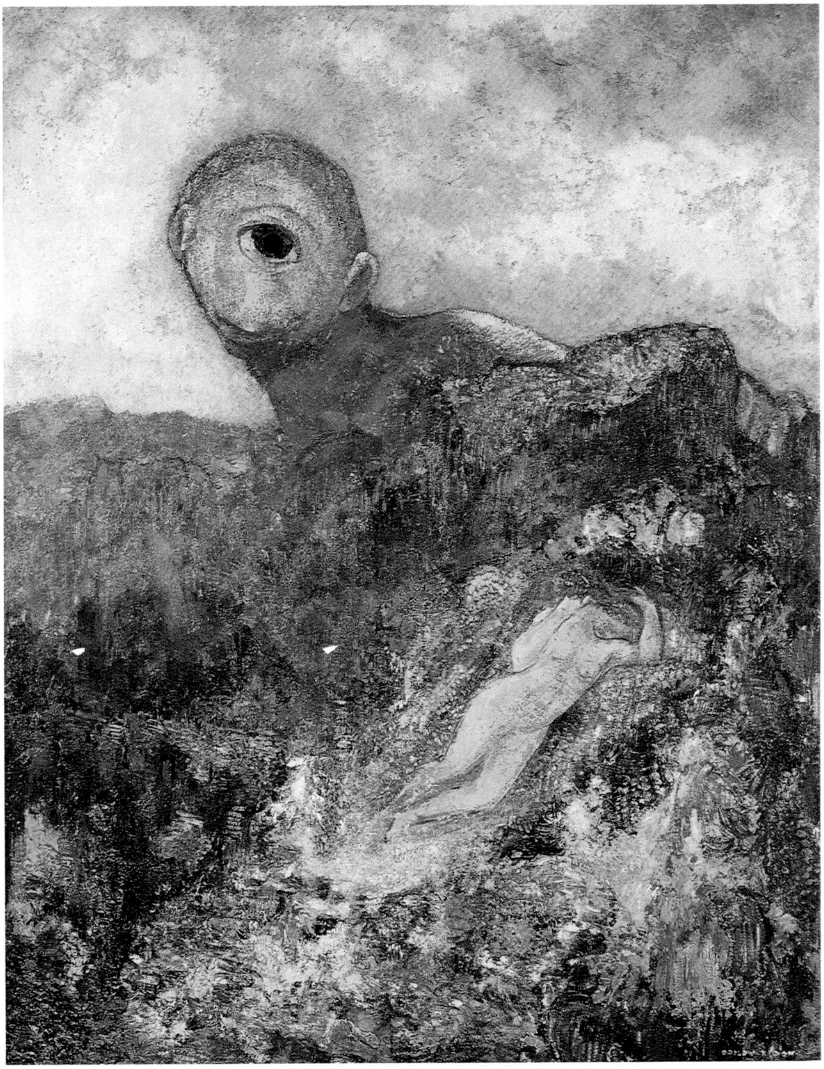

The Cyclops, c. 1914 (oil on canvas) by Odilon Redon (1840-1916)
Rijksmuseum Kroller-Muller, Otterlo, Netherlands /Bridgeman Art Library

Outline

This part of the book concentrates on the geometry of a single perspective camera. It contains three chapters.

Chapter 6 describes the projection of 3D scene space onto a 2D image plane. The camera mapping is represented by a matrix, and in the case of mapping points it is a 3×4 matrix $\mathtt{P}$ which maps from homogeneous coordinates of a world point in 3-space to homogeneous coordinates of the imaged point on the image plane. This matrix has in general 11 degrees of freedom, and the properties of the camera, such as its centre and focal length, may be extracted from it. In particular the internal camera parameters, such as the focal length and aspect ratio, are packaged in a 3×3 matrix $\mathtt{K}$ which is obtained from $\mathtt{P}$ by a simple decomposition. There are two particularly important classes of camera matrix: finite cameras, and cameras with their centre at infinity such as the *affine camera* which represents parallel projection.

Chapter 7 describes the estimation of the camera matrix $\mathtt{P}$, given the coordinates of a set of corresponding world and image points. The chapter also describes how constraints on the camera may be efficiently incorporated into the estimation, and a method of correcting for radial lens distortion.

Chapter 8 has three main topics. First, it covers the action of a camera on geometric objects other than finite points. These include lines, conics, quadrics and points at infinity. The image of points/lines at infinity are vanishing points/lines. The second topic is camera calibration, in which the internal parameters $\mathtt{K}$ of the camera matrix are computed, without computing the entire matrix $\mathtt{P}$. In particular the relation of the internal parameters to the image of the absolute conic is described, and the calibration of a camera from vanishing points and vanishing lines. The final topic is the *calibrating conic*. This is a simple geometric device for visualizing camera calibration.

6

Camera Models

A camera is a mapping between the 3D world (object space) and a 2D image. The principal camera of interest in this book is *central projection*. This chapter develops a number of camera *models* which are matrices with particular properties that represent the camera mapping.

It will be seen that all cameras modelling central projection are specializations of the *general projective camera*. The anatomy of this most general camera model is examined using the tools of projective geometry. It will be seen that geometric entities of the camera, such as the projection centre and image plane, can be computed quite simply from its matrix representation. Specializations of the general projective camera inherit its properties, for example their geometry is computed using the same algebraic expressions.

The specialized models fall into two major classes – those that model cameras with a finite centre, and those that model cameras with centre "at infinity". Of the cameras at infinity the *affine camera* is of particular importance because it is the natural generalization of parallel projection.

This chapter is principally concerned with the projection of points. The action of a camera on other geometric entities, such as lines, is deferred until chapter 8.

6.1 Finite cameras

In this section we start with the most specialized and simplest camera model, which is the basic pinhole camera, and then progressively generalize this model through a series of gradations.

The models we develop are principally designed for CCD like sensors, but are also applicable to other cameras, for example X-ray images, scanned photographic negatives, scanned photographs from enlarged negatives, etc.

The basic pinhole model. We consider the central projection of points in space onto a plane. Let the centre of projection be the origin of a Euclidean coordinate system, and consider the plane $\mathrm{Z} = f$, which is called the *image plane* or *focal plane*. Under the pinhole camera model, a point in space with coordinates $\mathbf{X} = (\mathrm{X}, \mathrm{Y}, \mathrm{Z})^\mathsf{T}$ is mapped to the point on the image plane where a line joining the point $\mathbf{X}$ to the centre of projection meets the image plane. This is shown in figure 6.1. By similar triangles, one quickly

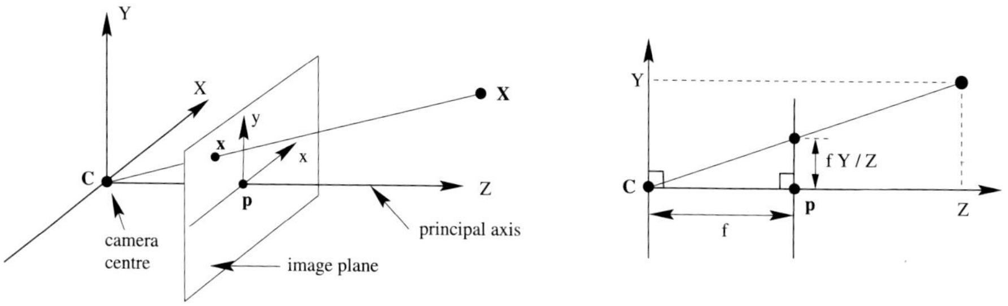

Fig. 6.1. **Pinhole camera geometry.** **C** *is the camera centre and* **p** *the principal point. The camera centre is here placed at the coordinate origin. Note the image plane is placed in front of the camera centre.*

computes that the point $(X, Y, Z)^T$ is mapped to the point $(fX/Z, fY/Z, f)^T$ on the image plane. Ignoring the final image coordinate, we see that

$$(X, Y, Z)^T \mapsto (fX/Z, fY/Z)^T \tag{6.1}$$

describes the central projection mapping from world to image coordinates. This is a mapping from Euclidean 3-space $\mathbb{R}^3$ to Euclidean 2-space $\mathbb{R}^2$.

The centre of projection is called the *camera centre*. It is also known as the *optical centre*. The line from the camera centre perpendicular to the image plane is called the *principal axis* or *principal ray* of the camera, and the point where the principal axis meets the image plane is called the *principal point*. The plane through the camera centre parallel to the image plane is called the *principal plane* of the camera.

Central projection using homogeneous coordinates. If the world and image points are represented by homogeneous vectors, then central projection is very simply expressed as a linear mapping between their homogeneous coordinates. In particular, (6.1) may be written in terms of matrix multiplication as

$$\begin{pmatrix} X \\ Y \\ Z \\ 1 \end{pmatrix} \mapsto \begin{pmatrix} fX \\ fY \\ Z \end{pmatrix} = \begin{bmatrix} f & & & 0 \\ & f & & 0 \\ & & 1 & 0 \end{bmatrix} \begin{pmatrix} X \\ Y \\ Z \\ 1 \end{pmatrix}. \tag{6.2}$$

The matrix in this expression may be written as $\text{diag}(f, f, 1)[\mathtt{I} \mid \mathbf{0}]$ where $\text{diag}(f, f, 1)$ is a diagonal matrix and $[\mathtt{I} \mid \mathbf{0}]$ represents a matrix divided up into a 3×3 block (the identity matrix) plus a column vector, here the zero vector.

We now introduce the notation $\mathbf{X}$ for the world point represented by the homogeneous 4-vector $(X, Y, Z, 1)^T$, $\mathbf{x}$ for the image point represented by a homogeneous 3-vector, and $\mathtt{P}$ for the 3×4 homogeneous *camera projection matrix*. Then (6.2) is written compactly as

$$\mathbf{x} = \mathtt{P}\mathbf{X}$$

which defines the camera matrix for the pinhole model of central projection as

$$\mathtt{P} = \text{diag}(f, f, 1)\,[\mathtt{I} \mid \mathbf{0}].$$

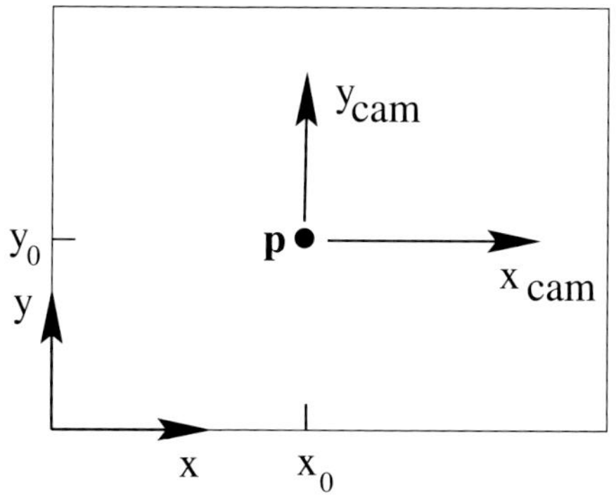

Fig. 6.2. *Image* (x, y) *and camera* $(x_{\text{cam}}, y_{\text{cam}})$ *coordinate systems.*

Principal point offset. The expression (6.1) assumed that the origin of coordinates in the image plane is at the principal point. In practice, it may not be, so that in general there is a mapping

$$(\mathrm{X}, \mathrm{Y}, \mathrm{Z})^{\mathsf{T}} \mapsto (f\mathrm{X}/\mathrm{Z} + p_x, f\mathrm{Y}/\mathrm{Z} + p_y)^{\mathsf{T}}$$

where $(p_x, p_y)^{\mathsf{T}}$ are the coordinates of the principal point. See figure 6.2. This equation may be expressed conveniently in homogeneous coordinates as

$$\begin{pmatrix} \mathrm{X} \\ \mathrm{Y} \\ \mathrm{Z} \\ 1 \end{pmatrix} \mapsto \begin{pmatrix} f\mathrm{X} + \mathrm{Z}p_x \\ f\mathrm{Y} + \mathrm{Z}p_y \\ \mathrm{Z} \end{pmatrix} = \begin{bmatrix} f & & p_x & 0 \\ & f & p_y & 0 \\ & & 1 & 0 \end{bmatrix} \begin{pmatrix} \mathrm{X} \\ \mathrm{Y} \\ \mathrm{Z} \\ 1 \end{pmatrix}. \tag{6.3}$$

Now, writing

$$\mathtt{K} = \begin{bmatrix} f & & p_x \\ & f & p_y \\ & & 1 \end{bmatrix} \tag{6.4}$$

then (6.3) has the concise form

$$\mathbf{x} = \mathtt{K}[\mathtt{I} \mid \mathbf{0}]\mathbf{X}_{\text{cam}}. \tag{6.5}$$

The matrix $\mathtt{K}$ is called the *camera calibration matrix.* In (6.5) we have written $(\mathrm{X}, \mathrm{Y}, \mathrm{Z}, 1)^{\mathsf{T}}$ as $\mathbf{X}_{\text{cam}}$ to emphasize that the camera is assumed to be located at the origin of a Euclidean coordinate system with the principal axis of the camera pointing straight down the Z-axis, and the point $\mathbf{X}_{\text{cam}}$ is expressed in this coordinate system. Such a coordinate system may be called the *camera coordinate frame*.

Camera rotation and translation. In general, points in space will be expressed in terms of a different Euclidean coordinate frame, known as the *world coordinate frame*. The two coordinate frames are related via a rotation and a translation. See figure 6.3. If $\widetilde{\mathbf{X}}$ is an inhomogeneous 3-vector representing the coordinates of a point in the world coordinate frame, and $\widetilde{\mathbf{X}}_{\text{cam}}$ represents the same point in the camera coordinate frame, then we may write $\widetilde{\mathbf{X}}_{\text{cam}} = \mathtt{R}(\widetilde{\mathbf{X}} - \widetilde{\mathbf{C}})$, where $\widetilde{\mathbf{C}}$ represents the coordinates of the camera

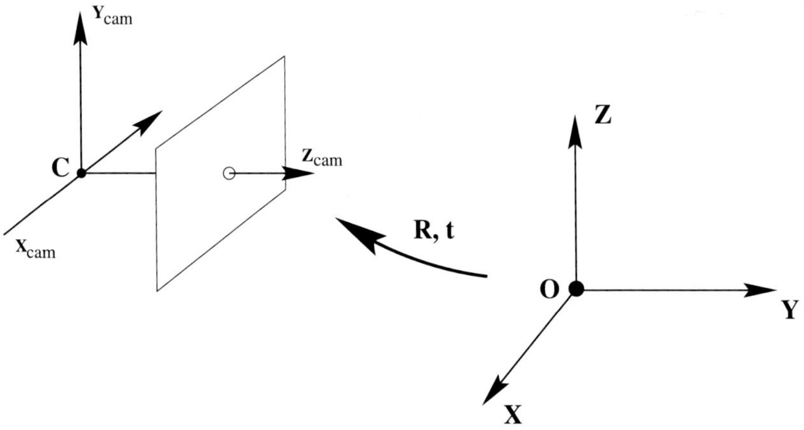

Fig. 6.3. *The Euclidean transformation between the world and camera coordinate frames.*

centre in the world coordinate frame, and $\mathtt{R}$ is a 3×3 rotation matrix representing the orientation of the camera coordinate frame. This equation may be written in homogeneous coordinates as

$$\mathbf{X}_{\text{cam}} = \begin{bmatrix} \mathtt{R} & -\mathtt{R}\widetilde{\mathtt{C}} \\ 0 & 1 \end{bmatrix} \begin{pmatrix} \mathtt{X} \\ \mathtt{Y} \\ \mathtt{Z} \\ 1 \end{pmatrix} = \begin{bmatrix} \mathtt{R} & -\mathtt{R}\widetilde{\mathtt{C}} \\ 0 & 1 \end{bmatrix} \mathbf{X}. \tag{6.6}$$

Putting this together with (6.5) leads to the formula

$$\mathbf{x} = \mathtt{KR}[\mathtt{I} \mid -\widetilde{\mathtt{C}}]\mathbf{X} \tag{6.7}$$

where $\mathbf{X}$ is now in a world coordinate frame. This is the general mapping given by a pinhole camera. One sees that a general pinhole camera, $\mathtt{P} = \mathtt{KR}[\mathtt{I} \mid -\widetilde{\mathtt{C}}]$, has 9 degrees of freedom: 3 for $\mathtt{K}$ (the elements f, p_x, p_y), 3 for $\mathtt{R}$, and 3 for $\widetilde{\mathtt{C}}$. The parameters contained in $\mathtt{K}$ are called the *internal* camera parameters, or the *internal orientation* of the camera. The parameters of $\mathtt{R}$ and $\widetilde{\mathtt{C}}$ which relate the camera orientation and position to a world coordinate system are called the *external* parameters or the *exterior orientation*.

It is often convenient not to make the camera centre explicit, and instead to represent the world to image transformation as $\widetilde{\mathbf{X}}_{\text{cam}} = \mathtt{R}\widetilde{\mathbf{X}} + \mathbf{t}$. In this case the camera matrix is simply

$$\mathtt{P} = \mathtt{K}[\mathtt{R} \mid \mathbf{t}] \tag{6.8}$$

where from (6.7) $\mathbf{t} = -\mathtt{R}\widetilde{\mathtt{C}}$.

CCD cameras. The pinhole camera model just derived assumes that the image coordinates are Euclidean coordinates having equal scales in both axial directions. In the case of CCD cameras, there is the additional possibility of having non-square pixels. If image coordinates are measured in pixels, then this has the extra effect of introducing unequal scale factors in each direction. In particular if the number of pixels per unit distance in image coordinates are m_x and m_y in the x and y directions, then the transformation from world coordinates to pixel coordinates is obtained by multiplying (6.4) on the left by an extra factor $\text{diag}(m_x, m_y, 1)$. Thus, the general form of the calibration matrix of a CCD camera is

$$\mathtt{K} = \begin{bmatrix} \alpha_x & & x_0 \\ & \alpha_y & y_0 \\ & & 1 \end{bmatrix} \tag{6.9}$$

where $\alpha_x = fm_x$ and $\alpha_y = fm_y$ represent the focal length of the camera in terms of pixel dimensions in the x and y direction respectively. Similarly, $\tilde{\mathbf{x}}_0 = (x_0, y_0)$ is the principal point in terms of pixel dimensions, with coordinates $x_0 = m_x p_x$ and $y_0 = m_y p_y$. A CCD camera thus has 10 degrees of freedom.

Finite projective camera. For added generality, we can consider a calibration matrix of the form

$$\mathtt{K} = \begin{bmatrix} \alpha_x & s & x_0 \\ & \alpha_y & y_0 \\ & & 1 \end{bmatrix}. \tag{6.10}$$

The added parameter s is referred to as the *skew* parameter. The skew parameter will be zero for most normal cameras. However, in certain unusual instances which are described in section 6.2.4, it can take non-zero values.

A camera

$$\mathtt{P} = \mathtt{KR}[\mathtt{I} \mid -\widetilde{\mathbf{C}}] \tag{6.11}$$

for which the calibration matrix $\mathtt{K}$ is of the form (6.10) will be called a *finite projective* camera. A finite projective camera has 11 degrees of freedom. This is the same number of degrees of freedom as a 3×4 matrix, defined up to an arbitrary scale.

Note that the left hand 3×3 submatrix of $\mathtt{P}$, equal to $\mathtt{KR}$, is non-singular. Conversely, any 3×4 matrix $\mathtt{P}$ for which the left hand 3×3 submatrix is non-singular is the camera matrix of some finite projective camera, because $\mathtt{P}$ can be decomposed as $\mathtt{P} = \mathtt{KR}[\mathtt{I} \mid -\widetilde{\mathbf{C}}]$. Indeed, letting $\mathtt{M}$ be the left 3×3 submatrix of $\mathtt{P}$, one decomposes $\mathtt{M}$ as a product $\mathtt{M} = \mathtt{KR}$ where $\mathtt{K}$ is upper-triangular of the form (6.10) and $\mathtt{R}$ is a rotation matrix. This decomposition is essentially the RQ matrix decomposition, described in section A4.1.1(*p*579), of which more will be said in section 6.2.4. The matrix $\mathtt{P}$ can therefore be written $\mathtt{P} = \mathtt{M}[\mathtt{I} \mid \mathtt{M}^{-1}\mathbf{p}_4] = \mathtt{KR}[\mathtt{I} \mid -\widetilde{\mathbf{C}}]$ where $\mathbf{p}_4$ is the last column of $\mathtt{P}$. In short

- *The set of camera matrices of finite projective cameras is identical with the set of homogeneous* 3×4 *matrices for which the left hand* 3×3 *submatrix is non-singular.*

General projective cameras. The final step in our hierarchy of projective cameras is to remove the non-singularity restriction on the left hand 3×3 submatrix. A *general projective* camera is one represented by an arbitrary homogeneous 3×4 matrix of rank 3. It has 11 degrees of freedom. The rank 3 requirement arises because if the rank is

Camera centre. The camera centre is the 1-dimensional right null-space $\mathbf{C}$ of $\mathtt{P}$, i.e. $\mathtt{P}\mathbf{C} = \mathbf{0}$. ◇ **Finite camera** ($\mathtt{M}$ is not singular) $\mathbf{C} = \begin{pmatrix} -\mathtt{M}^{-1}\mathbf{p}_4 \\ 1 \end{pmatrix}$ ◇ **Camera at infinity** ($\mathtt{M}$ is singular) $\mathbf{C} = \begin{pmatrix} \mathbf{d} \\ 0 \end{pmatrix}$ where $\mathbf{d}$ is the null 3-vector of $\mathtt{M}$, i.e. $\mathtt{M}\mathbf{d} = \mathbf{0}$. **Column points.** For $i = 1, \ldots, 3$, the column vectors $\mathbf{p}_i$ are vanishing points in the image corresponding to the X, Y and Z axes respectively. Column $\mathbf{p}_4$ is the image of the coordinate origin. **Principal plane.** The principal plane of the camera is $\mathbf{P}^3$, the last row of $\mathtt{P}$. **Axis planes.** The planes $\mathbf{P}^1$ and $\mathbf{P}^2$ (the first and second rows of $\mathtt{P}$) represent planes in space through the camera centre, corresponding to points that map to the image lines $x = 0$ and $y = 0$ respectively. **Principal point.** The image point $\mathbf{x}_0 = \mathtt{M}\mathbf{m}^3$ is the principal point of the camera, where $\mathbf{m}^{3\mathsf{T}}$ is the third row of $\mathtt{M}$. **Principal ray.** The principal ray (axis) of the camera is the ray passing through the camera centre $\mathbf{C}$ with direction vector $\mathbf{m}^{3\mathsf{T}}$. The principal axis vector $\mathbf{v} = \det(\mathtt{M})\mathbf{m}^3$ is directed towards the front of the camera.

Table 6.1. *Summary of the properties of a projective camera* $\mathtt{P}$. *The matrix is represented by the block form* $\mathtt{P} = [\mathtt{M} \mid \mathbf{p}_4]$.

less than this then the range of the matrix mapping will be a line or point and not the whole plane; in other words not a 2D image.

6.2 The projective camera

A general projective camera $\mathtt{P}$ maps world points $\mathbf{X}$ to image points $\mathbf{x}$ according to $\mathbf{x} = \mathtt{P}\mathbf{X}$. Building on this mapping we will now dissect the camera model to reveal how geometric entities, such as the camera centre, are encoded. Some of the properties that we consider will apply only to finite projective cameras and their specializations, whilst others will apply to general cameras. The distinction will be evident from the context. The derived properties of the camera are summarized in table 6.1.

6.2.1 Camera anatomy

A general projective camera may be decomposed into blocks according to $\mathtt{P} = [\mathtt{M} \mid \mathbf{p}_4]$, where $\mathtt{M}$ is a 3×3 matrix. It will be seen that if $\mathtt{M}$ is non-singular, then this is a finite camera, otherwise it is not.

Camera centre. The matrix $\mathtt{P}$ has a 1-dimensional right null-space because its rank is 3, whereas it has 4 columns. Suppose the null-space is generated by the 4-vector $\mathbf{C}$, that is $\mathtt{P}\mathbf{C} = \mathbf{0}$. It will now be shown that $\mathbf{C}$ is the camera centre, represented as a homogeneous 4-vector.

Consider the line containing $\mathbf{C}$ and any other point $\mathbf{A}$ in 3-space. Points on this line may be represented by the join

$$\mathbf{X}(\lambda) = \lambda\mathbf{A} + (1 - \lambda)\mathbf{C} \ .$$

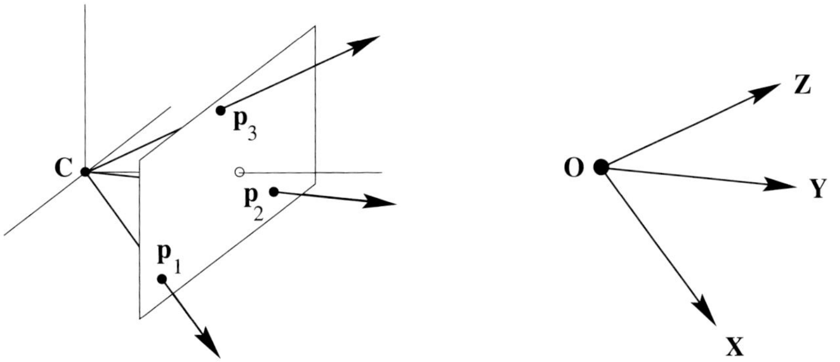

Fig. 6.4. *The three image points defined by the columns $\mathbf{p}_i, i = 1, \ldots, 3$, of the projection matrix are the vanishing points of the directions of the world axes.*

Under the mapping $\mathbf{x} = \mathtt{P}\mathbf{X}$ points on this line are projected to

$$\mathbf{x} = \mathtt{P}\mathbf{X}(\lambda) = \lambda\mathtt{P}\mathbf{A} + (1-\lambda)\mathtt{P}\mathbf{C} = \lambda\mathtt{P}\mathbf{A}$$

since $\mathtt{P}\mathbf{C} = \mathbf{0}$. That is all points on the line are mapped to the same image point $\mathtt{P}\mathbf{A}$, which means that the line must be a ray through the camera centre. It follows that $\mathbf{C}$ is the homogeneous representation of the camera centre, since for all choices of $\mathbf{A}$ the line $\mathbf{X}(\lambda)$ is a ray through the camera centre.

This result is not unexpected since the image point $(0,0,0)^\mathsf{T} = \mathtt{P}\mathbf{C}$ is not defined, and the camera centre is the unique point in space for which the image is undefined. In the case of finite cameras the result may be established directly, since $\mathbf{C} = (\widetilde{\mathbf{C}}^\mathsf{T}, 1)^\mathsf{T}$ is clearly the null-vector of $\mathtt{P} = \mathtt{KR}[\mathtt{I} \mid -\widetilde{\mathbf{C}}]$. The result is true even in the case where the first 3×3 submatrix $\mathtt{M}$ of $\mathtt{P}$ is singular. In this singular case, though, the null-vector has the form $\mathbf{C} = (\mathbf{d}^\mathsf{T}, 0)^\mathsf{T}$ where $\mathtt{M}\mathbf{d} = \mathbf{0}$. The camera centre is then a point at infinity. Camera models of this class are discussed in section 6.3.

Column vectors. The columns of the projective camera are 3-vectors which have a geometric meaning as particular image points. With the notation that the columns of $\mathtt{P}$ are $\mathbf{p}_i, i = 1, \ldots, 4$, then $\mathbf{p}_1, \mathbf{p}_2, \mathbf{p}_3$ are the vanishing points of the world coordinate $\mathtt{X}$, $\mathtt{Y}$ and $\mathtt{Z}$ axes respectively. This follows because these points are the images of the axes' directions. For example the x-axis has direction $\mathbf{D} = (1,0,0,0)^\mathsf{T}$, which is imaged at $\mathbf{p}_1 = \mathtt{P}\mathbf{D}$. See figure 6.4. The column $\mathbf{p}_4$ is the image of the world origin.

Row vectors. The rows of the projective camera (6.12) are 4-vectors which may be interpreted geometrically as particular world planes. These planes are examined next. We introduce the notation that the rows of $\mathtt{P}$ are $\mathbf{P}^{i\mathsf{T}}$ so that

$$\mathtt{P} = \begin{bmatrix} p_{11} & p_{12} & p_{13} & p_{14} \\ p_{21} & p_{22} & p_{23} & p_{24} \\ p_{31} & p_{32} & p_{33} & p_{34} \end{bmatrix} = \begin{bmatrix} \mathbf{P}^{1\mathsf{T}} \\ \mathbf{P}^{2\mathsf{T}} \\ \mathbf{P}^{3\mathsf{T}} \end{bmatrix}. \tag{6.12}$$

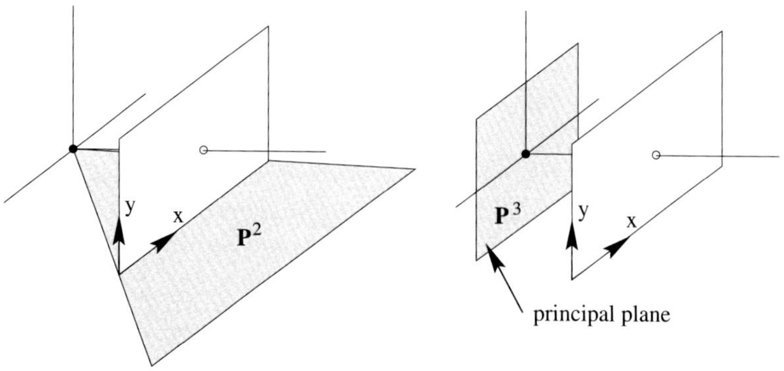

Fig. 6.5. *Two of the three planes defined by the rows of the projection matrix.*

The principal plane. The principal plane is the plane through the camera centre parallel to the image plane. It consists of the set of points $\mathbf{X}$ which are imaged on the line at infinity of the image. Explicitly, $\mathtt{P}\mathbf{X} = (x, y, 0)^\mathsf{T}$. Thus a point lies on the principal plane of the camera if and only if $\mathbf{P}^{3\mathsf{T}}\mathbf{X} = 0$. In other words, $\mathbf{P}^3$ is the vector representing the principal plane of the camera. If $\mathbf{C}$ is the camera centre, then $\mathtt{P}\mathbf{C} = \mathbf{0}$, and so in particular $\mathbf{P}^{3\mathsf{T}}\mathbf{C} = 0$. That is $\mathbf{C}$ lies on the principal plane of the camera.

Axis planes. Consider the set of points $\mathbf{X}$ on the plane $\mathbf{P}^1$. This set satisfies $\mathbf{P}^{1\mathsf{T}}\mathbf{X} = 0$, and so is imaged at $\mathtt{P}\mathbf{X} = (0, y, w)^\mathsf{T}$ which are points on the image y-axis. Again it follows from $\mathtt{P}\mathbf{C} = \mathbf{0}$ that $\mathbf{P}^{1\mathsf{T}}\mathbf{C} = 0$ and so $\mathbf{C}$ lies also on the plane $\mathbf{P}^1$. Consequently the plane $\mathbf{P}^1$ is defined by the camera centre and the line $x = 0$ in the image. Similarly the plane $\mathbf{P}^2$ is defined by the camera centre and the line $y = 0$.

Unlike the principal plane $\mathbf{P}^3$, the axis planes $\mathbf{P}^1$ and $\mathbf{P}^2$ are dependent on the image x- and y-axes, i.e. on the choice of the image coordinate system. Thus they are less tightly coupled to the natural camera geometry than the principal plane. In particular the line of intersection of the planes $\mathbf{P}^1$ and $\mathbf{P}^2$ is a line joining the camera centre and image origin, i.e. the back-projection of the image origin. This line will not coincide in general with the camera principal axis. The planes arising from $\mathbf{P}^i$ are illustrated in figure 6.5.

The camera centre $\mathbf{C}$ lies on all three planes, and since these planes are distinct (as the $\mathtt{P}$ matrix has rank 3) it must lie on their intersection. Algebraically, the condition for the centre to lie on all three planes is $\mathtt{P}\mathbf{C} = \mathbf{0}$ which is the original equation for the camera centre given above.

The principal point. The principal axis is the line passing through the camera centre $\mathbf{C}$, with direction perpendicular to the principal plane $\mathbf{P}^3$. The axis intersects the image plane at the principal point. We may determine this point as follows. In general, the normal to a plane $\boldsymbol{\pi} = (\pi_1, \pi_2, \pi_3, \pi_4)^\mathsf{T}$ is the vector $(\pi_1, \pi_2, \pi_3)^\mathsf{T}$. This may alternatively be represented by a point $(\pi_1, \pi_2, \pi_3, 0)^\mathsf{T}$ on the plane at infinity. In the case of the principal plane $\mathbf{P}^3$ of the camera, this point is $(p_{31}, p_{32}, p_{33}, 0)^\mathsf{T}$, which we denote $\widehat{\mathbf{P}}^3$. Projecting that point using the camera matrix $\mathtt{P}$ gives the principal point of the camera $\mathtt{P}\widehat{\mathtt{P}}^3$. Note that only the left hand 3×3 part of $\mathtt{P} = [\mathtt{M} \mid \mathbf{p}_4]$ is involved in this formula. In fact the principal point is computed as $\mathbf{x}_0 = \mathtt{M}\mathbf{m}^3$ where $\mathbf{m}^{3\mathsf{T}}$ is the third row of $\mathtt{M}$.

The principal axis vector. Although any point $\mathbf{X}$ not on the principal plane may be mapped to an image point according to $\mathbf{x} = \mathtt{P}\mathbf{X}$, in reality only half the points in space, those that lie in front of the camera, may be seen in an image. Let $\mathtt{P}$ be written as $\mathtt{P} = [\mathtt{M} \mid \mathbf{p}_4]$. It has just been seen that the vector $\mathbf{m}^3$ points in the direction of the principal axis. We would like to define this vector in such a way that it points in the direction towards the front of the camera (the *positive* direction). Note however that $\mathtt{P}$ is only defined up to sign. This leaves an ambiguity as to whether $\mathbf{m}^3$ or $-\mathbf{m}^3$ points in the positive direction. We now proceed to resolve this ambiguity.

We start by considering coordinates with respect to the camera coordinate frame. According to (6.5), the equation for projection of a 3D point to a point in the image is given by $\mathbf{x} = \mathtt{P}_{\text{cam}}\mathbf{X}_{\text{cam}} = \mathtt{K}[\mathtt{I} \mid \mathbf{0}]\mathbf{X}_{\text{cam}}$, where $\mathbf{X}_{\text{cam}}$ is the 3D point expressed in camera coordinates. In this case observe that the vector $\mathbf{v} = \det(\mathtt{M})\mathbf{m}^3 = (0, 0, 1)^\mathsf{T}$ points *towards the front of the camera* in the direction of the principal axis, irrespective of the scaling of $\mathtt{P}_{\text{cam}}$. For example, if $\mathtt{P}_{\text{cam}} \rightarrow k\mathtt{P}_{\text{cam}}$ then $\mathbf{v} \rightarrow k^4\mathbf{v}$ which has the same direction.

If the 3D point is expressed in world coordinates then $\mathtt{P} = k\mathtt{K}[\mathtt{R} \mid -\mathtt{R}\widetilde{\mathbf{C}}] = [\mathtt{M} \mid \mathbf{p}_4]$, where $\mathtt{M} = k\mathtt{K}\mathtt{R}$. Since $\det(\mathtt{R}) > 0$ the vector $\mathbf{v} = \det(\mathtt{M})\mathbf{m}^3$ is again unaffected by scaling. In summary,

- $\mathbf{v} = \det(\mathtt{M})\mathbf{m}^3$ *is a vector in the direction of the principal axis, directed towards the front of the camera.*

6.2.2 Action of a projective camera on points

Forward projection. As we have already seen, a general projective camera maps a point in space $\mathbf{X}$ to an image point according to the mapping $\mathbf{x} = \mathtt{P}\mathbf{X}$. Points $\mathbf{D} = (\mathbf{d}^\mathsf{T}, 0)^\mathsf{T}$ on the plane at infinity represent vanishing points. Such points map to

$$\mathbf{x} = \mathtt{P}\mathbf{D} = [\mathtt{M} \mid \mathbf{p}_4]\mathbf{D} = \mathtt{M}\mathbf{d}$$

and thus are only affected by $\mathtt{M}$, the first 3×3 submatrix of $\mathtt{P}$.

Back-projection of points to rays. Given a point $\mathbf{x}$ in an image, we next determine the set of points in space that map to this point. This set will constitute a ray in space passing through the camera centre. The form of the ray may be specified in several ways, depending on how one wishes to represent a line in 3-space. A Plücker representation is postponed until section 8.1.2(*p*196). Here the line is represented as the join of two points.

We know two points on the ray. These are the camera centre $\mathbf{C}$ (where $\mathtt{P}\mathbf{C} = \mathbf{0}$) and the point $\mathtt{P}^+\mathbf{x}$, where $\mathtt{P}^+$ is the pseudo-inverse of $\mathtt{P}$. The pseudo-inverse of $\mathtt{P}$ is the matrix $\mathtt{P}^+ = \mathtt{P}^\mathsf{T}(\mathtt{P}\mathtt{P}^\mathsf{T})^{-1}$, for which $\mathtt{P}\mathtt{P}^+ = \mathtt{I}$ (see section A5.2(*p*590)). Point $\mathtt{P}^+\mathbf{x}$ lies

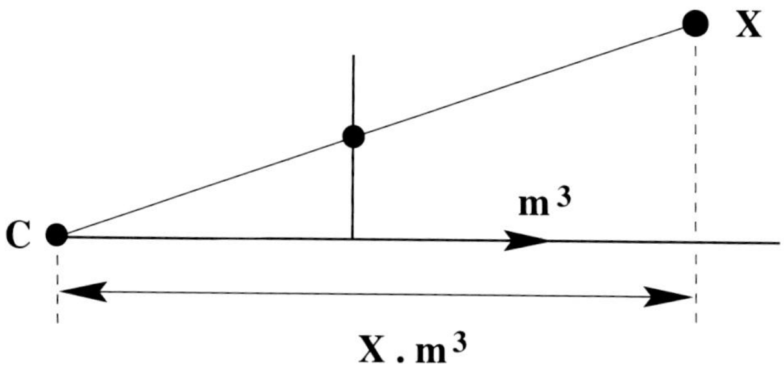

Fig. 6.6. *If the camera matrix* $\mathtt{P} = [\mathtt{M} \mid \mathbf{p}_4]$ *is normalized so that* $\|\mathbf{m}^3\| = 1$ *and* $\det \mathtt{M} > 0$*, and* $\mathbf{x} = w(x, y, 1)^\mathsf{T} = \mathtt{P}\mathbf{X}$*, where* $\mathbf{X} = (\mathrm{X}, \mathrm{Y}, \mathrm{Z}, 1)^\mathsf{T}$*, then* w *is the depth of the point* $\mathbf{X}$ *from the camera centre in the direction of the principal ray of the camera.*

on the ray because it projects to $\mathbf{x}$, since $\mathtt{P}(\mathtt{P}^+\mathbf{x}) = \mathtt{I}\mathbf{x} = \mathbf{x}$. Then the ray is the line formed by the join of these two points

$$\mathbf{X}(\lambda) = \mathtt{P}^+\mathbf{x} + \lambda\mathbf{C}. \tag{6.13}$$

In the case of finite cameras an alternative expression can be developed. Writing $\mathtt{P} = [\mathtt{M} \mid \mathbf{p}_4]$, the camera centre is given by $\widetilde{\mathbf{C}} = -\mathtt{M}^{-1}\mathbf{p}_4$. An image point $\mathbf{x}$ back-projects to a ray intersecting the plane at infinity at the point $\mathbf{D} = ((\mathtt{M}^{-1}\mathbf{x})^\mathsf{T}, 0)^\mathsf{T}$, and $\mathbf{D}$ provides a second point on the ray. Again writing the line as the join of two points on the ray,

$$\mathbf{X}(\mu) = \mu\begin{pmatrix} \mathtt{M}^{-1}\mathbf{x} \\ 0 \end{pmatrix} + \begin{pmatrix} -\mathtt{M}^{-1}\mathbf{p}_4 \\ 1 \end{pmatrix} = \begin{pmatrix} \mathtt{M}^{-1}(\mu\mathbf{x} - \mathbf{p}_4) \\ 1 \end{pmatrix}. \tag{6.14}$$

6.2.3 Depth of points

Next, we consider the distance a point lies in front of or behind the principal plane of the camera. Consider a camera matrix $\mathtt{P} = [\mathtt{M} \mid \mathbf{p}_4]$, projecting a point $\mathbf{X} = (\mathrm{X}, \mathrm{Y}, \mathrm{Z}, 1)^\mathsf{T} = (\widetilde{\mathbf{X}}^\mathsf{T}, 1)^\mathsf{T}$ in 3-space to the image point $\mathbf{x} = w(x, y, 1)^\mathsf{T} = \mathtt{P}\mathbf{X}$. Let $\mathbf{C} = (\widetilde{\mathbf{C}}, 1)^\mathsf{T}$ be the camera centre. Then $w = \mathbf{P}^{3\mathsf{T}}\mathbf{X} = \mathbf{P}^{3\mathsf{T}}(\mathbf{X} - \mathbf{C})$ since $\mathtt{P}\mathbf{C} = \mathbf{0}$ for the camera centre $\mathbf{C}$. However, $\mathbf{P}^{3\mathsf{T}}(\mathbf{X} - \mathbf{C}) = \mathbf{m}^{3\mathsf{T}}(\widetilde{\mathbf{X}} - \widetilde{\mathbf{C}})$ where $\mathbf{m}^3$ is the principal ray direction, so $w = \mathbf{m}^{3\mathsf{T}}(\widetilde{\mathbf{X}} - \widetilde{\mathbf{C}})$ can be interpreted as the dot product of the ray from the camera centre to the point $\mathbf{X}$, with the principal ray direction. If the camera matrix is normalized so that $\det \mathtt{M} > 0$ and $\|\mathbf{m}^3\| = 1$, then $\mathbf{m}^3$ is a unit vector pointing in the *positive* axial direction. Then w may be interpreted as the depth of the point $\mathbf{X}$ from the camera centre $\mathbf{C}$ in the direction of the principal ray. This is illustrated in figure 6.6.

Any camera matrix may be normalized by multiplying it by an appropriate factor. However, to avoid having always to deal with normalized camera matrices, the depth of a point may be computed as follows:

Result 6.1. *Let* $\mathbf{X} = (\mathrm{X}, \mathrm{Y}, \mathrm{Z}, \mathrm{T})^\mathsf{T}$ *be a 3D point and* $\mathtt{P} = [\mathtt{M} \mid \mathbf{p}_4]$ *be a camera matrix for a finite camera. Suppose* $\mathtt{P}(\mathrm{X}, \mathrm{Y}, \mathrm{Z}, \mathrm{T})^\mathsf{T} = w(x, y, 1)^\mathsf{T}$*. Then*

$$\operatorname{depth}(\mathbf{X}; \mathtt{P}) = \frac{\operatorname{sign}(\det \mathtt{M})w}{\mathrm{T}\|\mathbf{m}^3\|} \tag{6.15}$$

is the depth of the point $\mathbf{X}$ *in front of the principal plane of the camera.*

This formula is an effective way to determine if a point $\mathbf{X}$ is in front of the camera. One verifies that the value of $\text{depth}(\mathbf{X}; \mathtt{P})$ is unchanged if either the point $\mathbf{X}$ or the camera matrix $\mathtt{P}$ is multiplied by a constant factor k. Thus, $\text{depth}(\mathbf{X}; \mathtt{P})$ is independent of the particular homogeneous representation of $\mathbf{X}$ and $\mathtt{P}$.

6.2.4 Decomposition of the camera matrix

Let $\mathtt{P}$ be a camera matrix representing a general projective camera. We wish to find the camera centre, the orientation of the camera and the internal parameters of the camera from $\mathtt{P}$.

Finding the camera centre. The camera centre $\mathbf{C}$ is the point for which $\mathtt{P}\mathbf{C} = \mathbf{0}$. Numerically this right null-vector may be obtained from the SVD of $\mathtt{P}$, see section A4.4(*p*585). Algebraically, the centre $\mathbf{C} = (\mathrm{X}, \mathrm{Y}, \mathrm{Z}, \mathrm{T})^{\mathsf{T}}$ may be obtained as (see (3.5–*p*67))

$$\begin{aligned} \mathrm{X} &= \det([\mathbf{p}_2, \mathbf{p}_3, \mathbf{p}_4]) & \mathrm{Y} &= -\det([\mathbf{p}_1, \mathbf{p}_3, \mathbf{p}_4]) \\ \mathrm{Z} &= \det([\mathbf{p}_1, \mathbf{p}_2, \mathbf{p}_4]) & \mathrm{T} &= -\det([\mathbf{p}_1, \mathbf{p}_2, \mathbf{p}_3]). \end{aligned}$$

Finding the camera orientation and internal parameters. In the case of a finite camera, according to (6.11),

$$\mathtt{P} = [\mathtt{M} \mid -\mathtt{M}\widetilde{\mathbf{C}}] = \mathtt{K}[\mathtt{R} \mid -\mathtt{R}\widetilde{\mathbf{C}}].$$

We may easily find both $\mathtt{K}$ and $\mathtt{R}$ by decomposing $\mathtt{M}$ as $\mathtt{M} = \mathtt{KR}$ using the RQ-decomposition. This decomposition into the product of an upper-triangular and orthogonal matrix is described in section A4.1.1(*p*579). The matrix $\mathtt{R}$ gives the orientation of the camera, whereas $\mathtt{K}$ is the calibration matrix. The ambiguity in the decomposition is removed by requiring that $\mathtt{K}$ have positive diagonal entries.

The matrix $\mathtt{K}$ has the form (6.10)

$$\mathtt{K} = \begin{bmatrix} \alpha_x & s & x_0 \\ 0 & \alpha_y & y_0 \\ 0 & 0 & 1 \end{bmatrix}$$

where

- α_x is the scale factor in the x-coordinate direction,
- α_y is the scale factor in the y-coordinate direction,
- s is the skew,
- $(x_0, y_0)^{\mathsf{T}}$ are the coordinates of the principal point.

The *aspect ratio* is α_y/α_x.

Example 6.2. The camera matrix

$$\mathtt{P} = \begin{bmatrix} 3.53553\,e{+}2 & 3.39645\,e{+}2 & 2.77744\,e{+}2 & -1.44946\,e{+}6 \\ -1.03528\,e{+}2 & 2.33212\,e{+}1 & 4.59607\,e{+}2 & -6.32525\,e{+}5 \\ 7.07107\,e{-}1 & -3.53553\,e{-}1 & 6.12372\,e{-}1 & -9.18559\,e{+}2 \end{bmatrix}$$

with $\mathtt{P} = [\mathtt{M} \mid -\mathtt{M}\widetilde{\mathbf{C}}]$, has centre $\widetilde{\mathbf{C}} = (1000.0, 2000.0, 1500.0)^\mathsf{T}$, and the matrix $\mathtt{M}$ decomposes as

$$\mathtt{M} = \mathtt{KR} = \begin{bmatrix} 468.2 & 91.2 & 300.0 \\ & 427.2 & 200.0 \\ & & 1.0 \end{bmatrix} \begin{bmatrix} 0.41380 & 0.90915 & 0.04708 \\ -0.57338 & 0.22011 & 0.78917 \\ 0.70711 & -0.35355 & 0.61237 \end{bmatrix}.$$

△

When is $s \neq 0$? As was shown in section 6.1 a true CCD camera has only four internal camera parameters, since generally $s = 0$. If $s \neq 0$ then this can be interpreted as a skewing of the pixel elements in the CCD array so that the x- and y-axes are not perpendicular. This is admittedly very unlikely to happen.

In realistic circumstances a non-zero skew might arise as a result of taking an image of an image, for example if a photograph is re-photographed, or a negative is enlarged. Consider enlarging an image taken by a pinhole camera (such as an ordinary film camera) where the axis of the magnifying lens is not perpendicular to the film plane or the enlarged image plane.

The most severe distortion that can arise from this "picture of a picture" process is a planar homography. Suppose the original (finite) camera is represented by the matrix $\mathtt{P}$, then the camera representing the picture of a picture is $\mathtt{HP}$, where $\mathtt{H}$ is the homography matrix. Since $\mathtt{H}$ is non-singular, the left 3×3 submatrix of $\mathtt{HP}$ is non-singular and can be decomposed as the product $\mathtt{KR}$ – and $\mathtt{K}$ need not have $s = 0$. Note however that the $\mathtt{K}$ and $\mathtt{R}$ are no longer the calibration matrix and orientation of the original camera.

On the other hand, one verifies that the process of taking a picture of a picture does not change the apparent camera centre. Indeed, since $\mathtt{H}$ is non-singular, $\mathtt{HPC} = \mathbf{0}$ if and only if $\mathtt{PC} = \mathbf{0}$.

Where is the decomposition required? If the camera $\mathtt{P}$ is constructed from (6.11) then the parameters are known and a decomposition is clearly unnecessary. So the question arises – where would one obtain a camera for which the decomposition is not known? In fact cameras will be computed in myriad ways throughout this book and decomposing an unknown camera is a frequently used tool in practice. For example cameras can be computed directly by *calibration* – where the camera is computed from a set of world to image correspondences (chapter 7) – and indirectly by computing a multiple view relation (such as the fundamental matrix or trifocal tensor) and subsequently computing projection matrices from this relation.

A note on coordinate orientation. In the derivation of the camera model and its parametrization (6.10) it is assumed that the coordinate systems used in both the image and the 3D world are right handed systems, as shown in figure 6.1(p154). However, a common practice in measuring image coordinates is that the y-coordinate increases in the downwards direction, thus defining a left handed coordinate system, contrary to figure 6.1(p154). A recommended practice in this case is to negate the y-coordinate of the image point so that the coordinate system again becomes right handed. However, if the image coordinate system is left handed, then the consequences are not grave. The relationship between world and image coordinates is still expressed by a 3×4 camera matrix. Decomposition of this camera matrix according to (6.11) with $\mathtt{K}$ of the form (6.10) is still possible with α_x and α_y positive. The difference is that $\mathtt{R}$ now represents the orientation of the camera with respect to the negative $\mathtt{Z}$-axis. In addition, the depth of points given by (6.15) will be *negative* instead of positive for points in front of the camera. If this is borne in mind then it is permissible to use left handed coordinates in the image.

6.2.5 Euclidean vs projective spaces

The development of the sections to this point has implicitly assumed that the world and image coordinate systems are Euclidean. Ideas have been borrowed from projective geometry (such as directions corresponding to points on $\boldsymbol{\pi}_\infty$) and the convenient notation of homogeneous coordinates has allowed central projection to be represented linearly.

In subsequent chapters of the book we will go further and use a projective coordinate frame. This is easily achieved, for suppose the world coordinate frame is projective; then the transformation between the camera and world coordinate frame (6.6) is again represented by a 4×4 homogeneous matrix, $\mathbf{X}_{\text{cam}} = \mathtt{H}\mathbf{X}$, and the resulting map from projective 3-space $\mathbb{P}^3$ to the image is still represented by a 3×4 matrix $\mathtt{P}$ with rank 3. In fact, at its most general the projective camera is a map from $\mathbb{P}^3$ to $\mathbb{P}^2$, and covers the composed effects of a projective transformation of 3-space, a projection from 3-space to an image, and a projective transformation of the image. This follows simply by concatenating the matrices representing these mappings:

$$\mathtt{P} = [3 \times 3 \text{ homography}] \begin{bmatrix} 1 & 0 & 0 & 0 \\ 0 & 1 & 0 & 0 \\ 0 & 0 & 1 & 0 \end{bmatrix} [4 \times 4 \text{ homography}]$$

which results in a 3×4 matrix.

However, it is important to remember that cameras are Euclidean devices and simply because we have a projective model of a camera it does not mean that we should eschew notions of Euclidean geometry.

Euclidean and affine interpretations. Although a (finite) 3×4 matrix can always be decomposed as in section 6.2.4 to obtain a rotation matrix, a calibration matrix $\mathtt{K}$, and so forth, Euclidean interpretations of the parameters so obtained are only meaningful if the image and space coordinates are in an appropriate frame. In the decomposition case a Euclidean frame is required for both image and 3-space. On the other hand, the interpretation of the null-vector of $\mathtt{P}$ as the camera centre is valid even if both frames are projective – the interpretation requires only collinearity, which is a projective notion. The interpretation of $\mathbf{P}^3$ as the principal plane requires at least affine frames for the image and 3-space. Finally, the interpretation of $\mathbf{m}^3$ as the principal ray requires an affine image frame but a Euclidean world frame in order for the concept of orthogonality (to the principal plane) to be meaningful.

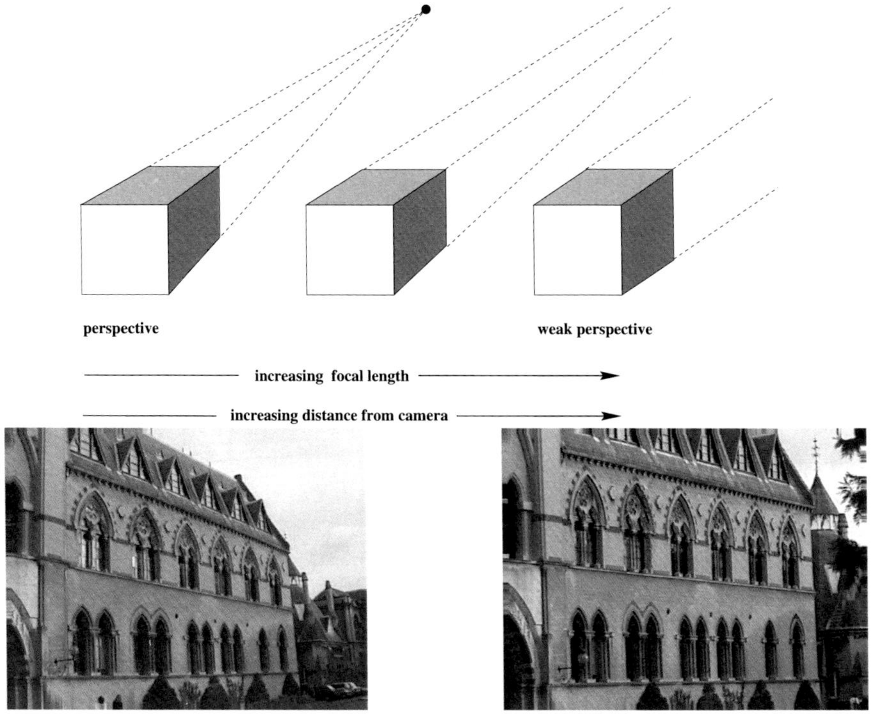

Fig. 6.7. *As the focal length increases and the distance between the camera and object also increases, the image remains the same size but perspective effects diminish.*

6.3 Cameras at infinity

We now turn to consider cameras with centre lying on the plane at infinity. This means that the left hand 3×3 block of the camera matrix $\mathtt{P}$ is singular. The camera centre may be found from $\mathtt{P}\mathbf{C} = \mathbf{0}$ just as with finite cameras.

Cameras at infinity may be broadly classified into two different types, *affine cameras* and *non-affine cameras*. We consider first of all the affine class of cameras which are the most important in practice.

Definition 6.3. An *affine* camera is one that has a camera matrix $\mathtt{P}$ in which the last row $\mathbf{P}^{3\mathsf{T}}$ is of the form $(0, 0, 0, 1)$.

It is called an affine camera because points at infinity are mapped to points at infinity.

6.3.1 Affine cameras

Consider what happens as we apply a cinematographic technique of tracking back while zooming in, in such a way as to keep objects of interest the same size[1]. This is illustrated in figure 6.7. We are going to model this process by taking the limit as both the focal length and principal axis distance of the camera from the object increase.

In analyzing this technique, we start with a finite projective camera (6.11). The

[1] See 'Vertigo' (Dir. Hitchcock, 1958) and 'Mishima' (Dir. Schrader, 1985).

camera matrix may be written as

$$\mathtt{P}_0 = \mathtt{KR}[\mathtt{I} \mid -\widetilde{\mathbf{C}}] = \mathtt{K}\begin{bmatrix} \mathbf{r}^{1\mathsf{T}} & -\mathbf{r}^{1\mathsf{T}}\widetilde{\mathbf{C}} \\ \mathbf{r}^{2\mathsf{T}} & -\mathbf{r}^{2\mathsf{T}}\widetilde{\mathbf{C}} \\ \mathbf{r}^{3\mathsf{T}} & -\mathbf{r}^{3\mathsf{T}}\widetilde{\mathbf{C}} \end{bmatrix} \tag{6.16}$$

where $\mathbf{r}^{i\mathsf{T}}$ is the i-th row of the rotation matrix. This camera is located at position $\widetilde{\mathbf{C}}$ and has orientation denoted by matrix $\mathtt{R}$ and internal parameters matrix $\mathtt{K}$ of the form given in (6.10–*p*157). From section 6.2.1 the principal ray of the camera is in the direction of the vector $\mathbf{r}^3$, and the value $d_0 = -\mathbf{r}^{3\mathsf{T}}\widetilde{\mathbf{C}}$ is the distance of the world origin from the camera centre in the direction of the principal ray.

Now, we consider what happens if the camera centre is moved backwards along the principal ray at unit speed for a time t, so that the centre of the camera is moved to $\widetilde{\mathbf{C}} - t\mathbf{r}^3$. Replacing $\widetilde{\mathbf{C}}$ in (6.16) by $\widetilde{\mathbf{C}} - t\mathbf{r}^3$ gives the camera matrix at time t:

$$\mathtt{P}_t = \mathtt{K}\begin{bmatrix} \mathbf{r}^{1\mathsf{T}} & -\mathbf{r}^{1\mathsf{T}}(\widetilde{\mathbf{C}} - t\mathbf{r}^3) \\ \mathbf{r}^{2\mathsf{T}} & -\mathbf{r}^{2\mathsf{T}}(\widetilde{\mathbf{C}} - t\mathbf{r}^3) \\ \mathbf{r}^{3\mathsf{T}} & -\mathbf{r}^{3\mathsf{T}}(\widetilde{\mathbf{C}} - t\mathbf{r}^3) \end{bmatrix} = \mathtt{K}\begin{bmatrix} \mathbf{r}^{1\mathsf{T}} & -\mathbf{r}^{1\mathsf{T}}\widetilde{\mathbf{C}} \\ \mathbf{r}^{2\mathsf{T}} & -\mathbf{r}^{2\mathsf{T}}\widetilde{\mathbf{C}} \\ \mathbf{r}^{3\mathsf{T}} & d_t \end{bmatrix} \tag{6.17}$$

where the terms $\mathbf{r}^{i\mathsf{T}}\mathbf{r}^3$ are zero for $i = 1, 2$ because $\mathtt{R}$ is a rotation matrix. The scalar $d_t = -\mathbf{r}^{3\mathsf{T}}\widetilde{\mathbf{C}} + t$ is the depth of the world origin with respect to the camera centre in the direction of the principal ray $\mathbf{r}^3$ of the camera. Thus

- *The effect of tracking along the principal ray is to replace the (3,4) entry of the matrix by the depth d_t of the camera centre from the world origin.*

Next, we consider zooming such that the camera focal length is increased by a factor k. This magnifies the image by a factor k. It is shown in section 8.4.1(*p*203) that the effect of zooming by a factor k is to multiply the calibration matrix $\mathtt{K}$ on the right by $\text{diag}(k, k, 1)$.

Now, we combine the effects of tracking and zooming. We suppose that the magnification factor is $k = d_t/d_0$ so that the image size remains fixed. The resulting camera matrix at time t, derived from (6.17), is

$$\mathtt{P}_t = \mathtt{K}\begin{bmatrix} d_t/d_0 & & \\ & d_t/d_0 & \\ & & 1 \end{bmatrix}\begin{bmatrix} \mathbf{r}^{1\mathsf{T}} & -\mathbf{r}^{1\mathsf{T}}\widetilde{\mathbf{C}} \\ \mathbf{r}^{2\mathsf{T}} & -\mathbf{r}^{2\mathsf{T}}\widetilde{\mathbf{C}} \\ \mathbf{r}^{3\mathsf{T}} & d_t \end{bmatrix} = \frac{d_t}{d_0}\mathtt{K}\begin{bmatrix} \mathbf{r}^{1\mathsf{T}} & -\mathbf{r}^{1\mathsf{T}}\widetilde{\mathbf{C}} \\ \mathbf{r}^{2\mathsf{T}} & -\mathbf{r}^{2\mathsf{T}}\widetilde{\mathbf{C}} \\ \mathbf{r}^{3\mathsf{T}}d_0/d_t & d_0 \end{bmatrix}$$

and one can ignore the factor d_t/d_0. When $t = 0$, the camera matrix $\mathtt{P}_t$ corresponds with (6.16). Now, in the limit as d_t tends to infinity, this matrix becomes

$$\mathtt{P}_\infty = \lim_{t\to\infty} \mathtt{P}_t = \mathtt{K}\begin{bmatrix} \mathbf{r}^{1\mathsf{T}} & -\mathbf{r}^{1\mathsf{T}}\widetilde{\mathbf{C}} \\ \mathbf{r}^{2\mathsf{T}} & -\mathbf{r}^{2\mathsf{T}}\widetilde{\mathbf{C}} \\ \mathbf{0}^{\mathsf{T}} & d_0 \end{bmatrix} \tag{6.18}$$

which is just the original camera matrix (6.16) with the first three entries of the last row set to zero. From definition 6.3 $\mathtt{P}_\infty$ is an instance of an affine camera.

6.3.2 Error in employing an affine camera

It may be noted that the image of any point on the plane through the world origin perpendicular to the principal axis direction $\mathbf{r}^3$ is unchanged by this combined zooming and motion. Indeed, such a point may be written as

$$\mathbf{X} = \begin{pmatrix} \alpha\mathbf{r}^1 + \beta\mathbf{r}^2 \\ 1 \end{pmatrix}.$$

One then verifies that $\mathtt{P}_0\mathbf{X} = \mathtt{P}_t\mathbf{X} = \mathtt{P}_\infty\mathbf{X}$ for all t, since $\mathbf{r}^{3\mathsf{T}}(\alpha\mathbf{r}^1 + \beta\mathbf{r}^2) = 0$.

For points not on this plane the images under $\mathtt{P}_0$ and $\mathtt{P}_\infty$ differ, and we will now investigate the extent of this error. Consider a point $\mathbf{X}$ which is at a perpendicular distance Δ from this plane. The 3D point can be represented as

$$\mathbf{X} = \begin{pmatrix} \alpha\mathbf{r}^1 + \beta\mathbf{r}^2 + \Delta\mathbf{r}^3 \\ 1 \end{pmatrix}$$

and is imaged by the cameras $\mathtt{P}_0$ and $\mathtt{P}_\infty$ at

$$\mathbf{x}_{\text{proj}} = \mathtt{P}_0\mathbf{X} = \mathtt{K}\begin{pmatrix} \tilde{x} \\ \tilde{y} \\ d_0 + \Delta \end{pmatrix} \qquad \mathbf{x}_{\text{affine}} = \mathtt{P}_\infty\mathbf{X} = \mathtt{K}\begin{pmatrix} \tilde{x} \\ \tilde{y} \\ d_0 \end{pmatrix}$$

where $\tilde{x} = \alpha - \mathbf{r}^{1\mathsf{T}}\tilde{\mathbf{C}},\ \tilde{y} = \beta - \mathbf{r}^{2\mathsf{T}}\tilde{\mathbf{C}}$. Now, writing the calibration matrix as

$$\mathtt{K} = \begin{bmatrix} \mathtt{K}_{2\times 2} & \tilde{\mathbf{x}}_0 \\ \tilde{\mathbf{0}}^\mathsf{T} & 1 \end{bmatrix},$$

where $\mathtt{K}_{2\times 2}$ is an upper-triangular 2×2 matrix, gives

$$\mathbf{x}_{\text{proj}} = \begin{pmatrix} \mathtt{K}_{2\times 2}\tilde{\mathbf{x}} + (d_0 + \Delta)\tilde{\mathbf{x}}_0 \\ d_0 + \Delta \end{pmatrix} \qquad \mathbf{x}_{\text{affine}} = \begin{pmatrix} \mathtt{K}_{2\times 2}\tilde{\mathbf{x}} + d_0\tilde{\mathbf{x}}_0 \\ d_0 \end{pmatrix}$$

The image point for $\mathtt{P}_0$ is obtained by dehomogenizing, by dividing by the third element, as $\tilde{\mathbf{x}}_{\text{proj}} = \tilde{\mathbf{x}}_0 + \mathtt{K}_{2\times 2}\tilde{\mathbf{x}}/(d_0 + \Delta)$, and for $\mathtt{P}_\infty$ the inhomogeneous image point is $\tilde{\mathbf{x}}_{\text{affine}} = \tilde{\mathbf{x}}_0 + \mathtt{K}_{2\times 2}\tilde{\mathbf{x}}/d_0$. The relationship between the two points is therefore

$$\tilde{\mathbf{x}}_{\text{affine}} - \tilde{\mathbf{x}}_0 = \frac{d_0 + \Delta}{d_0}(\tilde{\mathbf{x}}_{\text{proj}} - \tilde{\mathbf{x}}_0)$$

which shows that

- *The effect of the affine approximation* $\mathtt{P}_\infty$ *to the true camera matrix* $\mathtt{P}_0$ *is to move the image of a point* $\mathbf{X}$ *radially towards or away from the principal point* $\tilde{\mathbf{x}}_0$ *by a factor equal to* $(d_0 + \Delta)/d_0 = 1 + \Delta/d_0$.

This is illustrated in figure 6.8.

Affine imaging conditions. From the expressions for $\tilde{\mathbf{x}}_{\text{proj}}$ and $\tilde{\mathbf{x}}_{\text{affine}}$ we can deduce that

$$\tilde{\mathbf{x}}_{\text{affine}} - \tilde{\mathbf{x}}_{\text{proj}} = \frac{\Delta}{d_0}(\tilde{\mathbf{x}}_{\text{proj}} - \tilde{\mathbf{x}}_0) \tag{6.19}$$

which shows that the distance between the true perspective image position and the position obtained using the affine camera approximation $\mathtt{P}_\infty$ will be small provided:

(i) The depth relief (Δ) is small compared to the average depth (d_0), and
(ii) The distance of the point from the principal ray is small.

The latter condition is satisfied by a small field of view. In general, images acquired using a lens with a longer focal length tend to satisfy these conditions as both the field of view and the depth of field are smaller than those obtained by a short focal length lens with the same CCD array.

For scenes at which there are many points at different depths, the affine camera is not a good approximation. For instance where the scene contains close foreground as well as background objects, an affine camera model should not be used. However, a different affine model can be used for each region in these circumstances.

6.3.3 Decomposition of $\mathtt{P}_\infty$

The camera matrix (6.18) may be written as

$$\mathtt{P}_\infty = \begin{bmatrix} \mathtt{K}_{2\times 2} & \tilde{\mathbf{x}}_0 \\ \hat{\mathbf{0}}^\mathsf{T} & 1 \end{bmatrix} \begin{bmatrix} \hat{\mathtt{R}} & \hat{\mathbf{t}} \\ \mathbf{0}^\mathsf{T} & d_0 \end{bmatrix}$$

where $\hat{\mathtt{R}}$ consists of the two first rows of a rotation matrix, $\hat{\mathbf{t}}$ is the vector $(-\mathbf{r}^{1\mathsf{T}}\tilde{\mathbf{C}}, -\mathbf{r}^{2\mathsf{T}}\tilde{\mathbf{C}})^\mathsf{T}$, and $\hat{\mathbf{0}}$ the vector $(0,0)^\mathsf{T}$. The 2×2 matrix $\mathtt{K}_{2\times 2}$ is upper-triangular. One quickly verifies that

$$\mathtt{P}_\infty = \begin{bmatrix} \mathtt{K}_{2\times 2} & \tilde{\mathbf{x}}_0 \\ \hat{\mathbf{0}}^\mathsf{T} & 1 \end{bmatrix} \begin{bmatrix} \hat{\mathtt{R}} & \hat{\mathbf{t}} \\ \mathbf{0}^\mathsf{T} & d_0 \end{bmatrix} = \begin{bmatrix} d_0^{-1}\mathtt{K}_{2\times 2} & \tilde{\mathbf{x}}_0 \\ \hat{\mathbf{0}}^\mathsf{T} & 1 \end{bmatrix} \begin{bmatrix} \hat{\mathtt{R}} & \hat{\mathbf{t}} \\ \mathbf{0}^\mathsf{T} & 1 \end{bmatrix}$$

so we may replace $\mathtt{K}_{2\times 2}$ by $d_0^{-1}\mathtt{K}_{2\times 2}$ and assume that $d_0 = 1$. Multiplying out this product gives

$$\begin{aligned} \mathtt{P}_\infty &= \begin{bmatrix} \mathtt{K}_{2\times 2}\hat{\mathtt{R}} & \mathtt{K}_{2\times 2}\hat{\mathbf{t}} + \tilde{\mathbf{x}}_0 \\ \hat{\mathbf{0}}^\mathsf{T} & 1 \end{bmatrix} = \begin{bmatrix} \mathtt{K}_{2\times 2} & \hat{\mathbf{0}} \\ \hat{\mathbf{0}}^\mathsf{T} & 1 \end{bmatrix} \begin{bmatrix} \hat{\mathtt{R}} & \hat{\mathbf{t}} + \mathtt{K}_{2\times 2}^{-1}\tilde{\mathbf{x}}_0 \\ \mathbf{0}^\mathsf{T} & 1 \end{bmatrix} \\ &= \begin{bmatrix} \mathtt{K}_{2\times 2} & \mathtt{K}_{2\times 2}\hat{\mathbf{t}} + \tilde{\mathbf{x}}_0 \\ \hat{\mathbf{0}}^\mathsf{T} & 1 \end{bmatrix} \begin{bmatrix} \hat{\mathtt{R}} & \hat{\mathbf{0}} \\ \mathbf{0}^\mathsf{T} & 1 \end{bmatrix}. \end{aligned}$$

Thus, making appropriate substitutions for $\hat{\mathbf{t}}$ or $\tilde{\mathbf{x}}_0$, we can write the affine camera matrix in one of the two forms

$$\mathtt{P}_\infty = \begin{bmatrix} \mathtt{K}_{2\times 2} & \hat{\mathbf{0}} \\ \hat{\mathbf{0}}^\mathsf{T} & 1 \end{bmatrix} \begin{bmatrix} \hat{\mathtt{R}} & \hat{\mathbf{t}} \\ \mathbf{0}^\mathsf{T} & 1 \end{bmatrix} = \begin{bmatrix} \mathtt{K}_{2\times 2} & \tilde{\mathbf{x}}_0 \\ \hat{\mathbf{0}}^\mathsf{T} & 1 \end{bmatrix} \begin{bmatrix} \hat{\mathtt{R}} & \hat{\mathbf{0}} \\ \mathbf{0}^\mathsf{T} & 1 \end{bmatrix}. \tag{6.20}$$

Consequently, the camera $\mathtt{P}_\infty$ can be interpreted in terms of these decompositions in

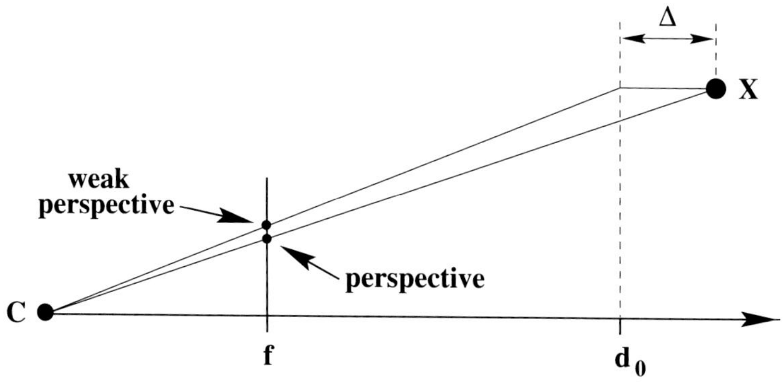

Fig. 6.8. **Perspective vs weak perspective projection.** *The action of the weak perspective camera is equivalent to orthographic projection onto a plane (at $Z = d_0$), followed by perspective projection from the plane. The difference between the perspective and weak perspective image point depends both on the distance Δ of the point $\mathbf{X}$ from the plane, and the distance of the point from the principal ray.*

one of two ways, either with $\tilde{\mathbf{x}}_0 = \mathbf{0}$ or with $\hat{\mathbf{t}} = \hat{\mathbf{0}}$. Using the second decomposition of (6.20), the image of the world origin is $\mathtt{P}_\infty(0,0,0,1)^\mathsf{T} = (\tilde{\mathbf{x}}_0^\mathsf{T}, 1)^\mathsf{T}$. Consequently, the value of $\tilde{\mathbf{x}}_0$ is dependent on the particular choice of world coordinates, and hence is not an intrinsic property of the camera itself. This means that the camera matrix $\mathtt{P}_\infty$ does not have a principal point. Therefore, it is preferable to use the first decomposition of $\mathtt{P}_\infty$ in (6.20), and write

$$\mathtt{P}_\infty = \begin{bmatrix} \mathtt{K}_{2\times 2} & \hat{\mathbf{0}} \\ \hat{\mathbf{0}}^\mathsf{T} & 1 \end{bmatrix} \begin{bmatrix} \hat{\mathtt{R}} & \hat{\mathbf{t}} \\ \mathbf{0}^\mathsf{T} & 1 \end{bmatrix} \tag{6.21}$$

where the two matrices represent the internal camera parameters and external camera parameters of $\mathtt{P}_\infty$.

Parallel projection. In summary the essential differences between $\mathtt{P}_\infty$ and a finite camera are:

- *The parallel projection matrix* $\begin{bmatrix} 1 & 0 & 0 & 0 \\ 0 & 1 & 0 & 0 \\ 0 & 0 & 0 & 1 \end{bmatrix}$ *replaces the canonical projection matrix* $[\mathtt{I} \mid \mathbf{0}]$ *of a finite camera (6.5–p155).*
- *The calibration matrix* $\begin{bmatrix} \mathtt{K}_{2\times 2} & \hat{\mathbf{0}} \\ \hat{\mathbf{0}}^\mathsf{T} & 1 \end{bmatrix}$ *replaces* $\mathtt{K}$ *of a finite camera (6.10–p157).*
- *The principal point is not defined.*

6.3.4 A hierarchy of affine cameras

In a similar manner to the development of the finite projection camera taxonomy in section 6.1 we can start with the basic operation of parallel projection and build a hierarchy of camera models representing progressively more general cases of parallel projection.

Orthographic projection. Consider projection along the Z-axis. This is represented by a matrix of the form

$$\mathtt{P} = \begin{bmatrix} 1 & 0 & 0 & 0 \\ 0 & 1 & 0 & 0 \\ 0 & 0 & 0 & 1 \end{bmatrix}. \tag{6.22}$$

This mapping takes a point $(\mathrm{X}, \mathrm{Y}, \mathrm{Z}, 1)^\mathsf{T}$ to the image point $(\mathrm{X}, \mathrm{Y}, 1)^\mathsf{T}$, dropping the Z-coordinate.

For a general orthographic projection mapping, we precede this map by a 3D Euclidean coordinate change of the form

$$\mathtt{H} = \begin{bmatrix} \mathtt{R} & \mathbf{t} \\ \mathbf{0}^\mathsf{T} & 1 \end{bmatrix}.$$

Writing $\mathbf{t} = (t_1, t_2, t_3)^\mathsf{T}$, we see that a general orthographic camera is of the form

$$\mathtt{P} = \begin{bmatrix} \mathbf{r}^{1\mathsf{T}} & t_1 \\ \mathbf{r}^{2\mathsf{T}} & t_2 \\ \mathbf{0}^\mathsf{T} & 1 \end{bmatrix}. \tag{6.23}$$

An orthographic camera has five degrees of freedom, namely the three parameters describing the rotation matrix $\mathtt{R}$, plus the two offset parameters t_1 and t_2. An orthographic projection matrix $\mathtt{P} = [\mathtt{M} \mid \mathbf{t}]$ is characterized by a matrix $\mathtt{M}$ with last row zero, with the first two rows orthogonal and of unit norm, and $t_3 = 1$.

Scaled orthographic projection. A scaled orthographic projection is an orthographic projection followed by isotropic scaling. Thus, in general, its matrix may be written in the form

$$\mathtt{P} = \begin{bmatrix} k & & \\ & k & \\ & & 1 \end{bmatrix} \begin{bmatrix} \mathbf{r}^{1\mathsf{T}} & t_1 \\ \mathbf{r}^{2\mathsf{T}} & t_2 \\ \mathbf{0}^\mathsf{T} & 1 \end{bmatrix} = \begin{bmatrix} \mathbf{r}^{1\mathsf{T}} & t_1 \\ \mathbf{r}^{2\mathsf{T}} & t_2 \\ \mathbf{0}^\mathsf{T} & 1/k \end{bmatrix}. \tag{6.24}$$

It has six degrees of freedom. A scaled orthographic projection matrix $\mathtt{P} = [\mathtt{M} \mid \mathbf{t}]$ is characterized by a matrix $\mathtt{M}$ with last row zero, and the first two rows orthogonal and of equal norm.

Weak perspective projection. Analogous to a finite CCD camera, we may consider the case of a camera at infinity for which the scale factors in the two axial image directions are not equal. Such a camera has a projection matrix of the form

$$\mathtt{P} = \begin{bmatrix} \alpha_x & & \\ & \alpha_y & \\ & & 1 \end{bmatrix} \begin{bmatrix} \mathbf{r}^{1\mathsf{T}} & t_1 \\ \mathbf{r}^{2\mathsf{T}} & t_2 \\ \mathbf{0}^\mathsf{T} & 1 \end{bmatrix}. \tag{6.25}$$

It has seven degrees of freedom. A weak perspective projection matrix $\mathtt{P} = [\mathtt{M} \mid \mathbf{t}]$ is characterized by a matrix $\mathtt{M}$ with last row zero, and first two rows orthogonal (but they need not have equal norm as is required in the scaled orthographic case). The geometric action of this camera is illustrated in figure 6.8.

The affine camera, $\mathtt{P}_{\mathrm{A}}$. As has already been seen in the case of $\mathtt{P}_\infty$, a general camera matrix of the affine form, and with no restrictions on its elements, may be decomposed as

$$\mathtt{P}_{\mathrm{A}} = \begin{bmatrix} \alpha_x & s & \\ & \alpha_y & \\ & & 1 \end{bmatrix} \begin{bmatrix} \mathbf{r}^{1\mathsf{T}} & t_1 \\ \mathbf{r}^{2\mathsf{T}} & t_2 \\ \mathbf{0}^{\mathsf{T}} & 1 \end{bmatrix}.$$

It has eight degrees of freedom, and may be thought of as the parallel projection version of the finite projective camera (6.11–*p*157).

In full generality an affine camera has the form

$$\mathtt{P}_{\mathrm{A}} = \begin{bmatrix} m_{11} & m_{12} & m_{13} & t_1 \\ m_{21} & m_{22} & m_{23} & t_2 \\ 0 & 0 & 0 & 1 \end{bmatrix}.$$

It has eight degrees of freedom corresponding to the eight non-zero and non-unit matrix elements. We denote the top left 2×3 submatrix by $\mathtt{M}_{2\times3}$. The sole restriction on the affine camera is that $\mathtt{M}_{2\times3}$ has rank 2. This arises from the requirement that the rank of $\mathtt{P}$ is 3.

The affine camera covers the composed effects of an affine transformation of 3-space, an orthographic projection from 3-space to an image, and an affine transformation of the image. This follows simply by concatenating the matrices representing these mappings:

$$\mathtt{P}_{\mathrm{A}} = [3 \times 3 \text{ affine}] \begin{bmatrix} 1 & 0 & 0 & 0 \\ 0 & 1 & 0 & 0 \\ 0 & 0 & 0 & 1 \end{bmatrix} [4 \times 4 \text{ affine}]$$

which results in a 3×4 matrix of the affine form.

Projection under an affine camera is a linear mapping on *inhomogeneous* coordinates composed with a translation:

$$\begin{pmatrix} x \\ y \end{pmatrix} = \begin{bmatrix} m_{11} & m_{12} & m_{13} \\ m_{21} & m_{22} & m_{23} \end{bmatrix} \begin{pmatrix} \mathrm{X} \\ \mathrm{Y} \\ \mathrm{Z} \end{pmatrix} + \begin{pmatrix} t_1 \\ t_2 \end{pmatrix}$$

which is written more concisely as

$$\tilde{\mathbf{x}} = \mathtt{M}_{2\times3}\tilde{\mathbf{X}} + \tilde{\mathbf{t}} \ . \qquad (6.26)$$

The point $\tilde{\mathbf{t}} = (t_1, t_2)^{\mathsf{T}}$ is the image of the world origin.

The camera models of this section are seen to be affine cameras satisfying additional constraints, thus the affine camera is an abstraction of this hierarchy. For example, in the case of the weak perspective camera the rows of $\mathtt{M}_{2\times3}$ are scalings of rows of a rotation matrix, and thus are orthogonal.

6.3.5 More properties of the affine camera

The plane at infinity in space is mapped to points at infinity in the image. This is easily seen by computing $\mathtt{P}_{\mathrm{A}}(\mathrm{X}, \mathrm{Y}, \mathrm{Z}, 0)^{\mathsf{T}} = (\mathrm{X}, \mathrm{Y}, 0)^{\mathsf{T}}$. Extending the terminology of finite projective cameras, we interpret this by saying that the principal plane of the camera is the plane at infinity. The optical centre, since it lies on the principal plane, must also lie on the plane at infinity. From this we have

(i) Conversely, any projective camera matrix for which the principal plane is the plane at infinity is an affine camera matrix.
(ii) Parallel world lines are projected to parallel image lines. This follows because parallel world lines intersect at the plane at infinity, and this intersection point is mapped to a point at infinity in the image. Hence the image lines are parallel.
(iii) The vector $\mathbf{d}$ satisfying $\mathtt{M}_{2\times3}\mathbf{d} = \mathbf{0}$ is the *direction* of parallel projection, and $(\mathbf{d}^\mathsf{T}, 0)^\mathsf{T}$ the camera centre since $\mathtt{P}_\mathtt{A}\begin{pmatrix}\mathbf{d}\\0\end{pmatrix} = \mathbf{0}$.

Any camera which consists of the composed effects of affine transformations (either of space, or of the image) with parallel projection will have the affine form. For example, *para-perspective* projection consists of two such mappings: the first is parallel projection onto a plane π through the centroid and parallel to the image plane. The direction of parallel projection is the ray joining the centroid to the camera centre. This parallel projection is followed by an affine transformation (actually a similarity) between π and the image. Thus a para-perspective camera is an affine camera.

6.3.6 General cameras at infinity

An affine camera is one for which the principal plane is the plane at infinity. As such, its camera centre lies on the plane at infinity. However, it is possible for the camera centre to lie on the plane at infinity without the whole principal plane being the plane at infinity.

A camera centre lies at infinity if $\mathtt{P} = [\mathtt{M} \mid \mathbf{p}_4]$ with $\mathtt{M}$ a singular matrix. This is clearly a weaker condition than insisting that the last row of $\mathtt{M}$ is zero, as is the case for affine cameras. If $\mathtt{M}$ is singular, but the last row of $\mathtt{M}$ is not zero, then the camera is not affine, but not a finite projective camera either. Such a camera is rather a strange object, however, and will not be treated in detail in this book. We may compare the properties of affine and non-affine infinite cameras:

	Affine camera	Non-affine camera
Camera centre on $\boldsymbol{\pi}_\infty$	yes	yes
Principal plane is $\boldsymbol{\pi}_\infty$	yes	no
Image of points on $\boldsymbol{\pi}_\infty$ on $\mathbf{l}_\infty$	yes	no in general

In both cases the camera centre is the direction of projection. Furthermore, in the case of an affine camera all non-infinite points are in front of the camera. For a non-affine camera space is partitioned into two sets of points by the principal plane.

A general camera at infinity could arise from a perspective image of an image produced by an affine camera. This imaging process corresponds to left-multiplying the

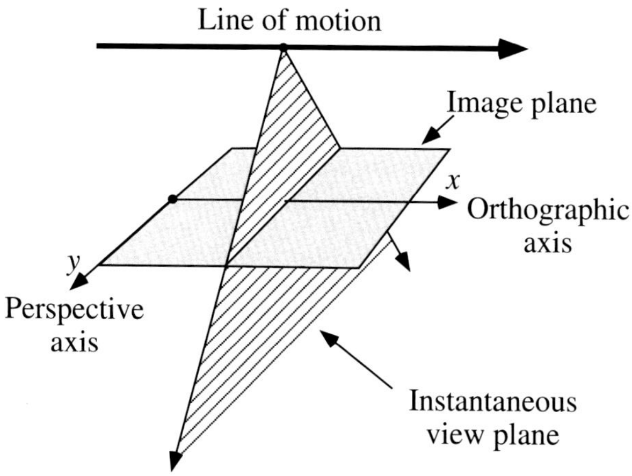

Fig. 6.9. *Acquisition geometry of a pushbroom camera.*

affine camera by a general 3×3 matrix representing the planar homography. The resulting 3×4 matrix is still a camera at infinity, but it does not have the affine form, since parallel lines in the world will in general appear as converging lines in the image.

6.4 Other camera models

6.4.1 Pushbroom cameras

The Linear Pushbroom (LP) camera is an abstraction of a type of sensor common in satellites, for instance the SPOT sensor. In such a camera, a linear sensor array is used to capture a single line of imagery at a time. As the sensor moves the sensor plane sweeps out a region of space (hence the name pushbroom), capturing the image a single line at a time. The second dimension of the image is provided by the motion of the sensor. In the linear pushbroom model, the sensor is assumed to move in a straight line at constant velocity with respect to the ground. In addition, one assumes that the orientation of the sensor array with respect to the direction of travel is constant. In the direction of the sensor, the image is effectively a perspective image, whereas in the direction of the sensor motion it is an orthographic projection. The geometry of the LP camera is illustrated in figure 6.9. It turns out that the mapping from object space into the image may be described by a 3×4 camera matrix, just as with a general projective camera. However, the way in which this matrix is used is somewhat different.

- *Let* $\mathbf{X} = (\mathrm{X}, \mathrm{Y}, \mathrm{Z}, 1)^\mathsf{T}$ *be an object point, and let* $\mathtt{P}$ *be the camera matrix of the LP camera. Suppose that* $\mathtt{P}\mathbf{X} = (x, y, w)^\mathsf{T}$*. Then the corresponding image point (represented as an inhomogeneous 2-vector) is* $(x, y/w)^\mathsf{T}$*.*

One must compare this with the projective camera mapping. In that case the point represented by $(x, y, w)^\mathsf{T}$ is $(x/w, y/w)^\mathsf{T}$. Note the difference that in the LP case, the coordinate x is not divided by the factor w to get the image coordinate. In this formula, the x-axis in the image is the direction of the sensor motion, whereas the y-axis is in the direction of the linear sensor array. The camera has 11 degrees of freedom.

Another way of writing the formula for LP projection is

$$\tilde{x} = x = \mathtt{P}^{1\mathsf{T}}\mathbf{X} \qquad \tilde{y} = y/z = \frac{\mathtt{P}^{2\mathsf{T}}\mathbf{X}}{\mathtt{P}^{3\mathsf{T}}\mathbf{X}} \tag{6.27}$$

where $(\tilde{x}, \tilde{y})$ is the image point.

Note that the $\tilde{y}$-coordinate behaves projectively, whereas the $\tilde{x}$ is obtained by orthogonal projection of the point $\mathbf{X}$ on the direction perpendicular to the plane $\mathtt{P}^1$. The vector $\mathtt{P}^1$ represents the sweep plane of the camera at time $t = 0$ – that is the moment when the line with coordinates $\tilde{x} = 0$ is captured.

Mapping of lines. One of the novel features of the LP camera is that straight lines in space are not mapped to straight lines in the image (they are mapped to straight lines in the case of a projective camera – see section 8.1.2). The set of points $\mathbf{X}$ lying on a 3D line may be written as $\mathbf{X}_0 + \alpha\mathbf{D}$, where $\mathbf{X}_0 = (\mathrm{X}, \mathrm{Y}, \mathrm{Z}, 1)^\mathsf{T}$ is a point on the line and $\mathbf{D} = (D_\mathrm{X}, D_\mathrm{Y}, D_\mathrm{Z}, 0)^\mathsf{T}$ is the intersection of this line with the plane at infinity. In this case, we compute from (6.27)

$$\begin{aligned} \tilde{x} &= \mathbf{P}^{1\mathsf{T}}(\mathbf{X}_0 + t\mathbf{D}) \\ \tilde{y} &= \frac{\mathbf{P}^{2\mathsf{T}}(\mathbf{X}_0 + t\mathbf{D})}{\mathbf{P}^{3\mathsf{T}}(\mathbf{X}_0 + t\mathbf{D})}. \end{aligned}$$

This may be written as a pair of equations $\tilde{x} = a+bt$ and $(c+dt)\tilde{y} = e+ft$. Eliminating t from these equations leads to an equation of the form $\alpha\tilde{x}\tilde{y} + \beta\tilde{x} + \gamma\tilde{y} + \delta = 0$, which is the equation of a hyperbola in the image plane, asymptotic in one direction to the line $\alpha\tilde{x} + \gamma = 0$, and in the other direction to the line $\alpha\tilde{y} + \beta = 0$. A hyperbola is made up of two curves. However, only one of the curves making up the image of a line actually appears in the image – the other part of the hyperbola corresponds to points lying behind the camera.

6.4.2 Line cameras

This chapter has dealt with the central projection of 3-space onto a 2D image. An analogous development can be given for the central projection of a plane onto a 1D line contained in the plane. See figure 22.1(*p*535). The camera model for this geometry is

$$\begin{bmatrix} x \\ y \end{bmatrix} = \begin{bmatrix} p_{11} & p_{12} & p_{13} \\ p_{21} & p_{22} & p_{23} \end{bmatrix} \begin{bmatrix} \mathrm{X} \\ \mathrm{Y} \\ \mathrm{Z} \end{bmatrix} = \mathtt{P}_{2\times 3}\mathbf{x}$$

which is a linear mapping from homogeneous representation of the plane to a homogeneous representation of the line. The camera has 5 degrees of freedom. Again the null-space, $\mathbf{c}$, of the $\mathtt{P}_{2\times 3}$ projection matrix is the camera centre, and the matrix can be decomposed in a similar manner to the finite projective camera (6.11–*p*157) as

$$\mathtt{P}_{2\times 3} = \mathtt{K}_{2\times 2}\mathtt{R}_{2\times 2}[\mathtt{I}_{2\times 2} \mid -\tilde{\mathbf{c}}]$$

where $\tilde{\mathbf{c}}$ is the inhomogeneous 2-vector representing the centre (2 dof), $\mathtt{R}_{2\times2}$ is a rotation matrix (1 dof), and

$$\mathtt{K}_{2\times2} = \begin{bmatrix} \alpha_x & x_0 \\ & 1 \end{bmatrix}$$

the internal calibration matrix (2 dof).

6.5 Closure

This chapter has covered camera models, their taxonomy and anatomy. The subsequent chapters cover the estimation of cameras from a set of world to image correspondences, and the action of a camera on various geometric objects such as lines and quadrics. Vanishing points and vanishing lines are also described in more detail in chapter 8.

6.5.1 The literature

[Aloimonos-90] defined a hierarchy of camera models including para-perspective. Mundy and Zisserman [Mundy-92] generalized this with the affine camera. Faugeras developed properties of the projective camera in his textbook [Faugeras-93]. Further details on the linear pushbroom camera are given in [Gupta-97], and on the 2D camera in [Quan-97b].

6.5.2 Notes and exercises

(i) Let I_0 be a projective image, and I_1 be an image of I_0 (an image of an image). Let the composite image be denoted by I'. Show that the apparent camera centre of I' is the same as that of I_0. Speculate on how this explains why a portrait's eyes "follow you round the room." Verify on the other hand that all other parameters of I' and I_0 may be different.

(ii) Show that the ray back-projected from an image point $\mathbf{x}$ under a projective camera $\mathtt{P}$ (as in (6.14–*p*162)) may be written as

$$\mathtt{L}^* = \mathtt{P}^\mathsf{T}[\mathbf{x}]_\times \mathtt{P} \tag{6.28}$$

where $\mathtt{L}^*$ is the dual Plücker representation of a line (3.9–*p*71).

(iii) **The affine camera.**

(a) Show that the affine camera is the most general linear mapping on homogeneous coordinates that maps parallel world lines to parallel image lines. To do this consider the projection of points on $\boldsymbol{\pi}_\infty$, and show that only if $\mathtt{P}$ has the affine form will they map to points at infinity in the image.

(b) Show that for parallel lines mapped by an affine camera the ratio of lengths on line segments is an invariant. What other invariants are there under an affine camera?

(iv) **The rational polynomial camera** is a general camera model, used extensively in the satellite surveillance community. Image coordinates are defined by the ratios

$$x = N_x(\mathbf{X})/D_x(\mathbf{X}) \quad y = N_y(\mathbf{X})/D_y(\mathbf{X})$$

where the functions N_x, D_x, N_y, D_y are homogeneous *cubic* polynomials in the 3-space point $\mathbf{X}$. Each cubic has 20 coefficients, so that overall the camera has 78 degrees of freedom. All of the cameras surveyed in this chapter (projective, affine, pushbroom) are special cases of the rational polynomial camera. Its disadvantage is that it is severely over-parametrized for these cases. More details are given in Hartley and Saxena [Hartley-97e].

(v) A finite projective camera (6.11–*p*157) $\mathtt{P}$ may be transformed to an orthographic camera (6.22) by applying a 4×4 homography $\mathtt{H}$ on the right such that

$$\mathtt{PH} = \mathtt{KR}[\mathtt{I} \mid -\widetilde{\mathbf{C}}]\mathtt{H} = \begin{bmatrix} 1 & 0 & 0 & 0 \\ 0 & 1 & 0 & 0 \\ 0 & 0 & 0 & 1 \end{bmatrix} = \mathtt{P}_{\text{orthog}} \ .$$

(the last row of $\mathtt{H}$ is chosen so that $\mathtt{H}$ has rank 4). Then since

$$\mathbf{x} = \mathtt{P}(\mathtt{HH}^{-1})\mathbf{X} = (\mathtt{PH})(\mathtt{H}^{-1}\mathbf{X}) = \mathtt{P}_{\text{orthog}}\mathbf{X}'$$

imaging under $\mathtt{P}$ is equivalent to first transforming the 3-space points $\mathbf{X}$ to $\mathbf{X}' = \mathtt{H}^{-1}\mathbf{X}$ and then applying an orthographic projection. Thus the action of any camera may be considered as a projective transformation of 3-space followed by orthographic projection.

7

Computation of the Camera Matrix P

This chapter describes numerical methods for estimating the camera projection matrix from corresponding 3-space and image entities. This computation of the camera matrix is known as *resectioning*. The simplest such correspondence is that between a 3D point $\mathbf{X}$ and its image $\mathbf{x}$ under the unknown camera mapping. Given sufficiently many correspondences $\mathbf{X}_i \leftrightarrow \mathbf{x}_i$ the camera matrix $\mathtt{P}$ may be determined. Similarly, $\mathtt{P}$ may be determined from sufficiently many corresponding world and image lines.

If additional constraints apply to the matrix $\mathtt{P}$, such as that the pixels are square, then a *restricted* camera matrix subject to these constraints may be estimated from world to image correspondences.

Throughout this book it is assumed that the map from 3-space to the image is linear. This assumption is invalid if there is lens distortion. The topic of radial lens distortion correction is dealt with in this chapter.

The internal parameters $\mathtt{K}$ of the camera may be extracted from the matrix $\mathtt{P}$ by the decomposition of section 6.2.4. Alternatively, the internal parameters can be computed directly, without necessitating estimating $\mathtt{P}$, by the methods of chapter 8.

7.1 Basic equations

We assume a number of point correspondences $\mathbf{X}_i \leftrightarrow \mathbf{x}_i$ between 3D points $\mathbf{X}_i$ and 2D image points $\mathbf{x}_i$ are given. We are required to find a camera matrix $\mathtt{P}$, namely a 3×4 matrix such that $\mathbf{x}_i = \mathtt{P}\mathbf{X}_i$ for all i. The similarity of this problem with that of computing a 2D projective transformation $\mathtt{H}$, treated in chapter 4, is evident. The only difference is the dimension of the problem. In the 2D case the matrix $\mathtt{H}$ has dimension 3×3, whereas in the present case, $\mathtt{P}$ is a 3×4 matrix. As one may expect, much of the material from chapter 4 applies almost unchanged to the present case.

As in section 4.1(*p*88) for each correspondence $\mathbf{X}_i \leftrightarrow \mathbf{x}_i$ we derive a relationship

$$\begin{bmatrix} \mathbf{0}^\mathsf{T} & -w_i\mathbf{X}_i^\mathsf{T} & y_i\mathbf{X}_i^\mathsf{T} \\ w_i\mathbf{X}_i^\mathsf{T} & \mathbf{0}^\mathsf{T} & -x_i\mathbf{X}_i^\mathsf{T} \\ -y_i\mathbf{X}_i^\mathsf{T} & x_i\mathbf{X}_i^\mathsf{T} & \mathbf{0}^\mathsf{T} \end{bmatrix} \begin{pmatrix} \mathbf{P}^1 \\ \mathbf{P}^2 \\ \mathbf{P}^3 \end{pmatrix} = \mathbf{0}. \tag{7.1}$$

where each $\mathbf{P}^{i\mathsf{T}}$ is a 4-vector, the i-th row of $\mathtt{P}$. Alternatively, one may choose to use only the first two equations:

$$\begin{bmatrix} \mathbf{0}^\mathsf{T} & -w_i\mathbf{X}_i^\mathsf{T} & y_i\mathbf{X}_i^\mathsf{T} \\ w_i\mathbf{X}_i^\mathsf{T} & \mathbf{0}^\mathsf{T} & -x_i\mathbf{X}_i^\mathsf{T} \end{bmatrix} \begin{pmatrix} \mathbf{P}^1 \\ \mathbf{P}^2 \\ \mathbf{P}^3 \end{pmatrix} = \mathbf{0} \tag{7.2}$$

since the three equations of (7.1) are linearly dependent. From a set of n point correspondences, we obtain a $2n \times 12$ matrix $\mathtt{A}$ by stacking up the equations (7.2) for each correspondence. The projection matrix $\mathtt{P}$ is computed by solving the set of equations $\mathtt{A}\mathbf{p} = \mathbf{0}$, where $\mathbf{p}$ is the vector containing the entries of the matrix $\mathtt{P}$.

Minimal solution. Since the matrix $\mathtt{P}$ has 12 entries, and (ignoring scale) 11 degrees of freedom, it is necessary to have 11 equations to solve for $\mathtt{P}$. Since each point correspondence leads to two equations, at a minimum $5\frac{1}{2}$ such correspondences are required to solve for $\mathtt{P}$. The $\frac{1}{2}$ indicates that only one of the equations is used from the sixth point, so one needs only to know the x-coordinate (or alternatively the y-coordinate) of the sixth image point.

Given this minimum number of correspondences, the solution is exact, i.e. the space points are projected exactly onto their measured images. The solution is obtained by solving $\mathtt{A}\mathbf{p} = \mathbf{0}$ where $\mathtt{A}$ is an 11×12 matrix in this case. In general $\mathtt{A}$ will have rank 11, and the solution vector $\mathbf{p}$ is the 1-dimensional right null-space of $\mathtt{A}$.

Over-determined solution. If the data is not exact, because of noise in the point coordinates, and $n \geq 6$ point correspondences are given, then there will not be an exact solution to the equations $\mathtt{A}\mathbf{p} = \mathbf{0}$. As in the estimation of a homography a solution for $\mathtt{P}$ may be obtained by minimizing an algebraic or geometric error.

In the case of algebraic error the approach is to minimize $\|\mathtt{A}\mathbf{p}\|$ subject to some normalization constraint. Possible constraints are

(i) $\|\mathbf{p}\| = 1$;
(ii) $\|\hat{\mathbf{p}}^3\| = 1$, where $\hat{\mathbf{p}}^3$ is the vector $(p_{31}, p_{32}, p_{33})^\mathsf{T}$, namely the first three entries in the last row of $\mathtt{P}$.

The first of these is preferred for routine use and will be used for the moment. We will return to the second normalization constraint in section 7.2.1. In either case, the residual $\mathtt{A}\mathbf{p}$ is known as the *algebraic error*. Using these equations, the complete DLT algorithm for computation of the camera matrix $\mathtt{P}$ proceeds in the same manner as that for $\mathtt{H}$ given in algorithm 4.1(*p*91).

Degenerate configurations. Analysis of the degenerate configurations for estimation of $\mathtt{P}$ is rather more involved than in the case of the 2D homography. There are two types of configurations in which ambiguous solutions exist for $\mathtt{P}$. These configurations will be investigated in detail in chapter 22. The most important critical configurations are as follows:

(i) The camera and points all lie on a twisted cubic.

(ii) The points all lie on the union of a plane and a single straight line containing the camera centre.

For such configurations, the camera cannot be obtained uniquely from the images of the points. Instead, it may move arbitrarily along the twisted cubic, or straight line respectively. If data is close to a degenerate configuration then a poor estimate for P is obtained. For example, if the camera is distant from a scene with low relief, such as a near-nadir aerial view, then this situation is close to the planar degeneracy.

Data normalization. It is important to carry out some sort of data normalization just as in the 2D homography estimation case. The points $\mathbf{x}_i$ in the image are appropriately normalized in the same way as before. Namely the points should be translated so that their centroid is at the origin, and scaled so that their RMS (root-mean-squared) distance from the origin is $\sqrt{2}$. What normalization should be applied to the 3D points $\mathbf{X}_i$ is a little more problematical. In the case where the variation in depth of the points from the camera is relatively slight it makes sense to carry out the same sort of normalization. Thus, the centroid of the points is translated to the origin, and their coordinates are scaled so that the RMS distance from the origin is $\sqrt{3}$ (so that the "average" point has coordinates of magnitude $(1, 1, 1, 1)^{\mathsf{T}}$). This approach is suitable for a compact distribution of points, such as those on the calibration object of figure 7.1.

In the case where there are some points that lie at a great distance from the camera, the previous normalization technique does not work well. For instance, if there are points close to the camera, as well as points that lie at infinity (which are imaged as vanishing points) or close to infinity, as may occur in oblique views of terrain, then it is not possible or reasonable to translate the points so that their centroid is at the origin. The normalization method described in exercise (iii) on page 128 would be more appropriately used in such a case, though this has not been thoroughly tested.

With appropriate normalization the estimate of P is carried out in the same manner as algorithm 4.2(p109) for H.

Line correspondences. It is a simple matter to extend the DLT algorithm to take account of line correspondences as well. A line in 3D may be represented by two points $\mathbf{X}_0$ and $\mathbf{X}_1$ through which the line passes. Now, according to result 8.2(p197) the plane formed by back-projecting from the image line $\mathbf{l}$ is equal to $\mathtt{P}^{\mathsf{T}}\mathbf{l}$. The condition that the point $\mathbf{X}_j$ lies on this plane is then

$$\mathbf{l}^{\mathsf{T}}\mathtt{P}\mathbf{X}_j = 0 \quad \text{for } j = 0, 1. \tag{7.3}$$

Each choice of j gives a single linear equation in the entries of the matrix P, so two equations are obtained for each 3D to 2D line correspondence. These equations, being linear in the entries of P, may be added to the equations (7.1) obtained from point correspondences and a solution to the composite equation set may be computed.

7.2 Geometric error

As in the case of 2D homographies (chapter 4), one may define geometric error. Suppose for the moment that world points $\mathbf{X}_i$ are known far more accurately than the

Objective

Given $n \geq 6$ world to image point correspondences $\{\mathbf{X}_i \leftrightarrow \mathbf{x}_i\}$, determine the Maximum Likelihood estimate of the camera projection matrix P, i.e. the P which minimizes $\sum_i d(\mathbf{x}_i, \mathtt{P}\mathbf{X}_i)^2$.

Algorithm

(i) **Linear solution.** Compute an initial estimate of P using a linear method such as algorithm 4.2(p109):

 (a) **Normalization:** Use a similarity transformation T to normalize the image points, and a second similarity transformation U to normalize the space points. Suppose the normalized image points are $\tilde{\mathbf{x}}_i = \mathtt{T}\mathbf{x}_i$, and the normalized space points are $\tilde{\mathbf{X}}_i = \mathtt{U}\mathbf{X}_i$.

 (b) **DLT:** Form the $2n \times 12$ matrix A by stacking the equations (7.2) generated by each correspondence $\tilde{\mathbf{X}}_i \leftrightarrow \tilde{\mathbf{x}}_i$. Write $\mathbf{p}$ for the vector containing the entries of the matrix $\tilde{\mathtt{P}}$. A solution of $\mathtt{A}\mathbf{p} = \mathbf{0}$, subject to $\|\mathbf{p}\| = 1$, is obtained from the unit singular vector of A corresponding to the smallest singular value.

(ii) **Minimize geometric error.** Using the linear estimate as a starting point minimize the geometric error (7.4):

$$\sum_i d(\tilde{\mathbf{x}}_i, \tilde{\mathtt{P}}\tilde{\mathbf{X}}_i)^2$$

over $\tilde{\mathtt{P}}$, using an iterative algorithm such as Levenberg–Marquardt.

(iii) **Denormalization.** The camera matrix for the original (unnormalized) coordinates is obtained from $\tilde{\mathtt{P}}$ as

$$\mathtt{P} = \mathtt{T}^{-1}\tilde{\mathtt{P}}\mathtt{U}.$$

Algorithm 7.1. *The Gold Standard algorithm for estimating* P *from world to image point correspondences in the case that the world points are very accurately known.*

measured image points. For example the points $\mathbf{X}_i$ might arise from an accurately machined calibration object. Then the geometric error in the image is

$$\sum_i d(\mathbf{x}_i, \hat{\mathbf{x}}_i)^2$$

where $\mathbf{x}_i$ is the measured point and $\hat{\mathbf{x}}_i$ is the point $\mathtt{P}\mathbf{X}_i$, i.e. the point which is the exact image of $\mathbf{X}_i$ under P. If the measurement errors are Gaussian then the solution of

$$\min_{\mathtt{P}} \sum_i d(\mathbf{x}_i, \mathtt{P}\mathbf{X}_i)^2 \qquad (7.4)$$

is the Maximum Likelihood estimate of P.

Just as in the 2D homography case, minimizing geometric error requires the use of iterative techniques, such as Levenberg–Marquardt. A parametrization of P is required, and the vector of matrix elements $\mathbf{p}$ provides this. The DLT solution, or a minimal solution, may be used as a starting point for the iterative minimization. The complete Gold Standard algorithm is summarized in algorithm 7.1.

Example 7.1. Camera estimation from a calibration object

We will compare the DLT algorithm with the Gold Standard algorithm 7.1 for data

Fig. 7.1. *An image of a typical calibration object. The black and white checkerboard pattern (a "Tsai grid") is designed to enable the positions of the corners of the imaged squares to be obtained to high accuracy. A total of 197 points were identified and used to calibrate the camera in the examples of this chapter.*

	f_y	f_x/f_y	skew	x_0	y_0	residual
linear	1673.3	1.0063	1.39	379.96	305.78	0.365
iterative	1675.5	1.0063	1.43	379.79	305.25	0.364

Table 7.1. *DLT and Gold Standard calibration.*

from the calibration object shown in figure 7.1. The image points $\mathbf{x}_i$ are obtained from the calibration object using the following steps:

(i) Canny edge detection [Canny-86].
(ii) Straight line fitting to the detected linked edges.
(iii) Intersecting the lines to obtain the imaged corners.

If sufficient care is taken the points $\mathbf{x}_i$ are obtained to a localization accuracy of far better than $1/10$ of a pixel. A rule of thumb is that for a good estimation the number of constraints (point measurements) should exceed the number of unknowns (the 11 camera parameters) by a factor of five. This means that at least 28 points should be used.

Table 7.1 shows the calibration results obtained by using the linear DLT method and the Gold Standard method. Note that the improvement achieved using the Gold Standard algorithm is very slight. The difference of residual of one thousandth of a pixel is insignificant. △

Errors in the world points

It may be the case that world points are not measured with "infinite" accuracy. In this case one may choose to estimate P by minimizing a 3D geometric error, or an image geometric error, or both.

If only errors in the world points are considered then the 3D geometric error is defined as

$$\sum_i d(\mathbf{X}_i, \widehat{\mathbf{X}}_i)^2$$

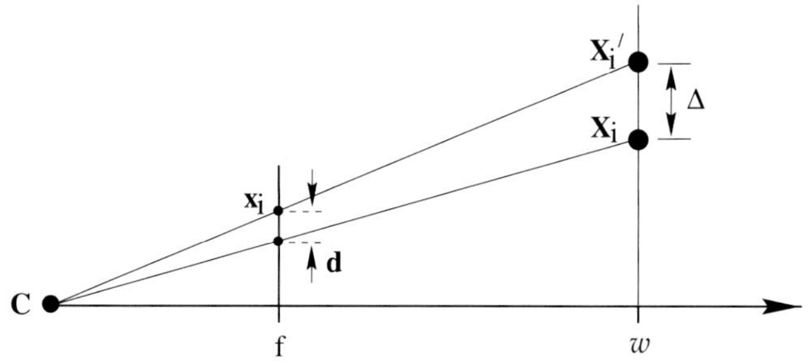

Fig. 7.2. *The DLT algorithm minimizes the sum of squares of geometric distance* Δ *between the point* $\mathbf{X}_i$ *and the point* $\mathbf{X}'_i$ *mapping exactly onto* $\mathbf{x}_i$ *and lying in the plane through* $\mathbf{X}_i$ *parallel to the principal plane of the camera. A short calculation shows that* $wd = f\Delta$.

where $\widehat{\mathbf{X}}_i$ is the closest point in space to $\mathbf{X}_i$ that maps exactly onto $\mathbf{x}_i$ via $\mathbf{x}_i = \mathtt{P}\widehat{\mathbf{X}}_i$.

More generally, if errors in both the world and image points are considered, then a weighted sum of world and image errors is minimized. As in the 2D homography case, this requires that one augment the set of parameters by including parameters $\widehat{\mathbf{X}}_i$, the estimated 3D points. One minimizes

$$\sum_{i=1}^{n} d_{\text{Mah}}(\mathbf{x}_i, \mathtt{P}\widehat{\mathbf{X}}_i)^2 + d_{\text{Mah}}(\mathbf{X}_i, \widehat{\mathbf{X}}_i)^2$$

where d_{Mah} represents Mahalanobis distance with respect to the known error covariance matrices for each of the measurements $\mathbf{x}_i$ and $\mathbf{X}_i$. In the simplest case, the Mahalanobis distance is simply a weighted geometric distance, where the weights are chosen to reflect the relative accuracy of measurements of the image and 3D points, and also the fact that image and world points are typically measured in different units.

7.2.1 Geometric interpretation of algebraic error

Suppose all the points $\mathbf{X}_i$ in the DLT algorithm are normalized such that $\mathbf{X}_i = (\mathrm{X}_i, \mathrm{Y}_i, \mathrm{Z}_i, 1)^\mathsf{T}$, and $\mathbf{x}_i = (x_i, y_i, 1)^\mathsf{T}$. In this case, it was seen in section 4.2.4-(*p*95) that the quantity being minimized by the DLT algorithm is $\sum_i (\hat{w}_i d(\mathbf{x}_i, \hat{\mathbf{x}}_i))^2$, where $\hat{w}_i(\hat{x}_i, \hat{y}_i, 1)^\mathsf{T} = \mathtt{P}\mathbf{X}_i$. However, according to (6.15–*p*162),

$$\hat{w}_i = \pm\|\hat{\mathbf{p}}^3\| \;\text{depth}(\mathbf{X};\mathtt{P}) \;\; .$$

Thus, the value $\hat{w}_i$ may be interpreted as the depth of the point $\mathbf{X}_i$ from the camera in the direction along the principal ray, provided the camera is normalized so that $\|\hat{\mathbf{p}}^3\|^2 = p_{31}^2 + p_{32}^2 + p_{33}^2 = 1$. Referring to figure 7.2 one sees that $\hat{w}_i d(\mathbf{x}_i, \hat{\mathbf{x}}_i)$ is proportional to $f d(\mathbf{X}', \mathbf{X})$, where f is the focal length and $\mathbf{X}'_i$ is a point mapping to $\mathbf{x}_i$ and lying in a plane through $\mathbf{X}_i$ parallel to the principal plane of the camera. Thus, the algebraic error being minimized is equal to $f \sum_i d(\mathbf{X}_i, \mathbf{X}'_i)^2$.

The distance $d(\mathbf{X}_i, \mathbf{X}'_i)$ is the correction that needs to be made to the measured 3D points in order to correspond precisely with the measured image points $\mathbf{x}_i$. The restriction is that the correction must be made in the direction perpendicular to the principal axis of the camera. Because of this restriction, the point $\mathbf{X}'_i$ is not the same as the closest point $\widehat{\mathbf{X}}_i$ to $\mathbf{X}_i$ that maps to $\mathbf{x}_i$. However, for points $\mathbf{X}_i$ not too far from the principal ray of the camera, the distance $d(\mathbf{X}_i, \mathbf{X}'_i)$ is a reasonable approximation to the distance $d(\mathbf{X}_i, \widehat{\mathbf{X}}_i)$. The DLT slightly weights the points farther away from the principal ray by minimizing the squared sum of $d(\mathbf{X}_i, \mathbf{X}'_i)$, which is slightly larger than $d(\mathbf{X}_i, \widehat{\mathbf{X}}_i)$. In addition, the presence of the focal length f in the expression for algebraic error suggests that the DLT algorithm will be biased towards minimizing focal length at a cost of a slight increase in 3D geometric error.

Transformation invariance. We have just seen that by minimizing $\|\mathtt{A}\mathbf{p}\|$ subject to the constraint $\|\hat{\mathbf{p}}^3\| = 1$ one may interpret the solution in terms of minimizing 3D geometric distances. Such an interpretation is not affected by similarity transformations in either 3D space or the image space. Thus, one is led to expect that carrying out translation and scaling of the data, either in the image or in 3D point coordinates, will not have any effect on the solutions. This is indeed the case as may be shown using the arguments of section 4.4.2(p105).

7.2.2 Estimation of an affine camera

The methods developed above for the projective cameras can be applied directly to affine cameras. An affine camera is one for which the projection matrix has last row $(0, 0, 0, 1)$. In the DLT estimation of the camera in this case one minimizes $\|\mathtt{A}\mathbf{p}\|$ subject to this condition on the last row of P. As in the case of computing 2D affine transformations, for affine cameras, algebraic error and geometric image error are equal. This means that geometric image distances may be minimized by a linear algorithm.

Suppose as above that all the points $\mathbf{X}_i$ are normalized such that $\mathbf{X}_i = (\mathrm{X}_i, \mathrm{Y}_i, \mathrm{Z}_i, 1)^\mathsf{T}$, and $\mathbf{x}_i = (x_i, y_i, 1)^\mathsf{T}$, and also that the last row of P has the affine form. Then (7.2) for a single correspondence reduces to

$$\begin{bmatrix} \mathbf{0}^\mathsf{T} & -\mathbf{X}_i^\mathsf{T} \\ \mathbf{X}_i^\mathsf{T} & \mathbf{0}^\mathsf{T} \end{bmatrix} \begin{pmatrix} \mathbf{P}^1 \\ \mathbf{P}^2 \end{pmatrix} + \begin{pmatrix} y_i \\ -x_i \end{pmatrix} = \mathbf{0} \tag{7.5}$$

which shows that the squared algebraic error in this case equals the squared geometric error

$$\|\mathtt{A}\mathbf{p}\|^2 = \sum_i \left(x_i - \mathbf{P}^{1\mathsf{T}}\mathbf{X}_i\right)^2 + \left(y_i - \mathbf{P}^{2\mathsf{T}}\mathbf{X}_i\right)^2 = \sum_i d(\mathbf{x}_i, \hat{\mathbf{x}}_i)^2.$$

This result may also be seen geometrically by comparison of figure 6.8(p170) and figure 7.2.

A linear estimation algorithm for an affine camera which minimizes geometric error is given in algorithm 7.2. Under the assumption of Gaussian measurement errors this is the Maximum Likelihood estimate of $\mathtt{P}_\mathrm{A}$.

7.3 Restricted camera estimation

The DLT algorithm, as it has so far been described, computes a general projective camera matrix P from a set of 3D to 2D point correspondences. The matrix P with centre at a finite point may be decomposed as $\mathtt{P} = \mathtt{K}[\mathtt{R} \mid -\mathtt{R}\widetilde{\mathbf{C}}]$ where R is a 3×3

Objective

Given $n \geq 4$ world to image point correspondences $\{\mathbf{X}_i \leftrightarrow \mathbf{x}_i\}$, determine the Maximum Likelihood Estimate of the affine camera projection matrix $\mathtt{P}_{\mathtt{A}}$, i.e. the camera $\mathtt{P}$ which minimizes $\sum_i d(\mathbf{x}_i, \mathtt{P}\mathbf{X}_i)^2$ subject to the affine constraint $\mathbf{P}^{3\mathsf{T}} = (0, 0, 0, 1)$.

Algorithm

(i) **Normalization:** Use a similarity transformation $\mathtt{T}$ to normalize the image points, and a second similarity transformation $\mathtt{U}$ to normalize the space points. Suppose the normalized image points are $\tilde{\mathbf{x}}_i = \mathtt{T}\mathbf{x}_i$, and the normalized space points are $\tilde{\mathbf{X}}_i = \mathtt{U}\mathbf{X}_i$, with unit last component.

(ii) Each correspondence $\tilde{\mathbf{X}}_i \leftrightarrow \tilde{\mathbf{x}}_i$ contributes (from (7.5)) equations

$$\begin{bmatrix} \tilde{\mathbf{X}}_i^{\mathsf{T}} & \mathbf{0}^{\mathsf{T}} \\ \mathbf{0}^{\mathsf{T}} & \tilde{\mathbf{X}}_i^{\mathsf{T}} \end{bmatrix} \begin{pmatrix} \tilde{\mathbf{P}}^1 \\ \tilde{\mathbf{P}}^2 \end{pmatrix} = \begin{pmatrix} \tilde{x}_i \\ \tilde{y}_i \end{pmatrix}$$

which are stacked into a $2n \times 8$ matrix equation $\mathtt{A}_8\mathbf{p}_8 = \mathbf{b}$, where $\mathbf{p}_8$ is the 8-vector containing the first two rows of $\tilde{\mathtt{P}}_{\mathtt{A}}$.

(iii) The solution is obtained by the pseudo-inverse of $\mathtt{A}_8$ (see section A5.2(p590))

$$\mathbf{p}_8 = \mathtt{A}_8^{+}\mathbf{b}$$

and $\tilde{\mathbf{P}}^{3\mathsf{T}} = (0, 0, 0, 1)$.

(iv) **Denormalization:** The camera matrix for the original (unnormalized) coordinates is obtained from $\tilde{\mathtt{P}}_{\mathtt{A}}$ as

$$\mathtt{P}_{\mathtt{A}} = \mathtt{T}^{-1}\tilde{\mathtt{P}}_{\mathtt{A}}\mathtt{U}$$

Algorithm 7.2. *The Gold Standard Algorithm for estimating an affine camera matrix* $\mathtt{P}_{\mathtt{A}}$ *from world to image correspondences.*

rotation matrix and $\mathtt{K}$ has the form (6.10–p157):

$$\mathtt{K} = \begin{bmatrix} \alpha_x & s & x_0 \\ & \alpha_y & y_0 \\ & & 1 \end{bmatrix}. \tag{7.6}$$

The non-zero entries of $\mathtt{K}$ are geometrically meaningful quantities, the internal calibration parameters of $\mathtt{P}$. One may wish to find the best-fit camera matrix $\mathtt{P}$ subject to restrictive conditions on the camera parameters. Common assumptions are

(i) The skew s is zero.
(ii) The pixels are square: $\alpha_x = \alpha_y$.
(iii) The principal point (x_0, y_0) is known.
(iv) The complete camera calibration matrix $\mathtt{K}$ is known.

In some cases it is possible to estimate a restricted camera matrix with a linear algorithm (see the exercises at the end of the chapter).

As an example of restricted estimation, suppose that we wish to find the best pinhole camera model (that is projective camera with $s = 0$ and $\alpha_x = \alpha_y$) that fits a set of point measurements. This problem may be solved by minimizing either geometric or algebraic error, as will be discussed next.

Minimizing geometric error. To minimize geometric error, one selects a set of parameters that characterize the camera matrix to be computed. For instance, suppose we wish to enforce the constraints $s = 0$ and $\alpha_x = \alpha_y$. One can parametrize the camera matrix using the remaining 9 parameters. These are x_0, y_0, α, plus 6 parameters representing the orientation $\mathtt{R}$ and location $\widetilde{\mathtt{C}}$ of the camera. Let this set of parameters be denoted collectively by $\mathbf{q}$. The camera matrix $\mathtt{P}$ may then be explicitly computed in terms of the parameters.

The geometric error may then be minimized with respect to the set of parameters using iterative minimization (such as Levenberg–Marquardt). Note that in the case of minimization of image error only, the size of the minimization problem is $9 \times 2n$ (supposing 9 unknown camera parameters). In other words the LM minimization is minimizing a function $f : \mathbb{R}^9 \rightarrow \mathbb{R}^{2n}$. In the case of minimization of 3D and 2D error, the function f is from $\mathbb{R}^{3n+9} \rightarrow \mathbb{R}^{5n}$, since the 3D points must be included among the measurements and minimization also includes estimation of the true positions of the 3D points.

Minimizing algebraic error. It is possible to minimize algebraic error instead, in which case the iterative minimization problem becomes much smaller, as will be explained next. Consider the parametrization map taking a set of parameters $\mathbf{q}$ to the corresponding camera matrix $\mathtt{P} = \mathtt{K}[\mathtt{R} \mid -\mathtt{R}\widetilde{\mathtt{C}}]$. Let this map be denoted by g. Effectively, one has a map $\mathbf{p} = g(\mathbf{q})$, where $\mathbf{p}$ is the vector of entries of the matrix $\mathtt{P}$. Minimizing algebraic error over all point matches is equivalent to minimizing $\|\mathtt{A}g(\mathbf{q})\|$.

The reduced measurement matrix. In general, the $2n \times 12$ matrix $\mathtt{A}$ may have a very large number of rows. It is possible to replace $\mathtt{A}$ by a square 12×12 matrix $\hat{\mathtt{A}}$ such that $\|\mathtt{A}\mathbf{p}\| = \mathbf{p}^{\mathsf{T}}\mathtt{A}^{\mathsf{T}}\mathtt{A}\mathbf{p} = \|\hat{\mathtt{A}}\mathbf{p}\|$ for any vector $\mathbf{p}$. Such a matrix $\hat{\mathtt{A}}$ is called a *reduced measurement matrix*. One way to do this is using the Singular Value Decomposition (SVD). Let $\mathtt{A} = \mathtt{U}\mathtt{D}\mathtt{V}^{\mathsf{T}}$ be the SVD of $\mathtt{A}$, and define $\hat{\mathtt{A}} = \mathtt{D}\mathtt{V}^{\mathsf{T}}$. Then

$$\mathtt{A}^{\mathsf{T}}\mathtt{A} = (\mathtt{V}\mathtt{D}\mathtt{U}^{\mathsf{T}})(\mathtt{U}\mathtt{D}\mathtt{V}^{\mathsf{T}}) = (\mathtt{V}\mathtt{D})(\mathtt{D}\mathtt{V}^{\mathsf{T}}) = \hat{\mathtt{A}}^{\mathsf{T}}\hat{\mathtt{A}}$$

as required. Another way of obtaining $\hat{\mathtt{A}}$ is to use the QR decomposition $\mathtt{A} = \mathtt{Q}\hat{\mathtt{A}}$, where $\mathtt{Q}$ has orthogonal columns and $\hat{\mathtt{A}}$ is upper triangular and square.

Note that the mapping $\mathbf{q} \mapsto \hat{\mathtt{A}}g(\mathbf{q})$ is a mapping from $\mathbb{R}^9$ to $\mathbb{R}^{12}$. This is a simple parameter-minimization problem that may be solved using the Levenberg–Marquardt method. The important point to note is the following:

- *Given a set of n world to image correspondences, $\mathbf{X}_i \leftrightarrow \mathbf{x}_i$, the problem of finding a constrained camera matrix $\mathtt{P}$ that minimizes the sum of algebraic distances $\sum_i d_{alg}(\mathbf{x}_i, \mathtt{P}\mathbf{X}_i)^2$ reduces to the minimization of a function $\mathbb{R}^9 \rightarrow \mathbb{R}^{12}$, independent of the number n of correspondences.*

Minimization of $\|\hat{\mathtt{A}}g(\mathbf{q})\|$ takes place over all values of the parameters $\mathbf{q}$. Note that if $\mathtt{P} = \mathtt{K}[\mathtt{R} \mid -\mathtt{R}\widetilde{\mathtt{C}}]$ with $\mathtt{K}$ as in (7.6) then $\mathtt{P}$ satisfies the condition $p_{31}^2 + p_{32}^2 + p_{33}^2 = 1$, since these entries are the same as the last row of the rotation matrix $\mathtt{R}$. Thus, minimizing $\mathtt{A}g(\mathbf{q})$ will lead to a matrix $\mathtt{P}$ satisfying the constraints $s = 0$ and $\alpha_x = \alpha_y$ and scaled such that $p_{31}^2 + p_{32}^2 + p_{33}^2 = 1$, and which in addition minimizes the algebraic error for all point correspondences.

Initialization. One way of finding camera parameters to initialize the iteration is as follows.

(i) Use a linear algorithm such as DLT to find an initial camera matrix.
(ii) Clamp fixed parameters to their desired values (for instance set $s = 0$ and set $\alpha_x = \alpha_y$ to the average of their values obtained using DLT).
(iii) Set variable parameters to their values obtained by decomposition of the initial camera matrix (see section 6.2.4).

Ideally, the assumed values of the fixed parameters will be close to the values obtained by the DLT. However, in practice this is not always the case. Then altering these parameters to their desired values results in an incorrect initial camera matrix that may lead to large residuals, and difficulty in converging. A method which works better in practice is to use *soft* constraints by adding extra terms to the cost function. Thus, for the case where $s = 0$ and $\alpha_x = \alpha_y$, one adds extra terms $ws^2 + w(\alpha_x - \alpha_y)^2$ to the cost function. In the case of geometric image error, the cost function becomes

$$\sum_i d(\mathbf{x}_i, \mathtt{P}\mathbf{X}_i)^2 + ws^2 + w(\alpha_x - \alpha_y)^2 \ .$$

One begins with the values of the parameters estimated using the DLT. The weights begin with low values and are increased at each iteration of the estimation procedure. Thus, the values of s and the aspect ratio are drawn gently to their desired values. Finally they may be clamped to their desired values for a final estimation.

Exterior orientation. Suppose that all the internal parameters of the camera are known, then all that remains to be determined are the position and orientation (or *pose*) of the camera. This is the "exterior orientation" problem, which is important in the analysis of calibrated systems.

To compute the exterior orientation a configuration with accurately known position in a world coordinate frame is imaged. The pose of the camera is then sought. Such a situation arises in hand–eye calibration for robotic systems, where the position of the camera is required, and also in model-based recognition using alignment where the position of an object relative to the camera is required.

There are six parameters that must be determined, three for the orientation and three for the position. As each world to image point correspondence generates two constraints it would be expected that three points are sufficient. This is indeed the case, and the resulting non-linear equations have four solutions in general.

Experimental evaluation

Results of constrained estimation for the calibration grid of example 7.1 are given in table 7.2.

Both the algebraic and geometric minimization involve an iterative minimization

	f_y	f_x/f_y	skew	x_0	y_0	residual
algebraic	1633.4	1.0	0.0	371.21	293.63	0.601
geometric	1637.2	1.0	0.0	371.32	293.69	0.601

Table 7.2. *Calibration for a restricted camera matrix.*

over 9 parameters. However, the algebraic method is far quicker, since it minimizes only 12 errors, instead of $2n = 396$ in the geometric minimization. Note that fixing skew and aspect ratio has altered the values of the other parameters (compare table 7.1) and increased the residual.

Covariance estimation. The techniques of covariance estimation and propagation of the errors into an image may be handled in just the same way as in the 2D homography case (chapter 5). Similarly, the minimum expected residual error may be computed as in result 5.2(p136). Assuming that all errors are in the image measurements, the expected ML residual error is equal to

$$\epsilon_{\text{res}} = \sigma(1 - d/2n)^{1/2} \ .$$

where d is the number of camera parameters being fitted (11 for a full pinhole camera model). This formula may also be used to estimate the accuracy of the point measurements, given a residual error. In the case of example 7.1 where $n = 197$ and $\epsilon_{\text{res}} = 0.365$ this results in a value of $\sigma = 0.37$. This value is greater than expected. The reason, as we will see later, lies in the camera model – we are ignoring radial distortion.

Example 7.2. Covariance ellipsoid for an estimated camera

Suppose that the camera is estimated using the Maximum Likelihood (Gold Standard) method, optimizing over a set of camera parameters. The estimated covariance of the point measurements can then be used to compute the covariance of the camera model by back-propagation, according to result 5.10(p142). This gives $\Sigma_{\text{camera}} = (\mathtt{J}^{\mathsf{T}}\Sigma_{\text{points}}^{-1}\mathtt{J})^{-1}$ where J is the Jacobian matrix of the measured points in terms of the camera parameters. Uncertainty in 3D world points may also be taken into account in this way. If the camera is parametrized in terms of meaningful parameters (such as camera position), then the variance of each parameter can be measured directly from the diagonal entries of the covariance matrix.

Knowing the covariance of the camera parameters, error bounds or ellipsoids can be computed. For instance, from the covariance matrix for all the parameters we may extract the subblock representing the 3×3 covariance matrix of the camera position, $\Sigma_{\mathbf{C}}$. A confidence ellipsoid for the camera centre is then defined by

$$(\mathbf{C} - \bar{\mathbf{C}})^{\mathsf{T}}\Sigma_{\mathbf{C}}^{-1}(\mathbf{C} - \bar{\mathbf{C}}) = k^2$$

where k^2 is computed from the inverse cumulative χ^2_n distribution in terms of the desired confidence level α: namely $k^2 = F_n^{-1}(\alpha)$ (see figure A2.1(p567)). Here n is the

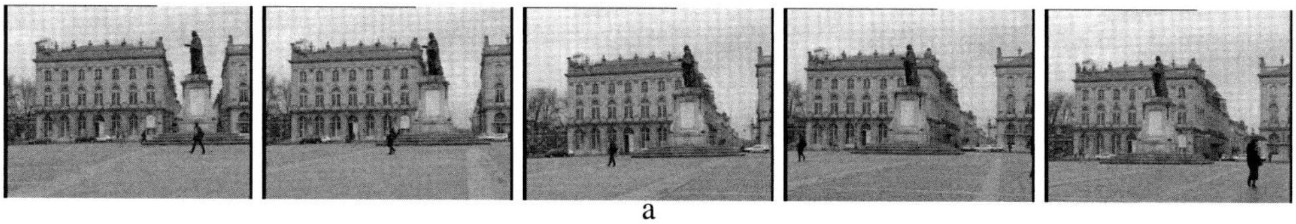
a

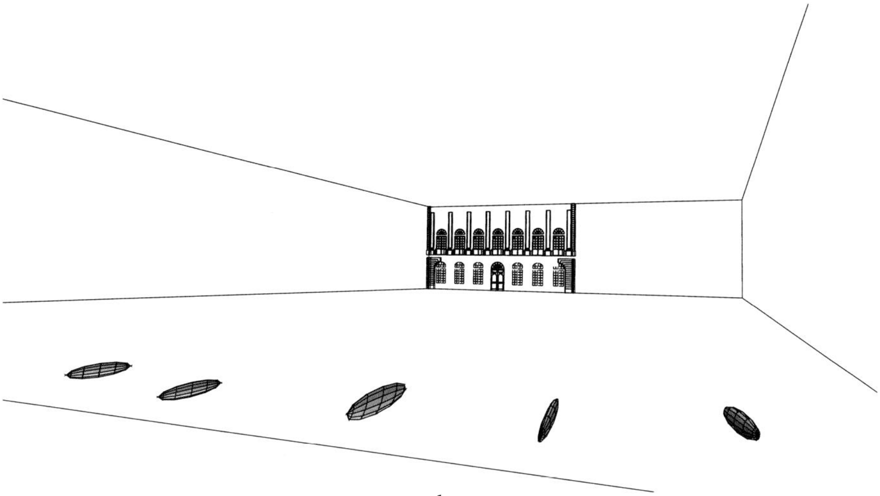
b

Fig. 7.3. **Camera centre covariance ellipsoids.** *(a) Five images of Stanislas square (Nancy, France), for which 3D calibration points are known. (b) Camera centre covariance ellipsoids corresponding to each image, computed for cameras estimated from the imaged calibration points. Note, the typical cigar shape of the ellipsoid aligned towards the scene data. Figure courtesy of Vincent Lepetit, Marie-Odile Berger and Gilles Simon.*

number of variables – that is 3 in the case of the camera centre. With the chosen level of certainty α, the camera centre lies inside the ellipsoid.

Figure 7.3 shows an example of ellipsoidal uncertainty regions for computed camera centres. Given the estimated covariance matrix for the computed camera, the techniques of section 5.2.6(p148) may be used to compute the uncertainty in the image positions of further 3D world points. △

7.4 Radial distortion

The assumption throughout these chapters has been that a linear model is an accurate model of the imaging process. Thus the world point, image point and optical centre are collinear, and world lines are imaged as lines and so on. For real (non-pinhole) lenses this assumption will not hold. The most important deviation is generally a radial distortion. In practice this error becomes more significant as the focal length (and price) of the lens decreases. See figure 7.4.

The cure for this distortion is to correct the image measurements to those that would have been obtained under a perfect linear camera action. The camera is then effectively again a linear device. This process is illustrated in figure 7.5. This correction must

Fig. 7.4. *(a) Short vs (b) long focal lengths. Note the curved imaged lines at the periphery in (a) which are images of straight scene lines.*

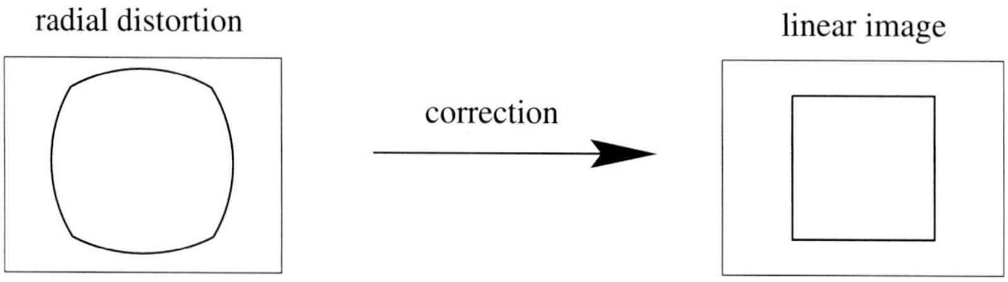

Fig. 7.5. *The image of a square with significant radial distortion is corrected to one that would have been obtained under a perfect linear lens.*

be carried out in the right place in the projection process. Lens distortion takes place during the initial projection of the world onto the image plane, according to (6.2–p154). Subsequently, the calibration matrix (7.6) reflects a choice of affine coordinates in the image, translating physical locations in the image plane to pixel coordinates.

We will denote the image coordinates of a point under ideal (non-distorted) pinhole projection by $(\tilde{x}, \tilde{y})$, measured in units of focal-length. Thus, for a point $\mathbf{X}$ we have (see (6.5–p155))

$$(\tilde{x}, \tilde{y}, 1)^{\mathsf{T}} = [\mathtt{I} \mid \mathbf{0}]\mathbf{X}_{\text{cam}}$$

where $\mathbf{X}_{\text{cam}}$ is the 3D point in camera coordinates, related to world coordinates by (6.6–p156). The actual projected point is related to the ideal point by a radial displacement. Thus, radial (lens) distortion is modelled as

$$\begin{pmatrix} x_d \\ y_d \end{pmatrix} = L(\tilde{r}) \begin{pmatrix} \tilde{x} \\ \tilde{y} \end{pmatrix} \tag{7.7}$$

where

- $(\tilde{x}, \tilde{y})$ is the ideal image position (which obeys linear projection).
- (x_d, y_d) is the actual image position, after radial distortion.
- $\tilde{r}$ is the radial distance $\sqrt{\tilde{x}^2 + \tilde{y}^2}$ from the centre for radial distortion.
- $L(\tilde{r})$ is a distortion factor, which is a function of the radius $\tilde{r}$ only.

Correction of distortion. In pixel coordinates the correction is written

$$\hat{x} = x_c + L(r)(x - x_c) \qquad \hat{y} = y_c + L(r)(y - y_c).$$

where (x, y) are the measured coordinates, $(\hat{x}, \hat{y})$ are the corrected coordinates, and (x_c, y_c) is the centre of radial distortion, with $r^2 = (x - x_c)^2 + (y - y_c)^2$. Note, if the aspect ratio is not unity then it is necessary to correct for this when computing r. With this correction the coordinates $(\hat{x}, \hat{y})$ are related to the coordinates of the 3D world point by a linear projective camera.

Choice of the distortion function and centre. The function $L(r)$ is only defined for positive values of r and $L(0) = 1$. An approximation to an arbitrary function $L(r)$ may be given by a Taylor expansion $L(r) = 1 + \kappa_1 r + \kappa_2 r^2 + \kappa_3 r^3 + \ldots$. The coefficients for radial correction $\{\kappa_1, \kappa_2, \kappa_3, \ldots, x_c, y_c\}$ are considered part of the interior calibration of the camera. The principal point is often used as the centre for radial distortion, though these need not coincide exactly. This correction, together with the camera calibration matrix, specifies the mapping from an image point to a ray in the camera coordinate system.

Computing the distortion function. The function $L(r)$ may be computed by minimizing a cost based on the deviation from a linear mapping. For example, algorithm 7.1(p181) estimates P by minimizing geometric image error for calibration objects such as the Tsai grids of figure 7.1. The distortion function may be included as part of the imaging process, and the parameters κ_i computed together with P during the iterative minimization of the geometric error. Similarly, the distortion function may be computed when estimating the homography between a single Tsai grid and its image.

A simple and more general approach is to determine $L(r)$ by the requirement that images of straight scene lines should be straight. A cost function is defined on the imaged lines (such as the distance between the line joining the imaged line's ends and its mid-point) after the corrective mapping by $L(r)$. This cost is iteratively minimized over the parameters κ_i of the distortion function and the centre of radial distortion. This is a very practical method for images of urban scenes since there are usually plenty of lines available. It has the advantage that no special calibration pattern is required as the scene provides the calibration entities.

Example 7.3. Radial correction. The function $L(r)$ is computed for the image of figure 7.6a by minimizing a cost based on the straightness of imaged scene lines. The image is 640×480 pixels and the correction and centre are computed as $\kappa_1 = 0.103689$, $\kappa_2 = 0.00487908$, $\kappa_3 = 0.00116894$, $\kappa_4 = 0.000841614$, $x_c = 321.87$, $y_c = 241.18$ pixels, where pixels are normalized by the average half-size of the image. This is a correction by 30 pixels at the image periphery. The result of warping the image is shown in figure 7.6b. △

Example 7.4. We continue with the example of the calibration grid shown in figure 7.1 and discussed in example 7.1(p181). Radial distortion was removed by the straight line

Fig. 7.6. **Radial distortion correction.** *(a) The original image with lines which are straight in the world, but curved in the image. Several of these lines are annotated by dashed curves. (b) The image warped to remove the radial distortion. Note that the lines in the periphery of the image are now straight, but that the boundary of the image is curved.*

method, and then the camera calibrated using the methods described in this chapter. The results are given in table 7.3.

Note that the residuals after radial correction are substantially smaller. Estimation of the error of point measurements from the residual leads to a value of $\sigma = 0.18$ pixels. Since radial distortion involves selective stretching of the image, it is quite plausible that the effective focal length of the image is changed, as seen here. △

	f_y	f_x/f_y	skew	x_0	y_0	residual
linear	1580.5	1.0044	0.75	377.53	299.12	0.179
iterative	1580.7	1.0044	0.70	377.42	299.02	0.179
algebraic	1556.0	1.0000	0.00	372.42	291.86	0.381
iterative	1556.6	1.0000	0.00	372.41	291.86	0.380
linear	1673.3	1.0063	1.39	379.96	305.78	0.365
iterative	1675.5	1.0063	1.43	379.79	305.25	0.364
algebraic	1633.4	1.0000	0.00	371.21	293.63	0.601
iterative	1637.2	1.0000	0.00	371.32	293.69	0.601

Table 7.3. **Calibration with and without radial distortion correction.** *The results above the line are after radial correction – the results below for comparison are without radial distortion (from the previous tables). The upper two methods in each case solve for the general camera model, the lower two are for a constrained model with square pixels.*

In correcting for radial distortion, it is often not actually necessary to warp the image. Measurements can be made in the original image, for example the position of a corner feature, and the measurement simply mapped according to (7.7). The question of where features *should* be measured does not have an unambiguous answer. Warping the image will distort noise models (because of averaging) and may well introduce aliasing effects. For this reason feature detection on the unwarped image will often be preferable. However, feature grouping, such as linking edgels into straight line primitives, is best performed after warping since thresholds on linearity may well be erroneously exceeded in the original image.

7.5 Closure

7.5.1 The literature

The original application of the DLT in [Sutherland-63] was for camera computation. Estimation by iterative minimization of geometric errors is a standard procedure of photogrammetrists, e.g. see [Slama-80].

A minimal solution for a calibrated camera (pose from the image of 3 points) was the original problem studied by Fischler and Bolles [Fischler-81] in their RANSAC paper. Solutions to this problem reoccur *often* in the literature; a good treatment is given in [Wolfe-91] and also [Haralick-91]. Quasi-linear solutions for one more than the minimum number of point correspondences $\mathbf{X}_i \leftrightarrow \mathbf{x}_i$ are in [Quan-98] and [Triggs-99a].

Another class of methods, which are not covered here, is the iterative estimation of a projective camera starting from an affine one. The algorithm of "Model based pose in 25 lines of code" by Dementhon and Davis [Dementhon-95] is based on this idea. A similar method is used in [Christy-96].

Devernay and Faugeras [Devernay-95] introduced a straight line method for computing radial distortion into the computer vision literature. In the photogrammetry literature the method is known as "plumb line correction", see [Brown-71].

7.5.2 Notes and exercises

(i) Given 5 world-to-image point correspondences, $\mathbf{X}_i \leftrightarrow \mathbf{x}_i$, show that there are in general four solutions for a camera matrix $\mathtt{P}$ *with zero skew* that exactly maps the world to image points.

(ii) Given 3 world-to-image point correspondences, $\mathbf{X}_i \leftrightarrow \mathbf{x}_i$, show that there are in general four solutions for a camera matrix $\mathtt{P}$ *with known calibration* $\mathtt{K}$ that exactly maps the world to image points.

(iii) Find a linear algorithm for computing the camera matrix $\mathtt{P}$ under each of the following conditions:

  (a) The camera location (but not orientation) is known.
  (b) The direction of the principal ray of the camera is known.
  (c) The camera location and the principal ray of the camera are known.
  (d) The camera location and complete orientation of the camera are known.
  (e) The camera location and orientation are known, as well as some subset of the internal camera parameters (α_x, α_y, s, x_0 and y_0).

(iv) **Conflation of focal length and position on principal axis.** Compare the imaged position of a point of depth d before and after an increase in camera focal length Δf, or a displacement Δt_3 of the camera backwards along the principal axis. Let $(x, y)^\mathsf{T}$ and $(x', y')^\mathsf{T}$ be the image coordinates of the point before and after the change. Following a similar derivation to that of (6.19–*p*169), show that

$$\begin{pmatrix} x' \\ y' \end{pmatrix} = \begin{pmatrix} x \\ y \end{pmatrix} + k \begin{pmatrix} x - x_0 \\ y - y_0 \end{pmatrix}$$

where $k^f = \Delta f/f$ for a focal length change, or $k^{t_3} = -\Delta t_3/d$ for a displacement (here skew $s = 0$, and $\alpha_x = \alpha_y = f$).
For a set of calibration points $\mathbf{X}_i$ with depth relief (Δ_i) small compared to the average depth (d_0),

$$k_i^{t_3} = -\Delta t_3/d_i = -\Delta t_3/(d_0 + \Delta_i) \approx -\Delta t_3/d_0$$

i.e. $k_i^{t_3}$ is approximately constant across the set. It follows that in calibrating from such a set, similar image residuals are obtained by changing the focal length k^f or displacing the camera k^{t_3}. Consequently, the estimated parameters of focal length and position on the principal axis are correlated.

(v) **Pushbroom camera computation.** The pushbroom camera, described in section 6.4.1, may also be computed using a DLT method. The x (orthographic) part of the projection matrix has 4 degrees of freedom which may be determined by four or more point correspondences $\mathbf{X}_i \leftrightarrow \mathbf{x}_i$; the y (perspective) part of the projection matrix has 7 degrees of freedom and may be determined from 7 correspondences. Hence, a minimal solution requires 7 points. Details are given in [Gupta-97].

8

More Single View Geometry

Chapter 6 introduced the projection matrix as the model for the action of a camera on points. This chapter describes the link between other 3D entities and their images under perspective projection. These entities include planes, lines, conics and quadrics; and we develop their forward and back-projection properties.

The camera is dissected further, and reduced to its centre point and image plane. Two properties are established: images acquired by cameras with the same centre are related by a plane projective transformation; and images of entities on the plane at infinity, π_∞, do not depend on camera position, only on camera rotation and internal parameters, $\mathtt{K}$.

The images of entities (points, lines, conics) on π_∞ are of particular importance. It will be seen that the image of a point on π_∞ is a vanishing point, and the image of a line on π_∞ a vanishing line; their images depend on both $\mathtt{K}$ and camera rotation. However, the image of the absolute conic, ω, depends only on $\mathtt{K}$; it is unaffected by the camera's rotation. The conic ω is intimately connected with camera calibration, $\mathtt{K}$, and the relation $\omega = (\mathtt{KK}^\mathsf{T})^{-1}$ is established. It follows that ω defines the angle between rays back-projected from image points.

These properties enable camera relative rotation to be computed from vanishing points independently of camera position. Further, since $\mathtt{K}$ enables the angle between rays to be computed from image points, in turn $\mathtt{K}$ may be computed from the known angle between rays. In particular $\mathtt{K}$ may be determined from vanishing points corresponding to orthogonal scene directions. This means that a camera can be calibrated from scene features, without requiring known world coordinates.

A final geometric entity introduced in this chapter is the calibrating conic, which enables a geometric visualization of $\mathtt{K}$.

8.1 Action of a projective camera on planes, lines, and conics

In this section (and indeed in most of this book) it is only the 3×4 *form* and rank of the camera projection matrix $\mathtt{P}$ that is important in determining its action. The particular properties and relations of its elements are often not relevant.

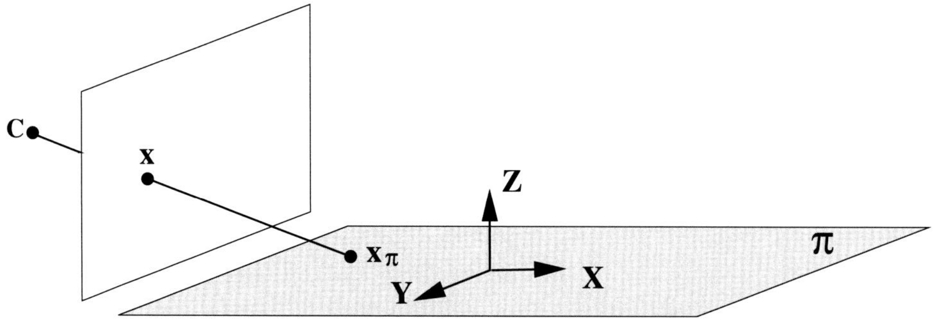

Fig. 8.1. **Perspective image of points on a plane.** *The* XY*-plane of the world coordinate frame is aligned with the plane* π. *Points on the image and scene planes are related by a plane projective transformation.*

8.1.1 On planes

The point imaging equation $\mathbf{x} = \mathtt{P}\mathbf{X}$ is a map from a point in a world coordinate frame, to a point in image coordinates. We have the freedom to choose the world coordinate frame. Suppose it is chosen such that the XY-plane corresponds to a plane $\boldsymbol{\pi}$ in the scene, so that points on the scene plane have zero Z-coordinate as shown in figure 8.1 (it is assumed that the camera centre does not lie on the scene plane). Then, if the columns of P are denoted as $\mathbf{p}_i$, the image of a point on $\boldsymbol{\pi}$ is given by

$$\mathbf{x} = \mathtt{P}\mathbf{X} = \begin{bmatrix} \mathbf{p}_1 & \mathbf{p}_2 & \mathbf{p}_3 & \mathbf{p}_4 \end{bmatrix} \begin{pmatrix} \mathrm{X} \\ \mathrm{Y} \\ 0 \\ 1 \end{pmatrix} = \begin{bmatrix} \mathbf{p}_1 & \mathbf{p}_2 & \mathbf{p}_4 \end{bmatrix} \begin{pmatrix} \mathrm{X} \\ \mathrm{Y} \\ 1 \end{pmatrix}.$$

So that the map between points $\mathbf{x}_\pi = (\mathrm{X}, \mathrm{Y}, 1)^\mathsf{T}$ on $\boldsymbol{\pi}$ and their image $\mathbf{x}$ is a general planar homography (a plane to plane projective transformation): $\mathbf{x} = \mathtt{H}\mathbf{x}_\pi$, with H a 3×3 matrix of rank 3. This shows that:

- *The most general transformation that can occur between a scene plane and an image plane under perspective imaging is a plane projective transformation.*

If the camera is affine, then a similar derivation shows that the scene and image planes are related by an affine transformation.

Example 8.1. For a calibrated camera (6.8–*p*156) $\mathtt{P} = \mathtt{K}[\mathtt{R} \mid \mathbf{t}]$, the homography between a world plane at $\mathrm{Z} = 0$ and the image is

$$\mathtt{H} = \mathtt{K}\left[\mathbf{r}_1, \mathbf{r}_2, \mathbf{t}\right] \tag{8.1}$$

where $\mathbf{r}_i$ are the columns of R. △

8.1.2 On lines

Forward projection. A line in 3-space projects to a line in the image. This is easily seen geometrically – the line and camera centre define a plane, and the image is the intersection of this plane with the image plane (figure 8.2) – and is proved algebraically

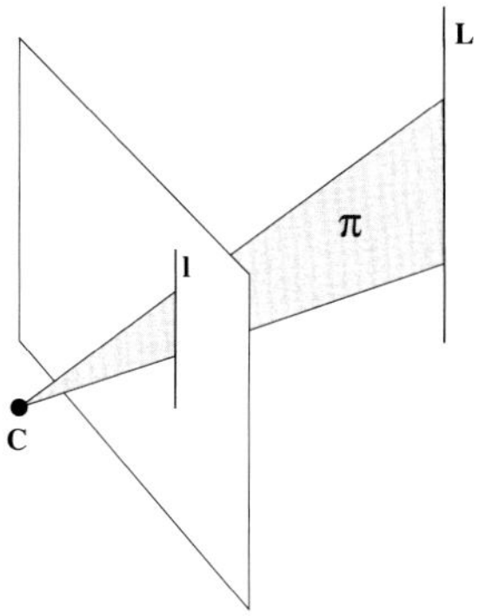

Fig. 8.2. **Line projection.** *A line* $\mathbf{L}$ *in 3-space is imaged as a line* $\mathbf{l}$ *by a perspective camera. The image line* $\mathbf{l}$ *is the intersection of the plane* $\boldsymbol{\pi}$*, defined by* $\mathbf{L}$ *and the camera centre* $\mathbf{C}$*, with the image plane. Conversely an image line* $\mathbf{l}$ *back-projects to a plane* $\boldsymbol{\pi}$ *in 3-space. The plane is the "pull-back" of the line.*

by noting that if $\mathbf{A}, \mathbf{B}$ are points in 3-space, and $\mathbf{a}, \mathbf{b}$ their images under $\mathtt{P}$, then a point $\mathbf{X}(\mu) = \mathbf{A} + \mu\mathbf{B}$ on a line which is the join of $\mathbf{A}, \mathbf{B}$ in 3-space projects to a point

$$\begin{aligned} \mathbf{x}(\mu) &= \mathtt{P}(\mathbf{A} + \mu\mathbf{B}) = \mathtt{P}\mathbf{A} + \mu\mathtt{P}\mathbf{B} \\ &= \mathbf{a} + \mu\mathbf{b} \end{aligned}$$

which is on the line joining $\mathbf{a}$ and $\mathbf{b}$.

Back-projection of lines. The set of points in space which map to a line in the image is a plane in space defined by the camera centre and image line, as shown in figure 8.2. Algebraically,

Result 8.2. *The set of points in space mapping to a line* $\mathbf{l}$ *via the camera matrix* $\mathtt{P}$ *is the plane* $\mathtt{P}^{\mathsf{T}}\mathbf{l}$.

Proof. A point $\mathbf{x}$ lies on $\mathbf{l}$ if and only if $\mathbf{x}^{\mathsf{T}}\mathbf{l} = 0$. A space point $\mathbf{X}$ maps to a point $\mathtt{P}\mathbf{X}$, which lies on the line if and only if $\mathbf{X}^{\mathsf{T}}\mathtt{P}^{\mathsf{T}}\mathbf{l} = 0$. Thus, if $\mathtt{P}^{\mathsf{T}}\mathbf{l}$ is taken to represent a plane, then $\mathbf{X}$ lies on this plane if and only if $\mathbf{X}$ maps to a point on the line $\mathbf{l}$. In other words, $\mathtt{P}^{\mathsf{T}}\mathbf{l}$ is the back-projection of the line $\mathbf{l}$. □

Geometrically there is a *star* (two-parameter family) of planes through the camera centre, and the three rows of the projection matrix $\mathbf{P}^{i\mathsf{T}}$ (6.12–*p*159) are a basis for this star. The plane $\mathtt{P}^{\mathsf{T}}\mathbf{l}$ is a linear combination of this basis corresponding to the element of the star containing the camera centre and the line $\mathbf{l}$. For example, if $\mathbf{l} = (0, 1, 0)^{\mathsf{T}}$ then the plane is $\mathbf{P}^2$, and is the back projection of the image x-axis.

Plücker line representation. *Understanding this material on Plücker line mapping is not required for following the rest of the book.*

We now turn to forward projection of lines. If a line in 3-space is represented by Plücker coordinates then its image can be expressed as a linear map on these coordinates. We will develop this map for both the 4×4 matrix and 6-vector line representations.

Result 8.3. *Under the camera mapping* $\mathtt{P}$*, a line in 3-space represented as a Plücker matrix* $\mathtt{L}$*, as defined in (3.8–p70), is imaged as the line* $\mathbf{l}$ *where*

$$[\mathbf{l}]_\times = \mathtt{P}\mathtt{L}\mathtt{P}^\mathsf{T}. \tag{8.2}$$

where the notation $[\mathbf{l}]_\times$ *is defined in (A4.5–p581).*

Proof. Suppose as above that $\mathbf{a} = \mathtt{P}\mathbf{A}$, $\mathbf{b} = \mathtt{P}\mathbf{B}$. The Plücker matrix $\mathtt{L}$ for the line through $\mathbf{A}, \mathbf{B}$ in 3-space is $\mathtt{L} = \mathbf{A}\mathbf{B}^\mathsf{T} - \mathbf{B}\mathbf{A}^\mathsf{T}$. Then the matrix $\mathtt{M} = \mathtt{P}\mathtt{L}\mathtt{P}^\mathsf{T} = \mathbf{a}\mathbf{b}^\mathsf{T} - \mathbf{b}\mathbf{a}^\mathsf{T}$ is 3×3 and antisymmetric, with null-space $\mathbf{a} \times \mathbf{b}$. Consequently, $\mathtt{M} = [\mathbf{a} \times \mathbf{b}]_\times$, and since the line through the image points is given by $\mathbf{l} = \mathbf{a} \times \mathbf{b}$, this completes the proof. □

It is clear from the form of (8.2) that there is a linear relation between the image line coordinates l_i and the world line coordinates L_{jk}, but that this relation is quadratic in the elements of the point projection matrix $\mathtt{P}$. Thus, (8.2) may be rearranged such that the map between the Plücker line coordinates, $\mathcal{L}$ (a 6-vector), and the image line coordinates $\mathbf{l}$ (a 3-vector) is represented by a single 3×6 matrix. It can be shown that

Definition 8.4. The *line projection matrix* $\mathcal{P}$ is the 3×6 matrix of rank 3 given by

$$\mathcal{P} = \begin{bmatrix} \mathbf{P}^2 \wedge \mathbf{P}^3 \\ \mathbf{P}^3 \wedge \mathbf{P}^1 \\ \mathbf{P}^1 \wedge \mathbf{P}^2 \end{bmatrix} \tag{8.3}$$

where $\mathbf{P}^{i\mathsf{T}}$ are the rows of the point camera matrix $\mathtt{P}$, and $\mathbf{P}^i \wedge \mathbf{P}^j$ are the Plücker line coordinates of the intersection of the planes $\mathbf{P}^i$ and $\mathbf{P}^j$.

Then the forward line projection is given by

Result 8.5. *Under the line projection matrix* $\mathcal{P}$*, a line in* $\mathbb{P}^3$ *represented by Plücker line coordinates* $\mathcal{L}$*, as defined in (3.11–p72), is mapped to the image line*

$$\mathbf{l} = \mathcal{P}\mathcal{L} = \begin{bmatrix} (\mathbf{P}^2 \wedge \mathbf{P}^3 | \mathcal{L}) \\ (\mathbf{P}^3 \wedge \mathbf{P}^1 | \mathcal{L}) \\ (\mathbf{P}^1 \wedge \mathbf{P}^2 | \mathcal{L}) \end{bmatrix} \tag{8.4}$$

where the product $(\mathcal{L}|\hat{\mathcal{L}})$ *is defined in (3.13–p72).*

Proof. Suppose the line in 3-space is the join of the points $\mathbf{A}$ and $\mathbf{B}$, and these project to $\mathbf{a} = \mathtt{P}\mathbf{A}, \mathbf{b} = \mathtt{P}\mathbf{B}$ respectively. Then the image line $\mathbf{l} = \mathbf{a} \times \mathbf{b} = (\mathtt{P}\mathbf{A}) \times (\mathtt{P}\mathbf{B})$. Consider the first element

$$\begin{aligned} l_1 &= (\mathbf{P}^{2\mathsf{T}}\mathbf{A})(\mathbf{P}^{3\mathsf{T}}\mathbf{B}) - (\mathbf{P}^{2\mathsf{T}}\mathbf{B})(\mathbf{P}^{3\mathsf{T}}\mathbf{A}) \\ &= (\mathbf{P}^2 \wedge \mathbf{P}^3 | \mathcal{L}) \end{aligned}$$

where the second equality follows from (3.14–*p*73). The other components follow in a similar manner. □

The line projection matrix $\mathcal{P}$ plays the same role for lines as $\mathtt{P}$ does for points. The rows of $\mathcal{P}$ may be interpreted geometrically as *lines*, in a similar manner to the interpretation of the rows of the point camera matrix $\mathtt{P}$ as *planes* given in section 6.2.1(*p*158). The rows $\mathbf{P}^{i\mathsf{T}}$ of $\mathtt{P}$ are the principal plane and axis planes of the camera. The rows of $\mathcal{P}$ are the lines of intersection of pairs of these camera planes. For example, the first row of $\mathcal{P}$ is $\mathbf{P}^2 \wedge \mathbf{P}^3$, and this is the 6-vector Plücker line representation of the line of intersection of the $y = 0$ axis plane, $\mathbf{P}^2$, and the principal plane, $\mathbf{P}^3$. The three lines corresponding to the three rows of $\mathcal{P}$ intersect at the camera centre. Consider lines $\mathcal{L}$ in 3-space for which $\mathcal{P}\mathcal{L} = \mathbf{0}$. These lines are in the null-space of $\mathcal{P}$. Since each row of $\mathcal{P}$ is a line, and from result 3.5(*p*72) the product $(\mathcal{L}_1|\mathcal{L}_2) = 0$ if two lines intersect, if follows that $\mathcal{L}$ intersects each of the lines represented by the rows of $\mathcal{P}$. These lines are the intersection of the camera planes, and the only point on all 3 camera planes is the camera centre. Thus we have

- *The lines $\mathcal{L}$ in $\mathbb{P}^3$ for which $\mathcal{P}\mathcal{L} = \mathbf{0}$ pass through the camera centre.*

The 3×6 matrix $\mathcal{P}$ has a 3-dimensional null-space. Allowing for the homogeneous scale factor, this null-space is a two-parameter family of lines containing the camera centre. This is to be expected since there is a star (two parameter family) of lines in $\mathbb{P}^3$ concurrent with a point.

8.1.3 On conics

Back-projection of conics. A conic $\mathtt{C}$ back-projects to a cone. A cone is a degenerate quadric, i.e. the 4×4 matrix representing the quadric does not have full rank. The cone vertex, in this case the camera centre, is the null-vector of the quadric matrix.

Result 8.6. *Under the camera $\mathtt{P}$ the conic $\mathtt{C}$ back-projects to the cone*

$$\mathtt{Q}_{\mathrm{co}} = \mathtt{P}^{\mathsf{T}}\mathtt{C}\mathtt{P}.$$

Proof. A point $\mathbf{x}$ lies on $\mathtt{C}$ if and only if $\mathbf{x}^{\mathsf{T}}\mathtt{C}\mathbf{x} = 0$. A space point $\mathbf{X}$ maps to a point $\mathtt{P}\mathbf{X}$, which lies on the conic if and only if $\mathbf{X}^{\mathsf{T}}\mathtt{P}^{\mathsf{T}}\mathtt{C}\mathtt{P}\mathbf{X} = 0$. Thus, if $\mathtt{Q}_{\mathrm{co}} = \mathtt{P}^{\mathsf{T}}\mathtt{C}\mathtt{P}$ is taken to represent a quadric, then $\mathbf{X}$ lies on this quadric if and only if $\mathbf{X}$ maps to a point on the conic $\mathtt{C}$. In other words, $\mathtt{Q}_{\mathrm{co}}$ is the back-projection of the conic $\mathtt{C}$. □

Note the camera centre $\mathbf{C}$ is the vertex of the degenerate quadric since $\mathtt{Q}_{\mathrm{co}}\mathbf{C} = \mathtt{P}^{\mathsf{T}}\mathtt{C}(\mathtt{P}\mathbf{C}) = \mathbf{0}$.

Example 8.7. Suppose that $\mathtt{P} = \mathtt{K}[\mathtt{I} \mid \mathbf{0}]$; then the conic $\mathtt{C}$ back-projects to the cone

$$\mathtt{Q}_{\mathrm{co}} = \begin{bmatrix} \mathtt{K}^{\mathsf{T}} \\ \mathbf{0}^{\mathsf{T}} \end{bmatrix} \mathtt{C}\,[\mathtt{K} \mid \mathbf{0}] = \begin{bmatrix} \mathtt{K}^{\mathsf{T}}\mathtt{C}\mathtt{K} & \mathbf{0} \\ \mathbf{0}^{\mathsf{T}} & 0 \end{bmatrix}.$$

The matrix $\mathtt{Q}_{\mathrm{co}}$ has rank 3. Its null-vector is the camera centre $\mathbf{C} = (0, 0, 0, 1)^{\mathsf{T}}$. △

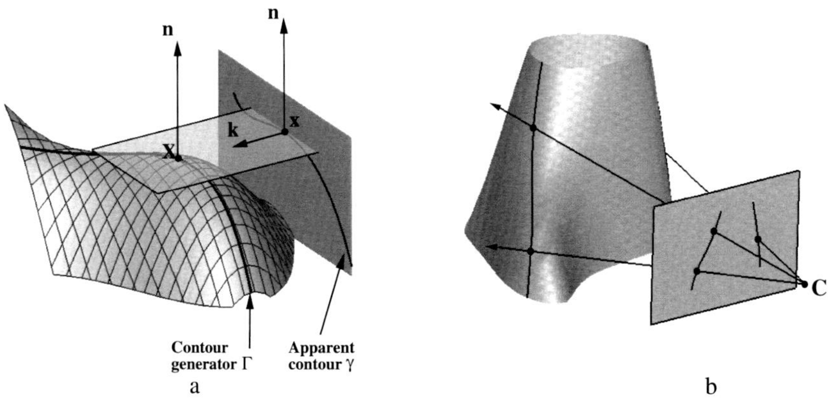

Fig. 8.3. **Contour generator and apparent contour.** *(a) for parallel projection; (b) for central projection. The ray from the camera centre through* $\mathbf{x}$ *is tangent to the surface at* $\mathbf{X}$. *The set of such tangent points* $\mathbf{X}$ *defines the contour generator, and their image defines the apparent contour. In general the contour generator is a space curve. Figure courtesy of Roberto Cipolla and Peter Giblin.*

8.2 Images of smooth surfaces

The image outline of a smooth surface S results from surface points at which the imaging rays are *tangent* to the surface, as shown in figure 8.3. Similarly, *lines* tangent to the outline back-project to planes which are *tangent planes* to the surface.

Definition 8.8. The *contour generator* Γ is the set of points $\mathbf{X}$ on S at which rays are tangent to the surface. The corresponding image *apparent contour* γ is the set of points $\mathbf{x}$ which are the image of $\mathbf{X}$, i.e. γ is the image of Γ.

The apparent contour is also called the "outline" and "profile". If the surface is viewed in the direction of $\mathbf{X}$ from the camera centre, then the surface appears to fold, or to have a boundary or occluding contour.

It is evident that the contour generator Γ depends only on the relative position of the camera centre and surface, not on the image plane. However, the apparent contour γ is defined by the intersection of the image plane with the rays to the contour generator, and so does depend on the position of the image plane.

In the case of parallel projection with direction $\mathbf{k}$, consider all the rays parallel to $\mathbf{k}$ which are tangent to S, see figure 8.3a. These rays form a "cylinder" of tangent rays, and the curve along which this cylinder is tangent to S is the contour generator Γ. The curve in which the cylinder meets the image plane is the apparent contour γ. Note that both Γ and γ depend in an essential way on $\mathbf{k}$. The set Γ slips over the surface as the direction of $\mathbf{k}$ changes. For example, with S a sphere, Γ is the great circle orthogonal to $\mathbf{k}$. In this case, the contour generator Γ is a plane curve, but in general Γ is a space curve.

We next describe the projection properties of quadrics. For this class of surface algebraic expressions can be developed for the contour generator and apparent contour.

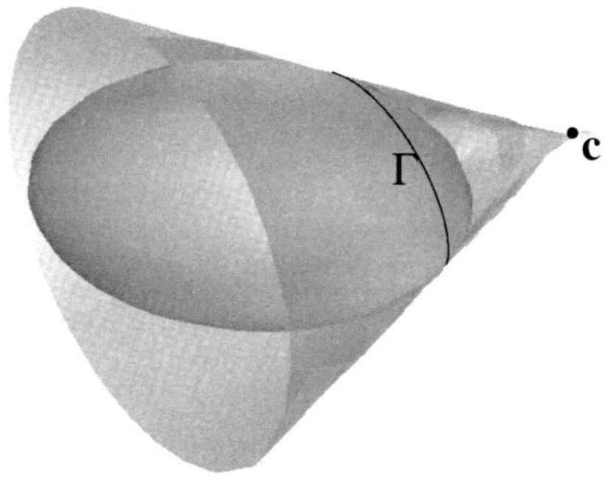

Fig. 8.4. **The cone of rays for a quadric.** *The vertex of the cone is the camera centre. (a) The contour generator* $\mathbf{\Gamma}$ *of a quadric is a plane curve (a conic) which is the intersection of the quadric with the polar plane of the camera centre,* $\mathbf{C}$.

8.3 Action of a projective camera on quadrics

A quadric is a smooth surface and so its outline curve is given by points where the back-projected rays are tangent to the quadric surface as shown in figure 8.4.

Suppose the quadric is a sphere, then the cone of rays between the camera centre and quadric is right-circular, i.e. the contour generator is a circle, with the plane of the circle orthogonal to the line joining the camera and sphere centres. This can be seen from the rotational symmetry of the geometry about this line. The image of the sphere is obtained by intersecting the cone with the image plane. It is clear that this is a classical conic section, so that the apparent contour of a sphere is a conic. In particular if the sphere centre lies on the principal ($\mathtt{Z}$) camera axis, then the conic is a circle.

Now consider a 3-space projective transformation of this geometry. Under this map the sphere is transformed to a quadric and the apparent contour to a conic. However, since intersection and tangency are preserved, the contour generator is a (plane) conic. Consequently, the apparent contour of a general quadric is a conic, and the contour generator is also a conic. We will now give algebraic representations for these geometric results.

Forward projection of quadrics. Since the outline arises from tangency, it is not surprising that the dual of the quadric, $\mathtt{Q}^*$, is important here since it defines the tangent planes to the quadric $\mathtt{Q}$.

Result 8.9. *Under the camera matrix* $\mathtt{P}$ *the outline of the quadric* $\mathtt{Q}$ *is the conic* $\mathtt{C}$ *given by*

$$\mathtt{C}^* = \mathtt{P}\mathtt{Q}^*\mathtt{P}^{\mathsf{T}}. \tag{8.5}$$

Proof. This expression is simply derived from the observation that lines $\mathbf{l}$ tangent to the conic outline satisfy $\mathbf{l}^{\mathsf{T}}\mathtt{C}^*\mathbf{l} = 0$. These lines back-project to planes $\boldsymbol{\pi} = \mathtt{P}^{\mathsf{T}}\mathbf{l}$ that are tangent to the quadric and thus satisfy $\boldsymbol{\pi}^{\mathsf{T}}\mathtt{Q}^*\boldsymbol{\pi} = 0$. Then it follows that for each line

$$\begin{aligned} \boldsymbol{\pi}^{\mathsf{T}}\mathtt{Q}^*\boldsymbol{\pi} &= \mathbf{l}^{\mathsf{T}}\mathtt{P}\mathtt{Q}^*\mathtt{P}^{\mathsf{T}}\mathbf{l} \\ &= \mathbf{l}^{\mathsf{T}}\mathtt{C}^*\mathbf{l} = 0 \end{aligned}$$

and since this is true for all lines tangent to $\mathtt{C}$ the result follows. □

Note the similarity of (8.5) with the projection of a line represented by a Plücker matrix (8.2). An expression for the projection of the point quadric $\mathtt{Q}$ can be derived from (8.5) but it is quite complicated. However, the plane of the contour generator is easily expressed in terms of $\mathtt{Q}$:

- *The plane of* Γ *for a quadric* $\mathtt{Q}$ *and camera with centre* $\mathbf{C}$ *is given by* $\boldsymbol{\pi}_\Gamma = \mathtt{Q}\mathbf{C}$.

This result follows directly from the pole–polar relation for a point and quadric of section 3.2.3(*p*73). Its proof is left as an exercise. Note, the intersection of a quadric and plane is a conic. So Γ is a conic and its image γ, which is the apparent contour, is also a conic as has been seen above.

We may also derive an expression for the cone of rays formed by the camera centre and quadric. This cone is a degenerate quadric of rank 3.

Result 8.10. *The cone with vertex* $\mathbf{V}$ *and tangent to the quadric* $\mathtt{Q}$ *is the degenerate quadric*

$$\mathtt{Q}_{\text{co}} = (\mathbf{V}^{\mathsf{T}}\mathtt{Q}\mathbf{V})\mathtt{Q} - (\mathtt{Q}\mathbf{V})(\mathtt{Q}\mathbf{V})^{\mathsf{T}}.$$

Note that $\mathtt{Q}_{\text{co}}\mathbf{V} = \mathbf{0}$, so that $\mathbf{V}$ is the vertex of the cone as required. The proof is omitted.

Example 8.11. We write the quadric in block form:

$$\mathtt{Q} = \begin{bmatrix} \mathtt{Q}_{3\times3} & \mathbf{q} \\ \mathbf{q}^{\mathsf{T}} & q_{44} \end{bmatrix}.$$

Then if $\mathbf{V} = (0,0,0,1)^{\mathsf{T}}$, which corresponds to the cone vertex being at the centre of the world coordinate frame,

$$\mathtt{Q}_{\text{co}} = \begin{bmatrix} q_{44}\mathtt{Q}_{3\times3} - \mathbf{q}\mathbf{q}^{\mathsf{T}} & \mathbf{0} \\ \mathbf{0}^{\mathsf{T}} & 0 \end{bmatrix}$$

which is clearly a degenerate quadric. △

8.4 The importance of the camera centre

An object in 3-space and camera centre define a set of rays, and an image is obtained by intersecting these rays with a plane. Often this set is referred to as a *cone* of rays, even though it is not a classical cone. Suppose the cone of rays is intersected by two planes, as shown in figure 8.5, then the two images, I and I', are clearly related by a perspective map. This means that images obtained with the same camera centre may be mapped to one another by a plane projective transformation, in other words they are projectively equivalent and so have the same projective properties. A camera can thus be thought of as a projective imaging device – measuring projective properties of the cone of rays with vertex the camera centre.

The result that the two images I and I' are related by a homography will now be derived algebraically to obtain a formula for this homography. Consider two cameras

$$\mathtt{P} = \mathtt{K}\mathtt{R}[\mathtt{I} \mid -\widetilde{\mathbf{C}}], \quad \mathtt{P}' = \mathtt{K}'\mathtt{R}'[\mathtt{I} \mid -\widetilde{\mathbf{C}}]$$

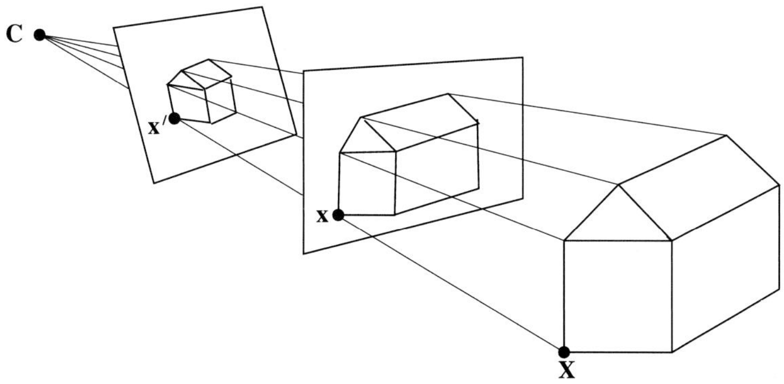

Fig. 8.5. **The cone of rays with vertex the camera centre.** *An image is obtained by intersecting this cone with a plane. A ray between a 3-space point* $\mathbf{X}$ *and the camera centre* $\mathbf{C}$ *pierces the planes in the image points* $\mathbf{x}$ *and* $\mathbf{x}'$*. All such image points are related by a planar homography,* $\mathbf{x}' = \mathtt{H}\mathbf{x}$.

with the same centre. Note that since the cameras have a common centre there is a simple relation between them, namely $\mathtt{P}' = (\mathtt{K}'\mathtt{R}')(\mathtt{K}\mathtt{R})^{-1}\mathtt{P}$. It then follows that the images of a 3-space point $\mathbf{X}$ by the two cameras are related as

$$\mathbf{x}' = \mathtt{P}'\mathbf{X} = (\mathtt{K}'\mathtt{R}')(\mathtt{K}\mathtt{R})^{-1}\mathtt{P}\mathbf{X} = (\mathtt{K}'\mathtt{R}')(\mathtt{K}\mathtt{R})^{-1}\mathbf{x}.$$

That is, the corresponding image points are related by a planar homography (a 3×3 matrix) as $\mathbf{x}' = \mathtt{H}\mathbf{x}$, where $\mathtt{H} = (\mathtt{K}'\mathtt{R}')(\mathtt{K}\mathtt{R})^{-1}$.

We will now investigate several cases of moving the image plane whilst fixing the camera centre. For simplicity the world coordinate frame will be chosen to coincide with the camera's, so that $\mathtt{P} = \mathtt{K}[\mathtt{I} \mid \mathbf{0}]$ (and it will be assumed that the image plane never contains the centre, as the image would then be degenerate).

8.4.1 Moving the image plane

Consider first an increase in focal length. To a first approximation this corresponds to a displacement of the image plane along the principal axis. The image effect is a simple magnification. This is only a first approximation because with a compound lens zooming will perturb both the principal point and the effective camera centre. Algebraically, if $\mathbf{x}$, $\mathbf{x}'$ are the images of a point $\mathbf{X}$ before and after zooming, then

$$\begin{aligned} \mathbf{x} &= \mathtt{K}[\mathtt{I} \mid \mathbf{0}]\mathbf{X} \\ \mathbf{x}' &= \mathtt{K}'[\mathtt{I} \mid \mathbf{0}]\mathbf{X} = \mathtt{K}'\mathtt{K}^{-1}(\mathtt{K}[\mathtt{I} \mid \mathbf{0}]\mathbf{X}) = \mathtt{K}'\mathtt{K}^{-1}\mathbf{x} \end{aligned}$$

so that $\mathbf{x}' = \mathtt{H}\mathbf{x}$ with $\mathtt{H} = \mathtt{K}'\mathtt{K}^{-1}$. If only the focal lengths differ between $\mathtt{K}$ and $\mathtt{K}'$ then a short calculation shows that

$$\mathtt{K}'\mathtt{K}^{-1} = \begin{bmatrix} k\mathtt{I} & (1-k)\tilde{\mathbf{x}}_0 \\ \mathbf{0}^{\mathsf{T}} & 1 \end{bmatrix}.$$

where $\tilde{\mathbf{x}}_0$ is the inhomogeneous principal point, and $k = f'/f$ is the magnification factor. This result follows directly from similar triangles: the effect of zooming by a

a b c

Fig. 8.6. *Between images (a) and (b) the camera rotates about the camera centre. Corresponding points (that is images of the same 3D point) are related by a plane projective transformation. Note that 3D points at different depths which are coincident in image (a), such as the mug lip and cat body, are also coincident in (b), so there is no motion parallax in this case. However, between images (a) and (c) the camera rotates about the camera centre* and *translates. Under this general motion coincident points of differing depth in (a) are imaged at different points in (c), so there* is *motion parallax in this case due to the camera translation.*

factor k is to move the image point $\tilde{\mathbf{x}}$ on a line radiating from the principal point $\tilde{\mathbf{x}}_0$ to the point $\tilde{\mathbf{x}}' = k\tilde{\mathbf{x}} + (1-k)\tilde{\mathbf{x}}_0$. Algebraically, using the most general form (6.10–*p*157) of the calibration matrix $\mathtt{K}$, we may write

$$\begin{aligned} \mathtt{K}' &= \begin{bmatrix} k\mathtt{I} & (1-k)\tilde{\mathbf{x}}_0 \\ \mathbf{0}^\mathsf{T} & 1 \end{bmatrix} \mathtt{K} = \begin{bmatrix} k\mathtt{I} & (1-k)\tilde{\mathbf{x}}_0 \\ \mathbf{0}^\mathsf{T} & 1 \end{bmatrix} \begin{bmatrix} \mathtt{A} & \tilde{\mathbf{x}}_0 \\ \mathbf{0}^\mathsf{T} & 1 \end{bmatrix} \\ &= \begin{bmatrix} k\mathtt{A} & \tilde{\mathbf{x}}_0 \\ \mathbf{0}^\mathsf{T} & 1 \end{bmatrix} = \mathtt{K} \begin{bmatrix} k\mathtt{I} & \\ & 1 \end{bmatrix}. \end{aligned}$$

This shows that

- *The effect of zooming by a factor k is to multiply the calibration matrix $\mathtt{K}$ on the right by* $\mathrm{diag}(k, k, 1)$.

8.4.2 Camera rotation

A second common example is where the camera is rotated about its centre with no change in the internal parameters. Examples of this "pure" rotation are given in figure 8.6 and figure 8.9. Algebraically, if $\mathbf{x}$, $\mathbf{x}'$ are the images of a point $\mathbf{X}$ before and after the pure rotation

$$\begin{aligned} \mathbf{x} &= \mathtt{K}[\mathtt{I} \mid \mathbf{0}]\mathbf{X} \\ \mathbf{x}' &= \mathtt{K}[\mathtt{R} \mid \mathbf{0}]\mathbf{X} = \mathtt{KRK}^{-1}\mathtt{K}[\mathtt{I} \mid \mathbf{0}]\mathbf{X} = \mathtt{KRK}^{-1}\mathbf{x} \end{aligned}$$

so that $\mathbf{x}' = \mathtt{H}\mathbf{x}$ with $\mathtt{H} = \mathtt{KRK}^{-1}$. This homography is a *conjugate rotation* and is discussed further in section A7.1(*p*628). For now, we mention a few of its properties by way of an example.

Example 8.12. Properties of a conjugate rotation

The homography $\mathtt{H} = \mathtt{KRK}^{-1}$ has the same eigenvalues (up to scale) as the rotation matrix, namely $\{\mu, \mu e^{i\theta}, \mu e^{-i\theta}\}$, where μ is an unknown scale factor (if $\mathtt{H}$ is scaled such that $\det \mathtt{H} = 1$, then $\mu = 1$). Consequently the angle of rotation between views may be computed directly from the phase of the complex eigenvalues of $\mathtt{H}$. Similarly, it can be

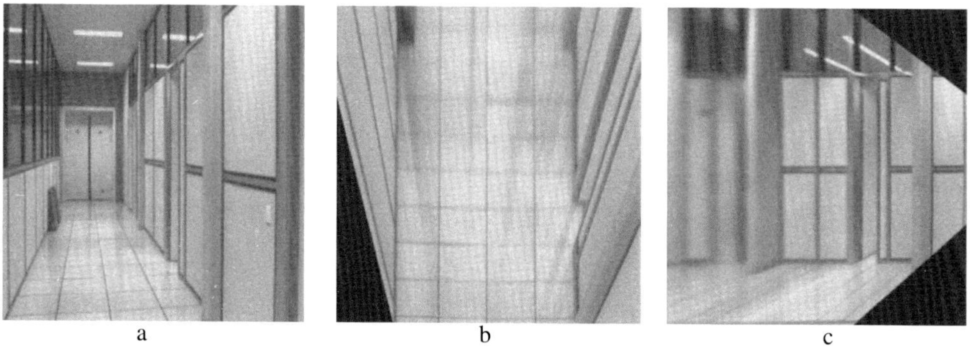

Fig. 8.7. **Synthetic views.** *(a) Source image. (b) Fronto-parallel view of the corridor floor generated from (a) using the four corners of a floor tile to compute the homography. (c) Fronto-parallel view of the corridor wall generated from (a) using the four corners of the door frame to compute the homography.*

shown (see exercises) that the eigenvector of $\mathtt{H}$ corresponding to the real eigenvalue is the vanishing point of the rotation axis.

For example, between images (a) and (b) of figure 8.6 there is a pure rotation of the camera. The homography $\mathtt{H}$ is computed by algorithm 4.6(*p*123), and from this the angle of rotation is estimated as $4.66°$, and the axis vanishing point as $(-0.0088, 1, 0.0001)^{\mathsf{T}}$, i.e. virtually at infinity in the y direction, so the rotation axis is almost parallel to the y-axis. △

The transformation $\mathtt{H} = \mathtt{KRK}^{-1}$ is an example of the *infinite homography* mapping $\mathtt{H}_{\infty}$, that will appear many times through this book. It is defined in section 13.4(*p*338). The conjugation property is used for auto-calibration in chapter 19.

8.4.3 Applications and examples

The homographic relation between images with the same camera centre can be exploited in several ways. One is the creation of synthetic images by projective warping. Another is mosaicing, where panoramic images can be created by using planar homographies to "sew" together views obtained by a rotating camera.

Example 8.13. Synthetic views

New images corresponding to different camera orientations (with the same camera centre) can be generated from an existing image by warping with planar homographies.

In a fronto-parallel view a rectangle is imaged as a rectangle, and the world and image rectangle have the same aspect ratio. Conversely, a fronto-parallel view can be synthesized by warping an image with the homography that maps a rectangle imaged as a quadrilateral to a rectangle with the correct aspect ratio. The algorithm is:

(i) Compute the homography $\mathtt{H}$ which maps the image quadrilateral to a rectangle with the correct aspect ratio.

(ii) Projectively warp the source image with this homography.

Examples are shown in figure 8.7. △

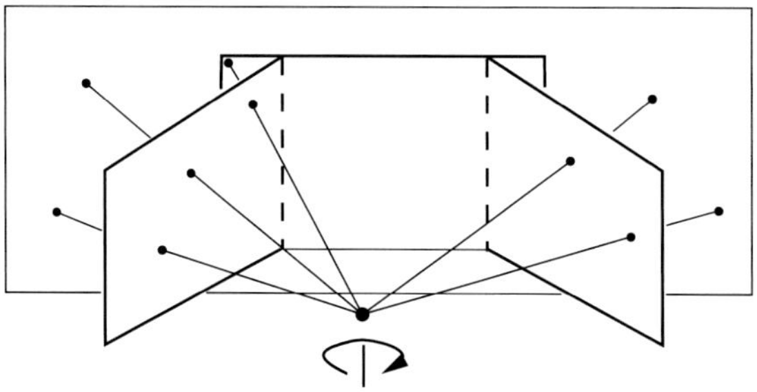

Fig. 8.8. *Three images acquired by a rotating camera may be registered to the frame of the middle one, as shown, by projectively warping the outer images to align with the middle one.*

Example 8.14. Planar panoramic mosaicing

Images acquired by a camera rotating about its centre are related to each other by a planar homography. A set of such images may be registered with the plane of one of the images by projectively warping the other images, as illustrated in figure 8.8.

Fig. 8.9. **Planar panoramic mosaicing.** *Eight images (out of thirty) acquired by rotating a camcorder about its centre. The thirty images are registered (automatically) using planar homographies and composed into the single panoramic mosaic shown. Note the characteristic "bow tie" shape resulting from registering to an image at the middle of the sequence.*

In outline the algorithm is:

(i) Choose one image of the set as a reference.
(ii) Compute the homography $\mathtt{H}$ which maps one of the other images of the set to this reference image.

(iii) Projectively warp the image with this homography, and augment the reference image with the non-overlapping part of the warped image.
(iv) Repeat the last two steps for the remaining images of the set.

The homographies may be computed by identifying (at least) four corresponding points, or by using the automatic method of algorithm 4.6(p123). An example mosaic is shown in figure 8.9. △

8.4.4 Projective (reduced) notation

It will be seen in chapter 20 that if canonical projective coordinates are chosen for world and image points, i.e.

$$\mathbf{X}_1 = (1,0,0,0)^\mathsf{T},\ \mathbf{X}_2 = (0,1,0,0)^\mathsf{T},\ \mathbf{X}_3 = (0,0,1,0)^\mathsf{T},\ \mathbf{X}_4 = (0,0,0,1)^\mathsf{T},$$

and

$$\mathbf{x}_1 = (1,0,0)^\mathsf{T},\ \mathbf{x}_2 = (0,1,0)^\mathsf{T},\ \mathbf{x}_3 = (0,0,1)^\mathsf{T},\ \mathbf{x}_4 = (1,1,1)^\mathsf{T},$$

then the camera matrix

$$\mathtt{P} = \begin{bmatrix} a & 0 & 0 & -d \\ 0 & b & 0 & -d \\ 0 & 0 & c & -d \end{bmatrix} \tag{8.6}$$

satisfies $\mathbf{x}_i = \mathtt{P}\mathbf{X}_i,\ i = 1,\ldots,4$, and also that $\mathtt{P}(a^{-1}, b^{-1}, c^{-1}, d^{-1})^\mathsf{T} = \mathbf{0}$, which means that the camera centre is $\mathbf{C} = (a^{-1}, b^{-1}, c^{-1}, d^{-1})^\mathsf{T}$. This is known as the *reduced* camera matrix, and it is clearly completely specified by the 3 degrees of freedom of the camera centre $\mathbf{C}$. This is a further illustration of the fact that all images acquired by cameras with the same camera centre are projectively equivalent – the camera has been reduced to its essence: a projective device whose action is to map $\mathbb{P}^3$ to $\mathbb{P}^2$ with only the position of the camera centre affecting the result. This camera representation is used in establishing duality relations in chapter 20.

8.4.5 Moving the camera centre

The cases of zooming and camera rotation illustrate that moving the image plane, whilst fixing the camera centre, induces a transformation between images that depends only on the image plane motion, but *not* on the 3-space structure. Conversely, no information on 3-space structure can be obtained by this action. However, if the camera centre is moved then the map between corresponding image points *does* depend on the 3-space structure, and indeed may often be used to (partially) determine the structure. This is the subject of much of the remainder of this book.

How can one determine from the images alone whether the camera centre has moved? Consider two 3-space points which have coincident images in the first view, i.e. the points are on the same ray. If the camera centre is moved (not along that ray) the image coincidence is lost. This relative displacement of previously coincident image points is termed *parallax*, and is illustrated in figure 8.6 and shown schematically in figure 8.10. If the scene is static and motion parallax is evident between two views then the camera centre has moved. Indeed, a convenient method for obtaining a camera

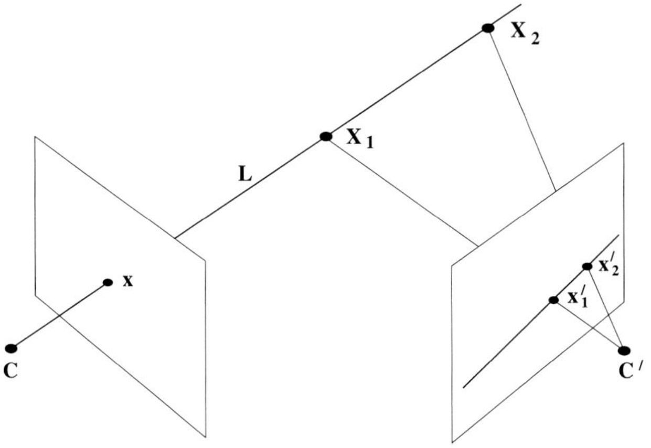

Fig. 8.10. **Motion parallax.** *The images of the space points* $\mathbf{X}_1$ *and* $\mathbf{X}_2$ *are coincident when viewed by the camera with centre* $\mathbf{C}$. *However, when viewed by a camera with centre* $\mathbf{C}'$, *which does not lie on the line* $\mathbf{L}$ *through* $\mathbf{X}_1$ *and* $\mathbf{X}_2$, *the images of the space points are not coincident. In fact the line through the image points* $\mathbf{x}'_1$ *and* $\mathbf{x}'_2$ *is the image of the ray* $\mathbf{L}$, *and will be seen in chapter 9 to be an* **epipolar line**. *The vector between the points* $\mathbf{x}'_1$ *and* $\mathbf{x}'_2$ *is the parallax.*

motion that is only a rotation about its centre (for example for a camera mounted on a robot head) is to adjust the motion until there is no parallax.

An important special case of 3-space structure is when all scene points are coplanar. In this case the images of corresponding points are related by a planar homography even if the camera centre is moved. The map between images in this case is discussed in detail in chapter 13 on planes. In particular vanishing points, which are images of points on the plane π_∞, are related by a planar homography for any camera motion. We return to this in section 8.6.

8.5 Camera calibration and the image of the absolute conic

Up to this point we have discussed projective properties of the forward and back-projection of various entities (point, lines, conics ...). These properties depend only on the 3×4 form of the projective camera matrix $\mathtt{P}$. Now we describe what is gained if the camera internal calibration, $\mathtt{K}$, is known. It will be seen that Euclidean properties, such as the angle between two rays, can then be measured.

What does calibration give? An image point $\mathbf{x}$ back-projects to a ray defined by $\mathbf{x}$ and the camera centre. Calibration relates the image point to the ray's *direction*. Suppose points on the ray are written as $\widetilde{\mathbf{X}} = \lambda \mathbf{d}$ in the camera Euclidean coordinate frame, then these points map to the point $\mathbf{x} = \mathtt{K}[\mathtt{I} \mid \mathbf{0}](\lambda \mathbf{d}^\mathsf{T}, 1)^\mathsf{T} = \mathtt{K}\mathbf{d}$ up to scale. Conversely the direction $\mathbf{d}$ is obtained from the image point $\mathbf{x}$ as $\mathbf{d} = \mathtt{K}^{-1}\mathbf{x}$. Thus we have established:

Result 8.15. *The camera calibration matrix* $\mathtt{K}$ *is the (affine) transformation between* $\mathbf{x}$ *and the ray's direction* $\mathbf{d} = \mathtt{K}^{-1}\mathbf{x}$ *measured in the camera's Euclidean coordinate frame.*

Note, $\mathbf{d} = \mathtt{K}^{-1}\mathbf{x}$ is in general *not* a unit vector.

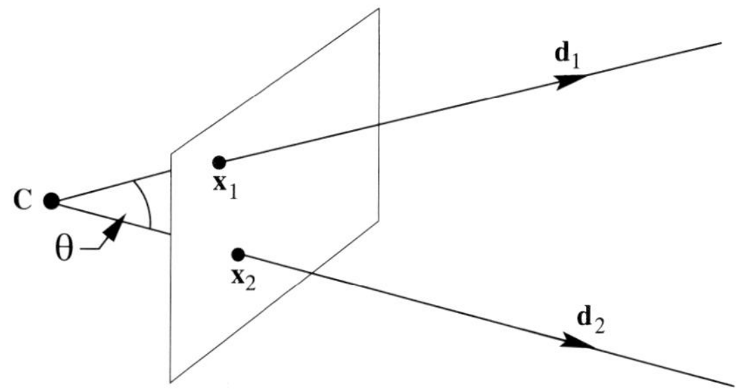

Fig. 8.11. *The angle θ between two rays.*

The angle between two rays, with directions $\mathbf{d}_1$, $\mathbf{d}_2$ corresponding to image points $\mathbf{x}_1, \mathbf{x}_2$ respectively, may be obtained from the familiar cosine formula for the angle between two vectors:

$$\begin{aligned}\cos\theta &= \frac{\mathbf{d}_1^{\mathsf{T}}\mathbf{d}_2}{\sqrt{\mathbf{d}_1^{\mathsf{T}}\mathbf{d}_1}\sqrt{\mathbf{d}_2^{\mathsf{T}}\mathbf{d}_2}} = \frac{(\mathtt{K}^{-1}\mathbf{x}_1)^{\mathsf{T}}(\mathtt{K}^{-1}\mathbf{x}_2)}{\sqrt{(\mathtt{K}^{-1}\mathbf{x}_1)^{\mathsf{T}}(\mathtt{K}^{-1}\mathbf{x}_1)}\sqrt{(\mathtt{K}^{-1}\mathbf{x}_2)^{\mathsf{T}}(\mathtt{K}^{-1}\mathbf{x}_2)}} \\ &= \frac{\mathbf{x}_1^{\mathsf{T}}(\mathtt{K}^{-\mathsf{T}}\mathtt{K}^{-1})\mathbf{x}_2}{\sqrt{\mathbf{x}_1^{\mathsf{T}}(\mathtt{K}^{-\mathsf{T}}\mathtt{K}^{-1})\mathbf{x}_1}\sqrt{\mathbf{x}_2^{\mathsf{T}}(\mathtt{K}^{-\mathsf{T}}\mathtt{K}^{-1})\mathbf{x}_2}}.\end{aligned} \tag{8.7}$$

The formula (8.7) shows that if $\mathtt{K}$, and consequently the matrix $\mathtt{K}^{-\mathsf{T}}\mathtt{K}^{-1}$, is known, then the angle between rays can be measured from their corresponding image points. A camera for which $\mathtt{K}$ is known is termed *calibrated*. A calibrated camera is a *direction sensor*, able to measure the direction of rays – like a 2D protractor.

The calibration matrix $\mathtt{K}$ also provides a relation between an image line and a scene plane:

Result 8.16. *An image line* $\mathbf{l}$ *defines a plane through the camera centre with normal direction* $\mathbf{n} = \mathtt{K}^{\mathsf{T}}\mathbf{l}$ *measured in the camera's Euclidean coordinate frame.*

Note, the normal $\mathbf{n}$ will not in general be a unit vector.

Proof. Points $\mathbf{x}$ on the line $\mathbf{l}$ back-project to directions $\mathbf{d} = \mathtt{K}^{-1}\mathbf{x}$ which are orthogonal to the plane normal $\mathbf{n}$, and thus satisfy $\mathbf{d}^{\mathsf{T}}\mathbf{n} = \mathbf{x}^{\mathsf{T}}\mathtt{K}^{-\mathsf{T}}\mathbf{n} = 0$. Since points on $\mathbf{l}$ satisfy $\mathbf{x}^{\mathsf{T}}\mathbf{l} = 0$, it follows that $\mathbf{l} = \mathtt{K}^{-\mathsf{T}}\mathbf{n}$, and hence $\mathbf{n} = \mathtt{K}^{\mathsf{T}}\mathbf{l}$. □

8.5.1 The image of the absolute conic

We now derive a very important result which relates the calibration matrix $\mathtt{K}$ to the image of the absolute conic, $\boldsymbol{\omega}$. First we must determine the map between the plane at infinity, $\boldsymbol{\pi}_\infty$, and the camera image plane. Points on $\boldsymbol{\pi}_\infty$ may be written as $\mathbf{X}_\infty = (\mathbf{d}^{\mathsf{T}}, 0)^{\mathsf{T}}$, and are imaged by a general camera $\mathtt{P} = \mathtt{KR}[\mathtt{I} \mid -\widetilde{\mathbf{C}}]$ as

$$\mathbf{x} = \mathtt{P}\mathbf{X}_\infty = \mathtt{KR}[\mathtt{I} \mid -\widetilde{\mathbf{C}}]\begin{pmatrix}\mathbf{d}\\0\end{pmatrix} = \mathtt{KR}\mathbf{d}.$$

This shows that

- *the mapping between π_∞ and an image is given by the planar homography* $\mathbf{x} = \mathtt{H}\mathbf{d}$ *with*

$$\mathtt{H} = \mathtt{KR}. \tag{8.8}$$

Note that this map is independent of the position of the camera, $\mathbf{C}$, and depends only on the camera internal calibration and orientation with respect to the world coordinate frame.

Now, since the absolute conic Ω_∞ (section 3.6(*p*81)) is on π_∞ we can compute its image under H, and find

Result 8.17. *The image of the absolute conic (the IAC) is the conic* $\omega = (\mathtt{KK}^\mathsf{T})^{-1} = \mathtt{K}^{-\mathsf{T}}\mathtt{K}^{-1}$.

Proof. From result 2.13(*p*37) under a point homography $\mathbf{x} \mapsto \mathtt{H}\mathbf{x}$ a conic C maps as $\mathtt{C} \mapsto \mathtt{H}^{-\mathsf{T}}\mathtt{C}\mathtt{H}^{-1}$. It follows that Ω_∞, which is the conic $\mathtt{C} = \Omega_\infty = \mathtt{I}$ on π_∞, maps to $\omega = (\mathtt{KR})^{-\mathsf{T}}\mathtt{I}(\mathtt{KR})^{-1} = \mathtt{K}^{-\mathsf{T}}\mathtt{R}\mathtt{R}^{-1}\mathtt{K}^{-1} = (\mathtt{KK}^\mathsf{T})^{-1}$. So the IAC $\omega = (\mathtt{KK}^\mathsf{T})^{-1}$. □

Like Ω_∞ the conic ω is an imaginary point conic with no real points. For the moment it may be thought of as a convenient algebraic device, but it will be used in computations later in this chapter, and also in chapter 19 on camera auto-calibration.
A few remarks here:

(i) The image of the absolute conic, ω, depends only on the internal parameters K of the matrix P; it does not depend on the camera orientation or position.

(ii) It follows from (8.7) that the angle between two rays is given by the simple expression

$$\cos\theta = \frac{\mathbf{x}_1^\mathsf{T}\omega\mathbf{x}_2}{\sqrt{\mathbf{x}_1^\mathsf{T}\omega\mathbf{x}_1}\sqrt{\mathbf{x}_2^\mathsf{T}\omega\mathbf{x}_2}}. \tag{8.9}$$

This expression is independent of the projective coordinate frame in the image, that is, it is unchanged under projective transformation of the image. To see this consider any 2D projective transformation, H. The points $\mathbf{x}_i$ are transformed to $\mathtt{H}\mathbf{x}_i$, and ω transforms (as any image conic) to $\mathtt{H}^{-\mathsf{T}}\omega\mathtt{H}^{-1}$. Thus, (8.9) is unchanged, and hence holds in any projective coordinate frame in the image.

(iii) A particularly important specialization of (8.9) is that if two image points $\mathbf{x}_1$ and $\mathbf{x}_2$ correspond to orthogonal directions then

$$\mathbf{x}_1^\mathsf{T}\omega\mathbf{x}_2 = 0. \tag{8.10}$$

This equation will be used at several points later in the book as it provides a linear constraint on ω.

(iv) We may also define the dual image of the absolute conic (the DIAC) as

$$\omega^* = \omega^{-1} = \mathtt{KK}^\mathsf{T}. \tag{8.11}$$

This is a dual (line) conic, whereas ω is a point conic (though it contains no real points). The conic ω^* is the image of $\mathtt{Q}_\infty^*$ and is given by (8.5) $\omega^* = \mathtt{P}\mathtt{Q}_\infty^*\mathtt{P}^\mathsf{T}$.

(v) Result 8.17 shows that once ω (or equivalently ω^*) is identified in an image then K is also determined. This follows because a symmetric matrix ω may be uniquely decomposed into a product $\omega^* = \mathtt{KK}^\mathsf{T}$ of an upper-triangular matrix with positive diagonal entries and its transpose by the Cholesky factorization (see result A4.5(*p*582)).

(vi) It was seen in chapter 3 that a plane π intersects π_∞ in a line, and this line intersects Ω_∞ in two points which are the circular points of π. The imaged circular points lie on ω at the points at which the vanishing line of the plane π intersects ω.

These final two properties of ω are the basis for a calibration algorithm, as shown in the following example.

Example 8.18. A simple calibration device

The image of three squares (on planes which are not parallel, but which need not be orthogonal) provides sufficiently many constraints to compute K. Consider one of the squares. The correspondences between its four corner points and their images define the homography H between the plane π of the square and the image. Applying this homography to circular points on π determines their images as $\mathtt{H}(1, \pm i, 0)^\mathsf{T}$. Thus we have two points on the (as yet unknown) ω. A similar procedure applied to the other squares generates a total of six points on ω, from which it may be computed (since five points are required to determine a conic). In outline the algorithm has the following steps:

(i) For each square compute the homography H that maps its corner points, $(0,0)^\mathsf{T}, (1,0)^\mathsf{T}, (0,1)^\mathsf{T}, (1,1)^\mathsf{T}$, to their imaged points. (The alignment of the plane coordinate system with the square is a similarity transformation and does not affect the position of the circular points on the plane).

(ii) Compute the imaged circular points for the plane of that square as $\mathtt{H}(1, \pm i, 0)^\mathsf{T}$. Writing $\mathtt{H} = [\mathbf{h}_1, \mathbf{h}_2, \mathbf{h}_3]$, the imaged circular points are $\mathbf{h}_1 \pm i\mathbf{h}_2$.

(iii) Fit a conic ω to the six imaged circular points. The constraint that the imaged circular points lie on ω may be rewritten as two real constraints. If $\mathbf{h}_1 \pm i\mathbf{h}_2$ lies on ω then $(\mathbf{h}_1 \pm i\mathbf{h}_2)^\mathsf{T}\, \omega\, (\mathbf{h}_1 \pm i\mathbf{h}_2) = 0$, and the imaginary and real parts give respectively:

$$\mathbf{h}_1^\mathsf{T} \omega \mathbf{h}_2 = 0 \quad \text{and} \quad \mathbf{h}_1^\mathsf{T} \omega \mathbf{h}_1 = \mathbf{h}_2^\mathsf{T} \omega \mathbf{h}_2 \tag{8.12}$$

which are equations linear in ω. The conic ω is determined up to scale from five or more such equations.

(iv) Compute the calibration K from $\omega = (\mathtt{KK}^\mathsf{T})^{-1}$ using the Cholesky factorization.

Figure 8.12 shows a calibration object consisting of three planes imprinted with squares, and the computed matrix K. For the purpose of internal calibration, the squares have the advantage over a standard calibration object (e.g. figure 7.1(*p*182)) that no measured 3D co-ordinates are required. △

$$K = \begin{bmatrix} 1108.3 & -9.8 & 525.8 \\ 0 & 1097.8 & 395.9 \\ 0 & 0 & 1 \end{bmatrix}$$

a b

Fig. 8.12. **Calibration from metric planes.** *(a) Three squares provide a simple calibration object. The planes need not be orthogonal. (b) The computed calibration matrix using the algorithm of example 8.18. The image size is* 1024×768 *pixels.*

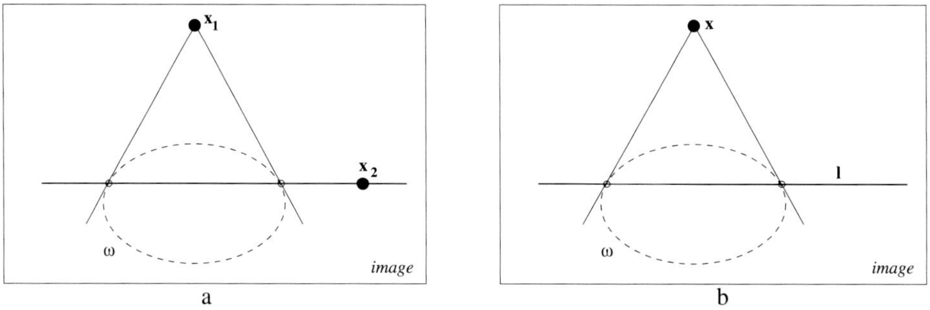

Fig. 8.13. **Orthogonality represented by conjugacy and pole–polar relationships.** *(a) Image points* $\mathbf{x}_1, \mathbf{x}_2$ *back-project to orthogonal rays if the points are conjugate with respect to* $\boldsymbol{\omega}$*, i.e.* $\mathbf{x}_1^\mathsf{T}\boldsymbol{\omega}\mathbf{x}_2 = 0$*. (b) The point* $\mathbf{x}$ *and line* $\mathbf{l}$ *back-project to a ray and plane that are orthogonal if* $\mathbf{x}$ *and* $\mathbf{l}$ *are pole–polar with respect to* $\boldsymbol{\omega}$*, i.e.* $\mathbf{l} = \boldsymbol{\omega}\mathbf{x}$*. For example (see section 8.6.3), the vanishing point of the normal direction to a plane and the vanishing line of the plane are pole–polar with respect to* $\boldsymbol{\omega}$*.*

We will return to camera calibration in section 8.8, where vanishing points and lines provide constraints on K. The geometric constraints that are used in example 8.18 are discussed further in section 8.8.1.

8.5.2 Orthogonality and $\boldsymbol{\omega}$

The conic $\boldsymbol{\omega}$ is a device for representing orthogonality in an image. It has already been seen (8.10) that if two image points $\mathbf{x}_1$ and $\mathbf{x}_2$ back-project to orthogonal rays, then the points satisfy $\mathbf{x}_1^\mathsf{T}\boldsymbol{\omega}\mathbf{x}_2 = 0$. Similarly, it may be shown that

Result 8.19. *A point* $\mathbf{x}$ *and line* $\mathbf{l}$ *back-projecting to a ray and plane respectively that are orthogonal are related by* $\mathbf{l} = \boldsymbol{\omega}\mathbf{x}$.

Geometrically these relations express that image points back-projecting to orthogonal rays are conjugate with respect to $\boldsymbol{\omega}$ ($\mathbf{x}_1^\mathsf{T}\boldsymbol{\omega}\mathbf{x}_2 = 0$), and that a point and line back-projecting to an orthogonal ray and plane are in a pole–polar relationship ($\mathbf{l} = \boldsymbol{\omega}\mathbf{x}$). See section 2.8.1(*p*58). A schematic representation of these two relations is given in figure 8.13.

These geometric representations of orthogonality, and indeed the projective representation (8.9) of the angle between two rays measured from image points, are simply specializations and a recapitulation of relations derived earlier in the book. For example, we have already developed a projective representation (3.23–*p*82) of the angle between two lines in 3-space, namely

$$\cos\theta = \frac{\mathbf{d}_1^\mathsf{T}\Omega_\infty\mathbf{d}_2}{\sqrt{\mathbf{d}_1^\mathsf{T}\Omega_\infty\mathbf{d}_1}\sqrt{\mathbf{d}_2^\mathsf{T}\Omega_\infty\mathbf{d}_2}}$$

where $\mathbf{d}_1$ and $\mathbf{d}_2$ are the directions of the lines (which are the points at which the lines intersect π_∞). Rays are lines in 3-space which are coincident at the camera centre, and so (3.23–*p*82) may be applied directly to rays. This is precisely what (8.9) does – it is simply (3.23–*p*82) computed in the image.

Under the map (8.8) $\mathtt{H} = \mathtt{KR}$, which is the homography between the plane π_∞ in the world coordinate frame and the image plane, $\Omega_\infty \mapsto \mathtt{H}^\mathsf{T}\omega\mathtt{H} = (\mathtt{KR})^\mathsf{T}\omega(\mathtt{KR})$ and $\mathbf{d}_i = \mathtt{H}^{-1}\mathbf{x}_i = (\mathtt{KR})^{-1}\mathbf{x}_i$. Substituting these relations into (3.23–*p*82) gives (8.9). Similarly the conjugacy and pole–polar relations for orthogonality in the image are a direct image of those on π_∞, as can be seen by comparing figure 3.8(*p*83) with figure 8.13.

In practice these orthogonality results find greatest application in the case of vanishing points and vanishing lines.

8.6 Vanishing points and vanishing lines

One of the distinguishing features of perspective projection is that the image of an object that stretches off to infinity can have finite extent. For example, an infinite scene line is imaged as a line terminating in a *vanishing point*. Similarly, parallel world lines, such as railway lines, are imaged as converging lines, and their image intersection is the vanishing point for the direction of the railway.

8.6.1 Vanishing points

The perspective geometry that gives rise to vanishing points is illustrated in figure 8.14. It is evident that geometrically the vanishing point of a line is obtained by intersecting the image plane with a ray parallel to the world line and passing through the camera centre. Thus a vanishing point depends only on the *direction* of a line, not on its position. Consequently a set of parallel world lines have a common vanishing point, as illustrated in figure 8.16.

Algebraically the vanishing point may be obtained as a limiting point as follows: Points on a line in 3-space through the point $\mathbf{A}$ and with direction $\mathbf{D} = (\mathbf{d}^\mathsf{T}, 0)^\mathsf{T}$ are written as $\mathbf{X}(\lambda) = \mathbf{A} + \lambda\mathbf{D}$, see figure 8.14b. As the parameter λ varies from 0 to ∞ the point $\mathbf{X}(\lambda)$ varies from the finite point $\mathbf{A}$ to the point $\mathbf{D}$ at infinity. Under a projective camera $\mathtt{P} = \mathtt{K}[\mathtt{I} \mid \mathbf{0}]$, a point $\mathbf{X}(\lambda)$ is imaged at

$$\mathbf{x}(\lambda) = \mathtt{P}\mathbf{X}(\lambda) = \mathtt{P}\mathbf{A} + \lambda\mathtt{P}\mathbf{D} = \mathbf{a} + \lambda\mathtt{K}\mathbf{d}$$

where $\mathbf{a}$ is the image of $\mathbf{A}$. Then the vanishing point $\mathbf{v}$ of the line is obtained as the

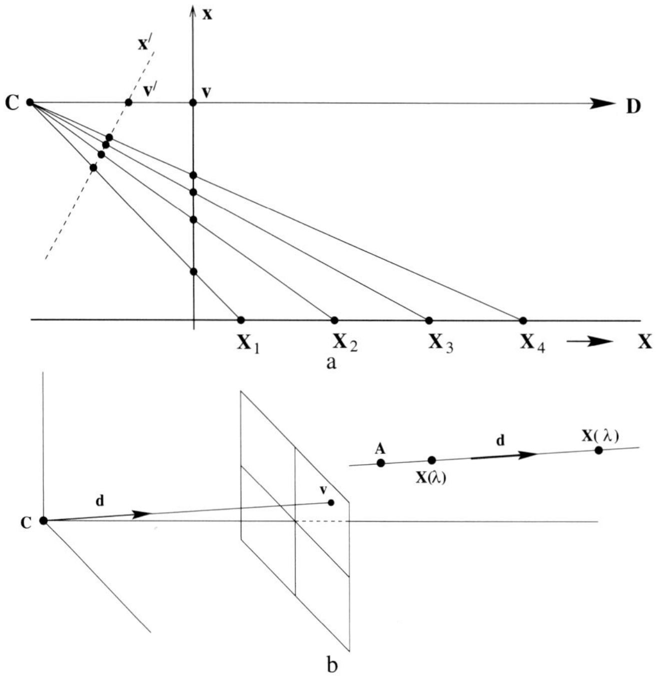

Fig. 8.14. **Vanishing point formation.** *(a) Plane to line camera. The points $\mathbf{X}_i, i = 1, \ldots, 4$ are equally spaced on the world line, but their spacing on the image line monotonically decreases. In the limit $\mathbf{X} \rightarrow \infty$ the world point is imaged at $\mathbf{x} = \mathbf{v}$ on the vertical image line, and at $\mathbf{x}' = \mathbf{v}'$ on the inclined image line. Thus the vanishing point of the world line is obtained by intersecting the image plane with a ray parallel to the world line through the camera centre $\mathbf{C}$. (b) 3-space to plane camera. The vanishing point, $\mathbf{v}$, of a line with direction $\mathbf{d}$ is the intersection of the image plane with a ray parallel to $\mathbf{d}$ through $\mathbf{C}$. The world line may be parametrized as $\mathbf{X}(\lambda) = \mathbf{A} + \lambda\mathbf{D}$, where $\mathbf{A}$ is a point on the line, and $\mathbf{D} = (\mathbf{d}^\mathsf{T}, 0)^\mathsf{T}$.*

limit

$$\mathbf{v} = \lim_{\lambda \to \infty} \mathbf{x}(\lambda) = \lim_{\lambda \to \infty} (\mathbf{a} + \lambda \mathtt{K}\mathbf{d}) = \mathtt{K}\mathbf{d}.$$

From result 8.15, $\mathbf{v} = \mathtt{K}\mathbf{d}$ means that the vanishing point $\mathbf{v}$ back-projects to a ray with direction $\mathbf{d}$. Note that $\mathbf{v}$ depends only on the direction $\mathbf{d}$ of the line, not on its position specified by $\mathbf{A}$.

In the language of projective geometry this result is obtained directly: In projective 3-space the plane at infinity $\boldsymbol{\pi}_\infty$ is the plane of directions, and all lines with the same direction intersect $\boldsymbol{\pi}_\infty$ in the same point (see chapter 3). The vanishing point is simply the image of this intersection. Thus if a line has direction $\mathbf{d}$, then it intersects $\boldsymbol{\pi}_\infty$ in the point $\mathbf{X}_\infty = (\mathbf{d}^\mathsf{T}, 0)^\mathsf{T}$. Then $\mathbf{v}$ is the image of $\mathbf{X}_\infty$

$$\mathbf{v} = \mathtt{P}\mathbf{X}_\infty = \mathtt{K}[\mathtt{I} \mid \mathbf{0}] \begin{pmatrix} \mathbf{d} \\ 0 \end{pmatrix} = \mathtt{K}\mathbf{d}.$$

To summarize:

Result 8.20. *The vanishing point of lines with direction $\mathbf{d}$ in 3-space is the intersection*

$\mathbf{v}$ *of the image plane with a ray through the camera centre with direction* $\mathbf{d}$*, namely* $\mathbf{v} = \mathtt{K}\mathbf{d}$.

Note, lines parallel to the image plane are imaged as parallel lines, since $\mathbf{v}$ is at infinity in the image. However, the converse – that parallel image lines are the image of parallel scene lines – does not hold since lines which intersect on the principal plane are imaged as parallel lines.

Example 8.21. Camera rotation from vanishing points
Vanishing points are images of points at infinity, and provide orientation (attitude) information in a similar manner to that provided by the fixed stars. Consider two images of a scene obtained by calibrated cameras, where the two cameras differ in orientation *and position.* The points at infinity are part of the scene and so are independent of the camera. Their images, the vanishing points, are not affected by the change in camera position, but are affected by the camera rotation. Suppose both cameras have the same calibration matrix $\mathtt{K}$, and the camera rotates by $\mathtt{R}$ between views.

Let a scene line have vanishing point $\mathbf{v}_i$ in the first view, and $\mathbf{v}'_i$ in the second. The vanishing point $\mathbf{v}_i$ has direction $\mathbf{d}_i$ measured in the first camera's Euclidean coordinate frame, and the corresponding vanishing point $\mathbf{v}'_i$ has direction $\mathbf{d}'_i$ measured in the second camera's Euclidean coordinate frame. These directions can be computed from the vanishing points, for example $\mathbf{d}_i = \mathtt{K}^{-1}\mathbf{v}_i / \|\mathtt{K}^{-1}\mathbf{v}_i\|$, where the normalizing factor $\|\mathtt{K}^{-1}\mathbf{v}_i\|$ is included to ensure that $\mathbf{d}_i$ is a unit vector. The directions $\mathbf{d}_i$ and $\mathbf{d}'_i$ are related by the camera rotation as $\mathbf{d}'_i = \mathtt{R}\mathbf{d}_i$, which represents two independent constraints on $\mathtt{R}$. Thus the rotation matrix $\mathtt{R}$ can be computed from two such corresponding directions. △

The angle between two scene lines. We have seen that the vanishing point of a scene line back-projects to a ray parallel to the scene line. Consequently (8.9), which determines the angle between rays back-projected from image points, enables the angle between the directions of two scene lines to be measured from their vanishing points:

Result 8.22. *Let* $\mathbf{v}_1$ *and* $\mathbf{v}_2$ *be the vanishing points of two lines in an image, and let* $\boldsymbol{\omega}$ *be the image of the absolute conic in the image. If* θ *is the angle between the two line directions, then*

$$\cos\theta = \frac{\mathbf{v}_1^\mathsf{T}\boldsymbol{\omega}\mathbf{v}_2}{\sqrt{\mathbf{v}_1^\mathsf{T}\boldsymbol{\omega}\mathbf{v}_1}\sqrt{\mathbf{v}_2^\mathsf{T}\boldsymbol{\omega}\mathbf{v}_2}} \,. \tag{8.13}$$

A note on computing vanishing points

Often vanishing points are computed from the image of a set of parallel line segments, though they may be determined in other ways for example by using equal length intervals on a line as described in example 2.18(*p*50) and example 2.20(*p*51). In the case of imaged parallel line segments the objective is to estimate their common image intersection – which is the image of the direction of the parallel scene lines. Due to measurement noise the imaged line segments will generally *not* intersect in a unique

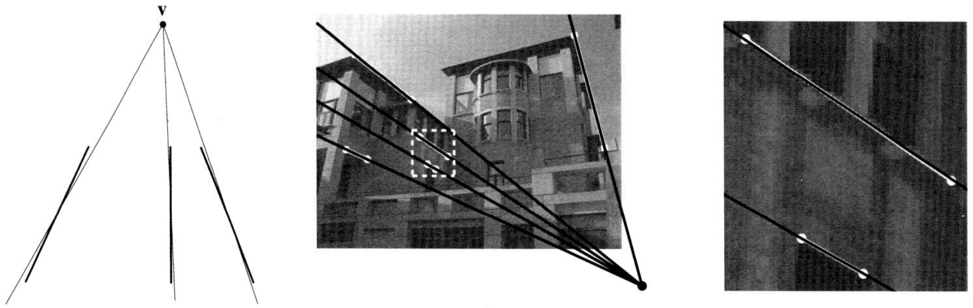

Fig. 8.15. **ML estimate of a vanishing point from imaged parallel scene lines.** *(a) Estimating the vanishing point* $\mathbf{v}$ *involves fitting a line (shown thin here) through* $\mathbf{v}$ *to each measured line (shown thick here). The ML estimate of* $\mathbf{v}$ *is the point which minimizes the sum of squared orthogonal distances between the fitted lines and the measured lines' end points. (b) Measured line segments are shown in white, and fitted lines in black. (c) A close-up of the dashed square in (b). Note the very slight angle between the measured and fitted lines.*

point. Commonly the vanishing point is then computed by intersecting the lines pairwise and using the centroid of these intersections, or finding the closest point to all the measured lines. However, these are *not* optimal procedures.

Under the assumption of Gaussian measurement noise, the maximum likelihood estimate (MLE) of the vanishing point *and* line segments is computed by determining a set of lines that do intersect in a single point, and which minimize the sum of squared orthogonal distances from the endpoints of the measured line segments as shown in figure 8.15(a). This minimization may be computed numerically using the Levenberg–Marquardt algorithm (section A6.2(*p*600)). Note that if the lines are defined by fitting to many points, rather than just their end points, one can use the method described in section 16.7.2(*p*404) to reduce each line to an equivalent pair of weighted end points which can then be used in this algorithm. Figure 8.15(b)(c) shows an example of a vanishing point computed in this manner. It is evident that the residuals between the measured and fitted lines are very small.

8.6.2 Vanishing lines

Parallel planes in 3-space intersect π_∞ in a common line, and the image of this line is the vanishing line of the plane. Geometrically the vanishing line is constructed, as shown in figure 8.16, by intersecting the image with a plane parallel to the scene plane through the camera centre. It is clear that a vanishing line depends only on the *orientation* of the scene plane; it does not depend on its position. Since lines parallel to a plane intersect the plane at π_∞, it is easily seen that the vanishing point of a line parallel to a plane lies on the vanishing line of the plane. An example is shown in figure 8.17.

If the camera calibration $\mathtt{K}$ is known then a scene plane's vanishing line may be used to determine information about the plane, and we mention three examples here:

(i) The plane's orientation relative to the camera may be determined from its vanishing line. From result 8.16 a plane through the camera centre with normal

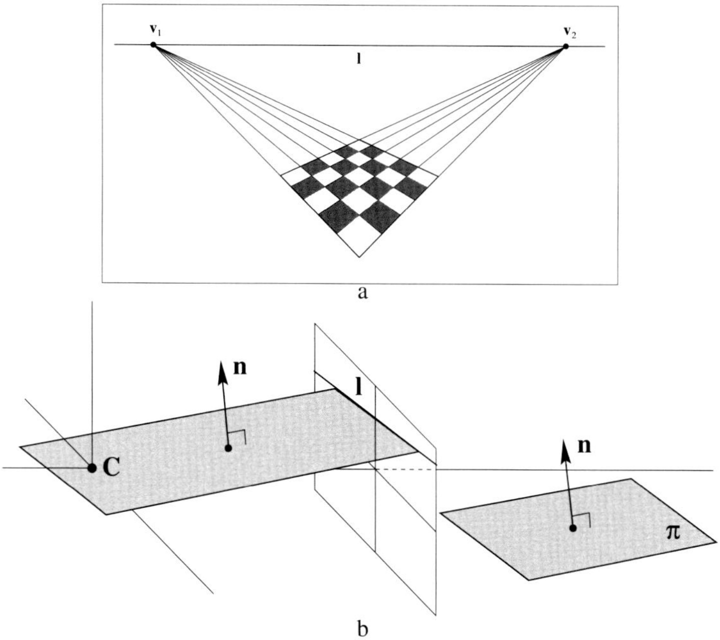

Fig. 8.16. **Vanishing line formation.** *(a) The two sets of parallel lines on the scene plane converge to the vanishing points* $\mathbf{v}_1$ *and* $\mathbf{v}_2$ *in the image. The line* $\mathbf{l}$ *through* $\mathbf{v}_1$ *and* $\mathbf{v}_2$ *is the vanishing line of the plane. (b) The vanishing line* $\mathbf{l}$ *of a plane* π *is obtained by intersecting the image plane with a plane through the camera centre* $\mathbf{C}$ *and parallel to* π.

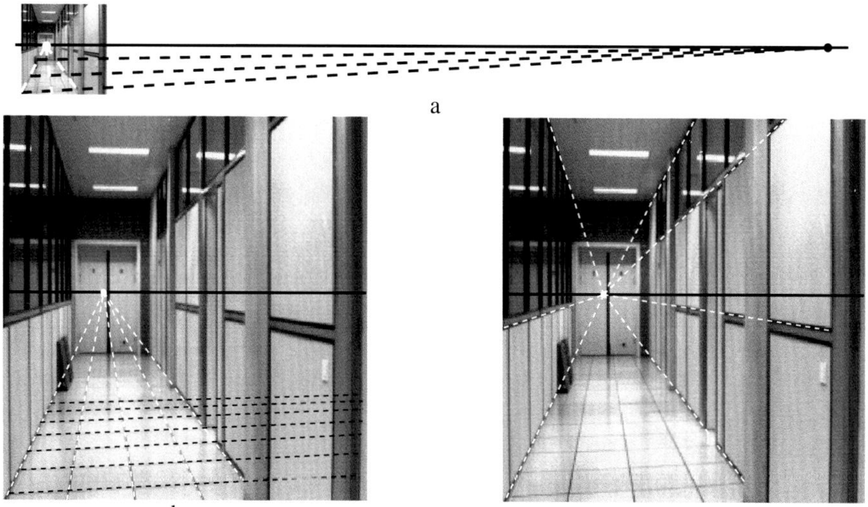

Fig. 8.17. **Vanishing points and lines.** *The vanishing line of the ground plane (the horizon) of the corridor may be obtained from two sets of parallel lines on the plane. (a) The vanishing points of lines which are nearly parallel to the image plane are distant from the finite (actual) image. (b) Note the monotonic decrease in the spacing of the imaged equally spaced parallel lines corresponding to the sides of the floor tiles. (c) The vanishing point of lines parallel to a plane (here the ground plane) lies on the vanishing line of the plane.*

direction $\mathbf{n}$ intersects the image plane in the line $\mathbf{l} = \mathtt{K}^{-\mathsf{T}}\mathbf{n}$. Consequently, $\mathbf{l}$ is the vanishing line of planes perpendicular to $\mathbf{n}$. Thus a plane with vanishing line $\mathbf{l}$ has orientation $\mathbf{n} = \mathtt{K}^{\mathsf{T}}\mathbf{l}$ in the camera's Euclidean coordinate frame.

(ii) The plane may be metrically rectified given only its vanishing line. This can be seen by considering a synthetic rotation of the camera in the manner of example 8.13(*p*205). Since the plane normal is known from the vanishing line, the camera can be synthetically rotated by a homography so that the plane is fronto-parallel (i.e. parallel to the image plane). The computation of this homography is discussed in exercise (ix).

(iii) The angle between two scene planes can be determined from their vanishing lines. Suppose the vanishing lines are $\mathbf{l}_1$ and $\mathbf{l}_2$, then the angle θ between the planes is given by

$$\cos\theta = \frac{\mathbf{l}_1^{\mathsf{T}}\boldsymbol{\omega}^*\mathbf{l}_2}{\sqrt{\mathbf{l}_1^{\mathsf{T}}\boldsymbol{\omega}^*\mathbf{l}_1}\sqrt{\mathbf{l}_2^{\mathsf{T}}\boldsymbol{\omega}^*\mathbf{l}_2}}. \tag{8.14}$$

The proof is left as an exercise.

Computing vanishing lines

A common way to determine a vanishing line of a scene plane is first to determine vanishing points for two sets of lines parallel to the plane, and then to construct the line through the two vanishing points. This construction is illustrated in figure 8.17. Alternative methods of determining vanishing points are shown in example 2.19(*p*51) and example 2.20(*p*51).

However, the vanishing line may be determined directly, without using vanishing points as an intermediate step. For example, the vanishing line may be computed given an imaged set of equally spaced coplanar parallel lines. This is a useful method in practice because such sets commonly occur in man-made structures, such as: stairs, windows on the wall of a building, fences, radiators and zebra crossings. The following example illustrates the projective geometry involved.

Example 8.23. The vanishing line given the image of three coplanar equally spaced parallel lines

A set of equally spaced lines on the scene plane may be represented as $ax' + by' + \lambda = 0$, where λ takes integer values. This set (a pencil) of lines may be written as $\mathbf{l}'_n = (a, b, n)^{\mathsf{T}} = (a, b, 0)^{\mathsf{T}} + n(0, 0, 1)^{\mathsf{T}}$, where $(0, 0, 1)^{\mathsf{T}}$ is the line at infinity on the scene plane. Under perspective imaging the point transformation is $\mathbf{x} = \mathtt{H}\mathbf{x}'$, and the corresponding line map is $\mathbf{l}_n = \mathtt{H}^{-\mathsf{T}}\mathbf{l}'_n = \mathbf{l}_0 + n\mathbf{l}$, where $\mathbf{l}$, the image of $(0, 0, 1)^{\mathsf{T}}$, is the vanishing line of the plane. The imaged geometry is shown in figure 8.18(c). Note all lines $\mathbf{l}_n$ intersect in a common vanishing point (which is given by $\mathbf{l}_i \times \mathbf{l}_j$, for $i \neq j$) and the spacing decreases monotonically with n. The vanishing line $\mathbf{l}$ may be determined from three lines of the set provided their index (n) is identified. For example, from the image of three equally spaced lines, $\mathbf{l}_0, \mathbf{l}_1$ and $\mathbf{l}_2$, the closed form solution for the vanishing line is:

$$\mathbf{l} = \left((\mathbf{l}_0 \times \mathbf{l}_2)^{\mathsf{T}}(\mathbf{l}_1 \times \mathbf{l}_2)\right)\mathbf{l}_1 + 2\left((\mathbf{l}_0 \times \mathbf{l}_1)^{\mathsf{T}}(\mathbf{l}_2 \times \mathbf{l}_1)\right)\mathbf{l}_2. \tag{8.15}$$

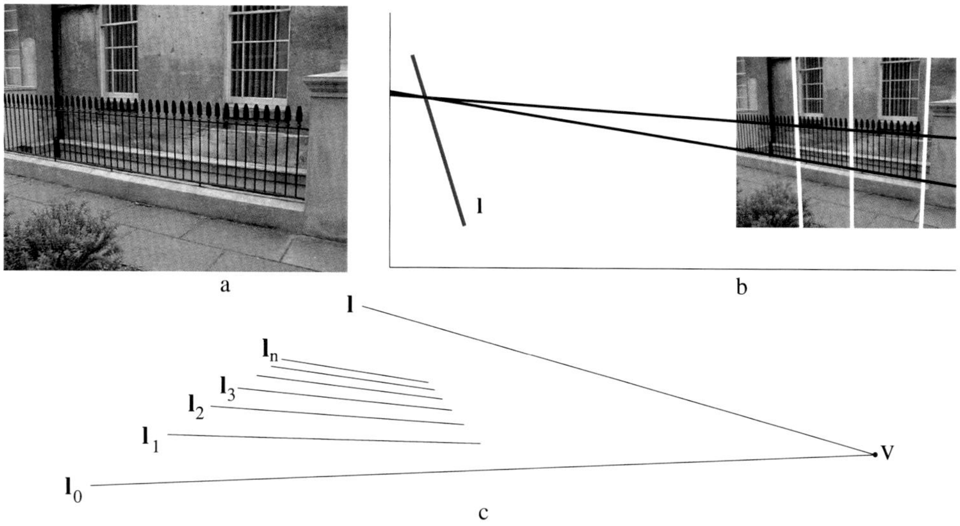

Fig. 8.18. **Determining a planes vanishing line from imaged equally spaced parallel lines.** *(a) Image of a vertical fence with equally spaced bars. (b) The computed vanishing line* $\mathbf{l}$ *from three equally spaced bars (12 apart). Note the vanishing point of the horizontal lines lies on this vanishing line. (c) The spacing between the imaged lines* $\mathbf{l}_n$ *monotonically decreases with* n.

The proof is left as an exercise. Figure 8.18(b) shows a vanishing line computed in this way. △

8.6.3 Orthogonality relationships amongst vanishing points and lines

It is often the case in practice that the lines and planes giving rise to vanishing points are orthogonal. In this case there are particularly simple relationships amongst their vanishing points and lines involving $\boldsymbol{\omega}$, and furthermore these relations can be used to (partially) determine $\boldsymbol{\omega}$, and consequently the camera calibration $\mathtt{K}$ as will be seen in section 8.8.

It follows from (8.13) that the vanishing points, $\mathbf{v}_1, \mathbf{v}_2$, of two perpendicular world lines satisfy $\mathbf{v}_1^{\mathsf{T}}\boldsymbol{\omega}\mathbf{v}_2 = 0$. This means that the vanishing points are conjugate with respect to $\boldsymbol{\omega}$, as illustrated in figure 8.13. Similarly it follows from result 8.19 that the vanishing point $\mathbf{v}$ of a direction perpendicular to a plane with vanishing line $\mathbf{l}$ satisfies $\mathbf{l} = \boldsymbol{\omega}\mathbf{v}$. This means that the vanishing point and line are in a pole–polar relation with respect to $\boldsymbol{\omega}$, as is also illustrated in figure 8.13. Summarizing these image relations:

(i) The vanishing points of lines with perpendicular directions satisfy

$$\mathbf{v}_1^{\mathsf{T}}\boldsymbol{\omega}\mathbf{v}_2 = 0. \tag{8.16}$$

(ii) If a line is perpendicular to a plane then their respective vanishing point $\mathbf{v}$ and vanishing line $\mathbf{l}$ are related by

$$\mathbf{l} = \boldsymbol{\omega}\mathbf{v} \tag{8.17}$$

and inversely $\mathbf{v} = \boldsymbol{\omega}^*\mathbf{l}$.

(iii) The vanishing lines of two perpendicular planes satisfy $\mathbf{l}_1^{\mathsf{T}}\boldsymbol{\omega}^*\mathbf{l}_2 = 0$.

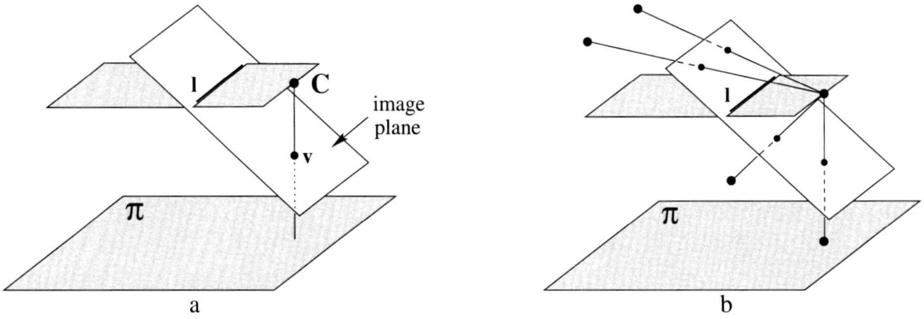

Fig. 8.19. **Geometry of a vertical vanishing point and ground plane vanishing line.** *(a) The vertical vanishing point* $\mathbf{v}$ *is the image of the vertical "footprint" of the camera centre on the ground plane* π. *(b) The vanishing line* $\mathbf{l}$ *partitions all points in scene space. Any scene point projecting onto the vanishing line is at the same distance from the plane* π *as the camera centre; if it lies "above" the line it is farther from the plane, and if "below" then it is closer to the plane than the camera centre.*

For example, suppose the vanishing line $\mathbf{l}$ of the ground plane (the horizon) is identified in an image, and the internal calibration matrix $\mathtt{K}$ is known, then the vertical vanishing point $\mathbf{v}$ (which is the vanishing point of the normal direction to the plane) may be obtained from $\mathbf{v} = \omega^*\mathbf{l}$.

8.7 Affine 3D measurements and reconstruction

It has been seen in section 2.7.2(*p*49) that identifying a scene plane's vanishing line allows affine properties of the scene plane to be measured. If in addition a vanishing point for a direction not parallel to the plane is identified, then affine properties can be computed for the 3-space of the perspectively imaged scene. We will illustrate this idea for the case where the vanishing point corresponds to a direction orthogonal to the plane, although orthogonality is not necessary for the construction. The method described in this section does not require that the internal calibration of the camera $\mathtt{K}$ be known.

It will be convenient to think of the scene plane as the horizontal ground plane, in which case the vanishing line is the *horizon*. Similarly, it will be convenient to think of the direction orthogonal to the scene plane as vertical, so that $\mathbf{v}$ is the vertical vanishing point. This situation is illustrated in figure 8.19.

Suppose we wish to measure the relative lengths of two line segments in the vertical direction as shown in figure 8.20(a). We will show the following result:

Result 8.24. *Given the vanishing line of the ground plane* $\mathbf{l}$ *and the vertical vanishing point* $\mathbf{v}$, *then the relative length of vertical line segments can be measured provided their end point lies on the ground plane.*

Clearly the relative lengths cannot be measured directly from their imaged lengths because as a vertical line recedes deeper into the scene (i.e. further from the camera) then its imaged length decreases. The construction to determine the relative lengths proceeds in two steps:

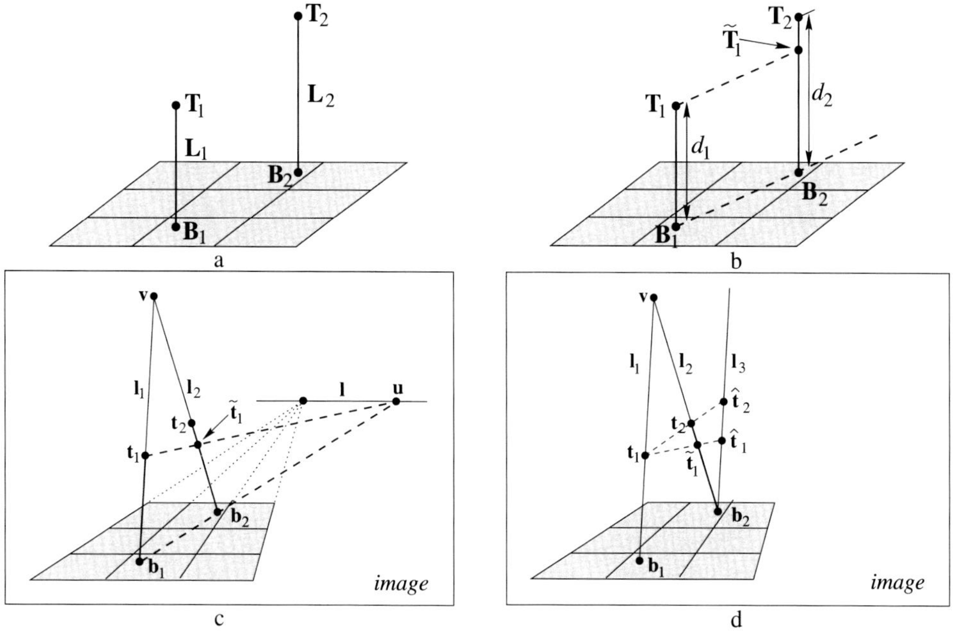

Fig. 8.20. **Computing length ratios of parallel scene lines.** *(a)* **3D geometry:** *The vertical line segments* $\mathbf{L}_1 = \langle \mathbf{B}_1, \mathbf{T}_1 \rangle$ *and* $\mathbf{L}_2 = \langle \mathbf{B}_2, \mathbf{T}_2 \rangle$ *have length* d_1 *and* d_2 *respectively. The base points* $\mathbf{B}_1, \mathbf{B}_2$ *are on the ground plane. We wish to compute the scene length ratio* $d_1 : d_2$ *from the imaged configuration. (b) In the scene the length of the line segment* $\mathbf{L}_1$ *may be transferred to* $\mathbf{L}_2$ *by constructing a line parallel to the ground plane to generate the point* $\widetilde{\mathbf{T}}_1$*. (c)* **Image geometry:** $\mathbf{l}$ *is the ground plane vanishing line, and* $\mathbf{v}$ *the vertical vanishing point. A corresponding parallel line construction in the image requires first determining the vanishing point* $\mathbf{u}$ *from the images* $\mathbf{b}_i$ *of* $\mathbf{B}_i$*, and then determining* $\tilde{\mathbf{t}}_1$ *(the image of* $\widetilde{\mathbf{T}}_1$*) by the intersection of* $\mathbf{l}_2$ *and the line* $\langle \mathbf{t}_1, \mathbf{u} \rangle$*. (d) The line* $\mathbf{l}_3$ *is parallel to* $\mathbf{l}_1$ *in the image. The points* $\hat{\mathbf{t}}_1$ *and* $\hat{\mathbf{t}}_2$ *are constructed by intersecting* $\mathbf{l}_3$ *with the lines* $\langle \mathbf{t}_1, \tilde{\mathbf{t}}_1 \rangle$ *and* $\langle \mathbf{t}_1, \mathbf{t}_2 \rangle$ *respectively. The distance ratio* $d(\mathbf{b}_2, \hat{\mathbf{t}}_1) : d(\mathbf{b}_2, \hat{\mathbf{t}}_2)$ *is the computed estimate of* $d_1 : d_2$*.*

Step 1: Map the length of one line segment onto the other. In 3D the length of $\mathbf{L}_1$ may be compared to $\mathbf{L}_2$ by constructing a line parallel to the ground plane in the direction $\langle \mathbf{B}_1, \mathbf{B}_2 \rangle$ that transfers $\mathbf{T}_1$ onto $\mathbf{L}_2$. This transferred point will be denoted $\widetilde{\mathbf{T}}_1$ (see figure 8.20(b)). In the image a corresponding construction is carried out by first determining the vanishing point $\mathbf{u}$ which is the intersection of $\langle \mathbf{b}_1, \mathbf{b}_2 \rangle$ with $\mathbf{l}$. Now any scene line parallel to $\langle \mathbf{B}_1, \mathbf{B}_2 \rangle$ is imaged as a line through $\mathbf{u}$, so in particular the image of the line through $\mathbf{T}_1$ parallel to $\langle \mathbf{B}_1, \mathbf{B}_2 \rangle$ is the line through $\mathbf{t}_1$ and $\mathbf{u}$. The intersection of the line $\langle \mathbf{t}_1, \mathbf{u} \rangle$ with $\mathbf{l}_2$ defines the image $\tilde{\mathbf{t}}_1$ of the transferred point $\widetilde{\mathbf{T}}_1$ (see figure 8.20(c)).

Step 2: Determine the ratio of lengths on the scene line. We now have four collinear points on an imaged scene line and wish to determine the actual length ratio in the scene. The four collinear image points are $\mathbf{b}_2, \tilde{\mathbf{t}}_1, \mathbf{t}_2$ and $\mathbf{v}$. These may be treated as images of scene points at distances $0, d_1, d_2$ and ∞, respectively, along the scene line. The affine ratio $d_1 : d_2$ may be obtained by applying a projective transfor-

Objective

Given the vanishing line of the ground plane $\mathbf{l}$ and the vertical vanishing point $\mathbf{v}$ and the top $(\mathbf{t}_1, \mathbf{t}_2)$ and base $(\mathbf{b}_1, \mathbf{b}_2)$ points of two line segments as in figure 8.20, compute the ratio of lengths of the line segments in the scene.

Algorithm

(i) Compute the vanishing point $\mathbf{u} = (\mathbf{b}_1 \times \mathbf{b}_2) \times \mathbf{l}$.

(ii) Compute the transferred point $\tilde{\mathbf{t}}_1 = (\mathbf{t}_1 \times \mathbf{u}) \times \mathbf{l}_2$ (where $\mathbf{l}_2 = \mathbf{v} \times \mathbf{b}_2$).

(iii) Represent the four points $\mathbf{b}_2, \tilde{\mathbf{t}}_1, \mathbf{t}_2$ and $\mathbf{v}$ on the image line $\mathbf{l}_1$ by their distance from $\mathbf{b}_2$, as $0, \tilde{t}_1, t_2$ and v respectively.

(iv) Compute a 1D projective transformation $\mathtt{H}_{2\times 2}$ mapping homogeneous coordinates $(0,1) \mapsto (0,1)$ and $(v,1) \mapsto (1,0)$ (which maps the vanishing point $\mathbf{v}$ to infinity). A suitable matrix is given by

$$\mathtt{H}_{2\times 2} = \begin{bmatrix} 1 & 0 \\ 1 & -v \end{bmatrix}.$$

(v) The (scaled) distance of the scene points $\widetilde{\mathbf{T}}_1$ and $\mathbf{T}_2$ from $\mathbf{B}_2$ on $\mathbf{L}_2$ may then be obtained from the position of the points $\mathtt{H}_{2\times 2}(\tilde{t}_1, 1)^\mathsf{T}$ and $\mathtt{H}_{2\times 2}(t_2, 1)^\mathsf{T}$. Their distance ratio is then given by

$$\frac{d_1}{d_2} = \frac{\tilde{t}_1(v - t_2)}{t_2(v - \tilde{t}_1)}$$

Algorithm 8.1. *Computing scene length ratios from a single image.*

mation to the image line which maps $\mathbf{v}$ to infinity. A geometric construction of this projectivity is shown in figure 8.20(d) (see example 2.20(p51)).

Details of the algorithm to carry out these two steps are given in algorithm 8.1.

Note, no knowledge of the camera calibration $\mathtt{K}$ or pose is necessary to apply the algorithm. In fact, the position of the camera centre relative to the ground plane can also be computed. The algorithm is well conditioned even when the vanishing point and/or line are at infinity in the image. For example, under affine image conditionings, or if the image plane is parallel to the vertical scene direction (so that $\mathbf{v}$ is at infinity). In these cases the distance ratio simplifies to $\frac{d_1}{d_2} = \frac{\tilde{t}_1}{t_2}$.

Example 8.25. Measuring a person's height in a single image

Suppose we have an image which contains sufficient information to compute the ground plane vanishing line and the vertical vanishing point, and also one object of known height for which the top and base are imaged. Then the height of a person standing on the ground plane can be measured anywhere in the scene provided that their head and feet are both visible. Figure 8.21(a) shows an example. The scene contains plenty of horizontal lines from which to compute a horizontal vanishing point. Two such vanishing points determine the vanishing line of the floor (which is the horizon for this image). The scene also contains plenty of vertical lines from which to compute a vertical vanishing point (figure 8.21(c)). Assuming that the two people are standing vertically, then their relative height may be computed directly from their length ratio using algorithm 8.1. Their absolute height may be determined by comput-

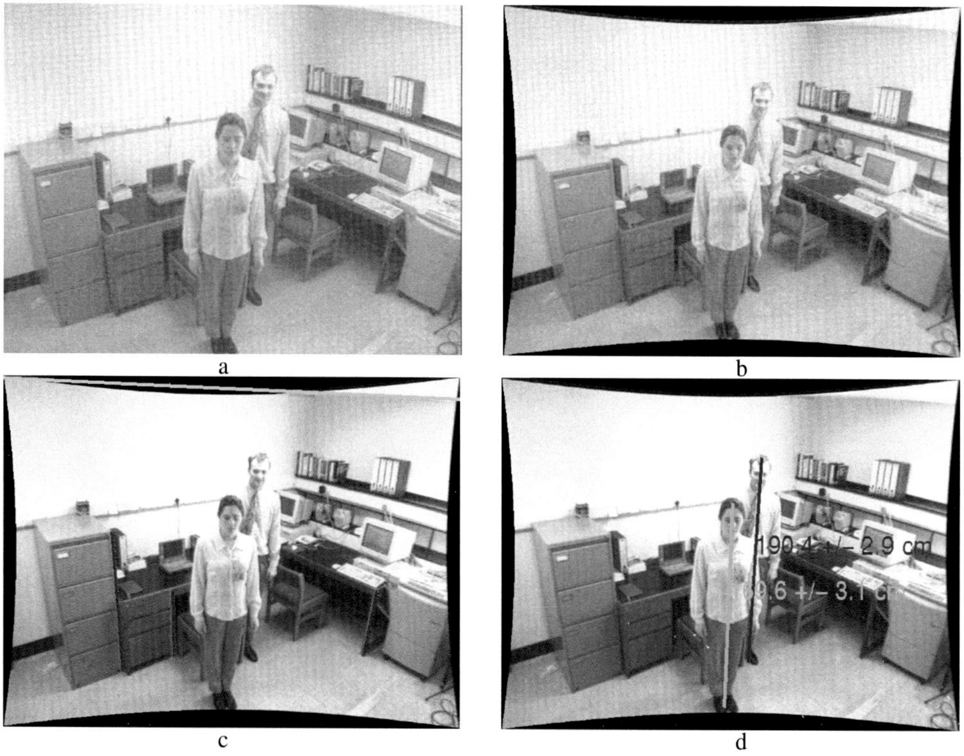

Fig. 8.21. **Height measurements using affine properties.** *(a) The original image. We wish to measure the height of the two people. (b) The image after radial distortion correction (see section 7.4(p189)). (c) The vanishing line (shown) is computed from two vanishing points corresponding to horizontal directions. The lines used to compute the vertical vanishing points are also shown. The vertical vanishing point is not shown since it lies well below the image. (d) Using the known height of the filing cabinet on the left of the image, the absolute height of the two people are measured as described in algorithm 8.1. The measured heights are within 2cm of ground truth. The computation of the uncertainty is described in [Criminisi-00].*

ing their height relative to an object on the ground plane with known height. Here the known height is provided by the filing cabinet. The result is shown in figure 8.21(d). △

8.8 Determining camera calibration K from a single view

We have seen that once ω is known the angle between rays can be measured. Conversely if the angle between rays is known then a constraint is placed on ω. Each known angle between two rays gives a constraint of the form (8.13) on ω. Unfortunately, for arbitrary angles, and known $\mathbf{v}_1$ and $\mathbf{v}_2$, this gives a quadratic constraint on the entries of ω. If the lines are perpendicular, however, (8.13) reduces to (8.16) $\mathbf{v}_1^\mathsf{T}\omega\mathbf{v}_2 = 0$, and the constraint on ω is linear.

A linear constraint on ω also results from a vanishing point and vanishing line arising from a line and its orthogonal plane. A common example is a vertical direction and horizontal plane as in figure 8.19. From (8.17) $\mathbf{l} = \omega\mathbf{v}$. Writing this as $\mathbf{l} \times (\omega\mathbf{v}) = \mathbf{0}$

Condition	constraint	type	# constraints
vanishing points $\mathbf{v}_1, \mathbf{v}_2$ corresponding to orthogonal lines	$\mathbf{v}_1^{\mathsf{T}} \boldsymbol{\omega} \mathbf{v}_2 = 0$	linear	1
vanishing point $\mathbf{v}$ and vanishing line $\mathbf{l}$ corresponding to orthogonal line and plane	$[\mathbf{l}]_\times \boldsymbol{\omega} \mathbf{v} = \mathbf{0}$	linear	2
metric plane imaged with known homography $\mathtt{H} = [\mathbf{h}_1, \mathbf{h}_2, \mathbf{h}_3]$	$\mathbf{h}_1^{\mathsf{T}} \boldsymbol{\omega} \mathbf{h}_2 = 0$ $\mathbf{h}_1^{\mathsf{T}} \boldsymbol{\omega} \mathbf{h}_1 = \mathbf{h}_2^{\mathsf{T}} \boldsymbol{\omega} \mathbf{h}_2$	linear	2
zero skew	$\omega_{12} = \omega_{21} = 0$	linear	1
square pixels	$\omega_{12} = \omega_{21} = 0$ $\omega_{11} = \omega_{22}$	linear	2

Table 8.1. **Scene and internal constraints on $\boldsymbol{\omega}$.**

removes the homogeneous scaling factor and results in three homogeneous equations linear in the entries of $\boldsymbol{\omega}$. These are equivalent to two independent constraints on $\boldsymbol{\omega}$.

All these conditions provide linear constraints on $\boldsymbol{\omega}$. Given a sufficient number of such constraints $\boldsymbol{\omega}$ may be computed and hence the camera calibration $\mathtt{K}$ also follows since $\boldsymbol{\omega} = (\mathtt{K}\mathtt{K}^{\mathsf{T}})^{-1}$.

The number of entries of $\boldsymbol{\omega}$ that need be determined from scene constraints of this sort can be reduced if the calibration matrix $\mathtt{K}$ has a more specialized form than (6.10–*p*157). In the case where $\mathtt{K}$ is known to have zero skew ($s = 0$), or square pixels ($\alpha_x = \alpha_y$ and $s = 0$), we can take advantage of this condition to help find $\boldsymbol{\omega}$. In particular, it is quickly verified by direct computation that:

Result 8.26. *If* $s = \mathtt{K}_{12} = 0$ *then* $\omega_{12} = \omega_{21} = 0$. *If in addition* $\alpha_x = \mathtt{K}_{11} = \mathtt{K}_{22} = \alpha_y$, *then* $\omega_{11} = \omega_{22}$.

Thus, in solving for the image of the absolute conic, one may easily take into account the zero-skew or square-aspect ratio constraint on the camera, if such a constraint is known to exist. One may also verify that no such simple connection as result 8.26 exists between the entries of $\mathtt{K}$ and those of $\boldsymbol{\omega}^* = \mathtt{K}\mathtt{K}^{\mathsf{T}}$.

We have now seen three sources of constraints on $\boldsymbol{\omega}$:

(i) metric information on a plane imaged with a known homography, see (8.12–*p*211)
(ii) vanishing points and lines corresponding to perpendicular directions and planes, (8.16)
(iii) "internal constraints" such as zero skew or square pixels, as in result 8.26

These constraints are summarized in table 8.1. We now describe how these constraints may be combined to estimate $\boldsymbol{\omega}$ and thence $\mathtt{K}$.

Since all the above constraints (including the internal constraints) are described algebraically as linear equations on $\boldsymbol{\omega}$, it is a simple matter to combine them as rows of

Objective

Compute K via $\boldsymbol{\omega}$ by combining scene and internal constraints.

Algorithm

(i) Represent $\boldsymbol{\omega}$ as a homogeneous 6-vector $\mathbf{w} = (w_1, w_2, w_3, w_4, w_5, w_6)^\mathsf{T}$ where:

$$\boldsymbol{\omega} = \begin{bmatrix} w_1 & w_2 & w_4 \\ w_2 & w_3 & w_5 \\ w_4 & w_5 & w_6 \end{bmatrix}$$

(ii) Each available constraint from table 8.1 may be written as $\mathbf{a}^\mathsf{T}\mathbf{w} = 0$. For example, for the orthogonality constraint $\mathbf{u}^\mathsf{T}\boldsymbol{\omega}\mathbf{v} = 0$, where $\mathbf{u} = (u_1,\ u_2,\ u_3)^\mathsf{T}$ and $\mathbf{v} = (v_1,\ v_2,\ v_3)^\mathsf{T}$, the 6-vector $\mathbf{a}$ is given by

$$\mathbf{a} = (v_1u_1, v_1u_2 + v_2u_1, v_2u_2, v_1u_3 + v_3u_1, v_2u_3 + v_3u_2, v_3u_3)^\mathsf{T}.$$

Similar constraints vectors are obtained from the other sources of scene and internal constraints. For example a metric plane generates two such constraints.

(iii) Stack the equations $\mathbf{a}^\mathsf{T}\mathbf{w} = 0$ from each constraint in the form $\mathtt{A}\mathbf{w} = \mathbf{0}$, where A is a $n \times 6$ matrix for n constraints.

(iv) Solve for $\mathbf{w}$ using the SVD as in algorithm 4.2(p109). This determines $\boldsymbol{\omega}$.

(v) Decompose $\boldsymbol{\omega}$ into K using matrix inversion and Cholesky factorization (see section A4.2.1(p582)).

Algorithm 8.2. *Computing* K *from scene and internal constraints.*

a constraint matrix. All constraints may be collected together so that for n constraints the system of equations may be written as $\mathtt{A}\mathbf{w} = \mathbf{0}$, where A is a $n \times 6$ matrix and $\mathbf{w}$ is a 6-vector containing the six distinct homogeneous entries of $\boldsymbol{\omega}$. With a minimum of 5 constraint equations an exact solution is found. With more than five equations, a least-squares solution is found by algorithm A5.4(p593). The method is summarized in algorithm 8.2.

With more than the minimum required five constraints, we have the option to apply some of the constraints as hard constraints – that is, constraints that will be satisfied exactly. This can be done by parametrizing $\boldsymbol{\omega}$ so that the constraints are satisfied explicitly (for instance setting $\omega_{21} = \omega_{12} = 0$ for the zero skew constraint, and also $\omega_{11} = \omega_{22}$ for the square-pixel constraint). The minimization method of algorithm A5.5(p594) may also be used to enforce hard constraints. Otherwise, treating all constraints as soft constraints and using algorithm A5.4(p593) will produce a solution in which the constraints are not satisfied exactly in the presence of noise – for instance, pixels may not be quite square.

Finally, an important issue in practice is that of degeneracy. This occurs when the combined constraints are not independent and results in the matrix A dropping rank. If the rank is less than the number of unknowns, then a parametrized family of solutions for $\boldsymbol{\omega}$ (and hence K) is obtained. Also, if conditions are near degenerate then the solution is ill-conditioned and the particular member of the family is determined by "noise". These degeneracies can often be understood geometrically – for example in example 8.18 if the three metric planes are parallel then the three pairs of imaged

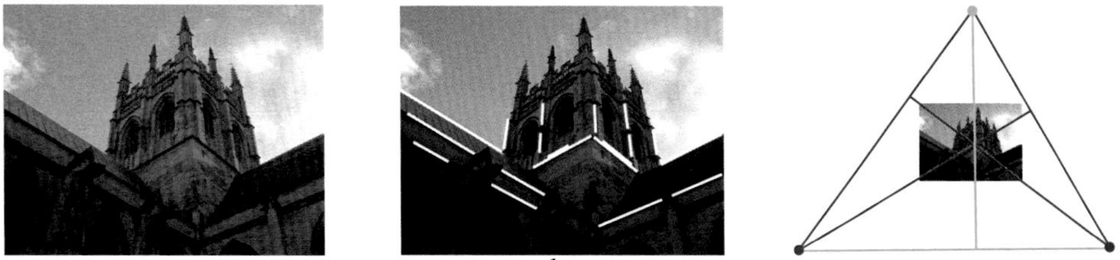

Fig. 8.22. *For the case that image skew is zero and the aspect ratio unity* **the principal point is the orthocentre of an orthogonal triad of vanishing points**. *(a) Original image. (b) Three sets of parallel lines in the scene, with each set having direction orthogonal to the others. (c) The principal point is the orthocentre of the triangle with the vanishing points as vertices.*

circular points are coincident and only provide a total of two constraints instead of six. A pragmatic solution to the problem of degeneracy, popularized by Zhang [Zhang-00], is to image a metric plane many times in varying positions. This reduces the chances of degeneracy occurring, and also provides a very over-determined solution.

Example 8.27. Calibration from three orthogonal vanishing points
Suppose that it is known that the camera has zero skew, and that the pixels are square (or equivalently their aspect ratio is known). A triad of orthogonal vanishing point directions supplies three more constraints. This gives a total of 5 constraints – sufficient to compute $\boldsymbol{\omega}$, and hence $\mathtt{K}$.

In outline the algorithm has the following steps:

(i) In the case of square pixels $\boldsymbol{\omega}$ has the form

$$\boldsymbol{\omega} = \begin{bmatrix} w_1 & 0 & w_2 \\ 0 & w_1 & w_3 \\ w_2 & w_3 & w_4 \end{bmatrix}.$$

(ii) Each pair of vanishing points $\mathbf{v}_i, \mathbf{v}_j$ generates an equation $\mathbf{v}_i^{\mathsf{T}}\boldsymbol{\omega}\mathbf{v}_j = 0$, which is linear in the elements of $\boldsymbol{\omega}$. The constraints from the three pairs of vanishing points are stacked together to form an equation $\mathtt{A}\mathbf{w} = \mathbf{0}$, where $\mathtt{A}$ is a 3×4 matrix.

(iii) The vector $\mathbf{w}$ is obtained as the null vector of $\mathtt{A}$, and this determines $\boldsymbol{\omega}$. The matrix $\mathtt{K}$ is obtained from $\boldsymbol{\omega} = (\mathtt{KK}^{\mathsf{T}})^{-1}$ by Cholesky factorization of $\boldsymbol{\omega}$, followed by inversion.

An example is shown in figure 8.22(a). Vanishing points are computed corresponding to the three perpendicular directions shown in figure 8.22(b). The image is 1024×768 pixels, and the calibration matrix is computed to be

$$\mathtt{K} = \begin{bmatrix} 1163 & 0 & 548 \\ 0 & 1163 & 404 \\ 0 & 0 & 1 \end{bmatrix}.$$

△

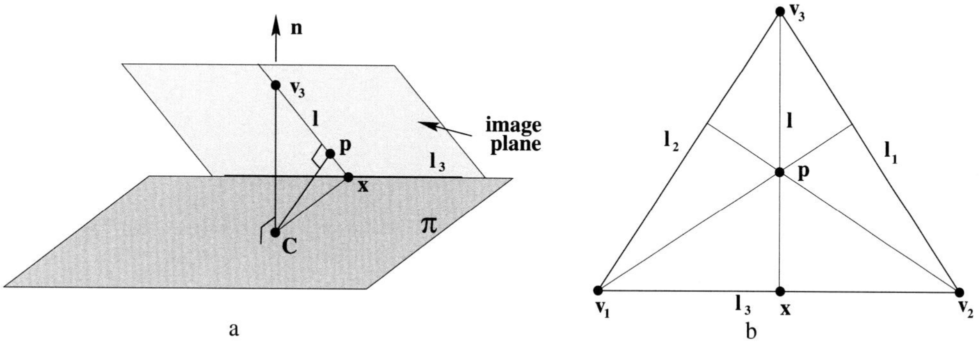

Fig. 8.23. **Geometric construction of the principal point.** *The vanishing line $\mathbf{l}_3$ back-projects to a plane π with normal $\mathbf{n}$. The vanishing point $\mathbf{v}_3$ back-projects to a line orthogonal to the plane π. (a) The normal $\mathbf{n}$ of the plane π through the camera centre $\mathbf{C}$ and the principal axis define a plane, which intersects the image in the line $\mathbf{l} = \langle \mathbf{v}_3, \mathbf{x} \rangle$. The line $\mathbf{l}_3$ is the intersection of π with the image plane, and is also its vanishing line. The point $\mathbf{v}_3$ is the intersection of the normal with the image plane, and is also its vanishing point. Clearly the principal point lies on $\mathbf{l}$, and $\mathbf{l}$ and $\mathbf{l}_3$ are perpendicular on the image plane. (b) The principal point may be determined from three such constraints as the orthocentre of the triangle.*

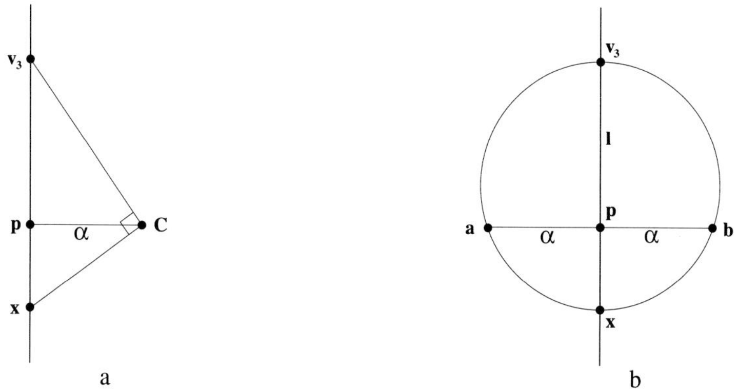

Fig. 8.24. **Geometric construction of the focal length.** *(a) Consider the plane defined by the camera centre $\mathbf{C}$, principal point and one of the vanishing points, e.g. $\mathbf{v}_3$ as shown in figure 8.23(a). The rays from $\mathbf{C}$ to $\mathbf{v}_3$ and $\mathbf{x}$ are perpendicular to each other. The focal length, α, is the distance from the camera centre to the image plane. By similar triangles, $\alpha^2 = d(\mathbf{p}, \mathbf{v}_3)d(\mathbf{p}, \mathbf{x})$, where $d(\mathbf{u}, \mathbf{v})$ is the distance between the points $\mathbf{u}$ and $\mathbf{v}$. (b) In the image a circle is drawn with diameter the line between $\mathbf{v}_3$ and $\mathbf{x}$. A line through $\mathbf{p}$ perpendicular to $\langle \mathbf{v}_3, \mathbf{x} \rangle$ meets the circle in two points $\mathbf{a}$ and $\mathbf{b}$. The focal length equals the distance $d(\mathbf{p}, \mathbf{a})$.*

The principal point and focal length may also be computed geometrically in this case. The principal point is the orthocentre of the triangle with vertices the vanishing points. Figure 8.23 shows that the principal point lies on the perpendicular line from one triangle side to the opposite vertex. A similar construction for the other two sides shows that the principal point is the orthocentre. An algebraic derivation of this result is left to the exercises. The focal length can also be computed geometrically as shown in figure 8.24.

As a cautionary note, this estimation method is degenerate if one of the vanishing

a b

Fig. 8.25. **Plane rectification via partial internal parameters** *(a) Original image. (b) Rectification assuming the camera has square pixels and principal point at the centre of the image. The focal length is computed from the single orthogonal vanishing point pair. The aspect ratio of a window in the rectified image differs from the ground truth value by 3.7%. Note that the two parallel planes, the upper building facade and the lower shopfront, are both mapped to fronto-parallel planes.*

points, say the vertical, is at infinity. In this case $\mathtt{A}$ drops rank to two, and there is a one-parameter family of solutions for ω and correspondingly for $\mathtt{K}$. This degeneracy can be seen geometrically from the orthocentre construction of figure 8.23. If $\mathbf{v}_3$ is at infinity then the principal point $\mathbf{p}$ lies on the line $\mathbf{l}_3 = \langle \mathbf{v}_1, \mathbf{v}_2 \rangle$, but its x position is not defined.

Example 8.28. Determining the focal length when the other internal parameters are known
We consider a further example of calibration from a single view. Suppose that it is known that the camera has zero skew, that the pixels are square (or equivalently their aspect ratio is known), and also that the principal point is at the image centre. Then only the focal length is unknown. In this case, the form of ω is very simple: it is a diagonal matrix $\text{diag}(1/f^2, 1/f^2, 1)$ with only one degree of freedom. Using algorithm 8.2, the focal length f may be determined from one further constraint, such as the one arising from two vanishing points corresponding to orthogonal directions.

An example is shown in figure 8.25(a). Here the vanishing points used in the constraint are computed from the horizontal edges of the windows and pavement, and the vertical edges of the windows. These vanishing points also determine the vanishing line $\mathbf{l}$ of the building facade. Given $\mathtt{K}$ and the vanishing line $\mathbf{l}$, the camera can be synthetically rotated such that the facade is fronto-parallel by mapping the image with a homography as in example 8.13(p205). The result is shown in figure 8.25(b). Note, in example 8.13 it was necessary to know the aspect ratio of a rectangle on the scene plane in order to rectify the plane. Here it is only necessary to know the vanishing line of the plane because the camera calibration $\mathtt{K}$ provides the additional information required for the homography. $\triangle$

8.8.1 The geometry of the constraints

Although the algebraic constraints given in table 8.1 appear to arise from distinct sources, they are in fact all equivalent to one of two simple geometric relations: two points lying on the conic ω, or conjugacy of two points with respect to ω.

For example, the zero skew constraint is an orthogonality constraint: it specifies that the image x and y axes are orthogonal. These axes correspond to rays with directions in the camera's Euclidean coordinate frame, $(1,0,0)^\mathsf{T}$ and $(0,1,0)^\mathsf{T}$, respectively, that are imaged at $\mathbf{v}_x = (1,0,0)^\mathsf{T}$ and $\mathbf{v}_y = (0,1,0)^\mathsf{T}$ (since the rays are parallel to the image plane). The zero skew constraint $\boldsymbol{\omega}_{12} = \boldsymbol{\omega}_{21} = 0$ is just another way of writing the orthogonality constraint (8.16) $\mathbf{v}_y^\mathsf{T}\boldsymbol{\omega}\mathbf{v}_x = 0$. Geometrically skew zero is equivalent to conjugacy of the points $(1,0,0)^\mathsf{T}$ and $(0,1,0)^\mathsf{T}$ with respect to $\boldsymbol{\omega}$.

The square pixel constraint may be interpreted in two ways. A square has the property of defining two sets of orthogonal lines: adjacent edges are orthogonal, and so are the two diagonals. Thus, the square pixel constraint may be interpreted as a pair of orthogonal line constraints. The diagonal vanishing points of a square pixel are $(1,1,0)^\mathsf{T}$ and $(-1,1,0)^\mathsf{T}$. The resulting orthogonality constraints lead to the square pixel constraints given in table 8.1.

Alternatively, the square pixel constraint can be interpreted in terms of two known points lying on the IAC. If the image plane has square pixels, then it has a Euclidean coordinate system and the circular points have known coordinates $(1,\pm i,0)^\mathsf{T}$. It may be verified that the two square pixel equations are equivalent to $(1,\pm i,0)\boldsymbol{\omega}(1,\pm i,0)^\mathsf{T} = 0$.

This is the most important geometric equivalence. In essence an image plane with square pixels acts as a metric plane in the scene. A square pixel image plane is equivalent to a metric plane imaged with a homography given by the identity. Indeed if the homography $\mathtt{H}$ in the "metric plane imaged with known homography" constraint of table 8.1 is replaced by the identity then the square pixel constraints are immediately obtained.

Thus, we see that all the constraints given in table 8.1 are derived either from known points lying on $\boldsymbol{\omega}$, or from pairs of points that are conjugate with respect to $\boldsymbol{\omega}$. Determining $\boldsymbol{\omega}$ may therefore be viewed as a conic fitting problem, given points on the conic and conjugate point pairs.

It is well to bear in mind that conic fitting is a delicate problem, often unstable ([Bookstein-79]) if the points are not well distributed on the conic. The same observation is true of the present problem, which we have seen is equivalent to conic fitting. The method given in algorithm 8.2 for finding the calibration from vanishing points amounts to minimization of algebraic error, and therefore does not give an optimal solution. For greater accuracy, the methods of chapter 4, for instance the Sampson error method of section 4.2.6(*p*98) should be used.

8.9 Single view reconstruction

As an application of the methods developed in this chapter we demonstrate now the 3D reconstruction of a texture mapped piecewise planar graphical model from a single image. The camera calibration methods of section 8.8 and the rectification method of example 8.28 may be combined to back project image regions to texture the planes of the model.

The method will be illustrated for the image of figure 8.26(a), where the scene contains three dominant and mutually orthogonal planes: the building facades on the left and right and the ground plane. The parallel line sets in three orthogonal directions de-

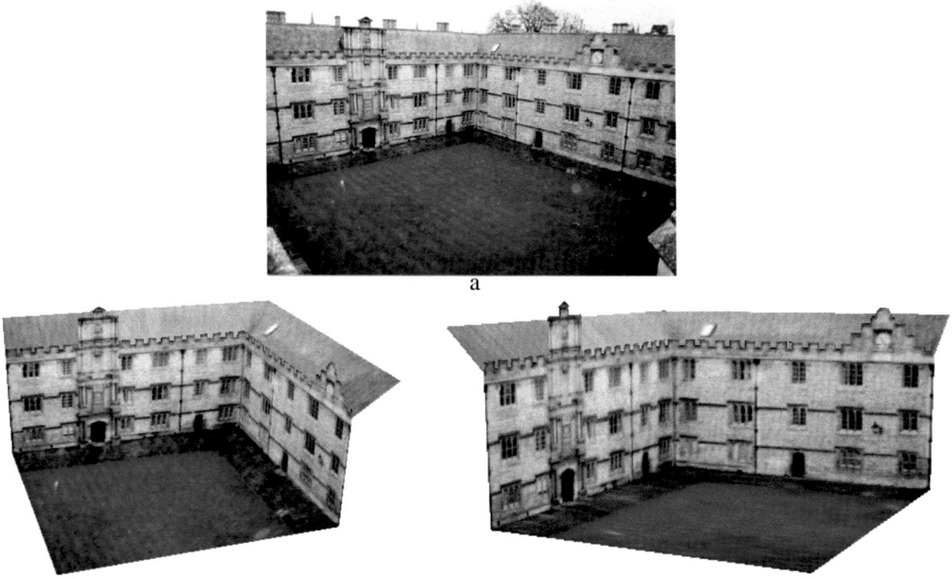

Fig. 8.26. **Single view reconstruction.** *(a) Original image of the Fellows quad, Merton College, Oxford. (b) (c) Views of the 3D model created from the single image. The vanishing line of the roof planes is computed from the repetition of the texture pattern.*

fine three vanishing points and together with the constraint of square pixels the camera calibration may be computed using the method described in section 8.8. From the vanishing lines of the three planes, likewise determined by the vanishing points, together with the computed ω, homographies may be computed to texture map the appropriate image regions onto the orthogonal planes of the model.

In more detail taking the left facade as a reference plane in figure 8.26(a), its correctly proportioned width and height are determined by the rectification. The right facade and ground planes define 3D planes orthogonal to the reference (we have assumed the orthogonality of the planes in computing the camera, so relative orientations are defined). Scaling of the right and ground planes is computed from the points common to the planes and this completes a three orthogonal plane model.

Having computed the calibration, the relative orientation of planes in the scene that are not orthogonal (such as the roof) can be computed if their vanishing lines can be found using (8.14–*p*218). Their relative positions and dimensions can be determined if the intersection of a pair of planes is visible in the image, so that there are points common to both planes. Relative size can be computed from the rectification of a distance between common points using the homographies of both planes. Views of the model, with texture mapped correctly to the planes, appear in figure 8.26(b) and (c).

8.10 The calibrating conic

The image of the absolute conic (IAC) is an imaginary conic in an image, and hence is not visible. Sometimes it is useful for visualization purposes to consider a different conic that is closely related to the calibration of the camera. Such a conic is the *calibrating conic*, which is the image of a cone with apex angle 45° and axis coinciding with the principal axis of the camera.

We wish to compute a formula for this cone in terms of the calibration matrix of the camera. Since the 45° cone moves with the camera, its image is clearly independent of the orientation and position of the camera. Thus, we may assume that the camera is located at the origin and oriented directly along the $\mathtt{Z}$-axis. Thus, let the camera matrix be $\mathtt{P} = \mathtt{K}[\mathtt{I} \mid \mathbf{0}]$. Now, any point on the 45° cone satisfies $\mathtt{X}^2 + \mathtt{Y}^2 = \mathtt{Z}^2$. Points on this cone map to points on the conic

$$\mathtt{C} = \mathtt{K}^{-\mathsf{T}} \begin{bmatrix} 1 & & \\ & 1 & \\ & & -1 \end{bmatrix} \mathtt{K}^{-1} \tag{8.18}$$

as one easily verifies from result 8.6(*p*199). This conic will be referred to as the calibrating conic of the camera. For a calibrated camera with identity calibration matrix $\mathtt{K} = \mathtt{I}$, the calibrating conic is a unit circle centred at the origin (which is the principal point of the image). The conic of (8.18) is simply this unit circle transformed by an affine transformation according to the conic transformation rule of result 2.13(*p*37): $(\mathtt{C} \mapsto \mathtt{H}^{-\mathsf{T}}\mathtt{C}\mathtt{H}^{-1})$. Thus the calibrating conic of a camera with calibration matrix $\mathtt{K}$ is the affine transformation of a unit circle centred on the origin by the matrix $\mathtt{K}$.

The calibration parameters are easily read from the calibrating conic. The principal point is the centre of the conic, and the scale factors and skew are easily identified, as in figure 8.27. In the case of zero skew, the calibrating conic has its principal axes aligned with the image coordinate axes. An example on a real image is shown in figure 8.29.

Example 8.29. Suppose $\mathtt{K} = \mathrm{diag}(f, f, 1)$, which is the calibration matrix for a camera of focal length f pixels, with no skew, square pixels, and image origin coincident with the principal point. Then from (8.18) the calibrating conic is $\mathtt{C} = \mathrm{diag}(1, 1, -f^2)$, which is a circle of radius f centred on the principal point. △

Orthogonality and the calibrating conic

A formula was given in (8.9–*p*210) for the angle between the rays corresponding to two image points. In particular the rays corresponding to two points $\mathbf{x}$ and $\mathbf{x}'$ are perpendicular when $\mathbf{x}'^{\mathsf{T}}\boldsymbol{\omega}\mathbf{x} = 0$. As shown in figure 8.13(*p*212) this may be interpreted as the point $\mathbf{x}'$ lying on the line $\boldsymbol{\omega}\mathbf{x}$, which is the polar of $\mathbf{x}$ with respect to the IAC.

We wish to carry out a similar analysis in terms of the calibrating conic. Writing $\mathtt{C} = \mathtt{K}^{-\mathsf{T}}\mathtt{D}\mathtt{K}^{-1}$, where $\mathtt{D} = \mathrm{diag}(1, 1, -1)$, we find

$$\mathtt{C} = (\mathtt{K}^{-\mathsf{T}}\mathtt{K}^{-1})(\mathtt{K}\mathtt{D}\mathtt{K}^{-1}) = \boldsymbol{\omega}\mathtt{S}$$

where $\mathtt{S} = \mathtt{K}\mathtt{D}\mathtt{K}^{-1}$. However, for any point $\mathbf{x}$, the product $\mathtt{S}\mathbf{x}$ represents the reflection of

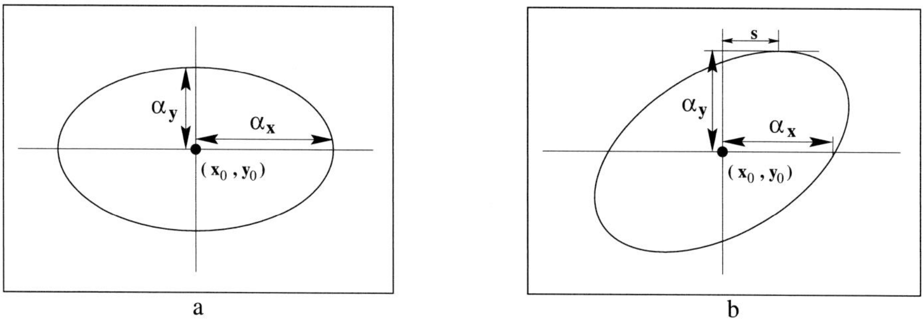

Fig. 8.27. **Reading the internal camera parameters K from the calibrating conic.** *(a) Skew s is zero. (b) Skew s is non-zero. The skew parameter of* K *(see (6.10–p157), is given by the x-coordinate of the highest point of the conic.*

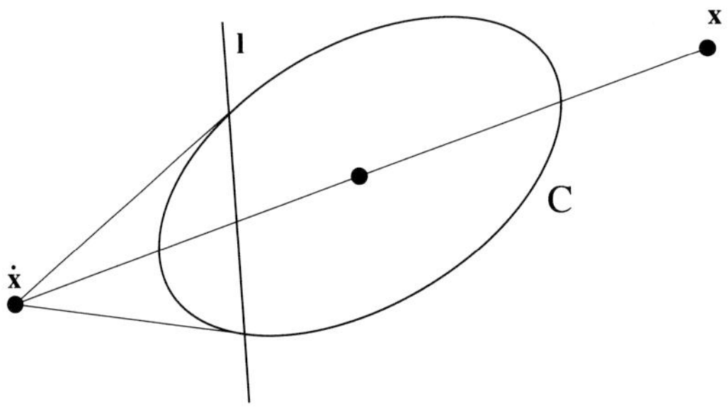

Fig. 8.28. *To construct the line perpendicular to the ray through image point* $\mathbf{x}$ *proceed as follows: (i) Reflect* $\mathbf{x}$ *through the centre of* C *to get point* $\dot{\mathbf{x}}$ *(i.e. at the same distance from the centre as* $\mathbf{x}$*). (ii) The desired line is the polar of* $\dot{\mathbf{x}}$*.*

the point $\mathbf{x}$ through the centre of the conic C, that is, the principal point of the camera. Representing this reflected point by $\dot{\mathbf{x}}$, one finds that

$$\mathbf{x}'^{\mathsf{T}}\omega\mathbf{x} = \mathbf{x}'^{\mathsf{T}}\mathtt{C}\dot{\mathbf{x}} \ . \tag{8.19}$$

This leads to the following geometric result:

Result 8.30. *The line in an image corresponding to the plane perpendicular to a ray through image point* $\mathbf{x}$ *is the polar* $\mathtt{C}\dot{\mathbf{x}}$ *of the reflected point* $\dot{\mathbf{x}}$ *with respect to the calibrating conic.*

This construction is illustrated in figure 8.28.

Example 8.31. The calibrating conic given three orthogonal vanishing points
The calibrating conic can be drawn directly for the example of figure 8.22. Again assume there is no skew and square pixels, then the calibrating conic is a circle. Now given three mutually perpendicular vanishing points, one can find the calibrating conic by direct geometric construction as shown in figure 8.29.

(i) First, construct the triangle with vertices the three vanishing points $\mathbf{v}_1$, $\mathbf{v}_2$ and $\mathbf{v}_3$.
(ii) The centre of C is the orthocentre of the triangle.

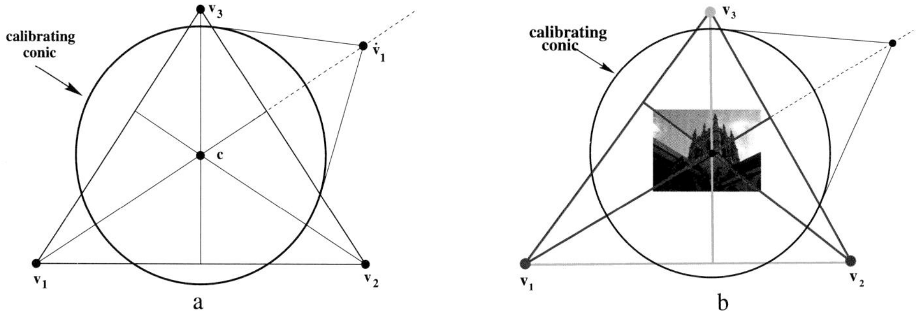

Fig. 8.29. *The calibrating conic computed from three orthogonal vanishing points. (a) The geometric construction. (b) The calibrating conic for the image of figure 8.22.*

(iii) Reflect one of the vanishing points (say $\mathbf{v}_1$) in the centre to get $\dot{\mathbf{v}}_1$.

(iv) The radius of C is determined by the condition that the polar of $\dot{\mathbf{v}}_1$ is the line passing though $\mathbf{v}_2$ and $\mathbf{v}_3$.

$\triangle$

8.11 Closure

8.11.1 The literature

Faugeras and Mourrain [Faugeras-95a], and Faugeras and Papadopoulo [Faugeras-97] develop the projection of lines using Plücker coordinates. Koenderink [Koenderink-84, Koenderink-90], and Giblin and Weiss [Giblin-87] give many properties of the contour generator and apparent contour, and their relation to the differential geometry of surfaces.

[Kanatani-92] gives an alternative, calibrated, treatment of vanishing points and lines, and of the result that images acquired by cameras with the same centre are related by a planar homography. Mundy and Zisserman [Mundy-92] showed this result geometrically, and [Hartley-94a] gave a simple algebraic derivation based on camera projection matrices. [Faugeras-92b] introduced the projective (reduced) camera matrix. The link between the image of the absolute conic and camera calibration was first given in [Faugeras-92a].

The computation of panoramic mosaics is described in [Capel-98, Sawhney-98, Szeliski-97]. The ML method of computing vanishing points is given in Liebowitz & Zisserman [Liebowitz-98]. Applications of automatic vanishing line estimation from coplanar equally spaced lines are given in [Schaffalitzky-00b] and also [Se-00]. Affine 3D measurements from a single view is described in [Criminisi-00, Proesmans-98].

The result that K may be computed from multiple scene planes on which metric structure (such as a square) is known was given in [Liebowitz-98]. Algorithms for this computation are given in [Liebowitz-99a, Sturm-99c, Zhang-00]. The advantage in using ω, rather than ω^*, when imposing the skew zero constraint was first noted in [Armstrong-96b]. The method of internal calibration using three vanishing points for orthogonal directions was given by Caprile and Torre [Caprile-90], though there is an earlier reference to this result in the photogrammetry literature [Gracie-68]. A simple formula for the focal length in this case is given in [Cipolla-99, Hartley-02b]. A discussion of the degeneracies that arise when combining multiple constraints is given in [Liebowitz-99b, Liebowitz-01]. Single view reconstruction is investigated in [Criminisi-99a, Criminisi-01, Horry-97, Liebowitz-99a, Sturm-99a].

8.11.2 Notes and exercises

(i) **Homography from a world plane.** Suppose $\mathtt{H}$ is computed (e.g. from the correspondence between four or more known world points and their images) and $\mathtt{K}$ known, then the pose of the camera $\{\mathtt{R}, \mathbf{t}\}$ may be computed from the camera matrix $[\mathbf{r}_1, \mathbf{r}_2, \mathbf{r}_1 \times \mathbf{r}_2, \mathbf{t}]$, where

$$[\mathbf{r}_1, \mathbf{r}_2, \mathbf{t}] = \pm \mathtt{K}^{-1}\mathtt{H}/\|\mathtt{K}^{-1}\mathtt{H}\|.$$

Note that there is a two-fold ambiguity. This result follows from (8.1–*p*196) which gives the homography between a world plane and calibrated camera $\mathtt{P} = \mathtt{K}[\mathtt{R} \mid \mathbf{t}]$.

Show that the homography $\mathbf{x} = \mathtt{H}\widetilde{\mathbf{X}}$ between points on a world plane $(\mathbf{n}^\mathsf{T}, d)^\mathsf{T}$ and the image may be expressed as $\mathtt{H} = \mathtt{K}(\mathtt{R} - \mathbf{t}\mathbf{n}^\mathsf{T}/d)$. The points on the plane have coordinates $\widetilde{\mathbf{X}} = (\mathrm{X}, \mathrm{Y}, \mathrm{Z})^\mathsf{T}$.

(ii) **Line projection.**

(a) Show that any line containing the camera centre lies in the null-space of the map (8.2–*p*198), i.e. it is projected to the line $\mathbf{l} = \mathbf{0}$.

(b) Show that the line $\mathcal{L} = \mathcal{P}^\mathsf{T}\mathbf{x}$ in $\mathbb{P}^3$ is the ray through the image point $\mathbf{x}$ and the camera centre. Hint: start from result 3.5(*p*72), and show that the camera centre $\mathbf{C}$ lies on $\mathcal{L}$.

(c) What is the geometric interpretation of the columns of $\mathcal{P}$?

(iii) **Contour generator of a quadric.** The contour generator $\boldsymbol{\Gamma}$ of a quadric consists of the set of points $\mathbf{X}$ on $\mathtt{Q}$ for which the tangent planes contain the camera centre, $\mathbf{C}$. The tangent plane at a point $\mathbf{X}$ on $\mathtt{Q}$ is given by $\boldsymbol{\pi} = \mathtt{Q}\mathbf{X}$, and the condition that $\mathbf{C}$ is on $\boldsymbol{\pi}$ is $\mathbf{C}^\mathsf{T}\boldsymbol{\pi} = \mathbf{C}^\mathsf{T}\mathtt{Q}\mathbf{X} = 0$. Thus points $\mathbf{X}$ on $\boldsymbol{\Gamma}$ satisfy $\mathbf{C}^\mathsf{T}\mathtt{Q}\mathbf{X} = 0$, and thus lie on the *plane* $\boldsymbol{\pi}_\Gamma = \mathtt{Q}\mathbf{C}$ since $\boldsymbol{\pi}_\Gamma^\mathsf{T}\mathbf{X} = \mathbf{C}^\mathsf{T}\mathtt{Q}\mathbf{X} = 0$. This shows that the contour generator of a quadric is a plane curve and furthermore, since $\boldsymbol{\pi}_\Gamma = \mathtt{Q}\mathbf{C}$, that the plane of $\boldsymbol{\Gamma}$ is the polar plane of the camera centre with respect to the quadric.

(iv) **Apparent contour of an algebraic surface.** Show that the apparent contour of a homogeneous algebraic surface of degree n is a curve of degree $n(n-1)$. For example, if $n = 2$ then the surface is a quadric and the apparent contour a conic. Hint: write the surface as $F(\mathrm{X}, \mathrm{Y}, \mathrm{Z}, \mathrm{W}) = 0$, then the tangent plane contains the camera centre $\mathbf{C}$ if

$$C_\mathrm{X}\frac{\partial F}{\partial \mathrm{X}} + C_\mathrm{Y}\frac{\partial F}{\partial \mathrm{Y}} + C_\mathrm{Z}\frac{\partial F}{\partial \mathrm{Z}} + C_\mathrm{W}\frac{\partial F}{\partial \mathrm{W}} = 0$$

which is a surface of a degree $n - 1$.

(v) **Rotation axis vanishing point for $\mathtt{H} = \mathtt{KRK}^{-1}$.** The homography of a conjugate rotation $\mathtt{H} = \mathtt{KRK}^{-1}$ has an eigenvector $\mathtt{K}\mathbf{a}$, where $\mathbf{a}$ is the direction of the rotation axis, since $\mathtt{HK}\mathbf{a} = \mathtt{KR}\mathbf{a} = \mathtt{K}\mathbf{a}$. The last equality follows because $\mathtt{R}\mathbf{a} = 1\mathbf{a}$, i.e. $\mathbf{a}$ is the unit eigenvector of $\mathtt{R}$. It follows that (a) $\mathtt{K}\mathbf{a}$ is a fixed point under the homography $\mathtt{H}$; and (b) from result 8.20(*p*215) $\mathbf{v} = \mathtt{K}\mathbf{a}$ is the vanishing point of the rotation axis.

(vi) **Synthetic rotations.** Suppose, as in example 8.12(*p*205), that a homography is estimated between two images related by a pure rotation about the camera centre. Then the estimated homography will be a conjugate rotation, so that $\mathtt{H} = \mathtt{KR}(\theta)\mathtt{K}^{-1}$ (though $\mathtt{K}$ and $\mathtt{R}$ are unknown). However, $\mathtt{H}^2$ applied to the first image generates the image that would have been obtained by rotating the camera about the same axis through twice the angle, since $\mathtt{H}^2 = \mathtt{KR}^2\mathtt{K}^{-1} = \mathtt{KR}(2\theta)\mathtt{K}^{-1}$.

More generally we may write $\mathtt{H}^\lambda$ to represent a rotation through any fractional angle $\lambda\theta$. To make sense of $\mathtt{H}^\lambda$, observe that the eigenvalue decomposition of $\mathtt{H}$ is $\mathtt{H}(\theta) = \mathtt{U}\,\mathrm{diag}(1, e^{i\theta}, e^{-i\theta})\,\mathtt{U}^{-1}$, and both θ and $\mathtt{U}$ may be computed from the estimated $\mathtt{H}$. Then

$$\mathtt{H}^\lambda = \mathtt{U}\,\mathrm{diag}(1, e^{i\lambda\theta}, e^{-i\lambda\theta})\,\mathtt{U}^{-1} = \mathtt{KR}(\lambda\theta)\mathtt{K}^{-1}.$$

which is the conjugate of a rotation through angle $\lambda\theta$. Writing ϕ instead of $\lambda\theta$, we may use this homography to generate synthetic images rotated through any angle ϕ. The images are interpolated between the original images (if $0 < \phi < \theta$), or extrapolated (if $\phi > \theta$).

(vii) Show that the imaged circular points of a perspectively imaged plane may be computed if any of the following are on the plane: (i) a square grid; (ii) two rectangles arranged such that the sides of one rectangle are not parallel to the sides of the other; (iii) two circles of equal radius; (iv) two circles of unequal radius.

(viii) Show that in the case of zero skew, $\boldsymbol{\omega}$ is the conic

$$\left(\frac{x - x_0}{\alpha_x}\right)^2 + \left(\frac{y - y_0}{\alpha_y}\right)^2 + 1 = 0$$

which may be interpreted as an ellipse aligned with the axes, centred on the principal point, and with axes of length $i\alpha_x$ and $i\alpha_y$ in the x and y directions respectively.

(ix) If the camera calibration $\mathtt{K}$ and the vanishing line $\mathbf{l}$ of a scene plane are known then the scene plane can be metric rectified by a homography corresponding to a synthetic rotation $\mathtt{H} = \mathtt{KRK}^{-1}$ that maps $\mathbf{l}$ to $\mathbf{l}_\infty$, i.e. it is required that $\mathtt{H}^{-\mathsf{T}}\mathbf{l} = (0, 0, 1)^\mathsf{T}$. This condition arises because if the plane is rotated such that its vanishing line is $\mathbf{l}_\infty$ then it is fronto-parallel. Show that $\mathtt{H}^{-\mathsf{T}}\mathbf{l} = (0, 0, 1)^\mathsf{T}$ is equivalent to $\mathtt{R}\mathbf{n} = (0, 0, 1)^\mathsf{T}$, where $\mathbf{n} = \mathtt{K}^\mathsf{T}\mathbf{l}$ is the normal to the scene plane. This is the condition that the scene normal is rotated to lie along the camera Z axis. Note the rotation is not uniquely defined since a rotation about the plane's normal does not affect its metric rectification. However, the last row of R equals $\mathbf{n}$, so that $\mathtt{R} = [\mathbf{r}_1, \mathbf{r}_2, \mathbf{n}]^\mathsf{T}$ where $\mathbf{n}, \mathbf{r}_1$ and $\mathbf{r}_2$ are a triad of orthonormal vectors.

(x) Show that the angle between two planes with vanishing lines $\mathbf{l}_1$ and $\mathbf{l}_2$ is

$$\cos\theta = \frac{\mathbf{l}_1^\mathsf{T}\boldsymbol{\omega}^*\mathbf{l}_2}{\sqrt{\mathbf{l}_1^\mathsf{T}\boldsymbol{\omega}^*\mathbf{l}_1}\sqrt{\mathbf{l}_2^\mathsf{T}\boldsymbol{\omega}^*\mathbf{l}_2}}.$$

(xi) Derive (8.15–*p*218). Hint, the line $\mathbf{l}$ lies in the pencil defined by $\mathbf{l}_1$ and $\mathbf{l}_2$, so it can be expressed as $\mathbf{l} = \alpha\mathbf{l}_1 + \beta\mathbf{l}_2$. Then use the relations $\mathbf{l}_n = \mathbf{l}_0 + n\mathbf{l}$ for $n = 1, 2$ to solve for α and β.

(xii) For the case of vanishing points arising from three orthogonal directions, and for an image with square pixels, show algebraically that the principal point is the orthocentre of the triangle with vertices the vanishing points. Hint: suppose the vanishing point at one vertex of the triangle is $\mathbf{v}$ and the line of the opposite side (through the other two vanishing points) is $\mathbf{l}$. Then from (8.17–*p*219) $\mathbf{v} = \boldsymbol{\omega}^*\mathbf{l}$ since $\mathbf{v}$ and $\mathbf{l}$ arise from an orthogonal line and plane respectively. Show that the principal point lies on the line from $\mathbf{v}$ to $\mathbf{l}$ which is perpendicular *in the image* to $\mathbf{l}$. Since this result is true for any vertex the principal point is the orthocentre of the triangle.

(xiii) Show that the vanishing points of an orthogonal triad of directions are the vertices of a self-polar triangle [Springer-64] with respect to $\boldsymbol{\omega}$.

(xiv) If a camera has square pixels, then the apparent contour of a sphere centred on the principal axis is a circle. If the sphere is translated parallel to the image plane, then the apparent contour deforms from a circle to an ellipse with the principal point on its major axis.

(a) How can this observation be used as a method of internal parameter calibration?

(b) Show by a geometric argument that the aspect ratio of the ellipse does not depend on the distance of the sphere from the camera.

If the sphere is now translated parallel to the principal axis the apparent contour can deform to a hyperbola, but only one branch of the hyperbola is imaged. Why is this?

(xv) Show that for a general camera the apparent contour of a sphere is related to the IAC as:

$$\boldsymbol{\omega} = \mathtt{C} + \mathbf{v}\mathbf{v}^\mathsf{T}$$

where C is the conic outline of the imaged sphere, and $\mathbf{v}$ is a 3-vector that depends on the position of the sphere. A proof is given in [Agrawal-03]. Note this relation places two constraints on $\boldsymbol{\omega}$, so that in principle $\boldsymbol{\omega}$, and hence the calibration K, may be computed from three images of a sphere. However, in practice this is not a well conditioned method for computing K because the deviation of the sphere's outline from a circle is small.

Part II

Two-View Geometry

The Birth of Venus (detail), c. 1485 (tempera on canvas) by Sandro Botticelli (1444/5-1510)
Galleria degli Uffizi, Florence, Italy/Bridgeman Art Library

Outline

This part of the book covers the geometry of two perspective views. These views may be acquired simultaneously as in a stereo rig, or acquired sequentially, for example by a camera moving relative to the scene. These two situations are geometrically equivalent and will not be differentiated here. Each view has an associated camera matrix, $\mathtt{P}, \mathtt{P}'$, where $'$ indicates entities associated with the second view, and a 3-space point $\mathbf{X}$ is imaged as $\mathbf{x} = \mathtt{P}\mathbf{X}$ in the first view, and $\mathbf{x}' = \mathtt{P}'\mathbf{X}$ in the second. Image points $\mathbf{x}$ and $\mathbf{x}'$ *correspond* because they are the image of the same 3-space point. There are three questions that will be addressed:

(i) **Correspondence geometry.** Given an image point $\mathbf{x}$ in the first view, how does this constrain the position of the corresponding point $\mathbf{x}'$ in the second view?

(ii) **Camera geometry (motion).** Given a set of corresponding image points $\{\mathbf{x}_i \leftrightarrow \mathbf{x}'_i\}, i = 1, \ldots, n$, what are the cameras $\mathtt{P}$ and $\mathtt{P}'$ for the two views?

(iii) **Scene geometry (structure).** Given corresponding image points $\mathbf{x} \leftrightarrow \mathbf{x}'$ and cameras $\mathtt{P}, \mathtt{P}'$, what is the position of (their pre-image) $\mathbf{X}$ in 3-space?

Chapter 9 describes the *epipolar geometry* of two views, and directly answers the first question: a point in one view defines an epipolar line in the other view on which the corresponding point lies. The epipolar geometry depends only on the cameras – their relative position and their internal parameters. It does *not* depend at all on the scene structure. The epipolar geometry is represented by a 3×3 matrix called the *fundamental matrix* $\mathtt{F}$. The anatomy of the fundamental matrix is described, and its computation from camera matrices $\mathtt{P}$ and $\mathtt{P}'$ given. It is then shown that $\mathtt{P}$ and $\mathtt{P}'$ may be computed from $\mathtt{F}$ up to a projective ambiguity of 3-space.

Chapter 10 describes one of the most important results in uncalibrated multiple view geometry – a *reconstruction* of both cameras and scene structure can be computed from image point correspondences alone; no other information is required. This answers both the second and third questions simultaneously. The reconstruction obtained from point correspondences alone is up to a projective ambiguity of 3-space, and this ambiguity can be resolved by supplying well defined additional information on the cameras or scene. In this manner an affine or metric reconstruction may be computed from uncalibrated images. The following two chapters then fill in the details and numerical algorithms for computing this reconstruction.

Chapter 11 describes methods for computing $\mathtt{F}$ from a set of corresponding image points $\{\mathbf{x}_i \leftrightarrow \mathbf{x}'_i\}$, even though the structure (3D pre-image $\mathbf{X}_i$) of these points is unknown and the camera matrices are unknown. The cameras $\mathtt{P}$ and $\mathtt{P}'$ may then be determined, up to a projective ambiguity, from the computed $\mathtt{F}$.

Chapter 12 then describes the computation of scene structure by *triangulation* given the cameras and corresponding image points – the point $\mathbf{X}$ in 3-space is computed as the intersection of rays back-projected from the corresponding points $\mathbf{x}$ and $\mathbf{x}'$ via their associated cameras $\mathtt{P}, \mathtt{P}'$. Similarly, the 3D position of other geometric entities, such as lines or conics, may also be computed given their image correspondences.

Chapter 13 covers the two-view geometry of planes. It provides an alternative answer to the first question: if scene points lie on a plane, then once the geometry of this plane is computed, the image $\mathbf{x}$ of a point in one image determines the position of $\mathbf{x}'$ in the other image. The points are related by a plane projective transformation. This chapter also describes a particularly important projective transformation between views – the *infinite homography*, which is the transformation arising from the plane at infinity.

Chapter 14 describes two-view geometry in the specialized case that the two cameras $\mathtt{P}$ and $\mathtt{P}'$ are affine. This case has a number of simplifications over the general projective case, and provides a very good approximation in many practical situations.

9

Epipolar Geometry and the Fundamental Matrix

The epipolar geometry is the intrinsic projective geometry between two views. It is independent of scene structure, and only depends on the cameras' internal parameters and relative pose.

The fundamental matrix F encapsulates this intrinsic geometry. It is a 3×3 matrix of rank 2. If a point in 3-space $\mathbf{X}$ is imaged as $\mathbf{x}$ in the first view, and $\mathbf{x}'$ in the second, then the image points satisfy the relation $\mathbf{x}'^{\mathsf{T}}\mathtt{F}\mathbf{x} = 0$.

We will first describe epipolar geometry, and derive the fundamental matrix. The properties of the fundamental matrix are then elucidated, both for general motion of the camera between the views, and for several commonly occurring special motions. It is next shown that the cameras can be retrieved from F up to a projective transformation of 3-space. This result is the basis for the projective reconstruction theorem given in chapter 10. Finally, if the camera internal calibration is known, it is shown that the Euclidean motion of the cameras between views may be computed from the fundamental matrix up to a finite number of ambiguities.

The fundamental matrix is independent of scene structure. However, it can be computed from correspondences of imaged scene points alone, without requiring knowledge of the cameras' internal parameters or relative pose. This computation is described in chapter 11.

9.1 Epipolar geometry

The epipolar geometry between two views is essentially the geometry of the intersection of the image planes with the pencil of planes having the baseline as axis (the baseline is the line joining the camera centres). This geometry is usually motivated by considering the search for corresponding points in stereo matching, and we will start from that objective here.

Suppose a point $\mathbf{X}$ in 3-space is imaged in two views, at $\mathbf{x}$ in the first, and $\mathbf{x}'$ in the second. What is the relation between the corresponding image points $\mathbf{x}$ and $\mathbf{x}'$? As shown in figure 9.1a the image points $\mathbf{x}$ and $\mathbf{x}'$, space point $\mathbf{X}$, and camera centres are coplanar. Denote this plane as $\boldsymbol{\pi}$. Clearly, the rays back-projected from $\mathbf{x}$ and $\mathbf{x}'$ intersect at $\mathbf{X}$, and the rays are coplanar, lying in $\boldsymbol{\pi}$. It is this latter property that is of most significance in searching for a correspondence.

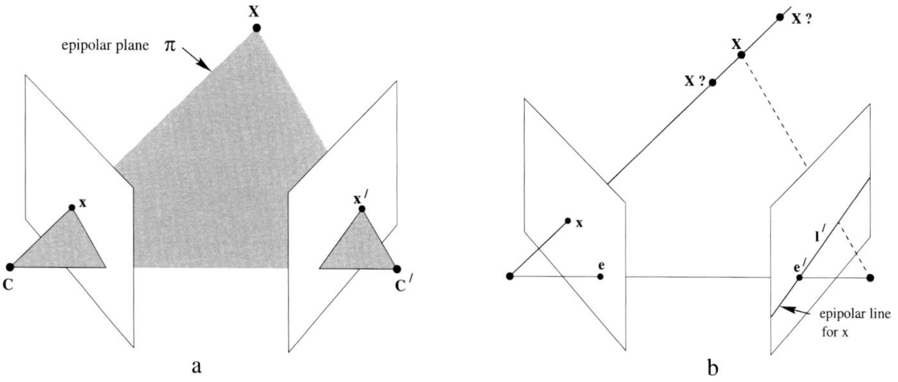

Fig. 9.1. **Point correspondence geometry.** *(a) The two cameras are indicated by their centres* $\mathbf{C}$ *and* $\mathbf{C}'$ *and image planes. The camera centres, 3-space point* $\mathbf{X}$*, and its images* $\mathbf{x}$ *and* $\mathbf{x}'$ *lie in a common plane* $\boldsymbol{\pi}$*. (b) An image point* $\mathbf{x}$ *back-projects to a ray in 3-space defined by the first camera centre,* $\mathbf{C}$*, and* $\mathbf{x}$*. This ray is imaged as a line* $\mathbf{l}'$ *in the second view. The 3-space point* $\mathbf{X}$ *which projects to* $\mathbf{x}$ *must lie on this ray, so the image of* $\mathbf{X}$ *in the second view must lie on* $\mathbf{l}'$.

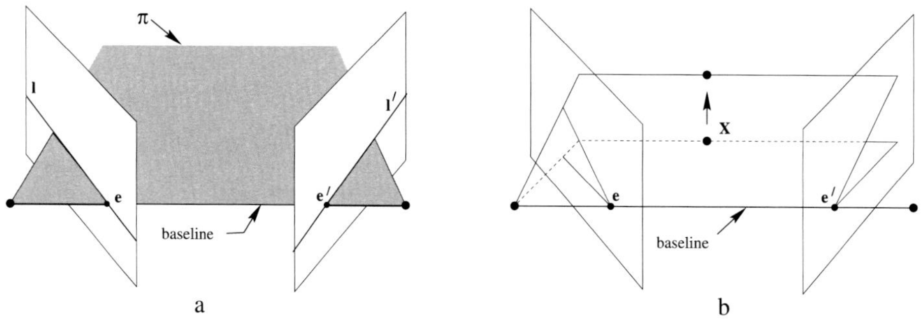

Fig. 9.2. **Epipolar geometry.** *(a) The camera baseline intersects each image plane at the epipoles* $\mathbf{e}$ *and* $\mathbf{e}'$*. Any plane* $\boldsymbol{\pi}$ *containing the baseline is an epipolar plane, and intersects the image planes in corresponding epipolar lines* $\mathbf{l}$ *and* $\mathbf{l}'$*. (b) As the position of the 3D point* $\mathbf{X}$ *varies, the epipolar planes "rotate" about the baseline. This family of planes is known as an epipolar pencil. All epipolar lines intersect at the epipole.*

Supposing now that we know only $\mathbf{x}$, we may ask how the corresponding point $\mathbf{x}'$ is constrained. The plane $\boldsymbol{\pi}$ is determined by the baseline and the ray defined by $\mathbf{x}$. From above we know that the ray corresponding to the (unknown) point $\mathbf{x}'$ lies in $\boldsymbol{\pi}$, hence the point $\mathbf{x}'$ lies on the line of intersection $\mathbf{l}'$ of $\boldsymbol{\pi}$ with the second image plane. This line $\mathbf{l}'$ is the image in the second view of the ray back-projected from $\mathbf{x}$. It is the *epipolar line* corresponding to $\mathbf{x}$. In terms of a stereo correspondence algorithm the benefit is that the search for the point corresponding to $\mathbf{x}$ need not cover the entire image plane but can be restricted to the line $\mathbf{l}'$.

The geometric entities involved in epipolar geometry are illustrated in figure 9.2. The terminology is

- The **epipole** is the *point* of intersection of the line joining the camera centres (the baseline) with the image plane. Equivalently, the epipole is the image in one view

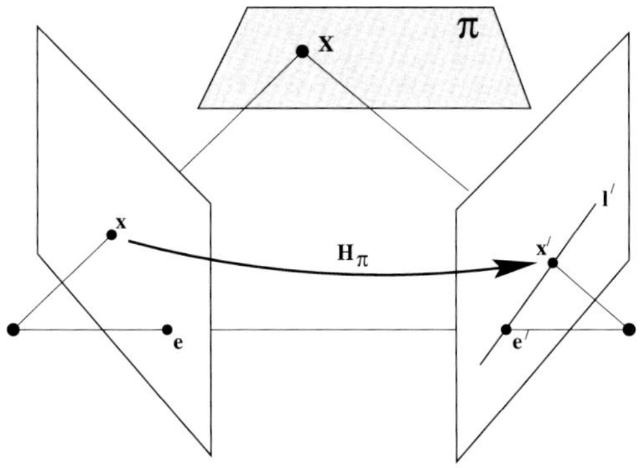

Fig. 9.5. *A point* $\mathbf{x}$ *in one image is transferred via the plane* $\boldsymbol{\pi}$ *to a matching point* $\mathbf{x}'$ *in the second image. The epipolar line through* $\mathbf{x}'$ *is obtained by joining* $\mathbf{x}'$ *to the epipole* $\mathbf{e}'$*. In symbols one may write* $\mathbf{x}' = \mathtt{H}_\pi \mathbf{x}$ *and* $\mathbf{l}' = [\mathbf{e}']_\times \mathbf{x}' = [\mathbf{e}']_\times \mathtt{H}_\pi \mathbf{x} = \mathtt{F}\mathbf{x}$ *where* $\mathtt{F} = [\mathbf{e}']_\times \mathtt{H}_\pi$ *is the fundamental matrix.*

figure 9.1b. The points $\mathbf{x}$ and $\mathbf{x}'$ are both images of the 3D point $\mathbf{X}$ lying on a plane. The set of all such points $\mathbf{x}_i$ in the first image and the corresponding points $\mathbf{x}'_i$ in the second image are projectively equivalent, since they are each projectively equivalent to the planar point set $\mathbf{X}_i$. Thus there is a 2D homography $\mathtt{H}_\pi$ mapping each $\mathbf{x}_i$ to $\mathbf{x}'_i$.

Step 2: Constructing the epipolar line. Given the point $\mathbf{x}'$ the epipolar line $\mathbf{l}'$ passing through $\mathbf{x}'$ and the epipole $\mathbf{e}'$ can be written as $\mathbf{l}' = \mathbf{e}' \times \mathbf{x}' = [\mathbf{e}']_\times \mathbf{x}'$ (the notation $[\mathbf{e}']_\times$ is defined in (A4.5–*p*581)). Since $\mathbf{x}'$ may be written as $\mathbf{x}' = \mathtt{H}_\pi \mathbf{x}$, we have

$$\mathbf{l}' = [\mathbf{e}']_\times \mathtt{H}_\pi \mathbf{x} = \mathtt{F}\mathbf{x}$$

where we define $\mathtt{F} = [\mathbf{e}']_\times \mathtt{H}_\pi$, the fundamental matrix. This shows

Result 9.1. *The fundamental matrix* $\mathtt{F}$ *may be written as* $\mathtt{F} = [\mathbf{e}']_\times \mathtt{H}_\pi$*, where* $\mathtt{H}_\pi$ *is the transfer mapping from one image to another via any plane* $\boldsymbol{\pi}$*. Furthermore, since* $[\mathbf{e}']_\times$ *has rank 2 and* $\mathtt{H}_\pi$ *rank 3,* $\mathtt{F}$ *is a matrix of rank 2.*

Geometrically, $\mathtt{F}$ represents a mapping from the 2-dimensional projective plane $\mathbb{P}^2$ of the first image to the pencil of epipolar lines through the epipole $\mathbf{e}'$. Thus, it represents a mapping from a 2-dimensional onto a 1-dimensional projective space, and hence must have rank 2.

Note, the geometric derivation above involves a scene plane $\boldsymbol{\pi}$, but a plane is *not* required in order for $\mathtt{F}$ to exist. The plane is simply used here as a means of defining a point map from one image to another. The connection between the fundamental matrix and transfer of points from one image to another via a plane is dealt with in some depth in chapter 13.

9.2.2 Algebraic derivation

The form of the fundamental matrix in terms of the two camera projection matrices, $\mathtt{P}, \mathtt{P}'$, may be derived algebraically. The following formulation is due to Xu and Zhang [Xu-96].

The ray back-projected from $\mathbf{x}$ by $\mathtt{P}$ is obtained by solving $\mathtt{P}\mathbf{X} = \mathbf{x}$. The one-parameter family of solutions is of the form given by (6.13–p162) as

$$\mathbf{X}(\lambda) = \mathtt{P}^{+}\mathbf{x} + \lambda\mathbf{C}$$

where $\mathtt{P}^{+}$ is the pseudo-inverse of $\mathtt{P}$, i.e. $\mathtt{P}\mathtt{P}^{+} = \mathtt{I}$, and $\mathbf{C}$ its null-vector, namely the camera centre, defined by $\mathtt{P}\mathbf{C} = \mathbf{0}$. The ray is parametrized by the scalar λ. In particular two points on the ray are $\mathtt{P}^{+}\mathbf{x}$ (at $\lambda = 0$), and the first camera centre $\mathbf{C}$ (at $\lambda = \infty$). These two points are imaged by the second camera $\mathtt{P}'$ at $\mathtt{P}'\mathtt{P}^{+}\mathbf{x}$ and $\mathtt{P}'\mathbf{C}$ respectively in the second view. The epipolar line is the line joining these two projected points, namely $\mathbf{l}' = (\mathtt{P}'\mathbf{C}) \times (\mathtt{P}'\mathtt{P}^{+}\mathbf{x})$. The point $\mathtt{P}'\mathbf{C}$ is the epipole in the second image, namely the projection of the first camera centre, and may be denoted by $\mathbf{e}'$. Thus, $\mathbf{l}' = [\mathbf{e}']_{\times}(\mathtt{P}'\mathtt{P}^{+})\mathbf{x} = \mathtt{F}\mathbf{x}$, where $\mathtt{F}$ is the matrix

$$\mathtt{F} = [\mathbf{e}']_{\times}\mathtt{P}'\mathtt{P}^{+}. \tag{9.1}$$

This is essentially the same formula for the fundamental matrix as the one derived in the previous section, the homography $\mathtt{H}_{\pi}$ having the explicit form $\mathtt{H}_{\pi} = \mathtt{P}'\mathtt{P}^{+}$ in terms of the two camera matrices. Note that this derivation breaks down in the case where the two camera centres are the same for, in this case, $\mathbf{C}$ is the common camera centre of both $\mathtt{P}$ and $\mathtt{P}'$, and so $\mathtt{P}'\mathbf{C} = \mathbf{0}$. It follows that $\mathtt{F}$ defined in (9.1) is the zero matrix.

Example 9.2. Suppose the camera matrices are those of a calibrated stereo rig with the world origin at the first camera

$$\mathtt{P} = \mathtt{K}[\mathtt{I} \mid \mathbf{0}] \qquad \mathtt{P}' = \mathtt{K}'[\mathtt{R} \mid \mathbf{t}].$$

Then

$$\mathtt{P}^{+} = \begin{bmatrix} \mathtt{K}^{-1} \\ \mathbf{0}^{\mathsf{T}} \end{bmatrix} \qquad \mathbf{C} = \begin{pmatrix} \mathbf{0} \\ 1 \end{pmatrix}$$

and

$$\begin{aligned} \mathtt{F} &= [\mathtt{P}'\mathbf{C}]_{\times}\mathtt{P}'\mathtt{P}^{+} \\ &= [\mathtt{K}'\mathbf{t}]_{\times}\mathtt{K}'\mathtt{R}\mathtt{K}^{-1} = \mathtt{K}'^{-\mathsf{T}}[\mathbf{t}]_{\times}\mathtt{R}\mathtt{K}^{-1} = \mathtt{K}'^{-\mathsf{T}}\mathtt{R}[\mathtt{R}^{\mathsf{T}}\mathbf{t}]_{\times}\mathtt{K}^{-1} = \mathtt{K}'^{-\mathsf{T}}\mathtt{R}\mathtt{K}^{\mathsf{T}}[\mathtt{K}\mathtt{R}^{\mathsf{T}}\mathbf{t}]_{\times} \end{aligned} \tag{9.2}$$

where the various forms follow from result A4.3(p582). Note that the epipoles (defined as the image of the other camera centre) are

$$\mathbf{e} = \mathtt{P}\begin{pmatrix} -\mathtt{R}^{\mathsf{T}}\mathbf{t} \\ 1 \end{pmatrix} = \mathtt{K}\mathtt{R}^{\mathsf{T}}\mathbf{t} \qquad \mathbf{e}' = \mathtt{P}'\begin{pmatrix} \mathbf{0} \\ 1 \end{pmatrix} = \mathtt{K}'\mathbf{t}. \tag{9.3}$$

Thus we may write (9.2) as

$$\mathtt{F} = [\mathbf{e}']_{\times}\mathtt{K}'\mathtt{R}\mathtt{K}^{-1} = \mathtt{K}'^{-\mathsf{T}}[\mathbf{t}]_{\times}\mathtt{R}\mathtt{K}^{-1} = \mathtt{K}'^{-\mathsf{T}}\mathtt{R}[\mathtt{R}^{\mathsf{T}}\mathbf{t}]_{\times}\mathtt{K}^{-1} = \mathtt{K}'^{-\mathsf{T}}\mathtt{R}\mathtt{K}^{\mathsf{T}}[\mathbf{e}]_{\times}. \tag{9.4}$$

△

The expression for the fundamental matrix can be derived in many ways, and indeed will be derived again several times in this book. In particular, (17.3–p412) expresses $\mathtt{F}$ in terms of 4×4 determinants composed from rows of the camera matrices for each view.

9.2.3 Correspondence condition

Up to this point we have considered the map $\mathbf{x} \rightarrow \mathbf{l}'$ defined by F. We may now state the most basic properties of the fundamental matrix.

Result 9.3. *The fundamental matrix satisfies the condition that for any pair of corresponding points* $\mathbf{x} \leftrightarrow \mathbf{x}'$ *in the two images*

$$\mathbf{x}'^{\mathsf{T}}\mathtt{F}\mathbf{x} = 0.$$

This is true, because if points $\mathbf{x}$ and $\mathbf{x}'$ correspond, then $\mathbf{x}'$ lies on the epipolar line $\mathbf{l}' = \mathtt{F}\mathbf{x}$ corresponding to the point $\mathbf{x}$. In other words $0 = \mathbf{x}'^{\mathsf{T}}\mathbf{l}' = \mathbf{x}'^{\mathsf{T}}\mathtt{F}\mathbf{x}$. Conversely, if image points satisfy the relation $\mathbf{x}'^{\mathsf{T}}\mathtt{F}\mathbf{x} = 0$ then the rays defined by these points are coplanar. This is a necessary condition for points to correspond.

The importance of the relation of result 9.3 is that it gives a way of characterizing the fundamental matrix without reference to the camera matrices, i.e. only in terms of corresponding image points. This enables F to be computed from image correspondences alone. We have seen from (9.1) that F may be computed from the two camera matrices, $\mathtt{P}, \mathtt{P}'$, and in particular that F is determined uniquely from the cameras, up to an overall scaling. However, we may now enquire how many correspondences are required to compute F from $\mathbf{x}'^{\mathsf{T}}\mathtt{F}\mathbf{x} = 0$, and the circumstances under which the matrix is uniquely defined by these correspondences. The details of this are postponed until chapter 11, where it will be seen that in general at least 7 correspondences are required to compute F.

9.2.4 Properties of the fundamental matrix

Definition 9.4. Suppose we have two images acquired by cameras with non-coincident centres, then the **fundamental matrix** F is the unique 3×3 rank 2 homogeneous matrix which satisfies

$$\mathbf{x}'^{\mathsf{T}}\mathtt{F}\mathbf{x} = 0 \tag{9.5}$$

for all corresponding points $\mathbf{x} \leftrightarrow \mathbf{x}'$.

We now briefly list a number of properties of the fundamental matrix. The most important properties are also summarized in table 9.1.

(i) **Transpose**: If F is the fundamental matrix of the pair of cameras $(\mathtt{P}, \mathtt{P}')$, then $\mathtt{F}^{\mathsf{T}}$ is the fundamental matrix of the pair in the opposite order: $(\mathtt{P}', \mathtt{P})$.

(ii) **Epipolar lines**: For any point $\mathbf{x}$ in the first image, the corresponding epipolar line is $\mathbf{l}' = \mathtt{F}\mathbf{x}$. Similarly, $\mathbf{l} = \mathtt{F}^{\mathsf{T}}\mathbf{x}'$ represents the epipolar line corresponding to $\mathbf{x}'$ in the second image.

(iii) The **epipole**: for any point $\mathbf{x}$ (other than $\mathbf{e}$) the epipolar line $\mathbf{l}' = \mathtt{F}\mathbf{x}$ contains the epipole $\mathbf{e}'$. Thus $\mathbf{e}'$ satisfies $\mathbf{e}'^{\mathsf{T}}(\mathtt{F}\mathbf{x}) = (\mathbf{e}'^{\mathsf{T}}\mathtt{F})\mathbf{x} = 0$ for all $\mathbf{x}$. It follows that $\mathbf{e}'^{\mathsf{T}}\mathtt{F} = \mathbf{0}$, i.e. $\mathbf{e}'$ is the left null-vector of F. Similarly $\mathtt{F}\mathbf{e} = \mathbf{0}$, i.e. $\mathbf{e}$ is the right null-vector of F.

- $\mathtt{F}$ is a rank 2 homogeneous matrix with 7 degrees of freedom.
- **Point correspondence**: If $\mathbf{x}$ and $\mathbf{x}'$ are corresponding image points, then $\mathbf{x}'^{\mathsf{T}}\mathtt{F}\mathbf{x} = 0$.
- **Epipolar lines**:
  - ◇ $\mathbf{l}' = \mathtt{F}\mathbf{x}$ is the epipolar line corresponding to $\mathbf{x}$.
  - ◇ $\mathbf{l} = \mathtt{F}^{\mathsf{T}}\mathbf{x}'$ is the epipolar line corresponding to $\mathbf{x}'$.
- **Epipoles**:
  - ◇ $\mathtt{F}\mathbf{e} = \mathbf{0}$.
  - ◇ $\mathtt{F}^{\mathsf{T}}\mathbf{e}' = \mathbf{0}$.
- **Computation from camera matrices** $\mathtt{P}, \mathtt{P}'$:
  - ◇ General cameras,
    $\mathtt{F} = [\mathbf{e}']_\times \mathtt{P}'\mathtt{P}^+$, where $\mathtt{P}^+$ is the pseudo-inverse of $\mathtt{P}$, and $\mathbf{e}' = \mathtt{P}'\mathbf{C}$, with $\mathtt{P}\mathbf{C} = \mathbf{0}$.
  - ◇ Canonical cameras, $\mathtt{P} = [\mathtt{I} \mid \mathbf{0}]$, $\mathtt{P}' = [\mathtt{M} \mid \mathbf{m}]$,
    $\mathtt{F} = [\mathbf{e}']_\times \mathtt{M} = \mathtt{M}^{-\mathsf{T}}[\mathbf{e}]_\times$, where $\mathbf{e}' = \mathbf{m}$ and $\mathbf{e} = \mathtt{M}^{-1}\mathbf{m}$.
  - ◇ Cameras not at infinity $\mathtt{P} = \mathtt{K}[\mathtt{I} \mid \mathbf{0}]$, $\mathtt{P}' = \mathtt{K}'[\mathtt{R} \mid \mathbf{t}]$,
    $\mathtt{F} = \mathtt{K}'^{-\mathsf{T}}[\mathbf{t}]_\times \mathtt{R}\mathtt{K}^{-1} = [\mathtt{K}'\mathbf{t}]_\times \mathtt{K}'\mathtt{R}\mathtt{K}^{-1} = \mathtt{K}'^{-\mathsf{T}}\mathtt{R}\mathtt{K}^{\mathsf{T}}[\mathtt{K}\mathtt{R}^{\mathsf{T}}\mathbf{t}]_\times$.

Table 9.1. *Summary of fundamental matrix properties.*

(iv) $\mathtt{F}$ has seven degrees of freedom: a 3×3 homogeneous matrix has eight independent ratios (there are nine elements, and the common scaling is not significant); however, $\mathtt{F}$ also satisfies the constraint $\det \mathtt{F} = 0$ which removes one degree of freedom.

(v) $\mathtt{F}$ is a *correlation*, a projective map taking a point to a line (see definition 2.29-(*p*59)). In this case a point in the first image $\mathbf{x}$ defines a line in the second $\mathbf{l}' = \mathtt{F}\mathbf{x}$, which is the epipolar line of $\mathbf{x}$. If $\mathbf{l}$ and $\mathbf{l}'$ are corresponding epipolar lines (see figure 9.6a) then any point $\mathbf{x}$ on $\mathbf{l}$ is mapped to the same line $\mathbf{l}'$. This means there is no inverse mapping, and $\mathtt{F}$ is not of full rank. For this reason, $\mathtt{F}$ is not a proper correlation (which would be invertible).

9.2.5 The epipolar line homography

The set of epipolar lines in each of the images forms a pencil of lines passing through the epipole. Such a pencil of lines may be considered as a 1-dimensional projective space. It is clear from figure 9.6b that corresponding epipolar lines are perspectively related, so that there is a homography between the pencil of epipolar lines centred at $\mathbf{e}$ in the first view, and the pencil centred at $\mathbf{e}'$ in the second. A homography between two such 1-dimensional projective spaces has 3 degrees of freedom.

The degrees of freedom of the fundamental matrix can thus be counted as follows: 2 for $\mathbf{e}$, 2 for $\mathbf{e}'$, and 3 for the epipolar line homography which maps a line through $\mathbf{e}$ to a line through $\mathbf{e}'$. A geometric representation of this homography is given in section 9.4. Here we give an explicit formula for this mapping.

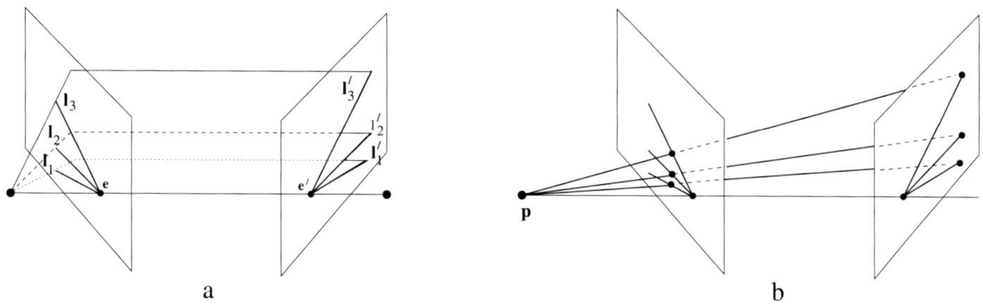

Fig. 9.6. **Epipolar line homography.** *(a) There is a pencil of epipolar lines in each image centred on the epipole. The correspondence between epipolar lines,* $\mathbf{l}_i \leftrightarrow \mathbf{l}'_i$, *is defined by the pencil of planes with axis the baseline. (b) The corresponding lines are related by a perspectivity with centre any point* $\mathbf{p}$ *on the baseline. It follows that the correspondence between epipolar lines in the pencils is a 1D homography.*

Result 9.5. *Suppose* $\mathbf{l}$ *and* $\mathbf{l}'$ *are corresponding epipolar lines, and* $\mathbf{k}$ *is any line not passing through the epipole* $\mathbf{e}$, *then* $\mathbf{l}$ *and* $\mathbf{l}'$ *are related by* $\mathbf{l}' = \mathtt{F}[\mathbf{k}]_\times \mathbf{l}$. *Symmetrically,* $\mathbf{l} = \mathtt{F}^\mathsf{T}[\mathbf{k}']_\times \mathbf{l}'$.

Proof. The expression $[\mathbf{k}]_\times \mathbf{l} = \mathbf{k} \times \mathbf{l}$ is the point of intersection of the two lines $\mathbf{k}$ and $\mathbf{l}$, and hence a point on the epipolar line $\mathbf{l}$ – call it $\mathbf{x}$. Hence, $\mathtt{F}[\mathbf{k}]_\times \mathbf{l} = \mathtt{F}\mathbf{x}$ is the epipolar line corresponding to the point $\mathbf{x}$, namely the line $\mathbf{l}'$. □

Furthermore a convenient choice for $\mathbf{k}$ is the line $\mathbf{e}$, since $\mathbf{k}^\mathsf{T}\mathbf{e} = \mathbf{e}^\mathsf{T}\mathbf{e} \neq 0$, so that the line $\mathbf{e}$ does not pass through the point $\mathbf{e}$ as is required. A similar argument holds for the choice of $\mathbf{k}' = \mathbf{e}'$. Thus the epipolar line homography may be written as

$$\mathbf{l}' = \mathtt{F}[\mathbf{e}]_\times \mathbf{l} \qquad \mathbf{l} = \mathtt{F}^\mathsf{T}[\mathbf{e}']_\times \mathbf{l}' \ .$$

9.3 Fundamental matrices arising from special motions

A special motion arises from a particular relationship between the translation direction, $\mathbf{t}$, and the direction of the rotation axis, $\mathbf{a}$. We will discuss two cases: *pure translation*, where there is no rotation; and *pure planar motion*, where $\mathbf{t}$ is orthogonal to $\mathbf{a}$ (the significance of the planar motion case is described in section 3.4.1(*p*77)). The 'pure' indicates that there is no change in the internal parameters. Such cases are important, firstly because they occur in practice, for example a camera viewing an object rotating on a turntable is equivalent to planar motion for pairs of views; and secondly because the fundamental matrix has a special form and thus additional properties.

9.3.1 Pure translation

In considering pure translations of the camera, one may consider the equivalent situation in which the camera is stationary, and the world undergoes a translation $-\mathbf{t}$. In this situation points in 3-space move on straight lines parallel to $\mathbf{t}$, and the imaged intersection of these parallel lines is the vanishing point $\mathbf{v}$ in the direction of $\mathbf{t}$. This is illustrated in figure 9.7 and figure 9.8. It is evident that $\mathbf{v}$ is the epipole for both views, and the imaged parallel lines are the epipolar lines. The algebraic details are given in the following example.

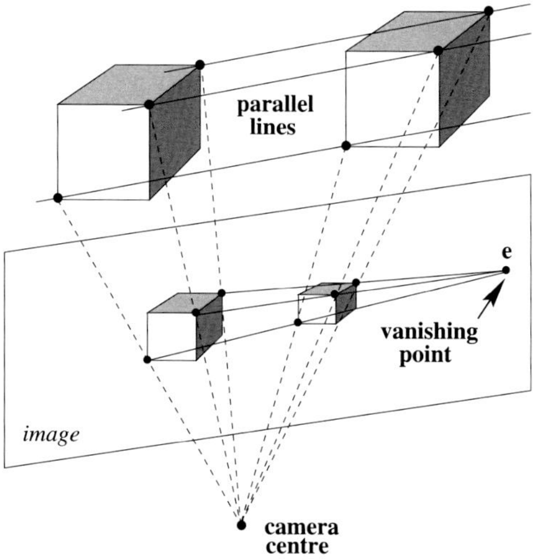

Fig. 9.7. *Under a pure translational camera motion, 3D points appear to slide along parallel rails. The images of these parallel lines intersect in a vanishing point corresponding to the translation direction. The epipole* $\mathbf{e}$ *is the vanishing point.*

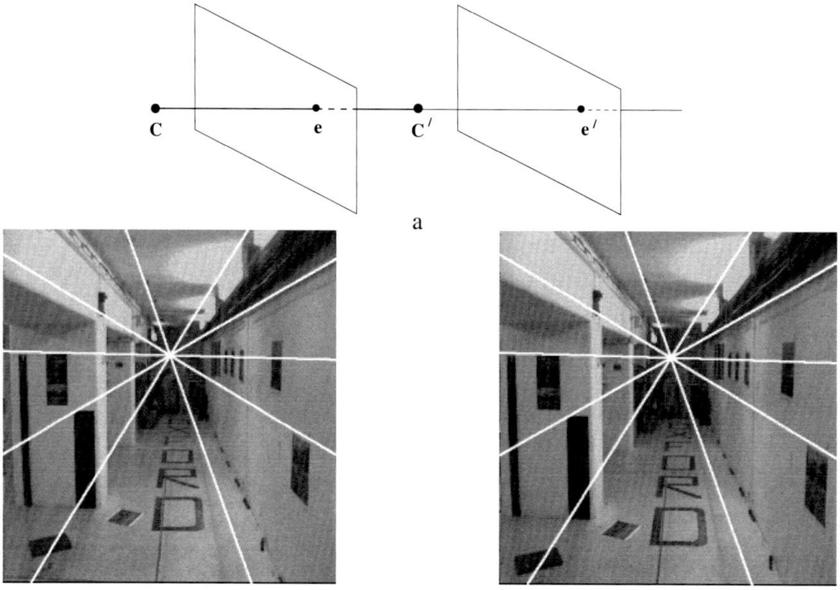

Fig. 9.8. **Pure translational motion.** *(a) under the motion the epipole is a fixed point, i.e. has the same coordinates in both images, and points appear to move along lines radiating from the epipole. The epipole in this case is termed the* Focus of Expansion *(FOE). (b) and (c) the same epipolar lines are overlaid in both cases. Note the motion of the posters on the wall which slide along the epipolar line.*

Example 9.6. Suppose the motion of the cameras is a pure translation with no rotation and no change in the internal parameters. One may assume that the two cameras are

$\mathtt{P} = \mathtt{K}[\mathtt{I} \mid \mathbf{0}]$ and $\mathtt{P}' = \mathtt{K}[\mathtt{I} \mid \mathbf{t}]$. Then from (9.4) (using $\mathtt{R} = \mathtt{I}$ and $\mathtt{K} = \mathtt{K}'$)

$$\mathtt{F} = [\mathbf{e}']_\times \mathtt{K}\mathtt{K}^{-1} = [\mathbf{e}']_\times.$$

If the camera translation is parallel to the x-axis, then $\mathbf{e}' = (1, 0, 0)^\mathsf{T}$, so

$$\mathtt{F} = \begin{bmatrix} 0 & 0 & 0 \\ 0 & 0 & -1 \\ 0 & 1 & 0 \end{bmatrix}.$$

The relation between corresponding points, $\mathbf{x}'^\mathsf{T}\mathtt{F}\mathbf{x} = 0$, reduces to $y = y'$, i.e. the epipolar lines are corresponding rasters. This is the situation that is sought by image rectification described in section 11.12(*p*302). △

Indeed if the image point $\mathbf{x}$ is normalized as $\mathbf{x} = (x, y, 1)^\mathsf{T}$, then from $\mathbf{x} = \mathtt{P}\mathbf{X} = \mathtt{K}[\mathtt{I} \mid \mathbf{0}]\mathbf{X}$, the space point's (inhomogeneous) coordinates are $(\mathtt{X}, \mathtt{Y}, \mathtt{Z})^\mathsf{T} = \mathtt{Z}\mathtt{K}^{-1}\mathbf{x}$, where $\mathtt{Z}$ is the depth of the point $\mathbf{X}$ (the distance of $\mathbf{X}$ from the camera centre measured along the principal axis of the first camera). It then follows from $\mathbf{x}' = \mathtt{P}'\mathbf{X} = \mathtt{K}[\mathtt{I} \mid \mathbf{t}]\mathbf{X}$ that the mapping from an image point $\mathbf{x}$ to an image point $\mathbf{x}'$ is

$$\mathbf{x}' = \mathbf{x} + \mathtt{K}\mathbf{t}/\mathtt{Z}. \tag{9.6}$$

The motion $\mathbf{x}' = \mathbf{x} + \mathtt{K}\mathbf{t}/\mathtt{Z}$ of (9.6) shows that the image point "starts" at $\mathbf{x}$ and then moves along the line defined by $\mathbf{x}$ and the epipole $\mathbf{e} = \mathbf{e}' = \mathbf{v}$. The extent of the motion depends on the magnitude of the translation $\mathbf{t}$ (which is not a homogeneous vector here) and the inverse depth $\mathtt{Z}$, so that points closer to the camera appear to move faster than those further away – a common experience when looking out of a train window.

Note that in this case of pure translation $\mathtt{F} = [\mathbf{e}']_\times$ is skew-symmetric and has only 2 degrees of freedom, which correspond to the position of the epipole. The epipolar line of $\mathbf{x}$ is $\mathbf{l}' = \mathtt{F}\mathbf{x} = [\mathbf{e}]_\times\mathbf{x}$, and $\mathbf{x}$ lies on this line since $\mathbf{x}^\mathsf{T}[\mathbf{e}]_\times\mathbf{x} = 0$, i.e. $\mathbf{x}$, $\mathbf{x}'$ and $\mathbf{e} = \mathbf{e}'$ are collinear (assuming both images are overlaid on top of each other). This collinearity property is termed *auto-epipolar*, and does not hold for general motion.

General motion. The pure translation case gives additional insight into the general motion case. Given two arbitrary cameras, we may rotate the camera used for the first image so that it is aligned with the second camera. This rotation may be simulated by applying a projective transformation to the first image. A further correction may be applied to the first image to account for any difference in the calibration matrices of the two images. The result of these two corrections is a projective transformation $\mathtt{H}$ of the first image. If one assumes these corrections to have been made, then the effective relationship of the two cameras to each other is that of a pure translation. Consequently, the fundamental matrix corresponding to the corrected first image and the second image is of the form $\hat{\mathtt{F}} = [\mathbf{e}']_\times$, satisfying $\mathbf{x}'^\mathsf{T}\hat{\mathtt{F}}\hat{\mathbf{x}} = 0$, where $\hat{\mathbf{x}} = \mathtt{H}\mathbf{x}$ is the corrected point in the first image. From this one deduces that $\mathbf{x}'^\mathsf{T}[\mathbf{e}']_\times\mathtt{H}\mathbf{x} = 0$, and so the fundamental matrix corresponding to the initial point correspondences $\mathbf{x} \leftrightarrow \mathbf{x}'$ is $\mathtt{F} = [\mathbf{e}']_\times\mathtt{H}$. This is illustrated in figure 9.9.

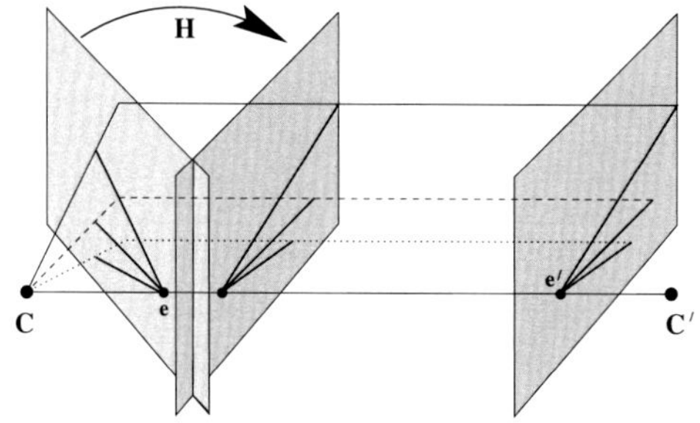

Fig. 9.9. **General camera motion.** *The first camera (on the left) may be rotated and corrected to simulate a pure translational motion. The fundamental matrix for the original pair is the product* $\mathtt{F} = [\mathbf{e}']_\times \mathtt{H}$, *where* $[\mathbf{e}']_\times$ *is the fundamental matrix of the translation, and* $\mathtt{H}$ *is the projective transformation corresponding to the correction of the first camera.*

Example 9.7. Continuing from example 9.2, assume again that the two cameras are $\mathtt{P} = \mathtt{K}[\mathtt{I} \mid \mathbf{0}]$ and $\mathtt{P}' = \mathtt{K}'[\mathtt{R} \mid \mathbf{t}]$. Then as described in section 8.4.2(*p*204) the requisite projective transformation is $\mathtt{H} = \mathtt{K}'\mathtt{R}\mathtt{K}^{-1} = \mathtt{H}_\infty$, where $\mathtt{H}_\infty$ is the infinite homography (see section 13.4(*p*338)), and $\mathtt{F} = [\mathbf{e}']_\times \mathtt{H}_\infty$.

If the image point $\mathbf{x}$ is normalized as $\mathbf{x} = (x, y, 1)^\mathsf{T}$, as in example 9.6, then $(\mathrm{X}, \mathrm{Y}, \mathrm{Z})^\mathsf{T} = \mathrm{Z}\mathtt{K}^{-1}\mathbf{x}$, and from $\mathbf{x} = \mathtt{P}'\mathbf{X} = \mathtt{K}'[\mathtt{R} \mid \mathbf{t}]\mathbf{X}$ the mapping from an image point $\mathbf{x}$ to an image point $\mathbf{x}'$ is

$$\mathbf{x}' = \mathtt{K}'\mathtt{R}\mathtt{K}^{-1}\mathbf{x} + \mathtt{K}'\mathbf{t}/\mathrm{Z}. \tag{9.7}$$

The mapping is in two parts: the first term depends on the image position alone, i.e. $\mathbf{x}$, but not the point's depth Z, and takes account of the camera rotation and change of internal parameters; the second term depends on the depth, but not on the image position $\mathbf{x}$, and takes account of camera translation. In the case of pure translation ($\mathtt{R} = \mathtt{I}, \mathtt{K} = \mathtt{K}'$) (9.7) reduces to (9.6). △

9.3.2 Pure planar motion

In this case the rotation axis is orthogonal to the translation direction. Orthogonality imposes one constraint on the motion, and it is shown in the exercises at the end of this chapter that if $\mathtt{K}' = \mathtt{K}$ then $\mathtt{F}_\mathrm{S}$, the symmetric part of $\mathtt{F}$, has rank 2 in this planar motion case (note, for a general motion the symmetric part of $\mathtt{F}$ has full rank). Thus, the condition that $\det \mathtt{F}_\mathrm{S} = 0$ is an additional constraint on $\mathtt{F}$ and reduces the number of degrees of freedom from 7, for a general motion, to 6 degrees of freedom for a pure planar motion.

9.4 Geometric representation of the fundamental matrix

This section is not essential for a first reading and the reader may optionally skip to section 9.5.

In this section the fundamental matrix is decomposed into its symmetric and skew-symmetric parts, and each part is given a geometric representation. The symmetric and skew-symmetric parts of the fundamental matrix are

$$\mathtt{F}_{\mathrm{S}} = \left(\mathtt{F} + \mathtt{F}^{\mathsf{T}}\right)/2 \qquad \mathtt{F}_{\mathrm{a}} = \left(\mathtt{F} - \mathtt{F}^{\mathsf{T}}\right)/2$$

so that $\mathtt{F} = \mathtt{F}_{\mathrm{S}} + \mathtt{F}_{\mathrm{a}}$.

To motivate the decomposition, consider the points $\mathbf{X}$ in 3-space that map to the same point in two images. These image points are fixed under the camera motion so that $\mathbf{x} = \mathbf{x}'$. Clearly such points are corresponding and thus satisfy $\mathbf{x}^{\mathsf{T}}\mathtt{F}\mathbf{x} = 0$, which is a necessary condition on corresponding points. Now, for any skew-symmetric matrix $\mathtt{A}$ the form $\mathbf{x}^{\mathsf{T}}\mathtt{A}\mathbf{x}$ is identically zero. Consequently only the symmetric part of $\mathtt{F}$ contributes to $\mathbf{x}^{\mathsf{T}}\mathtt{F}\mathbf{x} = 0$, which then reduces to $\mathbf{x}^{\mathsf{T}}\mathtt{F}_{\mathrm{S}}\mathbf{x} = 0$. As will be seen below the matrix $\mathtt{F}_{\mathrm{S}}$ may be thought of as a conic in the image plane.

Geometrically the conic arises as follows. The locus of all points in 3-space for which $\mathbf{x} = \mathbf{x}'$ is known as the *horopter* curve. Generally this is a twisted cubic curve in 3-space (see section 3.3(*p*75)) passing through the two camera centres [Maybank-93]. The image of the horopter is the conic defined by $\mathtt{F}_{\mathrm{S}}$. We return to the horopter in chapter 22.

Symmetric part. The matrix $\mathtt{F}_{\mathrm{S}}$ is symmetric and is of rank 3 in general. It has 5 degrees of freedom and is identified with a point conic, called the *Steiner conic* (the name is explained below). The epipoles $\mathbf{e}$ and $\mathbf{e}'$ lie on the conic $\mathtt{F}_{\mathrm{S}}$. To see that the epipoles lie on the conic, i.e. that $\mathbf{e}^{\mathsf{T}}\mathtt{F}_{\mathrm{S}}\mathbf{e} = 0$, start from $\mathtt{F}\mathbf{e} = \mathbf{0}$. Then $\mathbf{e}^{\mathsf{T}}\mathtt{F}\mathbf{e} = \mathbf{0}$ and so $\mathbf{e}^{\mathsf{T}}\mathtt{F}_{\mathrm{S}}\mathbf{e} + \mathbf{e}^{\mathsf{T}}\mathtt{F}_{\mathrm{a}}\mathbf{e} = 0$. However, $\mathbf{e}^{\mathsf{T}}\mathtt{F}_{\mathrm{a}}\mathbf{e} = 0$, since for any skew-symmetric matrix $\mathtt{S}$, $\mathbf{x}^{\mathsf{T}}\mathtt{S}\mathbf{x} = 0$. Thus $\mathbf{e}^{\mathsf{T}}\mathtt{F}_{\mathrm{S}}\mathbf{e} = 0$. The derivation for $\mathbf{e}'$ follows in a similar manner.

Skew-symmetric part. The matrix $\mathtt{F}_{\mathrm{a}}$ is skew-symmetric and may be written as $\mathtt{F}_{\mathrm{a}} = [\mathbf{x}_{\mathrm{a}}]_{\times}$, where $\mathbf{x}_{\mathrm{a}}$ is the null-vector of $\mathtt{F}_{\mathrm{a}}$. The skew-symmetric part has 2 degrees of freedom and is identified with the point $\mathbf{x}_{\mathrm{a}}$.

The relation between the point $\mathbf{x}_{\mathrm{a}}$ and conic $\mathtt{F}_{\mathrm{S}}$ is shown in figure 9.10a. The polar of $\mathbf{x}_{\mathrm{a}}$ intersects the Steiner conic $\mathtt{F}_{\mathrm{S}}$ at the epipoles $\mathbf{e}$ and $\mathbf{e}'$ (the pole–polar relation is described in section 2.2.3(*p*30)). The proof of this result is left as an exercise.

Epipolar line correspondence. It is a classical theorem of projective geometry due to Steiner [Semple-79] that for two line pencils related by a homography, the locus of intersections of corresponding lines is a conic. This is precisely the situation here. The pencils are the epipolar pencils, one through $\mathbf{e}$ and the other through $\mathbf{e}'$. The epipolar lines are related by a 1D homography as described in section 9.2.5. The locus of intersection is the conic $\mathtt{F}_{\mathrm{S}}$.

The conic and epipoles enable epipolar lines to be determined by a geometric construction as illustrated in figure 9.10b. This construction is based on the fixed point property of the Steiner conic $\mathtt{F}_{\mathrm{S}}$. The epipolar line $\mathbf{l} = \mathbf{x} \times \mathbf{e}$ in the first view defines an epipolar plane in 3-space which intersects the horopter in a point, which we will call $\mathbf{X}_{\mathrm{c}}$. The point $\mathbf{X}_{\mathrm{c}}$ is imaged in the first view at $\mathbf{x}_{\mathrm{c}}$, which is the point at which $\mathbf{l}$ intersects the conic $\mathtt{F}_{\mathrm{S}}$ (since $\mathtt{F}_{\mathrm{S}}$ is the image of the horopter). Now the image of $\mathbf{X}_{\mathrm{c}}$ is also $\mathbf{x}_{\mathrm{c}}$ in the second view due to the fixed-point property of the horopter. So $\mathbf{x}_{\mathrm{c}}$ is the

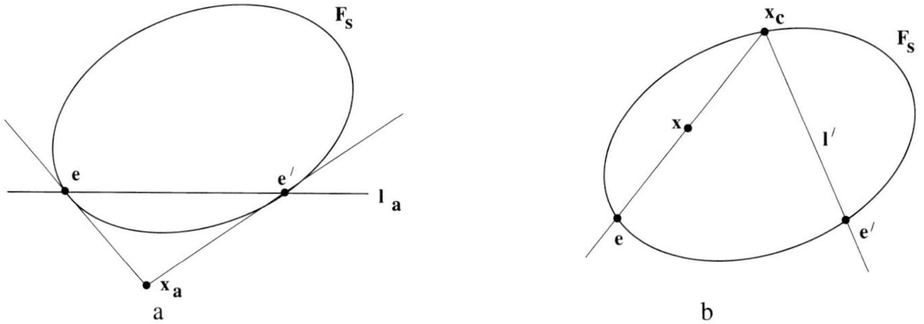

Fig. 9.10. **Geometric representation of** $\mathtt{F}$. *(a) The conic* $\mathtt{F_S}$ *represents the symmetric part of* $\mathtt{F}$*, and the point* $\mathbf{x_a}$ *the skew-symmetric part. The conic* $\mathtt{F_S}$ *is the locus of intersection of corresponding epipolar lines, assuming both images are overlaid on top of each other. It is the image of the horopter curve. The line* $\mathbf{l_a}$ *is the polar of* $\mathbf{x_a}$ *with respect to the conic* $\mathtt{F_S}$*. It intersects the conic at the epipoles* $\mathbf{e}$ *and* $\mathbf{e}'$*. (b) The epipolar line* $\mathbf{l}'$ *corresponding to a point* $\mathbf{x}$ *is constructed as follows: intersect the line defined by the points* $\mathbf{e}$ *and* $\mathbf{x}$ *with the conic. This intersection point is* $\mathbf{x}_c$*. Then* $\mathbf{l}'$ *is the line defined by the points* $\mathbf{x}_c$ *and* $\mathbf{e}'$*.*

image in the second view of a point on the epipolar plane of $\mathbf{x}$. It follows that $\mathbf{x}_c$ lies on the epipolar line $\mathbf{l}'$ of $\mathbf{x}$, and consequently $\mathbf{l}'$ may be computed as $\mathbf{l}' = \mathbf{x}_c \times \mathbf{e}'$.

The conic together with two points on the conic account for the 7 degrees of freedom of $\mathtt{F}$: 5 degrees of freedom for the conic and one each to specify the two epipoles on the conic. Given $\mathtt{F}$, then the conic $\mathtt{F_S}$, epipoles $\mathbf{e}, \mathbf{e}'$ and skew-symmetric point $\mathbf{x_a}$ are defined uniquely. However, $\mathtt{F_S}$ and $\mathbf{x_a}$ do not uniquely determine $\mathtt{F}$ since the identity of the epipoles is not recovered, i.e. the polar of $\mathbf{x_a}$ determines the epipoles but does not determine which one is $\mathbf{e}$ and which one $\mathbf{e}'$.

9.4.1 Pure planar motion

We return to the case of planar motion discussed above in section 9.3.2, where $\mathtt{F_S}$ has rank 2. It is evident that in this case the Steiner conic is degenerate and from section 2.2.3(*p*30) is equivalent to two non-coincident lines:

$$\mathtt{F_S} = \mathbf{l}_h \mathbf{l}_s^\mathsf{T} + \mathbf{l}_s \mathbf{l}_h^\mathsf{T}$$

as depicted in figure 9.11a. The geometric construction of the epipolar line $\mathbf{l}'$ corresponding to a point $\mathbf{x}$ of section 9.4 has a simple algebraic representation in this case. As in the general motion case, there are three steps, illustrated in figure 9.11b: first the line $\mathbf{l} = \mathbf{e} \times \mathbf{x}$ joining $\mathbf{e}$ and $\mathbf{x}$ is computed; second, its intersection point with the "conic" $\mathbf{x}_c = \mathbf{l}_s \times \mathbf{l}$ is determined; third the epipolar line $\mathbf{l}' = \mathbf{e}' \times \mathbf{x}_c$ is the join of $\mathbf{x}_c$ and $\mathbf{e}'$. Putting these steps together we find

$$\mathbf{l}' = \mathbf{e}' \times [\mathbf{l}_s \times (\mathbf{e} \times \mathbf{x})] = [\mathbf{e}']_\times [\mathbf{l}_s]_\times [\mathbf{e}]_\times \mathbf{x}.$$

It follows that $\mathtt{F}$ may be written as

$$\mathtt{F} = [\mathbf{e}']_\times [\mathbf{l}_s]_\times [\mathbf{e}]_\times. \tag{9.8}$$

The 6 degrees of freedom of $\mathtt{F}$ are accounted for as 2 degrees of freedom for each of the two epipoles and 2 degrees of freedom for the line.

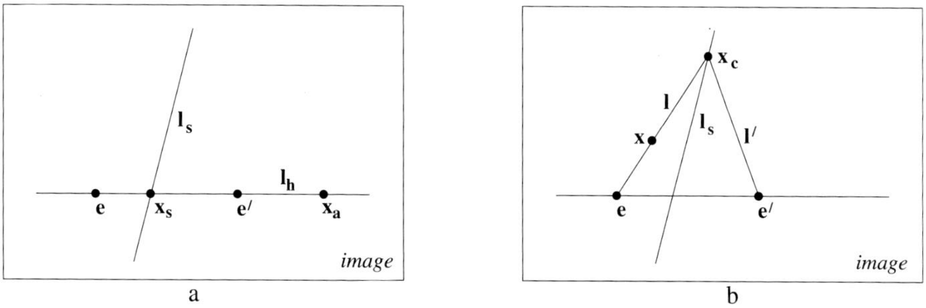

Fig. 9.11. **Geometric representation of F for planar motion.** *(a) The lines $\mathbf{l}_s$ and $\mathbf{l}_h$ constitute the Steiner conic for this motion, which is degenerate. Compare this figure with the conic for general motion shown in figure 9.10. (b) The epipolar line $\mathbf{l}'$ corresponding to a point $\mathbf{x}$ is constructed as follows: intersect the line defined by the points $\mathbf{e}$ and $\mathbf{x}$ with the (conic) line $\mathbf{l}_s$. This intersection point is $\mathbf{x}_c$. Then $\mathbf{l}'$ is the line defined by the points $\mathbf{x}_c$ and $\mathbf{e}'$.*

The geometry of this situation can be easily visualized: the horopter for this motion is a degenerate twisted cubic consisting of a circle in the plane of the motion (the plane orthogonal to the rotation axis and containing the camera centres), and a line parallel to the rotation axis and intersecting the circle. The line is the screw axis (see section 3.4.1(*p*77)). The motion is equivalent to a rotation about the screw axis with zero translation. Under this motion points on the screw axis are fixed, and consequently their images are fixed. The line $\mathbf{l}_s$ is the image of the screw axis. The line $\mathbf{l}_h$ is the intersection of the image with the plane of the motion. This geometry is used for auto-calibration in chapter 19.

9.5 Retrieving the camera matrices

To this point we have examined the properties of F and of image relations for a point correspondence $\mathbf{x} \leftrightarrow \mathbf{x}'$. We now turn to one of the most significant properties of F, that the matrix may be used to determine the camera matrices of the two views.

9.5.1 Projective invariance and canonical cameras

It is evident from the derivations of section 9.2 that the map $\mathbf{l}' = \mathtt{F}\mathbf{x}$ and the correspondence condition $\mathbf{x}'^{\mathsf{T}}\mathtt{F}\mathbf{x} = 0$ are *projective* relationships: the derivations have involved only projective geometric relationships, such as the intersection of lines and planes, and in the algebraic development only the linear mapping of the projective camera between world and image points. Consequently, the relationships depend only on projective coordinates in the image, and not, for example on Euclidean measurements such as the angle between rays. In other words the image relationships are projectively invariant: under a projective transformation of the image coordinates $\hat{\mathbf{x}} = \mathtt{H}\mathbf{x}, \hat{\mathbf{x}}' = \mathtt{H}'\mathbf{x}'$, there is a corresponding map $\hat{\mathbf{l}}' = \hat{\mathtt{F}}\hat{\mathbf{x}}$ with $\hat{\mathtt{F}} = \mathtt{H}'^{-\mathsf{T}}\mathtt{F}\mathtt{H}^{-1}$ the corresponding rank 2 fundamental matrix.

Similarly, F only depends on projective properties of the cameras P, P'. The camera matrix relates 3-space measurements to image measurements and so depends on both the image coordinate frame and the choice of world coordinate frame. F does not depend on the choice of world frame, for example a rotation of world coordinates changes $\mathtt{P}, \mathtt{P}'$, but not $\mathtt{F}$. In fact, the fundamental matrix is unchanged by a projective transformation of 3-space. More precisely,

Result 9.8. *If $\mathtt{H}$ is a 4×4 matrix representing a projective transformation of 3-space, then the fundamental matrices corresponding to the pairs of camera matrices $(\mathtt{P}, \mathtt{P}')$ and $(\mathtt{PH}, \mathtt{P}'\mathtt{H})$ are the same.*

Proof. Observe that $\mathtt{P}\mathbf{X} = (\mathtt{PH})(\mathtt{H}^{-1}\mathbf{X})$, and similarly for $\mathtt{P}'$. Thus if $\mathbf{x} \leftrightarrow \mathbf{x}'$ are matched points with respect to the pair of cameras $(\mathtt{P}, \mathtt{P}')$, corresponding to a 3D point $\mathbf{X}$, then they are also matched points with respect to the pair of cameras $(\mathtt{PH}, \mathtt{P}'\mathtt{H})$, corresponding to the point $\mathtt{H}^{-1}\mathbf{X}$. $\square$

Thus, although from (9.1–*p*244) a pair of camera matrices $(\mathtt{P}, \mathtt{P}')$ uniquely determine a fundamental matrix $\mathtt{F}$, the converse is not true. The fundamental matrix determines the pair of camera matrices at best up to right-multiplication by a 3D projective transformation. It will be seen below that this is the full extent of the ambiguity, and indeed the camera matrices are determined up to a projective transformation by the fundamental matrix.

Canonical form of camera matrices. Given this ambiguity, it is common to define a specific *canonical form* for the pair of camera matrices corresponding to a given fundamental matrix in which the first matrix is of the simple form $[\mathtt{I} \mid \mathbf{0}]$, where $\mathtt{I}$ is the 3×3 identity matrix and $\mathbf{0}$ a null 3-vector. To see that this is always possible, let $\mathtt{P}$ be augmented by one row to make a 4×4 non-singular matrix, denoted $\mathtt{P}^*$. Now letting $\mathtt{H} = \mathtt{P}^{*-1}$, one verifies that $\mathtt{PH} = [\mathtt{I} \mid \mathbf{0}]$ as desired.

The following result is very frequently used

Result 9.9. *The fundamental matrix corresponding to a pair of camera matrices $\mathtt{P} = [\mathtt{I} \mid \mathbf{0}]$ and $\mathtt{P}' = [\mathtt{M} \mid \mathbf{m}]$ is equal to $[\mathbf{m}]_\times \mathtt{M}$.*

This is easily derived as a special case of (9.1–*p*244).

9.5.2 Projective ambiguity of cameras given F

It has been seen that a pair of camera matrices determines a unique fundamental matrix. This mapping is not injective (one-to-one) however, since pairs of camera matrices that differ by a projective transformation give rise to the same fundamental matrix. It will now be shown that this is the only ambiguity. We will show that a given fundamental matrix determines the pair of camera matrices up to right multiplication by a projective transformation. Thus, the fundamental matrix captures the projective relationship of the two cameras.

Theorem 9.10. *Let $\mathtt{F}$ be a fundamental matrix and let $(\mathtt{P}, \mathtt{P}')$ and $(\tilde{\mathtt{P}}, \tilde{\mathtt{P}}')$ be two pairs of camera matrices such that $\mathtt{F}$ is the fundamental matrix corresponding to each of these pairs. Then there exists a non-singular 4×4 matrix $\mathtt{H}$ such that $\tilde{\mathtt{P}} = \mathtt{PH}$ and $\tilde{\mathtt{P}}' = \mathtt{P}'\mathtt{H}$.*

Proof. Suppose that a given fundamental matrix $\mathtt{F}$ corresponds to two different pairs of camera matrices $(\mathtt{P}, \mathtt{P}')$ and $(\tilde{\mathtt{P}}, \tilde{\mathtt{P}}')$. As a first step, we may simplify the problem by assuming that each of the two pair of camera matrices is in canonical form with $\mathtt{P} = \tilde{\mathtt{P}} = [\mathtt{I} \mid \mathbf{0}]$, since this may be done by applying projective transformations to each pair as necessary. Thus, suppose that $\mathtt{P} = \tilde{\mathtt{P}} = [\mathtt{I} \mid \mathbf{0}]$ and that $\mathtt{P}' = [\mathtt{A} \mid \mathbf{a}]$ and $\tilde{\mathtt{P}}' = [\tilde{\mathtt{A}} \mid \tilde{\mathbf{a}}]$. According to result 9.9 the fundamental matrix may then be written $\mathtt{F} = [\mathbf{a}]_\times \mathtt{A} = [\tilde{\mathbf{a}}]_\times \tilde{\mathtt{A}}$.
We will need the following lemma:

Lemma 9.11. *Suppose the rank 2 matrix* $\mathtt{F}$ *can be decomposed in two different ways as* $\mathtt{F} = [\mathbf{a}]_\times \mathtt{A}$ *and* $\mathtt{F} = [\tilde{\mathbf{a}}]_\times \tilde{\mathtt{A}}$*; then* $\tilde{\mathbf{a}} = k\mathbf{a}$ *and* $\tilde{\mathtt{A}} = k^{-1}(\mathtt{A} + \mathbf{a}\mathbf{v}^\mathsf{T})$ *for some non-zero constant* k *and 3-vector* $\mathbf{v}$.

Proof. First, note that $\mathbf{a}^\mathsf{T}\mathtt{F} = \mathbf{a}^\mathsf{T}[\mathbf{a}]_\times \mathtt{A} = \mathbf{0}$, and similarly, $\tilde{\mathbf{a}}^\mathsf{T}\mathtt{F} = \mathbf{0}$. Since $\mathtt{F}$ has rank 2, it follows that $\tilde{\mathbf{a}} = k\mathbf{a}$ as required. Next, from $[\mathbf{a}]_\times \mathtt{A} = [\tilde{\mathbf{a}}]_\times \tilde{\mathtt{A}}$ it follows that $[\mathbf{a}]_\times \left(k\tilde{\mathtt{A}} - \mathtt{A}\right) = 0$, and so $k\tilde{\mathtt{A}} - \mathtt{A} = \mathbf{a}\mathbf{v}^\mathsf{T}$ for some $\mathbf{v}$. Hence, $\tilde{\mathtt{A}} = k^{-1}(\mathtt{A} + \mathbf{a}\mathbf{v}^\mathsf{T})$ as required. □

Applying this result to the two camera matrices $\mathtt{P}'$ and $\tilde{\mathtt{P}}'$ shows that $\mathtt{P}' = [\mathtt{A} \mid \mathbf{a}]$ and $\tilde{\mathtt{P}}' = [k^{-1}(\mathtt{A}+\mathbf{a}\mathbf{v}^\mathsf{T}) \mid k\mathbf{a}]$ if they are to generate the same $\mathtt{F}$. It only remains now to show that these camera pairs are projectively related. Let $\mathtt{H}$ be the matrix $\mathtt{H} = \begin{bmatrix} k^{-1}\mathtt{I} & \mathbf{0} \\ k^{-1}\mathbf{v}^\mathsf{T} & k \end{bmatrix}$.
Then one verifies that $\mathtt{PH} = k^{-1}[\mathtt{I} \mid \mathbf{0}] = k^{-1}\tilde{\mathtt{P}}$, and furthermore,

$$\mathtt{P}'\mathtt{H} = [\mathtt{A} \mid \mathbf{a}]\mathtt{H} = [k^{-1}(\mathtt{A} + \mathbf{a}\mathbf{v}^\mathsf{T}) \mid k\mathbf{a}] = [\tilde{\mathtt{A}} \mid \tilde{\mathbf{a}}] = \tilde{\mathtt{P}}'$$

so that the pairs $\mathtt{P}, \mathtt{P}'$ and $\tilde{\mathtt{P}}, \tilde{\mathtt{P}}'$ are indeed projectively related. □

This can be tied precisely to a counting argument: the two cameras $\mathtt{P}$ and $\mathtt{P}'$ each have 11 degrees of freedom, making a total of 22 degrees of freedom. To specify a projective world frame requires 15 degrees of freedom (section 3.1(*p*65)), so once the degrees of freedom of the world frame are removed from the two cameras $22 - 15 = 7$ degrees of freedom remain – which corresponds to the 7 degrees of freedom of the fundamental matrix.

9.5.3 Canonical cameras given F

We have shown that $\mathtt{F}$ determines the camera pair up to a projective transformation of 3-space. We will now derive a specific formula for a pair of cameras with canonical form given $\mathtt{F}$. We will make use of the following characterization of the fundamental matrix $\mathtt{F}$ corresponding to a pair of camera matrices:

Result 9.12. *A non-zero matrix* $\mathtt{F}$ *is the fundamental matrix corresponding to a pair of camera matrices* $\mathtt{P}$ *and* $\mathtt{P}'$ *if and only if* $\mathtt{P}'^\mathsf{T}\mathtt{F}\mathtt{P}$ *is skew-symmetric.*

Proof. The condition that $\mathtt{P}'^\mathsf{T}\mathtt{F}\mathtt{P}$ is skew-symmetric is equivalent to $\mathbf{X}^\mathsf{T}\mathtt{P}'^\mathsf{T}\mathtt{F}\mathtt{P}\mathbf{X} = 0$ for all $\mathbf{X}$. Setting $\mathbf{x}' = \mathtt{P}'\mathbf{X}$ and $\mathbf{x} = \mathtt{P}\mathbf{X}$, this is equivalent to $\mathbf{x}'^\mathsf{T}\mathtt{F}\mathbf{x} = 0$, which is the defining equation for the fundamental matrix. □

One may write down a particular solution for the pairs of camera matrices in canonical form that correspond to a fundamental matrix as follows:

Result 9.13. *Let $\mathtt{F}$ be a fundamental matrix and $\mathtt{S}$ any skew-symmetric matrix. Define the pair of camera matrices*

$$\mathtt{P} = [\mathtt{I} \mid \mathbf{0}] \quad \textit{and} \quad \mathtt{P}' = [\mathtt{SF} \mid \mathbf{e}'],$$

where $\mathbf{e}'$ is the epipole such that $\mathbf{e}'^{\mathsf{T}}\mathtt{F} = \mathbf{0}$, and assume that $\mathtt{P}'$ so defined is a valid camera matrix (has rank 3). Then $\mathtt{F}$ is the fundamental matrix corresponding to the pair $(\mathtt{P}, \mathtt{P}')$.

To demonstrate this, we invoke result 9.12 and simply verify that

$$[\mathtt{SF} \mid \mathbf{e}']^{\mathsf{T}}\mathtt{F}[\mathtt{I} \mid \mathbf{0}] = \begin{bmatrix} \mathtt{F}^{\mathsf{T}}\mathtt{S}^{\mathsf{T}}\mathtt{F} & \mathbf{0} \\ \mathbf{e}'^{\mathsf{T}}\mathtt{F} & 0 \end{bmatrix} = \begin{bmatrix} \mathtt{F}^{\mathsf{T}}\mathtt{S}^{\mathsf{T}}\mathtt{F} & \mathbf{0} \\ \mathbf{0}^{\mathsf{T}} & 0 \end{bmatrix} \tag{9.9}$$

which is skew-symmetric.

The skew-symmetric matrix $\mathtt{S}$ may be written in terms of its null-vector as $\mathtt{S} = [\mathbf{s}]_\times$. Then $[[\mathbf{s}]_\times\mathtt{F} \mid \mathbf{e}']$ has rank 3 provided $\mathbf{s}^{\mathsf{T}}\mathbf{e}' \neq 0$, according to the following argument. Since $\mathbf{e}'\mathtt{F} = \mathbf{0}$, the column space (span of the columns) of $\mathtt{F}$ is perpendicular to $\mathbf{e}'$. But if $\mathbf{s}^{\mathsf{T}}\mathbf{e}' \neq 0$, then $\mathbf{s}$ is not perpendicular to $\mathbf{e}'$, and hence not in the column space of $\mathtt{F}$. Now, the column space of $[\mathbf{s}]_\times\mathtt{F}$ is spanned by the cross-products of $\mathbf{s}$ with the columns of $\mathtt{F}$, and therefore equals the plane perpendicular to $\mathbf{s}$. So $[\mathbf{s}]_\times\mathtt{F}$ has rank 2. Since $\mathbf{e}'$ is not perpendicular to $\mathbf{s}$, it does not lie in this plane, and so $[[\mathbf{s}]_\times\mathtt{F} \mid \mathbf{e}']$ has rank 3, as required.

As suggested by Luong and Viéville [Luong-96] a good choice for $\mathtt{S}$ is $\mathtt{S} = [\mathbf{e}']_\times$, for in this case $\mathbf{e}'^{\mathsf{T}}\mathbf{e}' \neq 0$, which leads to the following useful result.

Result 9.14. *The camera matrices corresponding to a fundamental matrix $\mathtt{F}$ may be chosen as $\mathtt{P} = [\mathtt{I} \mid \mathbf{0}]$ and $\mathtt{P}' = [[\mathbf{e}']_\times\mathtt{F} \mid \mathbf{e}']$.*

Note that the camera matrix $\mathtt{P}'$ has left 3×3 submatrix $[\mathbf{e}']_\times\mathtt{F}$ which has rank 2. This corresponds to a camera with centre on $\boldsymbol{\pi}_\infty$. However, there is no particular reason to avoid this situation.

The proof of theorem 9.10 shows that the four parameter family of camera pairs in canonical form $\tilde{\mathtt{P}} = [\mathtt{I} \mid \mathbf{0}]$, $\tilde{\mathtt{P}}' = [\mathtt{A} + \mathbf{a}\mathbf{v}^{\mathsf{T}} \mid k\mathbf{a}]$ have the same fundamental matrix as the canonical pair, $\mathtt{P} = [\mathtt{I} \mid \mathbf{0}]$, $\mathtt{P}' = [\mathtt{A} \mid \mathbf{a}]$; and that this is the most general solution. To summarize:

Result 9.15. *The general formula for a pair of canonic camera matrices corresponding to a fundamental matrix $\mathtt{F}$ is given by*

$$\mathtt{P} = [\mathtt{I} \mid \mathbf{0}] \quad \mathtt{P}' = [[\mathbf{e}']_\times\mathtt{F} + \mathbf{e}'\mathbf{v}^{\mathsf{T}} \mid \lambda\mathbf{e}'] \tag{9.10}$$

where $\mathbf{v}$ is any 3-vector, and λ a non-zero scalar.

9.6 The essential matrix

The essential matrix is the specialization of the fundamental matrix to the case of normalized image coordinates (see below). Historically, the essential matrix was introduced (by Longuet-Higgins) before the fundamental matrix, and the fundamental matrix may be thought of as the generalization of the essential matrix in which the (inessential) assumption of calibrated cameras is removed. The essential matrix has fewer degrees of freedom, and additional properties, compared to the fundamental matrix. These properties are described below.

Normalized coordinates. Consider a camera matrix decomposed as $\mathtt{P} = \mathtt{K}[\mathtt{R} \mid \mathbf{t}]$, and let $\mathbf{x} = \mathtt{P}\mathbf{X}$ be a point in the image. If the calibration matrix $\mathtt{K}$ is known, then we may apply its inverse to the point $\mathbf{x}$ to obtain the point $\hat{\mathbf{x}} = \mathtt{K}^{-1}\mathbf{x}$. Then $\hat{\mathbf{x}} = [\mathtt{R} \mid \mathbf{t}]\mathbf{X}$, where $\hat{\mathbf{x}}$ is the image point expressed in *normalized coordinates*. It may be thought of as the image of the point $\mathbf{X}$ with respect to a camera $[\mathtt{R} \mid \mathbf{t}]$ having the identity matrix $\mathtt{I}$ as calibration matrix. The camera matrix $\mathtt{K}^{-1}\mathtt{P} = [\mathtt{R} \mid \mathbf{t}]$ is called a *normalized camera matrix*, the effect of the known calibration matrix having been removed.

Now, consider a pair of normalized camera matrices $\mathtt{P} = [\mathtt{I} \mid \mathbf{0}]$ and $\mathtt{P}' = [\mathtt{R} \mid \mathbf{t}]$. The fundamental matrix corresponding to the pair of normalized cameras is customarily called the *essential matrix*, and according to (9.2–*p*244) it has the form

$$\mathtt{E} = [\mathbf{t}]_\times \mathtt{R} = \mathtt{R}\left[\mathtt{R}^\mathsf{T}\mathbf{t}\right]_\times .$$

Definition 9.16. The defining equation for the essential matrix is

$$\hat{\mathbf{x}}'^\mathsf{T}\mathtt{E}\hat{\mathbf{x}} = 0 \tag{9.11}$$

in terms of the normalized image coordinates for corresponding points $\mathbf{x} \leftrightarrow \mathbf{x}'$.

Substituting for $\hat{\mathbf{x}}$ and $\hat{\mathbf{x}}'$ gives $\mathbf{x}'^\mathsf{T}\mathtt{K}'^{-\mathsf{T}}\mathtt{E}\mathtt{K}^{-1}\mathbf{x} = 0$. Comparing this with the relation $\mathbf{x}'^\mathsf{T}\mathtt{F}\mathbf{x} = 0$ for the fundamental matrix, it follows that the relationship between the fundamental and essential matrices is

$$\mathtt{E} = \mathtt{K}'^\mathsf{T}\mathtt{F}\mathtt{K}. \tag{9.12}$$

9.6.1 Properties of the essential matrix

The essential matrix, $\mathtt{E} = [\mathbf{t}]_\times\mathtt{R}$, has only five degrees of freedom: both the rotation matrix $\mathtt{R}$ and the translation $\mathbf{t}$ have three degrees of freedom, but there is an overall scale ambiguity – like the fundamental matrix, the essential matrix is a homogeneous quantity.

The reduced number of degrees of freedom translates into extra constraints that are satisfied by an essential matrix, compared with a fundamental matrix. We investigate what these constraints are.

Result 9.17. *A 3×3 matrix is an essential matrix if and only if two of its singular values are equal, and the third is zero.*

Proof. This is easily deduced from the decomposition of $\mathtt{E}$ as $[\mathbf{t}]_\times \mathtt{R} = \mathtt{SR}$, where $\mathtt{S}$ is skew-symmetric. We will use the matrices

$$\mathtt{W} = \begin{bmatrix} 0 & -1 & 0 \\ 1 & 0 & 0 \\ 0 & 0 & 1 \end{bmatrix} \quad \text{and} \quad \mathtt{Z} = \begin{bmatrix} 0 & 1 & 0 \\ -1 & 0 & 0 \\ 0 & 0 & 0 \end{bmatrix}. \tag{9.13}$$

It may be verified that $\mathtt{W}$ is orthogonal and $\mathtt{Z}$ is skew-symmetric. From Result A4.1-(*p*581), which gives a block decomposition of a general skew-symmetric matrix, the 3×3 skew-symmetric matrix $\mathtt{S}$ may be written as $\mathtt{S} = k\mathtt{UZU}^\mathsf{T}$ where $\mathtt{U}$ is orthogonal. Noting that, up to sign, $\mathtt{Z} = \mathrm{diag}(1,1,0)\mathtt{W}$, then up to scale, $\mathtt{S} = \mathtt{U}\,\mathrm{diag}(1,1,0)\mathtt{WU}^\mathsf{T}$, and $\mathtt{E} = \mathtt{SR} = \mathtt{U}\,\mathrm{diag}(1,1,0)(\mathtt{WU}^\mathsf{T}\mathtt{R})$. This is a singular value decomposition of $\mathtt{E}$ with two equal singular values, as required. Conversely, a matrix with two equal singular values may be factored as $\mathtt{SR}$ in this way. □

Since $\mathtt{E} = \mathtt{U}\,\mathrm{diag}(1,1,0)\mathtt{V}^\mathsf{T}$, it may seem that $\mathtt{E}$ has six degrees of freedom and not five, since both $\mathtt{U}$ and $\mathtt{V}$ have three degrees of freedom. However, because the two singular values are equal, the SVD is not unique – in fact there is a one-parameter family of SVDs for $\mathtt{E}$. Indeed, an alternative SVD is given by $\mathtt{E} = (\mathtt{U}\,\mathrm{diag}(\mathtt{R}_{2\times 2}, 1))\,\mathrm{diag}(1,1,0)(\mathrm{diag}(\mathtt{R}_{2\times 2}^\mathsf{T}, 1))\mathtt{V}^\mathsf{T}$ for any 2×2 rotation matrix $\mathtt{R}$.

9.6.2 Extraction of cameras from the essential matrix

The essential matrix may be computed directly from (9.11) using normalized image coordinates, or else computed from the fundamental matrix using (9.12). (Methods of computing the fundamental matrix are deferred to chapter 11). Once the essential matrix is known, the camera matrices may be retrieved from $\mathtt{E}$ as will be described next. In contrast with the fundamental matrix case, where there is a projective ambiguity, the camera matrices may be retrieved from the essential matrix up to scale and a four-fold ambiguity. That is there are four possible solutions, except for overall scale, which cannot be determined.

We may assume that the first camera matrix is $\mathtt{P} = [\mathtt{I} \mid \mathbf{0}]$. In order to compute the second camera matrix, $\mathtt{P}'$, it is necessary to factor $\mathtt{E}$ into the product $\mathtt{SR}$ of a skew-symmetric matrix and a rotation matrix.

Result 9.18. *Suppose that the SVD of* $\mathtt{E}$ *is* $\mathtt{U}\,\mathrm{diag}(1,1,0)\mathtt{V}^\mathsf{T}$. *Using the notation of (9.13), there are (ignoring signs) two possible factorizations* $\mathtt{E} = \mathtt{SR}$ *as follows:*

$$\mathtt{S} = \mathtt{UZU}^\mathsf{T} \quad \mathtt{R} = \mathtt{UWV}^\mathsf{T} \;\; or \;\; \mathtt{UW}^\mathsf{T}\mathtt{V}^\mathsf{T}. \tag{9.14}$$

Proof. That the given factorization is valid is true by inspection. That there are no other factorizations is shown as follows. Suppose $\mathtt{E} = \mathtt{SR}$. The form of $\mathtt{S}$ is determined by the fact that its left null-space is the same as that of $\mathtt{E}$. Hence $\mathtt{S} = \mathtt{UZU}^\mathsf{T}$. The rotation $\mathtt{R}$ may be written as $\mathtt{UXV}^\mathsf{T}$, where $\mathtt{X}$ is some rotation matrix. Then

$$\mathtt{U}\,\mathrm{diag}(1,1,0)\mathtt{V}^\mathsf{T} = \mathtt{E} = \mathtt{SR} = (\mathtt{UZU}^\mathsf{T})(\mathtt{UXV}^\mathsf{T}) = \mathtt{U}(\mathtt{ZX})\mathtt{V}^\mathsf{T}$$

from which one deduces that $\mathtt{ZX} = \mathrm{diag}(1,1,0)$. Since $\mathtt{X}$ is a rotation matrix, it follows that $\mathtt{X} = \mathtt{W}$ or $\mathtt{X} = \mathtt{W}^\mathsf{T}$, as required. □

The factorization (9.14) determines the $\mathbf{t}$ part of the camera matrix $\mathtt{P}'$, up to scale, from $\mathtt{S} = [\mathbf{t}]_\times$. However, the Frobenius norm of $\mathtt{S} = \mathtt{UZU}^\mathsf{T}$ is $\sqrt{2}$, which means that if $\mathtt{S} = [\mathbf{t}]_\times$ *including scale* then $\|\mathbf{t}\| = 1$, which is a convenient normalization for the baseline of the two camera matrices. Since $\mathtt{S}\mathbf{t} = \mathbf{0}$, it follows that $\mathbf{t} = \mathtt{U}(0,0,1)^\mathsf{T} = \mathbf{u}_3$, the last column of $\mathtt{U}$. However, the sign of $\mathtt{E}$, and consequently $\mathbf{t}$, cannot be determined. Thus, corresponding to a given essential matrix, there are four possible choices of the camera matrix $\mathtt{P}'$, based on the two possible choices of $\mathtt{R}$ and two possible signs of $\mathbf{t}$. To summarize:

Result 9.19. *For a given essential matrix* $\mathtt{E} = \mathtt{U}\,\mathrm{diag}(1,1,0)\mathtt{V}^\mathsf{T}$, *and first camera matrix* $\mathtt{P} = [\mathtt{I} \mid \mathbf{0}]$, *there are four possible choices for the second camera matrix* $\mathtt{P}'$, *namely*

$$\mathtt{P}' = [\mathtt{UWV}^\mathsf{T} \mid +\mathbf{u}_3] \text{ or } [\mathtt{UWV}^\mathsf{T} \mid -\mathbf{u}_3] \text{ or } [\mathtt{UW}^\mathsf{T}\mathtt{V}^\mathsf{T} \mid +\mathbf{u}_3] \text{ or } [\mathtt{UW}^\mathsf{T}\mathtt{V}^\mathsf{T} \mid -\mathbf{u}_3].$$

9.6.3 Geometrical interpretation of the four solutions

It is clear that the difference between the first two solutions is simply that the direction of the translation vector from the first to the second camera is reversed.

The relationship of the first and third solutions in result 9.19 is a little more complicated. However, it may be verified that

$$[\mathtt{UW}^\mathsf{T}\mathtt{V}^\mathsf{T} \mid \mathbf{u}_3] = [\mathtt{UWV}^\mathsf{T} \mid \mathbf{u}_3] \begin{bmatrix} \mathtt{VW}^\mathsf{T}\mathtt{W}^\mathsf{T}\mathtt{V}^\mathsf{T} & \\ & 1 \end{bmatrix}$$

and $\mathtt{VW}^\mathsf{T}\mathtt{W}^\mathsf{T}\mathtt{V}^\mathsf{T} = \mathtt{V}\,\mathrm{diag}(-1,-1,1)\mathtt{V}^\mathsf{T}$ is a rotation through $180°$ about the line joining the two camera centres. Two solutions related in this way are known as a "twisted pair".

The four solutions are illustrated in figure 9.12, where it is shown that a reconstructed point $\mathbf{X}$ will be in front of both cameras in one of these four solutions only. Thus, testing with a single point to determine if it is in front of both cameras is sufficient to decide between the four different solutions for the camera matrix $\mathtt{P}'$.

Note. The point of view has been taken here that the essential matrix is a homogeneous quantity. An alternative point of view is that the essential matrix is defined exactly by the equation $\mathtt{E} = [\mathbf{t}]_\times\mathtt{R}$, (i.e. including scale), and is determined only up to indeterminate scale by the equation $\mathbf{x}'^\mathsf{T}\mathtt{E}\mathbf{x} = 0$. The choice of point of view depends on which of these two equations one regards as the defining property of the essential matrix.

9.7 Closure

9.7.1 The literature

The essential matrix was introduced to the computer vision community by Longuet-Higgins [LonguetHiggins-81], with a matrix analogous to $\mathtt{E}$ appearing in the photogrammetry literature, e.g. [VonSanden-08]. Many properties of the essential matrix have been elucidated particularly by Huang and Faugeras [Huang-89], [Maybank-93], and [Horn-90].

The realization that the essential matrix could also be applied in uncalibrated situations, as it represented a projective relation, developed in the early part of the 1990s,

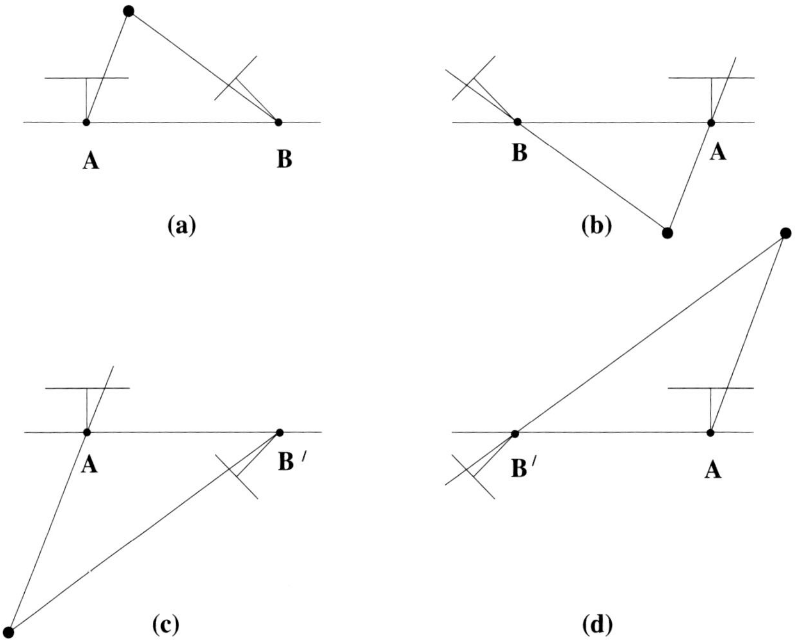

Fig. 9.12. **The four possible solutions for calibrated reconstruction from E.** *Between the left and right sides there is a baseline reversal. Between the top and bottom rows camera B rotates* 180° *about the baseline. Note, only in (a) is the reconstructed point in front of both cameras.*

and was published simultaneously by Faugeras [Faugeras-92b, Faugeras-92a], and Hartley *et al.* [Hartley-92a, Hartley-92c].

The special case of pure planar motion was examined by [Maybank-93] for the essential matrix. The corresponding case for the fundamental matrix is investigated by Beardsley and Zisserman [Beardsley-95a] and Viéville and Lingrand [Vieville-95], where further properties are given.

9.7.2 Notes and exercises

(i) **Fixating cameras.** Suppose two cameras fixate on a point in space such that their principal axes intersect at that point. Show that if the image coordinates are normalized so that the coordinate origin coincides with the principal point then the F_{33} element of the fundamental matrix is zero.

(ii) **Mirror images.** Suppose that a camera views an object and its reflection in a plane mirror. Show that this situation is equivalent to two views of the object, and that the fundamental matrix is skew-symmetric. Compare the fundamental matrix for this configuration with that of: (a) a pure translation, and (b) a pure planar motion. Show that the fundamental matrix is auto-epipolar (as is (a)).

(iii) Show that if the vanishing line of a plane contains the epipole then the plane is parallel to the baseline.

(iv) **Steiner conic.** Show that the polar of $\mathbf{x}_a$ intersects the Steiner conic F_s at the epipoles (figure 9.10a). Hint, start from $Fe = F_s e + F_a e = \mathbf{0}$. Since $\mathbf{e}$ lies on the conic $\mathtt{F_S}$, then $\mathbf{l}_1 = \mathtt{F_S}\mathbf{e}$ is the tangent line at $\mathbf{e}$, and $\mathbf{l}_2 = \mathtt{F_a}\mathbf{e} = [\mathbf{x_a}]_\times \mathbf{e} = \mathbf{x_a} \times \mathbf{e}$ is a line through $\mathbf{x_a}$ and $\mathbf{e}$.

(v) The affine type of the Steiner conic (hyperbola, ellipse or parabola as given in section 2.8.2(*p*59)) depends on the relative configuration of the two cameras. For example, if the two cameras are facing each other then the Steiner conic is a hyperbola. This is shown in [Chum-03] where further results on oriented epipolar geometry are given.

(vi) **Planar motion.** It is shown by [Maybank-93] that if the rotation axis direction is orthogonal or parallel to the translation direction then the symmetric part of the essential matrix has rank 2. We assume here that $\mathtt{K} = \mathtt{K}'$. Then from (9.12), $\mathtt{F} = \mathtt{K}^{-\mathsf{T}}\mathtt{E}\mathtt{K}^{-1}$, and so

$$\mathtt{F_S} = (\mathtt{F} + \mathtt{F}^{\mathsf{T}})/2 = \mathtt{K}^{-\mathsf{T}}(\mathtt{E} + \mathtt{E}^{\mathsf{T}})\mathtt{K}^{-1}/2 = \mathtt{K}^{-\mathsf{T}}\mathtt{E_S}\mathtt{K}^{-1}.$$

It follows from $\det(\mathtt{F_S}) = \det(\mathtt{K}^{-1})^2 \det(\mathtt{E_S})$ that the symmetric part of $\mathtt{F}$ is also singular. Does this result hold if $\mathtt{K} \neq \mathtt{K}'$?

(vii) Any matrix $\mathtt{F}$ of rank 2 is the fundamental matrix corresponding to some pair of camera matrices $(\mathtt{P}, \mathtt{P}')$ This follows directly from result 9.14 since the solution for the canonical cameras depends only on the rank 2 property of $\mathtt{F}$.

(viii) Show that the 3D points determined from one of the ambiguous reconstructions obtained from $\mathtt{E}$ are related to the corresponding 3D points determined from another reconstruction by either (i) an inversion through the second camera centre; or (ii) a harmonic homology of 3-space (see section A7.2(*p*629)), where the homology plane is perpendicular to the baseline and through the second camera centre, and the vertex is the first camera centre.

(ix) Following a similar development to section 9.2.2, derive the form of the fundamental matrix for two linear pushbroom cameras. Details of this matrix are given in [Gupta-97] where it is shown that affine reconstruction is possible from a pair of images.

10

3D Reconstruction of Cameras and Structure

This chapter describes how and to what extent the spatial layout of a scene and the cameras can be recovered from two views. Suppose that a set of image correspondences $\mathbf{x}_i \leftrightarrow \mathbf{x}'_i$ are given. It is assumed that these correspondences come from a set of 3D points $\mathbf{X}_i$, which are unknown. Similarly, the position, orientation and calibration of the cameras are not known. The reconstruction task is to find the camera matrices $\mathtt{P}$ and $\mathtt{P}'$, as well as the 3D points $\mathbf{X}_i$ such that

$$\mathbf{x}_i = \mathtt{P}\mathbf{X}_i \quad \mathbf{x}'_i = \mathtt{P}'\mathbf{X}_i \quad \text{for all } i.$$

Given too few points, this task is not possible. However, if there are sufficiently many point correspondences to allow the fundamental matrix to be computed uniquely, then the scene may be reconstructed up to a projective ambiguity. This is a very significant result, and one of the major achievements of the uncalibrated approach.

The ambiguity in the reconstruction may be reduced if additional information is supplied on the cameras or scene. We describe a two-stage approach where the ambiguity is first reduced to affine, and second to metric; each stage requiring information of the appropriate class.

10.1 Outline of reconstruction method

We describe a method for reconstruction from two views as follows.

(i) Compute the fundamental matrix from point correspondences.
(ii) Compute the camera matrices from the fundamental matrix.
(iii) For each point correspondence $\mathbf{x}_i \leftrightarrow \mathbf{x}'_i$, compute the point in space that projects to these two image points.

Many variants on this method are possible. For instance, if the cameras are calibrated, then one will compute the essential matrix instead of the fundamental matrix. Furthermore, one may use information about the motion of the camera, scene constraints or partial camera calibration to obtain refinements of the reconstruction.

Each of the steps of this reconstruction method will be discussed briefly in the following paragraphs. The method described is no more than a conceptual approach to reconstruction. The reader is warned not to implement a reconstruction method based solely on the description given in this section. For real images where measurements

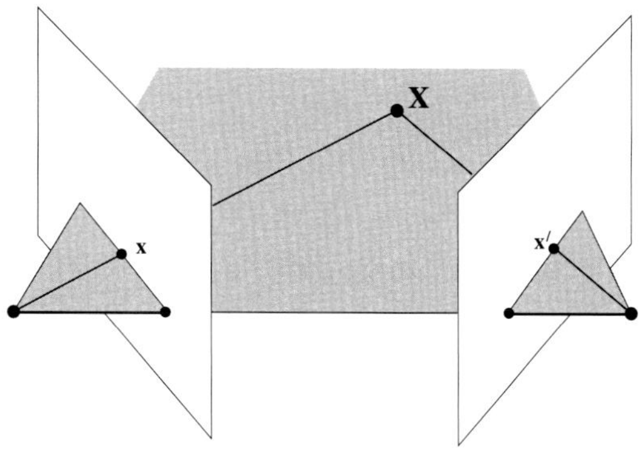

Fig. 10.1. **Triangulation.** *The image points* $\mathbf{x}$ *and* $\mathbf{x}'$ *back project to rays. If the epipolar constraint* $\mathbf{x}'^{\mathsf{T}}\mathtt{F}\mathbf{x} = 0$ *is satisfied, then these two rays lie in a plane, and so intersect in a point* $\mathbf{X}$ *in 3-space.*

are "noisy" preferred methods for reconstruction, based on this general outline, are described in chapter 11 and chapter 12.

Computation of the fundamental matrix. Given a set of correspondences $\mathbf{x}_i \leftrightarrow \mathbf{x}'_i$ in two images the fundamental matrix F satisfies the condition $\mathbf{x}'_i\mathtt{F}\mathbf{x}_i = 0$ for all i. With the $\mathbf{x}_i$ and $\mathbf{x}'_i$ known, this equation is linear in the (unknown) entries of the matrix F. In fact, each point correspondence generates one linear equation in the entries of F. Given at least 8 point correspondences it is possible to solve linearly for the entries of F up to scale (a non-linear solution is available for 7 point correspondences). With more than 8 equations a least-squares solution is found. This is the general principle of a method for computing the fundamental matrix.

Recommended methods of computing the fundamental matrix from a set of point correspondences will be described later in chapter 11.

Computation of the camera matrices. A pair of camera matrices P and P′ corresponding to the fundamental matrix F are easily computed using the direct formula in result 9.14.

Triangulation. Given the camera matrices P and P′, let $\mathbf{x}$ and $\mathbf{x}'$ be two points in the two images that satisfy the epipolar constraint, $\mathbf{x}'^{\mathsf{T}}\mathtt{F}\mathbf{x} = 0$. As shown in chapter 9 this constraint may be interpreted geometrically in terms of the rays in space corresponding to the two image points. In particular it means that $\mathbf{x}'$ lies on the epipolar line $\mathtt{F}\mathbf{x}$. In turn this means that the two rays back-projected from image points $\mathbf{x}$ and $\mathbf{x}'$ lie in a common epipolar plane, that is, a plane passing through the two camera centres. Since the two rays lie in a plane, they will intersect in some point. This point $\mathbf{X}$ projects via the two cameras to the points $\mathbf{x}$ and $\mathbf{x}'$ in the two images. This is illustrated in figure 10.1.

The only points in 3-space that cannot be determined from their images are points on the baseline between the two cameras. In this case the back-projected rays are collinear (both being equal to the baseline) and intersect along their whole length. Thus, the point

$\mathbf{X}$ cannot be uniquely determined. Points on the baseline project to the epipoles in both images.

Numerically stable methods of actually determining the point $\mathbf{X}$ at the intersection of the two rays back-projected from $\mathbf{x}$ and $\mathbf{x}'$ will be described later in chapter 12.

10.2 Reconstruction ambiguity

In this section we discuss the inherent ambiguities involved in reconstruction of a scene from point correspondences. This topic will be discussed in a general context, without reference to a specific method of carrying out the reconstruction.

Without some knowledge of a scene's placement with respect to a 3D coordinate frame, it is generally not possible to reconstruct the absolute position or orientation of a scene from a pair of views (or in fact from any number of views). This is true independently of any knowledge which may be available about the internal parameters of the cameras, or their relative placement. For instance the exact latitude and longitude of the scene in figure 9.8(*p*248) (or any scene) cannot be computed, nor is it possible to determine whether the corridor runs north-south or east-west. This may be expressed by saying that the scene is determined at best up to a Euclidean transformation (rotation and translation) with respect to the world frame.

Only slightly less obvious is the fact that the overall scale of the scene cannot be determined. Considering figure 9.8(*p*248) once more, it is impossible based on the images alone to determine the width of the corridor. It may be two metres, one metre. It is even possible that this is an image of a doll's house and the corridor is 10 cm wide. Our common experience leads us to expect that ceilings are approximately 3m from the floor, which allows us to perceive the real scale of the scene. This extra information is an example of subsidiary knowledge of the scene not derived from image measurements. Without such knowledge therefore the scene is determined by the image only up to a similarity transformation (rotation, translation and scaling).

To give a mathematical basis to this observation, let $\mathbf{X}_i$ be a set of points and $\mathtt{P}, \mathtt{P}'$ be a pair of cameras projecting $\mathbf{X}_i$ to image points $\mathbf{x}_i$ and $\mathbf{x}'_i$. The points $\mathbf{X}_i$ and the camera pair constitute a reconstruction of the scene from the image correspondences. Now let

$$\mathtt{H}_\mathrm{S} = \begin{bmatrix} \mathtt{R} & \mathbf{t} \\ \mathbf{0}^\mathsf{T} & \lambda \end{bmatrix}$$

be any similarity transformation: $\mathtt{R}$ is a rotation, $\mathbf{t}$ a translation and λ^{-1} represents overall scaling. Replacing each point $\mathbf{X}_i$ by $\mathtt{H}_\mathrm{S}\mathbf{X}_i$ and cameras $\mathtt{P}$ and $\mathtt{P}'$ by $\mathtt{PH}_\mathrm{S}^{-1}$ and $\mathtt{P}'\mathtt{H}_\mathrm{S}^{-1}$ respectively does not change the observed image points, since $\mathtt{P}\mathbf{X}_i = (\mathtt{PH}_\mathrm{S}^{-1})(\mathtt{H}_\mathrm{S}\mathbf{X}_i)$. Furthermore, if $\mathtt{P}$ is decomposed as $\mathtt{P} = \mathtt{K}[\mathtt{R}_\mathtt{P} \mid \mathbf{t}_\mathtt{P}]$, then one computes

$$\mathtt{PH}_\mathrm{S}^{-1} = \mathtt{K}[\mathtt{R}_\mathtt{P}\mathtt{R}^{-1} \mid \mathbf{t}']$$

for some $\mathbf{t}'$ that we do not need to compute more exactly. This result shows that multiplying by $\mathtt{H}_\mathrm{S}^{-1}$ does not change the calibration matrix of $\mathtt{P}$. Consequently this ambiguity of reconstruction exists even for calibrated cameras. It was shown by Longuet-Higgins

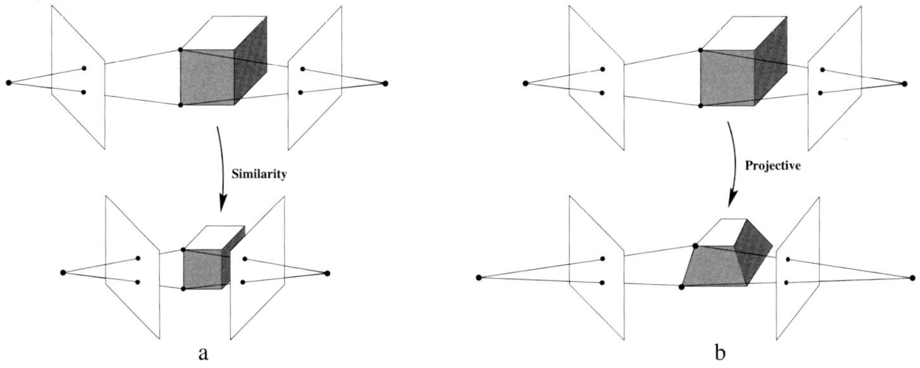

Fig. 10.2. **Reconstruction ambiguity.** *(a) If the cameras are calibrated then any reconstruction must respect the angle between rays measured in the image. A similarity transformation of the structure and camera positions does not change the measured angle. The angle between rays and the baseline (epipoles) is also unchanged. (b) If the cameras are uncalibrated then reconstructions must only respect the image points (the intersection of the rays with the image plane). A projective transformation of the structure and camera positions does not change the measured points, although the angle between rays is altered. The epipoles are also unchanged (intersection with baseline).*

([LonguetHiggins-81]) that for calibrated cameras, this is the only ambiguity of reconstruction. Thus for calibrated cameras, reconstruction is possible *up to a similarity transformation.* This is illustrated in figure 10.2a.

Projective ambiguity. If nothing is known of the calibration of either camera, nor the placement of one camera with respect to the other, then the ambiguity of reconstruction is expressed by an arbitrary projective transformation. In particular, if $\mathtt{H}$ is any 4×4 invertible matrix, representing a projective transformation of $\mathbb{P}^3$, then replacing points $\mathbf{X}_i$ by $\mathtt{H}\mathbf{X}_i$ and matrices $\mathtt{P}$ and $\mathtt{P}'$ by $\mathtt{PH}^{-1}$ and $\mathtt{P}'\mathtt{H}^{-1}$ (as in the previous paragraph) does not change the image points. This shows that the points $\mathbf{X}_i$ and the cameras can be determined at best only up to a projective transformation. It is an important result, proved in this chapter (section 10.3), that this is the only ambiguity in the reconstruction of points from two images. Thus reconstruction from uncalibrated cameras is possible *up to a projective transformation.* This is illustrated in figure 10.2b.

Other types of reconstruction ambiguity result from certain assumptions on the types of motion, or partial knowledge of the cameras. For instance,

(i) If the two cameras are related via a translational motion, without change of calibration, then reconstruction is possible up to an affine transformation.
(ii) If the two cameras are calibrated apart from their focal lengths, then reconstruction is still possible up to a similarity transformation.

These two cases will be considered later in section 10.4.1 and example 19.8(*p*472), respectively.

Terminology. In any reconstruction problem derived from real data, consisting of point correspondences $\mathbf{x}_i \leftrightarrow \mathbf{x}'_i$, there exists a **true** reconstruction consisting of the actual points $\bar{\mathbf{X}}_i$ and actual cameras $\bar{\mathtt{P}}, \bar{\mathtt{P}}'$ that generated the measured observations. The reconstructed point set $\mathbf{X}_i$ and cameras differ from the true reconstruction by a transformation belonging to a given class or group (for instance a similarity, projective or affine transformation). One speaks of *projective reconstruction*, *affine reconstruction*, *similarity reconstruction*, and so on, to indicate the type of transformation involved. However, the term *metric reconstruction* is normally used in preference to *similarity reconstruction*, being identical in meaning. The term indicates that metric properties, such as angles between lines and ratios of lengths, can be measured on the reconstruction and have their veridical values (since these are similarity invariants). In addition, the term *Euclidean reconstruction* is frequently used in the published literature to mean the same thing as a similarity or metric reconstruction, since true Euclidean reconstruction (including determination of overall scale) is not possible without extraneous information.

10.3 The projective reconstruction theorem

In this section the basic theorem of projective reconstruction from uncalibrated cameras is proved. Informally, the theorem may be stated as follows.

- *If a set of point correspondences in two views determine the fundamental matrix uniquely, then the scene and cameras may be reconstructed from these correspondences alone, and any two such reconstructions from these correspondences are projectively equivalent.*

Points lying on the line joining the two camera centres must be excluded, since such points cannot be reconstructed uniquely even if the camera matrices are determined. The formal statement is:

Theorem 10.1 (Projective reconstruction theorem). *Suppose that $\mathbf{x}_i \leftrightarrow \mathbf{x}'_i$ is a set of correspondences between points in two images and that the fundamental matrix* $\mathtt{F}$ *is uniquely determined by the condition $\mathbf{x}_i'^{\mathsf{T}}\mathtt{F}\mathbf{x}_i = 0$ for all i. Let $(\mathtt{P}_1, \mathtt{P}'_1, \{\mathbf{X}_{1i}\})$ and $(\mathtt{P}_2, \mathtt{P}'_2, \{\mathbf{X}_{2i}\})$ be two reconstructions of the correspondences $\mathbf{x}_i \leftrightarrow \mathbf{x}'_i$. Then there exists a non-singular matrix* $\mathtt{H}$ *such that $\mathtt{P}_2 = \mathtt{P}_1\mathtt{H}^{-1}$, $\mathtt{P}'_2 = \mathtt{P}'_1\mathtt{H}^{-1}$ and $\mathbf{X}_{2i} = \mathtt{H}\mathbf{X}_{1i}$ for all i,* **except** *for those i such that $\mathtt{F}\mathbf{x}_i = \mathbf{x}_i'^{\mathsf{T}}\mathtt{F} = \mathbf{0}$.*

Proof. Since the fundamental matrix is uniquely determined by the point correspondences, one deduces that $\mathtt{F}$ is the fundamental matrix corresponding to the camera pair $(\mathtt{P}_1, \mathtt{P}'_1)$ and also to $(\mathtt{P}_2, \mathtt{P}'_2)$. According to theorem 9.10(*p*254) there is a projective transformation $\mathtt{H}$ such that $\mathtt{P}_2 = \mathtt{P}_1\mathtt{H}^{-1}$ and $\mathtt{P}'_2 = \mathtt{P}'_1\mathtt{H}^{-1}$ as required.
As for the points, one observes that $\mathtt{P}_2(\mathtt{H}\mathbf{X}_{1i}) = \mathtt{P}_1\mathtt{H}^{-1}\mathtt{H}\mathbf{X}_{1i} = \mathtt{P}_1\mathbf{X}_{1i} = \mathbf{x}_i$. On the other hand $\mathtt{P}_2\mathbf{X}_{2i} = \mathbf{x}_i$, so $\mathtt{P}_2(\mathtt{H}\mathbf{X}_{1i}) = \mathtt{P}_2\mathbf{X}_{2i}$. Thus both $\mathtt{H}\mathbf{X}_{1i}$ and $\mathbf{X}_{2i}$ map to the same point $\mathbf{x}_i$ under the action of the camera $\mathtt{P}_2$. It follows that both $\mathtt{H}\mathbf{X}_{1i}$ and $\mathbf{X}_{2i}$ lie on the same ray through the camera centre of $\mathtt{P}_2$. Similarly, it may be deduced that these two points lie on the same ray through the camera centre of $\mathtt{P}'_2$. There are two possibilities: either $\mathbf{X}_{2i} = \mathtt{H}\mathbf{X}_{1i}$ as required, or they are distinct points lying on the line joining the two camera centres. In this latter case, the image points $\mathbf{x}_i$ and $\mathbf{x}'_i$ coincide with the epipoles in the two images, and so $\mathtt{F}\mathbf{x}_i = \mathbf{x}_i'^{\mathsf{T}}\mathtt{F} = \mathbf{0}$. □

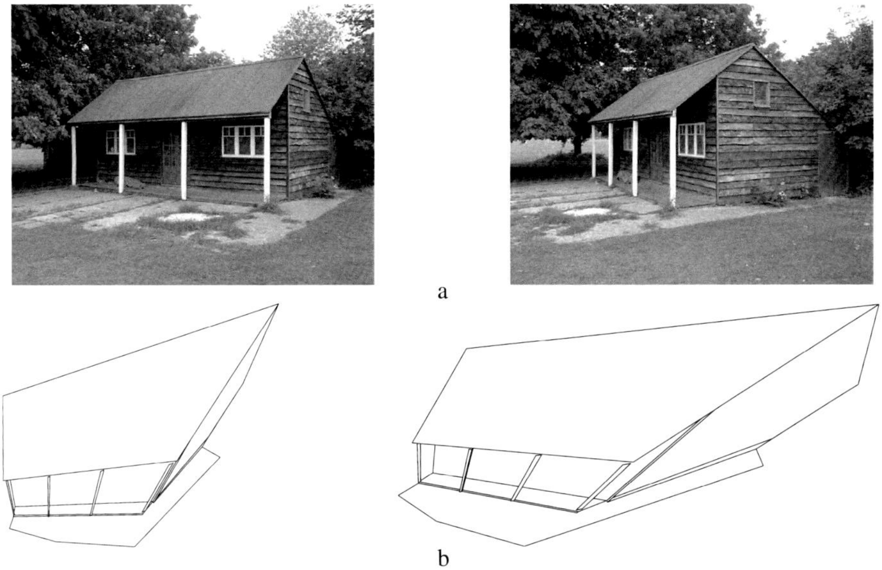

Fig. 10.3. **Projective reconstruction.** *(a) Original image pair. (b) 2 views of a 3D projective reconstruction of the scene. The reconstruction requires no information about the camera matrices, or information about the scene geometry. The fundamental matrix* F *is computed from point correspondences between the images, camera matrices are retrieved from* F*, and then 3D points are computed by triangulation from the correspondences. The lines of the wireframe link the computed 3D points.*

This is an enormously significant result, since it implies that one may compute a projective reconstruction of a scene from two views based on image correspondences alone, without knowing anything about the calibration or pose of the two cameras involved. In particular the true reconstruction is within a projective transformation of the projective reconstruction. Figure 10.3 shows an example of 3D structure computed as part of a projective reconstruction from two images.

In more detail suppose the true Euclidean reconstruction is $(\mathtt{P}_{\mathrm{E}}, \mathtt{P}'_{\mathrm{E}}, \{\mathbf{X}_{\mathrm{E}i}\})$ and the projective reconstruction is $(\mathtt{P}, \mathtt{P}', \{\mathbf{X}_i\})$, then the reconstructions are related by a non-singular matrix H such that

$$\mathtt{P}_{\mathrm{E}} = \mathtt{P}\mathtt{H}^{-1}, \ \ \mathtt{P}'_{\mathrm{E}} = \mathtt{P}'\mathtt{H}^{-1}, \text{ and } \mathbf{X}_{\mathrm{E}i} = \mathtt{H}\mathbf{X}_i \tag{10.1}$$

where H is a 4×4 homography matrix which is unknown but the same for all points.

For some applications projective reconstruction is all that is required. For example, questions such as "at what point does a line intersect a plane?", "what is the mapping between two views induced by particular surfaces, such as a plane or quadric?" can be dealt with directly from the projective reconstruction. Furthermore it will be seen in the sequel that obtaining a projective reconstruction of a scene is the first step towards affine or metric reconstruction.

10.4 Stratified reconstruction

The "stratified" approach to reconstruction is to begin with a projective reconstruction and then to refine it progressively to an affine and finally a metric reconstruction, if possible. Of course, as has just been seen, affine and metric reconstruction are not possible without further information either about the scene, the motion or the camera calibration.

10.4.1 The step to affine reconstruction

The essence of affine reconstruction is to locate the plane at infinity by some means, since this knowledge is equivalent to an affine reconstruction. This equivalence is explained in the 2D case in section 2.7(*p*47). To see this equivalence for reconstruction, suppose we have determined a projective reconstruction of a scene, consisting of a triple $(\mathtt{P}, \mathtt{P}', \{\mathbf{X}_i\})$. Suppose further that by some means a certain plane $\boldsymbol{\pi}$ has been identified as the true plane at infinity. The plane $\boldsymbol{\pi}$ is expressed as a 4-vector in the coordinate frame of the projective reconstruction. In the true reconstruction, $\boldsymbol{\pi}$ has coordinates $(0,0,0,1)^\mathsf{T}$, and we may find a projective transformation that maps $\boldsymbol{\pi}$ to $(0,0,0,1)^\mathsf{T}$. Considering the way a projective transformation acts on planes, we want to find $\mathtt{H}$ such that $\mathtt{H}^{-\mathsf{T}}\boldsymbol{\pi} = (0,0,0,1)^\mathsf{T}$. Such a transformation is given by

$$\mathtt{H} = \begin{bmatrix} \mathtt{I} \mid \mathbf{0} \\ \boldsymbol{\pi}^\mathsf{T} \end{bmatrix}. \tag{10.2}$$

Indeed, it is immediately verified that $\mathtt{H}^\mathsf{T}(0,0,0,1)^\mathsf{T} = \boldsymbol{\pi}$, and thus $\mathtt{H}^{-\mathsf{T}}\boldsymbol{\pi} = (0,0,0,1)^\mathsf{T}$, as desired. The transformation $\mathtt{H}$ is now applied to all points and the two cameras. Notice, however that this formula will not work if the final coordinate of $\boldsymbol{\pi}^\mathsf{T}$ is zero. In this case, one may compute a suitable $\mathtt{H}$ by computing $\mathtt{H}^{-\mathsf{T}}$ as a Householder matrix (A4.2–*p*580) such that $\mathtt{H}^{-\mathsf{T}}\boldsymbol{\pi} = (0,0,0,1)^\mathsf{T}$.

At this point, the reconstruction that one has is not necessarily the true reconstruction – all one knows is that the plane at infinity is correctly placed. The present reconstruction differs from the true reconstruction by a projective transformation that fixes the plane at infinity. However, according to result 3.7(*p*80), a projective transformation fixing the plane at infinity is an affine transformation. Hence the reconstruction differs by an affine transformation from the true reconstruction – it is an *affine reconstruction.*

An affine reconstruction may well be sufficient for some applications. For example, the mid-point of two points and the centroid of a set of points may now be computed, and lines constructed parallel to other lines and to planes. Such computations are not possible from a projective reconstruction.

As has been stated, the plane at infinity cannot be identified unless some extra information is given. We will now give several examples of the type of information that suffices for this identification.

Translational motion

Consider the case where the camera is known to undergo a purely translational motion. In this case, it is possible to carry out affine reconstruction from two views. A simple way of seeing this is to observe that a point $\mathbf{X}$ on the plane at infinity will map to the same point in two images related by a translation. This is easily verified formally. It is also part of our common experience that as one moves in a straight line (for instance in a car on a straight road), objects at a great distance (such as the moon) do not appear to move – only the nearby objects move past the field of view. This being so, one may invent any number of matched points $\mathbf{x}_i \leftrightarrow \mathbf{x}_i$ where a point in one image corresponds with the same point in the other image. Note that one does not actually have to observe such a correspondence in the two images – any point and the same point in the other image will do. Given a projective reconstruction, one may then reconstruct the point $\mathbf{X}_i$ corresponding to the match $\mathbf{x}_i \leftrightarrow \mathbf{x}_i$. Point $\mathbf{X}_i$ will lie on the plane at infinity. From three such points one can get three points on the plane at infinity – sufficient to determine it uniquely.

Although this argument gives a constructive proof that affine reconstruction is possible from a translating camera, this does not mean that this is the best way to proceed numerically. In fact in this case, the assumption of translational motion implies a very restricted form for the fundamental matrix – it is skew-symmetric as shown in section 9.3.1. This special form should be taken into account when solving for the fundamental matrix.

Result 10.2. *Suppose the motion of the cameras is a pure translation with no rotation and no change in the internal parameters. As shown in example 9.6(*p249*)* $\mathtt{F} = [\mathbf{e}]_\times = [\mathbf{e}']_\times$*, and for an affine reconstruction one may choose the two cameras as* $\mathtt{P} = [\mathtt{I} \mid \mathbf{0}]$ *and* $\mathtt{P}' = [\mathtt{I} \mid \mathbf{e}']$.

Scene constraints

Scene constraints or conditions may also be used to obtain an affine reconstruction. As long as three points can be identified that are known to lie on the plane at infinity, then that plane may be identified, and the reconstruction transformed to an affine reconstruction.

Parallel lines. The most obvious such condition is the knowledge that 3D lines are in reality parallel. The intersection of the two parallel lines in space gives a point on the plane at infinity. The image of this point is the vanishing point of the line, and is the point of intersection of the two imaged lines. Suppose that three sets of parallel lines can be identified in the scene. Each set intersects in a point on the plane at infinity. Provided each set has a different direction, the three points will be distinct. Since three points determine a plane, this information is sufficient to identify the plane $\boldsymbol{\pi}$.

The best way of actually computing the intersection of lines in space is a somewhat delicate problem, since in the presence of noise, lines that are intended to intersect rarely do. It is discussed in some detail in chapter 12. Correct numerical procedures for computing the plane are given in chapter 13. An example of an affine reconstruction computed from three sets of parallel scene lines is given in figure 10.4.

Note that it is not necessary to find the vanishing point in both images. Suppose the vanishing point $\mathbf{v}$ is computed from imaged parallel lines in the first image, and $\mathbf{l}'$ is a corresponding line in the second image. Vanishing points satisfy the epipolar constraint, so the corresponding vanishing point $\mathbf{v}'$ in the second image may be computed as the intersection of $\mathbf{l}'$ and the epipolar line $\mathtt{F}\mathbf{v}$ of $\mathbf{v}$. The construction of the

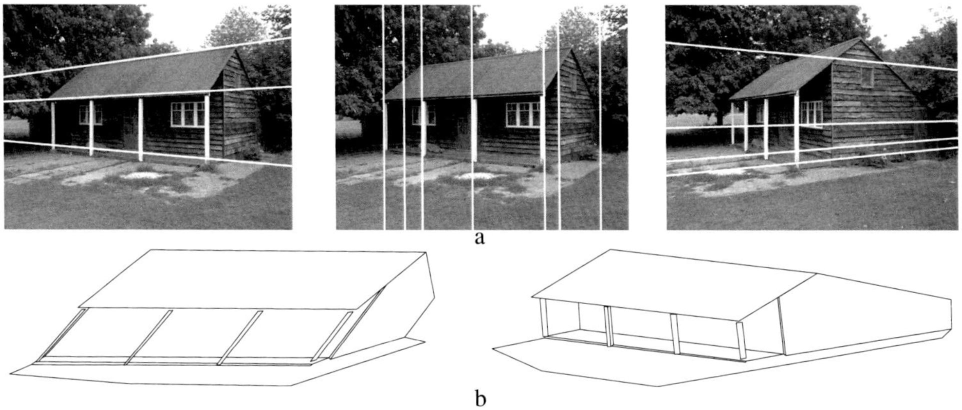

Fig. 10.4. **Affine reconstruction.** *The projective reconstruction of figure 10.3 may be upgraded to affine using parallel scene lines. (a) There are 3 sets of parallel lines in the scene, each set with a different direction. These 3 sets enable the position of the plane at infinity, π_∞, to be computed in the projective reconstruction. The wireframe projective reconstruction of figure 10.3 is then affinely rectified using the homography (10.2). (b) Shows two orthographic views of the wireframe affine reconstruction. Note that parallel scene lines are parallel in the reconstruction, but lines that are perpendicular in the scene are not perpendicular in the reconstruction.*

3-space point $\mathbf{X}$ can be neatly expressed algebraically as the solution of the equations $([\mathbf{v}]_\times \mathtt{P})\mathbf{X} = \mathbf{0}$ and $(\mathbf{l}'^{\mathsf{T}}\mathtt{P}')\mathbf{X} = 0$. These equations expresses the fact that $\mathbf{X}$ maps to $\mathbf{v}$ in the first image, and to a point on $\mathbf{l}'$ in the second image.

Distance ratios on a line. An alternative to computing vanishing points as the intersection of imaged parallel scene lines is to use knowledge of affine length ratios in the scene. For example, given two intervals on a line with a known length ratio, the point at infinity on the line may be determined. This means that from an image of a line on which a world distance ratio is known, for example that three points are equally spaced, the vanishing point may be determined. This computation, and other means of computing vanishing points and vanishing lines, are described in section 2.7(*p*47).

The infinite homography

Once the plane at infinity has been located, so that we have an affine reconstruction, then we also have an image-to-image map called the "infinite homography". This map, which is a 2D homography , is described in greater detail in chapter 13. Briefly, it is the map that transfers points from the $\mathtt{P}$ image to the $\mathtt{P}'$ image via the plane at infinity as follows: the ray corresponding to a point $\mathbf{x}$ is extended to meet the plane at infinity in a point $\mathbf{X}$; this point is projected to a point $\mathbf{x}'$ in the other image. The homography from $\mathbf{x}$ to $\mathbf{x}'$ is written as $\mathbf{x}' = \mathtt{H}_\infty \mathbf{x}$.

Having an affine reconstruction is equivalent to knowing the infinite homography as will now be shown. Given two cameras $\mathtt{P} = [\mathtt{M} \mid \mathbf{m}]$ and $\mathtt{P}' = [\mathtt{M}' \mid \mathbf{m}']$ of an affine reconstruction, the infinite homography is given by $\mathtt{H}_\infty = \mathtt{M}'\mathtt{M}^{-1}$. This is because a point $\mathbf{X} = (\tilde{\mathbf{X}}^{\mathsf{T}}, 0)^{\mathsf{T}}$ on the plane at infinity maps to $\mathbf{x} = \mathtt{M}\tilde{\mathbf{X}}$ in one image and $\mathbf{x}' = \mathtt{M}'\tilde{\mathbf{X}}$ in the other, so $\mathbf{x}' = \mathtt{M}'\mathtt{M}^{-1}\mathbf{x}$ for points on π_∞. Furthermore, it may be verified that this is unchanged by a 3-space affine transformation of the cameras. Hence, the infinite homography may be computed explicitly from an affine reconstruction, and vice versa:

Result 10.3. *If an affine reconstruction has been obtained in which the camera matrices are* $\mathtt{P} = [\mathtt{I} \mid \mathbf{0}]$ *and* $\mathtt{P}' = [\mathtt{M}' \mid \mathbf{e}']$*, then the infinite homography is given by* $\mathtt{H}_\infty = \mathtt{M}'$*. Conversely, if the infinite homography* $\mathtt{H}_\infty$ *has been obtained, then the cameras of an affine reconstruction may be chosen as* $\mathtt{P} = [\mathtt{I} \mid \mathbf{0}]$ *and* $\mathtt{P}' = [\mathtt{H}_\infty \mid \mathbf{e}']$.

The infinite homography may be computed directly from corresponding image entities, rather than indirectly from an affine reconstruction. For example, $\mathtt{H}_\infty$ can be computed from the correspondence of three vanishing points together with $\mathtt{F}$, or the correspondence of a vanishing line and vanishing point, together with $\mathtt{F}$. The correct numerical procedure for these computations is given in chapter 13. However, such direct computations are completely equivalent to determining $\boldsymbol{\pi}_\infty$ in a projective reconstruction.

One of the cameras is affine

Another important case in which affine reconstruction is possible is when one of the cameras is known to be an affine camera as defined in section 6.3.1(*p*166). To see that this implies that affine reconstruction is possible, refer to section 6.3.5(*p*172) where it was shown that the principal plane of an affine camera is the plane at infinity. Hence to convert a projective reconstruction to an affine reconstruction, it is sufficient to find the principal plane of the camera supposed to be affine and map it to the plane $(0, 0, 0, 1)^\mathsf{T}$. Recall (section 6.2(*p*158)) that the principal plane of a camera is simply the third row of the camera matrix. For example, consider a projective reconstruction with camera matrices $\mathtt{P} = [\mathtt{I} \mid \mathbf{0}]$ and $\mathtt{P}'$, for which the first camera is supposed to be affine. To map the third row of $\mathtt{P}$ to $(0, 0, 0, 1)$ it is sufficient to swap the last two columns of the two camera matrices, while at the same time swapping the 3rd and 4th coordinates of each $\mathbf{X}_i$. This is a projective transformation corresponding to a permutation matrix $\mathtt{H}$. This shows:

Result 10.4. *Let* $(\mathtt{P}, \mathtt{P}', \{\mathbf{X}_i\})$ *be a projective reconstruction from a set of point correspondences for which* $\mathtt{P} = [\mathtt{I} \mid \mathbf{0}]$*. Suppose in truth,* $\mathtt{P}$ *is known to be an affine camera, then an affine reconstruction is obtained by swapping the last two columns of* $\mathtt{P}$ *and* $\mathtt{P}'$ *and the last two coordinates of each* $\mathbf{X}_i$.

Note that the condition that one of the cameras is affine places no restriction on the fundamental matrix, since any canonical camera pair $\mathtt{P} = [\mathtt{I} \mid \mathbf{0}]$ and $\mathtt{P}'$ can be transformed to a pair in which $\mathtt{P}$ is affine. If both the cameras are known to be affine, then it will be seen that the fundamental matrix has the restricted form given in (14.1–*p*345). In this case, for numerical stability, one must solve for the fundamental matrix enforcing this special form of the fundamental matrix.

Of course there is no such thing as a real affine camera – the affine camera model is an approximation which is only valid when the set of points seen in the image has small depth variation compared with the distance from the camera. Nevertheless, an assumption of an affine camera may be useful to effect the significant restriction from projective to affine reconstruction.

10.4.2 The step to metric reconstruction

Just as the key to affine reconstruction is the identification of the plane at infinity, the key to metric reconstruction is the identification of the absolute conic (section 3.6-(*p*81)). Since the absolute conic, Ω_∞, is a planar conic, lying in the plane at infinity, identifying the absolute conic implies identifying the plane at infinity.

In a stratified approach, one proceeds from projective to affine to metric reconstruction, so one knows the plane at infinity before finding the absolute conic. Suppose one has identified the absolute conic on the plane at infinity. In principle the next step is to apply an affine transformation to the affine reconstruction such that the identified absolute conic is mapped to the absolute conic in the standard Euclidean frame (it will then have the equation $X_1^2 + X_2^2 + X_3^2 = 0$, on π_∞). The resulting reconstruction is then related to the true reconstruction by a projective transformation which fixes the absolute conic. It follows from result 3.9(*p*82) that the projective transformation is a similarity transformation, so we have achieved a metric reconstruction.

In practice the easiest way to accomplish this is to consider the image of the absolute conic in one of the images. The image of the absolute conic (as any conic) is a conic in the image. The back-projection of this conic is a cone, which will meet the plane at infinity in a single conic, which therefore defines the absolute conic. Remember that the image of the absolute conic is a property of the image itself, and like any image point, line or other feature, is not dependent on any particular reconstruction, hence it is unchanged by 3D transformations of the reconstruction.

Suppose that in the affine reconstruction the image of the absolute conic as seen by the camera with matrix $P = [M \mid \mathbf{m}]$ is a conic ω. We will show how ω may be used to define the homography H which transforms the affine reconstruction to a metric reconstruction:

Result 10.5. *Suppose that the image of the absolute conic is known in some image to be ω, and one has an affine reconstruction in which the corresponding camera matrix is given by $P = [M \mid \mathbf{m}]$. Then, the affine reconstruction may be transformed to a metric reconstruction by applying a 3D transformation of the form*

$$H = \begin{bmatrix} A^{-1} & \\ & 1 \end{bmatrix}$$

where A is obtained by Cholesky factorization from the equation $AA^\top = (M^\top \omega M)^{-1}$.

Proof. Under the transformation H, the camera matrix P is transformed to a matrix $P_M = PH^{-1} = [M_M \mid \mathbf{m}_M]$. If H^{-1} is of the form

$$H^{-1} = \begin{bmatrix} A & \mathbf{0} \\ \mathbf{0}^\top & 1 \end{bmatrix}$$

then $M_M = MA$. However, the image of the absolute conic is related to the camera matrix P_M of a Euclidean frame by the relationship

$$\omega^* = M_M M_M^\top \ .$$

This is because the camera matrix may be decomposed as $\mathtt{M}_{\mathrm{M}} = \mathtt{KR}$, and from (8.11–$p$210) $\boldsymbol{\omega}^* = \boldsymbol{\omega}^{-1} = \mathtt{KK}^\mathsf{T}$. Combining this with $\mathtt{M}_{\mathrm{M}} = \mathtt{MA}$ gives $\boldsymbol{\omega}^{-1} = \mathtt{MAA}^\mathsf{T}\mathtt{M}^\mathsf{T}$, which may be rearranged as $\mathtt{AA}^\mathsf{T} = (\mathtt{M}^\mathsf{T}\boldsymbol{\omega}\mathtt{M})^{-1}$. A particular value of $\mathtt{A}$ that satisfies this relationship is found by taking the Cholesky factorization of $(\mathtt{M}^\mathsf{T}\boldsymbol{\omega}\mathtt{M})^{-1}$. This latter matrix is guaranteed to be positive-definite (see result A4.5(p582)), otherwise no such matrix $\mathtt{A}$ will exist, and metric reconstruction will not be possible. □

This approach to metric reconstruction relies on identifying the image of the absolute conic. There are various ways of doing this and these are discussed next. Three sources of constraint on the image of the absolute conic are given, and in practice a combination of these constraints is used.

1. Constraints arising from scene orthogonality. Pairs of vanishing points, $\mathbf{v}_1$ and $\mathbf{v}_2$, arising from orthogonal scene lines place a single linear constraint on $\boldsymbol{\omega}$:

$$\mathbf{v}_1^\mathsf{T}\boldsymbol{\omega}\mathbf{v}_2 = 0.$$

Similarly, a vanishing point $\mathbf{v}$ and a vanishing line $\mathbf{l}$ arising from a direction and plane which are orthogonal place two constraints on $\boldsymbol{\omega}$:

$$\mathbf{l} = \boldsymbol{\omega}\mathbf{v}.$$

A common example is the vanishing point for the vertical direction and a vanishing line from the horizontal ground plane. Finally an imaged scene plane containing metric information, such as a square grid, places two constraints on $\boldsymbol{\omega}$.

2. Constraints arising from known internal parameters. If the calibration matrix of a camera is equal to $\mathtt{K}$, then the image of the absolute conic is $\boldsymbol{\omega} = \mathtt{K}^{-\mathsf{T}}\mathtt{K}^{-1}$. Thus, knowledge of the internal parameters (6.10–p157) contained in $\mathtt{K}$ may be used to constrain or determine the elements of $\boldsymbol{\omega}$. In the case where $\mathtt{K}$ is known to have zero skew ($s = 0$),

$$\omega_{12} = \omega_{21} = 0$$

and if the pixels are square (zero skew and $\alpha_x = \alpha_y$) then

$$\omega_{11} = \omega_{22}.$$

These first two sources of constraint are discussed in detail in section 8.8(p223) on single view calibration, where examples are given of calibrating a camera solely from such information. Here there is an additional source of constraints available arising from the multiple views.

3. Constraints arising from the same cameras in all images. One of the properties of the absolute conic is that its projection into an image depends only on the calibration matrix of the camera, and not on the position or orientation of the camera. In the case where both cameras $\mathtt{P}$ and $\mathtt{P}'$ have the same calibration matrix (usually meaning that both the images were taken with the same camera with different pose) one has that $\boldsymbol{\omega} = \boldsymbol{\omega}'$, that is the image of the absolute conic is the same in both images. Given

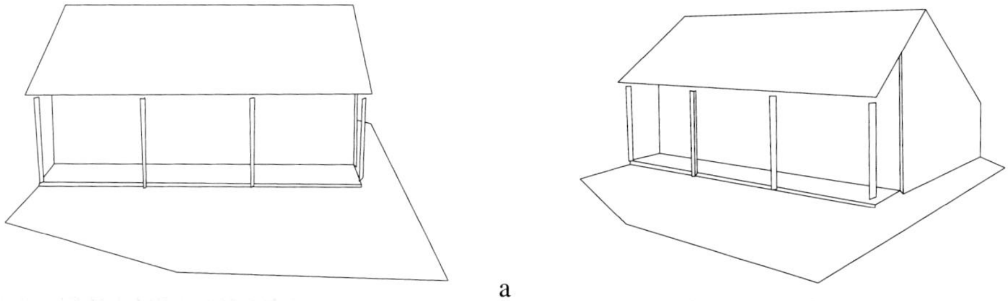

a

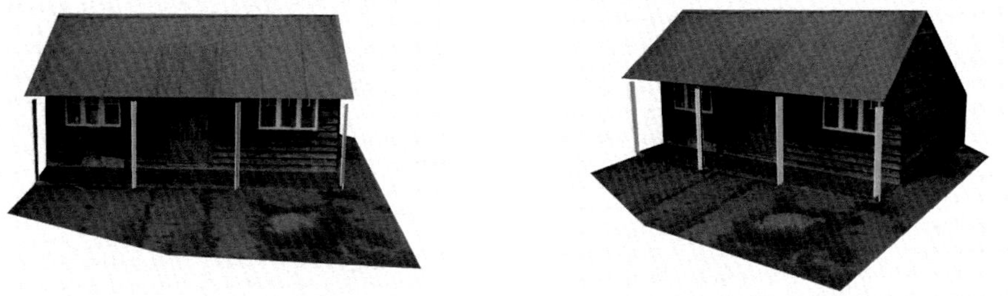

b

Fig. 10.5. **Metric reconstruction.** *The affine reconstruction of figure 10.4 is upgraded to metric by computing the image of the absolute conic. The information used is the orthogonality of the directions of the parallel line sets shown in figure 10.4, together with the constraint that both images have square pixels. The square pixel constraint is transferred from one image to the other using* $\mathtt{H}_\infty$. *(a) Two views of the metric reconstruction. Lines which are perpendicular in the scene are perpendicular in the reconstruction and also the aspect ratio of the sides of the house is veridical. (b) Two views of a texture mapped piecewise planar model built from the wireframes.*

sufficiently many images, one may use this property to obtain a metric reconstruction from an affine reconstruction. This method of metric reconstruction, and its use for self-calibration of a camera, will be treated in greater detail in chapter 19. For now, we give just the general principle.

Since the absolute conic lies on the plane at infinity, its image may be transferred from one view to the other via the infinite homography. This implies an equation (see result 2.13(*p*37))

$$\boldsymbol{\omega}' = \mathtt{H}_\infty^{-\mathsf{T}} \boldsymbol{\omega} \mathtt{H}_\infty^{-1} \tag{10.3}$$

where $\boldsymbol{\omega}$ and $\boldsymbol{\omega}'$ are images of Ω_∞ in the two views. In forming these equations it is necessary to have an affine reconstruction already, since the infinite homography must be known. If $\boldsymbol{\omega} = \boldsymbol{\omega}'$, then (10.3) gives a set of linear equations in the entries of $\boldsymbol{\omega}$. In general this set of linear equations places four constraints on $\boldsymbol{\omega}$, and since $\boldsymbol{\omega}$ has 5 degrees of freedom it is not completely determined. However, by combining these linear equations with those above provided by scene orthogonality or known internal parameters, $\boldsymbol{\omega}$ may be determined uniquely. Indeed (10.3) may be used to transfer constraints on $\boldsymbol{\omega}$ to constraints on $\boldsymbol{\omega}'$. Figure 10.5 shows an example of a metric reconstruction computed by combining constraints in this manner.

10.4.3 Direct metric reconstruction using ω

The previous discussion showed how knowledge of the image of the absolute conic (IAC) may be used to transform an affine to a metric reconstruction. However, knowing ω it is possible to proceed directly to metric reconstruction, given at least two views. This can be accomplished in at least two different ways. The most evident approach is to use the IAC to compute calibration of each of the cameras, and then carry out a calibrated reconstruction.

This method relies on the connection of ω to the calibration matrix $\mathtt{K}$, namely $\omega = (\mathtt{K}\mathtt{K}^{\mathsf{T}})^{-1}$. Thus one can compute $\mathtt{K}$ from ω by inverting it and then applying Cholesky factorization to obtain $\mathtt{K}$. If the IAC is known in each image, then both cameras may be calibrated in this way. Next with calibrated cameras, a metric reconstruction of the scene may be computed using the essential matrix, as in section 9.6. Note that four possible solutions may result. Two of these are just mirror images, but the other two are different, forming a twisted pair. (Though all solutions but one may be ruled out by consideration of points lying in front of the cameras.)

A more conceptual approach to metric reconstruction is to use knowledge of the IAC to directly determine the plane at infinity and the absolute conic. Knowing the camera matrices $\mathtt{P}$ and $\mathtt{P}'$ in a projective frame, and a conic (specifically the image of the absolute conic) in each image, then Ω_∞ may be explicitly computed in 3-space. This is achieved by back-projecting the conics to cones, which must intersect in the absolute conic. Thus, Ω_∞ and its support plane $\boldsymbol{\pi}_\infty$ are determined (see exercise (x) on page 342 for an algebraic solution). However, two cones will in general intersect in two different plane conics, each lying in a different support plane. Thus there are two possible solutions for the absolute conic, which one can identify as belonging to the two different reconstructions constituting the twisted pair ambiguity.

10.5 Direct reconstruction – using ground truth

It is possible to jump directly from a projective reconstruction to a metric reconstruction if "ground control points" (that is points with known 3D locations in a Euclidean world frame) are given. Suppose we have a set of n such ground control points $\{\mathbf{X}_{\mathrm{E}i}\}$ which are imaged at $\mathbf{x}_i \leftrightarrow \mathbf{x}'_i$. We wish to use these points to transform the projective reconstruction to metric.

The 3D location $\{\mathbf{X}_i\}$ of the control points in the projective reconstruction may be computed from their image correspondences $\mathbf{x}_i \leftrightarrow \mathbf{x}'_i$. Since the projective reconstruction is related by a homography to the true reconstruction we then have from (10.1) the equations:

$$\mathbf{X}_{\mathrm{E}i} = \mathtt{H}\mathbf{X}_i, \quad i = 1, \dots, n.$$

Each point correspondence provides 3 linearly independent equations on the elements of $\mathtt{H}$, and since $\mathtt{H}$ has 15 degrees of freedom a linear solution is obtained provided $n \geq 5$ (and no four of the control points are coplanar). This computation, and the proper numerical procedures, are described in chapter 4.

Alternatively, one may bypass the computation of the $\mathbf{X}_i$ and compute $\mathtt{H}$ by relating

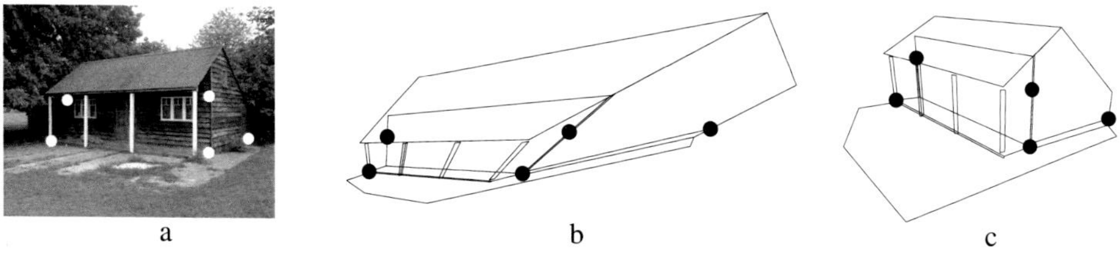

Fig. 10.6. **Direct reconstruction.** *The projective reconstruction of figure 10.3 may be upgraded to metric by specifying the position of five (or more) world points: (a) the five points used; (b) the corresponding points on the projective reconstruction of figure 10.3; (c) the reconstruction after the five points are mapped to their world positions.*

the known ground control points directly to image measurements. Thus as in the DLT algorithm for camera resection (section 7.1(p178)) the equation

$$\mathbf{x}_i = \mathtt{P}\mathtt{H}^{-1}\mathbf{X}_{\mathrm{E}i}$$

provides two linearly independent equations in the entries of the unknown $\mathtt{H}^{-1}$, all other quantities being known. Similarly equations may be derived from the other image if $\mathbf{x}'_i$ is known. It is not necessary for the ground control points to be visible in both images. Note however that if both $\mathbf{x}_i$ and $\mathbf{x}'_i$ *are* visible for a given control point $\mathbf{X}_{\mathrm{E}i}$ then because of the coplanarity constraint on $\mathbf{x}$ and $\mathbf{x}'$, the four equations generated in this way contain only three independent ones.

Once $\mathtt{H}$ has been computed it may be used to transform the cameras $\mathtt{P}, \mathtt{P}'$ of the projective reconstruction to their true Euclidean counterparts. An example of metric structure computed by this direct method is shown in figure 10.6.

10.6 Closure

In this chapter we have overviewed the steps necessary to produce a metric reconstruction from a pair of images. This overview is summarized in algorithm 10.1, and the computational procedures for these steps are described in the following chapters. As usual the general discussion has been restricted mainly to points, but the ideas (triangulation, ambiguity, stratification) apply equally to other image features such as lines, conics etc.

It has been seen that for a metric reconstruction it is necessary to identify two entities in the projective frame; these are the plane at infinity $\boldsymbol{\pi}_\infty$ (for affine), together with the absolute conic Ω_∞ (for metric). Conversely, given $\mathtt{F}$ and a pair of calibrated cameras then $\boldsymbol{\pi}_\infty$ and Ω_∞ may be explicitly computed in 3-space. These entities each have an image-based counterpart: specification of the infinite homography, $\mathtt{H}_\infty$, is equivalent to specifying $\boldsymbol{\pi}_\infty$ in 3-space; and specifying the image of the absolute conic, $\boldsymbol{\omega}$, in each view is equivalent to specifying $\boldsymbol{\pi}_\infty$ and Ω_∞ in 3-space. This equivalence is summarized in table 10.1.

Finally, it is worth noting that if metric precision is not the goal then an acceptable metric reconstruction is generally obtained directly from the projective if approximately correct internal parameters are guessed. Such a "quasi-Euclidean reconstruction" is often suitable for visualization purposes.

Objective

Given two uncalibrated images compute a metric reconstruction $(\mathtt{P}_{\mathrm{M}}, \mathtt{P}'_{\mathrm{M}}, \{\mathbf{X}_{\mathrm{M}i}\})$ of the cameras and scene structure, i.e. a reconstruction that is within a similarity transformation of the true cameras and scene structure.

Algorithm

(i) **Compute a projective reconstruction** $(\mathtt{P}, \mathtt{P}', \{\mathbf{X}_i\})$**:**

(a) **Compute the fundamental matrix** from point correspondences $\mathbf{x}_i \leftrightarrow \mathbf{x}'_i$ between the images.

(b) **Camera retrieval:** compute the camera matrices $\mathtt{P}, \mathtt{P}'$ from the fundamental matrix.

(c) **Triangulation:** for each point correspondence $\mathbf{x}_i \leftrightarrow \mathbf{x}'_i$, compute the point $\mathbf{X}_i$ in space that projects to these two image points.

(ii) **Rectify the projective reconstruction to metric:**

- either **Direct method:** Compute the homography $\mathtt{H}$ such that $\mathbf{X}_{\mathrm{E}i} = \mathtt{H}\mathbf{X}_i$ from five or more ground control points $\mathbf{X}_{\mathrm{E}i}$ with known Euclidean positions. Then the metric reconstruction is

$$\mathtt{P}_{\mathrm{M}} = \mathtt{P}\mathtt{H}^{-1}, \quad \mathtt{P}'_{\mathrm{M}} = \mathtt{P}'\mathtt{H}^{-1}, \quad \mathbf{X}_{\mathrm{M}i} = \mathtt{H}\mathbf{X}_i.$$

- or **Stratified method:**

(a) **Affine reconstruction:** Compute the plane at infinity, $\boldsymbol{\pi}_\infty$, as described in section 10.4.1, and then upgrade the projective reconstruction to an affine reconstruction with the homography

$$\mathtt{H} = \begin{bmatrix} \mathtt{I} \mid \mathbf{0} \\ \boldsymbol{\pi}_\infty^{\mathsf{T}} \end{bmatrix}.$$

(b) **Metric reconstruction:** Compute the image of the absolute conic, $\boldsymbol{\omega}$, as described in section 10.4.2, and then upgrade the affine reconstruction to a metric reconstruction with the homography

$$\mathtt{H} = \begin{bmatrix} \mathtt{A}^{-1} & \\ & 1 \end{bmatrix}$$

where $\mathtt{A}$ is obtained by Cholesky factorization from the equation $\mathtt{A}\mathtt{A}^{\mathsf{T}} = (\mathtt{M}^{\mathsf{T}}\boldsymbol{\omega}\mathtt{M})^{-1}$, and $\mathtt{M}$ is the first 3×3 submatrix of the camera in the affine reconstruction for which $\boldsymbol{\omega}$ is computed.

Algorithm 10.1. *Computation of a metric reconstruction from two uncalibrated images.*

10.6.1 The literature

Koenderink and van Doorn [Koenderink-91] give a very elegant discussion of stratification for affine cameras. This was extended to perspective in [Faugeras-95b], with developments given by Luong and Viéville [Luong-94, Luong-96]. The possibility of projective reconstruction given $\mathtt{F}$ appeared in [Faugeras-92b] and Hartley *et al.* [Hartley-92c].

The method of computing affine reconstruction from pure translation first appeared in Moons *et al.* [Moons-94]. Combining scene and internal parameter constraints over multiple views is described in [Faugeras-95c, Liebowitz-99b, Sturm-99c].

Image information provided	View relations and projective objects	3-space objects	Reconstruction ambiguity
Point correspondences	F		Projective
Point correspondences including vanishing points	F, H_∞	π_∞	Affine
Point correspondences and internal camera calibration	F, H_∞ ω, ω'	π_∞ Ω_∞	Metric

Table 10.1. *The two-view relations, image entities, and their 3-space counterparts for various classes of reconstruction ambiguity.*

10.6.2 Notes and exercises

(i) Using only (implicit) image relations (i.e. without an explicit 3D reconstruction) and given the images of a line $\mathbf{L}$ and point $\mathbf{X}$ (not on $\mathbf{L}$) in two views, together with H_∞ between the views, compute the image of the line in 3-space parallel to $\mathbf{L}$ and through $\mathbf{X}$. Other examples of this implicit approach to computation are given in [Zeller-96].

11

Computation of the Fundamental Matrix F

This chapter describes numerical methods for estimating the fundamental matrix given a set of point correspondences between two images. We begin by describing the equations on F generated by point correspondences in two images, and their minimal solution. The following sections then give linear methods for estimating F using algebraic distance, and then various geometric cost functions and solution methods including the MLE ("Gold Standard") algorithm, and Sampson distance.

An algorithm is then described for automatically obtaining point correspondences, so that F may be estimated directly from an image pair. We discuss the estimation of F for special camera motions.

The chapter also covers a method of image rectification based on the computed F.

11.1 Basic equations

The fundamental matrix is defined by the equation

$$\mathbf{x}'^{\mathsf{T}}\mathtt{F}\mathbf{x} = 0 \tag{11.1}$$

for any pair of matching points $\mathbf{x} \leftrightarrow \mathbf{x}'$ in two images. Given sufficiently many point matches $\mathbf{x}_i \leftrightarrow \mathbf{x}'_i$ (at least 7), equation (11.1) can be used to compute the unknown matrix F. In particular, writing $\mathbf{x} = (x, y, 1)^{\mathsf{T}}$ and $\mathbf{x}' = (x', y', 1)^{\mathsf{T}}$ each point match gives rise to one linear equation in the unknown entries of F. The coefficients of this equation are easily written in terms of the known coordinates $\mathbf{x}$ and $\mathbf{x}'$. Specifically, the equation corresponding to a pair of points $(x, y, 1)$ and $(x', y', 1)$ is

$$x'xf_{11} + x'yf_{12} + x'f_{13} + y'xf_{21} + y'yf_{22} + y'f_{23} + xf_{31} + yf_{32} + f_{33} = 0. \tag{11.2}$$

Denote by $\mathbf{f}$ the 9-vector made up of the entries of F in row-major order. Then (11.2) can be expressed as a vector inner product

$$(x'x, x'y, x', y'x, y'y, y', x, y, 1)\,\mathbf{f} = 0.$$

From a set of n point matches, we obtain a set of linear equations of the form

$$\mathtt{A}\mathbf{f} = \begin{bmatrix} x'_1x_1 & x'_1y_1 & x'_1 & y'_1x_1 & y'_1y_1 & y'_1 & x_1 & y_1 & 1 \\ \vdots & \vdots & \vdots & \vdots & \vdots & \vdots & \vdots & \vdots & \vdots \\ x'_nx_n & x'_ny_n & x'_n & y'_nx_n & y'_ny_n & y'_n & x_n & y_n & 1 \end{bmatrix} \mathbf{f} = \mathbf{0}. \tag{11.3}$$

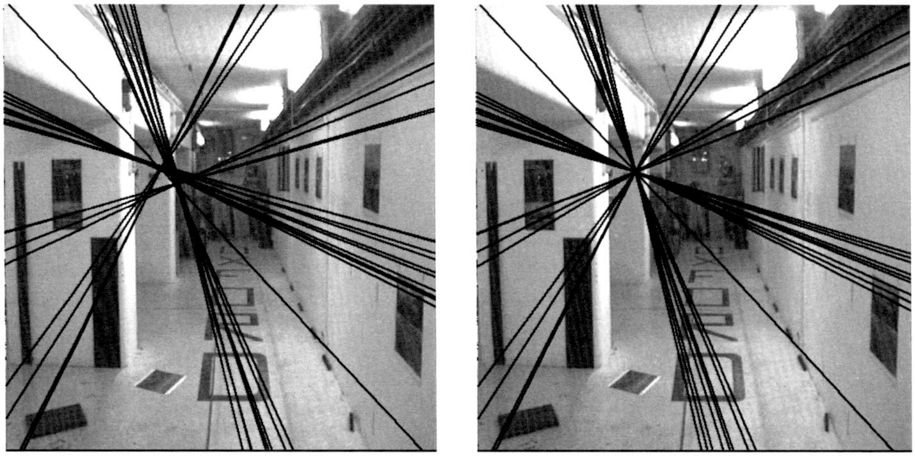

a b

Fig. 11.1. **Epipolar lines.** *(a) the effect of a non-singular fundamental matrix. Epipolar lines computed as* $\mathbf{l}' = \mathtt{F}\mathbf{x}$ *for varying* $\mathbf{x}$ *do not meet in a common epipole. (b) the effect of enforcing singularity using the SVD method described here.*

This is a homogeneous set of equations, and $\mathbf{f}$ can only be determined up to scale. For a solution to exist, matrix $\mathtt{A}$ must have rank at most 8, and if the rank is exactly 8, then the solution is unique (up to scale), and can be found by linear methods – the solution is the generator of the right null-space of $\mathtt{A}$.

If the data is not exact, because of noise in the point coordinates, then the rank of $\mathtt{A}$ may be greater than 8 (in fact equal to 9, since $\mathtt{A}$ has 9 columns). In this case, one finds a least-squares solution. Apart from the specific form of the equations (compare (11.3) with (4.3–*p*89)) the problem is essentially the same as the estimation problem considered in section 4.1.1(*p*90). Refer to the algorithm 4.1(*p*91). The least-squares solution for $\mathbf{f}$ is the singular vector corresponding to the smallest singular value of $\mathtt{A}$, that is, the last column of $\mathtt{V}$ in the SVD $\mathtt{A} = \mathtt{UDV}^\mathsf{T}$. The solution vector $\mathbf{f}$ found in this way minimizes $\|\mathtt{A}\mathbf{f}\|$ subject to the condition $\|\mathbf{f}\| = 1$. The algorithm just described is the essence of a method called the 8-point algorithm for computation of the fundamental matrix.

11.1.1 The singularity constraint

An important property of the fundamental matrix is that it is singular, in fact of rank 2. Furthermore, the left and right null-spaces of $\mathtt{F}$ are generated by the vectors representing (in homogeneous coordinates) the two epipoles in the two images. Most applications of the fundamental matrix rely on the fact that it has rank 2. For instance, if the fundamental matrix is not singular then computed epipolar lines are not coincident, as is demonstrated by figure 11.1. The matrix $\mathtt{F}$ found by solving the set of linear equations (11.3) will not in general have rank 2, and we should take steps to enforce this constraint. The most convenient way to do this is to correct the matrix $\mathtt{F}$ found by the SVD solution from $\mathtt{A}$. Matrix $\mathtt{F}$ is replaced by the matrix $\mathtt{F}'$ that minimizes the Frobenius norm $\|\mathtt{F} - \mathtt{F}'\|$ subject to the condition $\det \mathtt{F}' = 0$. A convenient method of doing this is to again use the SVD. In particular, let $\mathtt{F} = \mathtt{UDV}^\mathsf{T}$ be the SVD of F, where D is a diagonal matrix $\mathtt{D} = \text{diag}(r, s, t)$ satisfying $r \geq s \geq t$. Then $\mathtt{F}' = \mathtt{U}\text{diag}(r, s, 0)\mathtt{V}^\mathsf{T}$ minimizes the Frobenius norm of $\mathtt{F} - \mathtt{F}'$.

Thus, the 8-point algorithm for computation of the fundamental matrix may be formulated as consisting of two steps, as follows.

(i) **Linear solution.** A solution F is obtained from the vector $\mathbf{f}$ corresponding to the smallest singular value of A, where A is defined in (11.3).

(ii) **Constraint enforcement.** Replace F by $\mathtt{F}'$, the closest singular matrix to F under a Frobenius norm. This correction is done using the SVD.

The algorithm thus stated is extremely simple, and readily implemented, assuming that appropriate linear algebra routines are available. As usual normalization is required, and we return to this in section 11.2.

11.1.2 The minimum case – seven point correspondences

The equation $\mathbf{x}_i'^\mathsf{T}\mathtt{F}\mathbf{x}_i = 0$ gives rise to a set of equations of the form $\mathtt{A}\mathbf{f} = \mathbf{0}$. If A has rank 8, then it is possible to solve for $\mathbf{f}$ up to scale. In the case where the matrix A has rank seven, it is still possible to solve for the fundamental matrix by making use of the singularity constraint. The most important case is when only 7 point correspondences are known (other cases are discussed in section 11.9). This leads to a 7×9 matrix A, which generally will have rank 7.

The solution to the equations $\mathtt{A}\mathbf{f} = \mathbf{0}$ in this case is a 2-dimensional space of the form $\alpha\mathtt{F}_1 + (1-\alpha)\mathtt{F}_2$, where α is a scalar variable. The matrices $\mathtt{F}_1$ and $\mathtt{F}_2$ are obtained as the matrices corresponding to the generators $\mathbf{f}_1$ and $\mathbf{f}_2$ of the right null-space of A. Now, we use the constraint that $\det \mathtt{F} = 0$. This may be written as $\det(\alpha\mathtt{F}_1 + (1-\alpha)\mathtt{F}_2) = 0$. Since $\mathtt{F}_1$ and $\mathtt{F}_2$ are known, this leads to a cubic polynomial equation in α. This polynomial equation may be solved to find the value of α. There will be either one or three real solutions (the complex solutions are discarded [Hartley-94c]). Substituting back in the equation $\mathtt{F} = \alpha\mathtt{F}_1 + (1-\alpha)\mathtt{F}_2$ gives one or three possible solutions for the fundamental matrix.

This method of computing one or three fundamental matrices for the minimum number of points (seven) is used in the robust algorithm of section 11.6. We return to the issue of the number of solutions in section 11.9.

11.2 The normalized 8-point algorithm

The 8-point algorithm is the simplest method of computing the fundamental matrix, involving no more than the construction and (least-squares) solution of a set of linear equations. If care is taken, then it can perform extremely well. The original algorithm is due to Longuet-Higgins [LonguetHiggins-81]. The key to success with the 8-point algorithm is proper careful normalization of the input data before constructing the equations to solve. The subject of normalization of input data has applications to many of the algorithms of this book, and is treated in general terms in section 4.4-(p104). In the case of the 8-point algorithm, a simple transformation (translation and

Objective

Given $n \geq 8$ image point correspondences $\{\mathbf{x}_i \leftrightarrow \mathbf{x}'_i\}$, determine the fundamental matrix F such that $\mathbf{x}'^{\mathsf{T}}_i \mathtt{F}\mathbf{x}_i = 0$.

Algorithm

(i) **Normalization:** Transform the image coordinates according to $\hat{\mathbf{x}}_i = \mathtt{T}\mathbf{x}_i$ and $\hat{\mathbf{x}}'_i = \mathtt{T}'\mathbf{x}'_i$, where T and T′ are normalizing transformations consisting of a translation and scaling.

(ii) Find the fundamental matrix $\hat{\mathtt{F}}'$ corresponding to the matches $\hat{\mathbf{x}}_i \leftrightarrow \hat{\mathbf{x}}'_i$ by

(a) **Linear solution:** Determine $\hat{\mathtt{F}}$ from the singular vector corresponding to the smallest singular value of $\hat{\mathtt{A}}$, where $\hat{\mathtt{A}}$ is composed from the matches $\hat{\mathbf{x}}_i \leftrightarrow \hat{\mathbf{x}}'_i$ as defined in (11.3).

(b) **Constraint enforcement:** Replace $\hat{\mathtt{F}}$ by $\hat{\mathtt{F}}'$ such that $\det \hat{\mathtt{F}}' = 0$ using the SVD (see section 11.1.1).

(iii) **Denormalization:** Set $\mathtt{F} = \mathtt{T}'^{\mathsf{T}}\hat{\mathtt{F}}'\mathtt{T}$. Matrix F is the fundamental matrix corresponding to the original data $\mathbf{x}_i \leftrightarrow \mathbf{x}'_i$.

Algorithm 11.1. *The normalized 8-point algorithm for* F.

scaling) of the points in the image before formulating the linear equations leads to an enormous improvement in the conditioning of the problem and hence in the stability of the result. The added complexity of the algorithm necessary to do this transformation is insignificant.

The suggested normalization is a translation and scaling of each image so that the centroid of the reference points is at the origin of the coordinates and the RMS distance of the points from the origin is equal to $\sqrt{2}$. This is carried out for essentially the same reasons as in chapter 4. The basic method is analogous to algorithm 4.2(p109) and is summarized in algorithm 11.1.

Note that it is recommended that the singularity condition should be enforced before denormalization. For a justification of this, refer to [Hartley-97c].

11.3 The algebraic minimization algorithm

The normalized 8-point algorithm includes a method for enforcing the singularity constraint on the fundamental matrix. The initial estimate F is replaced by the singular matrix F′ that minimizes the difference $||\mathtt{F}' - \mathtt{F}||$. This is done using the SVD, and has the advantage of being simple and rapid.

Numerically, however, this method is not optimal, since all the entries of F do not have equal importance, and indeed some entries are more tightly constrained by the point-correspondence data than others. A more correct procedure would be to compute a covariance matrix from the entries of F in terms of the input data, and then to find the singular matrix F′ closest to F in terms of Mahalanobis distance with respect to this covariance. Unfortunately, minimization of the Mahalanobis distance $||\mathtt{F} - \mathtt{F}'||_\Sigma$ cannot be done linearly for a general covariance matrix Σ, so this approach is unattractive.

An alternative procedure is to find the desired singular matrix F′ directly. Thus, just as F is computed by minimizing the norm $||\mathtt{A}\mathbf{f}||$ subject to $||\mathbf{f}|| = 1$, so one should aim to find the *singular* matrix $\mathtt{F}'$ that minimizes $\|\mathtt{A}\mathbf{f}'\|$ subject to $\|\mathbf{f}'\| = 1$. It turns out not to be possible to do this by linear non-iterative means, chiefly because $\det \mathtt{F}' = 0$ is a cubic, rather than a linear constraint. Nevertheless, it will be seen that a simple iterative method is effective.

An arbitrary singular 3×3 matrix, such as the fundamental matrix $\mathtt{F}$, may be written as a product $\mathtt{F} = \mathtt{M}[\mathbf{e}]_\times$ where $\mathtt{M}$ is a non-singular matrix and $[\mathbf{e}]_\times$ is any skew-symmetric matrix, with $\mathbf{e}$ corresponding to the epipole in the first image.

Suppose we wish to compute the fundamental matrix $\mathtt{F}$ of the form $\mathtt{F} = \mathtt{M}[\mathbf{e}]_\times$ that minimizes the algebraic error $\|\mathtt{A}\mathbf{f}\|$ subject to the condition $\|\mathbf{f}\| = 1$. Let us assume for now that the epipole $\mathbf{e}$ is known. Later we will let $\mathbf{e}$ vary, but for now it is fixed. The equation $\mathtt{F} = \mathtt{M}[\mathbf{e}]_\times$ can be written in terms of the vectors $\mathbf{f}$ and $\mathbf{m}$ comprising the entries of $\mathtt{F}$ and $\mathtt{M}$ as an equation $\mathbf{f} = \mathtt{E}\mathbf{m}$ where $\mathtt{E}$ is a 9×9 matrix. Supposing that $\mathbf{f}$ and $\mathbf{m}$ contain the entries of the corresponding matrices in row-major order, then it can be verified that $\mathtt{E}$ has the form

$$\mathtt{E} = \begin{bmatrix} [\mathbf{e}]_\times & & \\ & [\mathbf{e}]_\times & \\ & & [\mathbf{e}]_\times \end{bmatrix}. \tag{11.4}$$

Since $\mathbf{f} = \mathtt{E}\mathbf{m}$, the minimization problem becomes: [1]

$$\text{Minimize } \|\mathtt{A}\mathtt{E}\mathbf{m}\| \text{ subject to the condition } \|\mathtt{E}\mathbf{m}\| = 1. \tag{11.5}$$

This minimization problem is solved using algorithm A5.6(*p*595). For the purposes of this algorithm one observes that $\text{rank}(\mathtt{E}) = 6$, since each of its diagonal blocks has rank 2.

11.3.1 Iterative estimation

The minimization (11.5) gives a way of computing an algebraic error vector $\mathtt{A}\mathbf{f}$ given a value for the epipole $\mathbf{e}$. This mapping $\mathbf{e} \mapsto \mathtt{A}\mathbf{f}$ is a map from $\mathbb{R}^3$ to $\mathbb{R}^9$. Note that the value of $\mathtt{A}\mathbf{f}$ is unaffected by scaling $\mathbf{e}$. Starting from an estimated value of $\mathbf{e}$ derived as the generator of the right null-space of an initial estimate of $\mathtt{F}$, one may iterate to find the final $\mathtt{F}$ that minimizes algebraic error. The initial estimate of $\mathtt{F}$ may be obtained from the 8-point algorithm, or any other simple algorithm. The complete algorithm for computation of $\mathtt{F}$ is given in algorithm 11.2.

Note the advantage of this method of computing $\mathtt{F}$ is that the iterative part of the algorithm consists of a very small parameter minimization problem, involving the estimation of only three parameters (the homogeneous coordinates of $\mathbf{e}$). Despite this, the algorithm finds the fundamental matrix that minimizes the algebraic error for all matched points. The matched points themselves do not come into the final iterative estimation.

[1] It does not do to minimize $\|\mathtt{A}\mathtt{E}\mathbf{m}\|$ subject to the condition $\|\mathbf{m}\| = 1$, since a solution to this occurs when $\mathbf{m}$ is a unit vector in the right null-space of $\mathtt{E}$. In this case, $\mathtt{E}\mathbf{m} = \mathbf{0}$, and hence $\|\mathtt{A}\mathtt{E}\mathbf{m}\| = 0$.

Objective

Find the fundamental matrix F that minimizes the algebraic error $\|\mathtt{A}\mathbf{f}\|$ subject to $\|\mathbf{f}\| = 1$ and $\det \mathtt{F} = 0$.

Algorithm

(i) Find a first approximation $\mathtt{F}_0$ for the fundamental matrix using the normalized 8-point algorithm 11.1. Then find the right null-vector $\mathbf{e}_0$ of $\mathtt{F}_0$.
(ii) Starting with the estimate $\mathbf{e}_i = \mathbf{e}_0$ for the epipole, compute the matrix $\mathtt{E}_i$ according to (11.4), then find the vector $\mathbf{f}_i = \mathtt{E}_i\mathbf{m}_i$ that minimizes $\|\mathtt{A}\mathbf{f}_i\|$ subject to $\|\mathbf{f}_i\| = 1$. This is done using algorithm A5.6(*p*595).
(iii) Compute the algebraic error $\epsilon_i = \mathtt{A}\mathbf{f}_i$. Since $\mathbf{f}_i$ and hence ϵ_i is defined only up to sign, correct the sign of ϵ_i (multiplying by minus 1 if necessary) so that $\mathbf{e}_i^\mathsf{T}\mathbf{e}_{i-1} > 0$ for $i > 0$. This is done to ensure that ϵ_i varies smoothly as a function of $\mathbf{e}_i$.
(iv) The previous two steps define a mapping $\mathbb{R}^3 \rightarrow \mathbb{R}^9$ mapping $\mathbf{e}_i \mapsto \epsilon_i$. Now use the Levenberg–Marquardt algorithm (section A6.2(*p*600)) to vary $\mathbf{e}_i$ iteratively so as to minimize $\|\epsilon_i\|$.
(v) Upon convergence, $\mathbf{f}_i$ represents the desired fundamental matrix.

Algorithm 11.2. *Computation of* F *with* $\det \mathtt{F} = 0$ *by iteratively minimizing algebraic error.*

11.4 Geometric distance

This section describes three algorithms which minimize a geometric image distance. The one we recommend, which is the Gold Standard method, unfortunately requires the most effort in implementation. The other algorithms produce extremely good results and are easier to implement, but are not optimal under the assumption that the image errors are Gaussian. Two important issues for each of the algorithms are the intitialization for the non-linear minimization, and the parametrization of the cost function. The algorithms are generally initialized by one of the linear algorithms of the previous section. An alternative, which is used in the automatic algorithm, is to select 7 correspondences and thus generate one or three solutions for F. Various parametrizations are discussed in section 11.4.2. In all cases we recommend that the image points be normalized by a translation and scaling. This normalization does not skew the noise characteristics, so does not interfere with the optimality of the Gold Standard algorithm, which is described next.

11.4.1 The Gold Standard method

The Maximum Likelihood estimate of the fundamental matrix depends on the assumption of an error model. We make the assumption that noise in image point measurements obeys a Gaussian distribution. In that case the ML estimate is the one that minimizes the geometric distance (which is reprojection error)

$$\sum_i d(\mathbf{x}_i, \hat{\mathbf{x}}_i)^2 + d(\mathbf{x}'_i, \hat{\mathbf{x}}'_i)^2 \tag{11.6}$$

where $\mathbf{x}_i \leftrightarrow \mathbf{x}'_i$ are the measured correspondences, and $\hat{\mathbf{x}}_i$ and $\hat{\mathbf{x}}'_i$ are estimated "true" correspondences that satisfy $\hat{\mathbf{x}}'^\mathsf{T}_i \mathtt{F}\hat{\mathbf{x}}_i = 0$ exactly for some rank-2 matrix F, the estimated fundamental matrix.

Objective

Given $n \geq 8$ image point correspondences $\{\mathbf{x}_i \leftrightarrow \mathbf{x}'_i\}$, determine the Maximum Likelihood estimate $\hat{\mathtt{F}}$ of the fundamental matrix.

The MLE involves also solving for a set of subsidiary point correspondences $\{\hat{\mathbf{x}}_i \leftrightarrow \hat{\mathbf{x}}'_i\}$, such that $\hat{\mathbf{x}}_i'^{\mathsf{T}}\hat{\mathtt{F}}\hat{\mathbf{x}}_i = 0$, and which minimizes

$$\sum_i d(\mathbf{x}_i, \hat{\mathbf{x}}_i)^2 + d(\mathbf{x}'_i, \hat{\mathbf{x}}'_i)^2.$$

Algorithm

(i) Compute an initial rank 2 estimate of $\hat{\mathtt{F}}$ using a linear algorithm such as algorithm 11.1.

(ii) Compute an initial estimate of the subsidiary variables $\{\hat{\mathbf{x}}_i, \hat{\mathbf{x}}'_i\}$ as follows:

  (a) Choose camera matrices $\mathtt{P} = [\mathtt{I} \mid \mathbf{0}]$ and $\mathtt{P}' = [[\mathbf{e}']_\times \hat{\mathtt{F}} \mid \mathbf{e}']$, where $\mathbf{e}'$ is obtained from $\hat{\mathtt{F}}$.

  (b) From the correspondence $\mathbf{x}_i \leftrightarrow \mathbf{x}'_i$ and $\hat{\mathtt{F}}$ determine an estimate of $\widehat{\mathbf{X}}_i$ using the triangulation method of chapter 12.

  (c) The correspondence consistent with $\hat{\mathtt{F}}$ is obtained as $\hat{\mathbf{x}}_i = \mathtt{P}\widehat{\mathbf{X}}_i,\ \hat{\mathbf{x}}'_i = \mathtt{P}'\widehat{\mathbf{X}}_i$.

(iii) Minimize the cost

$$\sum_i d(\mathbf{x}_i, \hat{\mathbf{x}}_i)^2 + d(\mathbf{x}'_i, \hat{\mathbf{x}}'_i)^2$$

over $\hat{\mathtt{F}}$ and $\widehat{\mathbf{X}}_i,\ i = 1, \ldots, n$. The cost is minimized using the Levenberg–Marquardt algorithm over $3n + 12$ variables: $3n$ for the n 3D points $\widehat{\mathbf{X}}_i$, and 12 for the camera matrix $\mathtt{P}' = [\mathtt{M} \mid \mathbf{t}]$, with $\hat{\mathtt{F}} = [\mathbf{t}]_\times \mathtt{M}$, and $\hat{\mathbf{x}}_i = \mathtt{P}\widehat{\mathbf{X}}_i,\ \hat{\mathbf{x}}'_i = \mathtt{P}'\widehat{\mathbf{X}}_i$.

Algorithm 11.3. *The Gold Standard algorithm for estimating* F *from image correspondences.*

This error function may be minimized in the following manner. A pair of camera matrices $\mathtt{P} = [\mathtt{I} \mid \mathbf{0}]$ and $\mathtt{P}' = [\mathtt{M} \mid \mathbf{t}]$ are defined. In addition one defines 3D points $\mathbf{X}_i$. Now letting $\hat{\mathbf{x}}_i = \mathtt{P}\mathbf{X}_i$ and $\hat{\mathbf{x}}'_i = \mathtt{P}'\mathbf{X}_i$, one varies $\mathtt{P}'$ and the points $\mathbf{X}_i$ so as to minimize the error expression. Subsequently $\mathtt{F}$ is computed as $\mathtt{F} = [\mathbf{t}]_\times \mathtt{M}$. The vectors $\hat{\mathbf{x}}_i$ and $\hat{\mathbf{x}}'_i$ will satisfy $\hat{\mathbf{x}}_i'^{\mathsf{T}}\mathtt{F}\hat{\mathbf{x}}_i = 0$. Minimization of the error is carried out using the Levenberg–Marquardt algorithm described in section A6.2(*p*600). An initial estimate of the parameters is computed using the normalized 8-point algorithm, followed by projective reconstruction, as described in chapter 12. Thus, estimation of the fundamental matrix using this method is effectively equivalent to projective reconstruction. The steps of the algorithm are summarized in algorithm 11.3.

It may seem that this method for computing $\mathtt{F}$ will be expensive in computing cost. However, the use of the sparse LM techniques means that it is not much more expensive than other iterative techniques, and details of this are given in section A6.5(*p*609).

11.4.2 Parametrization of rank-2 matrices

The non-linear minimization of the geometric distance cost functions requires a parametrization of the fundamental matrix which enforces the rank 2 property of the matrix. We describe three such parametrizations.

Over-parametrization. One way that we have already seen for parametrizing $\mathtt{F}$ is to write $\mathtt{F} = [\mathbf{t}]_\times \mathtt{M}$, where $\mathtt{M}$ is an arbitrary 3×3 matrix. This ensures that $\mathtt{F}$ is singular, since $[\mathbf{t}]_\times$ is. This way, $\mathtt{F}$ is parametrized by the nine entries of $\mathtt{M}$ and the three entries of $\mathbf{t}$ – a total of 12 parameters, more than the minimum number of parameters, which is 7. In general this should not cause a significant problem.

Epipolar parametrization. An alternative way of parametrizing $\mathtt{F}$ is by specifying the first two columns of $\mathtt{F}$, along with two multipliers α and β such that the third column may be written as a linear combination $\mathbf{f}_3 = \alpha\mathbf{f}_1 + \beta\mathbf{f}_2$. Thus, the fundamental matrix is parametrized as

$$\mathtt{F} = \begin{bmatrix} a & b & \alpha a + \beta b \\ c & d & \alpha c + \beta d \\ e & f & \alpha e + \beta f \end{bmatrix}. \tag{11.7}$$

This has a total of 8 parameters. To achieve a minimum set of parameters, one of the elements, for instance f, may be set to 1. In practice whichever of $a, \ldots, f$ has greatest absolute value is set to 1. This method ensures a singular matrix $\mathtt{F}$, while using the minimum number of parameters. The main disadvantage is that it has a singularity – it does not work when the first two columns of $\mathtt{F}$ are linearly dependent, for then it is not possible to write column 3 in terms of the first two columns. This problem can be significant, since it will occur in the case where the right epipole lies at infinity. For then $\mathtt{F}\mathbf{e} = \mathtt{F}(e_1, e_2, 0)^\mathsf{T} = \mathbf{0}$ and the first two columns are linearly dependent. Nevertheless, this parametrization is widely used and works well if steps are taken to avoid this singularity. Instead of using the first two columns as a basis, another pair of columns can be used, in which case the singularity occurs when the epipole is on one of the coordinate axes. In practice such singularities can be detected during the minimization and the parametrization switched to one of the alternative parametrizations.

Note that $(\alpha, \beta, -1)^\mathsf{T}$ is the right epipole for this fundamental matrix – the coordinates of the epipole occur explicitly in the parametrization. For best results, the parametrization should be chosen so that the largest entry (in absolute value) of the epipole is the one set to 1.

Note how the complete manifold of possible fundamental matrices is not covered by a single parametrization, but rather by a set of minimally parametrized patches. As a path is traced out through the manifold during a parameter minimization procedure, it is necessary to switch from one patch to another as the boundary between patches is crossed. In this case there are actually 18 different parameter patches, depending on which of $a, \ldots, f$ is greatest, and which pair of columns are taken as the basis.

Both epipoles as parameters. The previous parametrization uses one of the epipoles as part of the parametrization. For symmetry one may use both the epipoles as parameters. The resulting form of $\mathtt{F}$ is

$$\mathtt{F} = \begin{bmatrix} a & b & \alpha a + \beta b \\ c & d & \alpha c + \beta d \\ \alpha' a + \beta' c & \alpha' b + \beta' d & \alpha'\alpha a + \alpha'\beta b + \beta'\alpha c + \beta'\beta d \end{bmatrix}. \tag{11.8}$$

The two epipoles are $(\alpha, \beta, -1)^{\mathsf{T}}$ and $(\alpha', \beta', -1)^{\mathsf{T}}$. As above, one can set one of a, b, c, d to 1. To avoid singularities, one must switch between different choices of the two rows and two columns to use as the basis. Along with four choices of which of a, b, c, d to set to 1, there are a total of 36 parameter patches used to cover the complete manifold of fundamental matrices.

11.4.3 First-order geometric error (Sampson distance)

The concept of Sampson distance was discussed at length in section 4.2.6(*p*98). Here the Sampson approximation is used in the case of the variety defined by $\mathbf{x}'^{\mathsf{T}}\mathtt{F}\mathbf{x} = 0$ to provide a first-order approximation to the geometric error.

The general formula for the Sampson cost function is given in (4.13–*p*100). In the case of fundamental matrix estimation, the formula is even simpler, since there is only one equation per point correspondence (see also example 4.2(*p*100)). The partial-derivative matrix J has only one row, and hence $\mathtt{J}\mathtt{J}^{\mathsf{T}}$ is a scalar and (4.12–*p*99) becomes

$$\frac{\boldsymbol{\epsilon}^{\mathsf{T}}\boldsymbol{\epsilon}}{\mathtt{J}\mathtt{J}^{\mathsf{T}}} = \frac{(\mathbf{x}_i'^{\mathsf{T}}\mathtt{F}\mathbf{x}_i)^2}{\mathtt{J}\mathtt{J}^{\mathsf{T}}}.$$

From the definition of J and the explicit form of $\mathtt{A}_i = \mathbf{x}_i'^{\mathsf{T}}\mathtt{F}\mathbf{x}_i$ given in the left hand side of (11.2), we obtain

$$\mathtt{J}\mathtt{J}^{\mathsf{T}} = (\mathtt{F}\mathbf{x}_i)_1^2 + (\mathtt{F}\mathbf{x}_i)_2^2 + (\mathtt{F}^{\mathsf{T}}\mathbf{x}_i')_1^2 + (\mathtt{F}^{\mathsf{T}}\mathbf{x}_i')_2^2$$

where for instance $(\mathtt{F}\mathbf{x}_i)_j^2$ represents the square of the j-th entry of the vector $\mathtt{F}\mathbf{x}_i$. Thus, the cost function is

$$\sum_i \frac{(\mathbf{x}_i'^{\mathsf{T}}\mathtt{F}\mathbf{x}_i)^2}{(\mathtt{F}\mathbf{x}_i)_1^2 + (\mathtt{F}\mathbf{x}_i)_2^2 + (\mathtt{F}^{\mathsf{T}}\mathbf{x}_i')_1^2 + (\mathtt{F}^{\mathsf{T}}\mathbf{x}_i')_2^2}. \tag{11.9}$$

This gives a first-order approximation to geometric error, which may be expected to give good results if higher order terms are small in comparison to the first. The approximation has been used successfully in estimation algorithms by [Torr-97, Torr-98, Zhang-98]. Note that this approximation is undefined at the point in $\mathbb{R}^4$ determined by the two epipoles, as here $\mathtt{J}\mathtt{J}^{\mathsf{T}}$ is zero. This point should be avoided in any numerical implementation.

The key advantage of approximating the geometric error in this way is that the resulting cost function only involves the parameters of F. This means that to first-order the Gold Standard cost function (11.6) is minimized *without* introducing a set of subsidiary variables, namely the coordinates of the n space points $\mathbf{X}_i$. Consequently a minimization problem with $7 + 3n$ degrees of freedom is reduced to one with only 7 degrees of freedom.

Symmetric epipolar distance. Equation (11.9) is similar in form to another cost function

$$\sum_i \quad d(\mathbf{x}_i', \mathtt{F}\mathbf{x}_i)^2 + d(\mathbf{x}_i, \mathtt{F}^{\mathsf{T}}\mathbf{x}_i')^2$$

$$= \sum_i (\mathbf{x}_i'^\mathsf{T} \mathtt{F} \mathbf{x}_i)^2 \left(\frac{1}{(\mathtt{F}\mathbf{x}_i)_1^2 + (\mathtt{F}\mathbf{x}_i)_2^2} + \frac{1}{(\mathtt{F}^\mathsf{T}\mathbf{x}_i')_1^2 + (\mathtt{F}^\mathsf{T}\mathbf{x}_i')_2^2} \right) \quad (11.10)$$

which minimizes the distance of a point from its projected epipolar line, computed in each of the images. However, this cost function seems to give slightly inferior results to (11.9) (see [Zhang-98]), and hence is not discussed further.

11.5 Experimental evaluation of the algorithms

Three of the algorithms of the previous sections are now compared by estimating F from point correspondences for a number of image pairs. The algorithms are:

(i) The normalized 8-point algorithm (algorithm 11.1).
(ii) Minimization of algebraic error whilst imposing the singularity constraint (algorithm 11.2).
(iii) The Gold Standard geometric algorithm (algorithm 11.3).

The experimental procedure was as follows. For each pair of images, a number n of matched points were chosen randomly from the matches and the fundamental matrix estimated and residual error (see below) computed. This experiment was repeated 100 times for each value of n and each pair of images, and the average residual error plotted against n. This gives an idea of how the different algorithms behave as the number of points is increased. The number of points used, n, ranged from 8 up to three-quarters of the total number of matched points.

Residual error

The error is defined as

$$\frac{1}{N} \sum_i^N d(\mathbf{x}_i', \mathtt{F}\mathbf{x}_i)^2 + d(\mathbf{x}_i, \mathtt{F}^\mathsf{T}\mathbf{x}_i')^2$$

where $d(\mathbf{x}, \mathbf{l})$ here is the distance (in pixels) between a point $\mathbf{x}$ and a line $\mathbf{l}$. The error is the squared distance between a point's epipolar line and the matching point in the other image (computed for both points of the match), averaged over all N matches. Note the error is evaluated over *all* N matched points, and not just the n matches used to compute F. The residual error corresponds to the epipolar distance defined in (11.10). Note that this particular error is *not* minimized directly by any of the algorithms evaluated here.

The various algorithms were tried with 5 different pairs of images. The images are presented in figure 11.2 and show the diversity of image types, and placement of the epipoles. A few of the epipolar lines are shown in the images. The intersection of the pencil of lines is the epipole. There was a wide variation in the accuracy of the matched points for the different images, though mismatches were removed in a pre-processing step.

Results. The results of these experiments are shown and explained in figure 11.3. They show that minimizing algebraic error gives essentially indistinguishable results from minimizing geometric error.

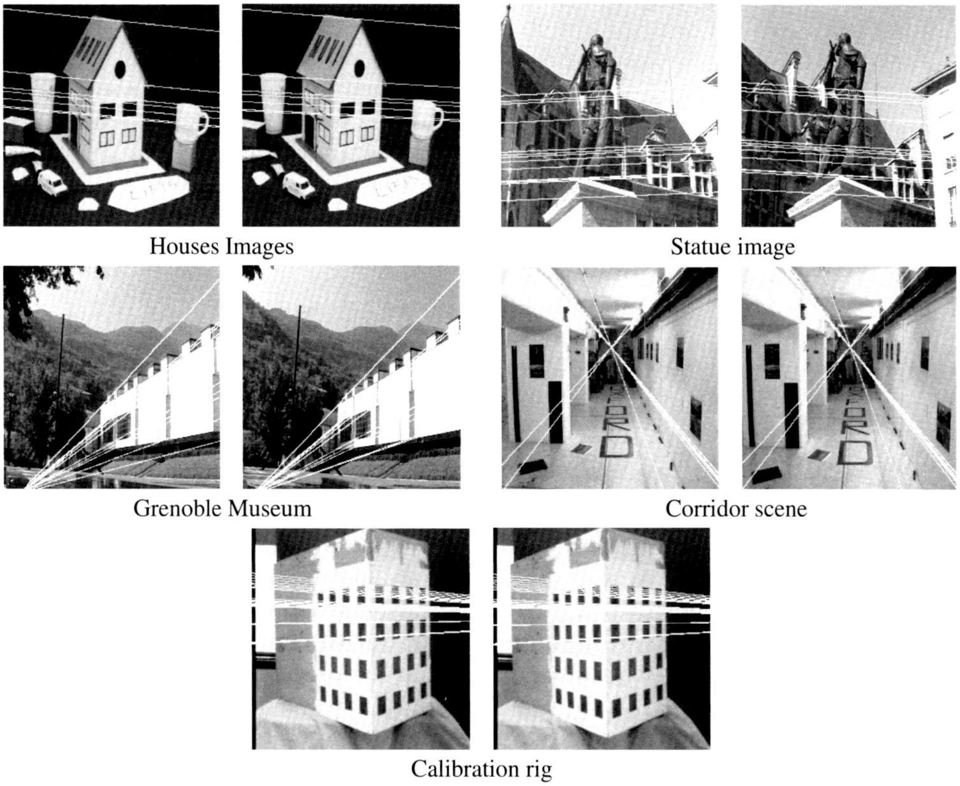

Fig. 11.2. *Image pairs used for the algorithm comparison. In the top two the epipoles are far from the image centres. In the middle two the epipoles are close (Grenoble) and in the image (Corridor). For the calibration images the matched points are known extremely accurately.*

11.5.1 Recommendations

Several methods of computing the fundamental matrix have been discussed in this chapter, and some pointers on which method to use are perhaps desirable. Briefly, these are our recommendations:

- Do not use the unnormalized 8-point algorithm.
- For a quick method, easy to implement, use the normalized 8-point algorithm 11.1. This often gives adequate results, and is ideal as a first step in other algorithms.
- If more accuracy is desired, use the algebraic minimization method, either with or without iteration on the position of the epipole.
- As an alternative that gives excellent results, use an iterative-minimization method that minimizes the Sampson cost function (11.9). This and the iterative algebraic method give similar results.
- To be certain of getting the best results, if Gaussian noise is a viable assumption, implement the Gold Standard algorithm.

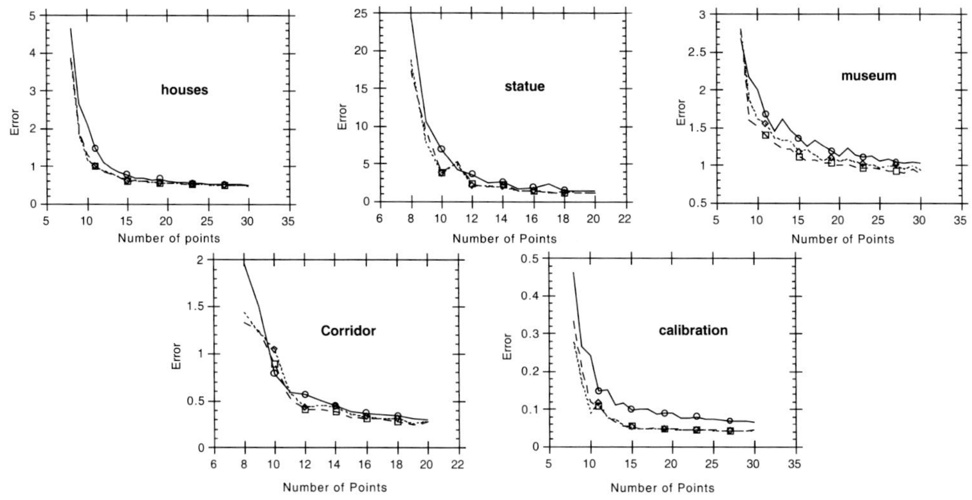

Fig. 11.3. **Results of the experimental evaluation of the algorithms.** *In each case, three methods of computing* F *are compared. Residual error is plotted against the number of points used to compute* F. *In each graph, the top (solid line) shows the results of the normalized 8-point algorithm. Also shown are the results of minimizing geometric error (long dashed line) and iteratively minimizing algebraic error subject to the determinant constraint (short dashed line). In most cases, the result of iteratively minimizing algebraic error is almost indistinguishable from minimizing geometric error. Both are noticeably better than the non-iterative normalized 8-point algorithm, though that algorithm also gives good results.*

11.6 Automatic computation of F

This section describes an algorithm to compute the epipolar geometry between two images automatically. The input to the algorithm is simply the pair of images, with no other *a priori* information required; and the output is the estimated fundamental matrix together with a set of interest points in correspondence.

The algorithm uses RANSAC as a search engine in a similar manner to its use in the automatic computation of a homography described in section 4.8(*p*123). The ideas and details of the algorithm are given there, and are not repeated here. The method is summarized in algorithm 11.4, with an example of its use shown in figure 11.4.

A few remarks on the method:

(i) **The RANSAC sample.** Only 7 point correspondences are used to estimate F. This has the advantage that a rank 2 matrix is produced, and it is not necessary to coerce the matrix to rank 2 as in the linear algorithms. A second reason for using 7 correspondences, rather than 8 say with a linear algorithm, is that the number of samples that must be tried in order to ensure a high probability of no outliers is exponential in the size of the sample set. For example, from table 4.3(*p*119) for a 99% confidence of no outliers (when drawing from a set containing 50% outliers) twice as many samples are required for 8 correspondences as for 7. The slight disadvantage in using 7 correspondences is that it may result in 3 real solutions for F, and all 3 must be tested for support.

Objective Compute the fundamental matrix between two images.

Algorithm

(i) **Interest points:** Compute interest points in each image.
(ii) **Putative correspondences:** Compute a set of interest point matches based on proximity and similarity of their intensity neighbourhood.
(iii) **RANSAC robust estimation:** Repeat for N samples, where N is determined adaptively as in algorithm 4.5(p121):
   (a) Select a random sample of 7 correspondences and compute the fundamental matrix F as described in section 11.1.2. There will be one or three real solutions.
   (b) Calculate the distance $d_\perp$ for each putative correspondence.
   (c) Compute the number of inliers consistent with F by the number of correspondences for which $d_\perp < t$ pixels.
   (d) If there are three real solutions for F the number of inliers is computed for each solution, and the solution with most inliers retained.

   Choose the F with the largest number of inliers. In the case of ties choose the solution that has the lowest standard deviation of inliers.
(iv) **Non-linear estimation:** re-estimate F from all correspondences classified as inliers by minimizing a cost function, e.g. (11.6), using the Levenberg–Marquardt algorithm of section A6.2(p600).
(v) **Guided matching:** Further interest point correspondences are now determined using the estimated F to define a search strip about the epipolar line.

The last two steps can be iterated until the number of correspondences is stable.

Algorithm 11.4. *Algorithm to automatically estimate the fundamental matrix between two images using RANSAC.*

(ii) **The distance measure.** Given a current estimate of F (from the RANSAC sample) the distance $d_\perp$ measures how closely a matched pair of points satisfies the epipolar geometry. There are two clear choices for $d_\perp$: reprojection error, i.e. the distance minimized in the cost function (11.6) (the value may be obtained using the triangulation algorithm of section 12.5); or the Sampson approximation to reprojection error ($d_\perp^2$ is given by (11.9)). If the Sampson approximation is used, then the Sampson cost function should be used to iteratively estimate F. Otherwise distances used in RANSAC and elsewhere in the algorithm will be inconsistent.

(iii) **Guided matching.** The current estimate of F defines a search band in the second image around the epipolar line $\mathrm{F}\mathbf{x}$ of $\mathbf{x}$. For each corner $\mathbf{x}$ a match is sought within this band. Since the search area is restricted a weaker similarity threshold can be employed, and it is not necessary to enforce a "winner takes all" scheme.

(iv) **Implementation and run details.** For the example of figure 11.4, the search window was ± 300 pixels. The inlier threshold was $t = 1.25$ pixels. A total of 407 samples were required. The RMS pixel error after RANSAC was 0.34 (for 99 correspondences), and after MLE and guided matching it was 0.33 (for 157 correspondences). The guided matching MLE required 10 iterations of the Levenberg–Marquardt algorithm.

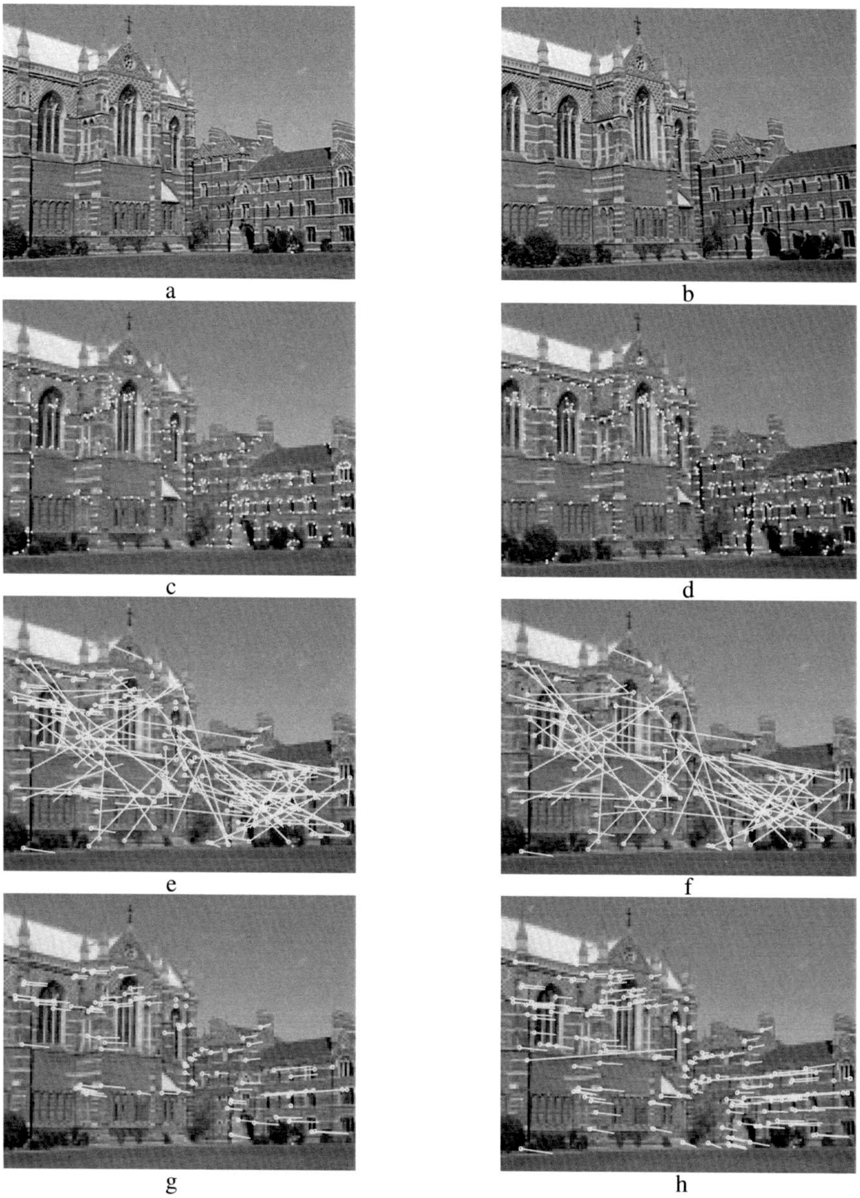

Fig. 11.4. **Automatic computation of the fundamental matrix between two images using RANSAC.** *(a) (b) left and right images of Keble College, Oxford. The motion between views is a translation and rotation. The images are* 640×480 *pixels. (c) (d) detected corners superimposed on the images. There are approximately 500 corners on each image. The following results are superimposed on the left image: (e) 188 putative matches shown by the line linking corners, note the clear mismatches; (f) outliers – 89 of the putative matches. (g) inliers – 99 correspondences consistent with the estimated* $\mathtt{F}$*; (h) final set of 157 correspondences after guided matching and MLE. There are still a few mismatches evident, e.g. the long line on the left.*

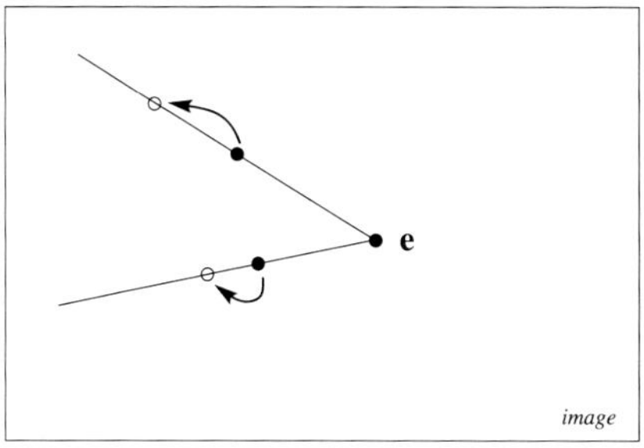

Fig. 11.5. *For a pure translation the epipole can be estimated from the image motion of two points.*

11.7 Special cases of F-computation

Certain special cases of motion, or partially known camera calibration, allow computation of the fundamental matrix to be simplified. In each case the number of degrees of freedom of the fundamental matrix is less than the 7 of general motion. We give three examples.

11.7.1 Pure translational motion

This is the simplest possible case. The matrix can be estimated linearly whilst simultaneously imposing the constraints that the matrix must satisfy, namely that it is skew-symmetric (see section 9.3.1(*p*247)), and thus has the required rank of 2. In this case $\mathtt{F} = [\mathbf{e}']_\times$, and has two degrees of freedom. It may be parametrized by the three entries of $\mathbf{e}'$.

Each point correspondence provides one linear constraint on the homogeneous parameters, as is clear from figure 11.5. The matrix can be computed uniquely from two point correspondences.

Note, in the general motion case if all 3D points are coplanar, which is a structure degeneracy (see section 11.9), the fundamental matrix cannot be determined uniquely from image correspondences. However, for pure translational motion this is not a problem (two 3D points are always coplanar). The only degeneracy is if the two 3D points are coplanar with both camera centres.

This special form also simplifies the Gold Standard estimation, and correspondingly triangulation for structure recovery. The Gold Standard estimation of the epipole from point correspondences under pure translation is identical to the estimation of a vanishing point given the end points of a set of imaged parallel lines, see section 8.6.1(*p*213).

11.7.2 Planar motion

In the case of planar motion, described in section 9.3.2(*p*250), we require that the symmetric part of F has rank 2, in addition to the standard rank 2 condition for the full matrix. It can be verified that the parametrization of (9.8–*p*252), namely $\mathtt{F} = [\mathbf{e}']_\times[\mathbf{l}_s]_\times[\mathbf{e}]_\times$, satisfies both these conditions. If unconstrained 3-vectors are used to represent $\mathbf{e}', \mathbf{l}_s$ and $\mathbf{e}$ then 9 parameters are used, whereas the fundamental matrix for planar motion has only 6 degrees of freedom. As usual this over-parametrization is not a problem.

An alternative parametrization with similar properties is

$$\mathtt{F} = \alpha[\mathbf{x_a}]_\times + \beta\left(\mathbf{l}_s\mathbf{l}_h^\mathsf{T} + \mathbf{l}_h\mathbf{l}_s^\mathsf{T}\right) \quad \text{with} \quad \mathbf{x_a}^\mathsf{T}\mathbf{l}_h = 0$$

where α and β are scalars, and the meaning of the 3-vectors $\mathbf{x_a}, \mathbf{l}_s$ and $\mathbf{l}_h$ is evident from figure 9.11(*p*253)(a).

11.7.3 The calibrated case

In the case of calibrated cameras normalized image coordinates may be used, and the essential matrix E computed instead of the fundamental matrix. As with the fundamental matrix, the essential matrix may be computed using linear techniques from 8 points or more, since corresponding points satisfy the defining equation $\mathbf{x}_i'^\mathsf{T}\mathtt{E}\mathbf{x}_i = 0$.

Where the method differs from the computation of the fundamental matrix is in the enforcement of the constraints. For, whereas the fundamental matrix satisfies $\det \mathtt{F} = 0$, the essential matrix satisfies the additional condition that its two singular values are equal. This constraint may be handled by the following result, which is offered here without proof.

Result 11.1. *Let* E *be a* 3×3 *matrix with SVD given by* $\mathtt{E} = \mathtt{UDV}^\mathsf{T}$, *where* $\mathtt{D} = \mathrm{diag}(a, b, c)$ *with* $a \geq b \geq c$. *Then the closest essential matrix to* E *in Frobenius norm is given by* $\hat{\mathtt{E}} = \mathtt{U}\hat{\mathtt{D}}\mathtt{V}^\mathsf{T}$, *where* $\hat{\mathtt{D}} = \mathrm{diag}((a+b)/2, (a+b)/2, 0)$.

If the goal is to compute the two normalized camera matrices P and P′ as part of a reconstruction process, then it is not actually necessary to compute $\hat{\mathtt{E}}$ by multiplying out $\hat{\mathtt{E}} = \mathtt{U}\hat{\mathtt{D}}\mathtt{V}^\mathsf{T}$. Matrix P′ can be computed directly from the SVD according to result 9.19-(*p*259). The choice between the four solutions for P′ is determined by the consideration that the visible points must lie in front of the two cameras, as explained in section 9.6.3-(*p*259).

11.8 Correspondence of other entities

So far in this chapter only point correspondences have been employed, and the question naturally arises: can F be computed from the correspondence of image entities other than points? The answer is yes, but not from all types of entities. We will now discuss some common examples.

Lines. The correspondence of image lines between views places *no* constraint at all on F. Here a line is an infinite line, not a line segment. Consider the case of corresponding image points: the points in each image back-project to rays, one through each camera centre, and these rays intersect at the 3-space point. Now in general two lines in 3-space are skew (i.e. they do not intersect); so the condition that the rays intersect places a constraint on the epipolar geometry. In contrast in the case of corresponding image lines, the back-projection is a plane from each view. However, two planes in 3-space always intersect so there is no constraint on the epipolar geometry (there is a constraint in the case of 3-views).

In the case of parallel lines, the correspondence of vanishing points does provide a

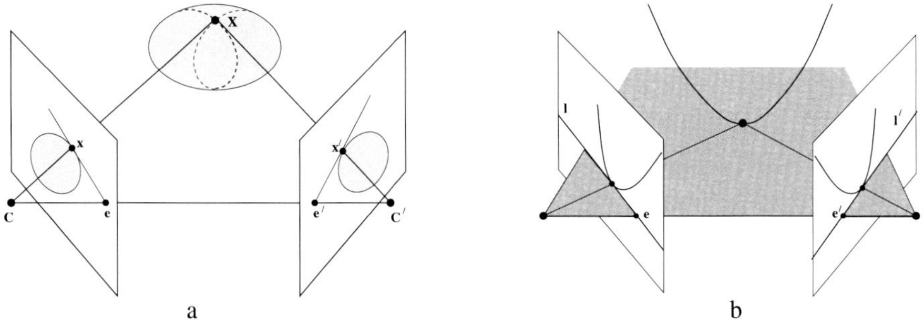

Fig. 11.6. **Epipolar tangency.** *(a) for a surface; (b) for a space curve – figure after Porrill and Pollard [Porrill-91]. In (a) the epipolar plane* $\mathbf{CC'X}$ *is tangent to the surface at* $\mathbf{X}$*. The imaged outline is tangent to the epipolar lines at* $\mathbf{x}$ *and* $\mathbf{x}'$ *in the two views. The dashed curves on the surface are the contour generators. In (b) the epipolar plane is tangent to the space curve. The corresponding epipolar lines* $\mathbf{l} \leftrightarrow \mathbf{l}'$ *are tangent to the imaged curve.*

constraint on $\mathtt{F}$. However, a vanishing point has the same status as any finite point, i.e. it provides one constraint.

Space curves and surfaces. As illustrated in figure 11.6, at points at which the epipolar plane is tangent to a space curve the imaged curve is tangent to the corresponding epipolar lines. This provides a constraint on the 2 view geometry, i.e. if an epipolar line is tangent to an imaged curve in one view, then the corresponding epipolar line must be tangent to the imaged curve in the other view. Similarly, in the case of surfaces, at points at which the epipolar plane is tangent to the surface the imaged outline is tangent to the corresponding epipolar lines. Epipolar tangent points act effectively as point correspondences and may be included in estimation algorithms as described by [Porrill-91].

Particularly important cases are those of conics and quadrics which are algebraic objects and so algebraic solutions can be developed. Examples are given in the notes and exercises at the end of this chapter.

11.9 Degeneracies

A set of correspondences $\{\mathbf{x}_i \leftrightarrow \mathbf{x}'_i, i = 1, \ldots, n\}$ is geometrically degenerate with respect to $\mathtt{F}$ if it fails to uniquely define the epipolar geometry, or equivalently if there exist linearly independent rank-2 matrices, $\mathtt{F}_j$, $j = 1, 2$, such that

$$\mathbf{x}_i'^{\mathsf{T}}\mathtt{F}_1\mathbf{x}_i = 0 \quad \text{and} \quad \mathbf{x}_i'^{\mathsf{T}}\mathtt{F}_2\mathbf{x}_i = 0 \qquad (1 \leq i \leq n) \ .$$

The subject of degeneracy is investigated in detail in chapter 22. However, a brief preview is given now for the two important cases of scene points on a ruled quadric, or on a plane.

Provided the two camera centres are not coincident the epipolar geometry *is* uniquely defined. It can always be computed from the camera matrices $\mathtt{P}, \mathtt{P}'$ as in (9.1–*p*244) for example. What is at issue here are configurations where the epipolar geometry cannot be estimated from point correspondences. An awareness of the degeneracies of

$\dim(N) = 1$: Unique solution – no degeneracy.	
	Arises from $n \geq 8$ point correspondences in general position. If $n > 8$ then the point correspondences must be perfect (i.e. noise-free).
$\dim(N) = 2$: 1 or 3 solutions.	
	Arises in the case of seven point correspondences, and also in the case of $n > 7$ perfect point correspondences where the 3D points and camera centres lie on a ruled quadric referred to as a critical surface. The quadric may be non-degenerate (a hyperboloid of one sheet) or degenerate.
$\dim(N) = 3$: Two-parameter family of solutions.	
	Arises if $n \geq 6$ perfect point correspondences are related by a homography, $\mathbf{x}'_i = \mathtt{H}\mathbf{x}_i$. • Rotation about the camera centre (a degenerate motion). • All world points on a plane (a degenerate structure).

Table 11.1. *Degeneracies in estimating* F *from point correspondences, classified by the dimension of the null-space* N *of* A *in (11.3–*p279*).*

estimation algorithms is important because configurations "close to" degenerate ones are likely to lead to a numerically ill-conditioned estimation. The degeneracies are summarized in table 11.1.

11.9.1 Points on a ruled quadric

It will be shown in chapter 22 that degeneracy occurs if both camera centres and all the 3D points lie on a (ruled) quadric surface referred to as the *critical surface* [Maybank-93]. A ruled quadric may be non-degenerate (a hyperboloid of one sheet – a cooling tower) or degenerate (for instance two planes, cones, and cylinders) – see section 3.2.4(*p*74); but a critical surface cannot be an ellipsoid or hyperboloid of two sheets. For a critical surface configuration there are three possible fundamental matrices.

Note that in the case of just 7 point correspondences, together with the two camera centres there are 9 points in total. A general quadric has 9 degrees of freedom, and one may always construct a quadric through 9 points. In the case where this quadric is a ruled quadric it will be a critical surface, and there will be three possible solutions for F. The case where the quadric is not ruled corresponds to the case where there is only one real solution for F.

11.9.2 Points on a plane

An important degeneracy is when all the points lie in a plane. In this case, all the points plus the two camera centres lie on a ruled quadric surface, namely the degenerate quadric consisting of two planes – the plane through the points, plus a plane passing through the two camera centres.

Two views of a planar set of points are related via a 2D projective transformation H. Thus, suppose that a set of correspondences $\mathbf{x}_i \leftrightarrow \mathbf{x}'_i$ is given for which $\mathbf{x}'_i = \mathtt{H}\mathbf{x}_i$. Any number of points $\mathbf{x}_i$ and the corresponding points $\mathbf{x}'_i = \mathtt{H}\mathbf{x}_i$ may be given.

The fundamental matrix corresponding to the pair of cameras satisfies the equation $\mathbf{x}_i'^{\mathsf{T}}\mathtt{F}\mathbf{x}_i = \mathbf{x}_i'^{\mathsf{T}}(\mathtt{FH}^{-1})\mathbf{x}_i' = 0$. This set of equations is satisfied whenever $\mathtt{FH}^{-1}$ is skew-symmetric. Thus, the solution for F is any matrix of the form $\mathtt{F} = \mathtt{SH}$, where S is skew-symmetric. Now, a 3×3 skew-symmetric matrix S may be written in the form $\mathtt{S} = [\mathbf{t}]_\times$, for any 3-vector $\mathbf{t}$. Thus, S has three degrees of freedom, and consequently so does F. More precisely, the correspondences $\mathbf{x}_i \leftrightarrow \mathbf{x}_i'$ lead to a three-parameter family of possible fundamental matrices F (note, one of the parameters accounts for scaling the matrix so there is only a *two*-parameter family of homogeneous matrices). The equation matrix A derived from the set of correspondences must therefore have rank no greater than 6.

From the decomposition of $\mathtt{F} = \mathtt{SH}$, it follows from result 9.9(*p*254) that the pair of camera matrices $[\mathtt{I} \mid \mathbf{0}]$ and $[\mathtt{H} \mid \mathbf{t}]$ correspond to the fundamental matrix F. Here, the vector $\mathbf{t}$ may take on any value. If point $\mathbf{x}_i = (x_i, y_i, 1)^{\mathsf{T}}$ and $\mathbf{x}_i' = \mathtt{H}\mathbf{x}_i$, then one verifies that the point $\mathbf{X}_i = (x, y, 1, 0)^{\mathsf{T}}$ maps to $\mathbf{x}_i$ and $\mathbf{x}_i'$ through the two cameras. Thus, the points $\mathbf{X}_i$ constitute a reconstruction of the scene.

11.9.3 No translation

If the two camera centres are coincident then the epipolar geometry is not defined. In addition, formulae such as result 9.9(*p*254) give a value of 0 for the fundamental matrix. In this case the two images are related by a 2D homography (see section 8.4.2(*p*204)).

If one attempts to find the fundamental matrix then, as shown above, there will be at least a 2-parameter family of solutions for F. Even if the camera motion involves no translation, then a method such as the 8-point algorithm used to compute the fundamental matrix will still produce a matrix F satisfying $\mathbf{x}_i'^{\mathsf{T}}\mathtt{F}\mathbf{x}_i = 0$, where F has the form $\mathtt{F} = \mathtt{SH}$, H is the homography relating the points, and S is an essentially arbitrary skew-symmetric matrix. Points $\mathbf{x}_i$ and $\mathbf{x}_i'$ related by H will satisfy this relationship.

11.10 A geometric interpretation of F-computation

The estimation of F from a set of image correspondences $\{\mathbf{x}_i \leftrightarrow \mathbf{x}_i'\}$ has many similarities with the problem of estimating a conic from a set of 2D points $\{x_i, y_i\}$ (or a quadric from a set of 3D points).

The equation $\mathbf{x}'^{\mathsf{T}}\mathtt{F}\mathbf{x} = 0$ is a single constraint in x, y, x', y' and so defines a surface (variety) $\mathcal{V}$ of codimension 1 (dimension 3) in $\mathbb{R}^4$. The surface is a quadric because the equation is quadratic in the coordinates x, y, x', y' of $\mathbb{R}^4$. There is a natural mapping from projective 3-space to the variety $\mathcal{V}$ that takes any 3D point to the quadruple $(x, y, x', y')^{\mathsf{T}}$ of the corresponding image points in the two views. The quadric form is evident if $\mathbf{x}'^{\mathsf{T}}\mathtt{F}\mathbf{x} = 0$ is rewritten as

$$\begin{pmatrix} x & y & x' & y' & 1 \end{pmatrix} \begin{bmatrix} 0 & 0 & f_{11} & f_{21} & f_{31} \\ 0 & 0 & f_{12} & f_{22} & f_{32} \\ f_{11} & f_{12} & 0 & 0 & f_{13} \\ f_{21} & f_{22} & 0 & 0 & f_{23} \\ f_{31} & f_{32} & f_{13} & f_{23} & 2f_{33} \end{bmatrix} \begin{pmatrix} x \\ y \\ x' \\ y' \\ 1 \end{pmatrix} = 0 .$$

The case of conic fitting is a good (lower-dimensional) model of F estimation. To

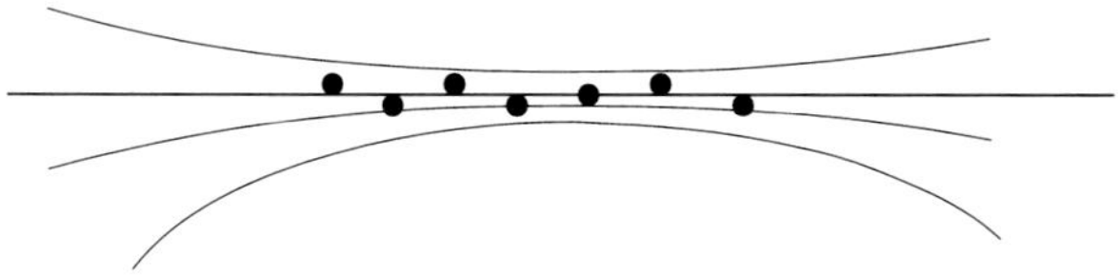

Fig. 11.7. *Estimating a conic from point data (shown as •) may be poorly conditioned. All of the conics shown have residuals within the point error distribution. However, even though there is ambiguity in the estimated conic, the tangent line is well defined, and can be computed from the points.*

bring out the analogy between the two estimation problems: a point (x_i, y_i) places one constraint on the 5 degrees of freedom of a conic as described in section 2.2.3(*p*30):

$$ax_i^2 + bx_iy_i + cy_i^2 + dx_i + ey_i + f = 0.$$

Similarly, a point correspondence (x_i, y_i, x'_i, y'_i) places one constraint on the (8) degrees of freedom of F as (11.2–*p*279):

$$x'_ix_if_{11} + x'_iy_if_{12} + x'_if_{13} + y'_ix_if_{21} + y'_iy_if_{22} + y'_if_{23} + x_if_{31} + y_if_{32} + f_{33} = 0.$$

It is not quite an exact analogy, since the defining relationship expressed by the fundamental matrix is bilinear in the two sets of indices, as is also evident from the zeros in the quadric matrix above, whereas in the case of a conic section the equation is an arbitrary quadratic. Also the surface defined by F must satisfy an additional constraint arising from $\det(\mathtt{F}) = 0$, and there is no such constraint in the conic fitting analogue.

The problems of extrapolation when data has only been fitted to a small section of a conic are well known, and similar issues arise in fitting the fundamental matrix to data. Indeed, there are cases where the data is sufficient to determine an accurate tangent line to the conic, but insufficient to determine the conic itself, see figure 11.7. In the case of the fundamental matrix the tangent plane to the quadric in $\mathbb{R}^4$ is the affine fundamental matrix (chapter 14), and this approximation may be fitted when perspective effects are small.

11.11 The envelope of epipolar lines

One of the uses of the fundamental matrix is to determine epipolar lines in a second image corresponding to points in a first image. For instance, if one is seeking matched points between two images, the match of a given point x in the first image may be found by searching along the epipolar line Fx in the second image. In the presence of noise, of course, the matching point will not lie precisely on the line Fx because the fundamental matrix will be known only within certain bounds, expressed by its covariance matrix. In general, instead of searching along the epipolar line only, it will be necessary to search in a region on either side of the line Fx. We will now consider how the covariance matrix of the fundamental matrix may be used to determine the region in which to search.

Let x be a point and F be a fundamental matrix for which one has computed a covariance matrix $\Sigma_{\mathtt{F}}$. The point x corresponds to an epipolar line $\mathbf{l} = \mathtt{F}\mathbf{x}$, and one may transfer the covariance matrix Σ_F to a covariance matrix Σ_l according to result 5.6-($p139$). Also by result 5.6($p139$), the mean value of the epipolar line is given by $\bar{l} = \bar{F}x$. To avoid singular cases, the vector l representing an epipolar line is normalized so that $||l|| = 1$. Then the mapping $x \mapsto l$ is given by $l = (Fx)/||Fx||$. If J is the Jacobian matrix of this mapping with respect to the entries of F, then J is a 3×9 matrix, and $\Sigma_l = J\Sigma_F J^T$.

Though the constraint $||l|| = 1$ is the most convenient constraint, the following analysis applies for any constraint used to confine the vector representing the epipolar line to vary on a 2-dimensional surface in $\mathbb{R}^3$. In this case, the covariance matrix Σ_l is singular, having rank 2, since no variation is allowed in the direction normal to the constraint surface. For a particular instance of l, the deviation from the mean, $\bar{l} - l$, must be along the constraint surface, and hence (in the linear approximation) perpendicular to the null-space of Σ_l.

For the remainder of this derivation, $\bar{l}$, the vector representing the mean epipolar line, will be denoted by m, so as to avoid confusing notation. Now, assuming a Gaussian distribution for the vectors l representing the epipolar line, the set of all lines having a given likelihood is given by the equation

$$(l - m)^T \Sigma_l^+ (l - m) = k^2 \tag{11.11}$$

where k is some constant. To analyze this further, we apply an orthogonal change of coordinates such that Σ_l becomes diagonal. Thus, one may write

$$U\Sigma_l U^T = \Sigma'_l = \begin{bmatrix} \tilde{\Sigma}'_l & \mathbf{0} \\ \mathbf{0}^T & 0 \end{bmatrix}$$

where $\tilde{\Sigma}'_l$ is a 2×2 non-singular diagonal matrix. Applying the same transformation to the lines, one defines 2-vectors $m' = Um$ and $l' = Ul$. Since $l' - m'$ is orthogonal to the null-space $(0, 0, 1)^T$ of Σ'_l, both m' and l' have the same third coordinate. By multiplying U by a constant as necessary, one may assume that this coordinate is 1. Thus we may write $l' = (\tilde{l}'^T, 1)^T$ and $m' = (\tilde{m}'^T, 1)^T$ for certain 2-vectors $\tilde{l}'$ and $\tilde{m}'$. Then, one verifies that

$$\begin{aligned} k^2 &= (l - m)^T \Sigma_l^+ (l - m) \\ &= (l' - m')^T \Sigma_l'^+ (l' - m') \\ &= (\tilde{l}' - \tilde{m}')^T \tilde{\Sigma}_l'^{-1} (\tilde{l}' - \tilde{m}'). \end{aligned}$$

This equation expands out to

$$\tilde{l}'^T \tilde{\Sigma}_l'^{-1} \tilde{l}' - \tilde{m}'^T \tilde{\Sigma}_l'^{-1} \tilde{l}' - \tilde{l}'^T \tilde{\Sigma}_l'^{-1} \tilde{m}' + \tilde{m}'^T \tilde{\Sigma}_l'^{-1} \tilde{m}' - k^2 = 0$$

which may be written as

$$(\tilde{l}'^T \ 1) \begin{bmatrix} \tilde{\Sigma}_l'^{-1} & -\tilde{\Sigma}_l'^{-1} \tilde{m}' \\ -\tilde{m}'^T \tilde{\Sigma}_l'^{-1} & \tilde{m}'^T \tilde{\Sigma}_l'^{-1} \tilde{m}' - k^2 \end{bmatrix} \begin{pmatrix} \tilde{l}' \\ 1 \end{pmatrix} = 0$$

or equivalently (as one may verify)

$$(\tilde{\mathbf{l}}'^{\mathsf{T}} \;\; 1) \begin{bmatrix} \tilde{\mathbf{m}}'\tilde{\mathbf{m}}'^{\mathsf{T}} - k^2\tilde{\Sigma}'_{\mathbf{l}} & \tilde{\mathbf{m}}' \\ \tilde{\mathbf{m}}'^{\mathsf{T}} & 1 \end{bmatrix}^{-1} \begin{pmatrix} \tilde{\mathbf{l}}' \\ 1 \end{pmatrix} = 0. \tag{11.12}$$

Finally, this is equivalent to

$$\mathbf{l}'^{\mathsf{T}}[\mathbf{m}'\mathbf{m}'^{\mathsf{T}} - k^2\Sigma'_{\mathbf{l}}]^{-1}\mathbf{l}' = 0. \tag{11.13}$$

This shows that the lines satisfying (11.11) form a line conic defined by the matrix $(\mathbf{m}'\mathbf{m}'^{\mathsf{T}} - k^2\Sigma'_{\mathbf{l}})^{-1}$. The corresponding point conic, which forms the envelope of the lines, is defined by the matrix $\mathbf{m}'\mathbf{m}'^{\mathsf{T}} - k^2\Sigma'_{\mathbf{l}}$. One may now transform back to the original coordinate system to determine the envelope of the lines in the original coordinate system. The transformed conic is

$$\mathtt{C} = \mathtt{U}^{\mathsf{T}}(\mathbf{m}'\mathbf{m}'^{\mathsf{T}} - k^2\Sigma'_{\mathbf{l}})\mathtt{U} = \mathbf{m}\mathbf{m}^{\mathsf{T}} - k^2\Sigma_{\mathbf{l}}. \tag{11.14}$$

Note that when $k = 0$, the conic $\mathtt{C}$ degenerates to $\mathbf{m}\mathbf{m}^{\mathsf{T}}$, which represents the set of points lying on the line $\mathbf{m}$. As k increases, the conic becomes a hyperbola the two branches of which lie on opposite sides of the line $\mathbf{m}$.

Suppose we want to choose k so that some fraction α of the epipolar lines lie inside the region bounded by this hyperbola. The value $k^2 = (\mathbf{l} - \mathbf{m})^{\mathsf{T}}\Sigma_{\mathbf{l}}^{+}(\mathbf{l} - \mathbf{m})$ of (11.11) follows a χ^2_n distribution, and the cumulative chi-squared distribution $F_n(k^2) = \int_0^{k^2} \chi^2_n(\xi)d\xi$ represents the probability that the value of a χ^2_n random variable is less than k^2 (the χ^2_n and F_n distributions are defined in section A2.2(*p*566)). Applying this to a random line $\mathbf{l}$, one sees that in order to ensure that a fraction α of lines lie within region bounded by the hyperbola defined by (11.14), one must choose k^2 such that $F_2(k^2) = \alpha$ ($n = 2$ since the covariance matrix $\Sigma_{\mathbf{l}}$ has rank 2). Thus, $k^2 = F_2^{-1}(\alpha)$, and for a value of $\alpha = 0.95$, for instance, one finds that $k^2 = 5.9915$. The corresponding hyperbola given by (11.14) is $\mathtt{C} = \mathbf{m}\mathbf{m}^{\mathsf{T}} - 5.9915\ \Sigma_{\mathbf{l}}$. To sum up this discussion:

Result 11.2. *If $\mathbf{l}$ is a random line obeying a Gaussian distribution with mean $\bar{\mathbf{l}}$ and covariance matrix $\Sigma_{\mathbf{l}}$ of rank 2, then the plane conic*

$$\mathtt{C} = \bar{\mathbf{l}}\bar{\mathbf{l}}^{\mathsf{T}} - k^2\Sigma_{\mathbf{l}} \tag{11.15}$$

represents an equal-likelihood contour bounding some fraction of all instances of $\mathbf{l}$. If $F_2(k^2)$ represents the cumulative χ^2_2 distribution, and k^2 is chosen such that $F_2^{-1}(k^2) = \alpha$, then a fraction α of all lines lie within the region bounded by $\mathtt{C}$. In other words with probability α the lines lie within this region.

In applying this formula, one must be aware that it represents only an approximation, since epipolar lines are not normally distributed. We have consistently made the assumption that the distributions may be correctly transformed using the Jacobian, that is an assumption of linearity. This assumption will be most reasonable for distributions with small variance, and close to the mean. Here, we are applying it to find the region in which as many as 95% of samples fall, namely almost the whole of the error distribution. In this case, the assumption of a Gaussian distribution of errors is less tenable.

11.11.1 Verification of epipolar line covariance

We now present some examples of epipolar line envelopes, confirming and illustrating the theory developed above. Before doing this, however, a direct verification of the theory will be given, concerning the covariance matrix of epipolar lines. Since the 3×3 covariance matrix of a line is not easily understood quantitatively, we consider the variance of the direction of epipolar lines. Given a line $\mathbf{l} = (l_1, l_2, l_3)^\mathsf{T}$, the angle representing its direction is given by $\theta = \arctan(-l_1/l_2)$. Letting $\mathtt{J}$ equal the 1×3 Jacobian matrix of the mapping $\mathbf{l} \rightarrow \theta$, one finds the variance of the angle θ to be $\sigma_\theta^2 = \mathtt{J}\Sigma_\mathbf{l}\mathtt{J}^\mathsf{T}$. This result may be verified by simulation, as follows.

One considers a pair of images for which point correspondences have been identified. The fundamental matrix is computed from the point correspondences and the points are then corrected so as to correspond precisely under the epipolar mapping (as described in section 12.3). A set of n of these corrected correspondences are used to compute the covariance matrix of the fundamental matrix $\mathtt{F}$. Then, for a further set of "test" corrected points $\mathbf{x}_i$ in the first image, the mean and covariance of the corresponding epipolar line $\mathbf{l}'_i = \mathtt{F}\mathbf{x}_i$ are computed, and subsequently the mean and variance of the orientation direction of this line are computed. This gives the theoretical values of these quantities.

Next, Monte Carlo simulation is done, in which Gaussian noise is added to the coordinates of the points used to compute $\mathtt{F}$. Using the computed $\mathtt{F}$, the epipolar lines corresponding to each of the test points are computed, and subsequently their angle, and the deviation of the angle from the mean. This is done many times, and the standard deviation of angle is computed, and finally compared with the theoretical value. The results of this are shown in figure 11.8 for the statue image pair of figure 11.2(*p*289).

Epipolar envelopes for statue image. The statue image pair of figure 11.2(*p*289) is interesting because of the large depth variation across the image. There are close points (on the statue) and distant points (on the building behind) in close proximity in the images. The fundamental matrix was computed from several points. A point in the first image (see figure 11.9) was selected and Monte Carlo simulation was used to compute several possible epipolar lines corresponding to a noise level of 0.5 pixels in each matched point coordinate. To test the theory, the mean and covariance of the epipolar line were next computed theoretically. The 95% envelope of the epipolar lines was computed and drawn in the second image. The results are shown in figure 11.10 for different numbers of points used to compute $\mathtt{F}$. The 95% envelope for $n = 15$ corresponds closely to the simulated envelope of the lines.

The results shown in figure 11.10 show the practical importance of computing the epipolar envelopes in point matching. Thus, suppose one is attempting to find a match for the foreground point in figure 11.9. If the epipolar line is computed from just 10 point matches, then epipolar search is unlikely to succeed, given the width of the

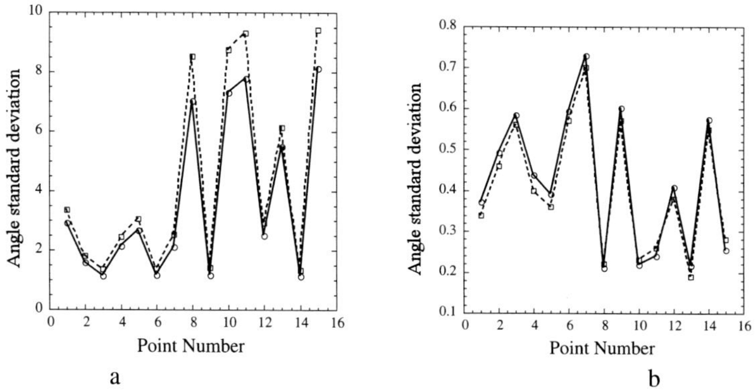

Fig. 11.8. *Comparison of theoretical and Monte Carlo simulated values of orientation angle of epipolar lines for 15 test points form the statue image pair of figure 11.2*(p289). *The horizontal axis represents the point number (1 to 15) and the vertical axis the standard deviation of angle. (a) the results when the epipolar structure (fundamental matrix) is computed from 15 points. (b) the results when 50 point matches are used.* **Note :** *the horizontal axis of these graphs represent discrete points numbered 1 to 15. The graphs are shown as a continuous curve only for visual clarity.*

envelope. Even for $n = 15$, the width of the envelope at the level of the correct match is several tens of pixels. For $n = 25$, the situation is more favourable. Note that this instability is inherent in the problem, and not the result of any specific algorithm for computing F.

An interesting point concerns the location of the narrowest point of the envelope. In this case, it appears to be close to the correct match position for the background point in figure 11.9. The match for the foreground point (leg of statue) lies far from the narrowest point of the envelope. Though the precise location of the narrow point of the envelope is not fully understood, it appears that in this case, most points used to the computation of F are on the background building. This biases towards the supposition that other matched points lie close to the plane of the building. The match for a point at significantly different depth is less precisely known.

Matching points close to the epipole – the corridor scene. In the case where the points to be matched are close to the epipole, then the determination of the epipolar line is more unstable, since any uncertainty in the position of the epipole results in uncertainty in the slope of the epipolar line. In addition, as one approaches this unstable position, the linear approximations implicit in the derivation of (11.14) become less tenable. In particular, the distribution of the epipolar lines deviates from a normal distribution.

11.12 Image rectification

This section gives a method for image rectification, the process of resampling pairs of stereo images taken from widely differing viewpoints in order to produce a pair of "matched epipolar projections". These are projections in which the epipolar lines run parallel with the x-axis and match up between views, and consequently disparities between the images are in the x-direction only, i.e. there is no y disparity.

Fig. 11.9. *(a) The point in the first image used to compute the epipolar envelopes in the second images. Note the ambiguity of which point is to be found in the second image. The marked point may represent the point on the statue's leg (foreground) or the point on the building behind the statue (background). In the second image, these two points are quite separate, and the epipolar line must pass through them both. (b) Computed corresponding epipolar lines computed from $n = 15$ point matches. The different lines correspond to different instances of injected noise in the matched points. Gaussian noise of 0.5 pixels in each coordinate was added to the ideal matched point positions before computing the epipolar line corresponding to the selected point. The ML estimator (Gold Standard algorithm) was used to compute* F. *This experiment shows the basic instability of the computation of the epipolar lines from small numbers of points. To find the point matching the selected point in the image at left, one needs to search over the regions covered by all these epipolar lines.*

The method is based on the fundamental matrix. A pair of 2D projective transformations are applied to the two images in order to match the epipolar lines. It is shown that the two transformations may be chosen in such a way that matching points have approximately the same x-coordinate as well. In this way, the two images, if overlaid on top of each other, will correspond as far as possible, and any disparities will be parallel to the x-axis. Since the application of arbitrary 2D projective transformations may distort the image substantially, the method for finding the pair of transformations subjects the images to a minimal distortion.

In effect, transforming the two images by the appropriate projective transformations reduces the problem to the epipolar geometry produced by a pair of identical cameras placed side by side with their principal axes parallel. Many stereo matching algorithms described in previous literature have assumed this geometry. After this rectification the search for matching points is vastly simplified by the simple epipolar structure and by the near-correspondence of the two images. It may be used as a preliminary step to comprehensive image matching.

11.12.1 Mapping the epipole to infinity

In this section we will discuss the question of finding a projective transformation H of an image that maps the epipole to a point at infinity. In fact, if epipolar lines are to be transformed to lines parallel with the x-axis, then the epipole should be mapped to

Fig. 11.10. *The 95% envelopes of epipolar lines are shown for a noise level of* 0.5 *pixels, with* F *being computed from* $n = 10, 15, 25$ *and* 50 *points. In each case, Monte Carlo simulated results agreed closely with these results (though not shown here). For the case* $n = 15$*, compare with figure 11.9. Note that for* $n = 10$*, the epipolar envelope is very wide (> 90 degrees), showing that one can have very little confidence in an epipolar line computed from 10 points in this case. For* $n = 15$*, the envelope is still quite wide. For* $n = 25$ *and* $n = 50$*, the epipolar line is known with quite good precision. Of course, the precise shape of the envelope depends strongly on just what matched points are used to compute the epipolar structure.*

the particular infinite point $(1, 0, 0)^{\mathsf{T}}$. This leaves many degrees of freedom (in fact four) open for H, and if an inappropriate H is chosen, severe projective distortion of the image can take place. In order that the resampled image should look somewhat like the original image, we may put closer restrictions on the choice of H.

One condition that leads to good results is to insist that the transformation H should act as far as possible as a rigid transformation in the neighbourhood of a given selected point $\mathbf{x}_0$ of the image. By this is meant that to first-order the neighbourhood of $\mathbf{x}_0$ may undergo rotation and translation only, and hence will look the same in the original and resampled images. An appropriate choice of point $\mathbf{x}_0$ may be the centre of the image. For instance, this would be a good choice in the context of aerial photography if the view is known not to be excessively oblique.

For the present, suppose $\mathbf{x}_0$ is the origin and the epipole $\mathbf{e} = (f, 0, 1)^{\mathsf{T}}$ lies on the

x-axis. Now consider the following transformation

$$\mathtt{G} = \begin{bmatrix} 1 & 0 & 0 \\ 0 & 1 & 0 \\ -1/f & 0 & 1 \end{bmatrix}. \tag{11.16}$$

This transformation takes the epipole $(f, 0, 1)^\mathsf{T}$ to the point at infinity $(f, 0, 0)^\mathsf{T}$ as required. A point $(x, y, 1)^\mathsf{T}$ is mapped by $\mathtt{G}$ to the point $(\hat{x}, \hat{y}, 1)^\mathsf{T} = (x, y, 1 - x/f)^\mathsf{T}$. If $|x/f| < 1$ then we may write

$$(\hat{x}, \hat{y}, 1)^\mathsf{T} = (x, y, 1 - x/f)^\mathsf{T} = (x(1 + x/f + \ldots), y(1 + x/f + \ldots), 1)^\mathsf{T}.$$

The Jacobian is

$$\frac{\partial(\hat{x}, \hat{y})}{\partial(x, y)} = \begin{bmatrix} 1 + 2x/f & 0 \\ y/f & 1 + x/f \end{bmatrix}$$

plus higher order terms in x and y. Now if $x = y = 0$ then this is the identity map. In other words, $\mathtt{G}$ is approximated (to first-order) at the origin by the identity mapping.

For an arbitrarily placed point of interest $\mathbf{x}_0$ and epipole $\mathbf{e}$, the required mapping $\mathtt{H}$ is a product $\mathtt{H} = \mathtt{GRT}$ where $\mathtt{T}$ is a translation taking the point $\mathbf{x}_0$ to the origin, $\mathtt{R}$ is a rotation about the origin taking the epipole $\mathbf{e}'$ to a point $(f, 0, 1)^\mathsf{T}$ on the x-axis, and $\mathtt{G}$ is the mapping just considered taking $(f, 0, 1)^\mathsf{T}$ to infinity. The composite mapping is to first-order a rigid transformation in the neighbourhood of $\mathbf{x}_0$.

11.12.2 Matching transformations

In the previous section it was shown how the epipole in one image may be mapped to infinity. Next, it will be seen how a map may be applied to the other image to match up the epipolar lines. We consider two images J and J'. The intention is to resample these two images according to transformations $\mathtt{H}$ to be applied to J and $\mathtt{H}'$ to be applied to J'. The resampling is to be done in such a way that an epipolar line in J is matched with its corresponding epipolar line in J'. More specifically, if $\mathbf{l}$ and $\mathbf{l}'$ are any pair of corresponding epipolar lines in the two images, then $\mathtt{H}^{-\mathsf{T}}\mathbf{l} = \mathtt{H}'^{-\mathsf{T}}\mathbf{l}'$. (Recall that $\mathtt{H}^{-\mathsf{T}}$ is the line map corresponding to the point map $\mathtt{H}$.) Any pair of transformations satisfying this condition will be called a *matched pair* of transformations.

Our strategy in choosing a matched pair of transformations is to choose $\mathtt{H}'$ first to be some transformation that sends the epipole $\mathbf{e}'$ to infinity as described in the previous section. We then seek a matching transformation $\mathtt{H}$ chosen so as to minimize the sum-of-squared distances

$$\sum_i d(\mathtt{H}\mathbf{x}_i, \mathtt{H}'\mathbf{x}'_i)^2. \tag{11.17}$$

The first question to be determined is how to find a transformation matching $\mathtt{H}'$. That question is answered in the following result.

Result 11.3. *Let J and J' be images with fundamental matrix $\mathtt{F} = [\mathbf{e}']_\times \mathtt{M}$, and let $\mathtt{H}'$ be a projective transformation of J'. A projective transformation $\mathtt{H}$ of J matches $\mathtt{H}'$ if and* *only if* H *is of the form*

$$\mathtt{H} = (\mathtt{I} + \mathtt{H}'\mathbf{e}'\mathbf{a}^{\mathsf{T}})\mathtt{H}'\mathtt{M} \tag{11.18}$$

for some vector $\mathbf{a}$.

Proof. If $\mathbf{x}$ is a point in J, then $\mathbf{e} \times \mathbf{x}$ is the epipolar line in the first image, and $\mathtt{F}\mathbf{x}$ is the epipolar line in the second image. Transformations $\mathtt{H}$ and $\mathtt{H}'$ are a matching pair if and only if $\mathtt{H}^{-\mathsf{T}}(\mathbf{e} \times \mathbf{x}) = \mathtt{H}'^{-\mathsf{T}}\mathtt{F}\mathbf{x}$. Since this must hold for all $\mathbf{x}$ we may write equivalently $\mathtt{H}^{-\mathsf{T}}[\mathbf{e}]_\times = \mathtt{H}'^{-\mathsf{T}}\mathtt{F} = \mathtt{H}'^{-\mathsf{T}}[\mathbf{e}']_\times\mathtt{M}$ or, applying result A4.3(*p*582),

$$[\mathtt{H}\mathbf{e}]_\times\mathtt{H} = [\mathtt{H}'\mathbf{e}']_\times\mathtt{H}'\mathtt{M}. \tag{11.19}$$

In view of lemma 9.11(*p*255), this implies $\mathtt{H} = (\mathtt{I} + \mathtt{H}'\mathbf{e}'\mathbf{a}^{\mathsf{T}})\mathtt{H}'\mathtt{M}$ as required.
To prove the converse, if (11.18) holds, then

$$\begin{aligned}\mathtt{H}\mathbf{e} &= (\mathtt{I} + \mathtt{H}'\mathbf{e}'\mathbf{a}^{\mathsf{T}})\mathtt{H}'\mathtt{M}\mathbf{e} = (\mathtt{I} + \mathtt{H}'\mathbf{e}'\mathbf{a}^{\mathsf{T}})\mathtt{H}'\mathbf{e}' \\ &= (1 + \mathbf{a}^{\mathsf{T}}\mathtt{H}'\mathbf{e}')\mathtt{H}'\mathbf{e}' = \mathtt{H}'\mathbf{e}'.\end{aligned}$$

This, along with (11.18), is sufficient for (11.19) to hold, and so $\mathtt{H}$ and $\mathtt{H}'$ are matching transformations. □

We are particularly interested in the case when $\mathtt{H}'$ is a transformation taking the epipole $\mathbf{e}'$ to a point at infinity $(1,0,0)^{\mathsf{T}}$. In this case, $\mathtt{I} + \mathtt{H}'\mathbf{e}'\mathbf{a}^{\mathsf{T}} = \mathtt{I} + (1,0,0)^{\mathsf{T}}\mathbf{a}^{\mathsf{T}}$ is of the form

$$\mathtt{H}_\mathrm{A} = \begin{bmatrix} a & b & c \\ 0 & 1 & 0 \\ 0 & 0 & 1 \end{bmatrix} \tag{11.20}$$

which represents an affine transformation. Thus, a special case of result 11.3 is

Corollary 11.4. *Let J and J' be images with fundamental matrix $\mathtt{F} = [\mathbf{e}']_\times\mathtt{M}$, and let $\mathtt{H}'$ be a projective transformation of J' mapping the epipole $\mathbf{e}'$ to the infinite point $(1,0,0)^{\mathsf{T}}$. A transformation $\mathtt{H}$ of J matches $\mathtt{H}'$ if and only if $\mathtt{H}$ is of the form $\mathtt{H} = \mathtt{H}_\mathrm{A}\mathtt{H}_0$, where $\mathtt{H}_0 = \mathtt{H}'\mathtt{M}$ and $\mathtt{H}_\mathrm{A}$ is an affine transformation of the form (11.20).*

Given $\mathtt{H}'$ mapping the epipole to infinity, we may use this corollary to make the choice of a matching transformation $\mathtt{H}$ to minimize the disparity. Writing $\hat{\mathbf{x}}'_i = \mathtt{H}'\mathbf{x}'_i$ and $\hat{\mathbf{x}}_i = \mathtt{H}_0\mathbf{x}_i$, the minimization problem (11.17) is to find $\mathtt{H}_\mathrm{A}$ of the form (11.20) such that

$$\sum_i d(\mathtt{H}_\mathrm{A}\hat{\mathbf{x}}_i, \hat{\mathbf{x}}'_i)^2 \tag{11.21}$$

is minimized.

In particular, let $\hat{\mathbf{x}}_i = (\hat{x}_i, \hat{y}_i, 1)^{\mathsf{T}}$, and let $\hat{\mathbf{x}}'_i = (\hat{x}'_i, \hat{y}'_i, 1)^{\mathsf{T}}$. Since $\mathtt{H}'$ and $\mathtt{M}$ are known, these vectors may be computed from the matched points $\mathbf{x}_i \leftrightarrow \mathbf{x}'_i$. Then the quantity to be minimized (11.21) may be written as

$$\sum_i (a\hat{x}_i + b\hat{y}_i + c - \hat{x}'_i)^2 + (\hat{y}_i - \hat{y}'_i)^2.$$

Since $(\hat{y}_i - \hat{y}'_i)^2$ is a constant, this is equivalent to minimizing

$$\sum_i (a\hat{x}_i + b\hat{y}_i + c - \hat{x}'_i)^2.$$

This is a simple linear least-squares parameter minimization problem, and is easily solved using linear techniques (see section A5.1(*p*588)) to find a, b and c. Then H_A is computed from (11.20) and $\mathtt{H}$ from (11.18). Note that a linear solution is possible because $\mathtt{H}_A$ is an affine transformation. If it were simply a projective transformation, this would not be a linear problem.

11.12.3 Algorithm outline

The resampling algorithm will now be summarized. The input is a pair of images containing a common overlap region. The output is a pair of images resampled so that the epipolar lines in the two images are horizontal (parallel with the x-axis), and such that corresponding points in the two images are as close to each other as possible. Any remaining disparity between matching points will be along the the horizontal epipolar lines. A top-level outline of the algorithm is as follows.

(i) Identify a seed set of image-to-image matches $\mathbf{x}_i \leftrightarrow \mathbf{x}'_i$ between the two images. Seven points at least are needed, though more are preferable. It is possible to find such matches by automatic means.

(ii) Compute the fundamental matrix $\mathtt{F}$ and find the epipoles $\mathbf{e}$ and $\mathbf{e}'$ in the two images.

(iii) Select a projective transformation $\mathtt{H}'$ that maps the epipole $\mathbf{e}'$ to the point at infinity, $(1, 0, 0)^\mathsf{T}$. The method of section 11.12.1 gives good results.

(iv) Find the matching projective transformation $\mathtt{H}$ that minimizes the least-squares distance

$$\sum_i d(\mathtt{H}\mathbf{x}_i, \mathtt{H}'\mathbf{x}'_i). \tag{11.22}$$

The method used is a linear method described in section 11.12.2.

(v) Resample the first image according to the projective transformation $\mathtt{H}$ and the second image according to the projective transformation $\mathtt{H}'$.

Example 11.5. Model house images

Figure 11.11(a) shows a pair of images of some wooden block houses. Edges and vertices in these two images were extracted automatically and a small number of common vertices were matched by hand. The two images were then resampled according to the methods described here. The results are shown in figure 11.11(b). In this case, because of the wide difference in viewpoint, and the three-dimensional shape of the objects, the two images even after resampling look quite different. However, it is the case that any point in the first image will now match a point in the second image with the same y-coordinate. Therefore, in order to find further point matches between the images only a 1-dimensional search is required. △

a b

Fig. 11.11. **Image rectification.** *(a) A pair of images of a house. (b) Resampled images computed from (a) using a projective transformation computed from* F. *Note, corresponding points in (b) match horizontally.*

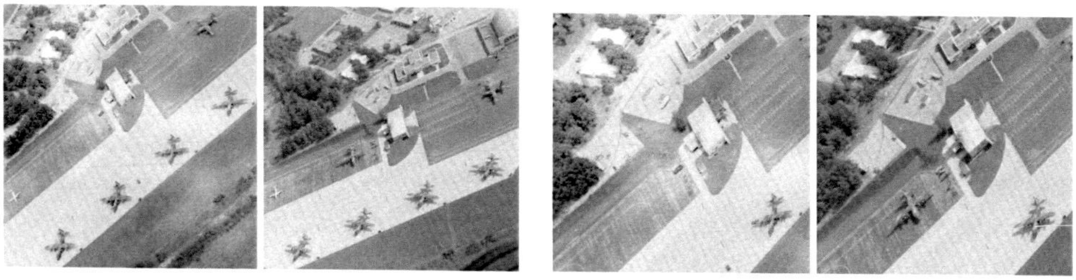

a b

Fig. 11.12. **Image rectification using affinities.** *(a) A pair of original images and (b) a detail of the images rectified using affine transformations. The average y-disparity after rectification is of the order of 3 pixels in a 512×512 image. (For correctly rectified images the y-disparity should be zero.)*

11.12.4 Affine rectification

The theory discussed in this section can equally be applied to affine resampling. If the two cameras can be well approximated by affine cameras, then one can rectify the images using just affine transformations. To do this, one uses the affine fundamental matrix (see section 14.2(*p*345)) instead of the general fundamental matrix. The above method with only minor variations can then be applied to compute a pair of matching affine transformations. Figure 11.12 shows a pair of images rectified using affine transformations.

11.13 Closure

11.13.1 The literature

The basic idea behind the computation of the fundamental matrix is given in [LonguetHiggins-81], which is well worth reading. It addresses the case of calibrated matrices only, but the principles apply to the uncalibrated case as well. A good reference for the uncalibrated case is [Zhang-98] which considers most of the best methods. In addition, that paper considers the uncertainty envelopes of epipolar lines, following earlier work by Csurka *et al.* [Csurka-97]. A more detailed study of the 8-point algorithm in the uncalibrated case is given in [Hartley-97c]. Weng *et al.* [Weng-89] used Sampson approximation for the fundamental matrix cost function. The SVD method of coercing the estimated F to have rank 2 was suggested by Tsai & Huang [Tsai-84].

There is a wealth of literature on conic fitting – minimizing algebraic distance

[Bookstein-79]; approximating geometric distance [Sampson-82, Pratt-87, Taubin-91]; optimal fitting [Kanatani-94]; and fitting special forms [Fitzgibbon-99].

11.13.2 Notes and exercises

(i) Six point correspondences constrain $\mathbf{e}$ and $\mathbf{e}'$ to a plane cubic in each image ([Faugeras-93], page 298). The cubic also passes through the six points in each image. A sketch derivation of these results follows. Given six correspondences, the null-space of $\mathtt{A}$ in (11.3–*p*279) will be 3-dimensional. Then the solution is $\mathtt{F} = \alpha_1\mathtt{F}_1 + \alpha_2\mathtt{F}_2 + \alpha_3\mathtt{F}_3$, where $\mathtt{F}_i$ denotes the matrices corresponding to the vectors spanning the null-space. The epipole satisfies $\mathtt{F}\mathbf{e} = \mathbf{0}$, so that $[(\mathtt{F}_1\mathbf{e}), (\mathtt{F}_2\mathbf{e}), (\mathtt{F}_3\mathbf{e})](\alpha_1, \alpha_2, \alpha_3)^\mathsf{T} = \mathbf{0}$. Since this equation has a solution it follows that $\det[(\mathtt{F}_1\mathbf{e}), (\mathtt{F}_2\mathbf{e}), (\mathtt{F}_3\mathbf{e})] = 0$ which is a cubic in $\mathbf{e}$.

(ii) Show that the image correspondence of four coplanar points and a quadric outline determines the fundamental matrix up to a two-fold ambiguity (Hint, see algorithm 13.2(*p*336)).

(iii) Show that the corresponding images of a (plane) conic are equivalent to two constraints on $\mathtt{F}$. See [Kahl-98b] for details.

(iv) Suppose that a stereo pair of images is acquired by a camera translating forward along its principal axis. Can the geometry of image rectification described in section 11.12 be applied in this case? See [Pollefeys-99a] for an alternative rectification geometry.

12

Structure Computation

This chapter describes how to compute the position of a point in 3-space given its image in two views and the camera matrices of those views. It is assumed that there are errors only in the measured image coordinates, not in the projection matrices $\mathtt{P}$, $\mathtt{P}'$.

Under these circumstances naïve triangulation by back-projecting rays from the measured image points will fail, because the rays will not intersect in general. It is thus necessary to *estimate* a best solution for the point in 3-space.

A best solution requires the definition and minimization of a suitable cost function. This problem is especially critical in affine and projective reconstruction in which there is no meaningful metric information about the object space. It is desirable to find a triangulation method that is invariant to projective transformations of space.

In the following sections we describe the estimation of $\mathbf{X}$ and of its covariance. An optimal (MLE) estimator for the point is developed, and it is shown that a solution can be obtained without requiring numerical minimization.

Note, this is the scenario where $\mathtt{F}$ is given *a priori* and then $\mathbf{X}$ is determined. An alternative scenario is where $\mathtt{F}$ and $\{\mathbf{X}_i\}$ are estimated simultaneously from the image point correspondences $\{\mathbf{x}_i \leftrightarrow \mathbf{x}'_i\}$, but this is not considered in this chapter. It may be solved using the Gold Standard algorithm of section 11.4.1, using the method considered in this chapter as an initial estimate.

12.1 Problem statement

It is supposed that the camera matrices, and hence the fundamental matrix, are provided; or that the fundamental matrix is provided, and hence a pair of consistent camera matrices can be constructed (as in section 9.5(*p*253)). In either case it is assumed that these matrices are known exactly, or at least with great accuracy compared with a pair of matching points in the two images.

Since there are errors in the *measured* points $\mathbf{x}$ and $\mathbf{x}'$, the rays back-projected from the points are skew. This means that there will *not* be a point $\mathbf{X}$ which exactly satisfies $\mathbf{x} = \mathtt{P}\mathbf{X}$, $\mathbf{x}' = \mathtt{P}'\mathbf{X}$; and that the image points do *not* satisfy the epipolar constraint $\mathbf{x}'^{\mathsf{T}}\mathtt{F}\mathbf{x} = 0$. These statements are equivalent since the two rays corresponding to a matching pair of points $\mathbf{x} \leftrightarrow \mathbf{x}'$ will meet in space if and only if the points satisfy the epipolar constraint. See figure 12.1.

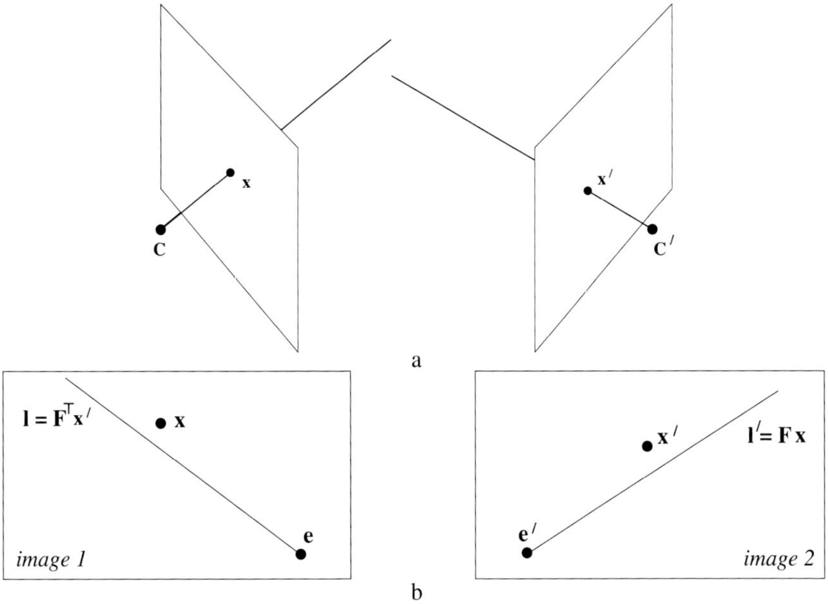

Fig. 12.1. *(a) Rays back-projected from imperfectly measured points* $\mathbf{x}, \mathbf{x}'$ *are skew in 3-space in general. (b) The epipolar geometry for* $\mathbf{x}, \mathbf{x}'$. *The measured points do not satisfy the epipolar constraint. The epipolar line* $\mathbf{l}' = \mathtt{F}\mathbf{x}$ *is the image of the ray through* $\mathbf{x}$, *and* $\mathbf{l} = \mathtt{F}^{\mathsf{T}}\mathbf{x}'$ *is the image of the ray through* $\mathbf{x}'$. *Since the rays do not intersect,* $\mathbf{x}'$ *does not lie on* $\mathbf{l}'$, *and* $\mathbf{x}$ *does not lie on* $\mathbf{l}$.

A desirable feature of the method of triangulation used is that it should be invariant under transformations of the appropriate class for the reconstruction – if the camera matrices are known only up to an affine (or projective) transformation, then it is clearly desirable to use an affine (resp. projective) invariant triangulation method to compute the 3D space points. Thus, denote by τ a triangulation method used to compute a 3D space point $\mathbf{X}$ from a point correspondence $\mathbf{x} \leftrightarrow \mathbf{x}'$ and a pair of camera matrices $\mathtt{P}$ and $\mathtt{P}'$. We write

$$\mathbf{X} = \tau(\mathbf{x}, \mathbf{x}', \mathtt{P}, \mathtt{P}').$$

The triangulation is said to be invariant under a transformation $\mathtt{H}$ if

$$\tau(\mathbf{x}, \mathbf{x}', \mathtt{P}, \mathtt{P}') = \mathtt{H}^{-1}\tau(\mathbf{x}, \mathbf{x}', \mathtt{P}\mathtt{H}^{-1}, \mathtt{P}'\mathtt{H}^{-1}).$$

This means that triangulation using the transformed cameras results in the transformed point.

It is clear, particularly for projective reconstruction, that it is inappropriate to minimize errors in the 3D projective space, $\mathbb{P}^3$. For instance, the method that finds the midpoint of the common perpendicular to the two rays in space is not suitable for projective reconstruction, since concepts such as distance and perpendicularity are not valid in the context of projective geometry. In fact, in projective reconstruction, this method will give different results depending on which particular projective reconstruction is considered – the method is not projective-invariant.

Here we will give a triangulation method that is projective-invariant. The key idea is to estimate a 3D point $\widehat{\mathbf{X}}$ which exactly satisfies the supplied camera geometry, so it projects as

$$\hat{\mathbf{x}} = \mathtt{P}\widehat{\mathbf{X}} \qquad \hat{\mathbf{x}}' = \mathtt{P}'\widehat{\mathbf{X}}$$

and the aim is to estimate $\widehat{\mathbf{X}}$ from the image measurements $\mathbf{x}$ and $\mathbf{x}'$. As described in section 12.3 the maximum likelihood estimate, under Gaussian noise, is given by the point $\widehat{\mathbf{X}}$ which minimizes the reprojection error – the (summed squared) distances between the projections of $\widehat{\mathbf{X}}$ and the measured image points.

Such a triangulation method is projective-invariant because only image distances are minimized, and the points $\hat{\mathbf{x}}$ and $\hat{\mathbf{x}}'$ which are the projections of $\widehat{\mathbf{X}}$ do not depend on the projective frame in which $\widehat{\mathbf{X}}$ is defined, i.e. a different projective reconstruction will project to the same points.

In the following sections simple linear triangulation methods are given. Then the MLE is defined, and it is shown that an optimal solution can be obtained via the root of a sixth-degree polynomial, thus avoiding a non-linear minimization of a cost function.

12.2 Linear triangulation methods

In this section, we describe simple linear triangulation methods. As usual the estimated point does not exactly satisfy the geometric relations, and is not an optimal estimate.

The linear triangulation method is the direct analogue of the DLT method described in section 4.1(*p*88). In each image we have a measurement $\mathbf{x} = \mathtt{P}\mathbf{X}$, $\mathbf{x}' = \mathtt{P}'\mathbf{X}$, and these equations can be combined into a form $\mathtt{A}\mathbf{X} = \mathbf{0}$, which is an equation linear in $\mathbf{X}$.

First the homogeneous scale factor is eliminated by a cross product to give three equations for each image point, of which two are linearly independent. For example for the first image, $\mathbf{x} \times (\mathtt{P}\mathbf{X}) = \mathbf{0}$ and writing this out gives

$$\begin{aligned} x(\mathbf{p}^{3\mathsf{T}}\mathbf{X}) - (\mathbf{p}^{1\mathsf{T}}\mathbf{X}) &= 0 \\ y(\mathbf{p}^{3\mathsf{T}}\mathbf{X}) - (\mathbf{p}^{2\mathsf{T}}\mathbf{X}) &= 0 \\ x(\mathbf{p}^{2\mathsf{T}}\mathbf{X}) - y(\mathbf{p}^{1\mathsf{T}}\mathbf{X}) &= 0 \end{aligned}$$

where $\mathbf{p}^{i\mathsf{T}}$ are the rows of $\mathtt{P}$. These equations are *linear* in the components of $\mathbf{X}$.

An equation of the form $\mathtt{A}\mathbf{X} = \mathbf{0}$ can then be composed, with

$$\mathtt{A} = \begin{bmatrix} x\mathbf{p}^{3\mathsf{T}} - \mathbf{p}^{1\mathsf{T}} \\ y\mathbf{p}^{3\mathsf{T}} - \mathbf{p}^{2\mathsf{T}} \\ x'\mathbf{p}'^{3\mathsf{T}} - \mathbf{p}'^{1\mathsf{T}} \\ y'\mathbf{p}'^{3\mathsf{T}} - \mathbf{p}'^{2\mathsf{T}} \end{bmatrix}$$

where two equations have been included from each image, giving a total of four equations in four homogeneous unknowns. This is a redundant set of equations, since the solution is determined only up to scale. Two ways of solving the set of equations of the form $\mathtt{A}\mathbf{X} = \mathbf{0}$ were discussed in section 4.1(*p*88) and will be considered again here.

Homogeneous method (DLT). The method of section 4.1.1(*p*90) finds the solution as the unit singular vector corresponding to the smallest singular value of $\mathtt{A}$, as shown in section A5.3(*p*592). The discussion in section 4.1.1 on the merits of normalization, and of including two or three equations from each image, applies equally well here.

Inhomogeneous method. In section 4.1.2(*p*90) the solution of this system as a set of inhomogeneous equations is discussed. By setting $\mathbf{X} = (\mathtt{X}, \mathtt{Y}, \mathtt{Z}, 1)^\mathsf{T}$ the set of homogeneous equations, $\mathtt{A}\mathbf{X} = \mathbf{0}$, is reduced to a set of four inhomogeneous equations in three unknowns. The least-squares solution to these inhomogeneous equations is described in section A5.1(*p*588). As explained in section 4.1.2, however, difficulties arise if the true solution $\mathbf{X}$ has last coordinate equal or close to 0. In this case, it is not legitimate to set it to 1 and instabilities can occur.

Discussion. These two methods are quite similar, but in fact have quite different properties in the presence of noise. The inhomogeneous method assumes that the solution point $\mathbf{X}$ is not at infinity, for otherwise we could not assume that $\mathbf{X} = (x, y, z, 1)^\mathsf{T}$. This is a disadvantage of this method when we are seeking to carry out a projective reconstruction, where reconstructed points may lie on the plane at infinity. Furthermore, neither of these two linear methods is quite suitable for projective reconstruction, since they are not projective-invariant. To see this, suppose that camera matrices $\mathtt{P}$ and $\mathtt{P}'$ are replaced by $\mathtt{PH}^{-1}$ and $\mathtt{P}'\mathtt{H}^{-1}$. One sees that in this case the matrix of equations, $\mathtt{A}$, becomes $\mathtt{AH}^{-1}$. A point $\mathbf{X}$ such that $\mathtt{A}\mathbf{X} = \epsilon$ for the original problem corresponds to a point $\mathtt{H}\mathbf{X}$ satisfying $(\mathtt{AH}^{-1})(\mathtt{H}\mathbf{X}) = \epsilon$ for the transformed problem. Thus, there is a one-to-one correspondence between points $\mathbf{X}$ and $\mathtt{H}\mathbf{X}$ giving the same error. However, neither the condition $\|\mathbf{X}\| = 1$ for the homogeneous method, nor the condition $\mathbf{X} = (\mathtt{X}, \mathtt{Y}, \mathtt{Z}, 1)^\mathsf{T}$ for the inhomogeneous method, is invariant under application of the projective transformation $\mathtt{H}$. Thus, in general the point $\mathbf{X}$ solving the original problem will not correspond to a solution $\mathtt{H}\mathbf{X}$ for the transformed problem.

For affine transformations, on the other hand, the situation is different. In fact, although the condition $\|\mathbf{X}\| = 1$ is not preserved under affine transformations, the condition $\mathbf{X} = (\mathtt{X}, \mathtt{Y}, \mathtt{Z}, 1)^\mathsf{T}$ is preserved, since for an affine transformation, $\mathtt{H}(\mathtt{X}, \mathtt{Y}, \mathtt{Z}, 1)^\mathsf{T} = (\mathtt{X}', \mathtt{Y}', \mathtt{Z}', 1)^\mathsf{T}$. This means that there is a one-to-one correspondence between a vector $\mathbf{X} = (\mathtt{X}, \mathtt{Y}, \mathtt{Z}, 1)^\mathsf{T}$ such that $\mathtt{A}(x, y, z, 1)^\mathsf{T} = \epsilon$ and the vector $\mathtt{H}\mathbf{X} = (\mathtt{X}', \mathtt{Y}', \mathtt{Z}', 1)^\mathsf{T}$ such that $(\mathtt{AH}^{-1})(\mathtt{X}', \mathtt{Y}', \mathtt{Z}', 1)^\mathsf{T} = \epsilon$. The error is the same for corresponding points. Thus, the points that minimize the error $\|\epsilon\|$ correspond as well. Hence, the inhomogeneous method is affine-invariant, whereas the homogeneous method is not.

In the remainder of this chapter we will describe a method for triangulation that is invariant to the projective frame of the cameras, and minimizes a geometric image error. This will be the recommended triangulation method. Nevertheless, the homogeneous linear method described above often provides acceptable results. Furthermore, it has the virtue that it generalizes easily to triangulation when more than two views of the point are available.

12.3 Geometric error cost function

A typical observation consists of a noisy point correspondence $\mathbf{x} \leftrightarrow \mathbf{x}'$ which does not in general satisfy the epipolar constraint. In reality, the correct values of the cor-

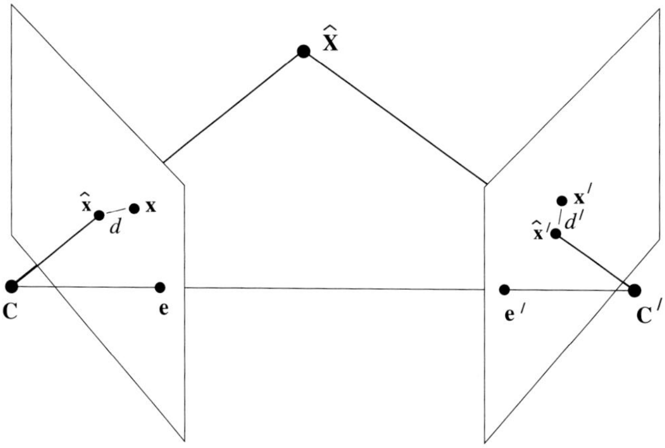

Fig. 12.2. **Minimization of geometric error.** *The estimated 3-space point $\widehat{\mathbf{X}}$ projects to the two images at $\hat{\mathbf{x}}, \hat{\mathbf{x}}'$. The corresponding image points $\hat{\mathbf{x}}, \hat{\mathbf{x}}'$ satisfy the epipolar constraint, unlike the measured points $\mathbf{x}$ and $\mathbf{x}'$. The point $\widehat{\mathbf{X}}$ is chosen so that the reprojection error $d^2 + d'^2$ is minimized.*

responding image points should be points $\bar{\mathbf{x}} \leftrightarrow \bar{\mathbf{x}}'$ lying close to the measured points $\mathbf{x} \leftrightarrow \mathbf{x}'$ and satisfying the epipolar constraint $\bar{\mathbf{x}}'^{\mathsf{T}}\mathtt{F}\bar{\mathbf{x}} = 0$ exactly.

We seek the points $\hat{\mathbf{x}}$ and $\hat{\mathbf{x}}'$ that minimize the function

$$\mathcal{C}(\mathbf{x}, \mathbf{x}') = d(\mathbf{x}, \hat{\mathbf{x}})^2 + d(\mathbf{x}', \hat{\mathbf{x}}')^2 \quad \text{subject to} \quad \hat{\mathbf{x}}'^{\mathsf{T}}\mathtt{F}\hat{\mathbf{x}} = 0 \tag{12.1}$$

where $d(*, *)$ is the Euclidean distance between the points. This is equivalent to minimizing the reprojection error for a point $\widehat{\mathbf{X}}$ which is mapped to $\hat{\mathbf{x}}$ and $\hat{\mathbf{x}}'$ by projection matrices consistent with F, as illustrated in figure 12.2.

As explained in section 4.3(*p*102), assuming a Gaussian error distribution, the points $\hat{\mathbf{x}}'$ and $\hat{\mathbf{x}}$ are Maximum Likelihood Estimates (MLE) for the true image point correspondences. Once $\hat{\mathbf{x}}'$ and $\hat{\mathbf{x}}$ are found, the point $\widehat{\mathbf{X}}$ may be found by any triangulation method, since the corresponding rays will meet precisely in space.

This cost function could, of course, be minimized using a numerical minimization method such as Levenberg–Marquardt (section A6.2(*p*600)). A close approximation to the minimum may also be found using a first-order approximation to the geometric cost function, namely the Sampson error, as described in the next section. However, in section 12.5 it is shown that the minimum can be obtained non-iteratively by the solution of a sixth-degree polynomial.

12.4 Sampson approximation (first-order geometric correction)

Before deriving the exact polynomial solution we develop the Sampson approximation, which is valid when the measurement errors are small compared with the measurements. The Sampson approximation to the geometric *cost* function in the case of the fundamental matrix has already been discussed in section 11.4.3. Here we are concerned with computing the *correction* to the measured points.

The Sampson correction $\boldsymbol{\delta}_{\mathbf{X}}$ to the measured point $\mathbf{X} = (x, y, x', y')^{\mathsf{T}}$ (note, in this section $\mathbf{X}$ does not denote a homogeneous 3-space point) is shown in section 4.2.6(*p*98)

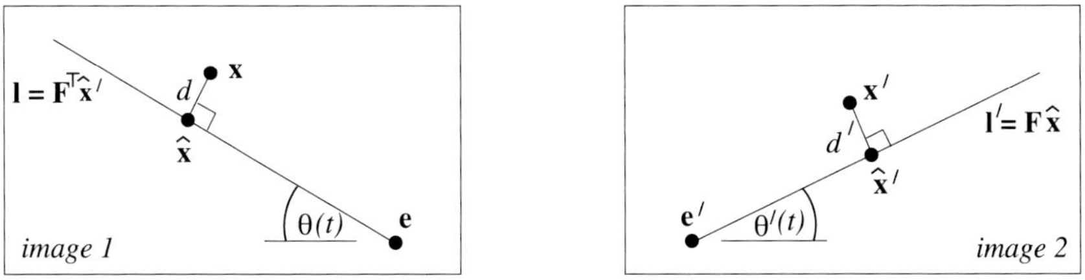

Fig. 12.3. *The projections* $\hat{\mathbf{x}}$ *and* $\hat{\mathbf{x}}'$ *of an estimated 3D point* $\widehat{\mathbf{X}}$ *lie on a pair of corresponding epipolar lines. The optimal* $\hat{\mathbf{x}}$ *and* $\hat{\mathbf{x}}'$ *will lie at the foot of the perpendiculars from the measured points* $\mathbf{x}$ *and* $\mathbf{x}'$. *Parametrizing the corresponding epipolar lines as a one-parameter family, the optimal estimation of* $\widehat{\mathbf{X}}$ *is reduced to a one-parameter search for corresponding epipolar lines so as to minimize the squared sum of perpendicular distances* $d^2 + d'^2$.

to be (4.11–*p*99)

$$\boldsymbol{\delta}_{\mathbf{X}} = -\mathtt{J}^{\mathsf{T}}(\mathtt{J}\mathtt{J}^{\mathsf{T}})^{-1}\boldsymbol{\epsilon}$$

and the corrected point is

$$\widehat{\mathbf{X}} = \mathbf{X} + \boldsymbol{\delta}_{\mathbf{X}} = \mathbf{X} - \mathtt{J}^{\mathsf{T}}(\mathtt{J}\mathtt{J}^{\mathsf{T}})^{-1}\boldsymbol{\epsilon}.$$

As shown in section 11.4.3 in the case of the variety defined by $\mathbf{x}'^{\mathsf{T}}\mathtt{F}\mathbf{x} = 0$, the error $\boldsymbol{\epsilon} = \mathbf{x}'^{\mathsf{T}}\mathtt{F}\mathbf{x}$, and the Jacobian is

$$J = \partial\boldsymbol{\epsilon}/\partial x = [(\mathtt{F}^{\mathsf{T}}\mathbf{x}')_1, (\mathtt{F}^{\mathsf{T}}\mathbf{x}')_2, (\mathtt{F}\mathbf{x})_1, (\mathtt{F}\mathbf{x})_2]$$

where for instance $(\mathtt{F}^{\mathsf{T}}\mathbf{x}')_1 = f_{11}x' + f_{21}y' + f_{31}$, etc. Then the first-order approximation to the corrected point is simply

$$\begin{pmatrix} \hat{x} \\ \hat{y} \\ \hat{x}' \\ \hat{y}' \end{pmatrix} = \begin{pmatrix} x \\ y \\ x' \\ y' \end{pmatrix} - \frac{\mathbf{x}'^{\mathsf{T}}\mathtt{F}\mathbf{x}}{(\mathtt{F}\mathbf{x})_1^2 + (\mathtt{F}\mathbf{x})_2^2 + (\mathtt{F}^{\mathsf{T}}\mathbf{x}')_1^2 + (\mathtt{F}^{\mathsf{T}}\mathbf{x}')_2^2} \begin{pmatrix} (\mathtt{F}^{\mathsf{T}}\mathbf{x}')_1 \\ (\mathtt{F}^{\mathsf{T}}\mathbf{x}')_2 \\ (\mathtt{F}\mathbf{x})_1 \\ (\mathtt{F}\mathbf{x})_2 \end{pmatrix}.$$

The approximation is accurate if the correction in each image is small (less than a pixel), and is cheap to compute. Note, however, that the corrected points will *not* satisfy the epipolar relation $\hat{\mathbf{x}}'^{\mathsf{T}}\mathtt{F}\hat{\mathbf{x}} = 0$ exactly. The method of the following section computes the points $\hat{\mathbf{x}}, \hat{\mathbf{x}}'$ which do exactly satisfy the epipolar constraint, but is more costly.

12.5 An optimal solution

In this section, we describe a method of triangulation that finds the global minimum of the cost function (12.1) using a non-iterative algorithm. If the Gaussian noise model can be assumed to be correct, this triangulation method is then provably optimal.

12.5.1 Reformulation of the minimization problem

Given a measured correspondence $\mathbf{x} \leftrightarrow \mathbf{x}'$, we seek a pair of points $\hat{\mathbf{x}}'$ and $\hat{\mathbf{x}}$ that minimize the sum of squared distances (12.1) subject to the epipolar constraint $\hat{\mathbf{x}}'^{\mathsf{T}}\mathtt{F}\hat{\mathbf{x}} = 0$.

The following discussion relates to figure 12.3. Any pair of points satisfying the epipolar constraint must lie on a pair of corresponding epipolar lines in the two images. Thus, in particular, the optimum point $\hat{\mathbf{x}}$ lies on an epipolar line $\mathbf{l}$ and $\hat{\mathbf{x}}'$ lies on the corresponding epipolar line $\mathbf{l}'$. On the other hand, any other pair of points lying on the lines $\mathbf{l}$ and $\mathbf{l}'$ will also satisfy the epipolar constraint. This is true in particular for the point $\mathbf{x}_\perp$ on $\mathbf{l}$ lying closest to the measured point $\mathbf{x}$, and the correspondingly defined point $\mathbf{x}'_\perp$ on $\mathbf{l}'$. Of all pairs of points on the lines $\mathbf{l}$ and $\mathbf{l}'$, the points $\mathbf{x}_\perp$ and $\mathbf{x}'_\perp$ minimize the squared distance sum of (12.1). It follows that $\hat{\mathbf{x}}' = \mathbf{x}'_\perp$ and $\hat{\mathbf{x}} = \mathbf{x}_\perp$, where $\mathbf{x}_\perp$ and $\mathbf{x}'_\perp$ are defined with respect to a pair of matching epipolar lines $\mathbf{l}$ and $\mathbf{l}'$. Consequently, we may write $d(\mathbf{x}, \hat{\mathbf{x}}) = d(\mathbf{x}, \mathbf{l})$, where $d(\mathbf{x}, \mathbf{l})$ represents the perpendicular distance from the point $\mathbf{x}$ to the line $\mathbf{l}$. A similar expression holds for $d(\mathbf{x}', \hat{\mathbf{x}}')$.

In view of the previous paragraph, we may formulate the minimization problem differently as follows. We seek to minimize

$$d(\mathbf{x}, \mathbf{l})^2 + d(\mathbf{x}', \mathbf{l}')^2 \qquad (12.2)$$

where $\mathbf{l}$ and $\mathbf{l}'$ range over all choices of corresponding epipolar lines. The point $\hat{\mathbf{x}}$ is then the closest point on the line $\mathbf{l}$ to the point $\mathbf{x}$ and the point $\hat{\mathbf{x}}'$ is similarly defined.

Our strategy for minimizing (12.2) is as follows:

(i) Parametrize the pencil of epipolar lines in the first image by a parameter t. Thus an epipolar line in the first image may be written as $\mathbf{l}(t)$.

(ii) Using the fundamental matrix $\mathtt{F}$, compute the corresponding epipolar line $\mathbf{l}'(t)$ in the second image.

(iii) Express the distance function $d(\mathbf{x}, \mathbf{l}(t))^2 + d(\mathbf{x}', \mathbf{l}'(t))^2$ explicitly as a function of t.

(iv) Find the value of t that minimizes this function.

In this way, the problem is reduced to that of finding the minimum of a function of a single variable t, i.e.

$$\min_{\widehat{\mathbf{X}}} \mathcal{C} = d(\mathbf{x}, \hat{\mathbf{x}})^2 + d(\mathbf{x}', \hat{\mathbf{x}}')^2 = \min_t \mathcal{C} = d(\mathbf{x}, \mathbf{l}(t))^2 + d(\mathbf{x}', \mathbf{l}'(t))^2.$$

It will be seen that for a suitable parametrization of the pencil of epipolar lines the distance function is a rational polynomial function of t. Using techniques of elementary calculus, the minimization problem reduces to finding the real roots of a polynomial of degree 6.

12.5.2 Details of the minimization

If both of the image points correspond with the epipoles, then the point in space lies on the line joining the camera centres. In this case it is impossible to determine the position of the point in space. If only one of the corresponding points lies at an epipole, then we conclude that the point in space must coincide with the other camera centre. Consequently, we assume that neither of the two image points $\mathbf{x}$ and $\mathbf{x}'$ corresponds with an epipole.

In this case, we may simplify the analysis by applying a rigid transformation to each image in order to place both points $\mathbf{x}$ and $\mathbf{x}'$ at the origin, $(0, 0, 1)^\mathsf{T}$ in homogeneous coordinates. Furthermore, the epipoles may be placed on the x-axis at points $(1, 0, f)^\mathsf{T}$ and $(1, 0, f')^\mathsf{T}$ respectively. A value f equal to 0 means that the epipole is at infinity. Applying these two rigid transforms has no effect on the sum-of-squares distance function in (12.1), and hence does not change the minimization problem.

Thus, in future we assume that in homogeneous coordinates, $\mathbf{x} = \mathbf{x}' = (0, 0, 1)^\mathsf{T}$ and that the two epipoles are at points $(1, 0, f)^\mathsf{T}$ and $(1, 0, f')^\mathsf{T}$. In this case, since $\mathtt{F}(1, 0, f)^\mathsf{T} = (1, 0, f')\mathtt{F} = \mathbf{0}$, the fundamental matrix has a special form

$$\mathtt{F} = \begin{pmatrix} ff'd & -f'c & -f'd \\ -fb & a & b \\ -fd & c & d \end{pmatrix}. \tag{12.3}$$

Consider an epipolar line in the first image passing through the point $(0, t, 1)^\mathsf{T}$ (still in homogeneous coordinates) and the epipole $(1, 0, f)^\mathsf{T}$. We denote this epipolar line by $\mathbf{l}(t)$. The vector representing this line is given by the cross product $(0, t, 1) \times (1, 0, f) = (tf, 1, -t)$, so the squared distance from the line to the origin is

$$d(\mathbf{x}, \mathbf{l}(t))^2 = \frac{t^2}{1 + (tf)^2}.$$

Using the fundamental matrix to find the corresponding epipolar line in the other image, we see that

$$\mathbf{l}'(t) = \mathtt{F}(0, t, 1)^\mathsf{T} = (-f'(ct + d), at + b, ct + d)^\mathsf{T}. \tag{12.4}$$

This is the representation of the line $\mathbf{l}'(t)$ as a homogeneous vector. The squared distance of this line from the origin is equal to

$$d(\mathbf{x}', \mathbf{l}'(t))^2 = \frac{(ct + d)^2}{(at + b)^2 + f'^2(ct + d)^2}.$$

The total squared distance is therefore given by

$$s(t) = \frac{t^2}{1 + f^2t^2} + \frac{(ct + d)^2}{(at + b)^2 + f'^2(ct + d)^2}. \tag{12.5}$$

Our task is to find the minimum of this function.

We may find the minimum using techniques of elementary calculus, as follows. We compute the derivative

$$s'(t) = \frac{2t}{(1 + f^2t^2)^2} - \frac{2(ad - bc)(at + b)(ct + d)}{((at + b)^2 + f'^2(ct + d)^2)^2}. \tag{12.6}$$

Maxima and minima of $s(t)$ will occur when $s'(t) = 0$. Collecting the two terms in $s'(t)$ over a common denominator and equating the numerator to 0 gives a condition

$$\begin{aligned} g(t) &= t((at + b)^2 + f'^2(ct + d)^2)^2 \\ &\quad -(ad - bc)(1 + f^2t^2)^2(at + b)(ct + d) \\ &= 0. \end{aligned} \tag{12.7}$$

The minima and maxima of $s(t)$ will occur at the roots of this polynomial. This is a

Objective

Given a measured point correspondence $\mathbf{x} \leftrightarrow \mathbf{x}'$, and a fundamental matrix $\mathtt{F}$, compute the corrected correspondences $\hat{\mathbf{x}} \leftrightarrow \hat{\mathbf{x}}'$ that minimize the geometric error (12.1) subject to the epipolar constraint $\hat{\mathbf{x}}'^{\mathsf{T}}\mathtt{F}\hat{\mathbf{x}} = 0$.

Algorithm

(i) Define transformation matrices

$$\mathtt{T} = \begin{bmatrix} 1 & & -x \\ & 1 & -y \\ & & 1 \end{bmatrix} \text{ and } \mathtt{T}' = \begin{bmatrix} 1 & & -x' \\ & 1 & -y' \\ & & 1 \end{bmatrix}.$$

These are the translations that take $\mathbf{x} = (x, y, 1)^{\mathsf{T}}$ and $\mathbf{x}' = (x', y', 1)^{\mathsf{T}}$ to the origin.

(ii) Replace $\mathtt{F}$ by $\mathtt{T}'^{-\mathsf{T}}\mathtt{F}\mathtt{T}^{-1}$. The new $\mathtt{F}$ corresponds to translated coordinates.

(iii) Compute the right and left epipoles $\mathbf{e} = (e_1, e_2, e_3)^{\mathsf{T}}$ and $\mathbf{e}' = (e'_1, e'_2, e'_3)^{\mathsf{T}}$ such that $\mathbf{e}'^{\mathsf{T}}\mathtt{F} = \mathbf{0}$ and $\mathtt{F}\mathbf{e} = \mathbf{0}$. Normalize (multiply by a scale) $\mathbf{e}$ such that $e_1^2 + e_2^2 = 1$ and do the same to $\mathbf{e}'$.

(iv) Form matrices

$$\mathtt{R} = \begin{bmatrix} e_1 & e_2 & \\ -e_2 & e_1 & \\ & & 1 \end{bmatrix} \text{ and } \mathtt{R}' = \begin{bmatrix} e'_1 & e'_2 & \\ -e'_2 & e'_1 & \\ & & 1 \end{bmatrix}$$

and observe that $\mathtt{R}$ and $\mathtt{R}'$ are rotation matrices, and $\mathtt{R}\mathbf{e} = (1, 0, e_3)^{\mathsf{T}}$ and $\mathtt{R}'\mathbf{e}' = (1, 0, e'_3)^{\mathsf{T}}$.

(v) Replace $\mathtt{F}$ by $\mathtt{R}'\mathtt{F}\mathtt{R}^{\mathsf{T}}$. The resulting $\mathtt{F}$ must have the form (12.3).

(vi) Set $f = e_3$, $f' = e'_3$, $a = F_{22}$, $b = F_{23}$, $c = F_{32}$ and $d = F_{33}$.

(vii) Form the polynomial $g(t)$ as a polynomial in t according to (12.7). Solve for t to get 6 roots.

(viii) Evaluate the cost function (12.5) at the real part of each of the roots of $g(t)$ (alternatively evaluate at only the real roots of $g(t)$). Also, find the asymptotic value of (12.1) for $t = \infty$, namely $1/f^2 + c^2/(a^2 + f'^2c^2)$. Select the value t_{min} of t that gives the smallest value of the cost function.

(ix) Evaluate the two lines $\mathbf{l} = (tf, 1, -t)$ and $\mathbf{l}'$ given by (12.4) at t_{min} and find $\hat{\mathbf{x}}$ and $\hat{\mathbf{x}}'$ as the closest points on these lines to the origin. For a general line (λ, μ, ν), the formula for the closest point on the line to the origin is $(-\lambda\nu, -\mu\nu, \lambda^2 + \mu^2)$.

(x) Transfer back to the original coordinates by replacing $\hat{\mathbf{x}}$ by $\mathtt{T}^{-1}\mathtt{R}^{\mathsf{T}}\hat{\mathbf{x}}$ and $\hat{\mathbf{x}}'$ by $\mathtt{T}'^{-1}\mathtt{R}'^{\mathsf{T}}\hat{\mathbf{x}}'$.

(xi) The 3-space point $\widehat{\mathbf{X}}$ may then be obtained by the homogeneous method of section 12.2.

Algorithm 12.1. *The optimal triangulation method.*

polynomial of degree 6, which may have up to 6 real roots, corresponding to 3 minima and 3 maxima of the function $s(t)$. The absolute minimum of the function $s(t)$ may be found by finding the roots of $g(t)$ and evaluating the function $s(t)$ given by (12.5) at each of the real roots. More simply, one checks the value of $s(t)$ at the real part of each root (complex or real) of $g(t)$, which saves the trouble of determining if a root is real or complex. One should also check the asymptotic value of $s(t)$ as $t \to \infty$ to see if the minimum distance occurs when $t = \infty$, corresponding to an epipolar line $fx = 1$ in the first image.

The overall method is summarized in algorithm 12.1.

a b

Fig. 12.4. *(a) Example of a cost function with three minima. (b) This is the cost function for a perfect point match, which nevertheless has two minima.*

12.5.3 Local minima

The fact that $g(t)$ in (12.7) has degree 6 means that $s(t)$ may have as many as three minima. In fact, this is indeed possible, as the following case shows. Setting $f = f' = 1$ and

$$\mathrm{F} = \begin{pmatrix} 4 & -3 & -4 \\ -3 & 2 & 3 \\ -4 & 3 & 4 \end{pmatrix}$$

gives a function

$$s(t) = \frac{t^2}{1+t^2} + \frac{(3t+4)^2}{(2t+3)^2 + (3t+4)^2}$$

with graph as shown in figure 12.4a[1]. The three minima are clearly shown.

As a second example, we consider the case where $f = f' = 1$, and

$$\mathrm{F} = \begin{pmatrix} 0 & -1 & 0 \\ 1 & 2 & -1 \\ 0 & 1 & 0 \end{pmatrix}.$$

In this case, the function $s(t)$ is given by

$$s(t) = \frac{t^2}{t^2+1} + \frac{t^2}{t^2 + (2t-1)^2}$$

and both terms of the cost function vanish for a value of $t = 0$, which means that the corresponding points $\mathbf{x}$ and $\mathbf{x}'$ exactly satisfy the epipolar constraint. This can be verified by observing that $\mathbf{x}'^{\mathsf{T}}\mathrm{F}\mathbf{x} = 0$. Thus the two points are exactly matched. A graph of the cost function $s(t)$ is shown in figure 12.4b. Apart from the absolute minimum at $t = 0$ there is also a local minimum at $t = 1$. Thus, even in the case of perfect matches local minima may occur. This example shows that an algorithm that attempts to minimize the cost function in (12.1), or equivalently (12.2), by an iterative

[1] In this graph and also figure 12.4b we make the substitution $t = \tan(\theta)$ and plot for θ in the range $-\pi/2 \leq \theta \leq \pi/2$, so as to show the whole infinite range for t.

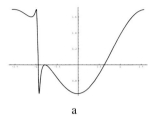

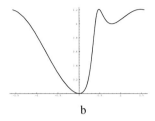

search beginning from an arbitrary initial point is in danger of finding a local minimum, even in the case of perfect point matches.

12.5.4 Evaluation on real images

An experiment was carried out using the calibration cube images shown in figure 11.2-(*p*289) with the goal of determining how the triangulation method effects the accuracy of reconstruction. A Euclidean model of the cubes, to be used as ground truth, was estimated and refined using accurate image measurements. The measured pixel locations were corrected to correspond exactly to the Euclidean model, requiring coordinate corrections averaging 0.02 pixels.

At this stage we had a model and a set of matched points corresponding exactly to the model. Next, a projective reconstruction of the points was computed and a projective transformation $\mathtt{H}$ computed that brought the projective reconstruction into agreement with the Euclidean model. Controlled zero-mean Gaussian noise was introduced into the point coordinates, and triangulation using two methods was carried out in the projective frame, the transformation $\mathtt{H}$ applied, and the error of each method was measured in the Euclidean frame. Figure 12.5 shows the results of this experiment for the two triangulation methods. The graph shows the average reconstruction error over all points in 10 separate runs at each chosen noise level. It clearly shows that the optimal method gives superior reconstruction results.

In this pair of images the two epipoles are distant from the image. For cases where the epipoles are close to the images, results on synthetic images show that the advantage of the polynomial method will be more pronounced.

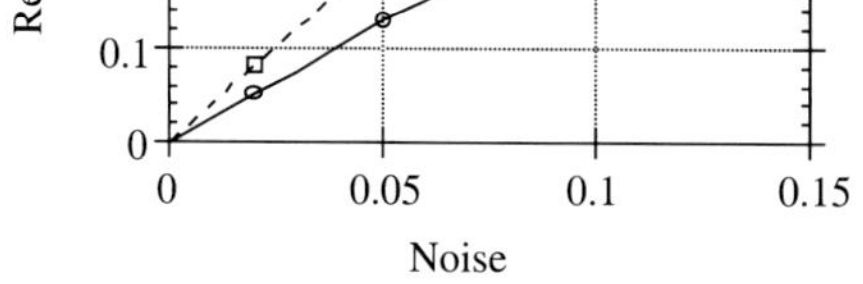

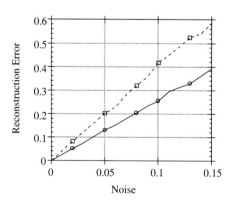

Fig. 12.5. **Reconstruction error comparison of triangulation methods.** *The graph shows the reconstruction error obtained using two triangulation methods: (i) selection of the midpoint of the common perpendicular to the rays in the projective frame (top curve), and (ii) the optimal polynomial method (lower curve). On the horizontal axis is the noise, on the vertical axis the reconstruction error. The units for reconstruction error are relative to a unit distance equal to the side of one of the dark squares in the calibration cube image figure 11.2(*p289*). Even for the best method the error is large for higher noise levels, because there is little movement between the images.*

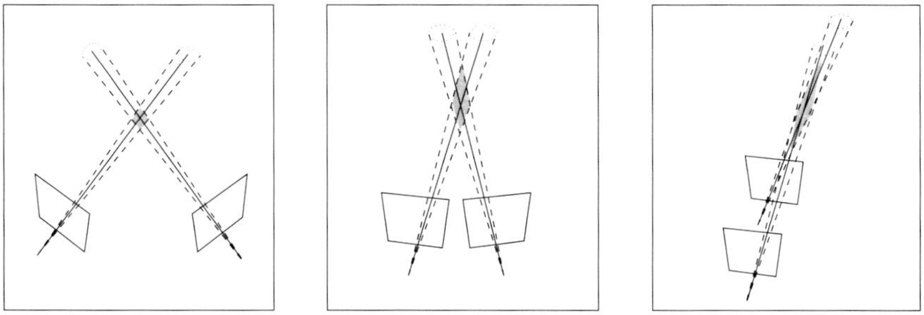

Fig. 12.6. **Uncertainty of reconstruction.** *The shaded region in each case illustrates the shape of the uncertainty region, which depends on the angle between the rays. Points are less precisely localized along the ray as the rays become more parallel. Forward motion in particular can give poor reconstructions since rays are almost parallel for much of the field of view.*

12.6 Probability distribution of the estimated 3D point

An illustration of the distribution of the reconstructed point is given in figure 12.6. A good rule of thumb is that the angle between the rays determines the accuracy of reconstruction. This is a better guide than simply considering the baseline, which is the more commonly used measure.

More formally the probability of a particular 3D point $\mathbf{X}$ depends on the probability of obtaining its image in each view. We will consider a simplified example where the objective is to estimate the probability that a point on a plane has position $\mathbf{X} = (\mathrm{X}, \mathrm{Y})^\mathsf{T}$ given its images $x = f(\mathbf{X})$ and $x' = f'(\mathbf{X})$ in two line cameras. (The projections f and f' are expressible in terms of 2×3 projection matrices $\mathtt{P}_{2\times3}$ and $\mathtt{P}'_{2\times3}$ respectively – see section 6.4.2(p175)). The imaging geometry is shown in figure 12.7(a).

Suppose that the measured image point is at x in the first image, and the measurement process is corrupted by Gaussian noise with mean zero and variance σ^2, then the probability of obtaining x, given that the true image point is $f(\mathbf{X})$, is given by

$$p(x|\mathbf{X}) = (2\pi\sigma^2)^{-1/2} \exp\left(-|f(\mathbf{X}) - x|^2/(2\sigma^2)\right).$$

with a similar expression for $p(x'|\mathbf{X})$. We wish to compute the *a posteriori* distribution:

$$p(\mathbf{X}|x, x') = p(x, x'|\mathbf{X})p(\mathbf{X})/p(x, x').$$

Assuming a uniform prior probability $p(\mathbf{X})$, and independent image measurements in the two images, it follows that

$$p(\mathbf{X}|x, x') \sim p(x, x'|\mathbf{X}) = p(x|\mathbf{X})p(x'|\mathbf{X}).$$

Figure 12.7 shows an example of this Probability Density Function (PDF). The bias and variance of this example is discussed in appendix 3(p568).

12.7 Line reconstruction

Suppose a line in 3-space is projected to lines in two views as $\mathbf{l}$ and $\mathbf{l}'$. The line in 3-space can be reconstructed by back-projecting each line to give a plane in 3-space, and intersecting the planes.

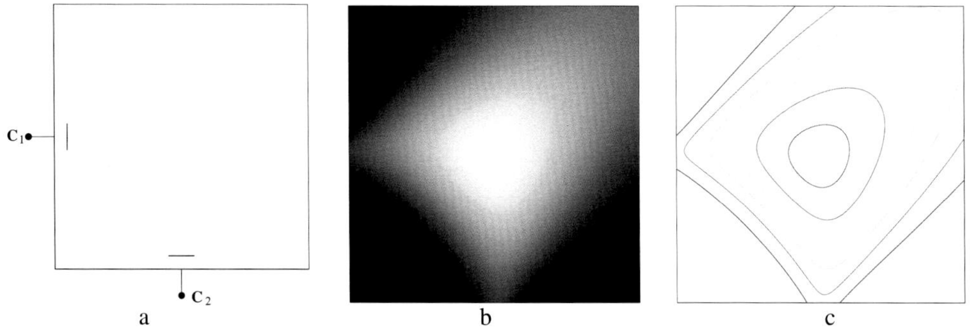

Fig. 12.7. PDF **for a triangulated point.** *(a) The camera configuration. There are two line cameras with centres at* $\mathbf{C}_1$ *and* $\mathbf{C}_2$*. The image lines are the left and lower edge of the square. The bar indicates the* 2σ *range of the noise. The plots show the* PDF *for a triangulated point computed from the two perspective projections. A large noise variance* σ^2 *is chosen to emphasize the effect. (b) The* PDF *shown as an image with white representing a higher value. (b) A contour plot of the* PDF*. Note that the* PDF *is not a Gaussian.*

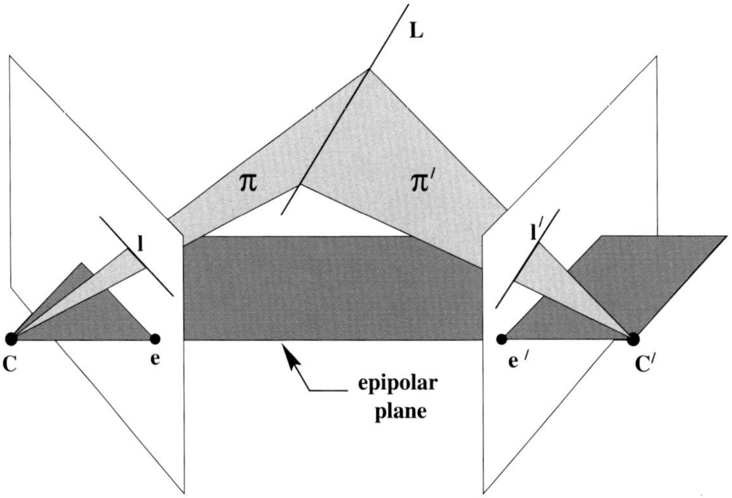

Fig. 12.8. **Line reconstruction.** *The image lines* $\mathbf{l}, \mathbf{l}'$ *back-project to planes* $\boldsymbol{\pi}, \boldsymbol{\pi}'$ *respectively. The plane intersection determines the line* $\mathbf{L}$ *in 3-space. If the line in 3-space lies on an epipolar plane then its position in 3-space cannot be determined from its images. In this case the epipoles lie on the image lines.*

The planes defined by the lines are $\boldsymbol{\pi} = \mathtt{P}^\mathsf{T}\mathbf{l}$ and $\boldsymbol{\pi}' = \mathtt{P}'^\mathsf{T}\mathbf{l}'$. It is often quite convenient in practice to parametrize the line in 3-space by the two planes defined by the image lines, i.e. to represent the line as the 2×4 matrix

$$\mathtt{L} = \begin{bmatrix} \mathbf{l}^\mathsf{T}\mathtt{P} \\ \mathbf{l}'^\mathsf{T}\mathtt{P}' \end{bmatrix}$$

as described in the span representation of section 3.2.2(*p*68). Then for example a point $\mathbf{X}$ lies on the line if $\mathtt{L}\mathbf{X} = \mathbf{0}$.

In the case of corresponding points the pre-image (i.e. the point in 3-space that projects to the image points) is over-determined since there are four measurements on the three degrees of freedom of the 3-space point. In contrast in the case of lines the pre-image is exactly determined because a line in 3-space has four degrees of freedom, and the image line provides two measurements in each view. Note, here we are considering the lines as infinite, and not using their endpoints.

Degeneracy. As illustrated in figure 12.8 lines in 3-space lying on epipolar planes cannot be determined from their images in two views. Such lines intersect the camera baseline. In practice, when there is measurement error, lines which are close to intersecting the baseline can be poorly localized in a reconstruction.

The degeneracy for lines is far more severe than for points: in the case of points there is a one-parameter family of points on the baseline which cannot be recovered. For lines there is a three-parameter family: one parameter for position on the baseline, and the other two for the star of lines through each point on the baseline.

Intersection of more than two planes

In later chapters (particularly chapter 15) we will be considering reconstruction from three or more views. To reconstruct the line that results from the intersection of several planes it is appropriate to proceed as follows. Represent each plane $\boldsymbol{\pi}_i$ by a 4-vector and form an $n \times 4$ matrix $\mathtt{A}$ for n planes with rows $\boldsymbol{\pi}_i^\mathsf{T}$. Let $\mathtt{A} = \mathtt{UDV}^\mathsf{T}$ be the singular value decomposition. The two columns of $\mathtt{V}$ corresponding to the two largest singular values span the best rank 2 approximation to $\mathtt{A}$ and may be used to define the line of intersection of the planes. If the planes are defined by back-projecting image lines, then the Maximum Likelihood estimate of the line $\mathbf{L}$ in 3-space is found by minimizing a geometric image distance between $\mathbf{L}$ projected into each image and the measured line in that image. This is discussed in section 16.4.1(*p*396).

12.8 Closure

It is not evident how to extend the polynomial method of triangulation to 3 or more views. However, the linear method extends in an obvious manner. More interestingly, the Sampson method also may be extended to 3 or more views, as is described in [Torr-97]. The disadvantage is that the computational cost (and also coding effort) increases noticeably with more views.

12.8.1 The literature

The optimal triangulation method was given by Hartley & Sturm [Hartley-97b].

12.8.2 Notes and exercises

(i) Derive a method for triangulation in the case of pure translational motion of the cameras. Hint, see figure 12.9. A closed form solution for the parameter θ is possible. This method was used in [Armstrong-94].

(ii) Adapt the polynomial triangulation method to a pair of affine cameras (or more generally, to cameras with the same principal plane). In this case, the fundamental matrix has a simple form, (14.1–*p*345), and the method reduces to a linear algorithm.

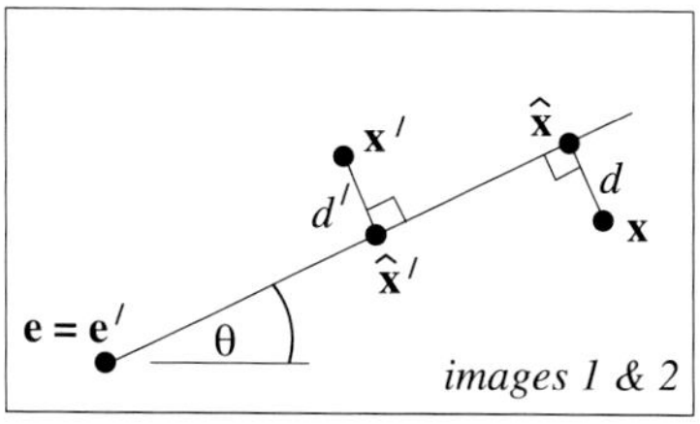

Fig. 12.9. **The epipolar geometry for pure translation.** *In this case, corresponding epipolar lines are identical (see section 11.7.1(p293)). The epipolar line (parametrized by θ) that minimizes $d^2 + d'^2$ can be computed directly.*

(iii) Show that the Sampson method (section 12.4) is invariant under Euclidean coordinate changes in the images (and the corresponding change in F).

(iv) Derive the analogue of the polynomial solution for triangulation in the case of a planar homography, i.e. given a measured correspondence $\mathbf{x} \leftrightarrow \mathbf{x}'$, compute points $\hat{\mathbf{x}}$ and $\hat{\mathbf{x}}'$ that minimize the function

$$\mathcal{C}(\mathbf{x}, \mathbf{x}') = d(\mathbf{x}, \hat{\mathbf{x}})^2 + d(\mathbf{x}', \hat{\mathbf{x}}')^2 \quad \text{subject to } \hat{\mathbf{x}}' = \mathtt{H}\hat{\mathbf{x}}.$$

See [Sturm-97b], where it is shown that the solution is a degree 8 polynomial in one variable.

13

Scene planes and homographies

This chapter describes the projective geometry of two cameras and a world plane.

Images of points on a plane are related to corresponding image points in a second view by a (planar) homography as shown in figure 13.1. This is a projective relation since it depends only on the intersections of planes with lines. It is said that the plane *induces* a homography between the views. The homography map *transfers* points from one view to the other as if they were images of points on the plane.

There are then two relations between the two views: first, through the epipolar geometry a point in one view determines a line in the other which is the image of the ray through that point; and second, through the homography a point in one view determines a point in the other which is the image of the intersection of the ray with a plane. This chapter ties together these two relations of 2-view geometry.

Two other important notions are described here: the parallax with respect to a plane, and the infinite homography.

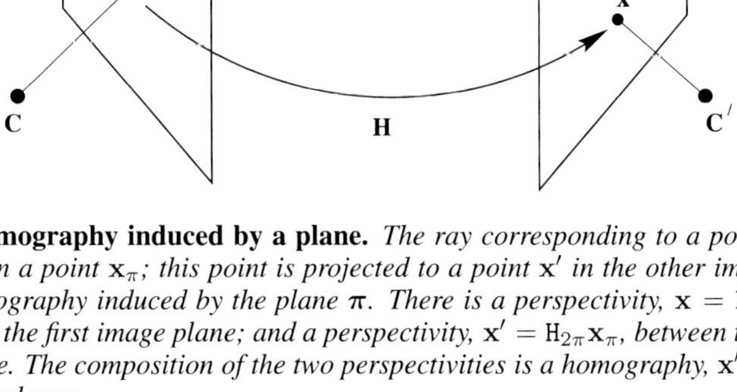

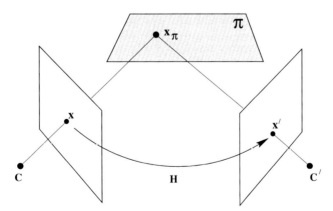

Fig. 13.1. **The homography induced by a plane.** *The ray corresponding to a point* $\mathbf{x}$ *is extended to meet the plane* $\boldsymbol{\pi}$ *in a point* $\mathbf{x}_\pi$*; this point is projected to a point* $\mathbf{x}'$ *in the other image. The map from* $\mathbf{x}$ *to* $\mathbf{x}'$ *is the homography induced by the plane* $\boldsymbol{\pi}$*. There is a perspectivity,* $\mathbf{x} = \mathtt{H}_{1\pi}\mathbf{x}_\pi$*, between the world plane* $\boldsymbol{\pi}$ *and the first image plane; and a perspectivity,* $\mathbf{x}' = \mathtt{H}_{2\pi}\mathbf{x}_\pi$*, between the world plane and second image plane. The composition of the two perspectivities is a homography,* $\mathbf{x}' = \mathtt{H}_{2\pi}\mathtt{H}_{1\pi}^{-1}\mathbf{x} = \mathtt{H}\mathbf{x}$*, between the image planes.*

13.1 Homographies given the plane and vice versa

We start by showing that for planes in general position the homography is determined uniquely by the plane and vice versa. General position in this case means that the plane does not contain either of the camera centres. If the plane does contain one of the camera centres then the induced homography is degenerate.

Suppose a plane π in 3-space is specified by its coordinates in the world frame. We first derive an explicit expression for the induced homography.

Result 13.1. *Given the projection matrices for the two views*

$$\mathtt{P} = [\mathtt{I} \mid \mathbf{0}] \qquad \mathtt{P}' = [\mathtt{A} \mid \mathbf{a}]$$

and a plane defined by $\boldsymbol{\pi}^{\mathsf{T}}\mathbf{X} = 0$ *with* $\boldsymbol{\pi} = (\mathbf{v}^{\mathsf{T}}, 1)^{\mathsf{T}}$, *then the homography induced by the plane is* $\mathbf{x}' = \mathtt{H}\mathbf{x}$ *with*

$$\mathtt{H} = \mathtt{A} - \mathbf{a}\mathbf{v}^{\mathsf{T}}. \tag{13.1}$$

We may assume that $\pi_4 = 1$ since the plane does not pass through the centre of the first camera at $(0, 0, 0, 1)^{\mathsf{T}}$.

Note, there is a three-parameter family of planes in 3-space, and correspondingly a three-parameter family of homographies between two views induced by planes in 3-space. These three parameters are specified by the elements of the vector $\mathbf{v}$, which is *not* a homogeneous 3-vector.

Proof. To compute H we back-project a point $\mathbf{x}$ in the first view and determine the intersection point $\mathbf{X}$ of this ray with the plane $\boldsymbol{\pi}$. The 3D point $\mathbf{X}$ is then projected into the second view.

For the first view $\mathbf{x} = \mathtt{P}\mathbf{X} = [\mathtt{I} \mid \mathbf{0}]\mathbf{X}$ and so any point on the ray $\mathbf{X} = (\mathbf{x}^{\mathsf{T}}, \rho)^{\mathsf{T}}$ projects to $\mathbf{x}$, where ρ parametrizes the point on the ray. Since the 3D point $\mathbf{X}$ is on $\boldsymbol{\pi}$ it satisfies $\boldsymbol{\pi}^{\mathsf{T}}\mathbf{X} = 0$. This determines ρ, and $\mathbf{X} = (\mathbf{x}^{\mathsf{T}}, -\mathbf{v}^{\mathsf{T}}\mathbf{x})^{\mathsf{T}}$. The 3D point $\mathbf{X}$ projects into the second view as

$$\begin{aligned} \mathbf{x}' &= \mathtt{P}'\mathbf{X} = [\mathtt{A} \mid \mathbf{a}]\mathbf{X} \\ &= \mathtt{A}\mathbf{x} - \mathbf{a}\mathbf{v}^{\mathsf{T}}\mathbf{x} = \left(\mathtt{A} - \mathbf{a}\mathbf{v}^{\mathsf{T}}\right)\mathbf{x} \end{aligned}$$

as required. □

Example 13.2. A calibrated stereo rig.

Suppose the camera matrices are those of a calibrated stereo rig with the world origin at the first camera

$$\mathtt{P}_{\mathrm{E}} = \mathtt{K}[\mathtt{I} \mid \mathbf{0}] \qquad \mathtt{P}'_{\mathrm{E}} = \mathtt{K}'[\mathtt{R} \mid \mathbf{t}],$$

and the world plane $\boldsymbol{\pi}_{\mathrm{E}}$ has coordinates $\boldsymbol{\pi}_{\mathrm{E}} = (\mathbf{n}^{\mathsf{T}}, d)^{\mathsf{T}}$ so that for points on the plane $\mathbf{n}^{\mathsf{T}}\widetilde{\mathbf{X}} + d = 0$. We wish to compute an expression for the homography induced by the plane.

From result 13.1, with $\mathbf{v} = \mathbf{n}/d$, the homography for the cameras $\mathtt{P} = [\mathtt{I} \mid \mathbf{0}]$, $\mathtt{P}' = [\mathtt{R} \mid \mathbf{t}]$ is

$$\mathtt{H} = \mathtt{R} - \mathbf{t}\mathbf{n}^{\mathsf{T}}/d.$$

Applying the transformations $\mathtt{K}$ and $\mathtt{K}'$ to the images we obtain the cameras $\mathtt{P}_{\mathrm{E}} = \mathtt{K}[\mathtt{I} \mid \mathbf{0}]$, $\mathtt{P}'_{\mathrm{E}} = \mathtt{K}'[\mathtt{R} \mid \mathbf{t}]$ and the resulting induced homography is

$$\mathtt{H} = \mathtt{K}' \left(\mathtt{R} - \mathbf{t}\mathbf{n}^{\mathsf{T}}/d \right) \mathtt{K}^{-1}. \tag{13.2}$$

This is a three-parameter family of homographies, parametrized by $\mathbf{n}/d$. It is defined by the plane, and the camera internal and relative external parameters. △

13.1.1 Homographies compatible with epipolar geometry

Suppose four points $\mathbf{X}_i$ are chosen on a scene plane. Then the correspondence $\mathbf{x}_i \leftrightarrow \mathbf{x}'_i$ of their images between two views defines a homography $\mathtt{H}$, which is the homography induced by the plane. These image correspondences also obey the epipolar constraint, i.e. $\mathbf{x}'^{\mathsf{T}}_i \mathtt{F} \mathbf{x}_i = 0$, since they arise from images of scene points. Indeed, the correspondence $\mathbf{x} \leftrightarrow \mathbf{x}' = \mathtt{H}\mathbf{x}$ obeys the epipolar constraint for *any* $\mathbf{x}$, since again $\mathbf{x}$ and $\mathbf{x}'$ are images of a scene point, in this case the point given by intersecting the scene plane with the ray back-projected from $\mathbf{x}$. The homography $\mathtt{H}$ is said to be consistent or *compatible* with $\mathtt{F}$.

Now suppose four *arbitrary* image points are chosen in the first view and four arbitrary image points chosen in the second. Then a homography $\tilde{\mathtt{H}}$ may be computed which maps one set of points into the other (provided no three are collinear in either view). However, correspondences $\mathbf{x} \leftrightarrow \mathbf{x}' = \tilde{\mathtt{H}}\mathbf{x}$ may *not* obey the epipolar constraint. If the correspondence $\mathbf{x} \leftrightarrow \mathbf{x}' = \tilde{\mathtt{H}}\mathbf{x}$ does not obey the epipolar constraint then there does not exist a scene plane which induces $\tilde{\mathtt{H}}$.

The epipolar geometry determines the projective geometry between two views, and can be used to define conditions on homographies which are induced by actual scene planes. Figure 13.2 illustrates several relations between epipolar geometry and scene planes which can be used to define such conditions. For example, since correspondences $\mathbf{x} \leftrightarrow \mathtt{H}\mathbf{x}$ obey the epipolar constraint if $\mathtt{H}$ is induced by a plane, then from $\mathbf{x}'^{\mathsf{T}}\mathtt{F}\mathbf{x} = 0$

$$(\mathtt{H}\mathbf{x})^{\mathsf{T}}\mathtt{F}\mathbf{x} = \mathbf{x}^{\mathsf{T}}\mathtt{H}^{\mathsf{T}}\mathtt{F}\mathbf{x} = 0.$$

This is true for all $\mathbf{x}$, so:

- *A homography* $\mathtt{H}$ *is compatible with a fundamental matrix* $\mathtt{F}$ *if and only if the matrix* $\mathtt{H}^{\mathsf{T}}\mathtt{F}$ *is skew-symmetric:*

$$\mathtt{H}^{\mathsf{T}}\mathtt{F} + \mathtt{F}^{\mathsf{T}}\mathtt{H} = 0 \tag{13.3}$$

The argument above showed that the condition was necessary. The fact that this is a sufficient condition was shown by Luong and Viéville [Luong-96]. Counting degrees of freedom, (13.3) places six homogeneous (five inhomogeneous) constraints on the 8 degrees of freedom of $\mathtt{H}$. There are therefore $8 - 5 = 3$ degrees of freedom remaining

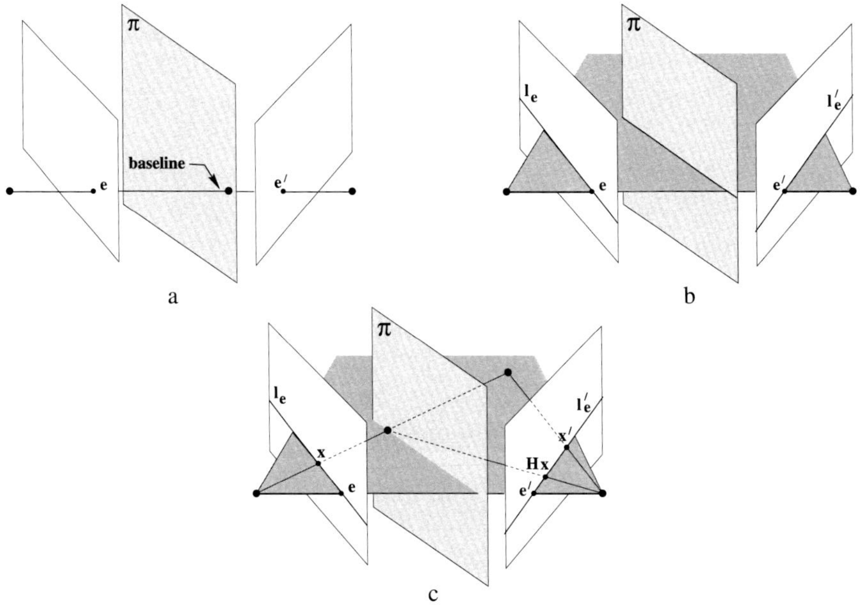

Fig. 13.2. **Compatibility constraints.** *The homography induced by a plane is coupled to the epipolar geometry and satisfies constraints. (a) The epipole is mapped by the homography, as* $\mathbf{e}' = \mathtt{H}\mathbf{e}$*, since the epipoles are images of the point on the plane where the baseline intersects* $\boldsymbol{\pi}$*. (b) Epipolar lines are mapped by the homography as* $\mathtt{H}^\mathsf{T}\mathbf{l}'_e = \mathbf{l}_e$*. (c) Any point* $\mathbf{x}$ *mapped by the homography lies on its corresponding epipolar line* $\mathbf{l}'_e$*, so* $\mathbf{l}'_e = \mathtt{F}\mathbf{x} = \mathbf{x}' \times (\mathtt{H}\mathbf{x})$.

for H; these 3 degrees of freedom correspond to the three-parameter family of planes in 3-space.

The compatibility constraint (13.3) is an implicit equation in H and F. We now develop an explicit expression for a homography H induced by a plane given F which is more suitable for a computational algorithm.

Result 13.3. *Given the fundamental matrix* F *between two views, the three-parameter family of homographies induced by a world plane is*

$$\mathtt{H} = \mathtt{A} - \mathbf{e}'\mathbf{v}^\mathsf{T} \tag{13.4}$$

where $[\mathbf{e}']_\times \mathtt{A} = \mathtt{F}$ *is any decomposition of the fundamental matrix.*

Proof. Result 13.1 has shown that given the camera matrices for the view pair $\mathtt{P} = [\mathtt{I} \mid \mathbf{0}]$, $\mathtt{P}' = [\mathtt{A} \mid \mathbf{a}]$ a plane $\boldsymbol{\pi}$ induces a homography $\mathtt{H} = \mathtt{A} - \mathbf{a}\mathbf{v}^\mathsf{T}$ where $\boldsymbol{\pi} = (\mathbf{v}^\mathsf{T}, 1)^\mathsf{T}$. However, according to result 9.9(*p*254), for the fundamental matrix $\mathtt{F} = [\mathbf{e}']_\times \mathtt{A}$ one can choose the two cameras to be $[\mathtt{I} \mid \mathbf{0}]$ and $[\mathtt{A} \mid \mathbf{e}']$. □

Remark. The above derivation, which is based on the projection of points on a plane, ensures that the homographies are compatible with the epipolar geometry. Algebraically, the homography (13.4) is compatible with the fundamental matrix since it obeys the necessary and sufficient condition (13.3) that $\mathtt{F}^\mathsf{T}\mathtt{H}$ is skew-symmetric. This follows from

$$\mathtt{F}^{\mathsf{T}}\mathtt{H} = \mathtt{A}^{\mathsf{T}}[\mathbf{e}']_\times \left(\mathtt{A} - \mathbf{e}'\mathbf{v}^{\mathsf{T}}\right) = \mathtt{A}^{\mathsf{T}}[\mathbf{e}']_\times \mathtt{A}$$

using $[\mathbf{e}']_\times \mathbf{e}' = \mathbf{0}$, since $\mathtt{A}^{\mathsf{T}}[\mathbf{e}']_\times \mathtt{A}$ is skew-symmetric.

Comparing (13.4) with the general decomposition of the fundamental matrix, as given in lemma 9.11(*p*255) or (9.10–*p*256) it is evident that they involve an identical formula (except for signs). In fact there is a one-to-one correspondence between decompositions of the fundamental matrix (up to the scale factor ambiguity k in lemma 9.11) and homographies induced by world planes, as stated here.

Corollary 13.4. *A transformation* H *is the homography between two images induced by some world plane if and only if the fundamental matrix* F *for the two images has a decomposition* $\mathtt{F} = [\mathbf{e}']_\times \mathtt{H}$.

This choice in the decomposition simply corresponds to the choice of projective world frame. In fact, H is the transformation with respect to the plane with coordinates $(0,0,0,1)^{\mathsf{T}}$ in the reconstruction with $\mathtt{P} = [\mathtt{I} \mid \mathbf{0}]$ and $\mathtt{P}' = [\mathtt{H} \mid \mathbf{e}']$.

Finding the plane that induces a given homography is a simple matter given a pair of camera matrices, as follows.

Result 13.5. *Given the cameras in the canonical form* $\mathtt{P} = [\mathtt{I} \mid \mathbf{0}]$, $\mathtt{P}' = [\mathtt{A} \mid \mathbf{a}]$, *then the plane* $\boldsymbol{\pi}$ *that induces a given homography* H *between the views has coordinates* $\boldsymbol{\pi} = (\mathbf{v}^{\mathsf{T}}, 1)^{\mathsf{T}}$ *where* $\mathbf{v}$ *may be obtained linearly by solving the equations* $\lambda\mathtt{H} = \mathtt{A} - \mathbf{a}\mathbf{v}^{\mathsf{T}}$, *which are linear in the entries of* $\mathbf{v}$ *and* λ.

Note, these equations have an exact solution only if H satisfies the compatibility constraint (13.3) with F. For a homography computed numerically from noisy data this will not normally be true, and the linear system is over-determined.

13.2 Plane induced homographies given F and image correspondences

A plane in 3-space can be specified by three points, or by a line and a point, and so forth. In turn these 3D elements can be specified by image correspondences. In section 13.1 the homography was computed from the coordinates of the plane. In the following the homography will be computed directly from the corresponding image elements that specify the plane. This is a quite natural mechanism to use in applications.

We will consider two cases: (i) three points; (ii) a line and a point. In each case the corresponding elements are sufficient to determine a plane in 3-space uniquely. It will be seen that in each case:

(i) The corresponding image entities have to satisfy *consistency constraints* with the epipolar geometry.

(ii) There are *degenerate configurations* of the 3D elements and cameras for which the homography is not defined. Such degeneracies arise from collinearities and coplanarities of the 3D elements and the epipolar geometry. There may also be degeneracies of the solution method, but these can be avoided.

The three-point case is covered in more detail.

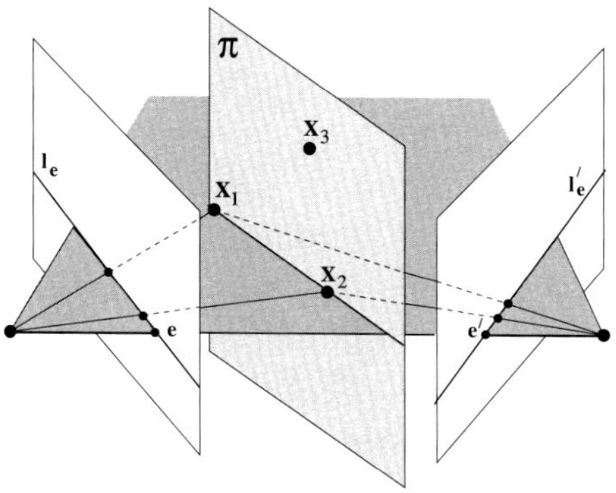

Fig. 13.3. **Degenerate geometry for an implicit computation of the homography.** *The line defined by the points* $\mathbf{X}_1$ *and* $\mathbf{X}_2$ *lies in an epipolar plane, and thus intersects the baseline. The images of* $\mathbf{X}_1$ *and* $\mathbf{X}_2$ *are collinear with the epipole, and* H *cannot be computed uniquely from the correspondences* $\mathbf{x}_i \leftrightarrow \mathbf{x}'_i, i \in \{1, \ldots, 3\}$, $\mathbf{e} \leftrightarrow \mathbf{e}'$. *This configuration is not degenerate for the explicit method.*

13.2.1 Three points

We suppose that we have the images in two views of three (non-collinear) points $\mathbf{X}_i$, and the fundamental matrix F. The homography H induced by the plane of the points may be computed in principle in two ways:

First, the position of the points $\mathbf{X}_i$ is recovered in a projective reconstruction (chapter 12). Then the plane $\boldsymbol{\pi}$ through the points is determined (3.3–*p*66), and the homography computed from the plane as in result 13.1. Second, the homography may be computed from four corresponding points, the four points in this case being the images of the three points $\mathbf{X}_i$ on the plane together with the epipole in each view. The epipole may be used as the fourth point since it is mapped between the views by the homography as shown in figure 13.2. Thus we have four correspondences, $\mathbf{x}'_i = \mathtt{H}\mathbf{x}_i, i \in \{1, \ldots, 3\}$, $\mathbf{e}' = \mathtt{H}\mathbf{e}$, from which H may be computed.

We thus have two alternative methods to compute H from three point correspondences, the first involving an *explicit* reconstruction, the second an *implicit* one where the epipole provides a point correspondence. It is natural to ask if one has an advantage over the other, and the answer is that the implicit method should **not** be used for computation as it has significant degeneracies which are not present in the explicit method.

Consider the case when two of the image points are collinear with the epipole (we assume for the moment that the measurements are noise-free). A homography H cannot be computed from four correspondences if three of the points are collinear (see section 4.1.3(*p*91)), so the implicit method fails in this case. Similarly if the image points are close to collinear with the epipole then the implicit method will give a poorly conditioned estimate for H. The explicit method has no problems when two points are collinear or close to collinear with the epipole – the corresponding image points define points in 3-space (the world points are on the same epipolar plane, but this is not a degenerate situation) and the plane $\boldsymbol{\pi}$ and hence homography can be computed. The configuration is illustrated in figure 13.3.

We now develop the algebra of the explicit method in more detail. It is not necessary to actually determine the coordinates of the points $\mathbf{X}_i$, all that is important is the constraint they place on the three-parameter family of homographies compatible with $\mathtt{F}$ (13.4), $\mathtt{H} = \mathtt{A} - \mathbf{e}'\mathbf{v}^\mathsf{T}$, parametrized by $\mathbf{v}$. The problem is reduced to that of solving for $\mathbf{v}$ from the three point correspondences. The solution may be obtained as:

Result 13.6. *Given* $\mathtt{F}$ *and the three image point correspondences* $\mathbf{x}_i \leftrightarrow \mathbf{x}'_i$, *the homography induced by the plane of the 3D points is*

$$\mathtt{H} = \mathtt{A} - \mathbf{e}'(\mathtt{M}^{-1}\mathbf{b})^\mathsf{T},$$

where $\mathtt{A} = [\mathbf{e}']_\times \mathtt{F}$ *and* $\mathbf{b}$ *is a 3-vector with components*

$$b_i = (\mathbf{x}'_i \times (\mathtt{A}\mathbf{x}_i))^\mathsf{T}(\mathbf{x}'_i \times \mathbf{e}')/\|\mathbf{x}'_i \times \mathbf{e}'\|^2,$$

and $\mathtt{M}$ *is a* 3×3 *matrix with rows* $\mathbf{x}_i^\mathsf{T}$.

Proof. According to result 9.14(*p*256), $\mathtt{F}$ may be decomposed as $\mathtt{F} = [\mathbf{e}']_\times \mathtt{A}$. Then (13.4) gives $\mathtt{H} = \mathtt{A} - \mathbf{e}'\mathbf{v}^\mathsf{T}$, and each correspondence $\mathbf{x}_i \leftrightarrow \mathbf{x}'_i$ generates a linear constraint on $\mathbf{v}$ as

$$\mathbf{x}'_i = \mathtt{H}\mathbf{x}_i = \mathtt{A}\mathbf{x}_i - \mathbf{e}'(\mathbf{v}^\mathsf{T}\mathbf{x}_i), \quad i = 1, \ldots, 3. \tag{13.5}$$

From (13.5) the vectors $\mathbf{x}'_i$ and $\mathtt{A}\mathbf{x}_i - \mathbf{e}'(\mathbf{v}^\mathsf{T}\mathbf{x}_i)$ are parallel, so their vector product is zero:

$$\mathbf{x}'_i \times (\mathtt{A}\mathbf{x}_i - \mathbf{e}'(\mathbf{v}^\mathsf{T}\mathbf{x}_i)) = (\mathbf{x}'_i \times \mathtt{A}\mathbf{x}_i) - (\mathbf{x}'_i \times \mathbf{e}')(\mathbf{v}^\mathsf{T}\mathbf{x}_i) = \mathbf{0}.$$

Forming the scalar product with the vector $\mathbf{x}'_i \times \mathbf{e}'$ gives

$$\mathbf{x}_i^\mathsf{T}\mathbf{v} = \frac{(\mathbf{x}'_i \times (\mathtt{A}\mathbf{x}_i))^\mathsf{T}(\mathbf{x}'_i \times \mathbf{e}')}{(\mathbf{x}'_i \times \mathbf{e}')^\mathsf{T}(\mathbf{x}'_i \times \mathbf{e}')} = b_i \tag{13.6}$$

which is linear in $\mathbf{v}$. Note, the equation is independent of the scale of $\mathbf{x}'$, since $\mathbf{x}'$ occurs the same number of times in the numerator and denominator. Each correspondence generates an equation $\mathbf{x}_i^\mathsf{T}\mathbf{v} = b_i$, and collecting these together we have $\mathtt{M}\mathbf{v} = \mathbf{b}$. □

Note, a solution cannot be obtained if $\mathtt{M}^\mathsf{T} = [\mathbf{x}_1, \mathbf{x}_2, \mathbf{x}_3]$ is not of full rank. Algebraically, $\det \mathtt{M} = 0$ if the three image points $\mathbf{x}_i$ are collinear. Geometrically, three collinear image points arise from collinear world points, or coplanar world points where the plane contains the first camera centre. In either case a full rank homography is not defined.

Consistency conditions. Equation (13.5) is equivalent to six constraints since each point correspondence places two constraints on a homography. Determining $\mathbf{v}$ requires only three constraints, so there are three constraints remaining which must be satisfied for a valid solution. These constraints are obtained by taking the cross product of (13.5) with $\mathbf{e}'$, which gives

$$\mathbf{e}' \times \mathbf{x}'_i = \mathbf{e}' \times \mathtt{A}\mathbf{x}_i = \mathtt{F}\mathbf{x}_i.$$

Objective

Given $\mathtt{F}$ and three point correspondences $\mathbf{x}_i \leftrightarrow \mathbf{x}'_i$ which are the images of 3D points $\mathbf{X}_i$, determine the homography $\mathbf{x}' = \mathtt{H}\mathbf{x}$ induced by the plane of $\mathbf{X}_i$.

Algorithm

(i) For each correspondence $\mathbf{x}_i \leftrightarrow \mathbf{x}'_i$ compute the corrected correspondence $\hat{\mathbf{x}}_i \leftrightarrow \hat{\mathbf{x}}'_i$ using algorithm 12.1(*p*318).

(ii) Choose $\mathtt{A} = [\mathbf{e}']_\times \mathtt{F}$ and solve linearly for $\mathbf{v}$ from $\mathtt{M}\mathbf{v} = \mathbf{b}$ as in result 13.6.

(iii) Then $\mathtt{H} = \mathtt{A} - \mathbf{e}'\mathbf{v}^\mathsf{T}$.

Algorithm 13.1. *The optimal estimate of the homography induced by a plane defined by three points.*

The equation $\mathbf{e}' \times \mathbf{x}'_i = \mathtt{F}\mathbf{x}_i$ is a *consistency constraint* between $\mathbf{x}_i$ and $\mathbf{x}'_i$, since it is independent of $\mathbf{v}$. It is simply a (disguised) epipolar constraint on the correspondence $\mathbf{x}_i \leftrightarrow \mathbf{x}'_i$: the LHS is the epipolar line through $\mathbf{x}'_i$, and the RHS is $\mathtt{F}\mathbf{x}_i$ which is the epipolar line for $\mathbf{x}_i$ in the second image, i.e. the equation enforces that $\mathbf{x}'_i$ lie on the epipolar line of $\mathbf{x}_i$, and hence the correspondence is consistent with the epipolar geometry.

Estimation from noisy points. The three point correspondences which determine the plane and homography must satisfy the consistency constraint arising from the epipolar geometry. Generally *measured* correspondences $\mathbf{x}_i \leftrightarrow \mathbf{x}'_i$ will not exactly satisfy this constraint. We therefore require a procedure for optimally correcting the measured points so that the estimated points $\hat{\mathbf{x}}_i \leftrightarrow \hat{\mathbf{x}}'_i$ satisfy the epipolar constraint. Fortunately, such a procedure has already been given in the triangulation algorithm 12.1(*p*318), which can be adopted here directly. We then have a Maximum Likelihood estimate of $\mathtt{H}$ and the 3D points under Gaussian image noise assumptions. The method is summarized in algorithm 13.1.

13.2.2 A point and line

In this section an expression is derived for a plane specified by a point and line correspondence. We start by considering only the line correspondence and show that this reduces the three-parameter family of homographies compatible with $\mathtt{F}$ (13.4) to a 1-parameter family. It is then shown that the point correspondence uniquely determines the plane and corresponding homography.

The correspondence of two image lines determines a line in 3-space, and a line in 3-space lies on a one parameter family (a pencil) of planes, see figure 13.4. This pencil of planes induces a pencil of homographies between the two images, and any member of this family will map the corresponding lines to each other.

Result 13.7. *The homography for the pencil of planes defined by a line correspondence* $\mathbf{l} \leftrightarrow \mathbf{l}'$ *is given by*

$$\mathtt{H}(\mu) = [\mathbf{l}']_\times \mathtt{F} + \mu \mathbf{e}' \mathbf{l}^\mathsf{T} \tag{13.7}$$

provided $\mathbf{l}'^\mathsf{T}\mathbf{e}' \neq 0$, *where* μ *is a projective parameter.*

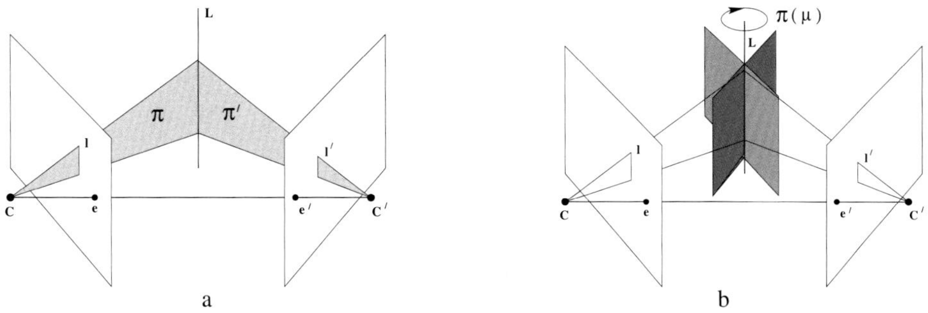

Fig. 13.4. *(a) Image lines* $\mathbf{l}$ *and* $\mathbf{l}'$ *determine planes* $\boldsymbol{\pi}$ *and* $\boldsymbol{\pi}'$ *respectively. The intersection of these planes defines the line* $\mathbf{L}$ *in 3-space. (b) The line* $\mathbf{L}$ *in 3-space is contained in a one parameter family of planes* $\boldsymbol{\pi}(\mu)$*. This family of planes induces a one parameter family of homographies between the images.*

Proof. From result 8.2(*p*197) the line $\mathbf{l}$ back-projects to a plane $\mathtt{P}^{\mathsf{T}}\mathbf{l}$ through the first camera centre, and $\mathbf{l}'$ back-projects to a plane $\mathtt{P}'^{\mathsf{T}}\mathbf{l}'$ through the second, see figure 13.4a. These two planes are the basis for a pencil of planes parametrized by μ. As in the proof of result 13.3 we may choose $\mathtt{P} = [\mathtt{I} \mid \mathbf{0}]$, $\mathtt{P}' = [\mathtt{A} \mid \mathbf{e}']$, then the pencil of planes is

$$\begin{aligned} \boldsymbol{\pi}(\mu) &= \mu \mathtt{P}^{\mathsf{T}}\mathbf{l} + \mathtt{P}'^{\mathsf{T}}\mathbf{l}' \\ &= \mu \begin{pmatrix} \mathbf{l} \\ 0 \end{pmatrix} + \begin{pmatrix} \mathtt{A}^{\mathsf{T}}\mathbf{l}' \\ \mathbf{e}'^{\mathsf{T}}\mathbf{l}' \end{pmatrix} \end{aligned}$$

From result 13.1 the induced homography is $\mathtt{H}(\mu) = \mathtt{A} - \mathbf{e}'\mathbf{v}(\mu)^{\mathsf{T}}$, with

$$\mathbf{v}(\mu) = (\mu\mathbf{l} + \mathtt{A}^{\mathsf{T}}\mathbf{l}')/(\mathbf{e}'^{\mathsf{T}}\mathbf{l}') \tag{13.8}$$

Using the decomposition $\mathtt{A} = [\mathbf{e}']_\times \mathtt{F}$ we obtain

$$\begin{aligned} \mathtt{H} &= \left((\mathbf{e}'^{\mathsf{T}}\mathbf{l}'\mathtt{I} - \mathbf{e}'\mathbf{l}'^{\mathsf{T}})[\mathbf{e}']_\times\mathtt{F} - \mu\mathbf{e}'\mathbf{l}^{\mathsf{T}}\right)/(\mathbf{e}'^{\mathsf{T}}\mathbf{l}') = -\left([\mathbf{l}']_\times[\mathbf{e}']_\times[\mathbf{e}']_\times\mathtt{F} + \mu\mathbf{e}'\mathbf{l}^{\mathsf{T}}\right)/(\mathbf{e}'^{\mathsf{T}}\mathbf{l}') \\ &= -\left([\mathbf{l}']_\times\mathtt{F} + \mu\mathbf{e}'\mathbf{l}^{\mathsf{T}}\right)/(\mathbf{e}'^{\mathsf{T}}\mathbf{l}') \end{aligned}$$

where the last equality follows from result A4.4(*p*582) that $[\mathbf{e}']_\times[\mathbf{e}']_\times\mathtt{F} = \mathtt{F}$. This is equivalent to (13.7) up to scale. □

The homography for a corresponding point and line. From the line correspondence we have that $\mathtt{H}(\mu) = [\mathbf{l}']_\times\mathtt{F} + \mu\mathbf{e}'\mathbf{l}^{\mathsf{T}}$, and now solve for μ using the point correspondence $\mathbf{x} \leftrightarrow \mathbf{x}'$.

Result 13.8. *Given* $\mathtt{F}$ *and a corresponding point* $\mathbf{x} \leftrightarrow \mathbf{x}'$ *and line* $\mathbf{l} \leftrightarrow \mathbf{l}'$*, the homography induced by the plane of the 3-space point and line is*

$$\mathtt{H} = [\mathbf{l}']_\times\mathtt{F} + \frac{(\mathbf{x}' \times \mathbf{e}')^{\mathsf{T}}(\mathbf{x}' \times ((\mathtt{F}\mathbf{x}) \times \mathbf{l}'))}{\|\mathbf{x}' \times \mathbf{e}'\|^2(\mathbf{l}^{\mathsf{T}}\mathbf{x})}\mathbf{e}'\mathbf{l}^{\mathsf{T}}.$$

The derivation is analogous to that of result 13.6. As in the three-point case, the image point correspondence must be consistent with the epipolar geometry. This means

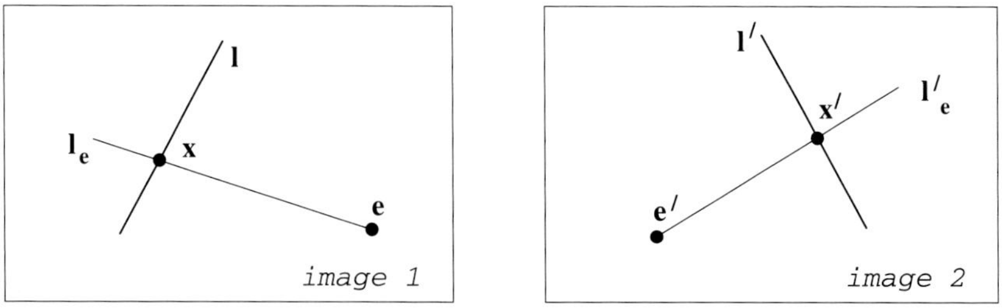

Fig. 13.5. *The epipolar geometry induces a homography between corresponding lines* $\mathbf{l} \leftrightarrow \mathbf{l}'$ *which are the images of a line* $\mathbf{L}$ *in 3-space. The points on* $\mathbf{l}$ *are mapped to points on* $\mathbf{l}'$ *as* $\mathbf{x}' = [\mathbf{l}']_\times \mathtt{F}\mathbf{x}$, *where* $\mathbf{x}$ *and* $\mathbf{x}'$ *are the images of the intersection of* $\mathbf{L}$ *with the epipolar plane corresponding to* $\mathbf{l}_e$ *and* $\mathbf{l}'_e$.

that the measured (noisy) points must be corrected using algorithm 12.1(p318) before result 13.8 is applied. There is no consistency constraint on the line, and no correction is available.

Geometric interpretation of the point map $\mathtt{H}(\mu)$**.** It is worth exploring the map $\mathtt{H}(\mu)$ further. Since $\mathtt{H}(\mu)$ is compatible with the epipolar geometry, a point $\mathbf{x}$ in the first view is mapped to a point $\mathbf{x}' = \mathtt{H}(\mu)\mathbf{x}$ in the second view on the epipolar line $\mathtt{F}\mathbf{x}$ corresponding to $\mathbf{x}$. In general the position of the point $\mathbf{x}' = \mathtt{H}(\mu)\mathbf{x}$ on the epipolar line varies with μ. However, if the point $\mathbf{x}$ lies on $\mathbf{l}$ (so that $\mathbf{l}^\mathsf{T}\mathbf{x} = 0$) then

$$\mathbf{x}' = \mathtt{H}(\mu)\mathbf{x} = ([\mathbf{l}']_\times \mathtt{F} + \mu \mathbf{e}'\mathbf{l}^\mathsf{T})\mathbf{x} = [\mathbf{l}']_\times \mathtt{F}\mathbf{x}$$

which is independent of the value of μ, depending only on $\mathtt{F}$. Thus as shown in figure 13.5 the epipolar geometry defines a point-to-point map for points on the line.

Degenerate homographies. As has already been stated, if the world plane contains one of the camera centres, then the induced homography is degenerate. The matrix representing the homography does not have full rank, and points on one plane are mapped to a line (if $\mathrm{rank}\,\mathtt{H} = 2$) or a point (if $\mathrm{rank}\,\mathtt{H} = 1$). However, an explicit expression can be obtained for a degenerate homography from (13.7). The degenerate (singular) homographies in this pencil are at $\mu = \infty$ and $\mu = 0$. These correspond to planes through the first and second camera centres respectively. Figure 13.6 shows the case where the plane contains the second camera centre, and intersects the image plane in the line $\mathbf{l}'$. A point $\mathbf{x}$ in the first view is imaged on $\mathbf{l}'$ at the point $\mathbf{x}'$ where

$$\mathbf{x}' = \mathbf{l}' \times \mathtt{F}\mathbf{x} = [\mathbf{l}']_\times \mathtt{F}\mathbf{x}.$$

The homography is thus $\mathtt{H} = [\mathbf{l}']_\times \mathtt{F}$. This is a rank 2 matrix.

13.3 Computing $\mathtt{F}$ given the homography induced by a plane

Up to now it has been assumed that $\mathtt{F}$ is given, and the objective is to compute $\mathtt{H}$ when various additional information is provided. We now reverse this, and show that if $\mathtt{H}$ is given then $\mathtt{F}$ may be computed when additional information is provided. We start by introducing an important geometric idea, that of parallax relative to a plane, which will make the algebraic development straightforward.

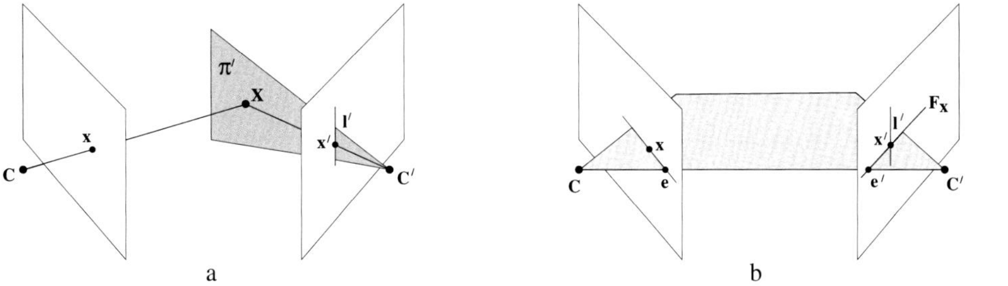

Fig. 13.6. **A degenerate homography.** *(a) The map induced by a plane through the second camera centre is a degenerate homography* $\mathtt{H} = [\mathbf{l}']_\times \mathtt{F}$. *The plane* $\boldsymbol{\pi}'$ *intersects the second image plane in the line* $\mathbf{l}'$. *All points in the first view are mapped to points on* $\mathbf{l}'$ *in the second. (b) A point* $\mathbf{x}$ *in the first view is imaged at* $\mathbf{x}'$, *the intersection of* $\mathbf{l}'$ *with the epipolar line* $\mathtt{F}\mathbf{x}$ *of* $\mathbf{x}$, *so that* $\mathbf{x}' = \mathbf{l}' \times \mathtt{F}\mathbf{x}$.

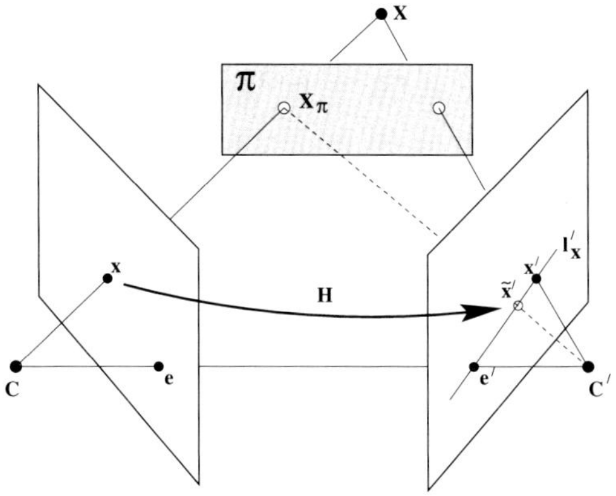

Fig. 13.7. **Plane induced parallax.** *The ray through* $\mathbf{X}$ *intersects the plane* $\boldsymbol{\pi}$ *at the point* $\mathbf{X}_\pi$. *The images of* $\mathbf{X}$ *and* $\mathbf{X}_\pi$ *are coincident points at* $\mathbf{x}$ *in the first view. In the second view the images are the points* $\mathbf{x}'$ *and* $\tilde{\mathbf{x}}' = \mathtt{H}\mathbf{x}$ *respectively. These points are not coincident (unless* $\mathbf{X}$ *is on* $\boldsymbol{\pi}$*), but both are on the epipolar line* $\mathbf{l}'_{\mathbf{x}}$ *of* $\mathbf{x}$. *The vector between the points* $\mathbf{x}'$ *and* $\tilde{\mathbf{x}}'$ *is the* parallax relative to the homography *induced by the plane* $\boldsymbol{\pi}$. *Note that if* $\mathbf{X}$ *is on the other side of the plane, then* $\tilde{\mathbf{x}}'$ *will be on the other side of* $\mathbf{x}'$.

Plane induced parallax. The homography induced by a plane generates a virtual parallax (see section 8.4.5(*p*207)) as illustrated schematically in figure 13.7 and by example in figure 13.8. The important point here is that in the second view $\mathbf{x}'$, the image of the 3D point $\mathbf{X}$, and $\tilde{\mathbf{x}}' = \mathtt{H}\mathbf{x}$, the point mapped by the homography, are on the epipolar line of $\mathbf{x}$; since both are images of points on the ray through $\mathbf{x}$. Consequently, the line $\mathbf{x}' \times (\mathtt{H}\mathbf{x})$ is an epipolar line in the second view and provides a constraint on the position of the epipole. Once the epipole is determined (two such constraints suffice), then as shown in result 9.1(*p*243) $\mathtt{F} = [\mathbf{e}']_\times \mathtt{H}$ where $\mathtt{H}$ is the homography induced by any plane. Similarly it can be shown that $\mathtt{F} = \mathtt{H}^{-\mathsf{T}}[\mathbf{e}]_\times$.

As an application of virtual parallax it is shown in algorithm 13.2 that $\mathtt{F}$ can be computed uniquely from the images of six points, four of which are coplanar and two are off the plane. The images of the four coplanar points define the homography, and the two points off the plane provide constraints sufficient to determine the epipole. The

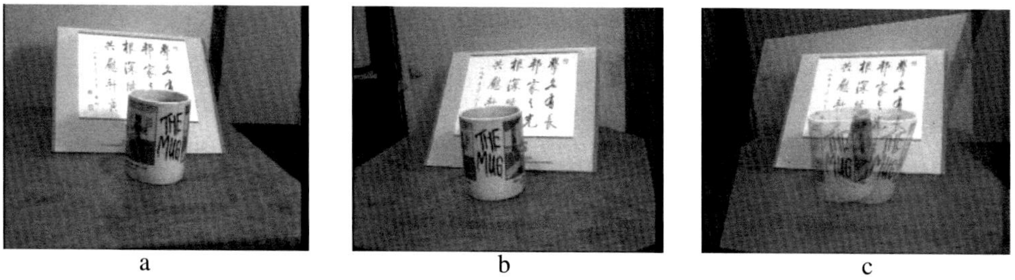

Fig. 13.8. **Plane induced parallax.** *(a) (b) Left and right images. (c) The left image is superimposed on the right using the homography induced by the plane of the Chinese text. The transferred and imaged planes exactly coincide. However, points off the plane (such as the mug) do not coincide. Lines joining corresponding points off the plane in the "superimposed" image intersect at the epipole.*

six-point result is quite surprising since for seven points in general position there are 3 solutions for F (see section 11.1.2(*p*281)).

<u>Objective</u>

Given six point correspondences $\mathbf{x}_i \leftrightarrow \mathbf{x}'_i$ which are the images of 3-space $\mathbf{X}_i$, with the first four 3-space points $i \in \{1, \ldots, 4\}$ coplanar, determine the fundamental matrix F.

<u>Algorithm</u>

(i) Compute the homography H, such that $\mathbf{x}'_i = \mathtt{H}\mathbf{x}_i, i \in \{1, \ldots, 4\}$.

(ii) Determine the epipole $\mathbf{e}'$ as the intersection of the lines $(\mathtt{H}\mathbf{x}_5) \times \mathbf{x}'_5$ and $(\mathtt{H}\mathbf{x}_6) \times \mathbf{x}'_6$.

(iii) Then $\mathtt{F} = [\mathbf{e}']_\times \mathtt{H}$.

See figure 13.9.

Algorithm 13.2. *Computing* F *given the correspondences of six points of which four are coplanar.*

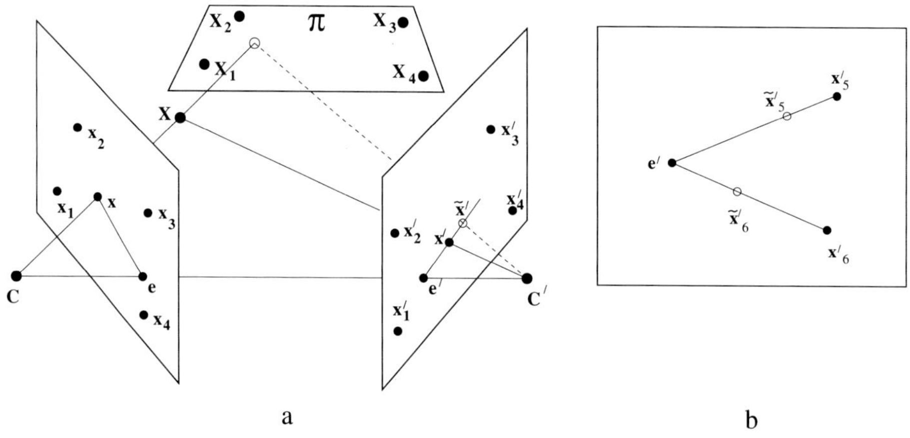

Fig. 13.9. *The fundamental matrix is defined uniquely by the image of six 3D points, of which four are coplanar. (a) The parallax for one point* $\mathbf{X}$*. (b) The epipole determined by the intersection of two parallax lines: the line joining* $\tilde{\mathbf{x}}'_5 = \mathtt{H}\mathbf{x}_5$ *to* $\mathbf{x}'_5$*, and the join of* $\tilde{\mathbf{x}}'_6 = \mathtt{H}\mathbf{x}_6$ *to* $\mathbf{x}'_6$.

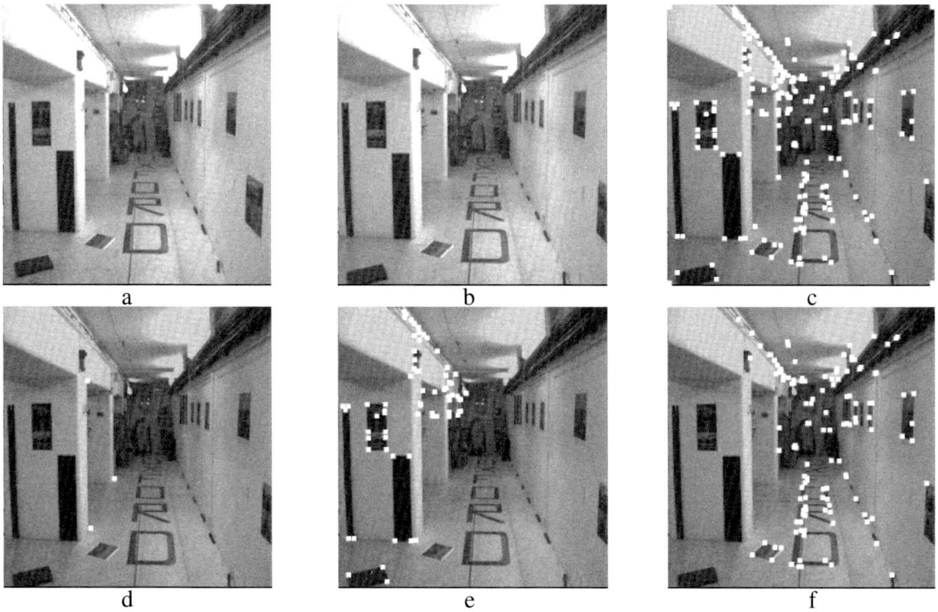

Fig. 13.10. **Binary space partition.** *(a) (b) Left and right images. (c) Points whose correspondence is known. (d) A triplet of points selected from (c). This triplet defines a plane. The points in (c) can then be classified according to their side of the plane. (e) Points on one side. (f) Points on the other side.*

Projective depth. A world point $\mathbf{X} = (\mathbf{x}^\mathsf{T}, \rho)^\mathsf{T}$ is imaged at $\mathbf{x}$ in the first view and at

$$\mathbf{x}' = \mathtt{H}\mathbf{x} + \rho\mathbf{e}' \tag{13.9}$$

in the second. Note that $\mathbf{x}'$, $\mathbf{e}'$ and $\mathtt{H}\mathbf{x}$ are collinear. The scalar ρ is the parallax *relative* to the homography $\mathtt{H}$, and may be interpreted as a "depth" relative to the plane $\boldsymbol{\pi}$. If $\rho = 0$ then the 3D point $\mathbf{X}$ is on the plane, otherwise the "sign" of ρ indicates which 'side' of the plane $\boldsymbol{\pi}$ the point $\mathbf{X}$ is (see figure 13.7 and figure 13.8). These statements should be taken with care because in the absence of oriented projective geometry the sign of a homogeneous object, and the side of a plane have no meaning.

Example 13.9. Binary space partition. The sign of the virtual parallax ($\text{sign}(\rho)$) may be used to compute a partition of 3-space by the plane $\boldsymbol{\pi}$. Suppose we are given $\mathtt{F}$ and three space points are specified by their corresponding image points. Then the plane defined by the three points can be used to partition all other correspondences into sets on either side of (or on) the plane. Figure 13.10 shows an example. Note, the three points need not actually correspond to images of physical points so the method can be applied to virtual planes. By combining several planes a region of 3-space can be identified. △

Two planes. Suppose there are two planes, $\boldsymbol{\pi}_1, \boldsymbol{\pi}_2$, in the scene which induce homographies $\mathtt{H}_1, \mathtt{H}_2$ respectively. With the idea of parallax in mind it is clear that because each plane provides off-plane information about the other, the two homographies

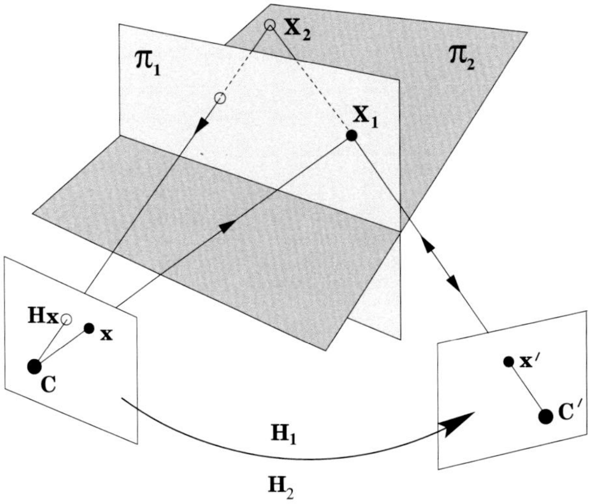

Fig. 13.11. *The action of the map* $\mathtt{H} = \mathtt{H}_2^{-1}\mathtt{H}_1$ *on a point* $\mathbf{x}$ *in the first image is first to transfer it to* $\mathbf{x}'$ *as though it were the image of the 3D point* $\mathbf{X}_1$*, and then map it back to the first image as though it were the image of the 3D point* $\mathbf{X}_2$*. Points in the first view which lie on the imaged line of intersection of the two planes will be mapped to themselves, so are fixed points under this action. The epipole* $\mathbf{e}$ *is also a fixed point under this map.*

should be sufficient to determine $\mathtt{F}$. Indeed $\mathtt{F}$ is over-determined by this configuration which means that the two homographies must satisfy consistency constraints.

Consider figure 13.11. The homography $\mathtt{H} = \mathtt{H}_2^{-1}\mathtt{H}_1$ is a mapping from the first image onto itself. Under this mapping the epipole $\mathbf{e}$ is a fixed point, i.e. $\mathtt{H}\mathbf{e} = \mathbf{e}$, so may be determined from the (non-degenerate) eigenvector of $\mathtt{H}$. The fundamental matrix may then be computed from result 9.1(*p*243) as $\mathtt{F} = [\mathbf{e}']_\times \mathtt{H}_i$, where $\mathbf{e}' = \mathtt{H}_i\mathbf{e}$ for $i = 1$ or 2. The map $\mathtt{H}$ has further properties which may be seen from figure 13.11. The map has a line of fixed points and a fixed point not on the line (see section 2.9(*p*61) for fixed points and lines). This means that two of the eigenvalues of $\mathtt{H}$ are equal. In fact $\mathtt{H}$ is a planar homology (see section A7.2(*p*629)). In turn, these properties of $\mathtt{H} = \mathtt{H}_2^{-1}\mathtt{H}_1$ define consistency constraints on $\mathtt{H}_1$ and $\mathtt{H}_2$ in order that their composition has these properties.

Up to this point the results of this chapter have been entirely projective. Now an affine element is introduced.

13.4 The infinite homography $\mathtt{H}_\infty$

The plane at infinity is a particularly important plane, and the homography induced by this plane is distinguished by a special name:

Definition 13.10. The infinite homography, $\mathtt{H}_\infty$, is the homography induced by the plane at infinity, $\boldsymbol{\pi}_\infty$.

The form of the homography may be derived by a limiting process starting from (13.2–*p*327), $\mathtt{H} = \mathtt{K}'\left(\mathtt{R} - \mathbf{t}\mathbf{n}^\mathsf{T}/d\right)\mathtt{K}^{-1}$, where d is the orthogonal distance of the plane from

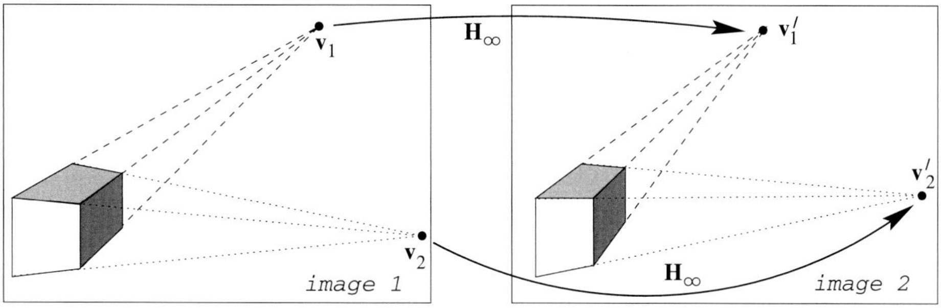

Fig. 13.12. *The infinite homography H_∞ maps vanishing points between the images.*

the first camera:

$$H_\infty = \lim_{d\to\infty} H = K'RK^{-1}.$$

This means that H_∞ does not depend on the translation between views, only on the rotation and camera internal parameters. Alternatively, from (9.7–*p*250) corresponding image points are related as

$$\mathbf{x}' = K'RK^{-1}\mathbf{x} + K'\mathbf{t}/Z = H_\infty\mathbf{x} + K'\mathbf{t}/Z \tag{13.10}$$

where Z is the depth measured from the first camera. Again it can be seen that points at infinity ($Z = \infty$) are mapped by H_∞. Note also that H_∞ is obtained if the translation $\mathbf{t}$ is zero in (13.10), which corresponds to a rotation about the camera centre. Thus H_∞ is the homography that relates image points of *any* depth if the camera rotates about its centre (see section 8.4(*p*202)).

Since $\mathbf{e}' = K'\mathbf{t}$, (13.10) can be written as $\mathbf{x}' = H_\infty\mathbf{x} + \mathbf{e}'/Z$, and comparison with (13.9) shows that $(1/Z)$ plays the role of ρ. Thus Euclidean inverse depth can be interpreted as parallax relative to $\boldsymbol{\pi}_\infty$.

Vanishing points and lines. Images of points on $\boldsymbol{\pi}_\infty$ are mapped by H_∞. These images are vanishing points, and so H_∞ maps vanishing points between images, i.e. $\mathbf{v}' = H_\infty\mathbf{v}$, where $\mathbf{v}'$ and $\mathbf{v}$ are corresponding vanishing points. See figure 13.12. Consequently, H_∞ can be computed from the correspondence of three (non-collinear) vanishing points together with F using result 13.6. Alternatively, H_∞ can be computed from the correspondence of a vanishing line and the correspondence of a vanishing point (not on the line), together with F, as described in section 13.2.2.

Affine and metric reconstruction. As we have seen in chapter 10, specifying $\boldsymbol{\pi}_\infty$ enables a projective reconstruction to be upgraded to an affine reconstruction. Not surprisingly, because of its association with $\boldsymbol{\pi}_\infty$, H_∞ arises naturally in the rectification. Indeed, if the camera matrices are chosen as $P = [I \mid \mathbf{0}]$ and $P' = [H_\infty \mid \lambda\mathbf{e}']$ then the reconstruction is affine.

Conversely, suppose the world coordinate system is affine (i.e. $\boldsymbol{\pi}_\infty$ has its canonical position at $\boldsymbol{\pi}_\infty = (0,0,0,1)^\mathsf{T}$); then H_∞ may be determined directly from the camera projection matrices. Suppose M, M' are the first 3×3 submatrix of P and P' respectively.

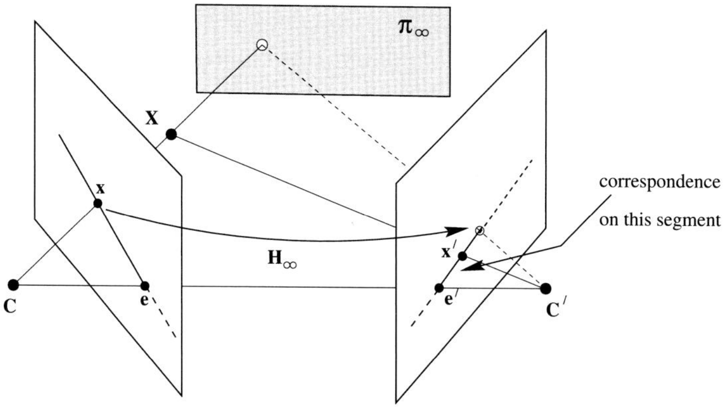

Fig. 13.13. **Reducing the search region using H_∞.** *Points in 3-space are no 'further' away than π_∞. H_∞ captures this constraint and limits the search on the epipolar line in one direction. The baseline between the cameras partitions each epipolar plane into two. A point on one "side" of the epipolar line in the left image will be imaged on the corresponding "side" of the epipolar line in the right image (indicated by the solid line in the figure). The epipole thus bounds the search region in the other direction.*

Then a point $\mathbf{X} = (\mathbf{x}_\infty^\mathsf{T}, 0)^\mathsf{T}$ on π_∞ is imaged at $\mathbf{x} = \mathtt{P}\mathbf{X} = \mathtt{M}\mathbf{x}_\infty$ and $\mathbf{x}' = \mathtt{P}'\mathbf{X} = \mathtt{M}'\mathbf{x}_\infty$ in the two views. Consequently $\mathbf{x}' = \mathtt{M}'\mathtt{M}^{-1}\mathbf{x}$ and so

$$\mathtt{H}_\infty = \mathtt{M}'\mathtt{M}^{-1}. \tag{13.11}$$

The homography $\mathtt{H}_\infty$ may be used to propagate camera calibration from one view to another. The absolute conic Ω_∞ resides on π_∞, and its image, ω, is mapped between images by $\mathtt{H}_\infty$ according to result 2.13(*p*37): $\omega' = \mathtt{H}_\infty^{-\mathsf{T}}\omega\mathtt{H}_\infty^{-1}$. Thus if $\omega = (\mathtt{K}\mathtt{K}^\mathsf{T})^{-1}$ is specified in one view, then ω', the image of Ω_∞ in a second view, can be computed via $\mathtt{H}_\infty$, and the calibration for that view determined from $\omega' = (\mathtt{K}'\mathtt{K}'^\mathsf{T})^{-1}$. Section 19.5.2(*p*475) describes applications of $\mathtt{H}_\infty$ to camera auto-calibration.

Stereo correspondence. $\mathtt{H}_\infty$ limits the search region when searching for correspondences. The region is reduced from the entire epipolar line to a bounded line. See figure 13.13. However, a correct application of this constraint requires oriented projective geometry.

13.5 Closure

This chapter has illustrated a raft of projective techniques for a plane that may be applied to many other surfaces. A plane is a simple parametrized surface with 3 degrees of freedom. A very similar development can be given for other surfaces where the degrees of freedom are determined from images of points on the surface. For example in the case of a quadric the surface can be determined both from images of points on its surface, and/or (an extension not possible for planes) from its outline in each view [Cross-98, Shashua-97]. The ideas of surface induced transfer, families of surfaces when the surface is not fully determined from its images, surface induced parallax, consistency constraints, implicit computations, degenerate geometries etc. all carry over to other surfaces.

13.5.1 The literature

The compatibility of epipolar geometry and induced homographies is investigated thoroughly by Luong & Viéville [Luong-96]. The six-point solution for $\mathtt{F}$ appeared in Beardsley *et al.* [Beardsley-92] and [Mohr-92]. The solution for $\mathtt{F}$ given two planes appeared in Sinclair [Sinclair-92]. [Zeller-96] gives many examples of configurations whose properties may be determined using only epipolar geometry and their image projections. He also catalogues their degenerate cases.

13.5.2 Notes and exercises

(i) **Homography induced by a plane (13.1–*p*326).**

(a) The inverse of the homography $\mathtt{H}$ is given by

$$\mathtt{H}^{-1} = \mathtt{A}^{-1}\left(\mathtt{I} + \frac{\mathbf{a}\mathbf{v}^{\mathsf{T}}\mathtt{A}^{-1}}{1 - \mathbf{v}^{\mathsf{T}}\mathtt{A}^{-1}\mathbf{a}}\right)$$

provided $\mathtt{A}^{-1}$ exists. This is sometimes called the Sherman-Morrison formula.

(b) Show that the homography $\mathtt{H}$ is degenerate if the plane contains the second camera centre. Hint, in this case $\mathbf{v}^{\mathsf{T}}\mathtt{A}^{-1}\mathbf{a} = 1$, and note that $\mathtt{H} = \mathtt{A}(\mathtt{I} - \mathtt{A}^{-1}\mathbf{a}\mathbf{v}^{\mathsf{T}})$.

(ii) Show that if the camera undergoes planar motion, i.e. the translation is parallel to the plane and the rotation is parallel to the plane normal, then the homography induced by the plane is conjugate to a planar Euclidean transformation. Show that the fixed points of the homography are the images of the plane's circular points.

(iii) Using (13.2–*p*327) show that if a camera undergoes a pure translation then the homography induced by the plane is a planar homology (as defined in section A7.2(*p*629)), with a line of fixed points corresponding to the vanishing line of the plane. Show further that if the translation is parallel to the plane then the homography is an elation (as defined in section A7.3(*p*631)).

(iv) Show that a necessary, but not sufficient, condition for two space lines to be coplanar is $(\mathbf{l}'_1 \times \mathbf{l}'_2)^{\mathsf{T}}\mathtt{F}(\mathbf{l}_1 \times \mathbf{l}_2) = 0$. Why is it not a sufficient condition?

(v) **Intersections of lines and planes.** Verify each of the following results by sketching the configuration assuming general position. In each case determine the degenerate configurations for which the result is not valid.

(a) Suppose the line $\mathbf{L}$ in 3-space is imaged as $\mathbf{l}$ and $\mathbf{l}'$, and the plane $\boldsymbol{\pi}$ induces the homography $\mathbf{x}' = \mathtt{H}\mathbf{x}$. Then the point of intersection of $\mathbf{L}$ with $\boldsymbol{\pi}$ is imaged at $\mathbf{x} = \mathbf{l} \times (\mathtt{H}^{\mathsf{T}}\mathbf{l}')$ in the first image, and at $\mathbf{x}' = \mathbf{l}' \times (\mathtt{H}^{-\mathsf{T}}\mathbf{l})$ in the second.

(b) The infinite homography may be used to find the vanishing point of a line seen in two images. If $\mathbf{l}$ and $\mathbf{l}'$ are corresponding lines in two images, and $\mathbf{v}, \mathbf{v}'$ their vanishing points in each image, then $\mathbf{v} = \mathbf{l} \times (\mathtt{H}_\infty^{\mathsf{T}}\mathbf{l}')$, $\mathbf{v}' = \mathbf{l}' \times (\mathtt{H}_\infty^{-\mathsf{T}}\mathbf{l})$.

(c) Suppose the planes $\boldsymbol{\pi}_1$ and $\boldsymbol{\pi}_2$ induce homographies $\mathbf{x}' = \mathtt{H}_1\mathbf{x}$ and $\mathbf{x}' = \mathtt{H}_2\mathbf{x}$ respectively. Then the image of the line of intersection of $\boldsymbol{\pi}_1$ with $\boldsymbol{\pi}_2$ in the first image obeys $\mathtt{H}_1^{\mathsf{T}}\mathtt{H}_2^{-\mathsf{T}}\mathbf{l} = \mathbf{l}$ and may be determined from the real eigenvector of the planar homology $\mathtt{H}_1^{\mathsf{T}}\mathtt{H}_2^{-\mathsf{T}}$ (see figure 13.11).

(vi) **Coplanarity of four points.** Suppose $\mathtt{F}$ is known, and four corresponding image points $\mathbf{x}_i \leftrightarrow \mathbf{x}'_i$ are supplied. How can it be determined whether their pre-images are coplanar? One possibility is to use three of the points to determine a homography via result 13.6(*p*331), and then measure the transfer error of the fourth point. A second possibility is to compute lines joining the image points, and determine if the line intersection obeys the epipolar constraint (see [Faugeras-92b]). A third possibility is to compute the cross-ratio of the four lines from the epipole to the image points – if the four scene points are coplanar then this cross-ratio will be the same in both images. Thus this equality is a necessary condition for co-planarity, but is it a sufficient condition also? What statistical tests should be applied when there is measurement error (noise)?

(vii) Show that the epipolar geometry can be computed uniquely from the images of four coplanar lines and two points off the plane of the lines. If two of the lines are replaced by points can the epipolar geometry still be computed?

(viii) Starting from the camera matrices $\mathtt{P} = [\mathtt{M} \mid \mathbf{m}]$, $\mathtt{P}' = [\mathtt{M}' \mid \mathbf{m}']$ show that the homography $\mathbf{x}' = \mathtt{H}\mathbf{x}$ induced by a plane $\boldsymbol{\pi} = (\tilde{\boldsymbol{\pi}}^{\mathsf{T}}, \pi_4)^{\mathsf{T}}$ is given by

$$\mathtt{H} = \mathtt{M}'(\mathtt{I} - \mathbf{t}\mathbf{v}^{\mathsf{T}})\mathtt{M}^{-1} \text{ with } \mathbf{t} = (\mathtt{M}'^{-1}\mathbf{m}' - \mathtt{M}^{-1}\mathbf{m}), \text{ and } \mathbf{v} = \tilde{\boldsymbol{\pi}}/(\pi_4 - \tilde{\boldsymbol{\pi}}^{\mathsf{T}}\mathtt{M}^{-1}\mathbf{m}).$$

(ix) Show that the homography computed as in result 13.6(*p*331) is independent of the scale of $\mathtt{F}$. Start by choosing an arbitrary fixed scale for $\mathtt{F}$, so that $\mathtt{F}$ is no longer a homogeneous quantity, but a matrix $\tilde{\mathtt{F}}$ with fixed scale. Show that if $\mathtt{H} = [\mathbf{e}']_\times\tilde{\mathtt{F}} - \mathbf{e}'(\mathtt{M}^{-1}\tilde{\mathbf{b}})^{\mathsf{T}}$ with $\tilde{\mathbf{b}}_i = \mathbf{c}_i'^{\mathsf{T}}(\tilde{\mathtt{F}}\mathbf{x}_i)$, then replacing $\tilde{\mathtt{F}}$ by $\lambda\tilde{\mathtt{F}}$ simply scales $\mathtt{H}$ by λ.

(x) Given two perspective images of a (plane) conic and the fundamental matrix between the views, then the plane of the conic (and consequently the homography induced by this plane) is defined up to a two-fold ambiguity. Suppose the image conics are $\mathtt{C}$ and $\mathtt{C}'$, then the induced homography is $\mathtt{H}(\mu) = [\mathtt{C}'\mathbf{e}']_\times\mathtt{F} - \mu\mathbf{e}'(\mathtt{C}\mathbf{e})^{\mathsf{T}}$, with the two values of μ obtained from

$$\mu^2\left[(\mathbf{e}^{\mathsf{T}}\mathtt{C}\mathbf{e})\mathtt{C} - (\mathtt{C}\mathbf{e})(\mathtt{C}\mathbf{e})^{\mathsf{T}}\right](\mathbf{e}'^{\mathsf{T}}\mathtt{C}'\mathbf{e}') = -\mathtt{F}^{\mathsf{T}}[\mathtt{C}'\mathbf{e}']_\times\mathtt{C}'[\mathtt{C}'\mathbf{e}']_\times\mathtt{F}.$$

Details are given in [Schmid-98].

(a) By considering the geometry, show that to be compatible with the epipolar geometry the conics must satisfy the consistency constraint that epipolar tangents are corresponding epipolar lines (see figure 11.6(*p*295)). Now derive this result algebraically starting from $\mathtt{H}(\mu)$ above.

(b) The algebraic expressions are not valid if the epipole lies on the conic (since then $\mathbf{e}^{\mathsf{T}}\mathtt{C}\mathbf{e} = \mathbf{e}'^{\mathsf{T}}\mathtt{C}'\mathbf{e}' = 0$). Is this a degeneracy of the geometry or of the expression alone?

(xi) **Fixed points of a homography induced by a plane.** A planar homography $\mathtt{H}$ has up to three distinct fixed points corresponding to the three eigenvectors of the 3×3 matrix (see section 2.9(*p*61)). The fixed points are images of points on the plane for which $\mathbf{x}' = \mathtt{H}\mathbf{x} = \mathbf{x}$. The horopter is the locus of *all* points in 3-space for which $\mathbf{x} = \mathbf{x}'$. It is a twisted cubic curve passing through the two camera centres. A twisted cubic intersects a plane in three points, and these are the three fixed points of the homography induced by that plane.

(xii) **Estimation.** Suppose $n > 3$ points $\mathbf{X}_i$ lie on a plane in 3-space and we wish to optimally estimate the homography induced by the plane given $\mathtt{F}$ and their image correspondences $\mathbf{x}_i \leftrightarrow \mathbf{x}'_i$. Then the ML estimate of the homography (assuming independent Gaussian measurement noise as usual) is obtained by estimating the plane $\hat{\boldsymbol{\pi}}$ (3 dof) and the n points $\widehat{\mathbf{X}}_i$ (2 dof each, since they lie on a plane) which minimizes reprojection error for the n points.

14

Affine Epipolar Geometry

This chapter recapitulates the developments and objectives of the previous chapters on two-view geometry, but here with affine cameras replacing projective cameras. The affine camera is an extremely usable and well conditioned approximation in many practical situations. Its great advantage is that, because of its linearity, many of the optimal algorithms can be implemented by linear algebra (matrix inverses, SVD etc.), whereas in the projective case solutions either involve high order polynomials (such as for triangulation) or are only possible by numerical minimization (such as in the Gold Standard estimation of $\mathtt{F}$).

We first describe properties of the epipolar geometry of two affine cameras, and its optimal computation from point correspondences. This is followed by triangulation, and *affine* reconstruction. Finally the ambiguities in reconstruction that result from parallel projection are sketched, and the non-ambiguous motion parameters are computed from the epipolar geometry.

14.1 Affine epipolar geometry

In many respects the epipolar geometry of two affine cameras is identical to that of two perspective cameras, for example a point in one view defines an epipolar line in the other view, and the pencil of such epipolar lines intersect at the epipole. The difference is that because the cameras are affine their centres are at infinity, and there is parallel projection from scene to image. This leads to certain simplifications in the affine epipolar geometry:

Epipolar lines. Consider two points, $\mathbf{x}_1$, $\mathbf{x}_2$, in the first view. These points back-project to rays which are *parallel* in 3-space, since all projection rays are parallel. In the second view an epipolar line is the image of a back-projected ray. The images of these two rays in the second view are also parallel since an affine camera maps parallel scene lines to parallel images lines. Consequently, all epipolar lines are parallel, as are the epipolar planes.

The epipoles. Since epipolar lines intersect in the epipole, and all epipolar lines are parallel, it follows that the epipole is at infinity.

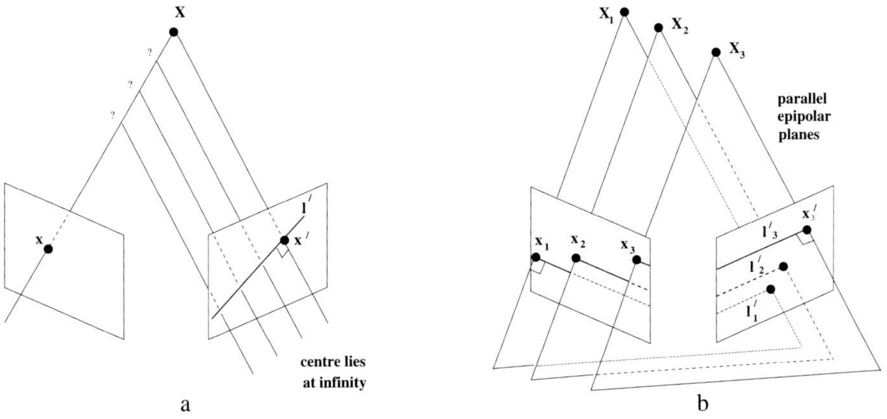

Fig. 14.1. **Affine epipolar geometry.** *(a) Correspondence geometry: Projection rays are parallel and intersect at infinity. A point* $\mathbf{x}$ *back-projects to a ray in 3-space defined by the first camera centre (at infinity) and* $\mathbf{x}$*. This ray is imaged as a line* $\mathbf{l}'$ *in the second view. The 3-space point* $\mathbf{X}$ *which projects to* $\mathbf{x}$ *lies on this ray, so the image of* $\mathbf{X}$ *in the second view lies on* $\mathbf{l}'$*. (b) Epipolar lines and planes are parallel.*

These points are illustrated schematically in figure 14.1, and examples on images are shown in figure 14.2.

14.2 The affine fundamental matrix

The affine epipolar geometry is represented algebraically by a matrix termed the *affine fundamental matrix*, $\mathtt{F}_A$. It will be seen in the following that:

Result 14.1. *The fundamental matrix resulting from two cameras with the affine form (i.e. the third row is* $(0, 0, 0, 1)$*) has the form*

$$\mathtt{F}_A = \begin{bmatrix} 0 & 0 & * \\ 0 & 0 & * \\ * & * & * \end{bmatrix}$$

where $*$ *indicates a non-zero entry.*

It will be convenient to write the five non-zero entries as

$$\mathtt{F}_A = \begin{bmatrix} 0 & 0 & a \\ 0 & 0 & b \\ c & d & e \end{bmatrix}. \tag{14.1}$$

Note that in general $\mathtt{F}_A$ has rank 2.

14.2.1 Derivation

Geometric derivation. This derivation is the analogue of that given in section 9.2.1-(*p*242) for a pair of projective cameras. The map from a point in one image to the corresponding epipolar line in the other image is decomposed into two steps, as illustrated in figure 14.5 on page 352:

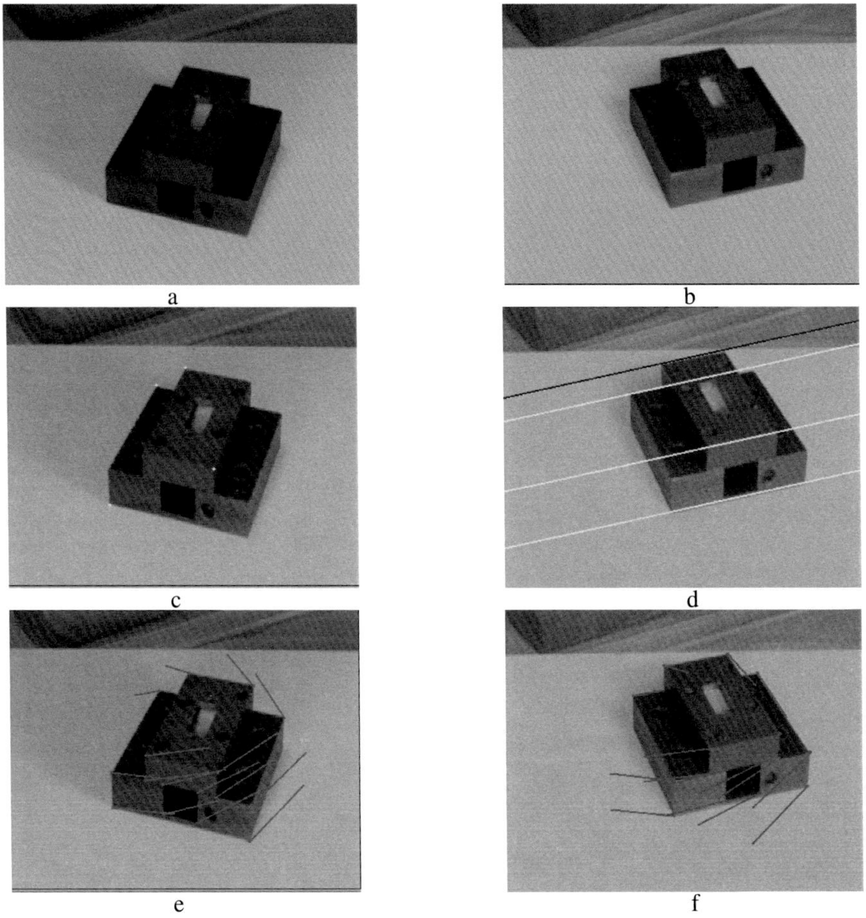

Fig. 14.2. **Affine epipolar lines.** *(a), (b) Two views of a hole punch acquired under affine imaging conditions. For the points marked in (c) the epipolar lines are superimposed on (d). Note that corresponding points lie on their epipolar lines, and that all epipolar lines are parallel. The epipolar geometry is computed from point correspondences using algorithm 14.1. (e) and (f) show the "flow" for selected points in the image (the lines link a point in one image to the point's position in the other image). This demonstrates that even though the epipolar lines are parallel the movement of imaged points between the views contains both rotational and translational components.*

(i) **Point transfer via a plane π.** Since both cameras are affine, points are mapped between an image and a scene plane by parallel projection, so the map between π and the images is a planar affine transformation; the composition of the affine transformations between the first view and π, and π and the second view, is also an affine transformation, i.e. $\mathbf{x}' = \mathtt{H}_A \mathbf{x}$.

(ii) **Constructing the epipolar line.** The epipolar line is obtained as the line through $\mathbf{x}'$ and the epipole $\mathbf{e}'$, i.e. $\mathbf{l}' = \mathbf{e}' \times \mathtt{H}_A \mathbf{x} = \mathtt{F}_A \mathbf{x}$, so that $\mathtt{F}_A = [\mathbf{e}']_\times \mathtt{H}_A$.

We now take note of the special forms of the affine matrix H_A, and the skew matrix $[\mathbf{e}']_\times$ when $\mathbf{e}'$ is at infinity, and so has a zero last element:

$$F_A = [\mathbf{e}']_\times H_A = \begin{bmatrix} 0 & 0 & * \\ 0 & 0 & * \\ * & * & 0 \end{bmatrix} \begin{bmatrix} * & * & * \\ * & * & * \\ 0 & 0 & 1 \end{bmatrix} = \begin{bmatrix} 0 & 0 & * \\ 0 & 0 & * \\ * & * & * \end{bmatrix} \tag{14.2}$$

where $*$ indicates a non-zero entry. This derives the affine form of F using only the geometric properties that the camera centres are on the plane at infinity.

Algebraic derivation. In the case that the cameras are both affine, the affine form of the fundamental matrix is obtained directly from the expression (9.1–*p*244) for F in terms of the pseudo-inverse, namely $F = [\mathbf{e}']_\times P'P^+$, where $\mathbf{e}' = P'\mathbf{C}$, with $\mathbf{C}$ the camera centre which is the null-vector of P. Details are left as an exercise. An elegant derivation of F_A in terms of determinants formed from rows of the affine camera matrices is given in section 17.1.2(*p*413).

14.2.2 Properties

The affine fundamental matrix is a homogeneous matrix with five non-zero elements, it thus has 4 degrees of freedom. These are accounted as: one for each of the two epipoles (the epipoles lie on $\mathbf{l}_\infty$, so only their direction need be specified); and two for the 1D affine transformation mapping the pencil of epipolar lines from one view to the other.

The geometric entities (epipoles etc.) are encoded in F_A in the same manner as their encoding in F. However, often the expressions are far simpler and so can be given explicitly.

The epipoles. The epipole in the first view is the right null-vector of F_A, i.e. $F_A\mathbf{e} = \mathbf{0}$. This determines $\mathbf{e} = (-d, c, 0)^\mathsf{T}$, which is a point (direction) on $\mathbf{l}_\infty$. Since all epipolar lines intersect the epipole this shows that all epipolar lines are parallel.

Epipolar lines. The epipolar line in the second view corresponding to $\mathbf{x}$ in the first is $\mathbf{l}' = F_A\mathbf{x} = (a, b, cx + dy + e)^\mathsf{T}$. Again it is evident that all epipolar lines are parallel since the line orientation, (a, b), is independent of (x, y).
These properties, and others, are summarized in table 14.1.

14.3 Estimating F_A from image point correspondences

The fundamental matrix is defined by the equation $\mathbf{x}'^\mathsf{T} F_A \mathbf{x} = 0$ for any pair of matching points $\mathbf{x} \leftrightarrow \mathbf{x}'$ in two images. Given sufficiently many point matches $\mathbf{x}_i \leftrightarrow \mathbf{x}'_i$, this equation can be used to compute the unknown matrix F_A. In particular, writing $\mathbf{x}_i = (x_i, y_i, 1)^\mathsf{T}$ and $\mathbf{x}'_i = (x'_i, y'_i, 1)^\mathsf{T}$ each point match gives rise to one linear equation

$$a x'_i + b y'_i + c x_i + d y_i + e = 0 \tag{14.3}$$

in the unknown entries $\{a, b, c, d, e\}$ of F_A.

- $\mathtt{F}_A$ is a rank 2 homogeneous matrix with 4 degrees of freedom. It has the form

$$\mathtt{F}_A = \begin{bmatrix} 0 & 0 & a \\ 0 & 0 & b \\ c & d & e \end{bmatrix}.$$

- **Point correspondence**: If $\mathbf{x}$ and $\mathbf{x}'$ are corresponding image points under an affine camera, then $\mathbf{x}'^{\mathsf{T}}\mathtt{F}_A\mathbf{x} = 0$. For finite points

$$ax' + by' + cx + dy + e = 0.$$

- **Epipolar lines**:
  - ◇ $\mathbf{l}' = \mathtt{F}_A\mathbf{x} = (a, b, cx + dy + e)^{\mathsf{T}}$ is the epipolar line corresponding to $\mathbf{x}$.
  - ◇ $\mathbf{l} = \mathtt{F}_A{}^{\mathsf{T}}\mathbf{x}' = (c, d, ax + by + e)^{\mathsf{T}}$ is the epipolar line corresponding to $\mathbf{x}'$.
- **Epipoles**:
  - ◇ From $\mathtt{F}_A\mathbf{e} = \mathbf{0}$, $\mathbf{e} = (-d, c, 0)^{\mathsf{T}}$.
  - ◇ From $\mathtt{F}_A{}^{\mathsf{T}}\mathbf{e}' = \mathbf{0}$, $\mathbf{e}' = (-b, a, 0)^{\mathsf{T}}$.
- **Computation from camera matrices** $\mathtt{P}_A, \mathtt{P}'_A$:
  - ◇ General cameras,
    $\mathtt{F}_A = [\mathbf{e}']_\times \mathtt{P}'_A\mathtt{P}_A^+$, where $\mathtt{P}_A^+$ is the pseudo-inverse of $\mathtt{P}_A$, and $\mathbf{e}'$ is the epipole defined by $\mathbf{e}' = \mathtt{P}'_A\mathbf{C}$, where $\mathbf{C}$ is the centre of the first camera.
  - ◇ Canonical cameras,

$$\mathtt{P}_A = \begin{bmatrix} 1 & 0 & 0 & 0 \\ 0 & 1 & 0 & 0 \\ 0 & 0 & 0 & 1 \end{bmatrix} \quad \mathtt{P}'_A = \left[\begin{array}{c|c} \mathtt{M}_{2\times 3} & \mathbf{t} \\ 0 \;\; 0 \;\; 0 & 1 \end{array}\right]$$

$$\begin{aligned} a &= m_{23}, \quad b = -m_{13}, \quad c = m_{13}m_{21} - m_{11}m_{23} \\ d &= m_{13}m_{22} - m_{12}m_{23}, \quad e = m_{13}t_2 - m_{23}t_1 \end{aligned}$$

Table 14.1. *Summary of affine fundamental matrix properties.*

14.3.1 The linear algorithm

In the usual manner a solution for $\mathtt{F}_A$ may be obtained by rewriting (14.3) as

$$(x'_i, y'_i, x_i, y_i, 1)\,\mathbf{f} = 0$$

with $\mathbf{f} = (a, b, c, d, e)^{\mathsf{T}}$. From a set of n point matches, we obtain a set of linear equations of the form $\mathtt{A}\mathbf{f} = \mathbf{0}$, where $\mathtt{A}$ is a $n \times 5$ matrix:

$$\begin{bmatrix} x'_1 & y'_1 & x_1 & y_1 & 1 \\ \vdots & \vdots & \vdots & \vdots & \vdots \\ x'_n & y'_n & x_n & y_n & 1 \end{bmatrix} \mathbf{f} = \mathbf{0}.$$

A minimal solution is obtained for $n = 4$ point correspondences as the right null-space of the 4×5 matrix $\mathtt{A}$. Thus $\mathtt{F}_A$ can be computed uniquely from only 4 point correspondences, provided the 3-space points are in general position. The conditions for general position are described in section 14.3.3 below.

If there are more than 4 correspondences, and the data is not exact, then the rank of A may be greater than 4. In this case, one may find a least-squares solution, subject to $\|\mathbf{f}\| = 1$, in essentially the same manner as that of section 4.1.1(*p*90), as the singular vector corresponding to the smallest singular value of A. Refer to algorithm 4.2(*p*109) for details. This linear solution is the equivalent of the 8-point algorithm 11.1(*p*282) for the computation of a general fundamental matrix. We do not recommend this approach for estimating F_A because the Gold Standard algorithm described below may be implemented with equal computational ease, and in general will have superior performance.

The singularity constraint. The form (14.1) of F_A ensures that the matrix has rank no greater than 2. Consequently, if F_A is estimated by the linear method above it is not necessary to subsequently impose a singularity constraint. This is a considerable advantage over the estimation of a general F by the linear 8-point algorithm, where the estimated matrix is not guaranteed to have rank 2, and thus must be subsequently corrected.

Geometric interpretation. As has been seen at several points in this book, computing a two-view relation from point correspondences is equivalent to fitting a surface (variety) to points x, y, x', y' in $\mathbb{R}^4$. In the case of the equation $\mathbf{x}'^{\mathsf{T}} F_A \mathbf{x} = 0$ the relation $ax'_i + by'_i + cx_i + dy_i + e = 0$ is *linear* in the coordinates, and the variety $\mathcal{V}_{F_A}$ defined by the affine fundamental matrix is a hyperplane.

This results in two simplifications: first, finding the best estimate of F_A may be formulated as a (familiar) plane-fitting problem; second, the Sampson error is identical to the geometric error, whereas in the case of a general (non-affine) fundamental matrix (11.9–*p*287) it is only a first-order approximation. As discussed in section 4.2.6-(*p*98) this latter property arises generally with affine (linear) relations because the tangent plane of the Sampson approximation is equivalent to the surface.

14.3.2 The Gold Standard algorithm

Given a set of n corresponding image points $\{\mathbf{x}_i \leftrightarrow \mathbf{x}'_i\}$, we seek the Maximum Likelihood estimate of F_A under the assumption that the noise in the image measurements obeys an isotropic, homogeneous Gaussian distribution. This estimate is obtained by minimizing a cost function on geometric image distances:

$$\min_{\{F_A, \hat{\mathbf{x}}_i, \hat{\mathbf{x}}'_i\}} \sum_i d(\mathbf{x}_i, \hat{\mathbf{x}}_i)^2 + d(\mathbf{x}'_i, \hat{\mathbf{x}}'_i)^2 \tag{14.4}$$

where as usual $\mathbf{x}_i \leftrightarrow \mathbf{x}'_i$ are the measured correspondences, and $\hat{\mathbf{x}}_i$ and $\hat{\mathbf{x}}'_i$ are estimated "true" correspondences that satisfy $\hat{\mathbf{x}}'^{\mathsf{T}}_i F_A \hat{\mathbf{x}}_i = 0$ exactly for the estimated affine fundamental matrix. The distances are illustrated in figure 14.3. The true correspondences are subsidiary variables that must also be estimated.

As discussed above, and in section 4.2.5(*p*96), minimizing the cost function (14.4)

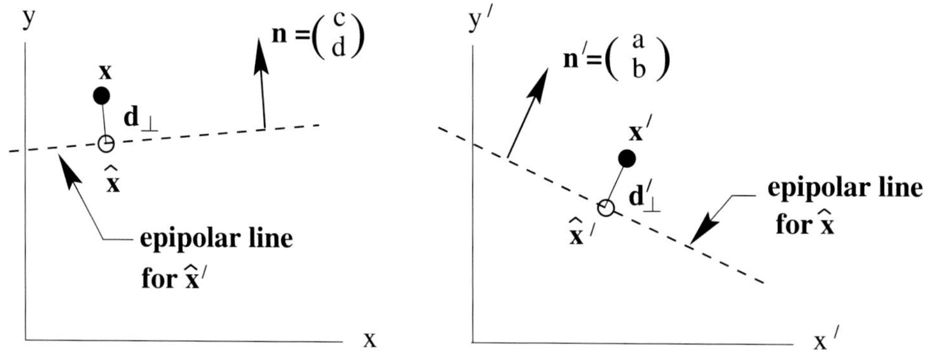

Fig. 14.3. *The MLE of* $\mathtt{F}_\mathrm{A}$ *from a set of measured corresponding points* $\{\mathbf{x}_i \leftrightarrow \mathbf{x}'_i\}$ *involves estimating the five parameters* a, b, c, d, e *together with a set of correspondences* $\{\hat{\mathbf{x}}_i \leftrightarrow \hat{\mathbf{x}}'_i\}$ *which exactly satisfy* $\hat{\mathbf{x}}_i'^{\mathsf{T}}\mathtt{F}_\mathrm{A}\hat{\mathbf{x}}_i = 0$. *There is a linear solution to this problem.*

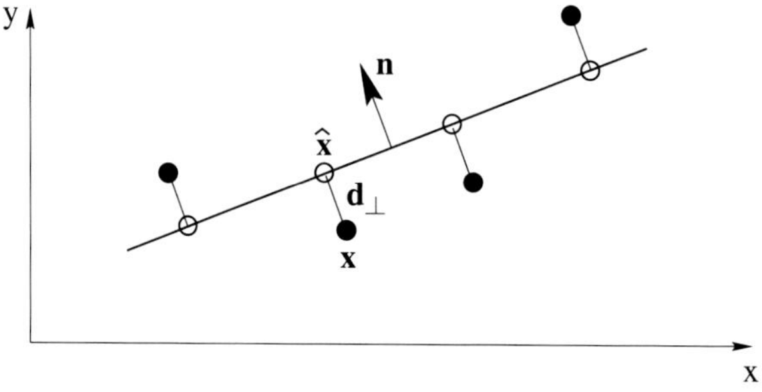

Fig. 14.4. *In 2D a line is the analogue of the hyperplane defined by* $\mathtt{F}_\mathrm{A}$, *and the problem of estimating the true correspondence given a measured correspondence, is the problem of determining the closest point* $(\hat{x}, \hat{y})$ *on the line* $ax + by + c$ *to a measurement point* (x, y). *The normal to the line has direction* (a, b), *and the perpendicular distance of the point* (x, y) *from the line is* $d_\perp = (ax + by + c)/\sqrt{a^2 + b^2}$, *so that* $(\hat{x}, \hat{y})^{\mathsf{T}} = (x, y)^{\mathsf{T}} - d_\perp \hat{\mathbf{n}}$, *where* $\hat{\mathbf{n}} = (a, b)/\sqrt{a^2 + b^2}$.

is equivalent to fitting a hyperplane to set of points $\mathbf{X}_i = (x'_i, y'_i, x_i, y_i)^{\mathsf{T}}$ in $\mathbb{R}^4$. The estimated points $\widehat{\mathbf{X}}_i = (\hat{\mathbf{x}}'_i, \hat{\mathbf{y}}'_i, \hat{\mathbf{x}}_i, \hat{\mathbf{y}}_i)^{\mathsf{T}}$ satisfy the equation $\hat{\mathbf{x}}_i'^{\mathsf{T}}\mathtt{F}_\mathrm{A}\hat{\mathbf{x}}_i = 0$ which may be written as $(\widehat{\mathbf{X}}_i^{\mathsf{T}}, 1)\mathbf{f} = 0$, where $\mathbf{f} = (a, b, c, d, e)^{\mathsf{T}}$. This is the equation of a point in $\mathbb{R}^4$ on the plane $\mathbf{f}$. We seek the plane $\mathbf{f}$ which minimizes the squared distance between the measured and estimated points, and consequently which minimizes the sum of squared perpendicular distances to the points $\mathbf{X}_i = (x'_i, y'_i, x_i, y_i)^{\mathsf{T}}$.

Geometrically the solution is very simple, and an analogue for line fitting in 2D is illustrated in figure 14.4. The perpendicular distance of a point $\mathbf{X}_i = (x_i, y_i, x'_i, y'_i)^{\mathsf{T}}$ from the plane $\mathbf{f}$ is

$$d_\perp(\mathbf{X}_i, \mathbf{f}) = \frac{ax'_i + by'_i + cx_i + dy_i + e}{\sqrt{a^2 + b^2 + c^2 + d^2}}.$$

Then the matrix $\mathtt{F}_\mathrm{A}$ which minimizes (14.4) is determined by minimizing the cost function

$$\mathcal{C} = \sum_i d_\perp(\mathbf{X}_i, \mathbf{f})^2 = \frac{1}{a^2 + b^2 + c^2 + d^2} \sum_i (ax'_i + by'_i + cx_i + dy_i + e)^2 \qquad (14.5)$$

Objective

Given $n \geq 4$ image point correspondences $\{\mathbf{x}_i \leftrightarrow \mathbf{x}'_i\}$, $i = 1, \ldots, n$, determine the Maximum Likelihood estimate F_A of the affine fundamental matrix.

Algorithm

A correspondence is represented as $\mathbf{X}_i = (x'_i, y'_i, x_i, y_i)^\mathsf{T}$.

(i) Compute the centroid $\overline{\mathbf{X}} = \frac{1}{n}\sum_i \mathbf{X}_i$ and centre the vectors $\Delta\mathbf{X}_i = \mathbf{X}_i - \overline{\mathbf{X}}$.
(ii) Compute the $n \times 4$ matrix $\mathtt{A}$ with rows $\Delta\mathbf{X}_i^\mathsf{T}$.
(iii) Then $\mathbf{N} = (a, b, c, d)^\mathsf{T}$ is the singular vector corresponding to the smallest singular value of $\mathtt{A}$, and $e = -\mathbf{N}^\mathsf{T}\overline{\mathbf{X}}$. The matrix F_A has the form (14.1).

Algorithm 14.1. *The Gold Standard algorithm for estimating* F_A *from image correspondences.*

over the 5 parameters $\{a, b, c, d, e\}$ of $\mathbf{f}$. Writing $\mathbf{N} = (a, b, c, d)^\mathsf{T}$ for the normal to the hyperplane then

$$\mathcal{C} = \frac{1}{\|\mathbf{N}\|^2}\sum_i \left(\mathbf{N}^\mathsf{T}\mathbf{X}_i + e\right)^2.$$

This cost function can be minimized by a very simple linear algorithm, equivalent to the classical problem of orthogonal regression to a plane. There are two steps:

The first step is to minimize $\mathcal{C}$ over the parameter e. We obtain

$$\frac{\partial \mathcal{C}}{\partial e} = \frac{1}{\|\mathbf{N}\|^2}\sum_i 2(\mathbf{N}^\mathsf{T}\mathbf{X}_i + e) = 0$$

and hence

$$e = -\frac{1}{n}\sum_i (\mathbf{N}^\mathsf{T}\mathbf{X}_i) = -\mathbf{N}^\mathsf{T}\overline{\mathbf{X}}$$

so the solution hyperplane passes through the data centroid $\overline{\mathbf{X}}$. Substituting for e in the cost function reduces $\mathcal{C}$ to

$$\mathcal{C} = \frac{1}{\|\mathbf{N}\|^2}\sum_i \left(\mathbf{N}^\mathsf{T}\Delta\mathbf{X}_i\right)^2$$

where $\Delta\mathbf{X}_i = \mathbf{X}_i - \overline{\mathbf{X}}$ is the vector $\mathbf{X}_i$ relative to the data centroid $\overline{\mathbf{X}}$.

The second step is to minimize this reduced cost function over $\mathbf{N}$. Writing $\mathtt{A}$ for the matrix with rows $\Delta\mathbf{X}_i^\mathsf{T}$, it is evident that

$$\mathcal{C} = \|\mathtt{A}\mathbf{N}\|^2 / \|\mathbf{N}\|^2.$$

Minimizing this expression is equivalent to minimizing $\|\mathtt{A}\mathbf{N}\|$ subject to $\|\mathbf{N}\| = 1$, which is our usual homogeneous minimization problem solved by the SVD. These steps are summarized in algorithm 14.1.

It is worth noting that the Gold Standard algorithm produces an identical estimate of F_A to that obtained by the factorization algorithm 18.1(*p*437) for an affine reconstruction from n point correspondences.

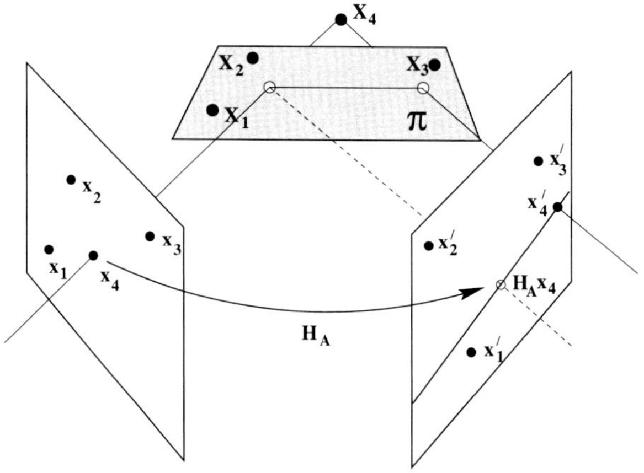

Fig. 14.5. *Computing the affine epipolar line for a minimal configuration of four points. The line is computed by the virtual parallax induced by the plane* π. *Compare figure 13.7(*p335*).*

Objective

Given four image point correspondences $\{\mathbf{x}_i \leftrightarrow \mathbf{x}'_i\}$, $i = 1, \ldots, 4$, compute the affine fundamental matrix.

Algorithm

The first three 3-space points $\mathbf{X}_i$, $i = 1, \ldots, 3$ define a plane $\boldsymbol{\pi}$. See figure 14.5.

(i) Compute the affine transformation matrix $\mathtt{H}_A$, such that $\mathbf{x}'_i = \mathtt{H}_A \mathbf{x}_i$, $i = 1, \ldots, 3$.
(ii) Determine the epipolar line in the second view from $\mathbf{l}' = (\mathtt{H}_A \mathbf{x}_4) \times \mathbf{x}'_4$. The epipole $\mathbf{e}' = (-l'_2, l'_1, 0)^{\mathsf{T}}$.
(iii) Then for any point $\mathbf{x}$ the epipolar line in the second view is $\mathbf{e}' \times (\mathtt{H}_A \mathbf{x}) = \mathtt{F}_A \mathbf{x}$. Hence $\mathtt{F}_A = [(-l'_2, l'_1, 0)^{\mathsf{T}}]_\times \mathtt{H}_A$.

Algorithm 14.2. *The computation of* $\mathtt{F}_A$ *for a minimal configuration of four point correspondences.*

14.3.3 The minimal configuration

We return to the minimal configuration for estimating $\mathtt{F}_A$, namely the corresponding images of four points in 3-space in general position. A geometric computation method of $\mathtt{F}_A$ for this configuration is described in algorithm 14.2. This minimal solution is useful in the case of robust estimation algorithms, such as RANSAC, and will be used here to illustrate degenerate configurations. Note that for this minimal configuration an exact solution is obtained for $\mathtt{F}_A$, and the linear algorithm of section 14.3.1, the Gold Standard algorithm 14.1, and the minimal algorithm 14.2 give an identical result.

General position. The configuration of four points shown in figure 14.5 demonstrates the conditions necessary for general position of the 3-space points when computing $\mathtt{F}_A$. Configurations for which $\mathtt{F}_A$ cannot be computed are degenerate. These fall into two classes: first, degenerate configurations depending only on the structure, for example if the four points are coplanar (so there is no parallax), or if the first three points are collinear (so that $\mathtt{H}_A$ can't be computed); second, those degeneracies which depend only on the cameras, for example if the two cameras have the same viewing direction (and so have common centres on the plane at infinity).

Note once again the importance of parallax – as the point $\mathbf{X}_4$ approaches the plane defined by the other three points in figure 14.5 the parallax vector, which determines the epipolar line direction, is monotonically reduced in length. Consequently, the accuracy of the line direction is correspondingly reduced. This result for the minimal configuration is true also of the Gold Standard algorithm 14.1: as relief reduces to zero, i.e. the point set approaches coplanarity, the covariance of the estimated $\mathtt{F}_A$ will increase.

14.4 Triangulation

Suppose we have a measured correspondence $(x, y) \leftrightarrow (x', y')$ and the affine fundamental matrix $\mathtt{F}_A$. We wish to determine the Maximum Likelihood estimate of the true correspondence, $(\hat{x}, \hat{y}) \leftrightarrow (\hat{x}', \hat{y}')$, under the usual assumption that image measurement error is Gaussian. The 3D point may then be determined from the ML estimate correspondence.

As we have seen earlier in chapter 12, the MLE involves determining a "true" correspondence which exactly obeys the affine epipolar geometry, i.e. $(\hat{x}', \hat{y}', 1)\mathtt{F}_A(\hat{x}, \hat{y}, 1)^\mathsf{T} = 0$, and also minimizes the image distance to the measured points,

$$(x - \hat{x})^2 + (y - \hat{y})^2 + (x' - \hat{x}')^2 + (y' - \hat{y}')^2.$$

Geometrically the solution is very simple, and is illustrated in 2D in figure 14.4. We seek the closest point on the hyperplane defined by $\mathtt{F}_A$ to the measured correspondence $\mathbf{X} = (x', y', x, y)^\mathsf{T}$ in $\mathbb{R}^4$. Again, the Sampson correction (4.11–*p*99) is exact in this case. Algebraically, the normal to the hyperplane has direction $\mathbf{N} = (a, b, c, d)^\mathsf{T}$ and the perpendicular distance of a point $\mathbf{X}$ to the hyperplane is given by $d_\perp = (\mathbf{N}^\mathsf{T}\mathbf{X}+e)/\|\mathbf{N}\|$, so that

$$\widehat{\mathbf{X}} = \mathbf{X} - d_\perp \frac{\mathbf{N}}{\|\mathbf{N}\|}$$

or in its full detail

$$\begin{pmatrix} \hat{x}' \\ \hat{y}' \\ \hat{x} \\ \hat{y} \end{pmatrix} = \begin{pmatrix} x' \\ y' \\ x \\ y \end{pmatrix} - \frac{(ax' + by' + cx + dy + e)}{(a^2 + b^2 + c^2 + d^2)} \begin{pmatrix} a \\ b \\ c \\ d \end{pmatrix}.$$

14.5 Affine reconstruction

Suppose we have $n \geq 4$ image point correspondences $\mathbf{x}_i \leftrightarrow \mathbf{x}'$, $i = 0, \ldots, n-1$, which for the moment will be assumed noise-free, then we may compute a reconstruction of the 3D points and cameras. In the case of projective cameras (with $n \geq 7$ points) the reconstruction was projective. In the affine case, not surprisingly, the reconstruction is *affine*. We will now give a simple constructive derivation of this result.

An affine coordinate frame in 3-space may be specified by four finite non-coplanar basis points $\mathbf{X}_i$, $i = 0, \ldots, 3$. As illustrated in figure 14.6 one point $\mathbf{X}_0$ is chosen as the

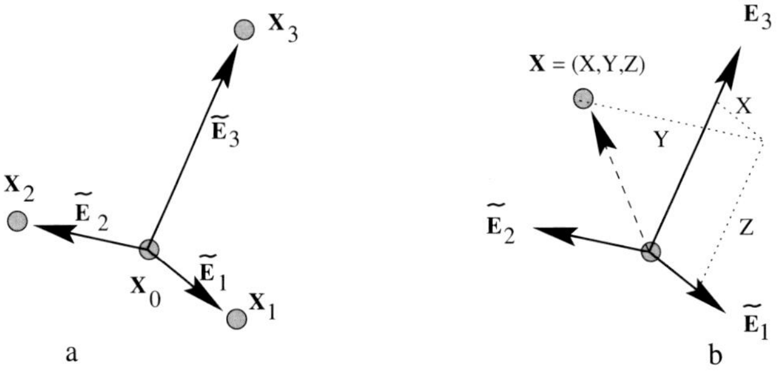

Fig. 14.6. **Affine coordinates.** *(a) four non-coplanar points in 3-space ($\mathbf{X}_1$, $\mathbf{X}_2$, $\mathbf{X}_3$ and origin $\mathbf{X}_0$) define a set of axes in terms of which other points $\mathbf{X}$ can be assigned affine coordinates $(\mathrm{X}, \mathrm{Y}, \mathrm{Z})$. (b) Each affine coordinate is defined by a ratio of lengths in parallel directions (which is an affine invariant). For example, X may be computed by the following two operations: first, $\mathbf{X}$ is projected parallel to $\widetilde{\mathbf{E}}_2$ onto the plane spanned by $\widetilde{\mathbf{E}}_1$ and $\widetilde{\mathbf{E}}_3$. Second, this projected point is projected parallel to $\widetilde{\mathbf{E}}_3$ onto the $\widetilde{\mathbf{E}}_1$ axis. The value of the coordinate X is the ratio of the length from the origin of this final projected point to the length of $\widetilde{\mathbf{E}}_1$.*

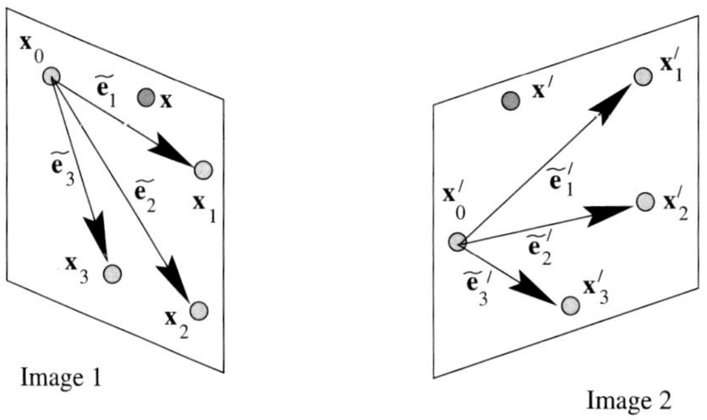

Fig. 14.7. **Reconstruction from two images.** *The affine coordinates of the 3D point $\mathbf{X}$ with image $\mathbf{x}, \mathbf{x}'$ in two views may be computed linearly from the projection of the basis points $\mathbf{x}_i$ and basis vectors $\tilde{\mathbf{e}}_i$ of figure 14.6.*

origin, and the three other points then define basis vectors $\widetilde{\mathbf{E}}_i = \widetilde{\mathbf{X}}_i - \widetilde{\mathbf{X}}_0, i = 1, \ldots, 3$, where $\widetilde{\mathbf{X}}_i$ is the inhomogeneous 3-vector corresponding to $\mathbf{X}_i$. The position of a point $\mathbf{X}$ may then be specified by simple vector addition as

$$\widetilde{\mathbf{X}} = \widetilde{\mathbf{X}}_0 + \mathrm{X}\widetilde{\mathbf{E}}_1 + \mathrm{Y}\widetilde{\mathbf{E}}_2 + \mathrm{Z}\widetilde{\mathbf{E}}_3$$

and $(\mathrm{X}, \mathrm{Y}, \mathrm{Z})$ are the affine coordinates of $\widetilde{\mathbf{X}}$ with respect to this basis. This means that the basis points $\mathbf{X}_i$ have the canonical coordinates $(\mathrm{X}, \mathrm{Y}, \mathrm{Z})^{\mathsf{T}}$:

$$\widetilde{\mathbf{X}}_0 = \begin{pmatrix} 0 \\ 0 \\ 0 \end{pmatrix} \quad \widetilde{\mathbf{X}}_1 = \begin{pmatrix} 1 \\ 0 \\ 0 \end{pmatrix} \quad \widetilde{\mathbf{X}}_2 = \begin{pmatrix} 0 \\ 1 \\ 0 \end{pmatrix} \quad \widetilde{\mathbf{X}}_3 = \begin{pmatrix} 0 \\ 0 \\ 1 \end{pmatrix}. \qquad (14.6)$$

Given the affine projection of the four basis points in two views, the 3D affine coordinates of any other point can be directly recovered from its image, as will now be demonstrated (see figure 14.7).

Projection with an affine camera may be represented as (6.26–p172)

$$\tilde{\mathbf{x}} = \mathtt{M}_{2\times3}\widetilde{\mathbf{X}} + \tilde{\mathbf{t}}$$

where $\tilde{\mathbf{x}} = (x, y)^\mathsf{T}$ is the inhomogeneous 2-vector corresponding to $\mathbf{x}$. Differences of vectors eliminate $\tilde{\mathbf{t}}$. For example the basis vectors project as $\tilde{\mathbf{e}}_i = \mathtt{M}_{2\times3}\widetilde{\mathbf{E}}_i,\ i = 1, \ldots, 3$. Consequently for any point $\mathbf{X}$, its image in the first view is

$$\tilde{\mathbf{x}} - \tilde{\mathbf{x}}_0 = \mathrm{X}\tilde{\mathbf{e}}_1 + \mathrm{Y}\tilde{\mathbf{e}}_2 + \mathrm{Z}\tilde{\mathbf{e}}_3 \qquad (14.7)$$

and similarly the image ($\tilde{\mathbf{x}}' = \mathtt{M}'_{2\times3}\widetilde{\mathbf{X}} + \tilde{\mathbf{t}}'$) in the second view is

$$\tilde{\mathbf{x}}' - \tilde{\mathbf{x}}'_0 = \mathrm{X}\tilde{\mathbf{e}}'_1 + \mathrm{Y}\tilde{\mathbf{e}}'_2 + \mathrm{Z}\tilde{\mathbf{e}}'_3. \qquad (14.8)$$

Each equation (14.7) and (14.8) imposes two linear constraints on the unknown affine coordinates $\mathrm{X}, \mathrm{Y}, \mathrm{Z}$ of the space point $\mathbf{X}$. All the other terms in the equations are known from image measurements (for example the image basis vectors $\tilde{\mathbf{e}}_i, \tilde{\mathbf{e}}'_i$ are computed from the projection of the four basis points $\widetilde{\mathbf{X}}_i,\ i = 0, \ldots, 3$). Thus, there are four linear simultaneous equations in the three unknowns $\mathrm{X}, \mathrm{Y}, \mathrm{Z}$, and the solution is straightforward. This demonstrates that the affine coordinates of a point $\mathbf{X}$ may be computed from its image in two views.

The cameras for the two views, $\mathtt{P}_\mathrm{A}, \mathtt{P}'_\mathrm{A}$, may be computed from the correspondences between the 3-space points $\widetilde{\mathbf{X}}_i$, with coordinates given in (14.6), and their measured images. For example, $\mathtt{P}_\mathrm{A}$ is computed from the correspondence $\tilde{\mathbf{x}}_i \leftrightarrow \widetilde{\mathbf{X}}_i,\ i = 0, \ldots, 3$.

The above development is not optimal, because the basis points are treated as exact, and all measurement error associated with the fifth point $\mathbf{X}$. An optimal reconstruction algorithm, where reprojection error is minimized over all points, is very straightforward in the affine case. However, its description is postponed until section 18.2(p436) because the factorization algorithm described there is applicable to any number of views.

Example 14.2. Affine reconstruction
A 3D reconstruction is computed for the hole punch images of figure 14.2 by choosing four points as the affine basis, and then computing the affine coordinates of each of the remaining points in turn by the linear method above. Two views of the resulting reconstruction are shown in figure 14.8. Note, however, that this five-point method is *not* recommended. Instead the optimal affine reconstruction algorithm 18.1(p437) should be used. △

14.6 Necker reversal and the bas-relief ambiguity

We have seen in the previous section that in the absence of any calibration information, an affine reconstruction is obtained from point correspondences alone. In this section we show that even if the camera calibration is known there remains a family of reconstruction ambiguities which cannot be resolved in the two-view case.

This situation differs from that of perspective projection where once the internal calibration is determined the camera motion is determined up to a finite number of

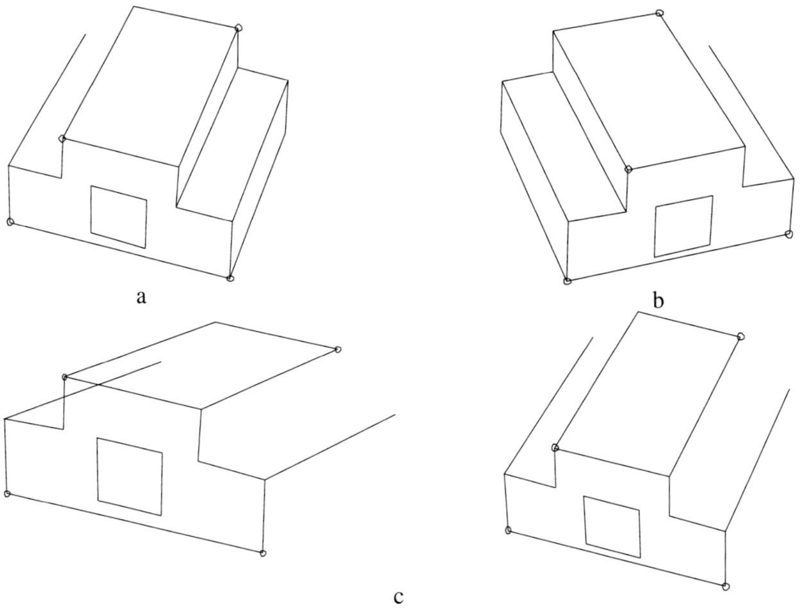

Fig. 14.8. **Affine reconstruction.** *(a)(b) Wireframe outline of the hole punch from the two images of figure 14.2. The circles show the points selected as the affine basis. The lines are for visualization only. (c) Two views of the 3D affine structure computed from the vertices of the wireframe.*

ambiguities (from the essential matrix, see section 9.6(p257)). For parallel projection there are two important additional ambiguities: a finite reflection ambiguity (Necker reversal); and a one-parameter family rotation ambiguity (the bas-relief ambiguity).

Necker reversal ambiguity. This arises because an object rotating by ρ and its mirror image rotating by $-\rho$ generate the same image under parallel projection, see figure 14.9(a). Thus, structure is only recovered up to a reflection about the frontal plane. This ambiguity is absent in the perspective case because the points have different depths in the two interpretations and so do not project to coincident image points.

The bas-relief ambiguity. This is illustrated in figure 14.9(b). Imagine a set of parallel rays from one camera, and consider adjusting a set of parallel rays from a second camera until each ray intersects its corresponding ray. The rays lie in a family of parallel epipolar planes, and there remains the freedom to rotate one camera about the normal to these planes whilst maintaining incidence of the rays. This *bas-relief* (or *depth–turn*) ambiguity is a one-parameter family of solutions for the rotation angle and depth. The parameters of depth, ΔZ, and rotation, $\sin \rho$, are confounded and cannot be determined individually – only their product can be computed. Consequently, a shallow object experiencing a large turn (i.e. small ΔZ and large ρ) generates the same image as a deep object experiencing a small turn (i.e. large ΔZ and small ρ). The name arises from bas-relief sculptures. Fixing the depth or the angle ρ determines the structure and the motion uniquely. Extra points cannot resolve this ambiguity, but an additional view (i.e. three views) will in general resolve it.

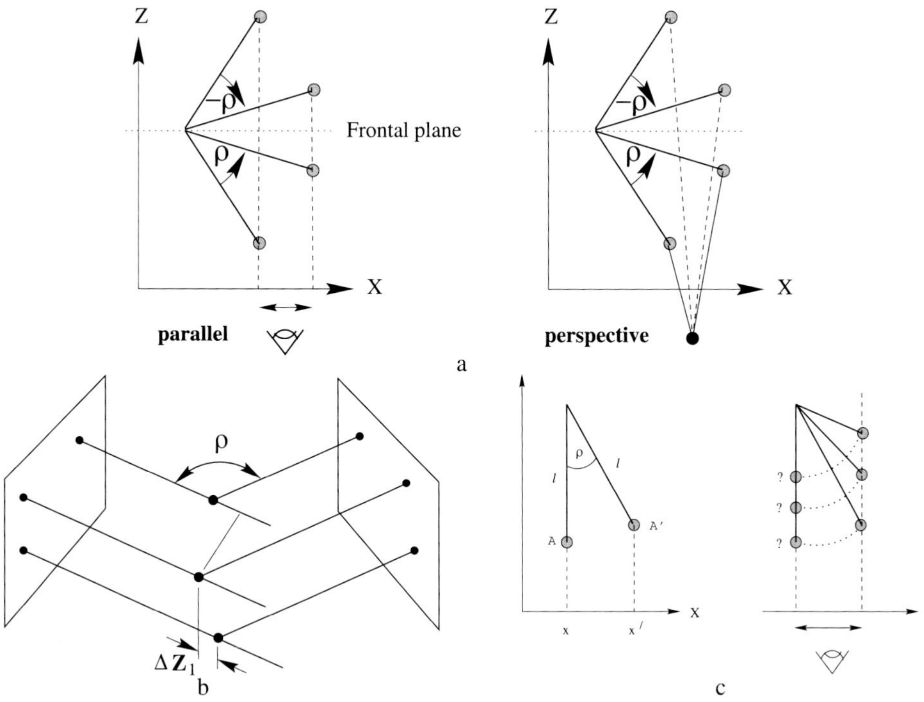

Fig. 14.9. **Motion ambiguities under parallel projection.** *(a) Necker reversal: a rotating object generates the same image as its mirror object rotating in the opposite sense. Under perspective projection the images are different. (b) The cameras can rotate (by ρ) and still preserve ray intersections. This cannot happen for perspective cameras. (c) The bas-relief ambiguity: consider a rod of length l, which rotates through an angle ρ. That is $x' - x = l \sin \rho$. This* bas–relief *(or* depth–turn*) ambiguity is so-named because a shallow object experiencing a large turn (i.e. small l and big ρ) generates the same image as a deep object experiencing a small turn (i.e. large l and small ρ).*

This ambiguity casts light on the stability of reconstruction from two perspective cameras: as imaging conditions approach affine the rotation angle will be poorly estimated, but the product of the rotation angle and depth will be stable.

14.7 Computing the motion

In this section expressions for computing the camera motion from $\mathtt{F}_\mathrm{A}$ will be given for the case of two weak perspective cameras (section 6.3.4(*p*170)). These cameras may be chosen as

$$\mathtt{P} = \begin{bmatrix} \alpha_x & & \\ & \alpha_y & \\ & & 1 \end{bmatrix} \begin{bmatrix} 1 & 0 & 0 & 0 \\ 0 & 1 & 0 & 0 \\ 0 & 0 & 0 & 1 \end{bmatrix} \quad \mathtt{P}' = \begin{bmatrix} \alpha'_x & & \\ & \alpha'_y & \\ & & 1 \end{bmatrix} \begin{bmatrix} \mathbf{r}^{1\mathsf{T}} & t_1 \\ \mathbf{r}^{2\mathsf{T}} & t_2 \\ \mathbf{0}^\mathsf{T} & 1 \end{bmatrix}$$

where $\mathbf{r}_1$ and $\mathbf{r}_2$ are the first and second rows of the rotation matrix $\mathtt{R}$ between the views. We will assume that the aspect ratio α_y/α_x is known in both cameras, but that the relative scaling $s = \alpha'_x/\alpha_x$ is unknown. $s > 1$ for a "looming" object and $s < 1$ for one that is "receding". As has been seen, the complete rotation $\mathtt{R}$ cannot be computed from two weak perspective views, resulting in the *bas-relief* ambiguity. Nevertheless

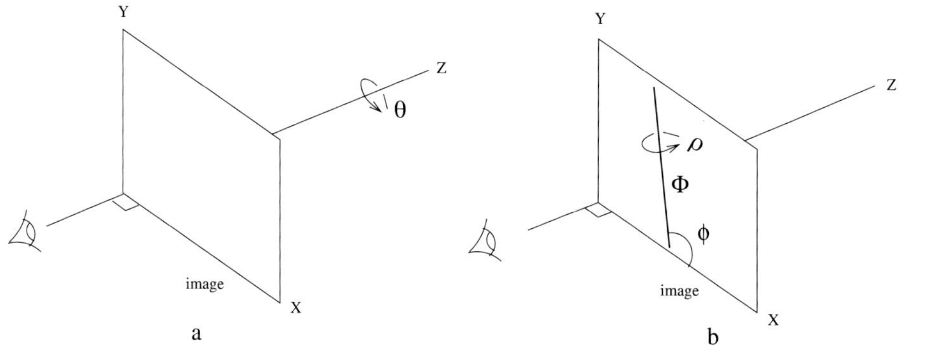

Fig. 14.10. **The rotation representation.** *(a) rotation by θ about the* Z*-axis; (b) subsequent rotation by ρ about a fronto–parallel axis $\mathbf{\Phi}$ angled at ϕ to the* X*-axis. The $\mathbf{\Phi}$-axis has components* $(\cos\phi, \sin\phi, 0)^{\mathsf{T}}$.

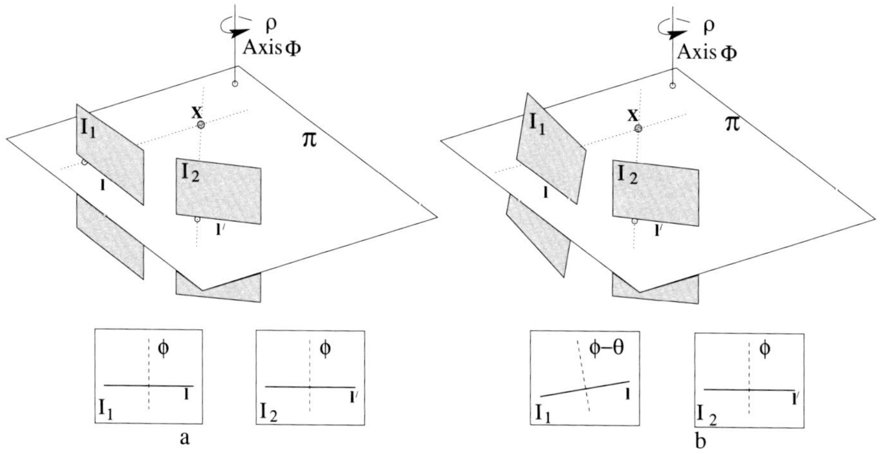

Fig. 14.11. *The camera rotates about the axis $\mathbf{\Phi}$ which is parallel to the image plane. The intersection of the epipolar plane π with the image planes gives epipolar lines* $\mathbf{l}$ *and* $\mathbf{l}'$*, and the projections of $\mathbf{\Phi}$ in the images are orthogonal to these epipolar lines: (a) no cyclotorsion occurs ($\theta = 0°$); (b) the camera counter-rotates by θ in I_1, so the orientation of the epipolar lines changes by θ.*

the remaining motion parameters can be computed from $\mathtt{F}_{\mathrm{A}}$, and their computation is straightforward.

To represent the motion we will use a rotation representation introduced by Koenderink and van Doorn [Koenderink-91]. As will be seen, this has the advantage that it isolates the parameter ρ of the bas-relief ambiguity, which cannot be computed from the affine epipolar geometry. In this representation the rotation $\mathtt{R}$ between the views is decomposed into two rotations (see figure 14.10),

$$\mathtt{R} = \mathtt{R}_\rho \, \mathtt{R}_\theta. \tag{14.9}$$

First, there is a cyclo-rotation $\mathtt{R}_\theta$ in the image plane through an angle θ (i.e. about the line of sight). This is followed by a rotation $\mathtt{R}_\rho$ through an angle ρ about an axis $\mathbf{\Phi}$ with direction parallel to the image plane, and angled at ϕ to the positive X-axis, i.e. a pure rotation *out of* the image plane.

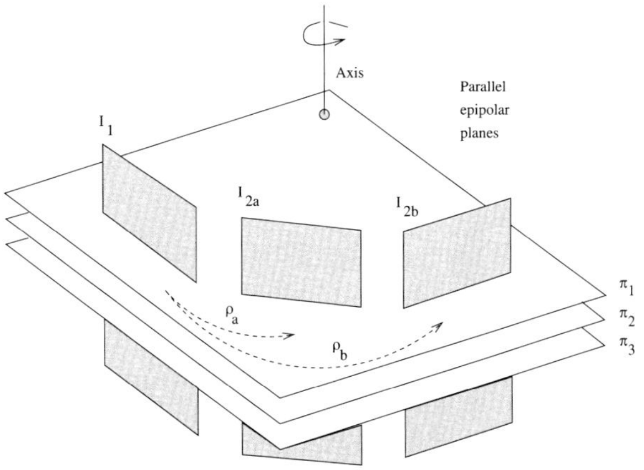

Fig. 14.12. *The scene can be sliced into parallel epipolar planes. The magnitude of ρ has no effect on the epipolar geometry (provided $\rho \neq 0$), so it is indeterminate from two views.*

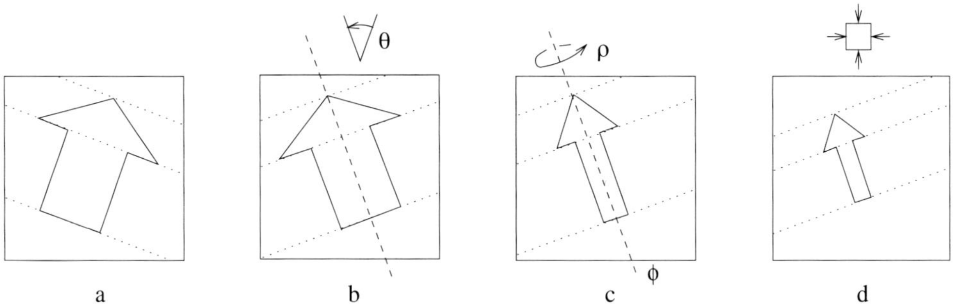

Fig. 14.13. *The effect of scale and rotation angles on the epipolar lines for an object moving relative to a stationary camera. This also illustrates the assumed sequence of events accounting for the transition from I_1 to I_2: (a) I_1; (b) cyclotorsion (θ); (c) rotation out of the plane (ϕ and ρ); (d) scaling, giving I_2.*

Solving for s, ϕ and θ. It is now shown that the scale factor (s), the projection of the axis of rotation (ϕ) and the cyclo-rotation angle (θ) may be computed directly from the affine epipolar geometry. The solution is preceded by a geometric explanation of how the epipolar lines relate to the unknown motion parameters.

Consider a camera rotating about an axis $\mathbf{\Phi}$ lying parallel to the image plane (figure 14.11(a)). The epipolar plane $\boldsymbol{\pi}$ is perpendicular to both this axis and the two images, and intersects the images in the epipolar lines $\mathbf{l}$ and $\mathbf{l}'$. Consequently:

- *The projection of the axis of rotation $\mathbf{\Phi}$ is perpendicular to the epipolar lines.*

This relation still holds if there is additionally a cyclotorsion θ in the image plane (figure 14.11(b)); the axis $\mathbf{\Phi}$ and intersection $\mathbf{l}'$ remain fixed in space, and are simply observed at a new angle in the image, maintaining the orthogonality between the epipolar lines and the projected axis. The orientations of the epipolar lines in the two images therefore differ by θ. Importantly, changing the magnitude of the turn angle ρ doesn't alter the epipolar geometry in any way (figure 14.12). This angle is therefore indeterminate from two views, a consequence of the bas-relief ambiguity.

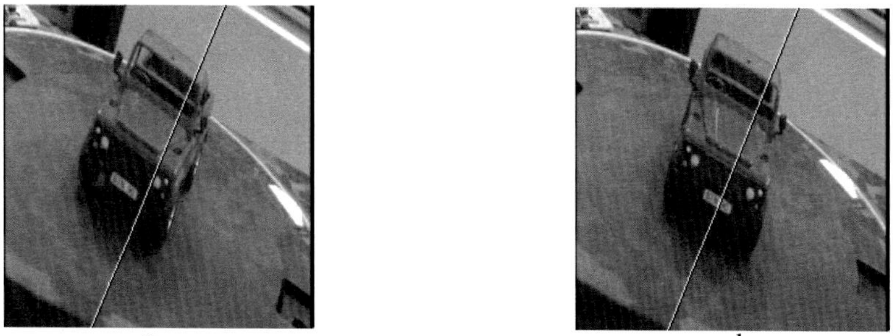

a b

Fig. 14.14. **Computing motion from affine epipolar geometry.** *(a)(b) Two views of a buggy rotating on a turntable. The computed rotation axis is superimposed on the image, drawn to pass through the image centre. The ground truth axis is, of course, perpendicular to the turntable in the world.*

Figure 14.13 illustrates the effect of scale. Consider a 3D object to be sliced into parallel epipolar planes, with each plane constraining how a particular slice of the object moves. Altering the effective size of the object (e.g. by moving closer to it) simply changes the relative spacing between successive epipolar planes.

In summary, cyclotorsion simply rotates the epipolar lines, rotation out of the plane causes foreshortening along the epipolar lines (orthogonal to $\mathbf{\Phi}$), and a scale change uniformly alters the epipolar line spacing (figure 14.13).

It can be shown (and is left as exercise) that s, θ and ϕ can be computed directly from the affine epipolar geometry as

$$\tan\phi = \frac{b}{a}, \quad \tan(\phi - \theta) = \frac{d}{c} \text{ and } s^2 = \frac{c^2 + d^2}{a^2 + b^2}, \tag{14.10}$$

with $s > 0$ (by definition). Note that ϕ is the angle of projection in I_2 of the axis of rotation out of the plane, while $(\phi - \theta)$ is its angle of projection in I_1.

Example 14.3. Motion computed from the affine fundamental matrix
figure 14.14 shows two images of a buggy rotating on a turntable. The image is 256×256 pixels with an aspect ratio of 0.65. The affine fundamental matrix is computed using algorithm 14.1, and the motion parameters computed from F_A using (14.10) above. The computed rotation axis is superimposed on the image. △

14.8 Closure

14.8.1 The literature

Koenderink and van Doorn [Koenderink-91] set the scene for affine reconstruction from two affine cameras. This paper should be read by all. The affine fundamental matrix was first defined in [Zisserman-92]. The computation of the motion parameters from F_A is described in Shapiro *et al.* [Shapiro-95], and in particular the cases where a third view does not resolve the bas–relief ambiguity. A helpful eigenvector analysis of the ambiguity is given in [Szeliski-96]. The three view affine motion case is treated quite elegantly in [Shimshoni-99].

14.8.2 Notes and exercises

(i) A scene plane induces an *affine* transformation between two affine cameras. There is a three-parameter family of such affinities defined by the three-parameter family of planes in $\mathbb{R}^3$. Given $\mathtt{F}_A$, this family of affinities may be written as (result 13.3(*p*328)) $\mathtt{H}_A = [\mathbf{e}']_\times \mathtt{F}_A + \mathbf{e}'\mathbf{v}^\mathsf{T}$, where $\mathtt{F}_A{}^\mathsf{T}\mathbf{e}' = \mathbf{0}$, and the 3-vector $\mathbf{v}$ parametrizes the family of planes. Conversely, show that given $\mathtt{H}_A$, the homography induced by a scene plane, then $\mathtt{F}_A$ is determined up to a one-parameter ambiguity.

(ii) Consider a perspective camera, i.e. the matrix does not have the affine form. Show that if the camera motion consists of a translation parallel to the image plane, and a rotation about the principal axis, then $\mathtt{F}$ has the affine form. This shows that a fundamental matrix with affine form does *not* imply that the imaging conditions are affine. Are there other camera motions which generate a fundamental matrix with the affine form?

(iii) Two affine cameras, $\mathtt{P}_A, \mathtt{P}'_A$, uniquely define an affine fundamental matrix $\mathtt{F}_A$ by (9.1–*p*244). Show that if the cameras are transformed on the right by a common affine transformation, i.e. $\mathtt{P}_A \mapsto \mathtt{P}_A\mathtt{H}_A, \mathtt{P}'_A \mapsto \mathtt{P}'_A\mathtt{H}_A$, the transformed cameras define the original $\mathtt{F}_A$. This shows that the affine fundamental matrix is invariant to an affine transformation of the world coordinates.

(iv) Suppose one of the cameras is affine and the other is a perspective camera. Show that in general in this case the epipoles in both views are finite.

(v) The 4×4 permutation homography

$$\mathtt{H} = \begin{bmatrix} 1 & 0 & 0 & 0 \\ 0 & 1 & 0 & 0 \\ 0 & 0 & 0 & 1 \\ 0 & 0 & 1 & 0 \end{bmatrix}$$

maps the canonical matrix of a finite projective camera $\mathtt{P} = [\mathtt{I} \mid \mathbf{0}]$ into the canonical matrix of parallel projection $\mathtt{P}_A$:

$$\mathtt{P}_A = [\mathtt{I} \mid \mathbf{0}]\,\mathtt{H} = \begin{bmatrix} 1 & 0 & 0 & 0 \\ 0 & 1 & 0 & 0 \\ 0 & 0 & 0 & 1 \end{bmatrix}.$$

Show, by applying this transformation to a pair of finite projective camera matrices, that the results of this chapter (such as the properties listed in table 14.1-(*p*348)) can be generated directly from their non-affine counterparts of the previous chapters. In particular derive an expression for a pair of affine cameras $\mathtt{P}_A, \mathtt{P}'_A$ consistent with $\mathtt{F}_A$.

Part III

Three-View Geometry

Lord Shiva, c. 1920-40 (print).

Shiva is depicted as having three eyes. The third eye in the centre of the forehead symbolizes spiritual knowledge and power.

Image courtesy of `http://www.healthyplanetonline.com`

Outline

This part contains two chapters on the geometry of three-views. The scene is imaged with three cameras perhaps simultaneously in a trinocular rig, or sequentially from a moving camera.

Chapter 15 introduces a new multiple view object – the trifocal tensor. This has analogous properties to the fundamental matrix of two-view geometry: it is independent of scene structure depending only on the (projective) relations between the cameras. The camera matrices may be retrieved from the trifocal tensor up to a common projective transformation of 3-space, and the fundamental matrices for view-pairs may be retrieved uniquely.

The new geometry compared with the two-view case is the ability to *transfer* from two views to a third: given a point correspondence over two views the position of the point in the third view is determined; and similarly, given a *line* correspondence over two views the position of the line in the third view is determined. This transfer property is of great benefit when establishing correspondences over multiple views.

If the essence of the epipolar constraint over two views is that rays back-projected from corresponding points are coplanar, then the essence of the trifocal constraint over three views is the geometry of a point–line–line correspondence arising from the image of a point on a line in 3-space: corresponding image lines in two views back-project to planes which intersect in a line in 3-space, and the ray back-projected from a corresponding image point in a third view must intersect this line.

Chapter 16 describes the computation of the trifocal tensor from point and *line* correspondences over three-views. Given the tensor, and thus the retrieved camera matrices, a projective reconstruction may be computed from correspondences over multiple views. The reconstruction may be upgraded to similarity or metric as additional information is provided in the same manner as in the two view case.

It is in reconstruction that there is another gain over two-view geometry. Given the cameras, in the two-view case each point correspondence provided four measurements on the three degrees of freedom (the position) of the point in 3-space. In three views there are six measurements on, again, three degrees of freedom. However, it is for lines that there is the more significant gain. In two-views the number of measurements equals the number of degrees of freedom of the line in 3-space, namely four. Consequently, there is no possibility of removing the effects of measurement errors. However, in three views there are six measurements on four degrees of freedom, so a scene line is over-determined and can be estimated by a suitable minimization over measurement errors.

15

The Trifocal Tensor

The trifocal tensor plays an analogous role in three views to that played by the fundamental matrix in two. It encapsulates all the (projective) geometric relations between three views that are independent of scene structure.

We begin this chapter with a simple introduction to the main geometric and algebraic properties of the trifocal tensor. A formal development of the trifocal tensor and its properties involves the use of tensor notation. To start, however, it is convenient to use standard vector and matrix notation, thus obtaining some geometric insight into the trifocal tensor without the additional burden of dealing with a (possibly) unfamiliar notation. The use of tensor notation will therefore be deferred until section 15.2.

The three principal geometric properties of the tensor are introduced in section 15.1. These are the homography between two of the views induced by a plane back-projected from a line in the other view; the relations between image correspondences for points and lines which arise from incidence relations in 3-space; and the retrieval of the fundamental and camera matrices from the tensor.

The tensor may be used to transfer points from a correspondence in two views to the corresponding point in a third view. The tensor also applies to lines, and the image of a line in one view may be computed from its corresponding images in two other views. Transfer is described in section 15.3.

The tensor only depends on the motion between views and the internal parameters of the cameras and is defined uniquely by the camera matrices of the views. However, it can be computed from image correspondences alone without requiring knowledge of the motion or calibration. This computation is described in chapter 16.

15.1 The geometric basis for the trifocal tensor

There are several ways that the trifocal tensor may be approached, but in this section the starting point is taken to be the incidence relationship of three corresponding lines.

Incidence relations for lines. Suppose a line in 3-space is imaged in three views, as in figure 15.1, what constraints are there on the corresponding image lines? The planes back-projected from the lines in each view must all meet in a single line in space, the 3D line that projects to the matched lines in the three images. Since in general three arbitrary planes in space do not meet in a single line, this geometric *incidence* condition

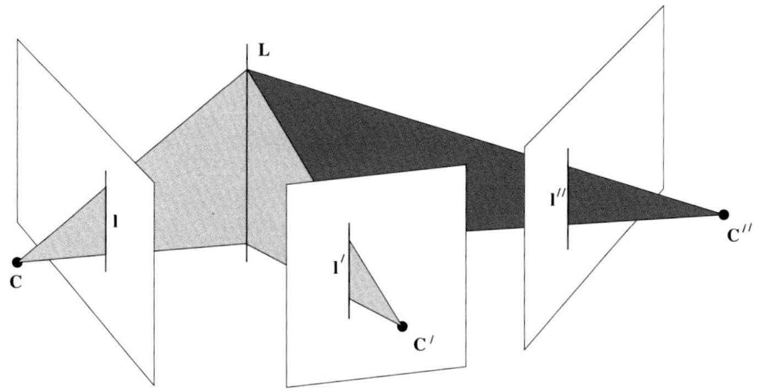

Fig. 15.1. *A line* $\mathbf{L}$ *in 3-space is imaged as the corresponding triplet* $\mathbf{l} \leftrightarrow \mathbf{l}' \leftrightarrow \mathbf{l}''$ *in three views indicated by their centres,* $\mathbf{C}, \mathbf{C}', \mathbf{C}''$*, and image planes. Conversely, corresponding lines back-projected from the first, second and third images all intersect in a single 3D line in space.*

provides a genuine constraint on sets of corresponding lines. We will now translate this geometric constraint into an algebraic constraint on the three lines.

We denote a set of corresponding lines as $\mathbf{l}_i \leftrightarrow \mathbf{l}'_i \leftrightarrow \mathbf{l}''_i$. Let the camera matrices for the three views be $\mathtt{P} = [\mathtt{I} \mid \mathbf{0}]$, as usual, and $\mathtt{P}' = [\mathtt{A} \mid \mathbf{a}_4]$, $\mathtt{P}'' = [\mathtt{B} \mid \mathbf{b}_4]$, where $\mathtt{A}$ and $\mathtt{B}$ are 3×3 matrices, and the vectors $\mathbf{a}_i$ and $\mathbf{b}_i$ are the i-th columns of the respective camera matrices for $i = 1, \ldots, 4$.

- $\mathbf{a}_4$ and $\mathbf{b}_4$ are the epipoles in views two and three respectively, arising from the first camera. These epipoles will be denoted by $\mathbf{e}'$ and $\mathbf{e}''$ throughout this chapter, with $\mathbf{e}' = \mathtt{P}'\mathbf{C}$, $\mathbf{e}'' = \mathtt{P}''\mathbf{C}$, where $\mathbf{C}$ is the first camera centre. (For the most part we will not be concerned with the epipoles between the second and third views).
- $\mathtt{A}$ and $\mathtt{B}$ are the infinite homographies from the first to the second and third cameras respectively.

As has been seen in chapter 9, any set of three cameras is equivalent to a set with $\mathtt{P} = [\mathtt{I} \mid \mathbf{0}]$ under projective transformations of space. In this chapter we will be concerned with properties (such as image coordinates and 3D incidence relations) that are invariant under 3D projective transforms, so we are free to choose the cameras in this form.

Now, each image line back-projects to a plane, as shown in figure 15.1. From result 8.2(*p*197) these three planes are

$$\boldsymbol{\pi} = \mathtt{P}^{\mathsf{T}}\mathbf{l} = \begin{pmatrix} \mathbf{l} \\ 0 \end{pmatrix} \quad \boldsymbol{\pi}' = \mathtt{P}'^{\mathsf{T}}\mathbf{l}' = \begin{pmatrix} \mathtt{A}^{\mathsf{T}}\mathbf{l}' \\ \mathbf{a}_4^{\mathsf{T}}\mathbf{l}' \end{pmatrix} \quad \boldsymbol{\pi}'' = \mathtt{P}''^{\mathsf{T}}\mathbf{l}'' = \begin{pmatrix} \mathtt{B}^{\mathsf{T}}\mathbf{l}'' \\ \mathbf{b}_4^{\mathsf{T}}\mathbf{l}'' \end{pmatrix}.$$

Since the three image lines are derived from a single line in space, it follows that these three planes are not independent but must meet in this common line in 3-space. This intersection constraint can be expressed algebraically by the requirement that the 4×3 matrix $\mathtt{M} = [\boldsymbol{\pi}, \boldsymbol{\pi}', \boldsymbol{\pi}'']$ has rank 2. This may be seen as follows. Points on the line of intersection may be represented as $\mathbf{X} = \alpha\mathbf{X}_1 + \beta\mathbf{X}_2$, with $\mathbf{X}_1$ and $\mathbf{X}_2$ linearly independent. Such points lie on all three planes and so $\boldsymbol{\pi}^{\mathsf{T}}\mathbf{X} = \boldsymbol{\pi}'^{\mathsf{T}}\mathbf{X} = \boldsymbol{\pi}''^{\mathsf{T}}\mathbf{X} = 0$. It follows that $\mathtt{M}^\mathsf{T}\mathbf{X} = \mathbf{0}$. Consequently $\mathtt{M}$ has a 2-dimensional null-space since $\mathtt{M}^\mathsf{T}\mathbf{X}_1 = \mathbf{0}$ and $\mathtt{M}^\mathsf{T}\mathbf{X}_2 = \mathbf{0}$.

This intersection constraint induces a relation amongst the image lines $\mathbf{l}, \mathbf{l}', \mathbf{l}''$. Since the rank of $\mathtt{M}$ is 2, there is a linear dependence between its columns $\mathbf{m}_i$. Denoting

$$\mathtt{M} = [\mathbf{m}_1, \mathbf{m}_2, \mathbf{m}_3] = \begin{bmatrix} 1 & \mathtt{A}^\mathsf{T}\mathbf{l}' & \mathtt{B}^\mathsf{T}\mathbf{l}'' \\ 0 & \mathbf{a}_4^\mathsf{T}\mathbf{l}' & \mathbf{b}_4^\mathsf{T}\mathbf{l}'' \end{bmatrix}$$

the linear relation may be written $\mathbf{m}_1 = \alpha\mathbf{m}_2 + \beta\mathbf{m}_3$. Then noting that the bottom left hand element of $\mathtt{M}$ is zero, it follows that $\alpha = k(\mathbf{b}_4^\mathsf{T}\mathbf{l}'')$ and $\beta = -k(\mathbf{a}_4^\mathsf{T}\mathbf{l}')$ for some scalar k. Applying this to the top 3-vectors of each column shows that (up to a homogeneous scale factor)

$$\mathbf{l} = (\mathbf{b}_4^\mathsf{T}\mathbf{l}'')\mathtt{A}^\mathsf{T}\mathbf{l}' - (\mathbf{a}_4^\mathsf{T}\mathbf{l}')\mathtt{B}^\mathsf{T}\mathbf{l}'' = (\mathbf{l}''^\mathsf{T}\mathbf{b}_4)\mathtt{A}^\mathsf{T}\mathbf{l}' - (\mathbf{l}'^\mathsf{T}\mathbf{a}_4)\mathtt{B}^\mathsf{T}\mathbf{l}''.$$

The i-th coordinate l_i of $\mathbf{l}$ may therefore be written as

$$l_i = \mathbf{l}''^\mathsf{T}(\mathbf{b}_4\mathbf{a}_i^\mathsf{T})\mathbf{l}' - \mathbf{l}'^\mathsf{T}(\mathbf{a}_4\mathbf{b}_i^\mathsf{T})\mathbf{l}'' = \mathbf{l}'^\mathsf{T}(\mathbf{a}_i\mathbf{b}_4^\mathsf{T})\mathbf{l}'' - \mathbf{l}'^\mathsf{T}(\mathbf{a}_4\mathbf{b}_i^\mathsf{T})\mathbf{l}''$$

and introducing the notation

$$\mathtt{T}_i = \mathbf{a}_i\mathbf{b}_4^\mathsf{T} - \mathbf{a}_4\mathbf{b}_i^\mathsf{T} \tag{15.1}$$

the incidence relation can be written

$$l_i = \mathbf{l}'^\mathsf{T}\mathtt{T}_i\mathbf{l}''. \tag{15.2}$$

Definition 15.1. The set of three matrices $\{\mathtt{T}_1, \mathtt{T}_2, \mathtt{T}_3\}$ constitute the *trifocal tensor* in matrix notation.

We introduce a further notation[1]. Denoting the ensemble of the three matrices $\mathtt{T}_i$ by $[\mathtt{T}_1, \mathtt{T}_2, \mathtt{T}_3]$, or more briefly $[\mathtt{T}_i]$, this last relation may be written as

$$\mathbf{l}^\mathsf{T} = \mathbf{l}'^\mathsf{T}[\mathtt{T}_1, \mathtt{T}_2, \mathtt{T}_3]\mathbf{l}'' \tag{15.3}$$

where $\mathbf{l}'^\mathsf{T}[\mathtt{T}_1, \mathtt{T}_2, \mathtt{T}_3]\mathbf{l}''$ is understood to represent the vector $(\mathbf{l}'^\mathsf{T}\mathtt{T}_1\mathbf{l}'', \mathbf{l}'^\mathsf{T}\mathtt{T}_2\mathbf{l}'', \mathbf{l}'^\mathsf{T}\mathtt{T}_3\mathbf{l}'')$.

Of course there is no intrinsic difference between the three views, and so by analogy with (15.3) there will exist similar relations $\mathbf{l}'^\mathsf{T} = \mathbf{l}^\mathsf{T}[\mathtt{T}'_i]\mathbf{l}''$ and $\mathbf{l}''^\mathsf{T} = \mathbf{l}^\mathsf{T}[\mathtt{T}''_i]\mathbf{l}'$. The three tensors $[\mathtt{T}_i]$, $[\mathtt{T}'_i]$ and $[\mathtt{T}''_i]$ exist, but are distinct. In fact, although all three tensors may be computed from any one of them, there is no very simple relationship between them. Thus, in fact there are three trifocal tensors existing for a given triple of views. Usually one will be content to consider only one of them. However, a method of computing the other trifocal tensors $[\mathtt{T}'_i]$ and $[\mathtt{T}''_i]$ given $[\mathtt{T}_i]$ is outlined in exercise (viii) on page 389.

Note that (15.3) is a relationship between image coordinates only, not involving 3D coordinates. Hence (as remarked previously), although it was derived under the assumption of a canonical camera set (that is $\mathtt{P} = [\mathtt{I} \mid \mathbf{0}]$), the value of the matrix elements $[\mathtt{T}_i]$ is independent of the form of the cameras. The particular simple formula (15.1) for the trifocal tensor given the camera matrices holds only in the case where

[1] This notation is somewhat cumbersome, and its meaning is not quite self-evident. It is for this reason that tensor notation is introduced in section 15.2.

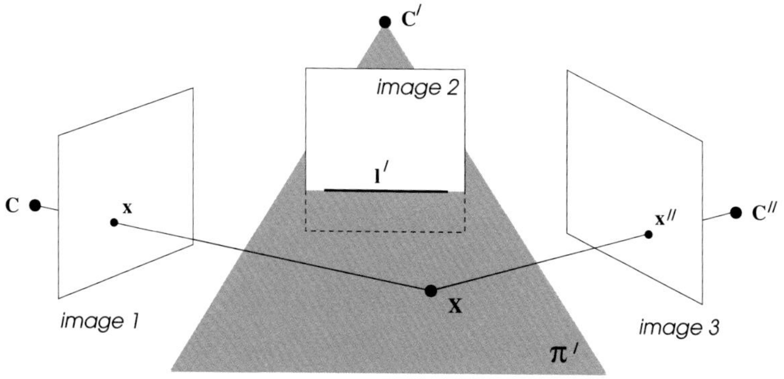

Fig. 15.2. **Point transfer.** *A line $\mathbf{l}'$ in the second view back-projects to a plane $\boldsymbol{\pi}'$ in 3-space. A point $\mathbf{x}$ in the first image defines a ray in 3-space which intersects $\boldsymbol{\pi}'$ in the point $\mathbf{X}$. This point $\mathbf{X}$ is then imaged as the point $\mathbf{x}''$ in the third view. Thus, any line $\mathbf{l}'$ induces a homography between the first and third views, defined by its back-projected plane $\boldsymbol{\pi}'$.*

$\mathtt{P} = [\mathtt{I} \mid \mathbf{0}]$, but a general formula (17.12–*p*415) for the trifocal tensor corresponding to any three cameras will be derived later.

Degrees of freedom. The trifocal tensor consists of three 3×3 matrices, and thus has 27 elements. There are therefore 26 independent ratios apart from the (common) overall scaling of the matrices. However, the tensor has only 18 independent degrees of freedom. In other words once 18 parameters are specified, all 27 elements of the tensor are determined up to a common scale. The number of degrees of freedom may be computed as follows. Each of 3 camera matrices has 11 degrees of freedom, which makes 33 in total. However, 15 degrees of freedom must be subtracted to account for the projective world frame, thus leaving 18 degrees of freedom. The tensor therefore satisfies $26 - 18 = 8$ independent algebraic constraints. We return to this point in chapter 16.

15.1.1 Homographies induced by a plane

A fundamental geometric property encoded in the trifocal tensor is the homography between the first view and the third induced by a line in the second image. This is illustrated in figure 15.2 and figure 15.3. A line in the second view defines (by back-projection) a plane in 3-space, and this plane induces a homography between the first and third views.

We now derive the algebraic representation of this geometry in terms of the trifocal tensor. The homography map between the first and third images, defined by the plane $\boldsymbol{\pi}'$ in figure 15.2 and figure 15.3, may be written as $\mathbf{x}'' = \mathtt{H}\mathbf{x}$ and (2.6–*p*36) $\mathbf{l} = \mathtt{H}^{\mathsf{T}}\mathbf{l}''$ respectively. Notice that the three lines $\mathbf{l}$, $\mathbf{l}'$ and $\mathbf{l}''$ in figure 15.3 are a corresponding line triple, the projections of the 3D line $\mathbf{L}$. Therefore, they satisfy the line incidence relationship $l_i = \mathbf{l}'^{\mathsf{T}}\mathtt{T}_i\mathbf{l}''$ of (15.2). Comparison of this formula and $\mathbf{l} = \mathtt{H}^{\mathsf{T}}\mathbf{l}''$ shows that

$$\mathtt{H} = [\mathbf{h}_1, \mathbf{h}_2, \mathbf{h}_3] \text{ with } \mathbf{h}_i = \mathtt{T}_i^{\mathsf{T}}\mathbf{l}'.$$

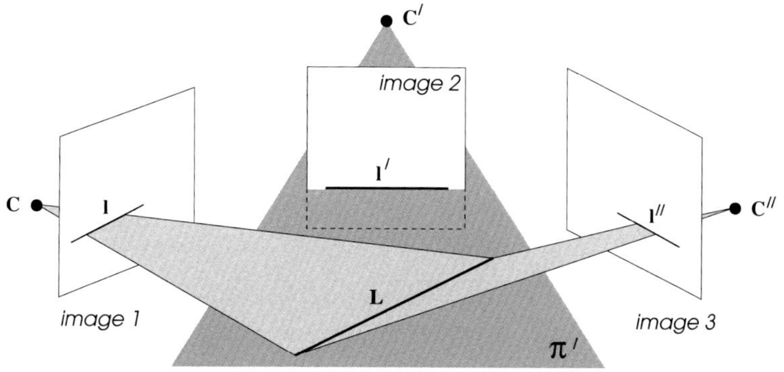

Fig. 15.3. **Line transfer.** *The action on lines of the homography defined by figure 15.2 may similarly be visualized geometrically. A line, $\mathbf{l}$, in the first image defines a plane in 3-space, which intersects π' in the line $\mathbf{L}$. This line $\mathbf{L}$ is then imaged as the line $\mathbf{l}''$ in the third view.*

Thus, $\mathtt{H}$ defined by the above formula represents the (point) homography $\mathtt{H}_{13}$ between views one and three specified by the line $\mathbf{l}'$ in view two.

The second and third views play similar roles, and the homography between the first and second views defined by a line in the third can be derived in a similar manner. These ideas are formalized in the following result.

Result 15.2. *The homography from the first to the third image induced by a line $\mathbf{l}'$ in the second image (see figure 15.2) is given by $\mathbf{x}'' = \mathtt{H}_{13}(\mathbf{l}')\,\mathbf{x}$, where*

$$\mathtt{H}_{13}(\mathbf{l}') = [\mathtt{T}_1^{\mathsf{T}}, \mathtt{T}_2^{\mathsf{T}}, \mathtt{T}_3^{\mathsf{T}}]\mathbf{l}'.$$

Similarly, a line $\mathbf{l}''$ in the third image defines a homography $\mathbf{x}' = \mathtt{H}_{12}(\mathbf{l}'')\,\mathbf{x}$ from the first to the second views, given by

$$\mathtt{H}_{12}(\mathbf{l}'') = [\mathtt{T}_1, \mathtt{T}_2, \mathtt{T}_3]\mathbf{l}''.$$

Once this mapping is understood the algebraic properties of the tensor are straightforward and can easily be generated. In the following section we deduce a number of incidence relations between points and lines based on (15.3) and result 15.2.

15.1.2 Point and line incidence relations

It is easy to deduce various linear relationships between lines and points in three images involving the trifocal tensor. We have seen one such relationship already, namely (15.3). This relation holds only up to scale since it involves homogeneous quantities. We may eliminate the scale factor by taking the vector cross product of both sides, which must be zero. This leads to the formula

$$(\mathbf{l}'^{\mathsf{T}}[\mathtt{T}_1, \mathtt{T}_2, \mathtt{T}_3]\mathbf{l}'')[\mathbf{l}]_\times = \mathbf{0}^{\mathsf{T}}, \tag{15.4}$$

where we have used the matrix $[\mathbf{l}]_\times$ to denote the cross product (see (A4.5–*p*581)), or more briefly $(\mathbf{l}'^{\mathsf{T}}[\mathtt{T}_i]\mathbf{l}'')[\mathbf{l}]_\times = \mathbf{0}^{\mathsf{T}}$. Note the symmetry between $\mathbf{l}'$ and $\mathbf{l}''$ – swapping the roles of these two lines is accounted for by transposing each $\mathtt{T}_i$, resulting in a relation $(\mathbf{l}''^{\mathsf{T}}[\mathtt{T}_i^{\mathsf{T}}]\mathbf{l}')[\mathbf{l}]_\times = \mathbf{0}^{\mathsf{T}}$.

Consider again figure 15.3. Now, a point $\mathbf{x}$ on the line $\mathbf{l}$ must satisfy $\mathbf{x}^{\mathsf{T}}\mathbf{l} = \sum_i x^i l_i = 0$ (using upper indices for the point coordinates, foreshadowing the use of tensor notation). Since $l_i = \mathbf{l}'^{\mathsf{T}}\mathtt{T}_i\mathbf{l}''$, this may be written as

$$\mathbf{l}'^{\mathsf{T}}(\sum_i x^i \mathtt{T}_i)\mathbf{l}'' = 0 \tag{15.5}$$

(note that $(\sum_i x^i \mathtt{T}_i)$ is simply a 3×3 matrix). This is an incidence relation in the first image: the relationship will hold for a point–line–line correspondence – that is whenever some 3D line $\mathbf{L}$ maps to $\mathbf{l}'$ and $\mathbf{l}''$ in the second and third images, and to a line passing through $\mathbf{x}$ in the first image. An important equivalent definition of a point–line–line correspondence for which (15.5) holds results from *an incidence relation in 3-space* – there exists a 3D point $\mathbf{X}$ mapping to $\mathbf{x}$ in the first image, and to points on the lines $\mathbf{l}'$ and $\mathbf{l}''$ in the second and third images as shown in figure 15.4(a).

From result 15.2 we may obtain relations involving points $\mathbf{x}'$ and $\mathbf{x}''$ in the second and third images. Consider a point–line–point correspondence as in figure 15.4(b) so that

$$\mathbf{x}'' = \mathtt{H}_{13}(\mathbf{l}')\,\mathbf{x} = [\mathtt{T}_1^{\mathsf{T}}\mathbf{l}', \mathtt{T}_2^{\mathsf{T}}\mathbf{l}', \mathtt{T}_3^{\mathsf{T}}\mathbf{l}']\,\mathbf{x} = (\sum_i x^i \mathtt{T}_i^{\mathsf{T}})\mathbf{l}'$$

which is valid for any line $\mathbf{l}'$ passing through $\mathbf{x}'$ in the second image. The homogeneous scale factor may be eliminated by (post-)multiplying the transpose of both sides by $[\mathbf{x}'']_\times$ to give

$$\mathbf{x}''^{\mathsf{T}}[\mathbf{x}'']_\times = \mathbf{l}'^{\mathsf{T}}(\sum_i x^i \mathtt{T}_i)[\mathbf{x}'']_\times = \mathbf{0}^{\mathsf{T}}, \tag{15.6}$$

A similar analysis may be undertaken with the roles of the second and third images swapped.

Finally, for a 3-point correspondence as shown in figure 15.4(c), there is a relation

$$[\mathbf{x}']_\times(\sum_i x^i \mathtt{T}_i)[\mathbf{x}'']_\times = \mathtt{0}_{3\times 3}. \tag{15.7}$$

Proof. The line $\mathbf{l}'$ in (15.6) passes through $\mathbf{x}'$ and so may be written as $\mathbf{l}' = \mathbf{x}' \times \mathbf{y}' = [\mathbf{x}']_\times \mathbf{y}'$ for some point $\mathbf{y}'$ on $\mathbf{l}'$. Consequently, from (15.6) $\mathbf{l}'^{\mathsf{T}}(\sum_i x^i \mathtt{T}_i)[\mathbf{x}'']_\times = \mathbf{y}'^{\mathsf{T}}[\mathbf{x}']_\times(\sum_i x^i \mathtt{T}_i)[\mathbf{x}'']_\times = \mathbf{0}^{\mathsf{T}}$. However, the relation (15.6) is true for *all* lines $\mathbf{l}'$ through $\mathbf{x}'$ and so is independent of $\mathbf{y}'$. The relation (15.7) then follows. □

The various relationships between lines and points in three views are summarized in table 15.1, and their properties are investigated further in section 15.2.1, once tensor notation has been introduced. Note that there are no relations listed for point–line–line correspondence in which the point is in the second or third view. Such simple relations do not exist in terms of the trifocal tensor in which the first view is the special view.

It is also worth noting that satisfying an image incidence relation does not guarantee incidence in 3-space, as illustrated in figure 15.5.

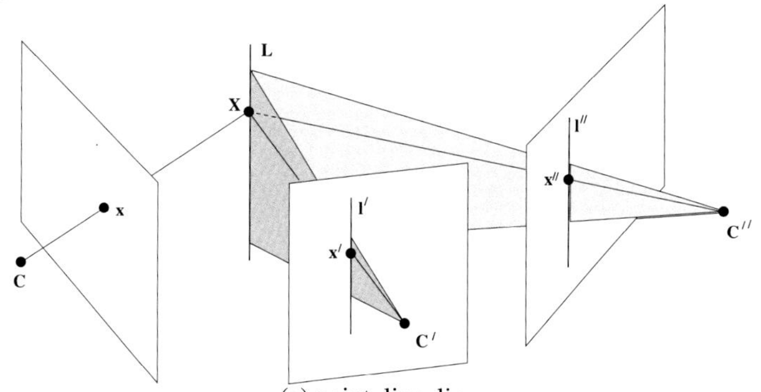

(a) point–line–line

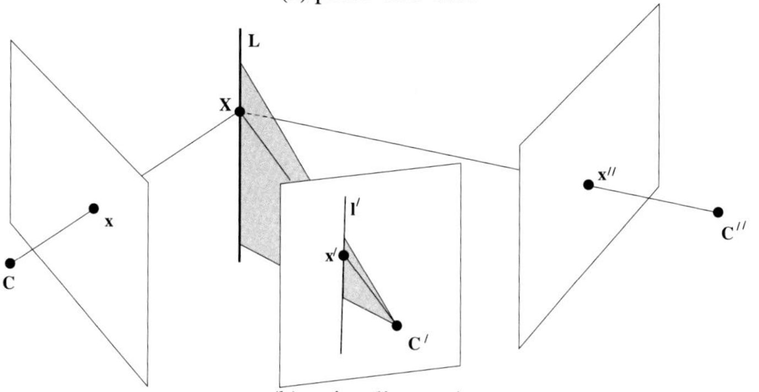

(b) point–line–point

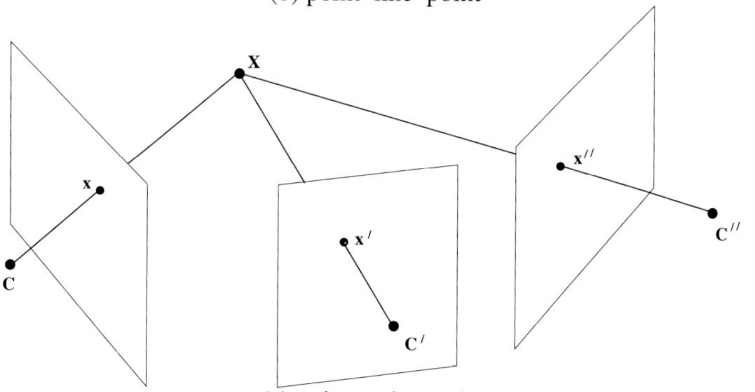

(c) point–point–point

Fig. 15.4. **Incidence relations.** *(a) Consider a 3-view point correspondence* $\mathbf{x} \leftrightarrow \mathbf{x}' \leftrightarrow \mathbf{x}''$. *If* $\mathbf{l}'$ *and* $\mathbf{l}''$ *are* **any** *two lines through* $\mathbf{x}'$ *and* $\mathbf{x}''$ *respectively, then* $\mathbf{x} \leftrightarrow \mathbf{l}' \leftrightarrow \mathbf{l}''$ *forms a point–line–line correspondence, corresponding to a 3D line* $\mathbf{L}$. *Consequently, (15.5) holds for any choice of lines* $\mathbf{l}'$ *through* $\mathbf{x}'$ *and* $\mathbf{l}''$ *through* $\mathbf{x}''$. *(b) The space point* $\mathbf{X}$ *is incident with the space line* $\mathbf{L}$. *This defines an incidence relation* $\mathbf{x} \leftrightarrow \mathbf{l}' \leftrightarrow \mathbf{x}''$ *between their images. (c) The correspondence* $\mathbf{x} \leftrightarrow \mathbf{x}' \leftrightarrow \mathbf{x}''$ *arising from the image of a space point* $\mathbf{X}$.

We now begin to extract the two-view geometry, the epipoles and fundamental matrix, from the trifocal tensor.

15.1.3 Epipolar lines

A special case of a point–line–line correspondence occurs when the plane π' back-projected from $\mathbf{l}'$ is an epipolar plane with respect to the first two cameras, and hence

(i) Line–line–line correspondence

$$\mathbf{l}'^{\mathsf{T}}[\mathtt{T}_1, \mathtt{T}_2, \mathtt{T}_3]\mathbf{l}'' = \mathbf{l}^{\mathsf{T}} \quad \text{or} \quad \left(\mathbf{l}'^{\mathsf{T}}[\mathtt{T}_1, \mathtt{T}_2, \mathtt{T}_3]\mathbf{l}''\right)[\mathbf{l}]_\times = \mathbf{0}^{\mathsf{T}}$$

(ii) Point–line–line correspondence

$$\mathbf{l}'^{\mathsf{T}}\left(\sum_i x^i \mathtt{T}_i\right)\mathbf{l}'' = 0 \text{ for a correspondence } \mathbf{x} \leftrightarrow \mathbf{l}' \leftrightarrow \mathbf{l}''$$

(iii) Point–line–point correspondence

$$\mathbf{l}'^{\mathsf{T}}\left(\sum_i x^i \mathtt{T}_i\right)[\mathbf{x}'']_\times = \mathbf{0}^{\mathsf{T}} \text{ for a correspondence } \mathbf{x} \leftrightarrow \mathbf{l}' \leftrightarrow \mathbf{x}''$$

(iv) Point–point–line correspondence

$$[\mathbf{x}']_\times\left(\sum_i x^i \mathtt{T}_i\right)\mathbf{l}'' = \mathbf{0} \text{ for a correspondence } \mathbf{x} \leftrightarrow \mathbf{x}' \leftrightarrow \mathbf{l}''$$

(v) Point–point–point correspondence

$$[\mathbf{x}']_\times\left(\sum_i x^i \mathtt{T}_i\right)[\mathbf{x}'']_\times = 0_{3\times 3}$$

Table 15.1. *Summary of trifocal tensor incidence relations using matrix notation.*

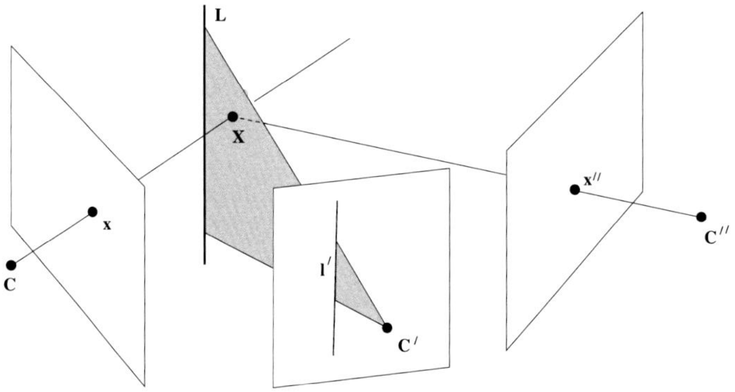

Fig. 15.5. **Non-incident configuration.** *The imaged points and lines of this configuration satisfy the point–line–point incidence relation of table 15.1. However, the space point* $\mathbf{X}$ *and line* $\mathbf{L}$ *are not incident. Compare with figure 15.4.*

passes through the camera centre $\mathbf{C}$ of the first camera. Suppose $\mathbf{X}$ is a point on the plane $\boldsymbol{\pi}'$; then the ray defined by $\mathbf{X}$ and $\mathbf{C}$ lies in this plane, and $\mathbf{l}'$ is the epipolar line corresponding to the point $\mathbf{x}$, the image of $\mathbf{X}$. This is shown in figure 15.6.

The plane $\boldsymbol{\pi}''$ back-projected from a line $\mathbf{l}''$ in the third image will intersect the plane $\boldsymbol{\pi}'$ in a line $\mathbf{L}$. Further, since the ray corresponding to $\mathbf{x}$ lies entirely in the plane $\boldsymbol{\pi}'$ it must intersect the line $\mathbf{L}$. This gives a 3-way intersection between the ray and planes back-projected from point $\mathbf{x}$ and lines $\mathbf{l}'$ and $\mathbf{l}''$, and so they constitute a point–line–line correspondence, satisfying $\mathbf{l}'^{\mathsf{T}}(\sum_i x^i \mathtt{T}_i)\mathbf{l}'' = 0$. The important point now is that this is true for *any* line $\mathbf{l}''$, and it follows that $\mathbf{l}'^{\mathsf{T}}(\sum_i x^i \mathtt{T}_i) = \mathbf{0}^{\mathsf{T}}$. The same argument holds with the roles of $\mathbf{l}'$ and $\mathbf{l}''$ reversed. To summarize:

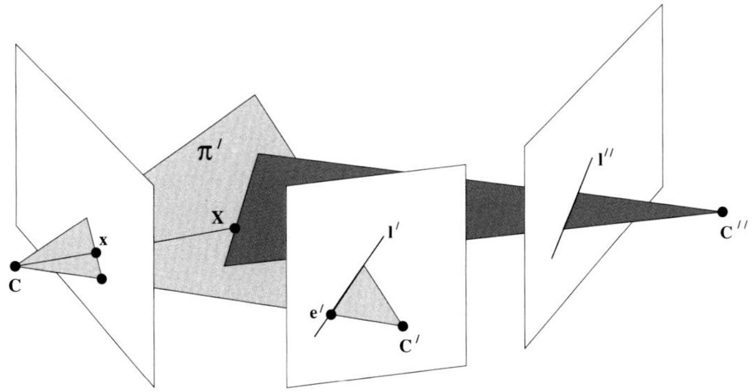

Fig. 15.6. *If the plane π' defined by $\mathbf{l}'$ is an epipolar plane for the first two views, then any line $\mathbf{l}''$ in the third view gives a point–line–line incidence.*

Result 15.3. *If $\mathbf{x}$ is a point and $\mathbf{l}'$ and $\mathbf{l}''$ are the corresponding epipolar lines in the second and third images, then*

$$\mathbf{l}'^{\mathsf{T}}(\sum_i x^i \mathtt{T}_i) = \mathbf{0}^{\mathsf{T}} \text{ and } (\sum_i x^i \mathtt{T}_i)\mathbf{l}'' = \mathbf{0}.$$

Consequently, the epipolar lines $\mathbf{l}'$ and $\mathbf{l}''$ corresponding to $\mathbf{x}$ may be computed as the left and right null-vectors of the matrix $\sum_i x^i \mathtt{T}_i$.

As the point $\mathbf{x}$ varies, the corresponding epipolar lines vary, but all epipolar lines in one image pass through the epipole. Thus, one may compute this epipole by computing the intersection of the epipolar lines for varying values of $\mathbf{x}$. Three convenient choices of $\mathbf{x}$ are the points represented by homogeneous coordinates $(1,0,0)^{\mathsf{T}}$, $(0,1,0)^{\mathsf{T}}$ and $(0,0,1)^{\mathsf{T}}$, with $\sum_i x^i \mathtt{T}_i$ equal to $\mathtt{T}_1$, $\mathtt{T}_2$ and $\mathtt{T}_3$ respectively for these three choices of $\mathbf{x}$. From this we deduce the following important result:

Result 15.4. *The epipole $\mathbf{e}'$ in the second image is the common intersection of the epipolar lines represented by the left null-vectors of the matrices $\mathtt{T}_i, i = 1, \ldots, 3$. Similarly the epipole $\mathbf{e}''$ is the common intersection of lines represented by the right null-vectors of the $\mathtt{T}_i$.*

Note that the epipoles involved here are the epipoles in the second and third images corresponding to the first image centre $\mathbf{C}$.

The usefulness of this result may not be apparent at present. However, it will be seen below that it is an important step in computing the camera matrices from the trifocal tensor, and in chapter 16 in the accurate computation of the trifocal tensor.

Algebraic properties of the $\mathtt{T}_i$ matrices. This section has established a number of algebraic properties of the $\mathtt{T}_i$ matrices. We summarize these here:

- Each matrix $\mathtt{T}_i$ has rank 2. This is evident from (15.1) since $\mathtt{T}_i = \mathbf{a}_i\mathbf{e}''^{\mathsf{T}} - \mathbf{e}'\mathbf{b}_i^{\mathsf{T}}$ is the sum of two outer products.
- The right null-vector of $\mathtt{T}_i$ is $\mathbf{l}''_i = \mathbf{e}'' \times \mathbf{b}_i$, and is the epipolar line in the third view for the point $\mathbf{x} = (1,0,0)^{\mathsf{T}}$, $(0,1,0)^{\mathsf{T}}$ or $(0,0,1)^{\mathsf{T}}$, as $i = 1, 2$ or 3 respectively.

- The epipole $\mathbf{e}''$ is the common intersection of the epipolar lines $\mathbf{l}''_i$ for $i = 1, 2, 3$.
- The left null-vector of $\mathtt{T}_i$ is $\mathbf{l}'_i = \mathbf{e}' \times \mathbf{a}_i$, and is the epipolar line in the second view for the point $\mathbf{x} = (1, 0, 0)^\mathsf{T}$, $(0, 1, 0)^\mathsf{T}$ or $(0, 0, 1)^\mathsf{T}$, as $i = 1, 2$ or 3 respectively.
- The epipole $\mathbf{e}'$ is the common intersection of the epipolar lines $\mathbf{l}'_i$ for $i = 1, 2, 3$.
- The *sum* of the matrices $\mathtt{M}(\mathbf{x}) = (\sum_i x^i \mathtt{T}_i)$ also has rank 2. The right null-vector of $\mathtt{M}(\mathbf{x})$ is the epipolar line $\mathbf{l}''$ of $\mathbf{x}$ in the third view, and its left null-vector is the epipolar line $\mathbf{l}'$ of $\mathbf{x}$ in the second view.

It's worth emphasizing again that although a particular canonical form of the camera matrices $\mathtt{P}, \mathtt{P}'$ and $\mathtt{P}''$ is used in the derivation, the epipolar properties of the $\mathtt{T}_i$ matrices are independent of this choice.

15.1.4 Extracting the fundamental matrices

It is simple to compute the fundamental matrices $\mathtt{F}_{21}$ and $\mathtt{F}_{31}$ between the first[1] and the other views from the trifocal tensor. It was seen in section 9.2.1(*p*242) that the epipolar line corresponding to some point can be derived by transferring the point to the other view via a homography and joining the transferred point to the epipole. Consider a point $\mathbf{x}$ in the first view. According to figure 15.2 and result 15.2, a line $\mathbf{l}''$ in the third view induces a homography from the first to the second view given by $\mathbf{x}' = ([\mathtt{T}_1, \mathtt{T}_2, \mathtt{T}_3]\mathbf{l}'')\,\mathbf{x}$. The epipolar line corresponding to $\mathbf{x}$ is then found by joining $\mathbf{x}'$ to the epipole $\mathbf{e}'$. This gives $\mathbf{l}' = [\mathbf{e}']_\times ([\mathtt{T}_1, \mathtt{T}_2, \mathtt{T}_3]\mathbf{l}'')\,\mathbf{x}$, from which it follows that

$$\mathtt{F}_{21} = [\mathbf{e}']_\times [\mathtt{T}_1, \mathtt{T}_2, \mathtt{T}_3]\mathbf{l}''.$$

This formula holds for any vector $\mathbf{l}''$, but it is important to choose $\mathbf{l}''$ to avoid the degenerate condition where $\mathbf{l}''$ lies in the null-space of any of the $\mathtt{T}_i$. A good choice is $\mathbf{e}''$ since as has been seen $\mathbf{e}''$ is perpendicular to the right null-space of each $\mathtt{T}_i$. This gives the formula

$$\mathtt{F}_{21} = [\mathbf{e}']_\times [\mathtt{T}_1, \mathtt{T}_2, \mathtt{T}_3]\mathbf{e}''. \tag{15.8}$$

A similar formula holds for $\mathtt{F}_{31} = [\mathbf{e}'']_\times [\mathtt{T}_1^\mathsf{T}, \mathtt{T}_2^\mathsf{T}, \mathtt{T}_3^\mathsf{T}]\mathbf{e}'$.

15.1.5 Retrieving the camera matrices

It was remarked that the trifocal tensor, since it expresses a relationship between image entities only, is independent of 3D projective transformations. Conversely, this implies that the camera matrices may be computed from the trifocal tensor only up to a projective ambiguity. It will now be shown how this may be done.

Just as in the case of reconstruction from two views, because of the projective ambiguity, the first camera may be chosen as $\mathtt{P} = [\mathtt{I} \mid \mathbf{0}]$. Now, since $\mathtt{F}_{21}$ is known (from (15.8)), we can make use of result 9.9(*p*254) to derive the form of the second camera as

$$\mathtt{P}' = [[\mathtt{T}_1, \mathtt{T}_2, \mathtt{T}_3]\mathbf{e}'' \mid \mathbf{e}']$$

and the camera pair $\{\mathtt{P}, \mathtt{P}'\}$ then has the fundamental matrix $\mathtt{F}_{21}$. It might be thought

[1] The fundamental matrix $\mathtt{F}_{21}$ satisfies $\mathbf{x}'^\mathsf{T}\mathtt{F}_{21}\mathbf{x} = 0$ for corresponding points $\mathbf{x} \leftrightarrow \mathbf{x}'$. The subscript notation refers to figure 15.8.

Given the trifocal tensor written in matrix notation as $[\mathtt{T}_1, \mathtt{T}_2, \mathtt{T}_3]$.

(i) **Retrieve the epipoles** $\mathbf{e}', \mathbf{e}''$
Let $\mathbf{u}_i$ and $\mathbf{v}_i$ be the left and right null-vectors respectively of $\mathtt{T}_i$, i.e. $\mathbf{u}_i^\mathsf{T}\mathtt{T}_i = \mathbf{0}^\mathsf{T}$, $\mathtt{T}_i\mathbf{v}_i = \mathbf{0}$. Then the epipoles are obtained as the null-vectors to the following 3×3 matrices:

$$\mathbf{e}'^\mathsf{T}[\mathbf{u}_1, \mathbf{u}_2, \mathbf{u}_3] = \mathbf{0} \text{ and } \mathbf{e}''^\mathsf{T}[\mathbf{v}_1, \mathbf{v}_2, \mathbf{v}_3] = \mathbf{0}.$$

(ii) **Retrieve the fundamental matrices** $\mathtt{F}_{21}, \mathtt{F}_{31}$

$$\mathtt{F}_{21} = [\mathbf{e}']_\times[\mathtt{T}_1, \mathtt{T}_2, \mathtt{T}_3]\mathbf{e}'' \text{ and } \mathtt{F}_{31} = [\mathbf{e}'']_\times[\mathtt{T}_1^\mathsf{T}, \mathtt{T}_2^\mathsf{T}, \mathtt{T}_3^\mathsf{T}]\mathbf{e}'.$$

(iii) **Retrieve the camera matrices** $\mathtt{P}', \mathtt{P}''$ **(with** $\mathtt{P} = [\mathtt{I} \mid \mathbf{0}]$**)**
Normalize the epipoles to unit norm. Then

$$\mathtt{P}' = [[\mathtt{T}_1, \mathtt{T}_2, \mathtt{T}_3]\mathbf{e}'' \mid \mathbf{e}'] \text{ and } \mathtt{P}'' = [(\mathbf{e}''\mathbf{e}''^\mathsf{T} - \mathtt{I})[\mathtt{T}_1^\mathsf{T}, \mathtt{T}_2^\mathsf{T}, \mathtt{T}_3^\mathsf{T}]\mathbf{e}' \mid \mathbf{e}''].$$

Algorithm 15.1. **Summary of $\mathtt{F}$ and $\mathtt{P}$ retrieval from the trifocal tensor.** *Note, $\mathtt{F}_{21}$ and $\mathtt{F}_{31}$ are determined uniquely. However, $\mathtt{P}'$ and $\mathtt{P}''$ are determined only up to a common projective transformation of 3-space.*

that the third camera could be chosen in a similar manner as $\mathtt{P}'' = [[\mathtt{T}_1^\mathsf{T}, \mathtt{T}_2^\mathsf{T}, \mathtt{T}_3^\mathsf{T}]\mathbf{e}' \mid \mathbf{e}'']$, but *this is incorrect.* This is because the two camera pairs $\{\mathtt{P}, \mathtt{P}'\}$ and $\{\mathtt{P}, \mathtt{P}''\}$ do not necessarily define the same projective world frame; although each pair is correct by itself, the triple $\{\mathtt{P}, \mathtt{P}', \mathtt{P}''\}$ is inconsistent.

The third camera cannot be chosen independently of the projective frame of the first two. To see this, suppose the camera pair $\{\mathtt{P}, \mathtt{P}'\}$ is chosen and points $\mathbf{X}_i$ reconstructed from their image correspondences $\mathbf{x}_i \leftrightarrow \mathbf{x}'_i$. Then the coordinates of $\mathbf{X}_i$ are specified in the projective world frame defined by by $\{\mathtt{P}, \mathtt{P}'\}$, and a consistent camera $\mathtt{P}''$ may be computed from the correspondences $\mathbf{X}_i \leftrightarrow \mathbf{x}''_i$. Clearly, $\mathtt{P}''$ depends on the frame defined by $\{\mathtt{P}, \mathtt{P}'\}$. However, it is not necessary to explicitly reconstruct 3D structure, a consistent camera triplet can be recovered from the trifocal tensor directly.

The pair of camera matrices $\mathtt{P} = [\mathtt{I} \mid \mathbf{0}]$ and $\mathtt{P}' = [[\mathtt{T}_1, \mathtt{T}_2, \mathtt{T}_3]\mathbf{e}'' \mid \mathbf{e}']$ are not the only ones compatible with the given fundamental matrix $\mathtt{F}_{21}$. According to (9.10–*p*256), the most general form for $\mathtt{P}'$ is

$$\mathtt{P}' = [[\mathtt{T}_1, \mathtt{T}_2, \mathtt{T}_3]\mathbf{e}'' + \mathbf{e}'\mathbf{v}^\mathsf{T} | \lambda\mathbf{e}']$$

for some vector $\mathbf{v}$ and scalar λ. A similar choice holds for $\mathtt{P}''$. To find a triple of camera matrices compatible with the trifocal tensor, we need to find the correct values of $\mathtt{P}'$ and $\mathtt{P}''$ from these families so as to be compatible with the form (15.1) of thc trifocal tensor.

Because of the projective ambiguity, we are free to choose $\mathtt{P}' = [[\mathtt{T}_1, \mathtt{T}_2, \mathtt{T}_3]\mathbf{e}''|\mathbf{e}']$, thus $\mathbf{a}_i = \mathtt{T}_i\mathbf{e}''$. This choice fixes the projective world frame so that $\mathtt{P}''$ is now defined uniquely (up to scale). Then substituting into (15.1) (observing that $\mathbf{a}_4 = \mathbf{e}'$ and $\mathbf{b}_4 = \mathbf{e}''$)

$$\mathtt{T}_i = \mathtt{T}_i\mathbf{e}''\mathbf{e}''^\mathsf{T} - \mathbf{e}'\mathbf{b}_i^\mathsf{T}$$

from which it follows that $\mathbf{e}'\mathbf{b}_i^\mathsf{T} = \mathtt{T}_i(\mathbf{e}''\mathbf{e}''^\mathsf{T} - \mathtt{I})$. Since the scale may be chosen such that $\|\mathbf{e}'\| = \mathbf{e}'^{\mathsf{T}}\mathbf{e}' = 1$, we may multiply on the left by $\mathbf{e}'^{\mathsf{T}}$ and transpose to get

$$\mathbf{b}_i = (\mathbf{e}''\mathbf{e}''^{\mathsf{T}} - \mathtt{I})\mathtt{T}_i^{\mathsf{T}}\mathbf{e}'$$

so $\mathtt{P}'' = [(\mathbf{e}''\mathbf{e}''^{\mathsf{T}} - \mathtt{I})[\mathtt{T}_1^{\mathsf{T}}, \mathtt{T}_2^{\mathsf{T}}, \mathtt{T}_3^{\mathsf{T}}]\mathbf{e}'|\mathbf{e}'']$. A summary of the steps involved in extracting the camera matrices from the trifocal tensor is given in algorithm 15.1.

We have seen that the trifocal tensor may be computed from the three camera matrices, and that conversely the three camera matrices may be computed, up to projective equivalence, from the trifocal tensor. Thus, the trifocal tensor completely captures the three cameras up to projective equivalence.

15.2 The trifocal tensor and tensor notation

The style of notation that has been used up to now for the trifocal tensor is derived from the standard matrix–vector notation. Since a matrix has two indices only, it is possible to distinguish between the two indices using the devices of matrix transposition and right or left multiplication, and in dealing with matrices and vectors, one can do without writing the indices explicitly. Because the trifocal tensor has three indices, instead of the two indices that a matrix has, it becomes increasingly cumbersome to persevere with this style of matrix notation, and we now turn to using standard tensor notation when dealing with the trifocal tensor. For those unfamiliar with tensor notation a gentle introduction is given in appendix 1(*p*562). This appendix should be read before proceeding with this chapter.

Image points and lines are represented by homogeneous *column* and *row* 3-vectors, respectively, i.e. $\mathbf{x} = (x^1, x^2, x^3)^{\mathsf{T}}$ and $\mathbf{l} = (l_1, l_2, l_3)$. The ij-th entry of a matrix $\mathtt{A}$ is denoted by a^i_j, index i being the contravariant (row) index and j being the covariant (column) index. We observe the convention that indices repeated in the contravariant and covariant positions imply summation over the range $(1, \ldots, 3)$ of the index. For example, the equation $\mathbf{x}' = \mathtt{A}\mathbf{x}$ is equivalent to $x'^i = \sum_j a^i_j x^j$, which may be written $x'^i = a^i_j x^j$.

We begin with the definition of the trifocal tensor given in (15.1). Using tensor notation, this becomes

$$\mathcal{T}_i^{jk} = a_i^j b_4^k - a_4^j b_i^k. \tag{15.9}$$

The positions of the indices in $\mathcal{T}_i^{jk}$ (two contravariant and one covariant) are dictated by the positions of the indices on the right side of the equation. Thus, the trifocal tensor is a mixed contravariant–covariant tensor. In tensor notation, the basic incidence relation (15.3) becomes

$$l_i = l'_j l''_k \mathcal{T}_i^{jk}. \tag{15.10}$$

Note that when multiplying tensors the order of the entries does not matter, in contrast with standard matrix notation. For instance the right side of the above expression is

$$l'_j l''_k \mathcal{T}_i^{jk} = \sum_{j,k} l'_j l''_k \mathcal{T}_i^{jk} = \sum_{j,k} l'_j \mathcal{T}_i^{jk} l''_k = l'_j \mathcal{T}_i^{jk} l''_k \ .$$

Definition. The trifocal tensor $\mathcal{T}$ is a valency 3 tensor $\mathcal{T}_i^{jk}$ with two contravariant and one covariant indices. It is represented by a homogeneous $3 \times 3 \times 3$ array (i.e. 27 elements). It has 18 degrees of freedom.

Computation from camera matrices. If the canonical 3×4 camera matrices are

$$\mathtt{P} = [\mathtt{I} \mid \mathbf{0}], \quad \mathtt{P}' = [a_j^i], \quad \mathtt{P}'' = [b_j^i]$$

then

$$\mathcal{T}_i^{jk} = a_i^j b_4^k - a_4^j b_i^k.$$

See (17.12–*p*415) for computation from three general camera matrices.

Line transfer from corresponding lines in the second and third views to the first.

$$l_i = l'_j l''_k \mathcal{T}_i^{jk}$$

Transfer by a homography.

(i) **Point transfer from first to third view via a plane in the second**
The contraction $l'_j \mathcal{T}_i^{jk}$ is a homography mapping between the first and third views induced by a plane defined by the back-projection of the line $\mathbf{l}'$ in the second view.

$$x''^k = h_i^k x^i \text{ where } h_i^k = l'_j \mathcal{T}_i^{jk}$$

(ii) **Point transfer from first to second view via a plane in the third**
The contraction $l''_k \mathcal{T}_i^{jk}$ is a homography mapping between the first and second views induced by a plane defined by the back-projection of the line $\mathbf{l}''$ in the third view.

$$x'^j = h_i^j x^i \text{ where } h_i^j = l''_k \mathcal{T}_i^{jk}$$

Table 15.2. *Definition and transfer properties of the trifocal tensor.*

The homography maps of figure 15.2 and figure 15.3 may be deduced from the incidence relation (15.10). In the case of the plane defined by back-projecting the line $\mathbf{l}'$,

$$l_i = l'_j l''_k \mathcal{T}_i^{jk} = l''_k (l'_j \mathcal{T}_i^{jk}) = l''_k h_i^k \text{ where } h_i^k = l'_j \mathcal{T}_i^{jk}$$

and h_i^k are the elements of the homography matrix $\mathtt{H}$. This homography maps points between the first and third view as

$$x''^k = h_i^k x^i.$$

Note that the homography is obtained from the tensor by contraction with a line (i.e. a summation over one contravariant (upper) index of the tensor, and the covariant (lower) index of the line), i.e. $\mathbf{l}'$ extracts a 3×3 matrix from the tensor – think of the trifocal tensor as an operator which takes a line and produces a homography matrix. Table 15.2 summarizes the definition and transfer properties of the trifocal tensor.

A pair of particularly important tensors are ϵ_{ijk} and its contravariant counterpart ϵ^{ijk}, defined in section A1.1(*p*563). This tensor is used to represent the vector product. For

(i) Line–line–line correspondence $$(l_r\epsilon^{ris})l'_jl''_k\mathcal{T}_i^{jk} = 0^s$$
(ii) Point–line–line correspondence $$x^il'_jl''_k\mathcal{T}_i^{jk} = 0$$
(iii) Point–line–point correspondence $$x^il'_j(x''^k\epsilon_{kqs})\mathcal{T}_i^{jq} = 0_s$$
(iv) Point–point–line correspondence $$x^i(x'^j\epsilon_{jpr})l''_k\mathcal{T}_i^{pk} = 0_r$$
(v) Point–point–point correspondence $$x^i(x'^j\epsilon_{jpr})(x''^k\epsilon_{kqs})\mathcal{T}_i^{pq} = 0_{rs}$$

Table 15.3. *Summary of trifocal tensor incidence relations – the trilinearities.*

instance, the line joining two points x^i and y^j is equal to the cross product $x^iy^j\epsilon_{ijk} = l_k$, and the skew-symmetric matrix $[\mathbf{x}]_\times$ is written as $x^i\epsilon_{irs}$ in tensor notation. It is now relatively straightforward to write down the basic incidence results involving the trifocal tensor given in table 15.1. The results are summarized in table 15.3. In this table, a notation such as 0_r represents an array of zeros.

The form of the relations in table 15.3 is more easily understood if one observes that three indices i, j and k in $\mathcal{T}_i^{jk}$ correspond to entities in the first, second and third views respectively. Thus for instance a partial expression such as $l''_j\mathcal{T}_i^{jk}$ cannot occur, because the index j belongs to the second view, and hence does not belong on the line $\mathbf{l}''$ in the third view. Repeated indices (indicating summation) must occur once as a contravariant (upper) index and once as a covariant (lower) index. Thus, we cannot write $x'^j\mathcal{T}_i^{jk}$, since the index j occurs twice in the upper position. Think of the ϵ tensor as being used to raise or lower indices, for instance by replacing $\mathbf{l}'_j$ by $\mathbf{x}^i\epsilon_{ijk}$. However, this may not be done arbitrarily, as pointed out in exercise (x) on page 389.

15.2.1 The trilinearities

The incidence relations in table 15.3 are *trilinear* relations or *trilinearities* in the coordinates of the image elements (points and lines). *Tri-* since every monomial in the relation involves a coordinate from each of the three image elements involved; and *linear* because the relations are linear in each of the algebraic entities (i.e. the three "arguments" of the tensor). For example in the point–point–point relation, $x^i(x'^j\epsilon_{jpr})(x''^k\epsilon_{kqs})\mathcal{T}_i^{pq} = 0_{rs}$, suppose both $\mathbf{x}_1$ and $\mathbf{x}_2$ satisfy the relation, then so does $\mathbf{x} = \alpha\mathbf{x}_1 + \beta\mathbf{x}_2$, i.e. the relation is linear in its first argument. Similarly, the relation is linear in the second and third argument. This multi-linearity is a standard property of tensors, and follows directly from the form $x^il'_jl''_k\mathcal{T}_i^{jk} = 0$ which is a contraction of the tensor over all three of its indices (arguments).

We will now describe the point–point–point trilinearities in more detail. There are nine of these trilinearities arising from the three choices of r and s. Geometrically these trilinearities arise from special choices of the lines in the second and third image for the point–line–line relation (see figure 15.4(a)). Choosing $r = 1, 2$ or 3 corresponds to a line parallel to the image x-axis, parallel to the image y-axis, or through the image coordinate origin (the point $(0, 0, 1)^\mathsf{T}$), respectively. For example, choosing $r = 1$ and expanding $x'^j \epsilon_{jpr}$ results in

$$l'_p = x'^j \epsilon_{jp1} = (0, -x'^3, x'^2)$$

which is a horizontal line in the second view through $\mathbf{x}'$ (since points of the form $\mathbf{y}' = (x'^1 + \lambda, x'^2, x'^3)^\mathsf{T}$ satisfy $\mathbf{y}'^\mathsf{T}\mathbf{l}' = 0$ for any λ). Similarly, choosing $s = 2$ in the third view results in the vertical line through $\mathbf{x}''$

$$l''_q = x''^k \epsilon_{kq2} = (x''^3, 0, -x''^1)$$

and the trilinear point relation expands to

$$\begin{aligned} 0 &= x^i x'^j x''^k \, \epsilon_{jp1}\epsilon_{kq2}\mathcal{T}_i^{pq} \\ &= x^i[-x'^3(x''^3\,\mathcal{T}_i^{21} - x''^1\,\mathcal{T}_i^{23}) + x'^2(x''^3\,\mathcal{T}_i^{31} - x''^1\,\mathcal{T}_i^{33})]. \end{aligned}$$

Of these nine trilinearities, four are linearly independent. This means that from a basis of four trilinearities all nine can be generated by linear combinations. The four degrees of freedom may be traced back to those of the point-line-line relation $x^i l'_j l''_k \mathcal{T}_i^{jk} = 0$ and are counted as follows. There is a one-parameter family of lines through $\mathbf{x}''$ in the third view. If $\mathbf{m}''$ and $\mathbf{n}''$ are two members of this family, then any other line through $\mathbf{x}''$ can be obtained from a linear combination of these:

$$\mathbf{l}'' = \alpha\mathbf{m}'' + \beta\mathbf{n}''.$$

The incidence relation is linear in $\mathbf{l}''$, so that given

$$\begin{aligned} l'_j m''_k \mathcal{T}_i^{jk} x^i &= 0 \\ l'_j n''_k \mathcal{T}_i^{jk} x^i &= 0 \end{aligned}$$

then the incidence relation for any other line $\mathbf{l}''$ can be generated by a linear combination of these two. Consequently, there are only two linearly independent incidence relations for $\mathbf{l}''$. Similarly there is a one-parameter family of lines through $\mathbf{x}'$, and the incidence relation is also linear in lines $\mathbf{l}'$ through $\mathbf{x}'$. Thus, there are a total of four linearly independent incidence relations between a point in the first view and lines in the second and third.

The main virtue of the trilinearities is that they are linear, otherwise their properties are often subsumed by transfer, as described in the following section.

15.3 Transfer

Given three views of a scene and a pair of matched points in two views one may wish to determine the position of the point in the third view. Given sufficient information about the placement of the cameras, it is usually possible to determine the location of

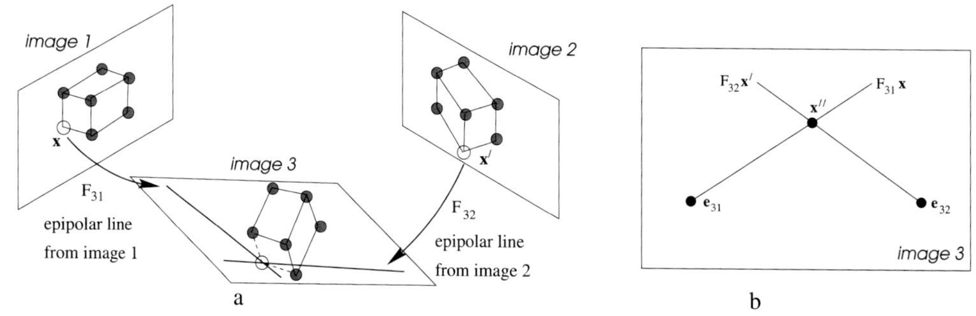

Fig. 15.7. **Epipolar transfer.** *(a) The image of* $\mathbf{X}$ *in the first two views is the correspondence* $\mathbf{x} \leftrightarrow \mathbf{x}'$. *The image of* $\mathbf{X}$ *in the third view may be computed by intersecting the epipolar lines* $F_{31}\mathbf{x}$ *and* $F_{32}\mathbf{x}'$. *(b) The configuration of the epipoles and transferred point* $\mathbf{x}''$ *as seen in the third image. Point* $\mathbf{x}''$ *is computed as the intersection of epipolar lines passing through the two epipoles* $\mathbf{e}_{31}$ *and* $\mathbf{e}_{32}$. *However, if* $\mathbf{x}''$ *lies on the line through the two epipoles, then its position cannot be determined. Points close to the line through the epipoles will be estimated with poor precision.*

the point in the third view without reference to image content. This is the point transfer problem. A similar transfer problem arises for lines.

In principle the problem can generally be solved given the cameras for the three views. Rays back-projected from corresponding points in the first and second view intersect and thus determine the 3D point. The position of the corresponding point in the third view is computed by projecting this 3D point onto the image. Similarly lines back-projected from the first and second image intersect in the 3D line, and the projection of this line in 3-space to the third image determines its image position.

15.3.1 Point transfer using fundamental matrices

The transfer problem may be solved using knowledge of the fundamental matrices only. Thus, suppose we know the three fundamental matrices F_{21}, F_{31} and F_{32} relating the three views, and let points $\mathbf{x}$ and $\mathbf{x}'$ in the first two views be a matched pair. We wish to find the corresponding point $\mathbf{x}''$ in the third image.

The required point $\mathbf{x}''$ matches point $\mathbf{x}$ in the first image, and consequently must lie on the epipolar line corresponding to $\mathbf{x}$. Since we know F_{31}, this epipolar line may be computed, and is equal to $F_{31}\mathbf{x}$. By a similar argument, $\mathbf{x}''$ must lie on the epipolar line $F_{32}\mathbf{x}'$. Taking the intersection of the epipolar lines gives

$$\mathbf{x}'' = (F_{31}\mathbf{x}) \times (F_{32}\mathbf{x}') \ .$$

See figure 15.7a.

Note that the fundamental matrix F_{21} is not used in this expression. The question naturally arises whether we can gain anything by knowledge of F_{21}, and the answer is yes. In the presence of noise, the points $\mathbf{x} \leftrightarrow \mathbf{x}'$ will not form an exact matched pair, meaning that they will not satisfy the equation $\mathbf{x}'^{\mathsf{T}} F_{21}\mathbf{x} = 0$ exactly. Given F_{21} one may use optimal triangulation as in algorithm 12.1(*p*318) to correct $\mathbf{x}$ and $\mathbf{x}'$, resulting in a pair $\hat{\mathbf{x}} \leftrightarrow \hat{\mathbf{x}}'$ that satisfies this relation. The transferred point may then be computed as $\mathbf{x}'' = (F_{31}\hat{\mathbf{x}}) \times (F_{32}\hat{\mathbf{x}}')$. This method of point transfer using the fundamental matrices will be called *epipolar transfer*.

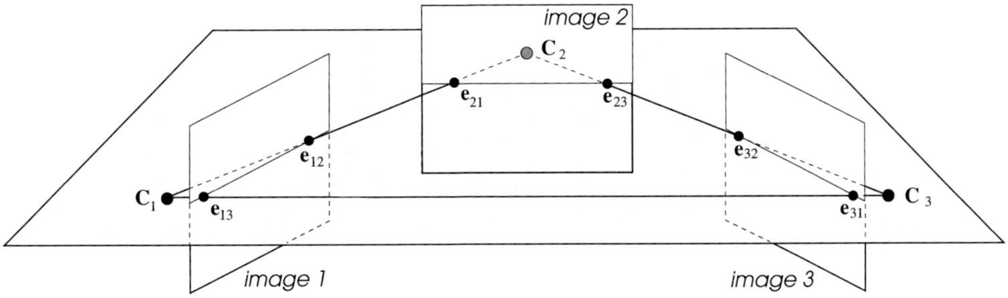

Fig. 15.8. **The trifocal plane** *is defined by the three camera centres. The notation for the epipoles is* $\mathbf{e}_{ij} = \mathtt{P}_i\mathbf{C}_j$. *Epipolar transfer fails for any point* $\mathbf{X}$ *on the trifocal plane. If the three camera centres are collinear then there is a one-parameter family of planes containing the three centres.*

Though at one time used for point transfer, epipolar transfer has a serious deficiency that rules it out as a practical method. This deficiency is due to the degeneracy that can be seen from figure 15.7(b): epipolar transfer fails when the two epipolar lines in the third image are coincident (and becomes increasingly ill-conditioned as the lines become less "transverse"). The degeneracy condition that $\mathbf{x}''$, $\mathbf{e}_{31}$ and $\mathbf{e}_{32}$ are collinear in the third image means that the camera centres $\mathbf{C}$ and $\mathbf{C}'$ and the 3D point $\mathbf{X}$ lie in a plane through the centre $\mathbf{C}''$ of the third camera; thus $\mathbf{X}$ lies on the *trifocal* plane defined by the three camera centres, see figure 15.8. Epipolar transfer will fail for points $\mathbf{X}$ lying on the trifocal plane and will be inaccurate for points lying near that plane. Note, in the special case that the three camera centres are collinear the trifocal plane is not uniquely defined, and epipolar transfer fails for all points. In this case $\mathbf{e}_{31} = \mathbf{e}_{32}$.

15.3.2 Point transfer using the trifocal tensor

The degeneracy of epipolar transfer is avoided by use of the trifocal tensor. Consider a correspondence $\mathbf{x} \leftrightarrow \mathbf{x}'$. If a line $\mathbf{l}'$ passing through the point $\mathbf{x}'$ is chosen in the second view, then the corresponding point $\mathbf{x}''$ may be computed by transferring the point $\mathbf{x}$ from the first to the third view using $x''^k = x^i l'_j \mathcal{T}_i^{jk}$, from table 15.2. It is clear from figure 15.4(*p*371)(b) that this transfer is not degenerate for general points $\mathbf{X}$ lying on the trifocal plane.

However, note from result 15.3 and figure 15.6 that if $\mathbf{l}'$ is the epipolar line corresponding to $\mathbf{x}$, then $x^i l'_j \mathcal{T}_i^{jk} = 0^k$, so the point $\mathbf{x}''$ is undefined. Consequently, the choice of line $\mathbf{l}'$ is important. To avoid choosing only an epipolar line, one possibility is to use two or three different lines passing through $\mathbf{x}'$, namely $l'_{jp} = x'^r \epsilon_{rjp}$ for the three choices of $p = 1, \ldots, 3$. For each such line, one computes the value of $\mathbf{x}''$ and retains the one that has the largest norm (i.e. is furthest from being zero). An alternative method entirely for finding $\mathbf{x}''$ is as the least-squares solution of the system of linear equations $x^i(x'^j \epsilon_{jpr})(x''^k \epsilon_{kqs})\mathcal{T}_i^{pq} = 0_{rs}$, but this method is probably an overkill.

The method we recommend is the following. Before attempting to compute the point $\mathbf{x}''$ transferred from a pair of points $\mathbf{x} \leftrightarrow \mathbf{x}'$, first correct the pair of points using the fundamental matrix $\mathtt{F}_{21}$, as described above in the case of epipolar transfer. If $\hat{\mathbf{x}}$ and $\hat{\mathbf{x}}'$

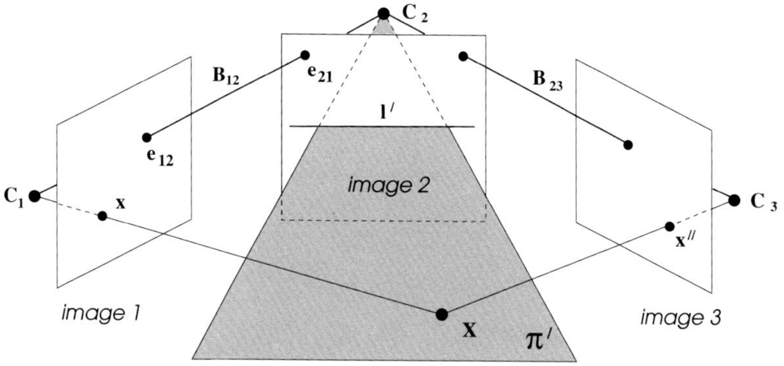

Fig. 15.9. **Degeneracy for point transfer using the trifocal tensor.** *The 3D point* $\mathbf{X}$ *is defined by the intersection of the ray through* $\mathbf{x}$ *with the plane* π'. *A point* $\mathbf{X}$ *on the baseline* B_{12} *between the first and second views cannot be defined in this manner. So a 3D point on the line* B_{12} *cannot be transferred to the third view via a homography defined by a line in the second view. Note that a point on the line* B_{12} *projects to* $\mathbf{e}_{12}$ *in the first image and* $\mathbf{e}_{21}$ *in the second image. Apart from the line* B_{12} *any point can be transferred. In particular there is not a degeneracy problem for points on the baseline* B_{23}, *between views two and three, or for any other point on the trifocal plane.*

are an exact match, then the transferred point $x''^k = \hat{x}^i l'_j \mathcal{T}_i^{jk}$ does not depend on the line $\mathbf{l}'$ chosen passing through $\hat{\mathbf{x}}'$ (as long as it is not the epipolar line). This may be verified geometrically by referring to figure 15.2(*p*368). A good choice is always given by the line perpendicular to $\mathtt{F}_{21}\hat{\mathbf{x}}$.

To summarize, a measured correspondence $\mathbf{x} \leftrightarrow \mathbf{x}'$ is transferred by the following steps:

(i) Compute $\mathtt{F}_{21}$ from the trifocal tensor (by the method given in algorithm 15.1), and correct $\mathbf{x} \leftrightarrow \mathbf{x}'$ to the exact correspondence $\hat{\mathbf{x}} \leftrightarrow \hat{\mathbf{x}}'$ using algorithm 12.1-(*p*318).
(ii) Compute the line $\mathbf{l}'$ through $\hat{\mathbf{x}}'$ and perpendicular to $\mathbf{l}'_e = \mathtt{F}_{21}\hat{\mathbf{x}}$. If $\mathbf{l}'_e = (l_1, l_2, l_3)^\mathsf{T}$ and $\hat{\mathbf{x}}' = (\hat{x}_1, \hat{x}_2, 1)^\mathsf{T}$, then $\mathbf{l}' = (l_2, -l_1, -\hat{x}_1 l_2 + \hat{x}_2 l_1)^\mathsf{T}$.
(iii) The transferred point is $x''^k = \hat{x}^i l'_j \mathcal{T}_i^{jk}$.

Degenerate configurations. Consider transfer to the third view via a plane, as shown in figure 15.9. The 3D point $\mathbf{X}$ is only undefined if it lies on the baseline joining the first and second camera centres. This is because rays through $\mathbf{x}$ and $\mathbf{x}'$ are collinear for such 3D points and so their intersection is not defined. In such a case, the points $\mathbf{x}$ and $\mathbf{x}'$ correspond with the epipoles in the two images. However, there is no problem transferring a point lying on the baseline between views two and three, or anywhere else on the trifocal plane. This is the key difference between epipolar transfer and transfer using the trifocal tensor. The former is undefined for *any* point on the trifocal plane.

15.3.3 Line transfer using the trifocal tensor

Using the trifocal tensor, it is possible to transfer lines from a pair of images to a third according to the line-transfer equation $l_i = l'_j l''_k \mathcal{T}_i^{jk}$ of table 15.2. This gives an explicit formula for the line in the first view, given lines in the other two views. Note however that if the lines $\mathbf{l}$ and $\mathbf{l}'$ are known in the first and second views then $\mathbf{l}''$ may be computed by solving the set of linear equations $(l_r \epsilon^{ris}) l'_j l''_k \mathcal{T}_i^{jk} = 0^s$, thereby transferring it into the third image. Similarly one may transfer lines into the second image. Line transfer is not possible using only the fundamental matrices.

Degeneracies. Consider the geometry of figure 12.8(*p*322). The line $\mathbf{L}$ in 3-space is defined by the intersection of the planes through $\mathbf{l}$ and $\mathbf{l}'$, namely $\boldsymbol{\pi}$ and $\boldsymbol{\pi}'$ respectively. This line is clearly undefined when the planes $\boldsymbol{\pi}$ and $\boldsymbol{\pi}'$ are coincident, i.e. in the case of epipolar planes. Consequently, lines cannot be transferred between the first and third image if both $\mathbf{l}$ and $\mathbf{l}'$ are corresponding epipolar lines for the first and second views. Algebraically, the line-transfer equation gives $l_i = l'_j l''_k \mathcal{T}_i^{jk} = \mathbf{0}$, and the equation matrix $(l_r \epsilon^{ris}) l'_j \mathcal{T}_i^{jk}$ used to solve for $\mathbf{l}''$ becomes zero. It is quite common for lines to be near epipolar, and their transfer is then inaccurate, so this condition should always be checked for. There is an equivalent degeneracy for line transfer between views one and two defined by a line in view three. Again, it occurs if the lines in views one and three are corresponding epipolar lines for these two views.

In general the epipolar geometries between views one and two, and one and three will differ, for instance the epipole $\mathbf{e}_{12}$ arising in the first view from view two will not coincide with the epipole $\mathbf{e}_{13}$ arising in the first view from view three. Thus an epipolar line in the first view for views one and two will not coincide with an epipolar line for views one and three. Consequently, when line transfer into the third view is degenerate, line transfer into the second view will not in general be degenerate. However, for lines in the trifocal plane transfer is degenerate (i.e. undefined) always.

15.4 The fundamental matrices for three views

The three fundamental matrices $\mathtt{F}_{21}, \mathtt{F}_{31}, \mathtt{F}_{32}$ are not independent, but satisfy three relations:

$$\mathbf{e}_{23}^{\mathsf{T}} \mathtt{F}_{21} \mathbf{e}_{13} = \mathbf{e}_{31}^{\mathsf{T}} \mathtt{F}_{32} \mathbf{e}_{21} = \mathbf{e}_{32}^{\mathsf{T}} \mathtt{F}_{31} \mathbf{e}_{12} = 0. \quad (15.11)$$

These relations are easily seen from figure 15.8. For example, $\mathbf{e}_{32}^{\mathsf{T}} \mathtt{F}_{31} \mathbf{e}_{12} = 0$ follows from the observation that $\mathbf{e}_{32}$ and $\mathbf{e}_{12}$ are matching points, corresponding to the centre of camera number 2.

Projectively, the three-camera configuration has 18 degrees of freedom counting 11 for each camera less 15 for an overall projective ambiguity. Alternatively, this may be accounted for as 21 for the 3×7 degrees of freedom of the fundamental matrices less 3 for the relations. The trifocal tensor also has 18 degrees of freedom and fundamental matrices computed from the trifocal tensor will automatically satisfy the three relations.

The counting argument implies that the three relations of (15.11) are sufficient to ensure consistency of three fundamental matrices. The counting argument alone is not a convincing proof of this, however, so a proof is given below.

Definition 15.5. Three fundamental matrices $\mathtt{F}_{21}$, $\mathtt{F}_{31}$ and $\mathtt{F}_{32}$ are said to be *compatible* if they satisfy the conditions (15.11).

In most cases, these conditions are sufficient to ensure that the three fundamental matrices correspond to some geometric configuration of cameras.

Theorem 15.6. *Let a set of three fundamental matrices* F_{21}, F_{31} *and* F_{32} *be given satisfying the conditions (15.11). Assume also that* $e_{12} \neq e_{13}$, $e_{21} \neq e_{23}$, *and* $e_{31} \neq e_{32}$. *Then there exist three camera matrices* P_1, P_2, P_3 *such that* F_{ij} *is the fundamental matrix corresponding to the pair* (P_i, P_j).

Note that the conditions $e_{ij} \neq e_{ik}$ in this theorem ensure that the three cameras are non-collinear. For this reason they will be referred to here as the *non-collinearity conditions*. One may show by example (left to the reader) that these conditions are necessary for the truth of the theorem.

Proof. In this proof, the indices i, j and k are intended to be distinct. We begin by choosing three points $\mathbf{x}_i; i = 1, \ldots, 3$, consistent with the three fundamental matrices. In other words, we require that $\mathbf{x}_i^\mathsf{T} F_{ij} \mathbf{x}_j = 0$ for all pairs (i, j). This is easily done by choosing first $\mathbf{x}_1$ and $\mathbf{x}_2$ to satisfy $\mathbf{x}_2^\mathsf{T} F_{21} \mathbf{x}_1 = 0$, and then defining $\mathbf{x}_3$ to be the intersection of the two epipolar lines $F_{32}\mathbf{x}_2$ and $F_{31}\mathbf{x}_1$.
In a similar manner, we choose a second set of points $\mathbf{y}_i; i = 1, \ldots, 3$ satisfying $\mathbf{y}_i^\mathsf{T} F_{ij} \mathbf{y}_j = 0$. This is done in such a way that the four points $\mathbf{x}_i, \mathbf{y}_i, \mathbf{e}_{ij}, \mathbf{e}_{ik}$ in each image i are in general position – that is no three are collinear. This is possible by the assumption that the two epipoles in each image are distinct.
Next we choose five world points $\mathbf{C}_1, \mathbf{C}_2, \mathbf{C}_3, \mathbf{X}, \mathbf{Y}$ in general position. For example, one could take the usual projective basis. We may now define the three camera matrices. Let the i-th camera matrix P_i satisfy the conditions

$$P_i \mathbf{C}_i = \mathbf{0}; \quad P_i \mathbf{C}_j = \mathbf{e}_{ij}; \quad P_i \mathbf{C}_k = \mathbf{e}_{ik}; \quad P_i \mathbf{X} = \mathbf{x}_i; \quad P_i \mathbf{Y} = \mathbf{y}_i.$$

In other words, the i-th camera has centre at $\mathbf{C}_i$ and maps the four other world points $\mathbf{C}_j, \mathbf{C}_k, \mathbf{X}, \mathbf{Y}$ to the four image points $\mathbf{e}_{ij}, \mathbf{e}_{ik}, \mathbf{x}_i, \mathbf{y}_i$. This uniquely determines the camera matrix since the points are in general position. To see this, recall that the camera matrix defines a homography between the image and the rays through the camera centre (a 2D projective space). The images of four points specify this homography completely. Let $\hat{F}_{ij}$ be the fundamental matrix defined by the pair of camera matrices P_i and P_j. The proof is completed by proving that $\hat{F}_{ij} = F_{ij}$ for all i, j.
The epipoles of $\hat{F}_{ij}$ and F_{ij} are the same, by the way that P_i and P_j are constructed. Consider the pencil of epipolar lines through $\mathbf{e}_{ij}$ in image i. This pencil forms a 1-dimensional projective space of lines, and the fundamental matrix F_{ij} induces a one-to-one correspondence (in fact a homography) between this pencil and the pencil of lines through $\mathbf{e}_{ji}$ in image j. The fundamental matrix $\hat{F}_{ij}$ also induces a homography between the same pencils. The two fundamental matrices are the same if the homographies they induce are the same.
Two 1-dimensional homographies are the same if they agree on three points (or in this case epipolar lines). The relation $\mathbf{x}_i^\mathsf{T} F_{ij} \mathbf{x}_j = 0$ means that the epipolar lines through $\mathbf{x}_i$ in image i and $\mathbf{x}_j$ in image j correspond under the homography induced by F_{ij}. By construction $\mathbf{x}_i \hat{F}_{ij} \mathbf{x}_j = 0$ as well, since $\mathbf{x}_i$ and $\mathbf{x}_j$ are the projections of the point $\mathbf{X}$ in

the two images. Thus, both homographies agree on this pair of epipolar lines. In the same way, the homographies induced by $\mathtt{F}_{ij}$ and $\hat{\mathtt{F}}_{ij}$ agree on the epipolar lines corresponding to the pairs $\mathbf{y}_i \leftrightarrow \mathbf{y}_j$ and $\mathbf{e}_{ik} \leftrightarrow \mathbf{e}_{jk}$. The two homographies therefore agree on three lines in the pencil and hence are equal; so are the corresponding fundamental matrices. (We are grateful to Frederik Schaffalitzky for this proof). □

15.4.1 Uniqueness of camera matrices given three fundamental matrices

The proof just given shows that there is at least one set of cameras corresponding to three compatible fundamental matrices (provided they satisfying the non-collinearity condition). It is important to know that the three fundamental matrices determine the configuration of the three cameras uniquely, at least up to the unavoidable projective ambiguity. This will be shown next.

The first two camera matrices P and P′ may be determined from the fundamental matrix $\mathtt{F}_{21}$ by two-view techniques (chapter 9). It remains to determine the third camera matrix P″ in the same projective frame. In principle, this may be done as follows.

(i) Select a set of matching points $\mathbf{x}_i \leftrightarrow \mathbf{x}'_i$ in the first two images, satisfying $\mathbf{x}'^{\mathsf{T}}_i \mathtt{F}_{21} \mathbf{x}_i = 0$, and use triangulation to determine the corresponding 3D points $\mathbf{X}_i$.

(ii) Use epipolar transfer to determine the corresponding points $\mathbf{x}''_i$ in the third image, using the fundamental matrices $\mathtt{F}_{31}$ and $\mathtt{F}_{32}$.

(iii) Solve for the camera matrix P″ from the set of 3D–2D correspondences $\mathbf{X}_i \leftrightarrow \mathbf{x}''_i$.

The second step in this algorithm will fail in the case where the point $\mathbf{X}_i$ lies in the trifocal plane. Such a point $\mathbf{X}_i$ is easily detected and discarded, since it projects into the first image as a point $\mathbf{x}_i$ lying on the line joining the two epipoles $\mathbf{e}_{12}$ and $\mathbf{e}_{13}$. Since there are infinitely many possible matched points, we can compute sufficiently many such points to compute P″.

The only situation in which this method will fail is when all space points $\mathbf{X}_i$ lie in a trifocal plane. This can occur only in the degenerate situation in which the three camera centres are collinear, in which case the trifocal plane is not uniquely determined. Thus, we see that unless the three camera centres are collinear, the three camera matrices may be determined from the fundamental matrices. On the other hand, if the three cameras are collinear, then there is no way to determine the relative spacings of the cameras along the line of their centres. This is because the length of the baseline cannot be determined from the fundamental matrices, and the three baselines (distances between the camera centres) may be arbitrarily chosen and remain consistent with the fundamental matrices. Thus we have demonstrated the following fact:

Result 15.7. *Given three compatible fundamental matrices* $\mathtt{F}_{21}$, $\mathtt{F}_{31}$ *and* $\mathtt{F}_{32}$ *satisfying the non-collinearity condition, the three corresponding camera matrices* P, P′ *and* P″ *are unique up to the choice of a* 3*D projective coordinate frame.*

15.4.2 Computation of camera matrices from three fundamental matrices

Given three compatible fundamental matrices, there exists a simple method for computing a corresponding set of three camera matrices. From the fundamental matrix F_{21}, one can compute a corresponding pair of camera matrices (P, P') using result 9.14-(*p*256). Next, according to result 9.12(*p*255) the third camera matrix P'' must satisfy the condition that $P''^{\mathsf{T}}F_{31}P$ and $P''^{\mathsf{T}}F_{32}P'$ be skew-symmetric. Each of these matrices gives rise to 10 linear equations in the entries of P'', a total of 20 equations in the 12 entries of P''. From these, P'' may be computed linearly.

If the three fundamental matrices are compatible in the sense of definition 15.5 and the non-collinearity condition of theorem 15.6 holds, then there will exist a solution, and it will be unique. If however the three fundamental matrices are computed independently from point correspondences, then they will not satisfy the compatibility conditions exactly. In this case it will be necessary to compute a least-squares solution to find P''. The error being minimized is not geometrically based. It is best to use this algorithm only when the fundamental matrices are known to be compatible.

One can think of doing three-view reconstruction by estimating the three fundamental matrices using pairwise point correspondences, then using the above algorithm to estimate the three camera matrices. This is not a very good strategy, for the following reasons.

(i) The method for computing the three camera matrices from the fundamental matrices assumes that the fundamental matrices are compatible. Otherwise, a least-squares problem involving a non-geometrically justified cost function is involved.

(ii) Although result 15.7 shows that three fundamental matrices may determine the camera geometry, and hence the trifocal tensor, this is only true when the cameras are not collinear. As they approach collinearity, the estimate of the relative camera placement becomes unstable.

The trifocal tensor is preferable to a triple of compatible fundamental matrices as a means of determining the geometry of three views. This is because the difficulty with the views being collinear is not an issue with the trifocal tensor. It is well defined and uniquely determines the geometry even for collinear cameras. The difference is that the fundamental matrices do not contain a direct constraint on the relative displacements between the three cameras, whereas this is built into the trifocal tensor.

Since the projective structure of the three cameras may be computed explicitly from the trifocal tensor, it follows that all three fundamental matrices for the three view pairs are determined by the trifocal tensor. In fact simple formulae, given in algorithm 15.1-(*p*375) exist for the two fundamental matrices F_{21} and F_{31}. The fundamental matrices determined from the trifocal tensor will satisfy the compatibility conditions (15.11).

15.4.3 Camera matrices compatible with two fundamental matrices

Suppose we are given only two fundamental matrices F_{21} and F_{31}. To what extent do these fix the geometry of the three cameras? It will be shown here that there are four degrees of freedom in the solution for the camera matrices, beyond the usual projective ambiguity.

From $\mathtt{F}_{21}$ one may compute a pair of camera matrices $(\mathtt{P}, \mathtt{P}')$, and from $\mathtt{F}_{31}$ the pair $(\mathtt{P}, \mathtt{P}'')$. In both cases we may choose $\mathtt{P} = [\mathtt{I} \mid \mathbf{0}]$, resulting in a triple of camera matrices $(\mathtt{P}, \mathtt{P}', \mathtt{P}'')$ compatible with the pair of fundamental matrices.

However, the choice of the three camera matrices is not unique, since for any matrices $\mathtt{H}_1$ and $\mathtt{H}_2$ representing 3D projective transforms, the pairs $(\mathtt{PH}_1, \mathtt{P}'\mathtt{H}_1)$ and $(\mathtt{PH}_2, \mathtt{P}''\mathtt{H}_2)$ are also compatible with the same fundamental matrices. In order to preserve the condition that $\mathtt{P}$ is equal to $[\mathtt{I} \mid \mathbf{0}]$ in each case, the form of $\mathtt{H}_i$ must be restricted to:

$$\mathtt{H}_i = \begin{bmatrix} \mathtt{I} & \mathbf{0} \\ \mathbf{v}_i^{\mathsf{T}} & k_i \end{bmatrix}.$$

We may now fix on a particular choice of the first two camera matrices $(\mathtt{P}, \mathtt{P}')$ compatible with $\mathtt{F}_{21}$. This is equivalent to fixing on a specific projective coordinate frame. The general solution for the camera matrices is then $(\mathtt{P}, \mathtt{P}', \mathtt{P}''\mathtt{H}_2)$, where $\mathtt{H}_2$ is of the form given above and the two pairs $(\mathtt{P}, \mathtt{P}')$ and $(\mathtt{P}, \mathtt{P}'')$ are compatible with the two fundamental matrices.

Allowing also for the overall projective ambiguity, the most general solution is $(\mathtt{PH}, \mathtt{P}'\mathtt{H}, \mathtt{P}''\mathtt{H}_2\mathtt{H})$, which gives a total of 19 degrees of freedom, 15 for the projective transformation $\mathtt{H}$ and 4 for the degrees of freedom of $\mathtt{H}_2$. The same number of degrees of freedom may be found using a counting argument as follows: two fundamental matrices have 7 degrees of freedom each, for a total of 14. Three arbitrary camera matrices on the other hand have $3 \times 11 = 33$ degrees of freedom. The 14 constraints imposed by the two fundamental matrices leave 19 remaining degrees of freedom for the three camera matrices.

15.5 Closure

The development of three-view geometry proceeds in an analogous manner to that of two-view geometry covered in part II of this book. The trifocal tensor may be computed from image correspondences over three views, and a projective reconstruction of the cameras and 3D scene then follows. This computation is described in chapter 16. The projective ambiguity may be reduced to affine or metric by supplying additional information on the scene or cameras in the same manner as that of chapter 10. A similar development to that of chapter 13 may be given for the relations between homographies induced by scene planes and the trifocal tensor.

15.5.1 The literature

With hindsight, the discovery of the trifocal tensor may be traced to [Spetsakis-91] and [Weng-88], where it was used for scene reconstruction from lines in the case of calibrated cameras. It was later shown in [Hartley-94d] to be equally applicable to projective scene reconstruction in the uncalibrated case. At this stage matrix notation was used, but [Vieville-93] used tensor notation for this problem.

Meanwhile in independent work, Shashua introduced trilinearity conditions relating the coordinates of corresponding points in three views with uncalibrated cameras [Shashua-94, Shashua-95a]. [Hartley-95b, Hartley-97a] then showed that Shashua's relation for points and scene reconstruction from lines both arise from a common tensor, and the trifocal tensor was explicitly identified.

In subsequent work properties of the tensor have been investigated, e.g. [Shashua-95b]. In particular [Triggs-95] described the mixed covariant–contravariant behaviour of the indices, and [Zisserman-96] described the geometry of the homographies encoded by the tensor. Faugeras and Mourrain [Faugeras-95a] gave enlightening new derivations of the trifocal tensor equations and considered the trifocal tensor in the context of general linear constraints involving multiple views. This approach will be discussed in chapter 17. Further geometric properties of the tensor were given in Faugeras & Papadopoulo [Faugeras-97].

Epipolar point transfer was described by [Barrett-92, Faugeras-94], and its deficiencies pointed out by [Zisserman-94], amongst others.

The trifocal tensor has been used for various applications including establishing correspondences in image sequences [Beardsley-96], independent motion detection [Torr-95a], and camera self-calibration [Armstrong-96a].

15.5.2 Notes and exercises

(i) The trifocal tensor is invariant to 3D projective transforms. Verify explicitly that if $\mathtt{H}_{4\times 4}$ is a transform preserving the first camera matrix $\mathtt{P} = [\mathtt{I} \mid \mathbf{0}]$, then the tensor defined by (15.1–*p*367) is unchanged.

(ii) In this chapter the starting point for the trifocal tensor derivation was the incidence property of three corresponding lines. Show that alternatively the starting point may be the homography induced by a plane.

Here is a sketch derivation: choose the camera matrices to be a canonical set $\mathtt{P} = [\mathtt{I} \mid \mathbf{0}], \mathtt{P}' = [\mathtt{A} \mid \mathbf{a}_4], \mathtt{P}'' = [\mathtt{B} \mid \mathbf{b}_4]$ and start from the homography $\mathtt{H}_{13}$ between the first and third views induced by a plane $\boldsymbol{\pi}'$. From result 13.1(*p*326) this homography may be written as $\mathtt{H}_{13} = \mathtt{B} - \mathbf{b}_4\mathbf{v}^\mathsf{T}$, where $\boldsymbol{\pi}'^\mathsf{T} = (\mathbf{v}^\mathsf{T}, 1)$. In this case the plane is defined by a line $\mathbf{l}'$ in the second view as $\boldsymbol{\pi}' = \mathtt{P}'^\mathsf{T}\mathbf{l}'$. Show that result 15.2(*p*369) follows.

(iii) Homographies involving the first view are simply expressed in terms of the trifocal tensor $\mathcal{T}_i^{jk}$ as given by result 15.2(*p*369). Investigate whether a simple formula exists for the homography $\mathtt{H}_{23}$ from the second to the third view, induced by a line $\mathbf{l}$ in the first image.

(iv) The contraction $x^i\mathcal{T}_i^{jk}$ is a 3×3 matrix. Show that this may be interpreted as a correlation (see definition 2.29(*p*59)) mapping between the second and third views induced by the line which is the back-projection of the point $\mathbf{x}$ in the first view.

(v) **Plane plus parallax over three views.** There is a rich geometry associated with the plane plus two points configuration (see figure 13.9(*p*336)) over three views: suppose the points off the (reference) plane are $\mathbf{X}$ and $\mathbf{Y}$. Project the point $\mathbf{X}$ onto the reference plane from each of the three camera centres to form a triangle $\mathbf{x}, \mathbf{x}', \mathbf{x}''$, and similarly project the point $\mathbf{Y}$ to the triangle $\mathbf{y}, \mathbf{y}', \mathbf{y}''$. Then the two triangles form a Desargues's configuration and are related by a planar homology (see section A7.2(*p*629)). A simple sketch shows that the lines joining corresponding triangle vertices, $(\mathbf{x}, \mathbf{y}), (\mathbf{x}', \mathbf{y}'), (\mathbf{x}'', \mathbf{y}'')$, are concurrent, and their intersection is the point at which the line joining $\mathbf{X}$ and $\mathbf{Y}$ pierces the reference plane. Similarly the intersection points of corresponding triangle sides are collinear, and the line so formed is the intersection of the trifocal plane of the cameras with the reference plane. Further details are given in [Criminisi-98, Irani-98, Triggs-00b].

(vi) In the case where two of the three cameras have the same camera centre, the trifocal tensor may be related to simpler entities. There are two cases.

(a) If the second and third camera have the same centre, then $\mathcal{T}_i^{jk} = \mathtt{F}_{ri}\mathtt{H}_s^k\epsilon^{rjs}$, where $\mathtt{F}_{ri}$ is the fundamental matrix for the first two views, and $\mathtt{H}$ is the homography from the second to the third view induced by the fact that they have the same centre.

(b) If the first and the second views have the same centre, then $\mathcal{T}_i^{jk} = \mathtt{H}_i^j\mathbf{e}''^k$, where $\mathtt{H}$ is the homography from the first to the second view and $\mathbf{e}''$ is the epipole in the third image.

Prove these relationships using the approach of chapter 17.

(vii) Consider the case of a small baseline between the cameras and derive a differential form of the trifocal tensor, see [Astrom-98, Triggs-99b].

(viii) There are actually three different trifocal tensors relating three views, depending on which of the three cameras corresponds to the covariant index. Given one such tensor $[\mathtt{T}_i]$, verify that the tensor $[\mathtt{T}'_i]$ may be computed in several steps, as follows:

(a) Extract the three camera matrices $\mathtt{P} = [\mathtt{I} \mid \mathbf{0}]$, $\mathtt{P}'$ and $\mathtt{P}''$ from the trifocal tensor.

(b) Find a 3D projective transformation $\mathtt{H}$ such that $\mathtt{P}'\mathtt{H} = [\mathtt{I} \mid \mathbf{0}]$, and apply it to each of $\mathtt{P}$ and $\mathtt{P}''$ as well.

(c) Compute the tensor $[\mathtt{T}'_i]$ by applying (15.1–*p*367).

(ix) Investigate the form and properties (e.g. rank of the matrices $\mathtt{T}_i$) of the trifocal tensor for the special motions (pure translation, planar motion) described in section 9.3(*p*247) for the fundamental matrix.

(x) Comparison of the incidence relationships of table 15.3(*p*378) indicates that one may replace a line l'_j by the expression $\epsilon_{jrs}x'^r$, and proceed similarly with l''_k. Also, one gets a three-view line equation by replacing x^i by $\epsilon^{irs}l_i$. Can both of these operations be carried out at once to obtain an equation

$$\left(\epsilon^{iru}l_i\right)\left(\epsilon_{jsv}x'^j\right)\left(\epsilon_{ktw}x''^k\right)\mathcal{T}_r^{st} = 0^u_{vw}?$$

Why, or why not?

(xi) **Affine trifocal tensor.** If the three cameras $\mathtt{P}, \mathtt{P}'$ and $\mathtt{P}''$ are all affine (definition 6.3(*p*166)), then the corresponding tensor $\mathcal{T}_{\text{A}}$ is the *affine trifocal tensor*. This affine specialization of the tensor has 12 degrees of freedom and 16 non-zero entries. The affine trifocal tensor was first defined in [Torr-95b], and has been studied in [Kahl-98a, Quan-97a, Thorhallsson-99]. It shares with the affine fundamental matrix (chapter 14) very stable numerical estimation behaviour. It has been shown to perform very well in tracking applications where the object of interest (for example a car) has small relief compared to the depth of the scene [Hayman-03, Tordoff-01].

16

Computation of the Trifocal Tensor $\mathcal{T}$

This chapter describes numerical methods for estimating the trifocal tensor given a set of point and line correspondences across three views. The development will be very similar to that for the fundamental matrix, using much the same techniques as those of chapter 11. In particular, five methods will be discussed:

(i) A linear method based on direct solution of a set of linear equations (after appropriate data normalization) (section 16.2).
(ii) An iterative method, that minimizes the algebraic error, while satisfying all appropriate constraints on the tensor (section 16.3).
(iii) An iterative method that minimizes geometric error (the "Gold Standard" method) (section 16.4.1).
(iv) An iterative method that minimizes the Sampson approximation to geometric error (section 16.4.3).
(v) Robust estimation based on RANSAC (section 16.6).

16.1 Basic equations

A complete set of the (tri-)linear equations involving the trifocal tensor is given in table 16.1. All of these equations are linear in the entries of the trifocal tensor $\mathcal{T}$.

Correspondence	Relation	Number of equations
three points	$x^i x'^j x''^k \epsilon_{jqs} \epsilon_{krt} \mathcal{T}_i^{qr} = 0_{st}$	4
two points, one line	$x^i x'^j l''_r \epsilon_{jqs} \mathcal{T}_i^{qr} = 0_s$	2
one point, two lines	$x^i l'_q l''_r \mathcal{T}_i^{qr} = 0$	1
three lines	$l_p l'_q l''_r \epsilon^{piw} \mathcal{T}_i^{qr} = 0^w$	2

Table 16.1. **Trilinear relations between point and line coordinates in three views.** *The final column denotes the number of linearly independent equations. The notation 0_{st} means a 2-dimensional tensor with all zero entries. Thus, the first line in this table corresponds to a set of 9 equations, one for each choice of s and t. However, among this set of 9 equations, only 4 are linearly independent.*

Given several point or line correspondences between three images, the complete set of equations generated is of the form $\mathtt{At} = \mathbf{0}$, where $\mathbf{t}$ is the 27-vector made up of the entries of the trifocal tensor. From these equations, one may solve for the entries of the tensor. Note that equations involving points may be combined with those involving lines – in general all available equations from table 16.1 may be used simultaneously. Since $\mathcal{T}$ has 27 entries, 26 equations are needed to solve for $\mathbf{t}$ up to scale. With more than 26 equations, a least-squares solution is computed. As with the fundamental matrix, one minimizes $\|\mathtt{At}\|$ subject to the constraint $\|\mathbf{t}\| = 1$ using algorithm A5.4(p593).

This gives a bare outline of a linear algorithm for computing the trifocal tensor. However, in order to build a practical algorithm out of this several issues, such as normalization, need to be addressed. In particular the tensor that is estimated must obey various constraints, and we consider these next.

16.1.1 The internal constraints

The most notable difference between the fundamental matrix and the trifocal tensor is the greater number of constraints that apply to the trifocal tensor. The fundamental matrix has a single constraint, namely $\det(\mathtt{F}) = 0$, leaving 7 degrees of freedom, discounting the arbitrary scale factor. The trifocal tensor, on the other hand, has 27 entries, but 18 parameters only are required to specify the equivalent camera configuration, up to projectivity. The elements of the tensor therefore satisfy 8 independent algebraic constraints. This condition is conveniently stated as follows.

Definition 16.1. A trifocal tensor $\mathcal{T}_i^{jk}$ is said to be "geometrically valid" or "satisfy all internal constraints" if there exist three camera matrices $\mathtt{P} = [\mathtt{I} \mid \mathbf{0}]$, $\mathtt{P}'$ and $\mathtt{P}''$ such that $\mathcal{T}_i^{jk}$ corresponds to the three camera matrices according to (15.9–p376).

Just as with the fundamental matrix it is important to enforce these constraints in some way so as to arrive at a geometrically valid trifocal tensor. If the tensor does not satisfy the constraints, there are consequences similar to a fundamental matrix which is not of rank 2 – where epipolar lines, computed as $\mathtt{F}\mathbf{x}$ for varying $\mathbf{x}$, do not intersect in a single point (see figure 11.1(p280)). For example, if the tensor does not satisfy the internal constraints and is used to transfer a point to a third view, given a correspondence over two views as described in section 15.3, then the position of the transferred point will vary depending on which set of equations from table 16.1 is used. In the following the objective is always to estimate a geometrically valid tensor.

The constraints satisfied by the trifocal tensor elements are not so simply expressed (as $\det = 0$), and some have thought this an impediment to accurate computation of the trifocal tensor. However, in reality, in order to work with or compute the trifocal tensor it is not necessary to express these constraints explicitly – rather they are implicitly enforced by an appropriate parametrization of the trifocal tensor, and rarely cause any trouble. We will return to the issue of parametrization in section 16.3 and section 16.4.2.

16.1.2 The minimum case – 6 point correspondences

A geometrically valid trifocal tensor may be computed from images of a 6 point configuration, provided the scene points are in general position. There are one or three real solutions. The tensor is computed from the three camera matrices which are obtained using algorithm 20.1(*p*511), as described in section 20.2.4(*p*510). This minimal six point solution is used in the robust algorithm of section 16.6.

16.2 The normalized linear algorithm

In forming the matrix equation $\mathtt{A}\mathbf{t} = \mathbf{0}$ from the equations on $\mathcal{T}$ in table 16.1 it is not necessary to use the complete set of equations derived from each correspondence, since not all of these equations are linearly independent. For instance in the case of a point–point–point correspondence (first row of table 16.1) all choices of s and t lead to a set of 9 equations, but only 4 of these equations are linearly independent, and these may be obtained by choosing two values for each of s and t, for instance 1 and 2. This point is discussed in more detail in section 17.7(*p*431).

The reader may verify that the three points equation obtained from table 16.1 for a given choice of s and t may be expanded as

$$x^k(x'^i x''^m \mathcal{T}_k^{jl} - x'^j x''^m \mathcal{T}_k^{il} - x'^i x''^l \mathcal{T}_k^{jm} + x'^j x''^l \mathcal{T}_k^{im}) = 0^{ijlm} \quad . \tag{16.1}$$

when $i, j \neq s$ and $l, m \neq t$. Equation (16.1) collapses for $i = j$ or $l = m$, and swapping i and j (or l and m) simply changes the sign of the equation. One choice of the four independent equations is obtained by setting $j = m = 3$, and letting i and l range freely. The coordinates x^3, x'^3 and x''^3 may be set to 1 to obtain a relationship between the observed image coordinates. Equation (16.1) then becomes

$$x^k(x'^i x''^l \mathcal{T}_k^{33} - x''^l \mathcal{T}_k^{i3} - x'^i \mathcal{T}_k^{3l} + \mathcal{T}_k^{il}) = 0. \tag{16.2}$$

The four different choices of $i, l = 1, 2$ give four different equations in terms of the observed image coordinates.

How to represent lines

The three lines correspondence equation of table 16.1 may be written in the form

$$l_i = l'_j l''_k \mathcal{T}_i^{jk},$$

where, as usual with homogeneous entities, the equality is up to scale. In the presence of noise, this relationship will only be approximately satisfied by the *measured* lines $\mathbf{l}$, $\mathbf{l}'$ and $\mathbf{l}''$, but will be satisfied exactly for three lines $\hat{\mathbf{l}}$, $\hat{\mathbf{l}}'$ and $\hat{\mathbf{l}}''$ that are close to the measured lines.

The question is whether two sets of homogeneous coordinates that differ by a small amount represent lines that are close to each other in some geometric sense. Consider the two vectors $\mathbf{l}_1 = (0.01, 0, 1)^\mathsf{T}$ and $\mathbf{l}_2 = (0, 0.01, 1)^\mathsf{T}$. Clearly as vectors they are not very different, and in fact $||\mathbf{l}_1 - \mathbf{l}_2||$ is small. On the other hand, $\mathbf{l}_1$ represents the line $x = 100$, and $\mathbf{l}_2$ represents the line $y = 100$. Thus in a geometric sense, these lines are totally different. Note that this problem is alleviated by scaling. If coordinates are

Objective

Given $n \geq 7$ image point correspondences across 3 images, or at least 13 line correspondences, or a mixture of point and line correspondences, compute the trifocal tensor.

Algorithm

(i) Find transformation matrices $\mathtt{H}$, $\mathtt{H}'$ and $\mathtt{H}''$ to apply to the three images.

(ii) Transform points according to $x^i \mapsto \hat{x}^i = \mathtt{H}^i_j x^j$, and lines according to $l_i \mapsto \hat{l}_i = (\mathtt{H}^{-1})^j_i l_j$. Points and lines in the second and third image transform in the same way.

(iii) Compute the trifocal tensor $\hat{\mathcal{T}}$ linearly in terms of the transformed points and lines using the equations in table 16.1 by solving a set of equation of the form $\mathtt{A}\mathbf{t} = \mathbf{0}$, using algorithm A5.4(*p*593).

(iv) Compute the trifocal tensor corresponding to the original data according to $\mathcal{T}_i^{jk} = \mathtt{H}^r_i (\mathtt{H}'^{-1})^j_s (\mathtt{H}''^{-1})^k_t \hat{\mathcal{T}}_r^{st}$.

Algorithm 16.1. *The normalized linear algorithm for computation of $\mathcal{T}$.*

scaled by a factor of 0.01, then the coordinates for the lines become $\mathbf{l}_1 = (1, 0, 1)^\mathsf{T}$ and $\mathbf{l}_2 = (0, 1, 1)^\mathsf{T}$, which are quite different.

Nevertheless, this observation indicates that care is needed when representing lines. Suppose one is given a correspondence between three lines $\mathbf{l}$, $\mathbf{l}'$ and $\mathbf{l}''$. Two points $\mathbf{x}_1$ and $\mathbf{x}_2$ lying on $\mathbf{l}$ are selected. Each of these points provides a correspondence $\mathbf{x}_s \leftrightarrow \mathbf{l}' \leftrightarrow \mathbf{l}''$, for $s = 1, 2$, between the three views, in the sense that there exists a 3D line that maps to $\mathbf{l}'$ and $\mathbf{l}''$ in the second and third images and to a line (namely $\mathbf{l}$) passing through $\mathbf{x}_s$ in the first image. Two equations of the form $x^i_s l'_j l''_k \mathcal{T}_i^{jk} = 0_s$ for $s = 1, 2$ result from these correspondences. In this way one avoids the use of lines in the first image, though not the other images. Often lines in images are defined naturally by a pair of points, possibly the two endpoints of the lines. Even lines that are defined as the best fit to a set of edge points in an image may be treated as if they were defined by just two points, as will be described in section 16.7.2.

Normalization

As in all algorithms of this type, it is necessary to carry out prenormalization of the input data before forming and solving the linear equation system. Subsequently, it is necessary to correct for this normalization to find the trifocal tensor for the original data. The recommended normalization is much the same as that given for the computation of the fundamental matrix. A translation is applied to each image such that the centroid of the points is at the origin, and then a scaling is applied so that the average (RMS) distance of the points from the origin is $\sqrt{2}$. In the case of lines, the transformation should be defined by considering each line's two endpoints (or some representative line points visible in the image). The transformation rule for the trifocal tensor under these normalizing transformations is given in section A1.2(*p*563). The normalized linear algorithm for computing $\mathcal{T}$ is summarized in algorithm 16.1.

This algorithm does not consider the constraints discussed in section 16.1.1 that should be applied to $\mathcal{T}$. These constraints ought to be enforced before the denormalization step (final step) in the above algorithm. Methods of enforcing these constraints will be considered next.

16.3 The algebraic minimization algorithm

The linear algorithm 16.1 will give a tensor not necessarily corresponding to any geometric configuration, as discussed in section 16.1.1. The next task is to correct the tensor to satisfy all required constraints.

Our task will be to compute a geometrically valid trifocal tensor $\mathcal{T}_i^{jk}$ from a set of image correspondences. The tensor computed will minimize the algebraic error associated with the input data. That is, we minimize $\|\mathtt{A}\hat{\mathbf{t}}\|$ subject to $\|\hat{\mathbf{t}}\| = 1$, where $\hat{\mathbf{t}}$ is the vector of entries of a geometrically valid trifocal tensor. The algorithm is quite similar to the algebraic algorithm (section 11.3(p282)) for computation of the fundamental matrix. Just as with the fundamental matrix, the first step is the computation of the epipoles.

Retrieving the epipoles

Let $\mathbf{e}'$ and $\mathbf{e}''$ be the epipoles in the second and third images corresponding to (that is being images of) the first camera centre. Recall from result 15.4(p373) that the two epipoles $\mathbf{e}'$ and $\mathbf{e}''$ are the common perpendicular to the left (respectively right) null-vectors of the three $\mathtt{T}_i$. In principle then, the epipoles may be computed from the trifocal tensor using the algorithm outlined in algorithm 15.1(p375). However, in the presence of noise, this translates easily into an algorithm for computing the epipoles based on four applications of algorithm A5.4(p593).

(i) For each $i = 1, \ldots, 3$ find the unit vector $\mathbf{v}_i$ that minimizes $\|\mathtt{T}_i \mathbf{v}_i\|$, where $\mathtt{T}_i = \mathcal{T}_i^{\cdot\cdot}$. Form the matrix $\mathtt{V}$, the i-th row of which is $\mathbf{v}_i^\mathsf{T}$.
(ii) Compute the epipole $\mathbf{e}''$ as the unit vector that minimizes $\|\mathtt{V}\mathbf{e}''\|$.

The epipole $\mathbf{e}'$ is computed similarly, using $\mathtt{T}_i^\mathsf{T}$ instead of $\mathtt{T}_i$.

Algebraic minimization

Having computed the epipoles the next step is to determine the remaining elements of the camera matrices $\mathtt{P}', \mathtt{P}''$ from which the trifocal tensor can be calculated. This step is linear.

From the form (15.9–p376) of the trifocal tensor, it may be seen that once the epipoles $\mathbf{e}'^j = a_4^j$ and $\mathbf{e}''^k = b_4^k$ are known, the trifocal tensor may be expressed linearly in terms of the remaining entries of the matrices a_i^j and b_i^k. This relationship may be written linearly as $\mathbf{t} = \mathtt{E}\mathbf{a}$ where $\mathbf{a}$ is the vector of the remaining entries a_j^i and b_j^i, $\mathbf{t}$ is the vector of entries of the trifocal tensor, and $\mathtt{E}$ is the linear relationship expressed by (15.9–p376). We wish to minimize the algebraic error $\|\mathtt{A}\mathbf{t}\| = \|\mathtt{AE}\mathbf{a}\|$ over all choices of $\mathbf{a}$ constrained such that $\|\mathbf{t}\| = 1$, that is $\|\mathtt{E}\mathbf{a}\| = 1$. This minimization problem is solved by algorithm A5.6(p595). The solution $\mathbf{t} = \mathtt{E}\mathbf{a}$ represents a trifocal tensor satisfying all constraints, and minimizing the algebraic error, subject to the given choice of epipoles.

Objective

Given a set of point and line correspondences in three views, compute the trifocal tensor.

Algorithm

(i) From the set of point and line correspondences compute the set of equations of the form $\mathtt{A}\mathbf{t} = \mathbf{0}$, from the relations given in table 16.1.

(ii) Solve these equations using algorithm A5.4(p593) to find an initial estimate of the trifocal tensor $\mathcal{T}_i^{jk}$.

(iii) Find the two epipoles $\mathbf{e}'$ and $\mathbf{e}''$ from $\mathcal{T}_i^{jk}$ as the common perpendicular to the left (respectively right) null-vectors of the three $\mathtt{T}_i$.

(iv) Construct the 27×18 matrix E such that $\mathbf{t} = \mathtt{E}\mathbf{a}$ where $\mathbf{t}$ is the vector of entries of $\mathcal{T}_i^{jk}$, $\mathbf{a}$ is the vector representing entries of a_i^j and b_i^k, and where E expresses the linear relationship $\mathcal{T}_i^{jk} = a_i^j e''^k - e'^j b_i^k$.

(v) Solve the minimization problem: minimize $\|\mathtt{AEa}\|$ subject to $\|\mathtt{E}\mathbf{a}\| = 1$, using algorithm A5.6($p$595). Compute the error vector $\boldsymbol{\epsilon} = \mathtt{AEa}$.

(vi) **Iteration:** The mapping $(\mathbf{e}', \mathbf{e}'') \mapsto \boldsymbol{\epsilon}$ is a mapping from $\mathbb{R}^6$ to $\mathbb{R}^{27}$. Iterate on the last two steps with varying $\mathbf{e}'$ and $\mathbf{e}''$ using the Levenberg–Marquardt algorithm to find the optimal $\mathbf{e}', \mathbf{e}''$. Hence find the optimal $\mathbf{t} = \mathtt{E}\mathbf{a}$ containing the entries of $\mathcal{T}_i^{jk}$.

Algorithm 16.2. **Computing the trifocal tensor minimizing algebraic error.** *The computation should be carried out on data normalized in the manner of algorithm 16.1. Normalization and denormalization steps are omitted here for simplicity. This algorithm finds the geometrically valid trifocal tensor that minimizes algebraic error. At the cost of a slightly inferior solution, the last iteration step may be omitted, providing a fast non-iterative algorithm.*

Iterative method

The two epipoles used to compute a geometrically valid tensor $\mathcal{T}_i^{jk}$ are determined using the estimate of $\mathcal{T}_i^{jk}$ obtained from the linear algorithm. Analogous to the case of the fundamental matrix, the mapping $(\mathbf{e}', \mathbf{e}'') \mapsto \mathtt{AE}\mathbf{a}$ is a mapping $\mathbb{R}^6 \rightarrow \mathbb{R}^{27}$. An application of the Levenberg–Marquardt algorithm to optimize the choice of the epipoles will result in an optimal (in terms of algebraic error) estimate of the trifocal tensor. Note that the iteration problem is of modest size, since only 6 parameters, the homogeneous coordinates of the epipoles, are involved in the iteration problem.

This contrasts with an iterative estimation of the optimal trifocal tensor in terms of geometric error, considered later. This latter problem requires estimating the parameters of the three cameras, plus the coordinates of all the points, a large estimation problem.

The complete algebraic method for estimating the trifocal tensor is summarized in algorithm 16.2.

16.4 Geometric distance

16.4.1 The Gold Standard method for the trifocal tensor

As with the computation of the fundamental matrix, best results may be expected from the maximum likelihood (or "Gold Standard") solution. Since this has been adequately described for the case of the fundamental matrix computation, little needs to be added for the three-view case.

Objective

Given $n \geq 7$ image point correspondences $\{\mathbf{x}_i \leftrightarrow \mathbf{x}'_i \leftrightarrow \mathbf{x}''_i\}$, determine the Maximum Likelihood Estimate of the trifocal tensor.

The MLE involves also solving for a set of subsidiary point correspondences $\{\hat{\mathbf{x}}_i \leftrightarrow \hat{\mathbf{x}}'_i \leftrightarrow \hat{\mathbf{x}}''_i\}$, which exactly satisfy the trilinear relations of the estimated tensor and which minimize

$$\sum_i d(\mathbf{x}_i, \hat{\mathbf{x}}_i)^2 + d(\mathbf{x}'_i, \hat{\mathbf{x}}'_i)^2 + d(\mathbf{x}''_i, \hat{\mathbf{x}}''_i)^2$$

Algorithm

(i) Compute an initial geometrically valid estimate of $\mathcal{T}$ using a linear algorithm such as algorithm 16.2.

(ii) Compute an initial estimate of the subsidiary variables $\{\hat{\mathbf{x}}_i, \hat{\mathbf{x}}'_i, \hat{\mathbf{x}}''_i\}$ as follows:

  (a) Retrieve the camera matrices $\mathtt{P}'$ and $\mathtt{P}''$ from $\mathcal{T}$.

  (b) From the correspondence $\mathbf{x}_i \leftrightarrow \mathbf{x}'_i \leftrightarrow \mathbf{x}''_i$ and $\mathtt{P} = [\mathtt{I} \mid \mathbf{0}], \mathtt{P}', \mathtt{P}''$ determine an estimate of $\widehat{\mathbf{X}}_i$ using the triangulation method of chapter 12.

  (c) The correspondence consistent with $\mathcal{T}$ is obtained as $\hat{\mathbf{x}}_i = \mathtt{P}\widehat{\mathbf{X}}_i,\ \hat{\mathbf{x}}'_i = \mathtt{P}'\widehat{\mathbf{X}}_i,\ \hat{\mathbf{x}}''_i = \mathtt{P}''\widehat{\mathbf{X}}_i$.

(iii) Minimize the cost

$$\sum_i d(\mathbf{x}_i, \hat{\mathbf{x}}_i)^2 + d(\mathbf{x}'_i, \hat{\mathbf{x}}'_i)^2 + d(\mathbf{x}''_i, \hat{\mathbf{x}}''_i)^2$$

over $\mathcal{T}$ and $\widehat{\mathbf{X}}_i, i = 1, \ldots, n$. The cost is minimized using the Levenberg–Marquardt algorithm over $3n + 24$ variables: $3n$ for the n 3D points $\widehat{\mathbf{X}}_i$, and 24 for the elements of the camera matrices $\mathtt{P}', \mathtt{P}''$.

Algorithm 16.3. *The Gold Standard algorithm for estimating $\mathcal{T}$ from image correspondences.*

Given a set of point correspondences $\{\mathbf{x}_i \leftrightarrow \mathbf{x}'_i \leftrightarrow \mathbf{x}''_i\}$ in three views, the cost function to be minimized is

$$\sum_i d(\mathbf{x}_i, \hat{\mathbf{x}}_i)^2 + d(\mathbf{x}'_i, \hat{\mathbf{x}}'_i)^2 + d(\mathbf{x}''_i, \hat{\mathbf{x}}''_i)^2 \qquad (16.3)$$

where the points $\hat{\mathbf{x}}_i, \hat{\mathbf{x}}'_i, \hat{\mathbf{x}}''_i$ satisfy a trifocal constraint (as in table 16.1) exactly for the estimated trifocal tensor. As in the case of the fundamental matrix one needs to introduce further variables corresponding to 3D points $\mathbf{X}_i$ and parametrize the trifocal tensor by the entries of the matrices $\mathtt{P}'$ and $\mathtt{P}''$ (see below). The cost function is then minimized over the position of the 3D points $\mathbf{X}_i$ and the two camera matrices $\mathtt{P}'$ and $\mathtt{P}''$ with $\hat{\mathbf{x}}_i = [\mathtt{I} \mid \mathbf{0}]\mathbf{X}_i,\ \hat{\mathbf{x}}'_i = \mathtt{P}'\mathbf{X}_i$, and $\hat{\mathbf{x}}''_i = \mathtt{P}''\mathbf{X}_i$. Essentially one is carrying out bundle adjustment over three views. The sparse matrix techniques of section A6.3-(*p*602) should be used.

A good way to find an initial estimate is the algebraic algorithm 16.2, though the final iterative step can be omitted. This algorithm gives a direct estimate of the entries of $\mathtt{P}'$ and $\mathtt{P}''$. The initial estimate of the 3D points $\mathbf{X}_i$ may be obtained using the linear triangulation method of section 12.2(*p*312). The steps of the algorithm are summarized in algorithm 16.3.

The technique can be extended to include line correspondences. To do this, one needs to find a representation of a 3D line convenient for computation. Given a 3-view line correspondence $\mathbf{l} \leftrightarrow \mathbf{l}' \leftrightarrow \mathbf{l}''$, the lines being perhaps defined by their endpoints in each image, a very convenient way to represent the 3D line during the LM parameter minimization is by its projections $\hat{\mathbf{l}}'$ and $\hat{\mathbf{l}}''$ in the second and third views. Given a candidate trifocal tensor, one can easily compute the projection of the 3D line into the first view using the line transfer equation $\hat{l}_i = \hat{l}'_j \hat{l}''_k \mathcal{T}_i^{jk}$. Then one minimizes the sum-of-squares line distance

$$\sum_i d(\mathbf{l}_i, \hat{\mathbf{l}}_i)^2 + d(\mathbf{l}'_i, \hat{\mathbf{l}}'_i)^2 + d(\mathbf{l}''_i, \hat{\mathbf{l}}''_i)^2$$

for some appropriate interpretation of the distance $d(\mathbf{l}'_i, \hat{\mathbf{l}}'_i)^2$ between the measured and estimated line. If the measured line is specified by its endpoints, then the obvious distance metric to use is the distance of the estimated line from the measured endpoints. In general a Mahalanobis distance may be used.

16.4.2 Parametrization of the trifocal tensor

If the tensor is parametrized simply by its 27 entries, then the estimated tensor will not satisfy the internal constraints. A parametrization which ensures that the tensor does satisfy its constraints, and so is geometrically valid, is termed *consistent*.

Since, from definition 16.1, a tensor is geometrically valid if it is generated from three camera matrices $\mathtt{P} = [\mathtt{I} \mid \mathbf{0}], \mathtt{P}', \mathtt{P}''$ by (15.9–*p*376), it follows that the three camera matrices give a consistent parametrization. Note that this is an *over*parametrization since it requires 24 parameters to be specified, namely the 12 entries each of the matrices $\mathtt{P}' = [\mathtt{A}|\mathbf{a}_4]$ and $\mathtt{P}'' = [\mathtt{B}|\mathbf{b}_4]$. There is no need to attempt to define a minimal set of (18) parameters, which is a difficult task. Any choice of cameras is a consistent parametrization, the particular projective reconstruction has no effect on the tensor.

Another consistent parametrization is obtained by computing the tensor from six point correspondences across three views as in section 20.2(*p*508). Then the position of the points in each image is the parametrization – a total of 6 (points) $\times 2$ (for x, y) $\times$ 3 (images) $= 36$ parameters. However, only a subset of the points need be varied during the minimization, or the movement of the points can be restricted to be perpendicular to the variety of trifocal tensors.

16.4.3 First-order geometric error (Sampson distance)

The trifocal tensor may be computed using a geometric cost function based on the Sampson approximation in a manner entirely analogous to the Sampson method used to compute the fundamental matrix (section 11.4.3(*p*287)). Again the advantage is that it is not necessary to introduce a set of subsidiary variables, as this first-order geometric error requires a minimization only over the parametrization of the tensor (e.g. only 24 parameters if $\mathtt{P}', \mathtt{P}''$ is used as above). The minimization can be carried out with a simple iterative Levenberg–Marquardt algorithm, and the method initialized by the iterative algebraic algorithm 16.2.

The Sampson cost function is a little more complex computationally than the corresponding cost function for the fundamental matrix (11.9–p287), because each point correspondence gives four equations, instead of just one for the fundamental matrix. The more general case was discussed in section 4.2.6(p98). The error function (4.13–p100) in the present case is

$$\sum_i \epsilon_i^{\mathsf{T}} (\mathtt{J}_i \mathtt{J}_i^{\mathsf{T}})^{-1} \epsilon_i \tag{16.4}$$

where ϵ_i is the algebraic error vector $\mathtt{A}_i\mathbf{t}$ corresponding to a single 3-view correspondence (a 4-vector in the case of 4 equations per point), and $\mathtt{J}$ is the 4×6 matrix of partial derivatives of ϵ with respect to the coordinates of each of the corresponding points $\mathbf{x}_i \leftrightarrow \mathbf{x}'_i \leftrightarrow \mathbf{x}''_i$. As in the programming hint given in exercise (vii) on page 129, the computation of the partial derivative matrix $\mathtt{J}$ may be simplified by observing that the cost function is multilinear in the coordinates of the points $\mathbf{x}_i, \mathbf{x}'_i, \mathbf{x}''_i$.

The Sampson error method has various advantages:

- It gives a good approximation to actual geometric error (the optimum), using a relatively simple iterative algorithm.
- As in the case of actual geometric error, non-isotropic and unequal error distributions may be specified for each of the points without significantly complicating the algorithm. See exercises in chapter 4.

16.5 Experimental evaluation of the algorithms

A brief comparison is now given of the results of the (iterative) algebraic algorithm 16.2 along with the Gold Standard algorithm 16.3 for computing the trifocal tensor. The algorithms are run on synthetic data with controlled levels of noise. This allows a comparison with the theoretically optimal ML results, and a determination of how well these algorithms are able to approximate the theoretical lower bound on residual error, achieved by an optimal ML algorithm.

Computer-generated data sets of 10, 15 and 20 points were used to test the algorithm, and the cameras were placed at random angles around the cloud of points. The camera parameters were chosen to approximate a standard 35mm camera, and the scale was chosen so that the size of the image was 600×600 pixels.

For a given level of added Gaussian noise in the image measurement, one may compute the expected residual achieved by an ML algorithm, according to result 5.2(p136). In this case, if n is the number of points, then the number of measurements is $N = 6n$, and the number of degrees of freedom in the fitting is $d = 18 + 3n$, where 18 represents the number of degrees of freedom of the three cameras (3×11 less 15 to account for projective ambiguity) and $3n$ represents the number of degrees of freedom of n points in space. Hence the ML residual is

$$\epsilon_{\text{res}} = \sigma(1 - d/N)^{1/2} = \sigma \left(\frac{n-6}{2n} \right)^{1/2}.$$

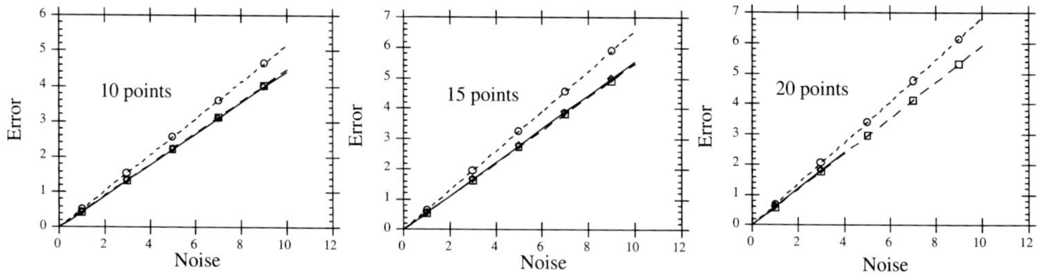

Fig. 16.1. **Comparison of trifocal tensor estimation algorithms.** *The residual error RMS-averaged over 100 runs is plotted against the noise level, for computation of the trifocal tensor using 10, 15 and 20 points. Each graph contains three curves. The top curve is the result of the algebraic error minimization, whereas the lower two curves, actually indistinguishable in the graphs, represent the theoretical minimum error, and the error obtained by the Gold Standard algorithm using the algebraic minimization as a starting point. Note that the residual errors are almost exactly proportional to added noise, as they should be.*

16.5.1 Results and recommendations

The results are shown in figure 16.1. We learn two things from these results. Minimization of the algebraic error achieves residual errors within about 15% of the optimal and using this estimate as a starting point for minimizing geometric error achieves a virtually optimal estimate.

All the algorithms developed above, except the linear method of section 16.1, enforce the internal constraints on the tensor. The linear method is not recommended for use on its own, but is necessary for initialization in most of the other methods. As in the case of estimating the fundamental matrix our recommendations are to use the iterative algebraic algorithm 16.2 or the Sampson geometric approximation of section 16.4.3. Both give excellent results. Again to be certain of getting the best results, if Gaussian noise is a viable assumption, implement the Gold Standard algorithm 16.3.

16.6 Automatic computation of $\mathcal{T}$

This section describes an algorithm to compute the trifocal geometry between three images automatically. The input to the algorithm is simply the triplet of images, with no other *a priori* information required; and the output is the estimated trifocal tensor together with a set of interest points in correspondence across the three images.

The fact that the trifocal tensor may be used to determine the exact image position of a point in a third view, given its image position in the other two views, means that there are fewer mismatches over three views than there are over two. In the two view case there is only the weaker geometric constraint of an epipolar line against which to verify a possible match.

The three-view algorithm uses RANSAC as a search engine in a similar manner to its use in the automatic computation of a homography described in section 4.8-(*p*123). The ideas and details of the algorithm are given there, and are not repeated here. The method is summarized in algorithm 16.4, with an example of its use shown

Objective Compute the trifocal tensor between three images.

Algorithm

(i) **Interest points:** Compute interest points in each image.
(ii) **Two-view correspondences:** Compute interest point correspondences (and F) between views 1 & 2, and 2 & 3 using algorithm 11.4(p291).
(iii) **Putative three-view correspondences:** Compute a set of interest point correspondences over three views by joining the two-view match sets.
(iv) **RANSAC robust estimation:** Repeat for N samples, where N is determined adaptively as in algorithm 4.5(p121):
   (a) Select a random sample of 6 correspondences and compute the trifocal tensor using algorithm 20.1(p511). There will be one or three real solutions.
   (b) Calculate the distance $d_\perp$ in $\mathbb{R}^6$ from each putative correspondence to the variety described by $\mathcal{T}$, as in section 16.6.
   (c) Compute the number of inliers consistent with $\mathcal{T}$ by the number of correspondences for which $d_\perp < t$.
   (d) If there are three real solutions for $\mathcal{T}$ the number of inliers is computed for each solution, and the solution with most inliers retained.

   Choose the $\mathcal{T}$ with the largest number of inliers. In the case of ties choose the solution that has the lowest standard deviation of inliers.
(v) **Optimal estimation:** Re-estimate $\mathcal{T}$ from all correspondences classified as inliers using the Gold Standard algorithm 16.3 or the Sampson approximation to this.
(vi) **Guided matching:** Further interest point correspondences are now determined using the estimated $\mathcal{T}$ as described in the text.

The last two steps can be iterated until the number of correspondences is stable.

Algorithm 16.4. *Algorithm to automatically estimate the trifocal tensor over three images using RANSAC.*

in figure 16.2, and additional explanation of the steps given below. Figure 16.3 shows a second example which includes automatically computed line matches.

The distance measure – reprojection error. Given the match $\mathbf{x} \leftrightarrow \mathbf{x}' \leftrightarrow \mathbf{x}''$ and the current estimate of $\mathcal{T}$ we need to determine the minimum of the reprojection error – $d_\perp^2 = d^2(\mathbf{x}, \hat{\mathbf{x}}) + d^2(\mathbf{x}', \hat{\mathbf{x}}') + d^2(\mathbf{x}'', \hat{\mathbf{x}}'')$, where the image points $\hat{\mathbf{x}}, \hat{\mathbf{x}}', \hat{\mathbf{x}}''$ are consistent with $\mathcal{T}$. As usual the consistent images points may be obtained from the projection of a 3-space point $\widehat{\mathbf{X}}$

$$\hat{\mathbf{x}} = [\mathtt{I} \mid \mathbf{0}]\widehat{\mathbf{X}}, \quad \hat{\mathbf{x}}' = \mathtt{P}'\widehat{\mathbf{X}}, \quad \hat{\mathbf{x}}'' = \mathtt{P}''\widehat{\mathbf{X}}$$

where the camera matrices $\mathtt{P}', \mathtt{P}''$ are extracted from $\mathcal{T}$. The distance $d_\perp^2$ is then obtained by determining the point $\widehat{\mathbf{X}}$ which minimizes the image distance between the measured points $\mathbf{x}, \mathbf{x}', \mathbf{x}''$ and the projected points.

Another way of obtaining this distance is to use the Sampson error (16.4), which is a first-order approximation to the geometric error. However, in practice it is quicker to estimate the error directly by non-linear least-squares iteration (a small Levenberg–Marquardt problem). Starting from an initial estimate of $\widehat{\mathbf{X}}$, one iterates varying the coordinates of $\widehat{\mathbf{X}}$ to minimize the reprojection error.

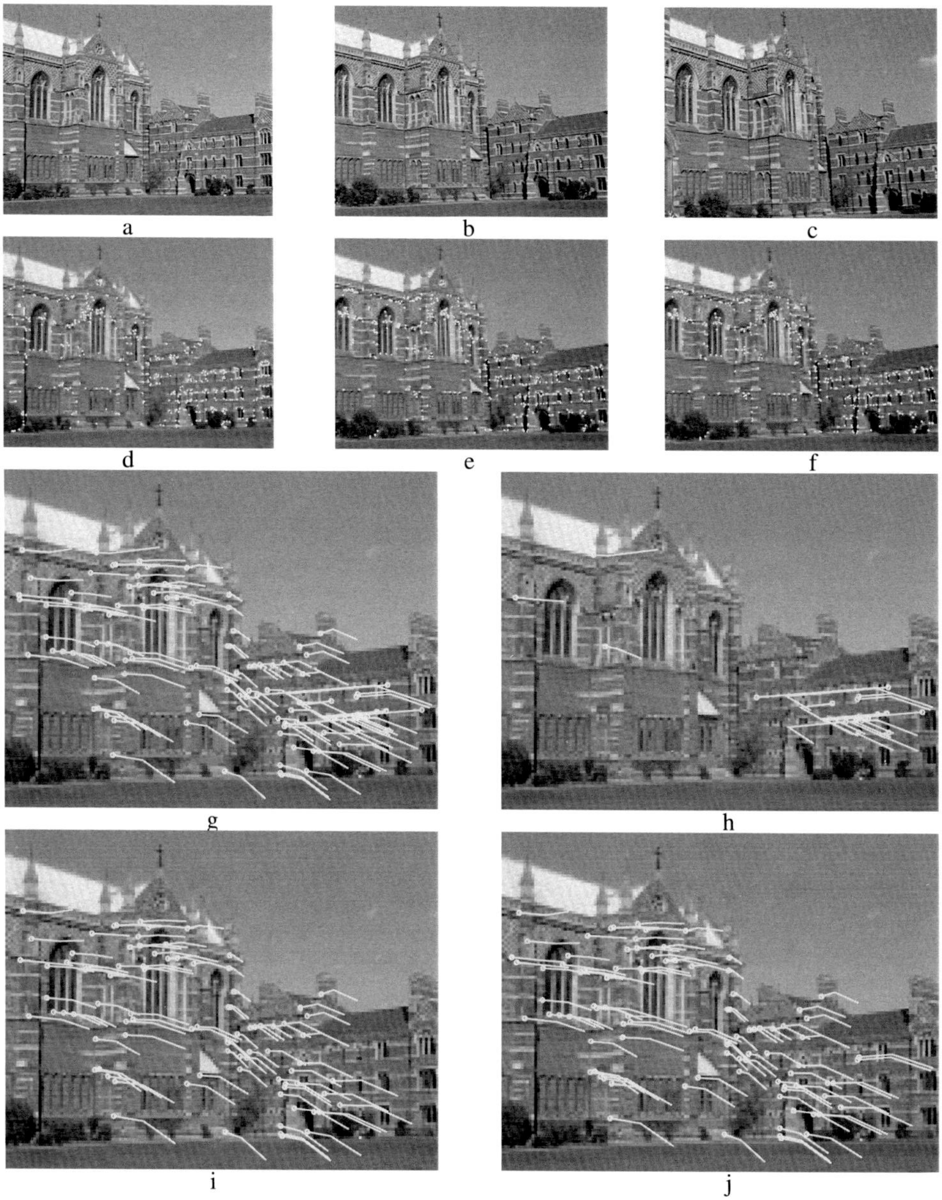

Fig. 16.2. **Automatic computation of the trifocal tensor between three images using RANSAC.** *(a - c) raw images of Keble College, Oxford. The motion between views consists of a translation and rotation. The images are* 640×480 *pixels. (d - f) detected corners superimposed on the images. There are approximately 500 corners on each image. The following results are superimposed on the (a) image: (g) 106 putative matches shown by the line linking corners, note the clear mismatches; (h) outliers – 18 of the putative matches. (i) inliers – 88 correspondences consistent with the estimated* $\mathcal{T}$*; (j) final set of 95 correspondences after guided matching and MLE. There are no mismatches.*

Guided matching. We have an initial estimate of $\mathcal{T}$ and wish to use this to generate and assess additional point correspondences across the three-views. The first step is to extract the fundamental matrix $\mathtt{F}_{12}$ between views 1 & 2 from $\mathcal{T}$. Then two-view

a

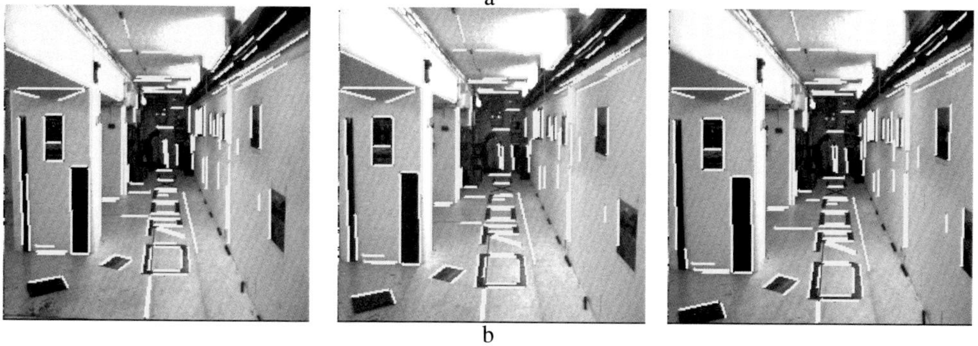

b

Fig. 16.3. **Image triplet matching.** *The trifocal tensor is computed automatically from interest points using algorithm 16.4, and subsequently used to match line features across views. (a) Three images of a corridor sequence. (b) Automatically matched line segments. The matching algorithm is described in [Schmid-97].*

guided matches are computed using loose thresholds on matching. Each two-view match is corrected using F_{12} to give points $\hat{x}, \hat{x}'$ which are consistent with F_{12}. These corrected two-view matches (together with $\mathcal{T}$) define a small search window in the third view in which the corresponding point is sought. Any three-view point correspondence is assessed by computing $d_\perp$, as described above. The match accepted if $d_\perp$ is less than the threshold t. Note, the same threshold is used for inlier detection within the RANSAC stage and guided matching.

In practice it is found that the stage of guided matching is more significant here, in that it generates additional correspondences, than in the case of homography estimation.

Implementation and run details. For the example of figure 16.2, the search window was ± 300 pixels. The inlier threshold was $t = 1.25$ pixels. A total of 26 samples were required. The RMS pixel error after RANSAC was 0.43 (for 88 correspondences), after MLE it was 0.23 (for 88 correspondences), and after MLE and guided matching it was 0.19 (for 95 correspondences). The MLE required 10 iterations of the Levenberg–Marquardt algorithm.

Note, RANSAC has to do far less work than in algorithm 11.4(*p*291) to estimate F and correspondences, because the two-view algorithm has already removed many outliers before the putative correspondences over three views are generated.

16.7 Special cases of $\mathcal{T}$-computation

16.7.1 Computing $\mathcal{T}_i^{jk}$ from a plane plus parallax

We describe here the computation of $\mathcal{T}_i^{jk}$ from the image of a special configuration consisting of a world plane (from which a homography between views can be computed) and two points off the plane. Of course, it is not necessary for the plane to actually be present. It may be virtual, or the homography may simply be specified by the images of four coplanar points or four coplanar lines. The method is the analogue of algorithm 13.2(*p*336) for the fundamental matrix.

The solution is obtained by constructing the three camera matrices (up to a common projective transformation of 3-space) and then computing the trifocal tensor from these matrices according to (15.9–*p*376). The homography induced by the world (reference) plane between the first and second view is $\mathtt{H}_{12}$, and between the first and third views is $\mathtt{H}_{13}$. As shown in section 13.3(*p*334) the epipole $\mathbf{e}'$ may be computed directly from the two point correspondences off the plane for the first and second views, and the camera matrices chosen as $\mathtt{P} = [\mathtt{I} \mid \mathbf{0}]$, $\mathtt{P}' = [\mathtt{H}_{12} \mid \mu\mathbf{e}']$, where μ is a scalar. Note the scale of both $\mathtt{H}_{12}$ and $\mathbf{e}'$ is considered fixed here, so they are no longer homogeneous quantities. Similarly, $\mathbf{e}''$ may be determined from the two point correspondences for views one and three and the camera matrices chosen as $\mathtt{P} = [\mathtt{I} \mid \mathbf{0}]$, $\mathtt{P}'' = [\mathtt{H}_{13} \mid \lambda\mathbf{e}'']$, where λ is a scalar.

It is then easily verified that a consistent set of cameras for the three views (see the discussion on consistent camera triplets on page 375) is given by

$$\mathtt{P} = [\mathtt{I} \mid \mathbf{0}], \quad \mathtt{P}' = [\mathtt{H}_{12} \mid \mathbf{e}'], \quad \mathtt{P}'' = [\mathtt{H}_{13} \mid \lambda\mathbf{e}''] \tag{16.5}$$

where μ has been set to unity. The value of λ is determined from one of the point correspondences over three views, and this is left as an exercise. For more on plane-plus-parallax reconstruction, see section 18.5.2(*p*450).

Note that the estimation of the trifocal tensor for this configuration is over-determined. In the case of the fundamental matrix over two views the homographies determine all but 2 degrees of freedom (the epipole), and each of the point correspondence provides one constraint, so that the number of constraints equals the number of degrees of freedom of the matrix. In the case of the trifocal tensor the homography determines all but 5 degrees of freedom (the two epipoles and their relative scaling). However, each point correspondence provides three constraints (there are six coordinate measurements less three for the point's position in 3-space), so that there are six constraints on 5 degrees of freedom. Since there are more measurements than degrees of freedom in this case, the tensor should be estimated by minimizing a cost function based on geometric error.

16.7.2 Lines specified by several points

In describing the reconstruction algorithm from lines, we have considered the case where lines are specified by their two endpoints. Another common way that lines may be specified in an image is as the best line fit to several points. It will be shown now how that case may easily be reduced to the case of a line defined by two endpoints. Consider a set of points $\mathbf{x}_i$ in an image, normalized to have third component equal to 1. Let $\mathbf{l} = (l_1, l_2, l_3)^\mathsf{T}$ be a line, which we suppose is normalized such that $l_1^2 + l_2^2 = 1$. In this case, the distance from a point $\mathbf{x}_i$ to the line $\mathbf{l}$ is equal to $\mathbf{x}_i^\mathsf{T}\mathbf{l}$. The squared distance may be written as $d^2 = \mathbf{l}^\mathsf{T}\mathbf{x}_i\mathbf{x}_i^\mathsf{T}\mathbf{l}$, and the sum-of-squares of all distances is

$$\sum_i \mathbf{l}^\mathsf{T}\mathbf{x}_i\mathbf{x}_i^\mathsf{T}\mathbf{l} = \mathbf{l}^\mathsf{T}(\sum_i \mathbf{x}_i\mathbf{x}_i^\mathsf{T})\mathbf{l} \ .$$

The matrix $\mathtt{E} = (\sum_i \mathbf{x}_i\mathbf{x}_i^\mathsf{T})$ is positive-definite and symmetric.

Lemma 16.2. *Matrix* $(\mathtt{E} - \epsilon_0\mathtt{J})$ *is positive-semidefinite, where* $\mathtt{J}$ *is the matrix* $\mathrm{diag}(1, 1, 0)$ *and* ϵ_0 *is the smallest solution to the equation* $\det(\mathtt{E} - \epsilon\mathtt{J}) = 0$.

Proof. We start by computing the vector $\mathbf{x} = (x_1, x_2, x_3)^\mathsf{T}$ that minimizes $\mathbf{x}^\mathsf{T}\mathtt{E}\mathbf{x}$ subject to the condition $x_1^2 + x_2^2 = 1$. Using the method of Lagrange multipliers, this comes down to finding the extrema of $\mathbf{x}^\mathsf{T}\mathtt{E}\mathbf{x} - \xi(x_1^2 + x_2^2)$, where ξ denotes the Lagrange coefficient. Taking the derivative with respect to $\mathbf{x}$ and setting it to zero, we find that $2\mathtt{E}\mathbf{x} - \xi(2x_1, 2x_2, 0)^\mathsf{T} = \mathbf{0}$. This may be written as $(\mathtt{E} - \xi\mathtt{J})\mathbf{x} = \mathbf{0}$. It follows that ξ is a root of the equation $\det(\mathtt{E} - \xi\mathtt{J}) = 0$ and $\mathbf{x}$ is the generator of the null-space of $\mathtt{E} - \xi\mathtt{J}$. Since $\mathbf{x}^\mathsf{T}\mathtt{E}\mathbf{x} = \xi\mathbf{x}^\mathsf{T}\mathtt{J}\mathbf{x} = \xi(x_1^2 + x_2^2) = \xi$, it follows that to minimize $\mathbf{x}^\mathsf{T}\mathtt{E}\mathbf{x}$ one must choose ξ to be the minimum root ξ_0 of the equation $\det(\mathtt{E} - \xi\mathtt{J}) = 0$. In this case one has $\mathbf{x}_0^\mathsf{T}\mathtt{E}\mathbf{x}_0 - \xi_0 = 0$ for the minimizing vector $\mathbf{x}_0$. For any other vector $\mathbf{x}$, not necessarily the minimizing vector, one has $\mathbf{x}^\mathsf{T}\mathtt{E}\mathbf{x} - \xi_0 \geq 0$. Then, $\mathbf{x}^\mathsf{T}(\mathtt{E} - \xi_0\mathtt{J})\mathbf{x} = \mathbf{x}^\mathsf{T}\mathtt{E}\mathbf{x} - \xi_0 \geq 0$, and so $\mathtt{E} - \xi_0\mathtt{J}$ is positive-semidefinite. □

Since the matrix $\mathtt{E} - \xi_0\mathtt{J}$ is symmetric it may be written in the form $\mathtt{E} - \xi_0\mathtt{J} = \mathtt{V}\mathrm{diag}(r, s, 0)\mathtt{V}^\mathsf{T}$ where $\mathtt{V}$ is an orthogonal matrix and r and s are positive. It follows that

$$\begin{aligned} \mathtt{E} - \xi_0\mathtt{J} &= \mathtt{V}\mathrm{diag}(r, 0, 0)\mathtt{V}^\mathsf{T} + \mathtt{V}\mathrm{diag}(0, s, 0)\mathtt{V}^\mathsf{T} \\ &= r\mathbf{v}_1\mathbf{v}_1^\mathsf{T} + s\mathbf{v}_2\mathbf{v}_2^\mathsf{T} \end{aligned}$$

where $\mathbf{v}_i$ is the i-th column of $\mathtt{V}$. Therefore $\mathtt{E} = \xi_0\mathtt{J} + r\mathbf{v}_1\mathbf{v}_1^\mathsf{T} + s\mathbf{v}_2\mathbf{v}_2^\mathsf{T}$. Then for any line $\mathbf{l}$ satisfying $l_1^2 + l_2^2 = 1$ we have

$$\begin{aligned} \sum_i (\mathbf{x}_i^\mathsf{T}\mathbf{l})^2 &= \mathbf{l}^\mathsf{T}\mathtt{E}\mathbf{l} \\ &= \xi_0 + r(\mathbf{v}_1^\mathsf{T}\mathbf{l})^2 + s(\mathbf{v}_2^\mathsf{T}\mathbf{l})^2. \end{aligned}$$

Thus, we have replaced the sum-of-squares of several points by a constant value ξ_0, which is not capable of being minimized, plus the weighted sum-of-squares of the distances to two points $\mathbf{v}_1$ and $\mathbf{v}_2$. To summarize: when forming the trifocal tensor equations involving a line defined by points $\mathbf{x}_i$, formulate two point equations expressed in terms of the points $\mathbf{v}_1$ and $\mathbf{v}_2$ with weights $\sqrt{r}$ and $\sqrt{s}$ respectively.

Orthogonal regression. In the proof of lemma 16.2 above, it was shown that the line $\mathbf{l}$ that minimizes the sum of squared distances to the set of all points $\mathbf{x}_i = (x_i, y_i, 1)^\mathsf{T}$ is obtained as follows.

(i) Define matrices $\mathtt{E} = \sum_i \mathbf{x}_i \mathbf{x}_i^\mathsf{T}$ and $\mathtt{J} = \text{diag}(1, 1, 0)$.
(ii) Let $\boldsymbol{\xi}_0$ be the minimum root of the equation $\det(\mathtt{E} - \xi \mathtt{J}) = 0$.
(iii) The required line $\mathbf{l}$ is the right null-vector of the matrix $\mathtt{E} - \xi_0 \mathtt{J}$.

This gives a least-squares best fit of a line to a set of points. This process is known as *orthogonal regression* and it extends in an obvious way to higher-dimensional fitting of a hyperplane to a set of points in a way that minimizes the sum of squared distances to the points.

16.8 Closure

16.8.1 The literature

A linear method for computing the trifocal tensor was first given in [Hartley-97a], where further experimental results of estimation using both point and line correspondences on real data are reported. An iterative algebraic method for estimating a consistent tensor was given in [Hartley-98d].

Torr and Zisserman [Torr-97] developed an automatic algorithm for estimating a consistent tensor $\mathcal{T}$ from three images. This paper also compared several parametrizations of the iterative minimization. Several methods of representing and imposing the constraints on the tensor are given by Faugeras and Papadopoulo [Faugeras-97].

[Oskarsson-02] gives minimal solutions for reconstruction for the two cases of "four points and three lines in three views", and "two points and six lines in three views".

16.8.2 Notes and exercises

(i) Consider the problem of estimating the 3-space point $\mathbf{X}$ which minimizes reprojection error from measured image points $\mathbf{x}, \mathbf{x}', \mathbf{x}''$, given the trifocal tensor. This is the analogue of the triangulation problem of chapter 12. Show that for general motion the one parameter family parametrization of epipolar lines developed in chapter 12 does not extend from two views to three. However, in the case that the three camera centres are collinear the two-view parametrization can be extended to three and a minimum determined by solving a polynomial in one variable. What is the degree of this polynomial?

(ii) An affine trifocal tensor may be computed from a minimal configuration of 4 points in general position. The computation is similar to that of algorithm 14.2-(*p*352), and the resulting tensor satisfies the internal constraints for an affine trifocal tensor. How many constraints are there in the affine case?

If more than 4 point correspondences are used in the estimation then a geometrically valid tensor is estimated using the factorization algorithm of section 18.2(*p*436).

(iii) The transformation rule for tensors is $\mathcal{T}_i^{jk} = \mathtt{A}_i^r (\mathtt{B}^{-1})_s^j (\mathtt{C}^{-1})_t^k \hat{\mathcal{T}}_r^{st}$. This may be computed easily as

```
Binv = B.inverse();
Cinv = C.inverse();

for (i=1; i<=3; i++) for (j=1; j<=3; j++) for (k=1; k<=3; k++)
{
  T[i][j][k] = 0.0;

  for (r=1; r<=3; r++) for (s=1; s<=3; s++) for (t=1; t<=3; t++)
    T[i][j][k] +=
             A[r][i] * Binv[j][s] * Cinv[k][t] * T_hat[r][s][t];
}
```

How many multiplications and loop iterations does this involve? Find a better way of computing this transformation.

(iv) In the computation of the trifocal tensor using plane plus parallax (section 16.7.1), show that if ρ is the projective depth of one of the points off the plane (i.e. $\mathbf{x}' = \mathtt{H}_{12}\mathbf{x} + \rho\mathbf{e}'$ see (13.9–*p*337)), then the scalar λ in (16.5) may be computed from the equation $\mathbf{x}'' = \mathtt{H}_{13}\mathbf{x} + \rho\lambda\mathbf{e}''$.

Part IV

N-View Geometry

Untitled 1947, (Oil on sackcloth) by Asger Jorn (1914-1973)

Outline

This part is partly a recapitulation and partly new material.

Chapter 17 is the recapitulation. We return to two- and three-view geometry but now within a more general framework which naturally extends to four- and n-views. The fundamental projective relations over multiple views arise from the intersection of lines (back-projected from points) and planes (back-projected from lines). These intersection properties are represented by the vanishing of determinants formed from the camera matrices of the views. The fundamental matrix, the trifocal tensor, and a new tensor for four views – the *quadrifocal tensor* – arise naturally from these determinants as the multiple view tensors for two, three, and four views respectively. The tensors are what remains when the 3D structure and non-essential part of the camera matrices are eliminated. The tensors stop at four views.

These tensors are unique for each set of views, and generate relationships which are multi-linear in the coordinates of the image measurements. The tensors can be computed from sets of image correspondences, and subsequently a camera matrix for each view can be computed from the tensor. Finally, the 3D structure can be computed from the retrieved cameras and image correspondences.

Chapter 18 covers the computation of a reconstruction from multiple views. In particular the important factorization algorithm is given for reconstruction from affine views. It is important because the algorithm is optimal, but is also non-iterative.

Chapter 19 describes the auto-calibration of a camera. These are a set of methods for computing the internal parameters of a camera based on constraints over multiple images. In contrast to the traditional approach to calibration described in chapter 7, no explicit scene calibration object is used, but simply constraints such as that the internal parameters are common across the images, or that the camera rotates about its centre and does not change aspect ratio.

Chapter 20 emphasises the duality between points and cameras, and how this links various configurations and algorithms that have been given throughout this book. This chapter contains an algorithm for computing a reconstruction of six points imaged in 3-views.

Chapter 21 investigates the issue of whether points are in front of or behind one or more cameras. This is an issue that goes beyond the homogeneous representation used throughout the book which does not distinguish the direction of a ray.

Chapter 22 covers the important topic of those configurations for which the estimation algorithms described in this book will fail. An example is for resectioning, where the camera matrix cannot be computed if all the 3D points and the camera centre lie on a twisted cubic.

17

N-Linearities and Multiple View Tensors

This chapter introduces the quadrifocal tensor Q^{ijkl} between four views, which is the analogue of the fundamental matrix for two and the trifocal tensor for three views. The quadrifocal tensor encapsulates the relationships between imaged points and lines seen in four views.

It is shown that multiple view relations may be derived directly and uniformly from the intersection properties of back-projected lines and points. From this analysis the fundamental matrix $\mathtt{F}$, trifocal tensor $\mathcal{T}_i^{jk}$, and quadrifocal tensor Q^{ijkl} appear in a common framework involving matrix determinants. Specific formulae are given for each of these tensors in terms of the camera matrices.

We also develop general counting arguments for the degrees of freedom of the tensors and the number of point and line correspondences required for tensor computation. These are given for configurations in general position and for the important special case where four or more of the elements are coplanar.

17.1 Bilinear relations

We consider first the relationship that holds between the coordinates of a point seen in two separate views. Thus, let $\mathbf{x} \leftrightarrow \mathbf{x}'$ be a pair of corresponding points which are the images of the same point $\mathbf{X}$ in space as seen in the two separate views. It will be convenient, for clarity of notation, to represent the two camera matrices by $\mathtt{A}$ and $\mathtt{B}$, instead of the usual notation, $\mathtt{P}$ and $\mathtt{P}'$. The projection from space to image can now be expressed as $k\mathbf{x} = \mathtt{A}\mathbf{X}$ and $k'\mathbf{x}' = \mathtt{B}\mathbf{X}$ where k and k' are two undetermined constants. This pair of equations may be written down as one equation

$$\begin{bmatrix} \mathtt{A} & \mathbf{x} & \mathbf{0} \\ \mathtt{B} & \mathbf{0} & \mathbf{x}' \end{bmatrix} \begin{pmatrix} \mathbf{X} \\ -k \\ -k' \end{pmatrix} = \mathbf{0}$$

and it may easily be verified that this is equivalent to the two equations. This can be written in a more detailed form by denoting the i-th row of the matrix $\mathtt{A}$ by $\mathbf{a}^i$, and similarly the i-th row of the matrix $\mathtt{B}$ by $\mathbf{b}^i$. We also write $\mathbf{x} = (x^1, x^2, x^3)^\mathsf{T}$ and

$\mathbf{x}' = (x'^1, x'^2, x'^3)^\top$. The set of equations is now

$$\left[\begin{array}{ccc} \mathbf{a}^1 & x^1 & \\ \mathbf{a}^2 & x^2 & \\ \mathbf{a}^3 & x^3 & \\ \hline \mathbf{b}^1 & & x'^1 \\ \mathbf{b}^2 & & x'^2 \\ \mathbf{b}^3 & & x'^3 \end{array}\right] \begin{pmatrix} \mathbf{X} \\ -k \\ -k' \end{pmatrix} = 0. \tag{17.1}$$

Now, this is a 6×6 set of equations which by hypothesis has a non-zero solution, the vector $(\mathbf{X}^\top, -k, -k')^\top$. It follows that the matrix of coefficients in (17.1) must have zero determinant. It will be seen that this condition leads to a bilinear relationship between the entries of the vectors $\mathbf{x}$ and $\mathbf{x}'$ expressed by the fundamental matrix $\mathtt{F}$. We will now look specifically at the form of this relationship.

Consider the matrix appearing in (17.1). Denote it by $\mathtt{X}$. The determinant of $\mathtt{X}$ may be written as an expression in terms of the quantities x^i and x'^i. Notice that the entries x^i and x'^i appear in only two columns of $\mathtt{X}$. This implies that the determinant of $\mathtt{X}$ may be expressed as a quadratic expression in terms of the x^i and x'^i. In fact, since all the entries x^i appear in the same column, there can be no terms of the form $x^i x^j$ or $x'^i x'^j$. Briefly, in terms of the x^i and x'^i, the determinant of $\mathtt{X}$ is a bilinear expression. The fact that the determinant is zero may be written as an equation

$$(x'^1, x'^2, x'^3)\mathtt{F}(x^1, x^2, x^3)^\top = x'^i x^j F_{ij} = 0 \tag{17.2}$$

where $\mathtt{F}$ is a 3×3 matrix, the fundamental matrix.

We may compute a specific formula for the entries of the matrix $\mathtt{F}$ as follows. The entry F_{ij} of $\mathtt{F}$ is the coefficient of the term $x'^i x^j$ in the expansion of the determinant of $\mathtt{X}$. In order to find this coefficient, we must eliminate the rows and columns of the matrix containing x'^i and x^j, take the determinant of the resulting matrix and multiply by ± 1 as appropriate. For instance, the coefficient of $x'^1 x^1$ is obtained by eliminating two rows and the last two columns of the matrix $\mathtt{X}$. The remaining matrix is

$$\begin{bmatrix} \mathbf{a}^2 \\ \mathbf{a}^3 \\ \mathbf{b}^2 \\ \mathbf{b}^3 \end{bmatrix}$$

and the coefficient of $x'^1 x^1$ is equal to the determinant of this 4×4 matrix. In general, we may write

$$F_{ji} = (-1)^{i+j} \det \begin{bmatrix} \sim\mathbf{a}^i \\ \sim\mathbf{b}^j \end{bmatrix}. \tag{17.3}$$

In this expression, the notation $\sim\mathbf{a}^i$ has been used to denote the matrix obtained from $\mathtt{A}$ by *omitting* the row $\mathbf{a}^i$. Thus the symbol $\sim$ may be read as *omit*, and $\sim\mathbf{a}^i$ represents two rows of $\mathtt{A}$. The determinant appearing on the right side of (17.3) is therefore a 4×4 determinant.

A different way of writing the expression for F_{ji} makes use of the tensor ϵ_{rst} (defined in section A1.1(*p*563)) as follows:[1]

$$F_{ji} = \left(\frac{1}{4}\right) \epsilon_{ipq}\epsilon_{jrs} \det \begin{bmatrix} \mathbf{a}^p \\ \mathbf{a}^q \\ \mathbf{b}^r \\ \mathbf{b}^s \end{bmatrix}. \tag{17.4}$$

To see this, note that F_{ji} is defined in (17.4) in terms of a sum of determinants over all values of p, q, r and s. However, for a given value of i, the tensor ϵ_{ipq} is zero unless p and q are different from i and from each other. This leaves only two remaining choices of p and q (for example if $i = 1$, then we may choose $p = 2,\ q = 3$ or $p = 3,\ q = 2$). Similarly, there are only two different choices of r and s giving rise to non-zero terms. Thus the sum consists of four non-zero terms only. Furthermore, the determinants appearing in these four terms consist of the same four rows of the matrices $\mathtt{A}$ and $\mathtt{B}$ and hence have equal values, except for sign. However, the value of $\epsilon_{ipq}\epsilon_{jrs}$ is such that the four terms all have the same sign and are equal. Thus, the sum (17.4) is equal to the single term appearing in (17.3).

17.1.1 Epipoles as tensors

The expression (17.3) for the fundamental matrix involves determinants of matrices containing two rows from each of $\mathtt{A}$ and $\mathtt{B}$. If we consider instead the determinants of matrices containing all three rows from one matrix and one row from the other matrix, the resulting determinants represent the epipoles. Specifically we have

$$e^i = \det \begin{bmatrix} \mathbf{a}^i \\ \mathtt{B} \end{bmatrix} \qquad e'^j = \det \begin{bmatrix} \mathtt{A} \\ \mathbf{b}^j \end{bmatrix} \tag{17.5}$$

where $\mathbf{e}$ and $\mathbf{e}'$ are the epipoles in the two images. To see this, note that the epipole is defined by $e^i = \mathbf{a}^i\mathbf{C}'$, where $\mathbf{C}'$ is the centre of the second camera, defined by $\mathtt{B}\mathbf{C}' = \mathbf{0}$. The formula (17.5) is now obtained by expanding the determinant by cofactors along the first row (in a similar manner to the derivation of (3.4–*p*67)).

17.1.2 Affine specialization

In the case where both the cameras are affine cameras, the fundamental matrix has a particularly simple form. Recall that an affine camera matrix is one for which the final row is $(0, 0, 0, 1)$. Now, note from (17.3) that if neither i nor j is equal to 3, then the third rows of both $\mathtt{A}$ and $\mathtt{B}$ are present in this expression for F_{ij}. The determinant has two equal rows, and hence equals zero. Thus, $\mathtt{F}$ is of the form

$$\mathtt{F}_{\mathtt{A}} = \begin{bmatrix} & & a \\ & & b \\ c & d & e \end{bmatrix}$$

[1] Of course the factor 1/4 is inessential since $\mathtt{F}$ is defined only up to scale. It is included here just to show the relationship to (17.3).

with all other entries being zero. Thus the affine fundamental matrix has just 5 non-zero entries, and hence 4 degrees of freedom. Its properties are described in section 14.2(p345).

Note that this argument relies solely on the fact that both cameras have the same third row. Since the third row of a camera matrix represents the principal plane of the camera (see section 6.2.1(p158)), it follows that the fundamental matrix for two cameras sharing the same principal plane is of the above form.

17.2 Trilinear relations

The determinant method of deriving the fundamental matrix can be used to derive relationships between the coordinates of points seen in three views. This analysis results in a formula for the trifocal tensor. Unlike the fundamental matrix, the trifocal tensor relates both lines and points in the three images. We begin by describing the relationships for corresponding points.

17.2.1 Trifocal point relations

Consider a point correspondence across three views: $\mathbf{x} \leftrightarrow \mathbf{x}' \leftrightarrow \mathbf{x}''$. Let the third camera matrix be $\mathtt{C}$ and let $\mathbf{c}^i$ be its i-th row. Analogous to (17.1) we can write an equation describing the projection of a point $\mathbf{X}$ into the three images as

$$\begin{bmatrix} \mathtt{A} & \mathbf{x} & & \\ \mathtt{B} & & \mathbf{x}' & \\ \mathtt{C} & & & \mathbf{x}'' \end{bmatrix} \begin{pmatrix} \mathbf{X} \\ -k \\ -k' \\ -k'' \end{pmatrix} = \mathbf{0}. \tag{17.6}$$

This matrix, which as before we will call $\mathtt{X}$, has 9 rows and 7 columns. From the existence of a solution to this set of equations, we deduce that its rank must be at most 6. Hence any 7×7 minor has zero determinant. This fact gives rise to the trilinear relationships that hold between the coordinates of the points $\mathbf{x}$, $\mathbf{x}'$ and $\mathbf{x}''$.

There are essentially two different types of 7×7 minors of $\mathtt{X}$. In choosing 7 rows of $\mathtt{X}$, we may choose either

(i) Three rows from each of two camera matrices and one row from the third, or
(ii) Three rows from one camera matrix and two rows from each of the two others.

Let us consider the first type. A typical such 7×7 minor of $\mathtt{X}$ is of the form

$$\begin{bmatrix} \mathtt{A} & \mathbf{x} & & \\ \mathtt{B} & & \mathbf{x}' & \\ \mathbf{c}^i & & & x''^i \end{bmatrix}. \tag{17.7}$$

Note that this matrix contains only one entry in the last column, namely x''^i. Expanding the determinant by cofactors down this last column reveals that the determinant is equal to

$$x''^i \det \begin{bmatrix} \mathtt{A} & \mathbf{x} & \\ \mathtt{B} & & \mathbf{x}' \end{bmatrix}.$$

Apart from the factor x''^i, this just leads to the bilinear relationship expressed by the fundamental matrix, as discussed in section 17.1.

The other sort of 7×7 minor is of more interest. An example of such a determinant is of the form

$$\det \begin{bmatrix} \mathtt{A} & \mathbf{x} & & \\ \mathbf{b}^j & & x'^j & \\ \mathbf{b}^l & & x'^l & \\ \mathbf{c}^k & & & x''^k \\ \mathbf{c}^m & & & x''^m \end{bmatrix} . \tag{17.8}$$

By the same sort of argument as with the bilinear relations it is seen that setting the determinant to zero leads to a trilinear relation of the form $f(\mathbf{x}, \mathbf{x}', \mathbf{x}'') = 0$. By expanding this determinant down the column containing x^i, we can find a specific formula as follows.

$$\det \mathtt{X}_{uv} = -\frac{1}{2} x^i x'^j x''^k \epsilon_{ilm} \epsilon_{jqu} \epsilon_{krv} \det \begin{bmatrix} \mathbf{a}^l \\ \mathbf{a}^m \\ \mathbf{b}^q \\ \mathbf{c}^r \end{bmatrix} = 0_{uv} \tag{17.9}$$

where u and v are free indices corresponding to the rows omitted from the matrices $\mathtt{B}$ and $\mathtt{C}$ to produce (17.8). We introduce the tensor

$$\mathcal{T}_i^{qr} = \frac{1}{2} \epsilon_{ilm} \det \begin{bmatrix} \mathbf{a}^l \\ \mathbf{a}^m \\ \mathbf{b}^q \\ \mathbf{c}^r \end{bmatrix} . \tag{17.10}$$

The trilinear relationship (17.9) may then be written

$$x^i x'^j x''^k \epsilon_{jqu} \epsilon_{krv} \mathcal{T}_i^{qr} = 0_{uv}. \tag{17.11}$$

The tensor $\mathcal{T}_i^{qr}$ is the trifocal tensor, and (17.11) is a trilinear relation such as those discussed in section 15.2.1(*p*378). The indices u and v are free indices, and each choice of u and v leads to a different trilinear relation.

Just as in the case of the fundamental matrix, one may write the formula for the tensor $\mathcal{T}_i^{qr}$ in a slightly different way

$$\mathcal{T}_i^{qr} = (-1)^{i+1} \det \begin{bmatrix} \sim\mathbf{a}^i \\ \mathbf{b}^q \\ \mathbf{c}^r \end{bmatrix} . \tag{17.12}$$

As in section 17.1, the expression $\sim\mathbf{a}^i$ means the matrix $\mathtt{A}$ with row i omitted. Note that we omit row i from the first camera matrix, but *include* rows q and r from the other two camera matrices.

In the often-considered case where the first camera matrix $\mathtt{A}$ has the canonical form $[\mathtt{I} \mid \mathbf{0}]$, the expression (17.12) for the trifocal tensor may be written simply as

$$\mathcal{T}_i^{qr} = b_i^q c_4^r - b_4^q c_i^r . \tag{17.13}$$

Note that there are in fact 27 possible trilinear relations that may be formed in this way (refer to (17.8)). Specifically, note that each relation arises from taking all three rows from one camera matrix along with two rows from each of the other two matrices. This gives the following computation.

- 3 ways to choose the first camera matrix from which to take all three rows.
- 3 ways to choose the row to omit from the second camera matrix.
- 3 ways to choose the row to omit from the third camera matrix.

This gives a total of 27 trilinear relations. However, among the 9 ways of choosing two rows from the second and third camera matrices, only 4 are linearly independent (we return to this in section 17.6). This means that there are a total of 12 linearly independent trilinear relations.

It is important to distinguish between the number of trilinear relations, however, and the number of different trifocal tensors. As is shown by (17.11), several different trilinear relations may be expressed in terms of just one trifocal tensor. In (17.11) each distinct choice of the free indices u and v gives rise to a different trilinear relation, all of which are expressible in terms of the same trifocal tensor $\mathcal{T}_i^{qr}$. On the other hand, in the definition of the trifocal tensor given in (17.10), the camera matrix $\mathtt{A}$ is treated differently from the other two, in that $\mathtt{A}$ contributes two rows (after omitting row i) to the determinant defining any given entry of $\mathcal{T}_i^{qr}$, whereas the other two camera matrices contribute just one row. This means that there are in fact three different trifocal tensors corresponding to the choice of which of the three camera matrices contributes two rows.

17.2.2 Trifocal line relations

A line in an image is represented by a covariant vector l_i, and the condition for a point $\mathbf{x}$ to lie on the line is that $l_i x^i = 0$. Let X^j represent a point $\mathbf{X}$ in space, and a_j^i represent a camera matrix $\mathtt{A}$. The 3D point X^j is mapped to the image point as $x^i = a_j^i \mathrm{X}^j$. It follows that the condition for the point X^j to project to a point on the line l_i is that $l_i a_j^i \mathrm{X}^j = 0$. Another way of looking at this is that $l_i a_j^i$ represents a plane consisting of all points that project onto the line l_i.

Consider the situation where a point X^j maps to a point x^i in one image and to some point on lines l'_q and l''_r in two other images. This may be expressed by equations

$$x^i = k a_j^i \mathrm{X}^j \quad l'_q b_j^q \mathrm{X}^j = 0 \quad l''_r c_j^r \mathrm{X}^j = 0.$$

These may be written as a single matrix equation of the form

$$\begin{bmatrix} \mathtt{A} & \mathbf{x} \\ l'_q \mathbf{b}^q & 0 \\ l''_r \mathbf{c}^r & 0 \end{bmatrix} \begin{pmatrix} \mathbf{X} \\ -k \end{pmatrix} = \mathbf{0}. \tag{17.14}$$

Since this set of equations has a solution, it follows that $\det \mathtt{X} = 0$, where $\mathtt{X}$ is the matrix on the left of the equation. Expanding this determinant down the last column gives

$$0 = -\det \mathtt{X} = \frac{1}{2} x^i \epsilon_{ilm} \det \begin{bmatrix} \mathbf{a}^l \\ \mathbf{a}^m \\ l'_q \mathbf{b}^q \\ l''_r \mathbf{c}^r \end{bmatrix} = \frac{1}{2} x^i l'_q l''_r \epsilon_{ilm} \det \begin{bmatrix} \mathbf{a}^l \\ \mathbf{a}^m \\ \mathbf{b}^q \\ \mathbf{c}^r \end{bmatrix}$$
$$= x^i l'_q l''_r \mathcal{T}_i^{qr}. \quad (17.15)$$

This shows the connection of the trifocal tensor with sets of lines. The two lines l'_q and l''_r back-project to planes meeting in a line in space. The image of this line in the first image is a line, which may be represented by l_i. For any point x^i on that line the relation (17.15) holds. It follows that $l'_q l''_r \mathcal{T}_i^{qr}$ is the representation of the line l_i. Thus, we see that for three corresponding lines in the three images

$$l_p = l'_q l''_r \mathcal{T}_p^{qr} \quad (17.16)$$

where, of course, the two sides are equal only up to a scale factor. Since the two sides of the relation (17.16) are vectors, this may be interpreted as meaning that the vector product of the two sides vanishes. Expressing this vector product using the tensor ϵ^{ijk}, we arrive at an equation

$$l_p l'_q l''_r \epsilon^{ipw} \mathcal{T}_i^{qr} = 0^w. \quad (17.17)$$

In an analogous manner to the derivation of (17.11) and (17.15) we may derive a relationship between corresponding points in two images and a line in a third image. In particular, if a point X^j in space maps to points x^i and x'^j in the first two images, and to some point on a line l''_r in the third image, then the relation is

$$x^i x'^j l''_r \epsilon_{jqu} \mathcal{T}_i^{qr} = 0_u. \quad (17.18)$$

In this relation, the index u is free, and there is one such relation for each choice of $u = 1, \ldots, 3$, of which two are linearly independent.

We summarize the results of this section in table 17.1, where the final column denotes the number of linearly independent equations.

Correspondence	Relation	Number of equations
three points	$x^i x'^j x''^k \epsilon_{jqu} \epsilon_{krv} \mathcal{T}_i^{qr} = 0_{uv}$	4
two points, one line	$x^i x'^j l''_r \epsilon_{jqu} \mathcal{T}_i^{qr} = 0_u$	2
one point, two lines	$x^i l'_q l''_r \mathcal{T}_i^{qr} = 0$	1
three lines	$l_p l'_q l''_r \epsilon^{piw} \mathcal{T}_i^{qr} = 0^w$	2

Table 17.1. *Trilinear relations (see also table 16.1(*p*391)).*

Note how the different equation sets are related to each other. For instance, the second line of the table is derived from the first by replacing $x''^k \epsilon_{krv}$ by the line l''_r and deleting the free index v.

17.2.3 Relations between two views and the trifocal tensor

To this point we have considered correspondences across three views and the trifocal tensor. Here we describe the constraints that arise if the correspondence is only across two views. From the two view case, where point correspondences constrain the fundamental matrix, we would expect some constraint on $\mathcal{T}$.

Consider the case of corresponding points x'^j and x''^k in the second and third images. This means that there is a point $\mathbf{X}$ in space mapping to the points x'^j and x''^k. The point $\mathbf{X}$ also maps to some point x^i in the first image, but x^i is not known. Nevertheless, there exists a relationship $x^i x'^j x''^k \epsilon_{jqu}\epsilon_{krv}\mathcal{T}_i^{qr} = 0_{uv}$ between these points. For each choice of u and v, denote $\mathtt{A}_{i,uv} = x'^j x''^k \epsilon_{jqu}\epsilon_{krv}\mathcal{T}_i^{qr}$. The entries of $\mathtt{A}_{i,uv}$ are linear expressions in the entries of $\mathcal{T}_i^{qr}$ that may be determined explicitly in terms of the known points x'^j and x''^k. There exists a point $\mathbf{x}$ such that $x^i \mathtt{A}_{i,uv} = 0$. For each choice of u, v we may consider $\mathtt{A}_{i,uv}$ as being a 3-vector indexed by i, and for the different choices of u and v, there are 4 linearly independent such expressions. Thus, $\mathtt{A}$ may be considered as a 3×4 matrix, and the condition that $x^i \mathtt{A}_{i,uv} = 0$ means that $\mathtt{A}_{i,uv}$ has rank 2. This means that every 3×3 subdeterminant of $\mathtt{A}$ is zero, which leads to cubic constraints on the elements of the trifocal tensor. For geometric reasons, it appears that the equations $x^i \mathtt{A}_{i,uv}$ are not algebraically independent for the four choices of u and v. Consequently we obtain a single cubic constraint on $\mathcal{T}_i^{jk}$ from a two-view point correspondence. Details are left to the reader.

In the case where the point correspondence is between the first and second (or third) views the analysis is slightly different. However, the result in each case is that although a point correspondence across two views leads to a constraint on the trifocal tensor, this constraint is not a linear constraint as it is in the case of correspondences across three views.

17.2.4 Affine trifocal tensor

In the case where all three cameras are affine, the trifocal tensor satisfies certain constraints. A camera matrix is affine if the last row is $(0, 0, 0, 1)$. It follows that if two of the rows in the matrix in (17.12) are of this form, then the corresponding element of $\mathcal{T}_i^{jk}$ is zero. This is the case for elements $\mathcal{T}_1^{j3}, \mathcal{T}_2^{j3}, \mathcal{T}_1^{3k}, \mathcal{T}_2^{3k}$ and $\mathcal{T}_3^{33}$ – a total of 11 elements. Thus the trifocal tensor contains 16 non-zero entries, defined up to scale. As in the case of the affine fundamental matrix, this analysis is equally valid for the case of cameras sharing the same principal plane.

17.3 Quadrilinear relations

Similar arguments work in the case of four views. Once more, consider a point correspondence across 4 views: $\mathbf{x} \leftrightarrow \mathbf{x}' \leftrightarrow \mathbf{x}'' \leftrightarrow \mathbf{x}'''$. With camera matrices $\mathtt{A}$, $\mathtt{B}$, $\mathtt{C}$ and $\mathtt{D}$, the projection equations may be written as

$$\begin{bmatrix} \mathtt{A} & \mathbf{x} & & & \\ \mathtt{B} & & \mathbf{x}' & & \\ \mathtt{C} & & & \mathbf{x}'' & \\ \mathtt{D} & & & & \mathbf{x}''' \end{bmatrix} \begin{pmatrix} \mathbf{X} \\ -k \\ -k' \\ -k'' \\ -k''' \end{pmatrix} = \mathbf{0}. \tag{17.19}$$

Since this equation has a solution, the matrix $\mathtt{X}$ on the left has rank at most 7, and so all 8×8 determinants are zero. As in the trilinear case, any determinant containing only one row from one of the camera matrices gives rise to a trilinear or bilinear relation between the remaining views. A different case occurs when we consider 8×8 determinants containing two rows from each of the camera matrices. Such a determinant leads to a new quadrilinear relationship of the form

$$x^i x'^j x''^k x'''^l \epsilon_{ipw} \epsilon_{jqx} \epsilon_{kry} \epsilon_{lsz} Q^{pqrs} = 0_{wxyz} \tag{17.20}$$

where each choice of the free variables w, x, y and z gives a different equation, and the 4-dimensional *quadrifocal tensor* Q^{pqrs} is defined by

$$Q^{pqrs} = \det \begin{bmatrix} \mathbf{a}^p \\ \mathbf{b}^q \\ \mathbf{c}^r \\ \mathbf{d}^s \end{bmatrix}. \tag{17.21}$$

Note that the four indices of the four-view tensor are contravariant, and there is no distinguished view as there is in the case of the trifocal tensor. There is only one four-view tensor corresponding to four given views, and this one tensor gives rise to 81 different quadrilinear relationships, of which 16 are linearly independent (see section 17.6).

As in the case of the trifocal tensor, there are also relations between lines and points in the case of the four-view tensor. Equations relating points are really just special cases of the relationship for lines. In the case of a 4-line correspondence, however, something different happens, as will now be explained. The relationship between a set of four lines and the quadrifocal tensor is given by the formula

$$l_p l'_q l''_r l'''_s Q^{pqrs} = 0 \tag{17.22}$$

for any set of corresponding lines l_p, l'_q, l''_r and l'''_s. However, the derivation shows that this condition will hold as long as there is a single point in space that projects onto the four image lines. It is not necessary that the four image lines correspond (in the sense that they are the image of a common line in space). This configuration is illustrated in figure 17.1a.

Now, consider the case where three of the lines (for instance l'_q, l''_r and l'''_s) correspond by deriving from a single 3D line (figure 17.1b). Now let l_p be any *arbitrary* line in the first image. The back-projection of this line is a plane, which will meet the 3D line in a single point, $\mathbf{X}$, and the conditions are present for (17.22) to hold. Since this is true for any arbitrary line l_p, it must follow that $l'_q l''_r l'''_s Q^{pqrs} = 0^p$. This gives three linearly independent equations involving l'_q, l''_r and l'''_s. However, given a set of corresponding

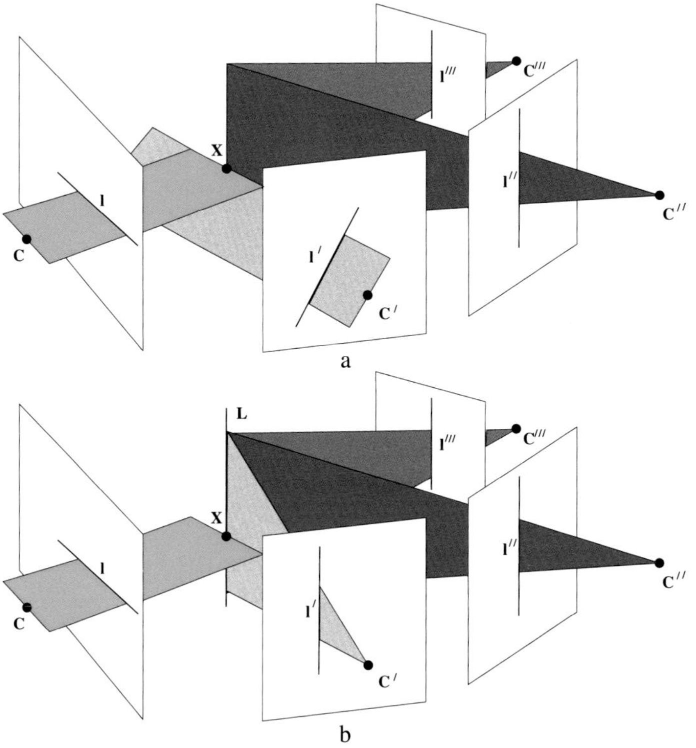

Fig. 17.1. **Four line "correspondence".** *The four lines* $\mathbf{l}, \mathbf{l}', \mathbf{l}'', \mathbf{l}'''$ *satisfy the quadrilinear relation (17.22) since their back-projections intersect in a common point* $\mathbf{X}$. *(a) No three planes intersect in a common line. (b) The three lines* $\mathbf{l}' \leftrightarrow \mathbf{l}'' \leftrightarrow \mathbf{l}'''$ *are the image of the same line* $\mathbf{L}$ *in 3-space.*

lines in four images, as above, we may choose a subset of three lines, and for each line-triplet obtain three equations in this way. Since there are four choices of line-triplets, the total number of equations is thus 12.

However only 9 of these equations are independent, and this may be seen as follows. Suppose that $\mathbf{l} = \mathbf{l}' = \mathbf{l}'' = \mathbf{l}''' = (1, 0, 0)^\mathsf{T}$. This is equivalent to the general situation since by applying projective transformations to each of the four images we can transform an arbitrary line correspondence to this case. Now the equation $l'_q l''_r l'''_s Q^{pqrs} = 0^p$ means that any element $Q^{p111} = 0$. Applying this argument to all four triplets of three views, we find that $Q^{pqrs} = 0$ whenever at least three of the indices are 1. There are a total of 9 such elements. Since the set of equations generated by the line correspondence is equivalent to setting each of these elements to zero, among the total of 12 equations there are just 9 independent ones.

The four-view relations are summarized in table 17.2. No equation is given here for the case of three lines and one point, since this gives no more restrictions on the tensor than just the three-line correspondence.

Correspondence	Relation	Number of equations
four points	$x^i x'^j x''^k x'''^l \epsilon_{ipw}\epsilon_{jqx}\epsilon_{kry}\epsilon_{lsz} Q^{pqrs} = 0_{wxyz}$	16
three points, one line	$x^i x'^j x''^k l'''_s \epsilon_{ipw}\epsilon_{jqx}\epsilon_{kry} Q^{pqrs} = 0_{wxy}$	8
two points, two lines	$x^i x'^j l''_r l'''_s \epsilon_{ipw}\epsilon_{jqx} Q^{pqrs} = 0_{wx}$	4
three lines	$l_p l'_q l''_r Q^{pqrs} = 0^s$	3
four lines	$l_p l'_q l''_r Q^{pqrs} = 0^s, \;\; l_p l'_q l'''_s Q^{pqrs} = 0^r, \;\; \ldots$	9

Table 17.2. *Quadrilinear relations.*

17.4 Intersections of four planes

The multi-view tensors may be given a different derivation, which sheds a little more light on their meaning. In this interpretation, the basic geometric property is the intersection of four planes. Four planes in space will generally not meet in a common point. A necessary and sufficient condition for them to do so is that the determinant of the 4×4 matrix formed from the vectors representing the planes should vanish.

Notation. In this section only we shall represent the determinant of a 4×4 matrix with rows $\mathbf{a}$, $\mathbf{b}$, $\mathbf{c}$ and $\mathbf{d}$ by $\mathbf{a} \wedge \mathbf{b} \wedge \mathbf{c} \wedge \mathbf{d}$. In a more general context, the symbol $\wedge$ represents the meet (or intersection) operator in the double algebra (see literature section of this chapter). However, for the present purposes the reader need only consider it as a shorthand for the determinant.

We start with the quadrifocal tensor for which the derivation is easiest. Consider four lines $\mathbf{l}$, $\mathbf{l}'$, $\mathbf{l}''$ and $\mathbf{l}'''$ in images formed from four cameras with camera matrices A, B, C and D. The back projection of a line $\mathbf{l}$ through camera A is written as the plane $l_i \mathbf{a}^i$, with notation as in (17.14). The condition that these four planes are coincident may be written as

$$(l_p \mathbf{a}^p) \wedge (l'_q \mathbf{b}^q) \wedge (l''_r \mathbf{c}^r) \wedge (l'''_s \mathbf{d}^s) = 0.$$

However, since the determinant is linear in each row, this may be written as

$$0 = l_p l'_q l''_r l'''_s (\mathbf{a}^p \wedge \mathbf{b}^q \wedge \mathbf{c}^r \wedge \mathbf{d}^s) \stackrel{\text{def}}{=} l_p l'_q l''_r l'''_s Q^{pqrs}. \tag{17.23}$$

This corresponds to the definition (17.21) and line relation (17.22) for the quadrifocal tensor. The basic geometric property is the intersection of the four planes in space.

Trifocal tensor derivation. Consider now a point–line–line relationship $x^i \leftrightarrow l'_j \leftrightarrow l''_k$ for three views and let l^1_p and l^2_q be two lines in the first image that pass through the image point $\mathbf{x}$. The planes back-projected from the four lines meet in a point (see figure 17.2). So we can write:

$$l^1_l l^2_m l'_q l''_r (\mathbf{a}^l \wedge \mathbf{a}^m \wedge \mathbf{b}^q \wedge \mathbf{c}^r) = 0\,.$$

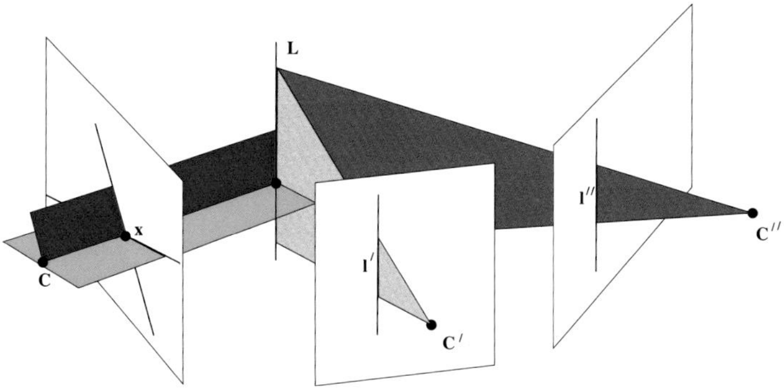

Fig. 17.2. *A point–line–line correspondence* $\mathbf{x} \leftrightarrow \mathbf{l}' \leftrightarrow \mathbf{l}''$ *involving three images may be interpreted as follows. Two arbitrary lines are chosen to pass through the point* $\mathbf{x}$ *in the first image. The four lines then back-project to planes that meet in a point in space.*

The next step is an algebraic trick – to multiply this equation by the $\epsilon^{ilm}\epsilon_{ilm}$. This is a scalar value (in fact equal to 6, the number of permutations of (ilm)). The result after regrouping is

$$\left(l^1_l l^2_m \epsilon^{ilm}\right) l'_q l''_r \epsilon_{ilm} \left(\mathbf{a}^l \wedge \mathbf{a}^m \wedge \mathbf{b}^q \wedge \mathbf{c}^r\right) = 0 \,.$$

Now the expression $l^1_l l^2_m \epsilon^{ilm}$ is simply the cross-product of the two lines l_l and l_m, in other words their intersection point, x^i. Thus finally we can write

$$0 = x^i l'_q l''_r \left(\epsilon_{ilm}(\mathbf{a}^l \wedge \mathbf{a}^m \wedge \mathbf{b}^q \wedge \mathbf{c}^r)\right) \stackrel{\text{def}}{=} x^i l'_q l''_r \mathcal{T}_i^{qr} \tag{17.24}$$

which are the definition (17.10) and basic incidence relation (17.15) for the trifocal tensor.

Fundamental matrix. We can derive the fundamental matrix in the same manner. Given a correspondence $\mathbf{x} \leftrightarrow \mathbf{x}'$, select pairs of lines l^1_p and l^2_q passing through $\mathbf{x}$, and l'^1_r and l'^2_s passing through $\mathbf{x}'$. The back-projected planes all meet in a point, so we write

$$l^1_p l^2_q l'^1_r l'^2_s (\mathbf{a}^p \wedge \mathbf{a}^q \wedge \mathbf{b}^r \wedge \mathbf{b}^s) = 0 \,.$$

Multiplying by $(\epsilon_{ipq}\epsilon^{ipq})(\epsilon_{jrs}\epsilon^{jrs})$ and proceeding as before leads to the coplanarity constraint

$$0 = x^i x'^j \left(\epsilon_{ipq}\epsilon_{jrs}(\mathbf{a}^p \wedge \mathbf{a}^q \wedge \mathbf{b}^r \wedge \mathbf{b}^s)\right) \stackrel{\text{def}}{=} x^i x'^j F_{ji} \tag{17.25}$$

which can be compared with (17.4).

17.5 Counting arguments

In this section we specify the number of points or lines required to carry out reconstruction from several views. This analysis is related to counting the number of degrees of freedom of the associated tensors. However, in doing this it is necessary to distinguish between the number of degrees of freedom of the tensor viewed as an unconstrained algebraic object, and the number of degrees of freedom that arises from a configuration of cameras and their camera matrices.

For instance, consider the fundamental matrix. At one level, the fundamental matrix may be considered as a homogeneous 3×3 matrix, and hence has 8 degrees of freedom (9 minus 1 for the indeterminate scale). On the other hand, the fundamental matrix arising from a pair of camera matrices according to (17.3–p412) must satisfy the additional constraint $\det \mathtt{F} = 0$. Hence, such a fundamental matrix has just 7 degrees of freedom. Since the camera matrices may be determined up to a 3D projectivity from the fundamental matrix (and vice versa), we may count the number of degrees of freedom of a fundamental matrix by counting the degrees of freedom of the camera matrices. Two camera matrices have a total of 22 degrees of freedom (two homogeneous 3×4 matrices). A 3D homography is represented by a 4×4 homogeneous matrix, and so has 15 degrees of freedom. This gives a total of $7 = 22 - 15$ degrees of freedom for the configuration of the two cameras, modulo a projective transformation. This agrees with the 7 degrees of freedom of the fundamental matrix, providing a check on the previous calculation.

Similarly, the trifocal tensor encodes the projective structure of three camera matrices, and hence has $18 = 3*11-15$ degrees of freedom. In the same way the quadrifocal tensor has $29 = 4*11 - 15$ degrees of freedom. Generally for m cameras, we have

$$\#\,\text{dof} = 11m - 15.$$

Since the trifocal and quadrifocal tensors, considered just as homogeneous algebraic arrays have 26 and 80 degrees of freedom respectively, they must satisfy an additional set of constraints, dictated by the camera geometry – 8 constraints for the trifocal tensor and 51 constraints for the quadrifocal tensor.

In computing geometric structure, we may use linear algebraic methods based on estimating the multifocal tensor by solving the constraints from the multi-linearities. The number of correspondences required is determined from the number of equations generated by each point or line correspondence. This *linear method* takes no account of the constraints imposed on the tensors by their geometry.

On the other hand, the number of correspondences required may be determined by counting the number of geometric constraints given by each correspondence and comparing with the total number of degrees of freedom of the system. Consider a configuration of n points in m views. The total number of degrees of freedom of this system is $11m - 15 + 3n$, since each of the n 3D points has 3 degrees of freedom. To estimate the projective structure the available data are the images of the n points in m images, a total of $2mn$ measurements (each 2D point having two coordinates). Thus for reconstruction to be possible, we require $2mn \geq 11m - 15 + 3n$, or $(2m-3)n \geq 11m - 15$. Thus the required number of points is

$$n \geq \frac{11m - 15}{2m - 3} = 5 + \frac{m}{2m - 3}.$$

One may also think of this by observing that each point correspondence contributes

# views	tensor	# elems	# dof	linear		non-linear	
				# points	# lines	# points	# lines
2	F	9	7	8	—	7*	—
3	$\mathcal{T}$	27	18	7	13	6*	9*?
4	Q	81	29	6	9	6	8?

Table 17.3. **Projective degrees of freedom and constraints.** *The linear column indicates the minimum number of correspondences across all views required to solve linearly for the tensor (up to scale). The non-linear is the minimum number of correspondences required. A star indicates multiple solutions, and a question-mark indicates that no practical reconstruction method is known.*

$2m - 3$ constraints on the cameras, that is $2m$ for the coordinates of the points in each view, less 3 for the added degree of freedom of the 3D point.

An analogous argument applies for line correspondences. A line has four degrees of freedom in 3-space, and its image line is described by 2 degrees of freedom, so that each line correspondence provides $2m - 4$ constraints and the number of lines l required is

$$l \geq \frac{11m - 15}{2m - 4}.$$

In either of these cases, if the number of constraints (equations) is equal to the number of degrees of freedom (unknowns) of the cameras and points or lines configuration, then we can in general expect multiple solutions, except in the linear case. However, if there are more equations than unknowns, the system is over-determined, and in the generic case there will exist a single solution.

Table 17.3 summarizes the number of correspondences required for reconstruction. A star (*) indicates that multiple solutions are expected. For the case of non-linear solutions, actual methods of solution are not always known, other than by brute-force generation and solution of a set of simultaneous polynomial equations. Situations where no simple method is known are marked with a question-mark. Note that not much is known about non-linear solutions for lines. Specific non-linear algorithms are:

(i) 7 points in 2 views: see section 11.1.2(p281). Three solutions are possible.

(ii) 6 points in 3 views: see section 20.2.4(p510). Three solutions are possible. This is the dual (see chapter 20) of the previous problem.

(iii) 6 points in 4 views. Solve using 6 points in 3 views, then use the camera resection DLT algorithm (section 7.1(p178)) to find the fourth view and eliminate all but one solution. However, unlike the previous two cases, the case of 6 points in 4 views is overdetermined, and this solution is only valid for perfect data. The estimation for noisy data is discussed in chapter 20.

# views	tensor	# non-zero elements	# dof	linear # points	linear # lines	non-linear # points	non-linear # lines
2	$\mathtt{F}_A$	5	4	4	—	4	—
3	$\mathcal{T}_A$	16	12	4	8	4	6*?
4	$\mathtt{Q}_A$	48	20	4	6	4	5*?

Table 17.4. **Affine degrees of freedom and constraints.** *The camera for each view is affine. See caption of table 17.3 for details.*

17.5.1 Affine cameras

For affine cameras, the reconstruction problem requires fewer correspondences. The plane at infinity may be identified in a reconstruction, being the principal plane of all of the cameras, and the reconstruction ambiguity is affine, not projective. The number of degrees of freedom for m affine cameras is

$$\# \text{dof} = 8m - 12.$$

Each view adds 8 degrees of freedom for the new 3×4 affine camera matrix, and we subtract 12 for the degrees of freedom of a 3D affine transformation.

As in the projective case a point correspondence imposes $2m - 3$ constraints, and a line correspondence $2m - 4$ constraints. As before the number of required points may be computed as $n(2m - 3) \geq 8m - 12$, i.e.

$$n \geq \frac{8m - 12}{2m - 3} = 4.$$

For lines the result is

$$l \geq \frac{8m - 12}{2m - 4} = 4 + \frac{2}{m - 2}.$$

As for linear methods, the number of elements in the tensor is 3^m. In the affine case the tensor is, as always, only defined up to scale, but additionally many of the elements are zero, as seen in section 17.1.2 and section 17.2.4. This cuts down on the required number of correspondences. Counting results are given in table 17.4. Note that for point correspondences, the linear algorithms apply with the minimum number of correspondences given by the above equation. Hence, the non-linear algorithms are the same as the linear ones.

17.5.2 Knowing four coplanar points – plane plus parallax

The previous counting arguments were for the case of points and lines in general position. Here we consider the important case that four or more of the 3D points are coplanar. It will be see that the computation of the tensors, and consequently projective structure, is significantly simplified. This discussion is given in terms of knowing

# views	tensor	# dof	points		lines	
			# points	# constraints	# lines	# constraints
2	F	2	2	2	—	
3	$\mathcal{T}$	5	2	5	5	5
4	Q	8	2	8	4	8

Table 17.5. *Number of additional correspondences required to compute projective structure given 2D homographies between the views, induced by a plane. The homographies may be computed from four or more point matches derived from coplanar points, or by any other means. Points used to compute the homographies are not counted in this table.*

four coplanar points in the images. However, all that is really important here is that inter-image homographies induced by a plane should be known.

Computation of the fundamental matrix knowing four coplanar points was considered in section 13.3(*p*334) (see algorithm 13.2(*p*336)), and for the trifocal tensor in section 16.7.1. Now, we consider the four-view case. From the correspondence of 4 (or more) points derived from 3D points in a plane, we can compute the homographies $\mathtt{H}'$, $\mathtt{H}''$ and $\mathtt{H}'''$ from the first view to the second, third and fourth views respectively, induced by the plane. In a projective reconstruction, we choose the plane containing the points as the plane at infinity, in which case $\mathtt{H}'$, $\mathtt{H}''$ and $\mathtt{H}'''$ are the infinite homographies. Assuming further that the first image is at the origin, the four camera matrices may now be written as

$$\mathtt{A} = [\mathtt{I} \mid \mathbf{0}] \quad \mathtt{B} = [\mathtt{H}'|\mathbf{t}'] \quad \mathtt{C} = [\mathtt{H}''|\mathbf{t}''] \quad \mathtt{D} = [\mathtt{H}'''|\mathbf{t}''']$$

The vectors $\mathbf{t}', \mathbf{t}'', \mathbf{t}'''$ may be determined only up to a common scale.

Since the left hand 3×3 blocks of the camera matrices are now known, it is easily seen from (17.21) that the entries of Q^{pqrs} are linear in the remaining entries $\mathbf{t}'$, $\mathbf{t}''$ and $\mathbf{t}'''$ of the camera matrices. Using (17.21) we can write down an expression for the entries of Q^{pqrs} in terms of the entries of $\mathbf{t}'$, $\mathbf{t}''$ and $\mathbf{t}'''$. In fact, we may write this explicitly as $\mathbf{q} = \mathtt{M}\mathbf{t}$, where $\mathtt{M}$ is an 81×9 matrix and $\mathbf{q}$ and $\mathbf{t}$ are vectors representing the entries of Q and $\mathbf{t}', \ldots, \mathbf{t}'''$. Thus, the quadrifocal tensor may be linearly parametrized in terms of 9 homogeneous coordinates and hence has 8 degrees of freedom.

Now, given a set of equations $\mathtt{E}\mathbf{q} = \mathbf{0}$ derived from correspondences as in table 17.2, they may be rewritten in terms of the minimal parameter set $\mathbf{t}$ by substituting $\mathbf{q} = \mathtt{M}\mathbf{t}$ arriving at $\mathtt{EM}\mathbf{t} = \mathbf{0}$. This allows a linear solution for $\mathbf{t}$ and hence the camera matrices, and (if desired) the tensor, $\mathbf{q} = \mathtt{M}\mathbf{t}$. Note the important advantage here that the tensor so obtained automatically corresponds to a set of camera matrices, and so satisfies all geometric constraints – the troublesome 51 constraints that must be satisfied by the quadrifocal tensor disappear into thin air.

The above analysis was for the computation of the quadrifocal tensor, but it applies equally well to the fundamental matrix and trifocal tensor as well.

Counting argument. We return to the general case of m views and consider the situation from a geometric point of view. The number of degrees of freedom parametrizing the tensor is equal to the number of geometric degrees of freedom remaining in the camera matrices, namely $3m - 4$ where m is the number of views. This arises from $3(m - 1)$ for the last column of each camera matrix apart from the first, less one for the common scaling.

Counting the number of constraints imposed by a point or a line correspondence is a little tricky, however, and shows that one must always be careful with counting arguments not to neglect hidden dependencies. First, consider a line correspondence $\mathbf{l} \leftrightarrow \mathbf{l}' \leftrightarrow \mathbf{l}''$ across three views – the argument will hold in general for $m \geq 3$ views. The question to be resolved is just how much information can be derived from the measurement of the image lines. Surprisingly, knowledge of the plane homographies between the images reduces the amount of information that a line correspondence provides. For simplicity of argument, we may assume that planar homographies have been applied to the images so that the four coplanar reference points map to the same point in each image. As a result any further point in the reference plane will map to the same point in each image. Now the 3D line $\mathbf{L}$ from which the line correspondence is derived must meet the reference plane in a point $\mathbf{X}$. Since it lies on the reference plane, $\mathbf{X}$ projects to the same point $\mathbf{x}$ in all images, and $\mathbf{x}$ must lie on all three image lines $\mathbf{l}, \mathbf{l}', \mathbf{l}''$. Thus, corresponding lines in the three views cannot be arbitrary – they must all pass through a common image point. In the general case the number of degrees of freedom of the measurements of the lines in m views is $m + 2$. To specify the point $\mathbf{x}$ requires 2 degrees of freedom, and each line through the point then has one remaining degree of freedom (its orientation). Subtracting 4 for the four added degrees of freedom of the line in space, we see

- *Each line correspondence across m views generates $m - 2$ constraints on the remaining degrees of freedom of the cameras.*

Note how the condition that the image lines must meet in a point restricts the number of equations generated by the line correspondence. Without observing this condition, one would expect $2m - 4$ constraints from each line. However, with perfect data the set of $2m - 4$ equations will have rank only $m - 2$. With noisy data the image lines will not be exactly coincident, and the system may have full rank, but this will be entirely due to noise, and the smallest singular values of the system will be essentially random. One should, however, include all available equations in solving the system, since this will diminish the noise effects.

For point correspondences the argument is similar. The line through any two image points is the image of a line in space. The projections of this 3D line are constrained as discussed in the preceding discussion, and this imposes constraints on the matching points. The measurements have $3m + 2$ degrees of freedom: 2 for the intersection point of the line with the plane and, in each view, one for the line orientation and two corresponding to the position of each of the two points on the line. Subtracting 6 for the degrees of freedom of the two points in 3-space, the result is

- *Two point correspondences across m views generate $3m - 4$ constraints on the remaining degrees of freedom of the cameras.*

Since this is the same as the number of degrees of freedom of the cameras, 2 points are sufficient to compute structure.

Since the number of geometric constraints on the cameras is the same as the number of degrees of freedom of the tensor, there is no distinction between constraints on the tensor and constraints on the geometry. Thus, point and line correspondences may be used to generate linear constraints on the tensor. There is no need for non-linear methods. The number of required correspondences is summarized in table 17.5.

17.6 Number of independent equations

It was asserted in table 17.2 that each four-view point correspondence gives rise to 16 linearly independent equations in the entries of the quadrifocal tensor. We now examine this point more closely.

Given sufficiently many point matches across four views, one may solve for the tensor Q^{pqrs}. Once Q is known, it is possible to solve for the camera matrices and hence compute projective structure. This was shown in [Heyden-95b, Heyden-97c, Hartley-98c] but is not discussed further in this book. A curious phenomenon occurs however when one counts the number of point matches necessary to do this. As indicated above, it appears to be the case that each point match gives 16 linearly independent equations in the entries of the tensor Q^{pqrs}, and it seems unlikely that the equations derived from two totally unrelated sets of point correspondences could have any dependencies. It would therefore appear that from five point correspondences one obtains 80 equations, which is enough to solve for the 81 entries of Q^{pqrs} up to scale. From this argument it would seem that it is possible to solve for the tensor from only five point matches across four views, and thence one may solve for the camera matrices, up to the usual projective ambiguity. This conclusion however is contradicted by the following remark.

- *It is not possible to determine the positions of four (or any number of) cameras from the images of five points.*

This follows from the counting arguments of section 17.5. Obviously there is some error in our counting of equations. The truth is contained in the following.

Result 17.1. *The full set of 81 linear equations (17.20) derived from a single point correspondence $\mathbf{x} \leftrightarrow \mathbf{x}' \leftrightarrow \mathbf{x}'' \leftrightarrow \mathbf{x}'''$ across four views contains 16 independent constraints on Q^{pqrs}. Furthermore, let the equations be written as $\mathtt{A}\mathbf{q} = \mathbf{0}$ where $\mathtt{A}$ is an 81×81 matrix and $\mathbf{q}$ is a vector containing the entries of Q^{pqrs}. Then the 16 non-zero singular values of $\mathtt{A}$ are all equal.*

What this result is saying is that indeed as expected one obtains 16 linearly independent equations from one point correspondence, and in fact it is possible to reduce this set of equations by an orthogonal transformation (multiplication of the equation matrix $\mathtt{A}$ on the left by an orthogonal matrix $\mathtt{U}$) to a set of 16 orthogonal equations. The proof is postponed until the end of this section. The surprising fact however is that the equation sets corresponding to two unrelated point correspondences have a dependency, as stated in the following result.

Result 17.2. *The set of equations (17.20–p419) derived from a set of n general point correspondences across four views has rank $16n - \binom{n}{2}$, for $n \leq 5$.*

The notation $\binom{n}{2}$ means the number of choices of 2 among n, specifically, $\binom{n}{2} = n(n-1)/2$. Thus for 5 points there are only 70 independent equations, not enough to solve for Q^{pqrs}. For $n = 6$ points, $16n - \binom{n}{2} = 81$, and we have enough equations to solve for the 81 entries of Q^{pqrs}.

We now prove the two results above. The key point in the proof of result 17.1 concerns the singular values of a skew-symmetric matrix (see result A4.1(p581)).

Result 17.3. *A 3×3 skew-symmetric matrix has two equal non-zero singular values.*

The rest of the proof of result 17.1 is quite straightforward as long as one does not get lost in notation.

Proof. (Result 17.1) The full set of 81 equations derived from a single point correspondence is of the form $x^i \epsilon_{ipw} x'^j \epsilon_{jqx} x''^k \epsilon_{kryv} x'''^l \epsilon_{lsz} Q^{pqrs} = 0_{wxyz}$. A total of 81 equations are generated by varying w, x, y, z over the range $1, \ldots, 3$. Thus, the equation matrix $\mathtt{A}$ may be written as

$$\mathtt{A}_{(wxyz)(pqrs)} = x^i \epsilon_{ipw} x'^j \epsilon_{jqx} x''^k \epsilon_{kry} x'''^l \epsilon_{lsz} \tag{17.26}$$

where the indices $(wxyz)$ index the row and $(pqrs)$ index the column of $\mathtt{A}$. We will consider a set of indices, such as $(wxyz)$ in this case, as a single index for the row or column of a matrix. This situation will be indicated by enclosing the indices in parentheses as here, and referring to them as a *combined index*.

We consider now the expression $x^i \epsilon_{ipw}$. This may be considered as a matrix indexed by the free indices p and w. Furthermore, since $x^i \epsilon_{ipw} = -x^i \epsilon_{iwp}$ we see that it is a skew-symmetric matrix, and hence has equal singular values. We denote this matrix by $\mathtt{S}_{wp}$. Writing result 17.3 using tensor notation, we have

$$\mathtt{U}_a^w \mathtt{S}_{wp} \mathtt{V}_e^p = k \mathtt{D}_{ae} \tag{17.27}$$

where the diagonal matrix $\mathtt{D}$ is as in result 17.3. The matrix $\mathtt{A}$ in (17.26) may be written as $\mathtt{A}_{(wxyz)(pqrs)} = \mathtt{S}_{wp} \mathtt{S}'_{xq} \mathtt{S}''_{yr} \mathtt{S}'''_{zs}$. Consequently, applying (17.27) we may write

$$\mathtt{U}_a^w \mathtt{U}_b'^x \mathtt{U}_c''^y \mathtt{U}_d'''^z \mathtt{A}_{(wxyz)(pqrs)} \mathtt{V}_e^p \mathtt{V}_f'^q \mathtt{V}_g''^r \mathtt{V}_h'''^s = k k' k'' k''' \mathtt{D}_{ae} \mathtt{D}_{bf} \mathtt{D}_{cg} \mathtt{D}_{dh}. \tag{17.28}$$

Now, writing

$$\hat{\mathtt{U}}_{(abcd)}^{(wxyz)} = \mathtt{U}_a^w \mathtt{U}_b'^x \mathtt{U}_c''^y \mathtt{U}_d'''^z \quad \hat{\mathtt{V}}_{(efgh)}^{(pqrs)} = \mathtt{V}_e^p \mathtt{V}_f'^q \mathtt{V}_g''^r \mathtt{V}_h'''^s \quad \hat{\mathtt{D}}_{(abcd)(efgh)} = \mathtt{D}_{ae} \mathtt{D}_{bf} \mathtt{D}_{cg} \mathtt{D}_{dh}$$

and $\hat{k} = k k' k'' k'''$ we see that (17.28) may be written as

$$\hat{\mathtt{U}}_{(abcd)}^{(wxyz)} \mathtt{A}_{(wxyz)(pqrs)} \hat{\mathtt{V}}_{(efgh)}^{(pqrs)} = \hat{k} \hat{\mathtt{D}}_{(abcd)(efgh)}. \tag{17.29}$$

As a matrix, $\mathtt{D}_{(abcd)(efgh)}$ is diagonal with 16 non-zero diagonal entries, all equal to unity. To show that (17.29) is the SVD of the matrix $\mathtt{A}_{(wxyz)(pqrs)}$, and hence to complete the proof, it remains only to show that $\mathtt{U}^{(wxyz)}_{(abcd)}$ and $\mathtt{V}^{(pqrs)}_{(efgh)}$ are orthogonal matrices. It is necessary only to show that the columns are orthonormal. This is straightforward and is left as an exercise. □

Proof. (Result 17.2) We consider two point correspondences across four views, namely $x^i \leftrightarrow x'^i \leftrightarrow x''^i \leftrightarrow x'''^i$ and $y^i \leftrightarrow y'^i \leftrightarrow y''^i \leftrightarrow y'''^i$. These give rise to two sets of equations $\mathtt{A}^{\mathbf{x}}\mathbf{q} = \mathbf{0}$ and $\mathtt{A}^{\mathbf{y}}\mathbf{q} = \mathbf{0}$ of the form (17.26). Each of these matrices has rank 16, and if the rows of $\mathtt{A}^{\mathbf{x}}$ are independent of the rows of $\mathtt{A}^{\mathbf{y}}$, then the rank of the combined set of equations is 32. However, if there is a linear dependence between the rows of $\mathtt{A}^{\mathbf{x}}$ and those of $\mathtt{A}^{\mathbf{y}}$ then their combined rank is at most 31.

We define a vector $\mathbf{s}_{\mathbf{x}}$ with combined index $(pqrs)$ by $\mathbf{s}_{\mathbf{x}}^{(pqrs)} = x^p x'^q x''^r x'''^s$. A vector $\mathbf{s}_{\mathbf{y}}$ is similarly defined. We will demonstrate that $\mathbf{s}_{\mathbf{y}}^{\mathsf{T}}\mathtt{A}^{\mathbf{x}} = \mathbf{s}_{\mathbf{x}}^{\mathsf{T}}\mathtt{A}^{\mathbf{y}}$, which means that the rows of $\mathtt{A}^{\mathbf{x}}$ and $\mathtt{A}^{\mathbf{y}}$ are linearly dependent.

Expanding $\mathbf{s}_{\mathbf{y}}^{\mathsf{T}}\mathtt{A}^{\mathbf{x}}$ gives

$$\begin{aligned}
\mathbf{s}_{\mathbf{y}}^{\mathsf{T}}\mathtt{A}^{\mathbf{x}} &= \mathbf{s}_{\mathbf{y}}^{(wxyz)}\mathtt{A}^{\mathbf{x}}_{(wxyz)(pqrs)} \\
&= (y^w y''^x y'''^y y''''^z) x^i \epsilon_{ipw} x'^j \epsilon_{jqx} x''^k \epsilon_{kry} x'''^l \epsilon_{lsz} \\
&= (x^i x''^j x'''^k x''''^l) y^w \epsilon_{wpi} y'^x \epsilon_{xqj} y''^y \epsilon_{yrk} y'''^z \epsilon_{zsl} \\
&= \mathbf{s}_{\mathbf{x}}^{\mathsf{T}}\mathtt{A}^{\mathbf{y}}.
\end{aligned}$$

This demonstrates that the rows of $\mathtt{A}^{\mathbf{x}}$ and $\mathtt{A}^{\mathbf{y}}$ are dependent, and their combined rank is at most 31. We now consider the possibility that the combined rank is less than 31. In such a case, all 31×31 subdeterminants of the matrix $[\mathtt{A}^{\mathbf{x}\mathsf{T}}, \mathtt{A}^{\mathbf{y}\mathsf{T}}]^{\mathsf{T}}$ must vanish. These subdeterminants may be expressed as polynomial expressions in the coefficients of the points $\mathbf{x}, \mathbf{x}', \mathbf{x}'', \mathbf{x}''', \mathbf{y}, \mathbf{y}', \mathbf{y}''$ and $\mathbf{y}'''$. These 24 coefficients together generate a 24-dimensional space. Thus, there is a function $f : \mathbb{R}^{24} \rightarrow \mathbb{R}^N$ for some N (equal to the number of such 31×31 subdeterminants), such that the equation matrix has rank less than 31 only on the set of zeros of the function f. Any arbitrarily chosen example (omitted) may be used to show that the function f is not identically zero. It follows that the set of point correspondences for which the set of equations has rank less than 31 is a variety in $\mathbb{R}^{24}$, and hence is nowhere dense. Thus, the set of equations generated by a general pair of point correspondences across four views has rank 31.

We now turn to the general case of n point correspondences across all four views. Note that the linear relationship that holds for two point correspondences is non-generic, but depends on the pair of correspondences. In general, therefore, given n point correspondences, there will be $\binom{n}{2}$ such relationships. This reduces the dimension of the space spanned by the set of equations to $16n - \binom{n}{2}$ as required. □

The three-view case. Similar arguments hold in the three-view case. It can be proved in the same manner that the nine equations arising from a point match contain four independent equations. This is left to an exercise (see page 432).

17.7 Choosing equations

In section 17.6 a proof was given that the singular values of the full set of equations derived from four point equations are all equal. The proof may easily be adapted to the three-view case as well (see exercise, page 432). The key point in the argument is that the two non-zero singular values of a 3×3 skew-symmetric matrix are equal. This proof may clearly be extended to apply to any of the other sets of equations derived from line or point correspondences given in sections 17.2 and 17.3.

We consider still the four-view case. The results on singular values show that it is in general advisable to include all 81 equations derived from this correspondence, rather than selecting just 16 independent equations. This will avoid difficulties with near singular situations. This conclusion is supported by experimental observation. Indeed, numerical examples show that the condition of a set of equations derived from several point correspondences is substantially better when all equations are included for each point correspondence. In this context, the condition of the equation set is given by the ratio of the first (largest) to the n-th singular value, where n is the number of linearly independent equations.

Including all 81 equations rather than just 16 means that the set of equations is larger, leading to increased complexity of solution. This can be remedied as follows. The basis for the equality of the singular values is that $\mathtt{S}_{wp} = x^i \epsilon_{ipw}$ and the other similarly defined terms are skew symmetric matrices, and hence have equal singular values. The same effect can be achieved by any other matrix $\mathtt{S}$ with equal singular values. We require only that the columns of $\mathtt{S}$ should represent lines passing through the point $\mathbf{x}$ (otherwise stated $\mathtt{S}_{wp} x^w = 0_p$). Matrix $\mathtt{S}$ will have equal singular values if its columns are orthonormal. These conditions may be achieved with $\mathtt{S}$ being a 3×2 matrix. If this is done for the point in each view the total number of equations will be reduced from $3^4 = 81$ to $2^4 = 16$, and the 16 equations will be orthogonal. A convenient way of choosing $\mathtt{S}$ is to use a Householder matrix (see section A4.1.2(p580)) as shown below.

This discussion also applies to the trifocal tensor, allowing us to reduce the number of equations from 9 to 4, while retaining equal singular values. Summarizing this discussion for the trifocal tensor case:

- *Given a point correspondence $\mathbf{x} \leftrightarrow \mathbf{x}' \leftrightarrow \mathbf{x}''$ across three views, generate equations of the form*

$$x^i \hat{l}'_{qx} \hat{l}''_{ry} \mathcal{T}_i^{qr} = 0_{xy} \textit{ for } x, y = 1, 2$$

where $\hat{l}'_{q1}$ and $\hat{l}'_{q2}$ are two lines through $\mathbf{x}'$ represented by orthonormal vectors (and similarly $\hat{l}''_{ry}$). A convenient way to find $\hat{l}'_{qx}$ and $\hat{l}''_{ry}$ is as follows.

  (i) *Find Householder matrices h'_{qx} and h''_{ry} such that $x'^q h'_{qx} = \delta_{3x}$ and $x''^r h'_{ry} = \delta_{3y}$.*

  (ii) *For $x, y = 1, 2$ set $\hat{l}'_{qx} = h'_{qx}$ and $\hat{l}''_{ry} = h''_{ry}$.*

It is evident that essentially this method will work for all the types of equations summarized in table 17.1(p417) and table 17.2(p421).

This chapter suggests that the most basic relations are the point–line–line correspondence equation $x^i l'_q l''_r \mathcal{T}_i^{qr} = 0$ in the three-view case, and the line-correspondence equation $l_p l'_q l''_r l'''_s Q^{pqrs} = 0$ for four views. Indeed numerical robustness may be enhanced by reducing other correspondences to this type of correspondence, for carefully selected lines.

17.8 Closure

17.8.1 The literature

Although using a slightly different approach, this chapter summarizes previous results of [Triggs-95] and Faugeras and Mourrain [Faugeras-95a] on the derivation of multilinear relationships between corresponding image coordinates. The formulae for relations between mixed point and line correspondences are extensions of the results of [Hartley-95b, Hartley-97a].

The enumeration of the complete set of multilinear relations given in table 17.1(*p*417) and table 17.2(*p*421), formulae for the multifocal tensors, and the analysis of the number of independent equations derived from point correspondences, are adapted from [Hartley-95a]. A similar analysis of the multifocal tensors has also appeared in [Heyden-98].

The quadrifocal tensor was probably first discovered by [Triggs-95]. The quadrilinear constraints and their associated tensor have been described in several papers [Triggs-95, Faugeras-95a, Shashua-95b, Heyden-95b, Heyden-97c].

The double (or Grassmann–Cayley) algebra was introduced into the computer vision literature in [Carlsson-93], see also [Faugeras-95a, Faugeras-97] for further applications.

An algorithm for computing the quadrifocal tensor and an algorithm for reconstructing it based on the reduced tensor was given in ([Heyden-95b, Heyden-97c]). A later paper [Hartley-98c] refined this algorithm.

17.8.2 Notes and exercises

(i) Determine the properties of the *affine quadrifocal tensor*, i.e. the quadrifocal tensor computed from affine camera matrices. In particular using the determinant definition of the tensor (17.21–*p*419), verify the number of non-zero elements given in table 17.4.

(ii) Show that the 9 linear equations (17.11–*p*415) derived from a single point correspondence $\mathbf{x} \leftrightarrow \mathbf{x}' \leftrightarrow \mathbf{x}''$ across three views contains 4 linearly independent equations. Furthermore, let the equations be written as $\mathtt{A}\mathbf{t} = \mathbf{0}$ where $\mathtt{A}$ is a 9×27 matrix. Then the 4 non-zero singular values of $\mathtt{A}$ are equal. Unlike the four-view case, the equations resulting from different point matches are linearly independent, so n point matches produce $4n$ independent equations.

(iii) If a canonical affine basis is chosen for the image coordinates such that three corresponding points have coordinates $(0,0), (1,0), (0,1)$ in each view, then the resulting tensors have a simpler form. These "reduced tensors" have a greater number of zero elements than the general form of the tensors. For example, in the case of the reduced fundamental matrix the diagonal elements are zero, and the reduced trifocal tensor has only 15 nonzero entries. Also the tensors are specified by fewer parameters, e.g. four in the case of the reduced fundamental matrix, as effectively the basis points specify the other parameters. Further details are given in [Heyden-95b, Heyden-95a].

(iv) Show that if the four camera centres are coplanar then the quadrifocal tensor has 28 geometric degrees of freedom.

18

N-View Computational Methods

This chapter describes computational methods for estimating a projective or affine reconstruction from a set of images – in particular where the number of views is large.

We start with the most general case which is that of bundle adjustment for a projective reconstruction. This is then specialized to affine cameras and the important factorization algorithm introduced. A generalization of this algorithm to non-rigid scenes is given. A second specialization of bundle adjustment is then described for the case of scenes containing planes. Finally we discuss methods for obtaining point correspondences throughout an image sequence and a projective reconstruction from these correspondences.

18.1 Projective reconstruction – bundle adjustment

Consider a situation in which a set of 3D points $\mathbf{X}_j$ is viewed by a set of cameras with matrices $\mathtt{P}^i$. Denote by $\mathbf{x}^i_j$ the coordinates of the j-th point as seen by the i-th camera. We wish to solve the following reconstruction problem: given the set of image coordinates $\mathbf{x}^i_j$ find the set of camera matrices, $\mathtt{P}^i$, and the points $\mathbf{X}_j$ such that $\mathtt{P}^i\mathbf{X}_j = \mathbf{x}^i_j$. Without further restriction on the $\mathtt{P}^i$ or $\mathbf{X}_j$, such a reconstruction is a projective reconstruction, because the points $\mathbf{X}_j$ may differ by an arbitrary 3D projective transformation from the true reconstruction.

Bundle adjustment. If the image measurements are noisy then the equations $\mathbf{x}^i_j = \mathtt{P}^i\mathbf{X}_j$ will not be satisfied exactly. In this case we seek the Maximum Likelihood (ML) solution assuming that the measurement noise is Gaussian: we wish to estimate projection matrices $\hat{\mathtt{P}}^i$ and 3D points $\widehat{\mathbf{X}}_j$ which project exactly to image points $\hat{\mathbf{x}}^i_j$ as $\hat{\mathbf{x}}^i_j = \hat{\mathtt{P}}^i\widehat{\mathbf{X}}_j$, and also minimize the image distance between the reprojected point and detected (measured) image points $\mathbf{x}^i_j$ for every view in which the 3D point appears, i.e.

$$\min_{\hat{\mathtt{P}}^i, \widehat{\mathbf{X}}_j} \sum_{ij} d(\hat{\mathtt{P}}^i\widehat{\mathbf{X}}_j, \mathbf{x}^i_j)^2 \qquad (18.1)$$

where $d(\mathbf{x}, \mathbf{y})$ is the geometric image distance between the homogeneous points $\mathbf{x}$ and $\mathbf{y}$. This estimation involving minimizing the reprojection error is known as *bundle adjustment* – it involves adjusting the bundle of rays between each camera centre and the set of 3D points (and equivalently between each 3D point and the set of camera centres).

Bundle adjustment should generally be used as a final step of any reconstruction algorithm. This method has the advantages of being tolerant of missing data while providing a true ML estimate. At the same time it allows assignment of individual covariances (or more general PDFs) to each measurement and may also be extended to include estimates of priors and constraints on camera parameters or point positions. In short, it would seem to be an ideal algorithm, except for the fact that: (i) it requires a good initialization to be provided, and (ii) it can become an extremely large minimization problem because of the number of parameters involved. We will discuss briefly these two points.

Iterative minimization. Since each camera has 11 degrees of freedom and each 3-space point 3 degrees of freedom, a reconstruction involving n points over m views requires minimization over $3n + 11m$ parameters. In fact, since entities are often over-parametrized (e.g. using 12 parameters for the homogeneous $\mathtt{P}$ matrix) this may be a lower bound. If the Levenberg–Marquardt algorithm is used to minimize (18.1) then matrices of dimension $(3n + 11m) \times (3n + 11m)$ must be factored (or sometimes inverted). As m and n increase this becomes extremely costly, and eventually impossible. There are several solutions to this problem:

(i) **Reduce n and/or m.** Do not include all the views or all the points, and fill these in later by resectioning or triangulation respectively; or, partition the data into several sets, bundle adjust each set separately and then merge. Such strategies are discussed further in section 18.6.

(ii) **Interleave.** Alternate minimizing reprojection error by varying the cameras with minimizing reprojection error by varying the points. Since each point is estimated independently given fixed cameras, and similarly each camera is estimated independently from fixed points, the largest matrix that must be inverted is the 11×11 matrix used to estimate one camera. Interleaving minimizes the same cost function as bundle adjustment, so the same solution should be obtained (provided there is a unique minimum), but it may take longer to converge. Interleaving is compared with bundle adjustment in [Triggs-00a].

(iii) **Sparse methods.** These are described in appendix 6(p597).

Initial solution. Several methods for initialization are described in the following sections. If the problem is restricted to affine cameras then factorization (section 18.2) gives a closed form optimal solution provided points are imaged in every view. Even with projective cameras there is an (iterative) factorization method (section 18.4) available provided points are imaged in every view. If there is more information available on the data, for example that it is partly coplanar, then again a closed form solution is possible (section 18.5). Finally, hierarchical methods can be used as described in section 18.6 for the case where points are not visible in every view.

18.2 Affine reconstruction – the factorization algorithm

In this section we describe reconstruction from a set of image point correspondences for images acquired by affine cameras. As described in section 17.5.1 the reconstruction in this case is affine.

The factorization algorithm of Tomasi and Kanade [Tomasi-92] to be presented below and summarized in algorithm 18.1 has the following property:

- *Under an assumption of isotropic mean-zero Gaussian noise independent and equal for each measured point, factorization achieves a Maximum Likelihood affine reconstruction.*

This fact was first pointed out by Reid and Murray [Reid-96]. However, the method requires a measurement of each point in all views. This is a limitation in practice, since matched points may be absent in some views.

An affine camera may be characterized by having its last row equal to $(0, 0, 0, 1)$. In this section, however, we will denote it somewhat differently, separating out the translation and the pure linear transformation part of the camera map. Thus we write

$$\begin{pmatrix} x \\ y \end{pmatrix} = \mathtt{M} \begin{pmatrix} \mathrm{X} \\ \mathrm{Y} \\ \mathrm{Z} \end{pmatrix} + \mathbf{t}$$

where $\mathtt{M}$ is a 2×3 matrix and $\mathbf{t}$ a 2-vector. From here on for ease of readability $\mathbf{x}$ represents an *in*homogeneous image point $\mathbf{x} = (x, y)^\mathsf{T}$, and $\mathbf{X}$ an *in*homogeneous world point $\mathbf{X} = (\mathrm{X}, \mathrm{Y}, \mathrm{Z})^\mathsf{T}$.

Our goal is to find a reconstruction to minimize geometric error in image coordinate measurements. That is, we wish to estimate cameras $\{\mathtt{M}^i, \mathbf{t}^i\}$ and 3D points $\{\mathbf{X}_j\}$ such that the distance between the estimated image points $\hat{\mathbf{x}}^i_j = \mathtt{M}^i\mathbf{X}_j + \mathbf{t}^i$ and measured image points $\mathbf{x}^i_j$ is minimized

$$\min_{\mathtt{M}^i, \mathbf{t}^i, \mathbf{X}_j} \sum_{ij} \left|\left|\mathbf{x}^i_j - \hat{\mathbf{x}}^i_j\right|\right|^2 = \min_{\mathtt{M}^i, \mathbf{t}^i, \mathbf{X}_j} \sum_{ij} \left|\left|\mathbf{x}^i_j - (\mathtt{M}^i\mathbf{X}_j + \mathbf{t}^i)\right|\right|^2. \tag{18.2}$$

As is common in such minimization problems the translation vector $\mathbf{t}^i$ can be eliminated in advance by choosing the centroid of the points as the origin of the coordinate system. This is a consequence of the geometric fact that an affine camera maps the centroid of a set of 3D points to the centroid of their projections. Thus, if the coordinate origin is chosen as the centroid of the 3D points and of each set of image points then it follows that $\mathbf{t}^i = \mathbf{0}$. This step requires that the same n points be imaged in all views, i.e. that there are no views in which the image coordinates of any point are unknown. An analytical derivation of this result goes like this. The minimization with respect to $\mathbf{t}^i$ requires that

$$\frac{\partial}{\partial \mathbf{t}^i} \sum_{kj} \left|\left|\mathbf{x}^k_j - (\mathtt{M}^k\mathbf{X}_j + \mathbf{t}^k)\right|\right|^2 = \mathbf{0}$$

which after a brief calculation reduces to $\mathbf{t}^i = \langle \mathbf{x}^i \rangle - \mathtt{M}^i\langle \mathbf{X} \rangle$, where the centroids are

Objective

Given $n \geq 4$ image point correspondences over m views $\mathbf{x}_j^i$, $j = 1, \ldots, n$; $i = 1, \ldots, m$, determine affine camera matrices $\{\mathtt{M}^i, \mathbf{t}^i\}$ and 3D points $\{\mathbf{X}_j\}$ such that the reprojection error

$$\sum_{ij} \left|\left|\mathbf{x}_j^i - (\mathtt{M}^i \mathbf{X}_j + \mathbf{t}^i)\right|\right|^2$$

is minimized over $\{\mathtt{M}^i, \mathbf{t}^i, \mathbf{X}_j\}$, with $\mathtt{M}^i$ a 2×3 matrix, $\mathbf{X}_j$ a 3-vector, and $\mathbf{x}_j^i = (x_j^i, y_j^i)^\mathsf{T}$ and $\mathbf{t}^i$ are 2-vectors.

Algorithm

(i) **Computation of translations.** Each translation $\mathbf{t}^i$ is computed as the centroid of points in image i, namely

$$\mathbf{t}^i = \langle \mathbf{x}^i \rangle = \frac{1}{n} \sum_j \mathbf{x}_j^i.$$

(ii) **Centre the data.** Centre the points in each image by expressing their coordinates with respect to the centroid:

$$\mathbf{x}_j^i \leftarrow \mathbf{x}_j^i - \langle \mathbf{x}^i \rangle.$$

Henceforth work with these centred coordinates.

(iii) **Construct the** $2m \times n$ **measurement matrix** $\mathtt{W}$ from the centred data, as defined in (18.5), and compute its SVD $\mathtt{W} = \mathtt{UDV}^\mathsf{T}$.

(iv) Then the matrices $\mathtt{M}^i$ are obtained from the first three columns of $\mathtt{U}$ multiplied by the singular values:

$$\begin{bmatrix} \mathtt{M}^1 \\ \mathtt{M}^2 \\ \vdots \\ \mathtt{M}^m \end{bmatrix} = \begin{bmatrix} \sigma_1 \mathbf{u}_1 & \sigma_2 \mathbf{u}_2 & \sigma_3 \mathbf{u}_3 \end{bmatrix}.$$

The vectors $\mathbf{t}^i$ are as computed in step (i) and the 3D structure is read from the first three columns of $\mathtt{V}$

$$\begin{bmatrix} \mathbf{X}_1 & \mathbf{X}_2 & \ldots & \mathbf{X}_n \end{bmatrix} = \begin{bmatrix} \mathbf{v}_1 & \mathbf{v}_2 & \mathbf{v}_3 \end{bmatrix}^\mathsf{T}.$$

Algorithm 18.1. *The factorization algorithm to determine the MLE for an affine reconstruction from n image correspondences over m views (under Gaussian image noise).*

$\langle \mathbf{x}^i \rangle = \frac{1}{n} \sum_j \mathbf{x}_j^i$ and $\langle \mathbf{X} \rangle = \frac{1}{n} \sum_j \mathbf{X}_j$. The origin of the 3D frame is arbitrary, so may be chosen to coincide with the centroid $\langle \mathbf{X} \rangle$, in which case $\langle \mathbf{X} \rangle = \mathbf{0}$ and

$$\mathbf{t}^i = \langle \mathbf{x}^i \rangle. \tag{18.3}$$

It follows that if we measure the image coordinates with respect to a coordinate origin based at the centroid of the projected points, then $\mathbf{t}^i = \mathbf{0}$. Thus, we replace each $\mathbf{x}_j^i$ by $\mathbf{x}_j^i - \langle \mathbf{x}^i \rangle$. Henceforth we will assume that this has been done, and work with the centred coordinates. With respect to these new coordinates $\mathbf{t}^i = \mathbf{0}$, and so (18.2) reduces to

$$\min_{\mathtt{M}^i, \mathbf{X}_j} \sum_{ij} \left|\left|\mathbf{x}_j^i - \hat{\mathbf{x}}_j^i\right|\right|^2 = \min_{\mathtt{M}^i, \mathbf{X}_j} \sum_{ij} \left|\left|\mathbf{x}_j^i - \mathtt{M}^i \mathbf{X}_j\right|\right|^2. \tag{18.4}$$

The minimization problem now has a very simple form when written as a matrix. The *measurement* matrix $\mathtt{W}$ is the $2m \times n$ matrix composed of the centred coordinates of the measured image points

$$\mathtt{W} = \begin{bmatrix} \mathbf{x}_1^1 & \mathbf{x}_2^1 & \dots & \mathbf{x}_n^1 \\ \mathbf{x}_1^2 & \mathbf{x}_2^2 & \dots & \mathbf{x}_n^2 \\ \vdots & \vdots & \ddots & \vdots \\ \mathbf{x}_1^m & \mathbf{x}_2^m & \dots & \mathbf{x}_n^m \end{bmatrix}. \tag{18.5}$$

Since each $\mathbf{x}_j^i = \mathtt{M}^i \mathbf{X}_j$, the complete set of equations may be written as

$$\mathtt{W} = \begin{bmatrix} \mathtt{M}^1 \\ \mathtt{M}^2 \\ \vdots \\ \mathtt{M}^m \end{bmatrix} \begin{bmatrix} \mathbf{X}_1 & \mathbf{X}_2 & \dots & \mathbf{X}_n \end{bmatrix}.$$

In the presence of noise this equation will not be satisfied exactly, so instead we seek a matrix $\hat{\mathtt{W}}$ as close as possible to $\mathtt{W}$ in Frobenius norm, such that $\hat{\mathtt{W}}$ may be decomposed as

$$\hat{\mathtt{W}} = \begin{bmatrix} \hat{\mathbf{x}}_1^1 & \hat{\mathbf{x}}_2^1 & \dots & \hat{\mathbf{x}}_n^1 \\ \hat{\mathbf{x}}_1^2 & \hat{\mathbf{x}}_2^2 & \dots & \hat{\mathbf{x}}_n^2 \\ \vdots & \vdots & \ddots & \vdots \\ \hat{\mathbf{x}}_1^m & \hat{\mathbf{x}}_2^m & \dots & \hat{\mathbf{x}}_n^m \end{bmatrix} = \begin{bmatrix} \mathtt{M}^1 \\ \mathtt{M}^2 \\ \vdots \\ \mathtt{M}^m \end{bmatrix} \begin{bmatrix} \mathbf{X}_1 & \mathbf{X}_2 & \dots & \mathbf{X}_n \end{bmatrix}. \tag{18.6}$$

In this case it may be verified that

$$\left|\left|\mathtt{W} - \hat{\mathtt{W}}\right|\right|_{\mathrm{F}}^2 = \sum_{ij} \left(\mathtt{W}_{ij} - \hat{\mathtt{W}}_{ij}\right)^2 = \sum_{ij} \left|\left|\mathbf{x}_j^i - \hat{\mathbf{x}}_j^i\right|\right|^2 = \sum_{ij} \left|\left|\mathbf{x}_j^i - \mathtt{M}^i\mathbf{X}_j\right|\right|^2$$

Comparing this with (18.4) we find that minimizing the required geometric error is equivalent to finding such a $\hat{\mathtt{W}}$ as close as possible to $\mathtt{W}$ in Frobenius norm.

Note that a matrix $\hat{\mathtt{W}}$ satisfying (18.6) is the product of a $2m \times 3$ *motion matrix* $\hat{\mathtt{M}}$, and a $3 \times n$ *structure matrix* $\hat{\mathtt{X}}$; consequently $\hat{\mathtt{W}} = \hat{\mathtt{M}}\hat{\mathtt{X}}$ has rank 3. In other words we seek a rank 3 matrix which is closest to $\mathtt{W}$ in Frobenius norm. Such a matrix may be determined by the SVD of $\mathtt{W}$ truncated to rank 3. In more detail, if the SVD of $\mathtt{W} = \mathtt{UDV}^\mathsf{T}$ then $\hat{\mathtt{W}} = \mathtt{U}_{2m\times3}\mathtt{D}_{3\times3}\mathtt{V}_{3\times n}^\mathsf{T}$ is the rank 3 matrix which is closest to $\mathtt{W}$ in the Frobenius norm, where $\mathtt{U}_{2m\times3}$ consists of the first 3 columns of $\mathtt{U}$, $\mathtt{V}_{3\times n}^\mathsf{T}$ consists of the first 3 rows of $\mathtt{V}^\mathsf{T}$, and $\mathtt{D}_{3\times3}$ is the diagonal matrix containing the first 3 singular values, $\mathtt{D}_{3\times3} = \mathrm{diag}(\sigma_1, \sigma_2, \sigma_3)$.

Note that the choice of $\hat{\mathtt{M}}$ and $\hat{\mathtt{X}}$ is not unique. For example $\hat{\mathtt{M}}$ may be chosen as $\hat{\mathtt{M}} = \mathtt{U}_{2m\times3}\mathtt{D}_{3\times3}$ and $\hat{\mathtt{X}} = \mathtt{V}_{3\times n}^\mathsf{T}$, or as $\hat{\mathtt{M}} = \mathtt{U}_{2m\times3}$, $\hat{\mathtt{X}} = \mathtt{D}_{3\times3}\mathtt{V}_{3\times n}^\mathsf{T}$ since in either case $\hat{\mathtt{W}} = \hat{\mathtt{M}}\hat{\mathtt{X}} = \mathtt{U}_{2m\times3}\mathtt{D}_{3\times3}\mathtt{V}_{3\times n}^\mathsf{T}$.

Affine ambiguity. In fact for any such choice there is an additional ambiguity since an arbitrary 3×3 rank 3 matrix $\mathtt{A}$ may be inserted in the decomposition as $\hat{\mathtt{W}} = \hat{\mathtt{M}}\mathtt{A}\mathtt{A}^{-1}\hat{\mathtt{X}} = (\hat{\mathtt{M}}\mathtt{A})(\mathtt{A}^{-1}\hat{\mathtt{X}})$. This means that the camera matrices $\mathtt{M}^i$, which are obtained from $\hat{\mathtt{M}}$, and the 3D points $\mathbf{X}_j$, which are obtained from $\hat{\mathtt{X}}$, are determined up to multiplication by a common matrix $\mathtt{A}$. In other words the MLE reconstruction is affine.

This affine reconstruction may be upgraded to a metric reconstruction by supplying metric information on the scene as described in section 10.4.2(*p*272), or by using auto-calibration methods as described in chapter 19, or a combination of the two. Note that in the case of affine cameras only three internal parameters need be specified (compared to five for projective cameras) and the auto-calibration task is correspondingly simpler.

18.2.1 Affine multiple view tensors

The factorization algorithm provides an optimal method for computing the affine multiview tensors from image point correspondences. These tensors are the affine fundamental matrix, affine trifocal tensor, and affine quadrifocal tensor. In each case the algorithm determines the camera matrices up to an overall affine ambiguity. The tensors may then be computed directly from the camera matrices (as for instance in chapter 17). The affine ambiguity of 3-space is irrelevant when computing the tensors since they are unaffected by affine transformations of 3-space. In fact it is not necessary to compute the full SVD of $\mathtt{W}$ since only the $\mathtt{U}$ part of the decomposition is required. If the number of points n is large compared with the number of views then very great savings can be made in the computation of the SVD by not determining $\mathtt{V}$ (see table A4.1(*p*587)).

An alternative to using the SVD is to use the eigenvalue decomposition of $\mathtt{W}\mathtt{W}^{\mathsf{T}}$, since $\mathtt{W}\mathtt{W}^{\mathsf{T}} = (\mathtt{U}\mathtt{D}\mathtt{V}^{\mathsf{T}})(\mathtt{U}\mathtt{D}\mathtt{V}^{\mathsf{T}})^{\mathsf{T}} = \mathtt{U}\mathtt{D}^2\mathtt{U}^{\mathsf{T}}$. In the case of three views (computation of the trifocal tensor) the matrix $\mathtt{W}\mathtt{W}^{\mathsf{T}}$ has dimension only 9×9. Thus this approach can mean significant savings. However, it is numerically inferior, since forming $\mathtt{W}\mathtt{W}^{\mathsf{T}}$ causes the condition number of the matrix to be squared (see the discussion of SVD in [Golub-89]). Since we need just the three largest eigenvectors, that may not be such a problem in this case. However, the savings of this approach will not be so great given an implementation of the SVD that avoids computing $\mathtt{V}$.

The factorization method may be used to compute any of the multiple-view affine tensors. For the affine fundamental matrix, however, algorithm 14.1(*p*351) described in chapter 14 is more direct. The results of both the methods are identical.

18.2.2 Triangulation and reprojection using subspaces

The factorization algorithm also provides an optimal method for computing the images of new points or of points not observed in all views. Again the affine ambiguity of 3-space is irrelevant.

A column of $\mathtt{W}$ is the set of all corresponding image points for the point $\mathbf{X}_j$ and is referred to as a point's *trajectory*. The rank 3 decomposition (18.6) of $\hat{\mathtt{W}}$ as $\hat{\mathtt{W}} = \hat{\mathtt{M}}\hat{\mathtt{X}}$ shows that all trajectories lie in a 3 dimensional subspace. In particular the trajectory (i.e. all image projections) of a new point $\mathbf{X}$ may be obtained as $\hat{\mathtt{M}}\mathbf{X}$. This is simply a linear weighting of the three columns of $\hat{\mathtt{M}}$.

Suppose we have observed a new point $\mathbf{X}$ in some (not all) views, and wish to predict its projection in the other views. This is carried out in two steps: first triangulation to find the pre-image $\mathbf{X}$, and then reprojection as $\hat{\mathtt{M}}\mathbf{X}$ to generate its image in all views. Note that the projected points will not coincide exactly with the measured (noisy) points. In the triangulation step we wish to find the point $\mathbf{X}$ that minimizes reprojection error, and this corresponds to finding the point in the linear subspace spanned by the columns of $\hat{\mathtt{M}}$ closest to the trajectory. This closest point is found by projecting the trajectory onto the subspace (in a similar manner to algorithm 4.7(p130)).

In more detail suppose we have computed a set of affine cameras $\{\mathtt{M}^i, \mathbf{t}^i\}$ then the triangulation problem may be solved linearly for any number of views. The image points $\mathbf{x}^i = \mathtt{M}^i\mathbf{X} + \mathbf{t}^i$ give a pair of linear equations $\mathtt{M}^i\mathbf{X} = \mathbf{x}^i - \mathbf{t}^i$ in the entries of $\mathbf{X}$. Given sufficiently many such equations (arising from known values of $\mathbf{x}^i$) one can find the linear least-squares solution for $\mathbf{X}$, using algorithm A5.1(p589), the pseudo-inverse (see result A5.1(p590)) or algorithm A5.3(p591). Note that if the data $\mathbf{x}^i$ is centred using the same transformation applied in step (ii) of algorithm 18.1, then the translation vectors $\mathbf{t}^i$ in the affine triangulation method may be taken to be zero.

In practice triangulation and reprojection provides a method of 'filling in' points that are missed during tracking or multiple view matching.

18.2.3 Affine Reconstruction by Alternation

Suppose a set of image coordinates $\mathbf{x}^i_j$ are given as in algorithm 18.1, and we wish to perform affine reconstruction. We have seen that affine triangulation may be carried out linearly. Thus, if the affine camera matrices represented by $\{\mathtt{M}^i, \mathbf{t}^i\}$ are known, then the optimal point positions $\mathbf{X}_j$ may be computed by a linear least-squares method such as the normal equations method of algorithm A5.3(p591).

Conversely, if the points $\mathbf{X}_j$ are known, then the equations $\mathbf{x}^i_j = \mathtt{M}^i\mathbf{X}_j + \mathbf{t}^i$ are linear in $\mathtt{M}^i$ and $\mathbf{t}^i$. So it is once again possible simply to solve for $\{\mathtt{M}^i, \mathbf{t}^i\}$ by linear least-squares.

This suggests a method of affine reconstruction in which linear least-squares methods are used to solve alternately for the points $\mathbf{X}_j$ and the cameras $\{\mathtt{M}^i, \mathbf{t}^i\}$. This method of alternation is not to be recommended as a general method for reconstruction, or for solving optimization problems in general. In the case of affine reconstruction, however, it can be proven to converge rapidly to the optimal solution, starting from a random starting point. This method of affine reconstruction has the advantage of working with missing data, or with covariance-weighted data which algorithm 18.1 will not, though in the missing data or covariance-weighted case, global optimal convergence is not guaranteed in all cases.

18.3 Non-rigid factorization

Throughout the book it has been assumed that we are viewing a rigid scene and that only the relative motion between the camera and scene is to be modelled. In this section we relax this assumption and consider the problem of recovering a reconstruction for a deforming object. It will be shown that if the deformation is modelled as a linear combination over basis shapes then the reconstruction *and the basis shapes* may be recovered with a simple modification of the factorization algorithm of section 18.2.

An example where this type of situation arises is in a sequence of images of a per-

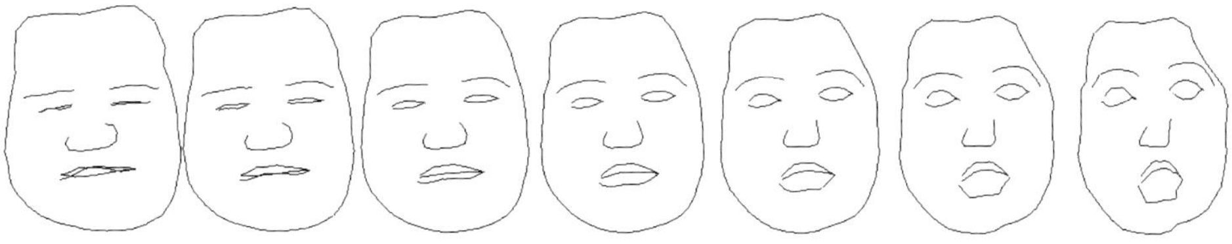

Fig. 18.1. **Shape basis.** *A face template is represented by N equally spaced 2D points (here $N = 140$). The central face of the seven is the mean shape and the faces to the left or right are generated by adding or subtracting, respectively, the basis shape that accounts for the maximum variation in the training set. In this case the basis spans expressions from surprised to disgruntled. Facial expressions are learnt by tracking the face of an actor with the template whilst he changes expression but does not vary his head pose. Each frame of the training sequence generates a set of N 2D points, and the coordinates of these are rewritten as a $2N$-vector. A $2N \times f$ matrix is then composed from these vectors, where f is the number of training frames, and the basis shapes are computed from the singular vectors of this matrix. Figure courtesy of Richard Bowden.*

son's head which moves and also changes expression. The motion of the head may be modelled as a rigid rotation, and the change of expression relative to the fixed head may be modelled as a linear combination over basis sets. For example the mouth outline may be represented by a set of points.

Suppose the set of n scene points $\mathbf{X}_j$ may be represented as a linear combination of l basis shapes $\mathtt{B}_k$ so that at a particular time i:

$$\begin{bmatrix} \mathbf{X}_1^i & \mathbf{X}_2^i & \dots & \mathbf{X}_n^i \end{bmatrix} = \sum_{k=1}^{l} \alpha_k^i \begin{bmatrix} \mathbf{B}_{1k} & \mathbf{B}_{2k} & \dots & \mathbf{B}_{nk} \end{bmatrix} = \sum_k \alpha_k^i \mathtt{B}_k$$

where here both the scene points $\mathbf{X}_j^i$ and the basis points $\mathbf{B}_{jk}$ are inhomogeneous points represented by 3-vectors, and $\mathtt{B}_k$ is a $3 \times n$ matrix. Typically the number of basis shapes, l, is much smaller than the number of points, n. The coefficients α_k^i may be different at each time i, and the resulting differing combination of basis shapes generates the deformation. An example is shown in figure 18.1.

In the forward model of image generation each view i is acquired by an affine camera and gives the image points

$$\mathbf{x}_j^i = \mathtt{M}^i \sum_k \alpha_k^i \mathbf{B}_{jk} + \mathbf{t}^i.$$

It will again be assumed that image point matches are available for all views. Our goal is to estimate cameras $\{\mathtt{M}^i, \mathbf{t}^i\}$ and 3D structure $\{\alpha_k^i, \mathbf{B}_{jk}\}$ from the measured image points $\{\mathbf{x}_j^i\}$, such that the distance between the estimated image points $\hat{\mathbf{x}}_j^i = \mathtt{M}^i \sum_k \alpha_k^i \mathbf{B}_{jk} + \mathbf{t}^i$ and measured image points is minimized

$$\min_{\mathtt{M}^i, \mathbf{t}^i, \alpha_k^i, \mathbf{B}_{jk}} \sum_{ij} \left\| \mathbf{x}_j^i - \hat{\mathbf{x}}_j^i \right\|^2 = \min_{\mathtt{M}^i, \mathbf{t}^i, \alpha_k^i, \mathbf{B}_{jk}} \sum_{ij} \left\| \mathbf{x}_j^i - (\mathtt{M}^i \sum_k \alpha_k^i \mathbf{B}_{jk} + \mathbf{t}^i) \right\|^2.$$

As in affine factorization the translation may be eliminated by centring the measured image points, and it will be assumed from here on that this has been done. Then the problem reduces to

$$\min_{\mathtt{M}^i,\alpha_k^i,\mathbf{B}_{jk}} \sum_{ij} \left\| \mathbf{x}_j^i - \hat{\mathbf{x}}_j^i \right\|^2 = \min_{\mathtt{M}^i,\alpha_k^i,\mathbf{B}_{jk}} \sum_{ij} \left\| \mathbf{x}_j^i - \mathtt{M}^i \sum_k \alpha_k^i \mathbf{B}_{jk} \right\|^2 . \tag{18.7}$$

The complete set of equations $\hat{\mathbf{x}}_j^i = \mathtt{M}^i \sum_k \alpha_k^i \mathbf{B}_{jk}$ may be written

$$\hat{\mathtt{W}} = \begin{bmatrix} \mathtt{M}^1 \left(\alpha_1^1 \mathtt{B}_1 + \alpha_2^1 \mathtt{B}_2 + \ldots \alpha_l^1 \mathtt{B}_l\right) \\ \mathtt{M}^2 \left(\alpha_1^2 \mathtt{B}_1 + \alpha_2^2 \mathtt{B}_2 + \ldots \alpha_l^2 \mathtt{B}_l\right) \\ \vdots \\ \mathtt{M}^m \left(\alpha_1^m \mathtt{B}_1 + \alpha_2^m \mathtt{B}_2 + \ldots \alpha_l^m \mathtt{B}_l\right) \end{bmatrix} = \begin{bmatrix} \alpha_1^1 \mathtt{M}^1 & \alpha_2^1 \mathtt{M}^1 & \ldots & \alpha_l^1 \mathtt{M}^1 \\ \alpha_1^2 \mathtt{M}^2 & \alpha_2^2 \mathtt{M}^2 & \ldots & \alpha_l^2 \mathtt{M}^2 \\ \vdots & \vdots & \ddots & \vdots \\ \alpha_1^m \mathtt{M}^m & \alpha_2^m \mathtt{M}^m & \ldots & \alpha_l^m \mathtt{M}^m \end{bmatrix} \begin{bmatrix} \mathtt{B}_1 \\ \mathtt{B}_2 \\ \vdots \\ \mathtt{B}_l \end{bmatrix} \tag{18.8}$$

This rearrangement shows that the $2m \times n$ matrix $\hat{\mathtt{W}}$ may be decomposed as a product of a $2m \times 3l$ motion matrix $\hat{\mathtt{M}}$ and $3l \times n$ structure matrix $\hat{\mathtt{B}}$, and consequently $\hat{\mathtt{W}}$ has maximum rank $3l$.

As in rigid factorization a rank $3l$ decomposition may be obtained from the measurement matrix $\mathtt{W}$ by truncating the SVD of $\mathtt{W}$ to rank $3l$. Also, as in rigid factorization, the decomposition $\hat{\mathtt{W}} = \hat{\mathtt{M}}\hat{\mathtt{B}}$ is not uniquely defined since an arbitrary $3l \times 3l$ rank $3l$ matrix $\mathtt{A}$ may be inserted in the decomposition as $\hat{\mathtt{W}} = \hat{\mathtt{M}}\mathtt{A}\mathtt{A}^{-1}\hat{\mathtt{B}} = (\hat{\mathtt{M}}\mathtt{A})(\mathtt{A}^{-1}\hat{\mathtt{B}})$. In the rigid case this resulted in a straightforward affine ambiguity in the reconstruction. However, in the non-rigid case there is the additional requirement that the motion matrix has the replicated block structure of (18.8), and we return to this below. This block structure is not required for determining a point's image motion, as will now be discussed.

18.3.1 Subspaces and tensors

In the case of rigid factorization (18.6), as discussed in section 18.2.2, the trajectories lie in a 3 dimensional subspace, and any trajectory may be generated as a linear combination of the columns of $\hat{\mathtt{M}}$ (the $2m \times 3$ motion matrix). Similarly in the case of non-rigid factorization, (18.8), the trajectories lie in a $3l$ dimensional subspace, and any trajectory may be generated as a linear combination of the columns of $\hat{\mathtt{M}}$ (the $2m \times 3l$ motion matrix).

Suppose we observe a new point in a subset of the views, how many images are required before its position can be predicted in all the other views? This is simply a question of triangulation: in rigid factorization a 3-space point has 3 degrees of freedom, and must be observed in two views to obtain the necessary 3 measurements. In non-rigid factorization we need to specify $3l$ degrees of freedom (the number of rows in the $\hat{\mathtt{B}}$ matrix), and this requires $3l/2$ images. For example, if $l = 2$ the subspace is six dimensional (the columns of the $\hat{\mathtt{B}}$ matrix are 6-vectors), and given the image position in three views, the image position in all views is then determined by an analogue of affine triangulation (section 18.2.2) even though the object is deforming.

Independently moving objects. Low-rank factorization methods also arise when there are independently moving objects in the scene. For instance suppose the scene is divided into two objects, each moving independently of the other, and viewed by

Fig. 18.2. **Non-rigid motion sequence.** *Top row: alternate frames from a sequence in which a giraffe gracefully walks and flexes its neck, whilst the camera pans to match its speed. Bottom row: point tracks showing the motion over (a) the 10 previous, and (b) the 10 forthcoming frames. These tracks are computed using non-rigid factorization and lie in a six dimensional subspace. Note the very different trajectories of the (rigid) background from the (deforming) foreground. Yet these are all spanned by the six basis vectors of the motion matrix. The rank can be accounted for as follows: the sequence motion is effectively that of two planes of points moving independently relative to the camera. The background is a rigid object represented by a plane and contributes 2 to the rank. The giraffe in the foreground is represented as a non-rigid object by a set of* $l = 2$ *planar basis shapes and contributes 4 to the rank. Figures courtesy of Andrew Fitzgibbon and Aeron Morgan.*

a moving affine camera. In this case, the columns of the measurement matrix corresponding to points on one object will have rank 3, and those corresponding to the other object will also have rank 3. The total rank of the measurement matrix will be 6. In degenerate configurations in which one object's points all lie in a plane, its contribution to the rank will be only 2. This multibody factorization problem has been studied in some depth in [Costeira-98].

An example of point tracks residing in a low dimensional subspace is shown in figure 18.2.

The existence of the analogue of the fundamental matrix and trifocal tensor depends on the dimension of the subspace. For example suppose the subspace has odd dimension (e.g. $l = 3$ so it is 9 dimensional) then given point measurements in $\lfloor 3l/2 \rfloor$ views (e.g. 4 views) the corresponding point in any other view is constrained to a line, the analogue of an epipolar line, since there is one fewer measurement than degrees of freedom of the subspace. However, if the dimension is even (e.g. $l = 2$ so it is 6 dimensional) then given point measurements in $l/2$ views (e.g. 3 views) the corresponding point in any other view is completely determined. Multi-view tensors can be built for the non-rigid $l > 1$ subspaces using methods similar to those developed in chapter 17 for $l = 1$ 3-space points.

18.3.2 Recovering the camera motion

In rigid-factorization the camera matrices are obtained relatively easily from the motion matrix $\hat{\mathtt{M}}$ – all that is required is to remove a global affine ambiguity specified by a 3×3 matrix $\mathtt{A}$ as described on page 438.

In the non-rigid case, the analogous problem is not so straightforward. It is a simple matter to obtain the motion matrix:

(i) Construct the $2m \times n$ measurement matrix $\mathtt{W}$ from the centred data, as defined in (18.5), and compute its SVD $\mathtt{W} = \mathtt{UDV}^{\mathsf{T}}$.
(ii) Then the motion matrix $\hat{\mathtt{M}}$ is obtained from the first $3l$ columns of $\mathtt{U}$ multiplied by the singular values as $\hat{\mathtt{M}} = \begin{bmatrix} \sigma_1 \mathbf{u}_1 & \sigma_2 \mathbf{u}_2 & \ldots & \sigma_{3l} \mathbf{u}_{3l} \end{bmatrix}$,

but the matrix obtained by this route will *not* in general have the block structure of (18.8). As in the case of rigid-factorization the motion matix is determined up to post-multiplication by a matrix $\mathtt{A}$, which here is $3l \times 3l$. The task is then to determine $\mathtt{A}$ such that $\hat{\mathtt{M}}\mathtt{A}$ has the required block structure of (18.8) *and* also to remove the usual affine ambiguity such that each block conforms to any available constraints on the camera calibration (for example identical internal parameters over all views).

Various methods for determining $\mathtt{A}$ have been investigated (see [Brand-01, Torresani-01]), but these do not impose the full block structure, and currently there is not a satisfactory solution to this problem. Once an initial solution has been obtained by some means, then the correct form can be imposed by bundle adjustment of (18.7).

18.4 Projective factorization

The affine factorization method does not apply directly to projective reconstruction. It was observed in [Sturm-96], however, that if one knows the "projective depth" of each of the points then the structure and camera parameters may be estimated by a simple factorization algorithm similar in style to the affine factorization algorithm.

Consider a set of image points $\mathbf{x}^i_j = \mathtt{P}^i \mathbf{X}_j$. This equation representing the projective mapping is to be interpreted as true only up to a constant factor. Writing these constant factors explicitly, we have $\lambda^i_j \mathbf{x}^i_j = \mathtt{P}^i \mathbf{X}_j$. In this equation, and henceforth in the description of the projective factorization algorithm, the notation $\mathbf{x}^i_j$ means the 3-vector $(x^i_j, y^i_j, 1)^{\mathsf{T}}$ representing an image point. Thus the third coordinate is equal to unity, and x^i_j and y^i_j are the actual measured image coordinates. Provided that each point is visible in every view, so that $\mathbf{x}^i_j$ is known for all i, j, the complete set of equations may be written as a single matrix equation as follows:

$$\begin{bmatrix} \lambda^1_1 \mathbf{x}^1_1 & \lambda^1_2 \mathbf{x}^1_2 & \ldots & \lambda^1_n \mathbf{x}^1_n \\ \lambda^2_1 \mathbf{x}^2_1 & \lambda^2_2 \mathbf{x}^2_2 & \ldots & \lambda^m_n \mathbf{x}^2_n \\ \vdots & \vdots & \ddots & \vdots \\ \lambda^m_1 \mathbf{x}^m_1 & \lambda^m_2 \mathbf{x}^m_2 & \ldots & \lambda^m_n \mathbf{x}^m_n \end{bmatrix} = \begin{bmatrix} \mathtt{P}^1 \\ \mathtt{P}^2 \\ \vdots \\ \mathtt{P}^m \end{bmatrix} [\mathbf{X}_1, \mathbf{X}_2, \ldots, \mathbf{X}_n] \ . \tag{18.9}$$

Objective

Given a set of n image points seen in m views:

$$\mathbf{x}_j^i \; ; \; i = 1, \ldots, m, \; j = 1, \ldots, n$$

compute a projective reconstruction.

Algorithm

(i) Normalize the image data using isotropic scaling as in section 4.4.4(*p*107).
(ii) Start with an initial estimate of the projective depths λ_j^i. This may be obtained by techniques such as an initial projective reconstruction, or else by setting all $\lambda_j^i = 1$.
(iii) Normalize the depths λ_j^i by multiplying rows and columns by constant factors. One method is to do a pass setting the norms of all rows to 1, then a similar pass on columns.
(iv) Form the $3m \times n$ measurement matrix on the left of (18.9), find its nearest rank-4 approximation using the SVD and decompose to find the camera matrices and 3D points.
(v) **Optional iteration.** Reproject the points into each image to obtain new estimates of the depths and repeat from step (ii).

Algorithm 18.2. *Projective reconstruction through factorization.*

This equation is true only if the correct weighting factors λ_j^i are applied to each of the measured points $\mathbf{x}_j^i$. For the present, let us assume that these depths are known. As with the affine factorization algorithm, we would like the matrix on the left – denote it by $\mathtt{W}$ – to have rank 4, since it is the product of two matrices with 4 columns and rows respectively. The actual measurement matrix can be corrected to have rank 4 by using the SVD. Thus, if $\mathtt{W} = \mathtt{UDV}^\mathsf{T}$, all but the first four diagonal entries of $\mathtt{D}$ are set to zero resulting in $\hat{\mathtt{D}}$. The corrected measurement matrix is $\hat{\mathtt{W}} = \mathtt{U}\hat{\mathtt{D}}\mathtt{V}^\mathsf{T}$. The camera matrices are retrieved from $[\mathtt{P}_1^\mathsf{T}, \mathtt{P}_2^\mathsf{T}, \ldots, \mathtt{P}_m^\mathsf{T}]^\mathsf{T} = \mathtt{U}\hat{\mathtt{D}}$ and the points from $[\mathbf{X}_1, \mathbf{X}_2, \ldots, \mathbf{X}_n] = \mathtt{V}^\mathsf{T}$. Note that this factorization is not unique, and in fact we may interpose an arbitrary 4×4 projective transformation $\mathtt{H}$ and its inverse between the two matrices on the right of (18.9), reflecting the fact that reconstruction has a projective ambiguity.

The steps of the projective factorization method are summarized in algorithm 18.2.

18.4.1 Choosing the depths

The weighting factors λ_j^i are called the *projective depths* of the points. The justification of this terminology is the relation of these λ_j^i to the actual depths if camera matrices are known in a Euclidean frame. Refer to section 6.2.3(*p*162) and in particular figure 6.6-(*p*162). The main difficulty with this projective factorization algorithm is that we need to know these projective depths up front, but we do not have this knowledge. There are various techniques to estimate the depths.

(i) Start with an initial projective reconstruction obtained by other means, such as those discussed in section 18.6 below. Then compute λ_j^i by reprojecting the 3D points.
(ii) Start with initial depths all equal to 1, compute the reconstruction and reproject to obtain a new estimate of the depths. This step may be repeated to obtain

improved estimates. However, there is no guarantee that the procedure will converge to a global minimum.

The original paper [Sturm-96] gives a method of computing the depths by stringing together pairwise estimates of the depth obtained from the fundamental matrix, or the trifocal tensor. This method is quite similar to obtaining an initial projective reconstruction by stringing together triples of images (see section 18.6), whilst ensuring that the scale factors are consistent for a common projective reconstruction.

18.4.2 What is being minimized?

In the case of noise, or incorrect values for λ^i_j, the equations (18.9) are not satisfied exactly. We determine a corrected measurement matrix $\hat{\mathtt{W}}$ that is closest to $\mathtt{W}$ in Frobenius norm, subject to having rank 4. Denoting the entries of this matrix as $\hat{\lambda}^i_j\hat{\mathbf{x}}^i_j$, then the computed solution minimizes the expression

$$\|\mathtt{W}-\hat{\mathtt{W}}\|^2=\sum_{ij}\|\lambda^i_j\mathbf{x}^i_j-\hat{\lambda}^i_j\hat{\mathbf{x}}^i_j\|^2=\sum_{ij}(\lambda^i_jx^i_j-\hat{\lambda}^i_j\hat{x}^i_j)^2+(\lambda^i_jy^i_j-\hat{\lambda}^i_j\hat{y}^i_j)^2+(\lambda^i_j-\hat{\lambda}^i_j)^2 \tag{18.10}$$

Because of the last term, at a minimum $\hat{\lambda}^i_j$ must be close to λ^i_j. Assuming they are equal, (18.10) reduces to $\sum_{ij}(\lambda^i_j)^2\|\mathbf{x}^i_j-\hat{\mathbf{x}}^i_j\|^2$. Noting that $\|\mathbf{x}^i_j-\hat{\mathbf{x}}^i_j\|$ is the geometric distance between the measured and estimated points, what is being minimized is a weighted sum-of-squares geometric distance, where each point is being weighted by λ^i_j. If all the geometric depths λ^i_j are close to equal, then the factorization method minimizes an approximation to geometric distance scaled by the common value of λ^i_j.

18.4.3 Normalizing the depths

Projective depths as defined here are not unique. Indeed suppose that $\lambda^i_j\mathbf{x}^i_j=\mathtt{P}^i\mathbf{X}_j$. If we replace $\mathtt{P}^i$ by $\alpha^i\mathtt{P}^i$ and $\mathbf{X}_j$ by $\beta_j\mathbf{X}_j$, then we find that

$$(\alpha^i\beta_j\lambda^i_j)\mathbf{x}^i_j=(\alpha^i\mathtt{P}^i)(\beta_j\mathbf{X}_j)\ .$$

In other words, the projective depths λ^i_j may be replaced by multiplying the i-th row of (18.9) by a factor α^i and the j-th column by a factor β_j. In the light of the previous paragraph, the closer all λ^i_j are to unity, the more exactly the error expression represents geometric distance. Therefore, it is advantageous to renormalize the values of the λ^i_j so that they are as close to unity as possible, by multiplying rows and columns of the measurement matrix by constant values α^i and β_j. A simple heuristic manner of doing this is to multiply each row by a factor α^i so that it has unit norm, followed by a similar pass normalizing the columns. The row and column passes may be iterated.

18.4.4 Normalizing the image coordinates

As with most numerical algorithms involving homogeneous representations of image coordinates described in this book, it is important to normalize the image coordinates. A reasonable scheme is the isotropic normalization method described in section 4.4.4-(p107). One can see the necessity of normalization quite clearly in this case. Consider two image points $\mathbf{x}=(200,300,1)^\mathsf{T}$ and $\hat{\mathbf{x}}=(250,375,1)^\mathsf{T}$. Obviously these points are very far apart in a geometric sense. However, the error expression (18.10) measures not geometric error, but the distance between homogeneous vectors $\|\lambda\mathbf{x} - \hat{\lambda}\hat{\mathbf{x}}\|$. Choosing $\lambda = 1.25$ and $\hat{\lambda} = 1.0$, the error is $\|(250, 375, 1.25)^\mathsf{T} - (250, 375, 1)^\mathsf{T}\|$ which is proportionally quite small. On the other hand, the distance between points $\mathbf{x} = (200, 300, 1)^\mathsf{T}$ and $\hat{\mathbf{x}} = (199, 301, 1)^\mathsf{T}$, which are much closer geometrically can not be made so small by choice of λ and $\hat{\lambda}$ (except for small values). The reader may observe that if the points are scaled down by a factor of 200, then this anomalous situation no longer occurs. In short, with normalized coordinates, the error is a closer approximation to geometric error.

18.4.5 When is the assumption $\lambda^i_j = 1$ reasonable?

According to result 6.1(*p*162), if camera matrices are normalized such that $p_{31}^2 + p_{32}^2 + p_{33}^2 = 1$, and 3D points are normalized to have last coordinate $\mathrm{T} = 1$, then λ_{ij} defined by $\lambda^i_j(x^i_j, y^i_j, 1) = \mathtt{P}^i\mathbf{X}_j$ are the true depths of the points from the camera in a Euclidean frame. If all points are equidistant from the cameras throughout a sequence then we may reasonably assume that each $\lambda^i_j = 1$, for (18.9) will have at least the solution where $\mathtt{P}^i$ and $\mathbf{X}_j$ are the true cameras and points, normalized in the manner just stated. More generally, suppose that points are located at different depths, but each point $\mathbf{X}_j$ remains at approximately the same depth d_j from the cameras through the whole sequence. In this case a solution will exist with all $\lambda^i_j = 1$ in which the computed $\mathbf{X}_j = d_j^{-1}(\mathrm{X}_j, \mathrm{Y}_j, \mathrm{Z}_j, 1)^\mathsf{T}$. Similarly, by allowing multiplication of the camera matrices by a factor, we find

- *If the ratios of true depths of the different 3D points $\mathbf{X}_j$ remain approximately constant during a sequence, then the assumption $\lambda^i_j = 1$ is a good first approximation to projective depth.*

This is for instance the case of an aerial image camera pointing straight down from constant altitude.

18.5 Projective reconstruction using planes

It was seen in section 17.5.2 that if four points visible in each view are known to be coplanar then the computation of the multifocal tensors relating the image points becomes significantly more simple. A major advantage is that a tensor satisfying all its constraints may be computed using a linear algorithm. We now continue with that particular line of investigation, and show that the use of linear techniques extends to estimation of motion and structure for any number of views.

The condition that four of the image correspondences are derived from coplanar points is equivalent to knowing the homographies between the images induced by a plane in space, since a homography may be computed from the four points. It is only the homographies that are important in the following approach. These homographies may be computed from four or more point correspondences, or line correspondences, or estimated directly from the images by direct correlation methods.

What do the plane-plane homographies tell us? The key to projective reconstruction using planes is the observation that knowledge of homographies between the images means we know the first 3×3 part of the camera matrices:

$$\mathtt{P} = \left[\begin{array}{c|c} & t_1 \\ \mathtt{M} & t_2 \\ & t_3 \end{array} \right]$$

Hence, it remains only to compute their last columns, namely the vectors $\mathbf{t}$.

Since we are interested at this point only in obtaining a *projective* reconstruction of the scene, we may suppose that the plane inducing the homographies is the plane at infinity, with points $\mathbf{X}_j = (\mathrm{X}_j, \mathrm{Y}_j, \mathrm{Z}_j, 0)^\mathsf{T}$. Camera matrices may be written in the form $\mathtt{P}^i = [\mathtt{M}^i | \mathbf{t}^i]$, where $\mathtt{M}$ is a 3×3 matrix and $\mathbf{t}^i$ is a column vector. A reasonable assumption is that the camera centres do not lie on the plane inducing the homographies (for otherwise the homographies will be degenerate). This means that the matrix $\mathtt{M}$ is non-singular. For simplicity, the first camera may be assumed to have the form $\mathtt{P}^1 = [\mathtt{I} \mid \mathbf{0}]$, where $\mathtt{I}$ is the identity matrix.

Now, if $\mathbf{x}^i_j$ is the point in image i corresponding to the 3D point $\mathbf{X}_j = (\mathrm{X}_j, \mathrm{Y}_j, \mathrm{Z}_j, 0)^\mathsf{T}$ lying on the homography-inducing plane, then

$$\mathbf{x}^1_j = \mathtt{P}^1 (\mathrm{X}_j, \mathrm{Y}_j, \mathrm{Z}_j, 0)^\mathsf{T} = (\mathrm{X}_j, \mathrm{Y}_j, \mathrm{Z}_j)^\mathsf{T}$$

whereas

$$\mathbf{x}^i_j = \mathtt{M}^i (\mathrm{X}_j, \mathrm{Y}_j, \mathrm{Z}_j)^\mathsf{T} = \mathtt{M}^i \mathbf{x}^1_j.$$

Thus $\mathtt{M}^i$ represents the homography from the first image to the i-th image induced by the plane. Conversely, if $\mathtt{M}^i$ is the known plane-induced homography that maps a point in the first image to its matching point in the i-th image, then the set of camera matrices can be assumed to have the form $\mathtt{P}^i = [\mathtt{M}^i | \mathbf{t}^i]$, where the $\mathtt{M}^i$ are known and their scale is fixed, but the final columns $\mathbf{t}^i$ are not.

Known camera orientation. We have just shown that knowledge of homographies implies the knowledge of the left-hand 3×3 submatrix of each camera matrix. The same will hold if we know the orientation (and calibration) of all the cameras. For instance, a reasonable approach to reconstruction, knowing the calibration of each camera, is to estimate the orientation of each camera separately from the translation (for example from two or more scene vanishing points). Once the orientation ($\mathtt{R}^i$) and calibration ($\mathtt{K}^i$) of each camera is known, the left-hand block of each camera matrix is $\mathtt{K}^i \mathtt{R}^i$.

18.5.1 Direct solution for structure and translation

We describe two separate methods for computation of the projective structure given plane-induced homographies between images. The first method solves for the 3D points and the camera motion simultaneously by solving a single linear system. Suppose point $\mathbf{X} = (\mathrm{X}, \mathrm{Y}, \mathrm{Z}, 1)^\mathsf{T}$ is not on the plane at infinity, that is, the plane inducing the homographies.

The equation for point projection is

$$\lambda \mathbf{x} = \mathtt{P}\mathbf{X} = [\mathtt{M}|\mathbf{t}]\mathbf{X} = [\mathtt{M}|\mathbf{t}] \begin{pmatrix} \widetilde{\mathbf{X}} \\ 1 \end{pmatrix}$$

where the (unknown) scale factor λ has been explicitly written. More precisely, we may write

$$\lambda \begin{pmatrix} x \\ y \\ 1 \end{pmatrix} = \begin{bmatrix} \mathbf{m}_1^\mathsf{T} & t_1 \\ \mathbf{m}_2^\mathsf{T} & t_2 \\ \mathbf{m}_3^\mathsf{T} & t_3 \end{bmatrix} \begin{pmatrix} \widetilde{\mathbf{X}} \\ 1 \end{pmatrix} = \begin{pmatrix} \mathbf{m}_1^\mathsf{T}\widetilde{\mathbf{X}} + t_1 \\ \mathbf{m}_2^\mathsf{T}\widetilde{\mathbf{X}} + t_2 \\ \mathbf{m}_3^\mathsf{T}\widetilde{\mathbf{X}} + t_3 \end{pmatrix}$$

where $\mathbf{m}_i^\mathsf{T}$ is the i-th row of the matrix $\mathtt{M}$.

The unknown scale factor λ may be eliminated by taking the vector product of the two sides of this equation, resulting in

$$\begin{pmatrix} x \\ y \\ 1 \end{pmatrix} \times \begin{pmatrix} \mathbf{m}_1^\mathsf{T}\widetilde{\mathbf{X}} + t_1 \\ \mathbf{m}_2^\mathsf{T}\widetilde{\mathbf{X}} + t_2 \\ \mathbf{m}_3^\mathsf{T}\widetilde{\mathbf{X}} + t_3 \end{pmatrix} = \mathbf{0}.$$

This provides two independent equations

$$\begin{aligned} x(\mathbf{m}_3^\mathsf{T}\widetilde{\mathbf{X}} + t_3) - (\mathbf{m}_1^\mathsf{T}\widetilde{\mathbf{X}} + t_1) &= 0 \\ y(\mathbf{m}_3^\mathsf{T}\widetilde{\mathbf{X}} + t_3) - (\mathbf{m}_2^\mathsf{T}\widetilde{\mathbf{X}} + t_2) &= 0 \end{aligned}$$

which are linear in the unknowns $\widetilde{\mathbf{X}} = (\mathrm{X}, \mathrm{Y}, \mathrm{Z})^\mathsf{T}$ and $\mathbf{t} = (t_1, t_2, t_3)^\mathsf{T}$. The equations may be written as

$$\begin{bmatrix} x\mathbf{m}_3^\mathsf{T} - \mathbf{m}_1^\mathsf{T} & -1 & 0 & x \\ y\mathbf{m}_3^\mathsf{T} - \mathbf{m}_2^\mathsf{T} & 0 & -1 & y \end{bmatrix} \begin{pmatrix} \widetilde{\mathbf{X}} \\ t_1 \\ t_2 \\ t_3 \end{pmatrix} = \mathbf{0}.$$

Thus, each measured point $\mathbf{x}_j^i = \mathtt{P}^i\mathbf{X}_j$ generates a pair of equations, and with m views involving n points a $2nm$ set of equations in $3n + 3m$ unknowns is generated in this way. These equations may be solved by linear or linear least-squares techniques to obtain the structure and motion.

A few remarks about this method are offered.

(i) In contrast to factorization methods (section 18.2) we do not need all points to be visible in all views. Only equations corresponding to the measured points are used.

(ii) Since it is assumed that points have final coordinate equal to one, it is necessary to exclude points that lie on the plane at infinity (the plane inducing the homography) which have final coordinate equal to zero. A test to detect points lying on or close to the plane is necessary.

(iii) Both points and cameras are computed at once. For a large number of points and cameras this may be a very large estimation problem. However, if the point tracks have a banded form, then sparse solution techniques may be used to solve the equation set efficiently, as in section A6.7(p613).

This method and its implementation are discussed in depth in [Rother-01, Rother-03]. The details given here are different from those given in [Rother-01], where the structure and motion computation is carried out in a specific projective frame related to the matched points on the plane, involving a coordinate change in the images.

18.5.2 Direct motion estimation

The second method for planar reconstruction knowing homographies solves for the camera matrices first and subsequently computes the point positions.

We start from the set of camera matrices which again can be assumed to have the form $\mathtt{P}^i = [\mathtt{H}^i|\mathbf{t}^i]$, where the $\mathtt{H}^i$ are known and their scale is fixed, but the final columns $\mathbf{t}^i$ are not. We may assume that $\mathtt{P}^1 = [\mathtt{I} \mid \mathbf{0}]$, so that $\mathbf{t}^1 = \mathbf{0}$. The set of all remaining $\mathbf{t}^i$ have $3m - 4$ degrees of freedom, since the $\mathbf{t}^i$ are defined only up to a common scale. Now assume that several point or line correspondences across two or more views are known (three views are required for lines). These correspondences must derive from 3D points or lines that do not lie in the reference plane (used to compute the $\mathtt{H}^i$). Each point correspondence across two views leads to a linear equation in the entries of the fundamental matrix. Similarly, correspondences of points or lines across three or four views lead to linear equations in the entries of the trifocal or quadrifocal tensor.

The key point (as explained in section 17.5.2) is that we may express the entries of the fundamental matrix (or trifocal or quadrifocal tensor) linearly in the entries of the vectors $\mathbf{t}^i$. Therefore each linear relation induced by a point or line correspondence may be related back to a linear relationship in terms of the entries of the $\mathbf{t}^i$. Thus, for example, a correspondence across views i, j and k gives rise to a set of linear equations in the entries of the three vectors $\mathbf{t}^i$, $\mathbf{t}^j$ and $\mathbf{t}^k$. A set of correspondences across many views can be broken down into correspondences across sets of consecutive views. Thus, for example, a single point correspondence across $m > 4$ views will give a set of equations of the form

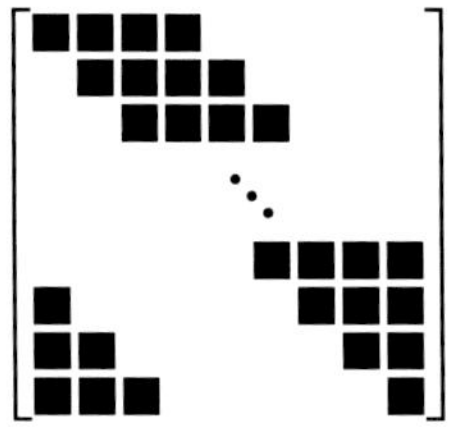

where each row represents a set of equations derived from a quadrifocal tensor relationship. Each black square represents a block with 3 columns corresponding to one of the vectors $\mathbf{t}^i$. In the diagram above, we choose to wrap the equations around from the last to the first view to add greater rigidity. Otherwise, the values of the $\mathbf{t}^i$ can drift from the first to the last view. Other schemes for selecting groups of views are possible, and it is not necessary to restrict to consecutive views.

Linear relations may be generated between any subset of sufficiently many images (2, 3 or 4 depending on which tensor is used to generate the equations). One must trade off the added stability of the solution against the added computational cost of adding more equations. A mixture of bifocal, trifocal and quadrifocal constraints may be used in generating the set of all equations, and it is not necessary that all points be visible in all views.

Numbers of equations generated. Let the total number of views be m. Consider a subset of s views ($s = 2, 3$ or 4) and let n point correspondences be given between these views. We briefly consider the problem of reconstruction from this subset of s views in isolation. From these point correspondences we can generate a set of equations $\mathtt{A}\mathbf{t}'$ between the entries $\mathbf{t}'$ of the s views, and thence estimate the values of the $3s$ entries of $\mathbf{t}'$. In doing this, we can assume that the first view has $\mathbf{t} = \mathbf{0}$, and the vectors $\mathbf{t}$ from the remaining $s - 1$ views are only determined up to a common scale. Thus, the $\mathtt{A}$ occurring in the equation set $\mathtt{A}\mathbf{t}'$ has a right null-space of dimension at least 4, corresponding to the 4 degrees of freedom of the solution. In general, then:

Result 18.1. *Ignoring the effects of noisy data, the total rank of the set of equations generated from $n \geq 2$ point correspondences in s views is $3s - 4$. This is independent of the number of point (or line) correspondences used to generate them.*

To be exact, the argument above showed that the rank was *at most* $3s - 4$. For 2-view, 3-view and 4-view correspondences this is equal to 2, 5 or 8 respectively. However, as long as there are two correspondences the maximum rank is achieved. This is because two points are sufficient for reconstruction from $s = 2, 3$ or 4 views as shown by the counting arguments of section 17.5.2.

Now consider the total set of m views. The total number of retrievable parameters of all the $\mathbf{t}^i$ is $3m - 4$. Therefore, for a solution to be possible, the number of equations must exceed $3m - 4$, which gives the following result.

Result 18.2. *If S subsets of s_k views are chosen from among m views, then in order to solve for all the vectors $\mathbf{t}^i$ representing final columns of the camera matrices, it is necessary that*

$$\sum_{k=1}^{S} (3s_k - 4) \geq 3m - 4 \ .$$

One can verify that if 2-view correspondences are to be used, involving equations derived from the fundamental matrix constraints, then it is not sufficient to use just pairs of consecutive views in a configuration such as

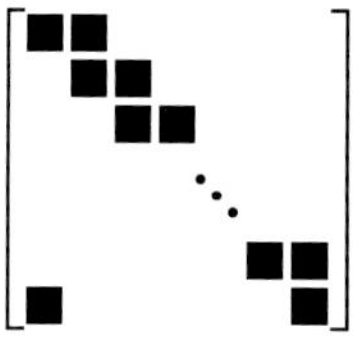

for in this case, the total number of equations generated is $m(3s - 4) = m(3 \cdot 2 - 4) = 2m$, whereas the total number of equations required is $3m - 4$. Thus for $m > 4$ there are not enough equations. This is related to the fact that the fundamental matrices between consecutive views are not sufficient to define the structure of the sequence of views. It is necessary to add additional constraints from non-consecutive views, such as

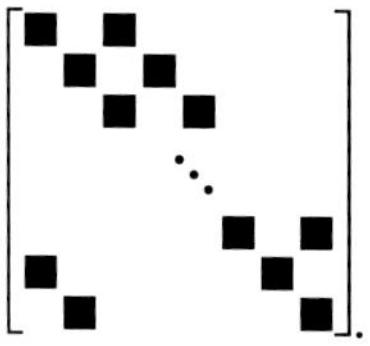

Note though that the discussion of section 15.4(*p*383) suggests that it is preferable to use trifocal or quadrifocal constraints over triplets or quadruplets of views. Implementation details for this method are given in [Kaucic-01].

18.6 Reconstruction from sequences

In this final section we bring together several ideas from earlier in the book. The objective here is to compute a reconstruction from a sequence of frames provided by a video. There are three stages to this problem: (i) compute corresponding features throughout the sequence; (ii) compute an initial reconstruction which may be used as a starting point for (iii) bundle adjustment (as described in section 18.1).

Here the features we will consider are interest points, though others such as lines could equally well be used. The correspondence problem is exacerbated because an interest point feature will generally not appear in all of the images, and often will be missing from consecutive images. Bundle adjustment, however, is not hindered by missing correspondences.

There are several advantages of a video sequence over an arbitrary set of images: (i) there is an ordering on the images; (ii) the distance between camera centres (the baseline) for successive frames is small. The small baseline is important because it enables possible feature matches between successive images to be obtained and assessed more easily. Matches are more easily obtained because the image points do not move "far" between views so a proximity search region can be employed; matches are more easily assessed (as to whether they arise from the same point in 3-space) because nearby images are similar in appearance. The disadvantage of a small baseline is that the 3D structure is estimated poorly. However, this disadvantage is mitigated by tracking over many views in the sequence so that the effective baseline is large.

An overview of the method is given in algorithm 18.3. There are several strategies that may be used to obtain the initial reconstruction, though this area is still to some extent a black art. Three possibilities are:

1. Extending the baseline. Suppose a reasonable number of scene points are visible throughout the sequence. Correspondences may be carried through from the first to the last frame using the pairwise matches (from $\mathtt{F}$), or the triplet matched points (from $\mathcal{T}$). Indeed if the baseline between consecutive frames is small (compared to the structure depth), then pairwise matches may be obtained using homography computation (algorithm 4.6(*p*123)) – this provides a stronger matching constraint (point to point) than $\mathtt{F}$ (point to line).

A trifocal tensor can then be estimated from corresponding points in the first, middle (say), and end frames of the sequence. This tensor determines a projective reconstruc-

Objective

Given a sequence of frames in a video, compute correspondences and a reconstruction of the scene structure and the camera for each frame.

Algorithm

(i) **Interest points:** Compute interest points in each image.
(ii) **2 view correspondences:** Compute interest point correspondences and F between consecutive frames using algorithm 11.4(*p*291) (frames may be omitted if the baseline motion is too small).
(iii) **3 view correspondences:** Compute interest point correspondences and $\mathcal{T}$ between all consecutive image triplets using algorithm 16.4(*p*401).
(iv) **Initial reconstruction:** See text.
(v) **Bundle adjust** the cameras and 3D structure for the complete sequence.
(vi) **Auto-calibration:** see chapter 19 (optional).

Algorithm 18.3. *Overview of reconstruction from a sequence of images.*

tion for those points and frames. The cameras for the intermediate frames may then be estimated by resectioning, and the scene points not visible throughout the sequence estimated by triangulation.

2. Hierarchical merging of sub-sequences. The idea here is to partition the sequence into manageable sub-sequences (there can be several hierarchical layers of partitioning). A projective reconstruction is then computed for each sub-sequence and these reconstructions are "zipped" (merged) together.

Consider the problem of merging two triplets which overlap by two views. It is a simple matter to extend the correspondences over the views: a correspondence which exists across the triplet 1-2-3 and also across the triplet 2-3-4 may be extended to the frames 1-2-3-4, since the pair 2-3 overlaps for the triplets. The camera matrices and 3D structure are then computed for the frames 1-2-3-4, for example by first resectioning and then bundle adjustment. This process is extended by merging neighbouring groups of frames until camera matrices and correspondences are established throughout the sequence. In this manner error can be distributed evenly over the sequence.

3. Incremental bundle adjustment. A fresh bundle adjustment is carried out as the correspondences from each new frame are added. The disadvantage of this method is the computational expense and also the possibility that error systematically accumulates.

Of course these three methods may be combined together. For example, the sequence can be partitioned into a sub-sequence where common points are visible, and a reconstruction built for the sub-sequence using the extended baseline method. These sub-sequences may then be combined hierarchically.

In this manner structure and cameras may be computed automatically for sequences consisting of hundreds of frames. These reconstructions may form the basis for such tasks as navigation (determining the camera/ego-position) and virtual model genera-

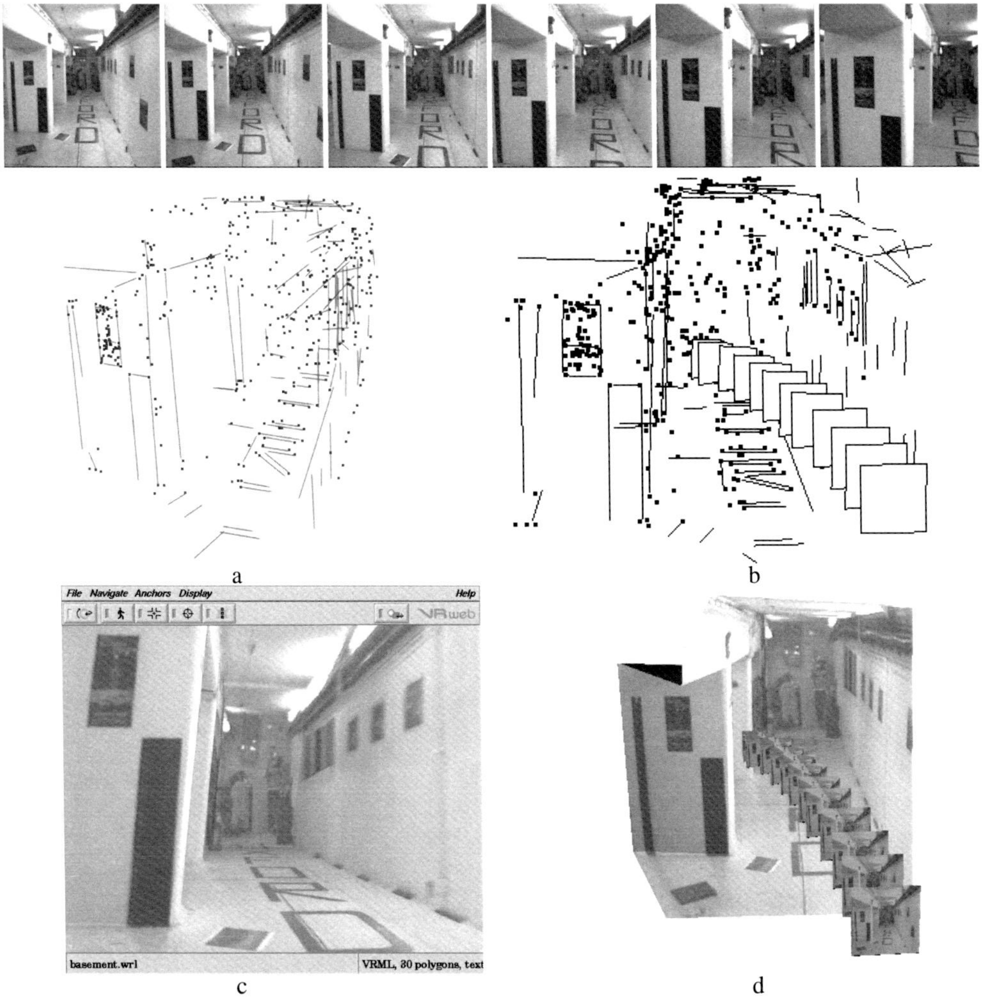

Fig. 18.3. **Corridor sequence**. *(a) A three dimensional reconstruction of points and lines in the scene, and (b) cameras (represented by their image planes) computed automatically from the images. A texture mapped triangulated graphical model is then automatically constructed as described in [Baillard-99]. (c) A rendering of the scene from a novel viewpoint, different from any in the sequence. (d) VRML model of the scene with the cameras represented by their image planes (texture mapped with the original images from the sequence).*

tion. Often it is necessary first to compute a metric reconstruction from the projective one, using the methods described in chapter 10 and chapter 19. Metric reconstruction and virtual model generation is illustrated in the following examples.

Example 18.3. Corridor sequence

A camera is mounted on a mobile vehicle for this sequence. The vehicle moves along the floor turning to the left. The forward translation in this sequence makes structure recovery difficult, due to the small baseline for triangulation. In this situation, the benefit of using all frames in the sequence is significant. Figure 18.3 shows the recovered structure. △

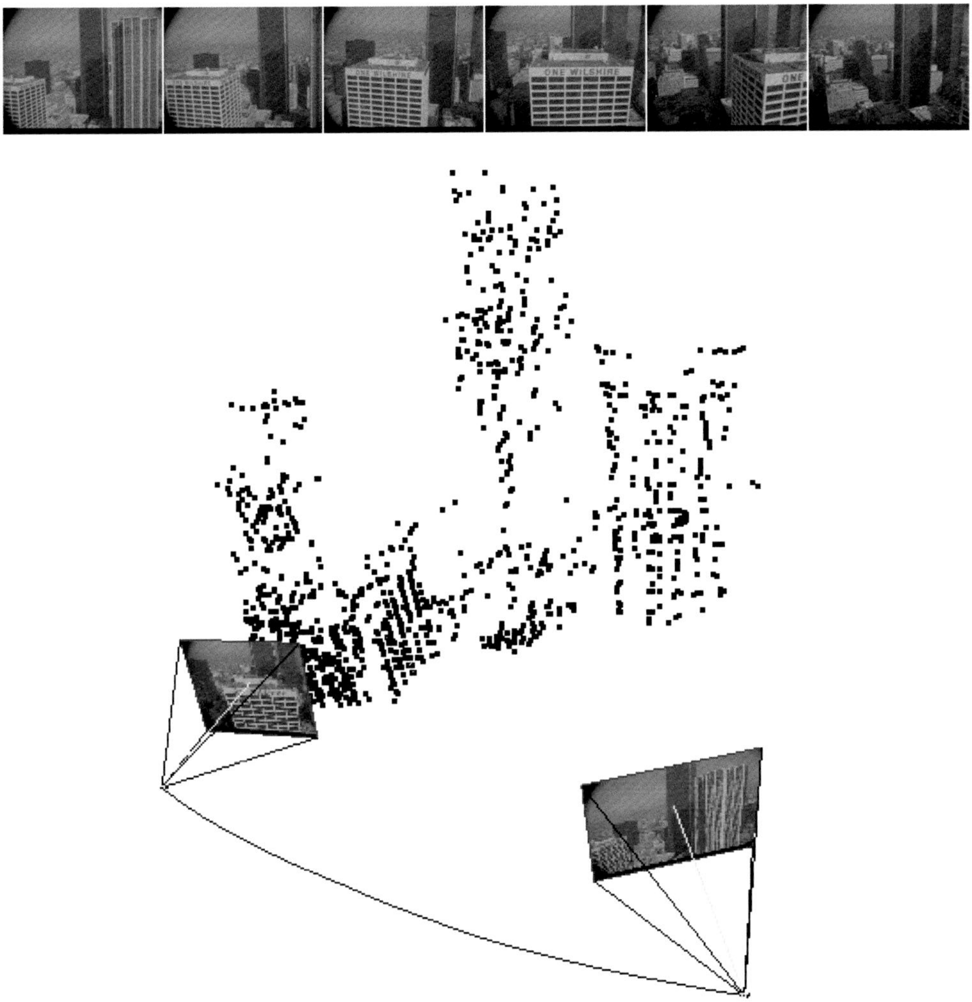

Fig. 18.4. **Wilshire:** *3D points and cameras for 350 frames of a helicopter shot. Cameras are shown for just the start and end frames for clarity, with the camera path plotted between.*

Example 18.4. "Wilshire" sequence

This is a helicopter shot of Wilshire Boulevard, Los Angeles. In this case reconstruction is hampered by the repeated structure in the scene – many of the feature points (for example those on the skyscraper windows) have very similar intensity neighbourhoods, so correlation-based tracking produces many false candidates. However, the robust geometry-guided matching successfully rejects the incorrect correspondences. Figure 18.4 shows the structure. △

18.7 Closure

It is probably fair to say that no fully satisfactory technique for reconstruction from a sequence of projective images is known, and many ad-hoc techniques have been used, with reasonable success. Four views is the limit for the closed-form solutions based on multiview tensors. For larger numbers of views there is no such neat mathematical formulation of the problem. One exception to this is the m-view technique based on duality (see chapter 20), but this techniques is limited to six to eight points, depending on which dual tensor (fundamental matrix, trifocal tensor or quadrifocal tensor) is used. Most sequences will contain many more matched points than this.

18.7.1 Literature

The Tomasi–Kanade algorithm was first proposed for orthographic projection, [Tomasi-92], but was later extended to paraperspective [Poelman-94]. It has been extended to lines and conics, e.g. [Kahl-98a], but the MLE property no longer applies, and it is unclear what is being minimized in the affine reconstruction. Others have investigated subspace methods for multiple affine views in the case of planes [Irani-99], and the case of multiple objects moving independently [Boult-91, Gear-98]. Non-rigid factorization was formulated by [Brand-01, Torresani-01], though the elements of the idea are present in [Bascle-98]. Affine reconstruction with uncertainty (covariance-weighted data) has been discussed by Irani and Anandan [Irani-00, Anandan-02] The method of affine reconstruction by alternating triangulation and camera estimation is mentioned in [Huynh-03], under the name "PowerFactorization."

The extension of factorization to projective cameras is due to Sturm and Triggs [Sturm-96]. Methods of iteration using this approach have been proposed by [Heyden-97a, Triggs-96].

A method of computing multiple cameras based on a plane homography was employed in [Cross-99], initializing the $\mathbf{t}^i$ vectors using planar auto-calibration.

Methods for obtaining an initial projective reconstruction from a sequence are described in [Avidan-98, Beardsley-94, Beardsley-96, Fitzgibbon-98a, Laveau-96a, Nister-00, Sturm-97b]. [Torr-99], and more recently [Pollefeys-02], discuss the important problem of scene and motion degeneracies that may be encounted in sequence reconstruction.

18.7.2 Notes and exercises

(i) The affine factorization algorithm can be applied to obtain a reconstruction in situations where a set of cameras $\{\mathtt{P}^i\}$ have a common third row, even though the cameras are not affine. The third row is the principal plane of the camera (see section 6.2(p158)) and the condition of a common third row is equivalent to coplanar principal planes. For example if a camera translates in a direction perpendicular to its principal axis, then all the camera centres will lie on a plane, and the principal planes are coplanar. The affine factorization algorithm can be applied in this case because the set of cameras can be transformed as $\mathtt{P}^i\mathtt{H}_{4\times 4}$ to the affine form by a 4×4 homography H satisfying $\mathbf{P}^3 \mathtt{H}_{4\times 4} = (0,0,0,1)$, where $\mathbf{P}^3$ is the last row of $\mathtt{P}^i$.

More generally, if the camera centres are restricted to a plane then the images may be synthetically rotated such that the cameras effectively have coplanar principal planes. For example in the case of planar motion (section 19.8) or single axis rotation (section 19.9(*p*490)) if all the images are rotated such that the principal axis is parallel to the rotation axis (by applying a homography to each image which maps the horizon to infinity in the case of a vertical rotation axis), then the principal planes of all the cameras are parallel. However, if the cameras are not actually affine, then the algorithm will not give the ML estimate of the reconstruction.

19

Auto-Calibration

Auto-calibration is the process of determining internal camera parameters directly from multiple uncalibrated images. Once this is done, it is possible to compute a metric reconstruction from the images. Auto-calibration avoids the onerous task of calibrating cameras using special calibration objects. This gives great flexibility since, for example, a camera can be calibrated directly from an image sequence despite unknown motion and changes in some of the internal parameters.

The root of the method is that a camera moves rigidly, so the absolute conic is fixed under the motion. Conversely, then, if a unique fixed conic in 3-space can be determined in some way from the images, this identifies Ω_∞. As we have seen in earlier chapters, once Ω_∞ is identified, the metric geometry can be computed. An array of auto-calibration methods are available for this task of identifying Ω_∞.

This chapter has four main parts. First we lay out the algebraic structure of the auto-calibration problem, and show how the auto-calibration equations are generated from constraints on the internal or external parameters. Second, we describe several *direct* methods for auto-calibration which involve computing the absolute conic or its image. These include estimating the absolute dual quadric over many views, or the Kruppa equations from view pairs. Third, are *stratified* methods for auto-calibration which involve two steps – first solving for the plane at infinity, then using this to solve for the absolute conic. The fourth part covers a number of special configurations including a camera rotating about its centre, a camera undergoing planar motion, and the motion of a stereo rig.

19.1 Introduction

Auto- (or self-) calibration is the computation of metric properties of the cameras and/or the scene from a set of uncalibrated images. This differs from conventional calibration where the camera calibration matrix $\mathtt{K}$ is determined from the image of a known calibration grid (chapter 7) or properties of the scene, such as vanishing points of orthogonal directions (chapter 8). Instead, in auto-calibration the metric properties are determined directly from constraints on the internal and/or external parameters.

For example, suppose we have a set of images acquired by a camera with fixed internal parameters, and that a projective reconstruction is computed from point correspondences across the image set. The reconstruction computes a projective camera matrix $\mathtt{P}^i$ for each view. Our constraint is that for the actual cameras the internal parameter matrix $\mathtt{K}$ is the same (but unknown) for each view. Now, each camera $\mathtt{P}^i$ of the projective reconstruction may be decomposed as $\mathtt{P}^i = \mathtt{K}^i[\mathtt{R}^i \mid \mathbf{t}^i]$ but in general the calibration matrix $\mathtt{K}^i$ will differ for each view. Thus the constraint will *not* be satisfied by the projective reconstruction.

However, we have the freedom to vary our projective reconstruction by transforming the camera matrices by a homography $\mathtt{H}$. Since the actual cameras have fixed internal parameters, there will exist a homography (or a family of homographies) such that the transformed cameras $\mathtt{P}^i\mathtt{H}$ do decompose as $\mathtt{P}^i\mathtt{H} = \mathtt{K}\mathtt{R}^i[\mathtt{I} \mid \mathbf{t}^i]$, with the same calibration matrix for each camera, so the reconstruction is consistent with the constraint. Provided there are sufficiently many views and the motion between the views is general (see later), then this consistency constrains $\mathtt{H}$ to the extent that the reconstruction transformed by $\mathtt{H}$ is within a similarity transformation of the actual cameras and scene, i.e. we achieve a metric reconstruction.

Although the particular constraints used to achieve a metric reconstruction may differ, this example illustrates the general approach:

(i) Obtain a projective reconstruction $\{\mathtt{P}^i, \mathbf{X}_j\}$.
(ii) Determine a rectifying homography $\mathtt{H}$ from auto-calibration constraints, and transform to a metric reconstruction $\{\mathtt{P}^i\mathtt{H}, \mathtt{H}^{-1}\mathbf{X}_j\}$.

Various flavours of auto-calibration will be covered in the following sections. They differ in the constraints used, and the methods whereby the homography $\mathtt{H}$ is determined. The methods may be divided into two classes: those that directly determine $\mathtt{H}$; and those that are stratified, determining first the projective and then the affine components of $\mathtt{H}$. The advantage of the latter approach is that once an affine reconstruction is achieved, i.e. $\boldsymbol{\pi}_\infty$ is known, the solution for a metric reconstruction is linear.

If camera calibration rather than metric scene reconstruction is the goal, then it is not always necessary to compute an explicit projective reconstruction, and sometimes the camera calibration may be computed more directly than via a rectifying transformation. This is the case, for instance, if a camera rotates about its centre without translation, as is discussed in section 19.6.

19.2 Algebraic framework and problem statement

Suppose we have a projective reconstruction $\{\mathtt{P}^i, \mathbf{X}_j\}$; then based on constraints on the cameras' internal parameters or motion we wish to determine a rectifying homography $\mathtt{H}$ such that $\{\mathtt{P}^i\mathtt{H}, \mathtt{H}^{-1}\mathbf{X}_j\}$ is a metric reconstruction.

We start from the true metric situation with calibrated cameras, and structure represented in a Euclidean world frame. Thus in actuality there are m cameras $\mathtt{P}^i_{\mathrm{M}}$ which project a 3D point $\mathbf{X}_{\mathrm{M}}$ to an image point $\mathbf{x}^i = \mathtt{P}^i_{\mathrm{M}}\mathbf{X}_{\mathrm{M}}$ in each view, where the subscript M indicates that the cameras are calibrated and the world frame is Euclidean. The cameras may be written as $\mathtt{P}^i_{\mathrm{M}} = \mathtt{K}^i[\mathtt{R}^i \mid \mathbf{t}^i]$ for $i = 1, \ldots, m$.

In a projective reconstruction we obtain cameras $\mathtt{P}^i$ which are related to $\mathtt{P}^i_{\mathrm{M}}$ by

$$\mathtt{P}^i_{\mathrm{M}} = \mathtt{P}^i\mathtt{H} \quad i = 1, \ldots, m \tag{19.1}$$

where $\mathtt{H}$ is an unknown 4×4 homography of 3-space. Our goal is to determine $\mathtt{H}$.

To be precise we are not concerned with the absolute rotation, translation and scale of the reconstruction, and we will now factor out this similarity component. We choose the world frame to coincide with the first camera, so that $\mathtt{R}^1 = \mathtt{I}$ and $\mathbf{t}^1 = \mathbf{0}$. Then $\mathtt{R}^i, \mathbf{t}^i$ specifies the Euclidean transformation between the i-th camera and the first, and $\mathtt{P}^1_{\mathrm{M}} = \mathtt{K}^1[\mathtt{I} \mid \mathbf{0}]$. Similarly, in the projective reconstruction we choose the usual canonical camera for the first view, so that $\mathtt{P}^1 = [\mathtt{I} \mid \mathbf{0}]$. Then writing $\mathtt{H}$ as

$$\mathtt{H} = \begin{bmatrix} \mathtt{A} & \mathbf{t} \\ \mathbf{v}^{\mathsf{T}} & k \end{bmatrix}$$

the condition $\mathtt{P}^1_{\mathrm{M}} = \mathtt{P}^1\mathtt{H}$ from (19.1) becomes $[\mathtt{K}^1 \mid \mathbf{0}] = [\mathtt{I} \mid \mathbf{0}]\mathtt{H}$, which implies that $\mathtt{A} = \mathtt{K}^1$ and $\mathbf{t} = \mathbf{0}$. In addition, since $\mathtt{H}$ is non-singular, k must be non-zero, so we may assume $k = 1$ (this fixes the scale of the reconstruction). This shows that $\mathtt{H}$ is of the form

$$\mathtt{H} = \begin{bmatrix} \mathtt{K}^1 & \mathbf{0} \\ \mathbf{v}^{\mathsf{T}} & 1 \end{bmatrix}.$$

This has factored out the similarity component.

The vector $\mathbf{v}$, together with $\mathtt{K}^1$, specifies the plane at infinity in the projective reconstruction since the coordinates of $\boldsymbol{\pi}_\infty$ are

$$\boldsymbol{\pi}_\infty = \mathtt{H}^{-\mathsf{T}} \begin{pmatrix} 0 \\ 0 \\ 0 \\ 1 \end{pmatrix} = \begin{bmatrix} (\mathtt{K}^1)^{-\mathsf{T}} & -(\mathtt{K}^1)^{-\mathsf{T}}\mathbf{v} \\ \mathbf{0} & 1 \end{bmatrix} \begin{pmatrix} 0 \\ 0 \\ 0 \\ 1 \end{pmatrix} = \begin{pmatrix} -(\mathtt{K}^1)^{-\mathsf{T}}\mathbf{v} \\ 1 \end{pmatrix}.$$

We will write $\boldsymbol{\pi}_\infty = (\mathbf{p}^{\mathsf{T}}, 1)^{\mathsf{T}}$ so that $\mathbf{p} = -(\mathtt{K}^1)^{-\mathsf{T}}\mathbf{v}$. To summarize so far we have shown:

Result 19.1. *A projective reconstruction $\{\mathtt{P}^i, \mathbf{X}_j\}$ in which $\mathtt{P}^1 = [\mathtt{I} \mid \mathbf{0}]$ can be transformed to a metric reconstruction $\{\mathtt{P}^i\mathtt{H}, \mathtt{H}^{-1}\mathbf{X}_j\}$ by a matrix $\mathtt{H}$ of the form*

$$\mathtt{H} = \begin{bmatrix} \mathtt{K} & \mathbf{0} \\ -\mathbf{p}^{\mathsf{T}}\mathtt{K} & 1 \end{bmatrix} \tag{19.2}$$

where $\mathtt{K}$ is an upper triangular matrix. Furthermore,

(i) $\mathtt{K} = \mathtt{K}^1$ *is the calibration matrix of the first camera.*
(ii) *The coordinates of the plane at infinity in the projective reconstruction are given by $\boldsymbol{\pi}_\infty = (\mathbf{p}^{\mathsf{T}}, 1)^{\mathsf{T}}$.*

Conversely, if the plane at infinity in the projective frame and the calibration matrix of the first camera are known, then the transformation $\mathtt{H}$ that converts the projective to a metric reconstruction is given by (19.2).

From this result it follows that to transform a projective to a metric reconstruction it is sufficient to specify 8 parameters – the three entries of $\mathbf{p}$ and five entries of $\mathtt{K}^1$. This agrees with a geometric counting argument. Finding metric structure is equivalent to specifying the plane at infinity and the absolute conic (three and five degrees of freedom respectively). In a metric reconstruction the calibration $\mathtt{K}^i$ of each camera, its rotation $\mathtt{R}^i$ relative to the first camera, and its translation $\mathbf{t}^i$ relative to the first camera up to a single common scaling, i.e. $\mathbf{t}^i \mapsto s\mathbf{t}^i$, are all determined.

We now develop the basic auto-calibration equations. We denote the cameras of the projective reconstruction as $\mathtt{P}^i = [\mathtt{A}^i \mid \mathbf{a}^i]$. Multiplying out (19.1) using (19.2) gives

$$\mathtt{K}^i\mathtt{R}^i = \left(\mathtt{A}^i - \mathbf{a}^i\mathbf{p}^\mathsf{T}\right)\mathtt{K}^1 \quad \text{for } i = 2, \ldots, m \tag{19.3}$$

which may be rearranged as $\mathtt{R}^i = (\mathtt{K}^i)^{-1}\left(\mathtt{A}^i - \mathbf{a}^i\mathbf{p}^\mathsf{T}\right)\mathtt{K}^1 \quad i = 2, \ldots, m$. Finally, the rotation $\mathtt{R}^i$ may be eliminated using $\mathtt{R}\mathtt{R}^\mathsf{T} = \mathtt{I}$, leaving

$$\mathtt{K}^i\mathtt{K}^{i\mathsf{T}} = \left(\mathtt{A}^i - \mathbf{a}^i\mathbf{p}^\mathsf{T}\right)\mathtt{K}^1\mathtt{K}^{1\mathsf{T}}\left(\mathtt{A}^i - \mathbf{a}^i\mathbf{p}^\mathsf{T}\right)^\mathsf{T}.$$

Note now that $\mathtt{K}^i\mathtt{K}^{i\mathsf{T}} = \boldsymbol{\omega}^*$, the dual image of the absolute conic (or DIAC) – see (8.11–*p*210). Making this substitution gives the basic equations for auto-calibration:

$$\begin{aligned} \boldsymbol{\omega}^{*i} &= \left(\mathtt{A}^i - \mathbf{a}^i\mathbf{p}^\mathsf{T}\right)\boldsymbol{\omega}^{*1}\left(\mathtt{A}^i - \mathbf{a}^i\mathbf{p}^\mathsf{T}\right)^\mathsf{T} \\ \boldsymbol{\omega}^i &= \left(\mathtt{A}^i - \mathbf{a}^i\mathbf{p}^\mathsf{T}\right)^{-\mathsf{T}}\boldsymbol{\omega}^1\left(\mathtt{A}^i - \mathbf{a}^i\mathbf{p}^\mathsf{T}\right)^{-1} \end{aligned} \tag{19.4}$$

the second equation being simply the inverse of the first, with $\boldsymbol{\omega}$ the image of the absolute conic (or IAC). These equations relate the unknown entries of $\boldsymbol{\omega}^{*i}$ or $\boldsymbol{\omega}^i$ $i = 1, \ldots, m$ and unknown parameters $\mathbf{p}$ with the *known* entries of the projective cameras $\mathtt{A}^i, \mathbf{a}^i$.

The art of auto-calibration is to use constraints on the $\mathtt{K}^i$, such as that one of the elements of $\mathtt{K}^i$ is zero, to generate equations on the eight parameters of $\mathbf{p}$ and $\mathtt{K}^1$ from (19.4). *All* auto-calibration methods are variations on solving these equations, and in the following sections we describe several of these methods. Generally methods proceed by computing $\boldsymbol{\omega}^i$ or $\boldsymbol{\omega}^{*i}$ first and extracting the values of the calibration matrices $\mathtt{K}^i$ from these – though iterative methods (such as bundle adjustment) may be parametrized by $\mathtt{K}^i$ directly. The equations (19.4) have a geometric interpretation as mappings on the absolute conic, and we will return to this in section 19.3 and section 19.5.2.

We start with a simple example to illustrate how equations on the eight parameters are generated from (19.4).

Example 19.2. Auto-calibration equations for identical $\mathtt{K}^i$

Suppose that all the cameras have the same internal parameters, so $\mathtt{K}^i = \mathtt{K}$, then (19.4) becomes

$$\mathtt{K}\mathtt{K}^\mathsf{T} = \left(\mathtt{A}^i - \mathbf{a}^i\mathbf{p}^\mathsf{T}\right)\mathtt{K}\mathtt{K}^\mathsf{T}\left(\mathtt{A}^i - \mathbf{a}^i\mathbf{p}^\mathsf{T}\right)^\mathsf{T} \quad i = 2, \ldots, m. \tag{19.5}$$

Each view $i = 2, \ldots, m$ provides an equation, and we can develop a counting argument for the number of views required (in principle) in order to be able to determine the 8 unknowns. Each view other than the first imposes 5 constraints since each side is a 3×3 symmetric matrix (i.e. 6 independent elements) and the equation is homogeneous. Assuming these constraints are independent for each view, a solution is determined provided $5(m-1) \geq 8$. Consequently, provided $m \geq 3$ a solution is obtained, at least in principle. Clearly, if m is much larger than 3 the unknowns $\mathtt{K}$ and $\mathbf{p}$ are very over-determined. △

One could imagine using (19.5) as a basis for a direct estimation of the rectifying transformation $\mathtt{H}$. This may be framed as a parametrized minimization problem in which the eight parameters of (19.2) are allowed to vary with the purpose of minimizing a cost function on how well the equations (19.4) are satisfied or measuring closeness to metric structure. Of course, a method of obtaining an initial solution would also be required. In essence these two steps, initial solution and iterative minimization, are what will be investigated in the following sections – though under constraints less restrictive than identical internal parameters.

19.3 Calibration using the absolute dual quadric

The absolute dual quadric, $\mathtt{Q}^*_\infty$ is a degenerate dual (i.e. plane) quadric represented by a 4×4 homogeneous matrix of rank 3. Its importance here is that $\mathtt{Q}^*_\infty$ encodes both $\boldsymbol{\pi}_\infty$ and Ω_∞ in a very concise fashion, for instance $\boldsymbol{\pi}_\infty$ is the null-vector of $\mathtt{Q}^*_\infty$, and it has an algebraically simple image projection:

$$\boldsymbol{\omega}^* = \mathtt{P}\mathtt{Q}^*_\infty\mathtt{P}^\mathsf{T} \tag{19.6}$$

which is simply the projection (8.5–*p*201) of a (dual) quadric. In words, $\mathtt{Q}^*_\infty$ projects to the dual image of the absolute conic $\boldsymbol{\omega}^* = \mathtt{K}\mathtt{K}^\mathsf{T}$.

The idea of auto-calibration based on $\mathtt{Q}^*_\infty$ is to use (19.6) to transfer a constraint on $\boldsymbol{\omega}^*$ to a constraint on $\mathtt{Q}^*_\infty$ via the (known) camera matrix $\mathtt{P}^i$. In this manner the matrix representing $\mathtt{Q}^*_\infty$ may be determined in the projective reconstruction from constraints on $\mathtt{K}^i$, as will be seen below. Indeed, $\mathtt{Q}^*_\infty$ was introduced as a convenient representation for auto-calibration in [Triggs-97].

Once $\mathtt{Q}^*_\infty$ has been determined, then the rectifying homography (19.2) $\mathtt{H}$ that we seek is also determined as shown below. Thus we have a general framework for auto-calibration based on specifying constraints on $\mathtt{K}^i$ to determine $\mathtt{Q}^*_\infty$, and then from $\mathtt{Q}^*_\infty$ determining $\mathtt{H}$. This general approach is summarized in algorithm 19.1. In section 19.3.1 we will concentrate on the second step of this algorithm, estimation of $\mathtt{Q}^*_\infty$. We first fill in some details.

Simple properties of the absolute dual quadric. Section 3.7(*p*83) gives a full description of $\mathtt{Q}^*_\infty$. For the purposes of auto-calibration particularly important properties are summarized here. In a Euclidean frame $\mathtt{Q}^*_\infty$ has the canonical form

$$\tilde{\mathtt{I}} = \begin{bmatrix} \mathtt{I}_{3\times 3} & \mathbf{0} \\ \mathbf{0}^\mathsf{T} & 0 \end{bmatrix}. \tag{19.7}$$

Objective

Given a set of matched points across several views and constraints on the calibration matrices $\mathtt{K}^i$, compute a metric reconstruction of the points and cameras.

Algorithm

(i) Compute a projective reconstruction from a set of views, resulting in camera matrices $\mathtt{P}^i$ and points $\mathbf{X}_j$.
(ii) Use (19.6) along with constraints on the form of the $\boldsymbol{\omega}^{*i}$ arising from $\mathtt{K}^i$ to estimate $\mathtt{Q}^*_\infty$.
(iii) Decompose $\mathtt{Q}^*_\infty$ as $\mathtt{H}\tilde{\mathtt{I}}\mathtt{H}^\mathsf{T}$, where $\tilde{\mathtt{I}}$ is the the matrix $\mathrm{diag}(1, 1, 1, 0)$.
(iv) Apply $\mathtt{H}^{-1}$ to the points and $\mathtt{H}$ to the cameras to get a metric reconstruction.
(v) Use iterative least-squares minimization to improve the solution (see section 19.3.3).

Alternatively, the calibration matrix of each camera may be computed directly:

(i) Compute $\boldsymbol{\omega}^{*i}$ for all i using (19.6).
(ii) Compute the calibration matrix $\mathtt{K}^i$ from the equation $\boldsymbol{\omega}^* = \mathtt{KK}^\mathsf{T}$ by Cholesky factorization.

Algorithm 19.1. *Auto-calibration based on* $\mathtt{Q}^*_\infty$.

In a projective coordinate frame $\mathtt{Q}^*_\infty$ has the form $\mathtt{Q}^*_\infty = \mathtt{H}\tilde{\mathtt{I}}\mathtt{H}^\mathsf{T}$, where $\tilde{\mathtt{I}}$ is the matrix in (19.7). This follows from the projective transformation rule (3.17–*p*74) for dual quadrics, $\mathtt{Q}^*_\infty \mapsto \mathtt{H}\mathtt{Q}^*_\infty\mathtt{H}^\mathsf{T}$. Consequently:

Result 19.3. *In an arbitrary projective frame, the dual absolute quadric is represented by a symmetric* 4×4 *matrix with the following properties.*

(i) *It is singular of rank 3, since* $\mathtt{Q}^*_\infty$ *is a degenerate conic.*
(ii) *Its null space is the vector representing the plane at infinity, since* $\mathtt{Q}^*_\infty\boldsymbol{\pi}_\infty = \mathbf{0}$.
(iii) *It is positive semi-definite (or negative – depending on the homogeneous scale).*

These properties are immediate for $\mathtt{Q}^*_\infty$ in its canonical form in a Euclidean frame, and easily extend to an arbitrary frame.

Extracting the rectifying homography from $\mathtt{Q}^*_\infty$. Given an estimated $\mathtt{Q}^*_\infty$ in a projective coordinate frame we wish to determine the homography $\mathtt{H}$. Extracting $\mathtt{H}$ is a simple matter of decomposing the expression as follows.

Result 19.4. *If* $\mathtt{Q}^*_\infty$ *is decomposed as* $\mathtt{Q}^*_\infty = \mathtt{H}\tilde{\mathtt{I}}\mathtt{H}^\mathsf{T}$ *(see notation above), then* $\mathtt{H}^{-1}$ *is a 3D (point) homography that takes the projective coordinate frame to a Euclidean frame.*

Note that a camera is transformed by the inverse of the transformation applied to points, so $\mathtt{H}$ is the correct matrix to apply to a camera to give $\mathtt{P}_\mathrm{M} = \mathtt{PH}$. Thus $\mathtt{H}$ is the rectifying transformation to apply to cameras. A decomposition of $\mathtt{Q}^*_\infty$ as $\mathtt{H}\tilde{\mathtt{I}}\mathtt{H}^\mathsf{T}$ may be easily computed from its eigenvalue decomposition (see section A4.2(*p*580) for Jacobi's algorithm for this).

Equivalence to auto-calibration equations. Equations (19.6) which describe the image projection of $\mathtt{Q}^*_\infty$ are simply a geometric representation of the auto-calibration equations (19.4) as will now be demonstrated.

The forms of $\boldsymbol{\omega} = (\mathtt{K}\mathtt{K}^\mathsf{T})^{-1}$ and $\boldsymbol{\omega}^* = \boldsymbol{\omega}^{-1} = \mathtt{K}\mathtt{K}^\mathsf{T}$ for a camera with calibration matrix K as in (6.10–p157) are

$$\boldsymbol{\omega}^* = \begin{bmatrix} \alpha_x^2 + s^2 + x_0^2 & s\alpha_y + x_0 y_0 & x_0 \\ s\alpha_y + x_0 y_0 & \alpha_y^2 + y_0^2 & y_0 \\ x_0 & y_0 & 1 \end{bmatrix} \tag{19.9}$$

and

$$\boldsymbol{\omega} = \frac{1}{\alpha_x^2\alpha_y^2} \begin{bmatrix} \alpha_y^2 & -s\alpha_y & -x_0\alpha_y^2 + y_0 s\alpha_y \\ -s\alpha_y & \alpha_x^2 + s^2 & \alpha_y s x_0 - \alpha_x^2 y_0 - s^2 y_0 \\ -x_0\alpha_y^2 + y_0 s\alpha_y & \alpha_y s x_0 - \alpha_x^2 y_0 - s^2 y_0 & \alpha_x^2\alpha_y^2 + \alpha_x^2 y_0^2 + (\alpha_y x_0 - s y_0)^2 \end{bmatrix} \tag{19.10}$$

If the skew is zero, i.e. $s = 0$, then the expressions simplify to

$$\boldsymbol{\omega}^* = \begin{bmatrix} \alpha_x^2 + x_0^2 & x_0 y_0 & x_0 \\ x_0 y_0 & \alpha_y^2 + y_0^2 & y_0 \\ x_0 & y_0 & 1 \end{bmatrix} \tag{19.11}$$

and

$$\boldsymbol{\omega} = \frac{1}{\alpha_x^2\alpha_y^2} \begin{bmatrix} \alpha_y^2 & 0 & -\alpha_y^2 x_0 \\ 0 & \alpha_x^2 & -\alpha_x^2 y_0 \\ -\alpha_y^2 x_0 & -\alpha_x^2 y_0 & \alpha_x^2\alpha_y^2 + \alpha_y^2 x_0^2 + \alpha_x^2 y_0^2 \end{bmatrix} \tag{19.12}$$

Table 19.1. *The image of the absolute conic, $\boldsymbol{\omega}$, and dual image of the absolute conic, $\boldsymbol{\omega}^*$, written in terms of the camera internal parameters.*

We have seen that in a projective frame $\mathtt{Q}_\infty^*$ has the form $\mathtt{H}\tilde{\mathtt{I}}\mathtt{H}^\mathsf{T}$. The projective reconstruction is related to the metric reconstruction by (19.2), so in detail

$$\mathtt{Q}_\infty^* = \mathtt{H}\tilde{\mathtt{I}}\mathtt{H}^\mathsf{T} = \begin{bmatrix} \mathtt{K}^1\mathtt{K}^{1\mathsf{T}} & -\mathtt{K}^1\mathtt{K}^{1\mathsf{T}}\mathbf{p} \\ -\mathbf{p}^\mathsf{T}\mathtt{K}^1\mathtt{K}^{1\mathsf{T}} & \mathbf{p}^\mathsf{T}\mathtt{K}^1\mathtt{K}^{1\mathsf{T}}\mathbf{p} \end{bmatrix} = \begin{bmatrix} \boldsymbol{\omega}^{*1} & -\boldsymbol{\omega}^{*1}\mathbf{p} \\ -\mathbf{p}^\mathsf{T}\boldsymbol{\omega}^{*1} & \mathbf{p}^\mathsf{T}\boldsymbol{\omega}^{*1}\mathbf{p} \end{bmatrix}. \tag{19.8}$$

On applying (19.6) with $\mathtt{P}^i = [\mathtt{A}^i \mid \mathbf{a}^i]$ we obtain once again the auto-calibration equations (19.4)

$$\boldsymbol{\omega}^{*i} = \mathtt{P}^i\mathtt{Q}_\infty^*\mathtt{P}^{i\mathsf{T}} = \left(\mathtt{A}^i - \mathbf{a}^i\mathbf{p}^\mathsf{T}\right)\boldsymbol{\omega}^{*1}\left(\mathtt{A}^i - \mathbf{a}^i\mathbf{p}^\mathsf{T}\right)^\mathsf{T}.$$

This is a geometric interpretation of (19.4) – $\mathtt{Q}_\infty^*$ is a fixed quadric under the Euclidean motion of the camera, and the DIAC $\boldsymbol{\omega}^{*i}$ is the image of $\mathtt{Q}_\infty^*$ in each view.

19.3.1 Linear solutions for $\mathtt{Q}_\infty^*$ from a set of images

The objective here is to estimate $\mathtt{Q}_\infty^*$ in a projective reconstruction directly from constraints on the internal parameters. We will start by describing three cases for which a linear solution may be obtained. It is convenient at this point to summarize the forms of the DIAC and also the IAC. Refer to table 19.1.

Specifying linear constraints on $\mathtt{Q}_\infty^*$. Linear constraints on $\mathtt{Q}_\infty^*$ may be obtained if the principal point is known. Assume that this point is known, then we may change the image coordinate system so that the origin coincides with the principal point. Then $x_0 = 0, y_0 = 0$, and from table 19.1 the DIAC becomes

$$\boldsymbol{\omega}^* = \begin{bmatrix} \alpha_x^2 + s^2 & s\alpha_y & 0 \\ s\alpha_y & \alpha_y^2 & 0 \\ 0 & 0 & 1 \end{bmatrix}. \tag{19.13}$$

The linear equations on $\mathtt{Q}_\infty^*$ are then generated from the zero entries in (19.13) by applying the projection equation (19.6) $\boldsymbol{\omega}^* = \mathtt{P}\mathtt{Q}_\infty^*\mathtt{P}^\mathsf{T}$ to each view i. For example the two equations

$$(\mathtt{P}^i\mathtt{Q}_\infty^*\mathtt{P}^{i\mathsf{T}})_{13} = 0 \text{ and } (\mathtt{P}^i\mathtt{Q}_\infty^*\mathtt{P}^{i\mathsf{T}})_{23} = 0 \tag{19.14}$$

follow immediately from ${\boldsymbol{\omega}^*}^i_{13} = {\boldsymbol{\omega}^*}^i_{23} = 0$.

If there are additional constraints on $\mathtt{K}^i$ which result in further relationship between the entries of $\boldsymbol{\omega}^*$, then these may provide additional linear equations. For instance, an assumption that skew is zero means that the (1,2)-entries of (19.13) vanish, which provides one more linear equation on the entries of $\mathtt{Q}_\infty^*$ similar to (19.14). Known aspect ratio provides a further constraint. Table 19.2 summarizes the possible constraints that may be used.

Condition	constraint	type	# constraints
zero skew	$\omega^*_{12}\omega^*_{33} = \omega^*_{13}\omega^*_{23}$	quadratic	m
principal point (p.p.) at origin	$\omega^*_{13} = \omega^*_{23} = 0$	linear	$2m$
zero skew (p.p. at origin)	$\omega^*_{12} = 0$	linear	m
fixed (unknown) aspect ratio (zero skew and p.p. at origin)	$\frac{{\omega^*}^i_{11}}{{\omega^*}^i_{22}} = \frac{{\omega^*}^j_{11}}{{\omega^*}^j_{22}}$	quadratic	$m-1$
known aspect ratio $r = \alpha_y/\alpha_x$ (zero skew and p.p. at origin)	$r^2\omega^*_{11} = \omega^*_{22}$	linear	m

Table 19.2. **Auto-calibration constraints derived from the DIAC**. *The number of constraints column gives the total number of constraints over m views, assuming the constraint is true for each view. Each additional item of information generates additional equations. For example, if the principal point is known and skew is zero then there are 3 constraints per view.*

Linear solution. Since it is symmetric, $\mathtt{Q}_\infty^*$ may be parametrized linearly by 10 homogeneous parameters, namely the 10 diagonal and above-diagonal entries. These 10 entries may be represented by a 10-vector $\mathbf{x}$. In the usual manner the linear equations on $\mathtt{Q}_\infty^*$ may be assembled into a matrix equation of the form $\mathtt{A}\mathbf{x} = \mathbf{0}$, and a least-squares solution for $\mathbf{x}$ obtained via the SVD. For example, the two equations (19.14) provide two rows of the matrix from each view. From five images a total of 10 equations are obtained (assuming only that principal point is known), and a linear solution is possible. From four images eight equations are generated. In the same way as with the computation of the fundamental matrix from seven points there is a 2-parameter family of solutions. The condition $\det \mathtt{Q}^*_\infty = 0$ gives a fourth-degree equation and so up to four solutions for $\mathtt{Q}^*_\infty$.

Example 19.5. Linear solution for variable focal length
Suppose the camera is calibrated apart from the focal length – the principal point is known, the aspect ratio is unity (if it is not the equations can be transformed so that it is unity from the known value), and skew is zero – the focal length is unknown and may vary between views. In this case from table 19.2 there are four linear constraints on $\mathtt{Q}^*_\infty$ available from each view. In the case of two views there are eight linear constraints and up to four solutions are obtained using the condition $\det \mathtt{Q}^*_\infty = 0$. If $m \geq 3$ a unique linear solution exists. △

More will be said about determination of focal lengths in this minimal case in example 19.8.

19.3.2 Non-linear solutions for $\mathtt{Q}^*_\infty$

We now describe various non-linear equations that can be obtained from the form of (19.6). It has been seen that each element of $\boldsymbol{\omega}^{*i} = \mathtt{P}^i\mathtt{Q}^*_\infty\mathtt{P}^{i\mathsf{T}}$ is expressible as a linear expression in terms of the parameters of $\mathtt{Q}^*_\infty$. It follows that any relationship between the entries of the various $\boldsymbol{\omega}^{*i}$ translates into an equation involving the entries of $\mathtt{Q}^*_\infty$. In particular, linear or quadratic relationships between entries of $\boldsymbol{\omega}^*$ generate respectively linear or quadratic relationships between entries of $\mathtt{Q}^*_\infty$. Given sufficiently many such equations, we may solve for $\mathtt{Q}^*_\infty$.

Constant internal parameters. If the internal parameters of all cameras are the same, then $\boldsymbol{\omega}^{*i} = \boldsymbol{\omega}^{*j}$ for all i and j, which expands to $\mathtt{P}^i\mathtt{Q}^*_\infty\mathtt{P}^{i\mathsf{T}} = \mathtt{P}^j\mathtt{Q}^*_\infty\mathtt{P}^{j\mathsf{T}}$. However, since these are homogeneous quantities, the equality holds only up to an unknown scale. A set of five equations are generated:

$$\boldsymbol{\omega}^{*i}_{11}/\boldsymbol{\omega}^{*j}_{11} = \boldsymbol{\omega}^{*i}_{12}/\boldsymbol{\omega}^{*j}_{12} = \boldsymbol{\omega}^{*i}_{13}/\boldsymbol{\omega}^{*j}_{13} = \boldsymbol{\omega}^{*i}_{22}/\boldsymbol{\omega}^{*j}_{22} = \boldsymbol{\omega}^{*i}_{23}/\boldsymbol{\omega}^{*j}_{23} = \boldsymbol{\omega}^{*i}_{33}/\boldsymbol{\omega}^{*j}_{33}.$$

This gives a set of quadratic equations in the entries of $\mathtt{Q}^*_\infty$. Given three views, a total of 10 equations result, which may be solved to find $\mathtt{Q}^*_\infty$.

Calibration assuming zero skew. Under the assumption of zero skew in each of the cameras, the form of the DIAC is simplified, as given in (19.11). In particular, we obtain the following constraints between the entries of $\boldsymbol{\omega}^*$ in the zero-skew case

$$\boldsymbol{\omega}^*_{12}\boldsymbol{\omega}^*_{33} = \boldsymbol{\omega}^*_{13}\boldsymbol{\omega}^*_{23}. \tag{19.15}$$

This gives a single quadratic equation in the entries of $\mathtt{Q}^*_\infty$. From a set of m views we obtain m quadratics. However there is also one extra equation $\det \mathtt{Q}^*_\infty = 0$ derived from the fact that the absolute dual quadric is degenerate. Since $\mathtt{Q}^*_\infty$ has 10 homogeneous linear parameters, it may be computed (at least in principle) from 8 views.

These different calibration constraints are also summarized in table 19.2.

19.3.3 Iterative methods

As we have seen on many occasions throughout this book there is a choice between minimizing an algebraic or geometric error. In this case a suitable algebraic error is provided by (19.4) In previous cases, such as (4.1–*p*89), the unknown scale factor has been eliminated by forming a cross product. Here the scale factor can be eliminated by using a matrix norm. The cost function is

$$\sum_i \|\mathtt{K}^i\mathtt{K}^{i\mathsf{T}} - \mathtt{P}^i\mathtt{Q}^*_\infty\mathtt{P}^{i\mathsf{T}}\|^2_{\mathrm{F}} \tag{19.16}$$

where $\|\mathtt{M}\|_{\mathrm{F}}$ is the Frobenius norm of $\mathtt{M}$, and $\mathtt{K}^i\mathtt{K}^{i\mathsf{T}}$ and $\mathtt{P}^i\mathtt{Q}^*_\infty\mathtt{P}^{i\mathsf{T}}$ are both normalized to have unit Frobenius norm. The cost function is parametrized by the (at most eight) unknown elements of $\mathtt{Q}^*_\infty$, and the unknown elements of each $\boldsymbol{\omega}^{*i} = \mathtt{K}^i\mathtt{K}^{i\mathsf{T}}$. It is possible to use the expansion (19.8) to parametrize the absolute dual quadric. For example, in the case of example 19.5 where the focal length is the only unknown per view, (19.16) would be minimized over $m+3$ parameters. These are the focal length f^i of each view, and the three components of $\mathbf{p}$. Note that this parametrization ensures that $\mathtt{Q}^*_\infty$ has rank 3 throughout the minimization.

Since the above cost function has no particular geometric meaning, it is advisable to follow this up with a complete bundle adjustment. In fact, given a good initial linear estimate one can proceed directly to bundle adjustment. There is no difficulty in incorporating assumptions on calibration parameters into a full bundle adjustment as described in section 18.1(*p*434).

Example 19.6. Metric reconstruction for general motion
Figure 19.1(a-c) shows views of an Indian temple acquired by a hand held camera. A projective reconstruction is computed from image point correspondences as described in section 18.6, and a metric reconstruction obtained using algorithm 19.1 under the constraint of constant camera parameters with known principal point. The computed cameras and 3D point cloud are shown in figure 19.1(d) and (e). △

19.3.4 A counting argument

The constraints we have seen have been of two types: a parameter has a known value; or a parameter is fixed across views but its value is unknown. The actual constraints that apply depend on the physical circumstances of the image production from acquisition by the camera, through digitization and cropping, to the final image. For example, for an image sequence in which the lens is zoomed it might be the case that the skew and aspect ratio are fixed (but unknown), but that the focal length and principal point vary through the sequence. Often it is the case that the pixels are square or have a known aspect ratio, so that both the skew (which is zero) and aspect ratio are known.

We will now consider the number of constraints that are required to determine a metric reconstruction fully.

The number of parameters that must be computed to perform calibration is 8. This is equal to the number of essential parameters of the absolute dual quadric, including the scale ambiguity and rank-3 constraint. Consider m views and suppose that k of the

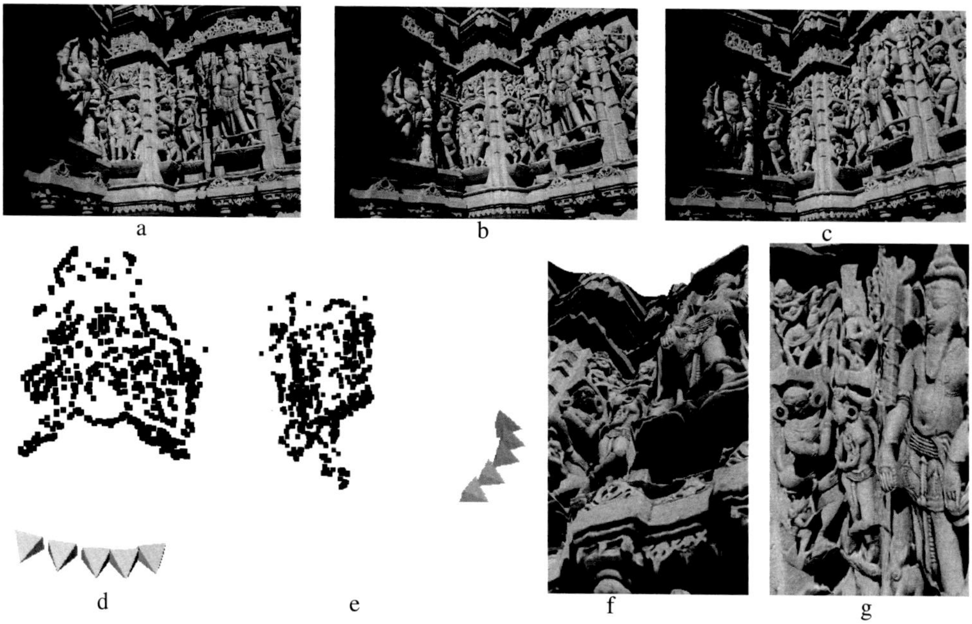

Fig. 19.1. **Metric reconstruction for general motion.** *(a)-(c) 3 views (of 5) acquired by a hand held camera. (d) and (e) Two views of a metric reconstruction computed from interest points matches over the five views. The cameras are represented by pyramids with apex at the computed camera centre. (f) and (g) two views of a texture mapped 3D model computed from the original images and reconstructed cameras using an area based stereo algorithm. Figures courtesy of Marc Pollefeys, Reinhard Koch, and Luc Van Gool.*

internal parameters are known in all views, and f are fixed over the views but unknown (where $k + f \leq 5$). A fixed and known calibration parameter provides one constraint per view via the condition $\omega^{*i} = \mathtt{P}^i \mathtt{Q}_\infty^* \mathtt{P}^{i\mathsf{T}}$, for a total of mk constraints. A fixed but unknown calibration parameter provides one fewer constraint, since just the value of the unknown parameter is missing. Thus f fixed parameters provide a total of $f(m-1)$ constraints. The requirement for calibration is then that

$$mk + (m-1)f \geq 8.$$

Table 19.3 gives values for m for several combinations of constraints. It is important to remember that degenerate configurations are of course possible in which some of the constraints are dependent. This will increase the number of required views.

19.3.5 Limitations of the absolute quadric approach to calibration

The following considerations apply to calibration using this method.

Limitations of least-squares algebraic solution. Since the least-squares solution (e.g. of $\mathtt{A}\mathbf{x} = \mathbf{0}$ in the linear solution for the ω^*) minimizes but does not enforce constraints, the solution obtained will not precisely satisfy the required conditions. This observation holds in over-constrained cases. For instance in the case of estimating focal lengths in example 19.5, the entries ${\omega^*}^i_{11}$ and ${\omega^*}^i_{22}$ will not be in the required

Condition	fixed f	known k	views m
Constant internal parameters	5	0	3
Aspect ratio and skew known, focal length and principal point vary	0	2	4*
Aspect ratio and skew constant, focal length and principal point vary	2	0	5*
Skew zero, all other parameters vary	0	1	8*
p.p. known all other parameters vary	0	2	4*, 5(linear)
p.p. known skew zero	0	3	3(linear)
p.p., skew and aspect ratio known	0	4	2, 3(linear)

Table 19.3. *The number of views m required under various conditions in order for there to be enough constraints for auto-calibration. For those cases marked with an asterisk there may be multiple solutions, even for general motion between views.*

ratio, nor will the off-diagonal entries be precisely zero. This means that the $\mathtt{K}^i$ will not be precisely of the desired form. The absolute dual quadric computed by linear means will not have rank 3 in general, since this is not enforced by the linear equations. A rank 3 matrix for $\mathtt{Q}^*_\infty$ can be obtained by setting the smallest eigenvalue to zero in its eigenvalue decomposition (in a similar manner to using the SVD to obtain a rank 2 matrix for $\mathtt{F}$ in the 8-point algorithm in section 11.1.1(*p*280)). This rank 3 matrix may then be directly decomposed to obtain the rectifying homography (19.2) using result 19.4. Alternatively, the rank 3 matrix can provide the starting point for an iterative minimization as described in section 19.3.3.

The positive-definiteness condition. The most troublesome failing of this method is the difficulty in enforcing the condition that $\mathtt{Q}^*_\infty$ is positive semi-definite, (or negative semi-definite if the sign is reversed). This is related to the condition that $\omega^* = \mathtt{P}\mathtt{Q}^*_\infty\mathtt{P}^\mathsf{T}$ should be positive-definite. If ω^* is not positive-definite, then it can not be decomposed using Cholesky factorization to compute the calibration matrix. This is a recurring problem with auto-calibration methods based on estimation of the IAC or DIAC. If the data is noisy, then this problem may occur indicating that the data are not consistent with metric reconstruction. It is not appropriate if this occurs to seek the closest positive-definite solution, since this will generally be a boundary case leading to a spurious calibration.

19.4 The Kruppa equations

A different method of auto-calibration involves the use of the Kruppa equations, which were originally introduced into computer vision by Faugeras, Luong and Maybank [Faugeras-92a] and historically are seen as the first auto-calibration method. They

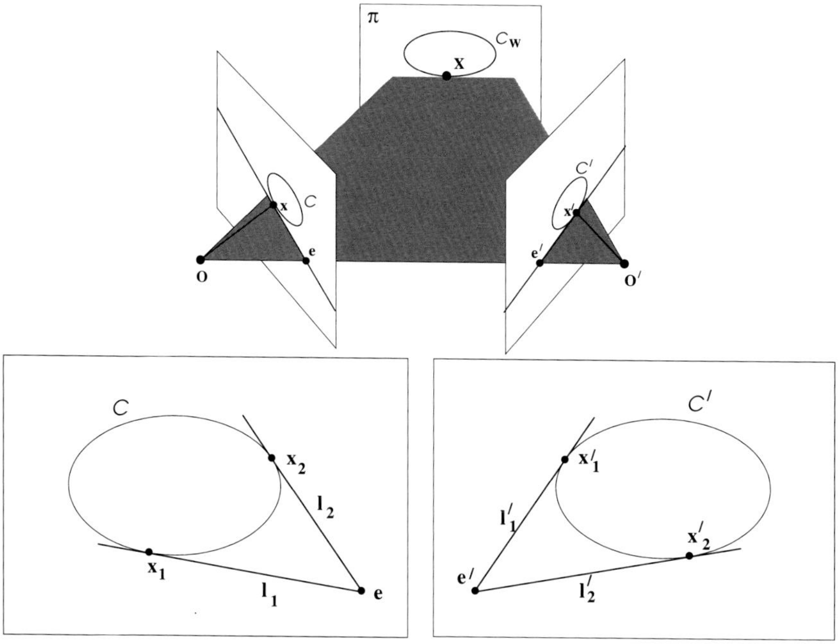

Fig. 19.2. **Epipolar tangency for a conic.** *A conic* $\mathtt{C}_\mathrm{W}$ *on a world plane* π *is imaged as corresponding conics* $\mathtt{C} \leftrightarrow \mathtt{C}'$ *in two views. The imaged conics are consistent with the epipolar geometry of the view pair. Upper: An epipolar plane tangent to the world conic* $\mathtt{C}_\mathrm{W}$ *defines corresponding epipolar lines which are tangent to the imaged conics. Lower: epipolar lines,* $\mathbf{l}_1, \mathbf{l}_2$ *tangent to the imaged conic in the first view correspond to the epipolar lines* $\mathbf{l}'_1, \mathbf{l}'_2$*, respectively, tangent to the imaged conic in the second.*

are two-view constraints that require only $\mathtt{F}$ to be known, and consist of two independent quadratic equations in the elements of $\boldsymbol{\omega}^*$.

The Kruppa equations are an algebraic representation of the correspondence of epipolar lines tangent to a conic. The geometry of this correspondence is illustrated in figure 19.2. Suppose the conics $\mathtt{C}$ and $\mathtt{C}'$ are the images of a conic $\mathtt{C}_\mathrm{W}$ on a world plane in the first and second views respectively, and that $\mathtt{C}^*$ and $\mathtt{C}^{*\prime}$ are their duals. In the first view the two epipolar tangent lines $\mathbf{l}_1$ and $\mathbf{l}_2$ may be combined into a single degenerate point conic (see example 2.8(*p*32)) as $\mathtt{C}_\mathrm{t} = [\mathbf{e}]_\times \mathtt{C}^* [\mathbf{e}]_\times$. (It may be verified that any point $\mathbf{x}$ on the lines $\mathbf{l}_1$ and $\mathbf{l}_2$ satisfies $\mathbf{x}^\mathsf{T}\mathtt{C}_\mathrm{t}\mathbf{x} = 0$). Similarly, in the second view the corresponding epipolar lines $\mathbf{l}'_1$ and $\mathbf{l}'_2$ may be written as $\mathtt{C}'_\mathrm{t} = [\mathbf{e}']_\times \mathtt{C}^{*\prime}[\mathbf{e}']_\times$. The epipolar tangent lines correspond under the homography $\mathtt{H}$ induced by any world plane $\boldsymbol{\pi}$. Since $\mathtt{C}_\mathrm{t}$ is a point conic it transforms according to result 2.13(*p*37) $\mathtt{C}'_\mathrm{t} = \mathtt{H}^{-\mathsf{T}}\mathtt{C}_\mathrm{t}\mathtt{H}^{-1}$, and the correspondence of the lines requires that

$$
\begin{aligned}
[\mathbf{e}']_\times \mathtt{C}^{*\prime}[\mathbf{e}']_\times &= \mathtt{H}^{-\mathsf{T}}[\mathbf{e}]_\times \mathtt{C}^*[\mathbf{e}]_\times \mathtt{H}^{-1} \\
&= \mathtt{F}\mathtt{C}^*\mathtt{F}^\mathsf{T} \qquad (19.17)
\end{aligned}
$$

the last equality following from $\mathtt{F} = \mathtt{H}^{-\mathsf{T}}[\mathbf{e}]_\times$ (see page 335). Note, this equation does not enforce the condition that the epipolar tangent lines map individually to their corresponding lines, only that their symmetric product maps to their symmetric product.

The development to this point applies to any conic. However, in the case of interest here the world conic is the absolute conic on the plane at infinity, so that $\mathtt{C}^* = \boldsymbol{\omega}^*$, $\mathtt{C}^{*\prime} = \boldsymbol{\omega}^{*\prime}$, (and $\mathtt{H} = \mathtt{H}_\infty$), and (19.17) specializes to

$$[\mathbf{e}']_\times \boldsymbol{\omega}^{*\prime} [\mathbf{e}']_\times = \mathtt{F}\boldsymbol{\omega}^* \mathtt{F}^\mathsf{T} \tag{19.18}$$

If the internal parameters are constant over the views then $\boldsymbol{\omega}^{*\prime} = \boldsymbol{\omega}^*$ and so $[\mathbf{e}']_\times \boldsymbol{\omega}^* [\mathbf{e}']_\times = \mathtt{F}\boldsymbol{\omega}^*\mathtt{F}^\mathsf{T}$, which are the Kruppa equations in a form originally given by Viéville [Vieville-95]. On eliminating the homogeneous scale factor, one obtains equations quadratic in the elements of $\boldsymbol{\omega}^*$.

Although (19.18) concisely expresses the Kruppa equations, it is not in a form that can be easily applied. A succinct and easily usable form of the Kruppa equations is now given. We show that the null-space of $[\mathbf{e}']_\times$, which is common to both sides of (19.18), can be eliminated leaving an equation between two 3-vectors.

Result 19.7. *The Kruppa equations (19.18) are equivalent to*

$$\begin{pmatrix} \mathbf{u}_2^\mathsf{T}\boldsymbol{\omega}^{*\prime}\mathbf{u}_2 \\ -\mathbf{u}_1^\mathsf{T}\boldsymbol{\omega}^{*\prime}\mathbf{u}_2 \\ \mathbf{u}_1^\mathsf{T}\boldsymbol{\omega}^{*\prime}\mathbf{u}_1 \end{pmatrix} \times \begin{pmatrix} \sigma_1^2\mathbf{v}_1^\mathsf{T}\boldsymbol{\omega}^*\mathbf{v}_1 \\ \sigma_1\sigma_2\mathbf{v}_1^\mathsf{T}\boldsymbol{\omega}^*\mathbf{v}_2 \\ \sigma_2^2\mathbf{v}_2^\mathsf{T}\boldsymbol{\omega}^*\mathbf{v}_2 \end{pmatrix} = \mathbf{0} \tag{19.19}$$

where $\mathbf{u}_i$, $\mathbf{v}_i$ and σ_i are the columns and singular values of the SVD of $\mathtt{F}$. *This provides three quadratic equations in the elements ω^*_{ij} of $\boldsymbol{\omega}^*$, of which two are independent.*

Proof. The fundamental matrix has rank 2, and thus has an SVD expansion

$$\mathtt{F} = \mathtt{UDV}^\mathsf{T} = \mathtt{U}\begin{bmatrix} \sigma_1 & & \\ & \sigma_2 & \\ & & 0 \end{bmatrix}\mathtt{V}^\mathsf{T}$$

where the null-vectors are $\mathtt{F}^\mathsf{T}\mathbf{u}_3 = \mathbf{0}$ and $\mathtt{F}\mathbf{v}_3 = \mathbf{0}$. This means that the epipoles are $\mathbf{e} = \mathbf{v}_3$ and $\mathbf{e}' = \mathbf{u}_3$. Substituting this expansion into (19.18) we obtain

$$[\mathbf{u}_3]_\times \boldsymbol{\omega}^{*\prime} [\mathbf{u}_3]_\times = \mathtt{UDV}^\mathsf{T}\boldsymbol{\omega}^*\mathtt{VDU}^\mathsf{T}. \tag{19.20}$$

We now use the property that $\mathtt{U}$ is an orthogonal matrix. On pre-multiplying (19.20) by $\mathtt{U}^\mathsf{T}$, and post-multiplying by $\mathtt{U}$, the LHS becomes

$$\begin{aligned} \mathtt{U}^\mathsf{T}[\mathbf{u}_3]_\times \boldsymbol{\omega}^{*\prime} [\mathbf{u}_3]_\times \mathtt{U} &= \begin{bmatrix} \mathbf{u}_2 & -\mathbf{u}_1 & \mathbf{0} \end{bmatrix}^\mathsf{T} \boldsymbol{\omega}^{*\prime} \begin{bmatrix} \mathbf{u}_2 & -\mathbf{u}_1 & \mathbf{0} \end{bmatrix} \\ &= \begin{bmatrix} \mathbf{u}_2^\mathsf{T}\boldsymbol{\omega}^{*\prime}\mathbf{u}_2 & -\mathbf{u}_2^\mathsf{T}\boldsymbol{\omega}^{*\prime}\mathbf{u}_1 & 0 \\ -\mathbf{u}_1^\mathsf{T}\boldsymbol{\omega}^{*\prime}\mathbf{u}_2 & \mathbf{u}_1^\mathsf{T}\boldsymbol{\omega}^{*\prime}\mathbf{u}_1 & 0 \\ 0 & 0 & 0 \end{bmatrix} \end{aligned}$$

and the RHS of (19.20) becomes

$$\begin{aligned} \mathtt{DV}^\mathsf{T}\boldsymbol{\omega}^*\mathtt{VD} &= \begin{bmatrix} \sigma_1 & & \\ & \sigma_2 & \\ & & 0 \end{bmatrix} \mathtt{V}^\mathsf{T}\boldsymbol{\omega}^*\mathtt{V} \begin{bmatrix} \sigma_1 & & \\ & \sigma_2 & \\ & & 0 \end{bmatrix} \\ &= \begin{bmatrix} \sigma_1^2\mathbf{v}_1^\mathsf{T}\boldsymbol{\omega}^*\mathbf{v}_1 & \sigma_1\sigma_2\mathbf{v}_1^\mathsf{T}\boldsymbol{\omega}^*\mathbf{v}_2 & 0 \\ \sigma_1\sigma_2\mathbf{v}_1^\mathsf{T}\boldsymbol{\omega}^*\mathbf{v}_2 & \sigma_2^2\mathbf{v}_2^\mathsf{T}\boldsymbol{\omega}^*\mathbf{v}_2 & 0 \\ 0 & 0 & 0 \end{bmatrix}. \end{aligned}$$

It is evident that both sides have reduced to symmetric matrices each with three independent elements. These three elements may be represented by a homogeneous 3-vector on each side:

$$\begin{aligned} \mathbf{x}_{\mathrm{LHS}}^{\mathsf{T}} &= \left(\mathbf{u}_2^{\mathsf{T}}\boldsymbol{\omega}^{*\prime}\mathbf{u}_2, \;\; -\mathbf{u}_1^{\mathsf{T}}\boldsymbol{\omega}^{*\prime}\mathbf{u}_2, \;\; \mathbf{u}_1^{\mathsf{T}}\boldsymbol{\omega}^{*\prime}\mathbf{u}_1 \right) \\ \mathbf{x}_{\mathrm{RHS}}^{\mathsf{T}} &= \left(\sigma_1^2\mathbf{v}_1^{\mathsf{T}}\boldsymbol{\omega}^{*}\mathbf{v}_1, \;\; \sigma_1\sigma_2\mathbf{v}_1^{\mathsf{T}}\boldsymbol{\omega}^{*}\mathbf{v}_2, \;\; \sigma_2^2\mathbf{v}_2^{\mathsf{T}}\boldsymbol{\omega}^{*}\mathbf{v}_2 \right). \end{aligned}$$

The two sides are only equal up to a scale factor. However, equalities are obtained in the usual way using a vector cross-product, $\mathbf{x}_{\mathrm{LHS}} \times \mathbf{x}_{\mathrm{RHS}} = \mathbf{0}$. An alternative derivation is given in [Hartley-97d]. □

Note, the Kruppa equations involve the DIAC, rather than the IAC, since they arise from tangent line constraints, and line constraints are more simply expressed using a dual (line) conic.

We now discuss the solution of the Kruppa equations, beginning with a simple example where all the internal parameters are known apart from the focal length. An alternative method for solving this problem using the absolute dual quadric was given in example 19.5.

Example 19.8. Focal lengths for a view pair

Suppose two cameras have zero skew and known principal point and aspect ratio, but unknown and different focal lengths (as in example 19.5). Then from (19.11) by a suitable change of coordinates their DIACs may be written as

$$\boldsymbol{\omega}^* = \mathrm{diag}(\alpha^2, \alpha^2, 1), \;\; \boldsymbol{\omega}^{*\prime} = \mathrm{diag}(\alpha'^2, \alpha'^2, 1)$$

where α, α' are the unknown focal lengths of the first and second view, respectively. Writing the Kruppa equations (19.19) as

$$\frac{\mathbf{u}_2^{\mathsf{T}}\boldsymbol{\omega}^{*\prime}\mathbf{u}_2}{\sigma_1^2\mathbf{v}_1^{\mathsf{T}}\boldsymbol{\omega}^{*}\mathbf{v}_1} = -\frac{\mathbf{u}_1^{\mathsf{T}}\boldsymbol{\omega}^{*\prime}\mathbf{u}_2}{\sigma_1\sigma_2\mathbf{v}_1^{\mathsf{T}}\boldsymbol{\omega}^{*}\mathbf{v}_2} = \frac{\mathbf{u}_1^{\mathsf{T}}\boldsymbol{\omega}^{*\prime}\mathbf{u}_1}{\sigma_2^2\mathbf{v}_2^{\mathsf{T}}\boldsymbol{\omega}^{*}\mathbf{v}_2}$$

it is evident that each numerator is linear in terms of α'^2 and each denominator linear in α^2. Cross-multiplying provides two simple quadratic equations in α^2 and α'^2 which are easily solved. The values of α and α' are found by taking the square roots. Note, if the internal parameters are the same for the two views (that is $\alpha = \alpha'$) then each equation of result 19.7 provides a quadratic in the single unknown α^2. △

Extending the Kruppa equations to multiple views. In the absence of knowledge of the internal parameters, other than that the parameters are constant across views, the Kruppa equations provide two independent constraints on the five unknown parameters. Thus given three views, with F known between each pair, there are in principle six quadratic constraints, which is sufficient to determine $\boldsymbol{\omega}^*$. Using any five of these equations results in five quadratics in five unknowns, a total of 2^5 possible solutions. Solving this set of equations is not a particularly promising approach, although solutions have been obtained by homotopy continuation [Luong-92] and by minimizing algebraic residuals using every view pair for a sequence of images [Zeller-96].

Ambiguities. If there is no rotation between views then the Kruppa equations provide no constraint on ω^*. This may be seen from (19.18) which, in the case of pure translation, reduces to $[\mathbf{e}']_\times \omega^* [\mathbf{e}']_\times = [\mathbf{e}']_\times \omega^* [\mathbf{e}']_\times$, since $\mathtt{F} = [\mathbf{e}']_\times$.

The Kruppa equations are closely related to the calibration constraint provided by the transfer of the IAC under the infinite homography, as discussed later in section 19.5.2. It will follow from that discussion that the constraint placed on ω^* by the Kruppa equations for a pair of views is weaker than that placed by the infinite homography constraint (19.25). Consequently ambiguities of ω^* imposed by the Kruppa equations are a superset of those imposed by (19.25).

The application of the Kruppa equations to three or more views provides weaker constraints than those obtained by other methods such as the modulus constraint (section 19.5.1) or the absolute dual quadric (section 19.3.1). This is because the Kruppa constraints are a view-pair constraint for *conics* obtained as a projection of a 3D (dual) *quadric*. They do not enforce that the (dual) quadric is degenerate, or equivalently do not enforce a common support plane for Ω_∞ over the multiple views. Consequently, there are additional ambiguous solutions as described in [Sturm-97b].

Although the application of the Kruppa equations to auto-calibration is chronologically the first example in the literature, the difficulty of their solution and the problem with ambiguities has seen them losing favour in the face of more tractable methods such as the dual quadric formulation. However, if only two views are given then the Kruppa equations are *the* constraint available on ω^*.

19.5 A stratified solution

Determining a metric reconstruction involves simultaneously obtaining both the camera calibration $\mathtt{K}$ and the plane at infinity, π_∞. An alternative approach is first to obtain by some means π_∞, or equivalently an affine reconstruction. The subsequent determination of $\mathtt{K}$ is then relatively simple because there exists a linear solution. This approach will now be described starting with methods of determining π_∞, and hence $\mathtt{H}_\infty$, and followed by methods of computing $\mathtt{K}$ given $\mathtt{H}_\infty$.

19.5.1 Affine reconstruction – determining π_∞

For general motion and constant internal parameters, (19.3–*p*461) can be rearranged into providing a constraint only on π_∞, known as the *modulus constraint*. This allows the coordinates $\mathbf{p}$ of π_∞ to be solved for directly, and is described below.

The modulus constraint

The modulus constraint is a polynomial equation in the coordinates of π_∞. Assume the internal parameters are constant; then from (19.3–*p*461) with $\mathtt{K}^i = \mathtt{K}$

$$\mathtt{A} - \mathbf{a}\mathbf{p}^\mathsf{T} = \mu \mathtt{K}\mathtt{R}\mathtt{K}^{-1} \tag{19.21}$$

where the scale factor μ is explicitly included, and for clarity the superscripts are omitted. Since $\mathtt{K}\mathtt{R}\mathtt{K}^{-1}$ is conjugate to a rotation, it has eigenvalues $\{1, e^{i\theta}, e^{-i\theta}\}$. Consequently, the eigenvalues of $(\mathtt{A} - \mathbf{a}\mathbf{p}^\mathsf{T})$ are $\{\mu, \mu e^{i\theta}, \mu e^{-i\theta}\}$, and thus have equal moduli. This is the modulus constraint on the coordinates of the plane at infinity, $\mathbf{p}$.

To develop this constraint further consider the characteristic polynomial of $\mathtt{A} - \mathbf{a}\mathbf{p}^\mathsf{T}$ which is

$$\begin{aligned}\det(\lambda \mathtt{I} - \mathtt{A} + \mathbf{a}\mathbf{p}^\mathsf{T}) &= (\lambda - \lambda_1)(\lambda - \lambda_2)(\lambda - \lambda_3) \\ &= \lambda^3 - f_1\lambda^2 + f_2\lambda - f_3\end{aligned}$$

where λ_i are the three eigenvalues, and

$$\begin{aligned}f_1 &= \lambda_1 + \lambda_2 + \lambda_3 = \mu(1 + 2\cos\theta) \\ f_2 &= \lambda_1\lambda_2 + \lambda_1\lambda_3 + \lambda_2\lambda_3 = \mu^2(1 + 2\cos\theta) \\ f_3 &= \lambda_1\lambda_2\lambda_3 = \mu^3.\end{aligned}$$

Eliminating the scalar μ and angle θ we obtain

$$f_3 f_1^3 = f_2^3.$$

Looking more closely at the characteristic polynomial we observe that $\mathbf{p}$ appears only as part of the rank-1 term $\mathbf{a}\mathbf{p}^\mathsf{T}$. This means that the elements of $\mathbf{p}$ appear only linearly in the determinant $\det(\lambda \mathtt{I} - \mathtt{A} + \mathbf{a}\mathbf{p}^\mathsf{T})$, and hence linearly in each of f_1, f_2, f_3. Hence the modulus constraint may be written as a *quartic* polynomial in the three elements p_i of $\mathbf{p}$. This polynomial equation is only a necessary condition for the eigenvalues to have equal moduli, not sufficient.

Each view pair generates a quartic equation in the coordinates of $\boldsymbol{\pi}_\infty$. Thus, in principle, three views determine $\boldsymbol{\pi}_\infty$, but only as the intersection of three quartics in three variables – a possible 4^3 solutions. However, for three views an additional cubic equation is available from the modulus constraint, and this equation can be used to eliminate many of the spurious solutions. This cubic equation is developed in [Schaffalitzky-00a]. The modulus constraint may also be combined with scene information. For example, if a corresponding vanishing line is available in two views, then $\boldsymbol{\pi}_\infty$ is determined up to a one-parameter ambiguity. Applying the modulus constraint resolves this ambiguity, and results in a quartic equation in one variable.

The modulus constraint may be considered the cousin of the Kruppa equations: the Kruppa equations are equations on $\boldsymbol{\omega}^*$ which do not involve $\boldsymbol{\pi}_\infty$; conversely, the modulus constraint is an equation on $\boldsymbol{\pi}_\infty$ which does not involve $\boldsymbol{\omega}^*$. Once one of $\boldsymbol{\omega}^*$ or $\boldsymbol{\pi}_\infty$ is known the other can subsequently be determined.

Other methods of finding $\boldsymbol{\pi}_\infty$

Because of the problem with solving sets of simultaneous quartic equations, the modulus constraint is not very satisfactory as a practical means of finding the plane at infinity. In fact, finding the plane at infinity is the hardest part of auto-calibration and the place where one is most likely to run into difficulties.

The plane at infinity may be identified by various other methods. Several of these are described in chapter 10. One straightforward method (which is outside the province of pure auto-calibration) is to use properties of the scene geometry. For example, the correspondence of a vanishing point between two views determines a point on $\boldsymbol{\pi}_\infty$, and three such correspondences determine $\boldsymbol{\pi}_\infty$ in a projective reconstruction. Indeed, a good approximation for π_∞ may well be obtained from the correspondence of three points that are distant in the scene. A second method is to employ a pure translation between two views, i.e. the camera translates but does not rotate or change internal parameters; π_∞ is determined uniquely by such a motion.

As seen in result 19.3(*p*463) the plane at infinity may also be computed from the absolute dual quadric and this method is quite attractive if the principal point is known. Methods of bounding the position of π_∞ using cheiral inequalities will be described in chapter 21. These use information about which points are in front of the cameras to get a *quasi-affine* reconstruction, which is close to an affine reconstruction. A method for finding the plane at infinity by iterative search from this initial quasi-affine reconstruction is described in [Hartley-94b]. More recently, the bounds imposed by cheirality have been used [Hartley-99] to define a rectangular region of 3D parameter space inside which the vector $\mathbf{p}$ representing the plane at infinity must lie. Then an exhaustive search is undertaken to find the elusive plane at infinity inside this region.

19.5.2 Affine to metric conversion – determining $\mathtt{K}$ given π_∞

Once the plane at infinity has been determined, an affine reconstruction is effectively known. The remaining step is to transform from affine to metric. It turns out that this is a far easier step than the step from projective to affine. In fact, a linear algorithm is available based on the transformation of the IAC or its dual.

The infinite homography. The infinite homography $\mathtt{H}_\infty$ is the plane projective transformation between two images induced by the plane at infinity π_∞ (see chapter 13). If the plane at infinity $\pi_\infty = (\mathbf{p}^\mathsf{T}, 1)^\mathsf{T}$ and camera matrices $[\mathtt{A}^i \mid \mathbf{a}^i]$ are known in any projective coordinate frame, an explicit formula for the infinite homography can be derived from result 13.1(*p*326)

$$\mathtt{H}^i_\infty = \mathtt{A}^i - \mathbf{a}^i\mathbf{p}^\mathsf{T} \tag{19.22}$$

where $\mathtt{H}^i_\infty$ represents the homography from a camera $[\mathtt{I} \mid \mathbf{0}]$ to the camera $[\mathtt{A}^i \mid \mathbf{a}^i]$. So $\mathtt{H}^i_\infty$ may be computed from a projective reconstruction once the plane at infinity is known.

If the first camera is not in the canonical form $[\mathtt{I} \mid \mathbf{0}]$, then one can still compute the homography $\mathtt{H}^i_\infty$ from the first image to the i-th by writing

$$\mathtt{H}^i_\infty = \left(\mathtt{A}^i - \mathbf{a}^i\mathbf{p}^\mathsf{T}\right)\left(\mathtt{A}^1 - \mathbf{a}^1\mathbf{p}^\mathsf{T}\right)^{-1}. \tag{19.23}$$

This is not strictly necessary, however, since one can *invent* a new view that *does* have camera matrix in the canonical form $[\mathtt{I} \mid \mathbf{0}]$, and express the infinite homographies with respect to this view. In the following discussion, we write $\mathtt{K}$ and $\boldsymbol{\omega}$ (without superscripts) to refer either to this reference view, or to the first view, if it is in canonical form.

The absolute conic lies on π_∞ so its image is mapped between views by $\mathtt{H}_\infty$. Under the point transformation $\mathbf{x}^i = \mathtt{H}^i_\infty\mathbf{x}$, where $\mathtt{H}^i_\infty$ is the infinite homography between the reference view and view i, the transformation rules for a dual conic (result 2.14(*p*37)) and a point conic (result 2.13(p37)) lead to the relations

$$\boldsymbol{\omega}^{*i} = \mathtt{H}_\infty^i \boldsymbol{\omega}^* \mathtt{H}_\infty^{i\,\mathsf{T}} \text{ and } \boldsymbol{\omega}^i = (\mathtt{H}_\infty^i)^{-\mathsf{T}} \boldsymbol{\omega} (\mathtt{H}_\infty^i)^{-1}. \quad (19.24)$$

where $\boldsymbol{\omega}^i$ is the IAC in the i-th view. It may be verified that these equations are precisely the auto-calibration equations (19.4–p461), and this is another geometric interpretation of those equations.

These are among the most important relationships for auto-calibration. They are the basis for obtaining metric reconstruction from affine reconstruction, and also for calibrating a non-translating camera, as will be seen later in section 19.6. The significance of this relation for auto-calibration is that if $\mathtt{H}_\infty^i$ is known, then these are *linear* relations between $\boldsymbol{\omega}^i$ and $\boldsymbol{\omega}$ (and similarly for $\boldsymbol{\omega}^*$). This means that constraints placed on $\boldsymbol{\omega}^i$ in one view can easily be transferred to another and in this manner sufficient constraints may be assembled to determine $\boldsymbol{\omega}$ by linear means. Once $\boldsymbol{\omega}$ is determined, then $\mathtt{K}$ follows by the Cholesky decomposition. We will illustrate this approach for the example of fixed internal parameters.

Sketch solution for identical internal parameters. If the internal parameters arc constant over m views then $\mathtt{K}^i = \mathtt{K}$ and $\boldsymbol{\omega}^{*i} = \boldsymbol{\omega}^*$ for $i = 1, \ldots, m$, and the $\boldsymbol{\omega}^*$ equation of (19.24) becomes

$$\boldsymbol{\omega}^* = \mathtt{H}_\infty^i \boldsymbol{\omega}^* \mathtt{H}_\infty^{i\,\mathsf{T}}. \quad (19.25)$$

A very important point here relates to the scale factors in the equation (19.25).

- *Although (19.25) is a relationship between homogeneous quantities, the scale factor in the homogeneous equation can be chosen as unity provided* $\mathtt{H}_\infty^i$ *is normalized as* $\det \mathtt{H}_\infty^i = 1$.

This results in six equations for the independent elements of the symmetric matrix $\boldsymbol{\omega}^*$. Then (19.25) can be written in a homogeneous *linear* form

$$\mathtt{A}\mathbf{c} = \mathbf{0}, \quad (19.26)$$

where $\mathtt{A}$ is a 6×6 matrix composed from the elements of $\mathtt{H}_\infty^i$, and $\mathbf{c}$ is the conic $\boldsymbol{\omega}^*$ written as a 6-vector. As discussed below, $\mathbf{c}$ is not uniquely determined by one such equation since $\mathtt{A}$ has at most rank 4. However, if linear equations (19.26) from $m \geq 2$ view pairs are combined, so that $\mathtt{A}$ is now a $6m \times 6$ matrix, and provided the rotations between the views are about different axes, then in general $\mathbf{c}$ is determined uniquely.

Related to the issue of uniqueness is the issue of numerical stability. Under a single motion the linear computation of $\mathtt{K}$ from $\mathtt{H}_\infty$ is extremely sensitive to the accuracy of $\mathtt{H}_\infty$. If $\mathtt{H}_\infty$ is inaccurate it is not always possible to obtain a positive-definite matrix $\boldsymbol{\omega}$ (or $\boldsymbol{\omega}^*$) and thus to apply the Cholesky decomposition to obtain $\mathtt{K}$. This sensitivity is reduced if further motions are made, and $\boldsymbol{\omega}$ obtained from the combined constraints of a number of $\mathtt{H}_\infty$'s.

Advantage of using the IAC. In an analogous manner to the linear solution for $\boldsymbol{\omega}^*$, a linear solution may be obtained for $\boldsymbol{\omega}$ starting from (19.24). In fact using the equations involving the IAC is attractive for the following reason. In the zero-skew case the form of (19.12–*p*464) for the IAC is simpler and more clearly reflects the role of each calibration parameter than does the corresponding formula (19.11–*p*464) for the DIAC. In order to obtain linear equations using the DIAC equations (19.11) it is necessary to assume that the principal point is known. This is not necessary for equations deriving from the IAC. An assumption of zero skew is quite natural and is a safe assumption for most imaging conditions. However, an assumption of known principal point is much less tenable. For this reason it is usually preferable to use the IAC constraints of (19.24) for auto-calibration rather than using the DIAC constraints.

Other calibration constraints. The algorithm just described was for constant but arbitrary internal parameters. If more is known about $\mathtt{K}$, such as the value of the aspect ratio or that the skew is zero, the corresponding constraints may be simply added to the set of equations on $\boldsymbol{\omega}$ (or $\boldsymbol{\omega}^*$), and imposed as soft constraints. The possible constraints are shown in table 19.2(*p*465) for the DIAC (the same constraints that are used to compute $\mathtt{Q}^*_\infty$ in section 19.3) and table 19.4 for the IAC.

As mentioned above, the constraints derived from the IAC are generally linear, whereas the constraints derived from the DIAC, are linear only under the assumption that the principal point is known (and at the origin).

Just as with the absolute dual quadric method, it is possible to allow varying internal parameters for the cameras, as long as sufficiently many constraints are imposed. The constraint of constant internal parameters for the cameras imposed a total of $5(m-1)$ constraints on the calibration parameters of the m views. We can make do with fewer constraints, letting certain parameters vary. The method of calibration with varying internal parameters is quite analogous to that used in the case of the absolute dual quadric. Each entry of $\boldsymbol{\omega}^i$ is expressible as a linear expression in the entries of $\boldsymbol{\omega}$ according to (19.24). A linear constraint on some entry of $\boldsymbol{\omega}^i$ therefore maps back to a linear constraint on the entries of $\boldsymbol{\omega}$.

Note: To avoid treating the first image differently, any constraints imposed on the first camera, such as $\omega^1_{12} = 0$ (camera 1 has zero skew) should be treated by adding this equation to the complete equation set, rather than by decreasing the number of parameters used to describe $\boldsymbol{\omega}^1$. The latter method would cause the zero-skew constraint to be enforced exactly in the first image (a hard constraint), but it would be a soft constraint in the other images.

Algorithm 19.2 summarizes the stratified method for both constant and varying parameters. One could imagine implementing this algorithm directly for a camera mounted on a robot: the camera is first moved by a pure translation in order to determine $\boldsymbol{\pi}_\infty$; and in subsequent motions the camera may both translate and rotate until sufficient rotations have accumulated to determine $\mathtt{K}$ uniquely.

Condition	constraint	type	# constraints
zero skew	$\omega_{12} = 0$	linear	m
principal point at origin	$\omega_{13} = \omega_{23} = 0$	linear	$2m$
known aspect ratio $r = \alpha_y / \alpha_x$ (assuming zero skew)	$\omega_{11} = r^2 \omega_{22}$	linear	m
fixed (unknown) aspect ratio (assuming zero skew)	$\omega^i_{11}/\omega^i_{22} = \omega^j_{11}/\omega^j_{22}$	quadratic	$m - 1$

Table 19.4. **Auto-calibration constraints derived from the IAC.** *These constraints are derived directly from the form of (19.10–p464) and (19.12–p464). The number of constraints column gives the total number of constraints over m views, assuming the constraint is true for each view.*

Using hard constraints. Algorithm 19.2 comes down to solving a homogeneous set of equations of the form $\mathtt{A}\mathbf{c} = \mathbf{0}$, where $\mathbf{c}$ represents $\boldsymbol{\omega}$ arranged as a 6-vector. Generally the supplied information on $\mathtt{K}$, such as that the skew is zero, will not be satisfied exactly. As discussed in section 8.8(*p*223) known information can be imposed as a hard constraint by parametrizing $\boldsymbol{\omega}^i$ in each view to satisfy this constraint. For instance if the camera is known to have square pixels then the remaining parameters for the IAC of each view can be represented by a homogeneous 4-vector. Linear equations for the unknown parameters in each view may again be obtained from (19.24). A homogeneous set of equations of the form $\mathtt{A}\mathbf{c} = \mathbf{0}$ may then be assembled, where $\mathbf{c}$ now represents the unknown parameters of $\boldsymbol{\omega}^i$ over all views, and a solution which minimizes $\|\mathtt{A}\mathbf{c}\|$ obtained in the usual manner via the SVD. An alternative is to include all the parameters in each view and use algorithm A5.5(*p*594) to minimize $\|\mathtt{A}\mathbf{c}\|$, while satisfying constraints $\mathtt{C}\mathbf{c} = \mathbf{0}$ exactly.

19.5.3 The ambiguities in using the infinite homography relation

In this section we describe the ambiguities in determining the internal parameters from (19.25) that occur if only a single rotation axis is used. It will be assumed that the internal parameters are unknown but fixed.

A rotation matrix $\mathtt{R}$ has an eigenvector $\mathbf{d}_\mathrm{r}$ with unit eigenvalue, $\mathtt{R}\mathbf{d}_\mathrm{r} = 1\mathbf{d}_\mathrm{r}$, where $\mathbf{d}_\mathrm{r}$ is the direction of the axis of the rotation. Consequently, the matrix $\mathtt{H}^i_\infty = \mathtt{K}\mathtt{R}^i\mathtt{K}^{-1}$ also has an eigenvector with unit eigenvalue (provided $\mathtt{H}^i_\infty$ is normalized as $\det \mathtt{H}^i_\infty = 1$). This eigenvector is $\mathbf{v}_\mathrm{r} = \mathtt{K}\mathbf{d}_\mathrm{r}$, and the image point $\mathbf{v}_\mathrm{r}$ corresponds to the vanishing point of the rotation axis direction. Suppose $\boldsymbol{\omega}^*_{\text{true}}$ is the true $\boldsymbol{\omega}^*$; then, it may be verified that if $\boldsymbol{\omega}^*_{\text{true}}$ satisfies (19.25) with $\mathtt{H}^i_\infty = \mathtt{K}\mathtt{R}^i\mathtt{K}^{-1}$, then so does the one-parameter family of (dual) conics

$$\boldsymbol{\omega}^*(\mu) = \boldsymbol{\omega}^*_{\text{true}} + \mu \mathbf{v}_\mathrm{r}\mathbf{v}_\mathrm{r}^\mathsf{T} \tag{19.27}$$

where μ parametrizes the family. In a similar manner there is a one parameter family (pencil) of solutions for the IAC equation of (19.24). This argument indicates that

Objective

Given a projective reconstruction $\{\mathtt{P}^i, \mathbf{X}_j\}$, where $\mathtt{P}^i = [\mathtt{A}^i \mid \mathbf{a}^i]$, determine a metric reconstruction via an intermediate affine reconstruction.

Algorithm

(i) **Affine rectification:** Determine the vector $\mathbf{p}$ that defines $\boldsymbol{\pi}_\infty$, using one of the methods described in section 19.5.1. At this point an affine reconstruction may be obtained as $\{\mathtt{P}^i\mathtt{H}_\mathrm{P}, \mathtt{H}_\mathrm{P}^{-1}\mathbf{X}_j\}$ with

$$\mathtt{H}_\mathrm{P} = \begin{bmatrix} \mathtt{I} & \mathbf{0} \\ -\mathbf{p}^\mathsf{T} & 1 \end{bmatrix}.$$

(ii) **Infinite homography:** Compute the infinite homography between the reference view and the others as

$$\mathtt{H}^i_\infty = \left(\mathtt{A}^i - \mathbf{a}^i\mathbf{p}^\mathsf{T}\right).$$

Normalize the matrix so that $\det \mathtt{H}^i_\infty = 1$.

(iii) **Compute $\boldsymbol{\omega}$:**

- In the case of constant calibration: rewrite the equations $\boldsymbol{\omega} = (\mathtt{H}^i_\infty)^{-\mathsf{T}}\boldsymbol{\omega}(\mathtt{H}^i_\infty)^{-1}$, $i = 1, \ldots, m$ as $\mathtt{A}\mathbf{c} = \mathbf{0}$ with $\mathtt{A}$ a $6m \times 6$ matrix, and $\mathbf{c}$ the elements of the conic $\boldsymbol{\omega}$ arranged as a 6-vector, **or**
- For variable calibration parameters, use the equation $\boldsymbol{\omega}^i = (\mathtt{H}^i_\infty)^{-\mathsf{T}}\boldsymbol{\omega}(\mathtt{H}^i_\infty)^{-1}$ to express linear constraints on entries of $\boldsymbol{\omega}^i$ (e.g. zero skew) as linear equations in the entries of $\boldsymbol{\omega}$.

(iv) Obtain a least-squares solution to $\mathtt{A}\mathbf{c} = \mathbf{0}$ via SVD.

(v) **Metric rectification:** Determine the camera matrix $\mathtt{K}$ from the Cholesky decomposition $\boldsymbol{\omega} = (\mathtt{K}\mathtt{K}^\mathsf{T})^{-1}$. Then a metric reconstruction is obtained as $\{\mathtt{P}^i\mathtt{H}_\mathrm{P}\mathtt{H}_\mathrm{A}, (\mathtt{H}_\mathrm{P}\mathtt{H}_\mathrm{A})^{-1}\mathbf{X}_j\}$ with

$$\mathtt{H}_\mathrm{A} = \begin{bmatrix} \mathtt{K} & \mathbf{0} \\ \mathbf{0}^\mathsf{T} & 1 \end{bmatrix}.$$

(vi) Use iterative least-squares minimization to improve the solution (see section 19.3.3).

Algorithm 19.2. *Stratified auto-calibration algorithm using IAC constraints.*

although the infinite homography constraint seemingly provides six constraints on the five degrees of freedom of $\boldsymbol{\omega}^*$, only four of these constraints are linearly independent.

Removing the ambiguity. The one-parameter ambiguity may be resolved in several ways. First, if there is another view available related by a rotation around an axis with a direction different to $\mathbf{d}_\mathrm{r}$, then the combination of both sets of constraints will not have this ambiguity. A linear solution is easily obtained in the manner of (19.26). Thus with a minimum of three views (i.e. more than one rotation) a unique solution can generally be obtained. A second method of resolving the ambiguity is to make assumptions on the internal parameters of the cameras: for instance an assumption of zero skew (see table 19.4). The equations enforcing zero skew may be added as hard constraints to the set of equations being solved.

An alternative (but equivalent) method enforces the constraints *a posteriori* in the following manner. An ambiguity in solving for $\mathbf{c}$, from the linear equation system

$\mathtt{Ac} = \mathbf{0}$, occurs when $\mathtt{A}$ has a 2-dimensional (or greater) right null-space. In this case in solving for $\boldsymbol{\omega}$ there would be a family of solutions of the form

$$\boldsymbol{\omega}(\alpha) = \boldsymbol{\omega}_1 + \alpha\boldsymbol{\omega}_2.$$

Here $\boldsymbol{\omega}_1$ and $\boldsymbol{\omega}_2$ are known from the null-space generators, and α must be determined. It remains simply to find the value of α that leads to a solution satisfying the chosen constraint condition in table 19.4. This is solved linearly. One could do the same thing solving for the DIAC, but then the constraint condition would be quadratic (see table 19.2(*p*465)), and one of the solutions would be spurious.

In certain cases, these additional constraints do not resolve the ambiguity. For example, skew-zero does not resolve the ambiguity if the rotation is about the image x- or y-axes. Such exceptions are described in more detail in [Zisserman-98], and we give a few commonly occurring examples now.

Typical ambiguities. The one-parameter family of solutions given in (19.27) for $\boldsymbol{\omega}^*(\mu)$ corresponds to a one-parameter family of calibration matrices obtained from $\boldsymbol{\omega}^*(\mu)$ as $\boldsymbol{\omega}^*(\mu) = \mathtt{K}(\mu)\mathtt{K}(\mu)^\mathsf{T}$. For simplicity we will assume that the true camera $\mathtt{K}$ (which is a member of this family) has skew zero, so $\mathtt{K}$ has four unknown parameters.

If the rotation axis is parallel to the camera X-axis, then $\mathbf{d}_\mathrm{r} = (1,0,0)^\mathsf{T}$ and $\mathbf{v}_\mathrm{r} = \mathtt{K}\mathbf{d}_\mathrm{r} = \alpha_x(1,0,0)^\mathsf{T}$. From the form (19.11–*p*464) of $\boldsymbol{\omega}^*$ with no skew, the family (19.27) is

$$\boldsymbol{\omega}^*(\mu) = \boldsymbol{\omega}^*_{\text{true}} + \mu\mathbf{v}_\mathrm{r}\mathbf{v}_\mathrm{r}^\mathsf{T} = \begin{bmatrix} \alpha_x^2(1+\mu) + x_0^2 & x_0y_0 & x_0 \\ x_0y_0 & \alpha_y^2 + y_0^2 & y_0 \\ x_0 & y_0 & 1 \end{bmatrix}. \quad (19.28)$$

Note that the entire family has skew-zero, and in this case only the element $\boldsymbol{\omega}^*_{11}$ is varying. This means that the principal point and α_y are unambiguously determined – since they may be read-off from elements which are unaffected by the ambiguity. However, it is apparent that α_x cannot be determined because it only appears in the varying element $\boldsymbol{\omega}^*_{11}(\mu)$. To summarize this, and two other canonical cases:

- *If* $\mathtt{K}$ *is computed from the infinite homography relation (19.25) assuming a zero-skew camera, then for some motions, there remains one undetermined calibration parameter. For rotation about various axes this ambiguity is as follows.*

  (i) X**-axis:** α_x *is undetermined;*

  (ii) Y**-axis:** α_y *is undetermined;*

  (iii) Z**-axis (principal axis):** α_x *and* α_y *are undetermined, but their ratio* α_y/α_x *is determined.*

Geometric note. These ambiguities are not limited to calibration from a pair of views, but apply to complete sequences. For instance if the set of rotations in a camera motion are all about the X-axis of the camera, then there will be a reconstruction ambiguity, and the same is true for Y-axis rotations. One can see this geometrically as follows. Consider a metric reconstruction of a scene from a sequence of images with only Y-axis rotations of the camera. One can define a coordinate system in which the world Y-axis is aligned with the direction of the camera's y-axis. Now, consider "squashing" the whole reconstruction (points and camera positions) so that their Y coordinate is multiplied by some factor k. From the imaging geometry, it is easy to see that this will have the effect of multiplying the y image coordinate of any imaged point by the same factor k, but not affecting the x-coordinate. However, this effect can be undone by multiplying the scale factor α_y of coordinates in the image by the inverse factor k^{-1}, thereby leaving image coordinates unchanged. This shows that α_y is not unambiguously determined, in fact it is unconstrained. In summary there is a one-parameter ambiguity parallel to the rotation axis in the metric reconstruction and a corresponding one-parameter ambiguity in the internal parameters. This argument shows that the problem of ambiguity is intrinsic to the motion, and not to any particular auto-calibration algorithm.

Relationship to the Kruppa equations. Writing (19.24) for two views as $\boldsymbol{\omega}^{*\prime} = \mathtt{H}_\infty \boldsymbol{\omega}^* \mathtt{H}_\infty^\mathsf{T}$ and multiplying before and after by the matrix $[\mathbf{e}']_\times$ leads to

$$[\mathbf{e}']_\times \boldsymbol{\omega}^{*\prime} [\mathbf{e}']_\times = [\mathbf{e}']_\times \mathtt{H}_\infty \boldsymbol{\omega}^* \mathtt{H}_\infty^\mathsf{T} [\mathbf{e}']_\times = \mathtt{F} \boldsymbol{\omega}^* \mathtt{F}^\mathsf{T}$$

since $\mathtt{F} = [\mathbf{e}']_\times \mathtt{H}_\infty$. This is simply the Kruppa equations (19.18–p471), which shows that they follow immediately from the infinite homography constraint. Since $[\mathbf{e}']_\times$ is not invertible, one can not go the other direction and derive the infinite homography constraint from the Kruppa equations. Thus, the Kruppa equations are a weaker constraint.

However the difference is that to apply (19.24) one needs to know the plane at infinity (and hence affine structure), since it is true only for the infinite homography, and not for an arbitrary H. The Kruppa equations, on the other hand, do not involve any knowledge of affine structure of the scene. Nevertheless, this relationship shows that for a sequence of images, any calibration ambiguity under the infinite homography relation is also an ambiguity of the Kruppa equations.

19.6 Calibration from rotating cameras

In this section, we begin consideration of calibration under special imaging conditions. The situation considered here is the one in which the camera rotates about its centre but does not translate. We will consider both the case of fixed internal parameters, and the case of some parameters known and fixed whilst others are unknown and varying.

This situation is one that occurs frequently. Examples include: pan–tilt and zoom surveillance cameras; cameras used for broadcasts of sporting events which are almost invariably fixed in location but free to rotate and zoom; and hand-held camcorders which are very often panned from a single viewpoint. Even though the rotation is not exactly about the centre, in practice the translation is generally negligible compared to the distance of scene points, and a fixed centre is an excellent approximation.

The calibration problem from rotating cameras is mathematically identical with the affine-to-metric calibration step in stratified reconstruction, as given in section 19.5.2.

Objective

Given $m \geq 2$ views acquired by a camera rotating about its centre with fixed or varying internal parameters, compute the parameters of each camera. It is assumed that the rotations are not all about the same axis.

Algorithm

(i) **Inter-image homographies:** Compute the homography $\mathtt{H}^i$ between each view i and a reference view such that $\mathbf{x}^i = \mathtt{H}^i\mathbf{x}$ using, for example, algorithm 4.6(p123). Normalize the matrices such that $\det \mathtt{H}^i = 1$.

(ii) **Compute $\boldsymbol{\omega}$:**
- In the case of constant calibration: rewrite the equations $\boldsymbol{\omega} = (\mathtt{H}^i)^{-\mathsf{T}}\boldsymbol{\omega}(\mathtt{H}^i)^{-1}$, $i = 1, \ldots, m$ as $\mathtt{A}\mathbf{c} = \mathbf{0}$ where $\mathtt{A}$ is a $6m \times 6$ matrix, and $\mathbf{c}$ the elements of the conic $\boldsymbol{\omega}$ arranged as a 6-vector, **or**
- For variable calibration parameters, use the equation $\boldsymbol{\omega}^i = (\mathtt{H}^i)^{-\mathsf{T}}\boldsymbol{\omega}(\mathtt{H}^i)^{-1}$ to express linear constraints on entries of $\boldsymbol{\omega}^i$ in table 19.4 (e.g. unit aspect ratio) as linear equations in the entries of $\boldsymbol{\omega}$.

(iii) **Compute $\mathtt{K}$:** Determine the Cholesky decomposition of $\boldsymbol{\omega}$ as $\boldsymbol{\omega} = \mathtt{U}\mathtt{U}^{\mathsf{T}}$, and thence $\mathtt{K} = \mathtt{U}^{-\mathsf{T}}$.

(iv) **Iterative improvement:** (Optional) Refine the linear estimate of $\mathtt{K}$ by minimizing

$$\sum_{i=2,m;\ j=1,n} d(\mathbf{x}_j^i, \mathtt{K}\mathtt{R}^i\mathtt{K}^{-1}\mathbf{x}_j)^2$$

over $\mathtt{K}$ and $\mathtt{R}^i$, where $\mathbf{x}_j, \mathbf{x}_j^i$ are the position of the j-th point measured in the first and i-th images respectively. Initial estimates for the minimization are obtained from $\mathtt{K}$ and $\mathtt{R}^i = \mathtt{K}^{-1}\mathtt{H}^i\mathtt{K}$.

Algorithm 19.3. *Calibration for a camera rotating about its centre.*

From a non-translating camera it is impossible to achieve an affine (or any) reconstruction, because there is no way to resolve depth. Nevertheless, we may compute the infinite homography between the images, which is all that is needed to determine the camera calibration.

As has been shown earlier (section 8.4(p202)) the images of two cameras with a common centre are related by a plane projective transformation. Indeed, if $\mathbf{x}^i$ and $\mathbf{x}$ are corresponding image points then they are related by $\mathbf{x}^i = \mathtt{H}^i\mathbf{x}$, where $\mathtt{H}^i = \mathtt{K}^i\mathtt{R}^i(\mathtt{K})^{-1}$, and $\mathtt{R}^i$ is the rotation between view i and the reference view. Furthermore, since this map is independent of the depth of the points imaged at $\mathbf{x}$, it applies also to points at infinity, so as shown in section 13.4(p338),

$$\mathtt{H}^i = \mathtt{H}^i_\infty = \mathtt{K}^i\mathtt{R}^i(\mathtt{K})^{-1}.$$

Thus we have a convenient means of measuring $\mathtt{H}_\infty$ directly from images.

Given $\mathtt{H}_\infty$ a solution for the calibration matrices $\mathtt{K}^i$ of all the images in the set acquired by the rotating camera may be obtained as described in section 19.5.2. The method may be applied to either fixed or variable internal parameters and is summarized in algorithm 19.3. We will illustrate this by a number of examples.

Fig. 19.3. **Calibrating a camera rotating about its centre.** *(***upper***) Five images of the US Capitol acquired by approximately rotating the camera about its centre. (***lower***) A mosaic image constructed from the five images (see example 8.14(*p207*)). The mosaic image shows very clearly the distortion effect of the infinite homography between the images. Analysis of this distortion provides the basis for the auto-calibration algorithm. The calibration is computed as described in algorithm 19.3.*

Example 19.9. Rotation about centre with fixed internal parameters

The images in figure 19.3 were obtained using a 35mm camera with ordinary black and white film to produce negatives. The camera was hand-held, and no particular care was taken to ensure that the camera centre remained stationary.

Prints enlarged from these negatives were digitized using a flat-bed scanner. The enlargement process can lead to a non-zero value of s and unequal values of α_x and α_y if the negative and print paper are not precisely parallel. The resulting image size was 776×536 pixels.

The constraint applied here is that the internal parameters are constant. The camera

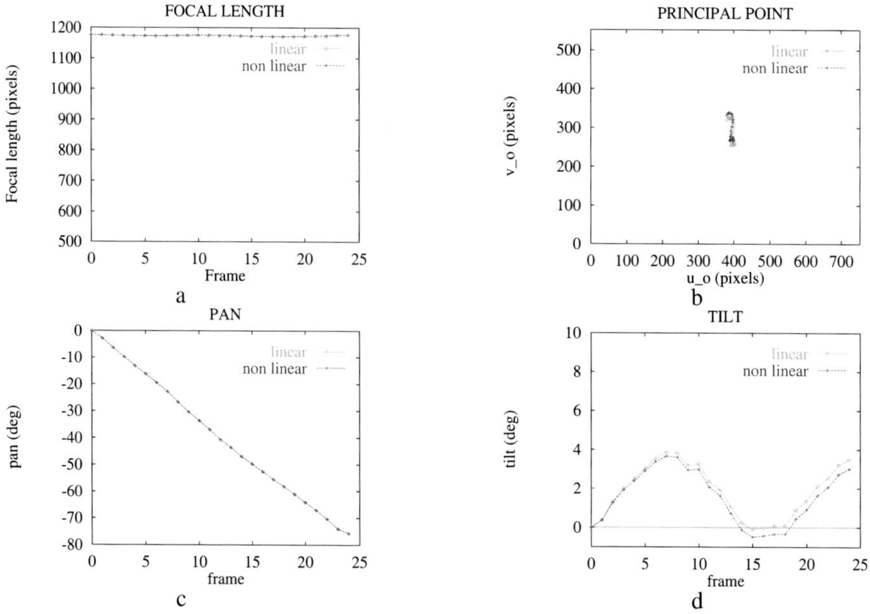

Fig. 19.4. **Rotation for varying internal parameters assuming square pixels.** *These are for the panned sequence of figure 8.9(*p206*). (a) Focal length. (b) Principal point. (c) Pan angle. (d) Tilt angle. Figures courtesy of Lourdes de Agapito Vicente.*

matrix computed as described in algorithm 19.3 is

$$\mathtt{K}_{\text{linear}} = \begin{bmatrix} 964.4 & -4.9 & 392.8 \\ & 966.4 & 282.0 \\ & & 1 \end{bmatrix} \quad \mathtt{K}_{\text{iterative}} = \begin{bmatrix} 956.8 & -6.4 & 392.0 \\ & 959.3 & 281.4 \\ & & 1 \end{bmatrix}.$$

There is little difference between the linear and iterative estimates, and the computed aspect ratio (virtually unity) and principal point are very reasonable. △

Example 19.10. Rotation about centre with varying internal parameters

The images in figure 8.9(*p*206) were acquired by panning a camcorder approximately about its centre. The camera was not zoomed, but due to auto-focus there might be slight variations in the focal length and principal point.

In this example the constraint used is that the pixels are square: i.e. that the skew is zero and the aspect ratio unity; but the focal length and principal point are unknown and not fixed. Then from table 19.4 we have two linear constraints on $\boldsymbol{\omega}$ from each view. From zero skew $(\mathtt{H}^{i}_{\infty}{}^{-\mathsf{T}}\,\boldsymbol{\omega}\,\mathtt{H}^{i}_{\infty}{}^{-1})_{12} = 0$, and from unit aspect ratio $(\mathtt{H}^{i}_{\infty}{}^{-\mathsf{T}}\,\boldsymbol{\omega}\,\mathtt{H}^{i}_{\infty}{}^{-1})_{11} = (\mathtt{H}^{i}_{\infty}{}^{-\mathsf{T}}\,\boldsymbol{\omega}\,\mathtt{H}^{i}_{\infty}{}^{-1})_{22}$. These constraints are assembled to give a linear system of equations on $\boldsymbol{\omega}$ as described in algorithm 19.3.

The internal parameters of the computed camera matrix for each view are shown in figure 19.4. It is evident that the recovered focal length and principal point are quite constant (even though this was not imposed), and the pan and tilt angles are very reasonable for this hand-held sequence. △

19.7 Auto-calibration from planes

For a set of images of a planar scene, the two-step approach of estimating a projective reconstruction followed by computation of a rectifying transformation to take it to metric does not work. This is because it is not possible to determine the cameras without depth relief. As seen in section 17.5.2(*p*425), a minimum of two points not lying on the plane are required. Nevertheless, auto-calibration from scene planes *is* possible. This was shown by [Triggs-98] who gave a solution in the case of constant internal parameters. The method is especially interesting from the point of view of potential applications. Scenes consisting of planes are extremely common in man-made environments, e.g. the ground plane. Furthermore, in aerial images acquired by a high-flying aircraft or a satellite, the depth-relief of the scene is small compared with the extent of the image, and the scene may be accurately approximated as a plane and the auto-calibration method will apply.

The starting point of the algorithm is a set of image–to–image homographies induced by the world plane. These can all be related back to the first image, providing a set of homographies $\mathtt{H}^i$. Geometrically auto-calibration from planes is then a marriage of two ideas. First, the circular points on the plane, which are the intersection of the absolute conic with the plane, are mapped from image to image via the homographies. Second, as we have seen in example 8.18(*p*211), the calibration matrix $\mathtt{K}$ may be determined from the imaged circular points of a plane (with two constraints provided by each image).

Thus suppose the images of the circular points (4 dof) are determined in the first image (by some means), then they may be transferred to the other views by the known $\mathtt{H}^i$. In each view then there are two constraints on $\boldsymbol{\omega}$, since the two imaged circular points lie on $\boldsymbol{\omega}$. In detail, if we denote the (at this stage unknown) imaged circular points in the first view by $\mathbf{c}_j, j = 1, 2$. Then the auto-calibration equations are

$$(\mathtt{H}^i\mathbf{c}_j)^\mathsf{T}\boldsymbol{\omega}^i(\mathtt{H}^i\mathbf{c}_j) = 0, \;\; i = 1, \ldots, m \;\; j = 1, 2 \qquad (19.29)$$

where $\mathtt{H}^1 = \mathtt{I}$. In solving these equations the unknowns are the coordinates of the circular points in the first image, and some number of unknown calibration parameters. Although the circular points are complex points, they are complex conjugates of each other, so 4 parameters suffice to describe them. If in addition there are a total of v unknowns in the internal parameters $\mathtt{K}^i$ of all m views, then a solution is possible provided $2m \geq v + 4$, since each view provides two equations.

Restrictions on the internal parameters of the cameras lead to further algebraic constraints according to table 19.4 and these are used to supplement the constraints imposed by (19.29). Various cases are considered in table 19.5. In most cases, calibration from a plane is a non-linear problem and nothing more will be said here about computational aspects of how to find the solution. Iterative methods are necessary, minimizing some cost function. See [Triggs-98] for more details of minimization methods.

Implementation. A considerable implementational advantage of this method is that it only requires the homography between planes, and not the point correspondences

Condition	dof(v)	views
Unknown but constant internal parameters	5	5
Constant known skew and aspect ratio. Constant unknown principal point and focal length	3	4
All internal parameters known except varying focal length	m	4
Varying focal length, all other internal parameters fixed but unknown	$m+4$	8

Table 19.5. **The number of views required for calibration from a plane under various conditions.** *Calibration is (in principle) possible if* $2m \geq v + 4$.

arising from 3-space points that are generally required to estimate multiple view tensors, such as the fundamental matrix. The matching transformation between planes is a much simpler, stabler and accurate computation because of the constrained nature of the inter-image transformation which is point-to-point. The method of algorithm 4.6-(p123) may be used to estimate this transformation between two images. Alternatively, correlation-based methods that estimate the parametrized homography directly from image intensity may be used.

Including additional information. If additional information is available on the plane or the motion then the complexity of auto-calibration using scene planes may be reduced. For example, if the vanishing line of the imaged plane can be determined then only two parameters are required to specify the circular points since the imaged circular points lie on the vanishing line. Indeed if the plane provides sufficient information to estimate its imaged circular points directly (such as a square grid) then the problem reduces to that of calibration from scene constraints discussed in section 8.8(p223).

Similarly constraints on the motion may be used to simplify the problem. One particular example is where the rotation axis describing the camera motion is parallel to the scene plane normal. In this case the imaged circular points may be computed directly from the fixed points of the homography and two linear constraints placed on $\boldsymbol{\omega}$. This situation is discussed further in Note (vii) at the end of the chapter. An example of such a motion is planar motion which is discussed in detail in the following section.

19.8 Planar motion

A case of some practical importance is that of a camera moving in a plane and rotating about an axis perpendicular to that plane. This is the case for a roaming vehicle moving on a ground plane, with a camera fixed with respect to the vehicle body. In this case, the camera must move in a plane parallel to the (horizontal) ground, and as the vehicle turns, the camera will rotate about a vertical axis. It is *not* assumed that the camera is pointing horizontally, or is in any other particular orientation with respect to the vehicle. However, we assume constant internal calibration for the camera. The constrained nature of the motion makes the calibration task significantly simpler.

It will be shown that given three or more images from a sequence of planar motions an affine reconstruction may be computed. To do this, we need to determine the plane at infinity. This will be done by identifying three points on the plane at infinity, thereby defining the plane. These points will be identified as being fixed points in the sequence of images.

Fixed image points under planar motion. According to section 3.4.1(*p*77), any rigid motion (for instance the camera motion) can be interpreted as a rotation about screw axis along with a translation along the direction of the axis. For a planar motion, the rotation axis is perpendicular to the plane of motion, and the translational part of the screw motion is zero. Think of the vehicle as being swung horizontally around the screw axis. The position of the screw axis with respect to the camera remains fixed, and so it will constitute a line of fixed points in the image. If a second motion takes place about a different axis, then the image of the second axis will be fixed in the second pair of images. The images of the two axes will in general be different, but will intersect in the image of the point where the two screw axes meet. Since the two axes are vertical, they are perforce parallel, and so will meet at their common direction on the plane at infinity. This direction projects into the images at the intersection of the images of the screw axes, which is the vanishing point of the screw axes direction. This image point is called the apex. We now have one fixed point over the views, and this will be used to determine one point on the plane at infinity in a projective reconstruction.

As we have seen the image of the screw axis is a line of fixed points for an image pair. There is also a fixed line which is identifiable from a pair of images as follows. Because the plane of motion of the camera (which will be called the ground plane) is fixed, the set of points in the plane is mapped to the same line in all the images. This line is called the horizon line and is the vanishing line of the ground plane. Since each of the cameras lie on the ground plane their epipoles must all lie on the horizon line. Unlike the image of the screw axis, the horizon line is a fixed line, but not a line of fixed points.

Although the horizon line is not fixed pointwise, it contains two points that are fixed in the image pair, namely the image of the two circular points on the ground plane. These circular points are the intersection of the absolute conic with the ground plane. Since the image of the absolute conic is fixed under rigid motion, and the image of the ground plane is fixed, the images of two circular points must be fixed. In fact, they will be fixed in all images from the planar motion sequence. This is illustrated in figure 19.5.

So far we have described the fixed points of the motion sequence. Computing these fixed points is equivalent to affine reconstruction, since we can back-project from the fixed image points to find the corresponding 3D points on the plane at infinity. Although the apex may be computed from two views; it requires three views to compute the imaged circular points.

Computing the fixed points. The set of points in space that map to the same image point in two images is called the horopter. In general, the horopter is a twisted cubic,

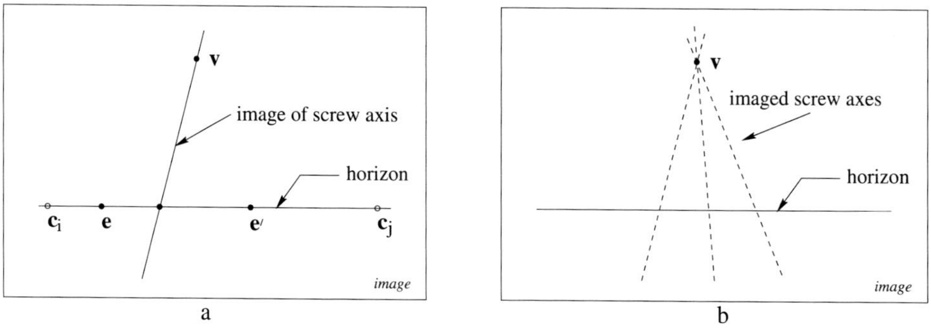

Fig. 19.5. **Fixed image entities for planar motion.** *(a) For two views the imaged screw axis is a line of fixed points in the image under the motion. The horizon is a fixed line under the motion. The epipoles* $\mathbf{e}, \mathbf{e}'$ *and imaged circular points of the ground plane* $\mathbf{c}_i, \mathbf{c}_j$ *lie on the horizon. (b) The relation between the fixed lines obtained pairwise for three images under planar motion. The image horizon lines for each pair are coincident, and the imaged screw axes for each pair intersect in the apex* $\mathbf{v}$*. All the epipoles lie on the horizon line.*

but in the case of planar motion it degenerates to a line (the screw axis) and a conic on the ground plane. The image of the horopter is the conic defined by $\mathtt{F} + \mathtt{F}^\mathsf{T}$, where $\mathtt{F}$ is the fundamental matrix (see section 9.4(p250)). In the case of planar motion this will be a degenerate conic consisting of two lines, the image of the screw axis and the horizon line (see figure 9.11(p253)). By decomposing the conic, these two lines are determined. From three images we can compute the image of the horopter for each of three pairs, and thereby obtain three sets of horizon lines and imaged axes. The horizon line will be a common component of these sets, and the other components (the images of the screw axes) will intersect in the image at the apex.

Now we turn to computing the circular points. It is useful to understand the geometry of a pair of horopters corresponding to two pairs of images. Let $\mathtt{C}^{12}$ be a conic representing the portion of the horopter for images 1 and 2, lying in the ground plane. This conic will pass through the two circular points, the two camera centres and the intersection of the screw axis with the ground plane. Since the conic contains the circular points it is a circle. Let $\mathtt{C}^{23}$ be the corresponding circle defined from images 2 and 3. The two circular points and the centre of the second camera will lie on both circles. Since two conics intersect in general in four points, there must be a further (real) intersection point. However, this can be discarded, since the points of interest are the two complex intersection points, namely the circular points on the ground plane.

In implementations, authors have chosen different ways of finding the two circular points. In [Armstrong-96b] the method is based on finding fixed lines in three views through the apex using the trifocal tensor. In [Faugeras-98, Sturm-97b] the method involves computing the trifocal tensor of a 1D camera, applied to imaging the 2D ground plane to a 1D image. In both cases the positions of the circular points on the horizon are obtained as the solution of a cubic in one variable.

The main steps of this affine calibration method are summarized in algorithm 19.4.

Objective

Given three (or more) images acquired by a camera with constant internal parameters undergoing planar motion compute an affine reconstruction.

Algorithm

(i) **Compute a projective reconstruction.** from the trifocal tensor $\mathcal{T}$ for the three views. The trifocal tensor may be computed by, e.g. algorithm 16.4(p401).
(ii) **Compute pairwise fundamental matrices from $\mathcal{T}$.** See algorithm 15.1(p375). Decompose the symmetric part of each fundamental matrix into two lines, a horizon and the image of the screw axes. See section 9.4.1(p252).
(iii) **Compute the apex.** Intersect the three imaged screw axes to determine the apex $\mathbf{v}$.
(iv) **Compute the horizon for the triplet.** Obtain the six epipoles from the three fundamental matrices, and determine the horizon by an orthogonal regression fit to these epipoles.
(v) **Compute the imaged circular points.** Compute the position of the imaged circular points on the horizon (see text) $\mathbf{c}_i, \mathbf{c}_j$.
(vi) **Compute the plane at infinity.** Triangulate points on the plane at infinity from the corresponding image points $\mathbf{x} \leftrightarrow \mathbf{x}'$, with $\mathbf{x} = \mathbf{x}'$ for each of $\mathbf{v}, \mathbf{c}_i, \mathbf{c}_j$. This determines three points on $\boldsymbol{\pi}_\infty$, and hence determines the plane.
(vii) **Compute an affine reconstruction.** Rectify the projective reconstruction using the computed $\boldsymbol{\pi}_\infty$ as in algorithm 19.2.

Algorithm 19.4. *Affine calibration for planar motion.*

Metric reconstruction. Once the apex and two circular points are found, the plane at infinity is computed, and the infinite homographies between the images can be computed. Calibration and metric reconstruction now proceeds in the usual way. However, it must be noted that the constrained nature of the motion means that there is a one-parameter family of solutions for the calibration because all the camera rotations are about the same axis. We have the sort of calibration ambiguity considered in section 19.5.3. It is necessary to make an assumption about internal calibration in order to find a unique result. If the y-axis of the camera is parallel with the rotation axis (which may be true in a practical situation), then we have seen that the zero-skew constraint is not sufficient. The best plan is to enforce a zero-skew and known aspect ratio constraint (e.g. if the pixels are square).

Example 19.11. Metric reconstruction for planar motion.
Figure 19.6(a) shows four of seven images of a planar motion sequence. For this sequence the elevation angle of the camera is approximately $20°$. The computed imaged screw axes and horizon lines using all possible pairs are shown in figure 19.6(b), with the resulting estimated apex and horizon line. The positions of the imaged circular points were estimated as $x = 104 \pm 362i,\ y = -86 \mp 2i$. Assuming an aspect ratio of 1.1, the internal parameters of the calibration matrix $\mathtt{K}$ were computed as $\alpha_x = 330, \alpha_y = 363, x_0 = 123, y_0 = 50$. The accuracy of the metric reconstruction was assessed by measuring metric invariants. Typical results are shown in figure 19.6(c). △

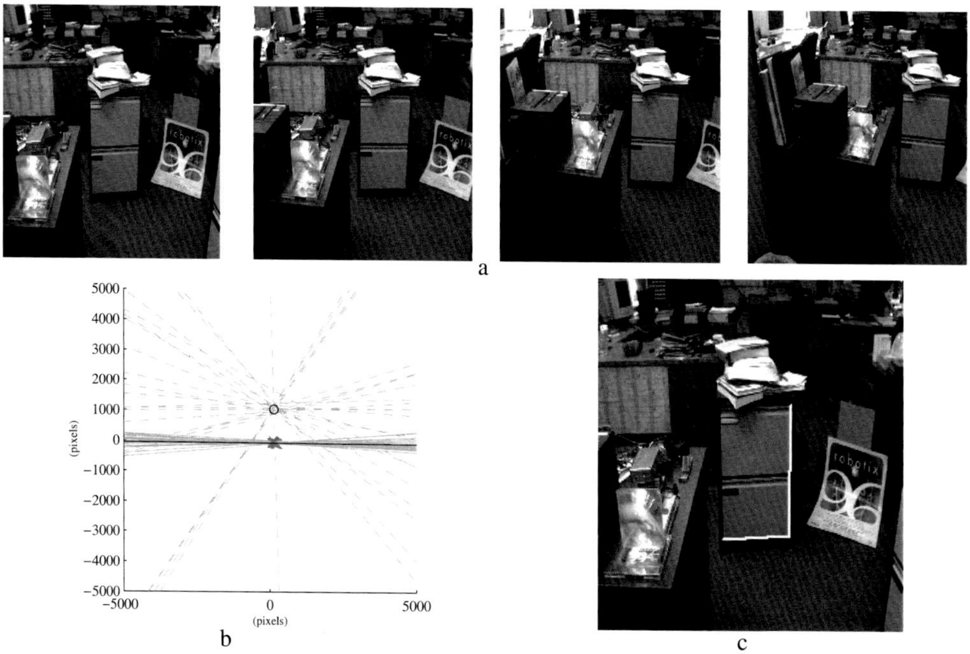

Fig. 19.6. **Planar motion sequence.** *(a) Four images (of seven used) acquired from a camera mounted on a vehicle moving on a plane. (b) The computed epipoles (×), horizon lines (grey solid), and imaged screw axes (grey dashed) for all image pairs. (c) Euclidean invariants measured in the metric reconstruction the right angle is measured as 89°, the ratio of the non-parallel lengths is measured as 0.61 (compared to the approximate veridical value of 0.65).*

19.9 Single axis rotation – turntable motion

In this section we discuss auto-calibration of single axis motions where the relative motion between scene and cameras is equivalent to a rotation about a single fixed axis. This is a specialization of the planar motion case of section 19.8 where here the screw axes for each motion are coincident. This situation occurs, for example, in the case of a static camera viewing an object rotating on a turntable. A second example is that of a camera rotating about a fixed axis (offset from its centre). A third example is that of a camera viewing a rotating mirror.

We will consider here turntable motion and for ease of discussion assume that the axis is vertical so that the motion occurs in a horizontal plane. Again it is *not* assumed that the camera is pointing horizontally, or is in any other particular orientation with respect to the axis. It is assumed that the internal calibration of the camera is constant.

The fixed image points under a sequence of single axis rotation are those of planar motion described in section 19.8, and shown in figure 19.5(a), with the addition that the imaged screw axis is a line of fixed points. The constraint of figure 19.5(b) is not available here as all the imaged screw axes are coincident. The consequence is that it is not possible to determine the apex $\mathbf{v}$ directly, and only the two circular points on π_∞ may be recovered from imaged fixed points. This means that the reconstruction, in the absence of constraints on the internal parameters, is not affine, but a particular parametrized projective transformation. Metric structure is known in the horizontal planes (since the circular points of these planes is known) but there is a 1D projective transformation in the vertical (Z) direction. The resulting ambiguity is the transformation $\mathbf{X}_P = \mathtt{H}\mathbf{X}_E$ where

$$\mathtt{H} = \begin{bmatrix} 1 & 0 & 0 & 0 \\ 0 & 1 & 0 & 0 \\ 0 & 0 & \gamma & 0 \\ 0 & 0 & \delta & 1 \end{bmatrix} \tag{19.30}$$

and γ and δ are scalars which determine the intersection of the Z axis with $\boldsymbol{\pi}_\infty$ and the relative scaling between the horizontal and vertical directions. An example of the projective transformations represented by family of mappings is shown in figure 1.4-(p16).

Computing the fixed points. One way to proceed is to determine the imaged circular points directly. As is evident from figure 19.7(b) the point tracks are ellipses which are images of circles. In 3-space these circles lie in parallel horizontal planes and intersect in the circular points on $\boldsymbol{\pi}_\infty$. In the image, ellipses may be fitted to these tracks, and the common intersection points of the image conics are the (complex conjugate) imaged circular points. The 3D circular points may then be determined by triangulation from two or more views. This is the approach taken by [Jiang-02].

An alternative more algebraic way to proceed is to model the camera matrices as $\mathtt{P}^i = \mathtt{H}_{3\times 3}[\mathtt{R}_Z(\theta^i) \mid \mathbf{t}]$ where

$$\mathtt{P}^i = \begin{bmatrix} & & \\ \mathbf{h}_1 & \mathbf{h}_2 & \mathbf{h}_3 \\ & & \end{bmatrix} \begin{bmatrix} \cos\theta^i & -\sin\theta^i & 0 & t \\ \sin\theta^i & \cos\theta^i & 0 & 0 \\ 0 & 0 & 1 & 0 \end{bmatrix} \tag{19.31}$$

with $\mathbf{h}_k$ the columns of $\mathtt{H}_{3\times 3}$. This division of the internal and external parameters means that $\mathtt{H}_{3\times 3}$ and $\mathbf{t}$ are fixed over the sequence, and only the angle of rotation, θ^i, about the Z axis varies for each camera $\mathtt{P}^i$.

Given this parametrization, the estimation problem can then be precisely stated as determining the common matrix $\mathtt{H}_{3\times 3}$ and the angles θ_i in order to estimate the set of cameras $\mathtt{P}^i$ for the sequence. Thus a total of $8 + m$ parameters must be estimated for m views, where 8 is the number of degrees of freedom of the homography $\mathtt{H}_{3\times 3}$. This is a considerable saving over the $11m$ that would be required for a projective reconstruction of a general motion sequence.

For single axis motion the fundamental matrix has the special form described in section 9.4.1(p252), and writing the matrix in terms of the camera matrices (19.31) gives

$$\mathtt{F} = \alpha[\mathbf{h}_2]_\times + \beta\left((\mathbf{h}_1 \times \mathbf{h}_3)(\mathbf{h}_1 \times \mathbf{h}_2)^\mathsf{T} + (\mathbf{h}_1 \times \mathbf{h}_2)(\mathbf{h}_1 \times \mathbf{h}_3)^\mathsf{T}\right)$$

which means that the columns of $\mathtt{H}_{3\times 3}$ are partially determined once the fundamental matrix is computed. This is the approach taken by [Fitzgibbon-98b] where a fundamental matrix of the special form is fitted to point correspondences (see section 11.7.2-(p293)). It may be shown that from 3 or more views the first two columns $\mathbf{h}_1, \mathbf{h}_2$ of

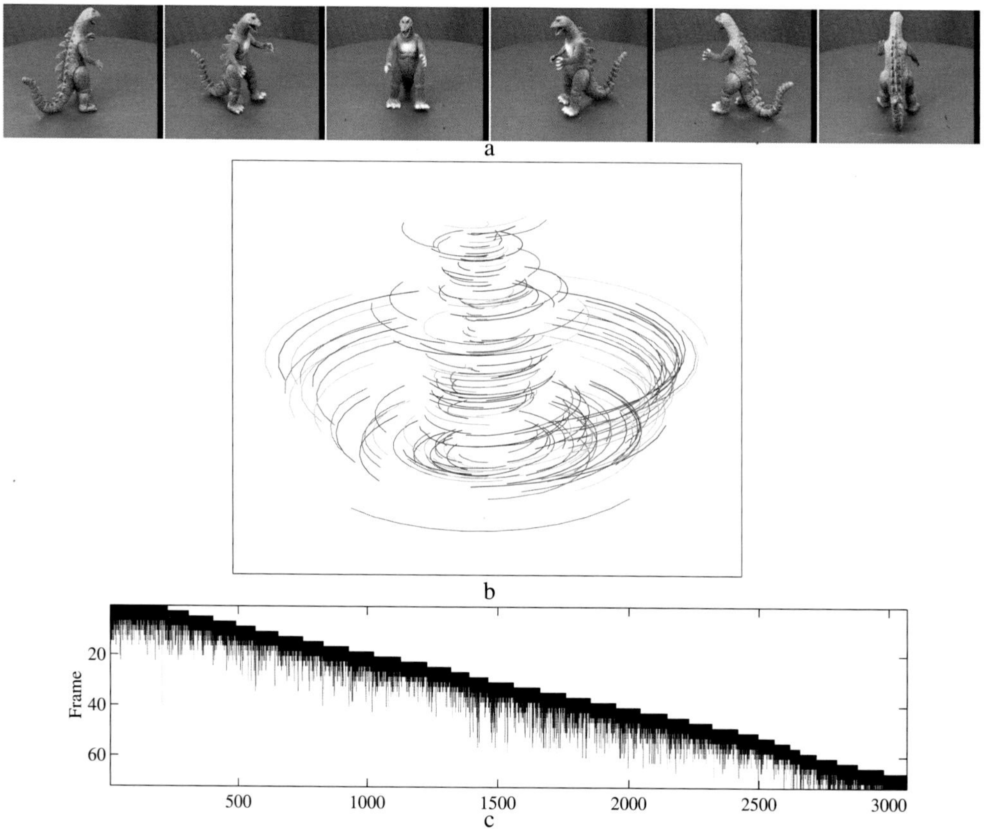

Fig. 19.7. **Dinosaur sequence and tracking:** *(a) six frames from a sequence of 36 of a dinosaur rotating on a turntable (Image sequence courtesy of the University of Hannover [Niem-94]). (b) A subset of the point tracks – only the 200 tracks which survived for longer than 7 successive views are shown. (c)* **Track lifetimes***: Each vertical bar corresponds to a single point track, extending from the first to last frame in which that point was seen. The horizontal ordering is according to where the point first appeared in the sequence. The measurement matrix is relatively sparse, and few points survive longer than 15 frames.*

$\mathtt{H}_{3\times3}$ and the angle θ^i can be fully determined, but $\mathbf{h}_3$ is only determined up to the two-parameter family corresponding to the ambiguity of (19.30).

Metric reconstruction. The two parameter ambiguity in the reconstruction given by (19.30) can be resolved by providing additional information on the internal parameters, for example that the pixels are square. However, if the camera is horizontal with image y axis parallel to the rotation axis, then square pixels only provides one additional constraint (from the aspect ratio, as the skew zero constraint does not provide an additional constraint). In this case further information on the camera is required (e.g. the y coordinate of the principal point) or the aspect ratio of the scene may be used.

Example 19.12. Reconstruction from a turntable sequence

Figure 19.7 shows frames from a sequence of a model dinosaur rotating on a turntable, and the resulting image point tracks. Feature extraction is performed on the luminance component of the colour signal. The projective geometry of the turntable motion is de-

Fig. 19.8. **Dinosaur:** *(a) 3D scene points (about 5000) and camera positions for the Dinosaur sequence. (b) The automatic computation of a 3D graphical model for this sequence is described in [Fitzgibbon-98b].*

termined from these tracks (and no other information) and the resulting reconstruction of cameras and 3D points is shown in figure 19.8. Effectively the camera circumnavigates the object. A 3D texture mapped graphical model may then be computed, in principle, by back-projecting cones defined by the dinosaur silhouette in each frame, and intersecting the set of cones to determine the visual hull of the 3D object. △

19.10 Auto-calibration of a stereo rig

In this section we describe a stratified method for calibrating a "fixed" two-camera stereo rig. Fixed here means that the relative orientation of the cameras on the rig is unchanged during the motion, and the internal parameters of each camera are also unchanged. It will be shown that from a single motion of the rig the plane at infinity is determined uniquely.

Suppose a fixed stereo rig undergoes a general motion. The projective structure of the scene can be obtained before ($\mathbf{X}$) and after ($\mathbf{X}'$) the motion. Since $\mathbf{X}$ and $\mathbf{X}'$ are two projective reconstructions of the same scene they are related by a 4×4 projective transformation $\mathtt{H}_{\mathrm{P}}$, as

$$\mathbf{X}' = \mathtt{H}_{\mathrm{P}}\mathbf{X}.$$

However, the actual motion of the rig is Euclidean, and it follows (see below) that the homography $\mathtt{H}_{\mathrm{P}}$ is conjugate to the Euclidean transformation representing the motion. Conjugacy is the key result because under a conjugacy relation fixed entities are mapped to fixed entities. Consequently the fixed entities of the Euclidean motion (in particular the plane at infinity) can be *accessed* from the fixed entities of the projective motion represented by $\mathtt{H}_{\mathrm{P}}$.

Conjugacy relation. Suppose $\mathbf{X}_{\mathrm{E}}$ represents a point in 3-space in a Euclidean coordinate frame attached to the rig, and $\mathbf{X}'_{\mathrm{E}}$ represents the same point after the motion of the rig. Then the points are related as

$$\mathbf{X}'_{\mathrm{E}} = \mathtt{H}_{\mathrm{E}}\mathbf{X}_{\mathrm{E}} \tag{19.32}$$

where $\mathtt{H}_{\mathrm{E}}$ is a non-singular 4×4 Euclidean transformation matrix that represents the rotation and translation of the rig. Suppose also that the point is represented in a projective coordinate frame attached to the rig (and which is obtained by a projective reconstruction); then

$$\mathbf{X}_{\mathrm{E}} = \mathtt{H}_{\mathrm{EP}}\mathbf{X} \quad \mathbf{X}'_{\mathrm{E}} = \mathtt{H}_{\mathrm{EP}}\mathbf{X}' \tag{19.33}$$

where $\mathtt{H}_{\mathrm{EP}}$ is a non-singular 4×4 matrix that relates projective to metric structure. An essential point to note here is that the two projective reconstructions, before and after the camera must be in the same projective coordinate frame, in other words, the same pair of cameras matrices must be used before and after.

From (19.32) and (19.33) if follows that

$$\mathtt{H}_{\mathrm{P}} = \mathtt{H}_{\mathrm{EP}}^{-1}\, \mathtt{H}_{\mathrm{E}}\, \mathtt{H}_{\mathrm{EP}} \tag{19.34}$$

so that $\mathtt{H}_{\mathrm{P}}$ is conjugate to a Euclidean transformation. There are two important properties of this conjugacy relation:

(i) $\mathtt{H}_{\mathrm{P}}$ and $\mathtt{H}_{\mathrm{E}}$ have the same eigenvalues.

(ii) If $\mathbf{E}$ is an eigenvector of $\mathtt{H}_{\mathrm{E}}$ then the corresponding eigenvector of $\mathtt{H}_{\mathrm{P}}$, with the same eigenvalue, is $(\mathtt{H}_{\mathrm{EP}}^{-1}\mathbf{E})$, i.e. the eigenvectors of $\mathtt{H}_{\mathrm{E}}$ are mapped to the eigenvectors of $\mathtt{H}_{\mathrm{P}}$ by the point transformation (19.33). This follows from (19.34), for if $\mathtt{H}_{\mathrm{E}}\mathbf{E} = \lambda\mathbf{E}$ then $\mathtt{H}_{\mathrm{EP}}\mathtt{H}_{\mathrm{P}}\mathtt{H}_{\mathrm{EP}}^{-1}\mathbf{E} = \lambda\mathbf{E}$, and pre-multiplying by $\mathtt{H}_{\mathrm{EP}}^{-1}$ gives the desired result.

Fixed points of a Euclidean transformation. Consider the Euclidean transformation represented by the matrix

$$\mathtt{H}_{\mathrm{E}} = \begin{bmatrix} \mathtt{R} & \mathbf{t} \\ \mathbf{0}^{\mathsf{T}} & 1 \end{bmatrix} = \begin{bmatrix} \cos\theta & -\sin\theta & 0 & 0 \\ \sin\theta & \cos\theta & 0 & 0 \\ 0 & 0 & 1 & 1 \\ 0 & 0 & 0 & 1 \end{bmatrix}.$$

This is a rotation by θ about the Z-axis together with a unit translation along the Z-axis (it is a general screw motion). The eigenvectors of $\mathtt{H}_{\mathrm{E}}$ are the fixed points under the transformation (refer to section 2.9(*p*61)). In this case the eigenvalues are $\{e^{i\theta}, e^{-i\theta}, 1, 1\}$ and the corresponding eigenvectors of $\mathtt{H}_{\mathrm{E}}$ are

$$\mathbf{E}_1 = \begin{pmatrix} 1 \\ i \\ 0 \\ 0 \end{pmatrix} \quad \mathbf{E}_2 = \begin{pmatrix} 1 \\ -i \\ 0 \\ 0 \end{pmatrix} \quad \mathbf{E}_3 = \begin{pmatrix} 0 \\ 0 \\ 1 \\ 0 \end{pmatrix} \quad \mathbf{E}_4 = \begin{pmatrix} 0 \\ 0 \\ 1 \\ 0 \end{pmatrix}.$$

All the eigenvectors lie on $\boldsymbol{\pi}_\infty$. This means that $\boldsymbol{\pi}_\infty$ is fixed as a set, but is *not* a plane of fixed points. The eigenvectors $\mathbf{E}_1$ and $\mathbf{E}_2$ are the circular points for planes perpendicular to the Z (rotation) axis. The other two (identical) eigenvectors $\mathbf{E}_3$ and $\mathbf{E}_4$ are the direction of the rotation axis.

Computing $\boldsymbol{\pi}_\infty$. If the point transformation matrix is $\mathtt{H}_{\mathrm{E}}$ then from (3.6–*p*68) the plane transformation matrix is $\mathtt{H}_{\mathrm{E}}^{-\mathsf{T}}$. The eigenvectors of $\mathtt{H}_{\mathrm{E}}^{-\mathsf{T}}$ are the fixed planes under the motion. The matrix $\mathtt{H}_{\mathrm{E}}^{-\mathsf{T}}$ also has two equal, unit eigenvalues and a single eigenvector corresponding to these which is the plane $\boldsymbol{\pi}_\infty$ as may easily be verified. The eigenvectors of $\mathtt{H}_{\mathrm{E}}^{-\mathsf{T}}$ are mapped to those of $\mathtt{H}_{\mathrm{P}}^{-\mathsf{T}}$, in the same manner as the mapping of eigenvectors of $\mathtt{H}_{\mathrm{E}}$ to those of $\mathtt{H}_{\mathrm{P}}$ described above. Consequently, $\boldsymbol{\pi}_\infty$ in the projective reconstruction is the eigenvector corresponding to the (double) real eigenvalue of $\mathtt{H}_{\mathrm{P}}^{-\mathsf{T}}$. Thus,

- $\boldsymbol{\pi}_\infty$ *may be computed uniquely as the real eigenvector of* $\mathtt{H}_{\mathrm{P}}^{-\mathsf{T}}$, *or equivalently, and more simply, as the real eigenvector of* $\mathtt{H}_{\mathrm{P}}^{\mathsf{T}}$.

We observe here that although the real eigenvalue has algebraic multiplicity of two, its geometric multiplicity (in the case of non-planar motions) is one. This is what enables us to find the plane at infinity.

The procedure for affine calibration is summarized in algorithm 19.5.

Metric calibration and ambiguities. Once $\boldsymbol{\pi}_\infty$ is identified, the metric calibration may proceed as described in the stratified algorithm 19.2(*p*479). Since the rig is fixed, the parameters of the left camera are unchanged during the motion (and similarly for the right camera). From a single motion the internal parameters of each camera are determined up to the one-parameter family resulting from a single rotation as described in section 19.5.3.

As usual the ambiguity from a single motion is removed by additional motions or

Objective

Given two (or more) stereo pairs of images acquired by a fixed stereo rig undergoing general motions (i.e. both $\mathtt{R}$ and $\mathbf{t}$ are non-zero, and $\mathbf{t}$ not perpendicular to the axis of $\mathtt{R}$), compute an affine reconstruction.

Algorithm

(i) **Compute an initial projective reconstruction X:** Using the first stereo pair compute a projective reconstruction $(\mathtt{P}^{\mathrm{L}}, \mathtt{P}^{\mathrm{R}}, \{\mathbf{X}_j\})$ as described in chapter 10. This involves computing the fundamental matrix $\mathtt{F}$ and point correspondences between the images of the first pair $x_j^{\mathrm{L}} \leftrightarrow x_j^{\mathrm{R}}$, e.g. use algorithm 11.4(*p*291).

(ii) **Compute a projective reconstruction X′ after the motion:** Compute correspondences between the images of the second stereo pair $x_j'^{\mathrm{L}} \leftrightarrow x_j'^{\mathrm{R}}$. Since both the internal and relative external parameters of the cameras are fixed, the second stereo pair has the same fundamental matrix $\mathtt{F}$ as the first. The same camera matrices $\mathtt{P}^{\mathrm{L}}, \mathtt{P}^{\mathrm{R}}$ are used for triangulating points $\mathbf{X}_j'$ in 3-space from the computed correspondences $x_j'^{\mathrm{L}} \leftrightarrow x_j'^{\mathrm{R}}$ in the second stereo pair.

(iii) **Compute the 4×4 matrix $\mathtt{H}_{\mathrm{P}}$ which relates X to X′:** Compute correspondences between the left images of the two stereo pairs $x_j^{\mathrm{L}} \leftrightarrow x_j'^{\mathrm{L}}$ (e.g. again use algorithm 11.4(*p*291)). This establishes correspondences between the space points $\mathbf{X}_j \leftrightarrow \mathbf{X}_j'$. The homography $\mathtt{H}_{\mathrm{P}}$ may be estimated linearly from five or more of these 3-space point correspondences, and then the estimate refined by minimizing a suitable cost function over $\mathtt{H}_{\mathrm{P}}$. For example, minimizing $\sum_j (d(x_j^{\mathrm{L}}, \mathtt{P}^{\mathrm{L}}\mathtt{H}\mathbf{X}_j')^2 + d(x_j^{\mathrm{r}}, \mathtt{P}^{\mathrm{R}}\mathtt{H}\mathbf{X}_j')^2)$ minimizes the distance between the measured and reprojected imagc points.

(iv) **Affine reconstruction:** Compute π_∞ from the real eigenvector of $\mathtt{H}_{\mathrm{P}}^{\mathsf{T}}$ and thence an affine reconstruction.

Algorithm 19.5. *Affine calibration of a fixed stereo rig.*

by supplying additional constraints, such as that the pixels are square. If there are additional motions then an improved estimate of π_∞ may also be computed. The outcome of metric calibration is the complete calibration of the rig (i.e. the relative external orientation of the cameras and their internal parameters).

Planar motion. In the special case of orthogonal (planar) motion, where the translation is orthogonal to the rotation axis direction, the space of eigenvectors corresponding to the repeated (real) eigenvalue is two-dimensional. Consequently, π_∞ is determined only up to a one-parameter family. We are therefore unable to find the plane at infinity uniquely (this is examined in detail in example 3.8(*p*81)). The ambiguity may be resolved by a second orthogonal motion about an axis with a different direction from the first.

Example 19.13. Auto-calibration from two stereo pairs

Figure 19.9(a)(b) shows the two stereo pairs used for the affine calibration of the stereo rig following the procedure of algorithm 19.5. The accuracy of the calibration is assessed by computing a vanishing point in the right image in two ways: first, as the intersection of imaged parallel lines; second, by determining the corresponding vanishing point in the left image (from images of the same parallel lines), and mapping this vanishing point to the right image using the infinite homography computed from

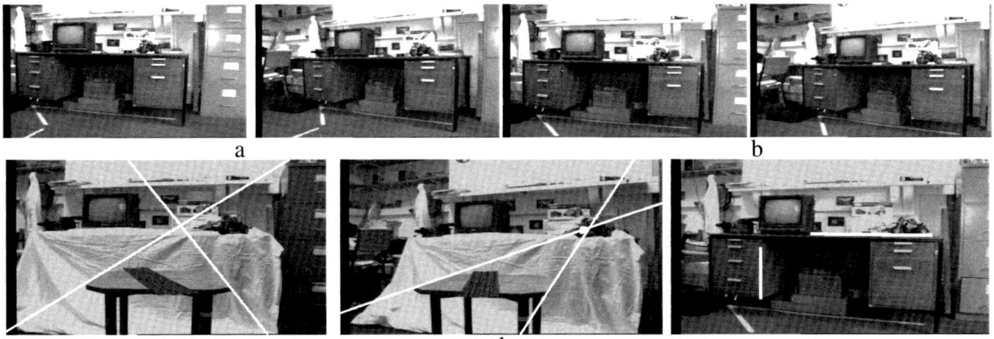

Fig. 19.9. **Auto-calibration of a stereo rig.** *The input stereo pairs before (a) and after (b) the motion of the rig. The stereo rig moves left by about 20 cm, pans by about* 10° *and changes elevation by about* 10°*. The accuracy of the computed* H_∞ *is assessed on another stereo pair acquired by the same rig as follows: In (c), the left image (of a stereo pair), a vanishing point is computed by intersecting the imaged sides of the table (which are parallel in the scene). In (d), the right image (of a stereo pair), the corresponding vanishing point is computed. The white square (near the line intersection) is the vanishing point from the left image mapped to the right using the computed* H_∞*. In the absence of error the points should be identical. (e) Following metric calibration the computed angle between the desk sides (shown in white) from the 3D reconstruction is* 90.7°*, in very good agreement with the veridical value.*

the eigenvector of H_P^T. The discrepancy between the vanishing points is a measure of the accuracy of the computed H_∞. The metric calibration uses the zero skew constraint to resolve the one-parameter ambiguity. Angles in the resulting metric reconstruction are accurate to within 1°. △

19.11 Closure

Research in the area of auto-calibration is still quite active, and better methods than those described in this chapter may yet be developed. There is still a lack of closed form solutions from multiview tensors, and of algorithms to automatically detect critical motion sequences (see below).

Critical motion sequences. It has been seen in this chapter that for certain classes of motion it is not possible to completely determine the rectifying homography H. The resulting reconstruction is then at some level between metric and projective. For example, for constant internal parameters in the case of planar motion there is a one-parameter scaling ambiguity parallel to the rotation axis; and for pure translation under constant internal parameters the reconstruction is affine. Sequences of camera motions for which such ambiguities arise are termed "Critical motion sequences" and have been systematically classified by Sturm [Sturm-97a, Sturm-97b] in the case of constant internal parameters. This classification has been extended to more general calibration constraints, such as varying focal lengths [Pollefeys-99b, Sturm-99b]. For recent work see [Kahl-99, Kahl-01b, Ma-99, Sturm-01].

Recommendations. It may seem that auto-calibration offers a complete solution to metric reconstruction. Calibrated cameras are not necessary and we can do with constraints as weak as the zero-skew constraint on the camera. Unfortunately one must be wary of putting complete trust in auto-calibration. Auto-calibration can work well in the right circumstances, but used recklessly it will fail. Several specific recommendations can be made.

(i) Take care to avoid ambiguous motion sequences. It has been seen that calibration degeneracies occur if the motion is too restricted, such as being about a single axis. The motion should not be too small, or cover too small a field of view. Auto-calibration often comes down to estimating the infinite homography, the effects of which are not apparent on small fields of view.

(ii) Use as much information as you have. Although it is possible to calibrate from minimal information such as zero skew, this should be avoided if other information is available. For instance the known aspect ratio constraint should be used if it is valid, as should the knowledge of the principal point. Even if the values are known only imprecisely, this information can be incorporated into a linear auto-calibration method by including an equation, but with low weight.

(iii) This recommendation relates to bundle adjustment as well. Generally it is best to finish off with a bundle adjustment. In doing this, it is recommended that the internal parameters of the camera not be left to float unbounded. For instance, even if the principal point is not known exactly, it is usually known within some reasonable bounds (it is not close to infinity for instance). Similarly, aspect ratio normally lies between 0.5 and 3. This knowledge should be incorporated in a bundle adjustment by adding further constraints to the cost function, with small weights (standard deviations) if necessary. This can give an enormous improvement in results where auto-calibration is poorly conditioned (and hence unstable) by preventing the solution from wandering off into remote regions of parameter space in quest of a minor and insignificant improvement in the cost function.

(iv) Methods that use restricted motions usually are more reliable than those that allow general motion. For instance the methods that involve a rotating but non-translating camera are generally much more reliable than general motion methods. The same is true of affine reconstruction from a translational motion.

19.11.1 The literature

The idea of auto calibrating a camera originated in Faugeras *et al.* [Faugeras-92a] where the Kruppa equations were used. The early papers considered the case of constant internal parameters. [Hartley-94b] and Mohr *et al.* [Mohr-93] investigated bundle-adjustment like methods for more than two views.

The affine reconstruction solution for the case of pure translation was given by Moons *et al.* [Moons-94], and was extended to a combination of pure translation followed by rotation for a full metric reconstruction by Armstrong *et al.* [Armstrong-94]. The case of auto-calibration for a camera rotating about its centre was given by [Hartley-94a]. The modulus constraint was first published by Pollefeys *et al.* [Pollefeys-96].

The original method for auto-calibration of a stereo rig was given by Zisserman *et al.* [Zisserman-95b], with alternative parametrizations given in Devernay and Faugeras [Devernay-96], and Horaud and Csurka [Horaud-98]. The special case of planar motion of a stereo rig is covered in [Beardsley-95b, Csurka-98]. For planar motion of a monocular camera the original method was published by Armstrong *et al.* [Armstrong-96b], and an alternative numerical solution was given in Faugeras *et al.* [Faugeras-98].

In more recent papers less restrictive constraints than constant internal parameters have been investigated. A number of "existence proofs" have been given: Heyden and Åström [Heyden-97b] showed that metric reconstruction is possible knowing only skew and aspect ratio, and [Pollefeys-98, Heyden-98] showed that skew-zero alone was sufficient.

Triggs [Triggs-97] introduced the absolute (dual) quadric as a numerical device for formulating auto-calibration problems, and applied both linear methods and sequential-quadratic programming to solve for Q^*_∞. Pollefeys *et al.* [Pollefeys-98] showed that computations based on Q^*_∞ could be used to compute metric reconstructions for varying focal length under general motion for real image sequences.

For the case of a rotating camera de Agapito *et al.* [DeAgapito-98] gave a non-linear solution for varying internal parameters based on the use of the DIAC. This was modified in [DeAgapito-99] to an IAC-based linear method.

19.11.2 Notes and exercises

(i) [Hartley-92a] first gave a solution for the extraction of focal lengths from the fundamental matrix, but the algorithm given there is unwieldy. A simple elegant formula is given in [Bougnoux-98]:

$$\alpha^2 = -\frac{\mathbf{p}'^{\mathsf{T}}[\mathbf{e}']_\times \tilde{\mathtt{I}}\mathtt{F}\mathbf{p}\mathbf{p}^{\mathsf{T}}\mathtt{F}^{\mathsf{T}}\mathbf{p}'}{\mathbf{p}'^{\mathsf{T}}[\mathbf{e}']_\times \tilde{\mathtt{I}}\mathtt{F}\tilde{\mathtt{I}}\mathtt{F}^{\mathsf{T}}\mathbf{p}'} \tag{19.35}$$

where $\tilde{\mathtt{I}}$ is the matrix $\text{diag}(1, 1, 0)$ and $\mathbf{p}$ and $\mathbf{p}'$ are the principal points in the two images. Unit aspect ratio and zero skew are assumed. The formula for α'^2 is given by reversing the roles of the two images (and transposing $\mathtt{F}$).

Note that the final step of the algorithm is to take a square root. It is assured that α^2 and α'^2 as computed by (19.35) are positive, *given good data and a good guess of the principal point.* However in practice this does not always pertain, and negative values can result. This is the same problem as mentioned previously in section 19.3.5(*p*468). In addition, as flagged in [Newsam-96], the method has an intrinsic degeneracy when the principal rays of the two cameras meet in space, in which case it is impossible to compute the focal lengths independently. This occurs when both cameras are trained on the same point, quite a common occurrence.

A further degeneracy occurs when the plane defined by the baseline and the principal ray of one camera is perpendicular to the plane defined by the baseline and principal ray of the other camera. Generally speaking, our opinion is that this method is of doubtful value as a means of computing focal lengths.

(ii) Show that if the internal parameters are constant then the constraints on $\mathtt{Q}^*_\infty$ obtained from two views (19.6–*p*462) are equivalent to the Kruppa equations (19.18–*p*471). Hint, from (9.10–*p*256) the cameras may be chosen as $\mathtt{P}^1 = [\mathtt{I} \mid \mathbf{0}]$, $\mathtt{P}^2 = [[\mathbf{e}']_\times \mathtt{F} \mid \mathbf{e}']$.

(iii) Show from (19.21–*p*473) that in the case of a camera translating with constant internal parameters and without rotating, then the plane at infinity may be computed directly from a projective reconstruction.

(iv) The infinite homography relation (19.24–*p*476) may be derived in two lines simply from the definition $\mathtt{H}^{ij}_\infty = \mathtt{K}^i \mathtt{R}^{ij} (\mathtt{K}^j)^{-1}$, in section 13.4(*p*338). This may be rearranged as $\mathtt{H}^{ij}_\infty \mathtt{K}^j = \mathtt{K}^i \mathtt{R}^{ij}$. Eliminating the rotation using orthogonality as $\mathtt{R}^{ij}\mathtt{R}^{ij\mathsf{T}} = \mathtt{I}$ gives $\mathtt{H}^{ij}_\infty (\mathtt{K}^j \mathtt{K}^{j\mathsf{T}}) \mathtt{H}^{ij\,\mathsf{T}}_\infty = (\mathtt{K}^i \mathtt{K}^{i\mathsf{T}})$.

(v) Under $\mathtt{H}_\mathrm{E}$, points on $\boldsymbol{\pi}_\infty$ (i.e. with $\mathrm{X}_4 = 0$) are mapped to points on $\boldsymbol{\pi}_\infty$ by the 3×3 homography $\mathbf{x}_\infty \mapsto \mathtt{R}\mathbf{x}_\infty$. Under this point transformation a conic on $\boldsymbol{\pi}_\infty$ maps according to result 2.13(*p*37) $\mathtt{C} \mapsto \mathtt{R}^{-\mathsf{T}}\mathtt{C}\mathtt{R}^{-1} = \mathtt{R}\mathtt{C}\mathtt{R}^\mathsf{T}$. The absolute conic Ω_∞ is fixed since $\mathtt{R}\mathtt{I}\mathtt{R}^\mathsf{T} = \mathtt{I}$. Now, denote by $\mathbf{a}$ the direction of the rotation axis, so that $\mathtt{R}\mathbf{a} = 1\mathbf{a}$. The (degenerate) point conic $\mathbf{a}\mathbf{a}^\mathsf{T}$ is also fixed. It follows that there is a pencil of fixed conics $\mathtt{C}_\infty(\mu) = \mathtt{I} + \mu\mathbf{a}\mathbf{a}^\mathsf{T}$ under the mapping since

$$\begin{aligned} \mathtt{R}(\Omega_\infty + \mu\mathbf{a}\mathbf{a}^\mathsf{T})\mathtt{R}^\mathsf{T} &= \mathtt{R}\mathtt{I}\mathtt{R}^\mathsf{T} + \mu\mathtt{R}\mathbf{a}\mathbf{a}^\mathsf{T}\mathtt{R}^\mathsf{T} \\ &= \Omega_\infty + \mu\mathbf{a}\mathbf{a}^\mathsf{T}. \end{aligned}$$

The scalar μ parametrizes the pencil. This shows that under a particular similarity there is a one-parameter family of fixed conics on $\boldsymbol{\pi}_\infty$. However, it is the case that Ω_∞ is the only conic fixed under any similarity.

(vi) A further calibration ambiguity exists for a common type of robot head, namely a pan-tilt (or alt-azimuth) head. In [DeAgapito-99] it was shown that since the camera may rotate about its X or Y axes its set of orientations form only a 2-parameter family, rather than a 3-parameter family of general rotations. This limitation causes an ambiguity in the aspect ratio α_x of the camera, and consequently of x_0 as well.

(vii) The method of auto-calibration from planes is generally non-linear. However, for special motions linear constraints on $\boldsymbol{\omega}$ can be obtained. Suppose we have two images of a plane that induces a planar homography $\mathtt{H}$ between views, and imagine that the motion of the camera relative to the plane is a general screw motion but with the screw axis parallel to the plane normal.

Consider the action of this screw motion on the plane. Since this action (a rotation about the plane's normal and a translation) does not change the plane's orientation, its line of intersection with the plane at infinity is unchanged (as a set). The absolute conic is fixed (as a set) under Euclidean motion. Consequently, the plane's intersection with the absolute conic, which defines the circular points for the plane, is also unchanged under the motion.

Consider now applying the action to the camera viewing the plane. Since the two circular points are fixed (as 3-space points) they have the same image before and after the motion. As the homography H maps points on the plane between images, the imaged circular points must correspond to two of its fixed points (see section 2.9(*p*61)) and can thus be determined directly from the homography. Each circular points places a linear constraint on ω. Further details of this method are given in [Knight-03].

20

Duality

It has been known since the work of Carlsson [Carlsson-95] and Weinshall *et al.* [Weinshall-95] that there is a dualization principle that allows one to interchange the role of points being viewed by several cameras and the camera centres themselves. In principle this implies the possibility of dualizing projective reconstruction algorithms to obtain new algorithms. In this chapter, this theme is developed to outline an explicit method for dualizing any projective reconstruction algorithm. At the practical implementation level, however, it is shown that there are difficulties which need to be overcome in order to allow application of this dualization method to produce working algorithms.

20.1 Carlsson–Weinshall duality

Let $\mathbf{E}_1 = (1,0,0,0)^\mathsf{T}$, $\mathbf{E}_2 = (0,1,0,0)^\mathsf{T}$, $\mathbf{E}_3 = (0,0,1,0)^\mathsf{T}$ and $\mathbf{E}_4 = (0,0,0,1)^\mathsf{T}$ form part of a projective basis for $\mathbb{P}^3$. Similarly, let $\mathbf{e}_1 = (1,0,0)^\mathsf{T}$, $\mathbf{e}_2 = (0,1,0)^\mathsf{T}$, $\mathbf{e}_3 = (0,0,1)^\mathsf{T}$ and $\mathbf{e}_4 = (1,1,1)^\mathsf{T}$ be a projective basis for the projective image plane $\mathbb{P}^2$.

Now, consider a camera with matrix $\mathtt{P}$. We assume that the camera centre $\mathbf{C}$ does not sit on any of the axial planes, that is none of the four coordinates of $\mathbf{C}$ is zero. In this case, no three of the points $\mathtt{P}\mathbf{E}_i$ for $i = 1, \ldots, 4$ are collinear in the image. Consequently, one may apply a projective transformation $\mathtt{H}$ to the image so that $\mathbf{e}_i = \mathtt{HP}\mathbf{E}_i$. We assume that this has been done, and henceforth denote $\mathtt{HP}$ simply by $\mathtt{P}$. Since $\mathtt{P}\mathbf{E}_i = \mathbf{e}_i$, the form of the matrix $\mathtt{P}$ is

$$\mathtt{P} = \begin{bmatrix} a & & & d \\ & b & & d \\ & & c & d \end{bmatrix}.$$

Definition 20.1. A camera matrix $\mathtt{P}$ is called a *reduced* camera matrix if it maps $\mathbf{E}_i$ to $\mathbf{e}_i$ for each $i = 1, \ldots, 4$. In other words $\mathbf{e}_i = \mathtt{P}\mathbf{E}_i$.

Now, for any point $\mathbf{X} = (\mathrm{X}, \mathrm{Y}, \mathrm{Z}, \mathrm{T})^\mathsf{T}$ one verifies that

$$\mathtt{P} = \begin{bmatrix} a & & & d \\ & b & & d \\ & & c & d \end{bmatrix} \begin{pmatrix} \mathrm{X} \\ \mathrm{Y} \\ \mathrm{Z} \\ \mathrm{T} \end{pmatrix} = \begin{pmatrix} a\mathrm{X} + d\mathrm{T} \\ b\mathrm{Y} + d\mathrm{T} \\ c\mathrm{Z} + d\mathrm{T} \end{pmatrix}. \tag{20.1}$$

Notice the symmetry in this equation between the entries of the camera matrix and the coordinates of the point. They may be interchanged as follows

$$\begin{bmatrix} a & & & d \\ & b & & d \\ & & c & d \end{bmatrix} \begin{pmatrix} \mathrm{X} \\ \mathrm{Y} \\ \mathrm{Z} \\ \mathrm{T} \end{pmatrix} = \begin{bmatrix} \mathrm{X} & & & \mathrm{T} \\ & \mathrm{Y} & & \mathrm{T} \\ & & \mathrm{Z} & \mathrm{T} \end{bmatrix} \begin{pmatrix} a \\ b \\ c \\ d \end{pmatrix}. \tag{20.2}$$

The interchange of the roles of cameras and points may be interpreted as a form of duality, which will be referred to as Carlsson–Weinshall duality, or more briefly Carlsson duality. The consequences of this duality will be explored in the rest of this chapter.

20.1.1 Dual algorithms

First of all, we will use it for deriving a dual algorithm from a given projective reconstruction algorithm. Specifically, it will be shown that if one has an algorithm for doing projective reconstruction from n views of $m + 4$ points, then there is an algorithm for doing projective reconstruction from m views of $n + 4$ points. This result, observed by Carlsson [Carlsson-95], will be made specific by explicitly describing the steps of the dual algorithm.

We consider a projective reconstruction problem, which will be referred to as $\mathcal{P}(m, n)$. It is the problem of doing reconstruction from m views of n points. We denote image points by $\mathbf{x}^i_j$, which represents the image of the j-th object space point in the i-th view. Thus, the upper index indicates the view number, and the lower index represents the point number. Such a set of points $\{\mathbf{x}^i_j\}$ is called *realizable* if there are a set of camera matrices $\mathtt{P}^i$ and a set of 3D points $\mathbf{X}_j$ such that $\mathbf{x}^i_j = \mathtt{P}^i\mathbf{X}_j$. The projective reconstruction problem $\mathcal{P}(m, n)$ is that of finding such camera matrices $\mathtt{P}^i$ and points $\mathbf{X}_j$ given a realizable set $\{\mathbf{x}^i_j\}$ for m views of n points. The set of camera matrices and 3D points together are called a *realization* (or *projective realization*) of the set of point correspondences.

Let $\mathcal{A}(n, m + 4)$ represent an algorithm for solving the projective reconstruction problem $\mathcal{P}(n, m + 4)$. An algorithm will now be exhibited for solving the projective reconstruction $\mathcal{P}(m, n + 4)$. This algorithm will be denoted $\mathcal{A}^*(m, n + 4)$, the dual of the algorithm $\mathcal{A}(n, m + 4)$.

Initially, the steps of the algorithm will be given without proof. In addition, difficulties will be glossed over so as to give the general idea without getting bogged down in details. In the description of this algorithm it is important to keep track of the range of the indices, and whether they index the cameras or the points. Thus, the following may help to keep track.

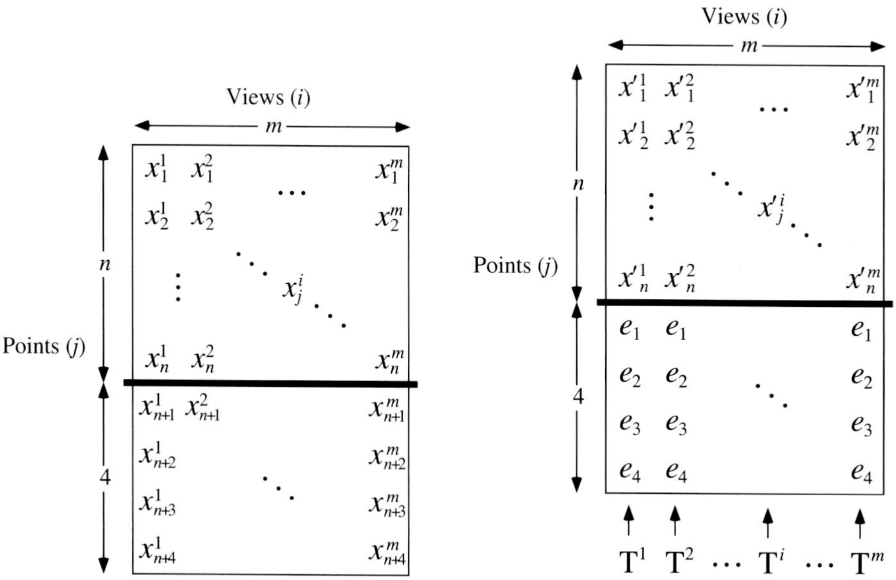

Fig. 20.1. **Left:** *Input to algorithm* $\mathcal{A}^*(m, n+4)$. **Right:** *Input data after transformation.*

- Upper indices represent the view number.
- Lower indices represent the point number.
- i ranges from 1 to m.
- j ranges from 1 to n.
- k ranges from 1 to 4.

The dual algorithm

Given an algorithm $\mathcal{A}(n, m+4)$ the goal is to exhibit a dual algorithm $\mathcal{A}^*(m, n+4)$.

Input:

The input to the algorithm $\mathcal{A}^*(m, n+4)$ consists of a realizable set of $n+4$ points seen in m views. This set of points can be arranged in a table as in figure 20.1(left).

In this table, the points $\mathbf{x}_{n+k}^i$ are separated from the other points $\mathbf{x}_j^i$, since they will receive special treatment.

Step 1: Transform

The first step is to compute, for each i, a transformation $\mathtt{T}^i$ that maps the points $\mathbf{x}_{n+k}^i$, $k = 1, \ldots, 4$ in the i-th view to the points $\mathbf{e}_k$ of a canonical basis for projective 2-space $\mathbb{P}^2$. The transformation $\mathtt{T}^i$ is applied also to each of the points $\mathbf{x}_j^i$ to produce transformed points $\mathbf{x}_j'^i = \mathtt{T}^i\mathbf{x}_j^i$. The result is the transformed point array shown in figure 20.1(right). A different transformation $\mathtt{T}^i$ is computed and applied to each column of the array, as indicated.

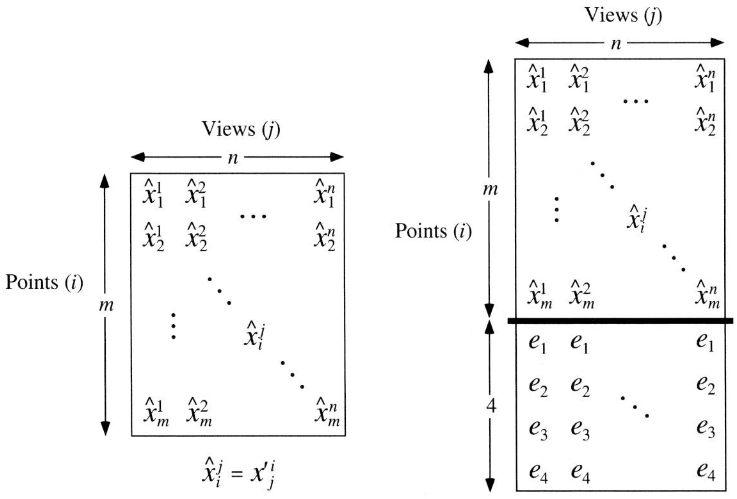

Fig. 20.2. **Left:** *Transposed data.* **Right:** *Transposed data extended by addition of extra points.*

Step 2: Transpose

The last four rows of the array are dropped, and the remaining block of the array is transposed. One defines $\hat{\mathbf{x}}_i^j = \mathbf{x}_j^{\prime i}$. At the same time, one does a mental switch of points and views. Thus the point $\hat{\mathbf{x}}_i^j$ is now conceived as being the image of the i-th point in the j-th view, whereas the point $\mathbf{x}_j^{\prime i}$ was the image of the j-th point in the i-th view. What is happening here effectively is that the roles of points and cameras are being swapped – the basic concept behind Carlsson duality expressed by (20.2). The resulting transposed array is shown in figure 20.2(left).

Step 3: Extend

The array of points is now extended by the addition of four extra rows containing points $\mathbf{e}_k$ in all positions of the $(m+k)$-th row of the array, as shown in figure 20.2(right). The purpose of this extension will be explained in section 20.1.2.

Step 4: Solve

The array of points resulting from the last step has $m+4$ rows and n columns, and may be regarded as the positions of $m+4$ points seen in n views. As such, it is a candidate for solution by the algorithm $\mathcal{A}(n, m+4)$, which we have assumed is given. Essential here is that the points in the array form a realizable set of point correspondences. Justification of this is deferred for now. The result of the algorithm $\mathcal{A}(n, m+4)$ is a set of cameras $\hat{\mathtt{P}}^j$ and points $\widehat{\mathbf{X}}_i$ such that $\hat{\mathbf{x}}_i^j = \hat{\mathtt{P}}^j \widehat{\mathbf{X}}_i$. In addition, corresponding to the last four rows of the array, there are points $\widehat{\mathbf{X}}_{m+k}$ such that $\mathbf{e}_k = \hat{\mathtt{P}}^j \widehat{\mathbf{X}}_{m+k}$ for all j.

Step 5: 3D transformation

Since the reconstruction obtained in the last step is a projective reconstruction, one may transform it (equivalently, choose a projective coordinate frame) such that the points

$\widehat{\mathbf{X}}_{m+k}$ are the four points $\mathbf{E}_k$ of a partial canonical basis for $\mathbb{P}^3$. The only requirement is that the points $\widehat{\mathbf{X}}_{m+k}$ obtained in the projective reconstruction are not coplanar. This assumption is validated later.

At this point, one sees that $\mathbf{e}_k = \hat{\mathtt{P}}^j \widehat{\mathbf{X}}_{m+k} = \hat{\mathtt{P}}^j \mathbf{E}_k$. From this it follows that $\hat{\mathtt{P}}^j$ has the special form

$$\hat{\mathtt{P}}^j = \begin{bmatrix} a^j & & & d^j \\ & b^j & & d^j \\ & & c^j & d^j \end{bmatrix} . \tag{20.3}$$

Step 6: Dualize

Let $\widehat{\mathbf{X}}_i = (\mathrm{X}_i, \mathrm{Y}_i, \mathrm{Z}_i, \mathrm{T}_i)^\mathsf{T}$, and $\hat{\mathtt{P}}^j$ be as given in (20.3). Now define points $\mathbf{X}_j = (a^j, b^j, c^j, d^j)^\mathsf{T}$ and cameras

$$\mathtt{P}'^i = \begin{bmatrix} \mathrm{X}_i & & & \mathrm{T}_i \\ & \mathrm{Y}_i & & \mathrm{T}_i \\ & & \mathrm{Z}_i & \mathrm{T}_i \end{bmatrix} .$$

Then one verifies that

$$\begin{aligned} \mathtt{P}'^i \mathbf{X}_j &= (\mathrm{X}_i a^j + \mathrm{T}_i d^j, \mathrm{Y}_i b^j + \mathrm{T}_i d^j, \mathrm{Z}_i c^j + \mathrm{T}_i d^j)^\mathsf{T} \\ &= \hat{\mathtt{P}}^j \widehat{\mathbf{X}}_i \\ &= \hat{\mathbf{x}}_i^j \\ &= \mathbf{x}'^i_j . \end{aligned}$$

If, in addition, one defines $\mathbf{X}_{n+k} = \mathbf{E}_k$ for $k = 1, \ldots, 4$, then $\mathtt{P}'^i \mathbf{X}_{n+k} = \mathbf{e}_k$. It is then evident that the cameras $\mathtt{P}'^i$ and points $\mathbf{X}_j$ and $\mathbf{X}_{n+k}$ form a projective realization of the transformed data array obtained in step 1 of this algorithm.

Step 7: Reverse transformation

Finally, defining $\mathtt{P}^i = (\mathtt{T}^i)^{-1}\mathtt{P}'^i$, and with the points $\mathbf{X}_j$ and $\mathbf{X}_{n+k}$ obtained in the previous step, one has a projective realization of the original data. Indeed, one verifies

$$\mathtt{P}^i \mathbf{X}_j = (\mathtt{T}^i)^{-1}\mathtt{P}'^i \mathbf{X}_j = (\mathtt{T}^i)^{-1} \mathbf{x}'^i_j = \mathbf{x}^i_j .$$

This completes the description of the algorithm. One can see that it takes place in various stages.

(i) In step 1, the data is transformed into canonical image reference frames based on the selection of four distinguished points.
(ii) In steps 2 and 3 the problem is mapped into the dual domain, resulting in a dual problem $\mathcal{P}(n, m+4)$.
(iii) The dual problem is solved in steps 4 and 5.
(iv) Step 6 maps the solution back into the original domain.
(v) Step 7 undoes the effects of the initial transformation.

20.1.2 Justification of the algorithm

To justify this algorithm, one needs to be sure that at step 4 there indeed exists a solution to the transformed problem. Before considering this, it is necessary to explain the purpose of step 3, which extends the data by the addition of rows of image points $\mathbf{e}_k$, and step 5, which transforms the arbitrary projective solution to one in which four points are equal to the 3D basis points $\mathbf{E}_k$.

The purpose of these steps is to ensure that one obtains a solution to the dual reconstruction problem in which $\hat{\mathtt{P}}^j$ has the special form given by (20.3) in which the camera matrix is parametrized by only 4 values. The dual algorithm is described in this manner so that it will work with any algorithm $\mathcal{A}(n, m + 4)$ whatever. However, both steps 3 and 5 may be eliminated if the known algorithm $\mathcal{A}(n, m+4)$ has the capability of enforcing this constraint on the camera matrices directly. Algorithms based on the fundamental matrix, trifocal or quadrifocal tensors may easily be modified in this way, as will be seen.

In the mean time, since $\hat{\mathtt{P}}^j$ of the form (20.3) is called a *reduced camera matrix*, we call any reconstruction of a set of image correspondences in which each camera matrix is of this form a *reduced reconstruction*. Not all sets of realizable point correspondences allow a reduced realization, however. The following result characterizes sets of point correspondences that do have this property.

Result 20.2. *A set of image points* $\{\mathbf{x}_j^i \;:\; i = 1, \ldots, m\;;\; j = 1, \ldots, n\}$ *admits a reduced realization if and only if it may be augmented with supplementary correspondences* $\mathbf{x}_{n+k}^i = \mathbf{e}_k$ *for* $k = 1, \ldots, 4$ *such that*

(i) *The total set of image correspondences is realizable, and*
(ii) *The reconstructed points* $\mathbf{X}_{n+k}$ *corresponding to the supplementary image correspondences are non-coplanar.*

Proof. The proof is straightforward enough. Suppose the set permits a reduced realization, and let $\mathtt{P}^i$ be the set of reduced camera matrices. Let points $\mathbf{X}_{n+k} = \mathbf{E}_k$ for $k = 1, \ldots, 4$ be projected into the m images. The projections are $\mathbf{x}_{n+k}^i = \mathtt{P}^i\mathbf{X}_{n+k} = \mathtt{P}^i\mathbf{E}_k = \mathbf{e}_k$ for all i.
Conversely, suppose the augmented set of points is realizable and the points $\mathbf{X}_{n+k}$ are non-coplanar. In this case, a projective basis may be chosen such that $\mathbf{X}_{n+k} = \mathbf{E}_k$. Then for each view, one has $\mathbf{e}_k = \mathtt{P}^i\mathbf{E}_k$ for all k. From this it follows that each $\mathtt{P}^i$ has the desired form (20.3). □

One other remark must be made before proving the correctness of the algorithm.

Result 20.3. *If a set of image points* $\{\mathbf{x}_j^i \;:\; i = 1, \ldots, m\;;\; j = 1, \ldots, n\}$ *permits a reduced realization then so does the transposed set* $\{\hat{\mathbf{x}}_i^j \;:\; j = 1, \ldots, n\;;\; i = 1, \ldots, m\}$ *where* $\hat{\mathbf{x}}_i^j = \mathbf{x}_j^i$ *for all* i *and* j.

This is the basic duality property, effectively proved by the construction given in step 6 of the algorithm above. Now it is possible to prove the correctness of the algorithm.

Result 20.4. *Let $\mathbf{x}_j^i$ and $\mathbf{x}_{n+k}^i$ as in figure 20.1(left) be a set of realizable image point correspondences, and suppose*

(i) *for each i, the four points $\mathbf{x}_{n+k}^i$ do not include three collinear points.*
(ii) *the four points $\mathbf{X}_{n+k}$ in a projective reconstruction are non-coplanar.*

Then the algorithm of section 20.1.1 will succeed.

Proof. Because of the first condition, transformations $\mathtt{T}^i$ exist for each i, transforming the input data to the form shown in figure 20.1(right). This transformed data is also realizable, since the transformed data differs only by a projective transformation of the image.
Now, according to result 20.2 applied to figure 20.1(right), the correspondences $\mathbf{x}_j'^i$ admit a reduced realization. By result 20.3 the transposed data figure 20.2(left) also admits a reduced realization. Applying result 20.2 once more shows that the extended data figure 20.2(right) is realizable. Furthermore, the points $\widehat{\mathbf{X}}_{m+k}$ are non-coplanar, and so step 5 is valid. The subsequent steps 6 and 7 go forward without problems. □

The first condition may be checked from the image correspondences $\mathbf{x}_j^i$. It may be thought that to check the second condition requires reconstruction to be carried out. It is, however, possible to check whether the reconstructed points will be coplanar without carrying out the reconstruction. This is left as an exercise for the reader (page 342).

20.2 Reduced reconstruction

In this section, we concentrate on and reevaluate steps 3 – 5 of the algorithm described in the preceding section. To recapitulate, the purpose of these steps is to obtain a reduced reconstruction from a set of image correspondences. Thus, the input is a set of image correspondences $\hat{\mathbf{x}}_i^j$ admitting a reduced realization (see figure 20.2(left)). The output is a set of *reduced* camera matrices $\hat{\mathtt{P}}^j$ and points $\widehat{\mathbf{X}}_i$ such that $\hat{\mathtt{P}}^j\widehat{\mathbf{X}}_i = \hat{\mathbf{x}}_i^j$ for all i, j.

As we have seen, one way to do this (as in steps 3 – 5) of the given algorithm is to augment the points by the addition of four extra synthetic point correspondences $\hat{\mathbf{x}}_{m+k}^j$, carrying out projective reconstruction, and then applying a 3D homography so that the 3D points $\widehat{\mathbf{X}}_{m+k}$ are mapped to the points $\mathbf{E}_k$ of a projective basis for $\mathbb{P}^3$. The problem with this is that in the presence of noise, the projective reconstruction is not exact. Thus, the camera matrices obtained by this method will map points $\mathbf{E}_k$ to points close to, but not identical with $\mathbf{e}_k$. This means that the camera matrices are not exactly in reduced form. Therefore, we now consider methods of computing a realization of the point correspondences in which the cameras are exactly reduced.

20.2.1 The reduced fundamental matrix

The most evident applications of these dual methods are to dualize the reconstruction algorithms involving the fundamental matrix and trifocal tensor. These will lead to reconstruction algorithms for 6 or 7 points (respectively) across N views. In this section, we consider reconstruction from 6 points. The dual of a reconstruction problem

$\mathcal{P}(N, 6)$ is a problem $\mathcal{P}(2, N+4)$, namely reconstruction from $N+4$ points in 2 views. The method of chapter 10 involving the fundamental matrix is a standard way of solving such a problem.

To this end we define a reduced fundamental matrix:

Definition 20.5. A fundamental matrix $\hat{\mathtt{F}}$ is called a *reduced* fundamental matrix if it satisfies the condition $\mathbf{e}_i^{\mathsf{T}}\hat{\mathtt{F}}\mathbf{e}_i = 0$ for $i = 1, \ldots, 4$.

It is evident that since a reduced fundamental matrix already satisfies constraints derived from four point correspondences, it may be computed from a small number of additional points, in fact linearly from four points, or non-linearly from three points.

20.2.2 Computation of the reduced fundamental matrix

For a reduced fundamental matrix, the condition $\mathbf{e}_i^{\mathsf{T}}\hat{\mathtt{F}}\mathbf{e}_i = 0$ for $i = 1, \ldots, 3$ implies that the diagonal entries of $\hat{\mathtt{F}}$ are zero. The requirement that $(1,1,1)\hat{\mathtt{F}}(1,1,1)^{\mathsf{T}} = 0$ gives the additional condition that the sum of entries of $\hat{\mathtt{F}}$ is zero. Thus one may write $\hat{\mathtt{F}}$ in the form

$$\hat{\mathtt{F}} = \begin{bmatrix} 0 & p & q \\ r & 0 & s \\ t & -(p+q+r+s+t) & 0 \end{bmatrix} \tag{20.4}$$

thereby parametrizing a fundamental matrix satisfying all the linear constraints (though not the condition $\det \hat{\mathtt{F}} = 0$). Now, a further point correspondence $\mathbf{x} \leftrightarrow \mathbf{x}'$ satisfying $\mathbf{x}'^{\mathsf{T}}\hat{\mathtt{F}}\mathbf{x} = 0$ is easily seen to provide a linear equation in the parameters $p, \ldots, t$ of $\hat{\mathtt{F}}$. Given at least four such correspondences, one may solve for these parameters, up to an inconsequential scale. Given only three such correspondences, the extra constraint $\det \hat{\mathtt{F}} = 0$ may be used to provide the extra constraint necessary to determine $\hat{\mathtt{F}}$. There may be one or three solutions. This computation is analogous to the method used in section 11.1.2(*p*281) to compute the fundamental matrix from seven point correspondences. With four correspondences $\mathbf{x}_i \leftrightarrow \mathbf{x}'_i$ or more, one finds a least-squares solution.

20.2.3 Retrieving reduced camera matrices

Computing a pair of reduced camera matrices that correspond to a reduced fundamental matrix is surprisingly tricky. One can not assume that the first camera is $[\mathtt{I} \mid \mathbf{0}]$ as in the usual projective camera case, since this is non-generic, the camera centre corresponding with the basis point $\mathbf{E}_4 = (0,0,0,1)^{\mathsf{T}}$. However, we may instead assume that the pair of cameras are of the form

$$\mathtt{P} = \begin{bmatrix} 1 & & & 1 \\ & 1 & & 1 \\ & & 1 & 1 \end{bmatrix} \text{ and } \mathtt{P}' = \begin{bmatrix} a & & & d \\ & b & & d \\ & & c & d \end{bmatrix} \tag{20.5}$$

since the centre of the first camera is $(1,1,1,1)^{\mathsf{T}}$ which is a generic point with respect to the basis points $\mathbf{E}_1, \ldots, \mathbf{E}_4$. Further, if $d \neq 0$, then we may assume that $d = 1$, but we prefer not to do this.

The reduced fundamental matrix corresponding to this pair of cameras is

$$\hat{\mathrm{F}} = \begin{bmatrix} 0 & b(d-c) & -c(d-b) \\ -a(d-c) & 0 & c(d-a) \\ a(d-b) & -b(d-a) & 0 \end{bmatrix} \tag{20.6}$$

which the reader may verify satisfies the four linear constraints as well as the zero-determinant condition. The task at hand is to retrieve the values of (a, b, c, d) given the fundamental matrix. This seemingly requires a solution of simultaneous quadratic equations, but there is a linear method as follows.

(i) The ratio $a : b : c$ may be found by solving the set of homogeneous linear equations

$$\begin{bmatrix} f_{12} & f_{21} & 0 \\ f_{13} & 0 & f_{31} \\ 0 & f_{23} & f_{32} \end{bmatrix} \begin{pmatrix} a \\ b \\ c \end{pmatrix} = \mathbf{0} \tag{20.7}$$

where f_{ij} is the ij-th entry of $\hat{\mathrm{F}}$. The matrix appearing here clearly has the same rank as $\hat{\mathrm{F}}$ (namely 2), so there is a unique solution (up to scale) to this equation set. The solution $a : b : c = A : B : C$ provides a set of homogeneous equations in a, b and c, namely $Ba = Ab$, $Ca = Ac$ and $Cb = Bc$, of which two are linearly independent.

(ii) Similarly, one may find the ratio $d - a : d - b : d - c$ by solving $(d - a, d - b, d - c)\hat{\mathrm{F}} = \mathbf{0}$. Once again, the solution is unique. This provides two more linear equations in the values of a, b, c, d.

(iii) From the set of equations one may solve for (a, b, c, d) up to scale, and hence reconstruct the second camera matrix according to (20.5).

20.2.4 Solving for six points in three views

The minimal case involving the computation of the reduced fundamental matrix involves three point, in which case there may be three solutions. By dualization, this leads to a solution to the reconstruction problem for six points in three views. Its use in outlier detection using the trifocal tensor has been described in algorithm 16.4(p401). Because of its intrinsic interest as a minimum-case solution, and because of its practical use, the algorithm is given explicitly as algorithm 20.1. The algorithm consists essentially of putting together what has been described previously. However there are a few minor variations.

In algorithm 20.1, the final estimation of the camera matrices takes place in the domain of the original point measurements. As an alternative, one could apply a DLT algorithm in the dual domain, as in the basic algorithm of section 20.1.1. However, the present method seems simpler. It has the advantage of avoiding the need for applying the inverse transformations $\mathrm{T}, \mathrm{T}', \mathrm{T}''$. More significantly the final computation of the camera matrices is carried out using the original data. This is important, because the transformations can severely skew the noise characteristics of the data.

The basis for this algorithm and the n-view case to follow is the dual fundamental

Objective Given a set of six point correspondences $\mathbf{x}_j \leftrightarrow \mathbf{x}'_j \leftrightarrow \mathbf{x}''_j$ across three views, compute a reconstruction from these points, consisting of the three camera matrices $\mathtt{P}$, $\mathtt{P}'$ and $\mathtt{P}''$ and the six 3D points $\mathbf{X}_1, \ldots, \mathbf{X}_6$.

Algorithm

(i) Select a set of four points no three of which are collinear in any of the three views. Let these be the correspondences $\mathbf{x}_{2+k} \leftrightarrow \mathbf{x}'_{2+k} \leftrightarrow \mathbf{x}''_{2+k}$ for $k = 1, \ldots, 4$.

(ii) For the first view, find a projective transformation $\mathtt{T}$ that maps each $\mathbf{x}_{2+k}$ to $\mathbf{e}_k$. Apply $\mathtt{T}$ to the other two points $\mathbf{x}_1$ and $\mathbf{x}_2$ resulting in points $\hat{\mathbf{x}}_1 = \mathtt{T}\mathbf{x}_1$ and $\hat{\mathbf{x}}_2 = \mathtt{T}\mathbf{x}_2$.

(iii) From the *dual correspondence* $\hat{\mathbf{x}}_1 \leftrightarrow \hat{\mathbf{x}}_2$ derive an equation in the entries p, q, r, s, t of the reduced fundamental matrix $\hat{\mathtt{F}}$ as in (20.4). The equation is derived from the relationship $\hat{\mathbf{x}}_2^{\mathsf{T}} \hat{\mathtt{F}} \hat{\mathbf{x}}_1 = 0$.

(iv) In the same way as in the last two steps, form two more equations from the points in the other two views. This results in a set of three homogeneous equations in five unknowns. There will be a two-parameter family of solutions for the reduced fundamental matrix, generated by two independent solutions $\hat{\mathtt{F}}_1$ and $\hat{\mathtt{F}}_2$.

(v) The general solution is $\hat{\mathtt{F}} = \lambda \hat{\mathtt{F}}_1 + \mu \hat{\mathtt{F}}_2$. From the requirement $\det \hat{\mathtt{F}} = 0$ one derives a homogeneous cubic equation in (λ, μ), which one may solve to find (λ, μ), and hence $\hat{\mathtt{F}}$. There will be 1 or 3 real solutions. Further steps are applied to each solution in turn.

(vi) Use the method of section 20.2.3 to extract the parameters $(a, b, c, d)^{\mathsf{T}}$ of the second reduced camera matrix $\hat{\mathtt{P}}'$ defined in (20.5).

(vii) We complete the reconstruction in the original measurement domain. The dual of camera $\hat{\mathtt{P}}'$ defined by (a, b, c, d) is the point $\mathbf{X}_2 = (a, b, c, d)^{\mathsf{T}}$. Thus the six 3D points are $\mathbf{X}_1 = (1, 1, 1, 1)^{\mathsf{T}}$, $\mathbf{X}_2 = (a, b, c, d)^{\mathsf{T}}$ and $\mathbf{X}_{2+k} = \mathbf{E}_k$ for $k = 1, \ldots, 4$. This gives the structure of the reconstructed scene. One may then compute the three camera matrices using the DLT algorithm for camera calibration described in section 7.1(p178). Since we require the camera matrices defined with respect to the original camera coordinates here, we use the original coordinates to solve for $\mathtt{P}$, $\mathtt{P}'$ and $\mathtt{P}''$ such that $\mathtt{P}\mathbf{X}_j = \mathbf{x}_j$, *etc.* Since the solution will be exact, the DLT solution will be sufficient.

Algorithm 20.1. *Algorithm for computing a projective reconstruction from six points in three views.*

matrix, $\hat{\mathtt{F}}$. Note how the dual fundamental matrix expresses a relationship between points in the same image. Indeed the equations used to solve for $\hat{\mathtt{F}}$ are constructed from points in the same image. This contrasts with the standard fundamental matrix where the relationships being encoded are between points seen in separate images.

20.2.5 Six points in n views

The method for six points in three views can be applied with little modification to the case of six points in many views. The main difference is that the reduced fundamental matrix $\hat{\mathtt{F}}$ will be uniquely determined by the data. Specifically at step 4 of the algorithm of section 20.2.4, each view will contribute one equation. With four views or more, this will be sufficient to determine $\hat{\mathtt{F}}$.

In this redundant-data case, one must be careful with the effects of noise. For this reason, it appears preferable to carry out the last step of the algorithm, as shown, with original untransformed points. This mitigates the effect of noise distortion that would result from working with transformed points.

20.2.6 Seven points in n views

The problem of seven points in n views is dual to the case of three views of $n+4$ points and is solved by computing the reduced trifocal tensor from n point correspondences.

Definition 20.6. A trifocal tensor $\mathcal{T}$ is called a *reduced trifocal tensor* if it satisfies the linear constraints imposed by synthetic point correspondences $\mathbf{e}_k \leftrightarrow \mathbf{e}'_k \leftrightarrow \mathbf{e}''_k$ for $i = 1, \ldots, 4$.

The general method for reconstruction from 7 points is similar to the method for six points in n views, except that the reduced trifocal tensor is used instead of the reduced fundamental matrix. There are, however some minor differences.

In computing the reduced trifocal tensor, the constraints corresponding to the synthetic correspondences $\mathbf{e}_j \leftrightarrow \mathbf{e}_j \leftrightarrow \mathbf{e}_j$ should be satisfied exactly, whereas the other correspondences used to compute the tensor are subject to noise, and will only be satisfied approximately. Otherwise the computed tensor will not be exactly in reduced form. In the case of the reduced fundamental matrix this was handled by giving a specific parametrization of the reduced fundamental matrix. That is, it was parametrized in such a way that the constraints generated by the synthetic correspondences were automatically satisfied (see (20.4)). In the case of the trifocal tensor, it is not obvious that such a convenient parametrization is possible. The synthetic constraints are of the form

$$e^i e^p e^q \epsilon_{jpr} \epsilon_{kqs} \mathcal{T}_i^{jk} = 0_{rs}$$

which is rather more complicated than the linear constraints on the reduced fundamental matrix. Instead, one may proceed in the following manner.

In the usual linear method of computing the trifocal tensor, one must solve a set of linear equations of the form $\mathtt{A}\mathbf{t} = \mathbf{0}$, or more precisely, find the vector $\mathbf{t}$ that minimizes $\|\mathtt{A}\mathbf{t}\|$ subject to $\|\mathbf{t}\| = 1$. In solving for the reduced trifocal tensor, the matrix $\mathtt{A}$ may be divided into two parts, corresponding to those constraints from the synthetic correspondences, which should be satisfied exactly, and the constraints from real correspondences, which must be satisfied in a least-squares sense. The first set of constraints are of the form $\mathtt{C}\mathbf{t} = \mathbf{0}$, and the second set may be written as $\hat{\mathtt{A}}\mathbf{t} = \mathbf{0}$. The problem becomes: find $\mathbf{t}$ that minimizes $\|\hat{\mathtt{A}}\mathbf{t}\|$ subject to $\|\mathbf{t}\| = 1$ and $\mathtt{C}\mathbf{t} = \mathbf{0}$. An algorithm for solving this problem is given as algorithm A5.5(*p*594).

For the problem of extracting the three camera matrices from the reduced tensor no simple method seems to be available, similar to that described in section 20.2.3 for the fundamental matrix. Instead, one may use the method described in steps 5 and 6 of the general dual algorithm (see page 505).

The minimal configuration of this type is seven points in two views. In this case, the problem is best solved directly by the method of section 11.1.2(*p*281), rather than by dualization to the case of three points in six views.

20.2.7 Performance issues

Dual reconstruction algorithms based on the reduced fundamental matrix and trifocal tensor have been implemented and tested. The results of these tests were contained in a student report presented in August 1996 by Gilles Debunne. Since this report is effectively unavailable, the results are summarized here.

The most serious difficulty is the distortion of the noise distribution by the application of projective transformations T^i to the images. Application of projective transformations to the image data has the effect of distorting any noise distribution that may apply to the data. The problem is related to the need to choose four points that are non-collinear in any of the images. If the points are close to collinear in any of the images, then the projective transformation applied to the image in step 1 of the algorithm may entail extreme distortion of the image. This sort of distortion can degrade performance of the algorithm severely.

Without special attention being paid to the noise-distortion, performance of the algorithms was generally unsatisfactory, Despite great care being taken to minimize errors due to noise in steps 4–6 of the algorithm (page $505ff$), when the inverse projective transformations are applied in step 7, the average error became very large. Some points retained quite small error, whereas in those images where distortion was significant, quite large errors resulted.

Normalization in the sense of section 4.4.4(p107) is also a problem. It has been shown to be essential for performance of the linear reconstruction algorithms to apply data normalization. However, what sort of normalization should be applied to the transformed data of figure 20.1(right), which is geometrically unrelated to actual image measurements, is a mystery.

To get good results, it would seem that one would need to propagate assumed error distributions forward in step 1 of the algorithm to get assumed error distributions for the transformed data figure 20.1(right), and then during reconstruction to minimize residual error relative to this propagated error distribution. Equivalently, cost functions being minimized during reconstruction must be related back to measurement error in the original image points. Recent work reported in [Hartley-00a, Schaffalitzky-00c] has shown that this indeed gives significantly improved results.

20.3 Closure

20.3.1 The literature

The idea behind Carlsson–Weinshall duality was first described in a pair of papers appearing simultaneously: [Carlsson-95] and Weinshall [Weinshall-95] and subsequently in a joint paper [Carlsson-98]. The treatment given here for the general method of dualizing an algorithm was given in [Hartley-98b], derived from these earlier papers. Details of methods for handling with noise propagation were given in [Hartley-00a], building on earlier implementations contained in an unavailable report by Gilles Debunne (August 1996).

The problem of reconstruction from six points in three views was perhaps first treated in a technical report [Hartley-92b] (later published as [Hartley-94c]) where the existence of up to eight solutions was shown. The problem was given a complete solution in [Quan-94] where it was shown that only three solutions are possible. This was also pointed out in [Ponce-94]. The paper [Carlsson-95] established that this problem is dual to the two-view, seven point problem for which a solution was known. This enabled the formulation of the method given in this chapter. The minimum six point configuration was used in [Torr-97] for robust estimation of the trifocal tensor. An alternative method for computing a reconstruction from six points in $n \geq 3$ views is given in [Schaffalitzky-00c]. This method does not require that images are first projectively transformed to a canonical basis.

20.3.2 Notes and Exercises

(i) In the dual algorithm of section 20.1.1 it was noted that the method will only work if the four points used to define the image transformations are non-coplanar. However, note that in this case, the algorithm of section 18.5.2(*p*450) will compute a projective reconstruction linearly.

(ii) If the four chosen points are coplanar, then the homographies $\mathtt{T}^i$ will map the plane to a common coordinate system. The transformed points $\mathbf{x}_j'^i$ will then satisfy the condition of section 17.5.2(*p*425), namely the lines joining any pair of points $\mathbf{x}_j'^i$ and $\mathbf{x}_k'^i$ (j and k fixed and a different line for each i) will meet in a common point. The duality in the case is described in [Criminisi-98, Irani-98].

(iii) Still in the case of the four chosen points being coplanar: after applying the $\mathtt{T}^i$, any point on the plane of the four points will map to the same point in all images. Thus, the fundamental matrix consistent with the point correspondences will be skew-symmetric.

21

Cheirality

When a projective reconstruction of a scene is carried out from a set of point correspondences, an important piece of information is typically ignored – if the points are visible in the images, then they must have been in front of the camera. In general, a projective reconstruction of a scene will not bear a close resemblance to the real scene when interpreted as if the coordinate frame were Euclidean. The scene is often split across the plane at infinity, as is illustrated in two dimensions by figure 21.1. It is possible to come much closer to at least an affine reconstruction of the scene by taking this simple constraint into account. The resulting reconstruction is called "quasi-affine" in that it lies part way between a projective and affine reconstruction. Scene objects are no longer split across the plane at infinity, though they may still suffer projective distortion.

Converting a projective reconstruction to quasi-affine is extremely simple if one neglects the cameras and requires only that the scene be of the correct quasi-affine form – in fact it can be accomplished in about two lines of programming (see corollary 21.9). To handle the cameras as well requires the solution of a linear programming problem.

21.1 Quasi-affine transformations

A subset B of $\mathbb{R}^n$ is called convex if the line segment joining any two points in B also lies entirely within B. The convex hull of B, denoted $\overline{B}$, is the smallest convex set containing B. Our main concern will be with 3-dimensional point sets, so $n = 3$. We view $\mathbb{R}^3$ as being a subset of $\mathbb{P}^3$, consisting of all non-infinite points. The infinite points constitute the plane at infinity, denoted $\boldsymbol{\pi}_\infty$. Thus, $\mathbb{P}^3 = \mathbb{R}^3 \cup \boldsymbol{\pi}_\infty$. A subset of $\mathbb{P}^3$ will be called convex if and only if it is contained in $\mathbb{R}^3$ and is convex in $\mathbb{R}^3$. Hence, according to this definition, a convex set does not contain any infinite points.

Definition 21.1. Consider a point set $\{\mathbf{X}_i\} \subset \mathbb{R}^3 \subset \mathbb{P}^3$. A projective mapping $h : \mathbb{P}^3 \rightarrow \mathbb{P}^3$ is said to preserve the convex hull of the points $\{\mathbf{X}_i\}$ if

(i) $h(\mathbf{X}_i)$ is a finite point for all i, and
(ii) h maps the convex hull of points $\{\mathbf{X}_i\}$ bijectively onto the convex hull of the points $\{h(\mathbf{X}_i)\}$.

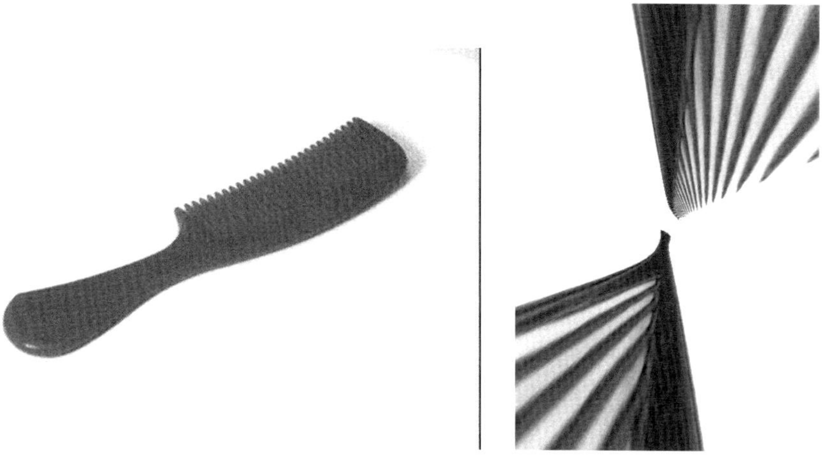

a b

Fig. 21.1. *(a) an image of a comb, and (b) the result of applying a projective transformation to the image. The projective transformation does not however preserve the convex hull of the set of points constituting the comb. In the original image, the convex hull of the comb is a finite set contained within the extent of the visible image. However, some of the points in this convex hull are mapped to infinity by the transformation.*

An example, shown in figure 21.1, may help in understanding this definition. The example deals with 2D point sets, but the principle is the same. The figure shows an image of a comb and the image resampled according to a projective mapping. The projective mapping does *not* however preserve the convex hull of the comb. Most people will agree that the resampled image is unlike any view of a comb seen by camera or human eye.

The property of preserving the convex hull of a set of points may be characterized in various different ways, as is shown by the theorem to be given shortly. In order to state this theorem, we introduce a new notation.

Notation. The symbol $\hat{\mathbf{X}}$ denotes a homogeneous representation of a point $\mathbf{X}$ in which the last coordinate is equal to 1.

Commonly in this chapter we will be interested in the exact equalities (not equalities up to scale) between vectors representing homogeneous quantities, such as points in 3D. Thus for instance if $\mathtt{H}$ is a projective transformation, we may write $\mathtt{H}\hat{\mathbf{X}} = \mathtt{T}'\hat{\mathbf{X}}'$ to mean that the transformation takes point $\hat{\mathbf{X}}$ to point $\hat{\mathbf{X}}'$, but that the scale factor $\mathtt{T}'$ is required to make this equality exact.

Now for the theorem.

Theorem 21.2. *Consider a projective transformation $h : \mathbb{P}^3 \rightarrow \mathbb{P}^3$ and a set of points $\{\mathbf{X}_i\}$. Let $\boldsymbol{\pi}_\infty$ be the plane mapped to infinity by h. The following statements are equivalent.*

(i) *h preserves the convex hull of the points $\{\mathbf{X}_i\}$.*
(ii) *$\tilde{\mathbf{X}} \cap \boldsymbol{\pi}_\infty = \emptyset$ for any point $\tilde{\mathbf{X}}$ in the convex hull of the points $\{\mathbf{X}_i\}$.*
(iii) *Let $\mathtt{H}$ be a matrix representing the transformation h, and suppose that $\mathtt{H}\hat{\mathbf{X}}_i = \mathtt{T}'_i\hat{\mathbf{X}}'_i$. Then the constants $\mathtt{T}'_i$ all have the same sign.*

Proof. This will be proved by showing that $(i) \Rightarrow (ii) \Rightarrow (iii) \Rightarrow (i)$.
$(i) \Rightarrow (ii)$. If h preserves the convex hull of the points, then $h(\tilde{\mathbf{X}})$ is a finite point for any point $\tilde{\mathbf{X}}$ in the convex hull of the $\mathbf{X}_i$. So $\tilde{\mathbf{X}} \cap \boldsymbol{\pi}_\infty = \emptyset$.
$(ii) \Rightarrow (iii)$. Consider the chord joining two points $\mathbf{X}_i$ and $\mathbf{X}_j$ and suppose that $\mathtt{T}'_i$ and $\mathtt{T}'_j$ (as in part (iii) of the theorem) have opposite signs. Since $\mathtt{T}'_i$ is a continuous function of the coordinates of $\mathbf{X}_i$, there must be a point $\tilde{\mathbf{X}}$ lying on the chord from $\mathbf{X}_i$ to $\mathbf{X}_j$ for which $\mathtt{T}'$ is equal to zero. This means that $\mathtt{H}\tilde{\mathbf{X}} = (\tilde{\mathtt{X}}', \tilde{\mathtt{Y}}', \tilde{\mathtt{Z}}', 0)^\mathsf{T}$. Since $\tilde{\mathbf{X}}$ is in the convex hull of the points $\{\mathbf{X}_i\}$, this contradicts (ii).
$(iii) \Rightarrow (i)$. We assume that there exist constants $\mathtt{T}'_i$ all of the same sign such that $\mathtt{H}\widehat{\mathbf{X}}_i = \mathtt{T}'_i\widehat{\mathbf{X}}'_i$. Let S be the subset of $\mathbb{R}^n$ consisting of all points $\mathbf{X}$ satisfying the condition $\mathtt{H}\widehat{\mathbf{X}} = \mathtt{T}'\widehat{\mathbf{X}}'$ such that $\mathtt{T}'$ has the same sign as the $\mathtt{T}'_i$. The set S contains $\{\mathbf{X}_i\}$. It will be shown that S is convex. If $\mathbf{X}_i$ and $\mathbf{X}_j$ are points in S with corresponding constants $\mathtt{T}'_i$ and $\mathtt{T}'_j$, then any intermediate point $\mathbf{X}$ between $\mathbf{X}_i$ and $\mathbf{X}_j$ must have $\mathtt{T}'$ value intermediate between $\mathtt{T}'_i$ and $\mathtt{T}'_j$. To see this, consider a point $\widehat{\mathbf{X}} = \alpha\widehat{\mathbf{X}}_i + (1-\alpha)\widehat{\mathbf{X}}_j$ where $0 \leq \alpha \leq 1$. This point lies between $\mathbf{X}_i$ and $\mathbf{X}_j$. Denote by $\mathbf{h}_4^\mathsf{T}$ the last row of $\mathtt{H}$. Then,

$$\begin{aligned}
\mathtt{T}' &= \mathbf{h}_4^\mathsf{T}\widehat{\mathbf{X}} \\
&= \mathbf{h}_4^\mathsf{T}(\alpha\widehat{\mathbf{X}}_i + (1-\alpha)\widehat{\mathbf{X}}_j) \\
&= \alpha\mathbf{h}_4^\mathsf{T}\widehat{\mathbf{X}}_i + (1-\alpha)\mathbf{h}_4^\mathsf{T}\widehat{\mathbf{X}}_j \\
&= \alpha\mathtt{T}'_i + (1-\alpha)\mathtt{T}'_j
\end{aligned}$$

which lies between $\mathtt{T}'_i$ and $\mathtt{T}'_j$ as claimed. Consequently, the value of $\mathtt{T}'$ must have the same sign as $\mathtt{T}'_i$ and $\mathtt{T}'_j$, and so $\mathbf{X}$ lies in S also. This shows that S is convex.
Now, let $\tilde{S}$ be a convex subset of S. It will be shown that $h(\tilde{S})$ is also convex. This is easily seen to be true, since h maps a line segment in $\tilde{S}$ to a line segment that does not cross the plane at infinity. Thus, h maps any convex set $\tilde{S}$ such that $S \supset \tilde{S} \supset \{\mathbf{X}_i\}$ to a convex set $\tilde{S}'$ such that $S' \supset \tilde{S}' \supset \{\mathbf{X}'_i\}$. However, if $\mathtt{H}$ satisfies condition (iii), then it is easily seen that $\mathtt{H}^{-1}$ does also. From this it follows that the above correspondence between convex sets $\tilde{S}$ and $\tilde{S}'$ is bijective. Since the convex hull of $\{\mathbf{X}_i\}$ (or $\{\mathbf{X}'_i\}$ respectively) is the intersection of all such convex sets, it follows that h preserves the convex hull of the points. □

The projective transformations that preserve the convex hull of a given set of points form an important class, and will be called *quasi-affine* transformations.

Definition 21.3. Let B be a subset of $\mathbb{R}^n$ and let h be a projectivity of $\mathbb{P}^n$. The projectivity h is said to be "quasi-affine" with respect to the set B if h preserves the convex hull of the set B.

It may be verified that if h is quasi-affine with respect to B, then h^{-1} is quasi-affine with respect to $h(B)$. Furthermore, if h is quasi-affine with respect to B and g is quasi-affine with respect to $h(B)$, then $g \circ h$ is quasi-affine with respect to B. Thus, quasi-affine projectivities may be composed in this fashion. Strictly speaking, however, quasi-affine projectivities with respect to a given fixed set of points do not form a group.

We will be considering sets of points $\{\mathbf{X}_i\}$ and $\{\mathbf{X}'_i\}$ that correspond via a projectivity. When we speak of the projectivity being *quasi-affine*, we will mean with respect to the set $\{\mathbf{X}_i\}$.

Two-dimensional quasi-affine mappings

Two-dimensional quasi-affine mappings arise as transformations between planar point sets in 3D and their image under a projective camera mapping, as stated formally below.

Theorem 21.4. *If B is a point set in a plane (the "object plane") in $\mathbb{R}^3$ and B lies entirely in front of a projective camera, then the mapping from the object plane to the image plane defined by the camera is quasi-affine with respect to B.*

Proof. That there is a projectivity h mapping the object plane to the image plane is well known. What is to be proved is that the projectivity is quasi-affine with respect to B. Let L be the line in which the principal plane of the camera meets the object plane. Since B lies entirely in front of the camera, L does not meet the convex hull of B. However, by definition of the principal plane $h(L) = L_\infty$, where L_∞ is the line at infinity in the image plane. Thus, one deduces that $h(\overline{B}) \cap L_\infty = \emptyset$, and hence by theorem 21.2 the transformation is quasi-affine with respect to B. □

Note that if points $\mathbf{x}_i$ are visible in an image, then the corresponding object points must lie in front of the camera. Applying theorem 21.4 to a sequence of imaging operations (for instance, a picture of a picture of a picture, etc.), it follows that the original and final images in the sequence are connected by a planar projectivity which is quasi-affine with respect to any point set in the object plane visible in the final image.

Similarly, if two images are taken of a set of points $\{\mathbf{X}_i\}$ in a plane, $\{\mathbf{x}_i\}$ and $\{\mathbf{x}'_i\}$ being corresponding points in the two images, then there is a quasi-affine mapping (with respect to the $\mathbf{x}_i$) mapping each $\mathbf{x}_i$ to $\mathbf{x}'_i$, and so theorem 21.2 applies, yielding the following:

Result 21.5. *If $\{\mathbf{x}_i\}$ and $\{\mathbf{x}'_i\}$ are corresponding points in two views of a set of object points $\{\mathbf{X}_i\}$ lying in a plane, then there is a matrix $\mathtt{H}$ representing a planar projectivity such that $\mathtt{H}\hat{\mathbf{x}}_i = w_i\hat{\mathbf{x}}'_i$ and all w_i have the same sign.*

21.2 Front and back of a camera

The depth of a point $\mathbf{X} = (\mathrm{X}, \mathrm{Y}, \mathrm{Z}, \mathrm{T})^\mathsf{T}$ with respect to a camera was shown in (6.15–*p*162) to be given by

$$\mathrm{depth}(\mathbf{X}; \mathtt{P}) = \frac{\mathrm{sign}(\det \mathtt{M})w}{\mathrm{T}\|\mathbf{m}^3\|} \tag{21.1}$$

where $\mathtt{M}$ is the left hand 3×3 block of $\mathtt{P}$, $\mathbf{m}^3$ is the third row of $\mathtt{M}$, and $\mathtt{P}\mathbf{X} = w\hat{\mathbf{x}}$. This expression is not dependent on the particular homogeneous representation of $\mathbf{X}$ or $\mathtt{M}$, that is it is unchanged by multiplication by non-zero scale factors. This definition of depth is used to determine whether a point is in front of a camera or not.

Result 21.6. *The point $\mathbf{X}$ lies in front of the camera $\mathtt{P}$ if and only if* $\mathrm{depth}(\mathbf{X}; \mathtt{P}) > 0$.

In fact, depth is positive for points in front of the camera, negative for points behind the camera, infinite on the plane at infinity and zero on the principal plane of the camera. If the camera centre or the point $\mathbf{X}$ is at infinity, then depth is not defined.

Usually, in this section we will only be concerned with the sign of depth and not its magnitude. We may then write

$$\text{depth}(\mathbf{X}; \mathtt{P}) \doteq w\mathtt{T} \det \mathtt{M} \tag{21.2}$$

where the symbol $\doteq$ indicates equality of sign. The quantity $\text{sign}(\text{depth}(\mathbf{X}; \mathtt{P}))$ will be referred to as the *cheirality* of the point $\mathbf{X}$ with respect to the camera $\mathtt{P}$. The cheirality of a point is said to be reversed by a transformation if it is swapped from 1 to -1 or vice versa.

21.3 Three-dimensional point sets

In this section the connection between cheirality of points with respect to a camera and convex hulls of point sets will be explained. The main result is stated now.

Theorem 21.7. *Let $\mathtt{P}^{\text{E}}$ and $\mathtt{P}'^{\text{E}}$ be two cameras, $\mathbf{X}_i^{\text{E}}$ a set of points lying in front of both cameras, and $\mathbf{x}_i$ and $\mathbf{x}'_i$ the corresponding image points. (The superscript E stands for Euclidean.)*

(i) *Let $(\mathtt{P}, \mathtt{P}', \{\mathbf{X}_i\})$ be any projective reconstruction from the image correspondences $\mathbf{x}_i \leftrightarrow \mathbf{x}'_i$, and let $\mathtt{P}\mathbf{X}_i = w_i\hat{\mathbf{x}}_i$ and $\mathtt{P}'\mathbf{X}_i = w'_i\hat{\mathbf{x}}'_i$. Then $w_iw'_i$ has the same sign for all i.*

(ii) *If each $\mathbf{X}_i$ is a finite point, and $\mathtt{P}\widehat{\mathbf{X}}_i = w_i\hat{\mathbf{x}}_i$ with w_i having the same sign for all i, then there exists a quasi-affine transformation $\mathtt{H}$ taking each $\mathbf{X}_i$ to $\mathbf{X}_i^{\text{E}}$.*

Of course, the existence of a projective transformation taking each $\mathbf{X}_i$ to $\mathbf{X}_i^{\text{E}}$ is guaranteed by theorem 10.1(*p*266). The current theorem gives the extra information that the transformation is quasi-affine, and hence one has a quasi-affine reconstruction.

Note that the condition that each $w_iw'_i$ have the same sign is unaffected by multiplying $\mathtt{P}$, $\mathtt{P}'$ or any of the points $\mathbf{X}_i$ by a scale factor, and hence is invariant of the choice of homogeneous representative for any of these quantities. In particular, if $\mathtt{P}$ is multiplied by a negative constant, then so is w_i for all i. Thus the sign of $w_iw'_i$ is inverted for each i, but they still all have the same sign. Similarly, if one point $\mathbf{X}_i$ is multiplied by a negative constant, then both w_i and w'_i change signs, and so the sign of $w_iw'_i$ is unchanged. In the same way, the condition that each w_i (in part (ii) of the theorem) have the same sign for all i is unaffected if the camera matrix is multiplied by a negative (or of course positive) constant.

Proof. The points $\mathbf{X}_i^{\text{E}}$ lie in front of the cameras $\mathtt{P}^{\text{E}}$ and $\mathtt{P}'^{\text{E}}$, and hence have positive depth with respect to these cameras. According to (21.2)

$$\text{depth}(\mathbf{X}_i^{\text{E}}; \mathtt{P}^{\text{E}}) \doteq \det(\mathtt{M}^{\text{E}})w_i\mathtt{T}_i^{\text{E}}.$$

Hence, $\det(\mathtt{M}^{\text{E}})w_i\mathtt{T}_i^{\text{E}} > 0$ for all i. Similarly for the second camera, $\det(\mathtt{M}'^{\text{E}})w'_i\mathtt{T}_i^{\text{E}} > 0$. Multiplying these expressions together, and cancelling $\mathtt{T}_i^{\text{E}}$ because it appears twice, gives $w_i w'_i \det \mathtt{M}^{\mathrm{E}} \det \mathtt{M}'^{\mathrm{E}} > 0$. Since $\det \mathtt{M}^{\mathrm{E}} \det \mathtt{M}'^{\mathrm{E}}$ is constant, this shows that $w_i w'_i$ has constant sign.

This was shown in terms of the true configuration. Note however that for any $\mathtt{H}$, one has $w_i \hat{\mathbf{x}}_i = \mathtt{P}^{\mathrm{E}} \mathbf{X}_i^{\mathrm{E}} = (\mathtt{P}^{\mathrm{E}} \mathtt{H}^{-1})(\mathtt{H}\mathbf{X}_i^{\mathrm{E}})$, and hence $w_i w'_i$ has the same sign for the projective reconstruction $(\mathtt{P}^{\mathrm{E}}\mathtt{H}^{-1}, \mathtt{P}'^{\mathrm{E}}\mathtt{H}^{-1}, \{\mathtt{H}\mathbf{X}_i^{\mathrm{E}}\})$. Since any projective reconstruction is of this form (except for homogeneous scale factors), and the condition that $w_i w'_i$ has the same sign is independent of choice of homogeneous representatives of $\mathbf{X}_i^{\mathrm{E}}$, $\mathtt{P}^{\mathrm{E}}$ and $\mathtt{P}'^{\mathrm{E}}$, it follows that in any projective reconstruction, $w_i w'_i$ has the same sign for all i. This proves the first part of the theorem.

To show the second part, suppose in the projective reconstruction $w_i \hat{\mathbf{x}}_i = \mathtt{P}\widehat{\mathbf{X}}$ all the w_i have the same sign. Since this is a projective reconstruction, there exists a transformation represented by $\mathtt{H}$ such that $\mathtt{H}\widehat{\mathbf{X}}_i = \eta_i \widehat{\mathbf{X}}_i^{\mathrm{E}}$ and $\mathtt{P}\mathtt{H}^{-1} = \epsilon \mathtt{P}^{\mathrm{E}}$ for some constants η_i and ϵ. Then,

$$w_i \hat{\mathbf{x}}_i = \mathtt{P}\widehat{\mathbf{X}}_i = (\mathtt{P}\mathtt{H}^{-1})(\mathtt{H}\widehat{\mathbf{X}}_i) = (\epsilon \mathtt{P}^{\mathrm{E}})(\eta_i \widehat{\mathbf{X}}_i^{\mathrm{E}}) \ .$$

and so

$$\mathtt{P}^{\mathrm{E}} \widehat{\mathbf{X}}_i^{\mathrm{E}} = (w_i / \epsilon \eta_i) \hat{\mathbf{x}}_i$$

for all i. However, since $\operatorname{depth}(\mathbf{X}_i^{\mathrm{E}}, \mathtt{P}^{\mathrm{E}}) > 0$, one has $\det(\mathtt{M}^{\mathrm{E}}) w_i / \epsilon \eta_i > 0$ for all i. Since $\det(\mathtt{M}^{\mathrm{E}})/\epsilon$ is constant, and by hypothesis w_i has the same sign for all i, it follows that η_i has the same sign for all i. Thus the mapping $\mathtt{H}$ such that $\mathtt{H}\widehat{\mathbf{X}}_i = \eta_i \widehat{\mathbf{X}}_i^{\mathrm{E}}$ is a quasi-affine map with respect to the points $\widehat{\mathbf{X}}_i$, according to theorem 21.2.

Note that the condition that w_i have the same sign for all i needs to be checked for one of the cameras only. However, defining $\mathtt{P}'\widehat{\mathbf{X}}_i = w'_i \hat{\mathbf{x}}'_i$, according to part (i) of the theorem, $w_i w'_i$ has the same sign for all i. Thus, if all w_i have the same sign, then so do all w'_i. □

21.4 Obtaining a quasi-affine reconstruction

According to theorem 21.7, any projective reconstruction in which $\mathtt{P}\widehat{\mathbf{X}}_i = w_i \hat{\mathbf{x}}_i$ and w_i has the same sign for all i is a quasi-affine reconstruction. The advantage of a quasi-affine reconstruction is that it gives a closer approximation to the true shape of the object than does an arbitrary projective transformation. It may be used as a stepping stone on the way to a metric reconstruction of the scene, as in [Hartley-94b]. In addition, one may retrieve the convex hull of the object or determine such questions as whether two points lie on the same side of a plane.

It turns out that quasi-affine reconstruction is extremely simple, given a projective reconstruction, as shown in the following theorem.

Theorem 21.8. *Any projective reconstruction in which one of the cameras is an affine camera is a quasi-affine reconstruction.*

Proof. Recall that an affine camera is one for which the last row is of the form $(0, 0, 0, 1)$. In this case, writing $w_i \hat{\mathbf{x}}_i = \mathtt{P}\widehat{\mathbf{X}}_i$, one immediately verifies that $w_i = 1$ for all i, and in particular they all have the same sign. According to theorem 21.2 this means that the reconstruction differs by a quasi-affine transformation from the truth. □

The following result follows immediately.

Corollary 21.9. *Let* $(\mathtt{P}, \mathtt{P}', \{\mathbf{X}_i\})$ *be a projective reconstruction of a scene in which* $\mathtt{P} = [\mathtt{I} \mid \mathbf{0}]$. *Then by swapping the last two columns of* P *and of* P′, *as well as the last two coordinates of each* $\mathbf{X}_i$, *one obtains a quasi-affine reconstruction of the scene.*

This is similar to result 10.4(*p*271), in which it was shown that if the camera P is known in reality to be an affine camera, then the above procedure provides an affine reconstruction.

21.5 Effect of transformations on cheirality

At this point, it is desirable to derive a slightly different form of the formula for depth defined in (21.2). Let P be a camera matrix. The centre of P is the unique point **C** such that $\mathtt{P}\mathbf{C} = \mathbf{0}$. One can write an explicit formula for **C** as follows.

Definition 21.10. Given a camera matrix P, we define $\mathbf{C}_\mathtt{P}^\mathsf{T}$ to be the vector (c_1, c_2, c_3, c_4), where

$$c_i = (-1)^i \det \hat{\mathtt{P}}^{(i)}$$

and $\hat{\mathtt{P}}^{(i)}$ is the matrix obtained by removing the i-th column of P.

We denote by $[\mathtt{P}/\mathbf{V}^\mathsf{T}]$ the 4×4 matrix made up of a 3×4 camera matrix P augmented with an final row $\mathbf{V}^\mathsf{T}$. Definition 21.10 leads to a simple formula for $\det[\mathtt{P}/\mathbf{V}^\mathsf{T}]$. Cofactor expansion of the determinant along the last row gives $\det[\mathtt{P}/\mathbf{V}^\mathsf{T}] = \mathbf{V}^\mathsf{T}\mathbf{C}_\mathtt{P}$ for any row vector $\mathbf{V}^\mathsf{T}$. As a special case, if $\mathbf{p}_i^\mathsf{T}$ is the i-th row of P, then

$$\mathbf{p}_i^\mathsf{T}\mathbf{C}_\mathtt{P} = \det[\mathtt{P}/\mathbf{p}_i^\mathsf{T}] = 0$$

where the last equality is true because the matrix has a repeated row. Since this is true for all i, it follows that $\mathtt{P}\mathbf{C}_\mathtt{P} = \mathbf{0}$, and so $\mathbf{C}_\mathtt{P}$ is the camera centre, as claimed.

Note that submatrix $\hat{\mathtt{P}}^{(4)}$ is the same as matrix M in the decomposition $\mathtt{P} = [\mathtt{M} \mid \mathbf{v}]$, and so $\det \mathtt{M} = c_4$. This allows us to reformulate (21.2), as follows.

$$\text{depth}(\mathbf{X}; \mathtt{P}) \doteq w(\mathbf{E}_4^\mathsf{T}\mathbf{X})(\mathbf{E}_4^\mathsf{T}\mathbf{C}_\mathtt{P}) \tag{21.3}$$

where $\mathbf{E}_4^\mathsf{T}$ is the vector $(0, 0, 0, 1)$. It is significant to note here that $\mathbf{E}_4$ is the vector representing the plane at infinity – a point **X** lies on the plane at infinity if and only if $\mathbf{E}_4^\mathsf{T}\mathbf{X} = 0$.

We now consider a projective transformation represented by matrix H. If $\mathtt{P}' = \mathtt{P}\mathtt{H}^{-1}$ and $\mathbf{X}' = \mathtt{H}\mathbf{X}$ then the image correspondences are preserved by this transformation. When speaking of a projective transformation being applied to a set of points and to a camera, it is meant that a point **X** is transformed to $\mathtt{H}\mathbf{X}$ and the camera matrix is transformed to $\mathtt{P}\mathtt{H}^{-1}$.

In this section we will consider such projective transformations and their effect on the cheirality of points with respect to a camera. First, we wish to determine what happens to $\mathbf{C}_\mathtt{P}$ when $\mathtt{P}$ is transformed to $\mathtt{PH}^{-1}$. To answer that question, consider an arbitrary 4-vector $\mathbf{V}$. We see that

$$\mathbf{V}^\mathsf{T}\mathtt{H}^{-1}\mathbf{C}_{\mathtt{PH}^{-1}} = \det(\mathtt{PH}^{-1}/\mathbf{V}^\mathsf{T}\mathtt{H}^{-1}) = \det(\mathtt{P}/\mathbf{V}^\mathsf{T})\det\mathtt{H}^{-1} = \mathbf{V}^\mathsf{T}\mathbf{C}_\mathtt{P}\det\mathtt{H}^{-1}.$$

Since this is true for all vectors $\mathbf{V}$, it follows that $\mathtt{H}^{-1}\mathbf{C}_{\mathtt{PH}^{-1}} = \mathbf{C}_\mathtt{P}\det\mathtt{H}^{-1}$, or

$$\mathbf{C}_{\mathtt{PH}^{-1}} = \mathtt{H}\mathbf{C}_\mathtt{P}\det\mathtt{H}^{-1}. \tag{21.4}$$

At one level, this formula is saying that the transformation $\mathtt{H}$ takes the camera centre $\mathbf{C} = \mathbf{C}_\mathtt{P}$ to the new location $\mathbf{C}_{\mathtt{PH}^{-1}} \approx \mathtt{H}\mathbf{C}$. However, we are interested in the exact coordinates of $\mathbf{C}_{\mathtt{PH}^{-1}}$, especially the sign of the last coordinate c_4 which appears in (21.3). Thus, the factor $\det\mathtt{H}^{-1}$ is significant.

Now, applying (21.4) to (21.3) gives

$$\begin{aligned}\mathrm{depth}(\mathtt{H}\mathbf{X};\mathtt{PH}^{-1}) &\doteq w(\mathbf{E}_4^\mathsf{T}\mathtt{H}\mathbf{X})(\mathbf{E}_4^\mathsf{T}\mathbf{C}_{\mathtt{PH}^{-1}})\\ &\doteq w(\mathbf{E}_4^\mathsf{T}\mathtt{H}\mathbf{X})(\mathbf{E}_4^\mathsf{T}\mathtt{H}\mathbf{C}_\mathtt{P})\det\mathtt{H}^{-1}\ .\end{aligned}$$

One may interpret the expression $\mathbf{E}_4^\mathsf{T}\mathtt{H}$ as being the plane $\boldsymbol{\pi}_\infty$ mapped to infinity by $\mathtt{H}$. This is because a point $\mathbf{X}$ lies on $\boldsymbol{\pi}_\infty$ if and only if the last coordinate of $\mathtt{H}\mathbf{X}$ is zero – that is $\mathbf{E}_4\mathtt{H}\mathbf{X} = 0$. On the other hand, $\mathbf{X}$ lies on $\boldsymbol{\pi}_\infty$ if and only if $\boldsymbol{\pi}_\infty^\mathsf{T}\mathbf{X} = 0$. Finally, denoting the fourth row of the transformation matrix $\mathtt{H}$ by $\mathbf{h}_4^\mathsf{T}$, and $\mathrm{sign}(\det\mathtt{H})$ by δ, we obtain

Result 21.11. *If $\boldsymbol{\pi}_\infty$ is the plane mapped to infinity by a projective transformation $\mathtt{H}$ and $\delta = \mathrm{sign}(\det\mathtt{H})$, then*

$$\mathrm{depth}(\mathtt{H}\mathbf{X};\mathtt{PH}^{-1}) \doteq w(\boldsymbol{\pi}_\infty^\mathsf{T}\mathbf{X})(\boldsymbol{\pi}_\infty^\mathsf{T}\mathbf{C}_\mathtt{P})\delta\ .$$

This equation will be used extensively. It may be considered to be a generalization of (21.3). It will be seen in the next section that $\delta = \mathrm{sign}(\det\mathtt{H})$ is an indicator of whether $\mathtt{H}$ is an orientation-reversing or orientation-preserving transformation. Thus, the effect on cheirality of applying a transformation $\mathtt{H}$ is determined only by the position of the plane mapped to infinity $\boldsymbol{\pi}_\infty$, and whether $\mathtt{H}$ preserves or reverses orientation.

We now consider the effect of different transformations on the cheirality of points with respect to a camera. The effect of an affine transformation is considered first.

Result 21.12. *An affine transformation with positive determinant preserves the cheirality of any point with respect to a camera. An affine transformation with negative determinant reverses cheirality.*

Proof. An affine transformation preserves the plane at infinity, hence $\boldsymbol{\pi}_\infty = \mathbf{E}_4$. The result then follows by comparing (21.3) and result 21.11. □

We now determine how an arbitrary projective transformation affects cheirality.

Result 21.13. *Let $\mathtt{H}$ represent a projective transformation with positive determinant, and let $\boldsymbol{\pi}_\infty$ be the plane in space mapped to infinity by $\mathtt{H}$. The cheirality of a point $\mathbf{X}$ is preserved by $\mathtt{H}$ if and only if $\mathbf{X}$ lies on the same side of the plane $\boldsymbol{\pi}_\infty$ as the camera centre.*

Proof. Since $\det \mathtt{H} > 0$, we see from (21.3) and result 21.11 that $\text{depth}(\mathbf{X}; \mathtt{P}) \doteq \text{depth}(\mathtt{H}\mathbf{X}; \mathtt{PH}^{-1})$ if and only if $(\boldsymbol{\pi}_\infty^\mathsf{T}\mathbf{X})(\boldsymbol{\pi}_\infty^\mathsf{T}\mathbf{C}) \doteq (\mathbf{E}_4^\mathsf{T}\mathbf{X})(\mathbf{E}_4^\mathsf{T}\mathbf{C})$. Suppose the point $\mathbf{X}$ and the camera $\mathtt{P}$ are located at finite points so that the cheirality is well defined, and let them be scaled so that both $\mathbf{X}$ and $\mathbf{C}$ have final coordinate equal to 1. In this case, $(\mathbf{E}_4^\mathsf{T}\mathbf{X})(\mathbf{E}_4^\mathsf{T}\mathbf{C}) = 1$ and we see that cheirality is preserved if and only if $(\boldsymbol{\pi}_\infty^\mathsf{T}\mathbf{X})(\boldsymbol{\pi}_\infty^\mathsf{T}\mathbf{C}) \doteq 1$, or otherwise expressed $\boldsymbol{\pi}_\infty^\mathsf{T}\mathbf{X} \doteq \boldsymbol{\pi}_\infty^\mathsf{T}\mathbf{C}$. This condition may be interpreted as meaning that the points $\mathbf{C}$ and $\mathbf{X}$ both lie on the same side of the plane $\boldsymbol{\pi}_\infty$. Hence, the cheirality of a point $\mathbf{X}$ is preserved by a transformation $\mathtt{H}$, if and only if it lies on the same side of the plane $\boldsymbol{\pi}_\infty$ as the camera centre. □

21.6 Orientation

We now consider the question of image orientation. A mapping h from $\mathbb{R}^n$ to itself is called orientation-preserving at points $\mathbf{X}$ where the Jacobian of h (the determinant of the matrix of partial derivatives) is positive, and orientation-reversing at points where the Jacobian is negative. Reflection of points of $\mathbb{R}^n$ with respect to a hyperplane (that is mirror imaging) is an example of an orientation-reversing mapping. A projectivity h from $\mathtt{P}^n$ to itself restricts to a mapping from $\mathbb{R}^n - \boldsymbol{\pi}_\infty$ to $\mathbb{R}^n$, where $\boldsymbol{\pi}_\infty$ is the hyperplane (line, plane) mapped to infinity by $\mathtt{H}$. Consider the case $n = 3$ and let $\mathtt{H}$ be a 4×4 matrix representing the projectivity h. We wish to determine at which points $\mathbf{X}$ in $\mathbb{R}^n - \boldsymbol{\pi}_\infty$ the map h is orientation-preserving. It may be verified (quite easily using Mathematica [Mathematica-92]) that if $\mathtt{H}\widehat{\mathbf{X}} = w\widehat{\mathbf{X}}'$ and $\mathtt{J}$ is the Jacobian matrix of h evaluated at $\mathbf{X}$, then $\det(\mathtt{J}) = \det(\mathtt{H})/w^4$. This gives the following result.

Result 21.14. *A projectivity h of $\mathbb{P}^3$ represented by a matrix $\mathtt{H}$ is orientation-preserving at any point in $\mathbb{R}^3 - \boldsymbol{\pi}_\infty$ if and only if $\det(\mathtt{H}) > 0$.*

Of course, the concept of orientability may be extended to the whole of $\mathbb{P}^3$, and it may be shown that h is orientation-preserving on the whole of $\mathbb{P}^3$ if and only if $\det(\mathtt{H}) > 0$. The essential feature here is that as a topological manifold, $\mathbb{P}^3$ is orientable.

Two sets of points $\{\mathbf{X}_i\}$ and $\{\overline{\mathbf{X}}_i\}$ that correspond via a quasi-affine transformation are said to be *oppositely oriented* if the transformation is orientation-reversing. As an example, consider the transformation given by a diagonal matrix $\mathtt{H} = \text{diag}(1, 1, -1, 1)$. This transformation has negative determinant, and hence is orientation-reversing. On the other hand, it is affine, and hence quasi-affine. Therefore, it is possible always to construct oppositely oriented quasi-affine reconstructions of a scene. It may appear therefore that the orientation of a scene may not be determined from a pair of images. Although this is sometimes true, it is sometimes possible to rule out one of the oppositely oriented quasi-affine reconstructions of a scene, and hence determine the true orientation of the scene.

Common experience provides some clues here. In particular a stereo pair may be viewed by presenting one image to one eye and the other image to the other eye. If this is done correctly, then the brain perceives a 3D reconstruction of the scene If, however, the two images are swapped and presented to the opposite eyes, then the perspective will be reversed – hills become valleys and vice versa. In effect, the brain is able to compute two oppositely oriented reconstructions of the image pair. It seems, therefore,

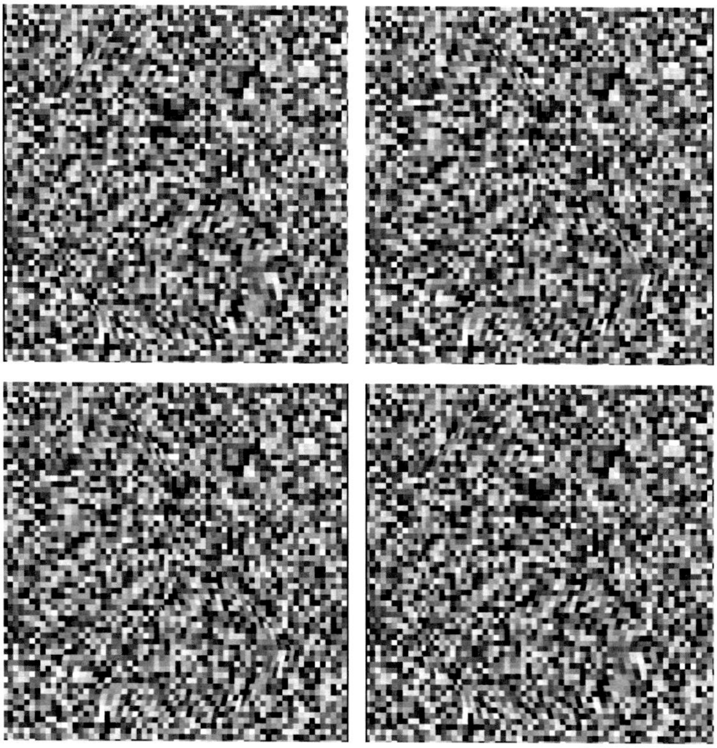

Fig. 21.2. *Stereo pairs of images that may be viewed by cross-fusing (the eyes are crossed so that the left eye sees the right image and vice versa). The two bottom images are the same as the top pair, except that they are swapped. In the top pair of images one sees an L-shaped region raised above a planar background. In the bottom pair of images the L-shaped region appears as an indentation. The two "reconstructions" differ by reflection in the background plane. This demonstrates that the same pair of images may give rise to two differently oriented projective reconstructions.*

that in certain circumstances, two oppositely oriented realizations of an image pair exist. This is illustrated in figure 21.2.

It may be surprising to discover that this is not always the case, as is shown in the following theorem. As used in this theorem and elsewhere in this chapter, a projective realization of a set of point correspondences is known as a *strong realization* if the reconstructed 3D points $\mathbf{X}_i$ are in front of all the cameras.

Theorem 21.15. *Let* $(\mathtt{P}, \mathtt{P}', \{\mathbf{X}_i\})$ *be a strong realization of a uniquely realizable set of point correspondences. There exists a different oppositely oriented strong realization* $(\overline{\mathtt{P}}, \overline{\mathtt{P}}', \{\overline{\mathbf{X}}_i\})$ *if and only if there exists a plane in* $\mathbb{R}^3$ *such that the perspective centres of both cameras* $\mathtt{P}$ *and* $\mathtt{P}'$ *lie on one side of the plane, and the points* $\mathbf{X}_i$ *lie on the other side.*

Proof. Consider one strong realization of the configuration. By definition, all the points lie in front of both cameras. Suppose that there exists a plane separating the points from the two camera centres. Let $\mathtt{G}$ be a projective transformation mapping the given plane to infinity and let $\mathtt{A}$ be an affine transformation. Suppose further that

$\det \mathtt{G} > 0$ and $\det \mathtt{A} < 0$. Let $\mathtt{H}$ be the composition $\mathtt{H} = \mathtt{AG}$. According to result 21.13 the transformation $\mathtt{G}$ is cheirality-reversing for the points, since the points are on the opposite side of the plane from the camera centres. According to result 21.12 $\mathtt{A}$ is also cheirality-reversing, since $\det \mathtt{A} < 0$. The composition $\mathtt{H}$ must therefore be cheirality-preserving, and it transforms the strong configuration to a different strong configuration. Since $\mathtt{H}$ has negative determinant, however, it is orientation-reversing, so the two strong realizations have opposite orientations.

Conversely, suppose that two strong oppositely oriented realizations exist and let $\mathtt{H}$ be the transformation taking one to the other. Since $\mathtt{H}$ is orientation-reversing, $\det \mathtt{H} < 0$. The mapping $\mathtt{H}$ is by definition cheirality-preserving on all points, with respect to both cameras. If $\boldsymbol{\pi}_\infty$ is the plane mapped to infinity by $\mathtt{H}$, then according to result 21.13 the points $\mathbf{X}$ must lie on the opposite side of the plane $\boldsymbol{\pi}_\infty$ from both camera centres. □

21.7 The cheiral inequalities

In section 21.4 a very simple method was given for obtaining a quasi-affine reconstruction of a scene directly from a projective reconstruction. However, the reconstruction obtained there did not respect the condition that the points must lie in front of all cameras. In fact, the first camera in this construction is an affine camera, for which front and back are not well defined. By taking full advantage of the fact that visible points must lie in front of the camera, it is possible to constrain the reconstruction more tightly, leading to a closer approximation to a true affine reconstruction of the scene.

The method will be given for the case of a reconstruction derived from several images. One is given a set of image points $\{\mathbf{x}_i^j\}$, where $\mathbf{x}_i^j$ is the projection of the i-th point in the j-th image. Not all points are visible in each image, so for some (i, j) the point $\mathbf{x}_i^j$ is not given, in which case it is not known whether the i-th point lies in front of the j-th camera or not. On the other hand, the existence of an image point $\mathbf{x}_i^j$ implies that the point lies in front of the camera.

We start from an assumed projective reconstruction of the scene, consisting of a set of 3D points $\mathbf{X}_i$ and cameras $\mathtt{P}^j$ such that $\mathbf{x}_i^j \approx \mathtt{P}^j\mathbf{X}_i$. Writing the implied scalar constant explicitly in this equation gives $w_i^j\hat{\mathbf{x}}_i^j = \mathtt{P}^j\mathbf{X}_i$. In this equation, $\mathtt{P}^j$ and $\mathbf{X}_i$ are arbitrarily chosen homogeneous representatives of the respective matrix or vector. Related to theorem 21.7 one may state for several views:

Result 21.16. *Consider a set of points $\mathbf{X}_i^{\mathrm{E}}$ and cameras $\mathtt{P}^{j\mathrm{E}}$, and let $\mathbf{x}_i^j = \mathtt{P}^{j\mathrm{E}}\mathbf{X}_i^{\mathrm{E}}$ be defined for some indices (i, j) such that point $\mathbf{X}_i^{\mathrm{E}}$ lies in front of camera $\mathtt{P}^{j\mathrm{E}}$. Let $(\mathtt{P}^j; \mathbf{X}_i)$ be a projective reconstruction from $\mathbf{x}_i^j$. Then there are camera matrices $\tilde{\mathtt{P}}^j = \pm\mathtt{P}^j$ and $\tilde{\mathbf{X}}_i = \pm\mathbf{X}_i$ such that for each (i, j) for which $\mathbf{x}_i^j$ is defined, one has*

$$\tilde{\mathtt{P}}^j\tilde{\mathbf{X}}_i = w_i^j\hat{\mathbf{x}}_i^j \;\; \text{with} \;\; w_i^j > 0.$$

Briefly stated, one can always adjust a projective reconstruction, multiplying camera matrices and points by -1 if necessary, so that w_i^j is positive whenever image point $\mathbf{x}_i^j$ exists. The simple proof is omitted. To find the matrices $\tilde{\mathtt{P}}^j$ and points $\tilde{\mathbf{X}}_i$, one may assume that one of the cameras $\tilde{\mathtt{P}}_1 = \mathtt{P}_1$, for otherwise all points and cameras may be multiplied by -1. The condition $\mathtt{P}_1\tilde{\mathbf{X}}_i = w_i^1\mathbf{x}_i^1$ with $w_i^1 > 0$ determines whether to choose $\tilde{\mathbf{X}}_i = \mathbf{X}_i$ or $-\mathbf{X}_i$ for all i such that $\mathbf{x}_i^1$ is defined. Each known $\tilde{\mathbf{X}}_i$ determines $\tilde{\mathtt{P}}^j$ for all j such that $\mathbf{x}_i^j$ is defined. Continuing in this way, one easily finds the factor ± 1 to apply to each $\mathtt{P}^j$ and $\mathbf{X}_j$ to find $\tilde{\mathtt{P}}^j$ and $\tilde{\mathbf{X}}_i$. We assume that this has been done, and replace each $\mathtt{P}^j$ by $\tilde{\mathtt{P}}^j$ and $\mathbf{X}_i$ by $\tilde{\mathbf{X}}_i$. In future we drop the tildes and continue to work with the corrected $\mathtt{P}^j$ and $\mathbf{X}_i$. We now know that $w_i^j > 0$ whenever image point $\mathbf{x}_i^j$ is given.

Now, we seek a transformation $\mathtt{H}$ that will transform the projective reconstruction to a quasi-affine reconstruction for which all points lie in front of the cameras as appropriate. Denoting by 4-vector $\mathbf{v}$ the plane $\boldsymbol{\pi}_\infty$ mapped to infinity by $\mathtt{H}$, this condition may be written as (see result 21.11):

$$\text{depth}(\mathbf{X}_i; \mathtt{P}^j) \doteq (\mathbf{v}^\mathsf{T}\mathbf{X}_i)(\mathbf{v}^\mathsf{T}\mathbf{C})\delta > 0$$

where $\delta = \text{sign}(\det \mathtt{H})$. This condition holds for all pairs (i, j) where $\mathbf{x}_i^j$ is given.

Since we are free to multiply $\mathbf{v}$ by -1 if necessary, we may assume that $(\mathbf{v}^\mathsf{T}\mathbf{C}^1)\delta > 0$ for the centre of the camera $\mathtt{P}^1$. The following inequalities now follow easily:

$$\begin{aligned} \mathbf{X}_i^\mathsf{T}\mathbf{v} &> 0 \quad \text{for all } i \\ \delta \mathbf{C}^{j\mathsf{T}}\mathbf{v} &> 0 \quad \text{for all } j. \end{aligned} \tag{21.5}$$

These equations (21.5) may be called the *cheiral inequalities*. Since the values of each $\mathbf{X}_i$, $\mathbf{C}$ and $\mathbf{C}'$ are known, they form a set of inequalities in the entries of $\mathbf{v}$. The value of δ is not known *a priori*, and so it is necessary to seek a solution for each of the two cases $\delta = 1$ and $\delta = -1$.

To find the required transformation $\mathtt{H}$, first of all we solve the cheiral inequalities to find a value of $\mathbf{v}$, either for $\delta = 1$ or $\delta = -1$. The required matrix $\mathtt{H}$ is any matrix having $\mathbf{v}^\mathsf{T}$ as its last row and satisfying the condition $\det \mathtt{H} \doteq \delta$. If the last component of $\mathbf{v}$ is non-zero, then $\mathtt{H}$ can be chosen to have the simple form in which the first three rows are of the form $\pm[\mathtt{I} \mid \mathbf{0}]$.

If a Euclidean reconstruction (or more specifically a quasi-affine reconstruction) is possible, then there must be a solution either for $\delta = 1$ or $\delta = -1$. In some cases there will exist solutions of the cheiral inequalities for both $\delta = 1$ and $\delta = -1$. This will mean that two oppositely oriented strong realizations exist. The conditions under which this may occur were discussed in section 21.6.

Solving the cheiral inequalities

Naturally, the cheiral inequalities may be solved using techniques of linear programming. As they stand however, if $\mathbf{v}$ is a solution then so is $\alpha\mathbf{v}$ for any positive factor α. In order to restrict the solution domain to be bounded, one may add additional inequalities. For instance, if $\mathbf{v} = (v_1, v_2, v_3, v_4)^\mathsf{T}$, then the inequalities $-1 < v_i < 1$ serve to restrict the solution domain to be a bounded polyhedron.

To achieve a unique solution we need to specify some goal function to be linearized. An appropriate strategy is to seek to maximize the extent to which each of the inequalities is satisfied. To do this, we introduce one further variable, d. Each of the inequalities $\mathbf{a}^\mathsf{T}\mathbf{v}$ of the form (21.5) for appropriate $\mathbf{a}$ is replaced by an inequality $\mathbf{a}^\mathsf{T}\mathbf{v} > d$. We seek to maximize d while satisfying all the inequalities. This is a standard linear programming problem, for which many methods of solution exist, such as the simplex method ([Press-88]).[1] If a solution is found for which $d > 0$ then this will be a desired solution.

Summary of the algorithm

Now, we give the complete algorithm for computing a quasi-affine reconstruction of a scene using the cheiral inequalities. The algorithm as outlined above was discussed for the case of two views. In the present case it will be presented for an arbitrary number of views. The extension to more views is straightforward.

Objective

Given a set of 3D points $\mathbf{X}_i$ and camera matrices $\mathtt{P}^j$ constituting a projective reconstruction from a set of image points, compute a projective transformation $\mathtt{H}$ transforming the projective to a quasi-affine reconstruction.

Algorithm

(i) For each pair (i, j) such that point $\mathbf{x}_i^j$ is given let $\mathtt{P}^j\mathbf{X}_i = w_i^j\hat{\mathbf{x}}_i^j$.
(ii) Replace some cameras $\mathtt{P}^j$ by $-\mathtt{P}^j$ and some points $\mathbf{X}_i$ by $-\mathbf{X}_i$ as required to ensure that each $w_i^j > 0$.
(iii) Form the cheiral inequalities (21.5) where $\mathbf{C}^j = \mathbf{C}_{\mathtt{P}^j}$ is defined by definition 21.10.
(iv) For each of the values $\delta = \pm 1$, choose a solution (if it exists) to the set of cheiral inequalities. Let the solution be $\mathbf{v}_\delta$. A solution must exist for at least one value of δ, sometimes for both values of δ.
(v) Define a matrix $\mathtt{H}_\delta$ having last row equal to $\mathbf{v}_\delta$ and such that $\det(\mathtt{H}) \doteq \delta$. The matrix $\mathtt{H}_\delta$ is the required transformation matrix. If both $\mathtt{H}_+$ and $\mathtt{H}_-$ exist, then they lead to two oppositely oriented quasi-affine reconstructions.

Algorithm 21.1. *Computing a quasi-affine reconstruction.*

Bounding the plane at infinity

A quasi-affine reconstruction is of course not unique, being defined only up to a quasi-affine transformation with respect to the points and camera centres. However, once one has been found, it is possible to set bounds on the coordinates of the plane at infinity. Thus, let $\mathtt{P}^j$ and $\mathbf{X}_i$ constitute a quasi-affine reconstruction of a scene. One may choose the sign of $\mathtt{P}^j$ and $\mathbf{X}_i$ such that the last coordinates of $\mathtt{X}_i$ and the determinants of each $\mathtt{M}^j$ are positive. One may apply a translation to the points and cameras so that the coordinate origin lies inside the convex hull of the points and camera centres. For simplicity, the centroid of these points may be placed at the origin.

It is possible to apply a further quasi-affine transformation $\mathtt{H}$ to obtain an alternative reconstruction. Let $\boldsymbol{\pi}_\infty$ be the plane mapped to infinity by $\mathtt{H}$. We confine our interest to orientation-preserving transforms, and wish to find constraints on the coordinates of $\boldsymbol{\pi}_\infty$ such that $\mathtt{H}$ is quasi-affine. A plane $\boldsymbol{\pi}_\infty$ has this property if and only if it lies entirely outside the convex hull of the points and camera centres. Since the plane $\boldsymbol{\pi}_\infty$

[1] The Simplex algorithm given in [Press-88] is not suitable for use as stands, since it makes the unnecessary assumption that all variables are non-negative. It needs to be modified to be used for this problem.

cannot cross the convex hull, it cannot pass through the origin. Representing π_∞ by the vector $\mathbf{v}$, this says that the last coordinate of $\mathbf{v}$ is non-zero. One may then write $\mathbf{v} = (v_1, v_2, v_3, 1)^\mathsf{T}$. Since the origin lies on the same side of the plane as all the points, the cheiral inequalities become

$$\begin{aligned} \mathbf{X}_i^\mathsf{T}\mathbf{v} &> 0 \text{ for all } i \\ \mathbf{C}^{j\mathsf{T}}\mathbf{v} &> 0 \text{ for all } j \end{aligned} \quad (21.6)$$

for $\mathbf{v} = (v_1, v_2, v_3, 1)^\mathsf{T}$. One may find upper and lower bounds for each v_i by solving the linear programming problem to maximize v_i or $-v_i$ subject to these constraints. None of the v_i can be unbounded, since otherwise the plane π_∞ represented by the vector $\mathbf{v}$ could lie arbitrarily close to the origin.

Before solving for this system, good practice is to apply an affine transformation to normalize the set of points and camera centres so that their centroid is at the origin and their principal moments are all equal to 1.

The complete algorithm for computing the bounds on the position of the plane at infinity is given in algorithm 21.2.

Objective

Given a quasi-affine reconstruction of a scene, establish bounds on the coordinates of the plane at infinity.

Algorithm

(i) Normalize the points $\mathbf{X}_i = (\mathtt{X}_i, \mathtt{Y}_i, \mathtt{Z}_i, \mathtt{T}_i)^\mathsf{T}$ so that $\mathtt{T}_i = 1$, and cameras $\mathtt{P}^j = [\mathtt{M}_j \mid \mathbf{t}^j]$ so that $\det \mathtt{M}^j = 1$.

(ii) Further normalize by replacing $\mathbf{X}_i$ by $\mathtt{H}^{-1}\mathbf{X}_i$ and $\mathtt{P}^j$ by $\mathtt{P}^j\mathtt{H}$, where $\mathtt{H}$ is an affine transformation moving the centroid to the origin and scaling in the principal axis directions so that is has equal principal axes.

(iii) Letting $\mathbf{v} = (v_1, v_2, v_3, 1)^\mathsf{T}$, form cheiral inequalities (21.6). Any orientation-preserving transformation $\mathtt{H}$ mapping the reconstruction to an affine reconstruction of the image must have the form

$$\mathtt{H} = \begin{bmatrix} \mathtt{I} & \mathbf{0} \\ v_1\ v_2\ v_3 & 1 \end{bmatrix}$$

for a vector $\mathbf{v}$ satisfying these inequalities.

(iv) Upper and lower bounds for each v_i may be found by running a linear programming problem six times. The coordinates of a desired transformation $\mathtt{H}$ must lie inside the box defined by these bounds.

Algorithm 21.2. *Establishing bounds on the plane at infinity.*

21.8 Which points are visible in a third view

Consider a scene reconstructed from two views. We consider now the question of determining which points are visible in a third view. Such a question arises when one is given two uncalibrated views of a scene and one seeks to synthesize a third view. This can be done by carrying out a projective reconstruction of the scene from the

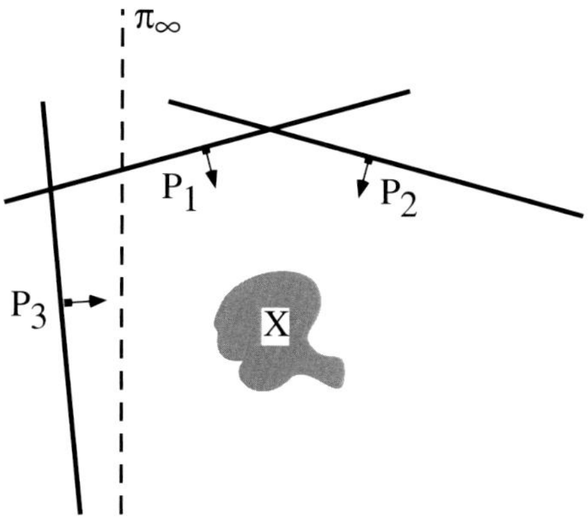

Fig. 21.3. *The point set* $\mathbf{X}$ *is in front of all three cameras as shown. However, if an orientation-preserving projective transformation* $\mathtt{H}$ *is applied taking the plane* π_∞ *to infinity, then the point set will subsequently lie in front of the cameras* $\mathtt{P}^1$ *and* $\mathtt{P}^2$ *but behind the camera* $\mathtt{P}^3$*. Thus, suppose the point set* $\mathbf{X}$ *is reconstructed from images captured by cameras* $\mathtt{P}^1$ *and* $\mathtt{P}^2$*, and let* $\mathtt{P}^3$ *be any other camera matrix. If a plane exists separating the centre of camera* $\mathtt{P}^3$ *from the other camera centres, and not meeting the convex hull of the point set* $\mathbf{X}$*, then it cannot be determined whether the points lie in front of* $\mathtt{P}^3$.

first two views and then projecting into the third view. In this case, it is important to determine if a point lies in front of the third camera and is hence visible, or not.

If the third view is given simply by specifying the camera matrix with respect to the frame of reference of some given reconstruction, then it may be impossible to determine whether points are in front of the third camera or behind it in the true scene. The basic ambiguity is illustrated in figure 21.3. Knowledge of a single point known to be visible in the third view serves to break the ambiguity, however, as the following result shows. By applying theorem 21.7(*p*519) to the first and third views, one obtains the following criterion.

Result 21.17. *Let points* $(\mathtt{P}^1, \mathtt{P}^2, \{\mathbf{X}_i\})$ *be a realization of a set of correspondences* $\mathbf{x}_i^1 \leftrightarrow \mathbf{x}_i^2$*. Let* $\mathtt{P}^3$ *be the camera matrix of a third view and suppose that* $w_j^i \hat{\mathbf{x}}_i = \mathtt{P}^i \mathbf{X}_j$ *for* $i = 1, \ldots, 3$*. Then* $w_j^1 w_j^3$ *has the same sign for all points* $\mathbf{X}_j$ *visible in the third view.*

In practice, it will usually be the case that one knows at least one point $\mathbf{X}_0$ visible in the third view. This serves to define the sign $w_0^1 w_0^3$, and any other point $\mathbf{X}_j$ will be in front of the camera $\mathtt{P}^3$ if and only if $w_j^1 w_j^3 \doteq w_0^1 w_0^3$.

As an example, once a projective reconstruction has been carried out using two views, the camera matrix of the third camera may be determined from the images of six or more points known to be in front of it by solving directly for the matrix $\mathtt{P}^3$ given the correspondences $\mathbf{x}_i^3 = \mathtt{P}^3 \mathbf{X}_i$ where points $\mathbf{X}_i$ are the reconstructed points. Then one can determine unambiguously which other points are in front of $\mathtt{P}^3$.

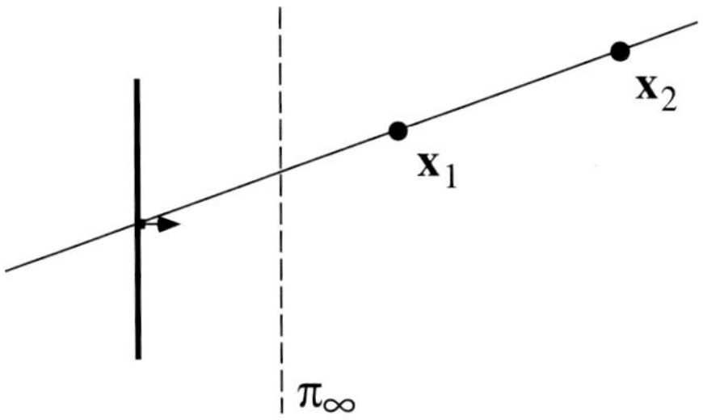

Fig. 21.4. *As shown, the point* $\mathbf{X}_1$ *is closer to the camera than* $\mathbf{X}_2$. *However, if an orientation-reversing projectivity is applied, taking* π_∞ *to infinity, then both* $\mathbf{X}_1$ *and* $\mathbf{X}_2$ *remain in front of the camera, but* $\mathbf{X}_2$ *is closer to the camera than* $\mathbf{X}_1$.

21.9 Which points are in front of which

When we are attempting to synthesize a new view of a scene that has been reconstructed from two or more uncalibrated views it is sometimes necessary to consider the possibility of points being obscured by other points. This leads to the question: given two points that project to the same point in the new view, which one is closer to the camera, and hence obscures the other? In the case where the possibility exists of oppositely oriented quasi-affine reconstructions it may once again be impossible to determine which of a pair of points is closer to the new camera. This is illustrated in figure 21.4. If a plane exists, separating the camera centres from the point set, then two oppositely oriented reconstructions exist, and one cannot determine which points are in front of which. The sort of ambiguity shown in figure 21.4 can only occur in the case where there exists a plane π_∞ that separates the camera centres from the set of all visible points. If this is not the case, then one can compute a quasi-affine reconstruction and the problem is easily solved. To avoid the effort of computing a quasi-affine reconstruction, however, we would like to solve this problem using only a projective reconstruction of the scene. How this may be done is explained next.

One may invert (21.1–*p*518) to get an expression for $\text{depth}^{-1}(\mathbf{X}; \mathtt{P}) = 1/\text{depth}(\mathbf{X}; \mathtt{P})$. This inverse depth function is infinite on the principal plane of the camera, zero on the plane at infinity, positive for points in front of the camera and negative for points behind the camera. For notational simplicity, we write $\chi(\mathbf{X}; \mathtt{P})$ instead of $\text{depth}^{-1}(\mathbf{X}; \mathtt{P})$.

For points $\mathbf{X}$ lying on a ray through the camera centre, the value of $\chi(\mathbf{X}; \mathtt{P})$ decreases monotonically along this ray, from zero at the camera centre, decreasing through positive values to zero at the plane at infinity, thence continuing to decrease through negative values to $-\infty$ at the camera centre. A point $\mathbf{X}_1$ lies closer to the front of the camera than $\mathbf{X}_2$ if and only if $\chi(\mathbf{X}_1) > \chi(\mathbf{X}_2)$. This is illustrated in figure 21.5.

Now, if the configuration undergoes an orientation-preserving transformation $\mathtt{H}$ taking the plane π_∞ to infinity, then the parameter χ will be replaced by a new parameter χ' defined by $\chi'(\mathbf{X}) = \chi(\mathtt{H}\mathbf{X}; \mathtt{PH}^{-1})$. The value of χ' must also vary monotonically along the ray. Since $\mathtt{H}$ is orientation-preserving, points just in front of the camera centre will remain in front of the camera after the transformation, because of result 21.13.

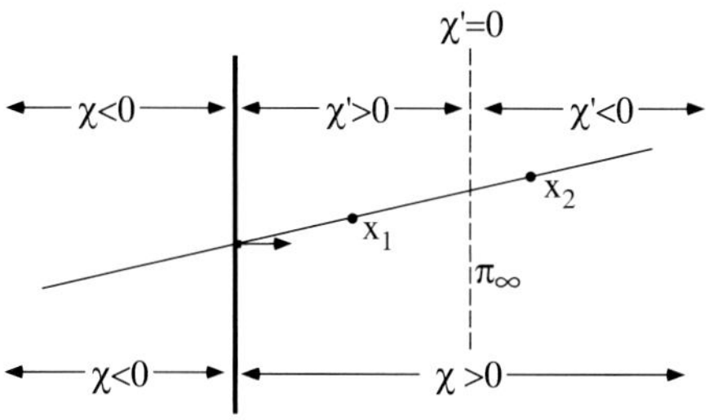

Fig. 21.5. *The parameter* χ.

Thus both χ and χ' decrease monotonically in the same direction along the ray. If $\mathbf{X}_1$ and $\mathbf{X}_2$ are two points on the line, then $\chi'(\mathbf{X}_1) > \chi'(\mathbf{X}_2)$ if and only if $\chi(\mathbf{X}_1) > \chi(\mathbf{X}_2)$.

In the case where the projective transformation has negative determinant, then the front and back of the camera are reversed locally. In this case the direction of increase of the parameter χ' will be reversed. Consequently, $\chi'(\mathbf{X}_1) > \chi'(\mathbf{X}_2)$ if and only if $\chi(\mathbf{X}_1) < \chi(\mathbf{X}_2)$.

In the case where the projective transformation transforms the scene to the "true" scene, of two points that project to the same point in the image, the one with the higher value of χ' is closer to the camera. This leads to the following result that allows us to determine from an arbitrary projective reconstruction which of two points is closer to the front of the camera.

Result 21.18. *Suppose that* $\mathbf{X}_1$ *and* $\mathbf{X}_2$ *are two points that map to the same point in an image. Consider a projective reconstruction of the scene and let the parameter* χ *be defined (by formula (21.3–*p521*)) in the frame of the projective reconstruction. If the projective reconstruction has the same orientation as the true scene, then the point that lies closer to the front of the camera in the true scene is the one that has the greater value of* χ. *On the other hand, if the projective transformation has the opposite orientation, then the point with smaller value of* χ *will lie closer to the front of the camera in the true scene.*

As remarked previously, unless there exists a plane separating the point set from the cameras used for the reconstruction, the orientation of the scene is uniquely determined, and one can determine whether the projective transformation of result 21.18 has positive or negative determinant. However, to do this may require one to compute a strong realization of the configuration by the linear programming method as described in section 21.7. If differently oriented strong realizations exist, then as illustrated by figure 21.4, there is an essential ambiguity. However, this ambiguity may be resolved by knowledge of the relative distance from the camera of a single pair of points.

21.10 Closure

21.10.1 The literature

The topic of this chapter belongs to *Oriented projective geometry*, which is treated in a standard and readable text [Stolfi-91]. Laveau and Faugeras apply the ideas of oriented projective geometry in [Laveau-96b]. The concepts of front and back of the camera were also used in [Robert-93] to compute convex hulls in projective reconstructions. This chapter derives from the paper [Hartley-98a] which also treats such topics of invariants for quasi-affine mappings and conditions under which arbitrary correspondences allow quasi-affine reconstructions.

Cheirality, and specifically the cheirality inequalities have been useful in determining quasi-affine reconstructions as an intermediate step towards affine and metric reconstruction in [Hartley-94b, Hartley-99]. More recently Werner and Pajdla in [Werner-01] have used oriented projective geometry to eliminate spurious line correspondences, and to constrain correspondences of five points [Werner-03], over two views.

22

Degenerate Configurations

In past chapters we have given algorithms for the estimation of various quantities associated with multiple images – the projection matrix, the fundamental matrix and the trifocal tensor. In each of these cases, linear and iterative algorithms were given, but little consideration was given to the possibility that these algorithms could fail. We now consider under what conditions this might happen.

Typically, if sufficiently many point correspondences are given in some sort of "general position" then the quantities in question will be uniquely determined, and the algorithms we have given will succeed. However, if there are too few point correspondences given, or else all the points lie in certain critical configurations, then there will not be a unique solution. Sometimes there will be a finite number of different solutions, and sometimes a complete family of solutions.

This chapter will concentrate on three of the main estimation problems that we have encountered in this book, camera resectioning, reconstruction from two views and reconstruction from three views. Some of the results given here are classical, particularly the camera resectioning and two-view critical surface problems. Others are more recent results. We consider the different estimation problems in turn.

22.1 Camera resectioning

We begin by considering the problem of computing the camera projection matrix, given a set of points in space and the corresponding set of points in the image. Thus, one is given a set of points $\mathbf{X}_i$ in space that are mapped to points $\mathbf{x}_i$ in the image by a camera with projection matrix $\mathtt{P}$. The coordinates of the points in space and the image are known, and the matrix $\mathtt{P}$ is to be computed. This problem was considered in chapter 7. Before considering the critical configurations for this problem, we will digress to look at an abstraction of the camera projection.

Cameras as points

Suppose the existence of a set of correspondences $\mathbf{X}_i \leftrightarrow \mathbf{x}_i$. Let us suppose that there is a unique camera matrix $\mathtt{P}$ such that $\mathbf{x}_i = \mathtt{P}\mathbf{X}_i$. Now, let $\mathtt{H}$ be a matrix representing a projective transformation of the image, and let $\mathbf{x}'_i = \mathtt{H}\mathbf{x}_i$ be the set of transformed image coordinates. Then it is clear that there is a unique camera matrix $\mathtt{P}'$ such that

$\mathbf{x}'_i = \mathtt{P}'\mathbf{X}_i$, namely the camera matrix $\mathtt{P}' = \mathtt{HP}$. Conversely, if there exists more than one camera matrix $\mathtt{P}$ mapping $\mathbf{X}_i$ to $\mathbf{x}_i$, then there exists more than one camera matrix $\mathtt{P}'$ mapping $\mathbf{X}_i$ to $\mathbf{x}'_i$. Thus, the existence or not of a unique solution to the problem of determining the projection matrix $\mathtt{P}$ is dependent on the image points $\mathbf{x}_i$ *only up to a projective transformation* $\mathtt{H}$ of the image.

Next, observe that applying a projective transformation $\mathtt{H}$ to a camera matrix $\mathtt{P}$ does not change the camera centre. Specifically, the point $\mathbf{C}$ is the camera centre if and only if $\mathtt{P}\mathbf{C} = \mathbf{0}$. However $\mathtt{P}\mathbf{C} = \mathbf{0}$ if and only if $\mathtt{HP}\mathbf{C} = \mathbf{0}$. Thus, the camera centre is preserved by a projective transformation of the image. Next, we show that this is essentially the only property of the camera that is preserved.

Result 22.1. *Let* $\mathtt{P}$ *and* $\mathtt{P}'$ *be two camera matrices with the same centre. Then there exists a projective image transformation represented by a non-singular matrix* $\mathtt{H}$ *such that* $\mathtt{P}' = \mathtt{HP}$.

Proof. If the centre $\mathbf{C}$ is not at infinity, then the camera matrices are of the form $\mathtt{P} = [\mathtt{M} \mid -\mathtt{M}\mathbf{c}]$ and $\mathtt{P}' = [\mathtt{M}' \mid -\mathtt{M}'\mathbf{c}]$, where $\mathbf{c}$ is the inhomogeneous 3-vector representing the camera centre. Then clearly, $\mathtt{P}' = \mathtt{M}'\mathtt{M}^{-1}\mathtt{P}$. If $\mathbf{C}$ is a point at infinity, then one chooses a 3D projective transformation $\mathtt{G}$ such that $\mathtt{G}\mathbf{C}$ is a finite point, say $\widehat{\mathbf{C}}$. In this case, the two camera matrices $\mathtt{PG}^{-1}$ and $\mathtt{P}'\mathtt{G}^{-1}$ both have the same centre, namely $\widehat{\mathbf{C}}$. It follows that $\mathtt{P}'\mathtt{G} = \mathtt{HPG}$ for some $\mathtt{H}$. Cancelling $\mathtt{G}$ gives $\mathtt{P}' = \mathtt{HP}$. □

This result may be interpreted as saying that an image is determined up to projectivity by the camera centre alone. Thus, we see that in considering the problem of uniqueness of the camera matrix, one may ignore all the parameters of the camera, except the camera centre, since this alone determines the projectivity type of the image, and hence the uniqueness or not of a solution.

Images as equivalence classes of rays

To gain insight into the critical configurations of camera resectioning, we turn first to consider 2-dimensional cameras, mapping $\mathbb{P}^2$ to $\mathbb{P}^1$. Consider a camera centre $\mathbf{c}$ and a set of points $\mathbf{x}_i$ in space. The rays $\overline{\mathbf{c}\mathbf{x}_i}$ intersect an image line $\mathbf{l}$ at a set of points $\bar{\mathbf{x}}_i$; thus points $\bar{\mathbf{x}}_i$ are the images of the points $\mathbf{x}_i$. The projection of the points $\mathbf{x}_i$ to points $\bar{\mathbf{x}}_i$ in the 1D image may be described by a 2×3 projection matrix as described in section 6.4.2(*p*175).

As shown in chapter 2, the projective equivalence type of the set of rays $\overline{\mathbf{c}\mathbf{x}_i}$ is the same as that of the image points $\bar{\mathbf{x}}_i$. This is illustrated in figure 22.1. Thus, instead of considering an image as being the set of points on the image line, the image may be thought of as the projective equivalence class of the set of rays from the camera centre through each of the image points. In the case of just 4 image points, the cross ratio of the points $\bar{\mathbf{x}}_i$ (or equivalently, the rays) characterizes their projective equivalence class. To give a specific notation, we denote by $\langle \mathbf{c}; \mathbf{x}_1, \ldots, \mathbf{x}_i, \ldots \mathbf{x}_n \rangle$ the projective equivalence class of the set of rays $\overline{\mathbf{c}\mathbf{x}_i}$.

The same remarks are valid for projections of 3D points into a 2-dimensional image. One may also extend the above notation by writing $\langle \mathbf{C}; \mathbf{X}_1, \ldots, \mathbf{X}_n \rangle$ to represent the

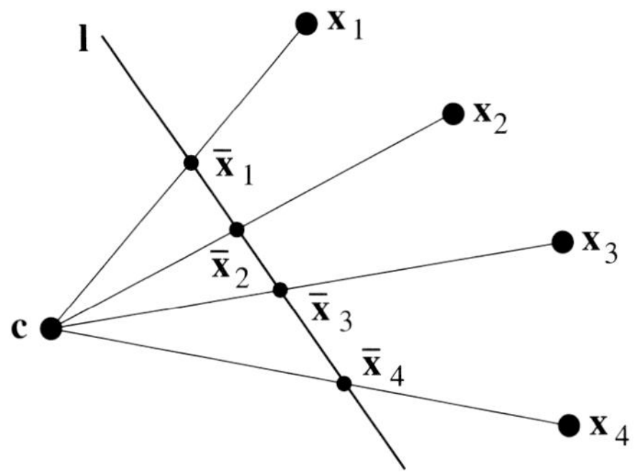

Fig. 22.1. *Projection of points in the plane using a 2D camera. A 1D image is formed by the intersection of the rays* $\mathbf{l}_i = \overline{\mathbf{c}\mathbf{x}_i}$ *with the image line* $\mathbf{l}$. *The set of image points* $\{\bar{\mathbf{x}}_i\}$ *is projectively equivalent to the set of rays* $\{\mathbf{l}_i\}$. *For four points, the projective equivalence class of the image is determined by the cross ratio of the points.*

projective equivalence class of all the rays $\overline{\mathbf{C}\mathbf{X}_i}$. As in the 2-dimensional case, this is an abstraction of the projection of the points $\mathbf{X}_i$ relative to a camera with centre at $\mathbf{C}$.

We will be considering configurations of camera centres and 3D points, which will be denoted by $\{\mathbf{C}_1, \ldots, \mathbf{C}_m; \mathbf{X}_1, \ldots, \mathbf{X}_n\}$ or variations thereof. Implicit is that the symbols appearing before the semicolon are camera centres, and those that come after are 3D points. In order to make the statements of derived results simple, the concept of *image equivalence* is defined.

Definition 22.2. Two configurations

$$\{\mathbf{C}_1, \ldots, \mathbf{C}_m; \mathbf{X}_1, \ldots, \mathbf{X}_n\} \text{ and } \{\mathbf{C}'_1, \ldots, \mathbf{C}'_m; \mathbf{X}'_1, \ldots, \mathbf{X}'_n\}$$

are called *image-equivalent* if $\langle \mathbf{C}_i; \mathbf{X}_1, \ldots, \mathbf{X}_n \rangle = \langle \mathbf{C}'_i; \mathbf{X}'_1, \ldots, \mathbf{X}'_n \rangle$ for all $i = 1, \ldots, m$.

The concept of image equivalence is distinct from projective equivalence of the sets of points and camera centres involved. Indeed, the relevance of this to reconstruction ambiguity is that if a configuration $\{\mathbf{C}_1, \ldots, \mathbf{C}_m; \mathbf{X}_1, \ldots, \mathbf{X}_n\}$ allows another image-equivalent set which is not projective equivalent, then this amounts to an ambiguity of the projective reconstruction problem, since the projective structure of the points and cameras is not uniquely defined by the set of images. In this case, we say that the configuration $\{\mathbf{C}_1, \ldots, \mathbf{C}_m; \mathbf{X}_1, \ldots, \mathbf{X}_n\}$ *allows an alternative reconstruction.*

22.1.1 Ambiguity in 2D – Chasles' theorem

Before considering the usual 3D cameras, we discuss the simpler case of 2D cameras. The analysis of the uniqueness of 2D camera projections involves planar conics. Ambiguity in determining the camera centre from the projection of a set of known points $\mathbf{x}_i$ means that the projection of the points is the same from two different camera centres $\mathbf{c}$ and $\mathbf{c}'$. The question is for what configurations of the points this may occur. The answer to this question is given by Chasles' Theorem.

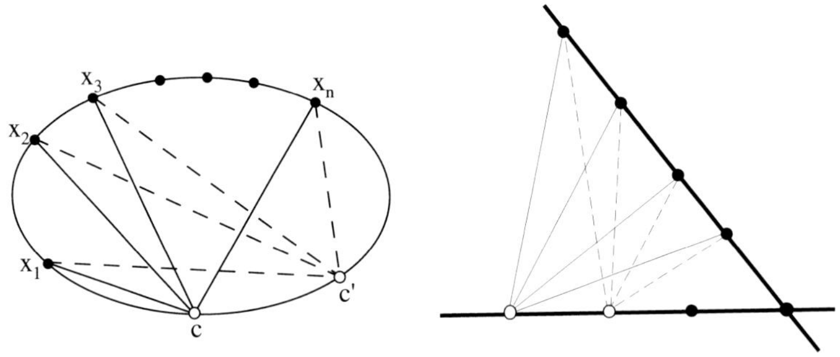

Fig. 22.2. *The points* $\mathbf{x}_1, \ldots, \mathbf{x}_n$ *project in equivalent ways to the two camera centres* $\mathbf{c}$ *and* $\mathbf{c}'$.

Theorem 22.3 Chasles' Theorem. *Let* $\mathbf{x}_i$ *be a set of* n *points and* $\mathbf{c}$ *and* $\mathbf{c}'$ *two camera centres, all lying in a plane. Then*

$$\langle \mathbf{c}; \mathbf{x}_1, \ldots, \mathbf{x}_n \rangle = \langle \mathbf{c}'; \mathbf{x}_1, \ldots, \mathbf{x}_n \rangle$$

if and only if one of the following conditions holds

(i) *The points* $\mathbf{c}$, $\mathbf{c}'$ *and all* $\mathbf{x}_i$ *all lie on a non-degenerate conic, or*
(ii) *All points lie on the union of two lines (a degenerate conic), both camera centres lying on the same line.*

These two configurations are shown in figure 22.2.

Note that as a simple corollary of this theorem, if $\mathbf{c}''$ is any other camera centre lying on the same component of a conic (degenerate or non-degenerate) as $\mathbf{c}$, $\mathbf{c}'$ and the $\mathbf{x}_i$, then the projection of the points to the centre $\mathbf{c}''$ is equivalent to their projection to the original camera centres. Furthermore, any number of extra points $\mathbf{x}_j$ may be added without breaking the ambiguity, as long as they lie on the same conic.

22.1.2 Ambiguity for 3D cameras

We now address the problem of ambiguity of camera resection in the case of full 3D cameras. Twisted cubics (described in section 3.3(*p*75)) play an analogous role in the 3D case to that played by conics in the case of 2D cameras. The degenerate form of a twisted cubic consisting of a conic plus a line intersecting the conic arises in this context; so does the degenerate cubic consisting of three lines. As in the 2D case, when ambiguity arises from points lying on a degenerate cubic, the camera centres must both lie on the same component.

A complete classification of the point and camera configurations leading to ambiguous camera resectioning is given in figure 22.3 and also in the following definition. For the present we describe the geometric configurations. The exact relevance to ambiguous camera configurations will be given afterwards.

Definition 22.4.
A *critical set* for camera resectioning consists of two parts:

(i) An algebraic curve $\mathcal{C}$ containing the camera centres, plus any number of the 3D points. This curve may be

  (a) a non-degenerate twisted cubic (degree 3),
  (b) a planar conic (degree 2),
  (c) a straight line (degree 1), or
  (d) a single point (degree 0).

(ii) A union of linear subspaces L (lines or planes) containing any number of 3D points.

The curve $\mathcal{C}$ and the linear subspaces satisfy three conditions:

(i) Each of the linear subspaces must meet the curve $\mathcal{C}$.
(ii) The sum of the degree of the curve $\mathcal{C}$ and the dimensions of the linear subspaces is at most 3.
(iii) Except in the case where $\mathcal{C}$ is a single point, the cameras do not lie at the intersection point of $\mathcal{C}$ and the linear subspaces.

The various possibilities are shown in figure 22.3, and it is easily verified that these completely enumerate all configurations in accordance with definition 22.4.

Result 22.5. *The different possible critical sets for camera resectioning are:*

(i) A non-degenerate twisted cubic $\mathcal{C}$ (degree 3).
(ii) A plane conic $\mathcal{C}$ (degree 2), plus a line (dimension 1) that meets the conic.
(iii) A line $\mathcal{C}$ (degree 1) plus up to two other lines (total dimension 2) that meet the first line.
(iv) A line $\mathcal{C}$ (degree 1), plus a plane (dimension 2).
(v) A point $\mathcal{C}$ (degree 0) and up to three lines passing through the point (total dimension 3).
(vi) A point $\mathcal{C}$ (degree 0) and a line and a plane both passing through this point.

The exact relationship of these critical sets to ambiguous camera resectioning is given by the following result.

Result 22.6. *Let $\mathtt{P}$ and $\mathtt{P}'$ be two different camera matrices with camera centres $\mathbf{C}_0$ and $\mathbf{C}_1$. Then the two camera centres and the points $\mathbf{X}_i$ that satisfy $\mathtt{P}\mathbf{X}_i = \mathtt{P}'\mathbf{X}_i$ all lie on a critical set as given by definition 22.4.*

Furthermore, if $\mathtt{P}_\theta = \mathtt{P} + \theta\mathtt{P}'$ has rank 3[1]*, then the camera centre of the camera defined by $\mathtt{P}_\theta$ lies on the component $\mathcal{C}$ of the critical set containing the two original camera centres $\mathbf{C}_0$ and $\mathbf{C}_1$, and $\mathtt{P}_\theta\mathbf{X} = \mathtt{P}\mathbf{X} = \mathtt{P}'\mathbf{X}$ for any point $\mathbf{X}$ in the critical set.*

Conversely, let $\mathtt{P}$ be a camera matrix with centre $\mathbf{C}_0$. Let $\mathbf{C}_0$ and a set of 3D points $\mathbf{X}_i$ lie in a critical set for camera resectioning. Let $\mathbf{C}_1$ be any other point lying on the component $\mathcal{C}$ of the critical set, with $\mathbf{C}_1 \neq \mathbf{C}_0$ unless $\mathcal{C}$ consists of a single point. Then there exists a camera matrix $\mathtt{P}'$ (different from $\mathtt{P}$) with camera centre $\mathbf{C}_1$ such that $\mathtt{P}\mathbf{X}_i = \mathtt{P}'\mathbf{X}_i$ for all points $\mathbf{X}_i$.

[1] We include the case $\mathtt{P}_\infty = \mathtt{P}'$.

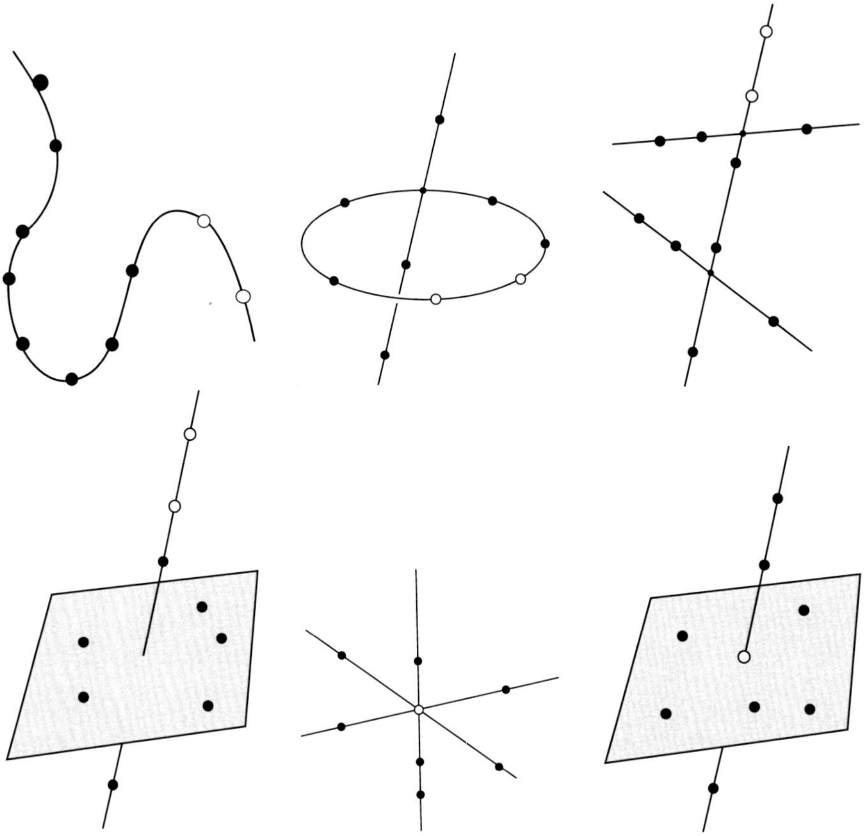

Fig. 22.3. *The different critical configurations for camera resectioning from a single view. The open circles represent centres of projection and the filled circles represent points. Each case consists of an algebraic curve (or single point) C containing the camera centres, plus a set of linear subspaces (lines or planes).*

Proof. An outline of the proof will be given, with details left for the reader to fill in. We temporarily need to distinguish between equality of homogeneous quantities up to a scale factor (which will be denoted by $\approx$) and absolute equality (which is denoted by $=$). Suppose that $\mathbf{X}$ maps to the same image point with respect to cameras $\mathtt{P}$ and $\mathtt{P}'$. One can write $\mathtt{P}\mathbf{X} \approx \mathtt{P}'\mathbf{X}$. Taking account of the scale factor, this can be written as $\mathtt{P}\mathbf{X} = -\theta\mathtt{P}'\mathbf{X}$ for some constant θ. From this it follows that $(\mathtt{P} + \theta\mathtt{P}')\mathbf{X} = \mathbf{0}$. Conversely, suppose that $(\mathtt{P} + \theta\mathtt{P}')\mathbf{X} = \mathbf{0}$. for some θ. It follows that $\mathtt{P}\mathbf{X} = -\theta\mathtt{P}'\mathbf{X}$, and so $\mathtt{P}\mathbf{X} \approx \mathtt{P}'\mathbf{X}$. Thus, the critical set is the set of points $\mathbf{X}$ in the right null-space of $\mathtt{P} + \theta\mathtt{P}'$ for some θ.

Define $\mathtt{P}_\theta = \mathtt{P} + \theta\mathtt{P}'$. The rest of the proof involves finding the set of all points $\mathbf{X}$ satisfying $\mathtt{P}_\theta\mathbf{X} = \mathbf{0}$ as θ runs over all values. If $\mathtt{P}_\theta$ is a camera matrix (has rank 3) then such an $\mathbf{X}$ is the centre of the camera $\mathtt{P}_\theta$. If however $\mathtt{P}_\theta$ is rank-deficient for some value of θ_i, then the set of points $\mathbf{X}$ such that $\mathbf{P}_{\theta_i}\mathbf{X} = \mathbf{0}$ is a linear space. The total critical set therefore consists of two parts:

(i) The locus of the camera centre of $\mathtt{P}_\theta$ over all values θ for which $\mathtt{P}_\theta$ has full rank (that is rank 3). This is a curve $\mathcal{C}$ containing the two camera centres $\mathbf{C}_0$ and $\mathbf{C}_1$.
(ii) A linear space (line or plane) corresponding to each value of θ for which $\mathtt{P}_\theta$ has rank 2 or less. If $\mathtt{P}_\theta$ has rank 2, the points such that $\mathtt{P}_\theta\mathbf{X} = \mathbf{0}$ form a line, and if it has rank 1, then they form a plane.

Let the 4-vector $\mathbf{C}_\theta$ be defined by $\mathbf{C}_\theta = (c_1, c_2, c_3, c_4)^\mathsf{T}$, where $c_i = (-1)^i \det \mathtt{P}_\theta^{(i)}$ and $\mathtt{P}_\theta^{(i)}$ is the matrix $\mathtt{P}_\theta$ with the i-th column removed. Since each $\mathtt{P}_\theta^{(i)}$ is a 3×3 matrix, and the entries of $\mathtt{P}_\theta$ are linear in θ, we see that each $c_i = (-1)^i \det \mathtt{P}_\theta^{(i)}$ is a cubic polynomial in θ. According to the discussion following definition 21.10(*p*521), $\mathtt{P}_\theta\mathbf{C}_\theta = \mathbf{0}$, hence if $\mathbf{C}_\theta \neq \mathbf{0}$ then it is the camera centre of $\mathtt{P}_\theta$, and as θ varies the point $\mathbf{C}_\theta$ traces out the curve $\mathcal{C}$. Since the coordinates of $\mathbf{C}_\theta$ are cubic polynomials, this is in general a twisted cubic. If however the four components of $\mathbf{C}_\theta$ have a simultaneous root θ_i, then the degree of the curve $\mathbf{C}_\theta$ is diminished. In this case $\mathtt{P}_{\theta_i}$ is rank-deficient, and there exists a linear space of points $\mathbf{X}$ such that $\mathtt{P}_{\theta_i}\mathbf{X} = \mathbf{0}$. Thus the linear subspace components of the critical set correspond to values of θ where $\mathbf{C}_\theta$ vanishes. Clearly there can be at most three such values. Further details are left to the reader.

The last part of the theorem provides a converse result – namely that if the points and one camera centre lie in a critical configuration, then there exist alternative resection solutions with the camera placed at any location in $\mathcal{C}$. The exact form of the camera matrix $\mathtt{P}$ is not important here, only its camera centre, as has been observed above. For most of the configurations in figure 22.3 it is clear enough geometrically that the image of the critical set is unchanged (up to projectivity) by moving the camera along the locus $\mathcal{C}$. In the case where $\mathcal{C}$ is a planar conic, this follows fairly easily from the 1D camera case (theorem 22.3). The exception is the twisted cubic case. It is illustrated graphically in figure 22.4. We leave this proof for now, and come back to it later (result 22.25(*p*551)). □

22.2 Degeneracies in two views

Notation. For the rest of this chapter, the camera matrices are represented by $\mathtt{P}$ and $\mathtt{Q}$, 3D points by $\mathbf{P}$ and $\mathbf{Q}$. Thus cameras and 3D points are distinguished only by their typeface. This may appear to be a little confusing, but the alternative of using subscripts or primes proved to be much more confusing. In the context of ambiguous reconstructions from image coordinates we distinguish the two reconstructions by using $\mathtt{P}$ and $\mathbf{P}$ for one, and $\mathtt{Q}$ and $\mathbf{Q}$ for the other.

Now we turn to the case of two views of an object. Given sufficiently many points placed in "general position" one may determine the placement of the two cameras, and reconstruct the point set up to a projective transformation. This may be done using one of the projective reconstruction algorithms discussed in chapter 10. We now wish to determine under what conditions this technique may fail.

Thus, we consider a set of image correspondences $\mathbf{x}_i \leftrightarrow \mathbf{x}'_i$. A realization of this set of correspondences consists of a pair of camera matrices $\mathtt{P}$ and $\mathtt{P}'$ and a set of 3D points $\mathbf{P}_i$ such that $\mathbf{x}_i = \mathtt{P}\mathbf{P}_i$ and $\mathbf{x}'_i = \mathtt{P}'\mathbf{P}_i$ for all i. Two realizations $\{\mathtt{P}, \mathtt{P}', \mathbf{P}_i\}$

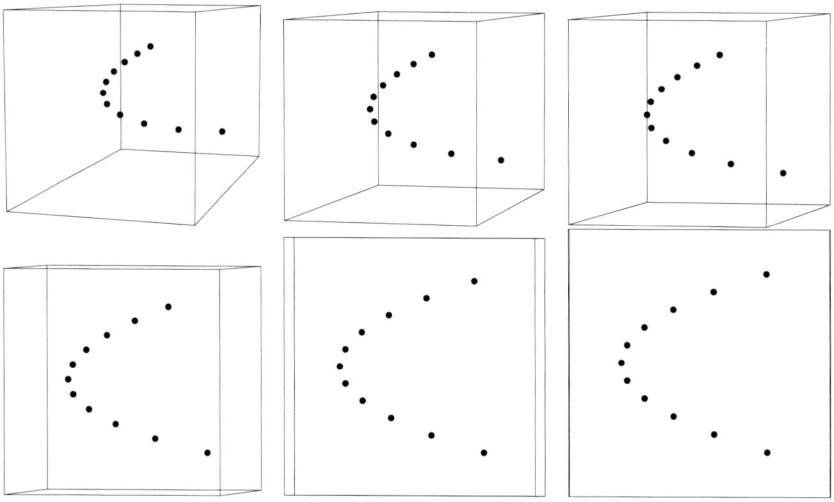

Fig. 22.4. *Separate views of a set of points on the twisted cubic* $(t^3, t^2, t, 1)^\mathsf{T}$ *as viewed from a centre of projection. The visible points are viewed from the points with* $t = 3, 4, 5, 10, 50, 1000$ *with the image suitably magnified to prevent the point set from becoming too small. As is plausible from the image, the sets of points differ by a projective transformation. From a viewpoint on a twisted cubic, the twisted cubic has the appearance of a conic, in this particular case a parabola.*

and $\{\mathtt{Q}, \mathtt{Q}', \mathbf{Q}_i\}$ are projectively equivalent if there is a 3D projective transformation, represented by a matrix $\mathtt{H}$ such that $\mathtt{Q} = \mathtt{PH}^{-1}$, $\mathtt{Q}' = \mathtt{P}'\mathtt{H}^{-1}$, and $\mathbf{Q}_i = \mathtt{H}\mathbf{P}_i$ for all i.

Because of a technicality, this definition of equivalence is not quite appropriate to the present discussion. Recall from the projective reconstruction theorem, theorem 10.1-(*p*266), that one cannot determine the position of a point lying on the line joining the two camera centres. Hence, non-projectively-equivalent reconstructions will always exist if some points lie on the line of camera centres, the two reconstructions differing only by the position of the points $\mathbf{P}_i$ and $\mathbf{Q}_i$ on this line. This type of reconstruction ambiguity is not of great interest, and so we will modify the notion of equivalence by defining two reconstructions to be equivalent if $\mathtt{H}$ exists such that $\mathtt{Q} = \mathtt{PH}^{-1}$ and $\mathtt{Q}' = \mathtt{P}'\mathtt{H}^{-1}$. As in the proof of the projective reconstruction theorem, such an $\mathtt{H}$ will also map $\mathbf{Q}_i$ to $\mathbf{P}_i$, except possibly for reconstructed points $\mathbf{Q}_i$ lying on the line of the camera centres. According to theorem 9.10(*p*254), this condition is also equivalent to the condition that $\mathtt{F}_{\mathtt{P}'\mathtt{P}} = \mathtt{F}_{\mathtt{Q}'\mathtt{Q}}$, where $\mathtt{F}_{\mathtt{P}'\mathtt{P}}$ and $\mathtt{F}_{\mathtt{Q}'\mathtt{Q}}$ are the fundamental matrices corresponding to the camera pairs $(\mathtt{P}, \mathtt{P}')$ and $(\mathtt{Q}, \mathtt{Q}')$. Accordingly, we make the following definition.

Definition 22.7. Two configurations of cameras and points $\{\mathtt{P}, \mathtt{P}', \mathbf{P}_i\}$ and $\{\mathtt{Q}, \mathtt{Q}', \mathbf{Q}_i\}$ are said to be *conjugate configurations* provided

(i) $\mathtt{P}\mathbf{P}_i = \mathtt{Q}\mathbf{Q}_i$ and $\mathtt{P}'\mathbf{P}_i = \mathtt{Q}'\mathbf{Q}_i$ for all i.
(ii) The fundamental matrices $\mathtt{F}_{\mathtt{Q}'\mathtt{Q}}$ and $\mathtt{F}_{\mathtt{Q}'\mathtt{Q}}$ corresponding to the two camera matrix pairs $(\mathtt{P}, \mathtt{P}')$ and $(\mathtt{Q}, \mathtt{Q}')$ are different.

A configuration $\{\mathtt{P}, \mathtt{P}', \mathbf{P}_i\}$ that allows a conjugate configuration is called *critical*.

An important remark is that being a critical configuration depends only on the camera centres and the points, and not on the particular cameras.

Result 22.8. *If* $\{\mathtt{P}, \mathtt{P}', \mathbf{P}_i\}$ *is a critical configuration and* $\hat{\mathtt{P}}$ *and* $\hat{\mathtt{P}}'$ *are two cameras with the same centres as* $\mathtt{P}$ *and* $\mathtt{P}'$ *respectively, then* $\{\hat{\mathtt{P}}, \hat{\mathtt{P}}', \mathbf{P}_i\}$ *is a critical configuration as well.*

Proof. This is easily seen as follows. Since $\{\mathtt{P}, \mathtt{P}', \mathbf{P}_i\}$ is a critical configuration there exists an alternative configuration $\{\mathtt{Q}, \mathtt{Q}', \mathbf{Q}_i\}$ such that $\mathtt{P}\mathbf{P}_i = \mathtt{Q}\mathbf{Q}_i$ and $\mathtt{P}'\mathbf{P}_i = \mathtt{Q}'\mathbf{Q}_i$ for all i. However, since $\mathtt{P}$ and $\hat{\mathtt{P}}$ have the same camera centre, $\hat{\mathtt{P}} = \mathtt{H}\mathtt{P}$ according to result 22.1 and similarly $\hat{\mathtt{P}}' = \mathtt{H}'\mathtt{P}'$. Therefore

$$\begin{aligned}\hat{\mathtt{P}}\mathbf{P}_i &= \mathtt{H}\mathtt{P}\mathbf{P}_i = \mathtt{H}\mathtt{Q}\mathbf{Q}_i \text{ and} \\ \hat{\mathtt{P}}'\mathbf{P}_i &= \mathtt{H}'\mathtt{P}'\mathbf{P}_i = \mathtt{H}'\mathtt{Q}'\mathbf{Q}_i.\end{aligned}$$

It follows that $\{\mathtt{H}\mathtt{Q}, \mathtt{H}'\mathtt{Q}', \mathbf{Q}_i\}$ is an alternative configuration to $\{\hat{\mathtt{P}}, \hat{\mathtt{P}}', \mathbf{P}_i\}$, which is therefore critical. □

The goal of this section is to determine under what conditions non-equivalent realizations of a set of point correspondences may occur. This question is completely resolved by the following theorem, which will be proved incrementally.

Theorem 22.9. (i) *Conjugate configurations of cameras and points generically come in triples. Thus a critical configuration* $\{\mathtt{P}, \mathtt{P}', \mathbf{P}_i\}$ *has two conjugates* $\{\mathtt{Q}, \mathtt{Q}', \mathbf{Q}_i\}$ *and* $\{\mathtt{R}, \mathtt{R}', \mathbf{R}_i\}$.

(ii) *If* $\{\mathtt{P}, \mathtt{P}', \mathbf{P}_i\}$ *is a critical configuration, then all the points* $\mathbf{P}_i$ *and the two camera centres* $\mathbf{C}_{\mathtt{P}}$ *and* $\mathbf{C}_{\mathtt{P}'}$ *lie on a ruled quadric surface* $\mathtt{S}_{\mathtt{P}}$.

(iii) *Conversely, suppose that the camera centres of* $\mathtt{P}$, $\mathtt{P}'$ *and a set of 3D points* $\mathbf{P}_i$ *lie on a ruled quadric (excluding the quadrics* (v) *and* (viii) *in result 22.11), then* $\{\mathtt{P}, \mathtt{P}', \mathbf{P}_i\}$ *is a critical configuration.*

By the words "ruled quadric" in this context is meant any quadric surface that contains a straight line. This includes various degenerate quadrics, as will be seen. A general discussion and classification of quadric surfaces has been given in section 3.2.4-(*p*74). A *quadric* is usually defined to be the set of points $\mathbf{X}$ such that $\mathbf{X}^\mathsf{T}\mathtt{S}\mathbf{X} = 0$, where $\mathtt{S}$ is a symmetric 4×4 matrix. However, if $\mathtt{S}$ is any 4×4 matrix, not necessarily symmetric, then one sees that for any point $\mathbf{X}$, one has $\mathbf{X}^\mathsf{T}\mathtt{S}\mathbf{X} = (\mathbf{X}^\mathsf{T}\mathtt{S}_{\text{sym}}\mathbf{X})$, where $\mathtt{S}_{\text{sym}} = (\mathtt{S} + \mathtt{S}^\mathsf{T})/2$ is the symmetric part of $\mathtt{S}$. Thus, $\mathbf{X}^\mathsf{T}\mathtt{S}\mathbf{X} = 0$ if and only if $\mathbf{X}^\mathsf{T}\mathtt{S}_{\text{sym}}\mathbf{X} = 0$, and so $\mathtt{S}$ defines the same quadric surface as $\mathtt{S}_{\text{sym}}$. In investigating reconstruction ambiguity, it will often be convenient to use non-symmetric matrices $\mathtt{S}$ to represent quadrics.

Proof. We begin by proving the first part of the theorem. Let $\mathtt{F}$ and $\mathtt{F}'$ be two distinct fundamental matrices satisfying the relation $\mathbf{x}_i'^\mathsf{T}\mathtt{F}\mathbf{x}_i = \mathbf{x}_i'\mathtt{F}'\mathbf{x}_i = 0$ for all correspondences $\mathbf{x}_i' \leftrightarrow \mathbf{x}_i$. Define $\mathtt{F}_\theta = \mathtt{F} + \theta\mathtt{F}'$. One easily verifies that $\mathbf{x}_i'^\mathsf{T}\mathtt{F}_\theta\mathbf{x}_i = 0$. However, $\mathtt{F}_\theta$ is a fundamental matrix only if $\det \mathtt{F}_\theta = 0$. Now, $\det \mathtt{F}(\theta)$ is generally a polynomial of degree 3 in θ. This polynomial has roots $\theta = 0$ and $\theta = 1$ corresponding to $\mathtt{F}$ and

F' respectively. The third root corresponds to a third fundamental matrix, and hence a third non-equivalent reconstruction. In special cases, $\det F(\theta)$ has degree 2 in θ and there are only two conjugate configurations. □

The second part of the theorem is concluded by proving the following lemma.

Lemma 22.10. *Consider two pairs of cameras* (P, P') *and* (Q, Q')*, with corresponding different fundamental matrices* $F_{P'P}$ *and* $F_{Q'Q}$*. Define quadrics* $S_P = P'^T F_{Q'Q} P$*, and* $S_Q = Q'^T F_{P'P} Q$.

(i) *The quadric* S_P *contains the camera centres of* P *and* P'*. Similarly,* S_Q *contains the camera centres of* Q *and* Q'.
(ii) S_P *is a ruled quadric.*
(iii) *If* $\mathbf{P}$ *and* $\mathbf{Q}$ *are 3D points such that* $P\mathbf{P} = Q\mathbf{Q}$ *and* $P'\mathbf{P} = Q'\mathbf{Q}$*, then* $\mathbf{P}$ *lies on the quadric* S_P*, and* $\mathbf{Q}$ *lies on* S_Q.
(iv) *Conversely, if* $\mathbf{P}$ *is a point lying on the quadric* S_P*, then there exists a point* $\mathbf{Q}$ *lying on* S_Q *such that* $P\mathbf{P} = Q\mathbf{Q}$ *and* $P'\mathbf{P} = Q'\mathbf{Q}$.

Proof. Recall that according to result 9.12(*p*255) the matrix F is the fundamental matrix corresponding to a pair of cameras (P, P') if and only if $P'^T F P$ is skew-symmetric. Since $F_{P'P} \neq F_{Q'Q}$, however, the matrices S_P and S_Q defined here are not skew-symmetric, and hence represent non-trivial quadrics.
We adopt a convention that a camera represented by a matrix such as P or P' has camera centre denoted by $\mathbf{C}_P$ or $\mathbf{C}_{P'}$.

(i) The camera centre of P satisfies $P\mathbf{C}_P = \mathbf{0}$. Then

$$\mathbf{C}_P^T S_P \mathbf{C}_P = \mathbf{C}_P^T (P'^T F_{Q'Q} P) \mathbf{C}_P = \mathbf{C}_P^T (P'^T F_{Q'Q}) P \mathbf{C}_P = 0$$

since $P\mathbf{C}_P = \mathbf{0}$. So, $\mathbf{C}_P$ lies on the quadric S_P. In a similar manner, $\mathbf{C}_{P'}$ lies on S_P.
(ii) Let $\mathbf{e}_Q$ be the epipole defined by $F_{Q'Q}\mathbf{e}_Q = \mathbf{0}$, and consider the ray passing through $\mathbf{C}_P$ consisting of all points such that $\mathbf{e}_Q = P\mathbf{X}$. Then for any such point, one verifies that $S_P\mathbf{X} = P'^T F_{Q'Q} P\mathbf{X} = P'^T F_{Q'Q} \mathbf{e}_Q = 0$. Thus the ray lies on S_P and so S_P is a ruled quadric.
(iii) Under the given conditions one sees that

$$\mathbf{P}^T S_P \mathbf{P} = \mathbf{P}^T P'^T F_{Q'Q} P\mathbf{P} = \mathbf{Q}^T (Q'^T F_{Q'Q} Q) \mathbf{Q} = 0$$

since $Q'^T F_{Q'Q} Q$ is skew-symmetric. Thus, $\mathbf{P}$ lies on the quadric S_P. By a similar argument, $\mathbf{Q}$ lies on S_Q.
(iv) Let $\mathbf{P}$ lie on S_P and define $\mathbf{x} = P\mathbf{P}$ and $\mathbf{x}' = P'\mathbf{P}$. Then, from $\mathbf{P}^T S_P \mathbf{P} = 0$ we deduce $0 = \mathbf{P}^T P'^T F_{Q'Q} P\mathbf{P} = \mathbf{x}'^T F_{Q'Q} \mathbf{x}$, and so $\mathbf{x} \leftrightarrow \mathbf{x}'$ are a corresponding pair of points with respect to $F_{Q'Q}$. Therefore, there exists a point $\mathbf{Q}$ such that $Q\mathbf{Q} = \mathbf{x} = P\mathbf{P}$, and $Q'\mathbf{Q} = \mathbf{x}' = P'\mathbf{P}$. From part (iii) of this lemma, $\mathbf{Q}$ must lie on S_Q.

□

This lemma completely describes the sets of 3D points giving rise to ambiguous image correspondences. Note that any two arbitrarily chosen camera pairs can give rise to ambiguous image correspondences, provided that the world points lie on the given quadrics.

22.2.1 Examples of ambiguity

At this point it remains to prove the converse of theorem 22.9. This needs to be done for all types of ruled quadrics and any placement of the two camera centres on the quadric. The different types of ruled quadrics, including degenerate cases, are (see section 3.2.4(*p*74)): a hyperboloid of one sheet; a cone; two (intersecting) planes; a single plane; a single line. A complete enumeration of the types of placement of two camera centres on a ruled quadric is given in the following result.

Result 22.11. *The possible configurations of two distinct points (particularly camera centres) on a ruled quadric surface are as enumerated:*

(i) *hyperboloid of one sheet, two points not on the same generator*
(ii) *hyperboloid of one sheet, two points on the same generator*
(iii) *cone, one point at the vertex and one not*
(iv) *cone, two points on different generators, neither one at the vertex*
(v) *cone, two points on the same generator, neither one at the vertex*
(vi) *pair of planes, two points on the intersection of the two planes*
(vii) *pair of planes, one point at the intersection and one not*
(viii) *pair of planes, neither point at the intersection, but points on different planes*
(ix) *pair of planes, neither point on the intersection, both points on the same plane*
(x) *single plane with two points*
(xi) *single line with two points*

Any two quadric/point-pairs in the same class are projectively equivalent.

It is clear by enumeration of cases that this list is complete. The only case in which it is not immediately obvious that any two configurations in the same category are projectively equivalent is in the non-degenerate case of the hyperboloid of one sheet. The proof of this fact is left as exercise (i) at the end of the chapter (page 559).

Now, consider an example of a critical configuration $\{\mathtt{P}, \mathtt{P}', \widehat{\mathbf{P}}_i\}$ in which all $\mathbf{P}_i$ lie on a quadric $\mathtt{S_P}$ also containing the two camera centres. The quadric and two camera centres belong to one of the categories given in result 22.11.

Let the centres of two new cameras $(\hat{\mathtt{P}}, \hat{\mathtt{P}}')$ and a set of points $\widehat{\mathbf{P}}_i$ lie on a quadric $\hat{\mathtt{S}}_\mathtt{P}$. Suppose that $\hat{\mathtt{S}}_\mathtt{P}$ and the two camera centres lie in the same category as the given example. Since two configurations in the same category are projectively equivalent, we may assume that $\hat{\mathtt{S}}_\mathtt{P} = \mathtt{S_P}$ and the centres of $\mathtt{P}$ and $\hat{\mathtt{P}}$ are the same, as are the centres of $\mathtt{P}'$ and $\hat{\mathtt{P}}'$. Since the points $\widehat{\mathbf{P}}_i$ lie on $\mathtt{S_P}$, it follows that $\{\mathtt{P}, \mathtt{P}', \widehat{\mathbf{P}}_i\}$ is a critical configuration, and hence by result 22.8 so is $\{\hat{\mathtt{P}}, \hat{\mathtt{P}}', \widehat{\mathbf{P}}_i\}$.

This shows that to demonstrate the converse section of theorem 22.9 it is sufficient merely to demonstrate an example of a critical configuration belonging to each of the categories given in result 22.11 (except for cases (v) and (viii)). Examples will be given for several of the categories, though not all. The fact that cases (v) and (viii) are not critical is not shown here. The remaining cases are left to the motivated reader.

Examples of critical configurations

Consider the case $\mathtt{P} = \mathtt{Q} = [\mathtt{I} \mid \mathbf{0}]$ and $\mathtt{P}' = [\mathtt{I} \mid \mathbf{t}_0]$. In this case, one sees that

$$\mathtt{S}_\mathtt{P} = \begin{bmatrix} \mathtt{I} \\ \mathbf{t}_0^\mathsf{T} \end{bmatrix} \mathtt{F}_{\mathtt{Q}'\mathtt{Q}}[\mathtt{I} \mid \mathbf{0}] = \begin{bmatrix} \mathtt{I} \\ \mathbf{t}_0^\mathsf{T} \end{bmatrix} [\mathtt{F}_{\mathtt{Q}'\mathtt{Q}} \mid \mathbf{0}] \ .$$

Consequently,

$$\mathtt{S}_{\mathtt{P}\mathrm{sym}} = \frac{1}{2} \begin{bmatrix} \mathtt{F}_{\mathtt{Q}'\mathtt{Q}} + \mathtt{F}_{\mathtt{Q}'\mathtt{Q}}^\mathsf{T} & \mathtt{F}_{\mathtt{Q}'\mathtt{Q}}^\mathsf{T}\mathbf{t}_0 \\ \mathbf{t}_0^\mathsf{T}\mathtt{F}_{\mathtt{Q}'\mathtt{Q}} & 0 \end{bmatrix} .$$

Given the fundamental matrix $\mathtt{F}_{\mathtt{Q}'\mathtt{Q}}$ of rank 2, and the camera matrix $\mathtt{Q} = [\mathtt{I} \mid \mathbf{0}]$, one may easily find the other camera matrix $\mathtt{Q}'$. This is done by using the formula of result 9.13(*p*256). We now consider several examples of critical configurations belonging to different categories of result 22.11.

Example 22.12. Hyperboloid of one sheet – two centres not on the same generator. We choose $\mathtt{F}_{\mathtt{Q}'\mathtt{Q}} = \begin{bmatrix} 1 & 0 & 1 \\ 0 & 1 & 0 \\ -1 & 0 & -1 \end{bmatrix}$ and $\mathbf{t}_0 = (0,2,0)^\mathsf{T}$. Then $\mathbf{t}_0^\mathsf{T}\mathtt{F}_{\mathtt{Q}'\mathtt{Q}} = (0,2,0)$ and we find that

$$\mathtt{S}_\mathrm{sym} = \begin{bmatrix} 1 & & & \\ & 1 & & 1 \\ & & -1 & \\ & 1 & & 0 \end{bmatrix} .$$

This is the quadric with equation $\mathrm{X}^2 + \mathrm{Y}^2 + 2\mathrm{Y} - \mathrm{Z}^2 = 0$, or $\mathrm{X}^2 + (\mathrm{Y}+1)^2 - \mathrm{Z}^2 = 1$. This is a hyperboloid of one sheet. Note that in this case, the camera centres are $\mathbf{C}_\mathtt{P} = \mathbf{C}_\mathtt{Q} = (0,0,0)^\mathsf{T}$ (in inhomogeneous coordinates). The camera centre $\mathbf{C}_{\mathtt{P}'} = (0,2,0)$. We note that the line from $\mathbf{C}_\mathtt{P}$ to $\mathbf{C}_{\mathtt{P}'}$ does not lie on the quadric surface. The camera centre $\mathbf{C}_{\mathtt{Q}'}$ is not uniquely determined by the information already given, since the fundamental matrix does not uniquely determine the two cameras. However, the epipole $\mathbf{e}$ such that $\mathtt{F}_{\mathtt{Q}'\mathtt{Q}}\mathbf{e} = \mathbf{0}$ is $\mathbf{e} = (1,0,-1)$. Since $\mathbf{e} = \mathtt{Q}\mathbf{C}_{\mathtt{Q}'}$, we see that $\mathbf{C}_{\mathtt{Q}'} = (1,0,-1,k^{-1})$. In inhomogeneous coordinates $\mathbf{C}_{\mathtt{Q}'} = k(1,0,-1)$ for any k. We verify that the complete line from $\mathbf{C}_\mathtt{P}$ to $\mathbf{C}_{\mathtt{Q}'}$ lies on the quadric, but $\mathbf{C}_{\mathtt{Q}'}$ may lie anywhere along this line. △

Example 22.13. Hyperboloid of one sheet, both centres on the same generator. We choose the same $\mathtt{F}_{\mathtt{Q}'\mathtt{Q}}$ as in the previous example, and and $\mathbf{t}_0 = (3,4,5)^\mathsf{T}$. Then $\mathbf{t}_0^\mathsf{T}\mathtt{F}_{\mathtt{Q}'\mathtt{Q}} = (-2,4,-2)$ and we find that

$$\mathtt{S}_\mathrm{sym} = \begin{bmatrix} 1 & & & -1 \\ & 1 & & 2 \\ & & -1 & -1 \\ -1 & 2 & -1 & 0 \end{bmatrix} .$$

This is the quadric with equation $(\mathrm{X}-1)^2 + (\mathrm{Y}+2)^2 - (\mathrm{Z}+1)^2 = 4$, which is once again a hyperboloid of one sheet. It may be verified that the line $(X, Y, Z) = (3t, 4t, 5t)$ lies entirely on the quadric and contains the two camera centres, $(0, 0, 0)^\mathsf{T}$ and $(3, 4, 5)^\mathsf{T}$. $\triangle$

Example 22.14. Cone – one centre at the vertex of the cone. We choose $F_{Q'Q}$ to be the same as in the previous example, but $\mathbf{t}_0 = (1, 0, 1)^\mathsf{T}$. In this case we see that $\mathbf{t}_0^\mathsf{T} F_{Q'Q} = \mathbf{0}^\mathsf{T}$, and so $S_{\text{sym}} = \text{diag}(1, 1, -1, 0)$. This is an example of a cone. The camera centre of both P and Q is at the vertex of the cone, namely the point $\mathbf{C}_P = (0, 0, 0, 1)^\mathsf{T}$. $\triangle$

Example 22.15. Cone – neither centre at the vertex of the cone. We choose $F_{Q'Q} = \text{diag}(1, 1, 0)$ and $\mathbf{t}_0 = (0, 2, 0)^\mathsf{T}$. In this case, we see that

$$S_{\text{sym}} = \begin{bmatrix} 1 & & & \\ & 1 & & 1 \\ & & 0 & \\ & 1 & & 0 \end{bmatrix}$$

This is the quadric with equation $x^2 + y^2 + 2y = 0$, or $x^2 + (y+1)^2 = 1$, which is a cylinder parallel with the Z-axis, thus projectively equivalent to the cone with vertex at the infinite point $(0, 0, 1, 0)^\mathsf{T}$. Neither of the camera centres lies at the vertex. $\triangle$

Example 22.16. Two planes. We choose $F_{Q'Q} = \text{diag}(1, -1, 0)$ and $\mathbf{t}_0 = (0, 0, 1)^\mathsf{T}$, so that $\mathbf{t}_0^\mathsf{T} F_{Q'Q} = \mathbf{0}^\mathsf{T}$. In this case, we see that $S_P = S_{\text{sym}} = \text{diag}(1, -1, 0, 0)$, which represents a pair of planes. In this case the camera centres are on the intersection of the two planes $\triangle$

Example 22.17. Single plane. We choose $F_{Q'Q} = \begin{bmatrix} 1 & 1 & 0 \\ -1 & 0 & 0 \\ 0 & 0 & 0 \end{bmatrix}$ and $\mathbf{t}_0 = (0, 0, 1)^\mathsf{T}$.
Then $S_{\text{sym}} = \text{diag}(1, 0, 0, 0)$, which represents a single plane, $x = 0$. $\triangle$

Example 22.18. Single line. We choose $F_{Q'Q} = \text{diag}(1, 1, 0)$ and $\mathbf{t}_0 = (0, 0, 1)^\mathsf{T}$. In this case, we see that $S_{\text{sym}} = \text{diag}(1, 1, 0, 0)$, which represents a single line – the Z-axis. All the points and the two camera centres lie on this single line. $\triangle$

Apart for the impossible cases (v) and (viii) this gives examples of all possible degenerate configurations except for cases (vii) and (ix) in result 22.11. These remaining cases are left for the reader.

Minimal case – seven points As seen in section 11.1.2(p281), seven is the minimum number of points in general position from which one can do projective reconstruction. The method comes down to solving a cubic equation, for which either one or three real solutions exist. Looked at from the point of view of critical surfaces, the seven points and two camera centres in one configuration must lie on a quadric surface (since 9 points lie on a quadric). If this quadric is ruled, then there will be three conjugate solutions. On the other hand, if it is not a ruled quadric (for instance an ellipsoid) then there will be only one solution. This shows that the distinction between the cases where the cubic equation has one or three solutions arises from the difference between the points and camera centres lying on a ruled or unruled quadric – a pleasing connection between the algebra and geometry.

22.3 Carlsson–Weinshall duality

The duality explored in chapter 20 between cameras and points may be exploited so as to dualize degeneracy results, as will be explained in this section. We give a more formal treatment of Carlsson–Weinshall duality here.

The basis of Carlsson–Weinshall duality is the equation

$$\begin{bmatrix} a & & & -d \\ & b & & -d \\ & & c & -d \end{bmatrix} \begin{pmatrix} \mathrm{X} \\ \mathrm{Y} \\ \mathrm{Z} \\ \mathrm{T} \end{pmatrix} = \begin{bmatrix} \mathrm{X} & & & -\mathrm{T} \\ & \mathrm{Y} & & -\mathrm{T} \\ & & \mathrm{Z} & -\mathrm{T} \end{bmatrix} \begin{pmatrix} a \\ b \\ c \\ d \end{pmatrix} .$$

The camera matrix on the left corresponds to a camera with centre $(a^{-1}, b^{-1}, c^{-1}, d^{-1})^\mathsf{T}$. We are interested in describing cameras in terms of their camera centres. As this shows, in swapping camera centres with 3D points, one must invert the coordinates of the camera centre and point. For instance, the point $(\mathrm{X}, \mathrm{Y}, \mathrm{Z}, \mathrm{T})^\mathsf{T}$ is dual to a camera with camera centre $(\mathrm{X}^{-1}, \mathrm{Y}^{-1}, \mathrm{Z}^{-1}, \mathrm{T}^{-1})^\mathsf{T}$.

We denote the reduced camera matrix

$$\mathtt{P} = \begin{bmatrix} a^{-1} & & & -d^{-1} \\ & b^{-1} & & -d^{-1} \\ & & c^{-1} & -d^{-1} \end{bmatrix} \tag{22.1}$$

with centre $\mathbf{C} = (a, b, c, d)^\mathsf{T}$ by $\mathtt{P}_\mathbf{C}$. Now, defining the points $\overline{\mathbf{X}} = (\mathrm{X}^{-1}, \mathrm{Y}^{-1}, \mathrm{Z}^{-1}, \mathrm{T}^{-1})^\mathsf{T}$ and $\overline{\mathbf{C}} = (a^{-1}, b^{-1}, c^{-1}, d^{-1})^\mathsf{T}$, one immediately verifies that

$$\mathtt{P}_\mathbf{C}\mathbf{X} = \mathtt{P}_{\overline{\mathbf{X}}}\overline{\mathbf{C}} \tag{22.2}$$

Thus, this transformation interchanges the results of 3D points and camera centres. Thus, a camera with centre $\mathbf{C}$ acting on $\mathbf{X}$ gives the same result as camera with centre $\overline{\mathbf{X}}$ acting on $\overline{\mathbf{C}}$.

This observation leads to the following definition

Definition 22.19. The mapping of $\mathbb{P}^3$ to itsclf given by

$$(\mathrm{X}, \mathrm{Y}, \mathrm{Z}, \mathrm{T})^\mathsf{T} \mapsto (\mathrm{YZT}, \mathrm{ZTX}, \mathrm{TXY}, \mathrm{XYZ})^\mathsf{T}$$

will be called the Carlsson–Weinshall map, and will be denoted by Γ. We denote the image of a point $\mathbf{X}$ under Γ by $\overline{\mathbf{X}}$. The image of an object under Γ is sometimes referred to as the *dual* object.

The Carlsson–Weinshall map is an example of a *Cremona* transformation. For more information on Cremona transformations, the reader is referred to Semple and Kneebone ([Semple-79]).

Note. If none of the coordinates of $\mathbf{X}$ is zero then we may divide $\overline{\mathbf{X}}$ by XYZT. Then Γ is equivalent to $(\mathrm{X}, \mathrm{Y}, \mathrm{Z}, \mathrm{T})^\mathsf{T} \mapsto (\mathrm{X}^{-1}, \mathrm{Y}^{-1}, \mathrm{Z}^{-1}, \mathrm{T}^{-1})^\mathsf{T}$. This is the form of the mapping that we will usually use. In the case where one of the coordinates of $\mathbf{X}$ is zero, then the mapping will be interpreted as in the definition. Note that any point $(0, \mathrm{Y}, \mathrm{Z}, \mathrm{T})^\mathsf{T}$ is mapped to the point $(1, 0, 0, 0)^\mathsf{T}$ by Γ, provided none of the other coordinates is zero. Thus, the mapping is not one-to-one.

If two of the coordinates of $\mathbf{X}$ are zero, then $\overline{\mathbf{X}} = (0, 0, 0, 0)^\mathsf{T}$, which is an undefined point. Thus, Γ is not defined at all points. In fact, there is no way to extend Γ continuously to such points.

Define the *reference tetrahedron* to be the tetrahedron with vertices $\mathbf{E}_1 = (1, 0, 0, 0)^\mathsf{T}$, $\mathbf{E}_2 = (0, 1, 0, 0)^\mathsf{T}$, $\mathbf{E}_3 = (0, 0, 1, 0)^\mathsf{T}$ and $\mathbf{E}_4 = (0, 0, 0, 1)^\mathsf{T}$. As we have just seen, Γ is one-to-one other than on the faces of the reference tetrahedron. It maps a face of the reference tetrahedron to the opposite vertex, and is undefined on the edges of the reference tetrahedron. Next, we investigate the way in which Γ acts on other geometric objects.

Theorem 22.20. *The Carlsson–Weinshall map, Γ acts in the following manner:*

- (i) *It maps a line passing through two general points $\mathbf{X}_0$ and $\mathbf{X}_1$ to the twisted cubic passing through $\overline{\mathbf{X}}_0, \overline{\mathbf{X}}_1$ and the four reference vertices $\mathbf{E}_1, \ldots, \mathbf{E}_4$.*
- (ii) *It maps a line passing through any of the points $\mathbf{E}_i$ to a line passing through the same $\mathbf{E}_i$. We exclude the lines lying on the face of the reference tetrahedron, since such lines will be mapped to a single point.*
- (iii) *It maps a quadric $\mathtt{S}$ passing through the four points $\mathbf{E}_i$, $i = 1, \ldots, 4$ to a quadric (denoted $\bar{\mathtt{S}}$) passing through the same four points. If $\mathtt{S}$ is a ruled quadric, then so is $\bar{\mathtt{S}}$. If $\mathtt{S}$ is degenerate then so is $\bar{\mathtt{S}}$.*

Proof.
(i) A line has parametric equation $(\mathrm{X}_0 + a\theta, \mathrm{Y}_0 + b\theta, \mathrm{Z}_0 + c\theta, \mathrm{T}_0 + d\theta)^\mathsf{T}$, and a point on this line is taken by the Carlsson–Weinshall map to the point

$$((\mathrm{Y}_0 + b\theta)(\mathrm{Z}_0 + c\theta)(\mathrm{T}_0 + d\theta), \ldots, (\mathrm{X}_0 + a\theta)(\mathrm{Y}_0 + b\theta)(\mathrm{Z}_0 + c\theta))^\mathsf{T} \ .$$

Thus, the entries of the vector are cubic functions of θ, and the curve is a twisted cubic. Now, setting $\theta = -\mathrm{X}_0/a$, the term $(\mathrm{X}_0 + a\theta)$ vanishes, and the corresponding dual point is $((\mathrm{Y}_0 + b\theta)(\mathrm{Z}_0 + c\theta)(\mathrm{T}_0 + d\theta), 0, 0, 0)^\mathsf{T} \approx (1, 0, 0, 0)^\mathsf{T}$. The first entry is the only one that does not contain $(\mathrm{X}_0 + a\theta)$, and hence the only one that does not vanish. This shows that the reference vertex $\mathbf{E}_1 = (1, 0, 0, 0)^\mathsf{T}$ is on the twisted cubic. By similar arguments, the other points $\mathbf{E}_2, \ldots, \mathbf{E}_4$ lie on the twisted cubic also. Note that a twisted cubic is defined by six points, and this twisted cubic is defined by the given six points $\mathbf{E}_i, \overline{\mathbf{X}}_0, \overline{\mathbf{X}}_1$ that lie on it, where $\mathbf{X}_0$ and $\mathbf{X}_1$ are any two points defining the line.
(ii) We prove this for lines passing through the point $\mathbf{E}_0 = (1, 0, 0, 0)^\mathsf{T}$. An analogous proof holds for the other points $\mathbf{E}_i$. Choose another point $\mathbf{X} = (\mathrm{X}, \mathrm{Y}, \mathrm{Z}, \mathrm{T})^\mathsf{T}$ on the line, such that $\mathbf{X}$ does not lie on any face of the reference tetrahedron. Thus $\mathbf{X}$ has no zero coordinate. Points on a line passing through $(1, 0, 0, 0)^\mathsf{T}$ and $\mathbf{X} = (\mathrm{X}, \mathrm{Y}, \mathrm{Z}, \mathrm{T})^\mathsf{T}$ are all of the form $(\alpha, \mathrm{Y}, \mathrm{Z}, \mathrm{T})^\mathsf{T}$ for varying values of α. These points are mapped by the transformation to $(\alpha^{-1}, \mathrm{Y}^{-1}, \mathrm{Z}^{-1}, \mathrm{T}^{-1})^\mathsf{T}$. This represents a line passing through the two points $(1, 0, 0, 0)^\mathsf{T}$ and $\overline{\mathbf{X}} = (\mathrm{X}^{-1}, \mathrm{Y}^{-1}, \mathrm{Z}^{-1}, \mathrm{T}^{-1})^\mathsf{T}$.

(iii) Since the quadric $\mathtt{S}$ passes through all the points $\mathbf{E}_i$, the diagonal entries of $\mathtt{S}$ must all be zero. This means that there are no terms involving a squared coordinate (such as X^2) in the equation for the quadric. Hence the equation for the quadric contains only mixed terms (such as XY, YZ or XT). Therefore, the quadric $\mathtt{S}$ may be defined by an equation $a\mathrm{XY} + b\mathrm{XZ} + c\mathrm{XT} + d\mathrm{YZ} + e\mathrm{YT} + f\mathrm{ZT} = 0$. Dividing this equation by XYZT, we obtain $a\mathrm{Z}^{-1}\mathrm{T}^{-1} + b\mathrm{Y}^{-1}\mathrm{T}^{-1} + c\mathrm{Y}^{-1}\mathrm{Z}^{-1} + d\mathrm{X}^{-1}\mathrm{T}^{-1} + e\mathrm{X}^{-1}\mathrm{Z}^{-1} + f\mathrm{X}^{-1}\mathrm{Y}^{-1} = 0$. Since $\overline{\mathbf{X}} = (\mathrm{X}^{-1}, \mathrm{Y}^{-1}, \mathrm{Z}^{-1}, \mathrm{T}^{-1})^\mathsf{T}$, this is a quadratic equation in the entries of $\overline{\mathbf{X}}$. Thus Γ maps quadric to quadric. Specifically, suppose $\mathtt{S}$ is represented by the matrix

$$\mathtt{S} = \begin{bmatrix} 0 & a & b & c \\ a & 0 & d & e \\ b & d & 0 & f \\ c & e & f & 0 \end{bmatrix} \quad \text{then } \bar{\mathtt{S}} = \begin{bmatrix} 0 & f & e & d \\ f & 0 & c & b \\ e & c & 0 & a \\ d & b & a & 0 \end{bmatrix}$$

and $\mathbf{X}^\mathsf{T}\mathtt{S}\mathbf{X} = 0$ implies $\overline{\mathbf{X}}^\mathsf{T}\bar{\mathtt{S}}\overline{\mathbf{X}} = 0$. If $\mathtt{S}$ is ruled, then it contains two generators passing through any point, and in particular through each $\mathbf{E}_i$. By part (ii), these are mapped to straight lines, which must lie on $\bar{\mathtt{S}}$. Thus $\bar{\mathtt{S}}$ is a ruled quadric. One may further verify that $\det \mathtt{S} = \det \bar{\mathtt{S}}$, which implies that if $\mathtt{S}$ is a non-degenerate quadric (that is $\det \mathtt{S} \neq 0$), then so is $\bar{\mathtt{S}}$. In this non-degenerate case, if $\mathtt{S}$ is a hyperboloid of one sheet, then $\det \mathtt{S} > 0$, from which it follows that $\det \bar{\mathtt{S}} > 0$. Thus $\bar{\mathtt{S}}$ is also a hyperboloid of one sheet. □

The action of Γ on other geometric entities is investigated in exercises (page 559);

We wish to interpret duality equation (22.2) in a coordinate-free manner. The matrix $\mathtt{P}_\mathbf{C}$ has by definition the form given in (22.1), and maps $\mathbf{E}_i$ to $\mathbf{e}_i$ for $i = 1, \ldots, 4$. The image $\mathtt{P}_\mathbf{C}\mathbf{X}$ is may be thought of as a representation of the projection of $\mathbf{X}$ relative to the projective basis $\mathbf{e}_i$ in the image. Alternatively, $\mathtt{P}_\mathbf{C}\mathbf{X}$ represents the projective equivalence class of the set of the five rays $\overline{\mathbf{CE}_1}, \ldots, \overline{\mathbf{CE}_4}, \overline{\mathbf{CX}}$. Thus $\mathtt{P}_\mathbf{C}\mathbf{X} = \mathtt{P}_{\mathbf{C}'}\mathbf{X}'$ if and only if the set of rays from $\mathbf{C}$ to $\mathbf{X}$ and the four vertices of the reference tetrahedron is projectively equivalent to the set of rays from $\mathbf{C}'$ to $\mathbf{X}'$ and the four reference vertices. In terms of the notation introduced earlier, we may write (22.2) in a different form as

$$\langle \mathbf{C}; \mathbf{E}_1, \ldots, \mathbf{E}_4, \mathbf{X} \rangle = \langle \overline{\mathbf{X}}; \mathbf{E}_1, \ldots, \mathbf{E}_4, \overline{\mathbf{C}} \rangle. \tag{22.3}$$

The duality principle

The basis of duality is (22.2) which states that $\mathtt{P}_\mathbf{C}\mathbf{X} = \mathtt{P}_{\overline{\mathbf{X}}}\overline{\mathbf{C}}$, with notation as in (22.2)

The notation $\mathtt{P}_\mathbf{C}\mathbf{X}$ represents the coordinates of the projection of point $\mathbf{X}$ with respect to the canonical image coordinate frame defined by the projections of the corners of the reference tetrahedron. Equivalently, $\mathtt{P}_\mathbf{C}$ may be considered as representing the projective equivalence class of the five projected points $\mathtt{P}_\mathbf{C}\mathbf{E}_i$ and $\mathtt{P}_\mathbf{C}\mathbf{X}$. In the notation of this chapter, this is $\langle \mathbf{C}; \mathbf{E}_1, \ldots, \mathbf{E}_4, \mathbf{X} \rangle$. Thus the duality relation may be written as

$$\langle \mathbf{C}; \mathbf{E}_1, \ldots, \mathbf{E}_4, \mathbf{X} \rangle = \langle \overline{\mathbf{X}}; \mathbf{E}_1, \ldots, \mathbf{E}_4, \overline{\mathbf{C}} \rangle \tag{22.4}$$

where the bar represents the Carlsson–Weinshall map.

Although $\mathtt{P}_\mathbf{C}$ was defined in terms of the canonical projective basis, there is nothing special about the four points $\mathbf{E}_1, \ldots, \mathbf{E}_4$ used as vertices of the reference tetrahedron, other than the fact that they are non-coplanar. Given any four non-coplanar points, one may define a projective coordinate system in which these four points are the points $\mathbf{E}_i$ forming part of a projective basis. The Carlsson–Weinshall map may then be defined with respect to this coordinate frame. The resulting map is called the Carlsson–Weinshall map with respect to the given reference tetrahedron.

To be more precise, it should be observed that five points (not four) define a projective coordinate frame in $\mathbb{P}^3$. In fact, there is more than one projective frame (in fact a 3-parameter family) for which four non-coplanar points have coordinates $\mathbf{E}_i$. Thus the Carlsson–Weinshall map with respect to a given reference tetrahedron is not unique. However, the mapping given by definition 22.19 with respect to any such coordinate frame may be used.

Given a statement or theorem concerning projections of sets of points with respect to one or more projection centres one may derive a dual statement. One requires that among the four points being projected, there are four non-coplanar points that may form a reference tetrahedron. Under a general duality mapping with respect to the reference tetrahedron

- (i) Points (other than those belonging to the reference tetrahedron) are mapped to centres of projection.
- (ii) Centres of projection are mapped to points.
- (iii) Straight lines are mapped to twisted cubics.
- (iv) Ruled quadrics containing the reference tetrahedron are mapped to ruled quadrics containing the reference tetrahedron. If the original quadric is non-degenerate, so is its image under the duality mapping.

Points lying on an edge of the reference tetrahedron should be avoided, since the Carlsson–Weinshall mapping is undefined for such points. Using this as a sort of translation table, one may dualize existing theorems about point projection, giving new theorems for which a separate proof is not needed.

Note. It is important to observe that only those points not belonging to the reference tetrahedron are mapped to camera centres by duality. The vertices of the reference tetrahedron remain points. In practice, in applying the duality principle, one may select any four points to form the reference tetrahedron, as long as they are non-coplanar. In general, in the results stated in the next section there will be an assumption (not always stated explicitly) that *point sets considered contain four non-coplanar points*, which may be taken as the reference tetrahedron.

22.3.1 Single view ambiguity

It will be shown in this section how various ambiguous reconstruction results may be derived simply from known or obvious geometric statements by applying duality.

Camera resectioning from five points

Five 3D–2D point correspondences are not sufficient for camera resectioning for projective cameras. It is interesting to know what one can determine from five point correspondences, however.

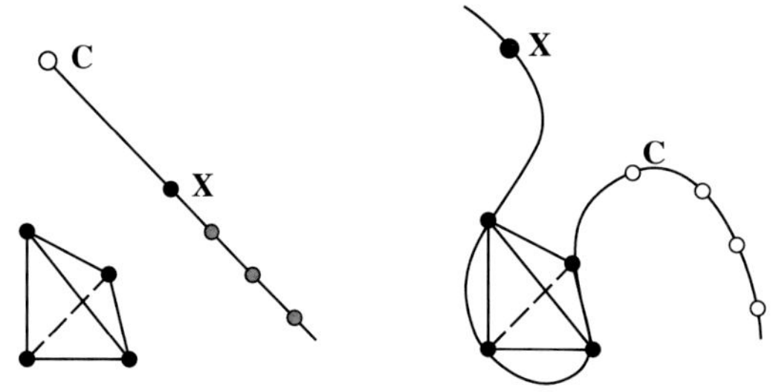

Fig. 22.5. **Left:** *Any point on the line passing through* **C** *and* **X** *is projected to the same point from projection centre* **C**. **Right:** *The dual statement – from any centre of projection* **C** *lying on a twisted cubic passing through* **X** *and the vertices of the reference tetrahedron, the five points are projected in the same way (up to projective equivalence). Thus a camera is constrained to lie on a twisted cubic by its image of five known points.*

As a simple example of what can be deduced using Carlsson duality, consider the following simple question: when do two points project to the same point in an image? The answer is obviously when the two points lie on the same ray (straight line) through the camera centre. Dualizing this simple observation, figure 22.5 shows that the centre of the camera constrained by five point 3D–2D correspondences must lie on a twisted cubic passing through the five 3D points.

The horopter

In a similar manner one may compute the form of the horopter determined by two cameras. The horopter is the set of space points that map to the same point in two images. The argument is illustrated in figure 22.6 and begins with a simple observation concerning straight lines.

Result 22.21. *Given points* $\mathbf{X}$ *and* $\mathbf{X}'$*, the locus of camera centres* $\mathbf{C}$ *such that*

$$\langle \mathbf{C}; \mathbf{E}_1, \ldots, \mathbf{E}_4, \mathbf{X} \rangle = \langle \mathbf{C}; \mathbf{E}_1, \ldots, \mathbf{E}_4, \mathbf{X}' \rangle$$

is the straight line passing through $\mathbf{X}$ *and* $\mathbf{X}'$.

This is illustrated in figure 22.6(left) The dual of this statement determines the horopter for a pair of cameras (see figure 22.6(right)).

Result 22.22. *Given projection centres* $\mathbf{C}$ *and* $\mathbf{C}'$*, non-collinear with the four points* $\mathbf{E}_i$ *of a reference tetrahedron, the set of points* $\mathbf{X}$ *such that* $\langle \mathbf{C}; \mathbf{E}_1, \ldots, \mathbf{E}_4, \mathbf{X} \rangle = \langle \mathbf{C}'; \mathbf{E}_1, \ldots, \mathbf{E}_4, \mathbf{X} \rangle$ *is a twisted cubic passing through* $\mathbf{E}_1, \ldots, \mathbf{E}_4$ *and the two projection centres* $\mathbf{C}$ *and* $\mathbf{C}'$.

Ambiguity of camera resection

Finally, we consider ambiguity of resection. This is very closely related to the horopter. To visualize this, the reader may refer again to figure 22.6, though it is not exactly pertinent in this situation.

Result 22.23. *Consider a set of camera centres* $\mathbf{C}_1, \ldots, \mathbf{C}_m$ *and a point* $\mathbf{X}_0$ *all lying on*

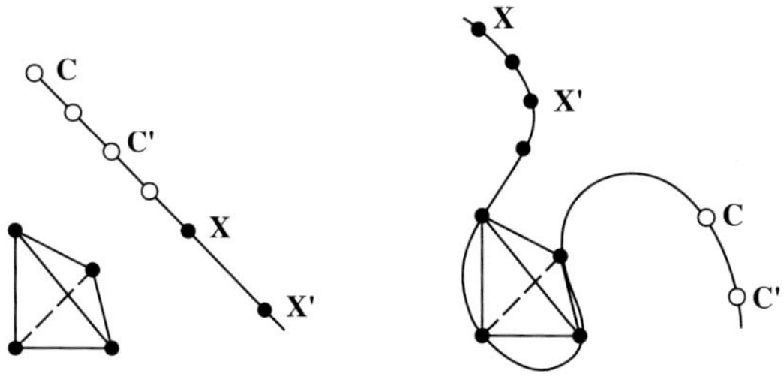

Fig. 22.6. **Left:** *From any centre of projection* $\mathbf{C}, \mathbf{C}', \ldots$ *lying on the line passing through* $\mathbf{X}$ *and* $\mathbf{X}'$*, the points* $\mathbf{X}$ *and* $\mathbf{X}'$ *are projected to the same ray. That is,* $\langle \mathbf{C}; \mathbf{E}_i, \mathbf{X} \rangle = \langle \mathbf{C}; \mathbf{E}_i, \mathbf{X}' \rangle$ *for all* $\mathbf{C}$ *on the line.* **Right:** *The dual statement – all points on the twisted cubic passing through* $\mathbf{C}$ *and* $\mathbf{C}'$ *and the vertices of the reference tetrahedron are projected in the same way relative to the two projection centres. That is,* $\langle \mathbf{C}; \mathbf{E}_i, \mathbf{X} \rangle = \langle \mathbf{C}'; \mathbf{E}_i, \mathbf{X} \rangle$ *for all* $\mathbf{X}$ *on the twisted cubic. This curve is called the* horopter *for the two centres of projection.*

a single straight line and let $\mathbf{E}_i, i = 1, \ldots, 4$ *be the vertices of a reference tetrahedron. Let* $\mathbf{X}$ *be another point. Then the two configurations*

$$\{\mathbf{C}_1, \ldots, \mathbf{C}_m; \mathbf{E}_1, \ldots, \mathbf{E}_4, \mathbf{X}\} \textit{ and } \{\mathbf{C}_1, \ldots, \mathbf{C}_m; \mathbf{E}_1, \ldots, \mathbf{E}_4, \mathbf{X}_0\}$$

are image-equivalent configurations if and only if $\mathbf{X}$ *lies on the same straight line as* $\mathbf{X}_0$ *and the cameras.*

In passing to the dual statement, according to theorem 22.20 the straight line becomes a twisted cubic through the four vertices of the reference tetrahedron. Thus the dual statement to result 22.23 is:

Result 22.24. *Consider a set of points* $\mathbf{X}_i$ *and a camera centre* $\mathbf{C}_0$ *all lying on a single twisted cubic also passing through four reference vertices* $\mathbf{E}_i$*. Let* $\mathbf{C}$ *be any other camera centre. Then the configurations*

$$\{\mathbf{C}; \mathbf{E}_1, \ldots, \mathbf{E}_4, \mathbf{X}_1, \ldots, \mathbf{X}_m\} \textit{ and } \{\mathbf{C}_0; \mathbf{E}_1, \ldots, \mathbf{E}_4, \mathbf{X}_1, \ldots, \mathbf{X}_m\}$$

are image-equivalent if and only if $\mathbf{C}$ *lies on the same twisted cubic.*

Since the points $\mathbf{E}_i$ may be any four non-coplanar points, and a twisted cubic cannot contain 4 coplanar points, one may state this last result in the following form:

Result 22.25. *Let* $\mathbf{X}_1, \ldots, \mathbf{X}_m$ *be a set of points and* $\mathbf{C}_0$ *a camera centre all lying on a twisted cubic. Then for any other camera centre* $\mathbf{C}$ *the configurations*

$$\{\mathbf{C}; \mathbf{X}_1, \ldots, \mathbf{X}_m\} \textit{ and } \{\mathbf{C}_0; \mathbf{X}_1, \ldots, \mathbf{X}_m\}$$

are image-equivalent if and only if $\mathbf{C}$ *lies on the same twisted cubic.*

This is illustrated in figure 22.6 (right). It shows that camera pose cannot be uniquely determined whenever all points and a camera centre lie on a twisted cubic. This gives an independent proof of result 22.6(*p*537) covering the case that was left unfinished previously.

Using similar methods one can show that this is one of only two possible ambiguous situations. The other case in which ambiguity occurs is when all points and the two camera centres lie in the union of a plane and a line. This arises as the dual of the case when the straight line through the camera centres meets one of the vertices of the reference tetrahedron. In this case, the dual of this line is also a straight line through the same reference vertex (see theorem 22.20), and all points must lie on this line or the opposite face of the reference tetrahedron.

Note in both these examples how the use of duality has taken intuitively obvious statements concerning projections of collinear points and derived a result somewhat less obvious about points lying on a twisted cubic.

22.3.2 Two-view ambiguity

The basic result theorem 22.9(*p*541) about critical surfaces from two views may be stated as follows.

Theorem 22.26. *A configuration* $\{\mathbf{C}_1, \mathbf{C}_2; \mathbf{X}_1, \ldots, \mathbf{X}_n\}$ *of two camera centres and* n *points allows an alternative reconstruction if and only if both camera centres* $\mathbf{C}_1, \mathbf{C}_2$ *and all the points* $\mathbf{X}_j$ *lie on a ruled quadric surface. If the quadric is non-degenerate (a hyperboloid of one sheet), then there will always exist a third distinct reconstruction.*

One may write down the dual statement straight away as follows.

Theorem 22.27. *A configuration* $\{\mathbf{C}_1, \ldots, \mathbf{C}_n; \mathbf{X}_1, \ldots, \mathbf{X}_6\}$ *of any number of cameras and six points allows an alternative reconstruction if and only if all camera centres* $\mathbf{C}_1, \ldots, \mathbf{C}_n$ *and all the points* $\mathbf{X}_1, \ldots, \mathbf{X}_6$ *lie on a ruled quadric surface.*[1] *If the quadric is non-degenerate (a hyperboloid of one sheet) then there will always exist a third distinct reconstruction.*

This result was originally proved in [Maybank-98]. Just to emphasize how a duality proof works, a proof for theorem 22.27 will be given.

Proof. Consider the configuration $\{\mathbf{C}_1, \ldots, \mathbf{C}_n; \mathbf{X}_1, \ldots, \mathbf{X}_6\}$. One renumbers the points so that the configuration is denoted by $\{\mathbf{C}_1, \ldots, \mathbf{C}_n; \mathbf{E}_1, \ldots, \mathbf{E}_4, \mathbf{X}_1, \mathbf{X}_2\}$ where $\mathbf{E}_1, \ldots, \mathbf{E}_4$ are four non-collinear points, taken to be the vertices of a reference tetrahedron. If this configuration has an alternative reconstruction, then there exists another configuration $\{\mathbf{C}'_1, \ldots, \mathbf{C}'_n; \mathbf{E}_1, \ldots, \mathbf{E}_4, \mathbf{X}'_1, \mathbf{X}'_2\}$ such that for all $i = 1, \ldots, n$ and $j = 1, 2$, one has $\langle \mathbf{C}_i; \mathbf{E}_1, \ldots, \mathbf{E}_4, \mathbf{X}_j \rangle = \langle \mathbf{C}'_i; \mathbf{E}_1, \ldots, \mathbf{E}_4, \mathbf{X}'_j \rangle$. Dualizing this using (22.3) yields

$$\langle \overline{\mathbf{X}}_j; \mathbf{E}_1, \ldots, \mathbf{E}_4, \overline{\mathbf{C}}_i \rangle = \langle \overline{\mathbf{X}}'_j; \mathbf{E}_1, \ldots, \mathbf{E}_4, \overline{\mathbf{C}}'_i \rangle \text{ for all } j = 1, 2 \text{ and } i = 1, \ldots, n.$$

Now, theorem 22.26 applies, and one deduces that the two camera centres $\overline{\mathbf{X}}_j$, the reference vertices $\mathbf{E}_1, \ldots, \mathbf{E}_4$ and the points $\overline{\mathbf{C}}_i$ all lie on a ruled quadric surface $\bar{\mathrm{S}}$. Applying the reverse dualization, using theorem 22.20(iii), one sees that the points $\mathbf{X}_1, \mathbf{X}_2$ and the camera centres $\mathbf{C}_i$ all lie on the quadric surface S. This proves the forward implication of the theorem. The reverse implication is handled in a similar manner.

[1] In this statement, it is assumed that the set of points $\mathbf{X}_1, \ldots, \mathbf{X}_6$ includes four non-coplanar points forming a reference tetrahedron and that none of the other two $\mathbf{X}_j$ nor any of the camera centres $\mathbf{C}_i$ lies on a face of this tetrahedron. Whether or not this condition is essential is not resolved.

The existence of a third distinct solution follows from the fact that the dual of a non-degenerate quadric is non-degenerate. □

The minimum interesting case of theorem 22.27 is when $n = 3$, as studied in section 20.2.4(p510). In this case there are nine points in total (three cameras and six points). One can construct a quadric surface passing through these nine points (a quadric is defined by nine points). If the quadric is a ruled quadric (a hyperboloid of one sheet in the non-degenerate case), then there are three possible distinct reconstructions. Otherwise the reconstruction is unique. As with reconstruction from seven points in two views, algorithm 20.1(p511) for six points in three views requires the solution of a cubic equation. As with seven points, the distinction between cases where the cubic has one or three real solutions is explained as the difference between whether the quadric is ruled or not.

22.4 Three-view critical configurations

We now turn to consider the ambiguous configurations that may arise in the three-view case.

In this section, to distinguish the three cameras, we use superscripts instead of primes. Thus, let $\mathtt{P}^0, \mathtt{P}^1, \mathtt{P}^2$ be three cameras and $\{\mathbf{P}_i\}$ be a set of points. We ask under what circumstances there exists another configuration consisting of three other camera matrices $\mathtt{Q}^0$, $\mathtt{Q}^1$ and $\mathtt{Q}^2$ and points $\{\mathbf{Q}_i\}$ such that $\mathtt{P}^j\mathbf{P}_i = \mathtt{Q}^j\mathbf{Q}_i$ for all i and j. We require that the two configurations be projectively inequivalent.

Various special ambiguous configurations exist.

Points in a plane

If all the points lie in a plane, and $\mathbf{P}_i = \mathbf{Q}_i$ for all i, then any of the cameras may be moved without changing the projective equivalence class of the projected points. It is possible to choose $\mathtt{P}^j$ and $\mathtt{Q}^j$ with centres at any two preassigned locations in such a way that $\mathtt{P}^j\mathbf{P}_i = \mathtt{Q}^j\mathbf{Q}_i$.

Points on a twisted cubic

A similar ambiguous situation arises when all the points plus one of the cameras, say $\mathtt{P}^2$, lie on a twisted cubic. In this case, we may choose $\mathtt{Q}^0 = \mathtt{P}^0$ and $\mathtt{Q}^1 = \mathtt{P}^1$ and the points $\mathbf{Q}_i = \mathbf{P}_i$ for all i. Then according to the ambiguity of camera resectioning for points on a twisted cubic, (section 22.1.2), for any point $\mathbf{C}^2_{\mathtt{Q}}$ on the twisted cubic a camera matrix $\mathtt{Q}^2$ may be chosen with centre at $\mathbf{C}^2_{\mathtt{Q}}$ such that $\mathtt{P}^2\mathbf{P}_i = \mathtt{Q}^2\mathbf{Q}_i$ for all i.

These examples of ambiguity are not very interesting, since they are no more than extensions of the one-view camera resectioning ambiguity. In the above examples, the points $\mathbf{P}_i$ and $\mathbf{Q}_i$ are the same in each case, and the ambiguity lies only in the placement of the cameras with respect to the points. More interesting ambiguities may also occur, as we consider next.

General three-view ambiguity

Suppose that the camera matrices $(\mathtt{P}^0, \mathtt{P}^1, \mathtt{P}^2)$ and $(\mathtt{Q}^0, \mathtt{Q}^1, \mathtt{Q}^2)$ are fixed, and we wish to find the set of all points such that $\mathtt{P}^i\mathbf{P} = \mathtt{Q}^i\mathbf{Q}$ for $i = 0, 1, 2$. Note that we are trying here to copy the two-view case in which both sets of camera matrices are chosen in advance. Later, we will turn to the less restricted case in which just one set of cameras is chosen in advance.

A simple observation is that a critical configuration for three views is also a critical set for each of the pairs of views. Thus one is led naturally to assume that the set of points for which $\{\mathtt{P}^0, \mathtt{P}^1, \mathtt{P}^2, \mathbf{P}_i\}$ is a critical configuration is simply the intersection of the point sets for which each of $\{\mathtt{P}^0, \mathtt{P}^1, \mathbf{P}_i\}$, $\{\mathtt{P}^1, \mathtt{P}^2, \mathbf{P}_i\}$ and $\{\mathtt{P}^0, \mathtt{P}^2, \mathbf{P}_i\}$ is a critical configuration. Since by lemma 22.10(*p*542) each of these point sets is a ruled quadric, one is led to assume that the critical point set in the three-view case is simply an intersection of three quadrics. Although this is not far from the truth, the reasoning is somewhat fuzzy. The crucial point missing in this argument is that the corresponding conjugate points may not be the same for each of the three pairs.

More precisely, corresponding to the critical configuration $\{\mathtt{P}^0, \mathtt{P}^1, \mathbf{P}_i\}$, there exists a conjugate configuration $\{\mathtt{Q}^0, \mathtt{Q}^1, \mathbf{Q}_i^{01}\}$ for which $\mathtt{P}^j\mathbf{P}_i = \mathtt{Q}^j\mathbf{Q}_i^{01}$ for $j = 0, 1$. Similarly, for the critical configuration $\{\mathtt{P}^0, \mathtt{P}^2, \mathbf{P}_i\}$, there exists a conjugate configuration $\{\mathtt{Q}^0, \mathtt{Q}^2, \mathbf{Q}_i^{02}\}$ for which $\mathtt{P}^j\mathbf{P}_i = \mathtt{Q}^j\mathbf{Q}_i^{02}$ for $j = 0, 2$. However, the points $\mathbf{Q}_i^{02}$ are not necessarily the same as $\mathbf{Q}_i^{01}$, so we cannot conclude that there exist points $\mathbf{Q}_i$ such that $\mathtt{P}^j\mathbf{P}_i = \mathtt{Q}^j\mathbf{Q}_i$ for all i and $j = 0, 1, 2$ – at least not immediately.

We now consider this a little more closely. Considering just the first pairs of cameras $(\mathtt{P}^0, \mathtt{P}^1)$ and $(\mathtt{Q}^0, \mathtt{Q}^1)$, lemma 22.10(*p*542) tells us that if $\mathbf{P}$ and $\mathbf{Q}$ are points such that $\mathtt{P}^j\mathbf{P} = \mathtt{Q}^j\mathbf{Q}$, then $\mathbf{P}$ must lie on a quadric surface $\mathtt{S}_\mathtt{P}^{01}$ determined by these camera matrices. Similarly, point $\mathbf{Q}$ lies on a quadric $\mathtt{S}_\mathtt{Q}^{01}$. Likewise considering the camera pairs $(\mathtt{P}^0, \mathtt{P}^2)$ and $(\mathtt{Q}^0, \mathtt{Q}^2)$ one finds that the point $\mathbf{P}$ must lie on a second quadric $\mathtt{S}_\mathtt{P}^{02}$ defined by these two camera pairs. Similarly, there exists a further quadric defined by the camera pairs $(\mathtt{P}^1, \mathtt{P}^2)$ and $(\mathtt{Q}^1, \mathtt{Q}^2)$ on which the point $\mathbf{P}$ must lie. Thus for points $\mathbf{P}$ and $\mathbf{Q}$ to exist such that $\mathtt{P}^j\mathbf{P} = \mathtt{Q}^j\mathbf{Q}$ for $j = 0, 1, 2$ it is necessary that $\mathtt{P}$ lie on the intersection of the three quadrics: $\mathbf{P} \in \mathtt{S}_\mathtt{P}^{01} \cap \mathtt{S}_\mathtt{P}^{02} \cap \mathtt{S}_\mathtt{P}^{12}$. It will now be seen that this is almost a necessary and sufficient condition.

Result 22.28. *Let* $(\mathtt{P}^0, \mathtt{P}^1, \mathtt{P}^2)$ *and* $(\mathtt{Q}^0, \mathtt{Q}^1, \mathtt{Q}^2)$ *be two triplets of camera matrices and assume* $\mathtt{P}^0 = \mathtt{Q}^0$. *For each of the pairs* $(i, j) = (0, 1), (0, 2)$ *and* $(1, 2)$, *let* $\mathtt{S}_\mathtt{P}^{ij}$ *and* $\mathtt{S}_\mathtt{Q}^{ij}$ *be the ruled quadric critical surfaces defined for camera matrix pairs* $(\mathtt{P}^i, \mathtt{P}^j)$ *and* $(\mathtt{Q}^i, \mathtt{Q}^j)$ *as in lemma 22.10(*p542*).*

(i) *The centre of camera* $\mathtt{P}^0$ *lies on* $\mathtt{S}_\mathtt{P}^{01} \cap \mathtt{S}_\mathtt{P}^{02}$, $\mathtt{P}^1$ *lies on* $\mathtt{S}_\mathtt{P}^{01} \cap \mathtt{S}_\mathtt{P}^{12}$, *and* $\mathtt{P}^2$ *lies on* $\mathtt{S}_\mathtt{P}^{12} \cap \mathtt{S}_\mathtt{P}^{02}$.

(ii) *If there exist points* $\mathbf{P}$ *and* $\mathbf{Q}$ *such that* $\mathtt{P}^i\mathbf{P} = \mathtt{Q}^i\mathbf{Q}$ *for all* $i = 0, 1, 2$, *then* $\mathbf{P}$ *must lie on the intersection* $\mathtt{S}_\mathtt{P}^{01} \cap \mathtt{S}_\mathtt{P}^{02} \cap \mathtt{S}_\mathtt{P}^{12}$ *and* $\mathbf{Q}$ *must lie on* $\mathtt{S}_\mathtt{Q}^{01} \cap \mathtt{S}_\mathtt{Q}^{02} \cap \mathtt{S}_\mathtt{Q}^{12}$.

(iii) *Conversely, if* $\mathbf{P}$ *is a point lying on the intersection of quadrics* $\mathtt{S}_\mathtt{P}^{01} \cap \mathtt{S}_\mathtt{P}^{02} \cap \mathtt{S}_\mathtt{P}^{12}$, but not on a plane containing the three camera centres $\mathbf{C}_\mathtt{Q}^0$, $\mathbf{C}_\mathtt{Q}^1$ and $\mathbf{C}_\mathtt{Q}^2$, *then there exists a point* $\mathbf{Q}$ *lying on* $\mathtt{S}_\mathtt{Q}^{01} \cap \mathtt{S}_\mathtt{Q}^{02} \cap \mathtt{S}_\mathtt{Q}^{12}$ *such that* $\mathtt{P}^i\mathbf{P} = \mathtt{Q}^i\mathbf{Q}$ *for all* $i = 0, 1, 2$.

Note that the condition that $\mathtt{P}^0 = \mathtt{Q}^0$ is not any restriction of generality, since the projective frames for the two configurations $(\mathtt{P}^0, \mathtt{P}^1, \mathtt{P}^2)$ and $(\mathtt{Q}^0, \mathtt{Q}^1, \mathtt{Q}^2)$ are independent. One may easily choose a projective frame for the second configuration in which this condition is true. This assumption is made simply so that one may consider the point $\mathbf{P}$ in relation to the projective frame of the second set of cameras.

The extra condition that the point $\mathbf{P}$ does not lie on the plane of camera centres $\mathbf{C}_{\mathtt{Q}}^i$ is necessary, however the reader is referred to [Hartley-00b] for justification of this claim. Note that this case will usually not arise, however, since the intersection point of the three quadrics with the trifocal plane will be empty, or in special cases consist of a finite number of points. Where it does arise is through the possibility that the three camera centres $\mathbf{C}_{\mathtt{Q}}^0$, $\mathbf{C}_{\mathtt{Q}}^1$ and $\mathbf{C}_{\mathtt{Q}}^2$ are collinear, in which case any other point is coplanar with these three camera centres.

Proof. The first statement follows directly from lemma 22.10(*p*542). For the second part, the fact that the points $\mathbf{P}$ and $\mathbf{Q}$ lie on the intersections of the three quadrics follows (as pointed out before the statement of the theorem) from lemma 22.10(*p*542) applied to each pair of cameras in turn.

To prove the final assertion, suppose that $\mathbf{P}$ lies on the intersection of the three quadrics. Then from lemma 22.10(*p*542), applied to each of the three quadrics $\mathtt{S}_{\mathtt{P}}^{ij}$, there exist points $\mathbf{Q}^{ij}$ such that the following conditions hold:

$$\begin{array}{ll} \mathtt{P}^0\mathbf{P} = \mathtt{Q}^0\mathbf{Q}^{01} & \mathtt{P}^1\mathbf{P} = \mathtt{Q}^1\mathbf{Q}^{01} \\ \mathtt{P}^0\mathbf{P} = \mathtt{Q}^0\mathbf{Q}^{02} & \mathtt{P}^2\mathbf{P} = \mathtt{Q}^2\mathbf{Q}^{02} \\ \mathtt{P}^1\mathbf{P} = \mathtt{Q}^1\mathbf{Q}^{12} & \mathtt{P}^2\mathbf{P} = \mathtt{Q}^2\mathbf{Q}^{12}. \end{array}$$

It is easy to be confused by the superscripts here, but the main point is that each line is precisely the result of lemma 22.10(*p*542) applied to one of the three pairs of camera matrices at a time. These equations may be rearranged as

$$\begin{aligned} \mathtt{P}^0\mathbf{P} &= \mathtt{Q}^0\mathbf{Q}^{01} = \mathtt{Q}^0\mathbf{Q}^{02} \\ \mathtt{P}^1\mathbf{P} &= \mathtt{Q}^1\mathbf{Q}^{01} = \mathtt{Q}^1\mathbf{Q}^{12} \\ \mathtt{P}^2\mathbf{P} &= \mathtt{Q}^2\mathbf{Q}^{02} = \mathtt{Q}^2\mathbf{Q}^{12}. \end{aligned}$$

Now, the condition that $\mathtt{Q}^1\mathbf{Q}^{01} = \mathtt{Q}^1\mathbf{Q}^{12}$ means that the points $\mathbf{Q}^{01}$ and $\mathbf{Q}^{12}$ are collinear with the camera centre $\mathbf{C}_{\mathtt{Q}}^1$ of $\mathtt{Q}^1$. Thus, assuming that the points $\mathbf{Q}^{ij}$ are distinct, they must lie in a configuration as shown in figure 22.7. One sees from the diagram that if two of the points are the same, then the third one is the same as the other two. If the three points are distinct, then the three points $\mathbf{Q}^{ij}$ and the three camera centres $\mathbf{C}_{\mathtt{Q}}^i$ are coplanar, since they all lie in the plane defined by $\mathbf{Q}^{01}$ and the line joining $\mathbf{Q}^{02}$ to $\mathbf{Q}^{12}$. Thus the three points all lie in the plane of the camera centres $\mathbf{C}_{\mathtt{Q}}^i$. However, since $\mathtt{P}^0\mathbf{P} = \mathtt{Q}^0\mathbf{Q}^{01} = \mathtt{Q}^0\mathbf{Q}^{02}$ it follows that $\mathbf{P}$ must lie along the same line as $\mathtt{Q}^{01}$ and $\mathtt{Q}^{02}$, and hence must lie in the same plane as the camera centres $\mathbf{C}_{\mathtt{Q}}^i$. □

Thus, this result shows that the points in a 3-view critical configuration lie on the intersection of three quadrics, whereas the camera centres lie on the intersections of

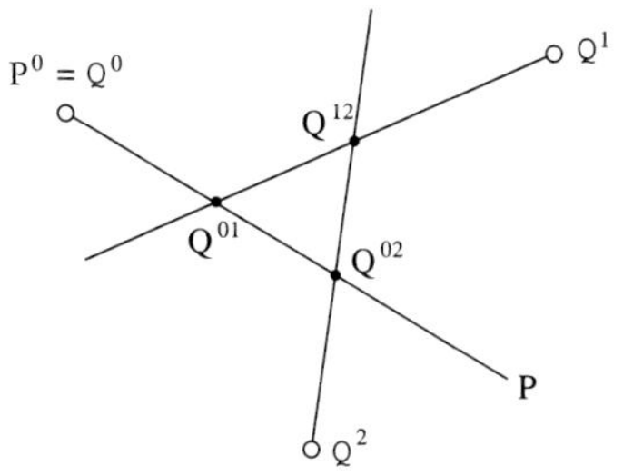

Fig. 22.7. *Configuration of the three camera centres and the three ambiguous points. If the three points* $\mathbf{Q}^{ij}$ *are distinct, then they all lie in the plane of the camera centres* $\mathbf{C}^i_{\mathtt{Q}}$.

pairs of the quadrics. In general, the intersection of three quadrics will consist of eight points. In this case, the critical set with respect to the two triplets of camera matrices will consist of these eight points, less any such points that lie on the plane of the three cameras $\mathtt{Q}^i$. In fact, it has been shown (in a longer unpublished version of [Maybank-98]) that of the eight points of intersection of three quadrics, only seven are critical, since the eighth point lies on the plane of the three cameras.

In some cases, however, the camera matrices may be chosen such that the three quadric surfaces meet in a curve. This will occur if the three quadrics $\mathtt{S}_{\mathtt{P}}^{ij}$ are linearly dependent. For instance if $\mathtt{S}_{\mathtt{P}}^{12} = \alpha \mathtt{S}_{\mathtt{P}}^{01} + \beta \mathtt{S}_{\mathtt{P}}^{02}$, then any point $\mathbf{P}$ that satisfies $\mathbf{P}^{\mathsf{T}} \mathtt{S}_{\mathtt{P}}^{01} \mathbf{P} = 0$ and $\mathbf{P}^{\mathsf{T}} \mathtt{S}_{\mathtt{P}}^{02} \mathbf{P} = 0$ will also satisfy $\mathbf{P}^{\mathsf{T}} \mathtt{S}_{\mathtt{P}}^{12} \mathbf{P} = 0$. Thus the intersection of the three quadrics is the same as the intersection of two of them. In this case, the three cameras must also lie on the same intersection curve. We define a non-degenerate *elliptic quartic* to be the intersection curve of two non-degenerate ruled quadrics, consisting of a single curve. This is a fourth-degree space curve. Other ways that two quadrics can intersect include a twisted-cubic plus a line, or two conics. Examples of elliptic quartics are shown in figure 22.8.

Example 22.29. Three-view critical configuration – the elliptic quartic.

We consider the quadrics represented by matrices $\mathtt{A}$ and $\mathtt{B} = \tilde{\mathtt{B}} + \tilde{\mathtt{B}}^{\mathsf{T}}$, where

$$\mathtt{A} = \begin{bmatrix} 0 & 1 & 0 & 0 \\ 1 & 0 & 0 & 0 \\ 0 & 0 & 0 & -1 \\ 0 & 0 & -1 & 0 \end{bmatrix} \quad \text{and } \tilde{\mathtt{B}} = \begin{bmatrix} p & q & s-t & -s-u \\ 0 & r & s+t & -s+u \\ 0 & 0 & -p-q-r & 0 \\ 0 & 0 & 0 & 0 \end{bmatrix}. \tag{22.5}$$

Thus, $\mathtt{B}$ is a member of a 5-parameter family of quadrics generated by $\{p, q, r, s, t, u\}$, (remembering that scale is irrelevant). The camera matrices

$$\mathtt{P}^0 = [\mathtt{I} \,|\, 0], \quad \mathtt{P}^1 = [\mathtt{I} \mid (-1, -1, -1)^{\mathsf{T}}] \quad \text{and} \quad \mathtt{P}^2 = [\mathtt{I} \mid (1, 1, -1)^{\mathsf{T}}]$$

have centres lying on the intersection of these three quadrics.

We show that a configuration consisting of these three cameras, and any number of points on the intersection of the two quadrics is critical. This is demonstrated by explicitly exhibiting two alternative configurations consisting of three cameras $\mathtt{Q}_i$ and for each point $\mathbf{P}$ lying on the intersection of the two quadrics, a conjugate point $\mathbf{Q}$ such

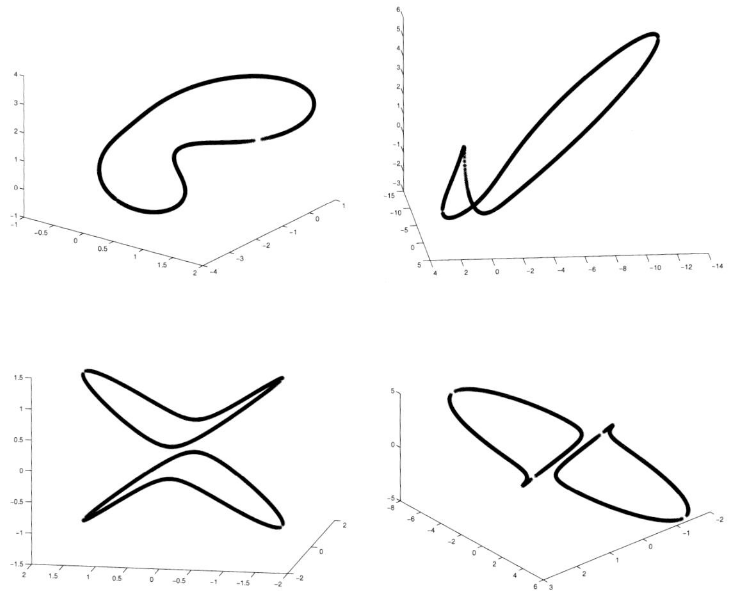

Fig. 22.8. *Examples of elliptic quartic curves generated as the intersection of two ruled quadrics.*

that $\mathtt{P}^i\mathbf{P} = \mathtt{Q}^i\mathbf{Q}$. In fact, two different conjugate configurations are given in table 22.1 and table 22.2.

It may be verified directly that $\mathtt{P}^i\mathbf{P} = \mathtt{Q}^i\mathbf{Q}$ for all points $\mathbf{P} = (x, y, xy, 1)^\mathsf{T}$ and corresponding points $\mathbf{Q}$, provided that $\mathbf{P}$ lies on the quadric $\mathtt{B}$. (It always lies on quadric $\mathtt{A}$). The easiest way to see this is to verify that $(\mathtt{P}^i\mathbf{P}) \times (\mathtt{Q}^i\mathbf{Q}) = 0$ for all such points. In fact for $i = 0, 1$, the cross-product is always zero, whereas for $i = 2$ it may be verified by direct computation that

$$(\mathtt{P}^2\mathbf{P}) \times (\mathtt{Q}^2\mathbf{Q}) = \left(\mathbf{P}^\mathsf{T}\mathtt{B}\mathbf{P}\right)(4, -4x, 4)^\mathsf{T}$$

for the first solution, and

$$(\mathtt{P}^2\mathbf{P}) \times (\mathtt{Q}^2\mathbf{Q}) = \left(\mathbf{P}^\mathsf{T}\mathtt{B}\mathbf{P}\right)(-4y, 4, 4)^\mathsf{T}$$

for the second solution. Thus $\mathtt{P}^2\mathbf{P} = \mathtt{Q}^2\mathbf{Q}$ if and only if $\mathbf{P}$ lies on $\mathtt{B}$.

Note that in this example, $\mathtt{A}$ is the matrix representing the quadric $\mathtt{S}_\mathtt{P}^{01}$. △

This example is quite general, since if $\mathtt{A}'$ and $\mathtt{B}'$ are two non-degenerate ruled quadrics containing the centres of three cameras, then by a projective transformation, we may map $\mathtt{A}'$ to $\mathtt{A}$ and the three camera centres to those of the given $\mathtt{P}^i$, provided only that no two of the camera centres lie on the same generator of $\mathtt{A}'$. In addition, $\mathtt{B}'$ will map to $\mathtt{A} + \lambda\mathtt{B}$ for some λ. Thus, the pencil generated by $\mathtt{A}'$ and $\mathtt{B}'$, and hence also their intersection curve, are projectively equivalent to those generated by $\mathtt{A}$ and $\mathtt{B}$.

The possibility that two of the camera centres lie on the same generator of $\mathtt{A}'$ is not a difficulty, since if the line of the camera centres lies on all quadrics in the pencil, then the quadric intersection can not be an non-degenerate elliptic quartic. Otherwise,

The camera matrices are

$$\mathtt{Q}^0 = \begin{bmatrix} 1 & 0 & 0 & 0 \\ 0 & 1 & 0 & 0 \\ 0 & 0 & 1 & 0 \end{bmatrix}, \quad \mathtt{Q}^1 = \begin{bmatrix} -4 & 0 & 0 & 0 \\ 0 & 0 & 2 & 1 \\ 0 & 0 & -2 & 1 \end{bmatrix}$$

and $\mathtt{Q}^2 =$

$$\begin{bmatrix} -4(2p+q-t+u) & 8r & 4(p+q+2r+s+t) & -2(p+q-s-t) \\ 0 & 8(r+s-u) & -2(q-t+u) & -q+t-u \\ 8p & -8r & -2(2p+q-2s+3t+3u) & 2p+q-2s-t-u \end{bmatrix}$$

The conjugate point to $\mathbf{P} = (x, y, xy, 1)^\mathsf{T}$ is

$$\mathbf{Q} = ((x-1)x, (x-1)y, (x-1)xy, -2x(-2+y+xy))^\mathsf{T}.$$

Table 22.1. *First conjugate solution to reconstruction problem for cameras* $\mathtt{P}^i$ *and points on the intersection of quadrics* $\mathtt{A}$ *and* $\mathtt{B}$ *given in (22.5).*

The camera matrices are

$$\mathtt{Q}^0 = \begin{bmatrix} 1 & 0 & 0 & 0 \\ 0 & 1 & 0 & 0 \\ 0 & 0 & 1 & 0 \end{bmatrix}, \quad \mathtt{Q}^1 = \begin{bmatrix} 0 & 0 & -2 & 1 \\ 0 & 4 & 0 & 0 \\ 0 & 0 & 2 & 1 \end{bmatrix}$$

and $\mathtt{Q}^2 =$

$$\begin{bmatrix} -8(p+s+u) & 0 & 2(q+t-u) & -q-t+u \\ -8p & 4(q+2r+t-u) & -4(2p+q+r+s-t) & -2(q+r-s+t) \\ 8p & -8r & 2(q+2r-2s-3t-3u) & q+2r-2s+t+u \end{bmatrix}$$

The conjugate point to $\mathbf{P} = (x, y, xy, 1)^\mathsf{T}$ is

$$\mathbf{Q} = ((y-1)x, (y-1)y, (y-1)xy, 2y(-2+x+xy))^\mathsf{T}.$$

Table 22.2. *Second conjugate solution to reconstruction problem.*

we can choose $\mathtt{A}'$ to be one of the quadrics not containing the line of the two camera centres. This demonstrates

Result 22.30. *Any configuration consisting of three cameras and any number of points lying on a non-degenerate elliptic quartic is critical.*

22.5 Closure

22.5.1 The literature

The twisted cubic as the critical curve for camera resectioning was brought to the attention of the computer-vision community by [Buchanan-88]. For more about critical sets of two views, the reader is referred to [Maybank-90] and the book [Maybank-93]. In both these cases, the critical point sets were known much earlier. In fact [Buchanan-88] refers the reader to the German photogrammetric literature [Krames-42, Rinner-72]. For two views, the result that (v) and (viii) are *not* critical in theorem 22.9(*p*541) is due to Fredrik Kahl (unpublished).

The discussion of critical configurations for three views given in this chapter is only a part of what is known about this topic. More can be found in [Hartley-00b, Hartley-02a, Kahl-01a]. In particular, the elliptic-quartic configuration is extended to any number of cameras in [Kahl-01a]. A critical configuration for any number of cameras, consisting of points on a twisted cubic and cameras on a straight line is considered in [Hartley-03]. Earlier work on this area includes an investigation of the critical camera positions for sets of six points in [Maybank-98], and an unpublished report [Shashua-96] deals with critical configurations in three views.

Nothing has been said here about critical configurations of lines in three or more views, but this topic has been treated in [Buchanan-92]. In addition, critical configuration for linear reconstruction from lines (the linear line complex) have been identified in [Stein-99].

22.5.2 Notes and exercises

(i) Fill out the details of the following sketch to prove that any two configurations consisting of a hyperboloid of one sheet and two points on the hyperboloid are projectively equivalent (via a projectivity of $\mathbb{P}^3$) provided that the points in both pairs either do or do not lie on the same generator.

Since any hyperboloid of one sheet is projectively equivalent to $\mathrm{X}^2 + \mathrm{Y}^2 - \mathrm{Z}^2 = 1$, any two hyperboloids of one sheet are projectively equivalent to each other, and also to the hyperboloid given by $\mathrm{Z} = \mathrm{XY}$. Define a 1D projective transformation $h_{\mathrm{X}}(\mathrm{X}) = \mathrm{X}' = (a\mathrm{X} + b)/(c\mathrm{X} + d)$. One computes that

$$\begin{bmatrix} a & & & b \\ & d & c & \\ & b & a & \\ c & & & d \end{bmatrix} \begin{pmatrix} \mathrm{X} \\ \mathrm{Y} \\ \mathrm{XY} \\ 1 \end{pmatrix} = \begin{pmatrix} \mathrm{X}' \\ \mathrm{Y} \\ \mathrm{X}'\mathrm{Y} \\ 1 \end{pmatrix} .$$

This is a 3D projective transformation taking the surface $\mathrm{Z} = \mathrm{XY}$ to itself. Composing this with a similar transformation of Y one finds a projective transformation that takes $(\mathrm{X}, \mathrm{Y}, \mathrm{XY}, 1)^\mathsf{T}$ to $(\mathrm{X}', \mathrm{Y}', \mathrm{X}'\mathrm{Y}', 1)^\mathsf{T}$ while fixing the quadric $\mathrm{Z} = \mathrm{XY}$. Since h_{X} and h_{Y} are arbitrary 1D projective transformations, this gives enough freedom to map any two points to two others.

(ii) Show that Γ maps a line that meets one of the edges of the reference tetrahedron to a conic.

(iii) Show that Γ maps a straight line meeting two opposite edges of the reference tetrahedron to a straight line meeting the same two edges.

(iv) How are these configurations related to degenerate configurations for camera resectioning, as shown in figure 22.3(*p*538).

(v) Two-view degeneracy occurs when all points and the two cameras lie on a ruled quadric. Given eight points on the corners of a Euclidean cube and two camera centres, show that these 10 points always lie on a quadric. If this is a ruled quadric, then the configuration is degenerate, and reconstruction is not possible from 8 points. Investigate under what conditions the quadric is ruled. *Hint:*

there is a two-parameter family of quadrics passing through the cube vertices. What does this two-parameter family look like?

(vi) Extend result 22.30 by showing that a configuration of any number of cameras and points lying on a non-degenerate elliptic quartic is critical. This does not require complex computations. If stuck, refer to [Kahl-01a].

Part V

Appendices

Portrait of the Countess D'Haussonville, 1845 (oil on canvas)
by Jean-Auguste-Dominique Ingres (1780-1867)
The Frick Collection, New York

Appendix 1

Tensor Notation

Since tensor notation is not commonly used in computer vision, it seems appropriate to give a brief introduction to its use. For more details, the reader is referred to [Triggs-95]. For simplicity, these concepts will be explained here in the context of low-dimensional projective spaces, rather than in their full generality. However, the ideas apply in arbitrary dimensional vector spaces.

Consider a set of basis vectors $\mathbf{e}_i$, $i = 1, \ldots, 3$ for a 2-dimensional projective space $\mathbb{P}^2$. For reasons to become clear, we will write the indices as subscripts. With respect to this basis, a point in $\mathbb{P}^2$ is represented by a set of coordinates x^i, which represents the point $\sum_{i=1}^3 x^i\, \mathbf{e}_i$. We write the coordinates with an upper index, as shown. Let $\mathbf{x}$ represent the triple of coordinates, $\mathbf{x} = (x^1, x^2, x^3)^\mathsf{T}$.

Now, consider a change of coordinate axes in which the basis vectors $\mathbf{e}_i$ are replaced by a new basis set $\hat{\mathbf{e}}_j$, where $\hat{\mathbf{e}}_j = \sum_i H^i_j\, \mathbf{e}_i$, and $\mathtt{H}$ is the basis transformation matrix with entries H^i_j. If $\hat{\mathbf{x}} = (\hat{x}^1, \hat{x}^2, \hat{x}^3)^\mathsf{T}$ are the coordinates of the vector with respect to the new basis, then we may verify that $\hat{\mathbf{x}} = \mathtt{H}^{-1}\mathbf{x}$. Thus, if the basis vectors transform according to $\mathtt{H}$ the coordinates of points transform according to the inverse transformation $\mathtt{H}^{-1}$.

Next, consider a line in $\mathbb{P}^2$ represented by coordinates $\mathbf{l}$ with respect to the original basis. With respect to the new basis, it may be verified that the line is represented by a new set of coordinates $\hat{\mathbf{l}} = \mathtt{H}^\mathsf{T}\mathbf{l}$. Thus coordinates of the line transform according to $\mathtt{H}^\mathsf{T}$.

As a further example, let $\mathtt{P}$ be a matrix representing a mapping between projective (or vector) spaces. If $\mathtt{G}$ and $\mathtt{H}$ represent basis transformations in the domain and range spaces, then with respect to the new bases, the mapping is represented by a new matrx $\hat{\mathtt{P}} = \mathtt{H}^{-1}\mathtt{P}\mathtt{G}$. Note in these examples that sometimes the matrix $\mathtt{H}$ or $\mathtt{H}^\mathsf{T}$ is used in the transformation, and sometimes $\mathtt{H}^{-1}$.

These three examples of coordinate transformations may be written explicitly as follows.

$$\hat{x}^i = (H^{-1})^i_j\, x^j \qquad \hat{l}_i = H^j_i\, l_j \qquad \hat{P}^i_j = (H^{-1})^i_k\, G^l_j\, P^k_l$$

where we use the tensor summation convention that an index repeated in upper and lower positions in a product represents summation over the range of the index. Note that those indices that are written as superscripts transform according to $\mathtt{H}^{-1}$, whereas those that are written as subscripts transform as $\mathtt{H}$ (or $\mathtt{G}$). Note that there is no distinction in tensor notation between indices that are transformed by $\mathtt{H}$, and those that are transformed by $\mathtt{H}^\mathsf{T}$. In general, tensor indices will transform by either $\mathtt{H}$ or $\mathtt{H}^{-1}$ – in fact this is the characteristic of a tensor. Those indices that transform according to $\mathtt{H}$ are known as *covariant* indices and are written as subscripts. Those indices that transform according to $\mathtt{H}^{-1}$ are known as *contravariant* indices, and are written as superscripts. The number of indices is the *valency* of the tensor. The sum over an index, e.g. $H_i^j\, l_j$, is referred to as a *contraction*, in this case the tensor H_i^j is contracted with the line l_j.

A1.1 The tensor ϵ_{rst}

The tensor ϵ_{rst} is defined for $r, s, t = 1, \ldots, 3$ as follows:

$$\epsilon_{rst} = \begin{cases} 0 \text{ unless } r,\ s \text{ and } t \text{ are distinct} \\ +1 \text{ if } rst \text{ is an even permutation of } 123 \\ -1 \text{ if } rst \text{ is an odd permutation of } 123 \end{cases}$$

The tensor ϵ_{ijk} (or its contravariant counterpart, ϵ^{ijk}) is connected with the cross product of two vectors. If $\mathbf{a}$ and $\mathbf{b}$ are two vectors, and $\mathbf{c} = \mathbf{a} \times \mathbf{b}$ is their cross product, then the following formula may easily be verified.

$$c_i = (\mathbf{a} \times \mathbf{b})_i = \epsilon_{ijk} a^j b^k .$$

Related to this is the expression (A4.5–*p*581) for the skew-symmetric matrix $[\mathbf{a}]_\times$. Using tensor notation one writes this as

$$([\mathbf{a}]_\times)_{ik} = \epsilon_{ijk} a^j .$$

Thus, one sees that if $\mathbf{a}$ is a contravariant vector, then $[\mathbf{a}]_\times$ is a matrix with two covariant indices. A similar formula holds for $[\mathbf{v}]_\times$ where $\mathbf{v}$ is covariant, namely $([\mathbf{v}]_\times)^{ik} = \epsilon^{ijk} v_j$.

Finally, the tensor ϵ_{ijk} is related to determinants: for three contravariant tensors a^i, b^j and c^k, one verifies that $a^i b^j c^k \epsilon_{ijk}$ is the determinant of the 3×3 matrix with rows a^i, b^j and c^k.

A1.2 The trifocal tensor

The trifocal tensor $\mathcal{T}_i^{jk}$ has one covariant and two contravariant indices. For vectors and matrices, such as x^i, l_i and P_j^i, it is possible to write the transformation rules using standard linear algebra notation, e.g. $\mathbf{x}' = \mathtt{H}\mathbf{x}$. However, for tensors with three or more indices, this cannot conveniently be done. There is really no choice but to use tensor notation when dealing with the trifocal tensor.

Transformation rule. The arrangement of indices for the trifocal tensor implies a transformation rule

$$\hat{\mathcal{T}}_i^{jk} = F_i^r \, (G^{-1})_s^j \, (H^{-1})_t^k \mathcal{T}_r^{st} \tag{A1.1}$$

with respect to changes of basis in the three images. It is worthwhile pointing out one possible source of confusion here. The transformation rule (A1.1) shows how the

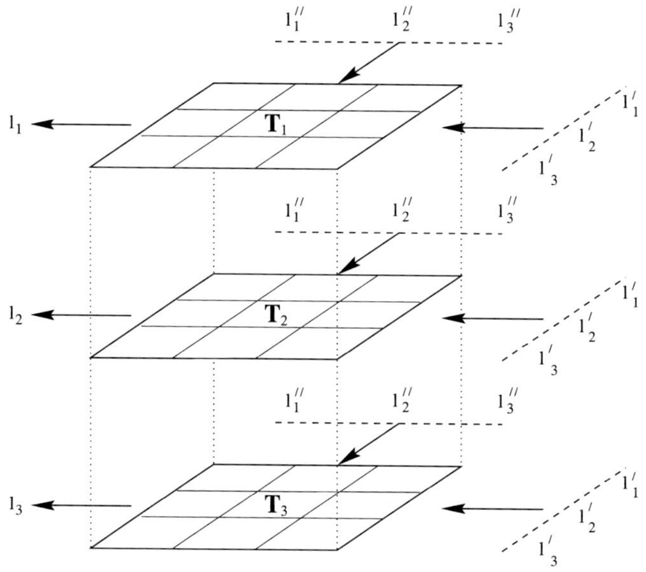

Fig. A1.1. **A 3-dimensional representation of the trifocal tensor** – *figure after Faugeras and Papadopoulo [Faugeras-97]. The picture represents* $l_i = l'_j l''_k \mathcal{T}_i^{jk}$, *which is the contraction of the tensor with the lines* $\mathbf{l}'$ *and* $\mathbf{l}''$ *to produce a line* $\mathbf{l}$. *In pseudo-matrix notation this can be written as* $l_i = \mathbf{l}'^{\mathsf{T}} \mathtt{T}_i \mathbf{l}''^{\mathsf{T}}$, *where* $(\mathtt{T}_i)_{jk} = \mathcal{T}_i^{jk}$.

tensor is transformed in terms of *basis* transformations in the three images. Often, we are concerned instead with point coordinate transformations. Thus, if $\mathtt{F}'$, $\mathtt{G}'$ and $\mathtt{H}'$ represent *coordinate* transformations in the images, in the sense that $\hat{x}^j = F'^j_i x^i$, and $\mathtt{G}'$ and $\mathtt{H}'$ are similarly defined for the other images, then the transformation rule may be written as

$$\hat{\mathcal{T}}_i^{jk} = (F'^{-1})_i^r \, G'^j_s \, H'^k_t \mathcal{T}_r^{st}.$$

Picture of tensors. A vector $\mathbf{x}$ may be thought of as a set of numbers arranged in a column or row, and a matrix $\mathtt{H}$ as a 2D array of numbers. Similarly, a tensor with three indices may be thought of as a 3D array of numbers. In particular the trifocal tensor is a $3 \times 3 \times 3$ cube of cells as illustrated in figure A1.1.

Appendix 2

Gaussian (Normal) and χ^2 Distributions

A2.1 Gaussian probability distribution

Given a vector $\mathbf{X}$ of random variables x_i for $i = 1, \ldots, N$, with mean $\overline{\mathbf{X}} = E[\mathbf{X}]$, where $E[\cdot]$ represents the expected value, and $\Delta\mathbf{X} = \mathbf{X} - \overline{\mathbf{X}}$, the covariance matrix Σ is an $N \times N$ matrix given by

$$\Sigma = E[\Delta\mathbf{X}\,\Delta\mathbf{X}^\mathsf{T}]$$

so that $\Sigma_{ij} = E[\Delta x_i \Delta x_j]$. The diagonal entries of the matrix Σ are the variances of the individual variables x_i, whereas the off-diagonal entries are the cross-covariance values.

The variables x_i are said to conform to a joint Gaussian distribution, if the probability distribution of $\mathbf{X}$ is of the form

$$P(\overline{\mathbf{X}} + \Delta\mathbf{X}) = (2\pi)^{-N/2}\det(\Sigma^{-1})^{1/2}\exp\left(-(\Delta\mathbf{X})^\mathsf{T}\Sigma^{-1}(\Delta\mathbf{X})/2\right) \tag{A2.1}$$

for some positive-semidefinite matrix Σ^{-1}. It may be verified that $\overline{\mathbf{X}}$ and Σ are the mean and covariance of the distribution. A Gaussian distribution is uniquely determined by its mean and covariance. The factor $(2\pi)^{-N/2}\det(\Sigma^{-1})^{1/2}$ is just the normalizing factor necessary to make the total integral of the distribution equal to 1.

In the special case where Σ is a scalar matrix $\Sigma = \sigma^2\mathrm{I}$ the Gaussian PDF takes a simple form

$$P(\mathbf{X}) = (\sqrt{2\pi}\sigma)^{-N}\exp\left(-\sum_{i=1}^{N}(x_i - \bar{x}_i)^2/2\sigma^2\right)$$

where $\mathbf{X} = (x_1, x_2, \ldots, x_N)^\mathsf{T}$. This distribution is called an *isotropic Gaussian distribution.*

Mahalanobis distance. Note that in this case the value of the PDF at a point $\mathbf{X}$ is simply a function of the Euclidean distance $\left(\sum_{i=1}^N(x_i - \bar{x}_i)^2\right)^{1/2}$ of the point $\mathbf{X}$ from the mean $\overline{\mathbf{X}} = (\bar{x}_1, \ldots, \bar{x}_N)^\mathsf{T}$. By analogy with this one may define the *Mahalanobis distance* between two vectors $\mathbf{X}$ and $\mathbf{Y}$ to be

$$\|\mathbf{X} - \mathbf{Y}\|_\Sigma = \left((\mathbf{X} - \mathbf{Y})^\mathsf{T}\Sigma^{-1}(\mathbf{X} - \mathbf{Y})\right)^{1/2}.$$

One verifies that for a positive-definite matrix Σ, this defines a metric on $\mathbb{R}^N$. Using this notation, the general form of the Gaussian PDF may be written as

$$P(\mathbf{X}) \approx \exp\left(-\|\mathbf{X} - \overline{\mathbf{X}}\|_{\Sigma}^2/2\right)$$

where the normalizing factor has been omitted. Thus, the value of the Gaussian PDF is a function of the Mahalanobis distance of the point $\mathbf{X}$ from the mean.

Change of coordinates. Since Σ is symmetric and positive-definite, it may be written as $\Sigma = \mathtt{U}^\mathsf{T}\mathtt{D}\mathtt{U}$, where $\mathtt{U}$ is an orthogonal matrix and $\mathtt{D} = (\sigma_1^2, \sigma_2^2, \ldots, \sigma_N^2)$ is diagonal. Writing $\mathbf{X}' = \mathtt{U}\mathbf{X}$ and $\overline{\mathbf{X}}' = \mathtt{U}\overline{\mathbf{X}}$, and substituting in (A2.1), leads to

$$\begin{aligned}
\exp\left(-(\mathbf{X} - \overline{\mathbf{X}})^\mathsf{T}\Sigma^{-1}(\mathbf{X} - \overline{\mathbf{X}})/2\right) &= \exp\left(-(\mathbf{X}' - \overline{\mathbf{X}}')^\mathsf{T}\mathtt{U}\Sigma^{-1}\mathtt{U}^\mathsf{T}(\mathbf{X}' - \overline{\mathbf{X}}')/2\right) \\
&= \exp\left(-(\mathbf{X}' - \overline{\mathbf{X}}')^\mathsf{T}\mathtt{D}^{-1}(\mathbf{X}' - \overline{\mathbf{X}}')/2\right)
\end{aligned}$$

Thus, the orthogonal change of coordinates from $\mathbf{X}$ to $\mathbf{X}' = \mathtt{U}\mathbf{X}$ transforms a general Gaussian PDF into one with diagonal covariance matrix. A further scaling by σ_i in each coordinate direction may be applied to transform it to an isotropic Gaussian distribution. Equivalently stated, a change of coordinates may be applied to transform Mahalanobis distance to ordinary Euclidean distance.

A2.2 χ^2 distribution

The χ_n^2 distribution is the distribution of the sum of squares of n independent Gaussian random variables. As applied to a Gaussian random vector $\mathbf{v}$ with non-singular covariance matrix Σ, the value of $(\mathbf{v} - \bar{\mathbf{v}})^\mathsf{T}\Sigma^{-1}(\mathbf{v} - \bar{\mathbf{v}})$ satisfies a χ_n^2 distribution, where n is the dimension of $\mathbf{v}$. If the covariance matrix Σ is singular, then we must replace Σ^{-1} with the pseudo-inverse Σ^+. In this case

- *If* $\mathbf{v}$ *is a Gaussian random vector with mean* $\bar{\mathbf{v}}$ *and covariance matrix* Σ*, then the value of* $(\mathbf{v} - \bar{\mathbf{v}})^\mathsf{T}\Sigma^+(\mathbf{v} - \bar{\mathbf{v}})$ *satisfies a* χ_r^2 *distribution, where* $r = \text{rank}\Sigma$.

The cumulative chi-squared distribution is defined as $F_n(k^2) = \int_0^{k^2} \chi_n^2(\xi)d\xi$. This represents the probability that the value of the χ_n^2 random variable is less than k^2. Graphs of the χ_n^2 distribution and inverse cumulative χ_n^2 distributions for $n = 1, \ldots, 4$ are shown in figure A2.1 A program for computing the cumulative chi-squared distribution $F_n(k^2)$ is given in [Press-88]. Since it is a monotonically increasing function, one may compute the inverse function by any simple technique such as subdivision, and values are tabulated in table A2.1 (compare with figure A2.1).

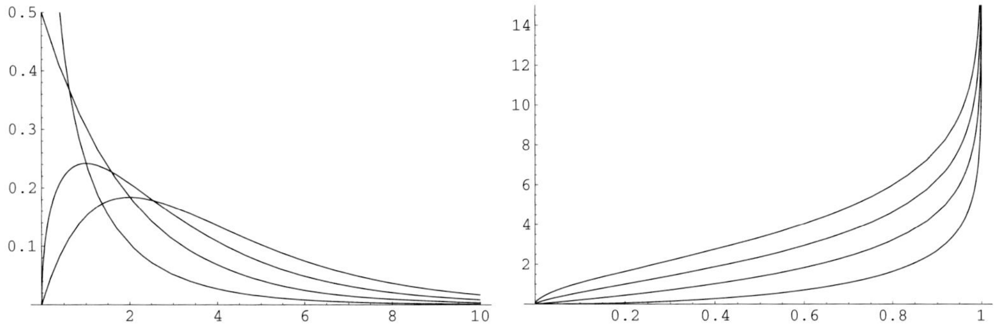

Fig. A2.1. *The χ^2_n distribution (left) and inverse cumulative χ^2_n distribution F_n^{-1} (right) for $n = 1, \ldots, 4$. In both cases, graphs are for $n = 1, \ldots, 4$ bottom to top (at middle point of horizontal axis).*

n	$\alpha = 0.95$	$\alpha = 0.99$
1	3.84	6.63
2	5.99	9.21
3	7.81	11.34
4	9.49	13.28

Table A2.1. *Values of k^2 for which $F_n(k^2)$, the cumulative χ^2 distribution with n degrees of freedom, equals α, i.e. $k^2 = F_n^{-1}(\alpha)$, where α is the probability.*

Appendix 3

Parameter Estimation

There is much theory about parameter estimation, dealing with properties such as the bias and variance of the estimate. This theory is based on analysis of the probability density functions of the measurements and the parameter space. In this appendix, we discuss such topics as bias of an estimator, the variance, the Cramér-Rao lower bound on the variance, and the posterior distribution. The treatment will be largely informal, based on examples, and exploring these concepts in the context of reconstruction.

The general lesson to be learnt from this discussion is that many of these concepts depend strongly on the particular parametrization of the model. In problems such as 3D projective reconstruction, where there is no preferred parametrization, these concepts are not well defined, or depend very strongly on assumed noise models.

A simple geometric estimation problem. The problem we shall consider is related to the triangulation problem of determining a point in space from its projection into two images. To simplify this problem, however, we consider its 2-dimensional analog. In addition, we fix one of the rays reducing the problem to one of estimating the position of a point along a known line from observing it in a single image.

Thus, consider a line camera (that is, one forming a 1D image as in section 6.4.2-(p175)) observing points on a single line. Let the camera be located at the origin $(0, 0)$ and point in the positive Y direction. Further, assume that it has unit focal length. Thus, the camera matrix for this camera is simply $[\mathtt{I}_{2\times 2}|\mathbf{0}]$. Now, suppose that the camera is observing points on the line $\mathrm{Y} = \mathrm{X}+1$ (the "world line"). A point $(\mathrm{X}, \mathrm{X}+1)$ on this line will be mapped to the image point $x = \mathrm{X}/(\mathrm{X} + 1)$. However, we assume that a point is measured with a certain inaccuracy, which may be modelled with a probability density function (PDF). The usual practice is to model the noise using a Gaussian distribution. Let us assume at least that the mode (maximum) of the distribution is at zero. The imaging setup is illustrated in figure A3.1.

The estimation problem we consider is the following: given the image coordinates of a point, estimate the position of the "world point" on the line $y = x + 1$. To consider a specific scenario, we may think of the line as a scintillator being flooded with gamma-rays. A camera is used to measure the location of each scintillation and determine its position along the line. The problem seems to be ridiculously simple, but it will turn out that there are some surprises.

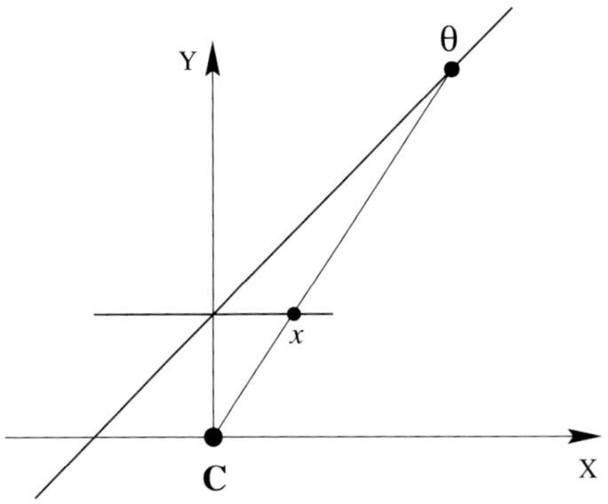

Fig. A3.1. *The imaging setup for a simple estimation problem. A point on the line* $Y = X + 1$ *is imaged by a line camera. The projection mapping is given by* $f : \theta \mapsto x = \theta/(1+\theta)$*, where* θ *parametrizes the points on the line* $Y = X + 1$*. Measurement is subject to noise with a zero-mode distribution.*

Probability density function. We start by parametrizing the world line $Y = X + 1$ by a parameter θ, where the most convenient parametrization is $\theta = X$ so that the 2D point parametrized by θ is $(\theta, \theta + 1)$. This point projects to $\theta/(\theta + 1)$. We denote this projection function from the world line to the image line by f, so that $f(\theta) = \theta/(\theta+1)$. The measurement of this point is corrupted by noise, resulting in a random variable x with probability distribution given by $p(x|\theta) = g(x - f(\theta))$. For instance, if g is a zero-mean Gaussian distribution with variance σ^2, then

$$p(x|\theta) = (2\pi\sigma^2)^{-1/2} \exp\left(-(x - f(\theta))^2/2\sigma^2\right).$$

Maximum Likelihood estimate. An estimate of the parameter vector θ given a measured value x is a function denoted $\hat{\theta}(x)$, assigning a parameter vector θ to a measurement x. The maximum likelihood (ML) estimate is given by

$$\hat{\theta}_{ML} = \arg\max_{\theta} p(x|\theta).$$

In the current estimation problem it is easily seen that the ML estimate is obtained simply by back-projecting the measured point x and selecting its intersection with the world line, according to the formula

$$\hat{\theta}(x) = f^{-1}(x) = x/(1 - x).$$

This is the ML estimate, because the resulting point, with parameter $\hat{\theta}(x)$, projects forward to x, hence $p(x|\hat{\theta}) = g(x-x) = g(0)$ which by assumption gives the maximum (mode) of the probability density function g. Any other choice of parameter θ will give a smaller value of $p(x|\theta)$.

A3.1 Bias

A desirable property of an estimator is that it can be expected to give the right answer on the average. Given a parameter θ, or equivalently in our case a point on the world line, we consider all possible measurements x and from them reestimate the parameter θ, namely $\hat{\theta}(x)$. The estimator is known as *unbiased* if on the average we obtain

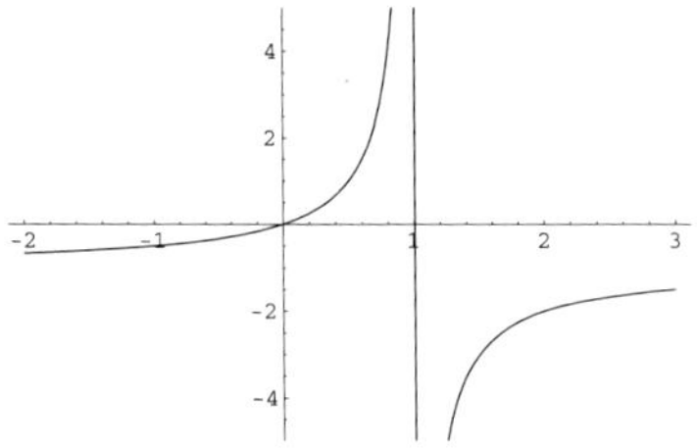

Fig. A3.2. *The ML estimate of the world-point position* $\hat{\theta}(x) = f^{-1}(x) = x/(1-x)$ *for different measurements of the image point* x. *Note that for values of* x *greater than 1, the ML estimate switches to "behind" the camera.*

the original parameter θ (the true value). In forming this average, we weight the measurements x according to their probability. More formally, the bias of the estimator is defined as

$$E_\theta[\hat{\theta}(x)] - \theta = \int_x p(x|\theta)\, \hat{\theta}(x) dx - \theta$$

and the estimator is unbiased if $E_\theta[\hat{\theta}(x)] = \theta$ for all θ. Here E_θ stands for the *expected value* given θ, defined as shown.

Another way of thinking of bias is in terms of repeating an experiment many times with identical model parameters and a different instance of the noise at each trial. The bias is the difference between the average value of the estimated parameters and the true parameter value. It is worth noting that for the bias to be defined, it is not necessary that the parameter space have an *a priori* distribution defined on it, not even that it be a measure space. It is necessary, however that it have some affine structure so that the average (or integral) can be formed.

Now, we determine whether the ML estimate of θ is unbiased in the case where $f(\theta) = \theta/(\theta+1)$. The integral becomes

$$\int_x p(x|\theta)\, \hat{\theta}(x) dx = \int_x \frac{1}{\sqrt{2\pi}\sigma} \exp\left(\frac{(x - \theta/(\theta+1))^2}{2\sigma^2}\right) \frac{x}{1-x} dx$$

It turns out that this integral diverges, and hence the bias is undefined. The difficulty is that with an assumed Gaussian distribution of noise, for any value of θ, there is always a finite (though perhaps very small) probability $p(x|\theta)$ that $x > 1$. For values of $x > 1$, the corresponding ray does not meet the world line in front of the camera (since the ray is parallel to the world line at $x = 1$). The estimate $\hat{\theta}(x)$ as a function of x is shown in figure A3.2, showing how it results in estimated world-points behind the camera. Even if values of $\hat{\theta}(x)$ behind the camera are ignored, the ML estimator has infinite bias, as is explained in figure A3.3.

Limiting the range of parameters. Since the range of the parameter θ is from -1 to ∞, it makes sense to limit its range. In fact, we may have knowledge that all "events" on the world-line lie in a more restricted range. As an example, suppose that we assume that θ lies in the range $-1 \leq \theta \leq 1$, and hence noise-free projected points are in the range $-\infty < x < 1/2$. In this case, the ML estimate for any image point $x > 1/2$ will

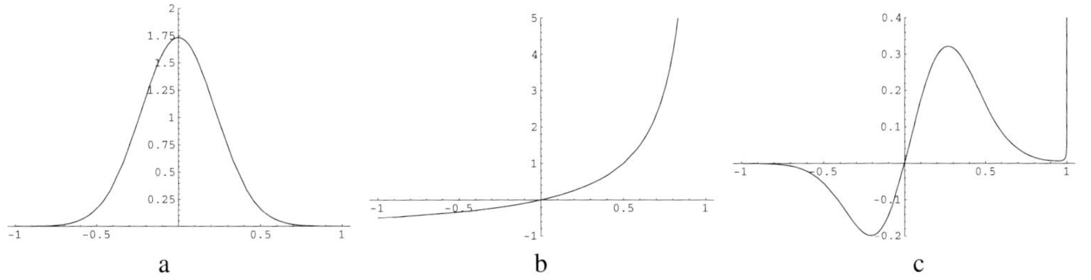

Fig. A3.3. **The reason that the ML estimate with Gaussian noise model has infinite bias.** *(a) The distribution of possible values of the image measurement given a world-point at* $x = 0, y = 1$ *assuming Gaussian noise distribution with* $\sigma = 0.4$ *– in symbols* $p(x|\theta = 0)$. *(b) The ML estimate of the world point for different values of the image point,* $\hat{\theta}(x) = x/(1-x)$. *Note that as the image point approaches* 1, *the estimated point on the world-line recedes to infinity. (c) Product* $\hat{\theta}(x)\ p(x|\theta = 0)$. *The integral of this function from* $x = -\infty$ *to* $x = 1$ *gives the bias of the ML estimator. Note that as* x *approaches* 1, *the graph increases abruptly to infinity. The integral is unbounded, meaning that the estimator has infinite bias.*

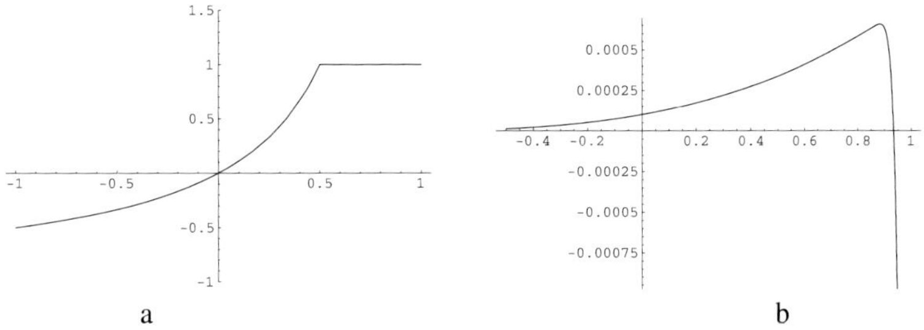

Fig. A3.4. *(a) If the range of possible values of the world-point parameter* θ *is limited to the range* $\theta \leq 1$, *then the ML estimate of any point* $x > 1/2$ *will be* $\theta = 1$. *This will prevent infinite bias in the estimate, but there will still be bias. (b) The bias* $E_\theta[\hat{\theta}(x)] - \theta = \int_x \hat{\theta}(x) p(x|\theta) dx - \theta$ *as a function of* θ. *Measurement noise is Gaussian with* $\sigma = 0.01$.

be at $\hat{\theta}(x) = 1$. With this restriction on the parameter θ, the ML estimate is still biased, as shown in figure A3.4.

If the noise-distribution has finite support, then the bias will also be finite for most values of θ, even if the range of the parameter θ is unrestricted. This is shown in figure A3.5. One learns from this that the bias of the estimator can be very dependent on the noise-model – a factor that is usually not within our control.

Dependency of bias on parametrization. The reason for the infinite bias for the ML estimator with Gaussian noise model in this example is the projective mapping between the world line and the image line. It is possible to parametrize the world line differently in a way that will change the bias.

Let the world line $\text{Y} = \text{X} + 1$ be parametrized in such a way that parameter θ represents the point $(\theta/(1-\theta), 1/(1-\theta))$ on the line. The part of the line in front of the camera (having positive y coordinate) is parametrized by θ in the range $-\infty < \theta < 1$. Under the projection $(\text{X}, \text{Y}) \mapsto \text{X}/\text{Y}$, the projection map f is given by $f(\theta) = \text{X}/\text{Y} = \theta$, thus the point with parameter θ maps to θ. In other words, points on the world line are

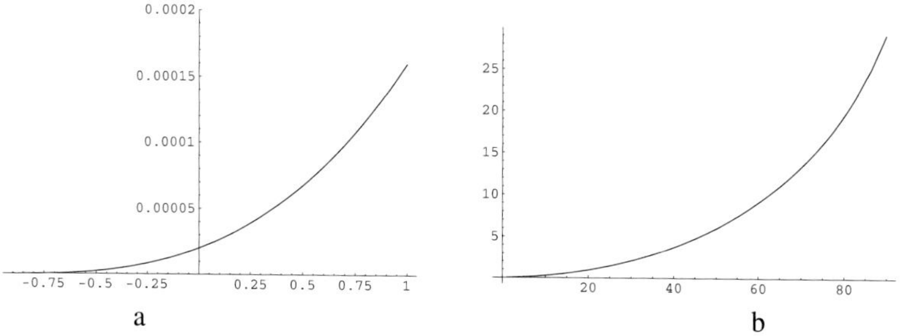

Fig. A3.5. *If the noise-model has finite support then the bias will be finite. In this example the noise model is* $3(1-(x/\sigma)^2)/4\sigma^2$, *for* $-\sigma \leq x \leq \sigma$, *where* $\sigma = 0.01$. *(a) Bias as a function of* θ *for small values of* θ. *(b) Percentage bias* $(E_\theta[\hat{\theta}(x)] - \theta)/\theta$. *The bias is relatively small for small values of* θ, *but larger (up to 20%) for large values. The position of the point along the world-line is always over-estimated.*

parametrized by the coordinate of the point that they project to under the camera mapping.

Now, in this case, the ML estimate is given by $\hat{\theta}(x) = f^{-1}(x) = x$, and the bias is

$$\begin{aligned}\int_x \hat{\theta}(x)p(x|\theta)dx - \theta &= \int_x xg(x - f(\theta))dx - \theta \\ &= \int_x (x + f(\theta))g(x)dx - \theta \\ &= \int_x xg(x)dx + f(\theta)\int_x g(x)dx - \theta \\ &= 0 + f(\theta) - \theta = 0\end{aligned}$$

Assuming that the distribution $g(x)$ is zero-mean. Note, this shows that the estimate of the *original* measurement x is unbiased.

Lessons about bias. By a change of parametrization of the world line, the bias has been changed from infinite to zero. In the present example, there is a natural affine parametrization of the world line, for which we have seen that the bias is infinite. However, if we are working in a projective context, then the parameter space has no natural affine parametrization. In this case, it is somewhat meaningless to speak of any absolute measurement of bias. A second lesson from the above example is that the ML estimate of the corrected measurement (as opposed to the world point) is unbiased.

It was also seen that the value of bias is strongly dependent on the noise distribution. Even the very small tails of the Gaussian distribution have a very large effect on the computed bias. Of course, a Gaussian distribution of the noise is only a convenient model for modelling image measurement errors. The exact distribution of image measurement noise is generally unknown, and the conclusion is inescapable that one can not theoretically compute an exact value for the bias of a given estimator, except for synthetic data with known noise model.

A3.2 Variance of an estimator

The other important attribute of an estimator is its variance. Consider an experiment being repeated many times with the same model parameters, but a different instantiation of the noise at each trial. Applying our estimator to the measured data, we obtain an estimate for each of these trials. The variance of the estimator is the variance (or covariance matrix) of the estimated values. More precisely, we can define the variance for an estimation problem involving a single parameter as

$$\text{Var}_\theta(\hat{\theta}) = E_\theta[(\hat{\theta}(x) - \bar{\theta})^2] = \int_x (\hat{\theta}(x) - \bar{\theta})^2 p(x|\theta)dx$$

where

$$\bar{\theta} = E_\theta[\hat{\theta}(x)] = \int_x \hat{\theta}(x)p(x|\theta)dx = \theta + \text{bias}(\hat{\theta})$$

In the case where the parameters θ form a vector, $\text{Var}_\theta(\hat{\theta})$ is the covariance matrix

$$\text{Var}_\theta(\hat{\theta}) = E_\theta[(\hat{\theta}(x) - \bar{\theta})(\hat{\theta}(x) - \bar{\theta})^\mathsf{T}] \tag{A3.1}$$

In many cases we might be more interested in the variability of the estimate with respect to the original parameter θ, which is the mean-squared error of the estimator. This is easily computed from

$$E_\theta[(\hat{\theta}(x) - \theta)(\hat{\theta}(x) - \theta)^\mathsf{T}] = \text{Var}_\theta(\hat{\theta}) + \text{bias}(\hat{\theta})\,\text{bias}(\hat{\theta})^\mathsf{T}.$$

It should be noted that, as with the bias, the variance of an estimator makes good sense only when there is a natural affine structure on the parameter set, at least locally.

Most estimation algorithms will give the right answer if there is no noise. If an algorithm performs badly when noise is added, this means that either the bias or variance of the algorithm is high. This is the case, for instance with the DLT algorithm 4.1(*p*91), or the unnormalized 8-point algorithm discussed in section 11.1(*p*279). The variance of the algorithm grows quickly with added noise.

The Cramér-Rao lower bound. It is evident that by adding noise to a set of measurements information is lost. Consequently, it is not to be expected that any estimator can have zero bias and variance in the presence of noise on the measurements. For unbiased estimators, this notion is formalized in the Cramér-Rao lower bound, which is a bound on the variance of an unbiased estimator. To explain the Cramér-Rao bound, we need a few definitions. Given a probability distribution $p(x|\theta)$, the Fisher score is defined as $V_\theta(x) = \partial_\theta \log p(x|\theta)$. The Fisher Information Matrix is defined to be

$$\begin{aligned} F(\theta) &= E_\theta[V_\theta(x)V_\theta(x)^\mathsf{T}] \\ &= \int_x V_\theta(x)V_\theta(x)^\mathsf{T} p(x|\theta)dx. \end{aligned}$$

The relevance of the Fisher Information Matrix is expressed in the following result.

Result A3.1. Cramér-Rao lower bound. *For an unbiased estimator* $\hat{\theta}(x)$*,*

$$\det(E[(\hat{\theta} - \theta)(\hat{\theta} - \theta)^\mathsf{T}]) \geq 1/\det F(\theta).$$

A Cramér-Rao lower bound may also be given in the case of a biased estimator.

A3.3 The posterior distribution

An alternative to the ML estimate is to consider the probability distribution for the parameters, given the measurements, namely $p(\theta|x)$. This is known as the posterior distribution, namely the distribution for the parameters *after* the measurements have been taken. To compute it, we need a *prior* distribution $p(\theta)$ for the parameters *before* any measurement has been taken. The posterior distribution can then be computed from Bayes Law

$$p(\theta|x) = \frac{p(x|\theta)\,p(\theta)}{p(x)}.$$

Since the measurement x is fixed, so is its probability $p(x)$, so we may ignore it, leading to $p(\theta|x) \approx p(x|\theta)\,p(\theta)$. The maximum of the posterior distribution is known as the Maximum A Posteriori (MAP) estimate.

Note. Though the MAP estimate may seem like a good idea, it is important to realize that it depends on the parametrization of the parameter space. The posterior probability distribution is proportional to $p(x|\theta)p(\theta)$. However, $p(\theta)$ is dependent on the parametrization of θ. For instance if $p(\theta)$ is a uniform distribution in one parametrization, it will not be a uniform distribution in a different parametrization that differs by a non-affine transformation. On the other hand, $p(x|\theta)$ does not depend on the parametrization of θ. Therefore, the result of a change of parametrization is to alter the posterior distribution in such a way that its maximum will change. If the parameter space does not have a natural affine coordinate system (for instance if the parameter space is projective) then the MAP estimate does not really make a lot of sense.

Other estimates based on the posterior distribution are also possible. Given a measurement x, and the posterior distribution $p(\theta|x)$, we may wish to make a different estimate of the parameter θ. One sensible choice is the estimate that minimizes the expected squared error in the estimate, namely

$$\hat{\theta}(x) = \text{argmin}_Y E[\|Y - \theta\|^2] = \text{argmin}_Y \int \|Y - \theta\|^2 p(\theta|x) d\theta,$$

which is the mean of the posterior distribution.

A further alternative is to minimize the expected absolute error

$$\hat{\theta}(x) = \text{argmin}_Y E[\|Y - \theta\|] = \text{argmin}_Y \int \|Y - \theta\| p(\theta|x) d\theta,$$

which is the median of the posterior distribution. Examples of these estimates are shown in figure A3.6 and figure A3.7.

More properties of these estimates are listed in the notes at the end of this appendix.

A3.4 Estimation of corrected measurements

We have seen that in geometric estimation problems, particularly those that involve projective models, concepts such as bias and variance of the estimator are dependent on the particular parametrization of the model, for instance a particular projective coordinate frame chosen. Even in cases where a natural affine parametrization of the model

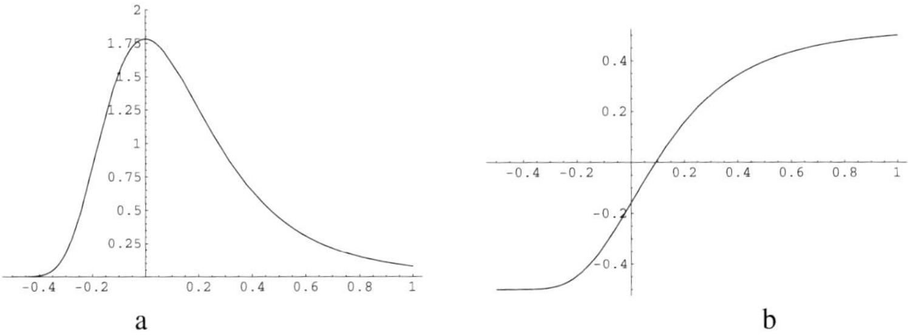

Fig. A3.6. **Different estimators for θ.** *(a) For the imaging setup of figure A3.1: the* a posteriori *distribution $p(\theta|x = 0)$ assuming a Gaussian noise distribution with $\sigma = 0.2$, and a prior distribution for θ, uniform on the interval $[-1/2, 1]$. The mode (maximum) of this distribution is the Maximal Apriori (MAP) estimate of θ, which is identical with the ML estimate, because of the assumed uniform distribution for θ. The mean of this distribution ($\theta = 0.1386$) is the estimate that minimizes the expected squared error $E[(\hat{\theta}(x) - \bar{\theta})^2]$ with respect to the true measurement $\bar{\theta}$. (b) The cumulative a posteriori distribution (offset by -0.5). The zero point of this graph is the median of the distribution, namely the estimate that minimizes $E[|\hat{\theta}(x) - \bar{\theta}|]$. The median lies at $\theta = 0.09137$.*

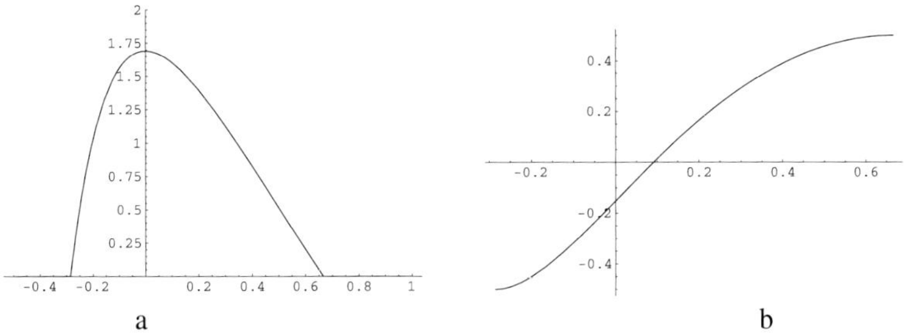

Fig. A3.7. **Different estimators with the parabolic noise model**. *The two graphs show the* a posteriori *distribution of θ and its cumulative distribution. In this example, the noise model is $3(1 - (x/\sigma)^2)/4\sigma^2$, for $-\sigma \leq x \leq \sigma$, where $\sigma = 0.4$. The mode of the distribution ($\theta = 0$) is the MAP estimate, identical with the ML estimate, the mean ($\theta = 0.1109$) minimizes the expected squared error in θ and the median ($\theta = 0.0911$) minimizes the expected absolute error.*

exists, it may be difficult to find an unbiased estimator. For instance, the ML estimator for problems such as triangulation is biased.

We saw however in the example of 1D back-projection discussed in section A3.1, that if instead of attempting to compute the model (namely the back-projected point) we estimate the corrected measurement instead, then the ML estimator is unbiased. We explore this notion further in this section, and show that in a general setting, the ML estimator of the corrected measurements is not only unbiased but attains the Cramér-Rao lower bound, when the noise-model is Gaussian.

Consider an estimation problem that involves fitting a parametrized model to a set of image measurements. As seen in section 5.1.3(p134) this problem may be viewed as an estimation problem in a high-dimensional Euclidean space $\mathbb{R}^N$, which is the space of all image measurements. This is illustrated in figure 5.2(p135). The estimation problem is, given a measurement vector $\mathbf{X}$, to find the closest point lying on a surface representing the set of all allowable exact measurements. The vector $\widehat{\mathbf{X}}$ represents the set of "corrected" image measurements that conform to the given model. The model itself may depend on a set of parameters θ, such as the fundamental matrix, hypothesized 3D points or other parameters appropriate to the problem.

The estimation of the parameters θ is subject to bias in the same way as we have seen with the simple problem discussed in section A3.1, and the exact degree of bias is dependent on the precise parametrization. Generally (for instance in projective-reconstruction problems) there is no natural affine coordinate system for the model parameters, though there is a natural affine coordinate system for the image plane.

If we think of the problem differently, as the problem of directly finding the corrected measurement vector $\widehat{\mathbf{X}}$, then we find a more favourable situation. The measurements are carried out in the images, which have a natural affine coordinate system, and so questions of bias in estimating the corrected measurements make more sense. We will show that, provided the measurement surface is well approximated by its tangent plane, the ML estimate of the corrected measurement vector is unbiased, provided the noise is zero-mean. In addition, if the noise is Gaussian and isotropic, then the ML estimate meets the Cramér-Rao lower-bound.

The geometric situation is follows. A point $\overline{\mathbf{X}}$ lies on a measurement surface, as shown in figure 5.2(*p*135). Noise is added to this point to obtain a measured point $\mathbf{X}$. The estimate $\widehat{\mathbf{X}}$ of the true point $\overline{\mathbf{X}}$ is obtained by selecting the closest point on the measurement surface to the measured point. We make an assumption that the measurement surface is effectively planar near $\mathbf{X}$.

We may choose a coordinate system in which the measurement surface close to $\overline{\mathbf{X}}$ is spanned by the first d coordinates. We may write $\overline{\mathbf{X}} = (\overline{\mathbf{X}}_1^\mathsf{T}, \mathbf{0}_{N-d}^\mathsf{T})^\mathsf{T}$, where $\overline{\mathbf{X}}_1$ is a d-vector. The measured point may similarly be written as $\mathbf{X} = (\mathbf{X}_1^\mathsf{T}, \mathbf{X}_2^\mathsf{T})^\mathsf{T}$, and its projection onto the tangent plane is $\widehat{\mathbf{X}} = (\mathbf{X}_1^\mathsf{T}, \mathbf{0}^\mathsf{T})^\mathsf{T} = (\widehat{\mathbf{X}}_1^\mathsf{T}, \mathbf{0}^\mathsf{T})^\mathsf{T}$. We suppose that the noise-distribution is given by $p(\mathbf{X}|\overline{\mathbf{X}}) = g(\mathbf{X} - \overline{\mathbf{X}})$. Now, the bias of the estimate $\widehat{\mathbf{X}}$ is

$$
\begin{aligned}
E[(\widehat{\mathbf{X}} - \overline{\mathbf{X}})] &= \int_{\mathbf{X}} (\widehat{\mathbf{X}} - \overline{\mathbf{X}}) p(\mathbf{X}|\overline{\mathbf{X}}) d\mathbf{X} = \int_{\mathbf{X}} (\widehat{\mathbf{X}} - \overline{\mathbf{X}}) g(\mathbf{X} - \overline{\mathbf{X}}) d\mathbf{X} \\
&= \int_{\mathbf{X}} \mathtt{J}(\mathbf{X} - \overline{\mathbf{X}}) g(\mathbf{X} - \overline{\mathbf{X}}) d\mathbf{X} \\
&= \mathtt{J} \int_{\mathbf{X}} (\mathbf{X} - \overline{\mathbf{X}}) g(\mathbf{X} - \overline{\mathbf{X}}) d\mathbf{X} \\
&= \mathbf{0}
\end{aligned}
$$

where J is the matrix $[\mathtt{I}_{d\times d}|\mathtt{0}_{d\times(N-d)}]$. This shows that the estimate of $\mathbf{X}$ is unbiased as long at g has zero-mean. The variance of the estimate is equal to

$$
\begin{aligned}
E[(\widehat{\mathbf{X}} - \overline{\mathbf{X}})(\widehat{\mathbf{X}} - \overline{\mathbf{X}})^\mathsf{T}] &= \int_{\mathbf{X}} (\widehat{\mathbf{X}} - \overline{\mathbf{X}})(\widehat{\mathbf{X}} - \overline{\mathbf{X}})^\mathsf{T} p(\mathbf{X}|\overline{\mathbf{X}}) d\mathbf{X} = \int_{\mathbf{X}} (\widehat{\mathbf{X}} - \overline{\mathbf{X}})(\widehat{\mathbf{X}} - \overline{\mathbf{X}})^\mathsf{T} g(\mathbf{X} - \overline{\mathbf{X}}) \\
&= \int_{\mathbf{X}} \mathtt{J}(\mathbf{X} - \overline{\mathbf{X}})(\mathbf{X} - \overline{\mathbf{X}})^\mathsf{T} \mathtt{J}^\mathsf{T} g(\mathbf{X} - \overline{\mathbf{X}}) d\mathbf{X} \\
&= \mathtt{J} \int_{\mathbf{X}} (\mathbf{X} - \overline{\mathbf{X}})(\mathbf{X} - \overline{\mathbf{X}})^\mathsf{T} g(\mathbf{X} - \overline{\mathbf{X}}) d\mathbf{X} \mathtt{J}^\mathsf{T} \\
&= \mathtt{J}\Sigma_g \mathtt{J}^\mathsf{T}
\end{aligned}
$$

where Σ_g is the covariance matrix of g.

We now compute the Cramér-Rao lower bound for this estimator, supposing that the distribution $g(\mathbf{X})$ is Gaussian defined by $g(\mathbf{X}) = k\exp(-\|\mathbf{X}\|^2/2\sigma^2)$. In this case, the variance of the estimator is simply $\sigma^2 \mathtt{I}_{d\times d}$.

We next compute the Fisher information matrix. The probability distribution is

$$\begin{aligned} p(\mathbf{X}|\overline{\mathbf{X}}) &= g(\mathbf{X}-\overline{\mathbf{X}}) = k\exp(-\|\mathbf{X}-\overline{\mathbf{X}}\|^2/2\sigma^2) \\ &= k\exp(-\|\mathbf{X}_1-\overline{\mathbf{X}}_1\|^2/2\sigma^2)\exp(-\|\mathbf{X}_2\|^2/2\sigma^2). \end{aligned}$$

Taking logarithms and derivatives with respect to $\overline{\mathbf{X}}_1$ gives

$$\partial_{\overline{\mathbf{X}}_1} \log p(\mathbf{X}|\overline{\mathbf{X}}) = -(\mathbf{X}_1 - \overline{\mathbf{X}}_1)/\sigma^2.$$

The Fisher information matrix is then

$$1/\sigma^2 \int (\mathbf{X}_1-\overline{\mathbf{X}}_1)(\mathbf{X}_1-\overline{\mathbf{X}}_1)^{\mathsf{T}} g(\mathbf{X}_1-\overline{\mathbf{X}}_1) g(\mathbf{X}_2) d\mathbf{X}_1 d\mathbf{X}_2 \; = \mathtt{I}_{d\times d}/\sigma^2.$$

Thus, the Fisher information matrix is the inverse of the covariance matrix for the estimator. Thus, for the case where the noise distribution is Gaussian, the ML estimator meets the Cramér-Rao lower bound, to the extent that the measurement surface is flat.

It should be noticed that the Fisher Information Matrix does not depend on the specific shape of the measurement surface, but only on its first-order approximation, the tangent plane. The properties of the estimate does however depend on the shape of the measurement surface, both as regards its bias and variance. It may also be shown that if the Cramér-Rao bound is met, then the noise distribution must be Gaussian. In other words, if the noise distribution is not Gaussian, then we can not meet the lower bound.

A3.5 Notes and exercises

(i) Show by a specific example that the a posteriori distribution is altered by a change of coordinates in the parameter space. Show also that the mean of the distribution may be altered by such a coordinate change. Thus the mode (MAP estimate) and mean of the posterior distribution are dependent on the choice of coordinates for the parameter space.

(ii) Show for any PDF $p(\theta)$ defined on $\mathbb{R}^n$, that $\mathrm{argmin}_Y \int \|Y-\theta\|^2 p(\theta)d\theta$ is the mean of the distribution.

(iii) Show for any PDF $p(\theta)$ defined on $\mathbb{R}$, that $\mathrm{argmin}_Y \int |Y-\theta| p(\theta)d\theta$ is the median of the distribution. In higher dimensions, show that $\int \|Y-\theta\| p(\theta)d\theta$ is a convex function of Y, and hence has a single minimum. The value of Y that minimizes this is a higher-dimensional generalization of the median of a 1-dimensional distribution.

(iv) Show that the median of a PDF defined on $\mathbb{R}$ is invariant to reparametrization of $\mathbb{R}$. Show by an example that this is not true in higher dimensions, however.

Appendix 4

Matrix Properties and Decompositions

In this appendix we discuss matrices with particular forms that occur throughout the book, and also various matrix decompositions.

A4.1 Orthogonal matrices

A square matrix $\mathtt{U}$ is known as *orthogonal* if its transpose is its inverse – symbolically $\mathtt{U}^\mathsf{T}\mathtt{U} = \mathtt{I}$, where $\mathtt{I}$ is the identity matrix. This means that the column vectors of $\mathtt{U}$ are all of unit norm and are orthogonal. This may be written $\mathbf{u}_i^\mathsf{T}\mathbf{u}_j = \delta_{ij}$. From the condition $\mathtt{U}^\mathsf{T}\mathtt{U} = \mathtt{I}$ one easily deduces that $\mathtt{U}\mathtt{U}^\mathsf{T} = \mathtt{I}$. Hence the row vectors of $\mathtt{U}$ are also of unit norm and are orthogonal. Consider once more the equation $\mathtt{U}^\mathsf{T}\mathtt{U} = \mathtt{I}$. Taking determinants leads to the equation $(\det \mathtt{U})^2 = 1$, since $\det \mathtt{U} = \det \mathtt{U}^\mathsf{T}$. Thus if $\mathtt{U}$ is orthogonal, then $\det \mathtt{U} = \pm 1$.

One easily verifies that the orthogonal matrices of a given fixed dimension form a group, denoted O_n, since if $\mathtt{U}$ and $\mathtt{V}$ are orthogonal, then $(\mathtt{U}\mathtt{V})^\mathsf{T}\mathtt{U}\mathtt{V} = \mathtt{V}^\mathsf{T}\mathtt{U}^\mathsf{T}\mathtt{U}\mathtt{V} = \mathtt{I}$. Furthermore, the orthogonal matrices of dimension n with positive determinant form a group, called SO_n. An element of SO_n is called an n-dimensional rotation.

Norm-preserving properties of orthogonal matrices. Given a vector $\mathbf{x}$, the notation $\|\mathbf{x}\|$ represents its Euclidean length. This can be written as $\|\mathbf{x}\| = (\mathbf{x}^\mathsf{T}\mathbf{x})^{1/2}$. An important property of orthogonal matrices is that multiplying a vector by an orthogonal matrix preserves its norm. This is easily seen by computing

$$(\mathtt{U}\mathbf{x})^\mathsf{T}(\mathtt{U}\mathbf{x}) = \mathbf{x}^\mathsf{T}\mathtt{U}^\mathsf{T}\mathtt{U}\mathbf{x} = \mathbf{x}^\mathsf{T}\mathbf{x}.$$

By the QR decomposition of a matrix is usually meant the decomposition of the matrix $\mathtt{A}$ into a product $\mathtt{A} = \mathtt{Q}\mathtt{R}$, where $\mathtt{Q}$ is orthogonal, and $\mathtt{R}$ is an upper-triangular matrix. The letter $\mathtt{R}$ stands for *Right*, meaning upper-triangular. Similar to the QR decomposition, there are also QL, LQ and RQ decompositions, where $\mathtt{L}$ denotes a *Left* or lower-triangular matrix. In fact, the RQ decomposition of a matrix is the one that will be of most use in this book, and which will therefore be discussed here. The most important case is the decomposition of a 3×3 matrix and we will concentrate on this in the following section.

A4.1.1 Givens rotations and RQ decomposition

A 3-dimensional Givens rotation is a rotation about one of the three coordinate axes. The three Givens rotations are

$$\mathtt{Q}_x = \begin{bmatrix} 1 & & \\ & c & -s \\ & s & c \end{bmatrix} \quad \mathtt{Q}_y = \begin{bmatrix} c & & s \\ & 1 & \\ -s & & c \end{bmatrix} \quad \mathtt{Q}_z = \begin{bmatrix} c & -s & \\ s & c & \\ & & 1 \end{bmatrix} \tag{A4.1}$$

where $c = \cos(\theta)$ and $s = \sin(\theta)$ for some angle θ and blank entries represent zeros.

Multiplying a 3×3 matrix $\mathtt{A}$ on the right by (for instance) $\mathtt{Q}_z$ has the effect of leaving the last column of $\mathtt{A}$ unchanged, and replacing the first two columns by linear combinations of the original two columns. The angle θ may be chosen so that any given entry in the first two columns becomes zero.

For instance, to set the entry $\mathtt{A}_{21}$ to zero, we need to solve the equation $ca_{21} + sa_{22} = 0$. The solution to this is $c = -a_{22}/(a_{22}^2 + a_{21}^2)^{1/2}$ and $s = a_{21}/(a_{22}^2 + a_{21}^2)^{1/2}$. It is required that $c^2 + s^2 = 1$ since $c = \cos(\theta)$ and $s = \sin(\theta)$, and the values of c and s given here satisfy that requirement.

The strategy of the RQ algorithm is to clear out the lower half of the matrix one entry at a time by multiplication by Givens rotations. Consider the decomposition of a 3×3 matrix $\mathtt{A}$ as $\mathtt{A} = \mathtt{RQ}$ where $\mathtt{R}$ is upper-triangular and $\mathtt{Q}$ is a rotation matrix. This may take place in three steps. Each step consists of multiplication on the right by a Givens rotation to set a chosen entry of the matrix $\mathtt{A}$ to zero. The sequence of multiplications must be chosen in such a way as not to disturb the entries that have already been set to zero. An implementation of the RQ decomposition is given in algorithm A4.1.

Objective

Carry out the RQ decomposition of a 3×3 matrix $\mathtt{A}$ using Givens rotations.

Algorithm

(i) Multiply by $\mathtt{Q}_x$ so as to set $\mathtt{A}_{32}$ to zero.
(ii) Multiply by $\mathtt{Q}_y$ so as to set $\mathtt{A}_{31}$ to zero. This multiplication does not change the second column of $\mathtt{A}$, hence $\mathtt{A}_{32}$ remains zero.
(iii) Multiply by $\mathtt{Q}_z$ so as to set $\mathtt{A}_{21}$ to zero. The first two columns are replaced by linear combinations of themselves. Thus, $\mathtt{A}_{31}$ and $\mathtt{A}_{32}$ remain zero.

Algorithm A4.1. *RQ decomposition of a* 3×3 *matrix.*

Other sequences of Givens rotations may be chosen to give the same result. As a result of these operations, we find that $\mathtt{AQ}_x\mathtt{Q}_y\mathtt{Q}_z = \mathtt{R}$ where $\mathtt{R}$ is upper-triangular. Consequently, $\mathtt{A} = \mathtt{RQ}_z^\mathsf{T}\mathtt{Q}_y^\mathsf{T}\mathtt{Q}_x^\mathsf{T}$, and so $\mathtt{A} = \mathtt{RQ}$ where $\mathtt{Q} = \mathtt{Q}_z^\mathsf{T}\mathtt{Q}_y^\mathsf{T}\mathtt{Q}_x^\mathsf{T}$ is a rotation. In addition, the angles θ_x, θ_y and θ_z associated with the three Givens rotations provide a parametrization of the rotation by three Euler angles, otherwise known as roll, pitch and yaw angles.

It should be clear from this description of the decomposition algorithm how similar QR, QL and LQ factorizations may be carried out. Furthermore, the algorithm is easily generalized to higher dimensions.

A4.1.2 Householder matrices and QR decomposition

For matrices of larger dimension, the QR decomposition is more efficiently carried out using Householder matrices. The symmetric matrix

$$\mathtt{H}_{\mathbf{v}} = \mathtt{I} - 2\mathbf{v}\mathbf{v}^{\mathsf{T}}/\mathbf{v}^{\mathsf{T}}\mathbf{v} \tag{A4.2}$$

has the property that $\mathtt{H}_{\mathbf{v}}^{\mathsf{T}}\mathtt{H}_{\mathbf{v}} = \mathtt{I}$, and so $\mathtt{H}_{\mathbf{v}}$ is orthogonal.

Let $\mathbf{e}_1$ be the vector $(1, 0, \ldots, 0)^{\mathsf{T}}$, and let $\mathbf{x}$ be any vector. Let $\mathbf{v} = \mathbf{x} \pm \|\mathbf{x}\|\mathbf{e}_1$. One easily verifies that $\mathtt{H}_{\mathbf{v}}\mathbf{x} = \mp\|\mathbf{x}\|\mathbf{e}_1$; thus $\mathtt{H}_{\mathbf{v}}$ is an orthogonal matrix that transforms the vector $\mathbf{x}$ to a multiple of $\mathbf{e}_1$. Geometrically $\mathtt{H}_{\mathbf{v}}$ is a reflection in the plane perpendicular to $\mathbf{v}$, and $\mathbf{v} = \mathbf{x} \pm \|\mathbf{x}\|\mathbf{e}_1$ is a vector that bisects $\mathbf{x}$ and $\pm\|\mathbf{x}\|\mathbf{e}_1$. Thus reflection in the $\mathbf{v}$ direction takes $\mathbf{x}$ to $\mp\|\mathbf{x}\|\mathbf{e}_1$. For reasons of stability, the sign ambiguity in defining $\mathbf{v}$ should be resolved by setting

$$\mathbf{v} = \mathbf{x} + \text{sign}(x_1)\|\mathbf{x}\|\mathbf{e}_1. \tag{A4.3}$$

If $\mathtt{A}$ is a matrix, $\mathbf{x}$ is the first column of $\mathtt{A}$, and $\mathbf{v}$ is defined by (A4.3), then forming the product $\mathtt{H}_{\mathbf{v}}\mathtt{A}$ will clear out the first column of the matrix, replacing the first column by $(\|\mathbf{x}\|, 0, 0, \ldots, 0)^{\mathsf{T}}$. One continues left multiplication by orthogonal Householder matrices to clear out the below-diagonal part of the matrix $\mathtt{A}$. In this way, one finds that eventually $\mathtt{QA} = \mathtt{R}$, where $\mathtt{Q}$ is a product of orthogonal matrices and $\mathtt{R}$ is an upper-triangular matrix. Therefore, one has $\mathtt{A} = \mathtt{Q}^{\mathsf{T}}\mathtt{R}$. This is the QR decomposition of the matrix $\mathtt{A}$.

When multiplying by Householder matrices it is inefficient to form the Householder matrix explicitly. Multiplication by a vector $\mathbf{a}$ may be carried out most efficiently as

$$\mathtt{H}_{\mathbf{v}}\mathbf{a} = (\mathtt{I} - 2\mathbf{v}\mathbf{v}^{\mathsf{T}}/\mathbf{v}^{\mathsf{T}}\mathbf{v})\mathbf{a} = \mathbf{a} - 2\mathbf{v}(\mathbf{v}^{\mathsf{T}}\mathbf{a})/\mathbf{v}\mathbf{v}^{\mathsf{T}} \tag{A4.4}$$

and the same holds for multiplication by a matrix $\mathtt{A}$. For more about Householder matrices and the QR decomposition, the reader is referred to [Golub-89].

Note. In the QR or RQ decomposition, R refers to an upper-triangular matrix and Q refers to an orthogonal matrix. In the notation used elsewhere in this book, $\mathtt{R}$ refers usually to a rotation (hence orthogonal) matrix.

A4.2 Symmetric and skew-symmetric matrices

Symmetric and skew-symmetric matrices play an important role in this book. A matrix is called *symmetric* if $\mathtt{A}^{\mathsf{T}} = \mathtt{A}$ and *skew-symmetric* if $\mathtt{A}^{\mathsf{T}} = -\mathtt{A}$. The eigenvalue decompositions of these matrices are summarized in the following result.

Result A4.1. Eigenvalue decomposition.

(i) *If* $\mathtt{A}$ *is a real symmetric matrix, then* $\mathtt{A}$ *can be decomposed as* $\mathtt{A} = \mathtt{UDU}^{\mathsf{T}}$, *where* $\mathtt{U}$ *is an orthogonal matrix and* $\mathtt{D}$ *is a real diagonal matrix. Thus, a real symmetric matrix has real eigenvalues, and the eigenvectors are orthogonal.*

(ii) *If* $\mathtt{S}$ *is real and skew-symmetric, then* $\mathtt{S} = \mathtt{UBU}^{\mathsf{T}}$ *where* $\mathtt{B}$ *is a block-diagonal matrix of the form* $\mathrm{diag}(a_1\mathtt{Z}, a_2\mathtt{Z}, \ldots, a_m\mathtt{Z}, 0, \ldots, 0)$, *where* $\mathtt{Z} = \begin{bmatrix} 0 & 1 \\ -1 & 0 \end{bmatrix}$. *The eigenvectors of* $\mathtt{S}$ *are all purely imaginary, and a skew-symmetric matrix of odd order is singular.*

A proof of this result is given in [Golub-89].

Jacobi's method. In general, eigenvalue extraction from arbitrary matrices is a difficult numerical problem. For real symmetric matrices however, a very stable method exists: Jacobi's method. An implementation of this algorithm is given in [Press-88].

Cross products

Of particular interest are 3×3 skew-symmetric matrices. If $\mathtt{a} = (a_1, a_2, a_3)^\mathsf{T}$ is a 3-vector, then one defines a corresponding skew-symmetric matrix as follows:

$$[\mathbf{a}]_\times = \begin{bmatrix} 0 & -a_3 & a_2 \\ a_3 & 0 & -a_1 \\ -a_2 & a_1 & 0 \end{bmatrix}. \tag{A4.5}$$

Note that any skew-symmetric 3×3 matrix may be written in the form $[\mathbf{a}]_\times$ for a suitable vector $\mathbf{a}$. Matrix $[\mathbf{a}]_\times$ is singular, and $\mathbf{a}$ is its null-vector (right or left). Hence, a 3×3 skew-symmetric matrix is defined up to scale by its null-vector.

The cross product (or vector product) of two 3-vectors $\mathbf{a} \times \mathbf{b}$ (sometimes written $\mathbf{a} \wedge \mathbf{b}$) is the vector $(a_2b_3 - a_3b_2, a_3b_1 - a_1b_3, a_1b_2 - a_2b_1)^\mathsf{T}$. The cross product is related to skew-symmetric matrices according to

$$\mathbf{a} \times \mathbf{b} = [\mathbf{a}]_\times \mathbf{b} = \left(\mathbf{a}^\mathsf{T}[\mathbf{b}]_\times\right)^\mathsf{T}. \tag{A4.6}$$

Cofactor and adjoint matrices. Let $\mathtt{M}$ be a square matrix. By $\mathtt{M}^*$ is meant the matrix of cofactors of $\mathtt{M}$. That is, the (ij)-th entry of the matrix $\mathtt{M}^*$ is equal to $(-1)^{i+j} \det \hat{\mathtt{M}}_{ij}$, where $\hat{\mathtt{M}}_{ij}$ is the matrix obtained from $\mathtt{M}$ by striking out the i-th row and j-th column. The transpose of the cofactor matrix $\mathtt{M}^*$ is known as the *adjoint* of $\mathtt{M}$, and denoted $\mathrm{adj}(\mathtt{M})$.

If $\mathtt{M}$ is invertible, then it is well known that

$$\mathtt{M}^* = \det(\mathtt{M})\,\mathtt{M}^{-\mathsf{T}} \tag{A4.7}$$

where $\mathtt{M}^{-\mathsf{T}}$ is the inverse transpose of $\mathtt{M}$. This formula does not hold for non-invertible matrices, but $\mathrm{adj}(\mathtt{M})\,\mathtt{M} = \mathtt{M}\,\mathrm{adj}(\mathtt{M}) = \det(\mathtt{M})\,\mathtt{I}$ is always valid.

The cofactor matrix is related to the way matrices distribute with respect to the cross product.

Lemma A4.2. *If* $\mathtt{M}$ *is any* 3×3 *matrix (invertible or not), and* $\mathbf{x}$ *and* $\mathbf{y}$ *are column vectors, then*

$$(\mathtt{M}\mathbf{x}) \times (\mathtt{M}\mathbf{y}) = \mathtt{M}^*(\mathbf{x} \times \mathbf{y}). \tag{A4.8}$$

This equation may be written as $[\mathbf{Mx}]_\times \mathtt{M} = \mathtt{M}^*[\mathbf{x}]_\times$, dropping $\mathbf{y}$ which is inessential. Now, putting $\mathbf{t} = \mathtt{M}\mathbf{x}$ and assuming $\mathtt{M}$ is invertible, one obtains a rule for commuting a skew-symmetric matrix $[\mathbf{t}]_\times$ with any non-singular matrix $\mathtt{M}$. One may write (A4.8) as follows.

Result A4.3. *For any vector* $\mathbf{t}$ *and non-singular matrix* $\mathtt{M}$ *one has*

$$[\mathbf{t}]_\times \mathtt{M} = \mathtt{M}^*[\mathtt{M}^{-1}\mathbf{t}]_\times = \mathtt{M}^{-\mathsf{T}}[\mathtt{M}^{-1}\mathbf{t}]_\times \text{ (up to scale).}$$

Note (see result 9.9(*p*254)) that $[\mathbf{t}]_\times \mathtt{M}$ is the form of the fundamental matrix for a pair of cameras $\mathtt{P} = [\mathtt{I} \mid \mathbf{0}]$ and $\mathtt{P}' = [\mathtt{M}|\mathbf{t}]$. The formula of result A4.3 is used in deriving alternative forms (9.2–*p*244) for the fundamental matrix.

A curious property of 3×3 skew-symmetric matrices is that up to scale, $[\mathbf{a}]_\times = [\mathbf{a}]_\times [\mathbf{a}]_\times [\mathbf{a}]_\times$ (including scale $[\mathbf{a}]_\times^3 = -\|\mathbf{a}\|^2 [\mathbf{a}]_\times$). This is easily verified, since the right hand side is clearly skew-symmetric and its null-space generator is $\mathbf{a}$. The next result follows immediately:

Result A4.4. *If* $\mathtt{F} = [\mathbf{e}']_\times \mathtt{M}$ *is a fundamental matrix (a* 3×3 *singular matrix), then* $[\mathbf{e}']_\times [\mathbf{e}']_\times \mathtt{F} = \mathtt{F}$ *(up to scale). Hence one may decompose* $\mathtt{F}$ *as* $\mathtt{F} = [\mathbf{e}']_\times \mathtt{M}$*, where* $\mathtt{M} = [\mathbf{e}']_\times \mathtt{F}$.

A4.2.1 Positive-definite symmetric matrices

The special class of real symmetric matrices that have positive real eigenvalues are called *positive-definite* symmetric matrices. We list some of the important properties of a positive-definite symmetric real matrix.

Result A4.5. Positive-definite symmetric real matrix.

(i) *A symmetric matrix* $\mathtt{A}$ *is positive-definite if and only if* $\mathbf{x}^\mathsf{T}\mathtt{A}\mathbf{x} > 0$ *for any non-zero vector* $\mathbf{x}$.

(ii) *A positive-definite symmetric matrix* $\mathtt{A}$ *may be uniquely decomposed as* $\mathtt{A} = \mathtt{K}\mathtt{K}^\mathsf{T}$ *where* $\mathtt{K}$ *is an upper-triangular real matrix with positive diagonal entries.*

Proof. The first part of this result follows almost immediately from the decomposition $\mathtt{A} = \mathtt{UDU}^\mathsf{T}$. As for the second part, since $\mathtt{A}$ is symmetric and positive-definite, it may be written as $\mathtt{A} = \mathtt{UDU}^\mathsf{T}$ where $\mathtt{D}$ is diagonal, real and positive and $\mathtt{U}$ is orthogonal. We may take the square root of $\mathtt{D}$, writing $\mathtt{D} = \mathtt{EE}^\mathsf{T}$ where $\mathtt{E}$ is diagonal. Then $\mathtt{A} = \mathtt{VV}^\mathsf{T}$ where $\mathtt{V} = \mathtt{UE}$. The matrix $\mathtt{V}$ is not upper-triangular. However, we may apply the RQ-decomposition (section A4.1.1) to write $\mathtt{V} = \mathtt{KQ}$ where $\mathtt{K}$ is upper-triangular and $\mathtt{Q}$ is orthogonal. Then $\mathtt{A} = \mathtt{VV}^\mathsf{T} = \mathtt{KQQ}^\mathsf{T}\mathtt{K}^\mathsf{T} = \mathtt{KK}^\mathsf{T}$. This is the Cholesky factorization of $\mathtt{A}$. One may ensure that the diagonal entries of $\mathtt{K}$ are all positive by multiplying $\mathtt{K}$ on the right by a diagonal matrix with diagonal entries equal to ± 1. This will not change the product $\mathtt{KK}^\mathsf{T}$.

Now, we prove uniqueness of the factorization. Specifically, if $\mathtt{K}_1$ and $\mathtt{K}_2$ are two upper-triangular matrices satisfying $\mathtt{K}_1\mathtt{K}_1^\mathsf{T} = \mathtt{K}_2\mathtt{K}_2^\mathsf{T}$ then $\mathtt{K}_2^{-1}\mathtt{K}_1 = \mathtt{K}_2^\mathsf{T}\mathtt{K}_1^{-\mathsf{T}}$. Since the left side of this equation is upper-triangular, and the right side is lower-triangular, they must both in fact be diagonal. Thus $\mathtt{D} = \mathtt{K}_2^{-1}\mathtt{K}_1 = \mathtt{K}_2^\mathsf{T}\mathtt{K}_1^{-\mathsf{T}}$. However, $\mathtt{K}_2^{-1}\mathtt{K}_1$ is the inverse transpose of $\mathtt{K}_2^\mathsf{T}\mathtt{K}_1^{-\mathsf{T}}$, and so $\mathtt{D}$ is equal to its own inverse transpose, and hence is a diagonal matrix with diagonal entries equal to ± 1. If both $\mathtt{K}_1$ and $\mathtt{K}_2$ have positive diagonal entries then $\mathtt{D} = \mathtt{I}$, and $\mathtt{K}_1 = \mathtt{K}_2$. □

The above proof gives a constructive method for computing the Cholesky factorization. There is, however, a very simple and more efficient direct method for computing the Cholesky factorization. See [Press-88] for an implementation.

A4.3 Representations of rotation matrices

A4.3.1 Rotations in n-dimensions

Given a matrix $\mathtt{T}$, we define $e^\mathtt{T}$ to be the sum of the series

$$e^\mathtt{T} = \mathtt{I} + \mathtt{T} + \mathtt{T}^2/2! + \ldots + \mathtt{T}^k/k! + \ldots$$

This series converges absolutely for all values of $\mathtt{T}$. Now, we consider powers of a skew-symmetric matrix. According to result A4.1 a skew-symmetric matrix can be written as $\mathtt{S} = \mathtt{UBU}^\mathsf{T}$ where $\mathtt{B}$ is block diagonal of the form $\mathtt{B} = \mathrm{diag}(a_1\mathtt{Z}, a_2\mathtt{Z}, \ldots, a_m\mathtt{Z}, 0, \ldots, 0)$, matrix $\mathtt{U}$ is orthogonal, and $\mathtt{Z}^2 = -\mathtt{I}_{2\times 2}$. We observe that the powers of $\mathtt{Z}$ are

$$\mathtt{Z}^2 = -\mathtt{I}\ ;\ \mathtt{Z}^3 = -\mathtt{Z}\ ;\ \mathtt{Z}^4 = \mathtt{I}$$

and so on. Thus,

$$e^\mathtt{Z} = \mathtt{I} + \mathtt{Z} - \mathtt{I}/2! - \mathtt{Z}/3! + \ldots \quad = \quad \cos(1)\mathtt{I} + \sin(1)\mathtt{Z} \quad = \quad \mathtt{R}_{2\times 2}(1)$$

Where $\mathtt{R}_{2\times 2}(1)$ means the 2×2 matrix representing a rotation through 1 radian. More generally,

$$e^{a\mathtt{Z}} = \cos(a)\mathtt{I} + \sin(a)\mathtt{Z} = \mathtt{R}_{2\times 2}(a)\ .$$

With $\mathtt{S} = \mathtt{UBU}^\mathsf{T}$ as above, it now follows that

$$e^\mathtt{S} \quad = \quad \mathtt{U}e^\mathtt{B}\mathtt{U}^\mathsf{T} \quad = \quad \mathtt{U}\,\mathrm{diag}(\mathtt{R}(a_1), \mathtt{R}(a_2), \ldots, \mathtt{R}(a_m), 1, \ldots, 1)\,\mathtt{U}^\mathsf{T}$$

Thus $e^\mathtt{S}$ is a rotation matrix. On the other hand, any rotation matrix may be written in the block-diagonal form $\mathtt{U}\,\mathrm{diag}(\mathtt{R}(a_1), \mathtt{R}(a_2), \ldots, \mathtt{R}(a_m), 1, \ldots, 1)\,\mathtt{U}^\mathsf{T}$, and it follows that the matrices $e^\mathtt{S}$ where $\mathtt{S}$ is an $n\times n$ skew-symmetric are exactly the set of n-dimensional rotation matrices.

A4.3.2 Rotations in 3-dimensions

If $\mathbf{t}$ is a 3-vector, then $[\mathbf{t}]_\times$ is a skew-symmetric matrix, and any 3×3 skew-symmetric matrix is of this form. Consequently, any 3-dimensional rotation can be written as $e^{[\mathbf{t}]_\times}$. We seek to describe the rotation $e^{[\mathbf{t}]_\times}$.

Let $[\mathbf{t}]_\times = \mathtt{U}\,\mathrm{diag}(a\mathtt{Z}, 0)\,\mathtt{U}^\mathsf{T}$. Then by matching the Frobenius norms of the matrices on both sides, we see that $a = \|\mathbf{t}\|$. Thus,

$$e^{[\mathbf{t}]_\times} = \mathtt{U}\,\mathrm{diag}(\mathtt{R}(\|\mathbf{t}\|), 1)\,\mathtt{U}^\mathsf{T} \ .$$

Thus, $e^{[\mathbf{t}]_\times}$ represents a rotation through an angle $\|\mathbf{t}\|$. It is easily verified that $\mathbf{u}_3$, the 3-rd column of $\mathtt{U}$ is the eigenvector of $\mathtt{U}\,\mathrm{diag}(\mathtt{R}, 1)\,\mathtt{U}^\mathsf{T}$ with unit eigenvector, hence the axis of rotation. However, $[\mathbf{t}]_\times \mathbf{u}_3 = \mathtt{U}\mathrm{diag}(a\mathtt{Z}, 0)\mathtt{U}^\mathsf{T}\mathbf{u}_3 = \mathtt{U}\,\mathrm{diag}(a\mathtt{Z}, 0)(0, 0, 1)^\mathsf{T} = 0$. Since $\mathbf{u}_3$ is the generator of the null space of $[\mathbf{t}]_\times$, it must be that $\mathbf{u}_3$ is a unit vector in the direction of $\mathbf{t}$. We have shown

Result A4.6. *The matrix $e^{[\mathbf{t}]_\times}$ is a rotation matrix representing a rotation through an angle $\|\mathbf{t}\|$ about the axis represented by the vector $\mathbf{t}$.*

This representation of a rotation is called the *angle-axis* representation.

We may write a specific formula for the rotation matrix corresponding to $e^{[\mathbf{t}]_\times}$. We observe that $[\mathbf{t}]_\times^3 = -\|\mathbf{t}\|^2\,[\mathbf{t}]_\times = -\|\mathbf{t}\|^3\,[\hat{\mathbf{t}}]_\times$, where $\hat{\mathbf{t}}$ represents a unit vector in the direction $\mathbf{t}$. Then, with $\mathrm{sinc}(\theta)$ representing $\sin(\theta)/\theta$, we have

$$\begin{aligned}
e^{[\mathbf{t}]_\times} &= \mathtt{I} + [\mathbf{t}]_\times + [\mathbf{t}]_\times^2/2! + [\mathbf{t}]_\times^3/3! + [\mathbf{t}]_\times^4/4! + \ldots \\
&= \mathtt{I} + \|\mathbf{t}\|\,[\hat{\mathbf{t}}]_\times + \|\mathbf{t}\|^2\,[\hat{\mathbf{t}}]_\times^2/2! - \|\mathbf{t}\|^3\,[\hat{\mathbf{t}}]_\times/3! - \|\mathbf{t}\|^4\,[\hat{\mathbf{t}}]_\times^2/4! + \ldots \\
&= \mathtt{I} + \sin\|\mathbf{t}\|\,[\hat{\mathbf{t}}]_\times + (1 - \cos\|\mathbf{t}\|)\,[\hat{\mathbf{t}}]_\times^2 \\
&= \mathtt{I} + \mathrm{sinc}\|\mathbf{t}\|\,[\mathbf{t}]_\times + \frac{1 - \cos\|\mathbf{t}\|}{\|\mathbf{t}\|^2}\,[\mathbf{t}]_\times^2 \qquad \text{(A4.9)} \\
&= \cos\|\mathbf{t}\|\mathtt{I} + \mathrm{sinc}\|\mathbf{t}\|\,[\mathbf{t}]_\times + \frac{1 - \cos\|\mathbf{t}\|}{\|\mathbf{t}\|^2}\,\mathbf{t}\mathbf{t}^\mathsf{T}
\end{aligned}$$

where the last line follows from the identity $[\mathbf{t}]_\times^2 = \mathbf{t}\mathbf{t}^\mathsf{T} - \|\mathbf{t}\|^2\mathtt{I}$.

Some properties of these representations:

(i) Extraction of the axis and rotation angle from a rotation matrix $\mathtt{R}$ is just a little tricky. The unit rotation axis $\mathbf{v}$ can be found as the eigenvector corresponding to the unit eigenvalue – that is by solving $(\mathtt{R} - \mathtt{I})\mathbf{v} = \mathbf{0}$. Next, it is easily seen from (A4.9) that the rotation angle ϕ satisfies

$$\begin{aligned}
2\cos(\phi) &= (\mathrm{trace}(\mathtt{R}) - 1) \\
2\sin(\phi)\mathbf{v} &= (\mathtt{R}_{32} - \mathtt{R}_{23}, \mathtt{R}_{13} - \mathtt{R}_{31}, \mathtt{R}_{21} - \mathtt{R}_{12})^\mathsf{T}. \qquad \text{(A4.10)}
\end{aligned}$$

Writing this second equation as $2\sin(\phi)\mathbf{v} = \hat{\mathbf{v}}$, we can then compute $2\sin(\phi) = \mathbf{v}^\mathsf{T}\hat{\mathbf{v}}$. Now, the angle ϕ can be computed from $\sin(\phi)$ and $\cos(\phi)$ using a two-argument $\arctan$ function (such as the C-language function atan2(y, x)).

It has often been written that ϕ can be computed directly from (A4.10) using $\arccos$ or $\arcsin$. However, this method is not numerically accurate, and fails to find the axis when $\phi = \pi$.

(ii) To apply a rotation $\mathtt{R}(\mathbf{t})$ to some vector $\mathbf{x}$, it is not necessary to construct the matrix representation of $\mathbf{t}$. In fact

$$\begin{aligned}\mathtt{R}(\mathbf{t})\mathbf{x} &= \left(\mathtt{I} + \mathrm{sinc}\|\mathbf{t}\|[\mathbf{t}]_\times + \frac{1-\cos\|\mathbf{t}\|}{\|\mathbf{t}\|^2}[\mathbf{t}]_\times^2\right)\mathbf{x} \\ &= \mathbf{x} + \mathrm{sinc}\|\mathbf{t}\|\mathbf{t}\times\mathbf{x} + \frac{1-\cos\|\mathbf{t}\|}{\|\mathbf{t}\|^2}\mathbf{t}\times(\mathbf{t}\times\mathbf{x}) \qquad \text{(A4.11)}\end{aligned}$$

(iii) If $\mathbf{t}$ is written as $\mathbf{t} = \theta\hat{\mathbf{t}}$, where $\hat{\mathbf{t}}$ is a unit vector in the direction of the axis, and $\theta = \|\mathbf{t}\|$ is the angle of rotation, then (A4.9) is equivalent to the Rodrigues formula for a rotation matrix:

$$\mathtt{R}(\theta, \hat{\mathbf{t}}) = \mathtt{I} + \sin\theta[\hat{\mathbf{t}}]_\times + (1-\cos\theta)[\hat{\mathbf{t}}]_\times^2 \qquad \text{(A4.12)}$$

A4.3.3 Quaternions

Three-dimensional rotations may also be represented by unit quaternions. A unit quaternion is a 4-vector and may be written in the form $\mathbf{q} = (\mathbf{v}\sin(\theta/2), \cos(\theta/2))^\mathsf{T}$, as may indeed any unit 4-vector. Such a quaternion represents a rotation about the vector $\mathbf{v}$ through the angle θ. This is a 2-to-1 representation in that both $\mathbf{q}$ and $-\mathbf{q}$ represent the same rotation. To check this, note that $-\mathbf{q} = (\mathbf{v}\sin(\theta/2+\pi), \cos(\theta/2+\pi))^\mathsf{T}$, which represents a rotation through $\theta + 2\pi = \theta$.

The relationship between the angle-axis representation of a rotation and the quaternion representation is easily determined. Given a vector $\mathbf{t}$, the angle-axis representation of a rotation, the corresponding quaternion is easily seen to be

$$\mathbf{t} \leftrightarrow \mathbf{q} = (\mathrm{sinc}(\|\mathbf{t}\|/2)\mathbf{t},\ \cos(\|\mathbf{t}\|/2))^\mathsf{T}$$

A4.4 Singular value decomposition

The singular value decomposition (SVD) is one of the most useful matrix decompositions, particularly for numerical computations. Its most common application is in the solution of over-determined systems of equations.

Given a square matrix $\mathtt{A}$, the SVD is a factorization of $\mathtt{A}$ as $\mathtt{A} = \mathtt{UDV}^\mathsf{T}$, where $\mathtt{U}$ and $\mathtt{V}$ are orthogonal matrices, and $\mathtt{D}$ is a diagonal matrix with non-negative entries. Note that it is conventional to write $\mathtt{V}^\mathsf{T}$ instead of $\mathtt{V}$ in this decomposition. The decomposition may be carried out in such a way that the diagonal entries of $\mathtt{D}$ are in descending order, and we will assume that this is always done. Thus a circumlocutory phrase such as "the column of $\mathtt{V}$ corresponding to the smallest singular value" is replaced by "the last column of $\mathtt{V}$."

The SVD also exists for non-square matrices $\mathtt{A}$. Of most interest is the case where $\mathtt{A}$ has more rows than columns. Specifically, let $\mathtt{A}$ be an $m \times n$ matrix with $m \geq n$. In this case $\mathtt{A}$ may be factored as $\mathtt{A} = \mathtt{UDV}^\mathsf{T}$ where $\mathtt{U}$ is an $m \times n$ matrix with orthogonal columns, $\mathtt{D}$ is an $n \times n$ diagonal matrix and $\mathtt{V}$ is an $n \times n$ orthogonal matrix. The fact that $\mathtt{U}$ has orthogonal columns means that $\mathtt{U}^\mathsf{T}\mathtt{U} = \mathtt{I}_{n\times n}$. Furthermore $\mathtt{U}$ has the norm-preserving property that $\|\mathtt{U}\mathbf{x}\| = \|\mathbf{x}\|$ for any vector $\mathbf{x}$, as one readily verifies. On the other hand, $\mathtt{UU}^\mathsf{T}$ is in general not the identity unless $m = n$.

Not surprisingly, one can also define a singular value decomposition for matrices with more columns than rows, but generally this will not be of interest to us. Instead on the occasional instances in this book where we need to take the singular value decomposition of a matrix $\mathtt{A}$ with $m < n$, it is appropriate to extend $\mathtt{A}$ by adding rows of zeros to obtain a square matrix, and then take the SVD of this resulting matrix. Usually this will be done without special remark.

Common implementations of the SVD, such as the one in [Press-88], assume that $m \geq n$. Since in this case the matrix $\mathtt{U}$ has the same dimension $m \times n$ as the input, matrix $\mathtt{A}$ may be overwritten by the output matrix $\mathtt{U}$.

Implementation of the SVD. A description of the singular value decomposition algorithm, or a proof of its existence, is not given in this book. For a description of how the algorithm works, the reader is referred to [Golub-89]. A practical implementation of the SVD is given in [Press-88]. However, the implementation of the SVD given in the first edition of "Numerical Recipes in C" can sometimes give incorrect results. The version of the algorithm given in the second edition [Press-88] of "Numerical Recipes in C" corrects mistakes in the earlier version.

Singular values and eigenvalues. The diagonal entries of matrix $\mathtt{D}$ in the SVD are non-negative. These entries are known as the singular values of the matrix $\mathtt{A}$. They are not the same thing as eigenvalues. To see the connection of the singular values of $\mathtt{A}$ with eigenvalues, we start with $\mathtt{A} = \mathtt{UDV}^\mathsf{T}$. From this it follows that $\mathtt{A}^\mathsf{T}\mathtt{A} = \mathtt{VDU}^\mathsf{T}\mathtt{UDV}^\mathsf{T} = \mathtt{VD}^2\mathtt{V}^\mathsf{T}$. Since $\mathtt{V}$ is orthogonal, $\mathtt{V}^\mathsf{T} = \mathtt{V}^{-1}$, and so $\mathtt{A}^\mathsf{T}\mathtt{A} = \mathtt{VD}^2\mathtt{V}^{-1}$. This is the defining equation for eigenvalues, indicating that the entries of $\mathtt{D}^2$ are the eigenvalues of $\mathtt{A}^\mathsf{T}\mathtt{A}$ and the columns of $\mathtt{V}$ are the eigenvectors of $\mathtt{A}^\mathsf{T}\mathtt{A}$. In short, the singular values of $\mathtt{A}$ are the square-roots of the eigenvalues of $\mathtt{A}^\mathsf{T}\mathtt{A}$.

Note, $\mathtt{A}^\mathsf{T}\mathtt{A}$ is symmetric and positive-semi-definite (see section A4.2.1 above), so its eigenvalues are real and non-negative. Consequently, singular values are real and non-negative.

Computational complexity of the SVD

The computational complexity of the SVD depends on how much information needs to be returned. For instance in algorithm A5.4 to be considered later, the solution to the problem is the last column of the matrix $\mathtt{V}$ in the SVD. The matrix $\mathtt{U}$ is not used, and does not need to be computed. On the other hand, algorithm A5.1 of section A5.1 requires the complete SVD to be computed. For systems of equations with many more rows than columns, the extra effort required to compute the matrix $\mathtt{U}$ is substantial.

Approximate numbers of floating-point operations (flops) required to compute the SVD of an $m \times n$ matrix are given in [Golub-89]. To find matrices $\mathtt{U}$, $\mathtt{V}$ and $\mathtt{D}$, a total of $4m^2n + 8mn^2 + 9n^3$ flops are needed. However, if only the matrices $\mathtt{V}$ and $\mathtt{D}$ are required, then only $4mn^2 + 8n^3$ flops are required. This is an important distinction, since this latter expression does not contain any term in m^2. Specifically, the number of operations required to compute $\mathtt{U}$ varies as the square of m, the number of rows. On the other hand, the complexity of computing $\mathtt{D}$ and $\mathtt{V}$ is linear in m. For cases where there are many more rows than columns, therefore, it is important (supposing computation time is an issue) to avoid computing the matrix $\mathtt{U}$ unless it is needed. To illustrate this point we consider the DLT algorithm for camera resection, described in chapter 7. In this algorithm a 3×4 camera matrix is computed from a set of n 3D to 2D point matches. The solution involves using algorithm A5.4, to solve a set of equations $\mathtt{A}\mathbf{p} = \mathbf{0}$ where $\mathtt{A}$ is a $2n \times 12$ matrix. The solution vector $\mathbf{p}$ is the last column of the matrix $\mathtt{V}$ in an SVD, $\mathtt{A} = \mathtt{UDV}^{\mathsf{T}}$. Thus the matrix $\mathtt{U}$ is not required. Table A4.1 gives the total number of flops for carrying out the SVD for six (the minimum number), 100 or 1000 point correspondences.

# points	# equations per point	# equations (m)	#unknowns (n)	# operations not computing $\mathtt{U}$	# operations computing $\mathtt{U}$
6	2	12	12	20,736	36,288
100	2	200	12	129,024	2,165,952
1000	2	2000	12	1,165,824	194,319,552

Table A4.1. *Comparison of the number of flops required to compute the SVD of a matrix of size $m \times n$, for varying values of m and for $n = 12$. Note that the computational complexity increases sub-linearly in the number of equations when $\mathtt{U}$ is not computed. On the other hand, the extra computational burden of computing $\mathtt{U}$ is very large, especially for large numbers of equations.*

Further reading. Two invaluable text books for this area are [Golub-89] and [Lutkepohl-96].

Appendix 5

Least-squares Minimization

In this appendix we discuss numerical algorithms for solving linear systems of equations under various constraints. As will be seen such problems are conveniently solved using the SVD.

A5.1 Solution of linear equations

Consider a system of equations of the form $\mathtt{A}\mathbf{x} = \mathbf{b}$. Let $\mathtt{A}$ be an $m \times n$ matrix. There are three possibilities:

(i) If $m < n$ there are more unknowns than equations. In this case, there will not be a unique solution, but rather a vector space of solutions.

(ii) If $m = n$ there will be a unique solution as long as $\mathtt{A}$ is invertible.

(iii) If $m > n$ then there are more equations than unknowns. In general the system will not have a solution unless by chance $\mathbf{b}$ lies in the span of the columns of $\mathtt{A}$.

Least-squares solutions: full-rank case. We consider the case $m \geq n$ and assume for the present that $\mathtt{A}$ is known to be of rank n. If a solution does not exist, then in many cases it still makes sense to seek a vector $\mathbf{x}$ that is closest to providing a solution to the system $\mathtt{A}\mathbf{x} = \mathbf{b}$. In other words, we seek $\mathbf{x}$ such that $\|\mathtt{A}\mathbf{x} - \mathbf{b}\|$ is minimized, where $\|\cdot\|$ represents the vector norm. Such an $\mathbf{x}$ is known as the *least-squares solution* to the over-determined system. The least-squares solution is conveniently found using the SVD as follows.

We seek $\mathbf{x}$ that minimizes $\|\mathtt{A}\mathbf{x}-\mathbf{b}\| = \|\mathtt{UDV}^\mathsf{T}\mathbf{x}-\mathbf{b}\|$. Because of the norm-preserving property of orthogonal transforms, $\|\mathtt{UDV}^\mathsf{T}\mathbf{x} - \mathbf{b}\| = \|\mathtt{DV}^\mathsf{T}\mathbf{x} - \mathtt{U}^\mathsf{T}\mathbf{b}\|$, and this is the quantity that we want to minimize. Writing $\mathbf{y} = \mathtt{V}^\mathsf{T}\mathbf{x}$ and $\mathbf{b}' = \mathtt{U}^\mathsf{T}\mathbf{b}$, the problem becomes one of minimizing $\|\mathtt{D}\mathbf{y} - \mathbf{b}'\|$ where $\mathtt{D}$ is an $m \times n$ matrix with vanishing off-diagonal entries. This set of equations is of the form

$$\begin{bmatrix} d_1 & & & \\ & d_2 & & \\ & & \ddots & \\ & & & d_n \\ \hline & & 0 & \end{bmatrix} \begin{pmatrix} y_1 \\ y_2 \\ \vdots \\ y_n \end{pmatrix} = \begin{pmatrix} b'_1 \\ b'_2 \\ \vdots \\ b'_n \\ \hline b'_{n+1} \\ \vdots \\ b'_m \end{pmatrix}.$$

Clearly, the nearest $\mathtt{D}y$ can approach to $\mathbf{b}'$ is the vector $(b'_1, b'_2, \ldots, b'_n, 0, \ldots, 0)^\mathsf{T}$, and this is achieved by setting $y_i = b'_i/d_i$ for $i = 1, \ldots, n$. Note that the assumption $\text{rank}\mathtt{A} = n$ ensures that $d_i \neq 0$. Finally, one retrieves $\mathbf{x}$ from $\mathbf{x} = \mathtt{V}\mathbf{y}$. The complete algorithm is

Objective

Find the least-squares solution to the $m \times n$ set of equations $\mathtt{A}\mathbf{x} = \mathbf{b}$, where $m > n$ and rank $\mathtt{A} = n$.

Algorithm

(i) Find the SVD $\mathtt{A} = \mathtt{UDV}^\mathsf{T}$.
(ii) Set $\mathbf{b}' = \mathtt{U}^\mathsf{T}\mathbf{b}$.
(iii) Find the vector $\mathbf{y}$ defined by $y_i = b'_i/d_i$, where d_i is the i-th diagonal entry of $\mathtt{D}$.
(iv) The solution is $\mathbf{x} = \mathtt{V}\mathbf{y}$.

Algorithm A5.1. *Linear least-squares solution to an over-determined full-rank set of linear equations.*

Deficient-rank systems. Sometimes one is called upon to solve a system of equations that is expected not to be of full column rank. Thus, let $r = \text{rank}\mathtt{A} < n$, where n is the number of columns of $\mathtt{A}$. It is possible that because of noise corruption, the matrix $\mathtt{A}$ actually has rank greater than r, but we wish to enforce the rank r constraint because of theoretical considerations, derived from the particular problem being considered. In this case, there will be an $(n-r)$-parameter family of solutions to the set of equations, where $r = \text{rank}\mathtt{A} < n$. This family of solutions is appropriately solved using the SVD, as follows:

This algorithm gives an $(n-r)$-parameter family (parametrized by the indeterminate values λ_i) of least-squares solutions to the deficient-rank system. The justification of this algorithm is similar to that of algorithm A5.1 for the least-squares solution of full-rank systems.

Systems of unknown rank. In most cases encountered in this book, the rank of a system of linear equations will be known theoretically in advance of solution. If the rank of the system of equations is not known, then one must guess at its rank. In this case, it is appropriate to set singular values that are small compared with the largest

Objective

Find the general solution to a set of equations $\mathtt{A}\mathbf{x} = \mathbf{b}$ where $\mathtt{A}$ is an $m \times n$ matrix of rank $r < n$.

Algorithm

(i) Find the SVD $\mathtt{A} = \mathtt{UDV}^\mathsf{T}$, where the diagonal entries d_i of $\mathtt{D}$ are in descending numerical order.
(ii) Set $\mathbf{b}' = \mathtt{U}^\mathsf{T}\mathbf{b}$.
(iii) Find the vector $\mathbf{y}$ defined by $y_i = b'_i/d_i$ for $i = 1, \ldots, r$, and $y_i = 0$ otherwise.
(iv) The solution $\mathbf{x}$ of minimum norm $\|\mathbf{x}\|$ is $\mathtt{V}\mathbf{y}$.
(v) The general solution is $\mathbf{x} = \mathtt{V}\mathbf{y} + \lambda_{r+1}\mathbf{v}_{r+1} + \ldots + \lambda_n\mathbf{v}_n$, where $\mathbf{v}_{r+1}, \ldots, \mathbf{v}_n$ are the last $n - r$ columns of $\mathtt{V}$.

Algorithm A5.2. *General solution to deficient-rank system*

singular value to zero. Thus, if $d_i/d_0 < \delta$ where δ is a small constant of the order of the machine precision[1] then one sets $y_i = 0$. A least-squares solution is then given by $\mathbf{x} = \mathtt{V}\mathbf{y}$ as before.

A5.2 The pseudo-inverse

Given a square diagonal matrix $\mathtt{D}$, we define its *pseudo-inverse* to be the diagonal matrix $\mathtt{D}^+$ such that

$$D^+_{ii} = \begin{cases} 0 & \text{if } D_{ii} = 0 \\ D_{ii}^{-1} & \text{otherwise.} \end{cases}$$

Now, consider an $m \times n$ matrix $\mathtt{A}$ with $m \geq n$. Let the SVD of $\mathtt{A}$ be $\mathtt{A} = \mathtt{UDV}^\mathsf{T}$. We define the *pseudo-inverse* of $\mathtt{A}$ to be the matrix

$$\mathtt{A}^+ = \mathtt{VD}^+\mathtt{U}^\mathsf{T}. \tag{A5.1}$$

One very simply verifies that the vector $\mathbf{y}$ in algorithm A5.1 or algorithm A5.2 is nothing more than $\mathtt{D}^+\mathbf{b}'$ where $\mathbf{b}' = \mathtt{U}^\mathsf{T}\mathbf{b}$. Thus,

Result A5.1. *The least-squares solution to an $m \times n$ system of equations $\mathtt{A}\mathbf{x} = \mathbf{b}$ of rank n is given by $\mathbf{x} = \mathtt{A}^+\mathbf{b}$. In the case of a deficient-rank system, $\mathbf{x} = \mathtt{A}^+\mathbf{b}$ is the solution that minimizes $\|\mathbf{x}\|$.*

As remarked when discussing the SVD, if $\mathtt{A}$ has fewer rows than columns, then this result may be applied after extending $\mathtt{A}$ to a square matrix by adding rows of zeros.

Symmetric matrices. For symmetric matrices, one may generalize the pseudo-inverse as follows. This generalization was used in chapter 5, section 5.2.3(*p*142) for discussing singular covariance matrices. If $\mathtt{A}$ is a non-invertible symmetric matrix, and $\mathtt{X}^\mathsf{T}\mathtt{AX}$ is invertible, then we write $\mathtt{A}^{+\mathtt{X}} \stackrel{\text{def}}{=} \mathtt{X}(\mathtt{X}^\mathsf{T}\mathtt{AX})^{-1}\mathtt{X}^\mathsf{T}$. One can see that this depends only on the span of the columns of $\mathtt{X}$. In other words, if $\mathtt{X}$ is replaced by $\mathtt{XB}$ for any invertible matrix $\mathtt{B}$, then $\mathtt{A}^{+\mathtt{X}} = \mathtt{A}^{+\mathtt{XB}}$. Otherwise stated, $\mathtt{A}^{+\mathtt{X}}$ depends only on the (left)

[1] Machine precision is the largest floating point value ϵ such that $1.0 + \epsilon = 1.0$.

null-space of $\mathtt{X}$, namely the space of vectors perpendicular to the columns of $\mathtt{X}$. Define the null-space $N_L\mathtt{X} = \{\mathbf{x}^\mathsf{T} \mid \mathbf{x}^\mathsf{T}\mathtt{X} = 0\}$. One finds that under a simple condition, $\mathtt{A}^{+\mathtt{X}}$ is the pseudo-inverse of $\mathtt{A}$:

Result A5.2. *Let* $\mathtt{A}$ *be a symmetric matrix, then* $\mathtt{A}^{+\mathtt{X}} \stackrel{\text{def}}{=} \mathtt{X}(\mathtt{X}^\mathsf{T}\mathtt{A}\mathtt{X})^{-1}\mathtt{X}^\mathsf{T} = \mathtt{A}^+$ *if and only if* $N_L(\mathtt{X}) = N_L(\mathtt{A})$.

Only a sketch proof is given. The necessity is obvious, since $N_L(\mathtt{X})$ and $N_L(\mathtt{A})$ are the null-spaces of the left and right sides of the equation. To prove the converse, one may assume that the columns of $\mathtt{X}$ are orthonormal, since as shown above, only the null-space of $\mathtt{X}$ is of importance. Thus, $\mathtt{X}$ may be extended by adding further columns $\mathtt{X}'$ to form an orthogonal matrix $\mathtt{U} = [\mathtt{X}|\mathtt{X}']$. Now, the rows of $\mathtt{X}'^\mathsf{T}$ span the null-space of $\mathtt{X}$, and hence, by assumption, of $\mathtt{A}$. Now, the proof is completed in a few lines by comparing the definition $\mathtt{A}^{+\mathtt{X}} \stackrel{\text{def}}{=} \mathtt{X}(\mathtt{X}^\mathsf{T}\mathtt{A}\mathtt{X})^{-1}\mathtt{X}^\mathsf{T}$ with the definition (A5.1) of the pseudo-inverse.

A5.2.1 Linear least-squares using normal equations

The linear least-squares problem may also be solved by a method involving the so-called *normal equations*. Once more, we consider the set of linear equations $\mathtt{A}\mathbf{x} = \mathbf{b}$ where $\mathtt{A}$ is an $m \times n$ matrix with $m > n$. In general, no solution $\mathbf{x}$ will exist for this set of equations. Consequently, the task is to find the vector $\mathbf{x}$ that minimizes the norm $\|\mathtt{A}\mathbf{x} - \mathbf{b}\|$. As the vector $\mathbf{x}$ varies over all values, the product $\mathtt{A}\mathbf{x}$ varies over the complete column space of $\mathtt{A}$, that is, the subspace of $\mathbb{R}^m$ spanned by the columns of $\mathtt{A}$. The task therefore is to find the closest vector to $\mathbf{b}$ that lies in the column space of $\mathtt{A}$, where closeness is defined in terms of vector norm. Let $\mathbf{x}$ be the solution to this problem; thus $\mathtt{A}\mathbf{x}$ is the closest point to $\mathbf{b}$. In this case, the difference $\mathtt{A}\mathbf{x} - \mathbf{b}$ must be a vector orthogonal to the column space of $\mathtt{A}$. This means, explicitly, that $\mathtt{A}\mathbf{x} - \mathbf{b}$ is perpendicular to each of the columns of $\mathtt{A}$, and hence $\mathtt{A}^\mathsf{T}(\mathtt{A}\mathbf{x} - \mathbf{b}) = \mathbf{0}$. Multiplying out and separating terms gives an equation

$$(\mathtt{A}^\mathsf{T}\mathtt{A})\mathbf{x} = \mathtt{A}^\mathsf{T}\mathbf{b}. \tag{A5.2}$$

This is a square $n \times n$ set of linear equations, called the *normal equations*. This set of equations may be solved to find the least-squares solution to the problem $\mathtt{A}\mathbf{x} = \mathbf{b}$. Even if $\mathtt{A}$ is not of full rank (rank n), this set of equations should have a solution, since $\mathtt{A}^\mathsf{T}\mathbf{b}$ lies in the column space of $\mathtt{A}^\mathsf{T}\mathtt{A}$. In the case where $\mathtt{A}$ has rank n, the matrix $\mathtt{A}^\mathsf{T}\mathtt{A}$ is

Objective

Find $\mathbf{x}$ that minimizes $\|\mathtt{A}\mathbf{x} - \mathbf{b}\|$.

Algorithm

(i) Solve the normal equations $\mathtt{A}^\mathsf{T}\mathtt{A}\mathbf{x} = \mathtt{A}^\mathsf{T}\mathbf{b}$.
(ii) If $\mathtt{A}^\mathsf{T}\mathtt{A}$ is invertible, then the solution is $\mathbf{x} = (\mathtt{A}^\mathsf{T}\mathtt{A})^{-1}\mathtt{A}^\mathsf{T}\mathbf{b}$.

Algorithm A5.3. *Linear least-squares using the normal equations.*

invertible, and so $\mathbf{x}$ may be found by $\mathbf{x} = (\mathtt{A}^\mathsf{T}\mathtt{A})^{-1}\mathtt{A}^\mathsf{T}\mathbf{b}$. Since $\mathbf{x} = \mathtt{A}^+\mathbf{b}$, this implies the following result, which is also easily verified directly:

Result A5.3. *If* $\mathtt{A}$ *is an* $m \times n$ *matrix of rank* n, *then* $\mathtt{A}^+ = (\mathtt{A}^\mathsf{T}\mathtt{A})^{-1}\mathtt{A}^\mathsf{T}$.

This result is useful in theoretical analysis, as well as being a computationally simpler method than using the SVD to compute a pseudo-inverse if n is small compared with m (so that computing the inverse of $(\mathtt{A}^\mathsf{T}\mathtt{A})$ is inexpensive compared to computing the SVD of $\mathtt{A}$).

Vector space norms. One sometimes wishes to minimize $\mathtt{A}\mathbf{x} - \mathbf{b}$ with respect to a different norm on the vector space $\mathbb{R}^n$. The usual norm in a vector space $\mathbb{R}^n$ is given in terms of the usual inner product. Thus, for two vectors $\mathbf{a}$ and $\mathbf{b}$ in $\mathbb{R}^n$ one may define the inner product $\mathbf{a} \cdot \mathbf{b}$ to be $\mathbf{a}^\mathsf{T}\mathbf{b}$. The norm of a vector $\mathbf{a}$ is then $\|\mathbf{a}\| = (\mathbf{a} \cdot \mathbf{a})^{1/2} = (\mathbf{a}^\mathsf{T}\mathbf{a})^{1/2}$. One notes the properties:

(i) The inner product is a symmetric bilinear form on $\mathbb{R}^n$.
(ii) $\|\mathbf{a}\| > 0$ for all non-zero vectors $\mathbf{a} \in \mathbb{R}^n$.

We say that the inner product is a positive-definite symmetric bilinear form. It is possible to define other inner products on a vector space $\mathbb{R}^n$. Let $\mathtt{C}$ be a real symmetric positive-definite matrix, and define a new inner product $\mathtt{C}(\mathbf{a}, \mathbf{b}) = \mathbf{a}^\mathsf{T}\mathtt{C}\mathbf{b}$. The symmetry of the inner product follows from the symmetry of $\mathtt{C}$. A norm may be defined by $\|\mathbf{a}\|_\mathtt{C} = (\mathbf{a}^\mathsf{T}\mathtt{C}\mathbf{a})^{1/2}$, and this is defined and positive-definite, because $\mathtt{C}$ is assumed to be a positive-definite matrix.

Weighted linear least-squares problems. Sometimes one desires to solve a weighted least-squares problem of the form $\mathtt{A}\mathbf{x} - \mathbf{b} = 0$ by minimizing the $\mathtt{C}$-norm $\|\mathtt{A}\mathbf{x} - \mathbf{b}\|_\mathtt{C}$ of the error. Here $\mathtt{C}$ is a positive-definite symmetric matrix defining an inner product and a norm $\| \cdot \|_\mathtt{C}$ on $\mathbb{R}^n$. As before, one can argue that the minimum error vector $\mathtt{A}\mathbf{x} - \mathbf{b}$ must be orthogonal in the inner product defined by $\mathtt{C}$ to the column space of $\mathtt{A}$. This leads to a requirement $\mathtt{A}^\mathsf{T}\mathtt{C}(\mathtt{A}\mathbf{x} - \mathbf{b}) = 0$. Rearranging this one obtains the weighted normal equations:

$$(\mathtt{A}^\mathsf{T}\mathtt{C}\mathtt{A})\mathbf{x} = \mathtt{A}^\mathsf{T}\mathtt{C}\mathbf{b}. \tag{A5.3}$$

The most common weighting will be where $\mathtt{C}$ is a diagonal matrix, corresponding to independent weights in each of the axial directions in $\mathbb{R}^n$. However, general weighting matrices $\mathtt{C}$ may be used also.

A5.3 Least-squares solution of homogeneous equations

Similar to the previous problem is that of solving a set of equations of the form $\mathtt{A}\mathbf{x} = \mathbf{0}$. This problem comes up frequently in reconstruction problems. We consider the case where there are more equations than unknowns – an over-determined set of equations. The obvious solution $\mathbf{x} = \mathbf{0}$ is not of interest – we seek a non-zero solution to the set of equations. Observe that if $\mathbf{x}$ is a solution to this set of equations, then so is $k\mathbf{x}$ for any scalar k. A reasonable constraint would be to seek a solution for which $\|\mathbf{x}\| = 1$.

In general, such a set of equations will not have an exact solution. Suppose $\mathtt{A}$ has dimension $m \times n$ then there is an exact solution if and only if $\text{rank}(\mathtt{A}) < n$ – the matrix $\mathtt{A}$ does not have full column rank. In the absence of an exact solution we will normally seek a least-squares solution. The problem may be stated as

- *Find the* $\mathbf{x}$ *that minimizes* $\|\mathtt{A}\mathbf{x}\|$ *subject to* $\|\mathbf{x}\| = 1$.

This problem is solvable as follows. Let $\mathtt{A} = \mathtt{UDV}^\mathsf{T}$. The problem then requires us to minimize $\|\mathtt{UDV}^\mathsf{T}\mathbf{x}\|$. However, $\|\mathtt{UDV}^\mathsf{T}\mathbf{x}\| = \|\mathtt{DV}^\mathsf{T}\mathbf{x}\|$ and $\|\mathbf{x}\| = \|\mathtt{V}^\mathsf{T}\mathbf{x}\|$. Thus, we need to minimize $\|\mathtt{DV}^\mathsf{T}\mathbf{x}\|$ subject to the condition $\|\mathtt{V}^\mathsf{T}\mathbf{x}\| = 1$. We write $\mathbf{y} = \mathtt{V}^\mathsf{T}\mathbf{x}$, and the problem is: minimize $\|\mathtt{D}\mathbf{y}\|$ subject to $\|\mathbf{y}\| = 1$. Now, $\mathtt{D}$ is a diagonal matrix with its diagonal entries in descending order. It follows that the solution to this problem is $\mathbf{y} = (0, 0, \ldots, 0, 1)^\mathsf{T}$ having one non-zero entry, 1 in the last position. Finally $\mathbf{x} = \mathtt{V}\mathbf{y}$ is simply the last column of $\mathtt{V}$. The method is summarized in algorithm A5.4.

<u>Objective</u>

Given a matrix $\mathtt{A}$ with at least as many rows as columns, find $\mathbf{x}$ that minimizes $\|\mathtt{A}\mathbf{x}\|$ subject to $\|\mathbf{x}\| = 1$.

<u>Solution</u>

$\mathbf{x}$ is the last column of $\mathtt{V}$, where $\mathtt{A} = \mathtt{UDV}^\mathsf{T}$ is the SVD of $\mathtt{A}$.

Algorithm A5.4. *Least-squares solution of a homogeneous system of linear equations.*

As mentioned in section A4.4 the last column of $\mathtt{V}$ may alternatively be described as the eigenvector of $\mathtt{A}^\mathsf{T}\mathtt{A}$ corresponding to the smallest eigenvalue.

A5.4 Least-squares solution to constrained systems

In the previous section, we considered a method of least-squares solution of equations of the form $\mathtt{A}\mathbf{x} = \mathbf{0}$. Such problems may arise from situations where measurements are made on a set of image features. With exact measurements and an exact imaging model the mathematical model predicts an exact solution to this system. In the case of inexact image measurements, or noise, there will not be an exact solution. In this case, it makes sense to find a least-squares solution.

On other occasions, however, some of the equations represented by rows of the matrix $\mathtt{A}$ are derived from precise mathematical constraints, and should be satisfied exactly. This set of constraints may be described by a matrix equation $\mathtt{C}\mathbf{x} = \mathbf{0}$, which should be satisfied exactly. Others of the equations are derived from image measurements and are subject to noise. This leads to a problem of the following sort:

- *Find the* $\mathbf{x}$ *that minimizes* $\|\mathtt{A}\mathbf{x}\|$ *subject to* $\|\mathbf{x}\| = 1$ *and* $\mathtt{C}\mathbf{x} = \mathbf{0}$.

This problem can be solved in the following manner. The condition that $\mathbf{x}$ satisfies $\mathtt{C}\mathbf{x} = \mathbf{0}$ means that $\mathbf{x}$ lies perpendicular to each of the rows of $\mathtt{C}$. The set of all such $\mathbf{x}$ is a vector space called the orthogonal complement of the row space of $\mathtt{C}$. We wish to find this orthogonal complement.

First, if $\mathtt{C}$ has fewer rows than columns, then extend it to a square matrix by adding rows of zero elements. This has no effect on the set of constraints $\mathtt{C}\mathbf{x} = \mathbf{0}$. Now, let $\mathtt{C} = \mathtt{UDV}^\mathsf{T}$ be the Singular Value Decomposition of $\mathtt{C}$, where $\mathtt{D}$ is a diagonal matrix with r non-zero diagonal entries. In this case, $\mathtt{C}$ has rank r and the row-space of $\mathtt{C}$ is generated by the first r rows of $\mathtt{V}^\mathsf{T}$. The orthogonal complement of the row-space of $\mathtt{C}$ consists of the remaining rows of $\mathtt{V}^\mathsf{T}$. Define $\mathtt{C}^\perp$ to be the matrix $\mathtt{V}$ with the first r columns deleted. Then $\mathtt{CC}^\perp = \mathtt{0}$, and so the set of vectors $\mathbf{x}$ satisfying $\mathtt{C}\mathbf{x} = \mathbf{0}$ is spanned by the columns of $\mathtt{C}^\perp$ and we may write any such $\mathbf{x}$ as $\mathbf{x} = \mathtt{C}^\perp\mathbf{x}'$ for suitable $\mathbf{x}'$. Since $\mathtt{C}^\perp$ has orthogonal columns, one observes that $\|\mathbf{x}\| = \|\mathtt{C}^\perp\mathbf{x}'\| = \|\mathbf{x}'\|$. The minimization problem now becomes

- *Find the* $\mathbf{x}'$ *that minimizes* $\|\mathtt{AC}^\perp\mathbf{x}'\|$ *subject to* $\|\mathbf{x}'\| = 1$.

This is simply an instance of the problem discussed in section A5.3, solved by algorithm A5.4. The complete algorithm for solution of the constrained minimization problem is given as algorithm A5.5.

Objective

Given an $m \times n$ matrix $\mathtt{A}$ with $m \geq n$, find the vector $\mathbf{x}$ that minimizes $\|\mathtt{A}\mathbf{x}\|$ subject to $\|\mathbf{x}\| = 1$ and $\mathtt{C}\mathbf{x} = \mathbf{0}$.

Algorithm

(i) If $\mathtt{C}$ has fewer rows than columns, then add zero-filled rows to $\mathtt{C}$ to make it square. Compute the SVD $\mathtt{C} = \mathtt{UDV}^\mathsf{T}$ where diagonal entries of $\mathtt{D}$ are sorted with non-zero ones first. Let $\mathtt{C}^\perp$ be the matrix obtained from $\mathtt{V}$ by deleting the first r columns of $\mathtt{V}$, where r is the number of non-zero entries in $\mathtt{D}$ (the rank of $\mathtt{C}$).

(ii) Find the solution to the minimization problem $\mathtt{AC}^\perp\mathbf{x}' = \mathbf{0}$ using algorithm A5.4. The solution is given by $\mathbf{x} = \mathtt{C}^\perp\mathbf{x}'$.

Algorithm A5.5. *Algorithm for constrained minimization.*

A5.4.1 More constrained minimization

A further constrained minimization problem arises in the algebraic estimation method used frequently throughout this book – for instance, for computation of the fundamental matrix (section 11.3(p282)) or the trifocal tensor (section 16.3(p395)).

The problem is:

- *Minimize* $\|\mathtt{A}\mathbf{x}\|$ *subject to* $\|\mathbf{x}\| = 1$ *and* $\mathbf{x} = \mathtt{G}\hat{\mathbf{x}}$ *for a given matrix* $\mathtt{G}$ *and some unknown vector* $\hat{\mathbf{x}}$.

Note that this is very similar to the previous minimization problem of section A5.4, which was reduced to the form of the present problem in which the matrix $\mathtt{G}$ had orthonormal columns. The condition that $\mathbf{x} = \mathtt{G}\hat{\mathbf{x}}$ for some $\hat{\mathbf{x}}$ means nothing more than that $\mathbf{x}$ lies in the span of the columns of $\mathtt{G}$. Thus, to solve the present problem using algorithm A5.5, we need only to replace $\mathtt{G}$ by a matrix with the same column space (i.e. the space spanned by the columns), but with orthonormal columns. If $\mathtt{G} = \mathtt{UDV}^\mathsf{T}$ where $\mathtt{D}$ has r non-zero entries (that is $\mathtt{G}$ has rank r), then let $\mathtt{U}'$ be the matrix consisting of the first r columns of $\mathtt{U}$. Then $\mathtt{G}$ and $\mathtt{U}'$ have the same column space. As in section A5.4 the solution is found by setting $\mathbf{x}'$ to be the unit vector that minimizes $\|\mathtt{A}\mathtt{U}'\mathbf{x}'\|$, then setting $\mathbf{x} = \mathtt{U}'\mathbf{x}'$.

If $\hat{\mathbf{x}}$ is also required, then it may be obtained by solving $\mathtt{G}\hat{\mathbf{x}} = \mathbf{x} = \mathtt{U}'\mathbf{x}'$. The solution is expressed in terms of the pseudo-inverse (section A5.2) as $\hat{\mathbf{x}} = \mathtt{G}^{+}\mathbf{x} = \mathtt{G}^{+}\mathtt{U}'\mathbf{x}'$; it may not be unique if $\mathtt{G}$ does not have full column rank. Since $\mathtt{G}^{+} = \mathtt{V}\mathtt{D}^{+}\mathtt{U}^{\mathsf{T}}$, we may write $\hat{\mathbf{x}} = \mathtt{V}\mathtt{D}^{+}\mathtt{U}^{\mathsf{T}}\mathtt{U}'\mathbf{x}'$, which simplifies to $\hat{\mathbf{x}} = \mathtt{V}'\mathtt{D}'^{-1}\mathbf{x}'$ where $\mathtt{V}'$ consists of the first r columns of $\mathtt{V}'$ and $\mathtt{D}'$ is the upper $r \times r$ block of $\mathtt{D}$.

The complete method is summarized in algorithm A5.6.

Objective

Find the vector $\mathbf{x}$ that minimizes $\|\mathtt{A}\mathbf{x}\|$ subject to the conditions $\|\mathbf{x}\| = 1$ and $\mathbf{x} = \mathtt{G}\hat{\mathbf{x}}$, where $\mathtt{G}$ has rank r.

Algorithm

(i) Compute the SVD $\mathtt{G} = \mathtt{U}\mathtt{D}\mathtt{V}^{\mathsf{T}}$, where the non-zero values of $\mathtt{D}$ appear first down the diagonal.
(ii) Let $\mathtt{U}'$ be the matrix comprising the first r columns of $\mathtt{U}$.
(iii) Find the unit vector $\mathbf{x}'$ that minimizes $\|\mathtt{A}\mathtt{U}'\mathbf{x}'\|$, using algorithm A5.4.
(iv) The required solution is $\mathbf{x} = \mathtt{U}'\mathbf{x}'$.
(v) If desired, one may compute $\hat{\mathbf{x}}$ as $\mathtt{V}'\mathtt{D}'^{-1}\mathbf{x}'$, where $\mathtt{V}'$ consists of the first r columns of $\mathtt{V}$ and $\mathtt{D}'$ is the upper $r \times r$ block of $\mathtt{D}$.

Algorithm A5.6. *Algorithm for constrained minimization, subject to a span-space constraint.*

A5.4.2 Yet another minimization problem

A very similar problem is

- *Minimize* $\|\mathtt{A}\mathbf{x}\|$ *subject to a condition* $\|\mathtt{C}\mathbf{x}\| = 1$.

This problem comes up for instance in the solution to the DLT camera calibration problem (section 7.3(p184)). In general it will be the case that rank$\mathtt{C} < n$ where n is the dimension of the vector $\mathbf{x}$. Geometrically the problem may be thought of as finding the “lowest” point on a quadratic surface (specified by $\mathbf{x}^{\mathsf{T}}\mathtt{A}^{\mathsf{T}}\mathtt{A}\mathbf{x}$), with the constraint that the point must lie on the (inhomogeneous) “conic” $\mathbf{x}^{\mathsf{T}}\mathtt{C}^{\mathsf{T}}\mathtt{C}\mathbf{x} = 1$.

We start by taking the SVD of the matrix $\mathtt{C}$, obtaining $\mathtt{C} = \mathtt{U}\mathtt{D}\mathtt{V}^{\mathsf{T}}$. The condition $\|\mathtt{U}\mathtt{D}\mathtt{V}^{\mathsf{T}}\mathbf{x}\| = 1$ is equivalent to $\|\mathtt{D}\mathtt{V}^{\mathsf{T}}\mathbf{x}\| = 1$, and it is not necessary to compute $\mathtt{U}$ explicitly. Then writing $\mathbf{x}' = \mathtt{V}^{\mathsf{T}}\mathbf{x}$, the problem becomes: minimize $\|\mathtt{A}\mathtt{V}\mathbf{x}'\|$ subject to the condition $\|\mathtt{D}\mathbf{x}'\| = 1$ Writing $\mathtt{A}' = \mathtt{A}\mathtt{V}$, this becomes: minimize $\|\mathtt{A}'\mathbf{x}'\|$ subject to $\|\mathtt{D}\mathbf{x}'\| = 1$. Thus we have reduced to the case where the constraint matrix is a diagonal matrix, $\mathtt{D}$.

We suppose that $\mathtt{D}$ has r non-zero diagonal entries, and s zero entries, where $r + s = n$, the non-zero entries appearing first on the diagonal of $\mathtt{D}$. Then the entries x'_i of $\mathbf{x}'$ for $i > r$ do not affect the value of $\|\mathtt{D}\mathbf{x}'_i\|$, since the corresponding diagonal entries of $\mathtt{D}$ are zero. Then, for a specific choice of the x'_i for $i = 1, \ldots, r$, the other entries x'_i,

$i = r + 1, \ldots, n$ should be chosen so as to minimize the value of $\|\mathtt{A}'\mathbf{x}'_i\|$. We write $\mathtt{A}' = [\mathtt{A}'_1 \mid \mathtt{A}'_2]$ where $\mathtt{A}'_1$ consists of the first r columns of $\mathtt{A}'$ and $\mathtt{A}'_2$ consists of the remaining s columns. Similarly, let $\mathbf{x}'_1$ be an r-vector consisting of the first r elements of $\mathbf{x}'$, and let $\mathbf{x}'_2$ consist of the remaining s elements of $\mathbf{x}'$. Further, let $\mathtt{D}_1$ be the $r \times r$ diagonal matrix consisting of the first r diagonal entries of $\mathtt{D}$. Then $\mathtt{A}'\mathbf{x}' = \mathtt{A}'_1\mathbf{x}'_1 + \mathtt{A}'_2\mathbf{x}'_2$, and the minimization problem is to minimize

$$\|\mathtt{A}'_1\mathbf{x}'_1 + \mathtt{A}'_2\mathbf{x}'_2\| \tag{A5.4}$$

subject to the condition $\|\mathtt{D}_1\mathbf{x}'_1\| = 1$. Now, temporarily fixing $\mathbf{x}'_1$, (A5.4) takes the form of a least-squares minimization problem of the type discussed in section A5.1. According to result A5.1, the value of $\mathbf{x}'_2$ that minimizes (A5.4) is $\mathbf{x}'_2 = -\mathtt{A}'^{+}_2\mathtt{A}'_1\mathbf{x}'_1$. Substituting this in (A5.4) gives $\|(\mathtt{A}'_2\mathtt{A}'^{+}_2 - \mathtt{I})\mathtt{A}'_1\mathbf{x}'_1\|$, which we are required to minimize, subject to the condition $\|\mathtt{D}_1\mathbf{x}'_1\| = 1$. Finally, writing $\mathbf{x}'' = \mathtt{D}_1\mathbf{x}'_1$, the problem reduces at last to a problem of the form of the familiar minimization problem of algorithm A5.4.

- *Minimize* $\|(\mathtt{A}'_2\mathtt{A}'^{+}_2 - \mathtt{I})\mathtt{A}'_1\mathtt{D}_1^{-1}\mathbf{x}''_1\|$, *subject to* $\|\mathbf{x}''\| = 1$.

We now summarize the algorithm.

Objective

Minimize $\|\mathtt{A}\mathbf{x}\|$ subject to $\|\mathtt{C}\mathbf{x}\| = 1$.

Algorithm

(i) Compute the SVD $\mathtt{C} = \mathtt{UDV}^\mathsf{T}$, and write $\mathtt{A}' = \mathtt{AV}$.
(ii) Suppose rank$\mathtt{D} = r$ and let $\mathtt{A}' = [\mathtt{A}'_1 \mid \mathtt{A}'_2]$ where $\mathtt{A}'_1$ consists of the first r columns of $\mathtt{A}'$, and $\mathtt{A}'_2$ is formed from the remaining columns.
(iii) Let $\mathtt{D}_1$ be the upper $r \times r$ minor of $\mathtt{D}$.
(iv) Compute $\mathtt{A}'' = (\mathtt{A}'_2\mathtt{A}'^{+}_2 - \mathtt{I})\mathtt{A}'_1\mathtt{D}_1^{-1}$. This is an $n \times r$ matrix.
(v) Minimize $\|\mathtt{A}''\mathbf{x}'\|$ subject to $\|\mathbf{x}''\| = 1$ using algorithm A5.4.
(vi) Set $\mathbf{x}'_1 = \mathtt{D}_1^{-1}\mathbf{x}''$, and $\mathbf{x}'_2 = -\mathtt{A}'^{+}_2\mathtt{A}'_1\mathbf{x}'_1$. Let $\mathbf{x}' = \begin{pmatrix} \mathbf{x}'_1 \\ \mathbf{x}'_2 \end{pmatrix}$.
(vii) The solution is given by $\mathbf{x} = \mathtt{V}\mathbf{x}'$.

Algorithm A5.7. *Least-squares solution of homogeneous equations subject to the constraint* $\|\mathtt{C}\mathbf{x}\| = 1$.

Appendix 6

Iterative Estimation Methods

In this appendix we describe the various components involved in building an efficient and robust iterative estimation algorithm.

We start with two of the most common iterative parameter minimization methods, namely Newton iteration (and the closely related Gauss-Newton method) and Levenberg–Marquardt iteration. The general idea of Newton iteration is familiar to most students of numerical methods as a way of finding the zeros of a function of a single variable. Its generalization to several variables and application to finding least-squares solutions rather than exact solutions to sets of equations is relatively straightforward. The Levenberg–Marquardt method is a simple variation on Newton iteration designed to provide faster convergence and regularization in the case of over-parametrized problems. It may be seen as a hybrid between Newton iteration and a gradient descent method.

For the type of problem considered in this book, important reductions of computational complexity are obtained by dividing the set of parameters into two parts. The two parts generally consist of a set of parameters representing camera matrices or homographies, and a set of parameters representing points. This leads to a sparse structure to the problem that is described starting at section A6.3.

We discuss two further implementation issues – the choice of cost function, with respect to their robustness to outliers and convexity (section A6.8); and the parametrization of rotations, and homogeneous and constrained vectors (section A6.9). Finally, those readers who want to learn more about iterative techniques and bundle-adjustment are referred to [Triggs-00a] for more details.

A6.1 Newton iteration

Suppose we are given a hypothesized functional relation $\mathbf{X} = \mathbf{f}(\mathbf{P})$ where $\mathbf{X}$ is a *measurement vector* and $\mathbf{P}$ is a *parameter vector* in Euclidean spaces $\mathbb{R}^N$ and $\mathbb{R}^M$ respectively. A measured value of $\mathbf{X}$ approximating the true value $\overline{\mathbf{X}}$ is provided, and we wish to find the vector $\widehat{\mathbf{P}}$ that most nearly satisfies this functional relation. More precisely, we seek the vector $\widehat{\mathbf{P}}$ satisfying $\mathbf{X} = \mathbf{f}(\widehat{\mathbf{P}}) - \epsilon$ for which $\|\epsilon\|$ is minimized. Note that the linear least-squares problem considered in section A5.1 is exactly of this type, the function $\mathbf{f}$ being defined as a linear function $\mathbf{f}(\mathbf{P}) = \mathtt{A}\mathbf{P}$.

To solve the case where $\mathbf{f}$ is not a linear function, we may start with an initial estimated value $\mathbf{P}_0$, and proceed to refine the estimate under the assumption that the function $\mathbf{f}$ is locally linear. Let $\boldsymbol{\epsilon}_0$ be defined by $\boldsymbol{\epsilon}_0 = \mathbf{f}(\mathbf{P}_0) - \mathbf{X}$. We assume that the function $\mathbf{f}$ is approximated at $\mathbf{P}_0$ by $\mathbf{f}(\mathbf{P}_0 + \boldsymbol{\Delta}) = \mathbf{f}(\mathbf{P}_0) + \mathtt{J}\boldsymbol{\Delta}$, where $\mathtt{J}$ is the linear mapping represented by the Jacobian matrix $\mathtt{J} = \partial\mathbf{f}/\partial\mathbf{P}$. We seek a point $\mathbf{f}(\mathbf{P}_1)$, with $\mathbf{P}_1 = \mathbf{P}_0 + \boldsymbol{\Delta}$, which minimizes $\mathbf{f}(\mathbf{P}_1) - \mathbf{X} = \mathbf{f}(\mathbf{P}_0) + \mathtt{J}\boldsymbol{\Delta} - \mathbf{X} = \boldsymbol{\epsilon}_0 + \mathtt{J}\boldsymbol{\Delta}$. Thus, it is required to minimize $\|\boldsymbol{\epsilon}_0 + \mathtt{J}\boldsymbol{\Delta}\|$ over $\boldsymbol{\Delta}$, which is a linear minimization problem. The vector $\boldsymbol{\Delta}$ is obtained by solving the *normal* equations (see (A5.2))

$$\mathtt{J}^\mathsf{T}\mathtt{J}\boldsymbol{\Delta} = -\mathtt{J}^\mathsf{T}\boldsymbol{\epsilon}_0 \tag{A6.1}$$

or by using the pseudo-inverse $\boldsymbol{\Delta} = -\mathtt{J}^+\boldsymbol{\epsilon}_0$. Thus, the solution vector $\widehat{\mathbf{P}}$ is obtained by starting with an estimate $\mathbf{P}_0$ and computing successive approximations according to the formula

$$\mathbf{P}_{i+1} = \mathbf{P}_i + \boldsymbol{\Delta}_i$$

where $\boldsymbol{\Delta}_i$ is the solution to the linear least-squares problem

$$\mathtt{J}\boldsymbol{\Delta}_i = -\boldsymbol{\epsilon}_i.$$

Matrix $\mathtt{J}$ is the Jacobian $\partial\mathbf{f}/\partial\mathbf{P}$ evaluated at $\mathbf{P}_i$ and $\boldsymbol{\epsilon}_i = \mathbf{f}(\mathbf{P}_i) - \mathbf{X}$. One hopes that this algorithm will converge to the required least-squares solution $\widehat{\mathbf{P}}$. Unfortunately, it is possible that this iteration procedure converges to a local minimum value, or does not converge at all. The behaviour of the iteration algorithm depends very strongly on the initial estimate $\mathbf{P}_0$.

Weighted iteration. As an alternative to all the dependent variables being equally weighted it is possible to provide a weight matrix specifying the weights of the dependent variables $\mathbf{X}$. To be more precise, one may assume that the measurement $\mathbf{X}$ satisfies a Gaussian distribution with covariance matrix $\Sigma_\mathbf{X}$, and one wishes to minimize the Mahalanobis distance $\|\mathbf{f}(\widehat{\mathbf{P}}) - \mathbf{X}\|_\Sigma$. This covariance matrix may be diagonal, specifying that the individual coordinates of $\mathbf{X}$ are independent, or more generally it may be an arbitrary symmetric and positive definite matrix. In this case, the normal equations become $\mathtt{J}^\mathsf{T}\Sigma^{-1}\mathtt{J}\boldsymbol{\Delta}_i = -\mathtt{J}^\mathsf{T}\Sigma^{-1}\boldsymbol{\epsilon}_i$. The rest of thc algorithm remains unchanged.

Newton's method and the Hessian. We pass now to consideration of finding minima of functions of many variables. For the present, we consider an arbitrary scalar-valued function $g(\mathbf{P})$ where $\mathbf{P}$ is a vector. The optimization problem is simply to minimize $g(\mathbf{P})$ over all values of $\mathbf{P}$. We make two assumptions: that $g(\mathbf{P})$ has a well-defined minimum value, and that we know a point $\mathbf{P}_0$ reasonably close to this minimum.

We may expand $g(\mathbf{P})$ about $\mathbf{P}_0$ in a Taylor series to get

$$g(\mathbf{P}_0 + \boldsymbol{\Delta}) = g + g_\mathbf{P}\boldsymbol{\Delta} + \boldsymbol{\Delta}^\mathsf{T} g_{\mathbf{PP}}\boldsymbol{\Delta}/2 + \ldots$$

where subscript $\mathbf{P}$ denotes differentiation, and the right hand side is evaluated at $\mathbf{P}_0$.

We wish to minimize this quantity with respect to $\mathbf{\Delta}$. To this end, we differentiate with respect to $\mathbf{\Delta}$ and set the derivative to zero, arriving at the equation $g_{\mathbf{P}} + g_{\mathbf{PP}}\mathbf{\Delta} = 0$ or

$$g_{\mathbf{PP}}\mathbf{\Delta} = -g_{\mathbf{P}}. \tag{A6.2}$$

In this equation, $g_{\mathbf{PP}}$ is the matrix of second derivatives, the *Hessian* of g, the (i, j)-th entry of which is $\partial^2 g/\partial p_i \partial p_j$, and p_i and p_j are the i-th and j-th parameters. Vector $g_{\mathbf{P}}$ is the gradient of g. The method of *Newton iteration* consists in starting at an initial value of the parameters, $\mathbf{P}_0$, and iteratively computing parameter increments $\mathbf{\Delta}$ using (A6.2) until convergence occurs.

Now we turn to the sort of cost function that arises in the least-squares minimization problem considered above. Specifically, $g(\mathbf{P})$ is the squared norm of an error function

$$g(\mathbf{P}) = \frac{1}{2}\|\boldsymbol{\epsilon}(\mathbf{P})\|^2 = \boldsymbol{\epsilon}(\mathbf{P})^\mathsf{T}\boldsymbol{\epsilon}(\mathbf{P})/2$$

where $\boldsymbol{\epsilon}(\mathbf{P})$ is a vector-valued function of the parameter vector $\mathbf{P}$. In particular, $\boldsymbol{\epsilon}(\mathbf{P}) = \mathbf{f}(\mathbf{P}) - \mathbf{X}$. The factor $1/2$ is present for simplifying the succeeding computations.

The gradient vector $g_{\mathbf{P}}$ is easily computed to be $\boldsymbol{\epsilon}_{\mathbf{P}}^\mathsf{T}\boldsymbol{\epsilon}$. However, we may write $\boldsymbol{\epsilon}_{\mathbf{P}} = \mathbf{f}_{\mathbf{P}} = \mathtt{J}$ using the notation introduced previously. In short $g_{\mathbf{P}} = \mathtt{J}^\mathsf{T}\boldsymbol{\epsilon}$. Differentiating $g_{\mathbf{P}} = \boldsymbol{\epsilon}_{\mathbf{P}}^\mathsf{T}\boldsymbol{\epsilon}$ a second time, we compute the following formula for the Hessian.[1]

$$g_{\mathbf{PP}} = \boldsymbol{\epsilon}_{\mathbf{P}}^\mathsf{T}\boldsymbol{\epsilon}_{\mathbf{P}} + \boldsymbol{\epsilon}_{\mathbf{PP}}^\mathsf{T}\boldsymbol{\epsilon}. \tag{A6.3}$$

Now, under the assumption that $\mathbf{f}(\mathbf{P})$ is linear, the second term on the right vanishes, leaving $g_{\mathbf{PP}} = \boldsymbol{\epsilon}_{\mathbf{P}}^\mathsf{T}\boldsymbol{\epsilon}_{\mathbf{P}} = \mathtt{J}^\mathsf{T}\mathtt{J}$. Now, substituting for the gradient and Hessian in (A6.2) yields $\mathtt{J}^\mathsf{T}\mathtt{J}\mathbf{\Delta} = -\mathtt{J}^\mathsf{T}\boldsymbol{\epsilon}$ which is nothing more than the normal equations (A6.1). Thus we have arrived at the same iterative procedure as previously solving the parameter estimation problem, under the assumption that $\mathtt{J}^\mathsf{T}\mathtt{J} = \boldsymbol{\epsilon}_{\mathbf{P}}^\mathsf{T}\boldsymbol{\epsilon}_{\mathbf{P}}$ is a reasonable approximation for the Hessian of the function $g(\mathbf{P})$. This procedure in which $\mathtt{J}^\mathsf{T}\mathtt{J}$ is used as an approximation for the Hessian is known as the *Gauss-Newton* method.

Gradient descent. The negative (or down-hill) gradient vector $-g_{\mathbf{P}} = -\boldsymbol{\epsilon}_{\mathbf{P}}^\mathsf{T}\boldsymbol{\epsilon}$ defines the direction of most rapid decrease of the cost function. A strategy for minimization of g is to move iteratively in the gradient direction. This is known as *gradient descent*. The length of the step may be computed by carrying out a line search for the function minimum in the negative gradient direction. In this case, the parameter increment $\mathbf{\Delta}$ is computed from the equation $\lambda\mathbf{\Delta} = -g_{\mathbf{P}}$, where λ controls the length of the step.

We may consider this as related to Newton iteration as expressed by the update equation (A6.2) in which the Hessian is approximated (somewhat arbitrarily) by the scalar matrix $\lambda\mathtt{I}$. Gradient descent by itself is not a very good minimization strategy, typically characterized by slow convergence due to zig-zagging. (See [Press-88] for a closer analysis.) It will be seen in the next section, however, that it can be useful in conjunction with Gauss-Newton iteration as a way of getting out of tight corners. The

[1] The last term in this formula needs some clarification. Since $\boldsymbol{\epsilon}$ is a vector, $\boldsymbol{\epsilon}_{\mathbf{PP}}$ is a 3-dimensional array (a tensor). The sum implied by the product $\boldsymbol{\epsilon}_{\mathbf{PP}}^\mathsf{T}\boldsymbol{\epsilon}$ is over the components of $\boldsymbol{\epsilon}$. It may be written more precisely as $\sum_i (\epsilon_i)_{\mathbf{PP}}\epsilon_i$ where ϵ_i is the i-th components of the vector $\boldsymbol{\epsilon}$, and $(\epsilon_i)_{\mathbf{PP}}$ is its Hessian.

Levenberg–Marquardt method is essentially a Gauss-Newton method that transitions smoothly to gradient descent when the Gauss-Newton updates fail.

To summarize, we have so far considered three methods of minimization of a cost function $g(\mathbf{P}) = \|\boldsymbol{\epsilon}(\mathbf{P})\|^2/2$:

(i) **Newton.** Update equation:

$$g_{\mathbf{PP}}\boldsymbol{\Delta} = -g_{\mathbf{P}}$$

where $g_{\mathbf{PP}} = \boldsymbol{\epsilon}_{\mathbf{P}}^{\mathsf{T}}\boldsymbol{\epsilon}_{\mathbf{P}} + \boldsymbol{\epsilon}_{\mathbf{PP}}^{\mathsf{T}}\boldsymbol{\epsilon}$ and $g_{\mathbf{P}} = \boldsymbol{\epsilon}_{\mathbf{P}}^{\mathsf{T}}\boldsymbol{\epsilon}$. Newton iteration is based on the assumption of an approximately quadratic cost function near the minimum, and will show rapid convergence if this condition is met. The disadvantage of this approach is that the computation of the Hessian may be difficult. In addition, far from the minimum the assumption of quadratic behaviour is probably invalid, so a lot of extra work is done with little benefit.

(ii) **Gauss-Newton.** Update equation:

$$\boldsymbol{\epsilon}_{\mathbf{P}}^{\mathsf{T}}\boldsymbol{\epsilon}_{\mathbf{P}}\boldsymbol{\Delta} = -\boldsymbol{\epsilon}_{\mathbf{P}}^{\mathsf{T}}\boldsymbol{\epsilon}$$

This is equivalent to Newton iteration in which the Hessian is approximated by $\boldsymbol{\epsilon}_{\mathbf{P}}^{\mathsf{T}}\boldsymbol{\epsilon}_{\mathbf{P}}$. Generally this is a good approximation, particularly close to a minimum, or when $\boldsymbol{\epsilon}$ is nearly linear in $\mathbf{P}$.

(iii) **Gradient descent.** Update equation:

$$\lambda\boldsymbol{\Delta} = -\boldsymbol{\epsilon}_{\mathbf{P}}^{\mathsf{T}}\boldsymbol{\epsilon} = -g_{\mathbf{P}}.$$

The Hessian in Newton iteration is replaced by a multiple of the identity matrix. Each update is in the direction of most rapid local decrease of the function value. The value of λ may be chosen adaptively, or by a line search in the downward gradient direction. Generally, gradient descent by itself is not recommended, but in conjunction with Gauss-Newton it yields the commonly used Levenberg–Marquardt method.

A6.2 Levenberg–Marquardt iteration

The Levenberg–Marquardt (abbreviated LM) iteration method is a slight variation on the Gauss-Newton iteration method. The normal equations $\mathtt{J}^{\mathsf{T}}\mathtt{J}\boldsymbol{\Delta} = -\mathtt{J}^{\mathsf{T}}\boldsymbol{\epsilon}$ are replaced by the *augmented normal equations* $(\mathtt{J}^{\mathsf{T}}\mathtt{J} + \lambda\mathtt{I})\boldsymbol{\Delta} = -\mathtt{J}^{\mathsf{T}}\boldsymbol{\epsilon}$, for some value of λ that varies from iteration to iteration. Here $\mathtt{I}$ is the identity matrix. A typical initial value of λ is 10^{-3} times the average of the diagonal elements of $\mathtt{N} = \mathtt{J}^{\mathsf{T}}\mathtt{J}$.

If the value of $\boldsymbol{\Delta}$ obtained by solving the augmented normal equations leads to a reduction in the error, then the increment is accepted and λ is divided by a factor (typically 10) before the next iteration. On the other hand if the value $\boldsymbol{\Delta}$ leads to an increased error, then λ is multiplied by the same factor and the augmented normal equations are solved again, this process continuing until a value of $\boldsymbol{\Delta}$ is found that gives rise to a decreased error. This process of repeatedly solving the augmented normal equations for different values of λ until an acceptable $\boldsymbol{\Delta}$ is found constitutes one iteration of the LM algorithm. An implementation of the LM algorithm is given in [Press-88].

Justification of LM. To understand the reasoning behind this method, consider what happens for different values of λ. When λ is very small, the method is essentially the same as Gauss-Newton iteration. If the error function $\|\boldsymbol{\epsilon}\|^2 = \|\mathbf{f}(\mathbf{P}) - \mathbf{X}\|^2$ is close to being quadratic in $\mathbf{P}$, then this method will converge fast to the minimum value. On the other hand when λ is large then the normal equation matrix is approximated by $\lambda\mathtt{I}$, and the normal equations become $\lambda\boldsymbol{\Delta} = -\mathtt{J}^\mathsf{T}\boldsymbol{\epsilon}$. Recalling that $\mathtt{J}^\mathsf{T}\boldsymbol{\epsilon}$ is simply the gradient vector of $\|\boldsymbol{\epsilon}\|^2$, we see that the direction of the parameter increment $\boldsymbol{\Delta}$ approaches that given by gradient descent. Thus, the LM algorithm moves seamlessly between Gauss-Newton iteration, which will cause rapid convergence in the neighbourhood of the solution, and a gradient descent approach, which will guarantee a decrease in the cost function when the going is difficult. Indeed, as λ becomes larger and larger, the length of the increment step $\boldsymbol{\Delta}$ decreases and eventually it will lead to a decrease of the cost function $\|\boldsymbol{\epsilon}\|^2$.

To demonstrate that the parameter increment $\boldsymbol{\Delta}$ obtained by solving the augmented normal equations for all values of λ is in the direction of decreasing cost, we will show that the inner product of $\boldsymbol{\Delta}$ and the negative gradient direction for the function $g(\mathbf{P}) = \|\boldsymbol{\epsilon}(\mathbf{P})\|^2$ is positive. This results from the following computation.

$$\begin{aligned} -g_\mathbf{P} \cdot \boldsymbol{\Delta} &= -g_\mathbf{P}^\mathsf{T}\boldsymbol{\Delta} \\ &= (\mathtt{J}^\mathsf{T}\boldsymbol{\epsilon})^\mathsf{T}(\mathtt{J}^\mathsf{T}\mathtt{J} + \lambda\mathtt{I})^{-1}\mathtt{J}^\mathsf{T}\boldsymbol{\epsilon} \end{aligned}$$

However, $\mathtt{J}^\mathsf{T}\mathtt{J} + \lambda\mathtt{I}$ is positive-definite for any value of λ, and so therefore is its inverse. By definition, this means that $(\mathtt{J}^\mathsf{T}\boldsymbol{\epsilon})^\mathsf{T}(\mathtt{J}^\mathsf{T}\mathtt{J} + \lambda\mathtt{I})^{-1}\mathtt{J}^\mathsf{T}\boldsymbol{\epsilon}$ is positive, unless $\mathtt{J}^\mathsf{T}\boldsymbol{\epsilon}$ is zero. Thus, the increment $\boldsymbol{\Delta}$ is in a direction of locally decreasing cost, unless of course the gradient $\mathtt{J}^\mathsf{T}\boldsymbol{\epsilon}$ is zero.

A different augmentation. In some implementations of Levenberg-Marquardt, notably that given in [Press-88], a different method of augmenting the normal equations is used. The augmented normal equation matrix $\mathtt{N}'$ is defined in terms of the matrix $\mathtt{N} = \mathtt{J}^\mathsf{T}\mathtt{J}$ by $\mathtt{N}'_{ii} = (1 + \lambda)\mathtt{N}_{ii}$ and $\mathtt{N}'_{ij} = \mathtt{N}_{ij}$ for $i \neq j$. Thus the diagonal of $\mathtt{N}$ is augmented by a multiplicative factor $(1 + \lambda)$ instead of an additive factor. As before, a small value of λ, results essentially in a Gauss-Newton update. For large λ, the off-diagonal entries of the normal equation matrix become insignificant with respect to the diagonal ones.

The i-th diagonal entry of $\mathtt{N}'$ is simply $(1 + \lambda)\mathbf{J}_i^\mathsf{T}\mathbf{J}_i$ where $\mathbf{J}_i = \partial\mathbf{f}/\partial p_i$, and p_i is the i-th parameter. The update equation is then $(1 + \lambda)\mathbf{J}_i^\mathsf{T}\mathbf{J}_i\delta_i = \mathbf{J}_i^\mathsf{T}\boldsymbol{\epsilon}$ where δ_i is the increment in the i-th parameter. Apart from the factor $(1 + \lambda)$, this is the normal equation that would result from minimizing the cost by varying only the i-th parameter δ_i. Thus, in the limit as λ becomes large, the increment to the parameters is the direction that would result from minimizing each one separately.

With this sort of augmentation, the parameter increments for large λ are not the same as for gradient descent. Nevertheless, the same analysis as before shows that the resulting increment is still in the down-hill direction for any value of λ.

One small problem may arise: if some parameter p_i has no effect on the value of the function $\mathbf{f}$, then $\mathbf{J}_i = \partial\mathbf{f}/\partial p_i$ is zero, and the i-th diagonal entry of $\mathtt{N}$ and hence $\mathtt{N}'$

is zero. The augmented normal equation matrix $\mathtt{N}'$ is then singular, which can cause trouble. In practice, this is a rare occurrence, but it can occur.

Implementation of LM. To carry out Levenberg–Marquardt minimization in its simplest form it is necessary only to provide a routine to compute the function being minimized, a goal vector $\widehat{\mathbf{X}}$ of observed or desired values of the function, and an initial estimate $\mathbf{P}_0$. Computation of the Jacobian matrix $\mathtt{J}$ may be carried out either numerically, or by providing a custom routine.

Numerical differentiation may be carried out as follows. Each independent variable x_i is incremented in turn to $x_i + \delta$, the resulting function value is computed using the routine provided for computing f and the derivative is computed as a ratio. Good results have been found by setting the value δ to the maximum of $|10^{-4} \times x_i|$ and 10^{-6}. This choice seemingly gives a good approximation to the derivative. In practice, there seems to be little disadvantage in using numerical differentiation, though for simple functions f one may prefer to provide a routine to compute $\mathtt{J}$, partly for aesthetic reasons, partly because of a possible slightly improved convergence and partly for speed.

A6.3 A sparse Levenberg–Marquardt algorithm

The LM algorithm as described above in section A6.2 is quite suitable for minimization with respect to a small number of parameters. Thus, in the case of 2D homography estimation (see chapter 4), for the simple cost functions (4.6–*p*94) and (4.7–*p*95) which are minimized with respect only to the entries of the homography matrix $\mathtt{H}$ the LM algorithm works well. However, for minimizing cost functions with respect to large numbers of parameters, the bare LM algorithm is not very suitable. This is because the central step of the LM algorithm, the solution of the normal equations (A5.2), has complexity N^3 in the number of parameters, and this step is repeated many times. However, in solving many estimation problems of the type considered in this book, the normal equation matrix has a certain sparse block structure that one may take advantage of to realize very great time savings.

An example of the situation in which this method is useful is the problem of estimating a 2D homography between two views assuming errors in both images, by minimizing the cost function (4.8–*p*95). This problem may be parametrized in terms of a set of parameters characterizing the 2D homography (perhaps the 9 entries of the homography matrix), plus parameters for each of the n points in the first view, a total of $2n + 9$ parameters.

Another instance where these methods are useful is the reconstruction problem in which one has image correspondences across two or more (let us say m) views and one wishes to estimate the camera parameters of all the cameras and also the 3D positions of all the points. One can assume arbitrary projective cameras or fully or partially calibrated cameras. Furthermore, to remove some of the incidental degrees of freedom one can fix one of the cameras. For instance in the projective reconstruction problem, the problem may be parametrized by the entries of all the camera matrices (a total of $12m$ or $11m$ parameters depending on how the cameras are parametrized), plus a set of $3n$ parameters for the coordinates of the 3D points.

The sparse LM algorithm is often perceived as complex and difficult to implement. To help overcome this, the algorithms are given cook-book style. Given a suitable library of standard matrix manipulation routines, a reader should be able to implement the algorithm without difficulty.

- **Notation:** *If* $\mathbf{a}_1, \mathbf{a}_2, \ldots, \mathbf{a}_n$ *are vectors, then the vector obtained by placing them one after the other in a single column vector is denoted by* $(\mathbf{a}_1^\mathsf{T}, \mathbf{a}_2^\mathsf{T}, \ldots, \mathbf{a}_n^\mathsf{T})^\mathsf{T}$. *A similar notation is used for matrices.*

A6.3.1 Partitioning the parameters in the LM method

The sparse LM method will be described primarily in terms of the reconstruction problem, since this is the archetypal problem to which this method relates. The estimation problem will be treated in general terms first of all, since this will illuminate the general approach without excessive detail. At this level of abstraction, the benefits of this approach may not be apparent, but they will become clearer in section A6.3.3. We start with the simple observation that the set of parameters in this problem may be divided up into two sets: a set of parameters describing the cameras, and a set of parameters describing the points. More formally, the "parameter vector" $\mathbf{P} \in \mathbb{R}^M$ may be partitioned into parameter vectors $\mathbf{a}$ and $\mathbf{b}$ so that $\mathbf{P} = (\mathbf{a}^\mathsf{T}, \mathbf{b}^\mathsf{T})^\mathsf{T}$. We are given a "measurement vector", denoted by $\mathbf{X}$ in a space $\mathbb{R}^N$. In the reconstruction problem, this consists of the vector of all image point coordinates. In addition let $\Sigma_\mathbf{X}$ be the covariance matrix for the measurement vector.[1] We consider a general function $f : \mathbb{R}^M \rightarrow \mathbb{R}^N$ taking the parameter vector $\mathbf{P}$ to the estimated measurement vector $\widehat{\mathbf{X}} = f(\mathbf{P})$. Denoting by $\boldsymbol{\epsilon}$ the difference $\mathbf{X} - \widehat{\mathbf{X}}$ between the measured and estimated quantities, one seeks the set of parameters that minimize the squared Mahalanobis distance $\|\boldsymbol{\epsilon}\|^2_{\Sigma_\mathbf{X}} = \boldsymbol{\epsilon}^\mathsf{T}\Sigma_\mathbf{X}^{-1}\boldsymbol{\epsilon}$.

Corresponding to the division of parameters $\mathbf{P} = (\mathbf{a}^\mathsf{T}, \mathbf{b}^\mathsf{T})^\mathsf{T}$, the Jacobian matrix $\mathtt{J} = [\partial\widehat{\mathbf{X}}/\partial\mathbf{P}]$ has a block structure of the form $\mathtt{J} = [\mathtt{A}|\mathtt{B}]$, where Jacobian submatrices are defined by

$$\mathtt{A} = \left[\partial\widehat{\mathbf{X}}/\partial\mathbf{a}\right]$$

and

$$\mathtt{B} = \left[\partial\widehat{\mathbf{X}}/\partial\mathbf{b}\right].$$

The set of equations $\mathtt{J}\boldsymbol{\delta} = \boldsymbol{\epsilon}$ solved as the central step in the LM algorithm (see section A6.2) now has the form

$$\mathtt{J}\boldsymbol{\delta} = [\mathtt{A}|\mathtt{B}]\begin{pmatrix}\boldsymbol{\delta}_\mathbf{a} \\ \hline \boldsymbol{\delta}_\mathbf{b}\end{pmatrix} = \boldsymbol{\epsilon}. \qquad \text{(A6.4)}$$

Then, the normal equations $\mathtt{J}^\mathsf{T}\Sigma_\mathbf{X}^{-1}\mathtt{J}\boldsymbol{\delta} = \mathtt{J}^\mathsf{T}\Sigma_\mathbf{X}^{-1}\boldsymbol{\epsilon}$ to be solved at each step of the LM algorithm are of the form

$$\left[\begin{array}{c|c}\mathtt{A}^\mathsf{T}\Sigma_\mathbf{X}^{-1}\mathtt{A} & \mathtt{A}^\mathsf{T}\Sigma_\mathbf{X}^{-1}\mathtt{B} \\ \hline \mathtt{B}^\mathsf{T}\Sigma_\mathbf{X}^{-1}\mathtt{A} & \mathtt{B}^\mathsf{T}\Sigma_\mathbf{X}^{-1}\mathtt{B}\end{array}\right]\begin{pmatrix}\boldsymbol{\delta}_\mathbf{a} \\ \hline \boldsymbol{\delta}_\mathbf{b}\end{pmatrix} = \begin{pmatrix}\mathtt{A}^\mathsf{T}\Sigma_\mathbf{X}^{-1}\boldsymbol{\epsilon} \\ \hline \mathtt{B}^\mathsf{T}\Sigma_\mathbf{X}^{-1}\boldsymbol{\epsilon}\end{pmatrix}. \qquad \text{(A6.5)}$$

[1] In the absence of other knowledge, one usually assumes that $\Sigma_\mathbf{X}$ is the identity matrix.

At this point in the LM algorithm the diagonal blocks of this matrix are augmented by multiplying their diagonal entries by a factor $1 + \lambda$, for the varying parameter λ. This augmentation alters the matrices $\mathtt{A}^\mathsf{T}\Sigma_{\mathbf{X}}^{-1}\mathtt{A}$ and $\mathtt{B}^\mathsf{T}\Sigma_{\mathbf{X}}^{-1}\mathtt{B}$. The resulting matrices will be denoted by $(\mathtt{A}^\mathsf{T}\Sigma_{\mathbf{X}}^{-1}\mathtt{A})^*$ and $(\mathtt{B}^\mathsf{T}\Sigma_{\mathbf{X}}^{-1}\mathtt{B})^*$. The reader may wish to look ahead to figure A6.1 and figure A6.2 which shows graphically the form of the Jacobian and normal equations in an estimation problem involving several cameras and points.

The set of equations (A6.5) may now be written in block form as

$$\begin{bmatrix} \mathtt{U}^* & \mathtt{W} \\ \mathtt{W}^\mathsf{T} & \mathtt{V}^* \end{bmatrix} \begin{pmatrix} \boldsymbol{\delta}_\mathbf{a} \\ \boldsymbol{\delta}_\mathbf{b} \end{pmatrix} = \begin{pmatrix} \boldsymbol{\epsilon}_\mathtt{A} \\ \boldsymbol{\epsilon}_\mathtt{B} \end{pmatrix}. \tag{A6.6}$$

As a first step to solving these equations, both sides are now multiplied on the left by $\begin{bmatrix} \mathtt{I} & -\mathtt{W}\mathtt{V}^{*-1} \\ 0 & \mathtt{I} \end{bmatrix}$ resulting in

$$\begin{bmatrix} \mathtt{U}^* - \mathtt{W}\mathtt{V}^{*-1}\mathtt{W}^\mathsf{T} & 0 \\ \mathtt{W}^\mathsf{T} & \mathtt{V}^* \end{bmatrix} \begin{pmatrix} \boldsymbol{\delta}_\mathbf{a} \\ \boldsymbol{\delta}_\mathbf{b} \end{pmatrix} = \begin{pmatrix} \boldsymbol{\epsilon}_\mathtt{A} - \mathtt{W}\mathtt{V}^{*-1}\boldsymbol{\epsilon}_\mathtt{B} \\ \boldsymbol{\epsilon}_\mathtt{B} \end{pmatrix}. \tag{A6.7}$$

This results in the elimination of the top right hand block. The top half of this set of equations is

$$(\mathtt{U}^* - \mathtt{W}\mathtt{V}^{*-1}\mathtt{W}^\mathsf{T})\boldsymbol{\delta}_\mathbf{a} = \boldsymbol{\epsilon}_\mathtt{A} - \mathtt{W}\mathtt{V}^{*-1}\boldsymbol{\epsilon}_\mathtt{B}. \tag{A6.8}$$

These equations may be solved to find $\delta_\mathbf{a}$. Subsequently, the value of $\delta_\mathbf{b}$ may be found by back-substitution, giving

$$\mathtt{V}^*\delta_\mathbf{b} = \boldsymbol{\epsilon}_\mathtt{B} - \mathtt{W}^\mathsf{T}\boldsymbol{\delta}_\mathbf{a}. \tag{A6.9}$$

As in section A6.2, if the newly computed value of the parameter vector $\mathbf{P} = ((\mathbf{a} + \delta_\mathbf{a})^\mathsf{T}, (\mathbf{b} + \delta_\mathbf{b})^\mathsf{T})^\mathsf{T}$ results in a diminished value of the error function, then one accepts the new parameter vector $\mathbf{P}$, diminishes the value of λ by a factor of 10, and proceeds to the next iteration. On the other hand if the error value is increased, then one rejects the new $\mathbf{P}$ and tries again with a new value of λ, increased by a factor of 10.

The complete partitioned Levenberg–Marquardt algorithm is given in algorithm A6.1.

Although in this method we solve first for $\boldsymbol{\delta}_\mathbf{a}$ and subsequently for $\boldsymbol{\delta}_\mathbf{b}$ based on the new value of $\mathbf{a}$, it should not be thought that the method amounts to no more than independent iterations over $\mathbf{a}$ and $\mathbf{b}$. If one were to solve for $\mathbf{a}$ holding $\mathbf{b}$ constant, then the normal equations used to solve for $\boldsymbol{\delta}_\mathbf{a}$ would take the simpler form $\mathtt{U}\boldsymbol{\delta}_\mathbf{a} = \boldsymbol{\epsilon}_\mathtt{A}$, compared with (A6.8). The method of alternating between solving for $\boldsymbol{\delta}_\mathbf{a}$ and $\boldsymbol{\delta}_\mathbf{b}$ is not recommended, however, because of potential slow convergence.

A6.3.2 Covariance

It was seen in result 5.12(*p*144) that the covariance matrix of the estimated parameters is given by

$$\Sigma_\mathbf{P} = (\mathtt{J}^\mathsf{T}\Sigma_{\mathbf{X}}^{-1}\mathtt{J})^+. \tag{A6.10}$$

Given A vector of measurements $\mathbf{X}$ with covariance matrix $\Sigma_{\mathbf{X}}$, an initial estimate of a set of parameters $\mathbf{P} = (\mathbf{a}^\mathsf{T}, \mathbf{b}^\mathsf{T})^\mathsf{T}$ and a function $f : \mathbf{P} \mapsto \widehat{\mathbf{X}}$ taking the parameter vector to an estimate of the measurement vector.

Objective Find the set of parameters $\mathbf{P}$ that minimizes $\epsilon^\mathsf{T}\Sigma_{\mathbf{X}}^{-1}\epsilon$ where $\epsilon = \mathbf{X} - \widehat{\mathbf{X}}$.

Algorithm

(i) Initialize a constant $\lambda = 0.001$ (typical value).

(ii) Compute the derivative matrices $\mathtt{A} = [\partial\widehat{\mathbf{X}}/\partial\mathbf{a}]$ and $\mathtt{B} = [\partial\widehat{\mathbf{X}}/\partial\mathbf{b}]$ and the error vector ϵ.

(iii) Compute intermediate expressions

$$\mathtt{U} = \mathtt{A}^\mathsf{T}\Sigma_{\mathbf{X}}^{-1}\mathtt{A} \quad \mathtt{V} = \mathtt{B}^\mathsf{T}\Sigma_{\mathbf{X}}^{-1}\mathtt{B} \quad \mathtt{W} = \mathtt{A}^\mathsf{T}\Sigma_{\mathbf{X}}^{-1}\mathtt{B}$$

$$\epsilon_\mathtt{A} = \mathtt{A}^\mathsf{T}\Sigma_{\mathbf{X}}^{-1}\epsilon \quad \epsilon_\mathtt{B} = \mathtt{B}^\mathsf{T}\Sigma_{\mathbf{X}}^{-1}\epsilon$$

(iv) Augment $\mathtt{U}$ and $\mathtt{V}$ by multiplying their diagonal elements by $1 + \lambda$.

(v) Compute the inverse $\mathtt{V}^{*-1}$, and define $\mathtt{Y} = \mathtt{W}\mathtt{V}^{*-1}$. The inverse may overwrite the value of $\mathtt{V}^*$ which will not be needed again.

(vi) Find $\boldsymbol{\delta}_\mathbf{a}$ by solving $(\mathtt{U}^* - \mathtt{Y}\mathtt{W}^\mathsf{T})\boldsymbol{\delta}_\mathbf{a} = \epsilon_\mathtt{A} - \mathtt{Y}\epsilon_\mathtt{B}$.

(vii) Find $\boldsymbol{\delta}_\mathbf{b}$ by back-substitution: $\delta_\mathbf{b} = \mathtt{V}^{*-1}(\epsilon_\mathtt{B} - \mathtt{W}^\mathsf{T}\boldsymbol{\delta}_\mathbf{a})$.

(viii) Update the parameter vector by adding the incremental vector $(\boldsymbol{\delta}_\mathbf{a}^\mathsf{T}, \boldsymbol{\delta}_\mathbf{b}^\mathsf{T})^\mathsf{T}$ and compute the new error vector.

(ix) If the new error is less than the old error, then accept the new values of the parameters, diminish the value of λ by a factor of 10, and start again at step (ii), or else terminate.

(x) If the new error is greater than the old error, then revert to the old parameter values, increase the value of λ by a factor of 10, and try again from step (iv).

Algorithm A6.1. *A partitioned Levenberg–Marquardt algorithm.*

In the over-parametrized case, the covariance matrix $\Sigma_\mathbf{P}$ given by (A6.10) is singular, and in particular, no variation in the parameters is allowed in directions perpendicular to the constraint surface – the variance is zero in these directions.

In the case where the parameter set is partitioned as $\mathtt{P} = (\mathbf{a}^\mathsf{T}, \mathbf{b}^\mathsf{T})^\mathsf{T}$, matrix $(\mathtt{J}^\mathsf{T}\Sigma_{\mathbf{X}}^{-1}\mathtt{J})$ has the block form given in (A6.5) and (A6.6) (but without augmentation, represented by stars). Thus we may write

$$\mathtt{J}^\mathsf{T}\Sigma_{\mathbf{X}}^{-1}\mathtt{J} = \begin{bmatrix} \mathtt{A}^\mathsf{T}\Sigma_{\mathbf{X}}^{-1}\mathtt{A} & \mathtt{A}^\mathsf{T}\Sigma_{\mathbf{X}}^{-1}\mathtt{B} \\ \mathtt{B}^\mathsf{T}\Sigma_{\mathbf{X}}^{-1}\mathtt{A} & \mathtt{B}^\mathsf{T}\Sigma_{\mathbf{X}}^{-1}\mathtt{B} \end{bmatrix} = \begin{bmatrix} \mathtt{U} & \mathtt{W} \\ \mathtt{W}^\mathsf{T} & \mathtt{V} \end{bmatrix}. \qquad \text{(A6.11)}$$

The covariance matrix $\Sigma_\mathbf{P}$ is the pseudo-inverse of this matrix. Under the assumption that $\mathtt{V}$ is invertible, redefine $\mathtt{Y} = \mathtt{W}\mathtt{V}^{-1}$. Then the matrix may be diagonalized according to

$$\mathtt{J}^\mathsf{T}\Sigma_{\mathbf{X}}^{-1}\mathtt{J} = \begin{bmatrix} \mathtt{U} & \mathtt{W} \\ \mathtt{W}^\mathsf{T} & \mathtt{V} \end{bmatrix} = \begin{bmatrix} \mathtt{I} & \mathtt{Y} \\ 0 & \mathtt{I} \end{bmatrix} \begin{bmatrix} \mathtt{U} - \mathtt{W}\mathtt{V}^{-1}\mathtt{W}^\mathsf{T} & 0 \\ 0 & \mathtt{V} \end{bmatrix} \begin{bmatrix} \mathtt{I} & 0 \\ \mathtt{Y}^\mathsf{T} & \mathtt{I} \end{bmatrix} \qquad \text{(A6.12)}$$

For matrices $\mathtt{G}$ and $\mathtt{H}$ with $\mathtt{G}$ invertible, we assume an identity

$$(\mathtt{G}\mathtt{H}\mathtt{G}^\mathsf{T})^+ = \mathtt{G}^{-\mathsf{T}}\mathtt{H}^+\mathtt{G}^{-1}$$

This identity is valid under conditions explored in the exercise at the end of this ap-

Objective Compute the covariance of the parameters $\mathbf{a}$ and $\mathbf{b}$ estimated using algorithm A6.1.

Algorithm

(i) Compute matrices $\mathtt{U}$, $\mathtt{V}$ and $\mathtt{W}$ as in algorithm A6.1, and also $\mathtt{Y} = \mathtt{W}\mathtt{V}^{-1}$.
(ii) $\Sigma_{\mathbf{a}} = (\mathtt{U} - \mathtt{W}\mathtt{V}^{-1}\mathtt{W}^{\mathsf{T}})^{+}$.
(iii) $\Sigma_{\mathbf{b}} = \mathtt{Y}^{\mathsf{T}}\Sigma_{\mathbf{a}}\mathtt{Y} + \mathtt{V}^{-1}$
(iv) The cross-covariance $\Sigma_{\mathbf{ab}} = -\Sigma_{\mathbf{a}}\mathtt{Y}$.

Algorithm A6.2. *Computation of the covariance matrix of the LM parameters.*

pendix. Applying this to (A6.12) and multiplying out provides a formula for the pseudo inverse

$$\Sigma_{\mathbf{P}} = (\mathtt{J}^{\mathsf{T}}\Sigma_{\mathbf{X}}^{-1}\mathtt{J})^{+} = \begin{bmatrix} \mathtt{X} & -\mathtt{X}\mathtt{Y} \\ -\mathtt{Y}^{\mathsf{T}}\mathtt{X} & \mathtt{Y}^{\mathsf{T}}\mathtt{X}\mathtt{Y} + \mathtt{V}^{-1} \end{bmatrix} \tag{A6.13}$$

where $\mathtt{X} = (\mathtt{U} - \mathtt{W}\mathtt{V}^{-1}\mathtt{W}^{\mathsf{T}})^{+}$.

The condition for this to be true is that $\text{span}(\mathtt{A}) \cap \text{span}(\mathtt{B}) = \emptyset$, where $\text{span}(\cdot)$ represents the span of the columns of the matrix. Here $\mathtt{A}$ and $\mathtt{B}$ are as in (A6.11). Proof of this fact and interpretation of the condition $\text{span}(\mathtt{A}) \cap \text{span}(\mathtt{B}) = \emptyset$ is outlined in exercise (i) on page 626.

The division of matrix $\mathtt{J}^{\mathsf{T}}\Sigma_{\mathbf{X}}^{-1}\mathtt{J}$ into blocks as in (A6.11) corresponds in (A6.5) to the division of $\mathbf{P}$ into parameters $\mathbf{a}$ and $\mathbf{b}$. Truncation of the covariance matrix for parameters $\mathbf{P}$ gives covariance matrices for parameters $\mathbf{a}$ and $\mathbf{b}$ separately. The result is summarized in algorithm A6.2.

A6.3.3 General sparse LM method

In the previous pages, a method has been described for carrying out LM iteration and computing covariances of the solution in the case where the parameter vector may be partitioned into two sub-vectors $\mathbf{a}$ and $\mathbf{b}$. It is not clear from the foregoing discussion that the methods described there actually give any computational advantage in the general case. However, such methods become important when the Jacobian matrix obeys a certain sparseness condition, as will be described now.

We suppose that the "measurement vector" $\mathbf{X} \in \mathbb{R}^N$ may broken up into pieces as $\mathbf{X} = (\mathbf{X}_1^{\mathsf{T}}, \mathbf{X}_2^{\mathsf{T}}, \ldots, \mathbf{X}_n^{\mathsf{T}})^{\mathsf{T}}$. Similarly, suppose that the "parameter vector" $\mathbf{P} \in \mathbb{R}^M$ may be divided up as $\mathbf{P} = (\mathbf{a}^{\mathsf{T}}, \mathbf{b}_1^{\mathsf{T}}, \mathbf{b}_2^{\mathsf{T}}, \ldots, \mathbf{b}_n^{\mathsf{T}})^{\mathsf{T}}$. The estimated values of $\mathbf{X}_i$ corresponding to a given assignment of parameters will be denoted by $\widehat{\mathbf{X}}_i$. We make the *sparseness assumption* that each $\widehat{\mathbf{X}}_i$ is dependent on $\mathbf{a}$ and $\mathbf{b}_i$ only, but not on the other parameters $\mathbf{b}_j$. In this case, $\partial\widehat{\mathbf{X}}_i/\partial\mathbf{b}_j = \mathtt{0}$ for $i \neq j$. No assumption is made about $\partial\widehat{\mathbf{X}}_i/\partial\mathbf{a}$. This situation arises in the reconstruction problem described at the start of this discussion, in which $\mathbf{b}_i$ is the vector of parameters of the i-th point, and $\widehat{\mathbf{X}}_i$ is the vector of measurements of the image of this point in all the views. In this case, since the image of a point does not depend on any other point, one sees that $\partial\widehat{\mathbf{X}}_i/\partial\mathbf{b}_j = 0$, as required, unless $i = j$.

Corresponding to this division, the Jacobian matrix $\mathtt{J} = [\partial\widehat{\mathbf{X}}/\partial\mathbf{P}]$ has a sparse block structure. We define Jacobian matrices by

$$\mathtt{A}_i = \left[\partial \widehat{\mathbf{X}}_i / \partial \mathbf{a}\right] \qquad \mathtt{B}_i = \left[\partial \widehat{\mathbf{X}}_i / \partial \mathbf{b}_i\right].$$

Given an error vector of the form $\boldsymbol{\epsilon} = (\boldsymbol{\epsilon}_1^\mathsf{T}, \ldots, \boldsymbol{\epsilon}_n^\mathsf{T})^\mathsf{T} = \mathbf{X} - \widehat{\mathbf{X}}$ the set of equations $\mathtt{J}\boldsymbol{\delta} = \boldsymbol{\epsilon}$ now has the form

$$\mathtt{J}\boldsymbol{\delta} = \left[\begin{array}{c|cccc} \mathtt{A}_1 & \mathtt{B}_1 & & & \\ \mathtt{A}_2 & & \mathtt{B}_2 & & \\ \vdots & & & \ddots & \\ \mathtt{A}_n & & & & \mathtt{B}_n \end{array}\right] \left(\begin{array}{c} \boldsymbol{\delta}_\mathbf{a} \\ \hline \boldsymbol{\delta}_{\mathbf{b}_1} \\ \vdots \\ \boldsymbol{\delta}_{\mathbf{b}_n} \end{array}\right) = \left(\begin{array}{c} \boldsymbol{\epsilon}_1 \\ \vdots \\ \boldsymbol{\epsilon}_n \end{array}\right). \qquad \text{(A6.14)}$$

We suppose further that all of the measurements $\mathbf{X}_i$ are independent with covariance matrices $\Sigma_{\mathbf{X}_i}$. Thus the covariance matrix for the complete measurement vector $\Sigma_\mathbf{X}$ has the block-diagonal form $\Sigma_\mathbf{X} = \operatorname{diag}(\Sigma_{\mathbf{X}_1}, \ldots, \Sigma_{\mathbf{X}_n})$.

In the notation of algorithm A6.1, we have

$$\begin{aligned} \mathtt{A} &= [\mathtt{A}_1^\mathsf{T}, \mathtt{A}_2^\mathsf{T}, \ldots, \mathtt{A}_n^\mathsf{T}]^\mathsf{T} \\ \mathtt{B} &= \operatorname{diag}(\mathtt{B}_1, \mathtt{B}_2, \ldots, \mathtt{B}_n) \\ \Sigma_\mathbf{X} &= \operatorname{diag}(\Sigma_{\mathbf{X}_1}, \ldots, \Sigma_{\mathbf{X}_n}) \\ \boldsymbol{\delta}_\mathbf{b} &= (\boldsymbol{\delta}_{\mathbf{b}_1}^\mathsf{T}, \boldsymbol{\delta}_{\mathbf{b}_2}^\mathsf{T}, \ldots, \boldsymbol{\delta}_{\mathbf{b}_n}^\mathsf{T})^\mathsf{T} \\ \boldsymbol{\epsilon} &= (\boldsymbol{\epsilon}_1^\mathsf{T}, \boldsymbol{\epsilon}_2^\mathsf{T}, \ldots, \boldsymbol{\epsilon}_n^\mathsf{T})^\mathsf{T} \end{aligned}$$

Now, it is a straightforward task to substitute these formulae into algorithm A6.1. The result of this substitution is given in algorithm A6.3, representing the computation of one step of the LM algorithm. The important observation is that in this form each step of the algorithm requires computation time linear in n. Without the advantage resulting from the sparse structure, the algorithm (for instance a blind adherence to algorithm A6.1) would have complexity of order n^3.

A6.4 Application of sparse LM to 2D homography estimation

We apply the foregoing discussion to the estimation of a 2D homography $\mathtt{H}$ given a set of corresponding image points $\mathbf{x}_i \leftrightarrow \mathbf{x}'_i$ in two images. The points in each image are subject to noise, and one seeks to minimize the cost function (4.8–*p*95). We define a measurement vector $\mathbf{X}_i = (\mathbf{x}_i^\mathsf{T}, \mathbf{x}_i'^\mathsf{T})^\mathsf{T}$. In this case, the parameter vector $\mathbf{P}$ may be divided up as $\mathbf{P} = (\mathbf{h}^\mathsf{T}, \hat{\mathbf{x}}_1^\mathsf{T}, \hat{\mathbf{x}}_2^\mathsf{T}, \ldots, \hat{\mathbf{x}}_n^\mathsf{T})^\mathsf{T}$, where the values $\hat{\mathbf{x}}_i$ are the estimated values of the image points in the first image, and $\mathbf{h}$ is a vector of entries of the homography $\mathtt{H}$. Thus, one must simultaneously estimate the homography $\mathtt{H}$ and the parameters of each point in the first image. The function f maps $\mathbf{P}$ to $(\widehat{\mathbf{X}}_1^\mathsf{T}, \widehat{\mathbf{X}}_2^\mathsf{T}, \ldots, \widehat{\mathbf{X}}_n^\mathsf{T})^\mathsf{T}$, where each $\widehat{\mathbf{X}}_i = (\hat{\mathbf{x}}_i^\mathsf{T}, \mathtt{H}\hat{\mathbf{x}}_i^\mathsf{T})^\mathsf{T} = (\hat{\mathbf{x}}_i^\mathsf{T}, \hat{\mathbf{x}}_i'^\mathsf{T})^\mathsf{T}$. Then algorithm A6.3 applies directly.

The Jacobian matrices have a special form in this case, since one observes that

$$\mathtt{A}_i = \partial \widehat{\mathbf{X}}_i / \partial \mathbf{h} = \left[\begin{array}{c} \mathtt{0} \\ \partial \hat{\mathbf{x}}'_i / \partial \mathbf{h} \end{array}\right]$$

Objective Formulate LM algorithm in the case where the parameter vector is partitioned as $\mathbf{P} = (\mathbf{a}^\top, \mathbf{b}_1^\top, \ldots, \mathbf{b}_n^\top)^\top$, and the measurement vector as $\mathbf{X} = (\mathbf{X}_1^\top, \ldots, \mathbf{X}_n^\top)^\top$, such that $\partial\widehat{\mathbf{X}}_i/\partial\mathbf{b}_j = 0$ for $i \neq j$.

Algorithm Steps (ii) to (vii) of algorithm A6.1 become:

(i) Compute the derivative matrices $\mathtt{A}_i = [\partial\widehat{\mathbf{X}}_i/\partial\mathbf{a}]$ and $\mathtt{B}_i = [\partial\widehat{\mathbf{X}}_i/\partial\mathbf{b}_i]$ and the error vectors $\boldsymbol{\epsilon}_i = \mathbf{X}_i - \widehat{\mathbf{X}}_i$.

(ii) Compute the intermediate values

$$\begin{aligned}
\mathtt{U} &= \sum_i \mathtt{A}_i^\top \Sigma_{\mathbf{X}_i}^{-1} \mathtt{A}_i \\
\mathtt{V} &= \text{diag}(\mathtt{V}_1, \ldots, \mathtt{V}_n) \text{ where } \mathtt{V}_i = \mathtt{B}_i^\top \Sigma_{\mathbf{X}_i}^{-1} \mathtt{B}_i \\
\mathtt{W} &= [\mathtt{W}_1, \mathtt{W}_2, \ldots, \mathtt{W}_n] \text{ where } \mathtt{W}_i = \mathtt{A}_i^\top \Sigma_{\mathbf{X}_i}^{-1} \mathtt{B}_i \\
\boldsymbol{\epsilon}_{\mathtt{A}} &= \sum_i \mathtt{A}_i^\top \Sigma_{\mathbf{X}_i}^{-1} \boldsymbol{\epsilon}_i \\
\boldsymbol{\epsilon}_{\mathtt{B}} &= (\boldsymbol{\epsilon}_{\mathtt{B}_1}^\top, \boldsymbol{\epsilon}_{\mathtt{B}_2}^\top, \ldots, \boldsymbol{\epsilon}_{\mathtt{B}_n}^\top)^\top \text{ where } \boldsymbol{\epsilon}_{\mathtt{B}_i} = \mathtt{B}_i^\top \Sigma_{\mathbf{X}_i}^{-1} \boldsymbol{\epsilon}_i \\
\mathtt{Y}_i &= \mathtt{W}_i \mathtt{V}_i^{*-1}.
\end{aligned}$$

(iii) Compute $\boldsymbol{\delta}_{\mathbf{a}}$ from the equation

$$(\mathtt{U}^* - \sum_i \mathtt{Y}_i \mathtt{W}_i^\top)\delta_{\mathbf{a}} = \epsilon_{\mathtt{A}} - \sum_i \mathtt{Y}_i \boldsymbol{\epsilon}_{\mathtt{B}_i}.$$

(iv) Compute each $\boldsymbol{\delta}_{\mathbf{b}_i}$ in turn from the equation

$$\delta_{\mathbf{b}_i} = \mathtt{V}_i^{*-1}(\boldsymbol{\epsilon}_{\mathtt{B}_i} - \mathtt{W}_i^\top \boldsymbol{\delta}_{\mathbf{a}}).$$

Covariance

(i) Redefine $\mathtt{Y}_i = \mathtt{W}_i \mathtt{V}_i^{-1}$

(ii) $\Sigma_{\mathbf{a}} = (\mathtt{U} - \sum_i \mathtt{Y}_i \mathtt{W}_i^\top)^+$

(iii) $\Sigma_{\mathbf{b}_i\mathbf{b}_j} = \mathtt{Y}_i^\top \Sigma_{\mathbf{a}} \mathtt{Y}_j + \delta_{ij} \mathtt{V}_i^{-1}$

(iv) $\Sigma_{\mathbf{a}\mathbf{b}_i} = -\Sigma_{\mathbf{a}} \mathtt{Y}_i$

Algorithm A6.3. *A sparse Levenberg–Marquardt algorithm.*

since $\hat{\mathbf{x}}_i$ is independent of $\mathbf{h}$. Also,

$$\mathtt{B}_i = \partial\widehat{\mathbf{X}}_i/\partial\hat{\mathbf{x}}_i = \begin{bmatrix} \mathtt{I} \\ \partial\hat{\mathbf{x}}_i'/\partial\hat{\mathbf{x}}_i \end{bmatrix}$$

because of the form of $\widehat{\mathbf{X}}_i = (\hat{\mathbf{x}}_i^\top, \hat{\mathbf{x}}_i'^\top)^\top$.

A6.4.1 Computation of the covariance

As an example of covariance computation, we consider the same problem as in section 5.2.4(*p*145), in which a homography is estimated from point correspondences. As in that example, we consider a case in which the estimated homography is actually the identity mapping, $\mathtt{H} = \mathtt{I}$. For the purposes of this example, the number of points or their distribution is not important. It will be assumed, however, that the errors of all point measurements are independent. We recall from (5.12–p146) that in the case of errors in the second image only, $\Sigma_{\mathbf{h}} = \left(\sum_i \mathtt{J}_i^\mathsf{T}\Sigma_i^{-1}\mathtt{J}_i\right)^+$, where $\mathtt{J}_i = [\partial\hat{\mathbf{x}}'_i/\partial\mathbf{h}]$.

We now proceed to compute the covariance of the camera parameter vector $\mathbf{h}$ in the case where the points in the first image are subject to noise as well. We assume further that $\Sigma_{\mathbf{x}_i}^{-1} = \Sigma_{\mathbf{x}'_i}^{-1}$, and denote them by $\mathtt{S}_i$. In this case, the inverse covariance matrix $\Sigma_{\mathbf{X}}^{-1}$ is block-diagonal, $\Sigma_{\mathbf{X}}^{-1} = \mathrm{diag}(\Sigma_{\mathbf{x}_i}^{-1}, \Sigma_{\mathbf{x}'_i}^{-1})$. Then, applying the steps of algorithm A6.3 to compute the covariance matrix for $\mathbf{h}$,

$$
\begin{aligned}
\mathtt{A}_i &= [\mathtt{0}^\mathsf{T}, \mathtt{J}_i^\mathsf{T}]^\mathsf{T} \\
\mathtt{B}_i &= [\mathtt{I}^\mathsf{T}, \mathtt{I}^\mathsf{T}]^\mathsf{T} \text{ since } \mathtt{H} = \mathtt{I} \\
\mathtt{U} &= \sum_i \mathtt{A}_i^\mathsf{T}\mathrm{diag}(\mathtt{S}_i, \mathtt{S}_i)\mathtt{A}_i = \sum_i \mathtt{J}_i^\mathsf{T}\mathtt{S}_i\mathtt{J}_i \\
\mathtt{V}_i &= \mathtt{B}_i^\mathsf{T}\mathrm{diag}(\mathtt{S}_i, \mathtt{S}_i)\mathtt{B}_i = 2\mathtt{S}_i \\
\mathtt{W}_i &= \mathtt{A}_i^\mathsf{T}\mathrm{diag}(\mathtt{S}_i, \mathtt{S}_i)\mathtt{B}_i = \mathtt{J}_i^\mathsf{T}\mathtt{S}_i \\
\mathtt{U} - \sum_i \mathtt{W}_i\mathtt{V}_i^{-1}\mathtt{W}_i^\mathsf{T} &= \sum_i \mathtt{J}_i^\mathsf{T}(\mathtt{S}_i - \mathtt{S}_i/2)\mathtt{J}_i = \sum_i \mathtt{J}_i^\mathsf{T}\mathtt{S}_i\mathtt{J}_i/2 \\
\Sigma_{\mathbf{h}} &= 2\left(\sum_i \mathtt{J}_i^\mathsf{T}\mathtt{S}_i\mathtt{J}_i\right)^+ .
\end{aligned}
$$

Hence, the covariance matrix for $\mathbf{h}$ is just twice the value of the covariance matrix for the case of error in one image. This is not generally true, and results from the fact that $\mathtt{H}$ is the identity mapping. As exercises, one may verify the following.

- *If* $\mathtt{H}$ *represents a scaling by a factor* s, *then* $\Sigma_{\mathbf{h}} = (s^2+1)\left(\sum_i \mathtt{J}_i^\mathsf{T}\mathtt{S}_i\mathtt{J}_i\right)^+$.
- *If* $\mathtt{H}$ *is an affine transformation and* $\mathtt{D}$ *is the upper* 2×2 *part of* $\mathtt{H}$ *(the non-translational part), and if* $\mathtt{S}_i = \mathtt{I}$ *for all* i *(isotropic and independent noise), then* $\Sigma_{\mathbf{h}} = \left(\sum_i \mathtt{J}_i^\mathsf{T}\left(\mathtt{I} - \mathtt{D}(\mathtt{I}+\mathtt{D}^\mathsf{T}\mathtt{D})^{-1}\mathtt{D}^\mathsf{T}\right)\mathtt{J}_i\right)^+$.

A6.5 Application of sparse LM to fundamental matrix estimation

In estimating the fundamental matrix and a set of 3D points, the algorithm is effectively that described in section A6.3.3, a sparse LM algorithm for the estimation of 2D homographies, but slightly modified to the present case. The analogy with the 2D homography estimation problem is as follows: in estimating 2D homographies, one has a mapping $\mathtt{H}$ that takes points $\mathbf{x}_i$ to corresponding points $\mathbf{x}'_i$; in the present problem, one has a mapping represented by a pair of camera matrices $\mathtt{P}$ and $\mathtt{P}'$ that map a 3D point to a pair of corresponding points $(\mathbf{x}_i, \mathbf{x}'_i)$.

For convenience, the notation of section A6.3.3 will be used here. In particular, note that in section A6.3.3, and here the notation $\mathbf{X}$ is used to denote the total measurement vector (in this case $(\mathbf{x}_1, \mathbf{x}'_1, \ldots, \mathbf{x}_n, \mathbf{x}'_n)$) and not a 3D point. Also, be careful to distinguish between $\mathbf{P}$ the parameter vector and $\mathtt{P}$ the camera matrix.

The parameter vector $\mathbf{P}$ is partitioned as $\mathbf{P} = (\mathbf{a}^\mathsf{T}, \mathbf{b}_1^\mathsf{T}, \ldots, \mathbf{b}_n^\mathsf{T})^\mathsf{T}$, where

(i) $\mathbf{a} = \mathbf{p}'$ is made up of the entries of camera matrix $\mathtt{P}'$, and

(ii) $\mathbf{b}_i = (\mathtt{X}_i, \mathtt{Y}_i, \mathtt{T}_i)^\mathsf{T}$ is a 3-vector, parametrizing the i-th 3D point $(\mathtt{X}_i, \mathtt{Y}_i, 1, \mathtt{T}_i)$.

Thus, there are a total of $3n+12$ parameters, where n is the number of points. Parameter vector $\mathbf{a}$ provides a parametrization for the camera $\mathtt{P}'$ and the other camera $\mathtt{P}$ is taken as $[\mathtt{I} \mid \mathbf{0}]$. Note also that it is convenient and permissible to set the third coordinate of the 3D space point to 1 as here, since a point $(\mathtt{X}_i, \mathtt{Y}_i, 0, \mathtt{T}_i)^\mathsf{T}$ maps to $(\mathtt{X}_i, \mathtt{Y}_i, 0)^\mathsf{T}$ which is an infinite point, not anywhere close to the measured point $(x_i, y_i, 1)^\mathsf{T}$.

The measurement vector $\mathbf{X}$ is partitioned as $\mathbf{X} = (\mathbf{X}_1^\mathsf{T}, \mathbf{X}_2^\mathsf{T}, \ldots, \mathbf{X}_n^\mathsf{T})^\mathsf{T}$, where each $\mathbf{X}_i = (\mathbf{x}_i^\mathsf{T}, \mathbf{x}_i'^\mathsf{T})^\mathsf{T}$, the measured images of the i-th point.

Now, the Jacobian matrices $\mathtt{A}_i = \partial\widehat{\mathbf{X}}_i/\partial\mathbf{a}$ and $\mathtt{B}_i = \partial\widehat{\mathbf{X}}_i/\partial\mathbf{b}_i$ may be computed and algorithm A6.3 applied to estimate the parameters, and hence $\mathtt{P}'$, from which $\mathtt{F}$ may be computed.

Partial derivative matrices

Since $\widehat{\mathbf{X}}_i = (\hat{\mathbf{x}}_i^\mathsf{T}, \hat{\mathbf{x}}_i'^\mathsf{T})^\mathsf{T}$ one may compute that $\mathtt{A}_i$ and $\mathtt{B}_i$ have a form similar to the Jacobian matrices in section A6.4:

$$\mathtt{A}_i = \begin{bmatrix} 0 \\ \partial\hat{\mathbf{x}}_i'/\partial\mathbf{a} \end{bmatrix} \qquad \mathtt{B}_i = \begin{bmatrix} \mathtt{I}_{2\times2}|\mathbf{0} \\ \partial\hat{\mathbf{x}}_i'/\partial\mathbf{b}_i \end{bmatrix}.$$

The covariance matrix $\Sigma_{\mathbf{X}_i}$ breaks up into diagonal blocks $\mathrm{diag}(\mathtt{S}_i, \mathtt{S}_i')$, where $\mathtt{S}_i = \Sigma_{\mathbf{x}_i}^{-1}$ and $\mathtt{S}_i' = \Sigma_{\mathbf{x}_i'}^{-1}$. Now, calculating the intermediate expressions in step 2 of algorithm A6.3, we find

$$\mathtt{V}_i = \mathtt{B}_i^\mathsf{T}\mathrm{diag}(\mathtt{S}_i, \mathtt{S}_i')\mathtt{B}_i = [\mathtt{I}_{2\times2} \mid \mathbf{0}]^\mathsf{T}\mathtt{S}_i[\mathtt{I}_{2\times2} \mid \mathbf{0}] + (\partial\hat{\mathbf{x}}_i'/\partial\mathbf{b})^\mathsf{T}\mathtt{S}_i'(\partial\hat{\mathbf{x}}_i'/\partial\mathbf{b}) \quad \text{(A6.15)}$$

The abstract form of $\mathtt{A}_i^\mathsf{T}\Sigma_{\mathbf{X}_i}^{-1}\mathtt{A}_i$ is the same as in the 2D homography case, and the other expressions $\mathtt{W}_i = \mathtt{A}_i^\mathsf{T}\Sigma_{\mathbf{X}_i}^{-1}\mathtt{B}_i$, $\epsilon_{\mathtt{B}_i} = \mathtt{B}_i^\mathsf{T}\Sigma_{\mathbf{X}_i}^{-1}\epsilon_i$, and $\epsilon_{\mathtt{A}_i} = \mathtt{A}_i^\mathsf{T}\Sigma_{\mathbf{X}_i}^{-1}\epsilon_i$ may easily be computed. The estimation procedure otherwise proceeds precisely as in algorithm A6.3.

Covariance of F

According to the discussion of section A6.3.3 and in particular algorithm A6.3, the covariance matrix of the camera parameters, namely the entries of $\mathtt{P}'$, is given by

$$\Sigma_{\mathtt{P}'} = (\mathtt{U} - \sum_i \mathtt{W}_i\mathtt{V}_i^{-1}\mathtt{W}_i^\mathsf{T})^+ \quad \text{(A6.16)}$$

with notation as in algorithm A6.3.

In computing this pseudo-inverse, it is useful to know the expected rank of $\Sigma_{\mathtt{P}'}$. In this case, this rank is 7, since the total number of degrees of freedom in the solution involving two cameras and n point matches is $3n + 7$. Looked at another way, $\mathtt{P}'$ is not determined uniquely, since if $\mathtt{P}' = [\mathtt{M} \mid \mathbf{m}]$, then any other matrix $[\mathtt{M} + \mathbf{t}\mathbf{m}^\mathsf{T} \mid \alpha\mathbf{m}]$ also determines the same fundamental matrix. Thus, in computing the pseudo-inverse appearing in the right hand side of (A6.16), one should set five of the singular values to zero.

The foregoing discussion shows how to compute the covariance matrix of the entries of $\mathtt{P}'$. We desire to compute the covariance matrix of the entries of $\mathtt{F}$. However, there is a simple formula for the entries of $\mathtt{F}$ in terms of the entries of $\mathtt{P}' = [\mathtt{M} \mid \mathbf{m}]$, namely

$\mathtt{F} = [\mathbf{m}]_\times \mathtt{M}$. If one desires to compute the covariance matrix of F normalized so that $\|\mathtt{F}\| = 1$, then one writes $\mathtt{F} = [\mathbf{m}]_\times \mathtt{M}/(\|[\mathbf{m}]_\times \mathtt{M}\|)$. Therefore, one may express the entries of F as a simple function in terms of the entries of $\mathtt{P}'$. Let J be the Jacobian matrix of this function. The covariance of F is then computed by propagating the covariance of $\mathtt{P}'$ using result 5.6(*p*139) to get

$$\Sigma_\mathtt{F} = \mathtt{J}\Sigma_{\mathtt{P}'}\mathtt{J}^\mathsf{T} = \mathtt{J}(\mathtt{U} - \sum_i \mathtt{W}_i \mathtt{V}_i^{-1} \mathtt{W}_i^\mathsf{T})^+ \mathtt{J}^\mathsf{T} \tag{A6.17}$$

where $\Sigma_{\mathtt{P}'}$ is given by (A6.16). This is the covariance of the fundamental matrix *estimated according to an ML algorithm* from the given point correspondences.

A6.6 Application of sparse LM to multiple image bundle adjustment

In the previous section, the application of the sparse Levenberg–Marquardt algorithm to the computation of the fundamental matrix was considered. This is essentially a reconstruction problem from two views. It should be clear how this may easily be extended to the computation of the trifocal tensor and the quadrifocal tensor. More generally, one may apply it to the simultaneous estimation of multiple camera and points to compute projective structure, or perhaps affine or metric structure given appropriate constraints. This technique is called *bundle adjustment*.

In the case of multiple cameras, one may also take advantage of the lack of interaction between parameters of the different cameras, as will be shown now. In the following discussion, for simplicity of notation it will be assumed that each point is visible in all the views. This is not at all necessary – points may in general be visible in some arbitrary subset of the available views.

We use the same notation as in section A6.3.3. The measurement data may be expressed as a vector $\mathbf{X}$, which may be divided up into parts $\mathbf{X}_i$, representing the measured image coordinates of some 3D point in all views. One may further subdivide $\mathbf{X}_i$ writing $\mathbf{X}_i = (\mathbf{x}_{i1}^\mathsf{T}, \mathbf{x}_{i2}^\mathsf{T}, \ldots, \mathbf{x}_{im}^\mathsf{T})^\mathsf{T}$ where $\mathbf{x}_{ij}$ is the image of the i-th point in the j-th image. The parameter vector $\mathbf{a}$ (camera parameters) may correspondingly be partitioned as $\mathbf{a} = (\mathbf{a}_1^\mathsf{T}, \mathbf{a}_2^\mathsf{T}, \ldots, \mathbf{a}_m^\mathsf{T})^\mathsf{T}$, where $\mathbf{a}_j$ are the parameters of the j-th camera. Since the image point $\mathbf{x}_{ij}$ does not depend on the parameters of any but the j-th camera, one observes that $\partial\hat{\mathbf{x}}_{ij}/\partial\mathbf{a}_k = 0$ unless $j = k$. In a similar way for derivatives with respect to the parameters $\mathbf{b}_k$ of the k-th 3D point, one has $\partial\hat{\mathbf{x}}_{ij}/\partial\mathbf{b}_k = 0$ unless $i = k$.

The form of the Jacobian matrix J for this problem and the resulting normal equations $\mathtt{J}^\mathsf{T}\mathtt{J}\boldsymbol{\delta} = \mathtt{J}^\mathsf{T}\boldsymbol{\epsilon}$ are shown schematically in figure A6.1 and figure A6.2. Referring to the Jacobian matrices defined in algorithm A6.3, one sees that $\mathtt{A}_i = [\partial\widehat{\mathbf{X}}_i/\partial\mathbf{a}]$ is a block diagonal matrix $\mathtt{A}_i = \mathrm{diag}(\mathtt{A}_{i1}, \ldots, \mathtt{A}_{im})$, where $\mathtt{A}_{ij} = \partial\hat{\mathbf{x}}_{ij}/\partial\mathbf{a}_j$. Similarly, matrix $\mathtt{B}_i = [\partial\widehat{\mathbf{X}}_i/\partial\mathbf{b}_i]$ decomposes as $\mathtt{B}_i = [\mathtt{B}_{i1}^\mathsf{T}, \ldots, \mathtt{B}_{im}^\mathsf{T}]^\mathsf{T}$, where $\mathtt{B}_{ij} = \partial\hat{\mathbf{x}}_{ij}/\partial\mathbf{b}_i$. It may normally be assumed also that $\Sigma_{\mathbf{X}_i}$ has a diagonal structure $\Sigma_{\mathbf{X}_i} = \mathrm{diag}(\Sigma_{\mathbf{x}_{i1}}, \ldots, \Sigma_{\mathbf{x}_{im}})$, meaning that the measurements of the projected points in separate images are independent (or more precisely, uncorrelated). With these assumptions, one is easily able to adapt algorithm A6.3, as shown in algorithm A6.4, as the reader is left to verify.

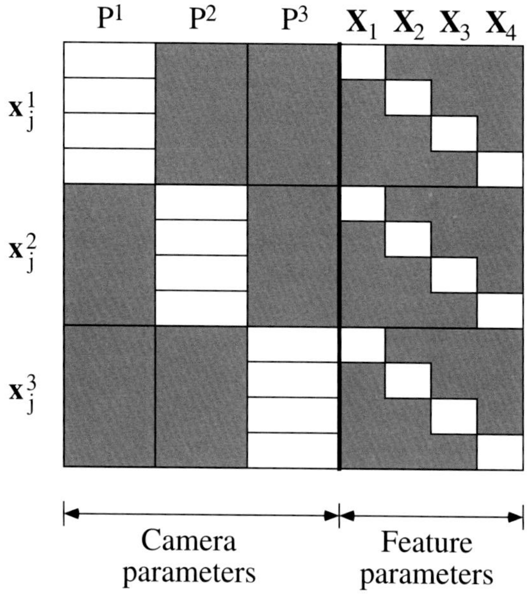

Fig. A6.1. *Form of the Jacobian matrix for a bundle-adjustment problem consisting of* 3 *cameras and* 4 *points.*

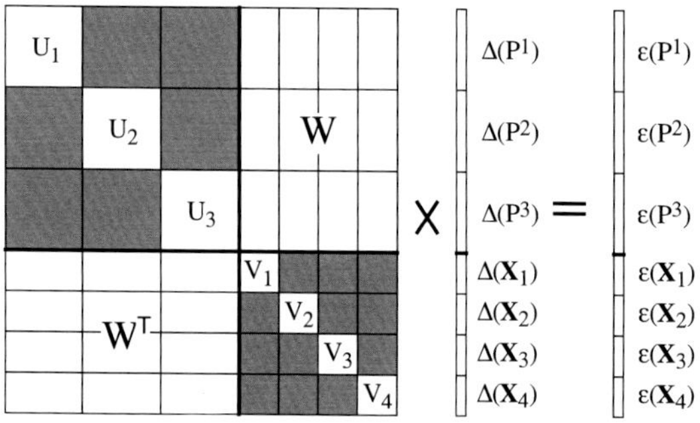

Fig. A6.2. *Form of the normal equations for the bundle-adjustment problem consisting of* 3 *cameras and* 4 *points.*

Missing data. Typically, in a bundle-adjustment problem some points are not visible in every image. Thus, some measurement $\mathbf{x}_{ij}$ may not exist, meaning that i-th point is not visible in the j-th image. Algorithm A6.4 is easily adapted to this situation, by ignoring terms subscripted by ij where the measurement $\mathbf{x}_{ij}$ does not exist. Such missing terms are simply omitted from the relevant summations. This includes all of $\mathtt{A}_{ij}$, $\mathtt{B}_{ij}$, $\Sigma_{\mathbf{x}_{ij}}^{-1}$, $\mathtt{W}_{ij}$ and $\mathtt{Y}_{ij}$. It may be seen that this is equivalent to setting $\mathtt{A}_{ij}$ and $\mathtt{B}_{ij}$ to zero, thus effectively giving zero weight to the missing measurements.

This is convenient when programming this algorithm, since the above quantities subscripted by ij may be associated only with existing measurements in a common data structure.

(i) Compute the derivative matrices $\mathtt{A}_{ij} = [\partial\hat{\mathbf{x}}_{ij}/\partial\mathbf{a}_j]$ and $\mathtt{B}_{ij} = [\partial\hat{\mathbf{x}}_{ij}/\partial\mathbf{b}_i]$ and the error vectors $\boldsymbol{\epsilon}_{ij} = \mathbf{x}_{ij} - \hat{\mathbf{x}}_{ij}$.

(ii) Compute the intermediate values

$$\mathtt{U}_j = \sum_i \mathtt{A}_{ij}^{\mathsf{T}}\Sigma_{\mathbf{x}_{ij}}^{-1}\mathtt{A}_{ij} \qquad \mathtt{V}_i = \sum_j \mathtt{B}_{ij}^{\mathsf{T}}\Sigma_{\mathbf{x}_{ij}}^{-1}\mathtt{B}_{ij} \qquad \mathtt{W}_{ij} = \mathtt{A}_{ij}^{\mathsf{T}}\Sigma_{\mathbf{x}_{ij}}^{-1}\mathtt{B}_{ij}$$

$$\boldsymbol{\epsilon}_{\mathbf{a}_j} = \sum_i \mathtt{A}_{ij}^{\mathsf{T}}\Sigma_{\mathbf{x}_{ij}}^{-1}\boldsymbol{\epsilon}_{ij} \qquad \boldsymbol{\epsilon}_{\mathbf{b}_i} = \sum_j \mathtt{B}_{ij}^{\mathsf{T}}\Sigma_{\mathbf{x}_{ij}}^{-1}\boldsymbol{\epsilon}_{ij} \qquad \mathtt{Y}_{ij} = \mathtt{W}_{ij}\mathtt{V}_i^{*-1}$$

where in each case $i = 1, \ldots, n$ and $j = 1, \ldots, m$.

(iii) Compute $\boldsymbol{\delta}_{\mathbf{a}} = (\boldsymbol{\delta}_{\mathbf{a}_1}^{\mathsf{T}}, \ldots, \boldsymbol{\delta}_{\mathbf{a}_m}^{\mathsf{T}})^{\mathsf{T}}$ from the equation

$$\mathtt{S}\delta_{\mathbf{a}} = (\mathbf{e}_1^{\mathsf{T}}, \ldots, \mathbf{e}_m^{\mathsf{T}})^{\mathsf{T}}$$

where $\mathtt{S}$ is an $m \times m$ block matrix with blocks $\mathtt{S}_{jk}$ defined by

$$\begin{aligned}\mathtt{S}_{jj} &= -\sum_i \mathtt{Y}_{ij}\mathtt{W}_{ij}^{\mathsf{T}} + \mathtt{U}_j^* \\ \mathtt{S}_{jk} &= -\sum_i \mathtt{Y}_{ij}\mathtt{W}_{ik}^{\mathsf{T}} \text{ if } j \neq k\end{aligned}$$

and

$$\mathbf{e}_j = \boldsymbol{\epsilon}_{\mathbf{a}_j} - \sum_i \mathtt{Y}_{ij}\boldsymbol{\epsilon}_{\mathbf{b}_i}$$

(iv) Compute each $\boldsymbol{\delta}_{\mathbf{b}_i}$ in turn from the equation

$$\delta_{\mathbf{b}_i} = \mathtt{V}_i^{*-1}(\boldsymbol{\epsilon}_{\mathbf{b}_i} - \sum_j \mathtt{W}_{ij}^{\mathsf{T}}\boldsymbol{\delta}_{\mathbf{a}_j})$$

<u>Covariance</u>

(i) Redefine $\mathtt{Y}_{ij} = \mathtt{W}_{ij}\mathtt{V}_i^{-1}$.

(ii) $\Sigma_{\mathbf{a}} = \mathtt{S}^+$, where $\mathtt{S}$ is defined as above, without the augmentation represented by the $*$.

(iii) $\Sigma_{\mathbf{b}_i\mathbf{b}_j} = \mathtt{Y}_i^{\mathsf{T}}\Sigma_{\mathbf{a}}\mathtt{Y}_j + \delta_{ij}\mathtt{V}_i^{-1}$.

(iv) $\Sigma_{\mathbf{a}\mathbf{b}_i} = -\Sigma_{\mathbf{a}}\mathtt{Y}_i$.

Algorithm A6.4. *General sparse Levenberg–Marquardt algorithm.*

A6.7 Sparse methods for equation solving

In a long sequence of images, it is rare for a point to be tracked through the whole sequence, and usually point tracks disappear and new ones start, causing the set of point tracks to have a banded structure, as seen in figure 19.7(*p*492)(c). This banded structure of the point track set leads to a banded structure for the set of equations that are solved to compute structure and motion – we refer here to the matrix $\mathtt{S}$ in algorithm A6.4. Thus, for bundle-adjustment problems with banded track structure, sparseness can appear at two levels, first at the level of independence of the individual point measurements, as exploited in algorithm A6.4, and secondly arising from the banded track structure as will be explained in this section.

Another similar context in which this will occur is solution for structure and motion in section 18.5.1(*p*448) or simply motion, as in section 18.5.2(*p*450). In both these methods, large sparse sets of equations may arise. In order for large problems of this kind to be tractable, it is necessary to take advantage of this sparse structure in order to minimize the amount of storage and computation involved. In this section, we will consider sparse matrix techniques that are valuable in this context.

A6.7.1 Banded structure in bundle-adjustment

The time-consuming step in finding the parameter increments in the iterative step of bundle-adjustment, as given in algorithm A6.4 is the solution of the equations $\mathtt{S}\delta_a = \mathbf{e}$ in step (iii) of the algorithm. As shown there, the matrix $\mathtt{S}$ is a symmetric matrix with off-diagonal blocks of the form $\mathtt{S}_{jk} = -\sum_i \mathtt{W}_{ij}\mathtt{V}_i^{*-1}\mathtt{W}_{ik}^{\mathsf{T}}$. We see that the block $\mathtt{S}_{jk}$ is non-zero only when for some i, both $\mathtt{W}_{ij}$ and $\mathtt{W}_{ik}$ are non-zero. Since $\mathtt{W}_{ij} = [\partial\hat{\mathbf{x}}_{ij}/\partial\mathbf{a}_j]^{\mathsf{T}}\Sigma_{\mathbf{x}_{ij}}^{-1}[\partial\hat{\mathbf{x}}_{ij}/\partial\mathbf{b}_i]$ it follows that $\mathtt{W}_{ij}$ is non-zero only when the corresponding measurement $\hat{\mathbf{x}}_{ij}$ depends on parameters $\mathbf{a}_j$ and $\mathbf{b}_i$. To be more concrete, if $\mathbf{a}_j$ represents the parameters of the j-th camera, and $\mathbf{b}_i$ represents the parameters of the i-th point, then $\mathtt{W}_{ij}$ is non-zero only when the i-th point is visible in the j-th image, and $\mathbf{x}_{ij}$ is its measured image position.

The condition that for some i both $\mathtt{W}_{ij}$ and $\mathtt{W}_{ik}$ are non-zero means that there exists some point with index i that is visible in both the j-th and k-th images. To summarize,

- *The block $\mathtt{S}_{jk}$ is non-zero only if there exists a point that is visible in both the j-th and k-th images.*

Thus, if point tracks extend only over consecutive views, then the matrix $\mathtt{S}$ will be banded. In particular, if no point track extends over more than B views (B representing *bandwidth*), then the block $\mathtt{S}_{jk}$ is zero unless $|j - k| < B$.

Consider tracking points over a long sequence, for instance along a path that may loop back and cross itself. In this case, it may be possible to recognize a point that had been seen previously in the sequence, and pick up its track again. The set of views in which a 3D point is seen will not be a consecutive set of views. This will destroy the banded nature of the matrix $\mathtt{S}$, by introducing non-zero blocks possibly far away from the central band. Nevertheless, if there is not too much filling-in of off-diagonal blocks, sparse solution techniques may still be utilized as we shall see later.

A6.7.2 Solution of symmetric linear equations

In solving a set of linear equations $\mathtt{A}\mathbf{x} = \mathbf{b}$ in which the matrix $\mathtt{A}$ is symmetric, it is best not to use a general purpose equation solver, such as Gaussian-elimination, but rather to take advantage of the symmetry of the matrix $\mathtt{A}$. One way of doing this is the use the $\mathtt{LDL}^{\mathsf{T}}$ decomposition of the matrix $\mathtt{A}$. This relies on the following observation:

Result A6.1. *Any positive-definite symmetric matrix $\mathtt{A}$ can be factored as $\mathtt{A} = \mathtt{LDL}^{\mathsf{T}}$, in which $\mathtt{L}$ is a lower-triangular matrix with unit diagonal entries, and $\mathtt{D}$ is diagonal.*

The reader is advised to consult [Golub-89] for details of efficient implementation and numeric properties of $\mathtt{LDL}^{\mathsf{T}}$ decomposition. The normal equations derived from structure and motion problems are always at least positive semi-definite, and with stabiliza-

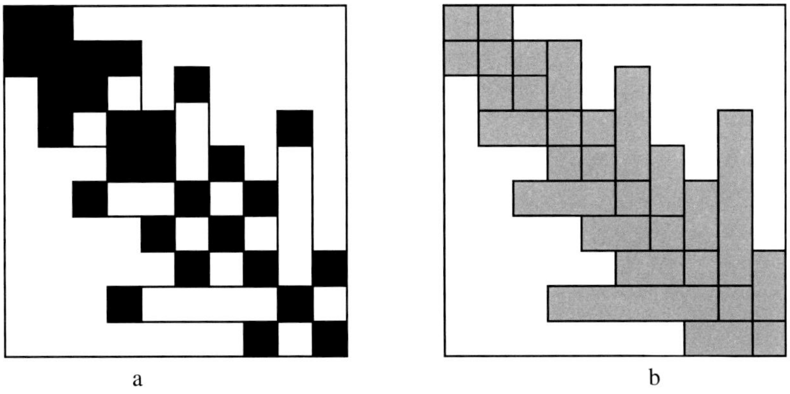

Fig. A6.3. *(a) A sparse matrix and (b) its corresponding "skyline" structure. Non-zero entries in the original matrix are shown in black. In the skyline format, all non-zero entries lie in the shaded area. For each row i, there is an integer m_i representing the first non-zero entry in that row. Note that non-zero off-diagonal elements cause "fill-in" of the skyline format for that row (or symmetric above-diagonal column). If such entries are relatively rare, the skyline format will remain sparse, and techniques for skyline matrices may be usefully applied. The* $\mathtt{LDL}^\mathsf{T}$ *decomposition of a matrix in skyline format has the same skyline structure. Thus, the* $\mathtt{LDL}^\mathsf{T}$ *decomposition of the original sparse matrix shown in (a), will have non-zero entries only within the shaded area of (b).*

tion through enhancement, they are positive-definite, and symmetric factorization is the recommended method of solution.

Given the $\mathtt{LDL}^\mathsf{T}$ factorization, the set of linear equations $\mathtt{A}\mathbf{x} = \mathtt{LDL}^\mathsf{T}\mathbf{x} = \mathbf{b}$ may be solved for $\mathbf{x}$ in three steps as (i) $\mathtt{L}\mathbf{x}' = \mathbf{b}$, (ii) $\mathbf{x}'' = \mathtt{D}^{-1}\mathbf{x}'$, (iii) $\mathtt{L}^\mathsf{T}\mathbf{x} = \mathbf{x}''$.

Solving the equations $\mathtt{L}\mathbf{x}' = \mathbf{b}$ is carried out by the process of "forward-substitution." In particular (bearing in mind that $\mathtt{L}$ has unit diagonal entries), the components of $\mathbf{x}$ may be computed in order as

$$\textit{forward-substitution:}\ \mathbf{x}'_i = \mathbf{b}_i - \sum_{j=1}^{i-1} L_{ij}\mathbf{x}'_j.$$

Since $\mathtt{L}^\mathsf{T}$ is upper-triangular, the second set of equations is solved in a similar fashion, except that the values $\mathbf{x}_i$ are computed in inverse order in a process known as "back-substitution."

$$\textit{back-substitution:}\quad \mathbf{x}_i = \mathbf{x}''_i - \sum_{j=i+1}^{n} L_{ji}\mathbf{x}_j.$$

The number of operations involved in this computation is given in [Golub-89], and is equal to $n^3/3$, where n is the dimension of the matrix.

A6.7.3 Solution of sparse symmetric linear systems

We consider a special type of sparse structure for a symmetric matrix, known as "skyline" format. This is illustrated in figure A6.3. An $n \times n$ symmetric matrix $\mathtt{A}$ in skyline format is characterized by the existence of an array of integers m_i for $i = 1, \dots, n$ such that $\mathtt{A}_{ij} = 0$ for $j < m_i$. A diagonally banded matrix is a special case of a matrix with skyline structure.

Although a diagonally banded or skyline matrix may be sparse, its inverse is not, and in fact will be completely filled out with non-zero elements. Thus, it is a very bad idea actually to compute the inverse of $\mathtt{A}$ to find the solution $\mathbf{x} = \mathtt{A}^{-1}\mathbf{b}$ to the set of equations. However, the importance of matrices in skyline (or banded) form is that skyline structure of the matrix *is preserved* by the $\mathtt{LDL}^\mathsf{T}$ decomposition, as expressed in the following result.

Result A6.2. *Let* $\mathtt{A}$ *be a symmetric matrix such that* $\mathtt{A}_{ij} = 0$ *for* $j < m_i$. *Let* $\mathtt{A} = \mathtt{LDL}^\mathsf{T}$. *Then* $\mathtt{L}_{ij} = 0$ *for* $j < m_i$.

In other words, the skyline structure of $\mathtt{L}$ is the same as that of $\mathtt{A}$.

Proof. Suppose that j is the smallest index such that $\mathtt{L}_{ij} = 0$. Then in multiplying out $\mathtt{A} = \mathtt{LDL}^\mathsf{T}$, it may be verified that only one product contributes to the (i, j)-th element of $\mathtt{A}_{ij}$. Specifically, $\mathtt{A}_{ij} = \mathtt{L}_{ij}\mathtt{D}_{jj}\mathtt{L}_{jj} \neq 0$. □

Thus, in computing the $\mathtt{LDL}^\mathsf{T}$ decomposition of $\mathtt{A}$ having a sparse skyline structure, we know in advance that many of the entries of $\mathtt{L}$ will be zero. The algorithm for computing the $\mathtt{LDL}^\mathsf{T}$ decomposition for such a matrix is much the same as the that for a full symmetric matrix, except that we do not need to consider the zero elements.

Forward and back substitution involving a matrix $\mathtt{L}$ with skyline structure easily take advantage of the sparse structure. In fact the forward substitution formula becomes

$$\mathbf{x}'_i = \mathbf{b}_i - \sum_{j=m_i}^{i-1} L_{ij}\mathbf{x}'_j .$$

Back-substitution is left for the reader to work out. More details of implementation are given in [Bathe-76].

A6.8 Robust cost functions

In estimation problems of the Newton or Levenberg-Marquardt type, an important decision to make is the precise form of the cost function. As we have seen, an assumption of Gaussian noise without outliers implies that the the Maximum Likelihood estimate is given by a least-squares cost function involving the predicted errors in the measurements, where the noise is introduced.

The same analysis may be carried out for other assumed probability models for the measurements. Thus, if all measurements are assumed to be independent, and $f(\delta)$ is the probability distribution of an error δ in the measurement, then the probability of a set of measurement with errors δ_i is given by $p(\delta_1, \ldots, \delta_n) = \prod_{i=1}^n f(\delta_i)$. Taking the negative logarithm gives $-\log(p(\delta_1, \ldots, \delta_n)) = -\sum_{i=1}^n \log(f(\delta_i))$ and the right-hand side of this expression is a suitable cost function for a set of measurements. It is usually appropriate to set the cost of an exact measurement to be zero, by subtracting $\log(f(0))$, though this is not strictly necessary if our purpose is cost minimization. Graphs of various specific cost functions to be discussed next are shown in figure A6.4.

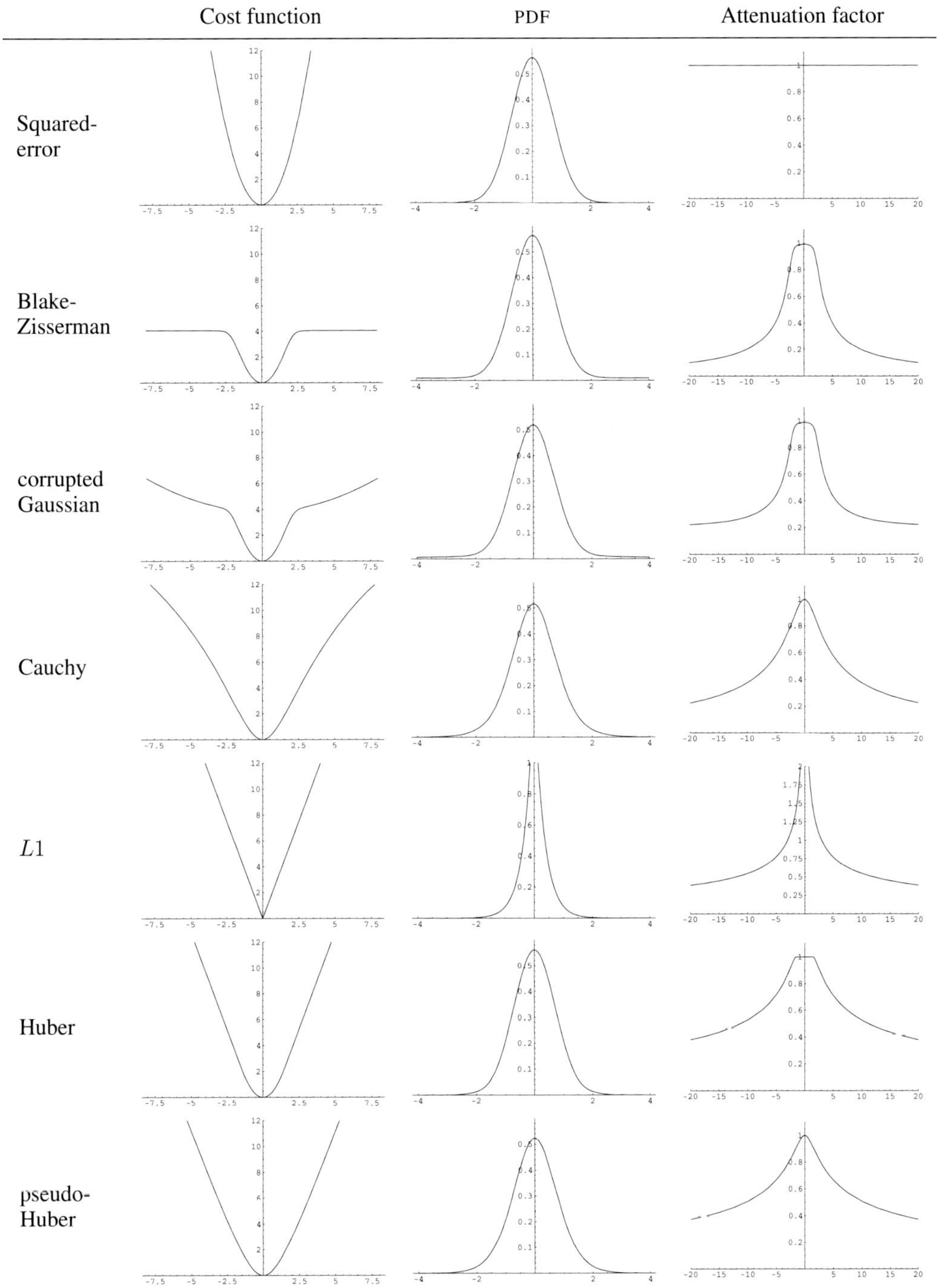

Fig. A6.4. *A comparison of different cost functions, $C(\delta)$, for robust estimation. Their corresponding* PDFs, $\exp(-C(\delta))$, *and attenuation factors ($w = C(\delta)^{1/2}/\delta$ see text) are also shown.*

Statistically based cost functions. Determination of a suitable cost function may be approached by estimating or guessing the distribution of errors for the particular measurement process involved, such as point extraction in an image. In the following list, for simplicity, we ignore the normalization constant for Gaussian distributions $(2\pi\sigma^2)^{-1/2}$, and assume that $2\sigma^2 = 1$.

(i) **Squared error.** Assuming the data is Gaussian distributed, the Probability Distribution Function (PDF) is $p(\delta) = \exp(-\delta^2)$ which leads to a cost function

$$C(\delta) = \delta^2.$$

(ii) **Blake-Zisserman.** The data is assumed to have a Gaussian distribution for inliers with a uniform distribution of outliers. The PDF is taken to be of the form $p(\delta) = \exp(-\delta^2) + \epsilon$. This is not actually a PDF, since it integrates to infinity. Nevertheless, it leads to a cost function of the form

$$C(\delta) = -\log(\exp(-\delta^2) + \epsilon).$$

For inliers (small δ), this approximates δ^2, whereas for outliers (large δ) the asymptotic cost is $-\log \epsilon$. Thus, the crossover point from inliers to outliers is given approximately by $\delta^2 = -\log \epsilon$. The actual cost function used by Blake and Zisserman in [Blake-87] was $\min(\delta^2, \alpha^2)$ and $\epsilon = \exp(-\alpha^2)$.

(iii) **Corrupted Gaussian.** The previous example has the theoretical disadvantage that it is not actually a PDF. An alternative is to model the outliers by a Gaussian with larger standard deviation, leading to a mixture model probability distribution of the form $p(\delta) = \alpha\ \exp(-\delta^2) + (1 - \alpha)\exp(\delta^2/w^2)/w$ where w is the ratio of standard deviations of the outliers to the inliers, and α is the expected fraction of inliers. Then

$$C(\delta) = -\log(\alpha \exp(-\delta^2) + (1 - \alpha)\exp(-\delta^2/w^2)/w).$$

Heuristic cost functions. Next we consider cost functions justified more by heuristics and required noise-immuneness properties than by adherence to a specific noise-distribution model. For this reason they will be introduced directly as a cost function, rather than a PDF.

(i) **Cauchy cost function.** The cost function is given by

$$C(\delta) = b^2 \log(1 + \delta^2/b^2)$$

for some constant b. For small values of δ, this curve approximates δ^2, and the value of b determines for what range of δ this approximation is close. The cost function is derived from the Cauchy distribution $p(\delta) = 1/(\pi(1 + \delta^2))$, which is a bell-curve similar to the Gaussian, but with heavier tails.

(ii) **The $L1$ cost function.** Instead of using the sum of squares, we use the sum of absolute errors. Thus,

$$C(\delta) = 2b|\delta|$$

where $2b$ is some positive constant (which normally could just be 1). This cost function is known as the *total variation*.

(iii) **Huber cost function.** This cost function is a hybrid between the $L1$ and least-squares cost function. Thus, we define

$$\begin{aligned} C(\delta) &= \delta^2 \text{ for } |\delta| < b \\ &= 2b|\delta| - b^2 \text{ otherwise} \end{aligned}$$

This cost function is continuous with continuous first derivative. The value of the threshold b is chosen approximately to equal the outlier threshold.

(iv) **Pseudo-Huber cost function.** The cost function

$$C(\delta) = 2b^2(\sqrt{1 + (\delta/b)^2} - 1)$$

is very similar to the Huber cost function, but has continuous derivatives of all orders. Note that it approximates δ^2 for small δ and is linear with slope $2b$ for large δ.

A6.8.1 Properties of the different cost functions

Squared error. The most basic cost function is the squared error $C(\delta) = \delta^2$. Its main drawback is that it is not robust to outliers in the measurements, as we shall see. Because of the rapid growth of the quadratic curve, distant outliers exert an excessive influence, and can draw the cost minimum well away from the desired value.

Non-convex cost functions. The Blake-Zisserman, corrupted Gaussian and Cauchy cost functions seek to mitigate the deleterious effect of outliers by giving them diminished weight. As is seen in the plot of the first two of these, once the error exceeds a certain threshold, it is classified as an outlier, and the cost remains substantially constant. The Cauchy cost function also seeks to deemphasize the cost of outliers, but this is done more gradually. These three cost functions are non-convex, which has important effects as we will see.

Asymptotically linear cost functions. The $L1$ cost function measures the absolute value of the error. The main effect of this is to give outliers less weight compared with the squared error. The key to understanding the performance of this cost function is to observe that it acts to find the *median* of a set of data. Consider a set of real valued data $\{a_i\}$ and a cost function defined by $C(x) = \sum_i |x - a_i|$. The minimum of this function is at the median of the set $\{a_i\}$. To see this, note that the derivative of $|x - a_i|$ with respect to x is $+1$ when $x > a_i$ and -1 when $x < a_i$. Thus, the derivative is zero when there are as many values of a_i less than x as there are greater than x. Thus, the cost is minimized at the median of the values a_i. Note that the median is immune to changes in the values of data a_i that lie far from the median. The value of the cost function changes, but not the position of its minimum.

For higher dimensional data $\mathbf{a}_i \in \mathbb{R}^n$, the minimum of the cost function $C(\mathbf{x}) = \sum_i \|\mathbf{x} - \mathbf{a}_i\|$ has similar stability properties. Note that $\|\mathbf{x} - \mathbf{a}_i\|$ is a *convex* function of x, and therefore so is a sum of such terms, $\sum_i \|\mathbf{x} - \mathbf{a}_i\|$. Consequently, this cost function has a single minimum (as do all convex functions).

The Huber cost function takes the form of a quadratic for small values of the error, δ, and becomes linear for values of δ beyond a given threshold. As such, it retains the outlier stability of the $L1$ cost function, while for inliers it reflects the property that the squared-error cost function gives the Maximum Likelihood estimate.

The Pseudo-Huber cost function is also near-quadratic for small δ, and linear for large δ. Thus, it may be used as a smooth approximation to the Huber cost function, and gives similar results. It is important to note that each of these three cost functions has the very desirable property of being convex.

A6.8.2 Performance of the different cost functions

To illustrate the properties of the different cost functions we will evaluate the cost $\sum_i C(x - a_i)$ for two synthetic example data sets $\{a_i\}$. Of the group of asymptotically linear cost functions, only the Huber cost function will be shown, since the other two ($L1$ and pseudo-Huber) give very similar results.

The data $\{a_i\}$ may be thought of as the outcome of an experiment to measure some quantity, with repeated measurements. The measurements are subject to random Gaussian noise, with outliers. The purpose of the estimation process is to estimate the value of the quantity by minimizing a cost function. The experiments and the results for the two data sets are described in the captions of figure A6.5 and figure A6.6.

Summary of findings. The squared-error cost function is generally very susceptible to outliers, and may be regarded as unusable as long as outliers are present. If outliers have been thoroughly eradicated, using for instance RANSAC, then it may be used.

The non-convex cost functions, though generally having a stable minimum, not much effected by outliers have the significant disadvantage of having local minima, which can make convergence to a global minimum chancy. The estimate is not strongly attracted to the minimum from outside of its immediate neighbourhood. Thus, they are not useful, unless (or until) the estimate is close to the final correct value.

The Huber cost function has the pleasant property of being convex, which makes convergence to a global minimum more reliable. The minimum is quite immune to the baleful influence of outliers since it represents a compromise between the Maximum Likelihood estimate of the inliers and the median of the outliers. The pseudo-Huber cost function is a good alternative to Huber, but use of $L1$ should be approached with care, because of its non-differentiablity at the origin.

These findings were illustrated on one-dimensional data, but they carry over to higher dimensional data also.

Parameter minimization. We have seen that the Huber and related cost functions are convex, and hence have a single minimum. We refer here to the cost $C(\delta)$ as a function of the error δ. In general in problems such as structure from motion, the error δ itself is a non-linear function of the parameters (such as camera and point positions). For this reason, the total cost expressed as a function of the motion and structure parameters

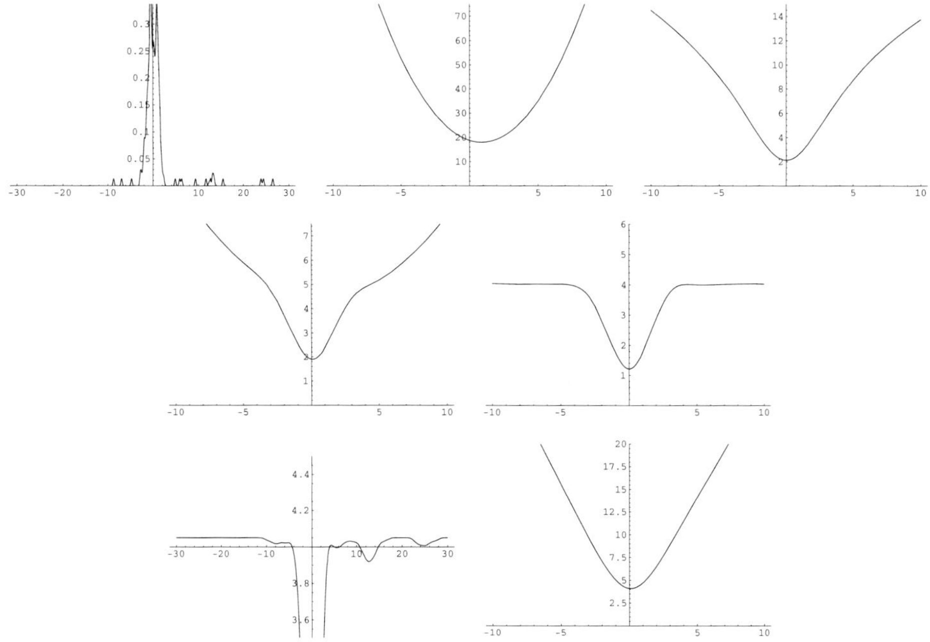

Fig. A6.5. *The data $\{a_i\}$ (illustrated in the top left graph) consists of a set of measurements centred around 0 with unit Gaussian noise, plus 10% of outliers biased towards the right of the true value. The graphs of $\sum_i C(|x - a_i|)$ correspond (left-to-right and top-to-bottom) to the cost functions Squared error, Cauchy, corrupted-Gaussian, Blake-Zisserman, a zoom of the Blake-Zisserman, and Huber cost functions. Note that the minimum of the squared-error cost function is pulled significantly to the right by the outliers, whereas the other cost-functions are relatively outlier-independent.*
The Blake-Zisserman cost function, which is based most nearly on the distribution of the data, has a very clear minimum. However, close examination (the zoomed plot) shows an undesirable characteristic, which is the presence of local minima near each of the outliers. An iterative method to find the cost minimum will fail if it is initiated outside the narrow basin of attraction surrounding the minimum.
By contrast, the Huber cost function is convex, which means the estimate will be drawn towards the single minimum from any initialization point.

can not be expected to be convex, and local minima are inevitable. Nevertheless, an important principle is:

- *choose a parameterization in which the error is as close as possible to being a linear function of the parameters, at least locally.*

Observing this principle will lead to simpler cost surfaces with fewer local minima, and generally quicker convergence.

Cost functions and least-squares. Usually cost functions of the type we have discussed are used in the context of a parameter minimization procedure, such as Levenberg-Marquardt or Newton iteration. Commonly, these procedures seek to minimize the norm of some vector $\boldsymbol{\Delta}$ depending on a set of parameters $\mathbf{p}$. Thus, they minimize $\|\boldsymbol{\Delta}(\mathbf{p})\|^2$ over all choices of the parameter vector $\mathbf{p}$. For instance in a structure and motion problem we may seek to minimize $\sum_i \|\mathbf{x}_i - \hat{\mathbf{x}}_i\|^2 = \sum_i \|\boldsymbol{\delta}_i\|^2 = \|\boldsymbol{\Delta}\|^2$ where the values $\mathbf{x}_i$ are measured image coordinates, the $\hat{\mathbf{x}}_i$ are the predicted values de-

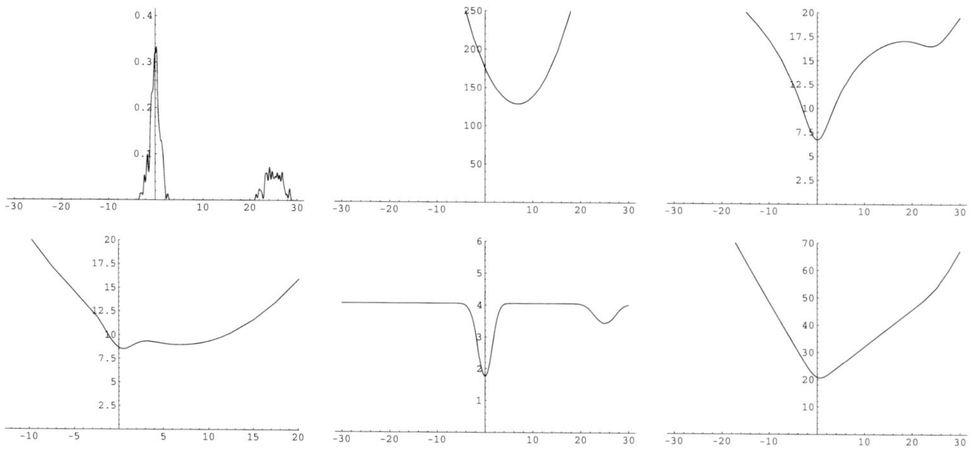

Fig. A6.6. *In this experiment, as in figure A6.5, the main part of the data (70%) is centred at the origin, with 30% of "outliers" concentrated in a block away from the origin (see top left graph). This type of measurement distribution is quite realistic in many imaging scenarios, for instance where point or edge measurement is confused by ghost edges. The cost functions in order from the top are: Square error, Cauchy, corrupted Gaussian, Blake-Zisserman and Huber.*
The Squared error cost function finds the mean of the measurement distribution, which is significantly pulled to the right by the block of outliers. The effect of the outlier block on the non-convex cost functions is also shown clearly here. Because of the non-convexity, the total cost function does not have a single minimum, but rather two minima around the separate blocks of measurements. Because of its convexity, the Huber cost function has a single minimum, which is located close to the median of the data, and is hardly influenced by the presence of the 30% of outliers.

rived from the current parameter values, and $\mathbf{\Delta}$ is the vector formed by concatenating the individual error vectors $\boldsymbol{\delta}_i$.

Since minimization of a squared vector norm $\|\mathbf{\Delta}\|^2$ is built into most implementations of Levenberg-Marquardt, we need to see how to apply the robust cost function in this case. The answer is to replace each vector $\boldsymbol{\delta}_i$ by a weighted vector $\boldsymbol{\delta}'_i = w_i \boldsymbol{\delta}_i$ such that

$$\|\boldsymbol{\delta}'_i\|^2 = w_i^2 \|\boldsymbol{\delta}_i\|^2 = C(\|\boldsymbol{\delta}_i\|)$$

for then $\sum_i C(\|\boldsymbol{\delta}_i\|) = \sum_i \|\boldsymbol{\delta}_i\|^2$ as desired. From this equality, we find

$$w_i = C(\|\boldsymbol{\delta}_i\|)^{1/2} / \|\boldsymbol{\delta}_i\|. \tag{A6.18}$$

Thus, the minimization problem is to minimize $\|\mathbf{\Delta}'\|^2$ where $\mathbf{\Delta}'$ is the vector obtained by concatenating the vectors $\boldsymbol{\delta}'_i = w_i \boldsymbol{\delta}_i$, and each w_i is computed from (A6.18). Note that w_i is a function of $\|\boldsymbol{\delta}_i\|$, which normally seeks to attenuate the cost of the outliers. This attenuation function is shown in the final column of figure A6.4 for the different cost functions. For the Squared error cost function, the attenuation factor is 1, meaning no attenuation occurs. For the other cost functions, there is little attenuation within an inlier region, and points outside this region are attenuated to different degrees.

A6.9 Parametrization

In the sort of iterative estimate problems we are considering here, an important consideration is how the solution space is to be parametrized. Most of the geometric entities that we consider do not have a simple Euclidean parametrization. For example, in solving a geometric optimization problem, we often wish to iterate over all camera orientations, represented by rotations. Rotations are most conveniently represented for computational purposes by rotation matrices, but this is a major overparametrization. The set of 3D rotations is naturally 3-dimensional (in fact, it forms a 3-dimensional Lie group, $SO(3)$), and we may wish to parametrize it with only 3 parameters.

Homogeneous vectors or matrices are another common type of representation. It is tempting to use a parametrization of a homogeneous n-vector just by using the components of the vector itself. However, there are really only $n-1$ degrees of freedom in a homogeneous n-vector, and it is sometimes advantageous to parametrize it with only $n-1$ parameters.

Gauge freedom. There has been much attention paid to *gauge freedom* and *gauge independence* in recent papers (for instance [McLauchlan-00]). In this context, the word gauge means a coordinate system for a parameter set, and gauge-freedom essentially refers to a change in the representation of the parameter set that does not essentially change the underlying geometry, and hence has no effect on the cost function. The most important gauge freedoms commonly encountered are projective or other ambiguities, such as those arising in reconstruction problems. However, the scale ambiguity of homogeneous vectors can be counted as gauge freedom also. Gauge freedoms in the parametrization of an optimization problem cause the normal equations to be singular, and hence allow multiple solutions. This problem is avoided by the regularization (or enhancement) step in Levenberg-Marquardt, but there is evidence that excessive gauge freedoms, causing slop in the parametrization, can lead to slower convergence. In addition, when gauge freedoms are present the covariance matrix of the estimated parameters is troublesome, in that there will be infinite variance in unconstrained parameter directions. For instance, it makes no sense to talk of the covariance matrix of an estimated homogeneous vector, unless the scale of the vector is constrained. Therefore, in the following pages, we will give some methods for obtaining minimal parametrizations for certain common geometric parameter sets.

What makes a good parametrization? The foremost requirement of a good parametrization is that it be singularity-free, at least in the areas that are visited during the course of an iterative optimization. This means that the parametrization should be locally continuous, differentiable and one-to-one – in short a diffeomorphism. A simple example of what is meant by this is given by the latitude-longitude parametrization of a sphere, that is, spherical-polar coordinates. This has a singularity at the poles, where the mapping from the lat-long coordinates to a neighbourhood of the pole is not one-to-one. The difficulty is that the point with coordinates (latitude = $89°$, longitude = $0°$) is very close to the point (latitude = $89°$, longitude = $90°$) – they are both points very close to the pole. However, they are a long way apart in parameter space. To see the effect of this, suppose that an optimization is taking place on the sphere, tracking down a minimum of a cost function, which exists at the point $(89^\circ, 90^\circ)$. If the current estimate is proceeding in the general direction of this minimum, up the line of zero longitude, when it gets near the pole it will find that although close to the minimum, it can not get there without a long detour in lat-long parameter space. The difficulty is that arbitrarily close points on the sphere, in the neighbourhood of the singularity (the pole) can have large differences in parameter values. The same sort of thing happens with representations of rotations using Euler angles.

Now, we move on to consider some specific parametrizations.

A6.9.1 Parametrization of 3D rotations

Using the angle-axis formula of (A4.9–*p*584) we may parametrize a 3×3 rotation by a 3-vector $\mathbf{t}$. This represents a rotation through an angle $\|\mathbf{t}\|$ about the axis determined by the vector $\mathbf{t}$. We denote the corresponding rotation matrix by $\mathtt{R}(\mathbf{t})$.

Regarding this representation, we may make certain simple observations:

(i) The identity map (no rotation) is represented by the zero vector $\mathbf{t} = \mathbf{0}$.

(ii) If some rotation $\mathtt{R}$ is represented by a vector $\mathbf{t}$, then the inverse rotation is represented by $-\mathbf{t}$. In symbols: $\mathtt{R}(\mathbf{t})^{-1} = \mathtt{R}(-\mathbf{t})$.

(iii) If $\mathbf{t}$ is small, then the rotation matrix is approximated by $\mathtt{I} + [\mathbf{t}]_\times$.

(iv) For small rotations represented by $\mathbf{t}_1$ and $\mathbf{t}_2$, the composite rotation is represented to first-order by $\mathbf{t}_1 + \mathbf{t}_2$. In other words $\mathtt{R}(\mathbf{t}_1)\mathtt{R}(\mathbf{t}_2) \approx \mathtt{R}(\mathbf{t}_1 + \mathbf{t}_2)$. Thus the mapping $\mathbf{t} \mapsto \mathtt{R}(\mathbf{t})$ is to first order a group isomorphism for small $\mathbf{t}$. In fact, for small $\mathbf{t}$, the map is an isometry (distance preserving map) in terms of the *distance* between two rotations $\mathtt{R}_1$ and $\mathtt{R}_2$ defined to equal to the angle of the rotation $\mathtt{R}_1\mathtt{R}_2^{-1}$.

(v) Any rotation may be represented as $\mathtt{R}(\mathbf{t})$ for some $\mathbf{t}$ such that $\|\mathbf{t}\| \leq \pi$. That is, any rotation is a rotation through an angle of at most π radians about some axis. The mapping $\mathbf{t} \mapsto \mathtt{R}(\mathbf{t})$ is one-to-one for $\|\mathbf{t}\| < \pi$ and two-to-one for $\|\mathbf{t}\| < 2\pi$. If $\|\mathbf{t}\| = 2\pi$, then $\mathtt{R}(\mathbf{t})$ is the identity map, regardless of $\mathbf{t}$. Thus, the parametrization has a singularity at $\|\mathbf{t}\| = 2\pi$.

(vi) **Normalization:** In parametrizing rotations by a vector $\mathbf{t}$ it is best to maintain the condition that $\|\mathbf{t}\| \leq \pi$, in order to keep away from the singularity when $\|\mathbf{t}\| = 2\pi$. If $\|\mathbf{t}\| > \pi$, then it may be replaced by the vector $(\|\mathbf{t}\| - 2\pi)\mathbf{t}/\|\mathbf{t}\| = \mathbf{t}(1 - 2\pi/\|\mathbf{t}\|)$, which represents the same rotation.

A6.9.2 Parametrization of homogeneous vectors

The quaternion representation of a rotation (section A4.3.3(*p*585)) is a redundant representation in that it contains 4 parameters where 3 will suffice. The angle-axis representation on the other hand is a minimum parametrization. Many entities in projective geometry are represented by homogeneous quantities, either vectors or matrices, for instance points in projective space or the fundamental matrix to name a few. For computational purposes, it is possible to represent such quantities as vectors with a minimum number of parameters in a similar way to which the angle-axis representation gives an alternative to the quaternion representation of a rotation.

Let $\mathbf{v}$ be a vector of any dimension, and represent by $\bar{\mathbf{v}}$ the unit vector $(\text{sinc}(\|\mathbf{v}\|/2)\mathbf{v}^\mathsf{T},\ \cos(\|\mathbf{v}\|/2))^\mathsf{T}$. This mapping $\mathbf{v} \mapsto \bar{\mathbf{v}}$ maps the disk of radius π (that is, the set of vectors of length at most π) smoothly and one-to-one onto the set of unit vectors $\bar{\mathbf{v}}$ with non-negative final coordinate. Thus, it provides a mapping onto the set of homogeneous vectors. The only difficult point with this mapping is that it takes any vector of length 2π to the same vector $(\mathbf{0}, -1)^\mathsf{T}$. However, this singular point may be avoided by renormalizing any vector $\mathbf{v}$ of length $\|\mathbf{v}\| > \pi$, replacing it with $(\|\mathbf{v}\| - 2\pi)\mathbf{v}/\|\mathbf{v}\|$ which represents the same homogeneous vector $\bar{\mathbf{v}}$.

A6.9.3 Parametrization of the n-sphere

Commonly it occurs in geometric optimization problems that some vector of parameters is required to lie on a unit sphere. As an example, consider a complete Euclidean bundle-adjustment with two views. The two cameras may be taken as $\mathtt{P} = [\mathtt{I} \mid \mathbf{0}]$ and $\mathtt{P}' = [\mathtt{R}|\mathbf{t}]$, where $\mathtt{R}$ is a rotation and $\mathbf{t}$ is a translation. In addition, 3D points $\mathbf{X}_i$ are defined, which are to map via the two camera matrices to image points. This defines an optimization problem in which the parameters are $\mathtt{R}$, $\mathbf{t}$ and the points $\mathbf{X}_i$, and the cost to be minimized is a geometric residual of the projections with respect to the image measurements. In this problem, there is an overall scale ambiguity, and this is conveniently resolved by requiring that $\|\mathbf{t}\| = 1$.

A minimum parametrization for the rotation matrix $\mathtt{R}$ is given by the rotation parametrization of section A6.9.1. Similarly, the points $\mathbf{X}_i$ are conveniently parametrized as homogeneous 4-vectors, using the parametrization of section A6.9.2. We consider in this section how one may parametrize the unit vector $\mathbf{t}$. Note that we can not simply parametrize $\mathbf{t}$ as a homogeneous vector, since change of sign of $\mathbf{t}$ changes the projection $\mathtt{P}'\mathbf{X} = [\mathtt{R}|\mathbf{t}]\mathbf{X}$.

The same problem arises in multiple-view Euclidean bundle-adjustment. In this case we have many camera matrices $\mathtt{P}^i = [\mathtt{R}^i|\mathbf{t}^i]$ and we may fix $\mathtt{P}^0 = [\mathtt{I} \mid \mathbf{0}]$. The set of translations $\mathbf{t}^i$ for all $i > 0$ are subject to scale ambiguity. We can minimally parametrize the translations by requiring that $\|\mathbf{T}\| = 1$, where $\mathbf{T}$ is the vector formed by concatenating all the $\mathbf{t}^i$ for $i > 0$.

There may be several ways of parametrizing a unit vector. We consider one particular parametrization here based on a local parametrization of the tangent plane to the unit sphere. We consider a sphere of dimension n, which consists of the set of $(n+1)$-vectors of unit length. Let $\mathbf{x}$ be a such a vector. Let $\mathtt{H}_{\mathbf{v}(\mathbf{x})}$ be a Householder matrix (see section A4.1.2(*p*580)) such that $\mathtt{H}_{\mathbf{v}(\mathbf{x})}\mathbf{x} = (0, \ldots, 0, 1)^\mathsf{T}$. Thus, we have transformed the vector $\mathbf{x}$ to lie along the coordinate axis. Now, we consider a parametrization of the unit sphere in the vicinity of $(0, \ldots, 0, 1)^\mathsf{T}$. Such a parametrization is a map $\mathbb{R}^n \rightarrow S^n$ that is well behaved in the vicinity of the origin. There are many choices, of which two possibilities are

(i) $f(\mathbf{y}) = \hat{\mathbf{y}}/\|\hat{\mathbf{y}}\|$ where $\hat{\mathbf{y}} = (\mathbf{y}^\mathsf{T}, 1)^\mathsf{T}$

(ii) $f(\mathbf{y}) = (\text{sinc}(\|\mathbf{y}\|/2)\mathbf{y}^\mathsf{T}, \cos(\|\mathbf{y}\|)/2)^\mathsf{T}$.

Both these functions map the origin $(0, \ldots, 0)^\mathsf{T}$ to $(0, \ldots, 0, 1)^\mathsf{T}$, and their Jacobian is $\partial f/\partial \mathbf{y} = [\mathtt{I}|\mathbf{0}]^\mathsf{T}$. Note that although we are interested in these functions just as local parametrizations, the first provides a parametrization for half the sphere, whereas for $\|\mathbf{y}\| \leq \pi$ the second map parametrizes the whole of the sphere with no singularity except at $\|\mathbf{y}\| = 2\pi$.

The composite map $\mathbf{y} \mapsto \mathtt{H}_{\mathbf{v}(\mathbf{x})} f(\mathbf{y})$ provides a local parametrization for a neighbourhood of the point $\mathbf{x}$ on the sphere (note here that we should write $\mathtt{H}^{-1}_{\mathbf{v}(\mathbf{x})}$, but $\mathtt{H}_{\mathbf{v}(\mathbf{x})} = \mathtt{H}^{-1}_{\mathbf{v}(\mathbf{x})}$). The Jacobian of this map is simply $\mathtt{H}_{\mathbf{v}(\mathbf{x})}[\mathtt{I}|\mathbf{0}]^\mathsf{T}$, which consists of the first n columns of the Householder matrix, and hence is easy to compute.

In minimization problems, we usually need to compute a Jacobian matrix $\partial C/\partial y$, of a vector valued cost function C with respect to a set of parameters $\mathbf{y}$. In the case where the parameters are constrainted to lie on a sphere S^n in $\mathbb{R}^{n+1}$ the cost function is nonetheless usually defined for all values of the parameter $\mathbf{x}$ in $\mathbb{R}^{n+1}$. As an example, in the Euclidean bundle-adjustment problem considered at the start of this section, the cost function (for instance residual reprojection error) can be defined for all pairs of cameras $\mathtt{P} = [\mathtt{I} \mid \mathbf{0}]$ and $\mathtt{P}' = [\mathtt{R}|\mathbf{t}]$ with $\mathbf{t}$ taking any value. Nevertheless, we may wish to minimize the cost function constraining $\mathbf{t}$ to lie on a sphere.

Thus, consider the case where a cost function $C(\mathbf{x})$ is defined for $\mathbf{x} \in \mathbb{R}^{n+1}$, but we parametrize $\mathbf{x}$ to lie on a sphere by setting $\mathbf{x} = \mathtt{H}_{\mathbf{v}(\mathbf{x})} f(\mathbf{y})$ with $\mathbf{y} \in \mathbb{R}^n$. In this case, we see that

$$\mathtt{J} = \frac{\partial C}{\partial \mathbf{y}} = \frac{\partial C}{\partial \mathbf{x}}\frac{\partial \mathbf{x}}{\partial \mathbf{y}} = \frac{\partial C}{\partial \mathbf{x}} \mathtt{H}_{\mathbf{v}(\mathbf{x})}[\mathtt{I}|\mathbf{0}]^\mathsf{T}.$$

In summary, by using local parametrizations, a parameter vector may be constrained to lie on an n-sphere with a modest added computational cost compared with the over-parametrization of allowing the vector to vary over the whole of $\mathbb{R}^{n+1}$. The key points of the method are as follows.

(i) Store the parameter vector $\mathbf{x} \in \mathbb{R}^{n+1}$, satisfying $\|\mathbf{x}\| = 1$.
(ii) In forming the linear update equations, compute the Jacobian matrix $\partial C/\partial \mathbf{x}$, and multiply it by $\mathtt{H}_{\mathbf{v}(\mathbf{x})}[\mathtt{I}|\mathbf{0}]^\mathsf{T}$ to obtain the Jacobian with respect to a minimal parameter set $\mathbf{y}$. Multiplication of $\partial C/\partial \mathbf{x}$ by $\mathtt{H}_{\mathbf{v}(\mathbf{x})}[\mathtt{I}|\mathbf{0}]^\mathsf{T}$ is efficiently carried out by the method of (A4.4–*p*580).
(iii) The iteration step provides an increment parameter vector $\boldsymbol{\delta}_\mathbf{y}$. Compute the new value of $\mathbf{x} = \mathtt{H}_{\mathbf{v}(\mathbf{x})} f(\boldsymbol{\delta}_\mathbf{y})$.

Essentially the same method of using local-parametrizations may be used more generally in other situations where a minimal parametrization is required. For instance, in section 11.4.2(*p*285) it was seen how the fundamental matrix may be parametrized locally with a minimum number of parameters, but no minimal parametrization can cover the whole set of fundamental matrices.

A6.10 Notes and exercises

(i) We prove in various steps the form of the pseudo-inverse of a block matrix given in (A6.13–*p*606).

(a) Recall that $\mathtt{H}^+ = \mathtt{G}(\mathtt{G}^\mathsf{T}\mathtt{H}\mathtt{G})^{-1}\mathtt{G}^\mathsf{T}$ if and only if $N_L(\mathtt{G}) = N_L(\mathtt{H})$ (see section A5.2(*p*590)).

(b) Let $\mathtt{G}$ be invertible. Then $(\mathtt{G}\mathtt{H}\mathtt{G}^\mathsf{T})^+ = \mathtt{G}^{-\mathsf{T}}\mathtt{H}^+\mathtt{G}^{-1}$ if and only if $N_L(\mathtt{H})\mathtt{G}^\mathsf{T} = N_L(\mathtt{H})\mathtt{G}^{-1}$.

(c) Applying this condition to (A6.12–*p*605) the necessary and sufficient condition for (A6.13–*p*606) to be valid is that $N_L(\mathtt{U} - \mathtt{W}\mathtt{V}^{-1}\mathtt{W}^\mathsf{T}) \subseteq N_L(\mathtt{Y}) = N_L(\mathtt{W})$.

(d) With $\mathtt{U}$, $\mathtt{V}$ and $\mathtt{W}$ defined in terms of $\mathtt{A}$ and $\mathtt{B}$ as in (A6.11–*p*605) this is equivalent to the condition $\text{span}(\mathtt{A}) \cap \text{span}(\mathtt{B}) = \emptyset$.

(ii) Investigate conditions under which the condition $\text{span}(\mathtt{A}) \cap \text{span}(\mathtt{B}) = \emptyset$ is true. It may be interpreted as meaning that the effects of varying the parameters $\mathbf{a}$ (for instance camera parameters) and the effects of varying $\mathbf{b}$ (point parameters) can not be complementary. Clearly this is not the case with (for instance) unconstrained projective reconstruction where both cameras and points may vary without affecting the measurements. In such a case, the variance of parameters $\mathbf{a}$ and $\mathbf{b}$ is infinite in directions $\delta_\mathbf{a}$ and $\delta_\mathbf{b}$ such that $\mathtt{A}\delta_\mathbf{a} = \mathtt{B}\delta_\mathbf{b}$.

Appendix 7

Some Special Plane Projective Transformations

Projective transformations (homographies) can be classified according to the algebraic and geometric multiplicity of their eigenvalues. The algebraic multiplicity of an eigenvalue is the number of times the root is repeated in the characteristic equation. The geometric multiplicity may be determined from the rank of the matrix $(\mathtt{H} - \lambda\mathtt{I})$, where $\mathtt{H}$ is the homography and λ the eigenvalue. A complete classification is given in projective geometry textbooks such as [Springer-64]. Here we mention several special cases which are important in practical situations, and occur at several points throughout this book. The description will be for plane transformations where $\mathtt{H}$ is a 3×3 matrix, but the generalization to 3-space transformations is straightforward.

The special forms are significant because $\mathtt{H}$ satisfies a number of relationships (remember the only restriction a general projective transformation is that it has full rank). Since $\mathtt{H}$ satisfies constraints it has fewer degrees of freedom, and consequently can be computed from fewer correspondences than a general projective transformation. The special transformations also have richer geometry and invariants than in the general case.

Note that unlike the special forms (affine etc.) discussed in chapter 2, which form subgroups, the following special projectivities do not form subgroups in general since they are not closed under multiplication. They do form a subgroup if all the elements have coincident fixed points and lines (i.e. differing only in their eigenvalues).

A7.1 Conjugate rotations

A rotation matrix $\mathtt{R}$ has eigenvalues $\{1, e^{i\theta}, e^{-i\theta}\}$, with corresponding eigenvectors $\{\mathbf{a}, \mathbf{I}, \mathbf{J}\}$, where $\mathbf{a}$ is the rotation axis, i.e. $\mathtt{R}\mathbf{a} = \mathbf{a}$, θ is the angle of rotation about the axis, and $\mathbf{I}$ and $\mathbf{J}$ (which are complex conjugate) are the circular points for the plane orthogonal to $\mathbf{a}$. Suppose a projective transformation between two planes has the form

$$\mathtt{H} = \mathtt{T}\mathtt{R}\mathtt{T}^{-1}$$

with $\mathtt{T}$ a general projective transformation; then $\mathtt{H}$ is a *conjugate rotation*. Eigenvalues are preserved under a conjugate relationship[1] so the eigenvalues of the projective transformation $\mathtt{H}$ are also $\{1, e^{i\theta}, e^{-i\theta}\}$ up to a common scale.

[1] Conjugacy is also referred to as a "similarity transformation". This meaning of "similarity" is unrelated to its use in this book as an isometry plus scaling transformation.

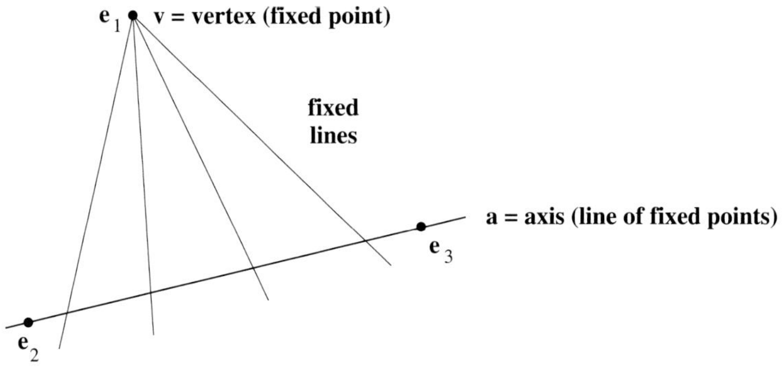

Fig. A7.1. **A planar homology**. *A planar homology is a plane projective transformation which has a line* $\mathbf{a}$ *of fixed points, called the* axis, *and a distinct fixed point* $\mathbf{v}$, *not on the line, called the* centre *or* vertex *of the homology. There is a pencil of fixed lines through the vertex. Algebraically, two of the eigenvalues of the transformation matrix are equal, and the fixed line corresponds to the 2D invariant space of the matrix (here the repeated eigenvalues are* λ_2 *and* λ_3*).*

Consider two images obtained by a camera rotating about its centre (as in figure 2.5-(p36)b); then as shown in section 8.4.2(p204), the images are related by a conjugate rotation. In this case the complex eigenvalues determine the angle (θ) through which the camera rotates, and the eigenvector corresponding to the real eigenvalue is the vanishing point of the rotation axis. Note that θ – a metric invariant – can be measured directly from the projective transformation.

A7.2 Planar homologies

A plane projective transformation $\mathtt{H}$ is a planar homology if it has a line of fixed points (called the *axis*), together with a fixed point (called the *vertex*) not on the line, see figure A7.1. Algebraically, the matrix has two equal and one distinct eigenvalues and the eigenspace corresponding to the equal eigenvalues is two-dimensional. The axis is the line through the two eigenvectors (i.e. points) spanning this eigenspace. The vertex corresponds to the other eigenvector. The ratio of the distinct eigenvalue to the repeated one is a characteristic invariant μ of the homology (i.e. the eigenvalues are, up to a common scale factor, $\{\mu, 1, 1\}$).

Properties of a planar homology include:

- Lines joining corresponding points intersect at the vertex, and corresponding lines (i.e. lines through two pairs of corresponding points) intersect on the axis. This is an example of Desargues' Theorem. See figure A7.2a.
- The cross ratios defined by the vertex, a pair of corresponding points, and the intersection of the line joining these points with the line of fixed points, are the same for all points related by the homology. See figure A7.2b.
- For curves related by a planar homology, corresponding tangents (the limit of neighbouring points defining corresponding lines) intersect on the axis.
- The vertex (2 dof), axis (2 dof) and invariant (1 dof) are sufficient to define the homology completely. A planar homology thus has 5 degrees of freedom.

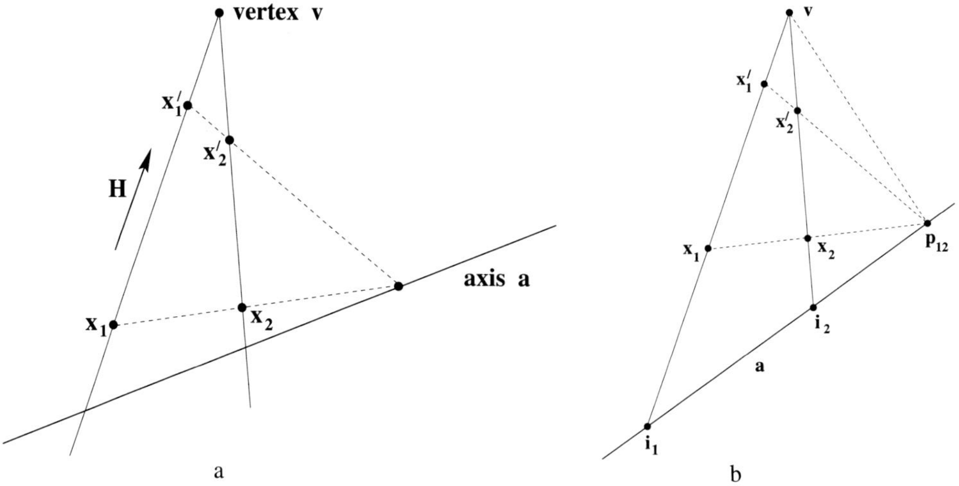

Fig. A7.2. **Homology transformation.** *(a) Under the transformation points on the axis are mapped to themselves; each point off the axis lies on a fixed line through* $\mathbf{v}$ *intersecting* $\mathbf{a}$ *and is mapped to another point on the line. Consequently, corresponding point pairs* $\mathbf{x} \leftrightarrow \mathbf{x}'$ *and the vertex of the homology are collinear. Corresponding lines – i.e. lines through pairs of corresponding points – intersect on the axis: for example, the lines* $\langle \mathbf{x}_1, \mathbf{x}_2 \rangle$ *and* $\langle \mathbf{x}'_1, \mathbf{x}'_2 \rangle$*. (b) The cross ratio defined by the vertex* $\mathbf{v}$*, the corresponding points* $\mathbf{x}, \mathbf{x}'$ *and the intersection of their join with the axis* $\mathbf{i}$*, is the characteristic invariant of the homology, and is the same for all corresponding points. For example, the cross ratios of the four points* $\{\mathbf{v}, \mathbf{x}'_1, \mathbf{x}_1, \mathbf{i}_1\}$ *and* $\{\mathbf{v}, \mathbf{x}'_2, \mathbf{x}_2, \mathbf{i}_2\}$ *are equal since they are perspectively related by lines concurrent at* $\mathbf{p}_{12}$*. It follows that the cross ratio is the same for all points related by the homology.*

- 3 matched points are sufficient to compute a planar homology. The 6 degrees of freedom of the point matches over-constrain the 5 degrees of freedom of the homology.

A planar homology arises naturally in an image of two planes related by a perspectivity of 3-space (i.e. lines joining corresponding points on the two planes are concurrent). An example is the transformation between the image of a planar object and the image of its shadow on a plane. In this case the axis is the imaged intersection of the two planes, and the vertex is the image of the light source, see figure 2.5(*p*36)c.

Parametrization. The projective transformation representing the homology can be parametrized directly in terms of the 3-vectors representing the axis $\mathbf{a}$ and vertex $\mathbf{v}$, and the characteristic ratio μ, as

$$\mathtt{H} = \mathtt{I} + (\mu - 1)\frac{\mathbf{v}\mathbf{a}^\mathsf{T}}{\mathbf{v}^\mathsf{T}\mathbf{a}}$$

where $\mathtt{I}$ is the identity. It is straightforward to verify that the inverse transformation is given by

$$\mathtt{H}^{-1} = \mathtt{I} + \left(\frac{1}{\mu} - 1\right)\frac{\mathbf{v}\mathbf{a}^\mathsf{T}}{\mathbf{v}^\mathsf{T}\mathbf{a}}.$$

The eigenvectors are

$$\{\mathbf{e}_1 = \mathbf{v}, \mathbf{e}_2 = \mathbf{a}_1^\perp, \mathbf{e}_3 = \mathbf{a}_2^\perp\}$$

with corresponding eigenvalues

$$\{\lambda_1 = \mu, \lambda_2 = 1, \lambda_3 = 1\}$$

where $\mathbf{a}_i^\perp$ are two vectors that span the space orthogonal to the 3-vector $\mathbf{a}$, i.e. $\mathbf{a}^\mathsf{T}\mathbf{a}_i^\perp = 0$ and $\mathbf{a} = \mathbf{a}_1^\perp \times \mathbf{a}_2^\perp$.

If the axis or the vertex is at infinity then the homology is an affine transformation. Algebraically, if $\mathbf{a} = (0, 0, 1)^\mathsf{T}$, then the axis is at infinity; or if $\mathbf{v} = (v_1, v_2, 0)^\mathsf{T}$, then the vertex is at infinity; and in both cases the transformation matrix $\mathtt{H}$ has last row $(0, 0, 1)$.

Planar harmonic homology. A specialization of a planar homology is the case that the cross ratio is harmonic ($\mu = -1$). This planar homology is called a planar harmonic homology and has 4 degrees of freedom since the invariant is known. The transformation matrix $\mathtt{H}$ obeys $\mathtt{H}^2 = \mathtt{I}$, i.e. the transformation is a square root of the identity, which is called an involution (also a collineation of period 2). The eigenvalues are, up to a common scale factor, $\{-1, 1, 1\}$. Two pairs of point correspondences determine $\mathtt{H}$.

In a perspective image of a plane object with a bilateral symmetry, corresponding points in the image are related by a planar harmonic homology. The axis of the homology is the image of the symmetry axis. Algebraically, $\mathtt{H}$ is a conjugate reflection where the conjugating element is a plane projective transformation. In an affine image (generated by an affine camera) the resulting transformation is a *skewed symmetry*, and the conjugating element is a plane affine transformation. For a skewed symmetry the vertex is at infinity, and the lines joining corresponding points are parallel.

The harmonic homology can be parametrized as

$$\mathtt{H} = \mathtt{H}^{-1} = \mathtt{I} - 2\frac{\mathbf{v}\mathbf{a}^\mathsf{T}}{\mathbf{v}^\mathsf{T}\mathbf{a}}.$$

Again, if the axis or vertex is at infinity then the transformation is affine.

A7.3 Elations

An elation has a line of fixed points (the axis), and a pencil of fixed lines intersecting in a point (the vertex) on the axis. It may be thought of as the limit of a homology where the vertex is on the line of fixed points. Algebraically, the matrix has three equal eigenvalues, but the eigenspace is 2-dimensional. It may be parametrized as

$$\mathtt{H} = \mathtt{I} + \mu\mathbf{v}\mathbf{a}^\mathsf{T} \quad \text{with} \quad \mathbf{a}^\mathsf{T}\mathbf{v} = 0 \tag{A7.1}$$

where $\mathbf{a}$ is the axis, and $\mathbf{v}$ the vertex. The eigenvalues are all unity. The invariant space of $\mathtt{H}$ is spanned by $\mathbf{a}_1^\perp, \mathbf{a}_2^\perp$. This is a line (pencil) of fixed points (which includes $\mathbf{v}$ since $\mathbf{a}^\mathsf{T}\mathbf{v} = 0$). The invariant space of $\mathtt{H}^\mathsf{T}$ is spanned by vectors $\mathbf{v}_1^\perp, \mathbf{v}_2^\perp$ orthogonal to $\mathbf{v}$. This is a pencil of fixed lines, $\mathbf{l} = \alpha\mathbf{v}_1^\perp + \beta\mathbf{v}_2^\perp$, for which $\mathbf{l}^\mathsf{T}\mathbf{v} = 0$, i.e. all lines of the pencil are concurrent at the point $\mathbf{v}$.

An elation has 4 degrees of freedom: one less than a homology due to the constraint $\mathbf{a}^\mathsf{T}\mathbf{v} = 0$. It is defined by the axis $\mathbf{a}$ (2 dof), the vertex $\mathbf{v}$ on $\mathbf{a}$ (1 dof) and the parameter μ (1 dof). It can be determined from 2 point correspondences.

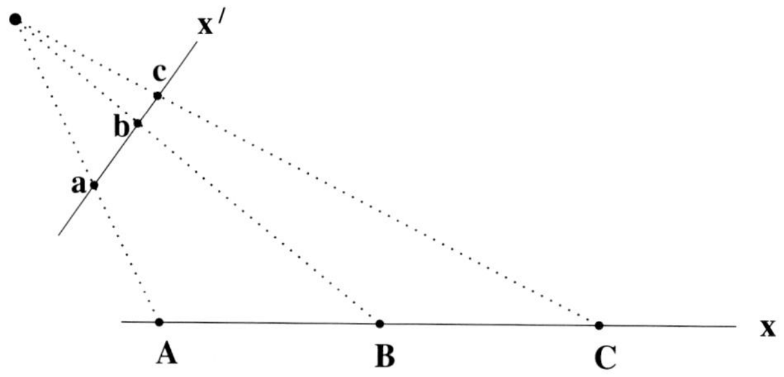

Fig. A7.3. **A line perspectivity**. *The lines joining corresponding points* ($\mathbf{a}, \mathbf{A}$ *etc.) are concurrent. Compare with figure A7.4.*

Elations often arise in practice as conjugate translations. Consider a pattern on a plane that repeats by a translation $\mathbf{t} = (t_x, t_y)^\mathsf{T}$, for example identical windows on the wall of a building. This action is represented on the plane of the wall as

$$\mathtt{H}_\mathrm{E} = \begin{bmatrix} \mathtt{I} & \mathbf{t} \\ \mathbf{0}^\mathsf{T} & 1 \end{bmatrix}$$

which is an elation where $\mathbf{v} = (t_x, t_y, 0)^\mathsf{T}$ is the translation direction of the repetition, and $\mathbf{a} = (0, 0, 1)^\mathsf{T}$ is the line at infinity. In an image of the wall the windows are related by a conjugate translation $\mathtt{H} = \mathtt{T}\,\mathtt{H}_\mathrm{E}\,\mathtt{T}^{-1}$, where $\mathtt{T}$ is the projectivity which maps the plane of the wall to the image. The image transformation $\mathtt{H}$ is also an elation. The vertex of this elation is the vanishing point of the translation direction, and the axis is the vanishing line of the wall plane.

A7.4 Perspectivities

One other special case of a projectivity is a *perspectivity*, which is shown in figure A7.3 for a 1D projectivity on the plane. The distinctive property of a perspectivity is that lines joining corresponding points are concurrent. The difference between a perspectivity and projectivity is made clear by considering the composition of two perspectivities. As shown in figure A7.4 the composition of two perspectivities is *not* in general a perspectivity. However, the composition *is* a projectivity because a perspectivity is a projectivity, and projectivities form a group (closed), so that the composition of two projectivities is a projectivity. To summarize:

- *The composition of two (or more) perspectivities is a projectivity, but not, in general, a perspectivity.*

A central projection image of a world plane, as in figure 2.3(*p*34), is an example of a 2D perspectivity between different planes. Notice that identifying the projectivity as a perspectivity requires the embedding of the planes in 3-space.

Finally, imagine that the planes and camera centre of figure 2.3(*p*34) are mapped (by another perspectivity) onto one of the planes. Then this imaged perspectivity is now a map between points on the same plane, and is seen to be a planar homology (section A7.2).

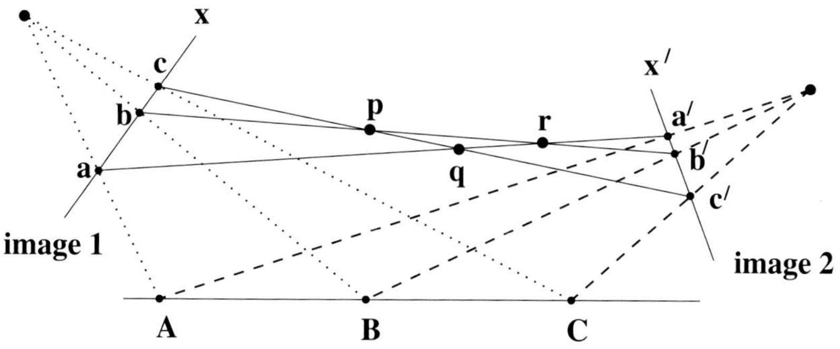

Fig. A7.4. **A line projectivity**. *Points* $\{\mathbf{a}, \mathbf{b}, \mathbf{c}\}$ *are related to points* $\{\mathbf{A}, \mathbf{B}, \mathbf{C}\}$ *by a line–to–line perspectivity. Points* $\{\mathbf{a}', \mathbf{b}', \mathbf{c}'\}$ *are also related to points* $\{\mathbf{A}, \mathbf{B}, \mathbf{C}\}$ *by a perspectivity. However, points* $\{\mathbf{a}, \mathbf{b}, \mathbf{c}\}$ *are related to points* $\{\mathbf{a}', \mathbf{b}', \mathbf{c}'\}$ *by a* projectivity*; they are* not *related by a perspectivity because lines joining corresponding points are* not *concurrent. In fact the pairwise intersections result in three distinct points* $\{\mathbf{p}, \mathbf{q}, \mathbf{r}\}$.

Further reading. [Springer-64] classifies projectivities and covers special cases, e.g. planar homologies. Planar homologies appear in many guises: modelling imaged shadow relations in [VanGool-98]; modelling imaged extruded surfaces in [Zisserman-95a]; and modelling relations for planar pose recovery in [Basri-99]. The parametrization of planar homologies is given in Viéville and Lingrand [Vieville-95]. Elations appear in the grouping of imaged repeated patterns on a plane [Schaffalitzky-99, Schaffalitzky-00b] and in 3-space they appear in the generalized bas-relief ambiguity [Kriegman-98].

Bibliography

[Agrawal-03] M. Agrawal and L. Davis. Camera calibration using spheres: A dual-space approach. Research Report CAR-TR-984, Center for Automation Research, University of Maryland, 2003.

[Aloimonos-90] J. Y. Aloimonos. Perspective approximations. *Image and Vision Computing*, 8(3):177–192, August 1990.

[Anandan-02] P. Anandan and M. Irani. Factorization with uncertainty. *International Journal of Computer Vision*, 49(2/3):101–116, 2002.

[Armstrong-94] M. Armstrong, A. Zisserman, and P. Beardsley. Euclidean reconstruction from uncalibrated images. In *Proc. British Machine Vision Conference*, pages 509–518, 1994.

[Armstrong-96a] M. Armstrong. *Self-Calibration from Image Sequences*. PhD thesis, University of Oxford, England, 1996.

[Armstrong-96b] M. Armstrong, A. Zisserman, and R. Hartley. Self-calibration from image triplets. In *Proc. European Conference on Computer Vision*, LNCS 1064/5, pages 3–16. Springer-Verlag, 1996.

[Astrom-98] K. Åström and A. Heyden. Continuous time matching constraints for image streams. *International Journal of Computer Vision*, 28(1):85–96, 1998.

[Avidan-98] S. Avidan and A. Shashua. Threading fundamental matrices. In *Proc. 5th European Conference on Computer Vision, Freiburg, Germany*, pages 124–140, 1998.

[Baillard-99] C. Baillard and A. Zisserman. Automatic reconstruction of piecewise planar models from multiple views. In *Proc. IEEE Conference on Computer Vision and Pattern Recognition*, pages 559–565, June 1999.

[Barrett-92] E. B. Barrett, M. H. Brill, N. N. Haag, and P. M. Payton. Invariant linear methods in photogrammetry and model-matching. In J. L. Mundy and A. Zisserman, editors, *Geometric invariance in computer vision*. MIT Press, Cambridge, 1992.

[Bascle-98] B. Bascle and A. Blake. Separability of pose and expression in facial tracing and animation. In *Proc. International Conference on Computer Vision*, pages 323–328, 1998.

[Basri-99] R. Basri and D. Jacobs. Projective alignment with regions. In *Proc. 7th International Conference on Computer Vision, Kerkyra, Greece*, pages 1158–1164, 1999.

[Bathe-76] K-J. Bathe and E. Wilson. *Numerical methods in finite element analysis*. Prentice Hall, 1976.

[Beardsley-92] P. A. Beardsley, D. Sinclair, and A. Zisserman. Ego-motion from six points. Insight meeting, Catholic University Leuven, February 1992.

[Beardsley-94] P. A. Beardsley, A. Zisserman, and D. W. Murray. Navigation using affine structure and motion. In *Proc. European Conference on Computer Vision*, LNCS 800/801, pages 85–96. Springer-Verlag, 1994.

[Beardsley-95a] P. A. Beardsley and A. Zisserman. Affine calibration of mobile vehicles. In *Europe–China workshop on Geometrical Modelling and Invariants for Computer Vision*, pages 214–221. Xidan University Press, Xi'an, China, 1995.

[Beardsley-95b] P. A. Beardsley, I. D. Reid, A. Zisserman, and D. W. Murray. Active visual navigation using non-metric structure. In *Proc. International Conference on Computer Vision*, pages 58–64, 1995.

[Beardsley-96] P. A. Beardsley, P. H. S. Torr, and A. Zisserman. 3D model aquisition from extended image sequences. In *Proc. 4th European Conference on Computer Vision, LNCS 1065, Cambridge*, pages 683–695, 1996.

[Blake-87] A. Blake and A. Zisserman. *Visual Reconstruction.* MIT Press, Cambridge, USA, August 1987.

[Boehm-94] W. Boehm and H. Prautzsch. *Geometric Concepts for Geometric Design.* A. K. Peters, 1994.

[Bookstein-79] F. Bookstein. Fitting conic sections to scattered data. *Computer Graphics and Image Processing*, 9:56–71, 1979.

[Bougnoux-98] S. Bougnoux. From Projective to Euclidean space under any practical situation, a criticism of self-calibration. In *Proc. 6th International Conference on Computer Vision, Bombay, India*, pages 790–796, January 1998.

[Boult-91] I. E. Boult and L. Gottesfeld Brown. Factorisation-based segmentation of motions. In *Proc. IEEE Workshop on Visual Motion*, 1991.

[Brand-01] M. Brand. Morphable 3d models from video. In *Proc. IEEE Conference on Computer Vision and Pattern Recognition*, pages II: 456–463, 2001.

[Brown-71] D. C. Brown. Close-range camera calibration. *Photogrammetric Engineering*, 37(8):855–866, 1971.

[Buchanan-88] T. Buchanan. The twisted cubic and camera calibration. *Computer Vision, Graphics and Image Processing*, 42:130–132, 1988.

[Buchanan-92] T. Buchanan. Critical sets for 3D reconstruction using lines. In *Proc. European Conference on Computer Vision*, LNCS 588, pages 730–738. Springer-Verlag, 1992.

[Canny-86] J. F. Canny. A computational approach to edge detection. *IEEE Transactions on Pattern Analysis and Machine Intelligence*, 8(6):679–698, 1986.

[Capel-98] D. Capel and A. Zisserman. Automated mosaicing with super-resolution zoom. In *Proc. IEEE Conference on Computer Vision and Pattern Recognition, Santa Barbara*, pages 885–891, June 1998.

[Caprile-90] B. Caprile and V. Torre. Using vanishing points for camera calibration. *International Journal of Computer Vision*, 4:127–140, 1990.

[Carlsson-93] S. Carlsson. Multiple image invariance using the double algebra. In *Applications of Invariance in Computer Vision*, volume SLN Comp. Science vol 825, pages 335–350, 1993.

[Carlsson-94] S. Carlsson. Multiple image invariance using the double algebra. In J. Mundy, A. Zisserman, and D. Forsyth, editors, *Applications of Invariance in Computer Vision LNCS 825*. Springer-Verlag, 1994.

[Carlsson-95] S. Carlsson. Duality of reconstruction and positioning from projective views. In *IEEE Workshop on Representation of Visual Scenes, Boston*, 1995.

[Carlsson-98] S. Carlsson and D. Weinshall. Dual computation of projective shape and camera positions from multiple images. *International Journal of Computer Vision*, 27(3):227–241, 1998.

[Christy-96] S. Christy and R. Horaud. Euclidean shape and motion from multiple perspective views by affine iteration. *IEEE Transactions on Pattern Analysis and Machine Intelligence*, 18(11):1098–1104, November 1996.

[Chum-03] O. Chum, T. Werner, and T. Pajdla. On joint orientation of epipoles. Research Report CTU–CMP–2003–10, Center for Machine Perception, K333 FEE Czech Technical University, Prague, Czech Republic, April 2003.

[Cipolla-99] R. Cipolla, T. Drummond, and D. Robertson. Camera calibration from vanishing points in images of architectural scenes. In *Proc. British Machine Vision Conference*, September 1999.

[Collins-93] R. T. Collins and J. R. Beveridge. Matching perspective views of coplanar structures using projective unwarping and similarity matching. In *Proc. IEEE Conference on Computer Vision and Pattern Recognition*, 1993.

[Costeira-98] J.P. Costeira and T. Kanade. A multibody factorization method for independently moving objects. *International Journal of Computer Vision*, 29(3):159–179, 1998.

[Criminisi-98] A. Criminisi, I. Reid, and A. Zisserman. Duality, rigidity and planar parallax. In *Proc.*

European Conference on Computer Vision, pages 846–861. Springer-Verlag, June 1998.

[Criminisi-99a] A. Criminisi, I. Reid, and A. Zisserman. Single view metrology. In *Proc. 7th International Conference on Computer Vision, Kerkyra, Greece*, pages 434–442, September 1999.

[Criminisi-99b] A. Criminisi, I. Reid, and A. Zisserman. A plane measuring device. *Image and Vision Computing*, 17(8):625–634, 1999.

[Criminisi-00] A. Criminisi, I. Reid, and A. Zisserman. Single view metrology. *International Journal of Computer Vision*, 40(2):123–148, November 2000.

[Criminisi-01] A. Criminisi. *Accurate Visual Metrology from Single and Multiple Uncalibrated Images.* Distinguished Dissertation Series. Springer-Verlag London Ltd., July 2001. ISBN: 1852334681.

[Cross-98] G. Cross and A. Zisserman. Quadric surface reconstruction from dual-space geometry. In *Proc. 6th International Conference on Computer Vision, Bombay, India*, pages 25–31, January 1998.

[Cross-99] G. Cross, A. W. Fitzgibbon, and A. Zisserman. Parallax geometry of smooth surfaces in multiple views. In *Proc. 7th International Conference on Computer Vision, Kerkyra, Greece*, pages 323–329, September 1999.

[Csurka-97] G. Csurka, C. Zeller, Z. Zhang, and O. D. Faugeras. Characterizing the uncertainty of the fundamental matrix. *Computer Vision and Image Understanding*, 68(1):18–36, October 1997.

[Csurka-98] G. Csurka, D. Demirdjian, A. Ruf, and R. Horaud. Closed-form solutions for the euclidean calibration of a stereo rig. In *Proc. 5th European Conference on Computer Vision, Freiburg, Germany*, pages 426–442, June 1998.

[DeAgapito-98] L. de Agapito, E. Hayman, and I. Reid. Self-calibration of a rotating camera with varying intrinsic parameters. In *Proc. 9th British Machine Vision Conference, Southampton*, 1998.

[DeAgapito-99] L. de Agapito, R. I. Hartley, and E. Hayman. Linear self-calibration of a rotating and zooming camera. In *Proc. IEEE Conference on Computer Vision and Pattern Recognition*, pages 15–21, 1999.

[Dementhon-95] D. Dementhon and L. Davis. Model based pose in 25 lines of code. *International Journal of Computer Vision*, 15(1/2):123–141, 1995.

[Devernay-95] F. Devernay and O. D. Faugeras. Automatic calibration and removal of distortion from scenes of structured environments. In *SPIE*, volume 2567, San Diego, CA, July 1995.

[Devernay-96] F. Devernay and O. D. Faugeras. From projective to euclidean reconstruction. In *Proc. IEEE Conference on Computer Vision and Pattern Recognition*, pages 264–269, 1996.

[Faugeras-90] O. D. Faugeras and S. J. Maybank. Motion from point matches: Multiplicity of solutions. *International Journal of Computer Vision*, 4:225–246, 1990.

[Faugeras-92a] O. D. Faugeras, Q. Luong, and S. Maybank. Camera self-calibration: Theory and experiments. In *Proc. European Conference on Computer Vision*, LNCS 588, pages 321–334. Springer-Verlag, 1992.

[Faugeras-92b] O. D. Faugeras. What can be seen in three dimensions with an uncalibrated stereo rig? In *Proc. European Conference on Computer Vision*, LNCS 588, pages 563–578. Springer-Verlag, 1992.

[Faugeras-93] O. D. Faugeras. *Three-Dimensional Computer Vision: a Geometric Viewpoint.* MIT Press, 1993.

[Faugeras-94] O. D. Faugeras and L. Robert. What can two images tell us about a third one. In J. O. Eckland, editor, *Proc. 3rd European Conference on Computer Vision, Stockholm*, pages 485–492. Springer-Verlag, 1994.

[Faugeras-95a] O. D. Faugeras and B. Mourrain. On the geometry and algebra of point and line correspondences between N images. In *Proc. International Conference on Computer Vision*, pages 951–962, 1995.

[Faugeras-95b] O. D. Faugeras. Stratification of three-dimensional vision: projective, affine, and metric representation. *Journal of the Optical Society of America*, A12:465–484, 1995.

[Faugeras-95c] O. D. Faugeras, S. Laveau, L. Robert, G. Csurka, and C. Zeller. 3-D reconstruction of urban scenes from sequences of images. Technical report, INRIA, 1995.

[Faugeras-97] O. D. Faugeras and T. Papadopoulo. Grassmann-Cayley algebra for modeling systems of cameras and the algebraic equations of the manifold of trifocal tensors. Technical Report 3225, INRIA, Sophia-Antipolis, France, 1997.

[Faugeras-98] O. D. Faugeras, L. Quan, and P. Sturm. Self-calibration of a 1D projective camera and its application to the self-calibration of a 2D projective camera. In *Proc. European Conference on Computer Vision*, pages 36–52, 1998.

[Fischler-81] M. A. Fischler and R. C. Bolles. Random sample consensus: A paradigm for model fitting with applications to image analysis and automated cartography. *Comm. Assoc. Comp. Mach.*, 24(6):381–395, 1981.

[Fitzgibbon-98a] A. W. Fitzgibbon and A. Zisserman. Automatic camera recovery for closed or open image sequences. In *Proc. European Conference on Computer Vision*, pages 311–326. Springer-Verlag, June 1998.

[Fitzgibbon-98b] A. W. Fitzgibbon, G. Cross, and A. Zisserman. Automatic 3D model construction for turn-table sequences. In R. Koch and L. Van Gool, editors, *3D Structure from Multiple Images of Large-Scale Environments, LNCS 1506*, pages 155–170. Springer-Verlag, June 1998.

[Fitzgibbon-99] A. W. Fitzgibbon, M. Pilu, and R. B. Fisher. Direct least-squares fitting of ellipses. *IEEE Transactions on Pattern Analysis and Machine Intelligence*, 21(5):476–480, May 1999.

[Gear-98] C. W. Gear. Multibody grouping from motion images. *International Journal of Computer Vision*, 29(2):133–150, 1998.

[Giblin-87] P. Giblin and R. Weiss. Reconstruction of surfaces from profiles. In *Proc. 1st International Conference on Computer Vision, London*, pages 136–144, London, 1987.

[Gill-78] P. E. Gill and W. Murray. Algorithms for the solution of the nonlinear least-squares problem. *SIAM J Num Anal*, 15(5):977–992, 1978.

[Golub-89] G. H. Golub and C. F. Van Loan. *Matrix Computations*. The Johns Hopkins University Press, Baltimore, MD, second edition, 1989.

[Gracie-68] G. Gracie. Analytical photogrammetry applied to single terrestrial photograph mensuration. In *XIth International Conference of Photogrammetry, Lausanne, Switzerland*, July 1968.

[Gupta-97] R. Gupta and R. I. Hartley. Linear pushbroom cameras. *IEEE Transactions on Pattern Analysis and Machine Intelligence*, September 1997.

[Haralick-91] R. M. Haralick, C. Lee, K. Ottenberg, and M. Nölle. Analysis and solutions of the three point perspective pose estimation problem. In *Proc. IEEE Conference on Computer Vision and Pattern Recognition*, pages 592–598, 1991.

[Harris-88] C. J. Harris and M. Stephens. A combined corner and edge detector. In *Proc. 4th Alvey Vision Conference, Manchester*, pages 147–151, 1988.

[Hartley-92a] R. I. Hartley. Estimation of relative camera positions for uncalibrated cameras. In *Proc. European Conference on Computer Vision*, LNCS 588, pages 579–587. Springer-Verlag, 1992.

[Hartley-92b] R. I. Hartley. Invariants of points seen in multiple images. GE internal report, GE CRD, Schenectady, NY 12301, USA, May 1992.

[Hartley-92c] R. I. Hartley, R. Gupta, and T. Chang. Stereo from uncalibrated cameras. In *Proc. IEEE Conference on Computer Vision and Pattern Recognition*, 1992.

[Hartley-94a] R. I. Hartley. Self-calibration from multiple views with a rotating camera. In *Proc. European Conference on Computer Vision*, LNCS 800/801, pages 471–478. Springer-Verlag, 1994.

[Hartley-94b] R. I. Hartley. Euclidean reconstruction from uncalibrated views. In J. Mundy, A. Zisserman, and D. Forsyth, editors, *Applications of Invariance in Computer Vision*, LNCS 825, pages 237–256. Springer-Verlag, 1994.

[Hartley-94c] R. I. Hartley. Projective reconstruction and invariants from multiple images. *IEEE Transactions on Pattern Analysis and Machine Intelligence*, 16:1036–1041, October 1994.

[Hartley-94d] R. I. Hartley. Projective reconstruction from line correspondence. In *Proc. IEEE Conference on Computer Vision and Pattern Recognition*, 1994.

[Hartley-95a] R. I. Hartley. Multilinear relationships between coordinates of corresponding image points and lines. In *Proceedings of the Sophus Lie Symposium, Nordfjordeid, Norway* (not published yet), 1995.

[Hartley-95b] R. I. Hartley. A linear method for reconstruction from lines and points. In *Proc. International Conference on Computer Vision*, pages 882–887, 1995.

[Hartley-97a] R. I. Hartley. Lines and points in three views and the trifocal tensor. *International Journal of Computer Vision*, 22(2):125–140, 1997.

[Hartley-97b] R. I. Hartley and P. Sturm. Triangulation. *Computer Vision and Image Understanding*, 68(2):146–157, November 1997.

[Hartley-97c] R. I. Hartley. In defense of the eight-point algorithm. *IEEE Transactions on Pattern Analysis and Machine Intelligence*, 19(6):580 – 593, October 1997.

[Hartley-97d] R. I. Hartley. Kruppa's equations derived from the fundamental matrix. *IEEE Transactions on Pattern Analysis and Machine Intelligence*, 19(2):133–135, 1997.

[Hartley-97e] R. I. Hartley and T. Saxena. The cubic rational polynomial camera model. In *Proc. DARPA Image Understanding Workshop*, pages 649 – 653, 1997.

[Hartley-98a] R. I. Hartley. Chirality. *International Journal of Computer Vision*, 26(1):41–61, 1998.

[Hartley-98b] R. I. Hartley. Dualizing scene reconstruction algorithms. In R. Koch and L. Van Gool, editors, *3D Structure from Multiple Images of Large-Scale Environments, LNCS 1506*, pages 14–31. Springer-Verlag, June 1998.

[Hartley-98c] R. I. Hartley. Computation of the quadrifocal tensor. In *Proc. European Conference on Computer Vision*, LNCS 1406, pages 20–35. Springer-Verlag, 1998.

[Hartley-98d] R. I. Hartley. Minimizing algebraic error in geometric estimation problems. In *Proc. International Conference on Computer Vision*, pages 469–476, 1998.

[Hartley-99] R. Hartley, L. de Agapito, E. Hayman, and I. Reid. Camera calibration and the search for infinity. In *Proc. 7th International Conference on Computer Vision, Kerkyra, Greece*, pages 510–517, September 1999.

[Hartley-00a] R. I. Hartley and N. Y. Dano. Reconstruction from six-point sequences. In *Proc. IEEE Conference on Computer Vision and Pattern Recognition*, pages II–480 – II–486, 2000.

[Hartley-00b] R. I. Hartley. Ambiguous configurations for 3-view projective reconstruction. In *Proc. 6th European Conference on Computer Vision, Part I, LNCS 1842, Dublin, Ireland*, pages 922–935, 2000.

[Hartley-02a] R. Hartley and F. Kahl. Critical curves and surfaces for euclidean reconstruction. In *Proc. 7th European Conference on Computer Vision, Part II, LNCS 2351, Copenhagen, Denmark*, pages 447–462, 2002.

[Hartley-02b] R. Hartley and R. Kaucic. Sensitivity of calibration to principal point position. In *Proc. 7th European Conference on Computer Vision, Copenhagen, Denmark*, volume 2, pages 433–446. Springer-Verlag, 2002.

[Hartley-03] R. Hartley and F. Kahl. A critical configuration for reconstruction from rectilinear motion. In *Proc. IEEE Conference on Computer Vision and Pattern Recognition*, 2003.

[Hayman-03] E. Hayman, T. Thórhallsson, and D.W. Murray. Tracking while zooming using affine transfer and multifocal tensors. *International Journal of Computer Vision*, 51(1):37–62, January 2003.

[Heyden-95a] A. Heyden. Reconstruction from image sequences by means of relative depths. In E. Grimson, editor, *Proc. 5th International Conference on Computer Vision, Boston*, Cambridge, MA, June 1995.

[Heyden-95b] A. Heyden. *Geometry and Algebra of Multiple Projective Transformations*. PhD thesis, Department of Mathematics, Lund University, Sweden, December 1995.

[Heyden-97a] A. Heyden. Projective structure and motion from image sequences using subspace methods. In *Scandinavian Conference on Image Analysis, Lappenraanta*, pages 963–968, 1997.

[Heyden-97b] A. Heyden and K. Åström. Euclidean reconstruction from image sequences with varying and unknown focal length and principal point. In *Proc. IEEE Conference on Computer Vision and Pattern Recognition*, 1997.

[Heyden-97c] A. Heyden. Reconstruction from multiple images by means of using relative depths. *International Journal of Computer Vision*, 24(2):155–161, 1997.

[Heyden-98] A. Heyden. Algebraic varieties in multiple view geometry. In *Proc. 5th European Conference on Computer Vision, Freiburg, Germany*, pages 3–19, 1998.

[Hilbert-56] D. Hilbert and S. Cohn-Vossen. *Geometry and the Imagination*. Chelsea, NY, 1956.

[Horaud-98] R. Horaud and G. Csurka. Self-calibration and Euclidean reconstruction using motions of a stereo rig. In *Proc. 6th International Conference on Computer Vision, Bombay, India*, pages 96–103, January 1998.

[Horn-90] B. K. P. Horn. Relative orientation. *International Journal of Computer Vision*, 4:59–78, 1990.

[Horn-91] B. K. P. Horn. Relative orientation revisited. *Journal of the Optical Society of America*, 8(10):1630–1638, 1991.

[Horry-97] Y. Horry, K. Anjyo, and K. Arai. Tour into the picture: Using a spidery mesh interface to make animation from a single image. In *Proceedings of the ACM SIGGRAPH Conference on Computer Graphics*, pages 225–232, 1997.

[Huang-89] T. S. Huang and O. D. Faugeras. Some properties of the E-matrix in two-view motion estimation. *IEEE Transactions on Pattern Analysis and Machine Intelligence*, 11:1310 – 1312, 1989.

[Huber-81] P. J. Huber. *Robust Statistics*. John Wiley and Sons, 1981.

[Huynh-03] D.Q. Huynh, R. Hartley, and A Heyden. Outlier correction of image sequences for the affine camera. In *Proc. 9th International Conference on Computer Vision, Vancouver, France*, 2003.

[Irani-98] M. Irani, P. Anandan, and D. Weinshall. From reference frames to reference planes: Multi-view parallax geometry and applications. In *Proc. European Conference on Computer Vision*, 1998.

[Irani-99] M. Irani. Multi-frame optical flow estimation using subspace contraints. In *Proc. International Conference on Computer Vision*, 1999.

[Irani-00] Michal Irani and P. Anandan. Factorization with uncertainty. In *Proc. 6th European Conference on Computer Vision, Part I, LNCS 1842, Dublin, Ireland*, pages 539 – 553, 2000.

[Jiang-02] G. Jiang, H. Tsui, L. Quan, and A. Zisserman. Single axis geometry by fitting conics. In *Proc. 7th European Conference on Computer Vision, Copenhagen, Denmark*, volume 1, pages 537–550. Springer-Verlag, 2002.

[Kahl-98a] F. Kahl and A. Heyden. Structure and motion from points, lines and conics with affine cameras. In *Proc. 5th European Conference on Computer Vision, Freiburg, Germany*, pages 327–341, 1998.

[Kahl-98b] F. Kahl and A. Heyden. Using conic correspondences in two images to estimate epipolar geometry. In *Proc. 6th International Conference on Computer Vision, Bombay, India*, pages 761–766, 1998.

[Kahl-99] F. Kahl. Critical motions and ambiguous euclidean reconstructions in auto-calibration. In *Proc. 7th International Conference on Computer Vision, Kerkyra, Greece*, pages 469–475, 1999.

[Kahl-01a] F. Kahl, R. Hartley, and K. Åström. Critical configurations for n-view projective reconstruction. In *Proc. IEEE Conference on Computer Vision and Pattern Recognition*, pages II–158 – II–163, 2001.

[Kahl-01b] F. Kahl. *Geometry and Critical Configurations of Multiple Views*. PhD thesis, Lund Institute of Technology, 2001.

[Kanatani-92] K. Kanatani. *Geometric computation for machine vision*. Oxford University Press, Oxford, 1992.

[Kanatani-94] K. Kanatani. Statistical bias of conic fitting and renormalization. *IEEE Transactions on Pattern Analysis and Machine Intelligence*, 16(3):320–326, 1994.

[Kanatani-96] K. Kanatani. *Statistical Optimization for Geometric Computation: Theory and Practice*. Elsevier Science, Amsterdam, 1996.

[Kaucic-01] R. Kaucic, R. I. Hartley, and N. Y. Dano. Plane-based projective reconstruction. In *Proc. 8th International Conference on Computer Vision, Vancouver, Canada*, pages I–420–427, 2001.

[Klein-39] F. Klein. *Elementary Mathematics from an Advanced Standpoint*. Macmillan, New York, 1939.

[Knight-03] J. Knight, A. Zisserman, and I. Reid. Linear auto-calibration for ground plane motion. In *Proc. IEEE Conference on Computer Vision and Pattern Recognition*, June 2003.

[Koenderink-84] J. J. Koenderink. What does the occluding contour tell us about solid shape? *Perception*, 13:321–330, 1984.

[Koenderink-90] J. Koenderink. *Solid Shape*. MIT Press, 1990.

[Koenderink-91] J. J. Koenderink and A. J. van Doorn. Affine structure from motion. *Journal of the Optical Society of America*, 8(2):377–385, 1991.

[Krames-42] J. Krames. Über die bei der Hauptaufgabe der Luftphotogrammetrie auftretenden "gefährlichen" Flächen. *Bildmessung und Luftbildwesen (Beilage zur Allg. Vermessungs-Nachr.)*, 17, Heft 1/2:1–18, 1942.

[Kriegman-98] D. J. Kriegman and P. Belhumeur. What shadows reveal about object structure. In *Proc. European Conference on Computer Vision*, pages 399–414, 1998.

[Laveau-96a] S. Laveau. *Géométrie d'un système de N caméras. Théorie, estimation et applications.* PhD thesis, INRIA, 1996.

[Laveau-96b] S. Laveau and O. D. Faugeras. Oriented projective geometry in computer vision. In *Proc. 4th European Conference on Computer Vision, LNCS 1065, Cambridge*, pages 147–156, Springer–Verlag, 1996. Buxton B. and Cipolla R.

[Liebowitz-98] D. Liebowitz and A. Zisserman. Metric rectification for perspective images of planes. In *Proc. IEEE Conference on Computer Vision and Pattern Recognition*, pages 482–488, June 1998.

[Liebowitz-99a] D. Liebowitz, A. Criminisi, and A. Zisserman. Creating architectural models from images. In *Proc. EuroGraphics*, volume 18, pages 39–50, September 1999.

[Liebowitz-99b] D. Liebowitz and A. Zisserman. Combining scene and auto-calibration constraints. In *Proc. 7th International Conference on Computer Vision, Kerkyra, Greece*, September 1999.

[Liebowitz-01] D. Liebowitz. *Camera Calibration and Reconstruction of Geometry from Images.* PhD thesis, University of Oxford, Dept. Engineering Science, June 2001. D.Phil. thesis.

[LonguetHiggins-81] H. C. Longuet-Higgins. A computer algorithm for reconstructing a scene from two projections. *Nature*, 293:133–135, September 1981.

[Luong-92] Q. Luong. *Matrice Fondamentale et Autocalibration en Vision par Ordinateur.* PhD thesis, Université de Paris-Sud, France, 1992.

[Luong-94] Q. T. Luong and T. Viéville. Canonic representations for the geometries of multiple projective views. In *Proc. 3rd European Conference on Computer Vision, Stockholm*, pages 589–599, May 1994.

[Luong-96] Q. T. Luong and T. Viéville. Canonical representations for the geometries of multiple projective views. *Computer Vision and Image Understanding*, 64(2):193–229, September 1996.

[Lutkepohl-96] H. Lutkepohl. *Handbook of Matrices.* Wiley, ISBN 0471970158, 1996.

[Ma-99] Y. Ma, S. Soatto, J. Kosecka, and S. Sastry. Euclidean reconstruction and reprojection up to subgroups. In *Proc. 7th International Conference on Computer Vision, Kerkyra, Greece*, pages 773–780, 1999.

[Mathematica-92] S. Wolfram. *Mathematica A System for Doing Mathematics by Computer second edition.* Addison-Wesley, 1992.

[Maybank-90] S. J. Maybank. The projective geometry of ambiguous surfaces. *Philosophical Transactions of the Royal Society of London, SERIES A*, A 332:1–47, 1990.

[Maybank-93] S. J. Maybank. *Theory of reconstruction from image motion.* Springer-Verlag, Berlin, 1993.

[Maybank-98] S. J. Maybank and A. Shashua. Ambiguity in reconstruction from images of six points. In *Proc. 6th International Conference on Computer Vision, Bombay, India*, pages 703–708, 1998.

[McLauchlan-00] P. F. McLauchlan. Gauge independence in optimization algorithms for 3D vision. In W. Triggs, A. Zisserman, and R. Szeliski, editors, *Vision Algorithms: Theory and Practice*, volume 1883 of *LNCS*, pages 183–199. Springer, 2000.

[Mohr-92] R. Mohr. Projective geometry and computer vision. In C. H. Chen, L. F. Pau, and P. S. P. Wang, editors, *Handbook of Pattern Recognition and Computer Vision.* World Scientific, 1992.

[Mohr-93] R. Mohr, F. Veillon, and L. Quan. Relative 3D reconstruction using multiple uncalibrated images. In *Proc. IEEE Conference on Computer Vision and Pattern Recognition*, pages 543–548, 1993.

[Moons-94] T. Moons, L. Van Gool, M. Van Diest, and E. Pauwels. Affine reconstruction from perspective image pairs. In J. Mundy, A. Zisserman, and D. Forsyth, editors, *Applications of Invariance in Computer Vision*, LNCS 825. Springer-Verlag, 1994.

[Muehlich-98] M. Mühlich and R. Mester. The role of total least squares in motion analysis. In *Proc. 5th European Conference on Computer Vision, Freiburg, Germany*, pages 305–321. Springer-Verlag,

1998.

[Mundy-92] J. Mundy and A. Zisserman. *Geometric Invariance in Computer Vision*. MIT Press, 1992.

[Newsam-96] G. Newsam, D. Q. Huynh, M. Brooks, and H. P. Pan. Recovering unknown focal lengths in self-calibration: An essentially linear algorithm and degenerate configurations. In *Int. Arch. Photogrammetry & Remote Sensing*, volume XXXI-B3, pages 575–80, Vienna, 1996.

[Niem-94] W. Niem and R. Buschmann. Automatic modelling of 3D natural objects from multiple views. In *European Workshop on Combined Real and Synthetic Image Processing for Broadcast and Video Production, Hamburg, Germany*, 1994.

[Nister-00] D. Nister. Reconstruction from uncalibrated sequences with a hierarchy of trifocal tensors. In *Proc. European Conference on Computer Vision*, 2000.

[Oskarsson-02] M. Oskarsson, A. Zisserman, and K. Åström. Minimal projective reconstruction for combinations of points and lines in three views. In *Proc. British Machine Vision Conference*, pages 62–72, 2002.

[Poelman-94] C. Poelman and T. Kanade. A paraperspective factorization method for shape and motion recovery. In *Proc. 3rd European Conference on Computer Vision, Stockholm*, volume 2, pages 97–108, 1994.

[Pollefeys-96] M. Pollefeys, L. Van Gool, and A. Oosterlinck. The modulus constraint: a new constraint for self-calibration. In *Proc. International Conference on Pattern Recognition*, pages 31–42, 1996.

[Pollefeys-98] M. Pollefeys, R. Koch, and L. Van Gool. Self calibration and metric reconstruction in spite of varying and unknown internal camera parameters. In *Proc. 6th International Conference on Computer Vision, Bombay, India*, pages 90–96, 1998.

[Pollefeys-99a] M. Pollefeys, R. Koch, and L. Van Gool. A simple and efficient rectification method for general motion. In *Proc. International Conference on Computer Vision*, pages 496–501, 1999.

[Pollefeys-99b] M. Pollefeys. *Self-calibration and metric 3D reconstruction from uncalibrated image sequences*. PhD thesis, ESAT-PSI, K.U.Leuven, 1999.

[Pollefeys-02] M. Pollefeys, F. Verbiest, and L. J. Van Gool. Surviving dominant planes in uncalibrated structure and motion recovery. In *ECCV (2)*, pages 837–851, 2002.

[Ponce-94] J. Ponce, D. H. Marimont, and T. A. Cass. Analytical methods for uncalibrated stereo and motion measurement. In *Proc. 3rd European Conference on Computer Vision, Stockholm*, volume 1, pages 463–470, 1994.

[Porrill-91] J. Porrill and S. B. Pollard. Curve matching and stereo calibration. *Image and Vision Computing*, 9(1):45–50, 1991.

[Pratt-87] V. Pratt. Direct least-squares fitting of algebraic surfaces. *Computer Graphics*, 21(4):145–151, 1987.

[Press-88] W. Press, B. Flannery, S. Teukolsky, and W. Vetterling. *Numerical Recipes in C*. Cambridge University Press, 1988.

[Pritchett-98] P. Pritchett and A. Zisserman. Wide baseline stereo matching. In *Proc. 6th International Conference on Computer Vision, Bombay, India*, pages 754–760, January 1998.

[Proesmans-98] M. Proesmans, T. Tuytelaars, and L. J. Van Gool. Monocular image measurements. Technical Report Improofs-M12T21/1/P, K.U.Leuven, 1998.

[Quan-94] L. Quan. Invariants of 6 points from 3 uncalibrated images. In J. O. Eckland, editor, *Proc. 3rd European Conference on Computer Vision, Stockholm*, pages 459–469. Springer-Verlag, 1994.

[Quan-97a] L. Quan and T. Kanade. Affine structure from line correspondences with uncalibrated affine cameras. *IEEE Transactions on Pattern Analysis and Machine Intelligence*, 19(8):834–845, August 1997.

[Quan-97b] L. Quan. Uncalibrated 1D projective camera and 3D affine reconstruction of lines. In *Proc. IEEE Conference on Computer Vision and Pattern Recognition*, pages 60–65, 1997.

[Quan-98] L. Quan and Z. Lan. Linear $n \geq 4$-point pose determination. In *Proc. 6th International Conference on Computer Vision, Bombay, India*, pages 778–783, 1998.

[Reid-96] I. D. Reid and D. W. Murray. Active tracking of foveated feature clusters using affine structure. *International Journal of Computer Vision*, 18(1):41–60, 1996.

[Rinner-72] K. Rinner and R. Burkhardt. Photogrammetrie. In *Handbuch der Vermessungskunde*, volume

Band III a/3. Jordan, Eggert, Kneissel, Stuttgart: J.B. Metzlersche Verlagsbuchhandlung, 1972.

[Robert-93] L. Robert and O. D. Faugeras. Relative 3D positioning and 3D convex hull computation from a weakly calibrated stereo pair. In *Proc. 4th International Conference on Computer Vision, Berlin*, pages 540–544, 1993.

[Rother-01] C. Rother and S. Carlsson. Linear multi view reconstruction and camera recovery. In *Proc. 8th International Conference on Computer Vision, Vancouver, Canada*, pages I–42–49, 2001.

[Rother-03] C. Rother. *Multi-View Reconstruction and Camera Recovery using a Real or Virtual Reference Plane*. PhD thesis, Computational Vision and Active Perception Laboratory, Kungl Tekniska Högskolan, 2003.

[Rousseeuw-87] P. J. Rousseeuw. *Robust Regression and Outlier Detection*. Wiley, New York, 1987.

[Sampson-82] P. D. Sampson. Fitting conic sections to 'very scattered' data: An iterative refinement of the Bookstein algorithm. *Computer Vision, Graphics, and Image Processing*, 18:97–108, 1982.

[Sawhney-98] H. S. Sawhney, S. Hsu, and R. Kumar. Robust video mosaicing through topology inference and local to global alignment. In *Proc. European Conference on Computer Vision*, pages 103–119. Springer-Verlag, 1998.

[Schaffalitzky-99] F. Schaffalitzky and A. Zisserman. Geometric grouping of repeated elements within images. In D.A. Forsyth, J.L. Mundy, V. Di Gesu, and R. Cipolla, editors, *Shape, Contour and Grouping in Computer Vision*, LNCS 1681, pages 165–181. Springer-Verlag, 1999.

[Schaffalitzky-00a] F. Schaffalitzky. Direct solution of modulus constraints. In *Proceedings of the Indian Conference on Computer Vision, Graphics and Image Processing, Bangalore*, pages 314–321, 2000.

[Schaffalitzky-00b] F. Schaffalitzky and A. Zisserman. Planar grouping for automatic detection of vanishing lines and points. *Image and Vision Computing*, 18:647–658, 2000.

[Schaffalitzky-00c] F. Schaffalitzky, A. Zisserman, R. I. Hartley, and P. H. S. Torr. A six point solution for structure and motion. In *Proc. European Conference on Computer Vision*, pages 632–648. Springer-Verlag, June 2000.

[Schmid-97] C. Schmid and A. Zisserman. Automatic line matching across views. In *Proc. IEEE Conference on Computer Vision and Pattern Recognition*, pages 666–671, 1997.

[Schmid-98] C. Schmid and A. Zisserman. The geometry and matching of curves in multiple views. In *Proc. European Conference on Computer Vision*, pages 394–409. Springer-Verlag, June 1998.

[Se-00] S. Se. Zebra-crossing detection for the partially sighted. In *Proc. IEEE Conference on Computer Vision and Pattern Recognition*, pages 211–217, 2000.

[Semple-79] J. G. Semple and G. T. Kneebone. *Algebraic Projective Geometry*. Oxford University Press, 1979.

[Shapiro-95] L. S. Shapiro, A. Zisserman, and M. Brady. 3D motion recovery via affine epipolar geometry. *International Journal of Computer Vision*, 16(2):147–182, 1995.

[Shashua-94] A. Shashua. Trilinearity in visual recognition by alignment. In *Proc. 3rd European Conference on Computer Vision, Stockholm*, volume 1, pages 479–484, May 1994.

[Shashua-95a] A. Shashua. Algebraic functions for recognition. *IEEE Transactions on Pattern Analysis and Machine Intelligence*, 17(8):779–789, August 1995.

[Shashua-95b] A. Shashua and M. Werman. On the trilinear tensor of three perspective views and its underlying geometry. In *Proc. 5th International Conference on Computer Vision, Boston*, 1995.

[Shashua-96] A. Shashua and S. J. Maybank. Degenerate N-point configurations of three views: Do critical surfaces exist? Technical Report TR 96-19, Hebrew University, Computer Science, November 1996.

[Shashua-97] A. Shashua and S. Toelg. The quadric reference surface: Theory and applications. *International Journal of Computer Vision*, 23(2):185–198, 1997.

[Shimshoni-99] I. Shimshoni, R. Basri, and E. Rivlin. A geometric interpretation of weak-perspective motion. Technical report, Technion, 1999.

[Sinclair-92] D. A. Sinclair. *Experiments in Motion and Correspondence*. PhD thesis, University of Oxford, 1992.

[Slama-80] C. Slama. *Manual of Photogrammetry*. American Society of Photogrammetry, Falls Church, VA, USA, 4th edition, 1980.

[Spetsakis-91] M. E. Spetsakis and J. Aloimonos. A multi-frame approach to visual motion perception. *International Journal of Computer Vision*, 16(3):245–255, 1991.

[Springer-64] C. E. Springer. *Geometry and Analysis of Projective Spaces*. Freeman, 1964.

[Stein-99] G. Stein and A. Shashua. On degeneracy of linear reconstruction from three views: Linear line complex and applications. *IEEE Transactions on Pattern Analysis and Machine Intelligence*, 21(3):244–251, 1999.

[Stolfi-91] J. Stolfi. *Oriented Projective Geometry*. Academic Press, 1991.

[Strecha-02] C.Strecha and L. Van Gool. PDE-based multi-view depth estimation. *1st Int. Symp. of 3D Data Processing Visualization and Transmission*, pages 416–425, 2002.

[Sturm-96] P. Sturm and W. Triggs. A factorization based algorithm for multi-image projective structure and motion. In *Proc. 4th European Conference on Computer Vision, Cambridge*, pages 709–720, 1996.

[Sturm-97a] P. Sturm. Critical motion sequences for monocular self-calibration and uncalibrated Euclidean reconstruction. In *Proc. IEEE Conference on Computer Vision and Pattern Recognition, Puerto Rico*, pages 1100–1105, June 1997.

[Sturm-97b] P. Sturm. *Vision 3D non calibrée: Contributions à la reconstruction projective et étude des mouvements critiques pour l'auto calibrage*. PhD thesis, INRIA Rhône-Alpes, 1997.

[Sturm-99a] P. Sturm and S. J. Maybank. A method for interactive 3D reconstruction of piecewise planar objects from single images. In *Proc. 10th British Machine Vision Conference, Nottingham*, 1999.

[Sturm-99b] P. Sturm. Critical motion sequences for the self-calibration of cameras and stereo systems with variable focal length. In *Proc. 10th British Machine Vision Conference, Nottingham*, pages 63–72, 1999.

[Sturm-99c] P. Sturm and S. Maybank. On plane based camera calibration: A general algorithm, singularities, applications. In *Proc. IEEE Conference on Computer Vision and Pattern Recognition*, pages 432–437, June 1999.

[Sturm-01] P. Sturm. On focal length calibration from two views. In *Proc. IEEE Conference on Computer Vision and Pattern Recognition*, pages 145–150, 2001.

[Sutherland-63] I. E. Sutherland. Sketchpad: A man-machine graphical communications system. Technical Report 296, MIT Lincoln Laboratories, 1963. Also published by Garland Publishing, New York, 1980.

[Szeliski-96] R. Szeliski and S. B. Kang. Shape ambiguities in structure from motion. In B. Buxton and Cipolla R., editors, *Proc. 4th European Conference on Computer Vision, LNCS 1064, Cambridge*, pages 709–721. Springer–Verlag, 1996.

[Szeliski-97] R. Szeliski and S. Heung-Yeung. Creating full view panoramic image mosaics and environment maps. In *Proceedings of the ACM SIGGRAPH Conference on Computer Graphics*, 1997.

[Taubin-91] G. Taubin. Estimation of planar curves, surfaces, and nonplanar space curves defined by implicit equations with applications to edge and range image segmentation. *PAMI*, 13(11):1115–1138, 1991.

[Thorhallsson-99] T. Thorhallsson and D.W. Murray. The tensors of three affine views. In *Proc. IEEE Conference on Computer Vision and Pattern Recognition*, 1999.

[Tomasi-92] C. Tomasi and T. Kanade. Shape and motion from image streams under orthography: A factorization approach. *International Journal of Computer Vision*, 9(2):137–154, November 1992.

[Tordoff-01] B. Tordoff and D.W. Murray. Reactive zoom control while tracking using an affine camera. In *Proc. British Machine Vision Conference*, volume 1, pages 53–62, 2001.

[Torr-93] P. H. S. Torr and D. W. Murray. Outlier detection and motion segmentation. In *Proc SPIE Sensor Fusion VI*, pages 432–443, Boston, September 1993.

[Torr-95a] P. H. S. Torr, A. Zisserman, and D. W. Murray. Motion clustering using the trilinear constraint over three views. In R. Mohr and C. Wu, editors, *Europe–China Workshop on Geometrical Modelling and Invariants for Computer Vision*, pages 118–125. Xidan University Press, 1995.

[Torr-95b] P. H. S. Torr. *Motion segmentation and outlier detection*. PhD thesis, Dept. of Engineering Science, University of Oxford, 1995.

[Torr-97] P. H. S. Torr and A. Zisserman. Robust parameterization and computation of the trifocal tensor.

Image and Vision Computing, 15:591–605, 1997.

[Torr-98] P. H. S. Torr and A. Zisserman. Robust computation and parameterization of multiple view relations. In *Proc. 6th International Conference on Computer Vision, Bombay, India*, pages 727–732, January 1998.

[Torr-99] P. H. S. Torr, A. W. Fitzgibbon, and A. Zisserman. The problem of degeneracy in structure and motion recovery from uncalibrated image sequences. *International Journal of Computer Vision*, 32(1):27–44, August 1999.

[Torresani-01] L. Torresani, D. Yang, G. Alexander, and C. Bregler. Tracking and modelling non-rigid objects with rank constraints. In *Proc. IEEE Conference on Computer Vision and Pattern Recognition*, pages I: 493–500, 2001.

[Triggs-95] W. Triggs. The geometry of projective reconstruction i: Matching constraints and the joint image. In *Proc. International Conference on Computer Vision*, pages 338–343, 1995.

[Triggs-96] W. Triggs. Factorization methods for projective structure and motion. In *Proc. IEEE Conference on Computer Vision and Pattern Recognition*, pages 845–851, 1996.

[Triggs-97] W. Triggs. Auto-calibration and the absolute quadric. In *Proc. IEEE Conference on Computer Vision and Pattern Recognition*, pages 609–614, 1997.

[Triggs-98] W. Triggs. Autocalibration from planar scenes. In *Proc. 5th European Conference on Computer Vision, Freiburg, Germany*, 1998.

[Triggs-99a] W. Triggs. Camera pose and calibration from 4 or 5 known 3D points. In *Proc. International Conference on Computer Vision*, pages 278–284, 1999.

[Triggs-99b] W. Triggs. Differential matching constraints. In *Proc. International Conference on Computer Vision*, pages 370–376, 1999.

[Triggs-00a] W. Triggs, P. F. McLauchlan, R. I. Hartley, and A. Fitzgibbon. Bundle adjustment for structure from motion. In *Vision Algorithms: Theory and Practice*. Springer-Verlag, 2000.

[Triggs-00b] W Triggs. Plane + parallax, tensors and factorization. In *Proc. European Conference on Computer Vision*, pages 522–538, 2000.

[Tsai-84] R. Y. Tsai and T. S. Huang. The perspective view of three points. *IEEE Transactions on Pattern Analysis and Machine Intelligence*, 6:13–27, 1984.

[VanGool-98] L. Van Gool, M. Proesmans, and A. Zisserman. Planar homologies as a basis for grouping and recognition. *Image and Vision Computing*, 16:21–26, January 1998.

[Vieville-93] T. Viéville and Q. Luong. Motion of points and lines in the uncalibrated case. Technical Report 2054, I.N.R.I.A., 1993.

[Vieville-95] T. Viéville and D. Lingrand. Using singular displacements for uncalibrated monocular vision systems. Technical Report 2678, I.N.R.I.A., 1995.

[VonSanden-08] H. von Sanden. *Die Bestimmung der Kernpunkte in der Photogrammetrie*. PhD thesis, Univ. Göttingen, December 1908.

[Weinshall-95] D. Weinshall, M. Werman, and A. Shashua. Shape descriptors: Bilinear, trilinear and quadrilinear relations for multi-point geometry and linear projective reconstruction algorithms. In *IEEE Workshop on Representation of Visual Scenes, Boston*, pages 58–65, 1995.

[Weng-88] J. Weng, N. Ahuja, and T. S. Huang. Closed-form solution and maximum likelihood : A robust approach to motion and structure estimation. In *Proc. IEEE Conference on Computer Vision and Pattern Recognition*, 1988.

[Weng-89] J. Weng, T. S. Huang, and N. Ahuja. Motion and structure from two perspective views: algorithms, error analysis and error estimation. *IEEE Transactions on Pattern Analysis and Machine Intelligence*, 11(5):451–476, 1989.

[Werner-01] T. Werner and T. Pajdla. Oriented matching constraints. In T Cootes and C Taylor, editors, *Proc. British Machine Vision Conference*, pages 441–450, London, UK, September 2001. British Machine Vision Association.

[Werner-03] T. Werner. A constraint on five points in two images. In *Proc. IEEE Conference on Computer Vision and Pattern Recognition*, June 2003.

[Wolfe-91] W. J. Wolfe, D. Mathis, C. Weber Sklair, and M. Magee. The perspective view of three points. *IEEE Transactions on Pattern Analysis and Machine Intelligence*, 13(1):66–73, January 1991.

[Xu-96] G. Xu and Z. Zhang. *Epipolar Geometry in Stereo, Motion and Object Recognition.* Kluwer Academic Publishers, 1996.

[Zeller-96] C. Zeller. *Projective, Affine and Euclidean Calibration in Computer Vision and the Application of Three Dimensional Perception.* PhD thesis, RobotVis Group, INRIA Sophia-Antipolis, 1996.

[Zhang-95] Z. Zhang, R. Deriche, O. D. Faugeras, and Q. Luong. A robust technique for matching two uncalibrated images through the recovery of the unknown epipolar geometry. *Artificial Intelligence*, 78:87–119, 1995.

[Zhang-98] Z. Zhang. Determining the epipolar geometry and its uncertainty – a review. *International Journal of Computer Vision*, 27(2):161–195, March 1998.

[Zhang-00] Z. Zhang. A flexible new technique for camera calibration. *IEEE Transactions on Pattern Analysis and Machine Intelligence*, 22(11):1330–1334, November 2000.

[Zisserman-92] A. Zisserman. Notes on geometric invariance in vision. Tutorial, British Machine Vision Conference, 1992.

[Zisserman-94] A. Zisserman and S. Maybank. A case against epipolar geometry. In J. Mundy, A. Zisserman, and D. Forsyth, editors, *Applications of Invariance in Computer Vision LNCS 825*. Springer-Verlag, 1994.

[Zisserman-95a] A. Zisserman, J. Mundy, D. Forsyth, J. Liu, N. Pillow, C. Rothwell, and S. Utcke. Class-based grouping in perspective images. In *Proc. International Conference on Computer Vision*, 1995.

[Zisserman-95b] A. Zisserman, P. Beardsley, and I. Reid. Metric calibration of a stereo rig. In *IEEE Workshop on Representation of Visual Scenes, Boston*, pages 93–100, 1995.

[Zisserman-96] A. Zisserman. A users guide to the trifocal tensor. Dept. of Engineering Science, University of Oxford, 1996.

[Zisserman-98] A. Zisserman, D. Liebowitz, and M. Armstrong. Resolving ambiguities in auto-calibration. *Philosophical Transactions of the Royal Society of London, SERIES A*, 356(1740):1193–1211, 1998.

Index

V

W

Z